PRODUCTION AND OPERATIONS MANAGEMENT

S. A. CHUNAWALLA
B.Com. (Hons.), D.Pharm., M.B.A.
Communication Consultant,
Benzer, Borivli, Mumbai - 400 103.
email: chunawalla@yahoo.com

D. R. PATEL
M.Com.
Formerly Reader, B.K. School of Business Management,
Gujarat University, Ahmedabad - 9.

Himalaya Publishing House
ISO 9001:2015 CERTIFIED

First Edition	:	**1994**
Second Edition	:	**1996**
Third Revised Edition	:	**1997**
Reprint	:	**1999**
Fourth Revised Edition	:	**2000**
Reprint	:	**2001, 2002**
Fifth Revised Edition	:	**2003**
Reprint	:	**2004, 2005**
Sixth Revised Edition	:	**2006**
Reprint	:	**2007**
Seventh Revised Edition	:	**2008**
Reprint	:	**2009**
Eighth Revised Edition	:	**2010**
Reprint	:	**2011**
Ninth Revised Edition	:	**2016**
Reprint	:	**2018, 2020**
Reprint	:	**2023, 2025**
Reprint	:	**2026**

Published by : Mrs. Meena Pandey
for **HIMALAYA PUBLISHING HOUSE PVT. LTD.,**
Vishal Industrial Estate, 1st Floor, Office No. 63/64,
Bhandup Village Road, Subhash Nagar (Opp. CEAT Tyres),
Nahur (W), Mumbai - 400 078. **Phone:** 022-35131464/65/66/67
E-mail: himpub@bharatmail.co.in; **Website:** www.himpub.com

Branch Offices :

New Delhi : Pooja Apartments, 4-B, Murari Lal Street, Ansari Road, Darya Ganj, New Delhi - 110 002. Phone: 011-23270392, 23278631; Fax: 011-23256286

Nagpur : Kundanlal Chandak Industrial Estate, Ghat Road, Nagpur - 440 018. Mobile: 09325409992, 09325908881

Bengaluru : Plot No. 91-33, 2nd Main Road, Seshadripuram, Behind Nataraja Theatre, Bengaluru - 560 020. Phone: 080-41138821; Mobile: 09379847017, 09379847005

Hyderabad : No. 3-4-184, Lingampally, Besides Raghavendra Swamy Matham, Kachiguda, Hyderabad - 500 027. Phone: 040-27560041, 27550139

Chennai : No. 34/44, Motilal Street, T. Nagar, Chennai - 600 017. Mobile: 09380460419

Pune : First Floor, Laksha Apartment, No. 527, Mehunpura, Shaniwarpeth (Near Prabhat Theatre), Pune - 411 030. Phone: 020-24496323, 24496333; Mobile: 09370579333

Cuttack : Plot No 5F-755/4, Sector-9, CDA Market Nagar, Cuttack - 753 014, Odisha. Mobile: 09338746007

Kolkata : 3, S.M. Bose Road, Near Gate No. 5, Agarpara Railway Station, North 24 Parganas, West Bengal - 700109. Mobile: 09674536325

DTP by : Sudhakar Shetty (HPH Pvt. Ltd., Bhandup)

Printed at : Geetanjali Press Pvt. Ltd., Nagpur. On behalf of HPH (P).

PREFACE TO THE NINTH EDITION

Manufacturing policy is under consideration. It envisages large manufacturing zones. In a globalised economy, the labour arbitrage can be availed of by the developed countries. Mostly components and assembly operations are outsourced. The demand keeps fluctuating and hence manufacturing should be flexible and nimble. There could be a conflict of interest between a firm operating at the microlevel interested in optimising costs and shareholder value and the country wedded to the goals of competitiveness and strategic capability within the country.

It is difficult to boost manufacturing's share in GDP to 25 per cent. The current rate of growth must be boosted to 15 per cent and must be sustained for a decade to make the difference This should get priority over other things.

Manufacturing has been considered inferior to other functions. Outsourcing to other countries has become the norm. The US outsourced semi-conductors from Taiwan, South Korea, Mexico and China. These countries benefitted in multiple ways. They became global semi-conductor hubs. Then they upgraded to manufacture flat panel displays. Later, they started producing LED lighting. Two new industries emanated from semi-conductors. It was not the R&D Centres in US who did these innovations. The outsourcing hubs upgraded in terms of value chain. It affected the US adversely in terms of jobs and inventiveness.

Design and fabrication move on simultaneously. These require inputs from the shop floor. These inputs shape the design on the drawing board. Outsourcing can be an interim measure. The country must keep its manufacturing capacity intact. Once damaged, it becomes irreversible. It affects the innovativeness adversely.

Global competitiveness is based on the state-of-the-art technology. The IT systems and robotics contribute to the technological power. The infrastructure must support the manufacturing system. All this creates manufacturing-led jobs. The manufacturing policy must provide a pool of employable manpower coming out of schools, colleges, and ITI-like training centres.

India has $41 billion worth of American treasury bills (or 1.89 lac crore). China tops the list in holding the US treasury bills — an investment of 1.15 trillion. India ranks 14th in terms of investment.

America has a national debt of $15 trillion, out of which $4.5 trillion is accounted for by the treasury bills held by the foreign governments. The US has to honour its commitment to pay the interest on these bills. If the US defaults, all these other nations will be adversely affected.

As S&P has downgraded AAA ranking of these bills to AA+, the RBI will have to take the remedial measures.

The question being asked is whether the world economy is stumbling towards another Lehman moment. Europe too is suffering from its sovereign debt crisis. Asian manufacturing is cooling off because of tighter monetary policies of their central banks.

India may continue to be one of the more resilient economies in the world, but it may be affected by the evolving crisis in the western economies.

The growth rate of Indian economy surged in the 1980s after the initiation of liberalisation for the first time. However, further liberalisation in the 1990s added little to the growth in the decade. The same applies to the Indian manufacturing sector. It is observed that productivity growth in the 1990s was lower than that in the 1980s. Kindly see further information on new products on www.marketingganga.com.

Is it an S-shaped learning curve where the initial rates fizzle out after a threshold? According to Arvind Virmani and Danish A. Hashim's research, the growth in manufacturing follows a J-curve pattern, slowing down in initial years after liberalisation, but picking up steam later.

The story differs from sector-to-sector. Some sectors have a hybrid J-cum-S curve pattern. This is expected as reforms are rolled out piecemeal rather than in one shot.

The question that remains unanswered is that when the J is in danger of becoming an S. Kindly see further information on new products on www.marketingganga.com

— Authors

PREFACE TO THE FIRST EDITION

This book has been designed as a basic text for students who have to study *Production and Operations Management* as a part of their commerce, or management or engineering or pharmacy curriculum. Production facilities and planning and control of production form the bed-rock of this subject. We have dealt with these two aspects in sufficient detail. Techniques of Method Study and Work Measurement help in managing production more effectively. These have been explained in a simplified but elaborate manner. Production and Materials are integrated functions, and so we have included chapters on purchasing, inventory, stores, codification and waste management.

The factory is the place where equipments are to be maintained and safety standards are to be followed. Both these areas have been incorporated. Besides, equipments require capital to be committed to them, and hence a chapter on Capital Budgeting has been included. Old equipments are replaced and our chapter on Equipment Replacement throws light on this. Most manpower of an organisation is to be found in its manufacturing unit. How are we to describe their jobs and specify their jobs? What compensation plans are in vogue to satisfy them? How jobs are evaluated? These are the personnel aspects which have been treated in this book.

In this competitive world, we have opening up our economy to the world. Quality considerations therefore have become all the more important. We have a comprehensive chapter on all aspects of quality in this book. Besides, the ISO-9000 Certification has been included as an appendix.

So far, Indian students had to depend on foreign textbooks which failed to meet their requirements. We have made an attempt to offer them a comprehensive book on production management custom-made to take care of their special needs.

We shall welcome suggestions for improvement the future editions of the book.

— Authors

CONTENTS

OPERATIONS/PRODUCTION MANAGEMENT — AN INTRODUCTION

Introduction

There are four functional areas in a business organization — marketing, production, finance and personnel. Production is the basic activity of all industrial units. All other activities revolve around this activity. The end-product of the production activity is the creation of goods and services for the satisfaction of human wants. These products could be tangible goods — such as beer bottles, laptops, cell phones or intangible services — such as insurance, education and aviation. Most products are a combination of both goods and services. McDonald's is known for its burgers and fast service. Maruti produces cars, but is also known for its after-sales service. The production activity is nothing but the step-by-step conversion of one form of materials into another, either chemically or mechanically. This is done in factories which house manufacturing processes. The basic inputs of the production processes are men, machines, plant, services and methods. The products of the mine, farm, sea and forest are used as raw materials on which the processing is done to create or enhance the form utility. It should be noted that the finished product of one manufacturing unit does not always furnish a ready-made product for the ultimate consumption. In a chain of manufacturing activities, the finished product of the processor sometimes becomes the raw material (or component) for the other manufacturing firms falling next in the sequence.

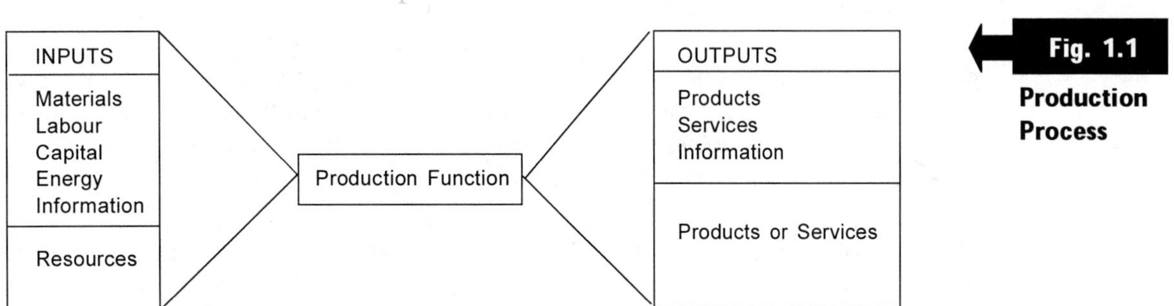

Fig. 1.1 Production Process

Production in other words, is a transformation system where inputs are converted into outputs. The transformation could be physical (manufacturing), locational (transport), exchange-based (retailing), storage-based (warehousing), physiological (hospitals) and informational (telecom).

The following table illustrates the input-output by transformation:

Organization	*Inputs*	*Resources*	*Transformation*	*Output*
Two-wheeler factory	Steel sheets, engine, tyres, control panel	Tools, dyes, workers	Fabrication and assembling	Motor bikes and scooters
Business School	Graduates	Faculty members, books, classes	Imparting knowledge and skills	MBAs
Supermarket	Shoppers	Displays. SKUs, sales persons	Attract shoppers, promote products, fill orders	Sales
Restaurant	Food-loving customers	Food, Chef, beverages, ambience, stewards, captains and wait staff	Food preparation, creating conducive environment	Satisfy customers
Hospital	Patients (In and out-patients)	Doctors, paramedical staff, pharmacy, medicines, medical equipment	Health care	Healthy individuals
Sales Depot	Stock Keeping Units (SKUs)	Storage bins, stockpickers	Storage and distribution	Fast delivery, availability of SKUs

Meaning

The meaning of the term "Production" and "Production management" should be noted carefully.

"Production" involves the step-by-step conversion of one form of materials into another through chemical or mechanical processing to create or enhance the utility of the products or services. According to economists, production is an activity through which the form utility is either created or enhanced, *e.g.,* a piece of wood has no doubt some utility. However, when it is converted into a chair with some mechanical processing, the utility of the material (*i.e.,* a piece of wood) would enhance substantially. According to **E.S. Buffa**, "production is a process by which goods and services are created."

These days, therefore both manufacturing and service organizations fall into the scope of production management. Thus production management which was formerly considered as manufacturing management only, now after inclusion of services into its scope, is broadly known as **operations management**. The core of every organisation consists of the activities that make the products. These activities are called 'operations.' In simple terms, operations describe what an organisation does. Operations at Apple make computers and iPods, operations at Jet Airways fly passengers, at Zee TV, they make TV programmes, at LIC they give insurance and at IIM they educate people to be executives. Many non-manufacturing organizations providing services like hospitals, banks, transportation, farming, warehousing etc. are now covered by operations management.

Operations by formal definition is a process of changing inputs into outputs, with the creation or adding of value to some entity. The process of alteration or transportation or storage or inspection or any combination thereof to add value to an entity is rightly called operations. The growth of service industry has brought with it the term 'operations management.' It is a general term these days.

Operations in the services organizations has some unique features, different from those which has manufacturing base. These are:

1. Non-inventoriable output of service, since generally no stock is produced.
2. Variable demand.
3. Labour-intensive operations mostly.
4. Location of service is dictated by the location of the users.

The word 'production management' arrived first with the emergence of manufacturing industry and the necessity to manage it as such. The meaning of the term **"production management"** is clarified in the following definitions:

(1) "Production management is the process of planning, organizing, directing and controlling the activities of the production function. Production function is the conversion of raw materials into finished products."

(2) **According to H.A. Harding,** "Production management is concerned with those processes which convert the inputs into outputs. The inputs are various resources like raw materials, men, machines, methods, etc. and the outputs are goods and services."

(3) **According to M.J.S. Harry,** the word **production** is often used to mean the same as manufacturing. In order to go through a process of manufacturing itself, we need basically three things: someone to do the job, his equipment and the necessary materials. To run production, we require **service activities** which make sure that the manufacturing activity can go on and **control** to make sure that it goes in the right direction.

(4) **According to E.S. Buffa,** "Production management deals with decision-making related to production processes so that the resulting goods or service is produced according to specifications, in the amounts and by the schedule demanded and at minimum cost."

The definition given by E.S. Buffa is simple, clear and exhaustive. It explains the following important aspects of production management:

(*a*) It is a decision-making managerial function;

(*b*) The decisions are made regarding the production processes required for converting the raw materials into finished products, and

(*c*) The production or output should be according to specifications, in the specified quantities, as per the schedule and at minimum cost.

(5) **According to Ray Wild,** 'Operations management is concerned with the design and operations of systems for manufacture, transport, supply or service.' In other words, it deals with an operating system which is a configuration of resources combined for the provision of goods and services. The operating system consists of manufacture, transport, supply and service.

There are some areas which facilitate the setting up of the production facilities such as method study, plant layout and work measurement. The production facilities are run by production planning and control (PPC), inventory control, quality control and maintenance. Collectively, these constitute what we call production management.

Both **'Production Management'** and **'Operations Management'** have been treated synonymously in this book.

OPERATIONS STRATEGY

These days corporates have to be globally competitive, and thus cannot just be content with what they produce. Organisations have to develop distinctive competence and should strive to do better by improving the products and processes of business.

Between 1945 and 1965, production/operations dominated the corporate strategy as the demand was greater than the world capacity. Between 1965 and 1980s, marketing came to centre stage and decided the corporate strategy due to imbalance between the available world capacity and world demand. Since early 80s till date, both marketing and finance contributed to the formulation of corporate strategy. Operations play a vital role in combination with other functions in the development of the corporate strategy.

Levels of Decisions

Managers, as we know, are decision makers. Some of these decisions are very significant and have long-term impact, whereas some are less significant and have effects lasting for a few days or even hours.

Strategic decisions are long-term decisions, and these require substantial deployment of resources. Tactical decisions are medium term decisions and require lesser deployment of resources, Strategic decisions are made by top-level and senior managers. Tactical decisions are made by the middle managers. Operational decisions are routine short-term decisions. Few resources are committed here. These are made by the junior executives.

A decision to start a new automobile plant in India is a strategic decision. A decision to introduce pension plans by an insurance company is a tactical decision. The tariff charged for Chennai-Mumbai routes in the peak season and lean season by an airline is an operational decision.

Decisions pass downwards through the scalar chain, and information about compliance and other feedback pass upwards.

IT has changed the traditional pattern of decision making. Top level and senior level managers have access to information for the whole organisation. They allow the managers closest to the scene of action to make the decision. Generally, the junior executive is best suited to do this. In the process, the middle level is undermined. Many organisations have adopted flat structures and reduced the organisation's layers.

Strategic Decisions

The three most strategic questions are where we are now, where we are headed and how to go about it. In practice, strategic decisions are complex and varied. Some prominent strategic decisions are:

- *Mission* that determines the overall direction of the organisation.
- *Corporate strategy* that spells out in detail how the mission could be achieved.
- *Business strategy* that shows how each business unit or vertical would contribute to the overall corporate strategy.
- *Competitive strategy* which is a part of business strategy and shows how business can compete effectively.
- *Functional strategy* which decides strategic directions of each function or department *e.g.*, operations strategy, marketing strategy, financial strategy etc.

Mission

Mission shows the overall of purpose of the organisation. It is a short statement. A financial institution, can define its mission as to be the leading provider of financial services in India. A pharmaceutical firm, can say its mission is 'health care — prevention, diagnosis, treatment and cure of diseases.' An auto company can spell out its mission as to make and market fuel-efficient, small, medium and big cars for all income groups. Mission can add some explanatory and qualifying statements. Mission provides the anchoring of the organisation, and ensures that all employees work towards achieving it. It enables the organisation to deploy resources sensibly towards a given focus, and thus prevents their frittering in many directions or in the wrong direction. Mission lends clarity to the business and avoids confusion and ambiguity about the direction the business takes. Mission requires brainstorming amongst the employees, and thus be clear about what the business is expected to do.

Corporate and Business Strategy

Mission enables contextualization of the next set of decisions — corporate strategy and business strategy. Corporate strategy spell out how the organisation will achieve its mission. There may be several business units within a corporation. Each such unit or vertical has its own business strategy that has to contribute to the achievement of the corporate strategy. These strategies are generally concerned with:

- The industry in which the organisation operates.
- The degree of diversification and integration.
- The product portfolio.
- The organisation structure.
- The business units or verticals
- The relationships with the stakeholders *e.g.,* customers, vendors, shareholders and other organisations.
- Geographic location.
- Competitive position
- Targets for profits, sales and other measures of performance.
- Innovations and adaptability of the organisation.

While designing corporate strategy and business strategy, management has to consider the mission, the business environment and the distinctive competence. The business environment consists of the customers, market conditions, technology, economic conditions, legal environment, competition, interest groups, social environment and political conditions.

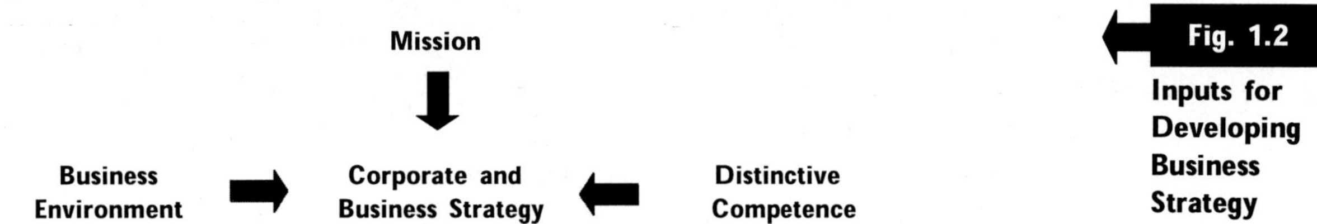

Fig. 1.2 **Inputs for Developing Business Strategy**

As the business environment is similar for all the organisations operating within that industry, the success of the business depends upon its distinctive competence. This includes those distinguishing factors that sets it apart from its competitors. These factors are within the control of the organisation. An innovative organisation puts forward new products faster. It is a part of its distinctive competence. Companies can base their distinctive competence on quality, costs or loyalty of the customers. A distinctive competence emanates from the assets of the organisation *e.g.,* customers, employees, finances, products, facilities, technology, suppliers, marketing and resources like patents and trade marks.

Competitive Strategy

We live in an age of cut throat competition. Our competitors sell products similar to our products, or are likely to do so in future. Competitive strategy especially requires dealing with the competitors.

Competitive strategy is developed taking into account the strengths and weaknesses of the business in relation to the competitors. If the company excels in product quality *vis-a-vis* its competitors, its competitive strategy focuses on quality excellence. There are retail outlets of big size called supermarkets and hypermarkets on the outskirts of the city, an organisation can have its competitive strategy where it sets up small convenience stores in the neighbourhood.

The competitive strategy succeeds if we make better products that serve the consumers needs and wans better. However, as consumers rate products on different criteria, it is difficult to define what is clearly better.

The product must first satisfy certain minimum criteria so that it comes into a consumer's consideration set. A consumer can forgo private transport if the public transport is better and economical. Out of the consideration set, the best product is chosen depending up certain winning factors. If all cars have the same features, a car that provides fuel efficiency is chosen.

Competitive strategy is woven around the qualifying factors and order winning factors. This is done either by cost leadership or product differentiation. Cost leaders make comparable or same products more economically. This can be done by manufacturing and technological efficiency, standardisation, getting economies of scale, using integration and efficient supply chain. Product differentiation makes the products unique. These products can be distinguished based on price, quality, performance and technology used. Other distinguishing features could be reliability, reputation accompanying services, availability and location.

An ideal situation is a combination of cost leadership and product differentiation. However, in practice, this does not work out.

Competitive strategy focuses on better products, and that in turn depends on better operations and processes. These are based on decisions made by the operations managers.

The next level of decisions are made at the operational or functional level. In this chapter, we are concerned with the operations strategy.

Operations Strategy

Operations strategy is concerned with all strategic operations decisions, overall policies of the operations. This provides the framework for detailed operations decisions.

Operations strategy is a link between the strategic plans and the final products. Corporate and business strategy decisions are holistic. The operations strategy involves the design of the products and processes so as to achieve the overall corporate strategy. Spice airways has business strategy of competing on price. Its operations strategy is to run a no-frill low cost flights easily affordable for the middle class. The operations strategy matches an organisation's capability with the customer needs and wants. Operations strategy answers the following questions:

- What should be our product mix?
- What should be the width and depth of our product line?
- What processes would be used to make the products?
- What technology should be used?
- What should be the level of quality?
- What should be our target market in terms of geography?
- How can we plan the production capacity and reap the benefits of scale?

Fig. 1.3
Operations Strategy Decisions

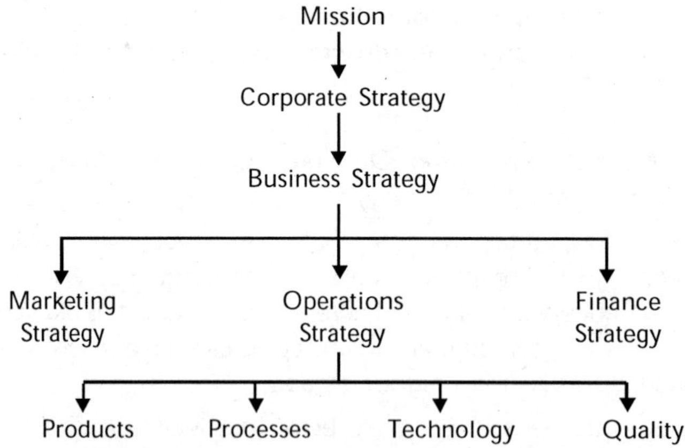

Formulation of Operations Strategy

Operations strategy can be formulated in a variety of ways. They are designed on the basis analysis, experience and logic. Some common considerations are:

- Examine business strategy from the view point of operations.
- Analyse the market conditions under which the operations strategy must work.
- Rank all the factors that can make successful products. Rank the features of the products.
- Examine the production processes which can deliver these products best. Examine capacity, flexibility and technology involved.

- Examine the organisational structure to support the process.
- Monitor the performance against planned performance. Examine performance against benchmarks of competitive performance. Examine the strengths and weaknesses of the business in comparison to our competitors. Improve the performance continuously.

Operations strategy is not formulated in isolation, but considers its linkages with other functional strategies such as finance, manpower, materials and marketing. Mass production strategy requires mass marketing strategy. It also calls for heavy investments in plant and machinery and advertising, promotion and distribution. Such co-ordination requires compromising conflicting goals. High profit business strategy requires low cost production and lesser number of products in the portfolio. However, marketing managers want additional sales and wider portfolio. These are conflicting aims resolved best by understanding which decisions contributes optimally to the mission, corporate and business strategies.

Other Operations Management Decisions

The operation strategy provides the direction to the operations.. The strategic decisions lead to tactical decisions for short term *e.g.*, facilities planning, product selection, process selection, quality control, production planning, make or buy decisions, manpower planning etc. These tactical decisions in turn lead to very short term operational decisions *e.g.*, scheduling of resources, stock control, purchasing etc. The hierarchy of decisions are shown in the following diagram:

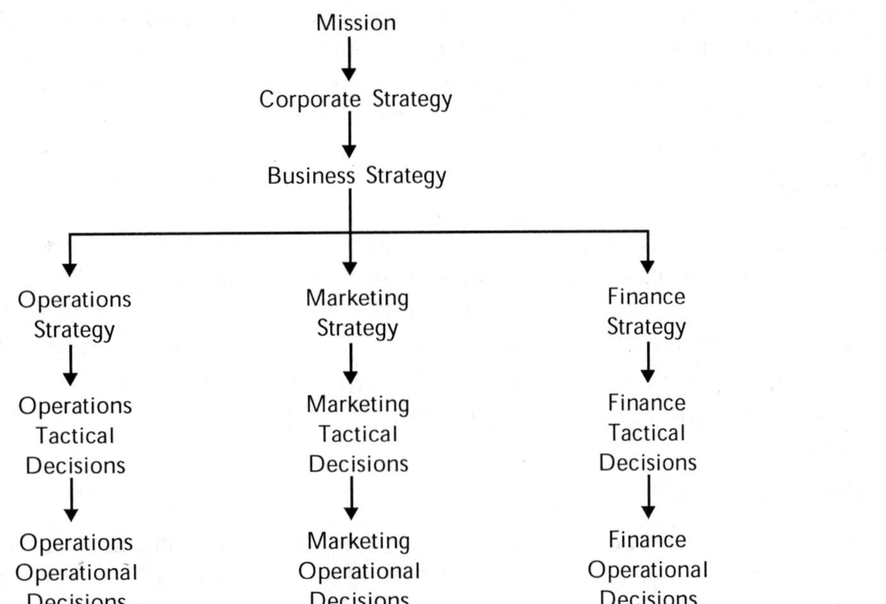

Fig. 1.4 **Hierarchy of Decisions in an Organisation**

The strategic and tactical content may overlap in certain decisions. *e.g.*, inventory decisions are strategic while deciding warehousing planning and location, tactical; when re-orders are issued and operational when orders are sent on weekly basis.

Operations managers in short make strategic decisions in consultation with the top management by providing strategic inputs from the operations view point, they design operations strategies to contribute to the overall corporate and business strategies, they design products and processes and emphasise on improving operations by better performance and remaining competitive.

Operations strategy is related operations functions, and contributes to the overall business strategy so as to give competitive advantage to business.

Strategic Link-up

Operational strategies have interface with business strategies. A product imitator strategy is cost-effective strategy that requires operational excellence plus marketing and finance support. Another strategy could be product innovation strategy where superior products are introduced as fast as possible.

Here operations must be kept flexible. Here also the support of marketing and finance function is necessary.

Strategies are successful if they receive support from all quarters. Hill talks about *order winners* and *order qualifiers*. An order winner wins orders from a particular segment of the market. Order qualifiers are elements such as flexibility, quality and delivery.

Terry Hill has coined these terms. An order-winner is a criterion that differentiates products of one organisation from another. The criterion could be cost, quality and reliability or anything else. An order qualifier is screening criterion that permits an organisation's products as possible candidates for purchase.

New Operational Strategies

Stalk and Hout put forward the concept of *time-based competition* (TBC) having two components — fast introduction of new products and faster delivery of existing products. *Agile Manufacturing* is responsible to any customer need quickly. Closely related strategy is that of *mass customization*. They are associated with the idea of flexibility.

Focused Operations

Skinner puts forward the concept of focused operation or focused factory. In order to avail the advantages of scale, we may lose focus in manufacturing plants. Even product proliferation leads to incompatible products being mixed in the same facility. We can instead think of a plant-within-a-plant (PWP). Though some economies of scale are compromised, the market requirements and profitability objectives are met better. Focus can have various dimensions — product or process, technology, volume, make-to-stock and made-to-order, new products and mature products. These dimensions can be combined while focussing operations.

Benchmarking

This approach came on the scene in the 80s. It enhances the competitive positioning of the companies. Here the organisation checks its performance against the best practices both within and outside the industry. That makes the comparative view possible in terms of the levels of performance so as to remain competitive right now and in years to come. It identifies the need to assess market requirements.

It makes the organisation outward-oriented. The company puts its products and practices against competitors and the leaders in any sector. By itself, this is not an end. It is a means to achieve higher levels of competitiveness.

Global Operations

Businesses were traditionally handled in several countries where the decisions were country-specific. A traditional company operates a country-specific business unit. In this age of globalization, a traditional company is at a disadvantage. What we require is a global corporation where decisions are to be taken for the corporation as a whole, *e.g.*, auto industry, electronic industry etc. Spares are sourced globally, and so do the services. The product design is universal and caters to global tastes. A local adaptation is treated as a variation, rather than a separate product. Demand measurement is done on a global basis. This results into economies of scale and lower costs. The supply chains and inventory management are global. The divisions of a global corporation have global responsibility. What is avoided is fragmentation.

Operations management in this context must have a global perspective. The distinctive competence should be developed on a global basis. The objectives and policies are formulated for global operations. All other operational decisions such as product design, facilities planning, HR do get affected. In short, business acquires global-orientation.

Operations Management and Strategic Planning

In the late forties and early sixties, planning was more or less production-oriented, since the output that was available would be easily sold off. During late sixties to early eighties, marketing occupied the centre stage, as companies experienced that selling products have become increasingly difficult. Planning thus became marketing-oriented. By early 80s and during the concluding decade of this century, both marketing and finance started to drive the strategy formulation. There are corporate failures, and financial problems. This led to finance contributing a great deal to strategy formulation.

It is now seen that critical operational inputs are not considered in strategic planning. Some of the reasons are historical, as we have already observed. There are other reasons too. Operations people are reluctant to put things in black and white. They are mostly reactive, rather than proactive. Their role is limited to short-term perspective, and is considered tactical. Operation management's inputs are thus considered too late in the strategy formulation process, which undermined their very contribution. Later, this may affect operations function, and may lead to conflicts. Besides, inappropriate strategies may shackle an organization for a long time, since large resources get committed to operations for a long time. We must, therefore, attempt an interface of operations and marketing.

Organizations must identify both technical and non-technical business specifications such as price, delivery, reliability, delivery speed and quality. Non-technical business specifications contribute a great deal to success. Operations have to provide both the technical and non-technical dimensions. The underlying link between marketing and operations is provided by the business we are in. Operations managers must be clear about corporate objectives, marketing strategy and the success criteria for products and services in the market place. Production/operations strategy in respect of process choice and infrastructure greatly affect the success criteria for products and services.

In the 80s, companies started comparing their own performance against best practice both within and outside industry. This is called *benchmarking*.

The Objectives of Production Management

Production is an organized activity in a manufacturing organization. Each organized activity must spell out its objectives so that its existence can be justified on the basis of the degree of the attainment of these objectives. Moreover, such identification of the objectives increases the consciousness of the personnel working in the respective organizations in checking their efforts by verifying whether they are in conformity with the stated objective of the organization. The objectives of the production function are classified as under: (1) Ultimate objectives, and (2) Intermediate objectives.

(1) Ultimate objectives: The primary responsibility of the manufacturing activity is to produce a product or products at (1) pre-established cost, (2) according to the specified quality, and (3) within the stipulated time schedule.

Thus the ultimate objectives can be sub-classified as under: (*i*) Manufacturing costs, (*ii*) Product quality, and (*iii*) Manufacturing time-schedule.

(i) Manufacturing costs: The unit cost of the product should be estimated carefully and every effort should be made to stick to the cost standards. For this purpose, the efforts should be made to segregate the costs into two — direct costs and variable costs. Efforts should be made for the following:

(*a*) Reduction in the variable costs.

(*b*) Reduction in the fixed costs.

(*c*) Increase in the volume of production, so that the fixed costs may be spread over more production resulting in the reduction in the per unit absorption.

(*d*) The allocation of the fixed overheads should be made on scientific basis.

(ii) Product quality: Generally, the product quality standards are often established by the product specifications or by the consumers. The manufacturing organization should try to translate such quality prescriptions into some measurable objectives. It should be noted that the product quality comes in conflict with the manufacturing cost objective and the manufacturing time-schedule. The maintenance of the quality should not result in increase in manufacturing costs or delay in the production. A proper balance must be maintained between quality and cost as well as quality and time-schedule.

(iii) Manufacturing schedule: There are many forces which compel side-tracking in the manufacturing activity. The time schedule should not be set for the shipment alone, it should be broken up into all the sub-systems like operating cycle time, inventory turnover rate, machine utilization rate, direct and indirect man-hours per unit, capacity utilization, machine and labour idle time, set-up, repair and maintenance time etc. Time schedule objective directly affects the cost, quality and the goodwill of the business in terms of regularity of shipment.

(2) Intermediate objectives: Production is the result of various types of inputs, like men, materials, machines and manufacturing services. The intermediate objectives strive to attain the optimum utilization of these various types of inputs. It should be noted that the output resulting out of the inputs is measured in terms of the cost, quality and time which relate to the prescription of aforesaid ultimate objectives. The intermediate goals can be spelled out as under: (*i*) Machinery and equipment, (*ii*) Materials, (*iii*) Manpower, and (*iv*) Manufacturing services.

(i) Machinery and equipment: The objectives in the area of machinery and equipment are divided into:

(*a*) Acquisition of machinery and equipment

(*b*) Utilization of machinery and equipment

The adequacy of the existing machinery should be considered and proper additions and replacements should be made according to the requirements. Efforts should also be made to increase the utilization rate of machinery through repair, maintenance and maximum occupancy of the machines.

(ii) Materials: The materials objectives must be prescribed in terms of units, rupee value and space requirements. The per unit material costs should be specified and efforts should be made to increase the inventory turnover of all types of inventories — raw materials, work-in-progress and finished goods.

(iii) Manpower: Manpower is an important as well as typical input in manufacturing activities. So the objectives of the production activities are as regards manpower must be closely allied with the objectives of selection, placement, training, rewarding and utilization of manpower. Usually, these objectives are considered in terms of employee turnover rates, safety measurements, industrial relations, absenteeism etc.

(iv) Manufacturing services: The provision of proper and adequate services directly affects the utilization of other inputs such as men, machines and materials. Proper objectives should be set for the installation of important facilities such as power, water supply, material handling etc. In a condensed form, it can be stated that the objectives of the manufacturing activities are — to manufacture a quality product, on schedule, at the lowest possible costs, with maximum asset turnover, to achieve consumer satisfaction. This statement is closely related to the ultimate and intermediate objectives of the production function.

To summarise, production has to

(*i*) Make sure that it develops a product which can function as expected, *i.e.*, product with the correct **Quality**,

(*ii*) Produce the product in correct **Quantity**,

(*iii*) Deliver the product in **Time** to the right **Place**,

(*iv*) And to perform these functions at the right **Price.**

Production System

The production system of an organization mainly uses facilities, equipment and operating methods to produce goods which the consumer demands. The production system can be classified on the basis of output — services or products, on the basis of flow — project, job shop, continuous, flow shop, or on the basis of specifications — customised or standardised.

National Manufacturing Policy

The National Manufacturing Policy has set in ambitious target of 25 per cent (from the current 16 per cent) as contribution of manufacturing to our GDP by 2025 and creation of 10 crore jobs. McKinsey study suggests India's manufacturing sector has the potential to grow six-fold by 2025 to $1 trillion. The growth will be driven by the rising demand in India and outsourcing by the MNCs.

The newly elected NDA government has made **'Make in India'**, a basic tenet of the manufaturing policy for which the government is committed to create a conducive environment and facilitate the ease of doing business. It also requires a huge investment into infrastructure of roads, railway, telecom and power. The government is thinking of public private partnership (PPP) model for this.

SCOPE OF OPERATIONS MANAGEMENT

Basically, this discipline has to decide about a production/operation system to generate customer satisfaction at optimum cost. In a one-man business, the three functions — manufacturing, servicing and control — will be carried out by one person. As the organisation grows, there are several separate departments. In a bigger organisation, each department has several sub-divisions. A typical production department can have sub-divisions such as production planning and control, production engineering, plant and maintenance and quality control. As such, there are certain long-term strategic decisions involved, influencing substantially the whole system. Mostly these decisions are with respect to the Design and Planning aspects.

To illustrate, let us examine some of these decisions.

Product Selection and Design: The product mix makes our system either efficient or inefficient. Choosing the right products, keeping the mission and overall objectives in mind is the key to success. Design of the product, which gives it enough functional and aesthetic value, is of paramount importance. It is the design of the product which makes us competitive or non-competitive. Value engineering does help us to retain enough of features, while eliminating the unnecessary cost increasing features.

Process Selection and Planning: Selection of a process involves taking decisions about technology, machines and equipment. We have to optimise the output from a given process. Process planning, detailing the stages of the process, give us an idea of optimum automation and mechanisation.

Location Facilities: Where can we locate our operations/production? It commits us at a location for a long time. So, a wrong decision may prove disastrous. Location should as far as possible cut down on production and distribution cost. Therefore, from the alternatives open to us, we have to evaluate and judge a suitable location for us. While evaluating, there are diverse factors to be considered.

Layout and Materials Handling Facilities: Plant layout deals with the arrangements of machines and plant facilities. The machines should be so arranged that the flow of production remains smooth. There should not be overlapping, duplication or interruption in production flow. Product layout, where machines are arranged in a sequence required for the processing of a particular product, and process layout — where machines performing similar processes are grouped together — are two popular methods of layout. The departments are laid out in such a way that the cost of material handling is reduced. There should be proper choice of materials handling equipment. These days, computer software is available for planning the process layout (*e.g.*, CRAFT, CORELAP etc.). Group Technology (G.T.), Cellular Manufacturing Systems (CMS) and Flexible Manufacturing Systems (FMS) have made our concepts of layout planning undergo a tremendous change.

Capacity Planning: This deals with the procurement of productive resources. Capacity refers to a level of output of the conversion process over a period of time. Full capacity indicates maximum level of output. Capacity is planned for short-term as well as for long-term. Process industries pose challenging problems in capacity planning, requiring in the long run, expansion and contraction of major facilities in the conversion process. Some tools that help us in capacity planning are marginal costing (BEA), learning curves, linear programming, and decision trees.

Operational or Short-term Decisions: These deal with short-term planning and control problems. Some illustrative decisions are:

(1) Production Planning: Planning is a pre-operation activity. It aims at anticipating the probable difficulties so that they can be eliminated before they materialise or be mitigated before they become grave. Production planning aims at setting the goals or targets and allocating the existing resources, *viz.*, men, machines, materials and plant services, among varied production operations so that their best possible use can be made in the light of the set goals or standards.

According to Bethel, Atwater, Smith and Stackman, "Production planning takes a given product or line of products and organizes in advance the manpower, materials, machines and money required for a predetermined output in a given period of time."

Thus, production planning is a management technique which attempts to gain the best utilization of a firm's manufacturing facilities. It is gained by the integration and co-ordination of the manpower, machines, materials and plant services employed in the manufacturing cycle.

(2) Production Control: Control is a management technique which aims to see that the activities are carried on in line with the predetermined standards. In case of production activities, production control tries to see that the actual manufacturing conforms to the predetermined standards and schedules of productions. Production Control controls the flow of jobs through manufacture. Production control is considered to have a wider scope and thus it includes production planning. In practice, a joint reference is made of production planning and control and it is popularly known as PPC.

According to Soriegel and Lansburgh, "Production control is the process of planning production in advance of operations; establishing the exact route of each individual item, part or assembly; setting, starting and finishing dates for each important item, assembly and the finished products; and releasing the necessary orders as well as initiating the required follow-up to effect the smooth functioning of the enterprise."

Thus, production control involves the following stages:

(*i*) Planning — setting targets of production.

(*ii*) Routing — to decide the route or flow-of production activity.

(*iii*) Dispatching — to issue materials and authorizations for the use of machines and plant services.

(*iv*) Follow-up — it compares the actual production with the targeted production. Deviations are found out and corrected and reasons are investigated.

(3) Inventory Control: Inventory control deals with the control over raw materials, work-in-progress, finished products, stores supplies, tools etc. The management of these items is closely related with the production function and so is included in production management.

The raw materials, supplies etc. should be purchased at right time, of right quality, in right quantity, from right source and at right price. These five 'Rs' consideration enables the scientific purchases.

Store-keeping is also an important aspect of inventory control. The raw materials, work-in-progress, finished goods, supplies, tools etc. should be stored efficiently. The different levels of inventory should be managed properly and the issue of materials to departments should be made promptly and effectively. Proper records should also be kept for various items of inventory control.

(4) Quality Control: The long-run success of the business largely depends on its ability to maintain the quality standards as decided by the management and accepted by customers. The quality standards are prescribed in terms of specifications like size, colour, shape, tastes etc. The quality control is maintained by testing the actual production and by ascertaining whether they conform to the set standards. The raw materials, work-in-progress, finished products etc., are inspected at various stages of production. There may be 100% quality control where each unit produced is inspected or there may be a policy of testing the samples where the entire lot produced is either passed or rejected on the basis of the tested samples. Various statistical techniques are used for the effective quality control.

(5) Method Study: Standard methods should be devised for performing the repetitive functions efficiently. Unnecessary movements should be eliminated and suitable positioning of the workers for different processes should be developed. Such methods should be devised with the help of time study and motion study. The workers should be trained accordingly.

(6) Maintenance and Replacement: In this we cover preventive methods to avoid machine breakdowns, scheduled and breakdowns maintenance, policies regarding repair and replacement decisions. Maintenance manpower is to be scheduled and repair jobs are to be sequenced. There are some preventive replacements also. Machine condition is to be constantly monitored. Effective maintenance is a crucial problem for India which can help better capacity utilisation and make our operations systems productive enough.

(7) Cost Reduction and Control: Cost reduction ultimately improves productivity. The industry becomes competitive. Essentially cost reduction and cost elimination are productivity techniques. Value engineering, budgetary control, standard costing, cost control of labour and materials etc. help us to keep our costs optimal.

All production decisions are subject to control measures, after receiving proper feedback. Control function is exercised over the quantity to be produced, quality expected, time needed, inventory consumed and carried and costs incurred. Control system is designed after due cost benefit analysis. Controls should be selective. A self-controlling cybernetic system though preferable is not possible in all complex industries.

Environmental changes ultimately affect all the systems of the organization. A dynamic environment makes it compulsory for us to adapt the production system to changes in technology and other factors of the environment. Product mix, composition of products, introduction of new products, changing the layout system are some of the representative decisions which respond to environmental feedback.

Types of Production Systems: When viewed from a different context, the operations/production system can be equated with the flow of materials — flow into, flow through and flow out of the conversion process. When we analyse the characteristics of this flow, we find in some systems it to be very smooth, whereas in others it is much more complex. The more difficult the materials flow, the more complex is the system to manage. Depending on the flow characteristics, there are four classes of the production system:

1. Mass production or flow-line production system
2. Batch production system
3. Job shop
4. Projects (unit manufacture)

Problems confronting a production man are relevant with reference to a particular system. Problems critical for mass production may not be at all important for batch production and so on. Thus, the system determines our focus of attention.

Mass Production System or Flow-Line Production Systems: In these systems, the flow is in a straight line. All facilities are arranged as per the sequence of operations. Output of one operation becomes the input for the subsequent operation. The system is cascaded. Some peculiar problems of this system are balancing of assembly line/production function. Maintenance must be very good to prevent the breakdown of the whole system. Raw material fed initially is very important since all the operations depend upon it. Balanced workload results in a smooth output rate. We will consider the methods and techniques to tackle these problems later in this book.

Batch Production System: In this system, a batch consisting of a certain quantity is made on a machine. The same machine then may be used for another product. Thus, here there are a variety of products; and it is not possible to maintain a separate assembly line for each product. Products compete for the share of the machine. Machines are for general purpose. Pharmaceutical companies make medicinal formulations by batch production system. Production problems are complex here. There is machine assignment problem. Again, what should be the size of each batch is another problem. Scheduling becomes more complex. Production planning, in response to demand, becomes challenging. Layout of the system also merits attention.

Job Shop: Here, the shop accepts customer's orders and executes them. It does not have its own product mix. Primarily, we have facilities and processes in a job shop to undertake a wide variety of customer jobs in different batch quantities. Each order may be unique — requiring its own planning and tooling. Here the flow of material is also complex. A busy job shop is a difficult system to plan and control. There is a need to prioritize different jobs for despatching to customers. At times, short-processing-time (SPT) becomes the yardstick to sequence the different jobs. Job shop is technically speaking a queuing problem. Simulation techniques do help in analysing it.

Projects: Consider the manufacturing of a ship. Such products are never made in large numbers. Manpower, facilities and other resources centre around such products. Each such product can therefore be treated as a project, requiring sequencing of certain activities either in series or concurrently. PERT/CPM or network analysis is a useful technique to plan and control such projects.

Operation Management Decisions

Operations managers make decisions regarding operations functions. The decision making in operations focus on four major areas — process, quality, capacity and inventory.

Process

It refers to the physical process or facility used to produce the product or service and the accompanying workforce practices. There are decisions about equipment, technology, layout, process flows, job design and workforce policies. Some decisions such as capital equipment, plant and machinery are long-term strategic decisions requiring capital commitment and deployment of workforce.

Process must be improved continuously after they are designed. It requires workers' participation. Capital budgeting for equipment is the preserve of the finance managers workforce decisions are taken by the HR managers. Most of the employment in an industry is in the operations function.

Quality

Operations is responsible for the quality of goods and services. This is not an isolated function, but requires the total support of the whole organisation.

Quality must be built into the product right from the design stage, and should be sustained at all other stages of production. Standards are set. Product or service is inspected. Quality is ensured.

Operations must produce the specified quality. Operations interfaces with the other functions in setting the specifications. Operations collaborates with other functions in defining the service expected. Quality improvement is an ongoing process.

Capacity

There should be the right capacity, at the right place, at the right time. Long-range capacity is function of the physical facilities and outsourcing policies. Short-term capacity can be expanded by hiring more space, by deploying more manpower or man-hours, and by sub-contracting. Capacity planning is matter of the size of the facilities and manpower planning. In the short-term, available capacity is allocated to different tasks and jobs. Therefore, manpower, equipment and facilities require scheduling.

Inventory

There are two major decisions — what quantity to order and when to order. Inventory control systems manage the raw material supplies, work-in-process and finished goods. Inventory managers store the inventory in warehouses. They manage the flow of inventories.

Supply Chain Management (SCM) is an integration of suppliers, producers and consumers. Here the flow of materials is considered right from the supply of raw materials, to production, to distribution and to final consumer.

Operations management as a subject can be studied under the above framework. As the syllabus prescribed contains many topics apart from these four areas, students get a feeling that operations management is a mix of several techniques and management. Mainstream operations management is confined to these four areas.

MATERIALS MANAGEMENT IN PRODUCTION SYSTEM

Introduction: All types of organizations, whether manufacturing, trading or even non-profit, are continuously involved in procurement, storage and stock replenishment of different types of materials. At different points of time many of the items are bought, stored and stocked either for immediate or future use. The function of buying or stocking is a result of decision-making process which may be simple or complex, intuitive or analytical, hasty or deliberate. In the manufacturing organizations materials management is relatively more important as well as complex. The cost of materials in the different industries ranges from 50% to 85% of the product cost. On an average about one-third of the total assets of a company represents the investments in inventories. Due to these reasons materials management assumed a greater importance since the inception of manufacturing activities. Materials is a fatty cost element. The slightest efficiency in its management results in substantial absolute cost advantage. With the growth of the specialized functions in the corporate organization materials management is given a distinct importance in modern management. In fact, it is recognized as one of the areas of management.

In the manufacturing organizations, the important inputs are — men, machines and materials which are the results of the monetary commitments. Materials being a key and inevitable input, directly affects the fundamental economic objective, *viz.*, profitability of any manufacturing organization. Efficient management of any of the input directly affects the output and results in the profitability of the organization. As materials consume lion's share of the investments and that too with a possibility of turnover, its efficient management directly contributes to the profitability of the organization.

Definition: APICS (American Production and Inventory Control Society). Dictionary defines materials management as under:

"*Materials Management* is a term to describe the grouping of management functions related to the complete cycle of material flow, from the purchase and internal control of production materials to the planning and control of work-in-progress, to the warehousing, shipping and distribution of the finished product. It differs from the materials control in that the latter term, traditionally is limited to the internal control of production materials."

Thus, materials management is concerned with those management functions circumscribed in the complete cycle of materials flow like purchasing, production and inventory control, material handling, packaging, traffic and distribution. All these related functions are grouped together and are put under the direct control of a line manager. All the sections of the materials management strive to attain the fundamental objectives of materials management. It should also be noted that inventory control is an integral part of materials management and it is confined to the internal control of the production materials.

Production Organization

In a small organization, production, servicing and control are handled by a single person. The larger the organization grows, the more complex the organization structure becomes and the functions are handled by different specialists. A typical factory may have the following organization structure:

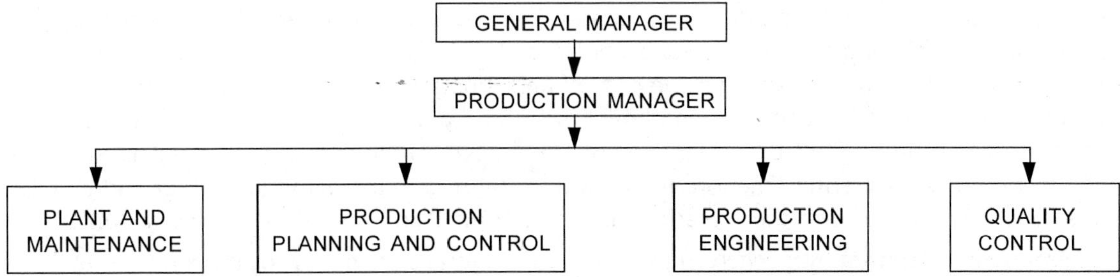

Services are provided by the human relations department and the maintenance department. Finance and accounts department provide the control ingredient. Control is also exercised by departments like production control.

Interface with other Departments

Production interfaces with several other departments. *Sales* department provides the present demand position and the future sales forecast to form the basis of production planning. *Design* gives an idea as to how the product should look like. Engineering drawing gives specifications, and guides production to develop a product. *Human relations* look after the welfare of the employees, resolves IR problems, and provides training inputs. *Accounts* spells out the availability of finance to do the tasks. Production and *materials* have very close interaction which is treated separately. Just as production depends upon the other departments in the organization, these other departments also derive useful information from the production department. Marketing and sales come to realise the productive capacity of the firm to make their plans. Human Relations need the data about the changes in production capacity to do the manpower planning.

Role of Materials Management

(1) Materials management as a prime corporate function: Where materials management holds a key role in the management of the organization and is considered as a prime or top-level corporate activity, it is placed in charge of the Materials Manager who directly reports to the Chief Executive. Like production, marketing, finance and personnel, it is treated as an important area of management, *e.g.*, in process industries where little layout is added to the raw materials for their conversion into finished products, the cost of the materials may be as high as 80% to 90% of the product cost. In such a situation financial considerations are greater than manufacturing responsibilities, and hence instead of considering the materials manager subordinate to the works manager, he is put at par with him.

Fig. 1.5 Organization of Materials Management

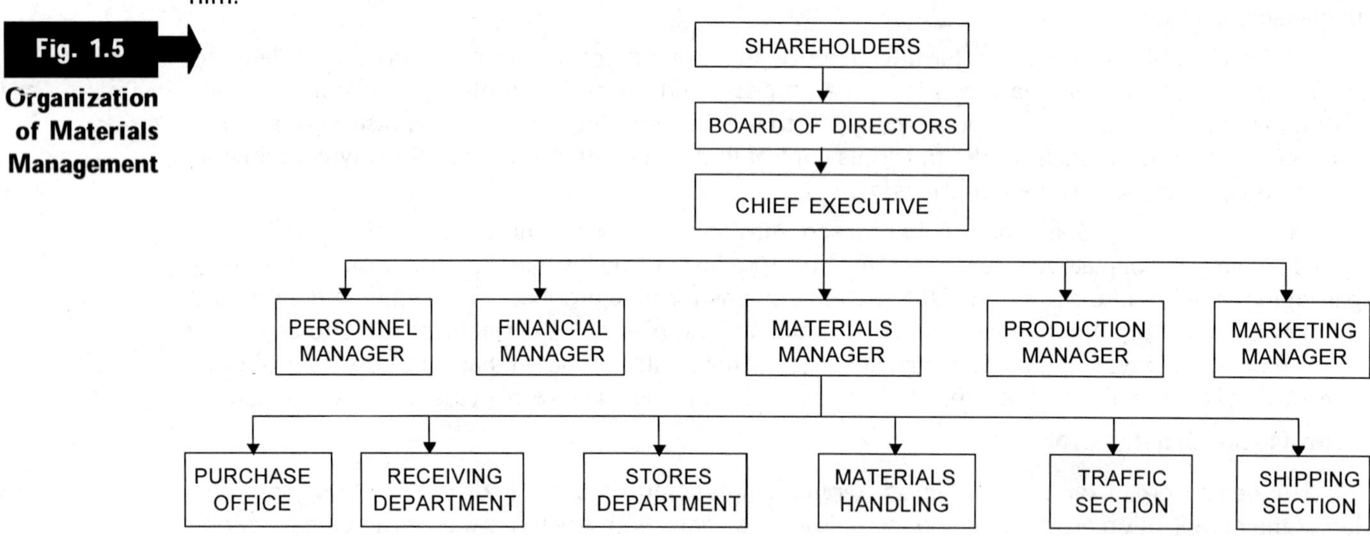

(2) Materials management as an operating function: Under this, the function of materials management is considered subordinate to the production function. The materials manager acts as a subordinate to the works manager. Materials management is considered as a service function to operations and is regulated with the other operations under the control and superintendence of the works manager. The splitting of the materials management department will largely depend on the quantum of the work of each section and the need of the organization. Whether the materials management is treated as a prime function or an operating function, the nature of splitting of the activities will be more or less the same. The usual splitting of the materials under the prime consideration is given as under:

(i) Production department: Regarding the flow of materials, selection of the supplier etc.

(ii) Marketing department: For converting the sales forecast into production schedule and giving delivery dates to customers etc.

(iii) Finance department: For maintaining the level of the stock, locking up of funds into inventory, tapping cash discount and quantity discounting, pledging or hypothecating the materials for working capital needs etc.

(iv) Engineering department: For the specification of materials, quality requirements, product research etc.

(v) Personnel department: For manning the materials management department, vendor relationships, advertising, public relations etc.

(vi) Top management: As an important profit centre, top management has a great concern for materials management.

Need for Integrated Approach to Materials Management

In order to be effective, we have to attain highest materials productivity (getting the most out of material investment). This is possible when there is co-ordination and integration of different areas in materials decision-making. Inventory control is dependent upon demand/supply management, lead-time, standardisation, codification and variety reduction. Thus the problems are inter-dependent and inter-related. Development of vendors affect the inventory control. The areas now integrated under the materials function are:

(1) Planning function: The planning part of materials management deals with the following issues:

(*i*) Translation of the sales projections into long-term requirements of materials.

(*ii*) The production plan is adjusted to the latest sales demand, and the materials are planned accordingly.

(*iii*) To project the facilities required for the materials management.

(2) Production control: The production control function develops the short-range operations plans and schedules from the long-range plans. The function of the production control is to direct and regulate the orderly movement of materials through the entire manufacturing cycle from the procurement of raw materials to the delivery of finished goods to the customers, minimum inventory investment and maximum manufacturing efficiency. This function deals with the following:

(*i*) To develop detailed plans for the production of parts or final products along with the needs of the materials.

(*ii*) To schedule the operations of parts and products on the basis of the availability of materials, operating cycle time, lead time, fluctuations in the sales etc.

(*iii*) To dispatch the materials to the production departments.

(*iv*) To expedite the operations so that the production may be completed according to the schedule along with the feedback variations.

(3) Inventory control: Materials control or inventory control is a systematic procedure for ensuring the availability of items necessary to meet the production requirements at optimum cost. It is concerned with the following issues:

(*i*) Requisition of the materials according to requirements at appropriate time.

(*ii*) Decision about the optimum size of the order which is popularly known as economic ordering quantity (EOQ).

(*iii*) To keep the updated records of the materials received, issued and held in balance.

(*iv*) To report the inventory data to those who use them as the decision tools.

(4) Purchasing: The basic objective of purchasing is to procure the materials of desired quality in time to meet the production specifications and at the lowest ultimate cost. The main activities of purchasing are as under:

(*i*) To select the acceptable supplier.

(*ii*) To place the purchase order with the selected supplier.

(*iii*) To expedite the delivery of materials to meet the inventory requirements.

(*iv*) To keep abreast of the market conditions for the new as well as reordered materials.

(5) Receiving and stores: The main activities of this section are as under:

(*i*) To accept the delivery of purchased materials, to verify them with the purchases order and packing slip, to inspect them and to prepare the 'goods received note' for stores and accounts, and to route the received materials to stores or to the using department according to the direction of the order.

(*ii*) To store the materials properly according to the policy and ensure their quick identification.

(*iii*) To issue the materials according to authorized requisition.

(*iv*) To verify the materials physically at periodic intervals and to record discrepancy if any, along with the reasons.

(6) Shipping: The shipping function is concerned with the distribution of the finished goods. It involves the following functions:

(*i*) To receive the finished goods from the production department and to verify the quantity.

(*ii*) To store the finished goods properly till they are distributed.

(*iii*) To pull the goods from the stores, to identify the customer, to pack and label them and to load into the vehicles for the transportation to customers.

(*iv*) To prepare shipping documents such as packing slip, bill of lading, railway receipt, lorry receipt or airways bill, etc., which are forwarded with the shipment.

(*v*) To report about the shipment to the accounting department for billing the customer, to sales department for order closing and customer notification.

(*vi*) To administer the fleet of the company vehicles used in shipment. If the services are to be hired then to negotiate with the outside carriers about freight, route etc.

(7) Material handling: The material handling function is sometimes grouped with the stores functions. Material handling as a distinct service involves the following functions:

(*i*) To handle in-plant materials though trucking, pallets, containers etc.

(*ii*) To maintain the material handling equipment and other incidental items like pallets, containers etc.

(8) Traffic: Traffic function is concerned with the incoming consignments of raw materials and outgoing shipments of finished goods. The former is sometimes attached to the receiving function and the latter to the shipment. However, when the company maintains its own traffic fleet or if the traffic services are hired on regular basis, it can exist as a separate function of materials management. It includes the following activities:

(*i*) To carry raw materials from the suppliers' plant or railway goods office or other such destinations.

(*ii*) To carry finished goods to customers, railway goods office, branch, wholesalers or retailers.

(*iii*) To administer freight rates, routes, etc., if transport services are hired.

(*iv*) To maintain the fleet of delivery vans, if vehicles are owned by the company.

(9) Waste management: Materials wastage is to be reduced as far as possible. Wastage is an index to our materials productivity. Minimum waste results in better productivity. An integrated approach to materials calls for co-ordination of all the above areas so as to optimise managerial effectiveness for this vital function.

Life Cycle Concept Extended to Production System

In marketing we have extensively adopted product life cycle approach in which a product over a period of time goes through several distinct stages: introduction, growth, maturity, decline and death. The marketing decisions at each stage of the product life cycle are typical. The same concept is extended to a production system as a whole. In the introduction stage of production, we have to select a product and its design. We have to set up facilities to manufacture it. All these decisions are major strategic decisions, taken by the promoters of an industry. Immediately thereafter, the production system becomes steady as most ongoing organizations are. Here the decisions are short-term tactical decisions. Here the system is influenced slightly by internal and external environmental changes. When there are radical changes in the external environment, and the production system finds it difficult to adapt to those changes, the system comes to an end. There is either liquidation or sale or merger. Sometimes, the system is phased out intentionally over a period of time. These days we also talk in terms of life cycle costing where we do not only consider the initial investment in a project but also the investment spread over a period of time in the form of maintenance cost to evaluate different competing project proposals.

Role of Scientific Methods in Operations Management

Scientific management techniques are much more relevant and widely used in operations management area than elsewhere. These techniques are an invaluable aid to decision-making. They modify the purely subjective judgement of the manager.

Industrial Engineering (IE) which is an integrated system of men, materials and machines helps production systems tremendously.

Modelling where reality is approximated by studying the relationship of certain variables so as to understand, explain, and predict the behaviour of the systems has done yeoman's service to production/ operations management. Of special interest are the optimisation techniques of OR like linear programming (LP), transportation, assignment, PERT/CPM etc. We also fall back upon statistical techniques like central tendency, sampling, quality control by control charts etc. Some of these will be discussed in this book at appropriate places.

Computers have given us software packages for all these useful techniques. Computers also help us in MIS. Computer based production systems with cybernetic control have also come in vogue.

Behavioural sciences with emphasis on human element enlighten us about morale and motivation, group dynamics, supervising styles, merit rating and performance appraisals. Thus, these also have a role to play in operations management.

Production and other Functional Areas

An organization is considered as a system having several sub-systems. Marketing sub-system has to make available the products to the consumers for their consumption. It receives sales orders, which are communicated to the production sub-system. Production utilises raw materials, which are processed on plant and machinery to turn out a value-added finished product. In other words, an organization utilises the available facilities to satisfy the market. While manufacturing products, the production function organizes its resources in accordance with the production plan. The finance function makes available finance necessary to carry out their functions to all other departments. Personnel is a support function which plans and provides manpower to all other sub-systems. It formulates suitable personnel policies.

All business sub-systems are inter-linked and inter-dependent. Marketing may fail, if the production does not fulfill the expectations of customers by providing suitably manufactured products. Production may fail in the absence of the working capital necessary to buy raw material for turning out the products. If skilled manpower is not available, all other plans will come to nought. The co-ordination amongst the various sub-systems is necessary for effective functioning of any organization.

Interface of Production and other Functions

Accountants have to understand the basic inventory management and capacity utilization.

Management Accountants must know process costing and variance analysis.

Financial Managers take capital budgeting decision based on production requirements. Cash flow statements and current asset management has to be examined in the light of production decisions. Make-or-buy or plant expansion has financial implications.

Marketing Managers have to understand production schedules to meet their delivery requirements. They should understand how products can be customised. Production has a great role to play in new product development. In service industries, marketing and operations overlap each other.

Personnel is interested in understanding job analysis, job descriptions, job specifications and job evaluation. They develop compensation plans and incentive systems, keeping production requirements in mind.

MIS has to install suitable control systems for production control which takes inputs from marketing information system and provides output to purchasing information system.

Entrepreneurs owe their success to successful production planning supported by working capital management and inventory management.

Responsibilities of a Production Manager

A typical duty chart of a production manager reads as follows:

1. He has to plan the production keeping in mind the demand forecast.
2. He has to utilise the resources in the most efficient and effective manner.
3. He has to exercise control over production costs.
4. He has to set up an efficient material handling system.
5. The production process is planned keeping in mind the industrial engineering techniques.
6. He has to improve employee productivity.
7. He has to manage the inventory both as inputs and outputs. He has to manage the work-in-process inventory.
8. He should be able to work as a member of a team. He has to motivate the team members.

OPERATIONS MANAGEMENT: HISTORICAL BACKGROUND

This management function is not very old. It can however be said that seminal concept of 'division of labour' propagated by Adam Smith (*Wealth of Nations, 1776*) led to the evolution of the present day operations management. Charles Babbage (1832) advocated the use of scientific methods for shop-floor problems. He also advanced the concept of specialisation in 1883. F.W. Taylor however could aptly be described as the pioneer in this field (1878), whose work and method study brought about significant changes in productivity. Taylorism consists of:

(*a*) Replacement of rule-of-thumb by scientific methods.

(*b*) Right selection for the right job, and training and development of the selected person on individual basis.

(*c*) Harmony between workers and management, the aim being maximisation of production, and better wages for the working class.

(*d*) Specialisation of workers and management, each doing the work in which they are most proficient.

The Principles of Scientific Management (1911) laid the foundations of operations management. Taylor also put forward the concept of functional management. Taylor's colleagues and contemporaries also deserve a mention.

Mr. and Mrs. Gilbreth contributed significantly to motion study. Frank Gilbreth developed the concept of Therblig (Gilbreth inverted) and chrono-cycle-graphs (1911). He classified motion into seventeen divisions called Therbligs. Lillian Gilbreth authored the book *The Psychology of Management.*

Henry Ford (1913) attempted mass production and arranged work stations into an assembly line, with the conveyor belt. In the same year (1913), Henry Gantt made known his studies of production scheduling. Gantt Charts are used even today.

H. Emerson (1913) applied Taylorism for the development of organizational structure and suggested staff functionaries for improving efficiency.

EOQ — Economic Order Quantity — Formula to control inventory was developed by F.W. Harris Wilson (1928). There were further refinements later in this formula.

Dodge, Roming and Shewhart (1931) put forward the concept of sample inspection and produced statistical tables. Prior to that in 1924, Stewhart developed control charts and laid the foundation of SQC — Statistical Quality Control.

Between 1933-39, Mayo and his associates conducted the famous Hawthorne Experiments emphasising the importance of the human element and informal groups to raise productivity. The behavioural school thus emerged with Mayo's work. Blake and Mouton's Managerial Grid, Douglas

McGregor's theory X & Y and Maslow's Need Hierarchy Theory were further developments in this area.

L.H.C. Tipett (1937) developed the concept of Work Sampling to set up work standards. One vitally important discipline in the meantime that happened to influence operations management most came on the scene in the form of Operations Research (OR) during the war time (1950). Mathematical models of optimisation and systems approach came to be applied extensively to resource allocation, scheduling, inventory control and location and layout problems of facilities.

Value engineering came forward as a cost reduction technique, trying to identify the unnecessary costs, not relevant to the functional utility of the product.

Computer applications in later years, especially for Industrial Engineering and OR problems, changed the very complexion of the Operations Management function.

Project Management techniques of PERT/CPM (1958) gave an effective tool of planning and control of large projects.

The fifties made production management as a science useful as a management function for diverse manufacturing organizations (like Petroleum, Chemical, Process Industries etc.). The sixties gave it a new status of Operations Management, embracing in its ambit the service sector of the economy also. The seventies gave us the Systems Approach, where the organization is treated as a whole consisting of several sub-systems.

Computer simulation, computer aided design and manufacturing (CAD/CAM), group technology (GT), cellular manufacturing system (CMS) are some of the recent developments making us optimistic about operations management's role and utility in future.

The following table summarises the evolution of operations management (OM).

Table 1.1 **Evolution of OM**

Year	*Concept*	*Contributor*	*Details*
1910s	Scientific Management Motion Study Moving Assembly Line	Taylor Gilbreth Ford and Gantt	Time and Work Study — Activity Scheduling Chart
1930s	EOQ Quality Control Hawthorne studies	Harris Shewhart, Dodge, Roming Elton Mayo	Economic Ordering Quantity SQC, Sampling, Inspection Worker Motivation
1940s	Linear Programming (LP)	Dantzig	—
1950s-60s	Operations Research (OR)	Many Researchers	Simulation, Waiting Line Theory, PERT-CPM, Programming.
1970s	Computerisation	—	Inventory Control, Scheduling, Forecasting, Project Management, MRP
1980s	JIT, TQC, Automation	—	Japanese Researchers, Deming and Juran
1990s	TQM Business Process Reengineering Internet-www Supply Chain Management (SCM)	— Hammer —	— SAP and Oracle

Shift from Agriculture to Production

Agriculture engages more than 60 per cent of people. The younger generation does not want to be in it because of uncertainties. There will be outflow of labour from agriculture. Services are stagnating. Therefore, manpower from agriculture will shift to manufacturing. Indian economy can be revived by depending on the manufacturing. The government is reviewing FTAs and SEZs because of that the manufacturing sector should be able to better utilise the FTAs. India is also looking at project exports in a big way. SEZ review focuses on access to non-exporters who engage with exporters, *e.g.*, courier service, hospital for staff welfare and housing.

Three Industrial Revolutions

The *first* Industrial Revolution was ushered in Britain on the advent of power-loom using textile-mills. The *second* Industrial Revolution was initiated by the large-scale production using the Assembly Line at Ford. The *third* industrial revolution in the pipeline is the digitization of the production process. The beginning has been made by the 3D printer. The unimaginable capacity of computers and new technologies will change the complexion of the production sector. The world will move again to the cottage industry. Production will be carried out at homes. Distance will, no longer be a hindrance. There will not be mining of ores. Biotech will make available the raw materials. There will be emphasis on the skills of workers, rather than on their numbers. Customisation will be at its peak.

LEAN PRODUCTION

Lean manufacturing is a performance-based strategy for maximising customer value by elimination of waste, while improving profitable growth of the organisation. The future of manufacturing is Lean. The survival aid growth of organisations will depend on how less waste is generated in the processes. For the lean manufacturer, waste is the sole enemy. It is viewed as a roadblock to customer satisfaction and company's profitable growth. Lean is the most effective way to eliminate waste and create wealth for the organisation.

The craftsman type of production was replaced by more efficient mass production on the eve of Industrial Revolution. Soon after World War II, the Japanese introduced a new approach to manufacturing called 'Lean Production.' It transfers the maximum number of tasks to those workers who actually created value on the line. It also has a fault finding system that traces the clause of fault. Lean production requires multi-skilled workers. And this places premium on training and development. In lean production, non-value adding functions are identified and discontinued. In lean production approach, there is focus on core competencies, flexibility, speed, integration of design and operations and the right people.

Tenets of Lean Production

- The product must always meet the customer needs at a specific price at a specific time.
- Produce with as few people, as little inventory and as little waste as possible.
- Each production stage processes exactly what the next stage wants, and when it wants it. The quality processed is exactly what the next stage wants.
- Variety in products can be accommodated avoiding the change-over costs involved in customised mass production.
- Sourcing, production, marketing, accounting and strategic planning — all these areas come under the purview of the lean concept. Lean is about changing he supplier management system, changing product development system changing production management system and changing what managers do the logic of supply chain should be to replenish what you have just used.
- Management should be about solving problems.

Lean Production is invented by Eiji Toyoda and Taiichi Ohno on the shop-floor of Toyota Motor Corp. Its objective is to build a lean-shopfloor — lean on people, on processes, on inventories and on time. Lean production can be adapted to our competitive strategy which could be either lowest-cost production or high-product variety. Its direct pay-off is the dramatically reduced costs.

Lean Manufacturing

Lean manufacturing concept was conceived by Toyota Corporation of Japan in the 1950s. Taiichi Ohno (1912-1990) is a symbol of Japan's manufacturing resurgence after the second World War. He

TOYOTA'S 'MILK RUN' AND LEAN IN WIPRO

Toyota Kirloskar Motors (TKM) has its manufacturing facilities at Bidadi, 45 kms off Bangalore. The operations are kept low-fat. The maximum amount of raw material at the factory at any point of time does not exceed two hours' production requirement. In India, 43 of its 57 vendors are as far away as Delhi, Chennai and Pune. But it still manages to source parts only as and when needed. All finished cars leave the factory within 48 hours, and no dealer is sent more than 15 days' stock. The secret lies in its famous 'milk run', which involves picking up small quantities of supplies from vendors throughout the day. Every morning small trucks leave a central stocking point (there is one each in Pune, Delhi and Chennai) picking up supplies from the local vendors. These trucks return to the hub, where the supplies are transferred to a bigger truck, which leaves for TKM every day. For vendors based in and around Bangalore, the milk runs are straight from the plant to the vendor and back. The cost implications of such lean manufacturing are huge.

Lean in Wipro

Traditionally, a manufacturing philosophy developed by Toyota, lean manufacturing is any activity or use of resources that does not deliver value for the customer and is wasteful. Wipro, the software solutions company from India has spent the last few years in applying and deploying the lean manufacturing principles to software development and management process. Toyota applied 'single machine exchange of dye' or SMED. Prior to SMED, Toyota kept the same dye running for long to make the best use of it, because the set up time for a dye is 24 hours. By working backwards, Toyota found that the job could be done offline. Wastes have been classified into two categories — one which can be eliminated, and the necessary waste that can be squeezed. In software services, dye is any process or line of code that can be used over and over again across different projects. Normally, at least 30-70 per cent work in most software projects can be standardised. In software testing, a machine is set up according to different projects. The common processes could be identified using Lean. The set up time could be reduced to an hour. Concurrent Engineering (CE) is the design in parallel and in sequence. Toyota uses CE to launch a new car every 36 months for which on an average GM takes 5 years. In software services, CE's use may generate lines that may not work together. Here they make use Eppinger's algorithm developed by MIT professor Steven D. Eppinger. Wipro eliminates non-core tasks. It reduces defect rates every thousand lines of codes. Earlier it was 18 per cent. It got reduced to 8 per cent. Wipro's example shows that Lean can work and become critical success factor. Wipro has moved over 25 customers to the Lean model. The project transition time from rivals to its own project team was reduced to 100 days from six months earlier. Wipro will have to evolve its own production system by taking bold initiatives.

is considered to be the father of the Toyota Production System, which became Lean Manufacturing in the US. Since then, it has been widely adopted by others. Daniel T. Jones, James P. Womack and Daniel Ross published their seminal book, *The Machine that Changed the World* in 1990. It made the world aware of the manufacturing revolution that had taken place at Toyota. Toyota had moved away from the conventional mass production to what the three researchers of MIT called 'Lean Production.' Lean starts with the customer and asks what the customer really needs. Lean is about tools that create goods and services that offer precise customer value with less of human effort, less apace, less capital an less time. It means less of everything: men, materials, money, time and even physical factory space. Lean makes a company flab-free. The next step is alignment of people with the tools. It requires an altogether new responsive management system. The next step is a alignment of people with the tools. It requires an altogether new responsive management system. Sundaram Brake Linings (SBL), Chennai employed in 1997 five workers on five different machines to produce 345 brake-linings per shift, and got a scrap of 10 out of every 1000 linings. Today, they put two workers on just four machines, and each worker generates an output of 1387 units, and the scrap rate is just one per 1000. This is achieved at a cost of ₹ 5 lakhs. Lean mathematics works by subtraction which actually results into additions. Process profitability is improved by reducing the workers operating a process. Inventory is reduced and so also the production cost by cutting the number of processes in manufacturing or product-design.

We become competitive by reducing the non-value-added activities in the supply chain. Lean redefines the corporation's means, methods and missions. Lean challenges what is being practised currently. Senior executives must be involved in shop-floor activity to introduce the lean philosophy. In lean pricing, the non-value added activities (NVAs) are excluded. To introduce the lean philosophy, a company must understand its value chain. In lean production, the daily production demand is synchronized with the total production time available. Lean also emphasises a single-piece flow by dividing its activities into cells, which typically employ U-shaped lines where a part goes through all intermediate processes necessary to turn it into a sub-assembly.

Here the problem remains confined to a specific cell only. Lean advocates defect detection by low-cost tools automatically to prevent defective items from flowing along. Lean integrates just-in-time supply of components. Lean also believes in *kaizen* — the continuous improvement philosophy.

James Womack came to India in 2002, and again in 2008. He is now the Chairman of the Lean Enterprise Institute.

It should be noted that Lean cannot bring a process under statistical control. Six sigma alone cannot dramatically improve process speed or reduce invested capital. What is required is the fusion of Lean and Six Sigma.

Distinction between Production Management and Engineering

Mostly production engineering and management are confused with each other. Production management, as we have observed at the beginning of this chapter, is involved in a conversion process, and its management. Production engineering is an advisory function. It provides expert support to run the equipment and carry out process technologies. Production management is a business function, and is not just an engineering function. In small businesses, perhaps both functions may merge with each other, but it is just an exception. Production management provides business orientation to the organization.

Distinction between Operations Management and Operations Research (OR)

Both operations management and operations research have a common term 'operations.' It is also true that most of the operations research techniques are used in the area of operations management. Operations research techniques are optimising techniques, *e.g.,* linear programming and are used extensively in production function. Though they have been treated in books of production management in pre-1980 period, their role and relevance have now been questioned in production management area, though a few of these techniques still cast their shadow on this area.

Remote Processing

Because of telecom revolution (Telegraph, 1833; Telephone, 1877; Television, 1928), it has now become possible to do remote processing of major operations several thousand miles away. A company in Gurgaon processes GE's credit cards in Europe. Several companies in India transcribe the doctor's prescriptions for the health care industry in the US. Several companies process loan applications for foreign companies. Call centres are established to answer customer queries. Many companies do data conversion work. Back office work is outsourced, *e.g.,* pay-roll accounting, internal auditing, credit appraisals. Legal deposition summaries can be prepared. Insurance claims are processed. Geographic information systems by digitised maps are created. Several thousand Indians do remote processing jobs for foreign companies. This number could go up in lacs, given the pace of development of this industry. In production/operations management, this will be a key area. Operations can be outsourced globally because of telecom development.

Cost Centre

Production function accounts for nearly 80% of all costs incurred by an organization. All direct costs related to employees and materials and part of overhead costs fall within its scope.

World Class Manufacturing

The economy is integrated to the global economy and industry is facing global competition. It is, therefore, necessary to improve performance. Performance measures indicate the real problems and how to overcome them. If a system does not deliver, the blame cannot be placed at the door of culture, level of technology, or labour. Mostly, it is due to faulty performance measures. Identification and definition of the right type of performance measure is thus a priority.

World Class Manufacturing (WCM) concept has emerged of late. The following characteristics of WCM are used to fulfil the consumer expectations:

1. Products of high quality.
2. Products at the right price.
3. Products with enhanced features.
4. Products in a wide variety.
5. Products delivered in time, in fact short time.
6. Products delivered with shorter lead times.
7. Flexibility in fulfilling the demand for the product.

The above-listed performance measures are external to the manufacturing system but are vital for the success of the organization. These can be measured internally. Such performance measures improve the acceptability of the product.

The success of an organization in this competitive environment is due as its superior performance measuring system in manufacturing. Under WCM, the products should have specifications closer to the customer needs.

Digital Manufacturing

Digital manufacturing systems combine advanced 3D simulation tools, product life-cycle management (PLM) software and virtual reality to manage a product visibly through the manufacturing process. Digital manufacturing puts the IT on the production floor. In a manufacturing company, production floor is the biggest cost centre. The whole success of the product depends on how fast and efficiently the production is managed, CAD/CAM makes design phase smooth. ERP makes the supply phase smooth and CRM takes care of sales. Manufacturing has yet to catch up the pace set up by the above three. Digital manufacturing can make production smoother. It can make production match the design and sales. Digital Manufacturing software covers the entire gamut of Part Manufacturing (define and verify component machining), Assembly Planning (create machine-line or assembly-line layouts, Resource Management (define and verify product assembly sequences), Plant Design and optimization (simulate specific operations and material flows to optimize the process), Human Performance (allocate the required time for each operation), Quality and Production Management (line performance and balancing, cost control, commission and programme production lines, execute and manage production process, track and trace specific customer orders). Simply put, the digital manufacturing software defines manufacturing process. Engineers can simulate on the computer what they want to achieve on the production floor. Digital manufacturing can be applied to existing factories and new facilities. Digital manufacturing can be justified if it reduces 'the cost per piece.'

Gandhian Engineering

This term is coined by Indian scientist R.A. Mashelkar on the lines of social engineering. It is a concept of doing more with less for more by more and more people. It is innovation-led inclusive growth. It uses the findings of science and technology in areas beneficial to many. Even a simple research can produce results that can have large scale impact by reaching out to masses and is affordable. Anything that is helpful to a large section of society right from the Jaipur foot that is affordable to the poor to the ₹ 1-lakh Tata Nano which is within the reach of the rising middle class in India constitute Gandhian engineering. The University of Mumbai will soon establish a chair in Gandhian engineering.

Additive Layer Manufacturing

This a groundbreaking technology. Scientists in Bristol designed a bike on the computer. It is sent to a printer which places layers of melted nylon powder on top of each other to build up the product. The final product is a single, one piece product. The bike can be built to the rider's specifications. The 3D printing method allows products to be made from a fine product of nylon, carbon-reinforced plastics or metals such as titanium, steel or aluminium. The technology may be used in aerospace, the motor industry and engineering.

3D printing

This process is also called Additive Manufacturing. It is not very different from printing a document digitally at home. The page is replaced by a 3D object. Instead of ink, layers upon successive layers of materials are put together to create the object. BMW has used it to manufacture jigs and fixtures. They have used a printer called Stratasys replacing the traditional CNC manufacturing techniques. The US Air Force is building many such 3D printed parts for its UAVs. It may help medical field. There could be bioprinting of organs and printing of bone scaffolds. In space exploration, a printer could be used to manufacture parts in zero gravity. Manufacturing will change a great deal. They will be able to produce complicated and unique items in just the quantity they need, thus avoiding waste. Companies can make prototypes. They can also make product parts quickly and on demand. The object today can be printed in 70 materials only. This limitation could be overcome in future. A consumer can copy copyrighted artworks. This problem will have to be addressed. 3D printing will open up imagination. Customised products could be offered. The prices of 3D printers are high today, but will drop soon to make them as common as home printers today are.

This process is also called Additive Manufacturing. It is not very different from printing a document digitally at home. The page is replaced by a 3D object. Instead of ink, layers upon successive layers of materials are put together to create the object. BMW has used it to manufacture jigs and fixtures. They have used a printer called Stratasys replacing the traditional CNC manufacturing techniques. The US Air Force is building many such 3D printed parts for its UAVs. It may help medical field. There could be bioprinting of organs and printing of bone scaffolds. In space exploration, a printer could be used to manufacture parts in zero gravity. Manufacturing will change a great deal. They will be able to produce what they need, thus avoiding waste. The object today can be printed in 70 materials only. This limitation could be overcome in future. A consumer can copy copyrighted artworks. This problem will have to be addressed. 3D printing will open up imaginations. Customised products could be offered. The prices of 3D printers are high today, but will drop soon to make them as common as home printers today are.

Biotz, a Kerala-based start-up set up by Anand has launched the most affordable 3D printer Makifyer in India. According to Anand, times are near when kids will print their toys home. 3D printing is increasingly gaining acceptability to design and build prototypes and functional parts. 3D printers work in additive manufacturing technology called **'fusion filament fabrication or FFF'**. Here the material is laid down in layers. A plastic filament or metal wire is unwound from a coil and supplies material to an extrusion nozzle, which can turn the flow on and off. The base model costs ₹ 1 lac. 3D printing is now moving from prototyping to large scale manufacturing. 3D printing will have applications in healthcare especially to develop prosthetics, in automobiles to recreate car parts and create futuristic car designs, in designing, in movies and TV and is useful for both researchers and do-it-yourself enthusiasts.

The 3D printing industry is predicted to worth over $ 8 billion by 2020. Physical products, mass produced and bought in outlet stores, will become *replicable* and *editable* by anyone with the knowledge of computer-aided drawing and access to a 3D printer.

Already, 3D printing technology is being used to manufacture a wide array of products from auto spares and prototypes to human skin and organs. In these days of mass manufacturing, 3D printing has influenced the thinking about production. There are going to new frontiers in global trade too. It is however, too early to describe the emergence of 3D printing as a new industrial revolution.

We have to see how small scale production could be made as efficient as large scale production. In designing and new product development, 3D printing will be of great help as it will allow the team to produce one-off products and prototypes. That will bring design and manufacturing closer. There will be more freedom for small firms to experiment with new ideas. It does not mean that 3D printing will replace traditional assembly lines or machining. It would complement the traditional manufacturing.

Scientists have moved a step closer to developing lab-grown meat using a new 3D printing technique. This could be used to create working artificial organs for transplants in the future. The blood vessels are printed first, and then, flesh is grown around them. The 'templates' of sugar are used, and meat is grown around them.

Daniel Nocera's Energy Device

Daniel Nocera, a professor of chemistry and energy, along with his group of scientists at MIT has attempted to mimic photosynthesis, the process by which plants breathe and produce energy while doing so. The water molecules are split to generate this energy. Though in electrolysis, water is split, the process requires clean water. Nocera's experiment can use even waste water. They plunged an artificial silicon 'leaf' coated with a proprietary solution of cobalt and phosphate into a jar of water, and made it to generate energy at efficiencies exceeding solar panels. Tata group has signed the MIT guru to get power from water. This can lead to a 'personalized energy box' that could power a small household and can revolutionize the rural electric supply. Nocera expects to develop a prototype in a year and half. The Tatas will take the technology to market. The technology is still at an early stage and is yet to be published.

Supramolecular Chemistry

Akzo Nobel, a chemical company and scientists at Eindhoven University of Technology, Netherlands are working on developing a supramolecular polymer that is able to heal itself. The new plastic called Supra B takes advantage of bonding that gives water its viscosity and surface tension. It is called hydrogen bonding that uses affinity between hydrogen and other atom such as oxygen and nitrogen. In Supra B, they have managed to quadruple the number of hydrogen bonds. It then does not require a chemical to join them together. It will provide a new scratch resistant coating for vehicles, lap tops and other portable equipments.

Flexible Electronics

After tile-like thin TV sets, we can soon have stretchable TV sets which can be rolled and bent. Stretchable electronics could become a reality by the successful development of elastic conductors using carbon nanotubes by a group of Japanese scientists. Researchers have integrated the conductor with organic transistors to make rubber-like integrated circuits (ICs) stretchable by 70 per cent without any mechanical or electronic degradation. ICs can be built on curved surface by this step. The surface then becomes 'smart' or 'intelligent'. The matrix is made of unique combination of elastic polymers and ionic liquids in which the carbon nanotubes are uniformly dispersed. These steps generate stretchable electronics — stretching axially and bi-axially without diluting electronic properties. The research will lead to large-area devices to become bendable and rollable. Applications can include wearable and washable electronics.

Munjal Global Manufacturing Institute (MGMI)

In collaboration with MIT and Sloan School of Management, an institute to teach manufacturing management is being set up on the campus of Indian School of Business (ISB), Mahali by Hero Motor Corp. Ltd. The institute will help the small and medium enterprises (SMEs) sector by developing case studies, giving field exposure and providing human resources to the sector. The areas the curriculum will cover are:

- operations management
- global supply chain networks.
- product innovation and development.
- manufacturing and operations innovation.

- lean production
- six sigma
- sustainable manufacturing and operations
- operations strategy
- pricing strategy and operations
- operations for entrepreneurs.
- performance management.

Apart from the courses, there will be project work.

Manufacturing Policy

This policy is a game changer. The National Investment and Manufacturing Zones (NIMZ) are planned. The clearance here will be through a single window mechanism. The master plan will be done by SPV. Zoning will be done by the states. Labour-related powers are delegated to the CEO of environmental issues. The power is delegated to an officer of State Pollution Control Board, on deputation to the SPV. There is a major thrust on training and development. There will be seven NIMZ. These will be standalone cities.

Big Data

There is huge amount of data around us and it keeps growing each nano-second. There is a digital trail of each online activity. That adds to this pool. At the same time, powerful tools employing complex algorithms are used to plough through this data. It would not have been possible to do so through traditional research methods. The mining of this data is called *Big Data.* It includes searching, capturing storing, analysing and eventually sharing relevant information with the target audience.

Big Data drives the business decisions and may actually shape the way the world functions — Big Data alters the way we process and perceive things. Big Data sample size is large and diverse. It cannot give the 'margin of error' which traditional surveys give. However, such exactness is not necessary. Insights obtained through Big Data could be far more useful. What is to be emphasised is correlations rather than causality.

However, there should not be over-reliance on Big Data especially while looking at sensitive issues such as crime. It is also not necessary to follow blindly what Big Data throws up. India's Aadhar card project is a Big Data project. It links an identification number to the demographic and biometric information.

University Research

We are mesmerised by the innovations in the corporate world but behind the success there of these corporate laboratories is a busy underpaid university scientist. In the corporate sector, is little room for fundamental research and that is why most Nobel laureates are from the universities. In university set up, you are prepared for years of failure, and risks can be taken. In corporate world, if you do not deliver in time, you will be asked to take risk. It is not always the Ivy League universities which corners all the glory, but many many non-Ivy League universities scattered all over. All chemistry research has been facilitated by Normal Allinger who is a guru to all those who use computer to figure out. National Institute of Health (NIH) of the US added to our understanding how the transport system in the cells work. This facilitates so much research in medicine. Though Steve Jobs was brilliant and audacious, yet without Alan Turing of National Physical Lab, UK and then the University of Manchester, there would neither be computer science, nor formalisation of the concept of 'algorithm'. Mark Zuckerberg may have leveraged the web, but the web was put in place by time Berners-Lee at CERN in 1989. CERN, Geneva is funded by 12 European countries and Berners-Lee is today a professor in the University of Southampton, UK.

As Indian universities are in bad shape, we do not think of pure science research in India. Though IIT, Mumbai is the best but ranks 251st in the world.

ഗ്ദ ര്ജ

2 PRODUCT PLANNING AND DESIGN

Products and Processes

Product planning and product design are important for operations management. Product planning is concerned with the introduction of new products, modifications of the existing products and phasing out the old products. Its primary aim is to ensure a steady flow of products that the customers want.

In practice, product design and the process to make it are inter-twined. The features of the product depend on the process used to make it. An assembly line meal is much different from a customised meal prepared by a mother. There are many services where it is not possible to separate the product and process — a courier company and the process used to deliver couriered articles.

It is nonetheless important to know the focus of an organisation — it could be a product focus or process focus. Product focus organisations see themselves primarily as making a product, whereas process focus organisation see themselves primarily as using a process.

A bottling plant of beverages company has a process focus. A plant that makes bottled apple juice has a product focus. Elite restaurants have a process focus — they cook meals. Pizza outlets have a product focus — they sell pizzas. A telecom company has a product focus, whereas a communication company has a process focus.

The distinction has significant influence on operations. A process focus organisation finds it easier to adjust production if the demand declines. An organisation having stable sales and demand is better organised around the product.

Product Life Cycle (PLC)

Customer demand keeps on changing and that is the main difficulty in product planning. Customers require the woollens in the winter and light clothes in the summer. There was a demand for cordless phones, but these days cell phones have overtaken them. Customers show different consumption patterns – may be due to fashion changes or the new environment. That results in demand fluctuations. Some changes in demand can be explained logically — the demand for pain balms and cough syrups in cold season. A demand pattern can be understood through the product life cycle (PLC) which traces the overall demand pattern from a product's introduction to its phasing out. There are five stages in a typical product life cycle as shown in Fig. 2.1.

(1) Introduction: Here a new product appears on the market. As people have to try it before adopting it for constant use, its demand is low. Blue discs are an example of the newly introduced product.

(2) Growth: Here new customers adopt the product. The demand keeps on rising. Internet banking is an example of a product in the growth stage.

(3) Maturity: Most of the potential customers know about the product and they continue to buy it steadily. Demand stabilizes and remains constant. Colour TVs have shown a stable demand.

(4) Decline: As alternative new products appear on the market, customers take to them, and abandon the older ones. As a result, sales fall. B&W TVs are in decline.

(5) Withdrawal: Demand declines to such a point that it is no longer worth making the product. Telegrams and typewriters are the examples.

The length of the life cycle is different for different products — a daily newspaper has a cycle lasting for a few hours, fashion clothing for a few weeks, consumer durables for a few years, and commodities for a few decades. Some products have extremely short life cycles, and some extremely long ones. Many products tend to remain at the mature stage for several years. Some products decline, and rejuvenate again. A new product life cycle can start again. *e.g.*, cinema attendances fell and then rose again after multiplexes came on the scene.

Fig. 2.1

Stages in a Product Life Cycle (PLC)

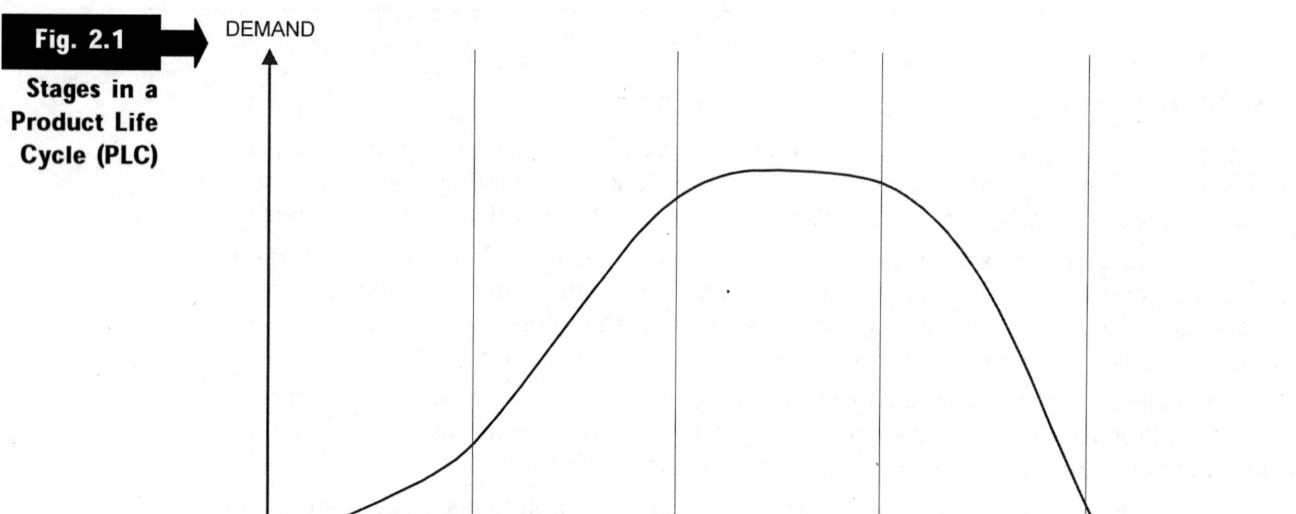

Operations and the Life Cycle

The PLC concept does influence operations:

- products at various stages of their PLC affect the operations and use different types of operations.
- at each stage, the financials of profits, costs and revenues change.
- organisations keep on introducing new products and withdraw the obsolete products.
- organisations make a range of products to smoothen the overall production.

Different Types of Operations During the Life Cycle

To innovate, an R&D department is maintained. The early research inputs are provided by the operations managers. At the introductory stage, the product is new and its demand has yet to build up. The operations are, therefore, small-scale. The initial design undergoes modifications in response to customer feedback. There should be enough flexibility in the operations to accommodate these changes. To build up the market share, a product must be of a specific quality and must follow a delivery schedule.

As product moves to the growth stage after some time, the product design becomes stable. Further improvements in the product are possible through process improvement. The typical change is to move from a manual process to an automatic one. The objective is to meet the demand, and be competitive by maintaining quality and price. Products form the finished product inventory which is used for satisfying orders as an when they come. Demand forecasting thus becomes important. The resources must be planned and scheduled accurately. The sourcing should be streamlined.

The maturity stage product has a stable demand. Production planning becomes routine. Some early competitors are no longer in the market. There are a few competitors who compete on the basis of price. Operations managers aim at cost reduction and efficient production. The process uses more automation and standardisation.

During the decline stage, many vendors drop out of the market. There could be excess capacity. The organisations try to revive the PLC by changing the product design and process. When this is not worthwhile, there would be termination procedures to stop the production.

Financials During the PLC

R&D costs are very heavy for the new products. The newly introduced products have to recover these costs and so they are priced higher. As the initial production runs are smaller, the per unit costs are higher. However, profits are made on account of premium prices. At the growth stage, revenues rise. As fixed costs are recovered, the profits are made. Revenues keep on rising, till the product reaches the maturity stage. Competitors make similar products by now. Demand does not show a surge. The unit price and revenue continue to fall. As product enters the decline stage, the demand is smaller and the capacity is higher. Profits fall. As the company has learnt production efficiency, there is higher productivity which offsets the decline. But as profits and demand continue to fall, the company decides to phase out the product. A company tries to revive the PLC by greater marketing and promotional efforts, finding new uses applications for the products, modifying the products, and entering the new geographical markets.

In electronics, the PLCs are very short. A handset manufacturer of mobiles can keep the prices low by having the best turnaround time, say either 2-3 months. It keeps the overheads low. The longer turnaround time keeps the resources blocked for just one model. It adds to the costs.

Range of Products Made

There are single product organisations where operations are routine and standardised. The employees become skilled. The production runs are long and this reduces equipment set up time. The inventory remains low and manageable. However, as there are customers who want differences in products, organisations make a range of products each of which have a different PLC. The overall demand is thus smooth. A narrow range makes the standard operations possible. A wider range satisfies a large number of customers. However, the organisation loses the efficiency that comes with standardisation.

Organisations do make different products, but they are similar to those they already make but are different enough to create new demands. However, conglomerates can make completely different types of products. *e.g.,* Tata Conglomerate is in the trucks, cars, telecom, steel, finance, chemicals, salt. These areas are organised as distinct businesses and are run independently.

However, the trend is to stick to one's knitting, and concentrate on core competencies. The unrelated businesses are hived off, and only the core businesses are retained.

Operations Strategy

Operations strategy is a package of plans and policies to utilise the resources of the organization to further the long-term competitive strategy. In other words, operations strategy is integrated is the overall corporate strategy. The strategy takes care of the changing environment by suitable adaptation.

Operations strategy touches upon the decisions of the *process design* and the *infrastructure* to sustain the process.

Process design consists of the choice of an appropriate technology, measuring the process over time, locating the process and logistical support of the process. The infrastructure refers to the planning and control systems, quality assurance and control, compensation methods and operations organization.

Operational objectives are correlated to the overall organizational objectives. Since the overall objectives change in response to the changing environment, so does the operational objectives.

Most of the US firms post-war were volume-driven to satisfy a large demand, whereas the Japanese firms were quality-driven. As such, we can say, priorities do change in formulating the operations strategy from country to country, and firm to firm. We have to appreciate the priorities and their consequences and the trade-offs involved.

The priorities generally include cost, quality, reliability, delivery speed, new product introduction speed and other criteria.

It should be appreciated that an operation could not excel at one and the same time on all performance measures, and hence the management changes the performance criteria critical to the success of the organization and concentrates its resources on these.

To illustrate, an organization committed to speedy delivery may compromise on product variety. A low-cost organization may not offer a premium quality. There are thus trade-offs of cost and quality.

An organization can have a plant within a plant where each facility carries separate product lines and unique operations strategy.

In these days of globalisation, there are companies who excel internationally and are called world-class manufacturers. They adopt a global perspective towards both operations and marketing.

The most important priorities for survival in business are conformance quality, product reliability and delivery dependability. The other priorities in 90s include low price, fast delivery, performance quality and speed to introduce new products. In the 90s, innovativeness and price-consciousness have acquired added importance.

These days customers want to derive *value* which means buying different benefits a product offers as against the cost thereof. Value improves when benefits are increased or cost is lowered or do both.

An organization has to identify its operations capability (producing right-hand or left-hand drive cars) and core capabilities or competencies. Core capabilities distinguish a firm from its competitors.

Product Selection

Conversion of inputs into outputs by adding value to them makes operations management an important function. Though the conversion process is taking place internally, the value added by it to products and services is perceived outside in the market by the consumers. Therefore, the operations manager has to be outward-oriented, conscious of consumer needs rather than inward-oriented, placing emphasis on the production process only.

To begin with, we talked of products and services. But these days the term product is used in a very comprehensive sense and includes services also. In fact a product is considered as a bundle of benefits that it offers to the customers. Thus a lipstick is not only a combination of a few chemicals, but is something that imparts beauty to the customers. Similarly, a tonic is not a mix of some vitamins, but something that promises health to an invalid, indisposed person. When products are thought of so broadly in terms of customer benefits, several services also become a part of products. Thus, when a computer is sold, we also sell a solution to customer, to his problem of handling data for information needs. Thus, it involves systems analysis and design, the hardware of adequate computing power, the software packages to help the customer for his information needs, the installation of the system and its maintenance as an after sales service. Part of the product is tangible, and part of it is in the form of intangible services. Similarly, a service centre like an orthopaedic hospital sells medical care and tangible products like artificial limbs. Thus, to a customer, a product is a bundle of benefits, a solution to his specific problems.

The above discussion points out the importance of deciding correct definitions of our products and organizational missions, which give a strategic dimension to our output selection decision. Thus when we say we are in the entertainment business, we not only think in terms of producing movies only, but also video-movies if the customer demands them for his entertainment needs.

Product mix is a selection of products we desire to produce, keeping our business mission in mind. It is a strategic decision. While deciding our product mix, we take into account our marketing and technological strengths, the potential demand, the history and traditions of our organization and the financial capability we have. Competition also shapes our product mix decision. Product selection is not a decision that could be taken by the operations management department alone, but requires interface with departments like marketing, finance, research and development, materials etc. It involves participation and support of the top management.

Once a product mix is chosen, we have to pay attention to the economics of producing each product, the design of the individual product, the quality and reliability of the products intended to be produced. We also consider *producibility* which means the ease and the speed with which the output can be generated. This is closely related to the plant and machinery and its sophistication level, engineering operations necessary, and flexibility with which we can adapt the facilities from producing one product to another product. Of course it is easier always to create a family of similar products. Dissimilar products may need creation of either facilities *de novo* entirely or in some sub-processes.

Main Factors to be Considered in Product Selection, Development and Design

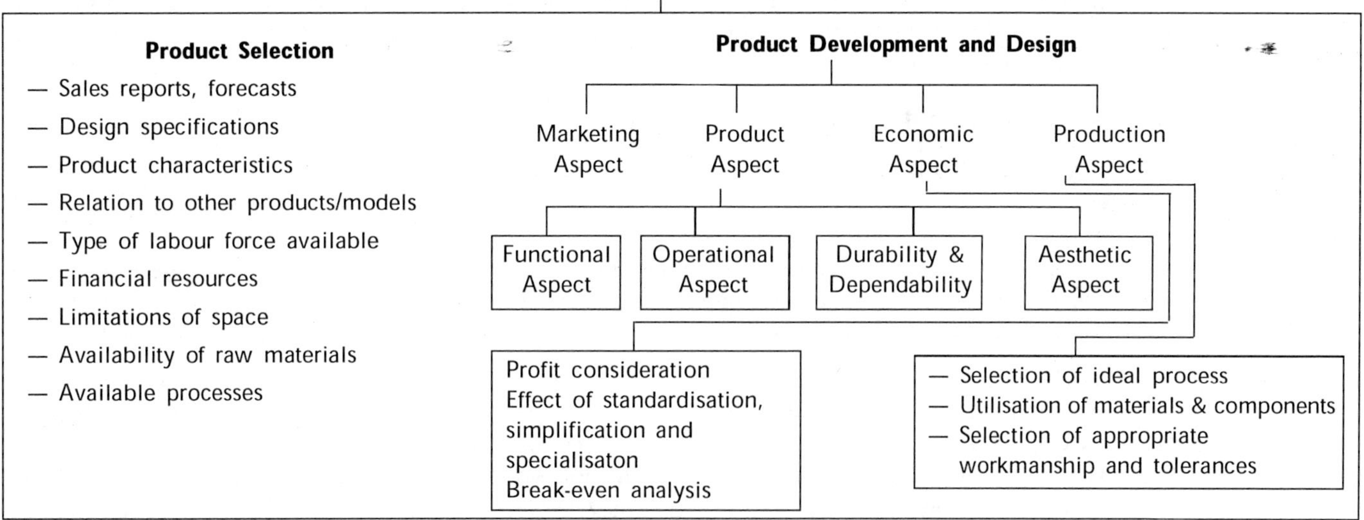

Product Selection Process

It is a part of product planning process which is a continuous activity in an organization involving marking out and supervising the search, screening, development and commercialisation of new products; the modification of existing lines and phasing out of the marginal or unprofitable lines. The most important part in product selection process is that of idea generation. Each new product, and this includes modification of an existing product, is developed from an idea. These ideas come from many sources. They come from unorganized sources like the wife of a chairman or for that matter even a salesman. They come on golf courses, at cocktail parties, in cafes and accidentally. The ideas may come from organized sources through consumers, scientists and technologists, research laboratories etc. They come in other words through pure and applied research. The ideas are also generated by the competitors, salesmen and distributors, consultants, bankers, patent office and foreign sources. These are special techniques of idea generation like attribute listing method, morphological analysis, brainstorming sessions, Delphi method and problem inventory analysis. The following diagram makes this discussion clear:

Ideas are not immediately converted into new products as shown in the above diagram. They are subjected to a screening process first.

Screening means critical evaluation of product ideas to select those that are suitable and viable and to reject others. The product ideas should satisfy consumer needs, sales volume criteria, profitability criteria, and company image criteria. They should be consistent with the overall marketing objectives

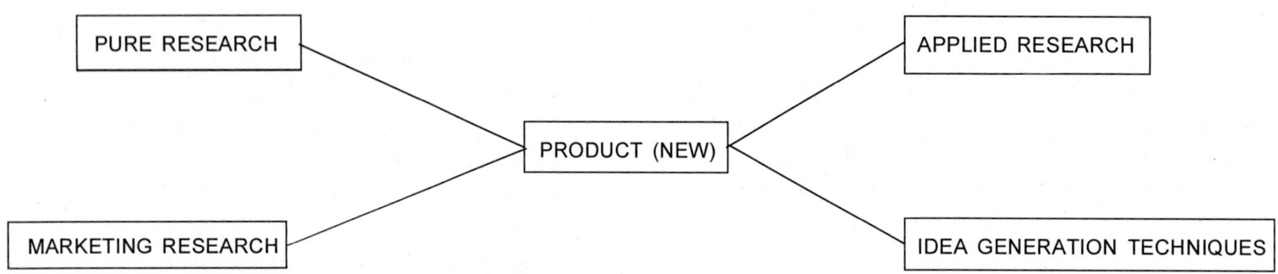

and organizational objectives of the company. Screening is done by check-list method, rating method of different kinds. Once the screening is over, we undertake a detailed business analysis of the ideas. Mostly this is financial analysis consisting of break-even analysis, cash flow (discounted) analysis, Bayesian Decision Theory and Risk Analysis.

Product development is the next stage at which the product idea takes a concrete shape, with all the attributes which the consumers desire it to possess. First, of course, on a small-scale, a prototype is developed. This is preceded by careful engineering aspects like development of drawings and designs or laboratory compounds. The prototype is so developed till it comes close to consumer preferences. Product development thus includes both process development and design and testing. Later it is test marketed and commercialised.

New Idea Mortality Curve

As you have learnt, each product idea has to cross several hurdles before commercialisation. At any stage, we have to abandon following the further stages of new product development. It is a 'go' -'no go' type of decision at each stage. The product idea mortality curve is a graphical representation of this simple principle. We start with a number of ideas. Initial screening itself reduces them by almost half or even less than that. Business analysis leaves us with some 3-4 ideas to be worked out further into a prototype. Further development reduces them till finally only a single product is left.

You will appreciate that there is a time lag between the start of development process and the final national launch of the product. The time lag depends upon the type of industry and the product, and may vary from 1 to 8 years. If the time lag is excessive, competitors may in the meantime launch their products or the product may become irrelevant when it finally sees the light of the day. Even undue haste may result in product failures. The time therefore should be optimal under given conditions. Each developmental stage costs us in terms of money and other resources. So when the product is finally in the market, the market has to bear this developmental cost. Many organizations work simultaneously on different product propositions and may be at different stages of development. Thus when some product ideas are generated and screened, another set of ideas might have reached prototype stage, and yet another set of ideas might have reached the commercialisation stage. This is a sign of an innovative organization, where product development is a continuous process. The students may kindly note that the few successful products have to absorb even the cost of their less fortunate brothers — the unsuccessful products.

Product development continues after the commercial introduction of the product throughout its life-cycle consisting of the stages of introduction, growth, maturity, and decline. Modifications and extensions at the stage of maturity in case of existing products lengthen the product life cycle, and prevent its decline. Of course, an organization also modifies the me-too products introduced by others as a part of developmental effort. On the innovative scale, the extreme point is that of a major technological breakthrough like the introduction of nylon, transistor, micro-processor, radio-transmission, laser, lithotripsy for kidney and gall-stones, oral polio vaccine etc. Such breakthroughs may bring about an altogether new industry. We await now major breakthroughs in the field of genetic engineering and bio-technology, super-conductivity, cancer therapy, AIDS therapy, organ transplants etc. All this is a result of basic and applied research, and later on development on commercial scale. There is a major thrust to technology advancement in recent years, and we are all in for a future shock. What is more important? Research or development? Perhaps, the decision is a trade-off and is a strategic decision.

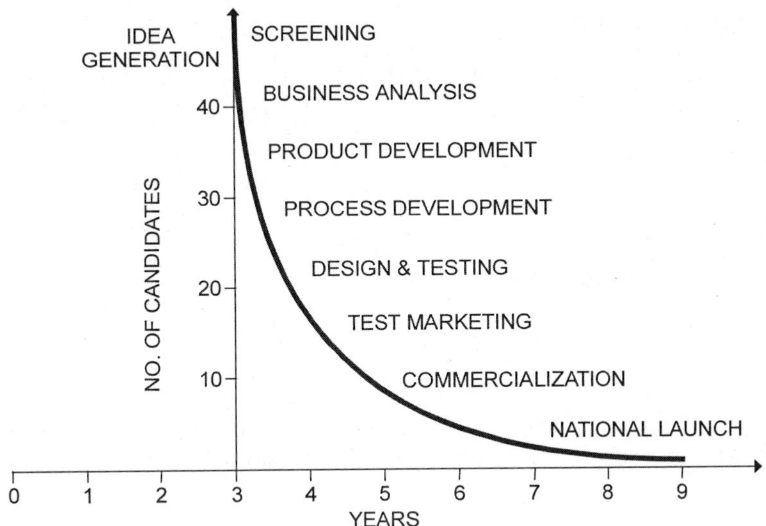

Fig. 2.2 **Product Idea Mortality Curve (After Meredith and Gibbs, 1984)**

Product Development

Product development has three components — developing new products, modifying existing products to meet the changing requirements of the consumers, and streamlining the product line by adding/ deleting the products to maintain profitability of the organisation.

Product development supplies the market with those products that satisfies its needs and wants, at the right time, and at right prices which cover the costs and leave a margin for the organisation.

Definition of an Innovation

Raghunath Anant Mashelkar defines innovation as 'the successful exploitation of a new idea.' The new idea could be new here in India or new abroad. Exploitation involves the actual use of the idea by the end customer. The idea must move to the field. The word successful indicates three factors — speed, scale and sustainability. The idea must move quickly from mind to market place. The innovation must sustain on its own — without any props or subsidies.

Innovation Culture

According to R.A. Mashelkar, the innovation culture must be promoted in India by believing that the 'I' in India stands for 'innovation'. Secondly, innovation must be directed to the national goal of inclusive growth by creating 'access equality' despite the 'income inequality'. Thirdly, the Indian innovation must move quickly from mind to market place. There are bottlenecks here. We must recognise that research labs need funding, and produce output. They thus convert money into knowledge. The real challenge comes after the research output is available again for conversion into money. Thus, we have to create monetisable knowledge. The skills in patenting too must be mastered. Fourthly, we must recognise the innovative potential of each Indian. Fifthly, we must build a national innovation ecosystem.

Introduction of New Products

A company has an existing line of products which is improved on a continuous basis to revive the products and to stimulate demand. However, in order to meet the competition effectively and stimulate further growth of the company, new products are introduced for which different ideas are explored. Here the company takes the advantage of the existing research elsewhere, or in-house, and the special skills available with the company. New products also satisfy the new requirements of the customers.

Developing New Products

New product development, as we have already observed, has six stages:

(*i*) generation of ideas
(*ii*) initial screening of ideas
(*iii*) technical evaluation
(*iv*) commercial evaluation
(*v*) final product development
(*vi*) launch of the product.

Generation of Ideas

Organisation search for business opportunities and ideas from the environment and from within the organisation. There are idea generation techniques like brainstorming which can be used to generate ideas.

Initial Screening of Ideas

As we have observed already, the ideas are screened to reject those which have flaws. Some ideas are not feasible. Some have been tried already, but have proved to be unsuccessful. Some ideas are beyond the organisation's present capabilities. Some ideas are similar to an already existing product. Ideas may not fit into the current operations. They may not have a good market potential. Some ideas are too risky, or financially unviable.

Technical Evaluation

Ideas after initial screening are converted into concepts and then tested. The usual considerations are whether the concept can be converted into a product. The legal and safety considerations are also taken into account. The technical feasibility of the proposed design, the producibility with available technology, the compatibility with current operations and the competence available to convert it into a product — all these considerations are examined.

A prototype is then made, and its trial is taken. It can be modified in the light of these trials. The process design is also considered.

Commercial Evaluation

Market and financial feasibility is studied. The projected profit and loss account is made. If the product is promising, further development is continued. The technical and commercial evaluation together form feasibility study.

Final Product Development

Those products which pass the feasibility test move to the design and testing stage. The final designs are made by using inputs from customer surveys and other relevant information. This stage gives the product offering meant for the consumer. It also spells out the process to be used to make the product.

Launch of the Product

Once the product and process designs are finalised, the product is ready for launching. The launch timing is considered carefully. It could be a national launch or a selective limited launch.

As we have seen, very few initial ideas survive all the stage — hardly 1-2 per cent.

Even after launch, very few ideas become successful products.

The whole process of product development has been treated in detail in an appendix at the end of the chapter.

PRODUCT DEVELOPMENT AND DESIGN

An organization has to survive in the fast changing and turbulent environment. The needs and expectations of the consumers must be met by introducing the relevant and innovative products. Product development is a continuous activity and is a link between the market and the production department. A product emerges as an idea which is developed into a concept. The concept is converted by suitable engineering into a prototype. The prototype is further improved by interacting with the process. The pilot production is the next step. The process is further refined and finally commercially the product is launched.

The development process is speeded by concurrent engineering (CE) which takes several steps simultaneously rather than in sequential form.

Product development team has to take care of the design, management and technical aspects.

Product design has to respond to the requirements of the customers. Many products have features which are never used by the customers. The customer and aesthetic-centred design is called *industrial design*.

Customer requirements can be ranked in the order of importance. Competitive product and the organization's product are compared. Technical specifications are developed. These should be related to the customers' requirements. This approach to involve the customer into design specification is called quality function deployment (QFD).

Reverse Innovation

Vijay Govindarajan, Tuck Centre for Global Leadership is an expert on strategy and innovation. He has written with Chris Thimble a book on reverse innovation. Traditionally, innovations have flowed from the rich countries to the poor ones. If they flow in the opposite direction from the poor countries to the rich, it is called reverse innovation. The term has been coined by Chris Thimble. In the first chapter of the book, an example of Gatorade has been cited as one of reverse innovation. The present day Bangladesh and the then East Pakistan had a cholera epidemic in the 1960s. The diarrhoea resulting from a cholera was treated by a drink containing carbs — coconut water, carrot juice, rice water, carb flour, dehydrated bananas. The Western opinion was not in favour of carbs as they were likely to multiply the cholera microbes. The absorption of carbs was quicker, and it rehydrated the patients. *Lancet* covered the treatment. A doctor at University of Florida took notice, and extended the treatment to football players. The concoction contained water, glucose, sodium, potassium and flavours. It replenished the electrolyte balance disturbed by sweating. The preparation was given the name Gatorade after the team's name — Florida Gators. Similarly chicken tikka masala travelled from India to the UK in 1990s. Yoga has similarly travelled to several countries abroad. There is a huge customer base in the poor countries. Here the companies can spot opportunities to innovate. Aliva introduced by Pepsi in India could travel to markets abroad. China has developed portable ultra-sound machine. A customised tractor for small plots of agricultural land has been developed. Narayana Hrudayalaya Hospital performs a worldclass open heart surgery for just $ 2000, and this has the potential to become a reverse innovation. Mahindra's tractors for small farms are being sold as hobby farming tractors in the US.

Product Design

In the development of the product, the design stage is the most crucial. Detailed specifications are listed for a product at this stage. These specifications ultimately result in product quality. The product's design is translated in quantitative terms here. Compiling specification is not an easy task. It requires a great deal of time. The profitability and competitiveness of the product depend upon its design which in turn depends upon specifications. And so specifications should be carefully developed. Properly formulated specifications have the potential of controlling costs at the design stage. The task of setting specifications is done in the face of sometimes conflicting views of different departments like sales, engineering and production. We cannot over-specify as well as under specify. We have also to ensure smoothness of the production line. Specifications are therefore clear and explicit, and preferably written.

Generally specifications are prepared by a multi-dimensional committee (consisting of the design engineers, the purchase officer, the marketing executive, the quality control executive etc.). Only after the approval of the committee, the design is finalised. In case of most widely used and highly competitive products, standard specifications are available. Drugs and pharmaceutical industry always falls in line with standard specifications given in official books like I.P., B.P., U.S.P., USSRP, BPC, N.F. etc. Specifications are technical type or performance type specifications. Sometimes specifications take the form of a blueprint, describing an item of special design, with descriptions of castings, forgings, tooling, machining etc. accurately. Specifications are frequently reviewed, considering the technological developments and marketing considerations.

The design field is primarily divided in two areas — industrial design and communication design. Industrial design covers product design, furniture design, and interior design. Engineers (mechanical) are suited for product design or transportation design. Architects are suited for furniture and interior design. Communication design covers graphics, animation, film and video design covering print/TV media. It generally caters to the field of advertising and promotion. Fine arts graduates are suited for this field. Communication design is further expanded to cover user interface design and new media design. Communication design applied no fashion industry is known as fashion communication. Product design applied to fashion industry is known as life style accessory design.

John Kenneth Galbraith on Design (November, 1978)

"India's great past skill has been in design. It was the design and the quality of Indian textile, and today the design and quality of Indian fabrics that gives India access to the world markets. We live in a time when the artist is probably more important than the engineer. The world market belongs not to the most technically accomplished goods but to the most appealing goods. After things work reasonably well, people are more interested in how they look. The great industrial success after World War II has been Italy, not because Italian technology is the best in the world, but because Italian design is the best in the world. Italy has had a better record than Germany."

Steve Jobs at Apple not only made great products, but made them beautifully just like the Italians. The Vespa scooter is a pleasure to ride and the Fiat car pleasure to drive. Ferragama shoes are a pleasure to wear. Steve jobs also focussed along with Jonathan Ive, the VP, Industrial Design to execute techno-art noeau zeal for each Apple product. Jonathan Ive was described as the "Armani of Apple" in a 2002 BBC profile. He is also called the 'spiritual partner' of Steve Jobs. As a technologist, Steve Jobs was different because he was not an engineer. It was his great strength. He was obsessed with product design and aesthetics. He made advanced technology simple to use. He took an existing half-formed idea and developed it properly, *e.g.*, the mouse-driven computer, the digital music player, the smartphone and the tablet computer.

Design

Design is an integral part of nature seen in the process of evolution where survival depended not only fitness but also on adaptation in terms of design. Frogs have some 3000 species, and they match their colour to their surroundings.

Though Dreyfuss made design popular in the US in the last century, design is woven informally into civilisation since long. Design came to be recognised as a discipline in the last 100 years. There are two reasons — technological advances occurred in the 19th century, and they were put to use by smart design. *e.g.*, rotary dial phones and toasters. A whole range of household products were designed in the first 20 years of the 20th century. Most all applications were made by adapting electricity to different uses. Design thus remained a handmaiden of technology.

Mass production and mass distribution made it necessary to bring the design element in the process of mass production itself to make it easier. Design along with production and marketing formed a trio of the modern business.

Design and manufacturing went hand-in-hand for nearly half the century. In 50s, Japan focussed extensively on design. Japanese companies were not only great manufacturing giants, they were good designers too *e.g.,* Sony, Toyota and Matsushita. Later in 80s, Korea improved its design capabilities. Recently, China has started concentrating on design.

If India is to get her place in the industrial world, she has to pay attention to her design capabilities. Indian companies like Tata Motors, Mahindra and Mahindra and the Hero group have become design conscious. India lags behind in machine tools as she is low on design consciousness.

Design has become a differentiator. Chrysler turned around its fortunes with a series of winning designs. Symphony in India put very good designs in the staid air-cooler market.

Design movement is still nascent in India. Capital equipment makers have started getting orders on the strength of their designs. One emerging area is interface design, essentially the skill of making customer interaction with technology pleasant. *Business World* and National Institute of Design (NID) have instituted Design Excellence Awards.

Design of capital equipment is perhaps the least sexy field in this discipline. It is a part of industrial design. The glamorous face of industrial design is the modelling of cars. Designers are responsible for skin-thin slimmest watches. Even interiors of the stores like Cafe Coffee invite the skills of a designer. Each designer has own style. A simple but sophisticated style is desirable. A design must also satisfy the future aspirations. A design should bestow a competitive edge to the product. As industrial design must find solutions for the masses, they are evaluated in terms of the impact they have. A designer must have the ability to mix and match to find interesting solutions. A design must not only look good, but it must work well too. A designer has to study materials which go to make a product.

Concept design is another hot area — a breakthrough concept that can be manufactured, can always be a potential best-seller. A lot of time is spent on stretching working on the renderings and visualising products. Indica has been indigenously designed. Kinetic Nova scooter is a two-wheeler designed in India. The design objective was to create a four-stroke gearless scooter with a target price of ₹ 35,000.

Though we are advised not to judge the book by its cover, yet most of us are swayed by the packaging of a product. In the cluttered market, innovative packaging is the only way to stand out. Packaging design is an important area.

Design should push the frontiers of technology, not follow it. It can change the quality of life. Good design is good business. It becomes the deciding factor for consumer choice. Before the product is developed, user research is conducted by multi-disciplinary teams who observe and interpret the everyday experience of target consumers from different vantage points. The team then identifies core motivations and aspirations behind the use of products. This understanding helps define the user-experience criteria for design. Participatory design (PD) is another approach that is receiving attention. Here end-users are involved in the design. Apart from PD, consumers are invited to project future experiences they desire to have within the environment in which a product is used, *e.g.,* ideas of ideal cooking experiences of the future. They can articulate their ideas through collage or blocks. Internal manpower also undertakes such studies. The ideas are later integrated. The design criteria of consumers' needs for desired experience around a product are synchronised with the company's vision and future profitability.

APPLE'S CELEBRATED DESIGN TEAM

Apple's celebrated design team is a group of around 16 'maniacal' individuals from all over the world who spends a lot of time brainstorming around a kitchen table. iPhone and iPad design features owes a great debt to creative guru Jonathan Ive and has cadre of designers assembled from Britain, Australia, the US, Japan, Germany over more than a decade. Their role is to imagine products that do not exist and guide them to life. Ive's team works out of a large, open studio on Apple's campus in Cupertino, California. Over the years, the team earned a reputation for blending the aesthetically appealing with the functional. Once a product design idea is solidified through a brainstorming session, the design team sketches those ideas and models it through a Computer Aided Design process

XUV 500 Design

A sports utility vehicle traditionally looks muscular with monstrous silhouettes and beefy grilles. It is a sign of ruggedness. This ruggedness is juxtaposed with subtle creases and deft touches by a woman designer Ramkripa Ananthan (40), heading the 20-member styling team, that worked on the XUV500. She is 'out-of-doors' type personality devoted to trekking and researching in the wilderness of Kenya and on the Masai Mara to get inspired for the exteriors and interiors for this SUV.

MAHINDRA AND MAHINDRA SUV DESIGN PLAN

Pawan Goenka led the design team at M&M resulting into the successful launch of an SUV — Scorpio. Abraham Joseph developed the engine for the Pulsar motorbike of Bajaj Auto. Rajan Wadhera is the lynchpin of Nano from Tata Motors. All these are gamechanging products. They are now collaborating to launch an SUV in the global market codenamed W201 and branded XUV500 read as XUV five double OL. It will be launched in South Africa and Western Europe, priced between ₹12 lac and ₹ 14 lac. It will be manufactured at Chakan plant, Pune. It will have monocoque (or unibody) design. All Mahindra UVs are body-on-frame vehicles, whereas the monocoque body is technologically superior. It is the most sophisticated SUV Mahindra has developed and it could be the next big thing after Scorpio.

The vehicle has been given a taut fender pounce, lean body and distinctive rear haunch. The design should reflect the global trend of 'feeling the power.' Amongst the various concepts, the cheetah metaphor influenced the team. It is an edgy design language and not machine-like. It avoids the conservative boxy or rounded shape. The team worked on a different exterior concepts and 17 interior concepts. Some of these concepts are translated into prototypes. For the interiors, the bright centre console seemingly flows from outside-in which makes a connect like the CNS of a beast. According to her, design is a feeling. It is a raw emotion. It has to show the skill sets of balance, proportion and conviction, She has also worked on the designs of Bolero, Scorpio and Xylo. She is a mechanical engineer from BITS-Pilani and a PG in Industrial Design from IIT-B. She joined M&M in 1997.

Companies operating globally introduced new products into emerging markets by selling products past their prime in developed markets while tinkering with them only cosmetically. To them it is an asset amortisation process. But these days such a simple approach may not work. Indigenous ideas must be integrated into the design conceptualisation process to satisfy the unique needs of these markets by developing customers' solutions.

A well engineered product provides a great customer experience. Add great design and it becomes an amazing customer experience. According to Steve Jobs, some people think design means how the product looks. However, if you dig deeper, it really means how the product works. In most people's vocabularies, design means veneer. It is the interior decorating. It is the fabric of the curtains and the sofa. But to Steve Jobs, nothing could be further from the meaning of design. Design is the soul of a man-made creation that expresses itself in successive layers of product. Design establishes the relationship between the company and the customers. The complete design incorporates what customers see, interact with and come in contact with. In fact, all things they experience about the company and use to form their opinions, and to create desire for the products. These touch points are not allowed to just happen. They must be designed and co-ordinated. Design also has an emotional side. It is good to have Indian design. We can make people spend more on the basis of design. Design can be a marketing and profit driving tool. According to Harry Cheng, Chief Operating Officer of Basco's, there is a lot of commonality between Indian and Japanese designs. Their spiritualities are tied together on the basis of Buddhism. Design can cost money, yet add value so much so that the consumer is motivated to buy the product. Indian design does not have its own identity. It has never recognised design as an important factor for products. Indian brands need to learn a lot on packaging.

Product design translates a product concept into tangible form by using different techniques. A concept is developed systematically and methodically. It is a balance of art, science and technology.

Most of the times an industrial design is considered a product design. Industrial design is an outcome of the product development process. It is mostly concerned with machining. It is more related to mechanism or working of the product. Product design is an outcome of the production process. It takes into account the end uses of the product and the nature of the product.

The concept could be based on necessity. It could be based on the needs of the consumers. It is further researched. It is subjected to technology. It takes into account ergonomics. The design could be user-based.

Product design is a team work that receives inputs from several experts.

Innovators may create designs that people come to accept. Steve Jobs believed that people are not expected to know what they want.

Interface Design

We access so many features from our cell phones conveniently and efficiently. The interface between a human being and a machine is a fascinating subject. It has spawned new superspecialisations like usability engineering. Interface design pertains to websites and technical products with embedded software. An interface designer solves the problem from a user's perspective — he could be a designer, or an artist or an engineer and a cognitive psychologist or a language specialist. India has good software code writing skills. But she requires interface design skills where software meets the users. Microsoft today employs 300 interface designers.

Design Movements Across the Globe

The following table summarises the design movements across the globe:

Country	***Type of Movement***	***Description***
Italy	Neo-modernism	Ornate, art and craft. Up-to-date styles of living. Irony, kitsch, strong colours and distortions of scale to undermine purely functional value. Elegance and good taste.
Germany	Bauhaus (1919)	Simplicity, straight edges and smooth forms. Steel as material for furniture. The Bauhaus went to the US after the Nazi's shut down the school. Technology — key to modernism.
Finland	Functional	Functionalism dominant. Clean sophistication that we now associate with Scandinavia.
Britain	Innovation-led design Creative workshop	The Royal College of Art was founded in 1837.
The USA	Modernists	Adopted Bauhaus School. Cleanliness, geometric forms and machined finishes. Autos reflect their philosophy — large and powerful.
Japan	Technology-led	Japan was virtually rebuilt after 1945. Delicacy and miniaturization. 'Retro' movement.
Korea	Aspiring leaders in design	Strong Japanese influence. Western aesthetic values.
India	New awakening	NID was set up in 1961. Graphic design, communication design, textile and fashion design. Liberalisation has brought an awakening about design, *e.g.*, Pulsar range of bikes from Bajaj and Titan Edge — the World's slimmest watch.

Product Design: Important Considerations

There are two apparently conflicting considerations that affect the product designing. We can standardise the products and improve the ease of their manufacture. On the other hand, we can offer a variety of products to meet different kinds of customers and their differing needs. There is a trade-off involved here.

When you buy a new electric bulb, you know it will screw into the socket all right, because the bulbs are standardized. There are only a few kinds of bases made. Standard is the word that denotes that there are only specific sizes made and sold. Some people call the process of cutting down on the number of sizes 'simplification.' Standardization, they say is the process of writing down the size, shape, performance and other attributes of the items you decide to concentrate on. The two concepts are closely related.

Standardization (including simplification) means that non-standard items will not be made except when the customer orders them specially, places a high order, and pays extra for non-standard items.

Sometimes standards have been enacted into law for safety or for health reasons. Mostly, though standardization is voluntary, industry wide standardization requires industry-wide co-operation.

Standardization reduces the kinds, types and sizes of raw materials that have to be bought. This lets you buy and so get lower prices per unit. Standardization also cuts down on your manufacturing costs because you get longer runs on the fewer kinds of products that you still make. You can cut set-up costs and use more specialised machines. You also need fewer patterns and tools. We would always be reordering larger quantities of fewer things and so holding down manufacturing costs.

In the markets, there is a demand for low volumes, and high variety. In such a situation, rigid standardisation is not the solution. The right approach could be to design a range of products that share parts, people and production processes.

New Thinking on Design

Karim Rashid, a prolific designer, who attended the India Design Forum in 2012 spoke about the change in design industry from designing for mass production to elitism to going back to a 'designocracy' as we are beginning to witness now. Rashid fails to appreciate sentimental design, *e.g.*, a restaurant serves innovative food, but makes you seat on a 16th century European chair. He is for beautiful objects that make our lives a simpler. Rashid created a bathing luxury — all in one TV-tub unit made of acrylic resin with a waterproof LCD-screen that allows you to watch TV and DVDs and listen to MP3 format music and surf the net. According to him, contemporary design has the power to shape the future. The role of a designer today is to make the world a better place by influencing our everyday behaviour — functionally and in everyday life. His best designs function both as sculptural and functional objects. Gaston Bachelard, a philosopher, called all objects obstacles in our experience of the world. Rashid evokes him and says that indeed we are living in a poorly designed world.

According to Lidewij Edelkoort, a trend forecaster, India urgently needs to create its own design language. Contemporary Indian design has completely distanced itself from the past. Design schools should take on this task.

International design moves along the continuum of lush-and-plush (Versace) to clean-and-simple (Apple). The extreme of less-is-more has found favour in recent times. Design itself has been used as a strategy by Steve Dieter Rams now 80 (2012), a German designer who wrote *As Little Design As Possible* and put forward the maxim good design is as little design as possible. It stands in sharp contrast to the complex and cluttered Indian design. We focus more on embellishment and less on functionality. A good design is holistic. It is balanced.

In India, we speak about designer dresses or sunglasses to distinguish these from overproduced banality. Design here defines consumer life style. Design makes the products desirable.

Modular Design

In order to get perceived variety or variety, designers resort to modular construction. Products are made mostly out of easily detachable sub-assemblies or sections. When an item fails they take out the whole component of which it is a part, and put in a new component. Later they can repair the removed unit or throw it away. Modular design is used extensively in computers. Besides different combinations of modules give a new variety of products. For instance, four dial shapes, four different colours, two dial movements and two dial sizes for each shape gives us 4 × 4 × 2 × 2 ×, *i.e.*, 64 varieties of wrist watches, still making some standard modules in large volumes.

Form and Functional Design

Product design deals with form and function. Form design deals with the product's shape and appearance. Functional design deals with how it works or performs. The need for functional design is obvious — the product has to work or it is useless. But how necessary is form design? When customers have no basis of functions, the eye appeal wins. Even machinery makers pay attention to form design, though functional utility is still uppermost. In most situations, it is a trade off between form and function.

Design and Production Costs

In designing products, we should keep in mind the production costs. Sometimes initial designs cost more to produce than the market can bear. It needs redesigning so that it costs less to produce. May be we will have to compromise quality in order to get costs down. It means exploring the sales possibilities of the low prices and lower quality product.

Design for Volume Production

Mass-produced items need to be designed so that they can be made at low cost. Products, sub-assemblies and parts are first designed so that they will perform. Then the possibilities of cost reduction and elimination are examined without affecting the functional utility.

Parts are so designed that they can be put on the machines for processing quickly. The sequence of operations should be integrated, if possible. Quality and speed is built into tools. Sub-assemblies are used for assembled products wherever possible.

Precision of parts is of utmost importance for high volume products.

Repairability

Easy repair is important in product design. Too much obsession with appearance sometimes comes in the way of easy repairs.

Redesign

Each product made can be improved by re-designing. Frequent redesigns are however avoided. There is however no constant design. Changes in design over a period of time are inevitable.

Miniaturization

More eloquently condenses the philosophy of miniaturization. An army expression says: 'If your product is room-size, make it desk-size; if it is desk-size make it portable. When you can't shrink it any more, pack twice as much power into it.' For industry in general we can say: "Make it smaller and lighter in weight."

Lap-top computers and palm pilot PCs are examples of miniaturization. Palm V succeeds Palm III, the earlier model. It costs around $450. It uses a rechargeable battery, which lasts about 21 hours between two charges.

Yet it isn't always so. Not everyone has to miniaturize. A half-size bed isn't much good to a full-sized person. And a desk has to stay desk-size and a book, book-size. Typewriter and calculators cannot be made smaller beyond a certain extent, or else we won't be able to use them.

But even where you can't miniaturize the whole product, it may be paying to miniaturize the parts. Miniaturization is very important in electronics.

Miniaturization is partly design and partly research. No one could make a finger nail-size hearing aid, for example, until germanium came out of research. The miniature products using germanium had to be developed, and finally, they had to be incorporated into the hearing aids.

Miniaturization always results in using less material (but it may be more expensive material). Saving space and weight is the main idea, particularly in air planes, space rockets, automation components and instrumentation.

There is more and more miniaturization on account of the developing science of micro-electronics. The revolution dates back to 1947 when transistor was developed as a major component in the micro-electronic circuit. Some 15 years ago, the dimension of a transistor was one micron (millionth of a metre. A single hair is 50 microns wide). It has since then reduced to 10th of that. We now speak in terms of nanos (a billionth of a metre, 10 times the size of an atom). Since the devices depend on the flow of electrons, the smaller they are, the lesser is the travelling distance, and the better they work.

Computer chips now have more capability due to reduced sizes. The photolithography process uses a laser beam (or electron beam). The sharper the beam, the finer the components. More is packed in a given surface.

We can build certain devices atom-by-atom. The STM: Scanning, Tunelling Microscope is compact but powerful enough to see an atom. It can examine surfaces, like that of a silicon, at atomic level. STM is also used as a showel to pick up clumps of silicon atoms and move them to another site.

Molecular Man

IBM scientists made a *molecular man* by spraying molecules of CO onto a platinum surface and then dragging them into shape using the STM tip. The molecular man was 20 atoms wide. (To surround a single strand of hair, 1,00,000 such men will be needed).

Further Miniaturization

IC's will shrink further as a result of this experiment. They will shrink further by 500 times. Nano-structures can be built atom by atom. Intel's latest chips are just 22 nanometres wide, not far off from the point where the rules of classical physics no longer apply. Ten nanometres is the absolute limit for transistor miniaturization — any smaller and you are getting close to the atomic level, where non-classical effects arise. Stacking chips will provide a third dimension for growth for some years to come. Molecular-sized nano-machines can be created to carry out repairs and do genetic engineering in human body.

Novel Materials and Quantum Effects

There is a possibility of making novel materials using quantum effects.

Further Applications

(*i*) quantum computer, much more powerful than the existing ones.
(*ii*) quantum sized particles for dirty tasks like decomposing toxic gases.
(*iii*) quantum particles for optical properties like night vision.
(*iv*) quantum particles to substitute silver halide in photographic film.
(*v*) optical switches in optical computers.

Design by Computers

Computers are doing both the calculating operations required in the design work and the actual making of engineering drawings. General Electric uses computers to design electric motors. GM uses them in automobile design. Air plane companies use them to compute the contours of the wings and to layout electronic circuits.

The key elements are thus function, cost, quality and reliability. Other elements that affect the design are appearance, safety, repairability, environmental impact, timing and accessibility.

These considerations sometimes require a trade-off. Marketing considerations like segmentation lead to specialised product versions (different TV sets from one manufacturer.)

Preferred Numbers

Many products can be made in a continuous series of sizes, from very small to extremely large, but to them such a series would be impractical. Electric light bulbs, motors, clothing, shoes, packaged food, tin cans, and many other items can be made in very small or very large sizes and in any number of in between sizes. Manufacturers of such products must decide upon certain particular sizes. Only in this way can enough volume be concentrated in particular sizes to permit economical manufacture and sale. Today the makers of the products listed above, and many others, make most of their products only in standard sizes.

Generally a geometric progression of size differences (1, 2, 4, 8, 16 etc.) is more satisfactory to customers, and meets their needs better, than an arithmetic progression (5, 10, 15, 20 etc.).

Institutes of Design

NID is a premier design training institution at Ahmedabad. It offers diploma courses in industrial design. Students first join a foundation course of two years, followed by a specialisation in textile design, product design, furniture design, ceramic design, graphic design. These days even IITs have included industrial design in their curricula. Symbiosis Institute of Design (SID), Viman Nagar, Pune offers Bachelor of Design (B.Des) courses in communication, product and fashion design. They also offer a course in fashion communication. MAEER's set up MIT Institute of Design at Rajbaug, next to Hapsar, Lonikalbhor, Pune that runs courses in transportation design, product design, inerior spaces, equipment design, graphics design, animation design, retail and exhibition design, film and video design and user experience design.

Industrial Design Centre (IDC)

The Central Government set up Industrial Design Centre (IDC) in 1969 under the auspices of Indian Institute of Technology, Mumbai. The aim was to produce the world-class designers. In this institute, there are P.G. Courses in Industrial Design, Visual Communication, Animation, Interaction Design, Mobility and Vehicle Design. There is a facility to do the doctoral research (Ph.D.) in design. The admissions are on the basis of an entrance test SEED which assesses visual perception ability, drawing skills, design aptitude and communication skills. The candidates are admitted for Master in Design course in the following institutes:

- Industrial Design Centre, IIT, Mumbai
- Instrument Design and Development Centre, IIT, Delhi
- Centre for Product Design and Manufacturing, IISC, Bangalore
- Design Programme, IIT, Kanpur.

Design and Costs

The lab is the place where cost control starts. If our design itself is cost conscious, the assembly becomes cheaper. Like quality, costs are built into design. Almost 70 per cent of the eventual cost of a product is decided at the design stage itself. To begin with, the development process can be geared to meet only the customer needs, and little else. All frills can be eliminated. The cost-consciousness of the design should be carried to procurement and manufacturing operations by using low-cost components and production methods. Lastly, the product must be off the drawing board quickly, and should be produced in such a way that it does not need to return to the lab. Designing should be accelerated to cut the development costs. However, there is a trade-off sometimes when development process is speeded up, product performance could suffer and *vice versa.* The factory should turn out a product that performs what it promises, within the cost parameters set and must reach the market before competition does. In the market, it must make money. Success lies in how a company transits from the chaos of the invention to the daily discipline of the production department (Preston G. Smith). It should be remembered that 80 per cent of costs are committed at the design stage. Even when the market wants a product with enhanced features, it does not ignore product-price equation you give and that which your competition gives.

Condom Design and Vespas Design

The very fact that condoms are unpopular can be attributed to their no-good-feel design. Bill and Melinda Gates Foundation has offered a grant of $ 100,000 to anyone who can design a superior condom — one that actually enhances pleasure and makes user to look forward to slipping one on. Condoms have been in use for about 400 years, but they have not undergone major technological improvements. Some minor improvements have happened in the last 50 years. The world needs a Next Generation Condom. They have praised Origami condoms being designed by a California-based company. The Japanese paper folding technique is exploited to create collapsible condoms that fold up rather than roll up. The pleasure sensation is retained, as the loose-fitting sheath moves with the natural movement of the body.

Vespa's Design

Corradino D'Ascanio designed Vespa. He is also responsible for the design of Italy's helicopter around World War II. He had dislike for motorcycles, which he believed were bulky, uncomfortable and unreliable. Enrico Piaggio, the Italian industrialist found the design resembles a wasp and hence the name Vespa. Vespa has featured in movies such as *Roman Holiday, The Talented Mr. Ripley* and *Larry Crowne.* The first design of Vespa was done after drawing a person sitting comfortably on a sofa in his drawing room, and the scooter was designed around him. The first Vespa model was called Paperino, Italian for Donald Duck. Vespa's new Indian version has Italian looks and a stylish retro design with glittering chrome finish.

Computers and Design

These days computers aid the designing process. The state-of-the-art CAD software has reduced the time to finalise a product's design. The software has 3D capability. CAD has moved into rapid prototyping too. Real prototyping is time consuming and expensive. BHEL builds parts with components tested by computers. A turbine's butter-fly valve, tailor-made for each turbine, is tested by simulating the environment in which the valve will function, and by permutations and combinations of the design parameters under different conditions. Another model tests the valve in its interface with other components of the turbine. Thus, prior to manufacturing, the product is tested under different conditions. The product development then including manufacturing is completed in four months. Computer software enables product design flexibility. Many companies use optimisation technique, simulating operating conditions, through a large number of input variables (such as weight, performance, aesthetics, price, reliability, noise levels, maintainability, delivery, logistics, tooling and machinery). The modelling responses are recorded for different product designs. After several alterations, using different mix of inputs, the best least-cost design can be chosen.

Graphic Design

A graphic designer is not only concerned with the design, but also with the contemporary society, history and research. This is a field which allows the candidates to create new designs based on their study of culture, economics and social norms. A graphic designer uses computer technology in such a way that the outcome becomes visually appealing. These designers have great demand in publishing houses and advertising. A designer can set up his own free lance consultancy services. In the courses of graphic design, they cover the subjects of studio art, the principles of design, computerized design, commercial graphic, production, print technology and web site design. The liberal subjects of history, writing, psychology, sociology, foreign language, marketing and commercial practices can be added. Even then the institutes must concentrate more on the use of computers in graphic design. Graphic design is a component of communication design. A student is exposed to typography, types of designs, illustration, photography, packaging, print design and IT. This helps them in computer graphics and multimedia. Those who are creative and have a sense of visualisation can succeed a lot in this field after studying design principles.

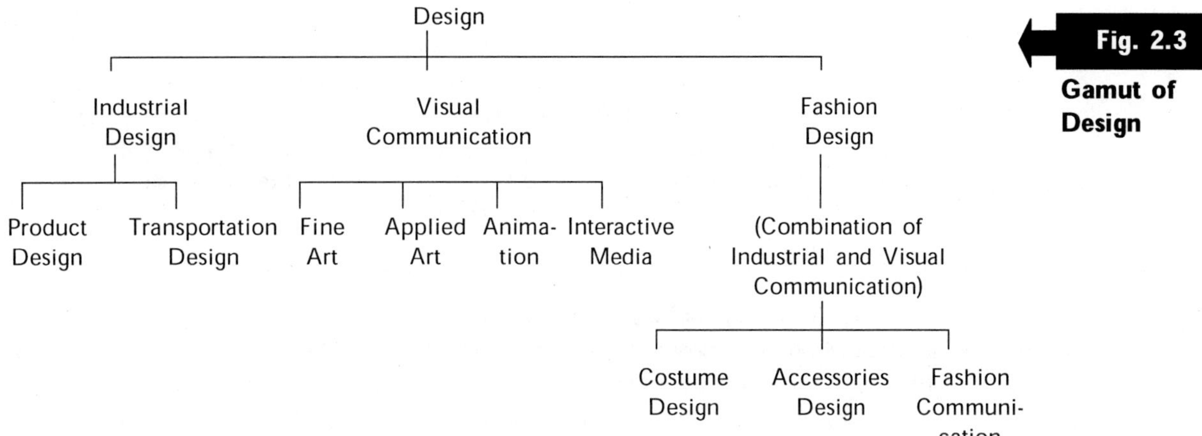

Fig. 2.3
Gamut of Design

Characteristics of a Good Design

1. Simplification: A simple design ensures easy producibility. The lesser is the cost of production. The performance is reliable.

2. Producibility: A well-designed product is easy to produce at competitive cost. A product must be made using the least operations so as to be easy on production and cost. A different technology sometimes achieves this purpose. *e.g.*, instead of a machined part, a moulded part can be used. The work content of the job must be reduced. The printed circuit boards in the instrumental penal in autos reduce the wiring work. A multiple pin plug serves the purpose.

3. Function: Products should be designed in such a way that they should be functionally useful. A match stick must burn on striking against a surface and a scooter must start when the electronic switch is pressed. Kodak used to say, just click, and leave the rest to us.

4. Reliability: A reliable product is hassle-free over a period of time. Reliability is achieved by a suitable design. It is necessary to conform to specifications in order to attain reliability. Reliability is affected by the number of components and the way they are configured. These aspects are considered while designing.

5. Maintainability: A product may develop faults, but its repair and replacements of parts must be easy. The down time is thus reduced.

6. Product Standardisation and Variety Reduction: Consumer require a wide choice of products, and so a variety of products are introduced. It is also to meet the competition. Modular design offers variety. Standardisation makes economies of scale possible.

7. Cost: Design affects the manufacturing cost. Good design ensures the least possible cost for the target audience. The scope of saving at the design stage has been discussed separately.

8. Quality: The individual components that make up the final product affect the quality of the final product. Each component must conform to specifications. Quality is thus built at the design stage itself.

Design Factors Affecting Manufacturing Cost

Design has the potential to optimise the manufacturing costs. It is better to exercise cost control over the product at the design stage itself. After the product has been designed, the scope to reduce the cost is minimal. The areas which can save costs at the design stage are discussed hereunder.

Materials

The major cost contribution to the total cost is that of material. It offers the greatest scope for saving costs. The selection of materials is crucial appropriate material must be chosen. If less costly material could work effectively, there is no point in selecting the costlier material. The ready availability of material must be considered. It is better to use standard material, as non-standard sizes push up costs.

Machinability

At the design stage, it is necessary to consider the machinability of the material before selecting. The materials which can be subjected to unit operations like cutting easily are chosen because costs can be saved due to wear and tear of the tools. Even if easily machinable material is slightly costly, it is chosen, as machining cost reduces. As compared to brass or aluminium, steel is difficult to machine and so may not be chosen, though it is less costly.

Tolerances

Exact dimension of each piece in production may not be possible. Tolerances provide a necessary fit between the mating parts, ensure their interchangeability and achieve this at the lowest cost. Tolerances are specified by the designer. Very close tolerances do require skilled operators, high quality materials, good tools and precision machines. This makes the whole thing costly. Machines will have to be often reset, and inspection becomes more frequent.

It is necessary to know the costing of a particular tolerance. Different manufacturing operations throw up different production costs.

Make-or-Buy Decisions

Any product is not 100 per cent made at one factory. It has components bought from outside, or outsourced. It is necessary to analyse at the design stage which components will be made in the factory and which will be outsourced. A part is made in-house if we have the technical know-how and economical to make. Outsourcing is resorted to make the product competitive and to avail of the know-how of the outsiders.

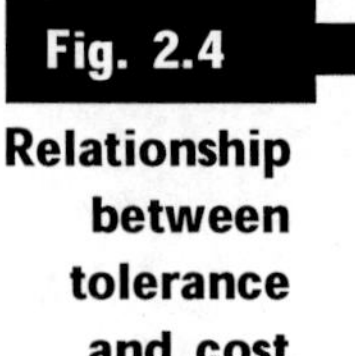

Relationship between tolerance and cost

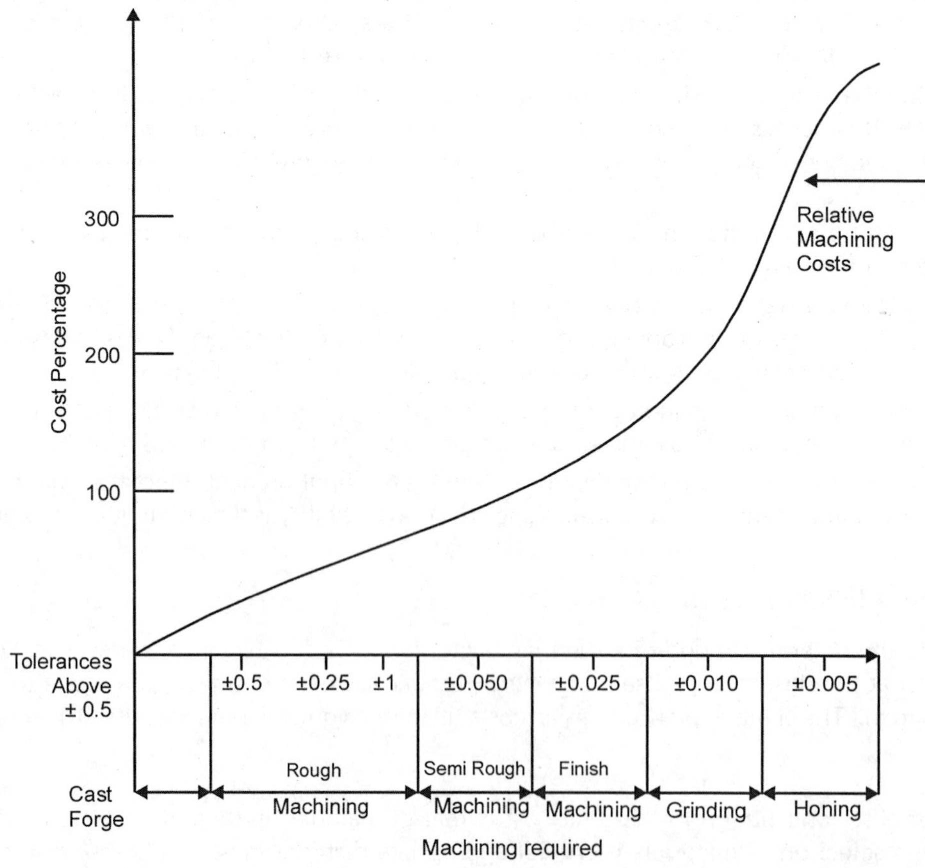

Use of Standard Parts

Use of standard parts reduces the cost. We can use vendor's specialty products. They come at a low cost. Non-standard parts should be reserved for special cases. Standard parts are also easy to procure. If some vendor is already making the standard part for some others, we can also contact him to take advantage of lower costs. Sometimes, a standard part bought from others can be modified to our requirements.

Tool Design

Design should be able to take the maximum advantage of the current facilities available with us.

Variety Reduction

Here unnecessary variety in product range is curtailed. It means lower manufacturing cost, inventory cost and labour cost. We can make a product using as few parts as possible. It improves the reliability of the product. It reduces the probability of a break down.

Microfluidics

Microfluidics is the science of designing, manufacturing and formulating devices and processes that deal with the volumes of fluid on the order of nanoliters (symbolized *nl* and representing units of 10-9 liter) or picoliters (symbolized *pl* and representing units of 10-12 liter). Such systems have wide industrial applications — pharma industry, printers like ink-jets, blood-cell separation equipment, biochemical assays, chemical synthesis, genetic analysis, drug screening, electro-chromatography, surface micromachining, laser ablation and mechanical micromilling. This technology minimizes reagent use.

New Promising Technologies

Nanotech denotes a billionth of a metre — 1/80000th the width of a human hair. Any product that has a characteristic that involves measurement at or below 100 nanometres falls under nanotechnology. In India, about 20 nano patents are filed every year. We are behind the rest of the world by at least six years. Nanotech products has applications in genetics, pharmaceuticals, cancer treatment, coatings etc.

Bioinformatics is the development of new tools to analyze an explosion of data from molecular biology, like genome data base. It is a combination of biology and powerful software.

Biotechnology is the application of a collection of techniques using cells and biological molecules to make antibiotics, insulin or even fix genetic defects. India holds 120 biotech patents. Biocon, an Indian company has filed for 270 patents. The Centre for Cellular and Molecular Biology, Hyderabad has filed 60 national and international patents over the past three years. Biotech has led to personalized medicine.

Wearable Technology

It is predicted that the next era of computing will be wearables. The speculation is about the nature of these wearables on the wrist. And wearables on the face, just like the glasses. It is possible that the future gadgets will be stretchable, bendable and thinner. They can adhere to the skin like tattoos or attach to the body like a Band-Aid strip. All these attachable computers will have sensors. They can collect a lot of health-related data. They will look like body art. Scientists are working on e-skin that sits on the body. It may lead to life-like prosthetics. Apple Watch has been launched in 2015. It is an example of wearable technology.

New Enabling technologies

Digital business is being facilitated by new enabling technologies such as 3D Printing, IoT and smart machines. We have already discussed 3D Printing. IoT represents a nature of devices connected to the Internet. These are embedded with sensors and are mainly used to collect data. These can be controlled remotely. IoT can be controlled remotely. IoT can be used by incorporating it in a machine to minimise cost. Smart machines represent new mobile robots which can do an array of jobs, unlike the industrial robots which are often designed to do one type of job. Further smart machines also mean machines with cognitive computer systems, with advanced artificial intelligence. These can be used to perform complete tasks, traditionally performed by human beings.

The 3D Printing affects the Product Life Cycle theory. Before scaling we can put short product runs with 3D printing. Later there will be traditional manufacturing. A 3D printed product can be made available even after the traditional manufacturing discontinues its production. In leasing decisions, there was reliance on depreciation. But thanks to IoT, companies can have data on the asset usage, and this enables a more realistic assessment of residual values. The workforce in future will be a hybrid workforce — people, augmented workers and smart machines. The augmentation devices could be wearables such as Google Glass. A resource planner will have to find the right balance of workers and machines.

Synthetic Biology

Synthetic biology is a rapidly expanding discipline that uses synthesized DNA, the genes of the most living organisms, to create biological functions not found in nature. These genes are edited (using a computer) and then synthesized from scratch (using chemicals). In future, genes could be designed and printed. There are possibilities of finding solutions to problems of environmental pollution, shortage of food and energy. It is expected that synthetic biology would create food and fuel, drugs and chemicals. Scientists have found a way to write, erase and rewrite information into the DNA of bacteria called E. coli. This ability to programme DNA could one day let us switch off cells when they become cancerous. Artemisin, anti-malarial drug, is currently extracted from plants. Funded by Bill and Melinda Gates Foundation, the drug is created by inserting genes from various organisms into E. coli. This is a big milestone for synthetic biology, as the plants from which it is extracted are short in supply and grow slowly.

Viruses are seen as apps of biology providing infinite possibilities for us to create new living systems. Viruses are chemical codes that add features to organisms they infect. A bacteriophase is a bacterium infected by a virus. Viruses can be used as diagnostic tools, as gene therapy.

Scaling is a big challenge for every synthetic biology application. Synthetic biology is drawing big research funds.

Bionics

Bionics is a combination of biology and electronics. It implies technology transfer between living organisms and mechanical products. It tries to develop engineering solutions from biological models. It is used mainly in medical science to develop artificial limbs. It is estimated that the orthopaedic prosthetic market alone would be around $20 billion by 2015.

Graphene: The New Wonder Material

Graphene is a single layer of carbon atoms networked in a honey-comb structure. It shows remarkable electric and optical properties. It is being used experimentally in labs to make transistors, memory devices, displays, batteries, solar cells, energy storage devices and several other things. We have yet to develop graphene manufacturing technology. Since its discovery in 2004, over 200 patents have been granted on graphene. However, graphene is unlikely to replace silicon in the near future. Electrons in graphene travel 100 times faster than those in silicon. Graphene can be interspersed with other materials which can then be used from food packaging to aircraft parts.

The Impact of Product Innovation on Process Innovation

There is a strong link between the product design and the process which turns it out. There are instances where the process generates new product designs. Just as a product undergoes different shapes in its life-cycle, a process also passes through these stages. The following graph shows process life cycle.

To begin with, as you can see from the Fig. 2.5, innovativeness in products is need-based. We try to maximise a product's performance. The process is not at all co-ordinated there. We improve the process to generate more output.

CASELET: TURNING IDEAS INTO REALITY

It is often said that Japan is not as strong in basic research as it is in applied research. It takes original ideas either from Europe or the US. While this is true on the face of it, nevertheless the country has seven Nobel prizes. Of course, the number of Nobel laureates in Physics is higher in U.K. and the number of Nobel laureates in all subjects is highest in the US. But there is also a steady increase in the number of Japanese papers cited as references in prestigious publications. From 3 p.c. in 1960 references to Japanese research papers have gone up to 30 p.c. today. Japan's unique skill in turning ideas into reality on the production line swiftly, which has helped her so far to be in the forefront of technology, may receive a boost with the country becoming more and more involved in basic research.

We invite readers to think how the Eastern tiger nations like Singapore, Hong Kong have taken rapid strides in technology on borrowed concepts. We also would like you to ponder over the changing role of Japan which so far adapted research to one which does basic research itself. What lessons do you see for India in all this?

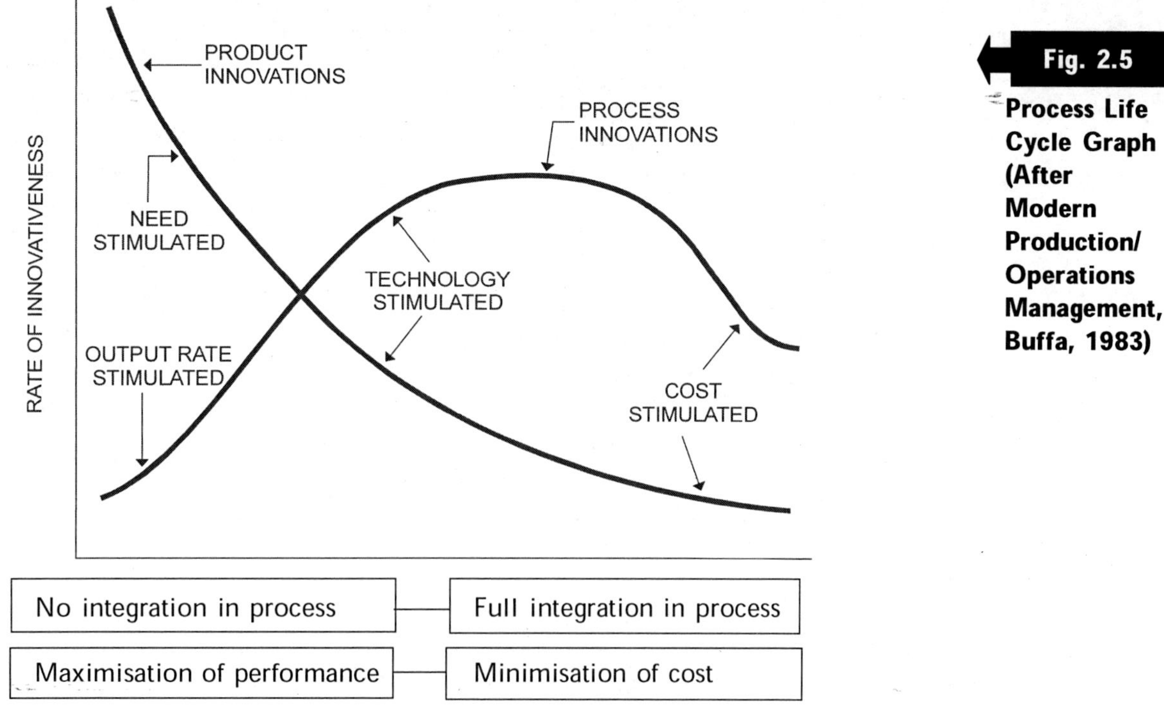

Fig. 2.5 **Process Life Cycle Graph (After Modern Production/ Operations Management, Buffa, 1983)**

In due course, there are lesser product innovations. Exactly there, process innovation gets more emphasis.

The second stage is marked by both product and process innovation which are technology-based. Our attention is directed towards a product system that minimises cost. This is necessary in view of the growing competition. Process innovations now dominate over product innovations. Again this is to gain cost advantage.

In the third stage, the product reaches maturity. If there are innovations, they are all cost-based. The process of production becomes highly integrated. There are plants of large capacities and product-based operations. It helps achieve economies of scale.

Process Innovation

Ice cream milk can be chilled with liquid nitrogen at –20°C and we get ice cream balls with liquid crystals which are 80 creamier and tasty. This ice cream is available under the brand name Dipping Dots. Slow Churned is a low fat ice cream on account of process innovation.

Design

Design has become a differentiator for products. Scorpio an SUV from Mahindra has tasted success with design. Bajaj Pulsar which is a successful two-wheeler has also the design as a differentiator. Design also saves costs. It makes a huge difference to any area where technology has stabilised. Gillette has leveraged its design of Mach 3 and Turbo. Though 97% people still use double-edged shaving products, the new systems are used only by 3%. But the design allows the companies to get out of the price trap. Vector plus is a revolution in terms of product design. It has a twin-blade with a lubra strip and push-clean button. Fusion, a five-blade shaving system will be introduced by Gillette shortly. Oral B for the first time in 1997 introduced indicator property with Oral B plus advising the time to change the brush. Anchor has created its identity on the basis of design for its product — the electrical switches. Honda Activa and Kinetic Nova have won on account of their designs. Nokia also follows design-based strategy. Honda City's design has scored over Hyundai Accent in the C-segment of cars. Design is the next big P of marketing — Product design.

	DESIGNING CAREER	
Position	***Job***	***Remuneration***
Junior Designer	A beginner working under a senior designer. He is a member of a team. He uses digital tools.	₹ 3-5 lakh a year
Lead Designer	Experience in the field of 2-4 years. Leads a design team.	₹ 6-8 lakh a year
Project Leader	Experience of 4-6 years in the field. He manages all aspects of the project and interacts with the client.	₹ 8-10 lakh a year
Design Director	Experience of 5-8 years in the field. He formulates design strategies. He manages high value large team projects.	₹ 10-20 lakh a year
Chief Designer	Experience of 8-12 years in the field. Responsible for brand/product strategies. He manages in-house designs and manufacturing designs.	₹ 25 lakh a year.

Design Thinking

SAP has trained and put together a pool of 1000 people who are practitioners of design thinking. It is a new approach to product innovation. Here the primary figure is not an engineer but a designer. The idea is to create desirable products. There are small teams each having a designer-in-residence. He initiates the process by interviewing the end user in terms of his expectations. The inputs are used before building a prototype. To set the content, they work like start-ups in their own space, away from cubicles and processes. All people in the organisation are not involved in design thinking — just 10-20 per cent of the people to overcome the innovator's dilemma.

Global Product Design

These are the days of multinational companies. Since the cost of supplying the product to the distant markets would be prohibitive, MNCs undertake the production locally. Mostly such local operations are done by a suitable technical, financial and administrative tie-up. Such a tie-up can lead to a joint venture where the MNC and the local partner form an independent company. The local partner is carefully chosen by identifying its production capability. The foreign company has to fill the gap in the product portfolio of the local company. The foreign company generally concentrates on product and process design. It also enhances the marketing clout of the local partner. The local partner suggests the adaptation of the product to the local needs. A moderately complex product is structured as a service of modules. Common processes can be developed for these modules. Some customised modules can be developed for local adaptation.

Design of Lota

The *lota*, a spherical water vessel, was admired by the American designer Charles Eames who said that it stands out as perhaps the greatest and the most useful object. The NID was setup in Gujarat in 1961 thanks to his comments in the *India Report*.

Universal Design

Ronald L. Mace, an architect coined this term in 1985. It is an environment that allows all people equal access, regardless of their level of mobility or disability. Accessibility must be incorporated into building design. Developers are not sensitised to this concept. Anyone can be subjected to a circumstance where accessibility is required, *e.g.*, an accident, temporary disability, permanent disability, age-related issue. At times, we have to sacrifice space to make this happen. How a person enters a building? How he navigates the different levels or use common facilities? To negotiate levels, we must have ramps. The tactile surface on which people walk should also be considered. The door knobs, light switches, lift panels must be within reach. A friendly wheel chair or a car or a stick with GPS — all this must be designed properly. Velcro and Google electric toothbrushes are examples of universal design.

Design and Structural Engineering

In construction, the architect is the designer. However, these designs are translated into reality by the structural engineer. It is an integrated discipline. It deals with the analysis and design of structures that supports or resists the loads. Beyond buildings, structural engineers are involved in non-building projects, *e.g.*, the design of machinery, medical equipment, vehicles or any item where structural integrity affects the item's function or safety. Today, structural engineering has to oversee the optimal usage of materials consistent with constructibility needs to get incorporated within the structural design. This is true for all turn-key projects. Structural engineering is driven by creative manipulation of materials and forms, mass, space, volume, texture and light so as to achieve an aesthetic, functional and artistic end.

Heritage Design Reshaped

Most clothing and accessory brands of today have history of 100-200 years. These are centred around creative craftsmen founders from Europe. Hermes, Louis Vuitton, Chanel, Dior, Armani, Cartier, Versace are luxury icons of this type. Similarly, Swiss watch and jewellery brands, Italian coachbuilders turned car designers have been around for a couple of hundred years and were also founded by visionary craftsmen *par excellence*. These brands have been continuously reinvented through storytelling and modern design.

Thus, we have inherited the heritage model of luxury which is reshaped by geographic, technological and ecological forces. Fashion labels are quick to change to keep pace with the times, but other products and automobiles are evolving quite slowly.

A buyer group is emerging in the developing countries which demands original stories which, and not just be content with the brand heritage. Thus luxury industry is experiencing a shift from exclusive to inclusive design. A new idiom of 'affordable luxury' has emerged. Instead of elitist brands, consumers responsible brands. Yes, there is resistance to change. Some do not want to change. However, the rigid need socially and ecologically will become irrelevant.

Concurrent Engineering (CE)

The design and production of a product is accomplished in three stages — conceptual stage where functional requirements of a product are specified and product idea is established to fulfill these, functional design stage and production design stage. The tool engineer tries to achieve the production at optimal cost. At the drawing stage itself, it is determined whether functionwise there is producibility. If a part is to be produced by machining, the designer must envisage how the job will be machined and minor alterations if any are made so that machining is facilitated. There should be proper attention to casting, forging, and the use of moulded plastic parts. The entire design process for production is called **Design for Manufacturability (DFM)** or **Concurrent Engineering (CE)**.

CE requires us to consider both the product and process design simultaneously, rather than sequentially. All constraints are taken into account. *e.g.*, assembly requirements, information flow regarding materials, material handling requirements. This leads to design optimisation. CF enables the design team to consider all aspects of design and production at earlier stages so that modifications can be effected easily. The following diagram illustrates the CE approach.

Fig. 2.6

Concurrent Engineering Approach

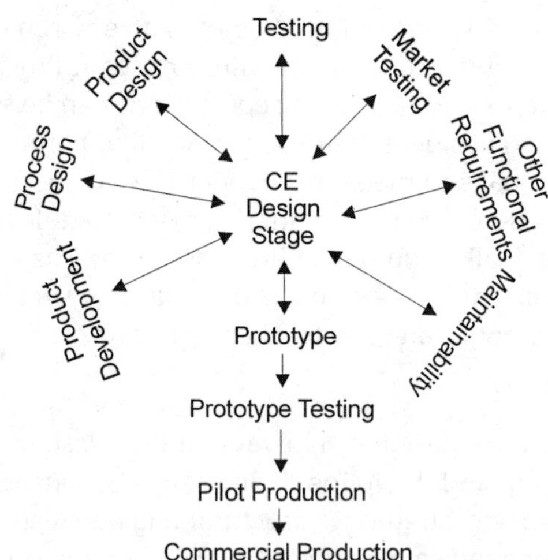

KARBONN HANDSETS

Till 2011, Karbonn had only a design house. It used to design its products and use the OEMs (original equipment manufacturers) in Taiwan, Korea and China to manufacture them. For instance, Taiwan is good for high-end like Android phones. Korea is best for sliders and flip and touch phones, while China is for low end. Karbonn uses all of them. They propose to set up their own manufacturing facilities at Chennai with a capacity of 5 lac phones per month very fast.

Appendix - I

Technology in Operations

A very vital role is played by technology in operations, business bottom-line and growth. Technology is also a change agent. Technology provides competitive edge to the businesses and nations. An innovative organization uses technology to develop products faster. Information technology (IT) has changed the complexion of the business itself. It has generated information systems so useful in decision making. Technology encompasses new products, new methods, new materials and new frontiers such as genetic engineering. Technology also helps the recycling, of materials and management of wastages. Global positioning system (GPS), cellular phone technology and HDTV — all these have potential to affect life and living a great deal.

Technology in Production

Manufacturing has come to benefit from technological changes. We have prefabricated materials for construction, for instance. We can have a car wholly made by recycling the parts of a previous car. In manufacturing, there are two types of technologies at work — the hardware technologies and the software technologies. Hardware relates to automation and machine-substitution for human labour. CNC and DNC machines, robots and automatic materials handling system are examples of hardware technologies. Software technologies are aids in the design and manufacturing of products. They also enable the production function — CAD and CAM are examples of software related technologies.

In the services sector, we use technologies like office automation, image processing systems (credit card terminals, barcoding and scanning), electronic data interchange (EDI), decision support systems, and computer networking.

Oleds

LED light bulbs consume very less electricity and have long life span. Organic light emitting diodes (Oleds) are equally good. LEDs, however, provide points of light like incandescent lamps. Oleds create uniform diffuse light across ultra-thin sheets of material that can even be made flexible. GE is developing a roll-to-roll manufacturing process, similar to a photo film or food packet. Oled can be used for illumination. Oleds can supplement existing technologies. As oled is 0.07 inch thick, architect will be able to create ceilings with oled panels, and no holes for lighting fixtures. The prices for oleds are likely is come down as production increases.

Carbon-based Solar Cells

Typical solar cells use expensive rare earth minerals, *e.g.,* silicon-based solar cells. Researchers at Stanford University have come up with an alternative method of creating solar cells made entirely of carbon. It is thin film prototype made of carbon materials that can be coated from solution. In future, flexible carbon solar cells could be coated on the surface of buildings, on windows or on cars to generate electricity. It can lower manufacturing costs. In the solar cell, the electrodes are made of grapheme consisting carbon nanotubes which are 10,000 times narrower than a human hair. These have extraordinary electrical conductivity and light absorption properties. Carbon prototypes absorbs near intra-red wavelength of light, contributing to a laboratory efficiency of one per cent, much lower than commercially available solar cells. We have a long way to go.

TOP 10 ENGINEERING MARVELS

Name of the Structure	*Location*	*Remarks*
1. Burj Khalifa	Dubai, UAE	Tallest man-made structure in the world. 829.84 metres or 2,723 ft. high
2. Taipes 101 (Taipei World Financial Centre)	Taipie, Taiwan	Tallest till Burj Khalifa appeared (2004-2010)
3. The Petronas Towers (Petronas Twin Towers)	Kaula Lumpur, Malaysia	Tallest till 2004 (2004-2010)
4. Empire State Building	New York, USA	—
5. CN Tower	Canada	—
6. Channel Tunnel	France	—
7. Delta Works	Netherlands	Prevents storms, high sea levels
8. Itaipu Dam	Brazil	Hydraulic power plant
9. Panama Canal	Panama	Connects the Atlanta and Pacific California

Journey of Engineering

Traditional engineering has moved to smart engineering which uses insights to conceive, model and scale an appropriate solution to a problem or objective. It makes use of the other branches of knowledge in the process.

To begin with the society was agrarian. It focused on soil and irrigation. It then travelled from stone age to metal edge. They learnt to cook. It was a shift from agriculture to heavy engendering to electronics engineering. Here engineering evolved as the need-based discipline. Later improvised engineering made things sophisticated from measuring time based on the length of the shadow, we moved to the use of clocks and watches, first mechanical, and then digital to nuclear.

In industry, they dismantled a product to know how it works, and reconstruct it then. It is reverse engineering. Parts not contributing to functionalities were removed — it was frugal engineering. Collectively, reverse engineering and frugal engineering gave us strip-down engineering.

In cell phones, we have multi-core processors starting with a single core to increase the processing power. This is an example of performance boosting engineering. Intelligent systems such as driverless cars and fuzzy washing machines give us intellisys engineering.

When engineering combines multiple faculties such as biology, medicine and engineering, we get cross-pollination engineering. In scientific projects such as CERN that seeks to mimic the conditions after Big bang, engineering plays a supportive role or becomes auxiliary engineering.

Sustainable engineering enables us to design products that are energy-efficient and cause the least damage to environment. Engineering is inspired by nature and is also forward-looking.

We would like the students to remember what Freeman Dyson said about a scientist and an engineer. A good scientist is a person with original ideas. A good engineer is a person who makes a design with as few original ideas as possible. Robert A. Heinlein has rightly observed, "One man's *magic* is another man's engineering. *Supernatural* is a null word."

Central Institute of Tool Design, Hyderabad

The institute offers training programmes in mechanical, mechatronics, electrical, electronics and tool engineering. Master of Engineering in Mechanical — CAD/CAM Course (MECG), Master of Engineering in Tool Design (METD), M.Tech. in Mechatronics, P.G. Course in Tool, Die and Mould, P.G. Course in CAD/CAM for Tool Engineering, P.G. Course in Mechatronics, P.G. Course in VLSI and Embedded Systems, Post Diploma in Tool Design are offered by the Institute. The new programmes being considered are MS in Mechatronics. The institute's web-site is www.citdindia.org.

DESIGN COURSES

Institute	Course/Programme	Eligibility
Industrial Design Centre, IIT, Mumbai	Master of Design Ph.D. (Design)	B.Arch or B.E./B.Tech —
National Institute of Design, Ahmedabad	Diploma in Industrial Design	10 + 2 or equivalent
	P.G. Diploma in Industrial Design	B.Arch. or B.E.
Department of Design, IIT, Gauhati	Bachelor of Design	10 + 2
IIT, Delhi	Master of Design	Graduates of Design, B.Arch or B.E.
IIT, Kanpur	Master of Design	—
Centre for Product Design and Manufacturing, IISc., Bangalore	Master of Design	Graduates of Design B.Arch., B.E.
Departmental of Industrial Design School of Planning and Architecture New Delhi	Graduate Programme in Industrial Design	—
M.S. Ramaih School of Advanced Studies, Bangalore	M.Sc. Engineering in Product Design	—
NTTF School of P.G. Studies, P.G. Studies, Bangalore	P.G. Programme in Product Design and Engineering	B.E.
IILM School of Design, Gurgaon	Graduate Programme in Design P.G. Programme in Design	10 + 2 —
Symbiosis Centre of Design, Pune	Degree Programme in Design	10 + 2
College of Architecture, Nashik	Bachelor of Design	10 + 2

Appendix - II

NEW PRODUCTS: PLANNING AND DEVELOPMENT

In any marketing programme, the company has to segment the market, select some segments it will cater to, and then determine the positioning of the products it will adopt. The company is now all ready to plan, develop and launch new products. Marketing management has to play a crucial role in this process, though the actual development takes place within the R&D department. In each stage of product development, marketing management has to participate along with other departments.

What exactly is a new product? Are the new models introduced by the audio music companies new products? If a cosmetic company adds an anti-wrinkle cream to its product mix, does it become a new product? Or should an item be a hither-to-unknown entity to qualify for being a new product?

There are some categories of new products which have been accepted all over:

(1) ***Technological breakthroughs*** that give really a unique product, *e.g.*, an anti-cancer drug, an AIDS vaccine. These products are quite different from the existing products. Nylon or transistors when first introduced were technological breakthroughs. These products are new-to-the world, and will create their own market.

(2) ***Significant Improvements:*** These products are significant improvements over the existing products, *e.g.,* instant coffee replaces the usual brew coffee. These have greater perceived value.

(3) ***Modified Products:*** There are revisions in the existing product, *e.g.,* addition of a new flavour or perfume, a new package, a revised size etc.

(4) ***Products New to the Company:*** These products are new to the company but not new to the market. They are imitative products. These allow the company to enter an existing market with a *me-too* product.

(5) ***Repositioning:*** Existing products are targeted to new markets or market segments.

(6) ***Cost-Reductions:*** The products remain functionally the same, but the prices are reduced.

Booz, Allen and Hamilton have given the above six categories of innovativeness of the products. The innovativeness of the products is considered with reference to the company and the market. Market perception of the buyers is the ultimate test of the innovativeness. A new product becomes an existing product after some time *e.g.,* cellular or mobile phones are common abroad. A company has a mix of the above six categories. Really innovative products unknown to the world constitute only 10 per cent of total innovations. Most innovative products are restricted to product and process improvement. It is largely a process of improving the existing product rather than creating new products. Truly innovative products involve the greatest risk and cost. Their innovativeness is yet to be accepted by the market.

In order to survive in a competitive environment, a company must innovate. It is a choice between *innovate* or *perish.* Drucker recognises only two basic functions of an enterprise — marketing and innovation. Many companies get their substantial sales volume and profits through products that did not exist a decade ago. Growth industries are those that are oriented to new products.

Existing products have a life cycle. These products may be required to be phased out or repositioned or improved. The introduction of a new product at the right time maintains the desired level of company's profits. Shortened product life cycles do demand innovations on the part of the companies. The advances in technology, globalisation and the changing consumer needs are the factors that support innovativeness. Environmental factors like the conservation of energy, concern for pollution, the green movement, the shortage of natural resources — all these make it necessary for us to innovate new products.

Instead of developing new products by itself, the company can *acquire* existing businesses for adding new products, *e.g.,* P & G acquires Richardson-Vicks. Sometimes, instead of a whole business, a *patent* for a product is acquired. Still there is one more option — be a licensee or franchisee of an existing company.

Those companies which decide to develop new products may do so in-house in their own laboratories or they can contract outside researchers and laboratories.

Some companies adopt both the acquisition and new product development route for growth, depending upon the perception of opportunities by the management.

Product Modification

An organisation can choose to improve the product quality on a continuous basis. There should be control on costs and updation on styling the product. This is called product modification. An organisation has to see how the modified product is received by the customers and non-customers. Apart from the physical products, there are modifications possible in product offering, say change in distribution channels, price changes, promotional changes and service changes. A bouquet personally delivered becomes special. Car service becomes important if there is waiting lounge for the customers. Packaging and styling are integral to products. A package can be made environment-friendly.

Product Variants

Product variants are really speaking line extensions, taking advantage of the equity of the mother brand. There could be a product family with several relatives, each appealing to a different segment.

You can have 'your type of soap for your type of skin.' Thus multiple products cater to multiple segments. There is scope for price discrimination. Production and operations people tend to reduce multiple versions to bring in efficiency. There is a possibility of diluting the equity of the parent brand. Extensions are thus a trade off. There are customer-oriented and operations-oriented concerns.

A product variant may add new customers. Of course, there could be cannibalization, and dilution of brand equity. A product can be upgraded but its acceptance is difficult. A product can be stretched downwards and its acceptance is easier, though the equity is lowered.

Customers do need streamlined set of product variants, though they tend to avoid over-abundance.

A product variant is dropped when there is low sales or profits.

To Innovate or Not to Innovate Dilemma

If companies decide not to innovate in these competitive times, they are exposing themselves to a great risk. The existing product range needs a change to keep pace with the changing consumer needs, changing technology, the competitive pressures and ever-shortening product life cycles. Though innovation is necessary, it is not without its risks. The failure rate of new products introduced is very high. Even service industry's products like insurance plans, credit cards, loan schemes and brokerage deals also show a high failure rate. Most of the new products fail at the time of launch. Product failures are defined in financial terms — the products fail to generate the expected profits or do not generate profits at all.

Why do new products fail? Sentimental attachment to an idea being developed is one important cause. The executives find it difficult to abandon the non-viable idea. Perhaps, the idea is viable but it may not have a market potential. Perhaps, the product has certain inherent flaws. There may be problems of marketing mix — poor advertisement, poor pricing, incorrect positioning. New product development costs exceed the budgeted costs several times. Competitors give a tough fight sometimes.

What are the barriers to the successful development of new products?

Lack of Ideas: In certain areas, there are few ideas to develop the products further, *e.g.,* steel industry.

Social and Governmental Constraints: New drugs have to be cleared by FDA. It slows down innovation in pharma industry. Liquors cannot be advertised in press and on TV in India. It is a social constraint.

Prohibitive Costs of Development: Many ideas are screened to select a few viable ideas. The process of development is prohibitively costly. Even viable ideas cannot be researched adequately sometimes due to shortage of funds.

Niche and Fragmented Marketing: Instead of mass markets, these days a company caters to specialised segments which are smaller niches. It means lower sales and profits.

Development Time: Many companies may be working on similar ideas. Only those who can develop these ideas faster than the competitors have a chance to succeed.

Shortened PLC: Competitors imitate successful products thereby shortening their PLC. It becomes difficult to recover the development costs.

Any successful attempt to innovate basically depends upon the type of organisational arrangement made for managing the process of developing the new products.

Organisation for New Products

Any programme of innovation can be successful only when it gets top management support on a continuous basis and this support is not withheld even in the face of failure of some new product development efforts. It is for the top management to define the overall domain of the business for new product development. The top management may spell out the product categories it wishes to emphasise.

Top management has to set out the criteria against which new product ideas will be scrutinised. The top management might say a new product proposal is acceptable if the product can be introduced within three years, and has a market potential of at least ₹100 crore, and a growth rate of 10 p.c. Further, it should provide a return of 25 p.c. on sales and 35 p.c. on investment. A very significant decision is about the budgeting of the new product development. Some companies finance several projects at a time, considering the possibility of having a few successful products at the end of different time periods. Some companies allocate a percentage of sales to R&D efforts. Even competitive efforts are taken into account. One may first decide how many successful products a company must have and then calculating backwards the investment needed.

It is common experience for companies that out of several ideas considered for a new product, only a handful pass the idea-screening stage. Each idea reviewed, however, costs a lot to the company. Only 50 p.c. ideas of the screened out ideas might survive the concept testing stage, and only a half of these might reach the product development stage. There has to be budget for concept testing, and product testing stages. Hardly one or two ideas are then launched at an enormous launch cost. They may be successful or may not be. The total cost of developing the new product is thus the summation of the costs incurred at each stage of development. The company has to improve the pass ratio and reduce the costs at each stage to make the whole process cost effective. The average cost of an idea getting converted into a successful product can be calculated. The products needed for a company multiplied by the average cost thus gives the total budget for new product development.

Several organisational mechanisms are introduced to handle the development of new products. There is no 'one-best' organisational structure to do so. Some most widely used organisational structures are briefly explained here.

Product Planning Committee

In several companies, a committee is formed with representatives drawn from the top management for monitoring new product development. The committee usually consists of the chief executives and representatives from the marketing, financing, production and research departments. Once the product is developed, the marketing responsibility is assigned to either a product manager or a new product department. The committee is an effort to pool the combined wisdom of different people. A resulting new product thus has the approval of the concerned administrators who were a party to its developmental decision. Incidentally a committee type arrangement is a time consuming process, and is slow to arrive at decisions.

New Product Department

In large companies, a new product department under a senior manager vested with sufficient authority and having access to top management is created. The manager heads a department which is compact, consisting of 4-5 persons. This department spells out the new product programmes. It also monitors the development process of the new product. Once developed, the new product is assigned to the concerned operating department.

New product department in some firms is authorised to contract with outside parties to bring the new product on par with competitive products. New product department can be authorised to farm out ideas to outside specialist firms who specialise in product development process. The new product department keeps track of patents and revives old patents. The products developed may not be of immediate use to the company. The new product department can be authorised to sell off these products or technology to others at a price so as to cover the R&D costs.

Routinely, all new product departments co-ordinate with R&D, generate and screen new product ideas, and test and commercialise the ideas developed.

Product Manager

He may be named as a product manager or a brand manager or a merchandise manager. He is after all responsible for either a product or a group of related products. He mainly plans the strategies for *existing* products. He may be assigned the additional responsibility of developing and marketing and new products. However, as the product manager is over-burdened with his existing load, he may not do justice to the new product. At most, he can do brand or line extensions and slight product improvements. Besides, he may not have the competence to develop the new products. Being too close to the company's existing product line, he is also blinkered to the possibility of exploring new product ideas.

New Product Manager: To overcome the drawbacks of an arrangement whereby new products are made the responsibility of existing product managers, some firms create the post of a new product manager who has to consider only about the development of new products. This professionalises the new product function. The new product manager reports to the Group Product Manager.

New Product Venture Teams: Here the major development work of new products is assigned to a venture team which is a small, multi-disciplinary group organisationally segregated from the rest of the firm. The venture group looks after the whole new product development process right from idea generation to full-scale marketing. It consists of representatives from the operating departments like engineering, production, finance, marketing research etc. The team acts as an entrepreneur, within the organisation, as it is immune to organisational rules and regulations. It reports directly to top management, and has a single-minded commitment to enter a new market profitably. The group members are relieved of their other organisational duties. They are given a budget and a time-frame. Once a product is developed, it is turned over to the existing organisational arrangement or to a subsidiary company. The venture team is then disbanded.

Venture teams are organisations within organisations. They by-pass the traditional problems of bureaucratisation and red-tapism. Besides, in existing organisations, there is an inherent resistance to change. The existing arrangements lack the authority or the courage to see the product through all the developmental stages.

Randall (1980) has identified three main types of formal organisational mechanisms used for product innovation: (1) new-product committees, (2) project teams, and (3) new-product or venture departments. Souder (1978) has found the following nine organisational trappings behind the formal structure to organise product innovation.

1. New product department
2. Product committee
3. Commercial-product manager
4. Technical-project manager
5. Commercial-line manager
6. Technical-line manager
7. Commercial one-man show
8. Technical one-man show
9. Dyad

Each of these nine systems can fall into one of the three broad categories suggested by Randall. Souder scores by emphasising the power base which could either be commercial or technical. Though useful to understand the structure, still it does not enlighten us about the interactions amongst the participants in terms other than formal power. Stalker (1961) finds that less product-innovator firms use mechanistic structures and active product innovator firms use organic structures. But this explanation is also not satisfactory, because while *implementing,* active firms to exercise far greater control just like mechanistic structures than they do at the initiation stage. Surprisingly, the control was exercised without changing the formal job titles.

Why New Products Fail or Succeed?

It is a baffling question. Some new products fail. Some succeed. For a company, every new product that is developed is a star. But it may fade out. Some of the reasons for this are.

Lack of Organisational Team-work

In most of the organisations, there is a tradition to rely on R&D to come out with a bright idea and research it, which is then handed over to the design and production people. The ultimate end-product comes to marketing department for selling. There are many problems in this segmental approach. The design people may revert to R&D, if they find the product unviable. The production people may ask the design people to redesign if the product cannot be turned out at the budgeted cost. The design people take their own time to redesign. The marketing department ultimately gets a product that is not acceptable to the customers at a price quoted. Perhaps, their needs are not met. Each party places the blame at the door of the other party. The solution to this situation is to have *team-approach*. At each stage, there should be cross-functional approach, *e.g.*, marketing examining the product idea. New products should be linked to a strategic management process, and the new product development process should be under an effective organisational arrangement. A stage-gate process of development ensures that the product proceeds to the next stage only when cleared by a cross-functional team of gate-keepers. At each stage, while the gate-keepers decide whether to go further/no go and kill /no go and hold/recycle. The criteria are decided by the project leader for each stage. This is different from the department-to-department approach; where leaders change often. Thus, if marketing research into consumer's wants and needs does not support a product, the product does not go ahead from the *business planning* stage to *product development* stage. *Simultaneous product development* by a cross-functional team turns out products quicker. It may be risky to do so. But where product life cycles are shorter, quick development of new products offers far more benefits than the risks associated with it.

Technical Problems: Too complicated a product or poor performance of a product that is not superior to any of the existing products may fail.

Poor Timing: Philips was too slow to bring improved generations of VCRs after it put its new product in 1972. In the meantime, Japanese companies put at least three generations of VCRs. Delay in introduction of new products may affect the marketing chances of a company. Even rushing a product in the market too quickly is not advisable. Hima Peas introduced by Lever several years back were not accepted by Indian consumers, who were not ready to accept packaged branded commodities then. In this age of working women, many fast-food items may become acceptable, though it was unthinkable to expect so a few years ago.

Let us now examine why new products succeed.

(*i*) Any product, whether new or existing, has to satisfy a consumer need or more than one consumer need.

(*ii*) The *product advantage* of being superior goes a long way in making the product successful. Xerox — a copying machine succeeded because it copied anything in seconds without any chemical/special paper. Polaroid succeeded as it took a picture, developed it, and gave a print in 60 seconds flat.

(*iii*) The product must be competitive cost-wise. It must be compatible with the distinctive competence of a company. It must be supported by top management. The environment should be conducive to developing new products. The management must be alive to new-product opportunities.

(*iv*) The product must have a *marketing advantage e.g.*, Avon is sold door-to-door or Barbie doll can get clothes to drape her in.

(*v*) The product must have a *creative advertising advantage*, *e.g.*, Maggie's two minute noodles emphasised the two-minute solution to satisfy the hunger of school going children.

Stages in the New Product Development Process

The overall guide to the new product development is the product strategy of the organisation. The development of new product proceeds in the following eight stages. At each stage, the firm has to decide whether to move ahead to the next stage or abandon the product or seek additional information. The eight stages, involved are: (*i*) Generation of new product ideas, (*ii*) Screening and evaluation of ideas; (*iii*) Concept development and testing; (*iv*) Marketing strategy; (*v*) Business analysis; (*vi*) Product development; (*vii*) Market Testing; (*viii*) Commercialisation.

The following diagram illustrates this.

The first three stages up to the concept development are the critical steps. These are the least expensive steps. Further steps are escalating in terms of costs and commitment of scarce resources. Most product failures are attributable to an unviable idea or faulty concept development. The stages help us to identify these situations. Activities in the development process can be co-ordinated and controlled by mathematical models like PERT/CPM.

First Stage

Generation of New Product Ideas

Idea Generation: A product that we use today was just an idea sometime back. It is the creative idea that gets eventually translated into the new product opportunity. Where do we find these ideas?

Sources of New Product Ideas: Ideas can come from a number of sources. Ideas can come from the R&D department. The chief executive himself can be a good source of ideas. The marketing people including the salesmen provide certain ideas. Outsiders like the suppliers, the dealers and the distributors, inventors and research agencies are fertile sources of new ideas. Technical people working in the company and outside are a good source of ideas. Companies get ideas from the competitors. The kith and kin of people interacting with the company, *e.g.*, Chairman's wife, may throw up bright ideas. Customers themselves are the most important source of new product ideas. Surveys of customers and feedback from the customers are treasure-mines for the companies. Ideas can be found in our country; or else we can be inspired by people and products abroad.

Though there are endless number of sources for new product ideas, what matters more is how seriously a company addresses itself to those new ideas. It is not possible to anticipate the sudden emerging idea. Sometimes, ideas occur accidentally. These must be accommodated. It is, however, unwise to rely on such accidental happenings. It is, therefore, desirable to have a systematic idea search programme.

There are two major sources of ideas as outlined in the following diagram:

Table 2.1
TWO MAJOR SOURCES OF IDEAS

A Real Problem	*Technological capability*
Market-driven External-orientation Good chances of success	Technology-driven Inward-orientation Poor chances of success.

These sources are the real need of the market and technological capability. There may be a situation when a new product is developed in response to a market problem as a solution, it has more chances of succeeding commercially. This is called a market pull development. Many such products are improvements on existing products in response to market pull. In another situation, ideas are derived from technological capability (technology push). These are less likely to be successful commercially. Here a solution is developed first which seeks a problem. Here we search for potential users where unmet needs could be satisfied at acceptable cost. On spotting such unmet need or creating it, the technology product may sometimes emerge as a winner, *e.g.,* 3M's Post-its.

Idea Generation Techniques

There are a number of techniques available to generate ideas. Apart from techniques, two other important factors in generating ideas are perspiration and inspiration.

Brainstorming Sessions

Alex Osborn is credited with this idea generating technique. It is a group exercise undertaken by six to ten people. They study a specific problem for sometime, say an hour. The chairman invites the participants to throw up ideas — any ideas, even the wildest. The emphasis is on quantity. There is no qualitative evaluation at this stage. The ideas flow — one leads to another, and then to the third and so on. Within an hour, a few hundred ideas may emerge. To make brainstorming effective, participants are encouraged to formulate new ideas from other participants' ideas, and build upon the ideas of others. Brainstorming sessions traditionally used are extremely rewarding if they are well-planned and conducted properly. The group should consist of people with different backgrounds and from different disciplines, *e.g.,* a brainstorming session on new financial product must have executives from the operational department of the bank, the marketing executives, the computer specialists, the clerical staff in direct contact with the customers, the market researcher and one or two potential customers. They should all be lively, bubbling over with ideas. They should articulate their ideas even at the risk of appearing stupid. They should be properly briefed beforehand. It is only at the end when all possible ideas are squeezed out of the group that it may be worthwhile to examine them critically, see the more promising ones and develop the best ones from just a short description to more of a concept.

Interaction with Various Groups

New product ideas can come from our customers, employees, distributors, salespeople, competitors, scientists and members of the top management. We can assess customer needs and wants to generate new product ideas. We can analyse the competitor's products to get good ideas. Sales representatives and distributors are also good sources of new product ideas. They are every close to the customers and are the first to learn about the competitors' moves. Top management is always on the look out for new product ideas to take the company ahead. We can source new product ideas from the academic field, research labs, patent attorneys, consultants, MR agencies and research publications. Amongst these varied sources, ideas are available in plenty. There should be someone in the organisation who takes the role of *product champion* to take note of these ideas.

Creativity Techniques

Some of the techniques to stimulate creativity are:

Attribute Listing

Here products are broken down into specific parts, qualities or attributes. For instance, a screw driver is a round, steel shank, a manually operated handle, a wedged end to engage a slot in the screw and torgue provided by twisting action. An individual or group can modify each attribute, *e.g.* the wooden handle of the screw driver can be converted into a plastic handle, the round shank can be made hexagonal to provide better grip, or a application of wrench to provide better torgue, or replacement of manual power by electric power and so on.

A toothpaste can be thought of in terms of the tooth whitening, breath freshing, decay preventing, taste specific and price specific product. All these attributes can be modified. Each attribute has three levels — high, medium and low. In all, there can be 243 combinations to choose from

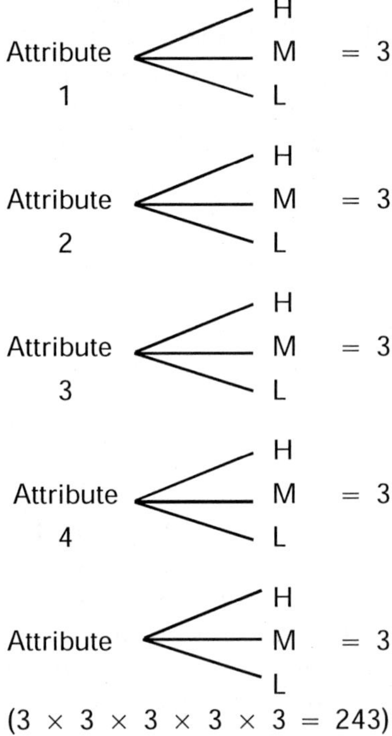

$(3 \times 3 \times 3 \times 3 \times 3 = 243)$

Osborn has suggested several questions to modify the object and its attributes — put to other uses, adapt, magnify, minify, substitute, rearrange, reverse or combine.

Forced Relationships: In this techniques several ideas are put forward and then an attempt is made to establish relationship amongst them. We can think of furniture, say a cot and a sofa, and then combine these two to get a sofa-cum-bed. Similarly, one can have a TV and VCD player ion one single piece, and a table with bookcase.

Morphological Analysis: Here we spell out a problem, a material handling system to carry materials from one spot to another. The vehicle could have a round platform, a flat plank or a seat-type arrangement, a trailer, a side-car or a swing. It can move on plain surface or rails. It can use pneumatic, hydraulic, electric or magnetic energy. All these options can be combined to generate new possibilities.

New Contents: We know a hospital for health care of normal human beings. We can think of a hospital for vets or psychotic people. We are aware of human funeral. What about animal funeral? Students attend a class by going to the institute. The institute may come to the students to teach them, say in the form of a mobile van..

Map Mapping: We should put down a thought on a piece of paper. Let us say we write a motor cycle. Let us further think about bikes, and what strikes us is Bajaj. Let us associate Bajaj further to Pune. Each word leads to new associations. It might lead us to new ideas.

Synectics

Synectics is a further refinement of brainstorming. It is developed by William J.J. Gordon. Synectics believes that creative process is not logical. It is more of an accident. Inventions come about when a person has given much thought to a problem, though there is no solution in sight. Suddenly, a solution appears accidentally. It is seemingly an unrelated situation. When Archimedes was having a bath, he found the Archimedes' Principle — a solution to his problem. A falling apple led to the solution of Newton's problem. A mould on agar plate led to the discovery of penicillin.

Synectics was developed at Harvard in the 60s. Many different variations have been developed over a period of time. Whatever the synectic technique, the objective is to find an answer to a given problem through "limbering up," by discussing seemingly unrelated subjects and then by asking the participants to come back to the initial problem and trying to find original solutions through a "force-fit" discussions, *i.e.*, by relating to the original problem words and ideas from completely different word associations and thought processes.

A really expert leader and a group of six to eight suitable intelligent outgoing people will come up with excellent results. A synectic sessions with uncreative people will, however, be useless.

For an important project, it is worth the while to hold several brainstorming sessions and synectic sessions. A number of ideas generating sessions under different environments and with different people go a long way in the generation of viable ideas.

Reverse Assumption Analysis: Here, we write down all normal assumptions about an entity and then reverse these. Let us assume that a college has specialised courses, changes fees and offers university degrees after coaching for a particular tenure. A new college may decide to have broad-spectrum courses where the student has the liberty to move to arts, science, commerce, computers by juggling with the modules. It might pay students who are ready to coach others. A course can be completed in a flexible manner, and completion of each module leads to certification.

Choice of Idea Generation Technique

Anything in the world that we see around us starts as an idea. Similarly, the new product development process begins with the search for ideas. There are a variety of techniques to generate new product ideas. Each technique has its pros and cons and it cannot be said that one technique is superior to the other technique. Organisations follow a systematic market-directed approach. However, individual situations act as constraints. Managers choose the idea generation techniques which are consistent with the aims and objectives of the organisation and its future plans. An organisation may need some product modifications and may find morphological analysis quite useful. Another organisation likes to develop a new instrument of control, for which purpose the technique of synectics can be useful.

Large organisations use well-manned new product development departments and R&D labs, whereas small from rely more on individual creativity through brainstorming.

Idea Screening and Evaluation

It is relatively easy to find a large number of opportunities in the form of initial ideas. We have to consider now which of them are really worth the while for a follow-up. Which of these ideas are worth committing the corporate resources to them? These are fairly difficult decisions. Some of the ideas are rejected for obvious reasons like:

(*a*) lousy idea;
(*b*) unsuitable idea for the firm;
(*c*) obvious problems in production and marketing;
(*d*) too little potential;
(*e*) someone else is already exploiting it;
(*f*) others would be able to implement it better and quicker;
(*g*) no long-term potential;
(*h*) other reasons, *e.g.*, unsuitable for the main customers of the company.

It should be possible to reduce the ideas from several hundreds to thirty or forty having some *prima facie* merit. Later, further pruning is done more rigorously. While screening the ideas, the company should not dismiss an otherwise good idea — a drop-error. Carlson's copying machine was a good idea. Xerox exploited it while IBM could not. RCA exploited the radio while Victor Talking Machine Company could not. Too many drop-errors may prove to be disastrous for a company. Its standards perhaps are too conservative. On the other hand, some companies become victims of the go-error — they proceed to the next stage though the idea was worth dismissing. An early rejection proves less costly for the company, since with the progressive stages of development process, the costs escalate. It is wrong on management's part to allow poor ideas to reach so far. Management should not allow ego and arrogance to blind fold itself in carrying forward apparently poor ideas.

A numerical rating of the specific factors is often useful at this stage. A typical rating device is given below:

Factor	*Maximum Score*
Idea is unique	20
Non-capable	25
Wider appeal	20
Strong enough to induce trials and repeat purchases	25
Technically viable	25
Not price-sensitive	25
Compatible with corporate policy	25
Little need for consumer education	20
Likely to appeal to current customers	20
Suitable for development considering company's technical expertise	25
Relevant to production resources/know-how	15
Can use company's branding	20
Suitable with the present sales/distribution resources	20
Can exploit other resources (financial, personnel, international)	10
Can be tested in the market place	20
Can be marketed in a given time frame	20
	335

Adapted after Peter Krausher, *Practical Business Development* (1985), *Holt, Rienhart and Winston.*

The factors chosen and the scores assigned are based on judgement and experience. These are useful in prioritising the factors at this stage. A team uses the above screen and arrives at an agreed point of view.

Richman's product-idea rating device lists the factors like company resources, location, corporate personality and goodwill. All these factors are weighted. The company's competence level against each factor is jotted down. The overall rating is the summation of the product of relative weight of each factor and company's competence level. A minimum cut-off point for acceptance is indicated.

The rating devices make idea screening more systematic. However, it is just an aid to decision-making, and cannot substitute it.

Third Stage

Concept Development and Testing

Even the best ideas just give an inkling of the final product. Product ideas are just an offer, say a "disposable watch" or a "powder to add to nutritional value of milk and make it tastier" or "a new savings scheme for kids — a kiddy-bank" or "an apple-based drink — an alternative to cola." This initial idea is to be developed into a *product concept* or a *consumer proposition.* The idea becomes a concept when it is elaborated — it covers the consumer or the consumer benefit, the target market and the intended usage. Consumers do not buy product ideas — they actually buy product concepts.

One product idea can lead to several possible product concepts. Each variant is to be examined with care because of all the product stages, the concept stage is the most critical. Hurried and haphazard approach might lead to a loss of an opportunity or heading for a wrong path from which it is difficult to retreat.

Let us take the idea of the disposable watch (the Swatch). First, we should ask who the possible users of this watch could be. The watch could be targeted to children, adults, fashionable women, upper-class people. Secondly, what benefit is to be built into this product is a question to be answered. It could be a time-keeping device, a fashion accessory, a low-cost watch, a gift watch, a disposable watch. Thirdly, one can consider the occasion of the use of this product — birthdays, weddings, festive occasions, daily use, accessory matching the outfits etc. By asking these questions, a company formulates several concepts.

Concept 1: The ideal gift for children — tough, plastic, really water-proof.

Concept 2: The modern woman's fashion accessory — in plastic, the material of the 90s. It tells the time, but it is bought for its looks. This is a feminine appeal.

Concept 3: The tough watch for men who want to tell the time. It should be durable and when faulty, can be thrown off without bothering for repairs.

Concept 4: The low cost disposable watch for the whole family. Who bothers about expensive repairs these days? It is boring too. We should be able to change it at will.

Concept 5: The latest gift for upmarket people. Though expensive, they can throw it out when out of order or when it wears out. It should have expensive face and band.

Concept 6: The new up-market fashion accessory that tells the time. A range of beautifully designed straps for both men and women, made of expensive materials and with a disposable watch face inside.

Many more concepts can be developed around a disposable watch, but the above gives you an idea as to how slight variations can affect a concept significantly. Each concept is likely to be different in terms of the probable product design, the target market and the pricing. Each concept has different marketing implications and technical considerations.

The above concepts may also define a product's category — a children's gift watch will compete with toys and games. A woman's accessory would compete with jewellery, buttons, straps, laces, flowers, footwear, shoulder-bags etc. It is the product's category that ultimately decides its competition.

Suppose, out of several milk additives, we ultimately accept the concept of instant breakfast drink. It then competes with eggs, breakfast cereals, coffee and cakes and other breakfast products. How it stands in relation to these other products is shown in a *positioning map* having time and cost dimensions.

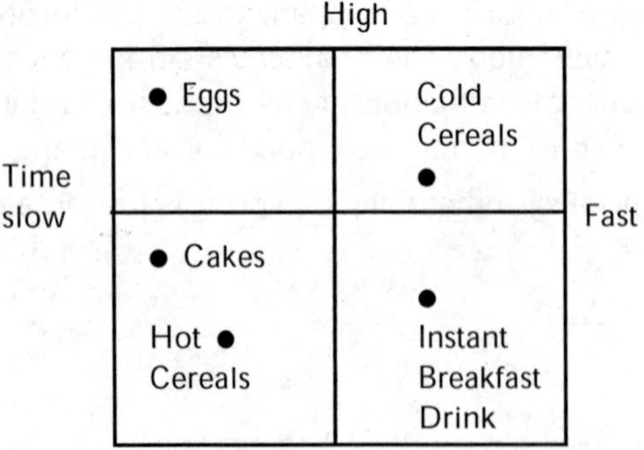

We have positioned instant breakfast drink as quick to make breakfast product which is low cost. Cold cereals are also quick to make but are not low cost. The product concept is then made a brand concept. Let us take three brands of breakfast drink and position them on price and nutritional value.

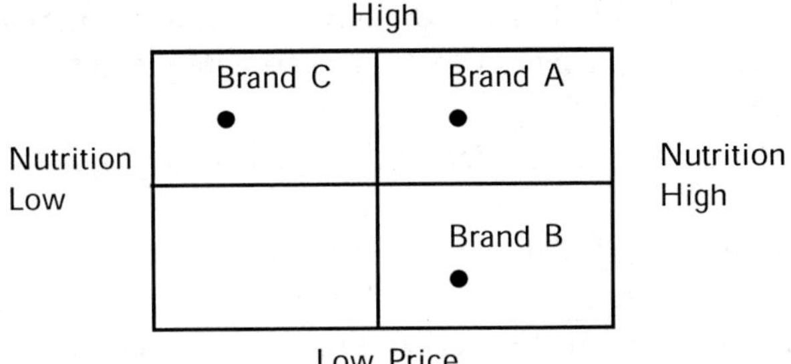

Our brand can be positioned as a moderately priced and moderately nutritive brand or low-priced and low nutritive brand.

Concept in certain markets, however, are relatively ephemeral. Concept is based on image factors rather than on factual service or product differentiation. This is particularly true of cosmetics, toiletries, household chemicals, cigarettes and even alcoholic beverages. Several pedestrian cosmetic products succeed due to image factors. The success of Dettol, Nivea, Marlboro, Brut after shave, Fa deodorants etc. is largely due to image: The image is created by consistent and heavy advertising. However, in the absence of any foundation on product attributes, if an image is built on advertising alone, it could prove risky, because the sales decline as soon as ad budget tapers off.

Concept Testing

Concepts developed painstakingly are tested on target audiences. The concepts are presented symbolically or physically. Maybe, a picture or verbal description suffices at this stage. However, concept test becomes more and more reliable when it is led from abstraction to concrete form. The consumer proposition should be informative. It just can't be like an ad copy "the best ice-cream in the world". It has got to be "a range of high-priced, high-quality ice-cream made from real cream and only with natural flavours and ingredients for those who like the best US or French ice-creams." The concept maybe backed up by illustrations and product prototypes, illustrating the claims in the proposition. The nearer the concept is to the final product or service, the better. However, in the case of durables, it is most likely to be an artists' impression. It is interesting to learn how much can be shown to consumers without spending money on prototype development. To illustrate, products already on the market can be chosen for comparison. Many straps and bracelets can be shown to the consumers for the watch concepts; without developing anything. It is, however, necessary that the customer understands what is being shown to him/her. Statements on a piece of paper may not be adequate. If the reaction is "it really depends on what the product looks like," the concept visualisation has failed.

Consumers are asked several questions while testing the concept:

(1) Are the benefits clear and credible?

(2) Will this solve your problem or satisfy your need?

(3) Are there existing products which satisfy the same need?

(4) Is the price fair?

(5) Do you intend to buy the product?

(6) Who would use this product and on what occasions?

In the light of these answers, the concepts are polished, revised. The testing and revising continue till the precious concept conforms to the consumer requirements. Once established finally, it is carried forward to other stages of development, without compromising anything.

Fourth Stage

Marketing Strategy Development

In order to put the product into the market, the company must develop its marketing strategy. The strategy developed initially is subject to revision later. The size of the market, the target market, and the financial goals sought to be achieved are specified. Thus, the target market for disposable watches will be families who will accept a new disposable watch which shows time, but, at the same time, is a fashion accessory. The watch will be moderately priced. The company initially intends to sell 5 lakh pieces. The profit margin expected is 15 p.c. of sales. The company plans to raise the sales to 35 lakh pieces in the next three years.

The second part of the strategy spells out product's price, distribution strategy and the promotional budget for the first year:

The watch will be given on plastic stand and will retail at ₹ 200 a piece. To begin with, dealers will be given one watch free for every few watches bought. To induce trials, coupons will be put in the press, giving a discount of 10 p.c. The promotional budget will be ₹ 50 lakhs. The budget will be split between 60 p.c. for TV and 40 p.c. for press. The theme of advertisement will be to emphasise the watch as a fashion accessory at a reasonable price. During the first year, ₹ 10 lakhs will be spent on marketing research.

The last part of the marketing strategy is to state the long term financial and marketing goals: The company intends to acquire a 30 p.c. market share of the total watch market and intends a rate of return on investment of 12 p.c. There will be further improvements in the product — straps and faces to match the current fashion trend. Price will be maintained at a low level. The promotional budget will be increased by 25 p.c. every year. Marketing research expenses will be reduced in future years.

Fifth Stage

Business Analysis

We have already developed the product concept and the marketing strategy. It is now time to examine the proposal's business or financial worth. Here projections are made about the sales, costs and profits to see whether these meet our objectives. If yes, the proposal proceeds to the prototype development stage.

Sales Estimation

It is important to know whether the product will generate sales enough to yield a satisfactory profit. Products are classified for such an estimation into three classes, a one-shot product, a frequently purchased product or an infrequently purchased product. The sales of a one time purchase product show a usual pattern. They rise, reach a peak and decline. If new buyers are added, the sales stabilise. Frequently purchased products are consumer nondurables or industrial products. First the sales rise as new buyers are attracted and then the sales fall. If the product is good, repeat purchases stabilise the sales. Infrequently purchased products like cars have two types of sales — first-time sales and replacement sales as the previous products become obsolete or depreciate due to wear and tear.

Estimating First Times Sales

We can use a *build-up* technique in which general estimates of future demand in the segments, likely to use the product are made. These are added to get the total forecast. It is also called a top-down approach.

First *market potential* for a product is estimated. It is the estimation of total market sales. To illustrate, a medical equipment may be sold to hospitals, laboratories and privates nursing homes. The existing facilities are accounted. They are reduced by the purchase probabilities for the new equipment. The sum gives the market potential. This market is to be penetrated. It is the *sales potential* that an individual company expects to achieve out of the market potential.

The company can make use of experience, judgement or statistical techniques to make the predictions.

Since replacement sales are difficult to predict before the product is in actual use, manufacturers base their new product's sales estimates on first-time sales.

Estimating Repeat Sales

This is necessary for frequently purchased products. A high repeat purchase rate shows satisfaction with the performance of the product. We have to estimate repeat purchases in each class, repeat purchase once, or twice or thrice and so on. Some products are abandoned after a few trials. It is necessary to estimate the rise or fall of repeat purchase ratio, and the rate of such rise and fall.

We can make use of the *derivation* method. To illustrate, we are interested to know the replacement demand for car tyres. First, it is estimated how many cars are candidates for the new tyres. Market research shows, on an average, a mileage of 10,000 miles per car per year, and tyres last for 30,000 miles. In 1995, all cars which have three-year old tyres are potential candidates for new tyres. We shall have to get the figure of cars sold in 1992. Further, in 1995, cars becoming 6 years old will be ready for the second replacement. The number of cars are put into age brackets. This number is multiplied by four (tyres per car). It gives market potential of replacement demand for car tyres in 1995. It should be noted that these are averages. All cars will not be driven for 10,000 miles a year.

Estimating Sales

Bass has used the following equation to estimate the probability of purchase at time (t).

$$P(t) = p + q\,[y(t) \div m)]$$

where p = probability of first purchase at $t = 0$ or the coefficient of innovation

q = coefficient of imitation

m = total number of potential adopters

$y(t)$ = adoption purchases by time (t) and

$y(t) \div m$ = fraction of potential adopters who have purchased

The number of adopters at t is

$$S(t) = pm + (q - p)\,y(t) - (q \div m)\,[y(t)2]$$

Maximum adoption will occur at t^+

$$t^+ = (p + q) \div m(q \div p)$$

and

$$S(t) = \frac{m(q+p)^2}{4q}$$

Fourt and Woodlock First-time Sales Model

New product penetration cumulative sales approach a limiting penetration level of less than 100 p.c. of all households. The subsequent incremental gain keeps on declining.

The equation is

$$q_t = rq\,(1 - r)^{t-l}$$

where q_1 = percentage of total households expected to try the product in period t

r = rate of penetration of untapped potential

q^- = percentage of total households who finally try the new product, and

t = time period

Say, it is estimated that 30% of all households will finally try a new product or $q^- = 0.3$. Also, during each period, 20% of the remaining households will be penetrated or $r = 0.2$. Therefore, the percentage of households trying the new product in the first four periods are:

$$q_l = rq^-\,(1 - r)^{l-l} = (0.2)\,(0.3)\,(0.8)^0 = 0.060$$

$$q_2 = rq^-\,(1 - r)^{2-1} = (0.2)\,(0.3)\,(0.8)^1 = 0.048$$

$$q_3 = rq^-\,(1 - r)^{3-1} = (0.2)\,(0.3)\,(0.8)^2 = 0.038$$

$$q_4 = rq^-\,(1 - r)^{4-1} = (0.2)\,(0.3)\,(0.8)^3 = 0.031$$

In other words, as time rolls on, the incremental trial purchase percentage moves to zero.

Estimation of Rupee Sales from New Buyers = qt (trial rate for any period) × total number of households × the expected first purchase expenditure household of the product.

Forecasting through Awareness - Trial-Repeat Purchase Rate

Consider a market of 6 million customers. The purchasing rate per customer is 10 units per annum organisation has the following data:

Awareness = 30 p.c. of customers

Trial = 25 p.c. of those who are aware

Repeat Purchase = 60 p.c. of those who have tried

To estimate sales, these rates can be multiplied

60,00,000 customers × 30% × 25% × 60%

= 2,70,000 customers are repeat buyers

2,70,000 × 10 units = 27,00,000 units sales per year

Therefore $\frac{27,00,000}{600,00,000}$ = 4.5% market share

(60m =6m × 10 units per annum = total unit market)

Survey of Buyer Intentions

Sales are commonly estimated by undertaking a survey of potential customers. The customers are asked whether they would buy a new product, and if yes, how much and how many times. Consumer panels might be maintained as a sounding board for new product ideas. It is to be noted that the consumers just *intend to buy*. It is open to question whether they would *actually buy* it. Perhaps, the survey might show inflated results.

Buyer behaviour may be studied for new technological breakthroughs and hitherto unheard products. What need is satisfied while the consumer may use this product? Products satisfying the same need already existing give an idea of the sales potential. The number of occasions a consumer cleans the toilet is a pointer to the possibility of use of a new toilet cleaner.

Estimating Costs and Profits

The costs are estimated by the marketing department in consultation with the production/engineering department and the costs/finance department. Afterwards, statements of estimated trading and P & L accounts are prepared for a specified future period, say of three to five years.

Proforma of Estimated Trading Account as on

To Cost of goods sold (estimated)	....	By Estimated sales	
To Estimated Profit			
transferred to P & L	....		
	....		....
	....		....
To Development Costs	....	By Estimated G.P.	....
To Marketing costs	....	By Estimated Other Income	
To Overheads allocated	....		
To Estimated Net Profit	....		....

The net profit estimated is subjected to the *discounted cash flow technique (DCF), viz.,* the present value of each year's net profit is discounted at an agreed rate of discount (say 15 p.c.). Alternatively, the company may use *pay-back period* method to know what time it will take to recover its investment.

Break-even analysis is another technique that is used to know what quantity of sales/production at which the company breaks even — no profit or no loss. *Risk analysis* using optimistic, pessimistic and *most likely* time estimates for a given uncertain variable are made to find out the possible outcomes. A rate-of-return probability distribution is computed, showing the possible rate of returns and their probabilities. The students are advised to consult a good text-book of Financial Management to master the details of these techniques.

Sixth Stage

Prototype Development

On passing the commercial tests, the product idea reaches a stage where it is converted into a physical product by the R&D and the engineering department. So far it was just a verbal or visual entity. Maybe, a crude mockup was made. However, its conversion into a physical product requires commitment of resources on a much larger scale than that at the earlier stages. The technically and commercially feasible product is developed at this stage. The firm may develop more than one prototypes. Prototype embodies the key features or attributes spelled out in the concept statement. The prototype should perform safely under normal conditions. It should also be made within the budgeted cost. Developing a prototype maybe a short process, hardly taking a few days or it may be a long process, taking several months or even years. In food products, it may take several months to develop a taste that corresponds to a taste demanded by the consumers. Even then, the desired product may become too costly. The prototype not only incorporates the physical attributes but also communicates the psychological aspects of the products through physical features. Perhaps, a green colour is perceived as being cool. A green mouthwash will be considered giving a cooling effect. To communicate that VIP is sturdy, it must be moulded out of the best ABS plastic. Marketing people have to communicate to the laboratory scientists as to what the consumers might expect of the product being developed.

Once the prototype is made, it is subjected to several tests — both functional testing and consumer testing. Functional tests are carried out in the lab, and data collected. In the case of pharmaceuticals, there are extensive tests — pharmoko-kinetic and toxicity tests. Consumer testing assumes various forms. The consumers might be invited into a lab. Sometimes, a product is placed at home to see how it is liked by the consumers. Consumer's preferences are solicited by techniques like ranking, paired comparisons and rating scales.

Test Marketing

The prototype may come up to the expectations of the firm. Then it is packaged properly, given a brand name and is tested in the market. Branding and packaging are discussed in detail in separate chapters. Test marketing tests the product in an actual market setting. It gives an idea about the reactions of the consumers to the product, the rate of trial and repeat purchases, the reactions of the distributors to the product and the potential market for the product.

All companies, however, do not opt for test marketing, and launch the product directly. Most companies, however, are convinced about the effectiveness of test marketing which enables the company to test the effectiveness of alternative marketing strategies. To what extent test marketing is to be resorted to we have to consider the risk involved in launching a product. The higher the risk, the greater is the need for test marketing. However, the time factor is an overall constraint. If competitors are likely to overtake the firm in putting a similar or better new product in the same category, it is better to dispense the testing. It is a choice between the risk of failure of the untested product and the risk of losing the market to the competitor who overtakes us.

Seventh Stage

Test Marketing Methods

The following methods are used in test marketing.

Consumer Goods Market Testing: Basically, we have to estimate the first trial purchase, the first repeat purchase, the adoption of the new product, and the purchase frequency. All these variables must be preferably at a high level. If it is observed that the consumers are buying the new product initially, but are not coming back to buy it again, then it clearly means that they are not satisfied with the performance of the product. There are situations when they come back for purchasing again, but the repurchasing rate later falls down. Sometimes, the product is adopted but the purchase frequency is less. Maybe, the buyers think that the product is for special occasion only. Though it is necessary to know about the repurchases it lengthens the test marketing period averages for two years. However, it seems preferable to settle for quickening of the time-scale like P&G which insists on one year's test marketing.

In durables, it maybe difficult to measure repeat purchase by means of test marketing.

Sales Wave Research

First, the product is offered free for trial. Then it is offered at a reduced price with an option to accept competitors product. The reoffering is done three to five times (sales waves). It is noted how many times the company's product is chosen and the level of satisfaction at each wave.

Sales wave research estimates the repeat purchase rate under conditions of freedom to spend money either on the firm's product or the products of the competitors.

Sales wave research can be used to test the advertising effectiveness of various themes of advertising. It can be seen how the theme affects the repeat purchases.

Sales wave research is easy to administer. It is however, is not useful to assess the trial rates, since the consumers are preselected to try the product.

Simulated Test Marketing: The consumers' simulated shopping exercise first exposes them to the ad copies including the one that advertises the new product. The consumers are given an amount to spend. They are invited to buy any items from a store. The new product is given free to even those who do not buy it. The company records how many consumers buy the new product and competeing brands. This indicates the effectiveness of the copy to induce a trial. The consumers are later telephonically interviewed to know their reactions. The results can be used as inputs in sales forecasts.

Controlled Test Marketing: A panel of stores participating in the exercise carry a stock of new product. The shelf position, the display method, the point of purchase promotion and prices are all pre-planned by the researcher. The sales results are analysed. This test enables us to know the impact of real-life in-store factors on buyer behaviour. Consumers are later interviewed for feedback. This technique, however, exposes the product to competition.

Selection of Test Markets: Test market ought to be a replica of the national market or full-scale market. Some cities are selected for test marketing — mostly 2-6 cities. No city can be an exact replica of the national market. Each company has to develop its own criteria for test-city selection. The city should have enough diversity, media availability, necessary retailing outlets, average competition and should not have been overtested.

Time of the Test Marketing: Test marketing ranges from a few months to several years. The test period corresponds to the average repurchasing period. The competitive activity calls for a shorter test marketing period.

Data Collected in Text Marketing: The data to be collected must be decided. Its cost and value trade off should be studied. Inventory levels will indicate weekly retail sales. Stores audits indicate retail sales of both the test-marketed product and the competitive product. Consumer panels are used to know the buying habits. Consumer surveys are carried out to collect data regarding attitudes, usage and satisfaction. Trade research is also carried out. Studies to assess effectiveness of promotional campaigns and retail distribution are also carried out.

Action Taken: "Success test marketing" means a high trial rate and repurchase rate. We can move further for a full-market launch. If there is high trial rate and low repurchase rate, it shows the dissatisfaction of the consumers with the product. The product needs modifications/redesigning. If there is low trial rate but high repurchase rate, it shows satisfaction with the performance of the product. But we should motivate more people to buy it by making promotion effective. If there is both low trial rate and repurchase rate, the product should be dropped.

Benefits of Test Marketing

(*i*) It is a value input to a sales forecast. Lower than the targeted sales in the test market indicates the dropping of the product or its modification. Even marketing programme will have to be reconsidered.

(*ii*) Test marketing enables us to compare alternative marketing plans. In each test market, a different marketing mix is used. The data are collected. The most beneficial marketing mix is chosen.

(*iii*) Test marketing may point out defect in a product, distribution problems and the different behaviour of buyers in various segments of the market.

Test Marketing Questioned: Though test marketing is a useful tool it alerts the competitors about a new product. Competitive activity may spoil test marketing itself. Several companies by-pass the test marketing route and resort to other methods of market testing like a launch in 25% of market or a launch in some countries.

Eighth Stage

Commercialisation

Test marketing feedback enables management to take a decision regarding the launching of a product. A product launch is the costliest stage of new product development. The company either sets up the manufacturing facilities for production itself and hires the same. As a precautionary measure, the company may set up a plant smaller than the one demanded by the sales forecast. Apart from production costs, the company has to bear heavy marketing costs — packaging, promotion, advertising, distribution etc. Marketing expenditures are the highest in the year of the launch, reaching in some cases almost 60 p.c. of sales.

Timing of the Launch: It is critical to time the entry of the new product correctly. When a competitor is also on the point of launching a rival product the company can decide to have the first entry and establish leadership or to enter the market simultaneously with the competitor or to have a late entry to have the benefit of hindsight. Soft drinks are generally launched in pre-summer months. The text-books are launched at the beginning of the academic section. The most likely question books are launched just before the exams. A product launch may be all delayed to clear first the previous stock.

Coverage: The product may be launched locally or in a region, or in several regions or nationally or internationally. Few companies have the marketing muscle and capability to undertake a national launch or a global launch. There is mostly a planned roll-out. They first do the local or regional launch and then expand gradually. Those companies which have national distribution network might launch their products nationally. In roll-out marketing, markets can be rated. In any roll-out marketing, the competitive scene is taken into account.

Target Markets: Each company identifies the main prospective users of its product. These are the prime prospects. They should ideally be early adopters, opinion leaders, be accessible at reasonable cost and heavy users.

Initial Marketing Strategy

An action-plan is put into effect in the roll-out market.

New Product Adoption

The new product's acceptance by the consumers is called its "adoption". It is a six-step process in which the consumer passes through the awareness, information, evaluation, trial, adoption and confirmation.

Stages	*Activities Involved*
(*i*) Awareness	Person is exposed to the new product. He becomes a prospect.
(*ii*) Interest	He develops interest in the new product solicits information about the new product.
(*iii*) Evaluation	He studies the merits of the new products mentally.
(*iv*) Trial	He tries the new product in a limited manner. He prefers a small quantity for trial.
(*v*) Adoption	Here he decides whether to accept the new product in a full-fledged manner.
(*vi*) Confirmation (Post-adoption)	The new product is adopted. He needs a constant reassurance about his choice.

The above progressive stages suggest that the marketer of a new product should facilitate the movement of the prospect through these stages. In India, many prospects are interested in a dish washer, say, a Maharaja Whiteline Dishwasher, but there is an uncertainty about its functioning. They may be given a demonstration of a dishwasher. A mail order company selling garments might induce the prospects to place a trial order, and may ask the consumers to return the goods if not satisfied within a specified time. A product may be offered on a trial basis with an option to buy if the results are satisfactory. It may be noted that the ultimate adoption or acceptance is a result of the adoption process.

Adopter Categories

Some people accept a new product quickly while others take time. There are some who never adopt a new product. Research studies put adopters into five categories depending upon the time taken to adopt a new product. The following diagram illustrates this:

The adoption process is represented as a normal distribution over time. First, there is a slow start. Increasing numbers adopt it later. The adoption reaches a peak. If then diminishes, leaving very few non-adopters.

Innovators: They are the first who venture to adopt a new product. They are likely to be younger. They may have a high social status. Their outlook is broad and cosmopolitan. They are venturesome to try out new ideas, taking some risk.

Early Adopters: This group consists more of opinion leaders. They are greatly respected in society. They adopt new ideas early but are careful. They are "change agents".

Early Majority: It is a *deliberate* group who accepts an innovation before the average person does so. It is a notch above average group. They themselves are not the leaders.

Late Majority: It is a *skeptical* group who adopt a new product out of necessity or social pressure. They adopt when so many others have done so before them.

Distribution of adopters of a New Product

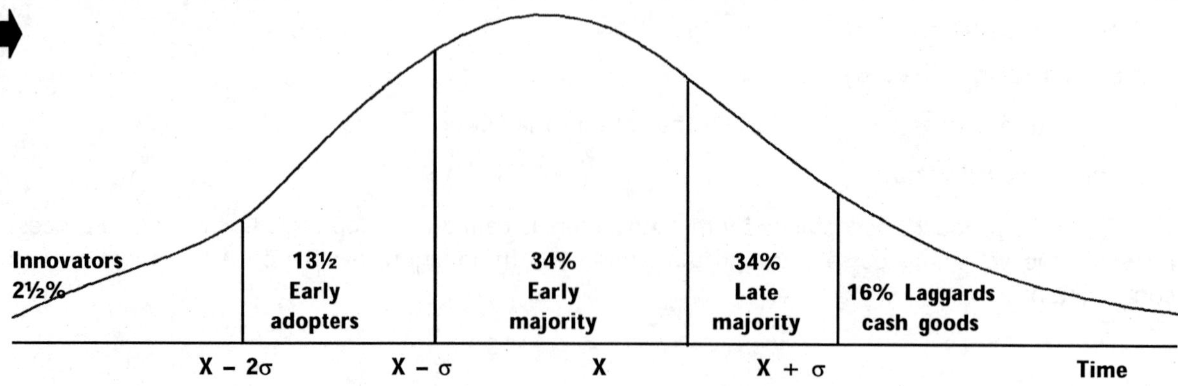

Laggards: They are a *tradition bound* group. They are the last to adopt a new product. They are suspicious of new products. When they finally accept a new product, it may so happen that the innovation might already have been discarded by the innovators. These people are comparatively older. They are at the lower end of social and economic scale.

These slots help the marketers to study the media habits of each slot differently. There is no overall innovative trait in an individual. He may be an innovator in certain areas and may be a laggard in others. A person may be conservative in dress habits, but may accept exotic dishes. Each marketer has to study the characteristics of likely early adopters in a given product category.

Characteristics of Innovation Affecting Adoption Role

According to Rogers, there are five characteristics of an innovation which affect its adoption rate.

Relative advantage: This is the degree to which a new product scores over the old ideas. It maybe the benefit of a lower cost or some other advantage. The greater the advantage, the faster the adoption.

Comparability: This is the degree to which the new product lives up to the cultural values and experiences of the prospects. A music system may be highly consistent with the life style of an upper middle class home.

Complexity: The degree or level of difficulty in using a new product or in understanding and mastering it. A professional camera may take a longer time for adoption since it is difficult to master its various functions.

Divisibility or trialability: This is the degree to which a new product may be tried in a limited manner. The hire purchase scheme increases the rate of adoption of an air-conditioner. Central air-conditioning system is having a lower trialability than a new variety of seed which can be tried on a small plot of land.

Communicability or Observability: This is the degree to which the results of the use of a new product can be observed or described. An innovation whose use can be demonstrated to others diffuses faster in the social system.

Apart from the above, personal influences, initial pricing, scientific credibility and social approval also affect the rate of adoption. All these factors must be carefully studied by the marketer, and are used as inputs while designing a new product.

Diffusion

Rogers has defined a diffusion. It is the spread of an innovation in the mass of ultimate users or adopters. Diffusion starts from the source of invention or creation and ends with the users or adopters. Diffusion is the process by which the innovation is communicated within the social system over time.

New Product Planning Process: Some Observations

There is no normative model of product planning process. It varies from company to company. Many companies do not use strategic planning much, and so also the marketing research inputs. This holds true especially in the idea generation and demand estimation stages. Criteria to appraise product proposals are neither fixed nor strategic concept testing is an extremely useful tool, but its use is an exception. Business analysis is just too elementary, and little effort is made to do detailed demand forecasting.

Some companies focus too much on engineering, and not only marketing. Their over-engineered products may be too expensive for the market.

There is a considerable gap between theory and practice, suggesting how complex the whole process is. The process tends to be disorderly, as it involves people with different skills, and varying perspectives. There is a further complication. In the new product development process, we deal with an intangible concept rather than a tangible product. It demands management of creativity. It is easy to become infatuated with technology. Engineers feel too competent to design anything. Scientists in the R&D are enamoured of their technological outcomes. They, as a result, are divorced from market realities. They come out with technological solutions to phantom problems.

The failure to provide strategic direction to the technical staff also results in a too technology-based approach. Creativity is the crux of the new product planning process, bur requires conducive organisational climate to flourish. Bureaucratisation stifles it.

A suitable organisational mechanism must be developed to do new product development. Many a time, management fails to provide such a mechanism. Technical personnel may lack a managerial perspective. Undue emphasis on consent rather than conflict also eliminates many potential new product ideas.

Improving the New Product Planning Process

According to Feldman and Page, product planning process improvement has three dimensions — strategic orientation, ordering the process and increasing information inputs.

Strategic nature of product decisions must be appreciated. It is essential to set up criteria against which the product decisions will be evaluated. Strategic direction must be given to the entire process. Or else we may venture deep into new product fields. Sometimes, we are anchored to the shallow waters of the current offerings, thus making us staid. The market may want us to brave the new areas.

Systematic product planning process pays off. There should be a method of evaluation of business proposals. The uniformity in the process should be seen both in contents and procedure. As it is a 'people process', it leads to a paradox. It fosters subjectivity, whereas the process should try to attain objectivity. Very few companies have a formal document spelling out the process. Criteria of evaluation must be carefully determined. The relative importance of these criteria must be known.

In business analysis stage, there is a tendency to equate it with screening while deciding its business viability. It may lead to a superficial appraisal which spills over from the screening stage, failing to understand deeper marketing realities. Marketing research inputs must be increased to improve the product planning process. It should be a continuous integration. It should be used more at the concept testing and product testing stage.

3

FACILITIES PLANNING: PROCESS PLANNING AND PROCESS FLOW ANALYSIS

Process Planning

Products can be made by several different processes. A chair can be turned out by a carpenter, or can be put together by combining different parts or modules, or can be made automatically by machines on an assembly line, or can be made by injection moulding machine from plastic. Each process vests a product with different characteristics. Operations managers thus have to select and design a process that turns out a product with planned features. This is called process planning.

A process is thus consists of operations used to make a product. Process planning are the decisions made about this process. A process is so designed that it makes the product effectively and efficiently.

As consumers, we are more concerned with the products we buy, rather than the process used to make it. It is, however, necessary to understand that the product and process are inseparable. In case of services, both the product and process are indistinguishable — banking service or cinema hall or cab service. It is important, therefore, to plan the process.

A product basically satisfies customer needs and wants. It has to be better than the competitive products. The process makes the product. The better the process, the better the product.

After the product has been designed, the process engineer takes over and develops a plan for the manufacture. Processing spells out how a product will be made. It is a question of selecting the right process, determining the tooling, gauges and equipment. There is a also cost estimation. Process planning is thus a systematic study of the methods by which a product will be made economically and competitively. It consists of:

- Devising, selecting and specifying processes.
- Determining machine tools and other equipment to convert raw material into finished products.
- Determine the optimal process for each job.

Expression of Process Plans

A process plan is expressed in a variety of ways. In a large organisation, process plans are recorded in some detail.

The media used are the routing or route sheet, process sheet, operation planning sheet and so on. These spell out and describe the operations of a process. Routings are written as briefly as possible. They outline departments, machine tools etc. The operation sheet used is different in different industries. A typical operation planning sheet is given below.

Fig. 3.1

Operation Planning Sheet

OPERATION PLANNING SHEET

Name of the Part	Material .... Material Specification					Part Number ....
Operation No.	Description of Operation	Machine	Tools	Jigs	Gauges	Time Analysis

Process Selection

The operations function essentially is a transformation process that accepts the inputs, and gives the outputs after adding value to these inputs. Process selection refers to the strategic decision of selecting which kind of production process to have in the plant, *e.g.*, batch production or assembly line production. Process selection is a major strategic decision as it involves allocation of man and material resources as well as financial commitments of a long nature. Corporate planning these days, gives enough importance to operations, along with marketing to which it plays a supportive role. The transformation process is expected to generate an output desired by the market, and this it should do in the most cost efficient way. We have to recognize that operations management is a business-related function, and is not a technical or engineering-driven function. Operations give outputs of products and services. Production engineering provide expert support services for these process selection has a technical dimension — process should be able to meet specifications. Process selection has a business dimension — to get into the market and stay there and once this is done to win orders.

We shall examine in this chapter the major considerations in the selection of the transformation process, the different types of processes available and the method of selecting the most appropriate process.

Adaptive Process

Process selection has to adapt itself to a number of changing factors like capacity, lead-time, flexibility, trade-offs between material, labour and capital, trade-offs between volume and variety, etc. Therefore, this decision is pretty complex. We cannot have the best process. It could only be the most acceptable process, given the different trade-offs. As the factors change with the passage of time, there could be a change in process selected too, leading to another appropriate process.

Environmental Effect

Process selection responds to environmental changes, especially changes in technology. The previous process may be replaced. They may become obsolete also. Even the technology involved in organizing the operations function tells upon the process selected. (Group Technology or Autonomous Working). The competitive environment also affects the process selection. If Amul has spray-dried milk, it also becomes necessary for Food Specialties Ltd. to have spray dried milk powder (Nespray). Non-price competition is also important in process selection.

Forms of Transformation Process

Process selection also refers to the selection of sub-processes, and the sub-processes of these sub-processes also. When the output consists of a product, there are assemblies and sub-assemblies and this break-up continues till the elemental level of components incapable of being broken down further. These components and sub-components can either be made by us or can be purchased from outside. We have to take a make or buy decision here. For those components which we are to make, we have to select the process — technology to be employed, sequence of operations, process, storage and transport from one work centre to another, plant and machinery for transformation process, manpower deployment, layout of the workplace, tooling, jigs and fixtures necessary etc. As we assemble certain products like transistor radios we have to outline in detail the assembly process. Here the point to be noted is that there is no ideal process for an ideal product — there is room for improvement in both the process used and the output generated.

Volume *vs.* Variety

It could be considered as a continuum (volume-variety). One extreme end of this continuum shows very high variety (and hence very low volume). The other extreme is that of low product variety but very high volumes. Variety requires skilled technicians, general purpose machines, and complex PPC. High volumes require automation, mass-producing special machines and simple PPC.

Produce-to-Stock *vs.* Produce-to-Order

One important consideration affecting selection of the process is that of making production first for storing in the storage for selling or receiving an order first from the customers, and then starting the production process. Standardisation and variety reduction leads to batch production which form the inventory from which stocks to sell are drawn, is replenished by further batch production once it reaches a minimum pre-determined level. The system produces here in anticipation of demand. There is no waiting time involved for the customer. Such products are inventoriable. The risk is much more in the case of perishable products and short shelf-life products.

Produce-to-order is customized producing where the manufacturing process or operation follow the receipt of customer's order. Yes, here there is a waiting time for the customer (delivery date). The time is proportional to the lead time of the operational process. Non-inventoriable services are always produced to order, taking care that the waiting time for the customer is as short as possible.

There could be a combination of both these: components and spares are produced to stock, and the assembly is carried out to order. In a restaurant, dishes are in the semi-cooked form (produced to stock) and are converted to dishes to be served on customer demand (produce-to-order).

Output Characteristics *vs.* Process Selection

The selection of process from project-type, intermittent-type, continuous-type or continuous-process type depends upon the characteristics of the output. Unique non-repetitive output like ship building requires project form. Assembly of ceiling fans may require interrupted form. Here the batch size is large. However, TV assembly may use continuous form, though interrupted form may be used if the batch size is small. There are products with no variety at all and are like genetic commodities — fertilizers, sugar, cement and others. They require a continuous process form.

Services may be on project form like that of an architect. Services from government are interrupted form. In high volume services, continuous form is used.

Types of Processes

Fundamentally, there are four types of processes:

Conversion processes convert the inputs into value-added outputs, *e.g.*, iron ore is converted into steel or a cough syrup is made from the listed ingredients on the label.

Fabrication processes change the input into a specific form, *e.g.*, sheet metal is turned into the car door or using plastic as replacement in the arthritic knee surgery.

Assembly processes are putting things together, *e.g.*, putting a medicinal cream into a carton or fixing a pilfer cap on a liquid medicine bottle or fixing a door to the body of the car.

Testing processes are for testing the effectiveness of the product as a whole, *e.g.*, testing the content of a particular ingredient in a cough syrup, testing the up-and-down movement of the spectacles frames to judge their strength, testing a bulb against fusing etc.

Process Selection: Products

The operations are essentially a transformation process that accepts the inputs and generates the outputs after adding value to these inputs. An organisation has to decide which type of process to use for such transformation. Indica cars at Tata Motors, Pune or Maruti cars at Gurgaon plant are made using assembly-line type of process. Sailboats are, however, made using batch production process. The selection of process depends upon several factors. The volume of the product and its nature do affect the decision. High volume standardized products are better suited to assembly-line, whereas, low-volume non-standardized products to batch production. Process selection decision is a major strategic decision as it involves allocation of scarce resources such as men, materials and money, and that too on a long-term basis.

In this chapter, we shall examine the available production processes for selection. Processes are classified on the basis of two criteria — the flow of the products, whether line, batch or project and the nature of the customer order, whether product is made-to-order or made-to-stock. We shall sum up by considering the dynamics of the process choice decisions.

Characteristics of Product Flow

Product flows are of of three types:

- Line flow
- Batch flow
- Project flow

In manufacturing industry, product flows correspond to materials flows, whereas in service industry, there could be flows of customers and information.

Line Flow

This type of flow shows a linear pattern. The product travels from step to step sequentially from the start to finish. Line flow is seen in car manufacturing, computer assembling, refrigerator manufacturing and many such mass-produced goods. The following figure illustrates the Line flow.

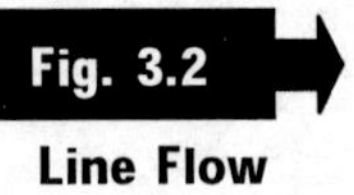

Line Flow

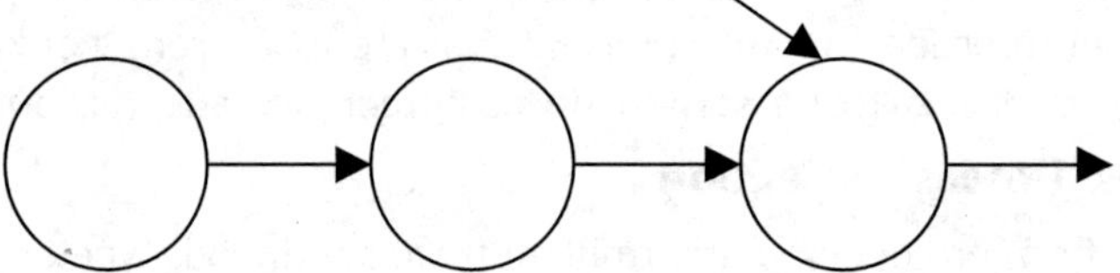

Where O denotes task or work-station
→ denotes product flow.

The entire manufacturing is broken down into operations but each limit moves or flows from one operation to the next individually. The process, as a result, generates mostly a single output, or may be with some additional options. The variety here is small but the volume is high. The facilities are arranged, therefore, in a linear sequence and consist of HS special machines. The material movement is minimized. Services traditionally do not use this type of flow since they are customer-based. However, on standardization, certain services can be given on a continuous basis — fast food outlets, auto service centre, etc.

Mass production and continuous flow are the terms which usually describe line flows. **Mass production** refers to the use of assembly lines to assembly discrete parts into a finished product, *e.g.*, a car. **Continuous process** refers to the so-called process industries like oil, paper, beer and electricity. The outputs of process industries are standardized. The process is automated. It generates a large volume.

Though this type of flow is very efficient, it is also inflexible since it is difficult to change the product or volume of flow. These days it is being attempted to individualise flexibility in line processes by using flexible equipment, labour assignments and computer automation. This has led to what is known as mass customization.

Line operations are capital extensive. Marketing must support the high volume products.

Batch Flow

This process is very suitable for large variety of outputs, each output taking a different route and hence operations, with different time requirements and sequence. In this process, different outputs are called batches or lots. Each batch of the product flows from one operation or work-centre to another. A work-centre is a group of similar machines or processes used to make the product, *e.g.*, metal-cutting machines, metal-grinding machines or painting facility. The following figure illustrates batch processing consisting of several work-centres and several products.

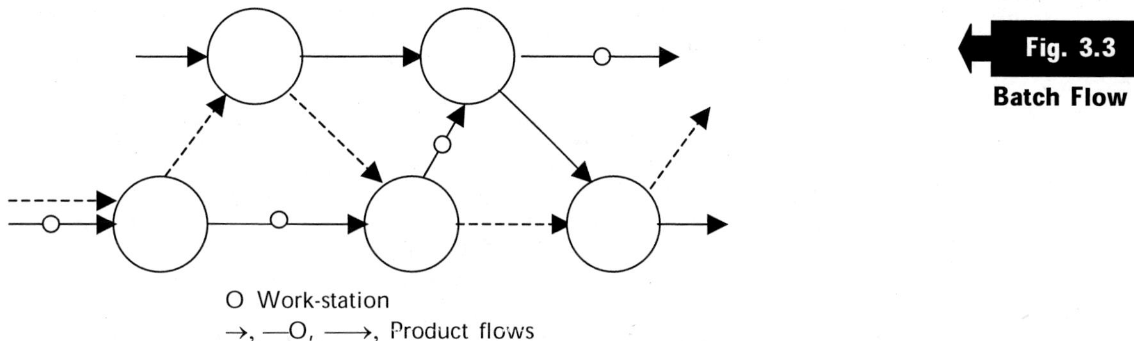

Fig. 3.3 Batch Flow

Every product follows a different path through the work-centres. There can be skipping of work-centres for certain products. The flow thus looks jumbled or intermittent. As against this, the line flow is regular and sequential.

This flow is flexible since it uses general purpose machines for a variety of outputs. The transformation process is organized around standard operations in the intermittent form *e.g.*, in a hospital we can have pathological lab, blood bank, radiography etc. In a bank, we can have savings account counter, current account counter, cash counter, advances and time-deposit departments. Each functional group is a specialist group.

There are complex problems of production planning and control as compared to continuous manufacturing. The scheduling function is performed according to the jobs on hand, their stage of completion and commitment for completion.

The dispatching also becomes complex. The job assignments to man and machines requires up-to-date information about the existing and probable work-loads.

The batch operations, when loaded to near full capacity, will typically have high inventories as jobs wait in line to be processed.

Efficiency of a batch process is given by **throughput ratio** (TR)

$$TR = \frac{\text{Total processing time for the job}}{\text{Total time in operations}} \times 100\%$$

Total processing time for the job includes only the time the job actually takes for being processed by machines or men and less any waiting time it takes between the operations. Total time in operations includes both processing and waiting time. Usually, TRs lie between 10 and 20 per cent, and rarely exceed 40 per cent. It means waiting time for a typical job is more than the actual processing time. As against this, line flow operations have TRs of 90 to 100 per cent.

Batch processing uses **process layout**, whereas line processing uses **product layout**. Layouts have been discussed in a separate chapter.

Batch operations are justified for low volume and large variety products. Furniture, boats, dishware, printing are processed in batches.

Project

This form is used for one-of-its-kind products or creative products. Some instances could be a construction project, a ship manufacturing, air-craft manufacturing or holding a concert. There are peculiar problems of planning and control as there could be no precedents. It is also difficult to automate projects. The equipment used is general purpose. Projects require skilled manpower. Strictly speaking projects have no project flow. However, a sequence of operations can be traced. This sequence is shown in the diagram below. There is predecessor-succession relationship between the tasks or activities.

Fig. 3.4

Project Flow

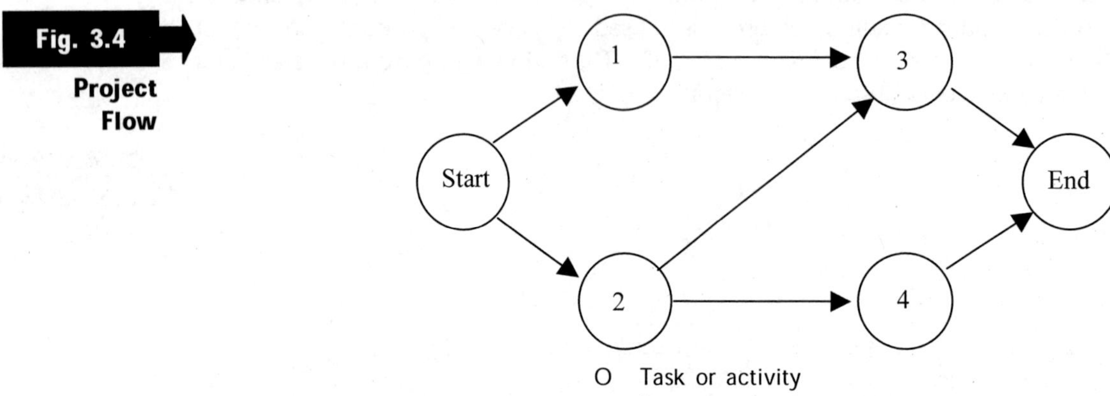

Projects are suitable for customized products. Production cost for projects is high. It is difficult to control costs. Managing projects require innovative steps all along.

Table 3.1 summarizes the characteristics of line, batch and project processes.

Table 3.1

Process Characteristics

Characteristic	***Line***	***Batch***	***Project***
Product			
Flow	Sequential	Jumbled	Sequential
Variety	Low	High	–
Market	Mass	Customized	Unique
Volume	High	Medium	Single unit
Manpower			
Skills	Low	High	High
Task	Competitive	Non-routine	Non-routine
Capital			
Investment	High	Medium	Low
Inventory	Low	High	Little
Equipment	Special purpose	General purpose	General purpose
Objective			
Flexibility	Low	Medium	High
Planning and Control			
Production Controls	Simple	Difficult	Difficult
Inventory	Simple	Difficult	Difficult

Classification by Customer Order

There are two process choices – produce-to-stock (PTS) and produce-to-order (PTO). PTS provides product from stock, and is thus faster in service. Standardisation and variety reduction leads to batch production which form the inventory from which the stocks to sell are drawn. Further batch production replenishes the stock once it reaches a minimum pre-determined level. The system produces here in anticipation of demand. There is no waiting time involved for the customer. There is a risk while selecting PTS for perishable products and short shelf-life products.

PTO is customized producing where the manufacturing process or operations follow the receipt of customer's order. There is a waiting time for the customer. The time is proportional to the lead time of the operational process. The waiting time should be kept as short as possible.

There can be combination of PTS and PTO. In a restaurant, dishes are kept in a semi-cooked form (produce-to-stock) and are converted into dishes to be served on customer demand (produce-to-order).

PTS is suitable for inexpensive products, whereas PTO for expensive products. PTS makes it compulsory to plan production and control inventory. PTO has to observe delivery discipline.

The following matrix covers all the characteristics of processes we have discussed so far.

MATRIX OF PROCESS CHARACTERISTICS

Type of Flow	*PTS*	*PTO*
Line	Oil refining	Cars
Batch	Fast food	Restaurant, Jewellery, Hospital
Project	Paintings	Movies, Bridges, Portraits, Aircrafts

The factors affecting process selection from the above matrix are market conditions, capital requirements, manpower requirements, managerial skills, raw materials and technology.

Product-Process Strategy

Process decisions are not static, but dynamic. Processes keep on evolving over a period of time. Process decisions are related to the product decisions. The relationship between process structures and volume requirements is depicted on product-process matrix proposed by Hayes and Wheelwright in 1979.

As the volume increases, the product line narrows. Then specialized equipment and standardized material flows become economically viable. The top of the matrix shows product side, evolving from left to right. The vertical side of the matrix shows process evolution evolving from top to bottom. Most organizations are positioned diagonally on the matrix indicating low-volume, high variety product being produced by jumbled flow at the top, while standardized, high volume being produced by continuous process at the bottom. The diagonal denotes the matching of product and process. Off the diagonal, the organization is probably having either the wrong product or process.

Process Selection-Service

The usual distinction between service and product is on the basis of tangibility. Services are intangible and cannot be easily quantified. Another way of looking at service is the simultaneous production and consumption of service. In a haircut, the service was received and produced at the same time. Later, only the result of the service could be seen.

Since the customer is in the production system while the service is produced, he introduces an element of uncertainty by putting demands on the producer. Service cannot be stored or transported.

Some services are personal, but many of them are professional.

The differences between services and manufacturing are tabulated below:

DISTINCTION BETWEEN MANUFACTURING AND SERVICES

Manufacturing	*Service*
Tangible product	Intangible
Transfer of title	Generally, not transferred
Resale possible	No resale
Demonstrable	No product exists before buying
Inventory possible	Non-inventoriable
Transportable	Non-transportable
Seller produces	Buyer is a part of production
Exportable	Non-exportable
Sales and production separated	Sales and production inseparable

Service-Product Bundle

A fast-food outlet serves a food product along with service. In a dentist's chamber, we use the dentist's chair along with the dental services. Thus, service-product bundles can have sensual service or psychological service along with facilitating goods. A cab drive has the cab as physical good, ambience of the cab as the sensual service, and a sense of security as the psychological service. It is important that service design does not get restricted to just facilitating goods and sensual service, but extends to the psychological service too. In a restaurant, sometimes food is not the most important thing, but the ambience and psychological service also count. In many cases the process is the product.

The following diagram illustrates the various service-product bundles.

Fig. 3.5

Service-goods Packages

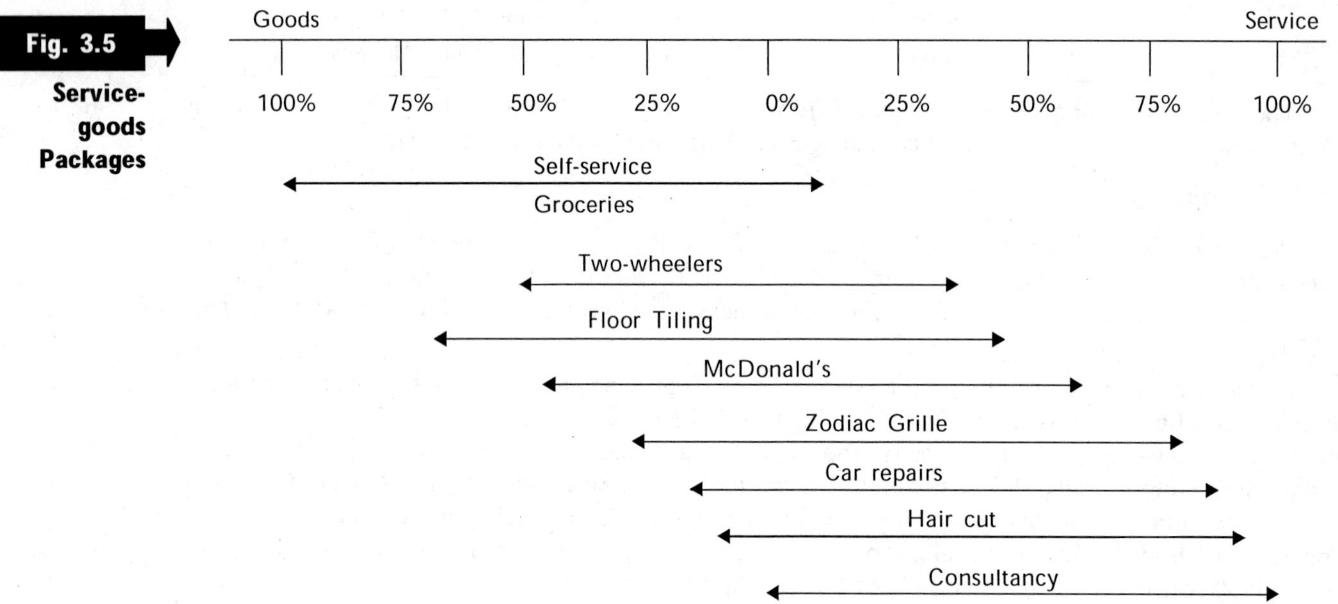

Service Recovery

In case there is service failure, the ability what the service provider does to compensate the failure and restore it, is known as service recovery *e.g.*, restoration of power when power fails, cleaning of clothes when something spills on it in a flight and the apology offered. Prompt and adequate response makes the failure acceptable.

Service Guarantees

Just as product guarantees are offered to ensure performance of the products, service guarantees are offered to ensure satisfactory delivery to the customer. There is a difference between product and service guarantees — products are returnable, whereas services are not. Service guarantees spell out what the service provider is to provide *e.g.*, a courier service guarantees next-day delivery, hotels provide free rooms if not satisfied, restaurants provide free food if not satisfied. Service guarantee must be substantial in order to be effective. Service guarantee helps the design of the service consistent with the service level promised.

Moments of Truth

In the entire cycle of service delivery, there are several points of interaction between the service provider and the customer. For instance, when we book a hotel room, the first contact is for reservation either by phone or through internet asking about the availability of rooms and tariff on a particular date. If the customer is satisfied, the reservation is confirmed. The customer then arrives at the destination on the appointed day. The service provider arranges to pick him up from the airport. As soon as customer arrives at the hotel, the doorkeeper has to welcome him by saluting. The attendant takes charge of his luggage. He is led to the reception for check-in. The check-in experience counts a lot. The customer is taken to the elevator. The waiting time involved matters. The customer is escorted to the room. Room-service is a point of contact. There are contact points at in-house restaurants. The check-out is the penultimate point of contact. Last, the customer is seen off. Each such contact is called a moment of truth. All the cumulative effect of these moments of truth defines the service provided. The entire chain forms the service cycle. Many positive experiences are cancelled out by one single bad moment of truth. It is better to prevent service failure, rather than attempt a service recovery. An organisation can count several thousand moments of truth each day. There are several lakh moments of truth in the hotel industry from several thousand employees. The magnitude of the service design can be understood from this. Perceived service is thus a function of all previous moments of truth. There are several departments involved in providing customer service. There should be proper co-ordination amongst them to ensure a seamless service experience.

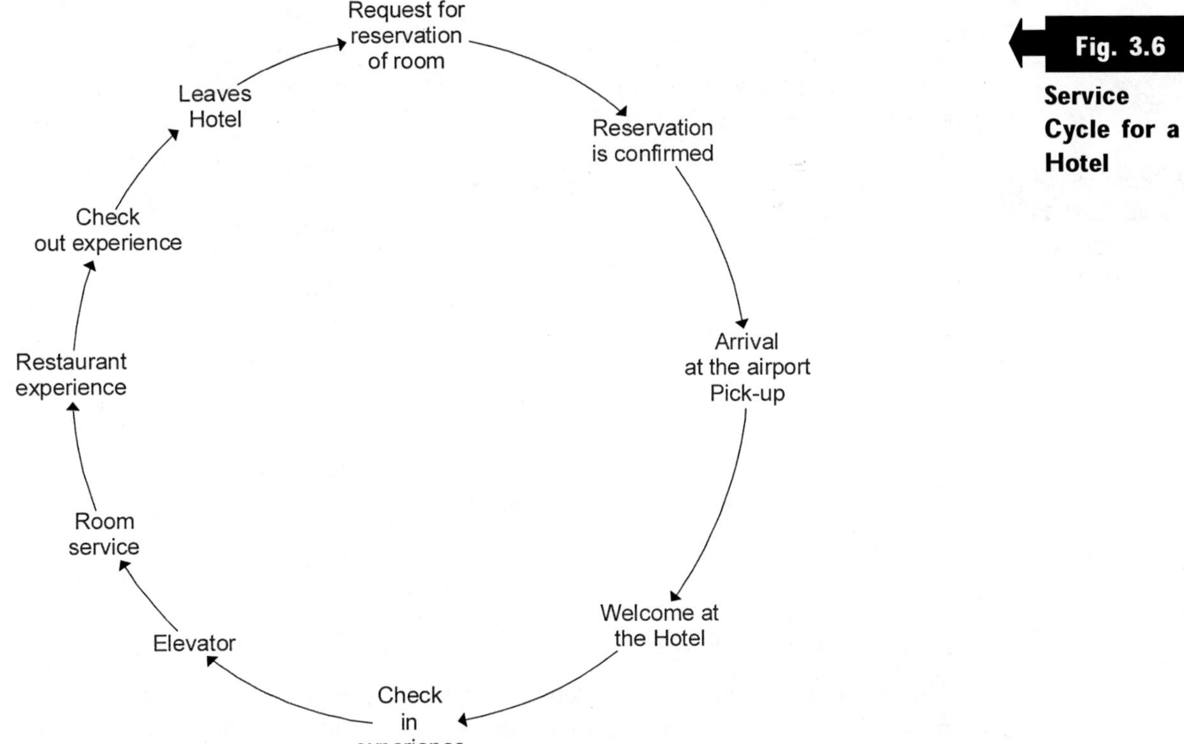

Fig. 3.6 **Service Cycle for a Hotel**

Customer contact can either be low or high in the production process. A low contact process such as ATM transactions or catalogue order processing makes it efficient and standardized. High contact systems are inefficient as the involvement of the customer brings special considerations or more processing time in the production of the service. A dentist's clinic, a hairdresser's salon and consultancy are examples of high contact systems. The potential inefficiency according to Chase and Tansik (1983) in high contact system is a function of the degree of customer contact. The amount of time the customer is in the system while the service is being rendered shows the degree of customer contact. Service systems with high contact or low contact should be separated, where high contact systems are front office operations and low contact system, the back-office operations. There is very high interaction with customers in front-office, whereas the back-office works like a factory.

The following table shows the distinction between high contact and low contact services.

Low Contact Services	***High Contact Services***
Used when personal interaction is not required. Employees must be skilled. Processing routinised and standardized. Work to average demand level peaks and valleys of demand are smoothened. Low/moderate prices.	Used to meet uncertain customer demands. Employees must have HR skills. Employees have to work with the customer with a smile. Response must be immediate to meet demand in peak situations. Higher prices. More customization.

What we must appreciate is that not only the customer contact, but the nature of uncertainty introduced by the customer is also of critical importance. Even in a high contact service, if the customer interface is standardized, efficiency can be achieved.

Service Matrix

Schemenner puts services along two dimensions — degree of interaction and customization and degree of labour intensity. (Fig. 3.7)

Fig. 3.7
Service Matrix

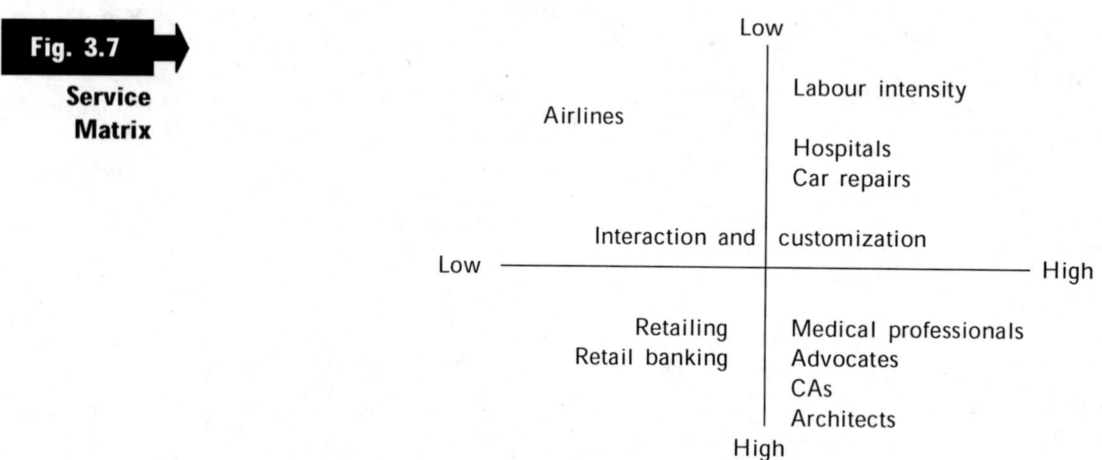

Adapted after Schemenner, *How can Service Business Survive and Prosper?* SMR, Spring, 1986.

Airlines hotels, resorts have low-labour intensity together with low customization and interaction and are service factories. Each customer receives standardized service. The production of service is highly customized. The upper left hand quadrant in the diagram shows this. The upper right hand quadrant shows health-care services and repair services. Here the service is highly customized. There is high degree is interaction with the client. But still there is scope for automation. We may call such establishments service shops. Lower, left-hand corner denotes mass service organization where labour intensity is high and customization is low. Retailing and academic institutions fall into this quadrant. As there is less automation possible, the efficiency of mass service is less than that of service factories located in the upper quadrant. Last, the lower right-hand quadrant shows professional service highly customized and interactive and least possible automation. The efficiency is the least, as there is no standardization. Service matrix enables us to classify and position the services.

Employees and Service

There is a linkage between the organisation's overall profitability and the quality of service.

Fig. 3.8
Service-Profit Chain

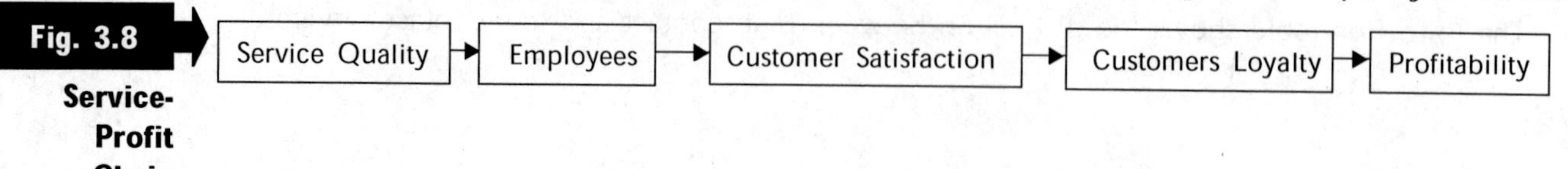

Front-line employees render the service. There should be supportive technology to facilitate service delivery. Employees must be trained to deliver the service. All this leads to customer satisfaction. Satisfied customers become loyal to the organisation and provide repeat business. They also attract new customers. All this leads to revenue growth and high profitability.

To Summarise

Intermittent manufacturing: Under this type of manufacturing, the product is processed in lots rather than on a continuous flow basis. The product design and the machines set-up are tailor-made to a particular lot production. It is the duty of the works manager or plant engineer to determine the economic manufacturing lot size for each component part, sub-assembly or assembly. Unlike the continuous flow production, the product design and the machine set-up changes as the lot changes. Generally, the general purpose machines are used in this type of manufacturing. It is desirable to arrange the machines on the process layout basis rather than on product layout which is more suited to continuous manufacturing.

The problem of production planning and control are relatively more complex as compared to continuous manufacturing. The routing function changes along with the change in the lot to be manufactured. The scheduling function is performed in the light of the jobs on hands, their stage of completion, commitment for completion etc. Unlike continuous manufacturing, it is relatively difficult to maintain the balance in the production line. The chances of waiting, rushing and bottlenecks are more, resulting in either idle capacity or pressure on existing production capacity. The dispatching also becomes a complex function. The job assignments to men and machines necessitates the up-to-date information about their existing and probable work loads. The investments in the inventories tend to be high due to the maintenance of reservoirs of materials in the sub-stores and the prolonged operating cycle. Due to all these factors, the follow-up function is difficult as well as inevitable in the intermittent manufacturing.

Job-lot manufacturing: Under the intermittent manufacturing system, the production is done for stock or according to a customer's order. When the manufacturing is carried on according to the specifications of the customer's order, it is popularly known as "job-lot manufacturing." Here the whole product is looked as one job which is to be completed before going on to the next. The job-lot manufacturing, signifies that the sales orders from the customers are obtained in advance and then they are translated into manufacturing operations. Generally, the job-lot production is undertaken by engineering firms who are manufacturing machines and equipment according to the specifications of the customers. The materials are procured on the basis of bills of materials prepared for each order. The cost of each job is ascertained on the basis of job costing. The orders may be of a repetitive or non-repetitive nature. In case of repetitive orders, the tools, patterns, dies etc. are stored and the product design is preserved for reproduction in the future. As repetitive orders ensure certain cost advantages to the manufacturing firm, a part of them are usually passed over to the customers in the form of reduced price for the jobs.

Advantages of the Intermittent Form

1. It is a trade-off between flexibility and efficiency. We opt for intermittent form when flexibility is more important than efficiency.
2. It gives us a variety at low cost, since it uses general purpose machines.
3. There is high capacity utilization.
4. There are staff advantages since each worker performs a complete operation giving him pride of workmanship and sense of responsibility.

Disadvantages of the Intermittent Form

1. It is expensive for high volumes since the variable costs are high for general purpose machines.
2. There is a problem of planning and control of complex jobs. There may be idling of resources.

3. There is a large in-process inventory and there is a heavy build-up of WIP if PPC is not well geared.
4. Material handling equipment are costly, and require more space.

New Frontiers of Intermittent Form

These days we have increasingly adopted Computerized Production and Inventory Controls Systems to enhance PPC function. There is Integrated Computer-Aided Manufacturing where computers are used not only to plan the operations but for the execution of operations too. Group Technology where groups are organized in the transaction process is picking up to tide over the demerits of intermittent form. Grouping is made for components, machines, equipment and people. The machines, equipment and groups are called 'cells.' Volumes through a cell are higher and variety lower. Each group gets the characteristics of continuous form. Besides it is cost effective and time effective since the nature of operations in a group are similar. There is reduced material handling since machines are close in a cell. The waiting period between operations is also reduced. This also results in a reduced WIP inventory.

Continuous Flow Processes

Unlike intermittent form, here the work-flow is continuous and all the outputs are treated alike. Here the manufacturing is broken down into operations but each unit moves or flows from one operation to the next individually and not as one of a batch. As a result, the process generates mostly a single output, may be with some additional options. The variety here is small, but the volume is high. The facilities are arranged therefore in a linear sequence, and consist of HS special machines. The material movement is minimized. This form was ruled out traditionally for services since they are customer-based. However, on standardisation, certain services can be given on continuous basis — (fast food outlets, auto services centres etc.).

In continuous manufacturing, the production of the standard products is carried on a flow basis at a predetermined rate. The mass production is carried on continuously for stock in anticipation of demand. Due to the production of the standardized products, the product design tends to be constant. The number of operations and the sequence of operations remain more or less same. The machines are arranged on the basis of product layout, *i.e.,* they are arranged in the sequence according to the operation sequence of the product. The material handling and positioning is mechanized mostly on the conveyor lines. The machines set-up remains unchanged for a longer time. Generally, the machines performing specific operations are used and are operated by semi-skilled operators.

The line-balancing is made by providing more machines performing production which is time synchronized. The entire production line is characterised by fixed rated capacity. Like intermittent production, the possibilities of waiting or rushing do not exist in continuous production. Though the production is made on continuous basis, the operating cycle time, *i.e.,* time required to convert the raw materials into finished products, is relatively short. Continuous manufacturing is most suitable to process industries such as the chemical industry, refineries, food processing etc. It is also applied to assembling industries such as automobiles, radios, refrigerators, typewriters etc. In the continuous assembling production, a constantly moving conveyor is employed. The base frame of the product starts from the first stage of the line and other component parts or sub-assemblies are added at subsequent stages of the line as the product moves. Thus, it grows on the line and is taken off at the final stage of the line.

As compared to intermittent production, the investments in the inventories are relatively less. This production system requires the standard materials and their requirements can be estimated reliably on the basis of the production schedule. It does not necessitate the sub-storing and reservoir of materials as required in case of intermittent production. In assembling industry, sometimes the fabrication of components are made in advance of production and they are kept as reservoirs. In fact, they serve as raw materials which are fed to the assembly line. In the continuous production, usually the production of the few standardized products is made on the large-scale for stock. However, sometimes the continuous production is also made according to the customer's order, provided it is of a fairly large size and is in consistency with the product line, *e.g.*, production of monopoly design of some customer in the textile industry, production of standardized engineering parts on a large-scale, say, 1,00,000 pieces etc. In such a situation, jobbing is nearer to continuous production.

The problems of production planning and control are relatively simplified as compared to intermittent production. The production schedule is based on the adjusted demand forecasting. The entire production activity is geared to the production schedule. The routing is simple due to the standard operations, preset sequence of operations and automatized material handling. The preparation of the route sheets and the duties of the route clerk are routine and mechanical. The scheduling function is also simple due to the synchronization of the operations. The periodic production is made according to the master schedule.

Some adjustments in the production schedule would be necessitated on the basis of the fluctuations in demand and the stockpiling of the finished products. In the assembling industry, where the parts and components are fabricated in the unit itself, proper scheduling would be required for the fabrication of such parts and components well in advance. Scheduling would also face a specific problem in case of interruption in production flow caused by machine breakdown, power cut, material shortage, labour trouble etc. Dispatching function stands to be easy due to standard machine set-up, standing instructions to the operators and use of standard materials and tools. The follow-up function does not see any special problem unless there are some interruptions in the production flow. The main task of the follow-up function is to see that the continuity of the flow is maintained. For the effective follow-up, the stand-by equipment are maintained for strategic operations and the reservoirs of the key material or parts are maintained. Sufficient attention is given to the quality of production, rate of rejections, oiling, cleaning, repairing and maintenance of machines and equipment.

Advantages of Continuous Form

In designing, the continuous form requires a considerable amount of effort. But once it sets going, it offers many simplicities in operations.

1. It has low unit cost per unit of production.
2. The machine operations are simpler. Maintenance however is difficult and complex.
3. The managerial control is simpler.

Disadvantages of the Continuous Form

Though cost-effective, it suffers from the following disadvantages:

1. It is difficult to adopt it to a different product line. It is also difficult to change the output rate.
2. Breakdown results in stoppage of line.
3. Line balancing responds to output rate of slowest work stations. The workers whose output rate is higher are therefore kept less busy.
4. The tasks are repetitive, and so monotonous. The process is dehumanizing. It affects morale of the workers.
5. Initial project cost is very high since special purpose machines are used. Maintenance is also expensive. Obsolescence of the process used is a big problem.

New Frontiers of Continuous Form

Numeric Control (NC) for machine control is the in-thing. CNC: Computer Numerical Control puts the instruction into computer memory (*e.g.*, CNC Lathes from HMT). In DNC: Direct Numeric Control, a single computer stores programmes for several NC machines. Automation by numeric control is soft automation. Robotics has come in a big way to move materials and parts and to manipulate them. Robotics helps the continuous form to switch over from one output to another. CAD: Computer Aided Design, CAM: Computer Aided Manufacturing and CAE: Computer Aided Engineering mean in the widest sense automation in all areas using computers as a tool from product concept to its final manufacture. In Flexible Manufacturing, we introduce flexibility in operations sequence, batch sizes and overall production capacity. It, therefore ties-up conventional automation with strategic merits of the intermediate form (more variety, customized response, up-to-date product designs etc.).

Characteristics of Intermittent and Continuous Manufacturing

Intermittent and continuous manufacturing are the mutually exclusive activities. The following comparison will clarify their true nature of operations:

Particulars	***Intermittent Manufacturing***	***Continuous Manufacturing***
1. Type of plant layout	Process layout is most suited.	Product layout designed according to a separate line for each product is considered.
2. Type of machines	As it necessitates frequent changes in the machine set-up required by the specifications of each order, the general purpose machines are more suitable.	As the production flow is permanently set in the form of product-line, the special purpose machines are used.
3. Type of labour	This type of production pre-supposes frequent changes in product design and machine set-up and thus requires highly skilled workers.	The manufacturing activity becomes a routine function and so is carried on by the unskilled workers. The specialized team of plant maintenance looks after the repair and maintenance of the machines.
4. No. of products and product designs	Wide range of products are manufactured in small quantities. The product design changes from lot to lot according to the product specifications.	Few standard products are manufactured in large quantities. Usually the product-line is geared to only two or three products of standard design.
5. Changes in the machines set-up	As the specifications of each order changes, the machines are set according to the requirements of each order. Thus, frequent changes in the machine set-up is a common phenomenon.	Under this type of manufacturing, the set-up of the machines remains unchanged for a longer period. The standard products are manufactured in a continuous flow.
6. Nature and size of the order	Generally the unrepeated small size of orders are received for unstandardized products. The order may involve the production of a single product or the identical products in limited lot. Usually the production is carried on according to the order. First the orders are received and then they are translated into the actual production.	Generally the production is carried on for stock. The production is made of standardized products and so they are produced in anticipation of demand. Like intermittent production, there does not arise any problem about non-repeat orders or orders for unstandardized products.
7. Investments in machines and equipment	As the machines are arranged according to process layout, less machines are required.	The machines are arranged according to the product layout. So it results in duplication of machines. Moreover, it is essential to maintain stand-by equipment to meet any breakdowns resulting in production stoppages. Thus investment in machines is fairly high.
8. Investment in inventories	It necessitates the reservoir of processed inventories and components in sub-stores. Moreover, waiting and bottlenecks slow down the operating cycle. As a result, the investment in inventories increase.	Due to continuous flow of production, the need for the sub-storing of processed inventories is reduced to the minimum. Similarly the operating cycle is very fast reducing the necessity for the locking-up of the in process inventories.

Particulars	***Intermittent Manufacturing***	***Continuous Manufacturing***
9. Material handling equipment	As the in-process materials are required to travel on varied routes, it is not feasible to employ mechanized material handling equipment.	Due to the movement of in-process materials between fixed points, it is possible to use mechanized material handling equipment. Mostly the materials are handled through conveyor belts, roller conveyors, pipelines, overhead cranes etc. Under the automation, the materials are automatically handled from one machine to the next one.
10. Material handling cost	The material handling cost tends to be high due to long distance, backtracking, movements of non-standard lots and lack of mechanization of material handling services.	The materials handling cost is less due to line balancing forward movement of materials and use of mechanized material handling equipment.
11. Plant maintenance services	It is desirable to have the plant maintenance services for repairs, maintenance and replacements. However, like continuous production, there is no danger of the stoppage of whole line.	It is highly essential to have a sound plant maintenance services with a view to avoid any interruptions in the production flow.
12. Balancing in the production capacity	The existence of imbalance in the production department is likely to exist in such production resulting in the underloading or overloading of work on men and machines.	It is possible to ensure the perfect balance in the production line. The chance of overloading or underloading on men and machines are very little.
13. The production planning and control	The function of routine scheduling, dispatching and follow-up become relatively complicated due to odd size of the order, non-repetitive nature of the order and awkward delivery dates resulting in imbalancing in the production capacity.	The routing, scheduling, despatching and follow-up functions are carried on smoothly due to the standard production under rated capacity carried on in anticipation of demand.

Processing Industries

The typical processing industries are bulk drugs plants, fertilizer plants, petrochemical plants and milk dairies which have highly automated systems and sophisticated controls. They are not labour-intensive and the worker is just an operator to monitor the system, and take corrective steps if called for. They are continuous process industries. In these industries a single input is processed generally to give one or more different products (*e.g.*, petroleum refinery gives from petroleum several products like diesel, petrol, kerosene, furnace oil, naphtha etc.) Processing industries are thus following analytical processes. In discrete manufacturing, continuous flow processing however uses synthetic processes. Here the plant installation also is more complex to begin with.

Batch

In this process, similar items needed in large volumes are produced. The process is divided into appropriate stages. Orders are processed stage by stage. Next stage is set when the first is completed. At each stage, the capacity is used and reused. Printing is an example of batch processing. The essential feature of batch production is to stop the first process and reset the whole thing to produce another product or provide another service.

Selection of the Process

You have to study the full text of this book to answer satisfactorily the question: Which process to choose? In practice, the process forms we have described (project, intermittent, continuous flow, continuous process) are not observed in pure extreme forms. More of these are combined to get different components and the final product. In auto industries the components are made by the intermittent form, and the vehicle is assembled on a continuous basis. Group Technology and FMS (flexible manufacturing system) referred to already are in fact attempts to combine the features of these forms.

Traditionally, services were offered on intermittent basis. However, services of an architect or a solicitor may be on project basis. In some countries, surgeries of certain natures like heart by-pass surgeries or eye surgeries have been so standardized that they can be given on continuous basis. Here the patient is passing along a health care line, where each surgeon performs a small task.

Product and process life cycles are related. Something may be started in an unorganized way on project basis. Soon there is batch production. Later in the growth phase, more and more sub-processes come into operation, thus resulting in adoption of continuous phase. Even in the maturity phase, it is better to use continuous form. Here the fixed costs of operations are high but per unit cost of output is low.

The whole thing is evolutionary — the process evolves with the market and the output. While choosing the process form, the organization also takes into account its distinctive competence — which ultimately decides its focus in operations. Process is a crucial ingredient of this focus.

Product-Process Matrix

We can match the process structures and product life cycle stage by forming a matrix.

Fig. 3.9

Product-Process Matrix

Process Structure	*PLC Stage*			
	Introduction	***Growth***	***Stability***	***Decline***
Job Shop Batch Assembly Line Continuous				

With the increase in volume, the product line narrows down. Processes use more specialised equipment, and material flow is standardised as we move vertically downwards. Process evolves over the PLC.

Process Flow Design

This spells out the flow of materials, parts and sub-assemblies as they move through the plant. The following tools are used to plan the process flow:

Tool	*Description*
Assembly Drawing	Exploded view of the product showing its components.
Assembly chart (Gozinto Chart)	Assembly drawing information is used. It defines how parts go together; their sequence, and the entire material flow.
Operation and Route Sheet	It spells out operations and routing for a particular part. It provides information such as the equipment used, tooling required, and operations required.

Process Analysis

A process consists of several tasks with a flow of material and information and the storage of material and information.

A task transforms the input into the desired output to some extent. The flow of material is from one task to the next one. The flow of information indicates the degree to which the transformation is accomplished from task to task. When there is no task performed and no part is being transferred, the part need to be stored. Goods stored thus form work-in-process (WIP) inventory.

Process-Centred Organisations

Organisations that focus on process of manufacturing are process-centred. Even the most advanced products are technologically copiable. It is therefore, necessary not to concentrate on current product designs but on the process having capability of delivering a stream of products. A process-centred organisation considers the whole cycle of satisfying customer demand. A specialised organisation divides a process into independent tasks — manufacturing, warehousing, transportation, accounting where each task is performed independently. The whole process is not appreciated. A process-centred organisation takes an integrated approach. The ultimate aim is to satisfy the customer demand. A process-centred organisation keeps customers actively involved in operations. The entire organisation works as a team, keeping the customer at the centre. Such an organisation can have a matrix-type of structure. The customer interface with the organisation is called the moment of truth. The empowered team is managed by a single operations manager called 'the process owner.' This manager is responsible for the design, development and smooth working of the process.

The process design considers the output of the process, its flexibility, the pay off, the optimal process, the automation involved and the layout of the process.

PROCESS-FLOW ANALYSIS

In production, as we know, there is transformation process where inputs are converted into outputs. Process flow analysis examines the flows of materials and information in the transformation process. Such an analysis gives insight to us to improve upon the methods and procedures.

Process flow analysis is done with the help of a flow chart. Flowcharts are not restricted to just process flows. They can also include customers, suppliers and employees. All these inputs when considered collectively are a great help in designing a better process.

Operations in the process flow analysis are generated as a system made up of parts. In a business system, there are sub-systems of operations, marketing, finance, HR and information. These interact amongst themselves and with the environment. They together achieve much more than they would have achieved individually. The **systems boundary** separates a system from its environment.

Process View

Business examined in terms of functions is a vertical view, and in terms of process is a horizontal view. A business decision is cross-functional, say it moves from function to function — marketing to operations to finance. While moving thus, it is possible to lose on time and information. Process view enables us to appreciate that operations are just a part of the larger organisation. Business decisions cannot be restricted to just one one function say operations. Operations decisions are related someway to other functions. The interface between operations and other parts of business must be streamlined. This leads us to flowcharting.

Flowchart Analysis

Flowcharts are employed to describe and improve the transformation process in business. They are a result of the systems view of business. Process elements of raw materials, product design, job design, management control, equipment and tools and vendors may be changed to improve the effectiveness.

Process flows are studied on a particular system – either a whole business or a part thereof. A cross-functional team is assigned to the task of improving the system. The objectives are set. The inputs and outputs are defined. The existing system is converted into flowcharts. An improved system is suggested and is also described by flowcharts. On getting management approval, it is implemented. If there is no existing process, the analysis starts from the desired process.

Materials Flow Analysis

Process flow analysis was employed to study the **materials flow** in the factories. It reduced the manufacturing throughput time or cycle time — the total time to order, manufacture and distribute a product from the start to the finish. The ultimate aim is to reduce waste in the process. Materials flow analysis is done through: assembly drawings, assembly charts, routing sheets and flow process charts.

Assembly Drawings

These show how parts fit together or are functionally related. Dimensions typically refer to relationships among parts. Often, a BOM (listing of all parts necessary to make up the assembly) is involved.

This is an important stage in the design process. It is used in the shop to guide the assembly process. It can also be used for maintenance purposes.

Assembly Chart

It shows the exact sequence of operations used to assemble a product. It is derived from the assembly drawing.

Routing Sheet

It is more elaborate than an assembly chart. It shows the operations and routing required for individual part. Along with the operations, the tools and equipment required are spelled out. Even time assigned for each operation can be listed.

Flow Process Chart

It is a process chart setting out the sequence of the flow of a produce or a procedure that records all events under review using the appropriate process chart symbols

(a) Man Type: A flow process chart which records what the worker does.

(b) Material Type: A flow process chart which records what happens to material.

(c) Equipment Type: A flow process chart which records how the equipment is used.

Flow Diagram: A diagram or model, substantially to scale, which shows the location of specific activities carried out and the routes followed by workers, materials, or equipment in their execution.

A flow process chart is very important in improving the flow of materials. By glancing over the flow chart, an analyst can combine certain operations, eliminate some others, simplify some operations and reduce throughput time. All this influences lay-out, equipment and work methods. Maybe, some product design changes may be required. Just a drawing of the flow process chart is not enough. These charts must be checked to answer the following questions:

1. What are the needs of the customers? To satisfy these needs, what operations are necessary? Could these operations be modified by elimination, combination or simplification?
2. Who would perform each operation? Can the operation be re-designed to make it less labour and skill intensive? Can we combine operations to enrich jobs? Which vendors are to be used and how? Which operations can be outsourced?
3. Where should the operation be conducted? Can there be layout modification?
4. When are the operations to be performed? Are there excessive delays? Are there bottlenecks? How could the waiting time be reduced?
5. How is the operation to be performed? Can we improve upon it? Can it be modified to make it efficient and effective?

Information Flow Analysis

The same method which we use to analyse materials flow can be used to analyse information flow too. Information flows may be recorded on a flow process chart. In addition, different flowcharting methods can be used to record information flows. The ultimate aim is to improve the efficiency and the effectiveness of the process.

There are two types of information flows. The first type of information flow is that where information flows from an operation *e.g.*, clerical processes in an office. The information flow is designed keeping in mind the customer contact points and moments of truth.

CASELET: PROCESS VS. PRODUCT

Though it is well-known that product development R&D is very heavy, the Asian countries piggy-back on successful products by adopting a different process of manufacturing without compensating the product patent holder for what is now known as intellectual property rights. It has happened glaringly in pharma industry, which took advantage of our process patent laws. Ciprofloxacin took ₹ 400 crores for development on the part of Bayer. Twenty-four Indian companies make this product. Nifedipine for cardio-vascular use from Bayer has 15 Indian clones. Ranbaxy, Cipla and Cadila have many such products for which there was no royalty outflow. MIMS estimated out of 900 molecules, only 28 are being paid for rights.

As soon as a new drug is discovered, a marginally different process is adopted by Indian companies to produce and market it. It is so far legal in India because the act here patents the process and not the product. The process-different product clones are naturally cheaper as there are no R&D costs involved.

India has been a signatory to GATT and India is now moving from process patents to product patents. A transitional period of 10 years has been given to us to shift to a new regime of product patents.

We would like you to appreciate the changing scenario. What strategies are available to us? Should we not develop more new products now rather than living off parasitically on products developed elsewhere? Should we concentrate on selling bulk products which go off patent? What steps should we take to protect our vast reservoir of herbal medicines from product patent sharks from abroad? Will not the Indian consumer pay higher prices for many products because of a shift in our patent law? Please consider the issue objectively from the view points of both the sides.

In the second type of information flow, the flow is used for management or control purposes *e.g.*, order entry, purchase documents and paperwork used in manufacturing. This is where information is used to control materials.

Materials flow analysis and information flow analysis must be done together or else there will be good materials flow, but there is no management control of the process.

So far materials flow analysis and information flow analysis were treated differently, perhaps due to the former being handled by the industrial engineers and the latter by computer specialists. These days systems analysts are considered as the engineers of the office.

Business Process Reengineering

Process flow principles are being applied as business process reengineering (BPR). The starting point is to consider the entire business and its critical processes to meet customer needs. These processes may cut across the functional areas of business. Major processes are redesigned and integrated to serve the customer better. BPR is a term coined by Hammer and Champy in their renowned book *Reengineering the Corporation* (1993). The concept is dealt with in detail in a separate chapter.

Fig. 3.10 **Flow Process Chart**

Flow Chart
Job: Cast, Turn, Drill

Method	: Present		**Location**	: Machine shop	
Charted by	: Ramesh Saxena		**Chart begins**	: Raw materials store	
Date	: 25th Jan., 2015		**Chart ends**	: Inspection pit	

SUMMARY

	Present		*Proposed*	
	Present	***Proposed***	***No.***	***Time***
○ Operations	3	120		
⇨ Transportation	2	Nil		
□ Inspections	1	20		
D Delays	2	40		
▽ Storages	3	Nil		
Distance Travelled	18	M		

Particular of Present/ Proposed Method	○ ***Operations***	⇨ ***Transportation***	□ ***Inspections***	**D** ***Delays***	▽ ***Storages***	***Distance* M**	**Q**	***Time***	***Remarks***
1. Raw Material Stores	○	⇨	□	D	▽				
2. Casting	○	⇨	□	D	▽			80	Improve
3. Storage of Casting	○	⇨	□	D	▽				
4. Sent to Turning	○	⇨	□	D	▽	12			
5. Delays at Lathe (M/C)	○	⇨	□	D	▽		10	25	
6. Turning	○	⇨	□	D	▽			20	
7. WIP storage	○	⇨	□	D	▽				
8. Sent to Drilling shop	○	⇨	□	D	▽	6			
9. Delay at Drilling	○	⇨	□	D	▽		8	15	Eliminate
10. Drilling	○	⇨	□	D	▽			20	Improve
11. Inspection	○	⇨	□	D	▽			20	

Appendix - I

Kaizen

Kaizen is a Japanese concept founded in 1986. Masaaki Imai has made it very popular. In a production process, one has to *anticipate the problems* which can turn up later in design and planning stage itself, and take the necessary steps *to prevent* them so as to *save* substantial costs. To implement this simple concept, it is necessary to become a hands-on manager and visit *gemba* or the workplace as often as one can. Many accidents can be prevented by *kaizen, e.g.*, a spanner falling into an assembly line. Every problem in the workplace is linked to the five 'M's — man, machine, material, method and measurement. We should follow *gemba gembutsu* approach, where gembutsu means a tangible thing like the customer, the product, the machine. Gembutsu has great relevance, since it helps designing a product with the customer in mind. Kaizen is a Japanese term used to describe the process of continuous improvement in production and every aspect of value added. Taiichi Ohno (1912-1990) laid out the fundamental philosophy of doing kaizen (continuous improvement) even in good times, in order to be always ready to compete with lowest cost production. In kaizen process, first the company is made 'normal' after removing problems, then it is made 'productive', and finally given 'longevity.' Imai's books on Kaizen are *Kaizen — The Key to Japan's Success* (1986) and *Gemba Kaizen — A Common Sense Low-cost Approach to Management* (1997).

CHOICE OF TECHNOLOGY

Managers are expected to choose an appropriate technology. We should not remain just the passive users of technology, but should become managers of technology. Technology is an applied science. The knowledge is applied to solve human problems. Viewed narrowly, technology is a set of processes, tools, methods and equipment used to produce goods and services.

After selecting the process, we have to choose a level of technology. Technology affects the jobs, and thus the human resources. Technology has social and human consequences.

As users of and managers of technology, we are concerned with the performance characteristics of technology and not its technical details, *e.g.*, we are concerned with the cooling effect of an AC rather than the technical specification of its compressor. Though technical specifications do affect performance but we as managers are more interested in the performance itself.

Technology decisions affect managers in other functional areas too. They should also contribute in choosing an appropriate technology.

Computer Integrated Manufacturing

We shall here talk about the **fully automated factory** of the future. The concept of the factory of the future has been developed in response to the change in the consumer preference in modern society characterized by shorter product life cycles. (Koren Y., 1983, *Computer Control of Manufacturing System,* McGraw Hill, Japan). The shorter product life cycles mean more competitive products, more phasing out of the existing products and consequently lower ordering quantities.

The popular concept of the factory of the future is robotized factory manned by steel collar workers. It will manufacture products according to coded instructions from the central computer to smart robots and machine tools. There will not be blue collar workers. The factory operations from concept to finished product will be monitored, controlled and managed by computers and performed by robots and intelligent systems. The essence is not automations and fewer people. It is a different type of automation organized around the computer. The factory of the future implies movement towards **computer integration of manufacturing** (CIM) functions. These include specification of the product, conceptual and final design, control of machines, handling of materials and control of production processes. These can be done through a common data-base which incorporates computer-assited design (CAD), computer-aided manufacturing (CAM), robotics and materials requirement planning (MRP). Computer database would provide automatic generation of production data using a CAD and a CAM system. Data generated may include programmes for NC machine tools, CNC or DNC inspection machines and industrial robots. One form of this fully automated factory is flexible manufacturing system (FMS).

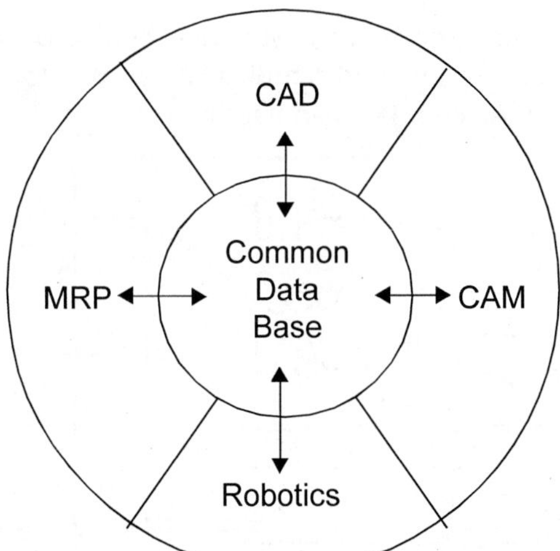

Fig. 4.1
Computer Integrated Manufacturing (CIM)

When computer integrated manufacturing encompasses other functions such as finance and accounts, order entries, sales, it becomes enterprise resource planning (ERP) system. It makes the whole business seamlessly integrated. It is discussed separately in this chapter.

Computer-Aided Design (CAD)

This term refers to the support the computer renders to the engineering design. The drawings are put into the computer through a terminal or directly on the screen. The printout of the drawing can be taken. The drawing can be linked to manufacturing or can be made stand-alone. A complete CAD system has three components — design calculations, parts classification and link to manufacturing. *Engineering design* calculations such as strength of materials (SOMs), stress analysis, thermal calculations can be made after storing part geometry in the computer. Design problems get simplified because of this, even though no prototypes are built. *Parts classification* codifies and classifies existing parts by using a coding system. The existing parts are identified by dimensions and functions. A numerical code is used; and parts can be accessed from database. Unnecessary parts are eliminated. The *link to manufacturing* is the last element of CAD. Manufacturing process and product design must be compatible. Proper machines and tooling are facilitative. Product geometry and specification in the computer database simplify the machining. Different machine processes can be tested for efficiency by simulations. Tools can be made compatible with product shape. The collaborative effect of engineering design and manufacturing leads to final design. Prior to this the different manufacturing steps are simulated. This is accomplished by the linkage of common database and design and manufacturing in a CIM factory.

CAD is extensively used in car manufacturing, aircraft manufacturing, shipbuilding, construction and electronics. It is labour saving. Redesign is achieved in reduced time. Design time is reduced. It makes the company competitive.

Computer-Aided Manufacturing (CAM)

In the 60s, researchers observed that it is possible to develop some means of automatically routing jobs through the manufacturing system from one machine to the next and some ways to reduce the set up time of jobs on a machine to a considerable extent. The joint effect would improve productivity in discrete parts manufacturing. To overcome the inherent limitation of conventional batch manufacturing system (small volumes, high producer variety, and a jumbled flow of materials), we can use computer-aided manufacturing which streamlines batch manufacturing.

CAM makes use of computers in process design, machine tool control and flow control. The machines can be changed rapidly while manufacturing small batches. Machines follow prescribed instructions. Materials move from one machine to the next under computer control. The products being produced are organised into groups or families. This approach is called **group technology** (GT)

While discussing CAD, we have examined classification and coding of similar parts. This is carried forward by organizing production machines by part families. When we dedicate machines to a group of parts, we follow group technology or cellular manufacturing.

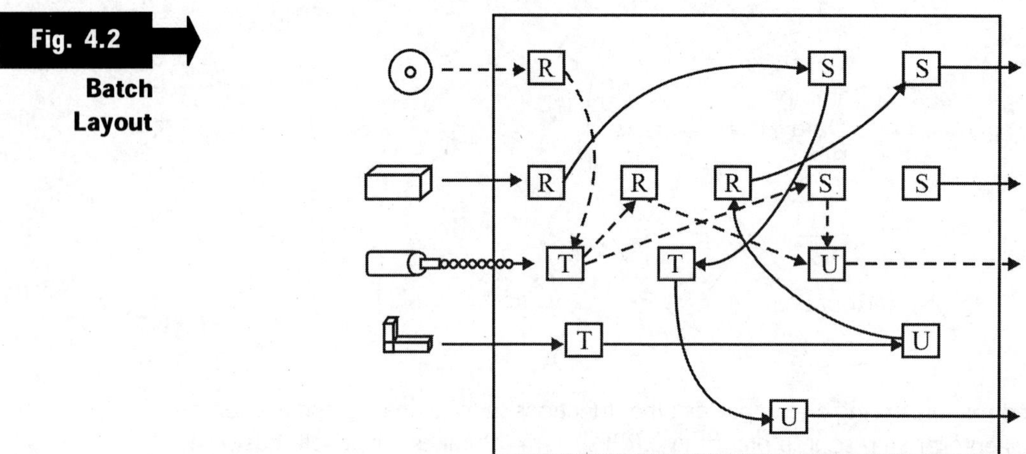

Fig. 4.2
Batch Layout

The above diagram shows batch layout. Here machines are grouped by similar type. Product follows a jumbled flow pattern.

The same facility is arranged in group technology format in the following diagram.

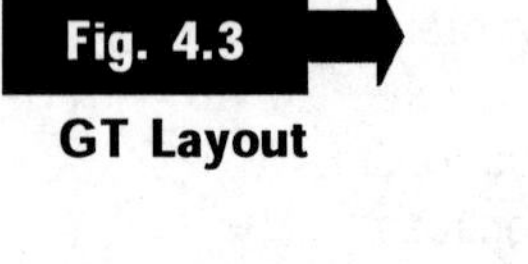

Fig. 4.3
GT Layout

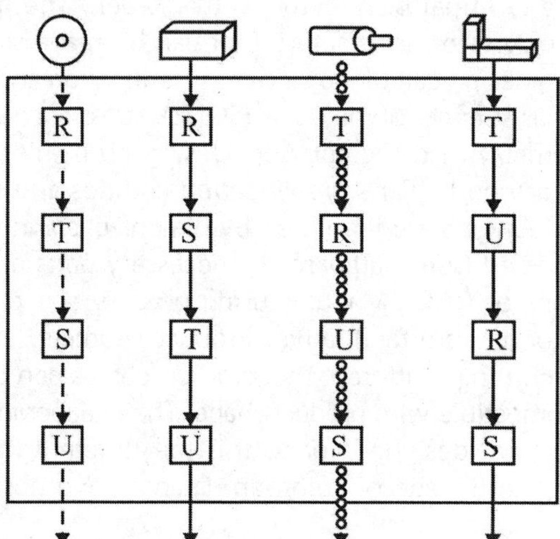

In GT layout, the machines required to produce a given part of a family are grouped together. A straight line flow is accomplished. Though there is some duplication of machines in the cells and probably less capacity utilization, the advantages of GT are too significant to ignore. It accelerates the production process. It lessens the WIP: work-in-process inventories. When GT layout is automated, it leads to **flexible manufacturing system (FMS).**

Flexible Manufacturing System (FMS)

The first FMS was installed in England in 1968. Many such systems have simple been installed all over. It has emerged as the most potential manufacturing system of the future. FMS is applied in metal cutting, electronic assembly, IC manufacturing and testing etc.

FMS is a mixture of traditional automation and state-of-the-art computer technology which essentially consists of a set of machine tools performing production operations linked up with material handling systems. All these are controlled by a central computer system.

The new era of automation started with numerical control (NC) based on digital computer principles. The logical extension of NC was computerized numerical control (CNC) for machine tools and simultaneous development of industrial robots in which minicomputers are used as an integral part of the control cabinet. CNC machine are on-line. DNC machines utilize a central computer to control several CNC machines at the same time.

The operation of several CNC machines and single robot can be incorporated into a system which produces a specific part or family with similar geometry. This structure, which substitutes for the DNC system, is called manufacturing cell. The computer of the cell is interfaced with the computers of the robot and CNC machines (Koren, 1983, *Computer Control of Manufacturing System,* McGraw Hill, Japan). The operation of many manufacturing cells can be co-ordinated by a central computer via the aid of a material handling system. This co-ordination between computer control and the operations of the manufacturing plant is called FMS.

The scheduling decisions are made based on the actual state of the system. FMS schedule must be capable of responding to real time decisions.

FMS has been classified based upon the number of CNC machines and their arrangements. There are five such groups.

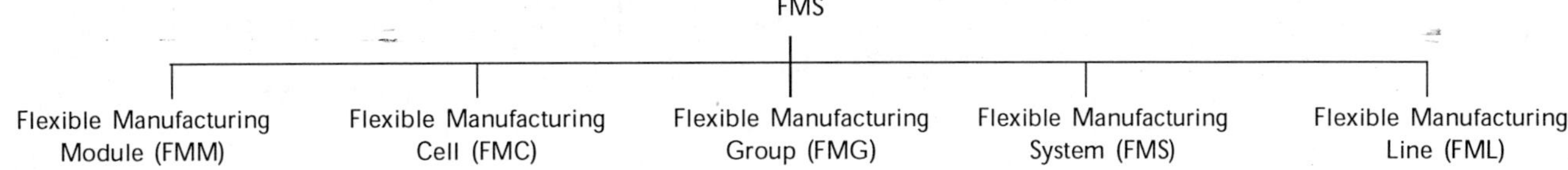

The following diagram illustrates the configuration of FMS for different production processes (from job to mass production of different parts).

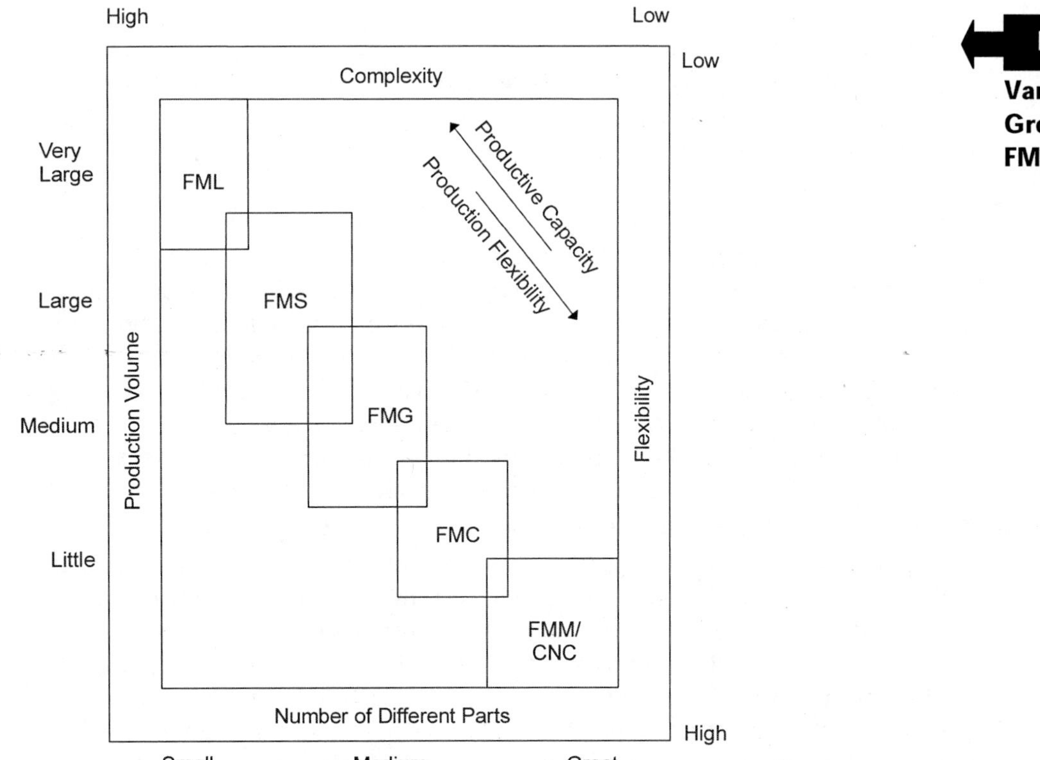

Fig. 4.4 Various Groups of FMS

Structure-wise, FMS has three sub-systems — fabrication, machining and assembly. Each subsystem has machines or work-stations having a range of flexibility. As they are equipped with numerical control, they do not require set-up time or change over time, and are capable of performing different operations. They are connected to storage/retrieval (AS/RS) to facilitate routing. The CAD/CAM systems are integrated with an FMS. FMS is also integrated to AS/RS. Integration between an FMS and AS/RS is often material handling system *e.g.,* an automated guided vehicle AGV or robot or conveyor and a computer system. Most of the literature focus on FMS for machining. FMS for assembly has developed independently. FMS for machining and FMS for assembly has a number of differences. It imposes unique requirements on flexible assembly systems (FAS). Flexible fabrication system (FFS) has attracted the least interest.

Fig. 4.5
Typical FMS

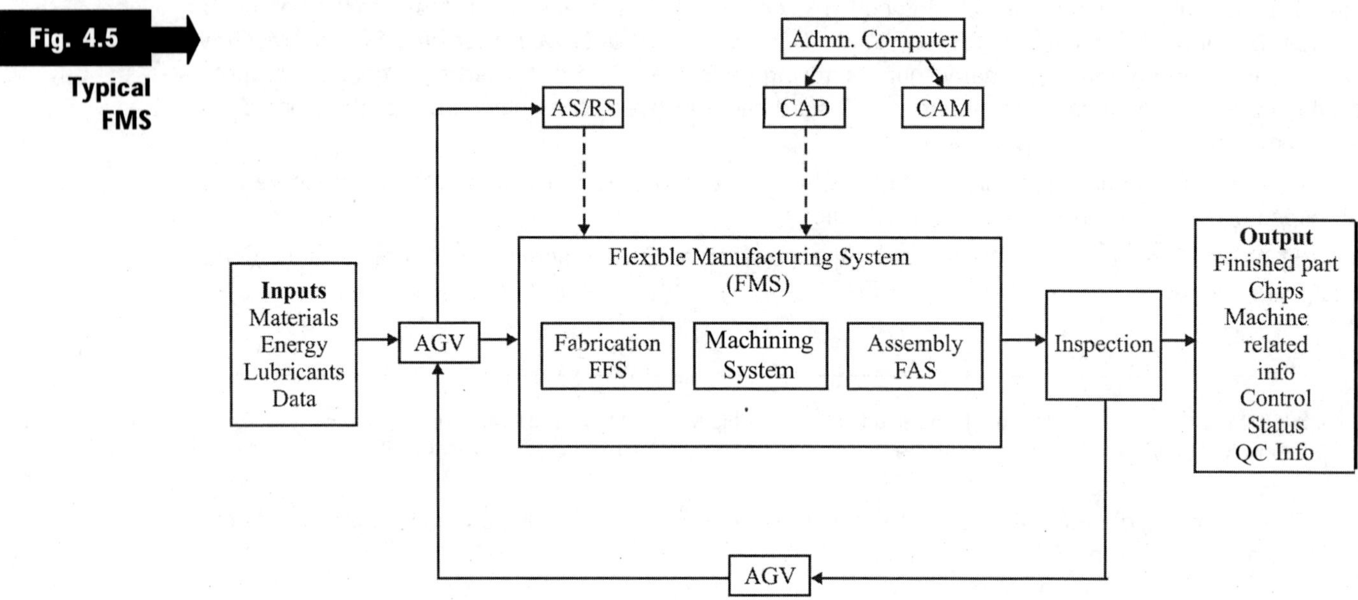

FMS is not a panacea for all the problems of conventional manufacturing. Volume and variety are the critical factors deciding the type of and amount of automation that can be justified.

CAM also uses computer-aided process planning (CAPP). The part design is downloaded from the CAD system. CAPP then decides routings, equipments and tools for producing that part.

Robotics

While a lay person would associate robotics with Isaac Asimov's human-like robots, the industrial robots do not look anything close to a human being. However, most are able to perform actions that a human being does, only with a greater control and precision. A robot is a computer-controlled machine. It is programmed to perform certain tasks. It can perform production tasks too. The arm of the robot assumes the movements of human hand. Robots were first used for heavy or dirty works. Later, robots came to be used for a variety of works *e.g.,* materials handling, assembly, welding, painting etc. The visual ability of the robots is now limited, but there are efforts is to improve it. Robots can save labour, introduce flexibility and perform hazardous tasks. The process to be robotized should be analysed carefully to integrate robots into it.

Robotics, according to Hugh Whyte, former professor of Mechatronic Engineering, Sydney University, is the intelligent connection of perception to action. An arm in a factory or a surgical robot do not have intelligence at all. They are just mechanical things, though it is clever mechanics. They are just machines. A robot is different from a machine on account of its ability to perceive its environment, understand it and make decisions on what to do. Each time the decision could be different. A robot has to understand a particular plant and all other plants. It has to do generalisation of the perceptual understanding. We human understand a tree, and all other trees. This is taken for granted. Robotics really asks that fundamental question — What makes us intelligent?

Though robots of future are feared, the real possibility of being scary comes from human clones, rather than electronic robots. Human clones are biological robots. Some countries think of robotising their armies in the next twenty years. Robotics should make the world safer and should not harm it. The choice is moral and not technical. Robotics is still at the stage computing was at when we had just mainframe computers. Robots are used commercially now, to automate the dirty or hard and to do the repetitive jobs such as cargo handling and agriculture. In medicine, robots are making a big impact. They are used in unmanned air vehicles. Several companies including Google and Apple are working on autonomous cars which will navigate without a driver on city streets. The technique should move in the direction of mini-computers and PCs being made in a robotic sense so that they can be used at home.

The cost has to come down. It is not a computing problem anymore. It is the physical costs of sensors and hardware holding it back. The breakthrough would be a low-cost 3D sense which will enable robots to understand its environment economically. It would enable a robot to do the household jobs such as serving tea.

Samsung, Noida and Robotics

Samsung makes a million mobile handsets a month in its Noida plant. There are robots along with the workers on the shopfloor. The coded matter on the handset is put by the printer-like surface mount technology. Then there is printed board assembly and the mainline. These are operated by compact robotic machines. In the packing area, each worker has two bins, each with a capacity of 50 handsets. A green alarm beeps when the capacity breaches 70. It calls for AGV or automated guided vehicle. The pre-programmed robot collects the handsets and transfers them to the delivery vans which carry them to the retailers.

Manufacturing in future will be more automated, robotised and decentralised.

Personal Robots

Luna has been developed as a personal robot in humanoid form. It is a completely programmable robot built on open source platform with Linux-based OS called Luna OS. Anyone can write applications for Luna. It costs initially $3000. A personal robotics industry is likely to emerge in a decade or so. Luna can perform some routine functions, like carrying a tray of drinks. It can be used for telepresence. It is hailed as future of work. Robots will sell better when they offer cleaning attachments. The success will depend on the robot-human interaction. Arkin from Georgia Tech is a robotic expert whom Sony consulted for its AIBO project, one of the earliest personal robot projects, now discontinued.

Office Technology

Office in the past had just one piece of machine — the ubiquitous typewriter. Most of the work was manual. Some machines like cyclostyle-machine, dictaphone and electric typewriters were being used. The advent of computer and networking changed all this. Office processes, messages, typing, copying, filing and scheduling — all this changed. In an automated office, a computer undertakes most of these tasks. The outward communication is through letters, typed with Microsoft Word, e-mails, cellular phones, landlines, electronic networks and internet. Offices tend to be more and more paperless as electronic media are used to store data. The errors are corrected on-line. Costs are reduced. Efficiency improves. Offices can be run off-sites and at homes. Offices are not restricted to central business district or skyscrapers. Banking and insurance have benefited most through on-line transactions. Office staff is not doing clerical or secretarial work. They are knowledge workers. The various tasks in the office are integrated.

Service Industries

Technology has tremendous impact on the services. In hospitals, we have CT and MRI scans and ICUs. In telecoms, we have GSM/CDMA phones, satellite communication and video-conferencing. In education there is interactive learning, e-books and internet. Retail is influenced by point-of-sale terminals, scanners, bar-coding and computerized inventory control. Legal services benefit by search engines, word processors and databases. In air-lines, there are computerized reservations and ATCs. Hotels boast of reservations, climate control systems with internet access, TV checkout and keycard securities.

Services are getting standardized. The delivery has improved. Service facilities are so designed that they become flawless. Deliveries are automated. Employees should be made focal point of service delivery system. Technology should assist the front-line employees. Human resources should be valued as assets. Their compensation should be performance-based.

Wireless Monitoring

The design, operation, maintenance and upgrading of industrial plants and mills are governed by wireless since it lowers the construction costs while greatly enhancing the ability of personnel to monitor and communicate with equipment in remote/inaccessible areas.

Iron and steel mills are the first to adopt wireless industrial networks. Here wireless field devices are used to monitor processes. Even equipment in hard-to-reach places are monitored. Remote parts of the mill are monitored.

Emerson's Smart Wireless technology was first launched in Europe and North America. In June 2007, it has been launched in Asia-Pacific region. Sensors will be installed virtually throughout the plant. Many equipment (which were previously not touched by data-retrieval network) including critical rotating network can now be tapped for data. There are various transmitters — vibration transmitters, pressure transmitters and temperature transmitters. The network will be further developed as new sensors become available.

Plant assets can be monitored cost effectively to return real-time data. Maintenance becomes reliability driven. Security is equally important. Wireless applications are subjected to the same scrutiny as the IT systems with respect to their security.

Reliability of wireless systems depends on having multiple paths of communication. If one device fails or is blocked, another path can automatically be taken. This is achieved through 'self-organising mesh network.' Another assurance of reliability is 'frequency hopping.' If one of the assigned frequencies is jammed or compromised, the wireless transmitter senses the problem and automatically uses another channel.

Wireless should not be viewed as direct replacement for wired instrumentation. Wireless is slower but are quickly installed. Wireless is easy to reposition.

Artificial Intelligence (AI)

Artificial Intelligence aims to create computers capable of performing tasks that humans do with the help of their intelligence. The cutting edge intelligence enables us to understand high level emotions and respond to these emotions in an appropriate manner. How easily we can be funny or loving or sexy. But in terms of behaviour, these are very sophisticated behaviours. We expect the computers to show similar capabilities. That makes them ideal for interaction with us. To understand emotion, one has to understand emotion, one has to understand the language. And language is the key to grasp knowledge.

There is progress in this field of developing AI. IBM's Watson computer is able to play the TV game of Jeopardy! which is a broad task involving complicated natural language queries. Watson acquires knowledge by reading Wikipedia and other encyclopedias. Google's self-driving car is another example of the application of AI. Apple's SIRI and Google Now answer questions.

Raw Kurzweil, director engineering, Google has written the best seller *The Singularity is Near.* He predicts that by 2045, 'singularity' will be achieved. This metaphor is borrowed from physics. It means that by 2045, we will have our intelligence multiplied a billion fold by merging it with AI we are creating. That is a profound transformation. By 2029, it is predicted that computers will match human intelligence. They will pass the 'Turing test'. It means they will be indistinguishable from human intelligence. Once this is achieved, the computers will exceed human intelligence. This does not mean they will compete with biological humans or displace them. They would rather enhance the biological beings. They are ready to do so, the caveat is that technology is a double-edged sword and must be used judiciously.

We can expect by 2030, technology will advance so much that for every passing year, one year will be added to human life by controlling genes and having nanobots in the blood stream to fight infections.

CHRONOLOGY: AI

Year	*Event*	*Remarks*
1950	Alan Turing, the British scientist introduces Turing Test.	It is a way of testing AI
1956	First international conference on Robotics in Dent mouth, US. Organised by Marvin Minsky and John McCarthy.	The term AI is coined
1963	Nobel for how brain cells communicate awarded.	Hodgkin Huxley and Eccles get this model.
1966	Machine translation report is negative	It kills Natural Language Processing (NLP) work for many years.
1973	Freddy — a Scottish robot built by Edinburgh University	It was capable of using vision to locate and assemble models
1975	First hierarchical neural networks built	—
1979	Hans Moravee — builds a computer-controlled vehicle Stanford Cart	—
1987	'The society of Mind' is published by Marvin Minsky.	—
1993	Polly — the first robot to navigate using vision and operate at animal-like speeds was created	Ian Horswill created it
1997	Deep Blue of IBM defeats world chess champion Garry Kasparov	—
2005	Blue Brain Project	Its simulator brain in molecular detail.
2011	SOINN (Self-Organising Incremental Neural Network) robot created. It learns functions it was not programmed to do	Osamu Hasegawa's research

Of course, neuroscience itself is still bit like physics before Newton. We gave understood only a fraction of how of brain functions. As more and more of the brain functions will be clear by advances in imaging technology, the feedback loop with computer scientists will expand. And so will the prospect of thinking machines.

Turing Test

If a human being cannot distinguish between a machine and a human through interaction, then that machine would be intelligent.

The experiment that is visualised runs like this, There is a computer in one room and a human with a computer. In another room, there is an interrogator — a human with a computer connected to both computers in another room. The interrogator interacts with both computers. He tries to guess which is run by a human and which one is running by itself.

When the computer manages to fool the interrogator into thinking that it is human, that is the point the intelligent machine is born. Despite the spectacular advances, no machine has come anywhere near passing the Turing test.

UNSUPERVISED NEURAL NETWORK

Andrew N. Ng and Jeff Dean working on a Google project developed an array of 16000 processors. This system was fed 10 million YouTube thumbnails so that it could 'watch' and categorise what it saw into 22000 categories like 'cats' 'humans', 'cars' and so on.

The way neurons are organs in the brain in a hierarchical fashion and are interconnected — in a similar way the system was organised — it was called 'unsupervised neural network.' Why unsupervised? Simply because it was not asked to identify 'cats' or anything like that. It was built to analyse and categorise. The system successfully identified cats and slotted them. Similarly, it identified humans. No computer had done so in unsupervised conditions. It was as if a 'learning machine' has been born.

ENTERPRISE RESOURCE PLANNING (ERP) SYSTEMS

This is a management technique in which every enterprise function (HR, finance, manufacturing, supplier chain and customers) is integrated in a seamless flow of information. This system integrates all facets of business including planning, manufacturing, sales and marketing. By integrating information, we can know what is going on in the company at any given point of time. Unnecessary meetings become redundant once ERP is installed. It is a planning tool that results in lower overheads, and reduced production costs. It improves profitability. In post-liberalisation period, ERP has become a necessity in India. ERP calls for re-engineering of processes, and getting the support of the managers. Currently, there are 2 lac companies in India of a size that will benefit from an ERP solution, less than 5,000 have it. The combined business of all major players like SAP, Oracle etc. will cover another 20000 companies over the two-three years. The market is huge. Bharat Goenka will introduce a Tally ERP which will be known for its flexibility, ease of implementation, ease of use and the ability to deploy continuously and scale without the need for a strong technical staff. They hope to get 1 lac customers for Tally ERP by 2011.

EVOLUTION OF ERP

Year	*System Evolved*	*Remarks*
1960s	Inventory Control	Customized software packages to handle inventory based on traditional inventory theory.
1970s	M.R.P: Material Requirement Planning	Master Schedule (MS) giving a detailed break-up of end items required. This list enabled computation of a time-table for procuring components of preparing sub-assemblies.
1980s	MRP II	MRP was extended on shop-floor and distribution management.
1990s	ERP — Enterprise Resources Planning	MRP II was extended to other areas like engineering, finance, human resources and projects management.

Supply Chain Management of Software (SCMS)

First let us understand what is meant by supply chain management. ERP package provides us control over materials and processes in our plants and offices. We, however, need to go beyond this. We should get control over the whole chain from raw material and component supplies to our plants and the retail store. This is implemented through a special software. Simplistically speaking, Supply Chain Management (SCM) is a method of creating products for the end user. It cuts across the suppliers of raw materials (vendors), the manufacturing unit, the warehouses, the transporters, the distributors, the retailers and the final sale. Market demand triggers off the supply chain. SCM could be defined as the delivery of enhanced customer and economic value through synchronized management of the flow of physical goods and associated information from sourcing through consumption.

Fig. 4.6

Supply Chain

Customer ➡	Retailer ➡	Distributor ➡	Warehouse ➡	Plant ➡	Vendors
(Marker Demand)	Data inputs at point of sales used to create demand forecast module	Data input on stock-levels and customer requirement	Data pass through the system	Components required are demanded	

The data from the vendors, the big distributors and retailers is constantly fed into the system enabling an appropriate response on the part of the marketing managers and production managers. SCMS makes us understand the demand pattern and we can align the product mix accordingly.

Out of 300 Indian companies which have installed ERP, most of them are thinking of installing SCMS also. The median price of a software is almost ₹ 1 crore.

Formerly, companies were integrated internally and externally by traditional devices like phone-lines, fax machines, VSATS. This integration which was mostly manual will now be software-based.

In SCM, the data is generated and analysed at several points on the chain. It takes into account any constraints which might affect the supply chain and incorporates this data for future forecasts. SCM rationalizes vendors, and reduces their numbers. Implementing SCM is not easy. Internal supply chains are integrated first. It calls for training personnel to log in data accurately and analyse the output. The success depends on the data input. There is often resistance to SCMS from the middle management. SCMS is revenue enhancer, makes a company learn by improved asset utilization, and decrease costs by removing inefficiencies.

A big company like Lever has to integrate its head office in Mumbai and 50 factories, 50 depots and 200 sites. It therefore needs a seamless supply chain software package. It recently launched and relaunched close to 70 products. SCM will enable it to monitor all its production lines, keeping in mind these launches. It will also enable to rearrange its distribution set-up to make way for a new product. The original supply chain of Lever consisted of suppliers to manufacturing centres, to storage points, to distributors, to retailers and to consumers. There was blockage of working capital in inventories to the extent of 20-25 per cent of turnover in 1995. After computerizing the supply chain, with more precise demand forecasting and daily stock, replenishment inventory came down to 5-6 per cent of turnover. High volume products are directly distributed, and buffer is created for lower volume brands.

Integrated Supply Chain Management (SCM) and real-time decisions-making are essential in order to keep pace with rapid changes in supply and demand. When data is shared with other players, the enterprise becomes extended. Integration is thus taken beyond the walls of the organisation itself. Here the company not only automates its own processes, but integrates them with the automated processes of supply chain partners. It is called Extended ERP system. It is necessary to come to an understanding of open standards across the industry to have an extended ERP system. Apart from open standards, we must have decision support tools that understand business relationship, and help automatically redefine and synchronise the business functions which support these relationships. One such tool is Advanced Planning and Scheduling (APS). It takes ERP beyond transaction data processing. APS considers various operating constraints. ERP is integrated with APS. Manufacturing then becomes customer-driven. There is better utilization of plant capacity, and materials. But this integration is not so easy. When ERP and APS tools are separate, the data must be synchronized between the two systems.

Oracle Supply Chain management (SCM) solutions is the software available to create a demand driven organisation by connecting and extending the values chain, streamling the business processes and eliminating non-value added activities. One can contact Oracles e-business solutions on 9622-123456.

Thermax Philips and Calcomp are companies which have installed ERP. ERP investment is a cost too. Its benefits must be greater than cost in installing it. We have a legacy of hardware. It is not always necessary to upgrade them. Instead, we can follow the low-cost route of running new software on already existing hardware.

ERP benefits are classifiable into two categories — the benefits of automation, like data entry elimination, fewer billing errors, pay roll and process cost avoidance and reduced account receivables and the benefits of transformation like reduced inventories, improved customer services, lower distribution costs and improved product margins.

Activities which add no value are eliminated. Along with these, the costs of performing these activities are also eliminated. Accurate demand forecasts integrate production to demand. It means lower inventories. Co-ordination amongst functional departments enable change occurring in one to be reflected as a change in all other processes. The costs of delay and confusion are avoided. The cycle times for manufacturing and distribution are reduced. This liberates capital. Customer service improves a great deal.

In EPP, infotech becomes the foundation for all functional departments. The basic objectives of ERP is to integrate all the information generated by different processes into a streamlined seamless flow. A piece of data just entered once if crucial, gets reflected in the information-flow everywhere in the organisation. To illustrate a new sales order is featured on the computer screen of every executive affected by it. Production department comes to know that it has to produce this. Purchase knows it has to take steps to keep stores ready. Logistics knows it has to gear up for delivery at a particular time. Accounts knows that it has to bill for the order. Instead of sequential processing there is parallel processing. This liberates cash from unproductive cells. ERP makes it possible to deliver to the customer the best quality at the lowest cost. Real-time information means we can act on market realities rather than depend on dated information and guesswork.

Enterprise System Management

You must have experienced what it is like when you enquire your current balance in the bank account, and the clerk gives you a sorry look as the system has blacked out. These days it is better to prevent such breakdowns, and be alerted about an impending breakdown. Enterprise System Management is an integrated solution that controls centrally all elements of the system like PCs, servers, network, and application software. It helps detect a flaw before it occurs. Unit Center TNG software package and Trivdli software package help prevent unscheduled breakdowns and loss of operation time. It ensures automatic data saving across all operating systems. It takes care of viruses. It takes care of security both internet as well as external. It has the capability to take the necessary corrective action on its own. It ensures 24-hour availability of IT system. Stanchart in India has introduced ESM. ESM is costly to install, say for 1,000 PCs, the software package costs ₹ 1 crore and implementation

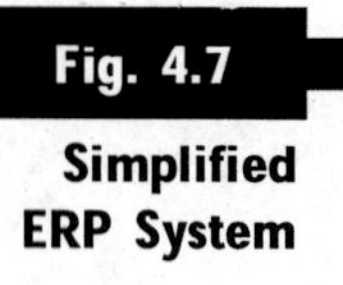

Simplified ERP System

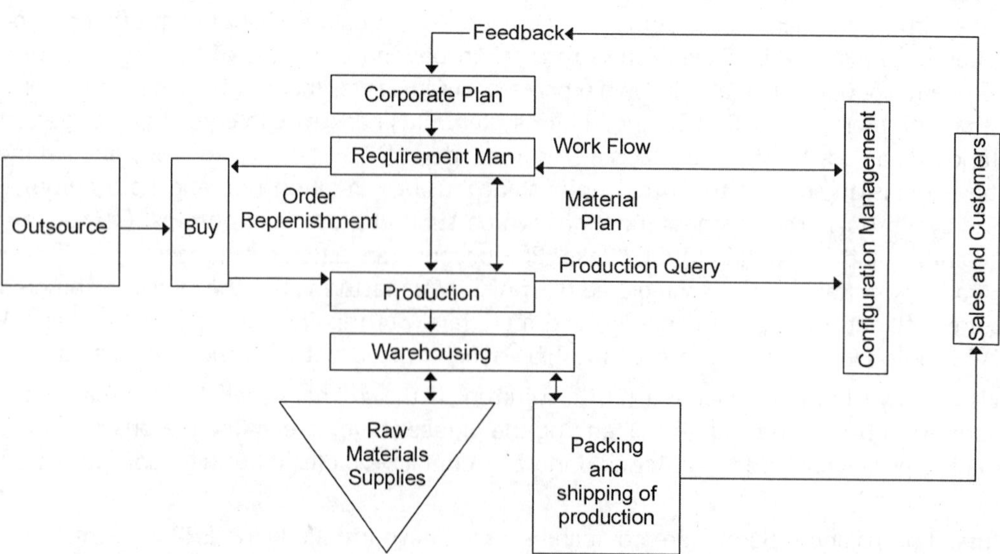

cost ₹ 20-30 lakhs. It is possible to design cheaper versions costing a few lakhs of rupees for medium and small firms.

These days most of the companies have gone in for the ERP. Once an ERP package is implemented, the company becomes wholly computerized. Even if one computer breaks down, the work in company gets paralysed. ESM, therefore, is a pre-requisite for proper working of ERP.

It is necessary to integrate the ERP project to Enterprise Product Information Management (EPIM). Most ERP packages tend to bypass product development activities. An additional module called Enterprise Product Data Management (EDPM) should be added to ERP. This will translate the design specifications into the raw materials needed to generate an appropriate Bill of Material. It can also enable product modification in response to the changing consumer needs, and this will be captured on the system at the shop-floor level. The assembly-line can thus be adjusted to the new design. EDPM is the link between product management to all other areas of business activity.

EPDM reduces the complexity at post-design stage and saves valuable time. Like ERP, the EDPM should also reflect how the company operates on day-to-day basis. It also makes available the information on any connected PC and information is just a click away. In this module we get a trinity of CAD/ CAE, computer-aided management and product data management. Product data affects all other functional areas. The design determines the manufacturing methods. Design specifications are pointers to the USPs around which marketing strategies are built. Product features determine how the product will be serviced, how many components go into the making of the products and what their designs are and how it affects the finance area and the make-or-buy decision, and quality control thereafter.

Inspite of all the benefits, many companies by-pass EDPM because its benefits are not visible immediately. Besides it is difficult to integrate the product development data into an ERP system.

ERP PACKAGES AVAILABLE

Vendor	*Software Package Available*
SAP	R/3
BaaN	Eponymous package
Oracle	Applications package
QAD	Mfg/Pro
Ramco	Marshall
Visesh	Movex
Eastern Software	Makes

Implementation of ERP

Each company is driven differently and so has to identify the objectives for using the ERP package and the results it wants to achieve by using such a package. It has also to list the strategic needs our data must serve. Sometimes the vendors promise too much but there is little by way of implementation. Some companies may not have any computerized system at all, not even a PC on MD's desk. Some have a semblance of MIS at least. ERP wants us to be online. ERP cost must be actually considered. It is not just the cost of the software package. We need to consider the cost of money that we must pour into the organisation to initiate changes in different parts of the organisation as per the demands of the ERP package. Sometimes, it takes a lot of money to keep ERP running considering the networking costs for different sites. When networking costs are high programmes like SAP's R/3 are not preferred, though they incorporate 1,000 best business practices around the world.

ERP must be developed for small enterprises. Even a 100-crore company is considered small for ERP purposes by the vendors. Some software like Mfg/Pro have low networking costs, and works on a dial-up network.

Vendors must understand the client's needs, his critical result areas, and the processes the organisation will adopt in future. The global package must be adapted to the local needs. India is a conglomerate

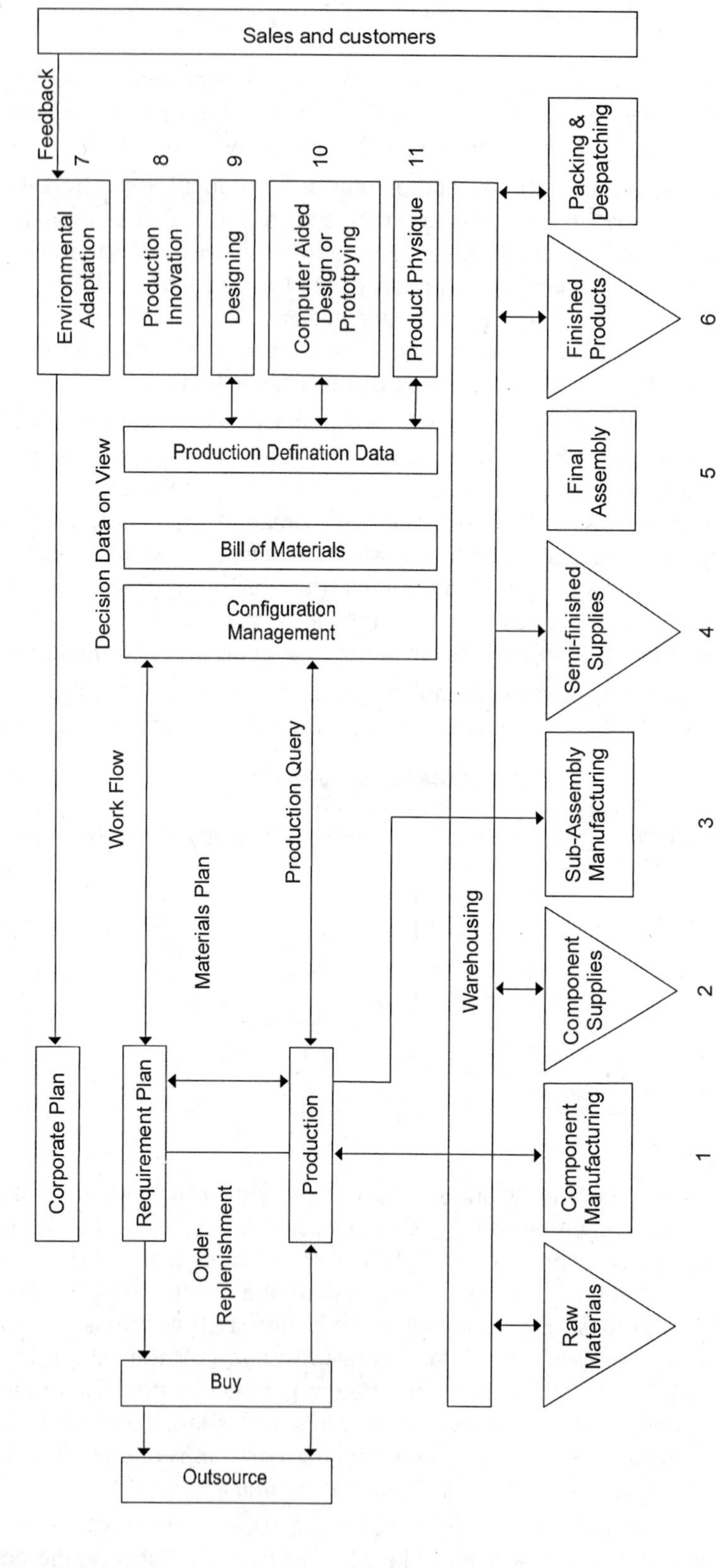

Fig. 4.8 **Integrated EPIM and ERP (Digits indicate EPIM System)**

of states with different distribution costs and varying local taxes. Oracle though a good package, has not been adapted to the Indian needs.

The functional core of an ERP package remains the same all over the world. Around this core we must put layers that are market specific. Ramco's Marshall is compatible with Indian laws. As most of the ERP packages are modular, re-layering as per local conditions is possible, But it entails some costs. We have to consider how much adaptation an ERP package will need. We must also consider what changes we must initiate in our processes to fit the ERP package. We may learn from the experience of the actual users.

Top management support is a must for the successful implementation of an ERP package. Oracle does not believe in adapting ERP beyond a point, since then it hinders implementation. A cross-functional cross-hierarchical ERP team is created, ERP is first tested at the laboratory level. A pilot project is run to realize the bottlenecks.

Training

Various training programmes are available for ERP training. NITTIE also conducts such programmes. Team SAP Academy Programme (Bangalore and Mumbai) is designed to provide structured training in current SAP R/3 business applications. Successful candidates will be Certified as SAP Certified Consultants. There are four application tracks each focusing on a specific function area. Candidates can only opt for any one of the four tracks. The four tracks are:

- ❒ Material Management.
- ❒ Production Planning.
- ❒ Financial Accounting.
- ❒ Sales and Distribution.

The course covers:

- ❑ SAP R/3 Overview.
- ❑ Specific Business Processes and Functions.
- ❑ Project Start Up and ASAP Overview
- ❑ Introduction to Indian Version.
- ❑ Short case study in a simulated environment to understand cross-functional aspects.
- ❑ Certification Examination.

One can contact Alka Saxena on telephone no. +91-22-4326943 or Fax +91-22-4326972 or e-mail alka.saxena@sap-ag de.

Is the Organisation Ready for ERP?

There are many cases of ERP disasters worldwide, and some of them have also started appearing in India. The basic question is to examine the readiness of the organisation for ERP. There is no known case of any organisation which could acquire competitive advantage on account of a ready-made ERP solution available from a vendor. We have to spell out our metrics in quantitative terms *i.e.,* to reduce order despatch time by 40 per cent or receivables by 50 per cent. Such quantification of expectation is necessary to justify the necessity of an ERP package. Even future business requirements must be taken into account. ERP itself has its own life-cycle and this varies from organisation to organisation. There should be process reviews. Just willingness to spend a particular quantity of money for buying an ERP package does not amount to top management support. We have to consider the changes that must be brought about before ERP can be implemented. In some organisations, a full-blown ERP package may not be necessary. We can do with a localized solution in one particular area. The applicability of ERP to organisation's goals should be seriously considered.

Those who implement ERP need better compensation package. A successful ERP programme requires staff retention policies, not only during project implementation stage but also through the life cycle of the system.

ERP *vs.* Groupware

In ERP-installed companies, there is a lot of paper work related to ISO:9000 compliance. Paper work can be reduced by restructuring the organisation, say by making it flatter rather than taller. The infotech solution to reduced paper work in a cost effective manner is the use of groupware which configures the work flows to any business process. The paper documents are converted into electronic documents. They are pushed into pre-assigned post-boxes. Paper is not circulated. This can be done at a fraction of a cost of an ERP solution. ERP is passive about the action taken by the managers on information sought. Groupware alerts the managers by charting a route a document should take to create a specific workflow creating an awareness regarding action. ERP solution is customized and hard and expensive to install. Groupware is compatible with different hardware system. It is quicker, cheaper and less-disruptive.

Most Implemented ERP Modules

1. Finance and Accounts
2. Materials Management
3. Inventory Control and Management
4. Production Planning and Control
5. Sales and Distribution
6. Supply Chain Management
7. Logistics
8. Quality Management
9. Human Resources Management
10. Plant Maintenance
11. Treasury
12. Project Management.

ERP Market Shares

Package	*Percentage Market Share*
SAP	20
JD Edwards	10
Mfg/Pro	10
BPCS	10
Marshal	9
Oracle Financials	7
BaaN	7
MAMIS	4
Others	22

Source: Dataquest Market Survey, 1999.

Components of ERP Expenditure

Component	*Expenditure (%)*
Software Package	53
Implementation	35
Pre-implementation	9
Post-implementation	3

Source: ERP Market Survey Dataquest, 1999.

Efficient Consumer Response (ECR)

This is a holistic strategy between the manufacturer and retailer to increase consumer value by removing non-value added cost from the entire supply chain.

ECR, according to Bhattacharya of P&G, India, has four basic elements.

1. Sorting of SKUs meaningfully to classify just extensions or 'flankers' and those that form an essential part of the product category.
2. Strategy of efficient replacement: Here the consumer demand pulls product through the chain. It is like just-in-time inventory management.
3. Strategy of efficient promotion: Maximize the total efficiency of trade and consumer promotions.
4. Strategy of new product introduction: Make innovations effectively.

ERP Journal

The Indian Express Group's business publication division has added ERP journal to its product portfolio. It is priced at ₹ 30 a copy. ERP is not covered adequately in mass media, Internet provides ERP information not relevant for India. Most ERP books are expensive. ERP seminars are held at metros. Marketing literature is available for specific product of a particular company. ERP journal has been launched (1999) to satisfy the need from 'authentic India-related in-depth low-cost information about ERP.' It is not positioned as an IT magazine. Its target audience is business managers, and not IT professionals. ERP may become outdated as a term but 'integrated information system' will not. There will be several industry specific issues. The sale will be subscription-based.

B2B Site of ERP

In Internet, B2C (business to consumer) model is difficult to make cost effective. However, B2B (business to business) model ensures disintermediation and consequent cost savings ensuring its success. Eastern Software Systems (ESS) is one of the first software companies to put ERP software on the Net under the brand name MakESS to cater specifically to small and medium enterprises. They are backed by venture capitalists. The software was launched in September 1999 and became the first ASP (Application Service Provider) in India. Ispat Steel, Indonesia is their largest customer on the Net. The rent is about ₹ 9,000 per month for MakESS. They have launched a site that caters to ERP on the Net called Ebizframe.com. They have just added Net-enabled applications to ERP, and they are renting it out for around ₹ 30,000 per customer per server.

ERP Revolution: The Microsoft Way

Microsoft Dynamics AX is an ERP solution that works like (and with) the familiar Microsoft Office software. This multi-language, multi-currency solution also integrates with Windows and other Microsoft products. ERP has now become a three horse race — Microsoft Dynamics, Oracle and SAP. Many small and mid-size businesses (SMBs) are expected to purchase new midmarket ERP applications to replace outdated Manufacturing Resource Planning (MRP II) systems. In larger decentralized companies, ERP suites are replacing older systems. ERP vendors have expanded product lines in areas such as Supply Chain Management (SCM), Customer Relationship management (CRM), Product Lifecycle Management (PLM) and Business Intelligence (BI). In India, Microsoft Dynamics has added more than 400 customers spanning across industry sectors. It has 2,75,000 customers worldwide. It has been introduced in 2004. They have a 60 plus partnership system. These partners customize the offerings.

CDMA TECHNOLOGY

Irwin Mark Jacobs, formerly of MIT and later of University of California set up a company called Qualcomm which developed a mobile technology CDMA: Code Division Multiple Access which was demonstrated to Hughes initially. In 1989, the industry thought of choosing between TDMA: Time Division Multiple Access and FDMA: Frequency Division

Multiple Access but did not find CDMA worth commercialisation. But CDMA had the possibility of offering at least 10-20 times **capacity improvement** than the others. In 1991, Qualcomm demonstrated this technology to a number of operators. The US chose to have two standards — TDMA and CDMA. In Europe, the countries are smaller and GSM suits them as it can be used in roaming. Besides, CDMA was welcomed as it is suited to 3G. The next technology will be to do packet switching with voice. Ultimately, 3G will be all packet switched. In future, a slightly bigger phone will serve as a computer with internet.

Irwin has written a textbook called *Principles of Engineering* that is taught till this day. He holds 13 patents.

Issue: How technology is chosen in the context of cellular telephony? How CDMA scores over GSM? How GSM is good for roaming?

Total Integrated Automation (TIA) Portal

It is a specially designed, efficient, intuitive and proven engineering framework that enables manufacturers to configure —

- all planning and production processes on a single screen.
- along the entire value creation chain (product design, production planning production engineering, production execution and specific services like consulting and maintenance).

Product Design

Innovation cycles have shortened very much. Software can be used to design and develop products speedily and at reduced costs.

Production Planning

Software enables the machine and factory design on screen. Production processes can be simulated and optimised.

Production Engineering

The greater use of hardware and software leads to better interface and communication of industrial systems with each other.

Production Execution

Automation and energy saving technology (use of energy efficient IE2 and IE3 motors than the usual IE1 motors) boost productivity.

Services

Services such as maintenance, support in planning, installation and operation and modernization. These play a central role in all phases of manufacturing.

Gartner's Application Maturity Model, 2007

This model assesses the capability of an organisation relative to an objective industry framework. It examines an organisation's overall application maturity and its maturity across eight critical disciplines. It is a measure of business alignment. This model is patterned after the CMM model. It identifies five levels of maturity.

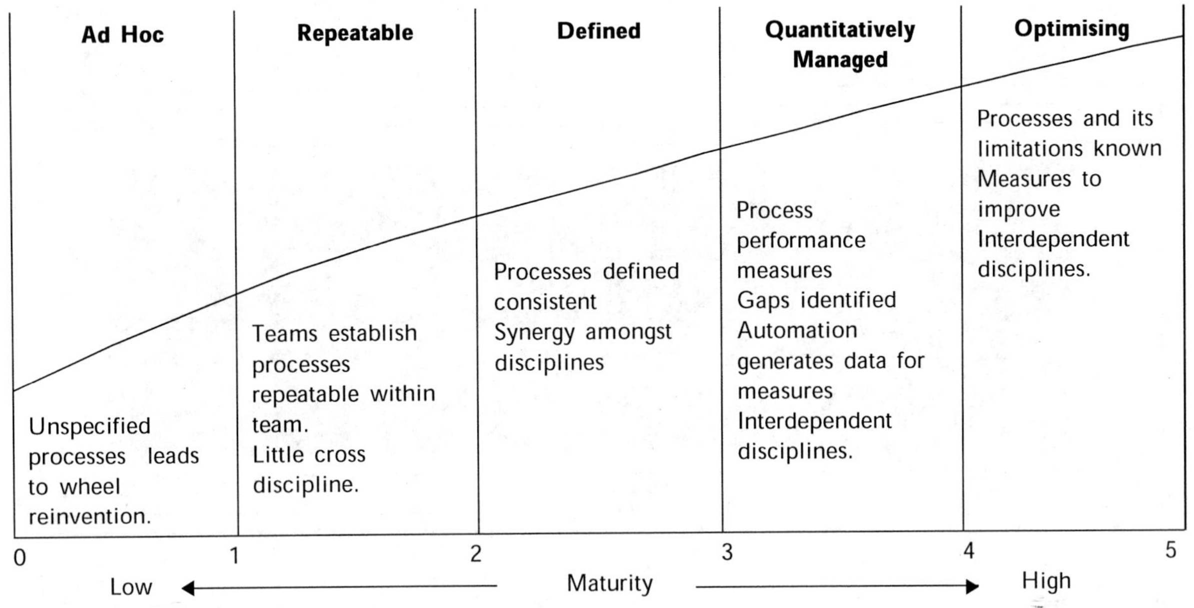

Source: Gartner, 2008.

The lowest level of maturity is called *ad hoc* where the score falls between zero and one. Processes are not specified. The managers are compelled to reinvent the wheel every time an application is initiated. The highest level of maturity is optimising where the organisation scores between four and five. Here processes are defined, and there are built-in measures to propel continuous improvement. Mature processes are repeatable, reliable predictable and measurable. They are subjected to continuous refinement. They ensure consistent delivery. People move freely. There is performance measurement. Mature application capability delivers optimal results even when the technology is not-so-modern.

The eight areas or disciplines whose maturity is understood are:

- *Application portfolio management* (APM) where performance and risk of its application assets are examined.
- *Project portfolio management* (PPTA) deals with deployment of scarce resources such as capital and manpower.
- *Staffing, skills and sourcing*
- *Financial analysis and budgets*
- Vendor management
- *Management of architecture* as related to business, information and technical
- *Software processes*
- *Operations and support.*

It is essential to look at industry benchmark averages for application maturity.

Chief Technology Officer (CTO)

These days companies appoint Chief Technology Officers (CTOs) just like Chief Operating Officers (COOs), Chief Marketing Officers (CMOs) and Chief Financial Officers (CFOs). The role of a CTO is very dynamic. It keeps on changing depending upon the needs of the company and the individual holding this post. It is also shaped by the environment and the technology deployed. A CTO could be a chief engineer, or an evangelist who preaches new disruption and fosters new ideas. A CTO improves R&D efficiency. He can design technology strategy and understand customer needs and the future needs. He constantly gets customer feedback. He looks for growth opportunities and resets the priorities in the organisation. He focuses on future growth and building the right products.

5

FACILITIES PLANNING: LOCATION

Introduction

Site selection is an important activity which decides the fate of the business. A good location may, reduce the cost of production and distribution to a considerable extent. The reduction of cost of production and distribution helps in elevating either the competitive strength or the profit margin of the business.

Locating a business involves a large, relatively permanent investment. If the site selection is not proper, all the money spent on factory building, machinery, and their installation will go in waste and the owner has to suffer a great loss. Therefore, the site for the factory should be selected very carefully. While selecting a site, it is necessary to consider technical, commercial and financial aspects and then select a site that may provide maximum advantages.

In 1902, J.N. Tata seeks the help of geologist Charles Page Parin to identity a site rich in resources such as iron and coal, to build India's first steel plant. The search starts in what is now Madhya Pradesh. In 1907, the team finally chooses Sakchi village in present-day Jharkhand, which has since grown into the steel town of Jamshedpur. The plant became operational in 1908. This shows how the sites are chosen for locating industries.

The need for selecting a suitable site or location to house the factory may arise in the following situations:

1. While starting a new factory.
2. During the expansion of the existing plant.
3. When the existing plant is to be re-located at some other place, to remove the drawbacks of the present location or to gain the benefits of a still better location.

The Problem of Location

The problem of site selection of a factory can be solved in the following three stages:

1. Selection of the region.
2. Selection of the locality.
3. Selection of actual site.

(1) Selection of the Region: Generally, the geographical area is divided on the basis of natural regions or political boundaries within the nation. (For example, Maharashtra State, U.P. etc.). The suitability of various regions is considered on the basis of comparative cost advantages available out of the possible regions.

(2) Selection of the Locality: After selecting the region, the specific locality within the region is considered. Generally, the following alternative are open in selecting the locality:

(*a*) Urban area

(*b*) Rural area

(*c*) Suburban area in the vicinity of the urban area. The comparative advantages of each locality are considered at this stage.

(3) Selection of the Site: While selecting the site, the type of development of land, cost of levelling etc., possibility of plant expansions, and other infrastructure facilities like transport, banking, power, communication, postal facilities etc. are considered.

Factors Affecting Size of the Firm

The size of firms is usually dependent on the following factors:

(1) Availability of Capital: The size of the firm depends upon the availability of capital. Every firm needs capital. Only large capital investment is made or small capital investment is made. The need of capital depends on size, type and nature of the firm. Industries which require large capital investment, *e.g.,* sugar refining, tend towards large scale. But business units requiring small capital and more labour and a few tools and machines can be started on a small scale.

(2) Entrepreneurial Ability and Efficiency: The ability, experiences and managerial efficiency of the entrepreneur is one of the important factors that determine the size of the business unit. As the firm continues to expand, the tasks of organization and co-ordination become more difficult. The entrepreneur is gradually overloaded with decisions which only he can take, so that he is unable to give enough time and thought to any one problem. The resulting inefficiency is reflected in rising cost. The inability of the entrepreneur to successfully co-ordinate and supervise a large unit is a factor that may check the expansion of the firm.

(3) Risk of Uncertainties: Risks of changes in demand have their impact on the trends in the size of the firms. Firms have to face fluctuations in demand for their products and accordingly adjust their policies and strategies in order to survive and maintain the position in the market. The firms should have the necessary strength to absorb the shocks of fluctuations in demand and they should be flexible enough to adapt to new trends in demand.

Variations in Demand are of Four Kinds

(i) Permanent change in demand may occur due to decline in the popularity of a product or due to a substitute. It may also be caused by changes in fashion, tastes, technology or methods of production so that the product that a firm was so far producing becomes outdated and hence unsalable.

(ii) Cyclical fluctuations in demand means imbalance in demand and supply for a short period. Trade cycles involving alternative phases of boom and depression are common phenomena.

(iii) Seasonal fluctuations changes in demand for certain products are seasonal in nature, *e.g.,* demand for woollen garments changes according to winter or summer. The same is the case with umbrellas, raincoats, fans etc.

(iv) Erratic fluctuations in the quantity demanded occur in industries where products are not manufactured according to individual orders and designs at different prices, *e.g.,* jewellery, furniture etc.

(4) Type of Organization: The size of the firm also depends on the type of organization, *e.g.,* sole trading business concern or individual proprietorship, partnership firm, private companies that are managing business on small and medium scale. Joint Stock Companies require capital on large scale. Thus, the size of the firm also depends on the convenience of the directors from the point of view of the organization and management.

(5) Availability of Inputs: The size can be large if the inputs are available on a large scale. Where the inputs will have to be transported from a distance and there is also some uncertainty, the size is bound to be small. It is for this reason that government has been locating super thermal power houses near the coal mines.

In urban areas many facilities are available whereas in rural areas the entrepreneur has to face many difficulties.

(6) Nature of Product: In the case of processing of raw materials resulting in the production of joint and by-products, the scale is naturally more if the entrepreneur decides to process all the products. In case of production of less standardised and more artistic products the size is bound to be small.

Similarly, if the expectations of the entrepreneur are limited, business can be started on small scale and, if his expectations are more such as reputation, or if a unit is catering to a big market, the size of the undertaking will be larger.

(7) Laws of Returns: Where an industry or its products is subject to decreasing returns, the increase of the product will mean higher cost. Such industries cannot grow beyond a certain size or become large. But where increasing returns apply, large production will result in lower cost, so that the firms can keep on growing larger in size provided the demand for the product is elastic.

(8) Government Regulation or Licensing Policy of Government: The size of the firm depends on the decision taken by the entrepreneur and on the attitude in the government. Large-scale firms are subject to much more rigorous state regulation than small ones. Licences have to be obtained, and they have to conform to a certain standard size. It is often desirable to start on a small-scale to take advantage of low taxes and then expand gradually.

Factors Affecting the Plant Location

Industry is an activity which converts raw materials and semi-finished goods into finished goods for sale. Industrial organization means the combination and co-ordination of capital, labour, machinery and raw materials. The objective of industrial organization is to minimise the cost of production and to achieve progress in that industry. This requires a predetermined and well thought out business policy, planning of machinery and plant layout, planning of purchases of raw materials, organization of distribution of goods and a planned sales organization. The success of business depends on the process of organization and planning.

As business grows, organization and planning become more necessary. When the location of an industrial unit is preplanned, many factors are taken into consideration, *e.g.,* adequate supply of raw materials, nearness to the market, transport facilities, supply of labourers, government facilities, land, climate, supply of power and water, etc. The consideration of these factors requires careful analysis because the location once chosen, cannot be changed often. Frequent changes in location lead to losses. Therefore, the location of an industry is determined by taking into consideration the following factors:

(A) Primary Factors

1. Supply of raw materials
2. Nearness to market
3. Transport facilities
4. Labour supply
5. Availability of power
6. Supply of capital

(B) Secondary Factors

7. Facilities
8. Natural factors
9. Political factors
10. Government subsidies and facilities

11. Historical and religious factors
12. Initial start and goodwill
13. Personal factors
14. Miscellaneous factors

FACTORS OF LOCALISATION

The factors of localisation can be divided into the following categories:

(A Primary Factors

(1) Supply of Raw Materials: It is necessary to consider the adequate supply of raw materials and the nature of raw materials. The cost of raw materials are an important element of the total cost of production. If the supply of raw materials is not regular, it may lead to frequent stoppages and breakages in production. The time and the cost of transporting raw materials is also important. Therefore, industrial units are located near sources of raw materials. When the raw materials are heavier than the finished product — *e.g.*, sugarcane — the factory is located near the raw material producing centre. Nearness to the source of raw materials reduces the cost of transportation. When the weight of the finished product is more than the weight of the raw materials, nearness to raw materials is not important because raw materials may be collected from several sources. Nearness to raw materials is important in case of industries such as sugar, cement, jute and cotton textiles.

(2) Nearness to Market: Every producer wants to sell his product in the market. Nearness to market is important from the point of view of his control over the market. In those industries where raw materials are obtained from different sources, nearness to the source of raw materials is not as important as nearness to the market. Nearness to the market is important for supplying goods to the customers in a minimum period of time adjusting supply according to changes in demand and gaining control over the market. Nearness to the market reduces the cost of transporting finished goods to the market and enhances taking advantage of favourable prices and demand in the market. The producers' survival capacity increases when the market is near the centre of production. Delay in transportation may lead to losses in the form of deterioration of goods. Nearness to market is an important factor in the case of industries producing light, delicate and perishable goods, *e.g.*, glass, cosmetics, food products, fashionable goods having a changing demand, etc.

(3) Transport Facilities: Speedy transport facilities are needed for the regular and timely supply of raw materials at low cost and for transporting finished products on time to the market. Transport facilities with a good speed and capacity are needed for transporting labourers and establishing contacts in the market, and controlling supply according to changes in demand. A producer has to choose a speedy and cheap means of transport after making a comparative cost study of different means of transport, *e.g.*, roads, railways, waterways, etc. Transport facilities are important for getting control over foreign markets.

(4) Supply of Labour: The supply of labour at low cost is important. The importance of labour supply has not lessened in spite of mechanisation. Labour costs are important. Machines cannot produce anything without the availability of skilled labourers. Nearness to the source of labour is, therefore, important. However, labourers are usually available at industrial centres. If the supply of labourers is not regular, manhours and machine-hours are lost forever. Due to labour legislation, trade unions, a dearth of skilled labourers and high absenteeism, the stability of a labour force is most important. Therefore, producers should try to regularise the supply of labourers by reducing absenteeism and strikes due to unsatisfactory working conditions.

(5) Power: Power is necessary for the process of production and for transporting finishing goods and raw materials. Power may be electrical, diesel and atomic energy. All types of power like electricity, diesel and atomic energy are localised and mobile. Power shortages lead to tremendous losses due to the stoppage of machinery. Therefore, industries must have a sufficient and regular supply of power if continuity in production is to be maintained and if industries are to operate at the full capacity.

Usually, heavy industries like machine tools and coal mining industries are located near sources of power. Industrialisation of villages depends on the local availability of electricity or diesel power in underdeveloped areas. All types of industries, whether big or small, require power.

(6) Supply of Capital: Industries require capital for initial promotion and expansion. Therefore, a capital market must be developed in industrial centres. Large-scale production, mechanisation and big industries require large amounts of equity capital and debenture capital for a long period. It is, therefore, necessary that development banks or long-term financing institutions (like the U.T.I., I.F.C., etc.) are developed. Commercial banks should also be developed for the supply of current, or short-term, or working capital. The capital market mobilises the small savings of the people for the purpose of industrialisation. Capital is more mobile than labour and, therefore, nearness to capital is not required for the purpose of industrialisation.

(B) Secondary Factors

(7) Facilities: An enterprising spirit, innovation, technical know-how and an industrious nature of population — all these factors taken together and a favourable government policy create a favourable atmosphere for the purpose of the establishment of industries. Heavy industries in India are the result of personal factors like enterprise, industrious nature of one man creating an industrial group or a family, *e.g.,* Tatas, Kirloskars, etc.

(8) Natural Factors: Land, water, climate, source of raw materials and agricultural climate are some natural factors which are important for some industries like cotton textiles, sugar and jute. These industries depend on a good climate and source of natural raw materials.

(9) Political Factors: The government's policy of licensing and encouraging the development of industries in underdeveloped regions determines the location of industries. Such a policy may cause the dispersal of industries. The location of defence industries depends on the political policy of the government. The government's policy of subsidising small industries in village areas will determine their location and dispersal in village areas. The government's policy of not allowing licences to big units in cities will cause the dispersal of industries to underdeveloped areas.

(10) Government Subsidies and Facilities: The government may encourage the dispersal of industries in underdeveloped areas by making capital, land, water and power available at subsidised rates. The government may give such facilities as development rebate, tax exemptions, price subsidies, banking, insurance and postal facilities at low rates, priority in transport and supply of raw materials, etc. By giving these facilities, the government may bring about the development of industries in backward areas and this will result in the regional balancing of industries.

(11) Historical and Religious Factors: Some industrial cities are of historical importance. Some of them are capital cities having religious importance, *e.g.,* Benaras, Prayag, Kolhapur, Nasik, etc. Industries grow at these religious centres because these are places of historical importance.

(12) Initial Start and Goodwill: Some industries get located at a place because some industrialists start the industry at that place at an early stage, *e.g.,* Jamshedpur (Tatas) was developed into an industrial city; the iron and steel industry received its initial start there. The motor car industry was started at a place where Mr. Ford started his workshop. Once one industry is started, other industries also develop at that place. Government restrictions play a negative role in the location decision. Industries are not permitted to be started or expanded in certain developed urban areas. So certain industries are relocated from urban areas to rural or less developed or the divisions or branches of the industries established in urban areas are started in such rural or undeveloped areas.

(13) Personal Factors: In business history, it is found that personal considerations have decidedly affected the location of certain industrial units. There is no rationale for such considerations, however, when there is a possibility of multiple locations, this factor plays a decisive role in locational consideration. Henry Ford started the automobile industry in Detroit (U.S.A.) because it was his home-town.

(14) Miscellaneous Factors: The following factors also affect the location of the industrial unit:

(*i*) Sufficient water supply, if water is consumed in large quantities in the production processes.

(*ii*) Disposal of waters.

(*iii*) Strategic factors like dangers of air-attacks.

(*iv*) Availability of fire-fighting facilities.

(*v*) Availability of recreational, medical and educational facilities.

(*vi*) Quality of life because of facilities like schools, hospitals, post-office, parks etc. enjoyed by the community.

(*vii*) Community attitudes.

(*viii*) Ecological and environmental considerations.

(*ix*) Regional aspirations of people and their political satisfaction.

Selection of Actual Site

The important factors in this respect are:

1. Availability of cheap land to build and expand this plant.
2. Cost of land development: The land should be flat and strong enough to sustain heavy machine installation. For agro-based industries the type of soil should also be considered.
3. Repair facilities: Facilities for upkeep and general maintenance should be available in nearby area.
4. Facilities for housing the workers and if necessary their transport from the place of residence to the work site.
5. Social and recreational facilities.
6. Post and telegraph facilities.
7. Cost of laying the water supply and providing sewage and disposal of waste.
8. Cheap facilities for disposing of trade waste.
9. Any restriction imposed by the town planning department, local bye-laws.
10. Taxes, fire protection facilities etc.

Economic Survey of Site Selection: The necessary factors in the selection of plant location vary from industry to industry and with changing technical and economic conditions. Therefore, a location survey must be carried out based on the specific requirements of a given enterprise.

The aim of such an economic survey is to find out whether or not the location meets first the primary, and then the secondary requirements. The relative importance of the necessary factors can be determined on the basis of their proportionate share in the unit cost of production and distribution. After the various factors have been weighed, suitable regions can be selected.

Computation of Investment and Cost of Production and Distribution: The required capital investment and the unit cost of production and distribution for a given volume of output should be computed for each prospective location. The ideal location is that which permits the lowest cost of production and its distribution. If the unit cost of production in the various locations is somewhat comparable, the location that requires the least capital or fixed investment will be preferred. The choice should be checked against detailed information obtained from local banks and government agencies.

Selection of Site (Urban, Rural or Suburban area)

There are broadly three possible alternatives open for the selection of the locality of the industrial unit:

(1) Urban or City area, (2) Rural area, (3) Suburban area.

The relative advantages and disadvantages of each area are discussed as under:

Table 6.1

Illustrating the Determination of Cost of Production and Distribution Fixed Capital Requirements in A			
Location	***A***	***B***	***C***
Land Building Improvement Equipment Total			
Unit Cost of Production and Distribution			
Location	***A***	***B***	***C***
Raw Materials **Fuel and Power** (*a*) Electricity (*b*) Coal (*c*) Water (*d*) Gas (*e*) Oil etc.			
Factory Expenses (*a*) Labour (*b*) Supervision (*c*) Inspection (*d*) Testing etc.			
General Expenses (*a*) Administration (*b*) Salaries (*c*) Taxes (*d*) Insurance (*e*) Postages etc.			
Distribution Expenses (*a*) Advertising (*b*) Packing (*c*) Stocking (*d*) Transport (*e*) Sales etc.			
Total cost per unit			

Urban or City Area

Due to certain typical advantages available only in the city area, promoters show preference for the city area as the location of the industrial unit.

Advantages of City Area

(*i*) Good transportation facilities are available for the movement of raw materials and finished products by rail and road and at times, by water and air.

(*ii*) Good and prompt postal and communication services are available.

(*iii*) Banking and credit facilities are available.

(*iv*) Services of insurance companies are available in city areas.

(*v*) Sufficient storing facilities including cold storage, are available.

(*vi*) Ample availability of skilled and unskilled workers.

(*vii*) Advantages of vicinity of the market for the product. Due to large population, the local demand for the product is fairly high.

(*viii*) Facility of the ancillary and service units, which develop around the industrial strip of the city area.

(*ix*) Sufficient passenger transport facilities by road and railways are available to employees.

(*x*) Development of the training institutes for workers and management institutes for executives put the city area units into privileged position.

(*xi*) Educational, medical and recreational institutes increase the amenities of life for the worker in the city area.

(*xii*) Certain specific municipal service facilities are available only in city areas, like water supply, drainage, fire fighting facilities, sufficient police protection etc.

Disadvantages of Urban or City Area

(*i*) The cost of land is very high as compared to rural areas.

(*ii*) Even at high cost, sufficient land is not available, which puts constraints on the arrangement of plants and machines. Sometimes multi-storey buildings are used which are not suitable for the installation of heavy plant and machines.

(*iii*) Due to high standard of living in city area, the cost of labour is relatively high.

(*iv*) Due to possibilities of changing jobs from one unit to another, and tendency of competitors to snatch away the good employees, the rate of labour turnover is very high in city area.

(*v*) The trade union movement is very strong in city area. Militant trade unionists disturb the amiable industrial relations, which give rise to strikes and lockouts.

(*vi*) Various types of taxes are levied in city areas. The rates of taxes are also relatively high, *e.g.,* Octroi is a typical tax of the city area which is not levied in rural areas.

(*vii*) Certain municipal restrictions put constraints and involve extra costs due to height of the building, disposal of waters, treatment of effluent water, elimination of air pollution caused by smoke etc.

(*viii*) The industrialization in the city area gives birth to slums and dirty residences which creates the typical problems of sanitation and health.

Rural Area

In certain situations, a rural area is also preferred as a site for the industrial unit. The following are its advantages and limitations:

Advantages of Rural Area

(*i*) As compared to the city area, the land is available at cheaper rates.

(*ii*) Large plots of the land are available which can be developed for a factory site, office buildings and residential quarters. Horizontal arrangement of plant and machines in the vast area of land is possible. Provisions can also be made for further expansion.

(*iii*) Due to lower standard of living, the rates of labour are relatively lower. Thus, labour cost is reduced substantially.

(*iv*) As compared to the city area, the labour force is more or less stable which reduces the rate of labour turnover.

(*v*) The industrial relations between labour and management are relatively amicable. The rural environment and residential staff quarters develop personal relations among employees.

(*vi*) The local taxes which are found in city areas are practically non-existent in rural areas.

(*vii*) The municipal restrictions which are found in city areas do not exist in rural areas, *e.g.*, height of building, constructed area in total land etc.

(*viii*) Slums and dirty residence are not found in rural areas. The rural environment is conducive to good health of workers.

(*ix*) Due to lack of congestion, there is no danger of fire caused by surrounding units.

(*x*) No danger of bombardment in war-time. Industrial city areas become the target of air-attacks in war time.

Limitations of Rural Area

(*i*) Transportation facilities are not available in good condition and sufficient quantities.

(*ii*) Sometimes the services of post and telegraph and means of communications are not available.

(*iii*) Banking and credit facilities are also not available. The indigenous moneylenders are charging exorbitantly for these services.

(*iv*) Absence of insurance facilities.

(*v*) Storing and warehouse facilities are also not available in rural areas.

(*vi*) Passenger transport facilities are not available, as are available in city area. If the unit is located at a distance from residential area, it becomes difficult for the workers to reach to the workplace.

(*vii*) Like city areas, the advantage of ancillary and service units is not available.

(*viii*) Such units are very far from the market place and this increases the cost of distribution of finished goods.

(*ix*) It is not possible to tap the advantage of industrial training institutes or management development programmes which is possible in city areas.

(*x*) It is generally not easy to get skilled workers in rural areas. In the city areas, it is not so difficult.

(*xi*) Municipal facilities like water supply, drainage, fire-fighting etc. are not available in rural areas.

(*xii*) There is absence of recreation facilities, good educational institutes, good and sufficient medical facilities etc.

Suburban Area

The city area as a location of industrial unit has got many negative aspects. The other extreme is the rural area, which again is not free from many limitations. The better compromise in the decision is the selection of suburban area as the location of the industrial unit. Suburban area is the area which is located on the outskirts of the city area. Suburban area matches the advantages of the rural area with those of city area which is located at a short distance, *e.g.*, Odhav, Narol, Kathawada, Naroda, Vatva are the suburban areas of Ahmedabad City.

Advantages of Suburban Area

(*i*) Land is available at a cheaper rate as compared to urban areas.

(*ii*) Adequate land is available for future expansion of the unit. The machines can be installed horizontally and still the provision for future expansion can be made.

(*iii*) Infrastructure facilities like road, water supply, drainage, banking, warehousing, insurance etc. are developed either by government, municipal authorities or industrial associations.

(*iv*) As the city area is nearest, the skilled and unskilled, both type of labour are available.

(*v*) It is possible to tap the advantage of industrial training institutes, management development programmes, research institutes etc. which are available in nearby city area.

(*vi*) The nearby city area provides a substantial market for the products of the unit. This reduces the cost of marketing the finished products and other ancillary advantages of marketing are available.

(*vii*) Educational institutes, medical facilities and other recreational facilities are available in the suburban area itself as well as in the nearby city area.

The limitation of suburban area as a site for industry is that in the development process, it may be converted into a part of the urban area with all its merits and demerits.

In general, the big city (urban area) offers particular benefits to the small enterprise. Rural areas offer benefits to a large manufacturing firm and suburban areas often suit the medium sized industries.

COMPARISON BETWEEN URBAN AND RURAL AREA IN CONNECTION WITH THE SELECTION OF SITE

Urban	*Rural*
1. *Availability of Local Market:* Due to large population the local demand for the product is fairly high.	The market place is far away from the industries, therefore cost of distribution of finished products is more.
2. *Labour:* Ample availability of diversified labour.	It is rather difficult to get skilled labour in rural areas.
3. *Transport Facilities:* Good transport facilities are available.	Adequate transport facilities are not available.
4. *Allied Industries:* Proximity to allied industries and service units.	Absence of allied industries.
5. *Availability of Educational Facilities:* Availability of educational, recreational and social facilities.	There are fewer educational, social and recreational facilities.
6. *Cost of Land:* The cost of land is high. Even at high cost, sufficient land is not available which puts constraints on the arrangement of plants and machines.	Sufficient land is available at cheaper rates.
7. *Restrictions on Constructions:* There are greater restrictions on the construction of factory buildings.	There are few restrictions on construction of factory buildings.
8. *Municipal and Public Utility Services:* Certain specific municipal facilities and public utility services such as water supply, drainage, fire fighting, police protection etc., are available.	Municipal facilities and public utility services are not available.
9. *Postal and Communication Service:* Good and prompt postal and communication services are available.	Prompt postal and communication services are not available.
10. *Rates of Taxes:* The rate of taxes are relatively high.	The rate of taxes are quite low.
11. *Cost of Labour:* Due to high standard of living, the cost of labour is relatively high.	Labour is available at cheaper rates.
12. *Availability of Facilities:* Banking facilities, credit facilities and insurance facilities are available.	Absence of banking facilities, credit facilities and insurance facilities.

Urban	*Rural*
13. ***Labour Turnover:*** High labour turnover because of large number of industries.	Labour force is more stable.
14. ***Trade Union Movement:*** The trade union movement is very strong which often results in strikes, lockouts etc.	Trade union movement is not very strong.
15. ***Training Facilities:*** Development of the training facilities for workers and management institutes for executives put the city area into privileged position.	Absence of training facilities and management institutes.
16. ***Transport Facilities:*** Sufficient passenger transport by road and railways are available to employees.	The passenger transport facilities are inadequate. If the factory is located at a large distance from the residential areas, it becomes difficult for the workers to reach the workplace.
17. ***Storage Facilities:*** Sufficient storage facilities including cold-storage are available.	Storing and warehouse facilities are not available.
18. ***Problems of Pollution:*** Concentration of many industries in urban areas creates problems of air pollution, water pollution, sanitation etc.	Problems of air pollution, water pollution etc. are less and the rural environment is conducive to good health of workers.
19. ***Danger of Bombardment in War Time:*** Industrial city areas become the target of air attacks in war time.	Less danger of bombardment in war time.
20. ***Government Policy:*** To avoid concentration of industries, government imposes restrictions for starting new industries in urban areas.	Government provides financial assistance and land at cheaper rates to attract the entrepreneurs to start industries in rural areas.

Recent Trends in the Location of Industries

The traditional factors like nearness of sources of raw materials, motive power, nearness of markets, labour supply etc. have no longer remained the effective pulling forces in the location of industries. The locational trends have changed substantially due to the development of substitute raw materials, network of electrification and transportation by roads and railway, mobility of the labour and persuasive and compulsive policies of the government for balanced regional development.

The recent trends in the selection of industrial location can be described as under:

(1) Priority for the suburban areas: The industrialists show their preference for the suburban area as the site for establishment of a new unit or relocation of the existing one. The industrial policy of the government does not permit the establishment of a new unit or expansion of an existing one in city areas. At the same time, infrastructure facilities are developed in the suburban areas.

(2) Industrial development in the notified backward areas: In order to have balanced regional development, the Central Government as well as the State Government has notified certain backward areas, *e.g.*, Panchamahals, Bharuch and Surendranagar are the centrally notified backward districts of Gujarat State. Similarly, Gujarat State Government has also notified certain backward talukas. Different types of incentives like cash subsidy, tax reliefs, concessional financial assistance, cheaper land and power supply etc. are provided. So, many such areas have been developed substantially in the recent times. An illustration can be cited for the industrial development of Halol in Panchamahals, Ankleshwar in Bharuch and Surendranagar.

(3) Establishment of industrial estate: Industrial estate is a piece of vast land sub-divided into different industrial plots wherein factory sheds are constructed. The Government of India has planned a national policy for the development of industrial estates. It assigned the responsibility of the development of industrial estates to State Governments. In each state, the State Development Corporation (S.D.C.) Gujarat Industrial Development Corporation (G.I.D.C.) has developed many industrial estates practically in all the districts of the state. Industrial estates have also been developed by private entrepreneurs and Chambers of Commerce. The plots of land along with factory sheds and infrastructure facilities are developed in the industrial estates and are sold to the prospective promoters. The establishment of industrial estates has greatly affected the location of industries.

(4) Decentralization of industries: Under the conscious industrial policy of the Government, concentration of industrial units is prevented through licensing policy. New units are not permitted to be started in certain industrially congested areas. Similarly, existing units either establish their additional plants in a less developed area or sometimes relocate the whole unit in such areas.

(5) Increased role of the Government in the decision of location of industries: Government through its persuasive and compulsive methods, greatly affects the locational decisions in recent times. It provides certain attractive incentives to the promoters to establish their units in less developed areas, at the same time it does not permit excessive industrialization in certain developed areas.

(6) Competition between Government and institutions: As industry provides job opportunities to the local population, many local organizations attempt to tempt the prospective promoters to establish the units in their areas. They provide different types of incentives like cheap land, relief in local taxes etc. Sometimes the objective of local organizations and the government, comes in conflict on the issue of location of industries. Thus, the whole pattern of decision about the location of industries has undergone substantial changes in recent times.

GOVERNMENT CONTROL ON LOCATION OF INDUSTRIES

The basic objective of the private sector is to obtain maximum profits out of the business operations. So private sector industries select such a site which reaps maximum economic advantage. Such a policy results in the concentration or localisation of industries in certain areas leaving the other areas underdeveloped. Such a policy distorts the quality of income, wealth and opportunities. So the government being the custodian of public interest, intervenes in the locational decisions as under:

1. Through the licensing policy, it restricts the concentration of industries in developed areas;
2. It provides certain tempting incentives for the spread of the industries in the industrially backward areas;
3. It establishes the giant public sector units in the relatively less developed areas.

The objectives of state intervention and control are:

1. To attain balanced regional development.
2. To narrow down the gap of inequality of income and wealth through creating and providing employment opportunities to less developed areas.
3. To reduce the concentration of population and congestion of industries in city areas.
4. As strategic defence policy, spread of industries reduces the chances of heavy losses in war time.

SUBJECTIVE, QUALITATIVE AND SEMI-QUANTITATIVE TECHNIQUES

In setting up industries, previous precedents have importance. At times, the location is governed by personal preference. Though very common in practice, the approach is not professional. In case of certain industries, there are dominant factors which influence the locational decision (refinery near the crude oil source). For evaluating these qualitative factors, ranking or rating methods are used. Let us examine some of these methods.

(1) Equal Weights Method: In this method, equal weights are assigned to different factors (F) and the sites (S) are evaluated among the factor scale. Himalaya, for instance, a manufacturer of auto spares chose three factors to rate four sites. The sites were assigned ratings between 0-10 points against each factor. The sum of the site ratings was used to compare it with the other sites.

Table 5.2 **Decision Matrix**

Factors		*Potential Sites*			
		S_1	S_2	S_3	S_4
F_1		3	6	8	2
F_2		4	5	9	3
F_3		7	2	6	3
Sum of site ratings		14	13	23	8

From the matrix, we can say site 3 has the highest rating (23), and deserves to be chosen.

(2) Variable Weights Method: In the equal weights method, just as equal weights were assigned to all the factors, in this method variable weights are assigned to each factor and sites are evaluated along the factor scale. For instance, factor F_1 may take 400 points, factor F_2 300 points and factor F_3 100 points. The scope of each site is jotted, out of maximum possible points assigned for that factor.

Table 5.3 **Decision Matrix**

Factors	*Maximum Points*	*Potential Sites*			
		S_1	S_2	S_3	S_4
F_1	400	300	350	350	200
F_2	300	150	200	150	100
F_3	100	50	75	80	40
Sum of Ratings		500	625	580	340

From the table, it is clear that site 2 has the highest rating of 625, and hence is chosen.

(3) Weight-cum-Rating Method: There is one more method of evaluating the potential of the site. Here, we assign variable weights to each factor. Thereafter, locations are rated along a common scale against each factor. The product of location rating and factor weight gives locational point assignment. For instance, we can allot weight between 1 to 5 amongst the three factors (F_1, F_2 and F_3 are assigned 2, 3, 5 respectively). Now as against each factor, the sites can get between 0-10 points. Each site rating is then computed.

Table 5.4 **Decision Matrix**

Factors	*Weight Assigned to factor*	*Potential Sites*			
		S_1	S_2	S_3	S_4
F_1	2	4	6	8	3
F_2	3	4	4	9	2
F_3	5	5	3	7	2
Site Rating		45	39	78	22

Illustrative Calculation

$45 = (2) \times 4 + (3) \times 4 + (5) \times 5$

As indicated by the Table, S_3 with the highest rating of 78 is chosen.

(4) Factor Point Rating Method: This is the last method we consider. Here we establish a subjective scale for all factors in common. The points are assigned to each factor along the subjective scale. Find out subjective rating for each factor. The subjective ratings, for example, could be: Poor, Fair, Adequate, Good and Excellent for evaluating each site for each factor. Adequate takes zero value, and to its left there are negative values and to its right positive values.

Table 5.5 Factor Point Ratings Sample

Factors	Poor	Fair	Adequate	Good	Excellent
F_1	–14	10	0	5	12
F_2	–2	–1	0	2	3

The weight that compares a factor to all other factors is the range between minimum and maximum weights assigned to a factor. Each site is then evaluated choosing the appropriate subjective rating for each factor for each location and the equivalent points of the subjective factor rating are assigned to the factor. The following table makes this clear:

Table 5.6 Decision Matrix

Factors	Potential Sites			
	S_1	S_2	S_3	S_4
F_1	0	– 10	5	0
F_2	0	– 2	3	1
F_3	0	0	0	0
Site Rating	0	–12	8	–1

Illustrative Calculation

$-12 = (-10) + (-2) + (0)$

Obviously, site 3 with the highest rating of 8 will be chosen.

The cost considerations are left to the management in the site evaluation scheme. The data, of course, is provided to the management, which then uses a composite measure method, an example of which follows:

Table 5.7

Factors	Site 'A'	Site 'B'	Site 'C'
1. Cost of land including development of land	50,000	49,000	45,000
2. Buildings	4,50,000	4,20,000	4,80,000
3. Labour charges	40,000	25,000	32,000
4. Power	10,000	9,000	10,000
5. Water	5,000	1,000	3,000
6. Cost of raw materials and other supplies	1,00,000	80,000	85,000
7. Freight:			
(*i*) Incoming	30,000	50,000	52,000
(*ii*) Outgoing	20,000	35,000	40,000
8. Local Taxes	5,000	NIL	3,000
Total Operating Cost	7,10,000	6,60,000	7,50,000
Other Factors:			
9. Cost of living	Very high	Low	Moderate
10. Housing facilities	Excellent	Poor	Good
11. Community facilities	Excellent	Poor	Good
12. Community attitude	Good	Encouraging	Indifferent

(5) Composite Measure Method

Illustration: Comparative appraisal of various plant sites with reference to the qualitative and quantitative factors affecting the locational decisions:

For the location of an engineering plant, three sites, A, B and C are under consideration. The costs of various factors and other relevant aspects in respect of each site are listed below. It is required to make the final selection of the site.

The observation of quantitative factors (from 1 to 8) reveals that site B avails substantial cost advantage over site 'A' and site 'C.' But in view of the qualitative factors (from 9 to 12) site 'A' is preferable.

The above-mentioned illustration is the most simplified version of the decision. In reality, the ascertainment of various costs largely depends on the types of production, scale of production, type of factory building, selection of plant and machines, plant layout, provisions of plant services and so on. It is also relatively difficult to quantify the qualitative considerations. However, the scientific analysis helps in arriving at good decisions.

Location Break-Even Analysis (BEA)

Break-Even Charts (BEC) are drawn for different locations to compare the sites. Fixed costs, variable costs and revenue/output are taken into account to do so. Mathematically, Break-Even volume is

$$\frac{\text{Fixed Costs}}{\text{Contribution}} \text{ or } \frac{\text{Fixed Costs}}{\text{Revenue/Unit} - \text{Variable Cost/Unit}}$$

We can draw up a Profit and Loss Account of different sites for comparison.

Quantitative Models of Location

A detailed discussion of quantitative models is beyond the scope of this book. We can make a brief reference to the models generally used. **Median Model** is based upon the assumption that movement of load is done on rectangular/rectilinear pattern. It is useful for a single new facilities location. The **Gravity Model** is an attempt to establish a 'Centre of Gravity' with respect to existing ancillary facilities (like sources of supply S_1, S_2 and distribution points like D_1, D_2 etc.). **Brown Gibsons Composite Model** provides a composite location model of the subjective and objective factors. **Bridgeman's Dimensional Analysis** is an optimisation model where different objectives are represented on different dimensions.

Government Steps to Ensure Regional Balanced Development

Concentration of industries in some cities in the West has already created serious problems for the socio-economic life of the people. Congested cities with insanitary working conditions make the city absolutely unhealthy. It creates problems for housing, transport, and education. Enemy bombing was also the result of high concentration of industries in big cities. In India, the political leaders from rural areas under pressure from their voters in the country, began to demand that industries be established in rural areas to provide opportunities of employment and higher incomes to people in those areas. Heavy concentration of industries in some pockets have economic, social and military evils. Decentralization of industries is the only solution to do away with such evils and to establish regional balance.

Government Measures for the Decentralization of Industries

1. Development and Regulation of Industries Act 1951, was passed with a view to prohibit the establishment or expansion of industries in developed areas by formulating the industrial licensing policy in India.
2. Encourage the establishment of industrial estates in rural and semi-urban areas with infra-structure facilities like factory sheds, water, electricity, transport, communication, warehousing etc. at concessional rates.
3. Establishment of public sector units in rural areas.
4. State Government followed it up with a package scheme of incentives for listed industries, if they are set up in underdeveloped areas.
5. Refund of capital gains tax paid on profits out of sale of factory premises in big cities, provided the sale proceeds of such land were invested in industrial units in the underdeveloped areas.
6. **Relief from duties and taxes:** Electricity Board offers rebate on its tariff to all new industries in the backward areas for five years. Public water sources exempt new industries in underdeveloped areas and state government subsidises them to the extent of 1.6% of the

value of such units. New units in backward regions are exempted from payment of non-agricultural assessment for a period of thirteen years from the date of licence or registration.

7. **Preference in Government purchases:** 33% of the government purchases shall be from new units in the developing areas at the lowest tendered process quoted in open competition for a period of 6 years from the date of production.
8. Industrial units which have to pay 25% of the cost of housing scheme under industrial housing scheme will be subsidised to the extent of 10% of their share to be paid up to the housing board.
9. Advance supply of building material to speed up industrial construction.
10. Assistance in technical training in technical high schools for personnel in these units.
11. State Industrial and Investment Corporation of Maharashtra (SICOM) assistance on plant location.
12. Government contribution to the extent of 75% of the cost feasibility study by government agencies.
13. **Financial assistance:** Interest free loan equal to the sales tax payable on purchase of raw materials and sale of finished goods for 13 years.
14. Refund of sales tax on certain conditions and clearance from SICOM.
15. Guaranteeing of loans to these new units.

Industrial Estates

An Industrial estate refers to the area or place, small or big, where a number of small manufacturers undertake their production activities because of certain facilities provided there. In a developing country like India, where there is a serious problem of unemployment due to lack of industrialization, industrial estate with infrastructural facilities like land, building or shed, water, power, transport, warehousing, communication, banking etc., will attract a large number of entrepreneurs to start industries. Industrial estates may be private, government or on a co-operative basis started in rural or semi-urban areas.

The main objectives of industrial estate are:

1. To help in the development of small industries.
2. To help regional and balanced development.
3. To help increase the production in the country.
4. To help reduce the problem of unemployment.
5. To attract new entrepreneurs to use modern methods and techniques in manufacturing.
6. To curb the environmental pollution in industrial cities.
7. To make use of the local resources to the maximum.

The inconvenient location and high cost of construction had created some difficulties in the initial stages. But the incentives and concessions provided by the government to business units located in industrial estates helped to attract a large number of small-scale industries. This already changed the face of many rural and semi-urban areas in India by providing more income and employment to the people.

Advantages of Industrial Estate

The advantages enjoyed by entrepreneurs from Industrial Estate are as under:

1. It provides basic common facilities at a reasonable price.
2. It provides well planned factory accommodation with water, electricity, roads etc.
3. It provides common facility services such as tool room, heat treatment, equipment, electro-plating units, testing laboratory etc.
4. All amenities are taken into consideration at the planning stage. The promotor of the industrial estate is specialised in this area.

Points to Remember

The following factors are responsible for the localisation of industries:

1. Raw materials, power, labour supply, technical knowledge, market, transport, water supply, machinery, capital etc.
2. **In India, industries are unevenly distributed because of the following reasons:**
   (*i*) Industries are localised mainly according to the availability of raw materials and power.
   (*ii*) These resources are concentrated in certain regions of the country, so industries dependent on these resources are localised in these regions only.
   (*iii*) Example: Iron ore is available in Orissa, Bihar and Madhya Pradesh. Coal is also available in the nearby areas. So centres of iron and steel industry are located in these states.
3. Principal raw materials needed for the manufacture of iron and steel are iron ore and coal.
4. **The following states in India have rich deposits of iron ore:**
   Orissa, Bihar and Madhya Pradesh.
5. **States and their Iron and Steel centres:**
   (*i*) Bihar — Jamshedpur, Bokaro
   (*ii*) West Bengal — Durgapur, Asansol
   (*iii*) Orissa — Rourkela
   (*iv*) Madhya Pradesh — Bhilai
   (*v*) Karnataka — Bhadravati
6. Iron and Steel centres in Bihar
7. **Cotton textile industry once developed very well in Mumbai because:**
   (*i*) The humid climate of Mumbai is suitable for cotton textile industry.
   (*ii*) The hinterland of Mumbai consists of cotton growing areas.
8. **Agro-based industry:** The industry for which the raw material comes from agriculture is called an agro-based industry.
9. Fruit canning industry, flour mills, jute mills, sugar mills are agro-based industries.
10. Sugar mills are raw material oriented due to the perishable nature of sugarcane.
11. Oil-refineries are located at the following places in India: Mumbai(Trombay), Koyali, Cochin, Chennai, Vishakhapatanam, Baramuni and Tejpur.
12. **Major sources of power in India are:**
    (*i*) Thermal power (*ii*) Hydel power (*iii*) Nuclear power.
13. **Major industrial regions in India are:**
    (*i*) Mumbai-Pune region, (*ii*) Jamshedpur-Kolkata region, (*iii*) Ahmedabad-Vadodara region, (*iv*) Chennai-Madurai region, (*v*) Coimbatore-Bangalore region.
14. **Attempts are being made by the Government of India to achieve the objective of balanced regional development in the following ways:**
    (*i*) The government is trying to establish new small-scale and cottage industries in the industrially backward areas.
    (*ii*) Through the small-scale and cottage and village industries, the local raw material and rural manpower can be used.

15. **States and their Small-scale Industries:**

Assam	Seri-culture
Bihar	Leather work
Gujarat	*Jari*-work
Himachal Pradesh	Sports material
Andhra Pradesh	Mat-making, Mirror-making
Jammu & Kashmir	Carpet-making
Madhya Pradesh	Statue-making
Tamil Nadu	*Bidi*-making
Punjab	Sports material, Bangles
Maharashtra	Handloom
Karnataka	Sandalwood carving
Manipur	Handloom
Orissa	Iron-casting
Rajasthan	Marble carving
Kerala	Coir industry
Tripura	Bamboo and cane work
West Bengal	Handmade paper

National Investment and Manufacturing Zones (NIMZs)

According to the policy document, NIMZs will be developed as integrated industrial townships with state-of-the-art infrastructure and land use on the basis of zoning, clean and energy efficient technology, necessary social infrastructure and skill development facilities. These NIMZs will be administered by SPVs that would take up master planning of the zone and get pre-clearances for setting up the industrial units in the zone. NIMZs will function as self-governing autonomous bodies as the state governments will designate them as industrial townships under article 243 Q(c) of the Constitution. This will promote world class manufacturing activity.

A typical NIMZ will be at least 5000 hectares in size. The preference will be for NA land with adequate water supply. NIMZ will put in place a comprehensive exit policy. The firms will have a job-loss policy to insure workers against loss of employment in the event of the closure or retrenchment. There will be deployment of labour from one unit to another in case of closures. There will be relief from capital gains tax on the sale of plant and machinery of a unit located in NIMZ provided the proceeds are used to invest in new plant and machinery in any other unit within a period of three years.

Appendix - I

THE RIGHT TO FAIR COMPENSATION AND TRANSPARENCY IN LAND ACQUISITION, REHABILITATION AND RESETTLEMENT BILL, 2012

This bill replaces the 120-year-old Land Acquisition Act, 1894. It makes mandatory rehabilitation and resettlement (R&R) of those whose lands are acquired and ensures fair compensation for them. However, the Bill also makes the land acquisition process more complicated, and could delay projects, and in the process may impact India's economic growth. Let us look at the key provisions of the new law.

Consent Clause

The state as well as private parties can acquire land. However, the consent of at least 80 per cent landowners or 70 per cent in case of PPP projects is mandatory. This may delay the project. The land records are often untraceable.

Compensation package

Landowners will be compensated *four times* the *market value* of the land acquired in rural India and *twice* the value in urban areas. Market value will be determined by the average sale price for similar kind of land in the nearest village of nearest vicinity area. The Bill also provides compensation to those dependent on the land for livelihood (non-owner stakeholders).

As land accounts for 20-25 per cent of a projects cost, higher compensation could raise project costs sharply. It is also difficult to estimate the market value in remote areas.

Applicability

The Bill is applicable in cases where land acquired is more than 100 acres in rural areas and 50 acres in urban areas.

Small projects are outside the purview of the Bill. Real estate projects will not be affected but large infrastructure projects will have to comply with the provisions.

State *vs.* Centre

As land acquisition is in the concurrent list, state governments can have their own laws for acquiring land. The state laws could bypass the compensation stipulations under the new Bill.

Retrospective Clause

The Bill will be applied to ongoing projects retrospectively.

Unutilised Land

If land remains unutilised for five years after acquisition, it has to be returned either to the owner or to the state land bank. If the new owner decides to sell the land, the original owner will get 40 per cent of the profit.

Multi-cropped Land

The new bill does not permit acquiring multi-cropped land keeping in mind food security. Acquisition of such land is restricted to only 5 per cent of the land required for a project.

The Bill was converted into an Act of parliament in 2013. There is a provision for assessment of social impact too in the Act. The newly elected NDA government has redrafted the Bill relaxing the provisions of assessment and consent, and has promulgated an ordnance thrice. It has yet to convert the ordnances in an Act.

cs so cs so

6

FACILITIES LAYOUT AND MATERIAL HANDLING

Introduction

A factory is a place where all the industrial activities are housed. After the selection of the factory site, the factory building is constructed at the selected site. The problem of arrangement of various departments inside the factory building arises only after the availability of the floor area covered by the walls and roofs forming the factory building. It should be noted that, though the problem of factory and plant layout arises only after the building facilities have been made available, they are considered along with the construction of the factory building. Certain specific requirements of the administrative departments and the characteristics of the production processes and plant services have a direct bearing on the construction of the factory building. Thus both factory building and factory layout are considered simultaneously. The architectural design and the exterior view of the factory is considered with the technical requirements of various departments. The emphasis is given to the technical aspects rather than the aesthetic considerations.

Factors like owned or hired building, new construction or readymade building, single storey or multi-storey building have a considerable effect on the decision of the arrangements of various departments inside the factory. A distinction between the factory layout and the plant layout should be noted carefully. The factory layout is a broad consideration and it decides about the housing of all the activities inside the factory. Generally, the activities are divided into the following groups:

1. Office area in which the administrative departments are housed;
2. Plant area which houses the following activities:
   (*i*) Production departments,
   (*ii*) Services departments,

(*a*) Technical Services — like receiving departments
store-room,
stock-room,
tool-room,
inspection department,
power house or boiler room,
material handling equipment,
shipping department, etc.

and

(*b*) Personal Services — like parking area,
timekeeper's office,
canteen and lunchroom,
recreation room,
toilets etc.

In relation to factory layout, plant layout is a narrow consideration and concentrates on the arrangements of production and service departments along with the location and sequence of machines and equipment.

Ideal Plant Layout

Plant layout is the overall arrangement of the production processes, storeroom, stockroom, toolroom, material handling equipment, aisles, racks and sub-stores, employee services and all other accessories required for facilitating the production in the factory. As it encompasses production and service facilities and provides for the most effective utilization of the men, materials and machines constituting the process, it is a master blueprint for co-ordinating all operations performed inside the factory.

According to *F.G. Moore,* "A good layout is one which allows materials rapidly and directly for processing. This reduces transport handling, clerical and other costs down per unit, space requirements are minimised and it reduces idle machine and idle man time."

Objectives of an Ideal Plant Layout

A good plant layout strives to attain the following objectives:

1. Minimisation of material handling.
2. Elimination of bottlenecks through balancing of plant capacities.
3. High material turnover through shorter operating cycle.
4. Effective utilization of installed capacity so that the returns on the investments may be maximised.
5. Effective utilization of cubic space of the factory area.
6. Effective utilization of manpower resources through elimination of idle time.
7. Elimination, improvement or confinement of objectionable operations, *e.g.,* operations with bad odour, vibrating operations etc.
8. Elimination of physical efforts required of operative workers.
9. Avoidance of industrial accidents.
10. Better working conditions for the employees like lighting, ventilation, control of noise and vibrations etc.
11. Decency and orderliness inside the plant area.
12. Better customer services through cheaper and better product supplies according to the delivery promises.

Factors Affecting the Plant Layout Decision

The decision of the plant layout is affected by the following factors:

(1) Type of production: The layout for an engineering unit will be quite different from that of a flour factory.

(2) Production system: The plant layout in a continuous production system will be totally different from that under the intermittent production system.

(3) Scale of production: The plant layout and material handling equipment in the large-scale organization will be different from that in the small-scale manufacturing activity.

(4) Type of machines: The use of single-purpose and multipurpose machines substantially affects the plant layout. Similarly noisy and vibrating machines require special attention in the plant layout decision.

(5) Type of building facilities: The plant layout in a single-storey building will be different from that in a multi-storey building.

(6) Availability of total floor area: The allocation of space for machines, work-benches, sub-stores, aisles, etc., is made on the basis of the available floor area. Use of overhead space is made in case of shortage of space.

(7) Possibility of future expansion: Plant layout is made in the light of the future requirements and installation of additional facilities.

(8) Arrangement of material handling equipment: The plant layout and the material handling services are closely related and the latter has a decisive effect on the arrangement of production process and plant services.

Material Flow System

Men, machines and materials are the three basic inputs in the manufacturing processes. Generally men and machines tend to remain static while the materials move from one work station to another for the purpose of processing. The raw materials pass through various paths till they are converted into finished products. The pattern of movement of materials inside the plant area is prescribed under different types of floor systems. The pattern of material flow is an important consideration in the plan layout decision because good layout aims at minimising the flow of materials. The pattern of the flow of the materials is largely decided by the type of layout. In the product layout, the material flow is short and smooth, while in the process layout it is long and involves many complexities. The flow pattern of the material is closely related to the type of the material handling equipment and the cost of material handling. It also decides the need for temporary storing, spots of bottlenecks or rushing. The operating cycle period has a close relation with the flow pattern of materials.

The flow pattern of the materials helps in eliminating bottlenecks, rushing, back-tracking and ensures good supervision and control. It also helps in minimizing the material handling cost, effective utilization of plant capacity, reduction in the operating cycle and resultantly profitable returns on the investments. Even without changing the process flow, the system can be speeded up, and waiting time reduced, by simple streamlining and de-bottlenecking the flow. If necessary, the shop-floor layout can be changed. The different activities on the shop-floor can be relocated. New lines can be added. We can introduce automation and re-prioritisation. In short, the flow of work can be re-organized.

The materials flow system is broadly divided into two on the basis of the nature of the availability of floor space as under:

(1) Horizontal flow system, (2) Vertical flow system.

(1) Horizontal Flow System: The horizontal flow systems are devised in the single storey building when the flat floor area is available. The starting point is the "receiving" (R) of raw materials and the terminal point is the "shipment" (S) of finished goods. In between these two points, the materials move from one work station to another for the purpose of processing. The horizontal flow system is denoted by the alphabetic letters as under:

Flow System | **Characteristics**

(*i*) "I" type flow:

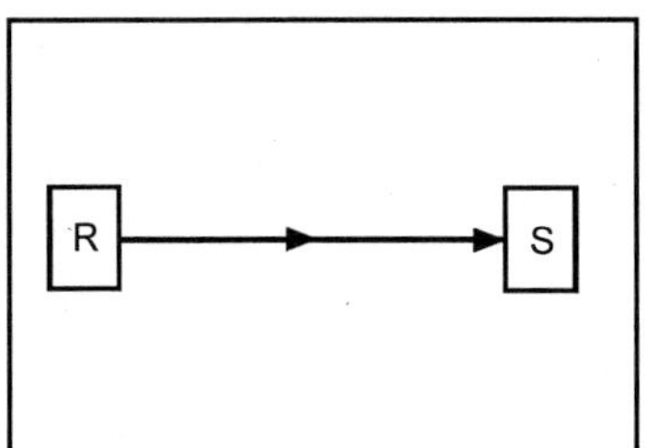

(*i*) Shortest route

(*ii*) Must have roads on both sides.

(*iii*) Plant area has long lengths but short width.

(*iv*) Difficulty in returning empty containers.

(*v*) Absence of rushing of outside transportation.

(*vi*) Unsuitable for longer production lines.

Fig. 6.1

Flow System **Characteristics**

(*ii*) "L" type flow

Fig. 6.2

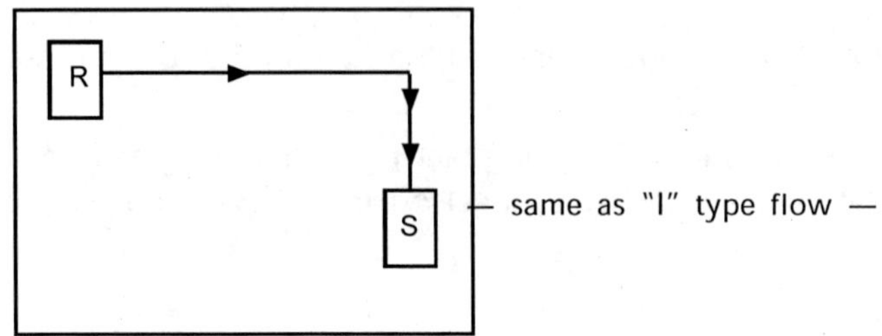

— same as "I" type flow —

(*iii*) "U" type flow

Fig. 6.3

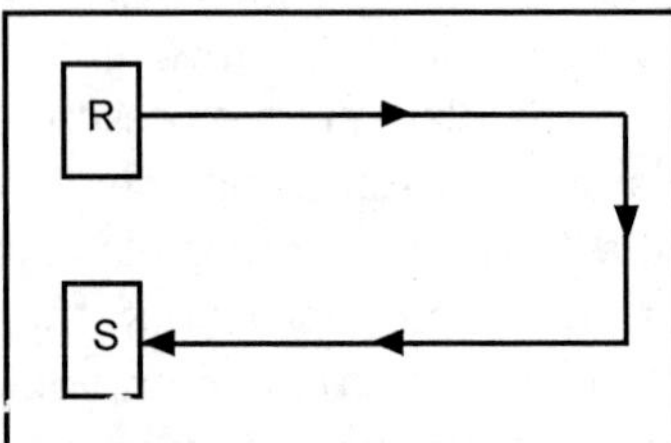

(*i*) One side road link will be required.
(*ii*) Less difficulty in returning the empty containers.
(*iii*) Possibility of rushing of outside transportation.
(*iv*) Suitable for longer production lines.
(*v*) Requires square-like floor area.

(*iv*) "S" or inverted "S" type flow

Fig. 6.4

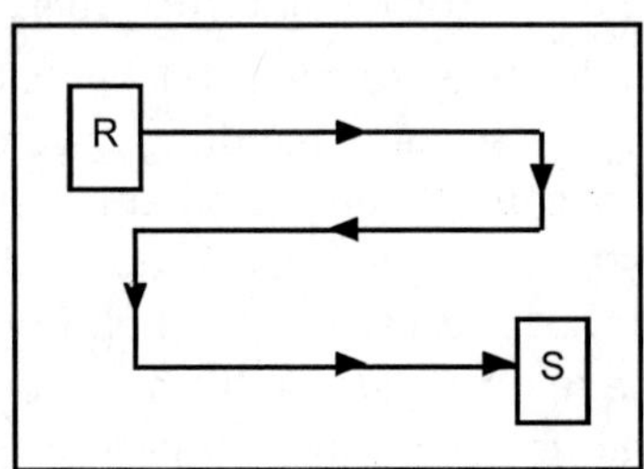

(*i*) Requires roads on both sides.
(*ii*) Absence of rushing of outside transportation.
(*iii*) Requires square-like floor area.
(*iv*) Difficulty in returning empty containers.
(*v*) Suitable for longer production lines.

(*v*) "O" type flow or Circular flow

Fig. 6.5

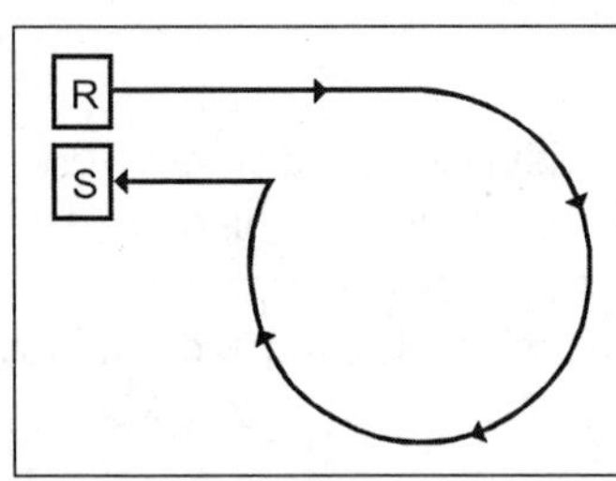

(*i*) One side road facility is required.
(*ii*) Heavy rush of outside transportation.
(*iii*) Ease in returning empty containers.
(*iv*) Requires square-like floor area.
(*v*) Suitable for longer production line.

(*vi*) Combination of "I" and "U" type flow

Fig. 6.6

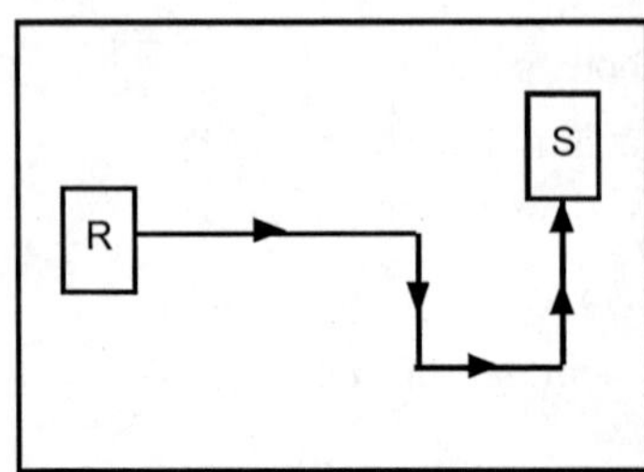

Combined characteristics of "I" and "U" type flow.

(*vii*) Combination of "I" and "S" type flow

R
S

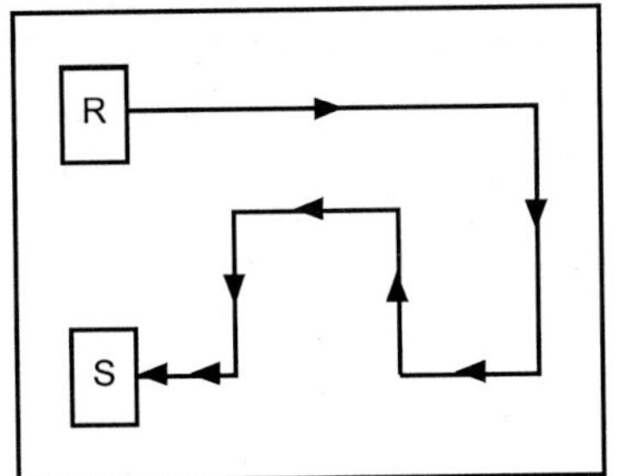

Fig. 6.7

Combined characteristics of "I" and "S" type flow.

(*vii*) Combination of "I" and "O" type flow

R
S

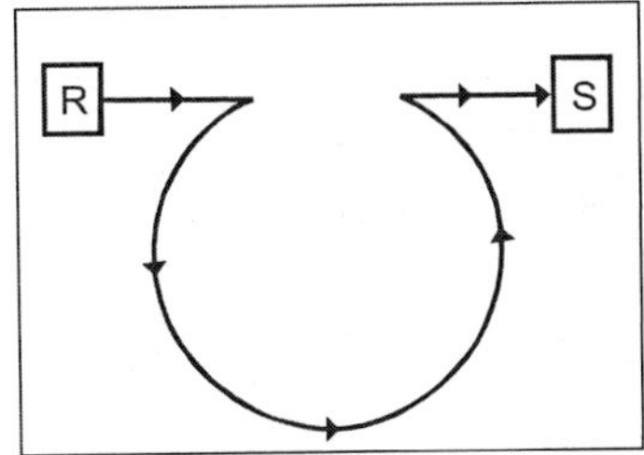

Fig. 6.8

Combined characteristics of "I" and "O" type flow.

(2) Vertical Flow System: The vertical flow system arises in case of multi-storey buildings. Multi-storey building are used where limited land area is available and the processing is done on light materials with the help of light machines. The advantages of gravity flow can be tapped, however, it first requires the availability of materials at the top floor.

Certain important vertical flow system are as under:

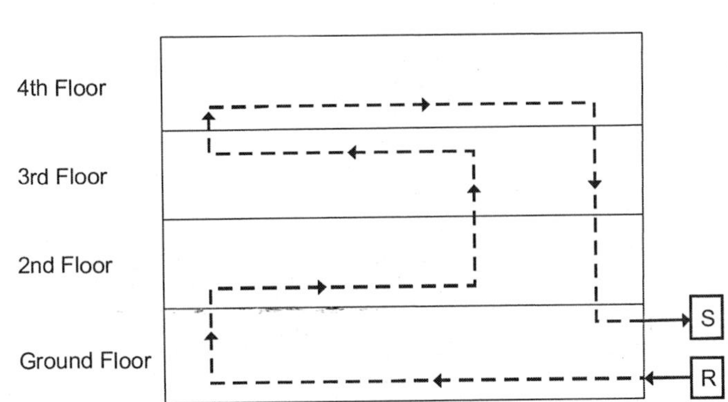

Fig. 6.9

4th Floor
3rd Floor
2nd Floor
Ground Floor
S
R

Fig. 6.10

4th Floor
3rd Floor
2nd Floor
Ground Floor
S
R

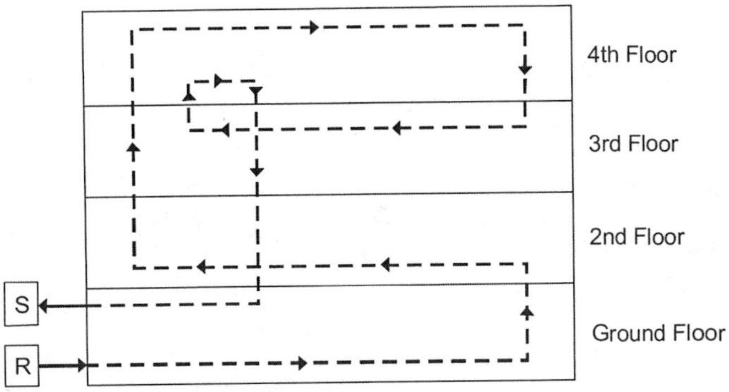

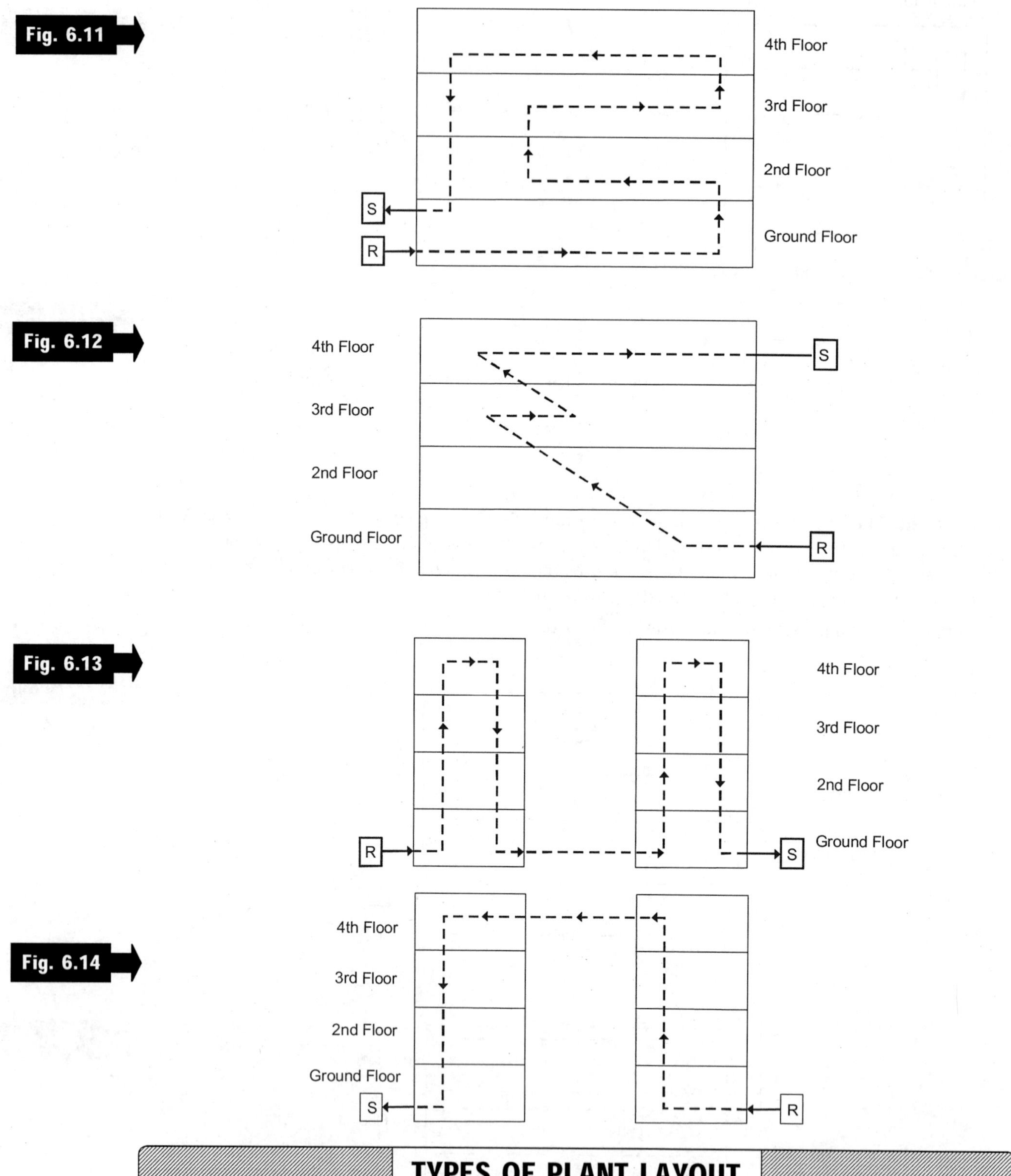

TYPES OF PLANT LAYOUT

The following are the popular types of plant layout:

(1) Process layout (2) Product layout (3) Combined layout (4) Static product layout or Project layout (5) Cellular layout (6) Job Shop layout. Each layout is explained in brief in the following paragraphs:

(1) Process layout: It is also called functional layout. Here, all similar types of operations are grouped together. All machines performing similar type of operations are grouped at one location in the process layout, *e.g.*, all lathes, milling machines, cutting machines etc., in the engineering shop will be clustered in their like groups. Thus all forging will be done in one area and all the lathes will be placed in another area. In this layout, several products may share a machine to make its full use. Here, different products use the same resources. The sequential arrangement of the machine group is generally, but not necessarily made on the basis of labour operations. Hospitals use a process layout and put all equipments for emergencies in one ward, surgical patients in another and paediatrics in another. Offices use this layout with people working in groups according to their skills — accountants work in one area, planners in another, IT professionals in the third. In this type of layout, the process rather than the product has a dominating role. The product is given secondary consideration and is moved for the purpose of operations to the process section with like machines stationed at a particular point. This type of process is more suitable to job order type of production. In such production the operations differ from product to product. So, it is desirable to arrange the machines on the basis of process rather than on the products.

The typical arrangement of the machines in the process layout will be as under:

Product 'A' and Product 'B' with their differential sequence will be routed for the processing in the manner as shown in the following figure:

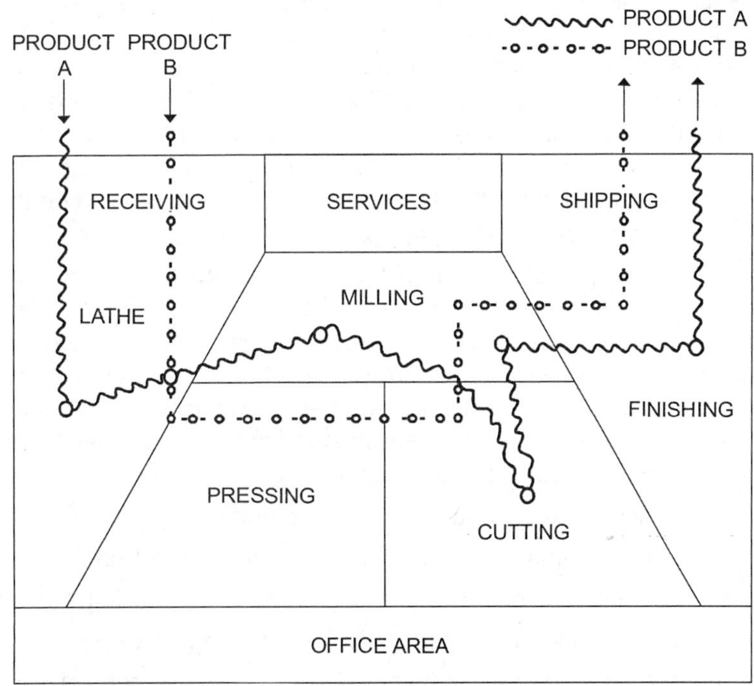

Fig. 6.15

Process Layout

Advantages: The process layout avails of the following advantages:

(*i*) Like product layout it eliminates the duplication of machines and enables the optimum use of installed capacity.

(*ii*) It facilitates the flexibility in production. It is more flexible than a line layout. Different products can be made without the changes in the arrangement of machine. The production capacity is not arranged in rigid sequence and fixed rated capacity with line balancing.

(*iii*) Like product layout, the breakdown of one machine does not interrupt the entire production flow.

(*iv*) Specialization in supervision becomes possible.

(*v*) Individual incentive schemes can be developed.

Disadvantages: The following are the main disadvantages of the process layout:

(*i*) Due to lack of straight line sequence of production, it is impossible to maintain the line-balancing in production. So the problems of bottleneck and waiting and idle capacity arise.

(*ii*) The cost of material handling increases due to long-routing and back-tracking between the processes.

(*iii*) The processing time is prolonged which reduces the inventory turnover and increases the investments in inventories.

(*iv*) The inspection cost increases. Due to frequent changes in the machine set-up, inspection is required at each stage of the process.

(*v*) The cost of supervision increases due to specialist supervisors and more number of supervisors are required at each process unit.

(*vi*) The production planning and control becomes difficult due to complexities arising in routing, scheduling, despatching and follow-up.

(*vii*) It is not possible to implement the group incentive schemes on the basis of quantity of the products manufacturing.

(*viii*) More space is required for internal storing, reservoir of materials and provision for the expansion of the particular process section.

(2) Product layout: In this type of layout, the machines are arranged in the sequence as required by the particular product. All operations used to make a particular product are grouped together. All machines as required to balance the particular product line are arranged in a sequential line but not necessarily in the straight line. It is also known as "the product-line layout." This layout is the basis for an assembly line or production line. In this layout, one product goes through all the machines lined up, in the order required by its manufacture (Fig. 6.16). The best-known example of this type of layout is seen in motor-car production. To make this layout successful, the work-load on the various machines must be balanced. The process of getting even loading at each stage of production is called *line balancing.*

In this type of layout, the product is dominating over the process, in the sense that the product is given the primary importance and the process machine must remain present at a point where the product needs its services. Thus, unlike the process layout, the process is given secondary importance in relation to the product. Product layout is more suitable for continuous flow-production with few items of production. It does not require frequent changes in machine set-up. The typical arrangement of the machines in the product with the separate independent product lines for the Product 'A' and Product 'B' will be as shown in the following figure:

Advantages: The product layout is advantageous as under:

(*i*) Reduced material handling cost due to straight-line production flow.

(*ii*) Mechanisation of material handling is possible due to handling between fixed points.

(*iii*) Line balancing may eliminate bottlenecks and idle capacity.

(*iv*) Shorter operating cycle due to shorter and speedier movement of materials.

(*v*) Maximum utilization of machine and labour capacity through developing proper balance between them.

(*vi*) Effective control over production with reduced supervision by generalists supervisors. By reducing the manufacturing to simple steps we can often use less skilled labour.

(*vii*) Effective quality control with reduced inspection points. It does not require frequent changes in machine set-up.

(*viii*) Effective production planning and control. Unlike process layout, the routing, scheduling, despatching and follow-up are relatively easier.

(*ix*) Maximum use of space due to straight production flow and reduced need of interim storing.

(*x*) It facilitates the implementation of the group incentive schemes for the workers.

(*xi*) It is relatively easy to control.

Disadvantages: The following are the main disadvantages of the product layout:

(*i*) The duplication of machines and equipment necessitates the increased investments in them sometime resulting in idle capacity.

(*ii*) The production flow is regulated through the straight line sequence and fixed rated capacity, and thus makes it highly inflexible.

(*iii*) The breakdown of one single machine in the line interrupts the entire production flow.

(*iv*) Unlike process layout, the benefits of specialized supervision is not possible.

(*v*) As the entire production is the result of the joint efforts of all operations in the line, it is difficult to implement individual incentive schemes.

(*vi*) They are less flexible than others. Any change in product requires re-balancing the line. If there is any trouble with one machine, the line goes out of balance.

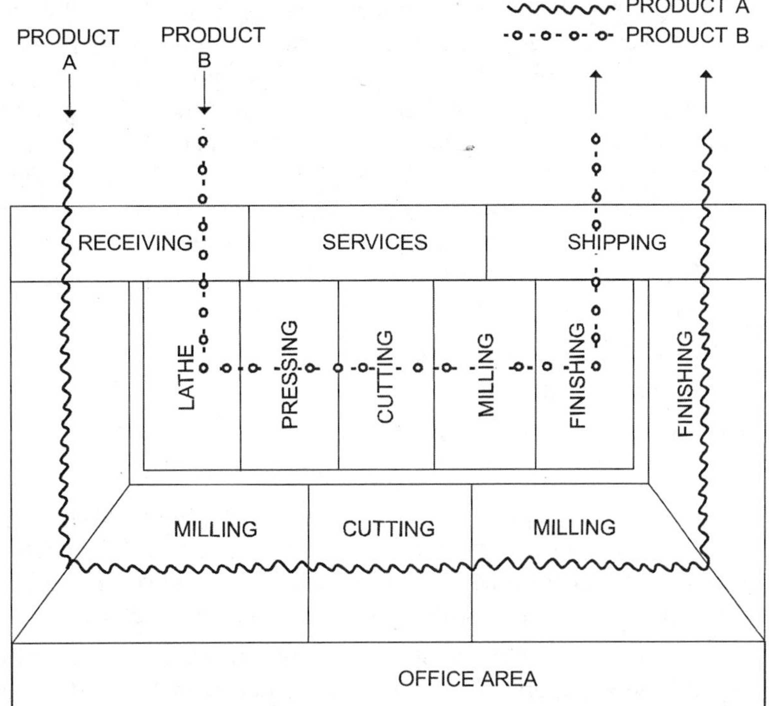

Fig. 6.16

(3) Mixed or Combined Layout: Generally pure process or pure layout is not found in practice. Both are mutually exclusive. A proper compromise reaping the benefits of both the layouts is possible to some extent. So efforts are made to have the combined layout incorporating the benefits of process and product layout. Combined layout is developed as under:

(*i*) Product layout for the main product with a process layout for joint or by-product tapping the idle capacity of product layout along with marginal investments required in process layout.

(*ii*) To diversify the production with a view to tap the idle capacity of the product layout. Products with complete negative correlation with the product-line can make the maximum use of idle capacity of the product layout.

(*iii*) In the product layout, some process may be segregated from the product-line, *e.g.*, objectionable, hazardous, requiring special treatment and repetitive performance etc.

An airport has a process layout with ticketing counters, check-in area, cafeteria, duty free shops and so on. However, customs clearance has a product layout. A fast food joint has a kitchen with process layout, but has an assembly line for hamburgers. A hospital has process layout wards, but in-patient admissions has a product layout.

(4) Static Product Layout or Project Layout: The manufacturing operations require the movements of men, machines and materials. Generally few inputs tend to be static while the others are moving. In the product layout and process layout generally the machines have fixed installations and the operators are static in terms of their specified work stations. It is only the materials which move from operation to operation for the purpose of processing. But where the product is large in size and heavy in weight, it tends to be static, *e.g.*, ship building. In such a production system, the product remains static and the men and machines move performing the operations on the product. The production characteristics are sufficient enough to treat it as a separate type of layout, *viz.*, static product layout.

In fixed position layouts, the product stays still and all operations are done on the same site. Apart from ship-building, other examples are construction sites and aeroplane assembly.

(5) Cellular or Group Layout: Here an attempt is made to introduce some of the advantages of a line layout into a situation where pure line layout is not practicable. Here machines are placed in groups. Each machine group makes a family of parts which require similar treatment. This layout lies between process layout and line layout. It is easier to control than a strictly process layout and has more flexibility than a line layout. These days there is a tendency to bring an element of flexibility into the manufacturing system as regards the batch size variations and the differing operations sequences. FMS — Flexible Manufacturing System was first installed in England in 1968. It employed group layout and is suitable for metal cutting, electronic assembly, IC manufacturing and testing etc. FMS is a mixture of traditional automation and state-of-the-art computer technology which essentially consist of a set of machine tools performing production operations linked up with material handling system. All these are controlled by a central computer system. FMS has several patterns of CNS: computerized numerical control machines.

1. Flexible Manufacturing Module (FMM)
2. Flexible Manufacturing Cell (FMC)
3. Flexible Manufacturing System (FMS)
4. Flexible Manufacturing Line (FML).

The grouping into cells enable the performance of similar type of functions for a group of products. A shop floor is converted into a collection of cells; one for each product. Every cell moves according to its own rhythm, producing complete product from scratch. There is no waiting time involved. This reduces costs. The money tied up in idle machinery or partly assembled products is released quickly.

(6) Job Shop Layout: Here there is processing of job production, and hence the system is very flexible. The layout depends upon the analysis of the universe of orders received and is a very complex affair.

Plant Layout Factors

There are a host of factors that affect the plant layout. It is necessary to optimise these to have an ideal layout. The factors have been grouped into the following clusters:

1. Manpower factors
2. Machinery factors
3. Movement factors
4. Material factors
5. Waiting factors
6. Service factors
7. Factory building factors
8. Change related factors.

All these groups have a number of features which are borne in mind before attempting the layout. The ultimate layout design is a compromise amongst the diverse factors.

Layout Design Procedure

The layout design moves from ideal to what is practical under the limitations given. The plan as a whole is made first, and details are added afterwards. The requirement of materials is central to all layout planning. The process and machinery may need modification in the light of the different factors affecting the layout plan. The following steps are followed in any layout plan:

1. Determine the objectives. Determine the limitations.
2. Collect the input data and study the activities involved. The input data may be about forecasts, work study, existing layout, charts etc.
3. Determine the flow of materials and activity relationships and form a relationship diagram. This is subject to space available and space required. What we ultimately get is a space relationship diagram.
4. The said space relationship diagram is modified in the light of various considerations and practical limitations.
5. Several alternative layouts emerge as a result. They are then evaluated.

Layout design can be classified into manual methods and computerised methods.

Manual Methods

We consider several traditional methods like flow and activity analysis, travel chart, REL chart and Systematic Layout Planning (SLP).

Flow and Activity Analysis

Data Collection: In order to design a sound layout plan, we require both qualitative and quantitative data about various factors affecting the plan like product attributes, output volume, and component parts. Data required is collected on a continuous basis through techniques like industrial engineering, quality control, marketing research, time and motion study etc. We need data regarding various materials and processes, flow and sequences, space required and activity relationships.

Process Charts: The most commonly used process charts are: (1) Operations Process Chart (2) Flow Process Chart.

(1) Operations process chart: It is a process chart which gives an overall picture by recording in sequence only the main operations (O) and inspections (□)

A specimen of an Operation Process Chart is given in Fig. 6.17.

Specify:

1. Type of chart.
2. Job concerned and whether it is the present or proposed method.
3. Date of study and name of the observer.
4. Where chart begins and ends.

Include

5. Adequate and accurate description of all activities on the right-hand side of the symbol concerned.
6. Number each activity for identification purposes by placing the number within the symbol. The convention for doing this is implied by the chart.
   (*a*) Each class of symbol is numbered in its own sequence.
   (*b*) Numbering begins on the main line of activities which is always placed on the right-hand side of the chart.
   (*c*) The numbering sequence continues until there is a junction with a subsidiary line, when it jumps to the top of this subsidiary and proceeds downwards from there. The same

convention is applied when meeting all other junctions. When combined symbols are used, the first number applies to the outer symbol.

7. Date concerning time, distance, weight, or quantity are shown on the left-hand side of the symbol it refers to.
8. A summary of activities is shown at the bottom left-hand side of the chart.
9. Use the same scale of breakdown in the analysis of activities so that the comparison of present and proposed methods will not be distorted by appearances.
10. Neatness and clarity in the layout of the chart help to simplify the process of critical examination.

Fig. 6.17 Operation Process Chart

RECONDITIONING BRAKE SHOES
OPERATION PROCESS CHART

METHOD: Present — **LOCATION:** Crossfield Garage

CHARTED BY: D.M. — **CHART BEGINS:** Inspection pit

DATE: 23 January 2015 — **CHART ENDS:** Road test

RIVETS AND LINING — **WORK BRAKE SHOE**

Rivets and lining:
- (4) REQUISITIONED
- (5) ISSUED

Work brake shoe:
- [1] INSPECTED ON BUS
- (1) REMOVED FROM BUS
- (2) CLEANED
- (3) WORN LINING REMOVED
- (6) NEW LINING FITTED

RECONDITIONED SHOE

- (7) FITTED TO BUS
- [2] ROAD TESTED

Summary

- ○ Operations 7
- □ Inspections 2

(2) Flow Process Chart: A process chart setting out the sequence of the flow of a product or a procedure by recording all events under review using the appropriate process chart symbols.

(*a*) Man Type : A flow process chart which records what the worker does.

(*b*) Material Type : A flow process chart which records what happens to material.

(*c*) Equipment Type : A flow process chart which records how the equipment is used.

Fig. 6.18

Flow Process Chart

FLOW PROCESS CHART
JOB: CAST, TURN, DRILL

METHOD	: Present	**LOCATION**	: Machines hop
CHARTED BY	: Ramesh Saxena	**CHART BEGINS**	: Raw Materials store
DATE	: 25th Jan., 2015	**CHART ENDS**	: Inspection pit

SUMMARY

		Present		Proposed	
		No.	**Time**	**No.**	**Time**
○	Operations	3	120		
⇨	Transportation	2	Nil		
□	Inspections	1	20		
D	Delays	2	40		
▽	Storages	3	Nil		
	Distance Travelled	18	M		

Flow Diagram: A diagram or model, substantially to scale, which shows the location of specific activities carried out and the routes followed by workers, materials, or equipment in their execution.

Particulars of Present/Proposed Method	○ *Operations*	⇨ *Transportation*	□ *Inspections*	D *Delays*	▽ *Storages*	*Distance M*	*Q*	*Time*	*Remarks*
1. Raw Material Store	○	⇨	□	D	▽			80	
2. Casting	○	⇨	□	D	▽				Improve
3. Storage of Casting	○	⇨	□	D	▽				
4. Sent to Turning	○	⇨	□	D	▽	12			
5. Delay at Lathe (M/C)	○	⇨	□	D	▽		10	25	
6. Turning	○	⇨	□	D	▽			20	
7. WIP Storage	○	⇨	□	D	▽				
8. Sent to Drilling Shop	○	⇨	□	D	▽	6			
9. Delay at Drilling	○	⇨	□	D	▽		8	15	Eliminate
10. Drilling	○	⇨	□	D	▽			20	Improve
11. Inspection	○	⇨	□	D	▽			20	

Travel Chart

It is also called ***From-To Chart***, since it depicts the entire material flow amongst the departments taken as source and destination. We present here in the Fig. 6.19 a typical travel chart. The travel chart is of significant help in process-type layout design. However, it has no importance in product layout. It shows the material interface between departments. The higher the interface, the closer the departments are placed. It avoids unnecessary materials handling. Though the theoretical ideal is not attainable in practice, it is approximated as far as possible. The travel-chart becomes a compact matrix of materials flow. It is possible to computerize it. It can carry additional details about bulk material handled, material handling equipment, method of material handling etc. to make it more helpful. The entries in the chart are scattered on both the sides of the diagonal. A to B and B to A departments' travel requirements may be different. The sum of each column (*i.e.*, jobs entering the department and leaving the same department are equal). It exercises a constraint on the continuity of the system. This is not valid for the first and last department. The sum of first and last row exactly balances the sum of first and last column.

Fig. 6.19 **Travel Chart**

To 'J'

	Casting	***Forging***	***Drilling***	***Machining***	***Metrolology***	***Elec.***	***Welding***	***Inspection***	***Total***
Casting			5	8	3	3	2	8	29
Forging			2	4			2	5	11
Drilling				2				8	10
Machining			3		4		2	5	14
Metro			M_{ij}					14	14
Elec.								3	3
Welding								6	6
Inspection					7				7
Total	0	0	10	14	14	3	6	49	

M_{ij} — No. of moves from *ith* to *jith* department

The entries in the chart are scattered on both the sides of the diagonal. A to B and B to A departments' travel requirements may be different. The sum of each row equals the sum of each column (*i.e.*, jobs entering the department and leaving the same department are equal). It exercises a constraint on the continuity of the system. This is not valid for the 1st and last row exactly balances the sum of 1st and last column. Travel chart has the following merits:

1. Useful tool of materials movement analysis.
2. Useful to locate activities.
3. Alternative flows and layouts could be compared.
4. Relationship of activities in terms of volume of movement becomes clear.
5. Shows quantitative relationship and hence useful in computerization/OR.

REL Chart

Expanded, it becomes a relationships chart denoting relationships amongst departments based on closeness of the activities in that department. The letters used in the chart stand for:

A : Absolutely essential

E : Essential

I : Important

O : Ordinary

U : Unimportant

X : Not desirable.

A typical REL chart is given below:

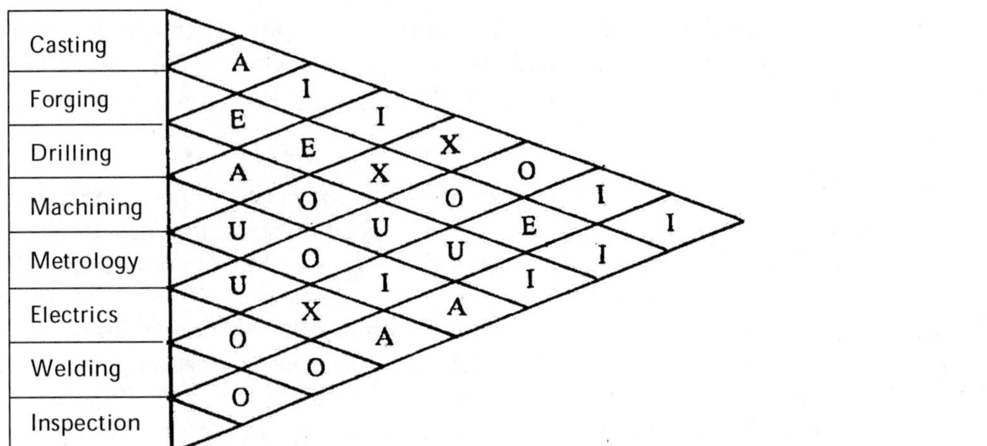

Fig. 6.20
REL Chart

Systematic Layout Planning (SLP) Procedure

Muther is credited with the work on the systematic approach to layout planning called SLP in short. The approach is graphically given in Fig. 6.21.

It is obvious that we have to develop a material flow analysis and activity analysis based upon appropriate data so as to generate a relationship chart. Ultimately, a space relationship chart is developed by matching the space considerations with the relationship chart. This can lead to a number of alternative layouts after suitable modifications and against practical constraints. The alternatives are finally evaluated. SLP starts after the problem is formulated.

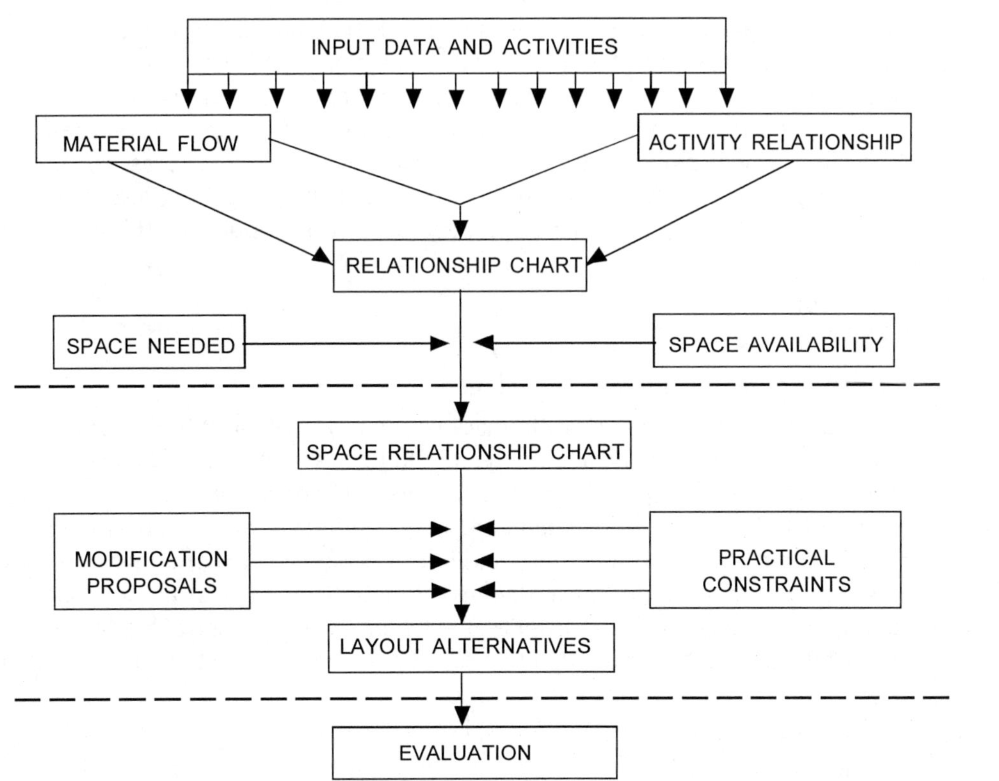

Fig. 6.21
Systematic Layout Planning (SLP) Procedure after Francis and White (74)

QTM and Layout

Quantitative Techniques in Management: QTM can be applied to layout problems. Some of the commonly used techniques for this purpose are: LP: Linear Programming, Transportation Problem, Assignment Technique, Dynamic Programming, Waiting Line Theory and Simulation.

Space Requirements

Plant layout primarily deals with the allocation of the total floor, rather cubic area among various production and service departments along with their specified stationing inside the plant area. The space for each work station is required for equipment, tools, loading and unloading work on machines, temporary material storage, benches, hoods, files, maintenance, clearance, operator work area etc. Moreover, space is also required for the movement of material handling equipment, aisles between the machines, inspection spots, safety spots, space for inspection, lubrication, repair and maintenance of machines etc. According to **James Lundy,** "Overall plant areas are generally about 150 to 200 sq. feet per employee for light manufacturing operations, 500 sq. feet for medium manufacturing and as high as 1,000 sq. feet for process industries." This estimate is just a guideline. In fact, the modern production systems with their varied and unique characteristics require separate independent solutions to this problem.

The area is to be allocated considering the needs of future expansion, and required flexibility. The area allocation is closely related to the type of material flow. 3D is used to allocate area. Area is earmarked for point-of-use and storage. There is also area left for aisles. The provision is made for column spacing.

Models of Plant Layout

We have to assemble three things before commencing production — the men, the machines and the materials. When these three are brought together, we create some kind of arrangement or *layout.*

It is inevitable to prepare the blueprints and models of the plant layout before the actual laying function begins. The location of the machines, equipment and plant facilities is the result of trial and error method backed up by varied considerations. They are arranged and rearranged until the most desirable setting is done. Templates or models represent the actual space requirements for each machine or service department along with their sequential relations, easy access to the same scale as the floor plan of the area in which they are to be installed. It is a good visual aid which helps in solving certain constraints in the layout before they arise. The popular methods of plant layout models are as under:

1. Square layout.
2. Template layout or two-dimensional layout.
3. Model layout or three-dimensional layout.

(1) Square layout: Square layout is a preliminary layout of the plant. It indicates the total square feet floor area and its allocation among various work stations and the plant facilities on the basis of some appropriate scale. It simply indicates the location of works station, plant facility and the flow patterns of the materials. Such floor charts are more helpful in arranging and rearranging the machines in terms of their impact on material handling. It is nothing but the blueprint of the plant layout. It is very simple to prepare and easy to understand. Duplicate copies can be made very easily. However, it does not provide any visual aid. Besides, the height considerations of the layout are ignored. The complex layout may distort the simplicity of its reading. However, it is the basis for the templates and model layouts.

(2) Template layout: This is the most common method of presenting the plant layout. They are two-dimensional and consider the height of the floor area. Generally, cardboard, hardboard, coloured papers, tapes etc., are used in presenting the building, walls, work stations, plant facilities etc. A template is generally prepared to a scale of 1/4 inch equal to one foot. They are characterised by their transparency. They are advantageous as under:

(*i*) It is cheaper as compared to model layout.

(*ii*) It is possible to produce duplicate copies thereof.

(*iii*) Its reading and interpretation is easy.

(*iv*) As compared to square layout, it considers the height of the layout and provides a visual aid in understanding the layout.

It has the following disadvantages:

(*i*) As compared to model layout, its interpretation is difficult for non-technical personnel.

(*ii*) It does consider height, but it is hard to visualize the impact of the overhead equipment on the plant and the process.

(3) Model layout: This model is also known as the three-dimensional model. The models of the plant and equipment with their appropriate scale are used in preparing the model layout. The models are obtained from the commercial suppliers. Sometimes the vendors also supply the scale models. Generally, model layouts are prepared to the same scale as template layout, *i.e.*, 1/4 inch equal to one foot. They are most expensive and are generally not used unless it is warranted by the complexities involved in the plant layout.

They are advantageous as under:

(*i*) It is easy to explain to the management.

(*ii*) It provides a visual aid in understanding the layout by non-technical personnel.

(*iii*) It is easy to shift the models for the study of the operational management.

(*iv*) It facilitates the study and checking of overhead structures.

(*v*) Different photographic situations can be developed for the purpose of comparing various alternative arrangements.

It suffers from the following disadvantages:

(*i*) It is costlier as compared to other forms of layout presentations.

(*ii*) Like blue prints, it cannot be folded and its movement for spot reference becomes difficult.

(*iii*) As they are large in size, it requires more storage area.

Layout Planning Methods

Traditional Methods

Though these methods seem to be very mundane as against contemporary theory, they still are valuable and time-tested. Visual aids facilitate layout planning, *e.g.* scale drawings, templates and 3D models. We also use charts and flow diagrams. These methods are criticised as they are based on the experience, knowledge and insight of the planner. But this is also an advantage. Though these methods lack the rigour, they consider all the relevant factors. While attempting to develop analytical methods of layout planning, the objective must be clearly spelled out. The common consideration in every type of layout is movement. It is thus obvious that minimization of movement is an important consideration. The additional objectives could be considered once the initial layout is obtained.

Cross and Relationship Charts

These are traditional methods of layout planning. These methods offer no solutions, they just organise the data in the layout planning process. Cross charts deal with movement. Relationship charts express relative locational preferences.

In Fig. 6.22, a cross chart is drawn to indicate the pattern amongst the ten departments. If it is a new layout, the routing will be obtained from the routing instructions, say from flow process charts and the quantities from output/throughput requirements. The figures represent the number of items/loads which move from department to department in a given period. If the layout exists already, this information is drawn by sampling of the activity occurring within the area. It is to be noted that the row and column totals may not tally. Some items may be consumed or combined. Then the row total may be less than the column totals. If there is no figure below the diagonal, it means none of the items backrack between the departments. If there is scatter above the diagonal, it means there is a varied movement pattern. In other words, there is processing of several types of product or customer. Some items follow a path through from department 1 to department 10, but based on the data alone, a 'product layout' appears impractical. There are various versions of the cross charts, but the principle remains the same. There is *weighted cross chart* to justify the extra effort involved. Instead of equal weight being given to movements of items between departments, each movement is weighted as per the significance of the item *e.g.,* its contribution to profit. Some charts consider only the principal goods.

Cross charts are used to collect and present information so that preferable departmental relationships can be established, Information so drawn can be summarised in a relationship chart as shown in Fig. 6.23.

Fig. 6.22

Cross Chart

To / From	Dept. No. 1	2	3	4	5	6	7	8	9	10	Total
Dept. No. 1		30				24	16	10			80
2			20	10							30
3				20							20
4					10	14		6			30
5						10					10
6							24				24
7								24	16		40
8									24	16	40
9										40	40
10											
Total		30	20	30	10	48	40	40	40	56	

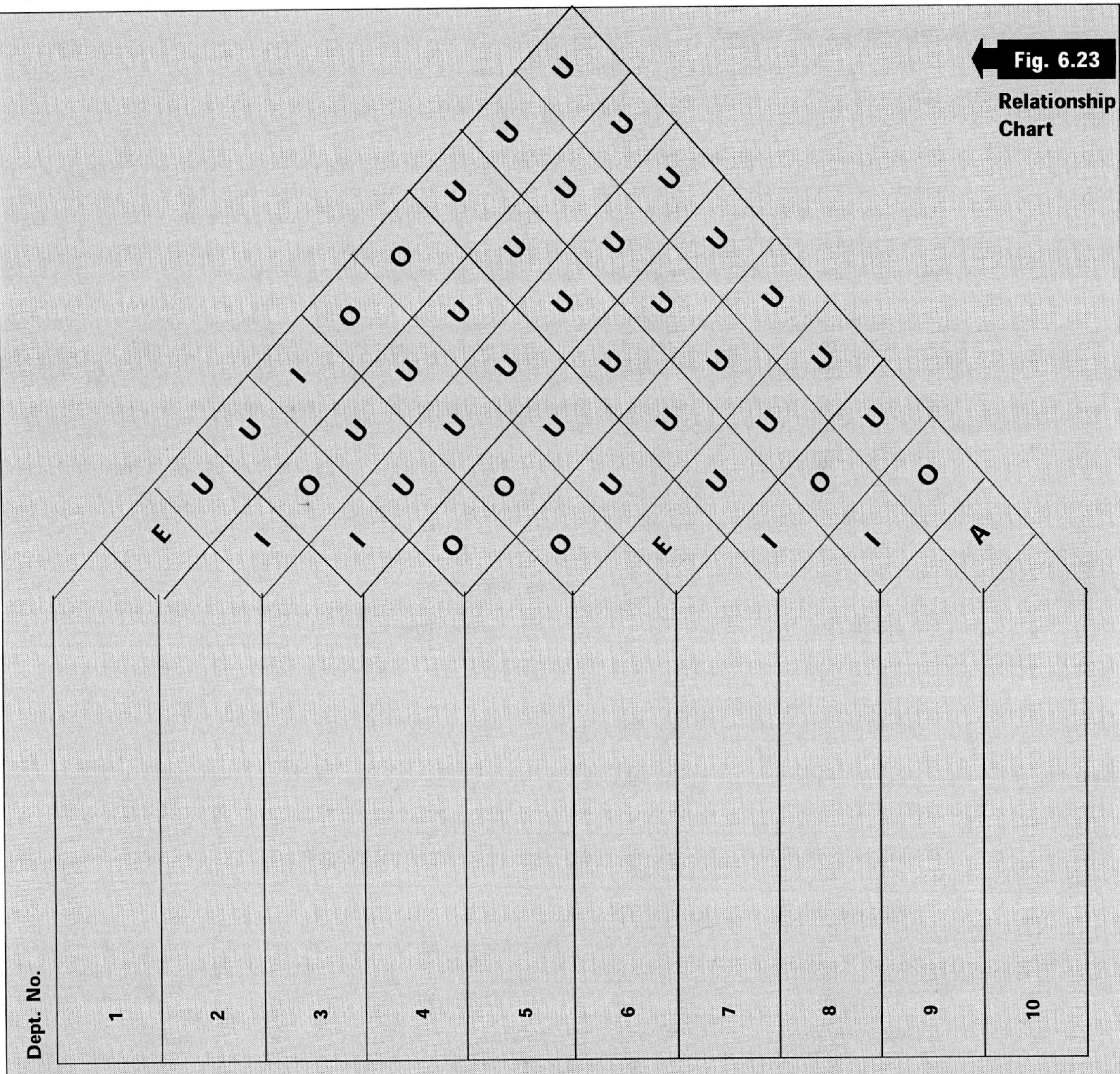

Fig. 6.23 **Relationship Chart**

Code	**Closeness**
A	Essential
E	Very Important
I	Important
O	Ordinary Close
U	Unimportant

The closeness required in the chart may reflect more than the needs for minimization of movements. A relationship chart is a summary of proximity requirements. At times, minimization of movement is not the primary objective.

Computer-based Layout

Two types of computer software are available: Construction Programmes and Improvement Programmes.

ADLEP and CORELAP are REL-based computer programmes to aid construction of a layout. (ADLEP: Automated Layout Design Programme, CORELAP: Computerized Relationship Layout Planning). CRAFT: Computerized Relative Allocation of Facilities Planning minimises a linear function of the movements amongst departments and thus is an improvement programme. It uses flow of material matrix and cost/unit moved/unit distance and space requirement data.

Computerised Relative Allocation of Facilities Technique (CRAFT)

Several computer programmes have been developed since 70s to devise process layouts. The most widely used programme called CRAFT has been developed by Armour and Buffa. It improves upon an initial layout with the interchange of departments in pairs to optimise the transport costs. It is an iterative programme which is continued till the further cost reductions are not possible. It is mainly a heuristic algorithm.

The first step in this algorithm is to have initial input in terms of the number of departments (say 4 or 5 and so on), the number of interchangeable departments, the initial layout, the cost matrix, the flow matrix and the area of departments.

The cost matrix may look as follows:

Cost Matrix (C_{ij})

From/To	***Departments***			
	1	***2***	***3***	***4***
1	—	1	1	1
2	1	—	1	1
3	1	1	—	1
4	1	1	1	—

In the above matrix, the cell values represent the transport cost per unit distance from department *i* to *j*.

The flow matrix may look as follows:

Flow Matrix (f_{ij})

From/To	***Departments***			
Departments	***1***	***2***	***3***	***4***
1	—	5	2	4
2	0	—	2	5
3	2	0	—	0
4	0	0	2	—

In the above matrix, the cell value represents the flow in terms of number of trips from department *i* to *j*.

Area of departments may be expressed in terms of square feet or metres.

In the second step, we have to compute centroids of all the departments in the initial lay-out. Here the left side of the layout is taken as Y-axis and the bottom side a X-axis. To illustrate,

$(X_1, Y_1) = 2, 6$

$(X_2, Y_2) = 2, 2$

$(X_3, Y_3) = 7, 2$

$(X_4, Y_4) = 8, 6$

In the third step, the distance matrix is developed. The distance between any two departments is the rectilinear distance between the centroids of these two departments.

$d_{ij} = (X_i - X_j) + (Y_i - Y_j)$

where (X_i, Y_i) and $(X_j\ Y_j)$ are the centroids of departments *i* and *j* respectively.

In step 4, the cost of the present layout is calculated.

$$\text{Total cost} = \sum_{i=1}^{4} \sum_{j=1}^{4} f_{ij} \times d_{ij} \times C_{ij}$$

where f_{ij} the flow from department *i* to department *j*

d_{ij} the distance from department *i* to department *j*

C_{ij} the cost/unit distance of travel or trip.

The total cost matrix is generated.

In step 5, we consider pairs of departments for interchange based upon common border or equal area. If there are N department, NC_2 pairwise interchanges are possible. Each interchange results in new centroids leading to a new distance matrix and total cost. A cost table for each interchange pair is developed. In step 6, that interchange which results in the least cost is selected for actual interchange in the layout. In step 7, proposed interchange cost and initial layout cost are compared. If it is less, we actually go ahead with the interchange. It results in a new layout (step 8). In step 9, we again calculate centroids, layout matrix and total cost matrix and repeat step 6. It is then taken as final layout.

CRAFT uses a benchmark of total cost reduction by considering one pair or two departments at a time. It may not generate an optimal layout. The initial layout influences the final layout. It can handle up to 40 departments. Mostly, there are 10 iterations before we arrive at a solution. The departments are combinations of square modules. CRAFT assumes variable path material handling equipments such as forklift trucks.

Computerized Relationship Layout Planning (CORELAP)

We have already studied Muther's SLP: Systematic Layout Planning. CORELAP algorithm is based upon SLP, and was developed by R.C. Lee, and its interactive version by James Moore. The input needed consists of the number of departments with their areas, REL-chart relationship and weighted ratings based on REL-chart. Additionally, we can have input of scale of output, length-to-width ratio, pre-assignment of departments.

The most critical department is placed at the centre. On placing it, the department with close relationship with other departments already placed is selected. It is placed near to the previously placed department. In this method, the layout is built from the centre, and the final layout looks rectangular. The score of the layout is obtained using the closeness values and the rectilinear distances amongst the different pairs of departments.

Automated Layout Design Programme (ALDEP)

This algorithm is constructed using the facilities data, and placing the departments successively in the layout. A score is calculated after all the departments are placed. The score is given by summing up the closeness values of different proximate departments. This algorithm is repeated a pre-determined number of times till we get the best layout giving the maximum possible score. The input consists of the data regarding the number, area, length-width ratio of departments, REL-chart, minimum department preference (MDP) value, sweep width, number of iterations and location and sizes of fixed departments.

Computer-aided Layout Planning

Layout planning manually is very cumbersome except in simplest possible situations. It is, therefore, necessary to develop computer-aided layout planning. Computer-aided approach is able to generate alternative layout plans quickly for evaluation and comparison purposes. In such a plan, there is an interactive approach which takes care of outputs without waiting till the layout is modified. Computer-based layout planning interfaces with other computer-based processes like material handling, maintenance, etc.

It was in the early 1960s that the first computer programmes for layout planning were developed. Since then, there are many changes, but even then the present-day software packages are a legacy of those days.

Two basic methodologies are behind the current computer-based layout planning procedures —

(*i*) Proximity maximization

(*ii*) Movement minimization

Proximity Maximisation

This approach is derived from the methodology of the relationship chart. Interdepartment closeness — desired or required — are rated or coded. They are expressed numerically. They form one type of input to the programme. The other inputs are department sizes and overall dimensions of the real estate used for such software are often based on CORELAP — Computerized Relationship Layout Planning discussed by Lee and Moore in the *Journal of Industrial Engineering,* 18(3) or ALDEP — Automated Layout Design Programme discussed by Seehof and Evans, in *Journal of Industrial Engineering 18(12).* CORELAP has more complex procedure. Here the layout department which has the highest total closeness rating is placed first. The other departments are added in descending order or total closeness rating so as to achieve, as far as possible, proximity to those departments with which they have a high closeness rating. This is subject to space constraints and order in which the departments are placed. The overall objective is to maximize total closeness score.

The ALDEP procedure also uses proximity rating approach. The programme generates a series of largely random layouts and chooses one with the best score. Alternatively ALDEP could generate one layout and then improves upon it incrementally by moving, exchanging departments.

Movement Minimization

The proximity maximization approach considers the need to minimise interdepartmental movement, since the closeness ratings consider often the movement along with other factors. Movement minimisation approach, however, is *mainly* concerned with this criterion. It aims to reduce the interdepartmental traffic.

Most widely used softwares are based on CRAFT developed in 1963 and discussed by Armour and Buff in *Management Science,* 9(1). Here, an initial layout is offered as an input. It can be considered as an improvement or modification procedure. The initial layout could be arbitrary, and is intended for the design of new layouts. In Fig. 6.24, a simple flow diagram for the software is shown.

The inputs are interdepartmental flow matrix, interdepartmental movement cost matrix, initial keyout configuration, and any constraints. The initial layout is improved upon by interchanging pairs of department. Each pair is examined and the effect of exchange on movement cost is computed. The pair cost reduction in terms of total (movement) cost is effected. This is repeated leads to any further reduction in cost. The algorithm is given below:

(*i*) Pairs chosen for interchange. Here adjacent, equal area departments, or departments bordering on common third department are chosen.

(*ii*) distance between departments is calculated. Here the centres of the department are considered for calculating the distances.

(*iii*) reduction in total (movement) cost after interchange of all possible departments is calculated.

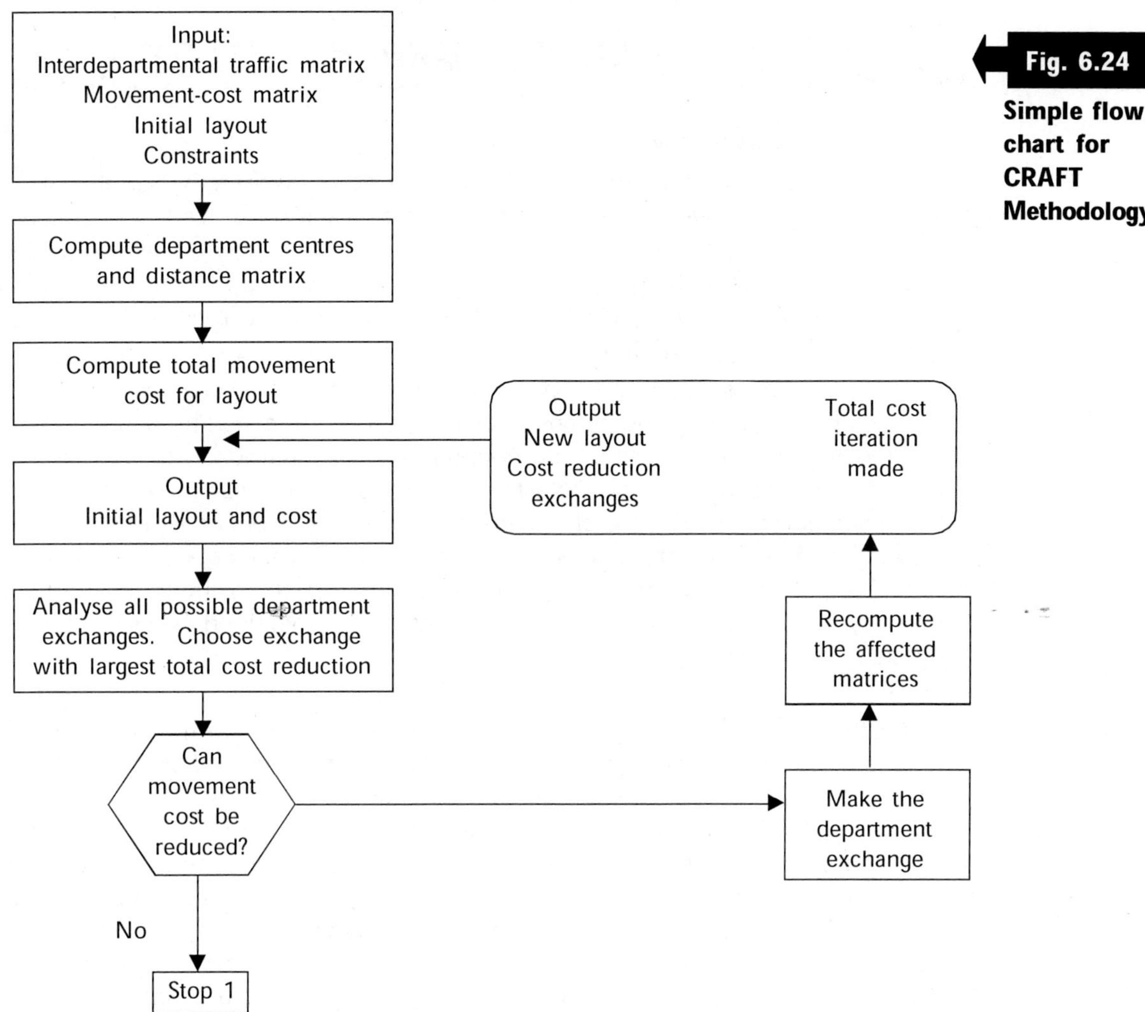

Fig. 6.24 **Simple flow chart for CRAFT Methodology**

(*iv*) Two departments which offer the highest saving in total (movement) cost are interchanged.

(*v*) Total (movement) cost is calculated and the revised layout print is taken.

This procedure is repeated till no further cost saving is possible. The final layout is then printed. CRAFT is extended to several applications.

Single Minute Exchange of Dies

Product-flow manufacturing system is in vogue in large, complex, multi-component product manufacturing units. An automobile on an average consists of 10,000 parts. Can you imagine how it can be produced in a cell? What is then the alternative? We have to do the assembly as done traditionally, but quicken the process. Quickness can cut costs. A solution is Single Minute Exchange of Dies (SMED). It compresses cycle-times (the time to produce a single unit of a product from start to finish). Hero Honda saves 29 minutes of die-exchange time at their Haryana plant.

MATERIAL HANDLING SYSTEMS

Meaning and Importance

In a manufacturing firm, the raw materials are obtained from the suppliers and are stored in the store-room. They are issued to production departments and are moved inside the plant area from one process to another for the purpose of processing till they are converted into finished products. Finished products are sent to the shipping section. The function of the material handling is confined only to the movement of raw materials from the store-room to the shipping section.

Thus material handling involves the movement of materials from one place to the another for the purpose of processing. They are moved either manually or mechanically with the help of different types of material handling equipment. The jobs tackled by material handling equipment include — lifting, moving, dropping, positioning, holding, releasing, stacking etc. They are moved as a single item or in a lot depending upon the size, weight etc., of the materials, the capacity of the material handling equipment and the type of the processing. Generally out of the men, machines and materials, the machines have fixed installations, men have specific working place on a shop floor area and their movements are mostly confined to the limited working space. While in case of materials, they travel extensively inside the plant area. So material handling is identified as one of the important functions of production engineering.

According to the American Material Handling Society, 'Materials handling is the art and science involving the movement, packing, and storing of substances in any form.' Thus material handling function includes all types of movements vertical, horizontal or combination of both and of all types of materials, fluid, semi-fluid and discrete items and of movements required for packaging and storing. The material handling function is considered as one of the most important activities of the production function, as out of the total time spent by the materials inside the plant area, about 20% of the time is utilized for the purpose of actual processing on them while the remaining 80% of the time is spent in moving from one place to another, waiting for the processing or finding place in the sub-stores. Moreover, about 20% of the total production cost is traceable as the material handling cost. Thus material handling function enjoys a pivotal role in production engineering. The relative percentage will vary according to the type of product, plant layout, production method, availability of resources like men, machines etc. The importance of material handling under the modern production system has increased to such an extent that, the production of material handling equipment itself has become a major industry of its own.

Material Handling and Plant Layout

The physical distance and the frequency of movements of the materials in between the process largely depends on the plant layout, *i.e.*, the arrangement of the machines and plant services inside the plant area. *The product layout* with continuous system of production will require less time and cost of material handling, while under the *process layout* with intermittent production system, the to-and-fro movement of the materials, possibility of waiting for the processing and necessity of the inspection for the purpose of quality control will increase the time-span of the material-stay as well as the cost of handling. A good layout is one which reduces the material handling to the minimum. Both functions are so closely connected with each other that they cannot be considered isolated.

Material Handling and Production Control

It should be noted that material handling is a distinct activity falling within the jurisdiction of production management. It is not a part of production control but it is closely associated with the function of production control. It is largely concerned with routing function of the production control activity and to some extent the scheduling of the production activity.

Analysis of the Material Handling Problem

The material handling is an inevitable function in the manufacturing process. The material handling problem is analysed as under:

(1) The establishment of objective, *e.g.*, to reduce the material handling cost.

(2) Collection of factual data, *e.g.*, type of materials to be handled, weight of materials, transportation area, type of material handling equipment and its capacity of handling.

(3) Analyzing the data, *i.e.*, if the objective is reduction of material handling cost then the collected data should be arranged in such a way that it brings out the cost advantage available by reducing the transportation distance or by handling the materials in the group. It should be noted that materials handling problem should not be considered isolated but in relation to other factors, *e.g.*, if the reduction in material handling cost increases the need for more investments in materials or reduces the quality of the product to be handled, then it should also be considered.

(4) Application of principles of material handling, *e.g.*, to minimise the movements, use of gravity principle, use of principle of containerization etc.

(5) The formulation of solution — in relation to the set objective — proper conclusions should be drawn.

Comprehensive Materials Handling Programme

The material handling problem is not considered isolated but is considered in the context of the following factors:

(1) Type of the product; (2) Plant layout; (3) Type of production system; (4) Factory building; (5) Production planning and control; (6) Packaging; (7) Material handling equipment.

(1) Type of the product: The material handling programme is largely affected by the characteristics of the product itself. The material handling services are largely governed by the bulk, shape, weight, fragility, liquidity etc. of the materials.

(2) Plant layout: Plant layout affects the material handling programme in terms of the sequence of the movement and the distance to be moved during the processing.

(3) Type of production system: As compared to the continuous production system, the intermittent production system poses the specific problems affecting the material handling programme. The problem of waiting (popularly known as bottlenecks) and rushing create the necessity for reservoir of materials in sub-stores or possibilities of slacks in the production. Both these situations have a direct bearing on the material handling programme.

(4) Factory building: The factory building with its various features like floor strength, ceiling heights, type and strength of roofs, door locations and sizes, partitions, stairs, width of the aisles etc., have a decisive effect on the material handling services.

(5) Production planning and control: Material handling function is not a part of production planning and control. However, the routing and scheduling functions of production control are closely related to the material handling services. The routing prescribes the sequence for the flow of the materials during the processing while the scheduling decides timings of the processing. Both these functions presuppose the availability of the efficient material handling system.

(6) Packaging: The handling of materials during the processing is facilitated through the pallets, while the finished products are packed in the specific containers. Generally, wooden-boxes, card-board cartons etc. are used for packaging the finished products. The packing of the finished products should be of a convenient size so that they can be handled easily.

(7) Material handling equipment: The material handling programme should be developed in the context of the existing material handling equipment. Their performances should be evaluated from time to time and necessary changes may be made in the light of the economic benefits availed from such changes. Thus material handling is not a sporadic piece-meal function, but a comprehensive programme having a close inter-dependence with many aspects of industrial management.

Principles of Material Handling

Material handling is a technique, the efficiency of which is governed by the following principles:

1. The first principle of material handling is not to handle the material at all. The materials should be moved as little as possible. The selection of production machinery and the type of the plant layout should be such that the material handling may be eliminated as far as possible.
2. The time of each move should be minimised. This can be attained through the shortest routes and use of mechanical material handling equipment in place of manual labour.
3. The distance of each move should be minimised. This can be attained through use of the shortest routes and elimination of back tracking.
4. The principle of "unit load" should be applied. According to this principle, the materials should be moved in lots rather than on individual basis. The optimum number of pieces should be moved in one unit. The concept of containerization and palletization is applied in deciding the unit load. The principle of unit load avails the economies in the form of reduced loading labour cost, packing cost, elimination of damage and pilferage, savings in time and the effective utilization of material handling equipment.
5. The gravity should be used wherever possible, as it is the cheapest source of motive power.
6. Re-handling and back-tracking of the materials should be avoided. This can be attained through proper layout and efficient routing and scheduling.
7. The appropriate material handling equipment should be selected so that the safety, efficiency and flexibility can be maintained.
8. The design of the container, pallets, drums etc., should be such that they may entail economy in handling, at the same time the material damages during the transit may be reduced.
9. The material handling service should not interfere with the production flow.
10. The safety of the people must be taken care of.
11. The provision of the stand-by facilities should be made so that the sudden breakdown may not paralyse the operations.
12. The check up, repairing and maintenance of the existing material handling equipment should be made periodically.
13. The material handling services should be evaluated periodically and necessary changes should be incorporated wherever it is possible.

Types of Material Handling Equipments

Various types of material handling services are required to be performed during the production processes, such as

(*i*) Lifting, Holding, Dropping;
(*ii*) Loading, Unloading;
(*iii*) Positioning;
(*iv*) Moving;
(*v*) Stacking etc.

All these services can be performed manually. However, in the modern complex production system, manual material handling is inefficient as compared to mechanized material handling. Moreover, it is more dangerous. So many types of material handling equipments have been developed to perform all these services. Various types of material handling equipments performing the different as well as similar types of functions are available. They can be classified on various bases, like:

(a) Types of equipment: (1) Cranes and hoists (2) Conveyors (3) Chutes (4) Trucks, Tractors and Trailers (5) Rails (6) Rope-ways and Cable-ways (7) Pipelines.

(b) Types of services: (1) Lifting (2) Moving (3) Positioning (4) Stacking.

(c) Space of movement of equipment: (1) On the floor (2) Above the floor (3) Overhead (4) Beneath the ground.

Relative Mobility of Equipment

(1) Travel between fixed points (2) Travel over wide areas.

For the purpose of simplified presentation, various types of material handling equipment have been explained in the following paragraphs on the basis of the above-mentioned classification (a) *viz.*, "Types of equipment."

Types of equipment: Some important types of material handling equipments are as under:

(1) Cranes and hoists: They lift and move the loads of varying size. The lifting capacity is subject to limitation. The service is available between the fixed points. They are operated hydraulically, pneumatically or electrically.

The important types of cranes and hoists are as under:

(*i*) Overhead bridge crane (Fig. 6.25)
(*ii*) Jib crane (Fig. 6.26)
(*iii*) Gantry crane (Fig. 6.27)
(*iv*) Electrical hoists
(*v*) Elevators
(*vi*) Stacker crane
(*vii*) Winches
(*viii*) Monorail

(2) Conveyors: Conveyors primarily perform the movement of uniform loads between fixed points. There may be fixed or portable conveyors, straight or circular ones. The materials are fed to the conveyor from some other source at the point of start. They are carried by the conveyor to the point of destination. They are dropped or fed to another conveyor with or without the change in the direction of the flow of materials. They are most suited where the flow of materials is continuous. The conveyors along with the movement of materials, also perform additional services like regulation of the pace of production of adjacent operations, positioning of materials during handling and temporary storing of materials between the injection and ejection points. They are driven with the help of power or without the power through gravity. The important types of conveyors are as under:

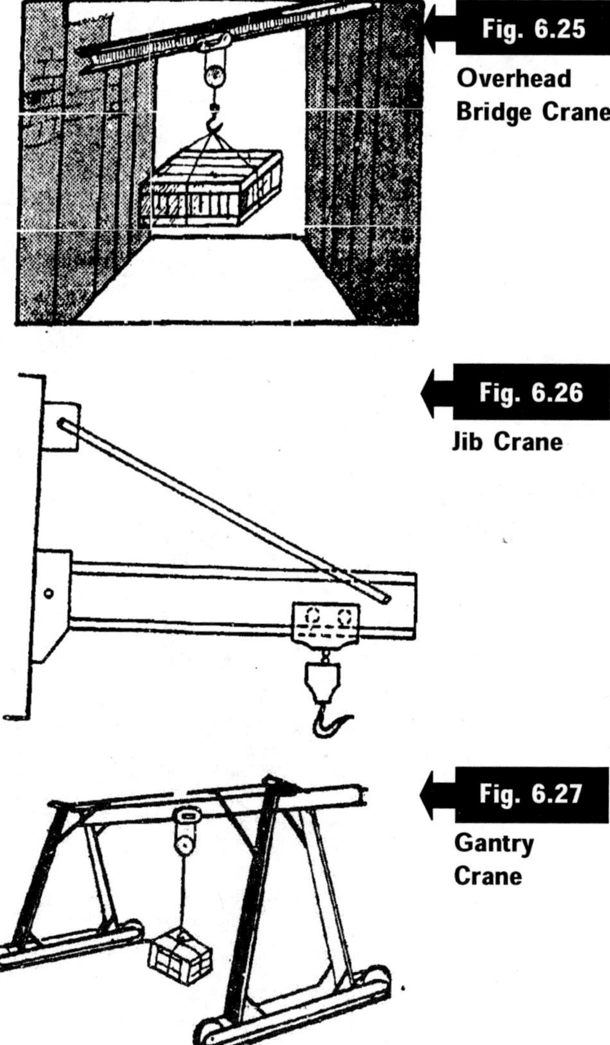

Fig. 6.25 Overhead Bridge Crane

Fig. 6.26 Jib Crane

Fig. 6.27 Gantry Crane

(i) Belt conveyors (Fig. 6.28): It may be flat or elevated with upward or downward flow of materials. The material of the belt should be suitable to the materials to be moved. Generally, rubber covered canvas, steel, plain fabric, perforated sheets or woven wires are used as belts. The fixed or portable belt conveyors are used according to the requirements of production processes and systems.

(ii) Roller conveyors (Fig. 6.29): Roller conveyors are flat, circular or spiral. They are driven through gravity. Generally materials having flat bottoms are moved, otherwise boxes or pellets are used.

(iii) Bucket conveyors: Bucket conveyors are used to move the granular, powdered or liquid materials. The movement may be vertical or flat. The vertical movement may be continuous wherein buckets are hooked in a sequential circular manner, or discrete where the buckets are hooked for lifting. These handling equipments are generally power-driven. The lift is a special type of bucket conveyor with a discrete vertical

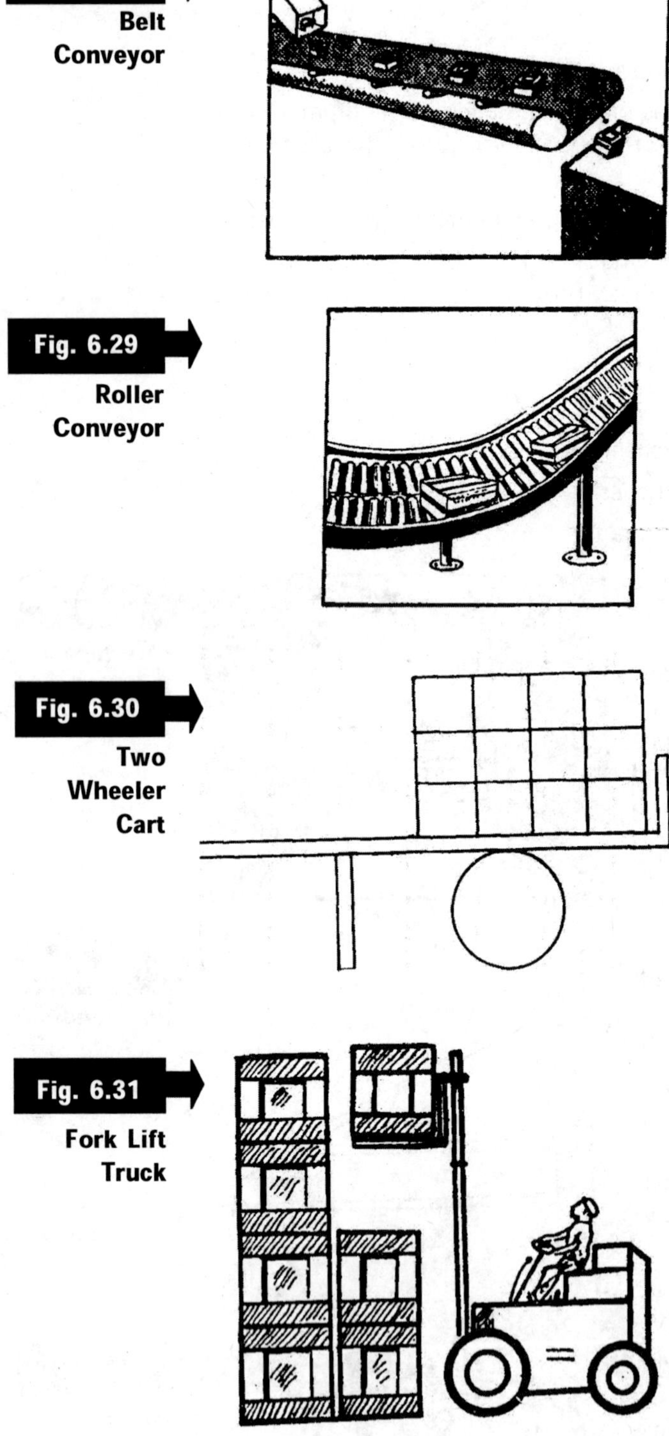

Fig. 6.28 Belt Conveyor

Fig. 6.29 Roller Conveyor

Fig. 6.30 Two Wheeler Cart

Fig. 6.31 Fork Lift Truck

movement. Generally, they are used for the processes housed in a multistory building. They are also used in super structure building construction. Generally, detachable trolleys are used in which the materials are moved. The trolleys are hooked in the lift for lifting or delifting. The movements may be made with the help of chains or ropes.

Some other conveyors in use are:

Chain conveyor, Trolley conveyor, Screw conveyor, Vibratory conveyor.

(3) Chutes: Chutes are the handling equipment which are static in nature. They handle the material between fixed points. They move the light material and small jobs which can slide down under the gravity. The previous process feeds the materials to the chutes which are slided down under the gravity. The chute may be straight or a spiral one. Where the sliding-down process tends to be slow, the vibrating chutes are used where the materials are moved downwards through vibrations.

(4) Trucks, Tractors and Trailers: The trucks are used to move the heavy materials over varying paths. They are either hand-driven or power-driven. Generally, two-wheeler (Fig. 6.31), three-wheeler or four or more wheeler trucks are used to carry and to move the heavy loads. They can move easily and effectively on the properly designed roads.

A special mention may be made of a fork-lift truck (Fig. 6.31) which is widely used by the industrial organizations. In the fork-lift truck, the fork is attached to the column on the truck. On the flat base of the fork the boxes or pallets are stacked. The fork generally moves vertically 4 to 5 feet high. The stacked pallets move along with the truck. The operator operates the truck as well as the fork till the materials are unloaded at the designated depository point.

Tractors perform the same role as trucks. Trailers containing materials are attached to the trucks or tractors and move along with them. Tractors are detachable. Trailers are generally two wheelers. They are nothing but large sized pallets or buckets. Dumpers are special types of trucks with a flexible base. The base is elevated to unload the materials. Generally, they are more suited for the granular materials.

(5) Rails: For the transportation of heavy materials inside the plant area locomotives are used as the material handling equipment. The two fixed points are joined by railway tracks. The wagons or trolleys containing the materials are moved by the locomotive between the two fixed points. This handling equipment is popularly used in steel industries where the materials to be handled are heavy and where the processes are located over vast areas.

(6) Ropeways and Cableways: Like railways the materials are moved with the help of rope or cable tracks. The trolleys are hung on the ropes and are moved vertically between two fixed points. It is an overhead device and is used in hilly areas. Where the space cannot be spared on the floor for the movement of material handling equipment, the overhead movement of materials with the help of ropeways or cableways can solve the problem to some extent.

(7) Pipelines: Pipelines are material handling devices popularly used for the movement of granular and liquid materials. Pipelines of various sizes are used for moving the liquid materials between the processes. Generally, the galvanized metal pipes, glass-lined or stainless steel pipelines are used according to the characteristics of the materials to be passed through them. Pipelines are installed between two fixed points. They are concealed inside the floors or walls or are exposed and installed on overhead space. Where the storage tanks are mounted on the ceiling area, then the liquid materials may first be pumped in the storage tanks and then are distributed by gravity flow to the point of use. The consumption can be controlled through the installation of meters. Pipelines can also be located inside the machines. They are popularly used in dairy industries, oil refineries, fertilizer industries, water supplies etc.

(8) Auxiliary Equipment: These are devices or attachments that accompany material handling equipment to enhance their usefulness and effectiveness.

Some of these are:

(*i*) Weighing equipment
(*ii*) Below the hook devices
(*iii*) Containers
(*iv*) Lift-truck attachments
(*v*) Positioners
(*vi*) Pallets and skids
(*vii*) Pallet loader and unloader
(*viii*) Dock-boards and levellers
(*ix*) Ramps.

Economics of Material Handling

The American Society of Mechanical Engineers (ASME) had developed certain formulas for estimating the economies that are possible with the application of certain equipment to a material handling problem. The following factors in the handling costs are taken into account are indicated by letters:

(*i*) A = Percentage allowance on investment.
(*ii*) B = Percentage allowance for insurance, taxes etc.
(*iii*) C = Percentage allowance for maintenance.
(*iv*) D = Percentage allowance for depreciation and obsolescence.
(*v*) E = Yearly cost of power, supplies and other items in dollars.
(*vi*) S = Yearly saving in direct labour cost in dollars.
(*vii*) T = Yearly saving in fixed charges, operating charges or burden in dollars.
(*viii*) U = Yearly saving or earning through increased production in dollars.
(*ix*) X = Percentage of year during which equipment is used.
(*x*) I = Initial cost of the equipment.

Formulae: The relations between these factors are expressed in following formulae:

(*i*) Maximum justifiable investment in dollars (*i.e.*, Z);

$$Z = \frac{(S+T+U-E)X}{A+B+C+D}$$

(*ii*) Yearly cost of maintaining the equipment (*i.e.*, Y);

$Y = 1(A + B + C + D)$

(*iii*) Yearly profit from the operation of the equipment, above simple interest (*i.e.*, V);

$V = [(S + T + U - E) X] - Y$

(*iv*) The estimated rate of profit (*i.e.*, P);

$$P = \frac{V}{I} + A$$

(*v*) Number of years required for amortization of investment out of earnings (*i.e.*, H);

$$H = \frac{100}{P+D}$$

Advantages of a Good Material Handling System

The following advantages are availed from an efficient material handling system:

1. A good material handling system minimizes the movement of material, moves them continuously and at maximum rate which is advantageous as under:
   (*i*) Shorter operating cycle.
   (*ii*) Reduction in handling cost.
2. It eliminates unproductive handling of materials like back-tracking, rehandling etc.
3. It reduces idle machine capacity thus ensuring better turnover of investment.
4. It reduces the idle time of labour. Workers are required to keep pace with the production processes supported by a good handling system. Moreover, they are freed from the physical work of moving and positioning materials.
5. It eliminates the factory hazards and thus increases the safety of the operators.
6. The quality of the materials is maintained through minimum human touches, elimination of breakages etc.
7. The factory area is used most effectively, unproductive overhead and floor areas are used most productively.
8. It avails of greater economy in store-room and facilitates material issues.
9. It helps in maintaining effective production control.
10. It helps in providing better customer services due to:
    (*i*) Reduced operating cost.
    (*ii*) Better quality of products, and
    (*iii*) Timely production.

Container Revolution

The cargo movement has been revolutionised with the arrival of a container. The development of shipping containers helped the post-World War II boom in global trade. The container has been described as the box that changed the world. Containers permit unit loads and are fit for inter-modal transport by road, rail, sea and air. ISO Container has the following dimensions.

Length : 5, 10, 20, 30, 40 feet

35 feet Sealand containers and 45 feet containers are becoming popular. 20 feet unit is popular in shipping.

Width : Common

Height : 8 feet - 9.6 feet

Details : Floor, walls and roof.

Opened at the end.

Some units permit entry from the side or top.

Insulated walls.

Refrigeration units.

Made of steel, aluminium or fire-board.

Cargo shifted manually or by fork-lifts.

Container are put on ship by container handling systems like counter-balanced trucks or reach stackers. There are straddle carriers and mobile lifting frames. These equipment operate in unrestricted area. Some equipment are operated in restricted area — gantry cranes and ship-to-shore cranes.

Fig. 6.32
A Container

If there is one area which can increase industrial productivity almost overnight, it is material handling. The term material handling relates to the art of sorting, packaging and moving materials from one place to another. A wise choice of techniques and equipments for material handling can bring about considerable saving of time and money.

Fig. 6.33
A Reach Stacker

Importance of Materials Handling

It is hard to realise how important is materials handling in the cost of operation because it is something that is quite common to everyone. But when once its nature is exposed it may be difficult to overlook it as a major potential of effecting cost reduction. Materials handling problems assume importance due to a number of factors:

1. Various studies made in different industries indicate that the cost of handling alone accounts for about 20-25% of total manufacturing costs. What the cost in any particular industry may be is largely the result of the methods and equipment used.
2. It is usually found that each part is handled 50-60 times while it passes through the chain of manufacture. Expressed in tonnes, it is found that on an average 59 tonnes of materials are handled for every tonne of finished product.
3. **Increased safety** — Materials handling account for 21% of the permanent disabilities and over 25% of the temporary disabilities.
4. **Reduce damage claims** — Modern handling methods have paid off in the reduction of damage in parts and materials.
5. **Ease drudgery for men** — Most of the jobs done by man handling are mere drudgery for men in the first place. Some of the mechanised handling jobs being done today would be a sheer physical impossibility for manual labour within the present economic frame work.
6. The field of materials handling remains still to be fully explored. Material handling techniques are not only industry's biggest opportunity — they are industry's biggest necessity. Competition is beginning to force this new technology upon industry.

Principles of Material Handling

These serve as guidelines for a material handling problem. They are not ready-made solutions, but are important considerations in taking material handling decisions.

1. Minimise handling or at best eliminate it wherever possible. No handling is the best handling.
2. Keep materials at a height at which they are to be worked upon, thus avoiding lifting up and down every time.
3. Avoid cross and back hauls.
4. As far as possible, try to handle in bulk.
5. The more the distance, the higher the handling cost.
6. Integrate handling with the production processes.
7. Keep gangways clear to avoid hold ups on account of obstructions.
8. Do not permit the handling of materials by direct operators at the cost of neglecting the main job.
9. Select the materials handling equipment on two considerations: cost and versality so that the equipment can be used for a variety of purposes.
10. To effect operating economy, reduce idle or terminal time of handling equipment to the minimum. Increase the size of the unit load. Employ powered mechanical equipment to perform the moving task. Increase the speed of the handling function.
11. Select the handling system that permits flexibility to accommodate changes in the layout or materials.
12. Ensure a higher ratio of equipment utilisation.
13. Nothing should be handled twice that can be handled very well only once. Each handling adds to cost and not to value.
14. Make the best possible use of natural resources like gravity in solving the handling problem.

Scope of Materials Handling

Materials handling is spread over to many different industries and fields of engineering. The following table gives its broad application:

Industry		***Remarks***
Manufacturing	:	Largest single field for application of materials handling. Wide range of materials handling equipment are used. Materials handling problems involve surveys, plant and equipment layouts, routing, packaging and storage of materials.
Processing	:	Handling of bulk materials (like gases, liquids, semi-liquids and bulk solids). Special handling problems affect the plant design.
Construction	:	Proper receiving, sorting, storing and moving materials. In heavy construction projects, there is now a chcice of special methods and equipment of materials handling. It influences the civil engineers in project planning.
Mining	:	In both underground mines and open pit operations, there is now a variety of equipment for extraction, handling and transportation of coal and ore. Cost of extracting the materials has been reduced to the minimum.
Power	:	Materials handling equipment for handling fuel and ash.
Machine Tools	:	The design of many processing machines is influenced by the need for integrating various material handling features or attachments to modern machine mechanisms.
Truck Building	:	The automotive engineer develops trucks and trailers as efficient materials handling vehicles, designed for speedy loading and unloading, proper securement of cargo, and safe transportation of a variety of materials.
Rail-Road Car Builders	:	Improved rail-road cars, development of terminal equipment, improvement in materials handling procedure for loading and securing freight and transferring or unloading it at terminals.
Barge and Ship Building	:	New handling devices and improved kinds of marine carriers.
Aircraft	:	Better cargo and storage methods for air transport. Cost efficient methods to handle cargo going into and out of the craft.

Modi, Hemant: *Material Handling Equipment, Purchase,* Vol. 9, No. 3, March 1986.

Machine Loading with Robots

A major growth area for industrial robot applications is that of automatic machine loading. Wherever there is a production machine that is 'operator-paced' or a grouping of two or more machine tools in a process, there is an opportunity for improvement using robots in the form of reduced direct labour costs, increased output from the machine or machines, better or more consistent quality of parts and improved capital equipment utilisation.

The robots are used to load, position and then unload and transfer work pieces. Even fully automated transfer lines are candidates for robot loading. In one of the typical applications, productivity has become 25% better than it was with manual handling. Equally important, the operator is now free to check and change tooling, watch automated gauging stations, and make necessary periodic adjustments.

Known as PUMA (Programmable Universal Manipulator for Assembly), a light-weight and highly precise industrial robot has been developed to operate on an assembly line side by side with human workers. The robot positions objects to an accuracy of 0.004 in (0.1 mm). It has five axes of motion corresponding to the human being's waist, shoulder and elbow rotation, wrist bend and hand rotation. Its load capacity is 7.7 lb (3.5 kgs). Microprocessor-controlled electric servos position the arm of the PUMA robot. The robot is taught a programme by either a teach module or computer terminal.

Other interesting development in field of mechanical handling have been "Pick-and-place" units and "Air-film transporter systems."

Two economically-priced, pneumatic transfer arms, designed to automate a wide range of routine 'pick-and-place' production operations are now available. Both are capable of automating such labour intensive operations as the selection of small-to-medium-sized components and positioning them accurately on jigs, fixtures, drilling tables, presses, conveyors, etc.

The larger unit, which can hold components up to 3.5 kgs provides five basic movements — clamping; horizontal extension up to 250 mm; lifting up to 50 mm; swinging up to 120 deg.; and rotation of the jaws through a maximum of 180 deg.

The smaller arm has a maximum working load of 0.5 kg and three movements — clamping, lifting up to 25 mm and swinging through 180 deg. maximum.

Both are powered by integral pneumatic actuators working from a standard factory air supply at 5.52 Bar (80 lb/in^2). The speed of movement can be adjusted by fitting restrictors to the control valves.

Air-film systems have been widely used in the United States for about 20 years. The system operates off a factory compressed air supply by creating a thin film of air between the factory floor and compliant inflated diaphragms which are built into transporters or sets of individual air stakes. Once floating on air the load can be moved with very little effort with equal ease in any direction.

Belt Conveyors

In mining, thermal power stations, cement ports, we come across large-scale material handling for which purpose, Belt Conveyor System can be employed.

Fig. 6.34 shows the general arrangement of conveyor belt system. The system can be designed for both huge boulders as well as pulverized material. German conveyor belts have a width of 3200 and a carrying capacity of 37500 tonnes per hour. The width and speed have a relationship. The wider the belt, the lower the speed needed or the speedier the belt, the lesser the width needed. Though single-length systems are better, there can be a number of conveyor belts, each having different feeding and loading points. Formerly, a conveyor belt length of 1 to 1.5 km was considered good. But now belts upto 30 km length from centre to centre and 100 kms running are available due to availability of better materials of making them such as steel-chords.

Formerly flat belts of leather were used. Later as other materials came on the scene, the belts were troughed from 20-25° to 60°. The carrying capacity increases due to troughing up to 57 and then declines. Belt speeds have now increased up to 7.2 m per second. The major cost of the conveyor

Fig. 6.34

Arrangement of Conveyor Belt System

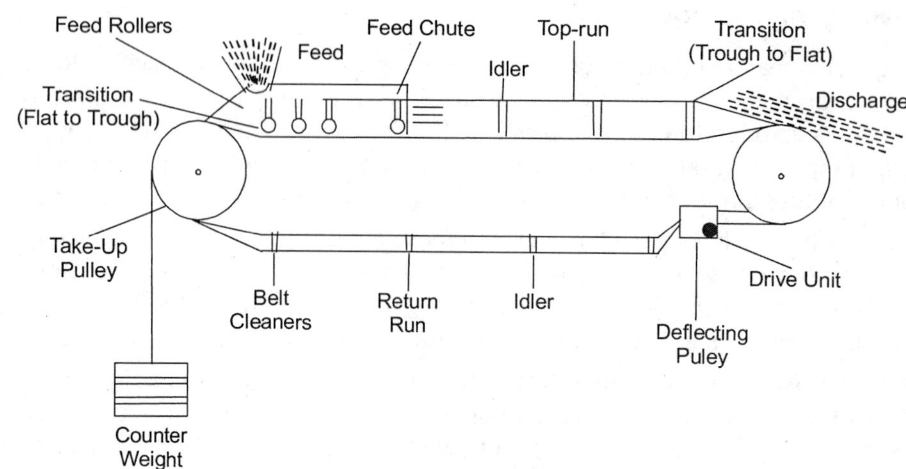

system is on account of conveyor rollers which need lubrication. In these rollers, ball-bearings and taper roller bearings are used. Belting is another major cost component. These days synthetic material is used for belting. Good material lessens the number of plies. Steel chords are used for belting. Armaid — a synthetic fibre has been developed as belt material. The belt is reconditioned to save cost. Reconditioning is equal to retreading of tyres.

In cable belt conveyors, the derive force is that of two wire ropes. It is an energy efficient system. To run the system on uneven ground and curves, they have developed stereoduct or curvoduct system. Pope conveyor is another modification to protect material being conveyed and to use in both horizontal and vertical conditions.

Automated Storage and Retrieval (ASR)

In supply chain management, manufacturing and distribution, automated storage and retrieval system is common. It provides for the automated storage of the inventory items and their automatic retrieval from stock. This system leads to better space utilisation and make the ASR system thus relevant in FMS and JIT manufacture. They are in vogue in food products warehouses, mass retail institutions and mail order houses. Automatic car parking in some cases resembles ASR. It is used in electronics industry alongside the assembly. It is valuable in holding and managing spares in maintenance organisations.

Components of ASR

It consists of (*i*) the storage area, (*ii*) the storage and retrieval machine, (*iii*) conveying devices (*iv*) and control computers. It is graphically shown in Fig. 6.35.

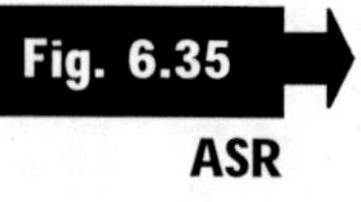

ASR

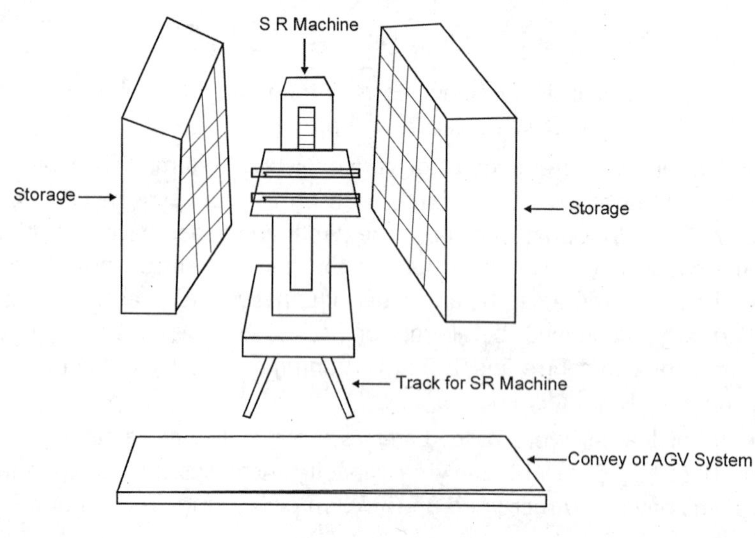

7 CAPACITY PLANNING

Creation of capacity means committing financial and other resources to it, mostly on substantial basis. It is an investment decision. It brings out the operational strategy of an organization. In service of organizations, it means creation of more space, furniture and other accessories and equipment.

Planning of capacity is in response to all that has gone into the previous chapters of this book. Capacity is to be planned keeping in mind our future growth and expansion plans, market trends, sales forecasting, multiple scenario analysis and our policy towards risk taking. Capacity planning decision has to decide a centralised capacity at one geographic location or a decentralised creation of plants at several locations.

Some other considerations also affect our capacity decisions. How to tide over a temporary deficit in capacity — by operating additional shifts giving over-time or holiday work? How much are we to make in our plants, and how much we are going to buy from outside? How best we should satisfy the market demand — either the demand is to be fully met or can we allow some lost sales? All these factors are a part of capacity planning.

Economic considerations of capacity are not difficult to arrive at, but strategic considerations do merit our attention. We shall discuss them in this chapter.

What is Capacity?

Capacity is elusive, and is therefore often qualified by terms like licensed capacity, installed capacity, rated capacity etc. It all depends on how we look at capacity.

Definition of Capacity

Capacity of a facility is its limiting capability to produce an output over a period of time. Thus the annual capacity of Bajaj is 7 lacs scooters currently. It means the production is limited to this productive capability over a period of time, here a year. The capacity however is subject to intensiveness of use of the facilities. It is possible to enhance capacity by working for more days or for more hours. Temporarily capacity can be increased to meet additional demand by these methods.

Imagine a transformation process having many sub-processes, each of them inter-linked. Here the capacity's limit is determined by the capacity of that sub-process which produces the least. If we want to upgrade the capacity, we can do so by balancing equipment to create a better balance amongst the sub-processes. The concept of capacity is thus invariably connected with the weakest link in the chain. This means that even when capacity is fully utilized in terms of the definition of capacity, there may be individual processes that may remain underutilized. In many cases, processes are partly manual and partly mechanical. Technology in many cases is indivisible.

Capacity has something to do with making in-house or buying or subcontracting from outside. We can buy certain components or even the entire production from elsewhere, when we do not have in-house capacity.

Process industries have an initial licensed capacity sanctioned by the government. At the time of installing the plant, the capacity that is installed is called installed capacity. When production is observed over a period of time, the highest rate is established by trial. It is called the rated capacity.

Various names and adjectives are associated with capacity. *Installed capacity* is determined on the basis of capacity as indicated by suppliers of plant and machinery in their technical quotations. We come across terms like *normal capacity, expected capacity, practical capacity* and *ideal capacity.* In power generation, we hear about *derated capacity.* In accounting parlance, *budgeted capacity* is a common term.

Normal capacity is calculated when normal conditions prevail and the enterprise works on a normal level of activity. It covers activity sufficient for meeting average sales demand over a period that is long enough to cover seasonal/cyclical variations. Practical capacity represents the maximum level of activity at which an enterprise can realistically operate at full efficiency. Estimated capacity is essentially for a short period for the next year. Ideal capacity indicates the maximum number of operating hours that would be available without taking into consideration stoppages. Budgeted capacity is more like estimated capacity, but is estimated for the budget period. Capacity is derated in conditions in which technically specified capacity can no longer operate.

Measurement of Capacity

In case of homogeneous tangible products which can be counted, the capacity is measured in terms of units of output per period of time. For example, electricity generation is measured in terms of MW, transistor radio in terms of number of sets per day, steel plant in terms of million of tonnes per year.

There are however complex situations. There could be multiple products, sharing common facilities. Job shop is an extreme example. In all these cases, capacity is very difficult to express. Here, then, we express capacity in terms of the constraints. For example, a job shop has maximum these many labour hours available per month could be a measure of its capacity. For hospitals, capacity is bed days/month.

Service Capacity

For countable homogeneous units of service like insurance policies, the capacity expression becomes number of policies serviced per year. In case of heterogeneous units, as explained above, capacity is expressed by referring to the constraints — man hours per month for a bank branch etc. However, since service output is not storable, planning capacity is always a challenging task. There are periods of peak demand (for plane seats, for banking services, for hotel rooms) and periods of average demand, which is much less than the peak demand. So most of these units produce an output on an average, which is less than its capacity. The problems of capacity utilization on the lower side, coupled with a problem of productivity deserve the attention of the business planning department.

Process of Capacity Planning

Capacity planning is concerned with assessing labour and capacity requirements to satisfy the current MPS (master production schedule) and long term future needs of the plant. Capacity planning is a several step process. After environmental analysis, we are in a position to predict future demands. We know our available capacity. We then try to prepare alternative capacity plans for our various predictions of demand. While doing this, we do a quantitative economic analysis of various capacity plans, and a qualitative analysis of risks and strategic consequences. The chosen course is then implemented. Let us now examine these steps in some detail.

Future Capacity Requirement: Prediction

Capacity plans are heavily dependent upon demand forecasting for our outputs. As we know, long-term forecasts of demand are so difficult to compute. Though there is secular trend and cyclical effect, there are contingencies difficult to foresee which affect the demand — these contingencies could be acts of God like droughts and floods or man made like wars, technological breakthrough, and oil embargoes. As a rule, however, mature products are subject to better prediction than the recent launches either in introductory or growth stages of PLC.

Multiple Outputs

There could be many products for which demand is to be forecast, and each product could be at different stages of PLC. The total demand for all outputs might not fluctuate much but individual outputs having different growth rates show demand fluctuations. In the long run, the output mix of the organization may change.

Multiple outputs insure us against uncertainties in environment, especially if each output were to have an independent demand. Segmentation of markets resulting in different brands for each segment results in a better planning of total capacity requirements.

In other words, demand forecasting for a flexible output is easier than that of a specific output of a continuous process or process industries.

Stabilized Demand for Mature Products

Electricity, cement, fertilizers, steel, health care and hospital services, textiles are some examples of products which have a long PLC and which are at maturity stage of their PLC. In these cases, the demand does not remain volatile.

Long-term Demand Forecasting

We use judgemental methods like Delphi, Executive Opinions and Expert Opinions. We may also use extension of past history methods like moving averages, exponential smoothing, or we can use causal forecasting models like Regression analysis and econometric models.

Regression analysis is a forecasting model that relates the dependent variable (sales, for example) to one or more independent variables (GNP disposable income, housing construction, road building, hospital services etc.). For example, the demand for refrigerators is a function of such independent variables as the new houses constructed in the previous years, new marriages solemnised during the previous years, disposable income available, and a seasonal and trend effect. We are here essentially developing a forecasting function called regression equation. It is a time-consuming process and also very costly process to assess and identify the various independent variables for developing a regression equation. For long-term forecasting, a forecast for each causal variable is needed.

Econometric forecasting is a further improvement on regression analysis. It consists of a system of simultaneous regression equations. For example, we can say demand for soaps is a function of its price and advertising and the personal disposable income of the consumer. However, price itself is a function of the total cost of production, selling and distribution and the mark-up desired. Production cost itself is a function of the manufacturing level and materials level. Similarly selling costs are a function of salesmen's salaries and commissions, cost of servicing the territories etc. We thus have to estimate several relationships simultaneously. These methods are expensive and time-consuming.

Judgemental methods are used when good data are not readily available. With the use of this method, we try to convert the qualitative data in the form of a subjective opinion into quantitative data that we can use for forecasting. Outside experts may be consulted, we can convene a panel of experts to make a forecast or we can refer the case to futurist organizations. In each case, reliance is being placed on human judgement to interpret past data and make projections about the future.

Marketing research on consumer behaviour, product, price distribution and ad research proves extremely useful in forecasting the long-term demand of product.

Historical analogy compares the life cycle of a product to that of another similar product to make predictions. (For example, demand for housemaids is related to demand for washing machines or demand for B&W TV sets is compared with demand for colour TVs).

While dealing with multiple outputs, the demand for each output is estimated independently and then summed up. If the outputs are heterogeneous, it may mean separate capacity planning for each sub-process. For multiple outputs, capacity gap or slack is computed for each sub-process.

In case of new outputs, the uncertainty of demand is higher. Hence the probability of demand distribution in the term of an optimistic forecast and pessimistic forecast are arrived at, over and above expected projected demand.

Capacity Plans: Generation Process

Capacity plans may not match the capacity required. We have to see what alternative capacity will be used or whether there is a provision of lost sales.

Capacity Enhancement: Size

To meet the growing demand, the added capacity is either added in small doses frequently or in large doses less frequently.

Capacity can be added in anticipation of the growing requirement or can wait till the requirement overtakes the available capacities.

There can be mixed options also. We can enhance the capacity substantially but as the demand is not static, soon it outstrips the available capacity thus leading to another enhancement on substantial basis.

Alternative Capacity Sources

It is not always necessary to create additional capacity. We can also use the facilities intensively (overtime, holiday work, additional shifts) and get more output. We can also sub-contract either fully or partly our work-load. In case of continuous process industry however, it is not feasible to have more intensiveness of use. So also sub-contracting is ruled out for sophisticated processing.

Whenever alternative capacity sources are possible to be tapped, we reduce the cost of carrying a high capacity, along with the attendant risk of not using it all along. Alternate capacity plans may have capacity gaps, which are to be filled up by alternative capacity sources.

Cost-Volume (CV) Relationships

There are two types of costs involved — fixed costs and variable costs. For a given volume of output, as we increase the output the variable costs do increase, but since the contribution is enough to cover fixed costs we get a lower cost per unit. Break-even volume is the volume where there is no profit and no loss (total costs and sales intersect on the graph).

Economies of Scale

High capacity plants have high fixed costs but since variable costs per unit are low, they offer economies of scale. Besides, there are other economies of scale (less investment in inventories, less investments in construction costs for a process industry).

Lost Sales

Lost sales result into losing our market share which might prove very risky as it could be permanent. Business organizations in the private sector therefore avoid less than required capacity. But in case of public utilities, like telephones, suburban trains, electricity boards, water supply, the facilities operate at less than required capacity which could not be built up due to infrastructure problems. Perhaps the culprit is the budgetary system where a particular amount only could be earmarked for a particular purpose. Even private sector business organizations encounter demand spurts leaving no other alternative than accepting the lost sales (thus loss in possible contribution).

Multiple and Anticyclic Outputs

In case of petroleum refineries, there are outputs at higher temperatures and lower temperatures in fractional distillation. Now the higher distillates and the lower distillates do not show the same pattern of demand, their PLC's being totally different. There the overall capacity does not show much fluctuation, but individual outputs do show them.

There are some products where there is a seasonal spurt in demand, *e.g.*, cough syrups and woollens in winter, electric fans and ACs in summer, electric heaters and convertors in winter etc. Fire-crackers are consumed only during festive Deepavali season and only occasionally in other months of the year. So also is the case of greeting cards, and account books. Here anticyclic production is built up over non-seasonal months (both ways, *e.g.*, produce more crackers throughout the year to accommodate Deepavali demand and/or produce non-crackers like match sticks using the same production facilities).

Evaluation of Alternative Plans

The various alternative capacity plans are to be evaluated for consequences in future which is uncertain. The plans have a different set of constraints. Certain effects in future are not easy to quantify. The analysis of risks and other consequences is therefore qualitative as well as quantitative.

Financial Analysis for Mature Outputs and Stabilized Demand

A capacity plan is an investment proposal that pays us (cash inflow) over a period of time in future. The future cash flows are however discounted at a particular rate to get their present value. The initial investment minus the sum of present values of future cash inflows is NPV: Net Present Value. The capacity plan with a higher net positive NPV is more attractive.

DCF (discounted cash-flow) can also be extended to analysis of multi-locational projects, and integrated projects (forward or backward integration).

Financial Analysis for Outputs where Demand is Uncertain

DCF can be applied here too, with the additional information of probability distribution of demand (pessimistic, optimistic and expected distribution), as NPV is calculated for each distribution separately. Decision free technique, a graphical description of sequential decisional problems, is also useful.

Risk Analysis

The predicted demand may not always turn out to be true, the actual demand may be higher than it or lower than it. If higher, there is under-capacity. If lower, there is over-capacity. Let us examine both the consequences of both these situations.

Factors which Favour Over-capacity (Rather than Under-capacity)

1. When there is an economic capacity size, below which the process is uneconomic.
2. Building capacity is not so costly.
3. Buying outside is not feasible.
4. Lead time to add capacity is long.
5. Demand growth approximates to the optimistic prediction.
6. Lost sales are viewed very negatively by trading circles, resulting in a big dip in the demand.

Factors which Favour Addition of Capacity on Conservative Basis

1. Alternative capacity plans are easily available.
2. Build up cost of capacity is low.
3. Lead time to build new capacity is short.
4. Lost sales have no disastrous results or the customers are prepared to wait.

Some of the factors could not be quantified. Judgement is taken as to how these affect the competitive position of the organization.

In short term capacity planning manpower studies, inventories and subcontracting are considered. In long term capacity planning, capital budgeting, investments and closure of facilities are considered.

Capacity Utilization

Machine Requirements

In a manufacturing concern, a substantial part of the financial resources are invested in the plant, machines and equipment.

The return on the investment can be maximized by:

(*i*) Making the optimum investment in the plant and machines, and

(*ii*) Making the optimum utilization of the installed production capacity.

The issue of "machine requirements" deals with above part (*i*) while the problem of "line-balance" is concerned with part (*ii*), Both these issues are explained in brief in the following paragraphs.

Machine requirements decide the desirable investment in plant and machines. Machine capacity is generally expressed in terms of machine hours. The time (in hours) necessary to complete an operation on the job, multiplied by total number of jobs that are required during a period of time, gives the total capacity required of the type of machine to be used. (This is expressed in "ST × MP" as denoted in the numerator of the following formula). The number of machines for the operation may be determined by dividing this figure by the number of hours that one machine will run during the period as adjusted to the per cent capacity utilization. (This is expressed in "MC × UC" as presented in the denominator of the following formula).

The relationship between these factors can be expressed as under:

$$N = \frac{ST \times MP}{MC \times UC}$$

N = The number of machines required for the particular operation.

ST = The standard time per job for the operation in hours.

MP = The maximum production required during the "specified time."

UC = Utilization of machine capacity in per cent.

Illustration: Job A is performed on Machine X. The relevant details are as under:

(*i*) Standard time per job for the operation is 6 minutes.

(*ii*) The maximum requirements of Job A is 70,000 per month.

(*iii*) The standard capacity of machine X is 2000 hr/month.

(*iv*) The average utilization of the machine capacity is 90%.

Ascertain the requirements of Machine X.

Requirement of Machine X

$$N = \frac{ST \times MP}{MC \times UC}$$

$$ST = 6 \text{ minutes} = \frac{6}{60} \text{ hrs. or } \frac{1}{10}$$

MP = 70,000 jobs

MC = 2,000 hr/month.

UC = 90%

$$N = \frac{\frac{1}{10} \times 70,000}{200 \times \frac{90}{100}} = \frac{7,000}{1,800} = 3.88\%$$

Hence 3.88 units of Machine X will be required. As the machine is the indivisible economic unit, 4 machines will be required.

Line Balancing

The problem of line balancing arises due to following factors:

1. The finished product is the result of many sequential operations.
2. The production capacity of each machine is not identical, *e.g.*, the production capacity of machine A, B and C is as under:

Machine A	100 pieces/hr
Machine B	50 pieces/hr
Machine C	25 pieces/hr

The technique of line balancing reduces the idle time of the installed production capacity and facilitates the intensive use of production capacity. Thus the turnover of the investments in plant and machines is geared up resulting in the increased profitability of the business.

The situation is explained in the most simplified way as under:

Hourly Production of Machines A, B and C

Now if only one machine is provided for the processes passing sequential through the machines A, B and C, then the contribution of each machine in the line will be decided on the basis of the machine with the least production capacity. In the above case Machine C produces only 25 units per hour. The production capacity of machine A and B will be confined to the production of 25 units per hour only. So in each hour machines A and B will remain idle for 45 and 30 minutes respectively. It should be noted that in the process layout such idle time or slacks can be minimized through proper routing and scheduling of other operations. However, under the product layout, due to the linear arrangements of the machines, the utilization of such idle capacity would be relatively difficult. The concept of line balancing would solve the problem of idle capacity to some extent as under:

The actual production in the line will be decided on the basis of the machine with the maximum production capacity. The production capacity of the other machines in the line will be adjusted through

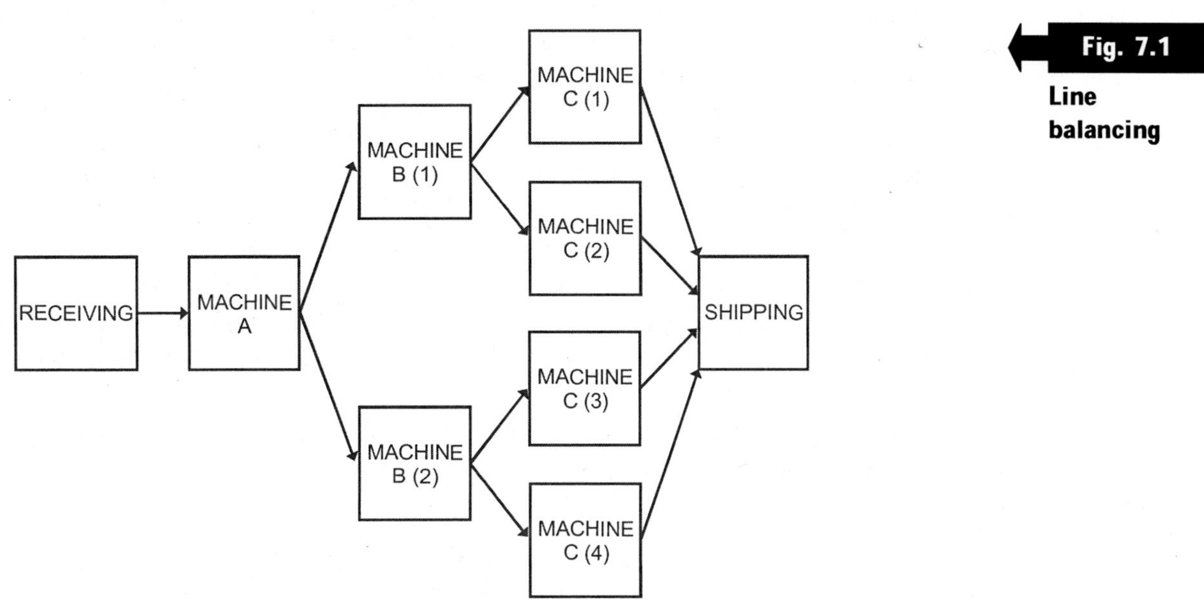

Fig. 7.1 **Line balancing**

the increase in the number of machines. In our case, Machine A produces 100 units/hr. So 100 units will be manufactured per hour with the help of two machines B and four machines C. The line balancing for the production of 100 units per hour will be made by employing one machine A, two machines B and four machines C. Thus the idle capacity will be totally eliminated.

It can be noted that any odd capacity of the different machines used in the line can be fully balanced with the help of a simple mathematical equation. However, in reality the problem is not simple. The main problem arising out of such simplified line balancing is the disposal of the large volume of production. In such a situation, the solution is sought with the help of the cost-benefit analysis. If the cost of overprotection exceeds the cost of idle capacity in the unbalanced line, then attempts are made to solve the problem in some other manner. The cost of idle capacity in the unbalanced line can be solved in the following manner:

1. Another product line enabling the use of idle capacity of the first line could be run close to it. However, sometimes such a solution may create more problems than what it can solve.
2. One more way of solving such a problem would be, to transfer the work elements from overloaded machines to some other machines and equipment somewhere else in the line, *i.e.*, the subsequent stages of work elements in the process may be performed first during the occupation of the overloaded machine by some other jobs. Such a solution has the following limitations:
   (*i*) Additional material handling cost.
   (*ii*) Increase in processing time.
   (*iii*) It is possible only where the sequence of work elements in the process is alterable, *e.g.*, the spray colouring cannot precede welding.
3. If negligible part of some machine capacity is required to be utilized, then the job may be performed with some outside jobbing firms. However, this will involve additional cost of handling, delay in the production line and uncertainty of jobbing contractors.
4. Alternatively, machines with lower capacity utilization rate, may be used to perform the jobs of other manufacturers through sub-contracting. This solution is also not free from varied constraints.

The problem of line balancing should be solved on the basis of cost-benefit analysis of the incremental production. Sophisticated techniques like linear programming, dynamic programming, PERT, CPM etc., are employed in the analysis. Only those solutions should be sought which command the maximum economic benefits.

Capacity decisions have their own dynamics. Installing new capacity, curtailing existing capacity and pricing have effects on the actions of the company and its competitors. These effects are more evident when installation of new capacity takes three or four years. While investing today, we expect profit given the current level of demand and pricing. However, if competitors also invest in capacity simultaneously, the utilisation will be lower than expected when all the plants are on stream later on. The prices start falling in a couple of years, as here is over capacity leading to a battle for market share.

Investments in high growth segments keep on rising to keep pace with the growing demand. The level of invested capital per ton cranks up. These areas also are vulnerable to competitive price-cutting.

Investing in a new capacity counter-cyclically (when there is a down-turn) can enhance a company's profitability substantially. The plant comes on stream during an upturn. This time the utilisation and prices will be high.

Modernising old equipment usually pays better returns than building new capacity. The re-build cost could be a fraction of the cost of new equipment.

Capacity Planning

The available capacity should match the forecast demand. That enables an organisation to design a schedule to show exactly when it will produce the output. This is what product planning is all about.

It must meet the long term demand, allow for variations in demand over a short term and remain within the available capacity. It then generates time tables for the manpower, equipment, purchases and the strategic level capacity plans to the detailed operations schedule. The following diagram illustrates this:

Fig. 7.2
Levels of Planning

Let us be clear about the terms used.

Capacity Plans:	They ensure that there is enough capacity to meet the long term demand
Aggregate Plans:	It shows the overall production for families of products within the physical capacity available. A typical aggregate plan is expressed in terms of a period of some months at each location. It also determines the workforce level.
Master Production Schedule (MPS):	It shows a detailed schedule of production of each product. It is a weekly schedule typically. It is constrained by aggregate planning
Short-term Schedules:	It shows detailed time table for jobs, equipment, people and other resources. It is a day-to-day plan.

Capacity of a Process

In common parlance, capacity refers to the holding capacity of something, say a container. Thus, we say that this perfume bottle has a capacity of 100 ml or this cinema hall has a capacity of 1000 seats. In production management, capacity refers to the maximum amount of product which can be produced in a given time. If at a college, an enquiry counter takes 4 minutes to deal with a student, it has a capacity of 15 students per hour. The capacity in a hospital is the maximum number of patients it can treat in a week. The capacity of a ship is the maximum load of cargo it can carry. The capacity of a scooter factory is the maximum number of scooters which can be produced per year. The capacity of an MBA class is the maximum seat intake it has per semester. Capacity measures **the rate of output** and refers to some relevant **time period.**

In short, the capacity of a process is the maximum amount of a product that can be made in a specific time under normal working conditions. Capacity planning includes all the decisions about the capacity of a process.

Capacity planning refers to a hierarchy of decisions regarding facilities, aggregate planning and scheduling. Facility planning establishes a physical capacity that cannot be exceeded by aggregate planning. The decisions proceed from the top down and there is a feedback loop from bottom up. Facilities decisions require capital investment, and are taken at the corporate level. Many such decisions are long term decisions. There are decisions of one-year time frame involving buildings and equipment which can be quickly constructed or leased. The five-year time-frame involves decisions for large and complex facilities such as oil refineries, steel mills, paper mills and electricity generation plants. There are some critical questions in facilities decisions.

1. **How much** total capacity is needed?
2. **How large** should each unit capacity be?
3. **When** is the capacity needed?
4. **What** type of facilities/capacity are needed?

All these questions can be separately considered, but they are often intertwined.

Capacity of an operator sometimes is obvious, say the number of beds in a hospital or seats in a cinema hall or tables in a restaurant. Sometimes, the capacity is not clear, *e.g.,* capacity of a warehouse, or a supermarket or a bank. There we have to use some **surrogate measure** *e.g.,* the number of customers per square metre of floor space. Such a figure is not just a matter of calculation. It is arrived at by using discussions and agreement. The maximum size of a class-room in colleges is an **agreed number** of students rather than a limit set by the building. The maximum number of spectators in a cricket stadium as set by safety regulations rather than by physical limitations of space.

Approach to Capacity Planning

As a matter of principle, capacity planning is simple to understand. It requires just a forecast of long-term demand and then building up of enough capacity to meet this demand.

If the capacity built is less, the demand cannot be met and there is a consequent loss of potential customers.

If the capacity built is more, even after meeting the demand, some capacity will remain spare with consequent extra costs and under-utilised resources:

We may enter a shop where there are not enough sales people to attend to us. Thus we are made to wait. The capacity of the shop is less than the demand. We are likely to move to a competitor where queues are shorter. Some shops have far too many sales people to attend to us. There are less customers, and so the sales people are under-used. Their salary bill is an extra cost.

Capacity Cushion

As we have already observed, the amount of capacity provided is in relation to the expected demand. Capacity cushion best describes this notion.

Capacity cushion = capacity – average demand

As capacity cushion is expressed relative to the average demand level, a positive value of the cushion provides excess capacity over the average demand and a negative value of the cushion means that the average demand exceeds the capacity. The ideal is to have no capacity cushion but it is not possible in view of the uncertain demand. There are three strategies which are adopted for the amount of capacity cushion.

1. **Attempt to prevent a run out:** Here we can use a positive capacity cushion. The organisation exceeds the forecast demand to have some additional capacity. In an expanding market or cost-effective capacity build up and operation, such a strategy is appropriate. Electricity generation plants are known to adopt this approach to prevent black-outs. Companies operating in a growth-oriented market tend to have such a positive cushion to capture market share ahead of their competitors. In such markets there is no risk of having idle capacity for long.
2. **Meet the average forecast:** This a conservative approach. There is a 0.5 probability of running out of capacity and 0.5 probability of having excess capacity. Such a strategy is useful when the run out costs approximate to the excess capacity costs.
3. **Maximise utilisation:** Here a negative cushion is used to maximize utilization. This strategy is apt when capacity build up cost is very high in relation to stock outs *e.g.,* oil refineries, paper-mills and capital-intensive industries. Such facilities show profits when capacity utilization rate touches 90 to 100 per cent. Though it improves short-term earings, it may harm the long-term marker share. This is likelier when competitors have larger capacity cushions and demand develops to use the excess capacity.

Effective Capacity

The capacity of a process is its maximum output under normal conditions. Normal conditions assume ideal conditions without any problems, interruption, maintenance or other stoppages. The designed capacity is then the maximum output under ideal conditions. But in practice, there are no ideal conditions. Thus, effective capacity is a more realistic measure. The designed capacity of a lift may be 100 people but it may not be its effective capacity. People arrive in smaller groups. People come in and get off at every floor, because of which there are interruptions. The effective capacity thus could be just 50 people. All the effective capacity may not be used. Products may use different amounts of resources. One product might consume the entire supply of a resource — say time on one machine. This is called a bottleneck. Here one machine works at full capacity, but all other resources have spare capacity. Bottlenecks limit the capacity of the overall process. In a restaurant, the chef can turn out 250 meals in the evening. But if the seating capacity is 100 only, this bottleneck limits the capacity. If a jeweller can make 30 bracelets everyday, but the gold available for manufacturing is just enough for 20 bracelets, the raw material supply limits the capacity. We have to identify correctly the limiting factors. A political party may have more leaders, whereas they lack the followers to spread its ideology. There is no point in expanding the area of waiting room when there are more patients. There should be more doctors to attend to the patients faster. An organisation may recruit more salespeople when there is a constraint on production output currently and the lead time is too long.

Steps in Capacity Planning

Capacity planning is both strategic and tactical. Facility planning decisions are mostly major strategic decisions. Short-term decisions pertain to hiring space or overtime work etc. Though there is no standard approach to capacity planning, the planners generally follow the steps such as:

1. Forecast the demand.
2. Convert this into a capacity requirement.
3. Assess capacity of existing facilities.
4. Assess the gap between the needed and available capacity.
5. Make alternative plans to fill the gap.
6. Compare these alternative plans and choose the best.
7. Implement the best plan and check and control its progress.

The above process is also described as **resource requirement planning**. Many a time, the steps may not work sequentially. There are so many plans many times. Comparisons may become difficult. The single procedure may be replaced by an iterative one where steps 5 and 6 are repeated till satisfactory results are obtained. Iterative process acknowledges that there is no single best plan. It is just a plan that is most acceptable. Different departments may have different perspectives, *e.g.*, a plan appealing to marketing executives may not find favour with the operations executive. The plans which are good for HR may turn out to be unacceptable for finance. Maybe, they are too expensive. The final plan is a compromise between conflicting objectives and subjective viewpoints. There are many factors which influence such a compromise:

- demand forecast, sales accomplished, back orders, demand variations.
- operations — machine capacity and utilization, capital budgeting plans, outstanding plans and productivity targets.
- materials — raw material availability, inventory policy, inventory levels and storage constraints.
- HR — manpower inventory, unemployment recruitment and selection and training.
- marketing — forecast reliability, new product arrangement and product substitution.

It is extremely difficult to balance all the factors, and the iterative process is the only way out till an acceptable plan emerges.

Adjustment to Capacity

Capacity planning is a strategic function but there should be enough flexibility to meet temporary mismatches between demand and supply in the short term *e.g.*, more number of people on weekends to see a blockbuster movie than the number of seats available. Such short-term adjustment can be done by two methods — demand management and capacity management.

Demand Management

Demand management is a short-term adjustment of demand with the available capacity by several methods.

Price Variations. Prices are increased to reduce demand at peak times and are reduced to increase demand at lean times.

Marketing Effort Variations. Marketing effort can be varied to match the demand and supply. We can demarket a scarce commodity like electricity by discouraging its enhanced consumption.

Incentivisation. Incentives can be given to encourage demand in the lean season.

Spare Units. We can keep a buffer stock to be used when the demand increases.

Lead Time Variation. By increasing the lead time, we make the customers wait for the product in short supply.

Rationing. We can use a reservation or appointment system.

There is active discouragement of customers or demarketing at the times of heavy demand. Professional courses have several hurdles to restrict entry to a select few. Discos do not permit people at peak times. Custom-made cars have long delivery dates. There is limited edition of high coutre outfits. Perfumes are charged a premium to prevent their being a mass market product.

Capacity Management

It refers to those short term adjustments in capacity so as to make it tally with the forecast demand. Working time is chosen for this. Overtime is used to increase the capacity and short-time to reduce it. There are a number of ways to effect capacity management.

Working Hours and Shift Management. We can change the working hours and shifts.

Scheduling Work Patterns. The total manpower available at any time varies with the demand when work patterns are so scheduled.

Part-time Staff. Such staff is used to meet the peak demand.

Outsourcing. We can outsource certain services. We can rent extra space.

Process Adjustment. The process is so adjusted that the set up time is reduced *e.g.*, making larger batches.

Adjusting Equipment and Processes. Work thus can be speeded up or slowed down.

Rescheduling Maintenance. Maintenance periods are rescheduled.

Self-Service. Let the customer do some work, use ATMS or pack their own bags in a hypermarket.

Such short-term adjustment have their **own costs**. These are temporary measures. Many options affect the manpower. These options are to be exercised sparingly. The lesson learnt is that a process runs more smoothly with a steady output rather than with wide variations.

Problems in Matching Capacity and Demand

Several problems are encountered in matching capacity and demand. Demand usually occurs in small quantities and can take any value. Capacity on the other hand comes in large discrete amounts.

Capacity can more or less match the demand. There may be at times some shortage or some spare capacity. Capacity can equal demand requiring more investment in facilities. It may lead to under-utilisation. Capacity can be deferred, and added only when it would be fully used. It requires less investment and high utilization. But it also restricts output.

There can be large expansion in size so that capacity always remains ahead of demand for a long time. There are economies of scale and less disruptions. But this involves high capital costs and under-utilisation. The demand may change, making the organisation vulnerable.

Changing Capacity Over Time

The capacity of a process changes over time. Sometimes, there are no changes but still we face short-term variations on account of operator's indisposition, break-downs, interruptions and such other problems. There are long-term changes too in capacity on account of learning curves and equipment ageing.

Repetitive activities provide an improvement in skills to operators, musicians, sports persons etc. As the repetitions increase, the time to perform the activities decrease. This is called the learning curve effect. It raises productivity over a period of time. The ageing of equipment brings about a fall in productivity due to break-downs, faults, slow downs, wearing out etc. The change may take place gradually *e.g.,* oil consumption of a car. What is required is the maintenance and replacement of worn out parts.

Aggregate Plans

Aggregate planning is concerned with matching the demand and supply of output over the medium range of time, say 12 months. It thus considers the forecast demand and planned capacity, to design a production plan for each family of products, typically for each of the following few months. Aggregate does connote planning for a single overall measure of output or at the most a few aggregated product categories. It is not concerned with the individual products. The objective is to develop a medium- to long-term statement of capacity requirements in aggregate terms. In other words, the plan indicates the amount of facilities to satisfy the total expected demand, period by period.

A ready-to-wear garment outfit may produce skirts and tops in different sizes and, colours and style. The aggregate plan would show the total production of skirts and tops. It avoids the details of sizes, colours and styles. A breweries total output of beer is considered and a publisher's total number of books to be printed. It ignores the different types of beers such as lagers and ales, dark and pale, diet and regular etc. It also ignores the various subjects of books or titles of books. Aggregate plans and master production schedule bridge the gap between strategic capacity plans and operational details.

The demand is assumed to be fluctuating, uncertain or seasonal. There is a possibility of changing both the demand and supply variables. Demand is modified by pricing, advertising and promotion, backlog or reservations, development of complementary products. Backlog means the customers will be asked to wait for their orders. Reservations mean reserving capacity in advance. Supply is modified by hiring and layoff of employees, using over-time and under-time, using part-time or temporary labour, carrying inventory, sub-contracting and making co-operative arrangements.

An organisation has to choose amongst the three basic strategies:

- **Produce at a constant rate:** The rate of regular output will be constant. Since the output is constant and demand is variable, the differences are met by using inventories, over-time, temporary workers, sub-contracting, customer's queues or similar arrangements.
- **Chase demand:** Here the workforce level is changed to meet the demand. That makes the production and demand equal. The workforce absorbs all the changes in demand.
- **Mixed policy:** it is a combination of the above two policies. There are some changes in production rate, but not every period. It aims at a fairly stable production, but leaving room for some changes. In practice, mixed strategy is extensively used.

The following table illustrates how costing of a typical aggregate planning is done.

AGGREGATE PLANNING COSTING

Months	*Jan.*	*Feb.*	*Mar.*	*Apr.*	*May.*	*June*	*Jul.*	*Aug.*	*Sept.*	*Oct.*	*Nov.*	*Dec.*
Resources Regular workers Overtime percentage Units produced Sales forecast Closing inventory (month end)												
Costs Regular time Overtime Hire/layoff Inventory carrying												
Total costs												

Methods of Designing Aggregate Plans

There are several methods to design aggregate plans.

Intuitive Approach: Here plans are extended from the previous plans, say last month's production would lead to next month's production and so on. It to convenient and easy to design plans this way. Experienced managers are put to design such plans.

Graphic Methods: A plan is visualized with the help of a graph. The most widely used methods is to plot cumulative demand over time and then add an aggregate plan as the line of cumulative supply. The cumulative supply line should be nearly straight, thus indicating constant production and as near to the cumulative demand line as possible. This method is easy to comprehend and use.

Expert Systems: Here a series of rules are used to imitate the thinking of a skilled scheduler. If not developed properly, the results are disappointing.

Spreadsheet Calculations: Alternative plans are composed by using spreadsheet calculation. One such format spells out resources (down on the left hand side) and demand (across the bottom). The matrix has two values – cost of using resources and the amount of resources actually used.

Simulations: It is a more formalized approach. It has realistic models of operation – a process is followed for a typical period and its performance is reported. The conditions and parameters are changed. It generates other plans. It is assessed how sensitive they are to the changes. Though a useful method, modelling realistically is difficult.

Mathematical Models: Optimal mathematical models can be used. They are difficult to use and may not present realistic picture of the situation.

Master Production Schedule (MPS)

Whereas the aggregate plan aggregates, the master production schedule **de-aggregates** what is aggregated by showing individual products to be produced, typically each week. It is a detailed time table of planned output for each product. An aggregate plan for shoes might show 10000 pairs of shoes being made next month, whereas the master production schedule gives the details of the sizes and colours of these pairs each week, say week one and two and so on. It is derived directly from the aggregate plan. Some variations may be due to incorrect forecasts and capacity constraints. Some orders may already have been received, and this must be factored in. Current stock-levels are considered as some demand can be met through it. MPS is more detailed down to the individual customer orders. It makes planning difficult and it tends to be subjective. Experienced schedulers design the MPS. The planning occurs in cycles, and so there is scope for modification of the previous schedules so as to draw up the new ones. It is an iterative approach. The plans are adjusted continually till they become accepted. It happens 3 weeks before the implementation of schedule. The consequent plan is used for scheduling other operations. It, therefore, must be frozen, at some stage and no changes are allowed. At this stage, schedulers design detailed time-tables for people, equipment, raw materials and other resources.

Gantt Charting

Gantt chart as a scheduling method has been used since 1917. It was put forward by Henry L. Gantt. Though several versions of the Gantt chart are in vogue, we shall discuss here its application to the batch facility scheduling problem. In the Gantt chart, the time is shown across the top and a scare resource (such as machines or people) along the side. In our illustration, we have taken machines as the scarce resource to be scheduled.

Illustration

There is a work-shop with three work-centres — A, B and C consisting of one machine each and five jobs (1, 2, 3, 4, and 5) are to be scheduled. The processing time of each job in each work centre is shown in Fig. 7.3. For instance job 2 is processed for 3 hours in work-shop B followed by 1 hour in C, and four hours in A.

Job	Work centre/Machine hours	Due date
1	A/2, B/4, C/3	3
2	B/3, C/1, A/4	2
3	C/2, B/3, A/2	4
4	B/4, A/3, C/6	4
5	A/2, B/1, C/2	2

Fig. 7.3 **Job Data for Scheduling**

The jobs are scheduled forward in time in finite capacity of one machine of each type – A, B and C. We assume arbitrarily that jobs are scheduled in the sequence 1,2,3,4 and 5.

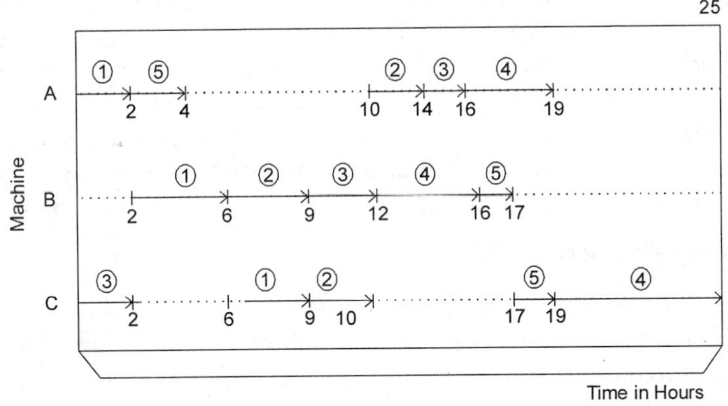

Fig. 7.4 **GANTT Chart jobs are sequenced in the order 1,2,3,4,5**

Machine	idle (hr)
A	12
B	10
C	11
	33
Make span = 25 hr	

Job time (hr)	Job waiting time (hr)	Delivery
1	0	9
2	6	14
3	0	7
4	12	25
5	2	7

Fig. 7.5

The Gantt chart resulting from the above data is presented as Fig. 7.4. This chart is constructed by scheduling job 1 on all three machines. Job 1 starts on machine A for two hours, then it is placed on machine B for four hours (from time 2 to 6) and finally it is placed on machine C for three hours (from time 6 to time 9). There is no waiting time for the first job scheduled. Next job 2 is scheduled on Gantt Chart for machines B, C and A. Job 2 can begin on machine B after 6 hours of waiting time from 6 to 9. It will be placed on machine C from 9 to 10 and on machine A from 10 to 14. Next Job 3 is scheduled on Gantt chart on machine C, B and A. It can start on machine C immediately. Machine B is already scheduled till time 9 and hence job 3 is scheduled from time 9 to 12. Machine A is busy till time 14 and so job three is scheduled from 14 to 16. This process of scheduling is continued till all the jobs are placed in the Gantt Chart.

After the construction of the Gantt Chart, it should be evaluated in terms of both the job and machine performance. Machine performance is given by the *make span* — the time it takes to complete all the work. In Fig. 7.5 the make span is 25 hours since it takes 25 hours to complete all the five jobs.

Another measure of evaluation is *machine utilization*. In Fig. 7.5, we add up the idle time for each machine (12+10+11) and that enables the computation of utilization or idle percentage. The idle time percentage is 33/75 = 44 per cent and the utilization percentage is 42/75 = 56 per cent. It is to be noted that utilization is closely related to the make span. In five jobs a total of 42 hours of processing time is required (add up machine time for all jobs from Fig. 7.5. The 42 hours of processing time is a constant regardless of the schedule used. It is to be noted that idle time = 3 [make span] – 42). Therefore, minimizing make span would also minimize machine idle time.

Job performance is measured in terms of the summation of the delivery time for each job. When we minimize the delivery time, it amounts to minimization of the total job waiting time. These two are complementary. In Fig. 7.5 both these times have been spelled out. These figures are drawn directly from the Gantt Chart. These timings are the result of the job sequence followed. As job 1 was scheduled first, it has no waiting time and is completed at the earliest. It got completed ahead of the due date. Job 2 which was sequenced later has a waiting time of 6 hours. Job 4 has considerable waiting time.

In general, the waiting times of jobs and machine utilization are dependent on the job sequencing. In our example, we have 5 jobs to schedule and the possible job sequences are 5! (five factorial) = 120. In order to determine the job sequence with minimum make span, or minimum total job waiting time, we will have to construct 120 Gantt Charts. The optimal sequence can be found by having all possible sequences which are equal to n! for n jobs This enumeration is not practical even with the help of a computer. In production management literature, optimal job algorithms have been developed to find an optimal solution by bypassing the necessity of enumerating all possible job sequences. These algorithms attempt to optimize one or more measures of schedule performance such as make span. They are governed by assumptions such as constant processing time, no passing of jobs, no job splitting and so on. One particular problem is called the **m x n machine scheduling problems**.

m x n Machine Scheduling Problem

Production scheduling involves resource allocation pertaining to the start and finish time of tasks. In this, various jobs are scheduled on a set of resources (machines) so as to optimize performance. m x n machine scheduling problem has *m* number of machines and *n* number of jobs. The m x n machine scheduling problem is solved for m = 1, 2 and 3 and arbitrary values of *n*. Efficient optimal algorithms have been developed for m < 3, as beyond this the possible sequence are far too many. However, heuristics offer good solutions for any values of *m* and *n*.

n jobs, One Machine Situation

This is the simplest m x n machine problem. Here there is a single machine and several jobs. Here the makespan and utilization are kept constant since several jobs are to be processed on a single machine. Makespan equals the sum of the processing times. Machine utilization is hundred per cent. We can minimize the sum of delivery dates (di) or the job waiting times (W_i). The rule used is the shortest possible time first to get the work done as soon as possible. We are reducing thereby the waiting time for other jobs. Thus *n* job one machine situation demands optimization of mean flow time.

The basic data necessary to describe jobs in a deterministic single machine scheduling problem.

- Processing time (t_i)
- Waiting time (W_i)
- Flow time (F_i)
- Competition time (C_i)
- Due delivery data (d_i)
- Lateness (L_i)
- Tardiness (T_i)*
- Ready time (r_i)
- Completion time (C_i)

Measure of Performance

Mean flow time = $\bar{F} = \frac{1}{n}\sum_{i=1}^{n} F_i$

Mean tardiness = $\bar{T} = \frac{1}{n}\sum_{i=1}^{n} T_i$

Shortest Processing Time (SPT) Rule to Minimize Mean Flow Time

In single-machine processing problem, jobs are sequenced in increasing order of processing time *i.e.,* one which takes the least time is taken first followed by one with the next smallest possible time. This sequencing is called SPT and it minimizes the mean flow time.

Illustration

Let us assume that there are four jobs to be scheduled on a single machine with the following processing times.

Table 7.1 **Processing Times**

Job i	*Processing time t_i*
1	3
2	6
3	2
4	1

Find the optimal sequence which will minimize the mean flow time and also obtain the corresponding minimum mean flow time.

Solution

For the above problem, these four jobs are arranged as per SPT ordering in the sequence of D, C, A, B, as follows.

Table 7.2 **Data as per SPT Ordering**

Job i	*Processing time t_i*
4	1
3	2
1	3
2	6

* Tardiness is the lateness of job if it fails to meet its due date. Otherwise, it is zero.

Computation of Optimal $\bar{F}$. The computation of flow time for the optimal sequence (4,3,1,2) are presented in the table below.

Table 7.3

Computation of Flow Time

Job i	*Processing time t_i*	*Competition time C_i (F_i)*
4	1	1
3	2	3
1	3	6
2	6	12

Since ready time (the time at which job is available for processing) in the basic model is zero for all values of *i* the flow time (*i*) = C_i for all *i*. Therefore,

$$\bar{F} = \frac{1}{4}\sum_{i=1}^{n} F_i$$

$$= \frac{1}{4}(1 + 3 + 6 + 12)$$

$$= \frac{1}{4}(22)$$

= 5.5 hours.

Therefore, the optimal mean flow time is 5.5 hours.

Weighted Shortest Processing Time (WSPT) Rule to Minimize Weighted Mean Flow Time

SPT is slightly modified by assigning weightages to the jobs as per their importance. The weight assigned is W_i. The mean time that is computed after incorporating W_i is called Weighted Mean Flow Time (WMFT). It is given by

$$\bar{F}_w = \frac{\sum_{i=1}^{n} W_i F_i}{\sum_{i=1}^{n} W_i}$$

While applying WSPT (Weighted Shortest Processing Time) Rule, n jobs are sequenced such that

$$\frac{t_{[1]}}{W_{[1]}} \le \frac{t_{[2]}}{W_{[2]}} \le \ldots \le \frac{t_{[n]}}{W_{[n]}}$$

where bracketed figures refer to the position of the job in the optimal sequence.

Illustration

Consider the following example with the additional data on weights assigned to different jobs as shown in the following table:

Table 7.4

Data

Job i	*Processing time t_i*	*Weight W_i*
1	2	1
2	6	2
3	12	3
4	1	1

Solution

The weighted processing time of the various jobs are summarized in the table below by using the formula t_i/w_i, j = A, B, C and D.

Job i	*Processing time* t_i	*Weight* w_i	T_i/W_i
1	2	1	2
2	6	2	3
3	12	3	4
4	1	1	1

Table 7.5
Details of Weighted Processing Time

Next the jobs are arranged in the increasing order of t_i/w_i (WSPT ordering). From the above table we can verify the following equation:

$$\frac{t_4}{w_4} \le \frac{t_1}{W_1} \le \frac{t_2}{W_2} \le \frac{t_3}{W_3}$$

Therefore, the optimal sequence which minimizes the WMFL is 4-1-2-3.

$\bar{F}_w$ Calculation

The details of WMFT calculations of the various jobs with respect to optimal sequence are given below:

Job i	*Processing time* t_i	*Ct* (F_i)	*Weight* w_i	$F_i\ W_i$
4	1	1	1	1
1	2	3	1	3
2	6	9	2	18
3	12	21	3	63

Table 7.6
Calculations of WMFT

Therefore,

$$\bar{F}_w = \frac{\sum_{i=1}^{4} W_i F_i}{\sum_{i=1}^{4} W_i} = \frac{1+3+18+63}{1+1+2+3} = 12.14 \text{ hours.}$$

Therefore, here WMFT is 12.14 hours

Processing with Due Dates

SPT discussed above minimizes the mean lateness of the jobs. The *lateness* of a job is defined as the difference between the completion time and due date of that job.

$L_i = C_i - d_i$

The earliest due date (EDD) rule states that the jobs are sequenced in order of increasing due dates. This helps in reducing maximum job lateness Lmax as well as maximum job tardiness.

N Jobs Two Machines Situation

This problem follows Johnson's Algorithm. Suppose *n* jobs are to be processed on two machines M_1 and later on M_2. The processing time of all jobs on both the machines are known. The minimum time to complete all jobs require a particular sequencing. The algorithm has the following steps:

(*a*) Jot down processing time of all jobs on M_1 and M_2.

(*b*) Assess the minimum processing time.

(*c*) If the minimum processing time is on M_1, place the corresponding job in the first available position (as early as possible in the sequence). If the minimum processing time is on Machine 2, place the associated job in the last available position (as late as possible in the sequence).

(*d*) Delete jobs already assigned (as a result of step c). Keep on repeating *b* and *c* till all the jobs are sequenced. Ties while applying step *c* may be broken randomly.

Johnson's Algorithm can be extended to *n* Jobs and Three Machines.

n Jobs and *m* Machines Situation

n Jobs m Machines situation can be addressed by branch-and-bound method and graphical method. Branch-and-bound method means curtailed enumeration techniques. Branching is the process of partitioning a large problem into two or more sub-problems and bounding is the process of calculating a lower bound on the optimal solution of a given sub-problem. A branch-and-bound method for a generalized *n* jobs and *m* machines was developed by Ignall and Scharge.

In the graphical method, we consider two jobs to be processed on m machines. The optimal sequencing so as to minimize the total processing time is derived graphically where

(*i*) On *x*-axis, processing time and sequencing of job 1 on machines are plotted.

(*ii*) On *y*-axis, job 2 is plotted. The scale is kept the same for both the jobs.

(*iii*) When a machines would be occupied by two jobs simultaneously, the region in the graph is shaded.

(*iv*) The processing of both the jobs is given by a continuous path having horizontal, vertical and diagonal segments. Diagonal lines are inclined at 45 degree. The line is drawn from the origin and continued to the upper-right corner by avoiding the shaded region. Diagonal segment means concurrent processing of the jobs. Vertical line means that job 1 keeps idle. Horizontal line means that job 2 keeps idle. Feasible path maximizes the diagonal movement and minimizes the makespan or total processing time.

We have to use the trial-and-error method to decide the optimal path — to draw the final line which has the maximum diagonal portion.

Two Jobs and *m* Machines Job Shop Scheduling

Two jobs and *m* machines problem is special kind of problem under Job Shop Scheduling. In this problem, we are to process two jobs, which require processing on *m* machines. The sequence in which the machines are required may not necessarily be the same. For example, the first job may require the machines in the order A,B and C, whereas the second job may require them in the order C,A and B. At times, it may happen that both the jobs require the same machine. So, we have to decide which job should be allowed to occupy the machine. Our aim would be optimize the processing time. So, to get the optimum schedule that corresponds to the optimal processing time, we use a graphical procedure as described below.

The graphical method contains the following steps:

Step 1: Construct a two-dimensional graph in which the X-axis represents the processing time of job 1, and the sequence of operations performed, and the Y-axis represents the processing time of job 2, and the sequence of operations performed.

Step 2: We shade or indicate the region where each machine is occupied by jobs simultaneously.

Step 3: The processing of jobs is shown by a horizontal, vertical and diagonal line (line inclined at 45 degrees to the horizontal). A line is drawn starting from the origin till the upper-right end corner, while avoiding the shaded regions. A horizontal or vertical line indicates that only one job is being processed. On the other hand, a diagonal line indicates that both the jobs are being processed. To optimize the processing time, we need to maximize the length of the diagonal line. This will minimize the makespan of the problem.

Using trial-and-error method, one can finally draw a line which has maximum diagonal length. This concept is illustrated with the help of an example.

Example

Consider a 'two jobs and *m* machines job shop scheduling' problem which is presented in Table 7.7. Use the graphical method to minimize the time needed to process the following jobs on the machines shown (*i.e.* for each machine find the job which should be scheduled first). Also, calculate the total time elapsed to complete both the jobs.

Job 1		Job 2	
Sequence	***Time(hrs)***	***Sequence***	***Time(hrs)***
A	2	C	6
B	6	B	5
C	5	D	7
D	4	A	4
E	7	E	8

Table 7.7

Sequence of Operations

Solution

As per the given procedure, the data presented in the above table is first represented visually in the form of a graph as shown in Fig. 7.6. The line from the origin to the upper-right end corner is shown in dark-gray. It indicates the makespan. The start and completion times of both the jobs are given in Table 7.8.

Based on the figure and the table, one can easily observe that the total idle time for Job 1 is 12 hours. Hence, the total time for completing Job 1 is its sum of processing times plus its idle time, that is

24 + 12 = 36 hours.

For Job 2, the idle time is 6 hours (2 + 4). Hence, the total time taken for completing the Job 2 is its own processing time plus its idle time, that is

30 + 6 = 36 hours.

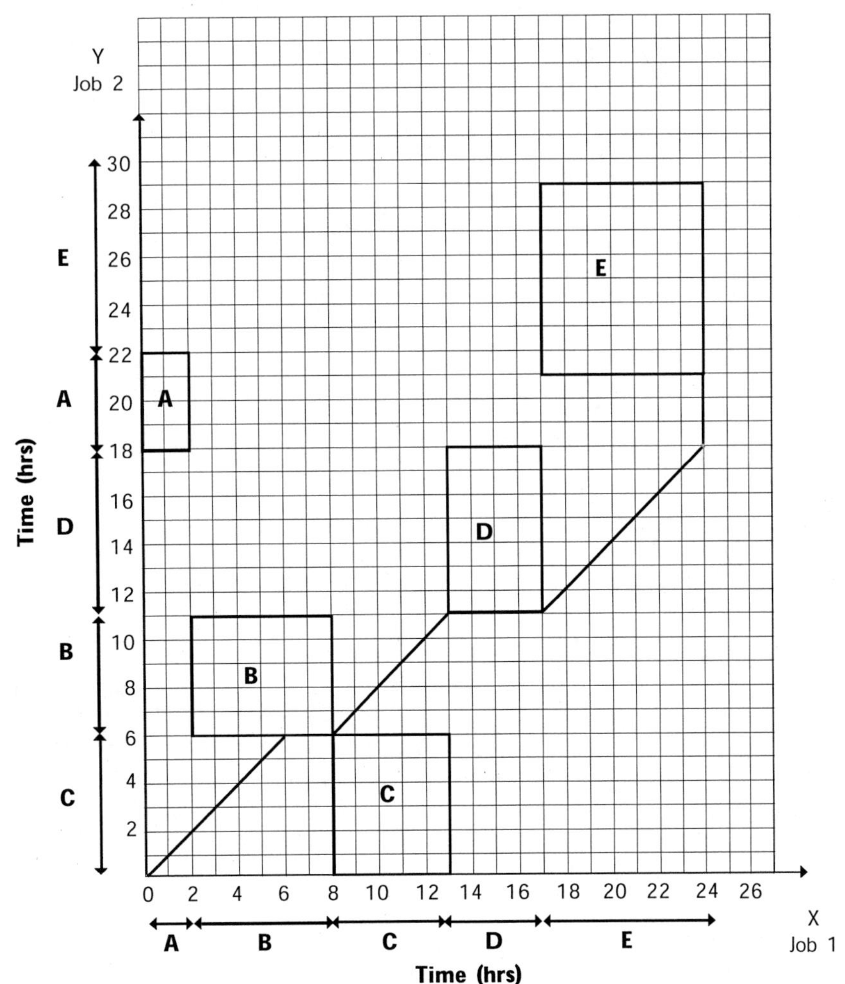

Fig 7.6

Graphical representation for the above example

The makespan is the maximum of these two quantities. That is,

$$\text{Max}(36, 36) = 36 \text{ hours.}$$

Therefore, the makespan (time taken to complete both the jobs) of the given problem is 36 hours.

Table 7.8 **Start and Completion Times of Jobs**

	Time for Job 1			*Time for Job 2*	
Machine	***Start***	***End***	***Machine***	***Start***	***End***
A	0	2	C	0	6
B	2	8	B	8	13
C	8	13	D	17	24
D	13	17	A	24	28
E	17	24	E	28	36

CAPACITY EXPANSION

Bharat Heavy Electricals Ltd. (BHEL) is the largest power equipment manufacturer in the country. It keeps on increasing its capacity to take care of the increased demand. Its current capacity is 15000 mw. This is flexible, and they can exceed it also. They can also outsource some of their work. In 2010, they are going to deliver 17,000 mw of equipment as against the capacity of 15000 mw. Beyond that, they are taking action to increase their capacity to 20,000 mw by March, 2012. As they move forward, they see the expansion in the market, and for that they need to ramp up their capacity continuously.

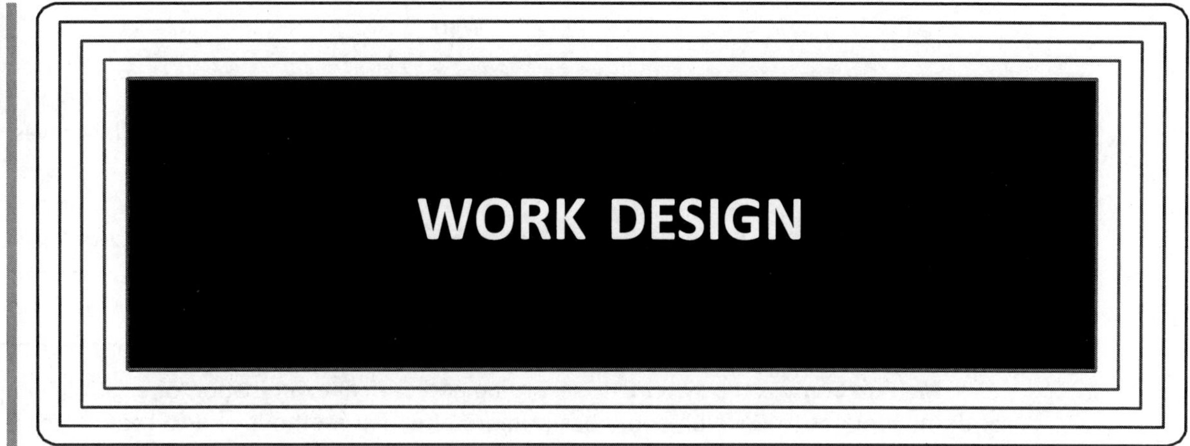

8 WORK DESIGN

Introduction

Work is the basic source of our livelihood. It also nourishes the human personality. We regard work differently at different points of time. Our attitude towards work changes from time to time, and is different from culture to culture. Perhaps these days in advanced societies, work has lost the central position it used to occupy in human life, thanks to other cultural, social, aesthetic and leisure pursuits. In India, however, work still is in the centre-stage, and, there is talk of making the right to work a fundamental constitutional right. Work systems set boundaries to what must be managed. Work systems result from people-machines interface or technical competence and equipment interface. This interface is in an organizational context to achieve certain objectives. **Work Design** is the study and design of a work system in an organizational context. Work to begin with, was considered in technological terms. Social scientists later modified the concept in favour of a behavioural angle. Technologically, work is viewed as tools, techniques and methods used for production of finished goods. The economic concept of work is associated with wages and employment. Work design seeks to increase productivity by seeking better and less expensive ways to perform the functions/tasks. Benefits of improved productivity are available to employees, managers, shareholders, consumers and people at large.

We assume in a production unit work exists and so do the work problems originating at individual work stations. The man-material-machine combination is the focus of any work problem. This is a part of the entire organization/work system. Work system is sub-system of a larger super system. Work systems mostly are open, and there are actions-reactions in them, depending upon the values associated with the work systems. Moreover, there is the work method which is important for Work Design. Work design is a systematic investigation of desired and present work systems to get the ideal work systems and methods.

Assumptions of Work Design

1. Work systems try to improve productivity and effectiveness.
2. Work systems are in the three states — design, betterment, improvement.
3. Work design considers all aspects of the work system.
4. Work design integrates abilities and talents.

Work design goes beyond a set of techniques, since work systems need continuous monitoring. A system is a collection of parts that form a whole. The objectives could be increased productivity and higher effectiveness. Work study is one of the techniques of enhancing productivity. Work study should be applied properly with due support from employees and management to enhance productivity. Work study guides us about how the jobs should be done and how long they should take.

Work Study Approach

Work study can be diagrammatically presented as follows:

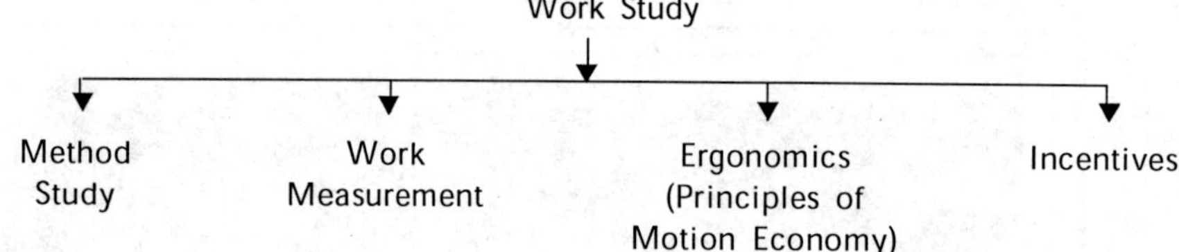

Work Study is defined as a technique that embraces method study and work measurement which are employed to ensure the best possible use of human and material resources in carrying out the specified activity.

The main objective of WS is to improve productivity of men, machines and materials.

Method Study is the systematic recording and critical examination of existing and proposed ways of doing work as to develop/apply easier/more effective methods and to reduce costs. It investigates how jobs are done and how the method of doing them can be improved.

Work Measurement is the application of techniques designed to establish the time for a qualified worker to carry out a specified job at a defined level of performance. It tries to estimate how long jobs should take once the method is decided.

Both the above concepts — Method Study and Work Measurement — are closely linked. The former intends to reduce the work-content, and the latter establishes time standards on the basis of work-content as determined by the former. Generally, a method study precedes work measurement. In some instances, time standards do indicate occurrence of ineffective time in work sampling for corrective action in anticipation of method study. Time study also enables comparison of alternative methods.

Purpose of Work Study

The objective of work study is to assist management to obtain the optimum use of the human and material resources available to an organization for the accomplishment of the work upon which it is engaged.

Fundamentally, this objective has 3 aspects:

1. The most effective use of plant and equipment.
2. The most effective use of human effort.
3. The evaluation of human work.

Work study is one of the major techniques in the group called as *"Productivity Science."* The other techniques are Organization and Methods, Operational Research, Network Analysis, Systems Analysis, Ergonomics and Value Engineering.

The function of work study is to obtain facts, and then to use those facts as a means of improvement. It may be regarded principally as a procedure for determining the truth about the activities of existing people and existing plant and equipment as a means to the improvement of these activities. It will provide the means of achieving higher productive efficiency under prevailing circumstances.

Definition

Work study, as the name implies, is the study of work of human work in the deepest sense and dignity of the word, and not merely in the special and more restricted meaning used in the physical sciences.

Work study is neither limited to the shop-floor, nor to manufacturing industry, it can be used in any situation where human work is performed.

The term "work study" as defined by British Glossary is:

"A management service based on those techniques, particularly method study a work measurement, which are used in the examination of human work in all its contexts and which lead to the systematic investigation of all the resources and factors which affects the efficiency and economy of the situation being reviewed in order to effect improvement."

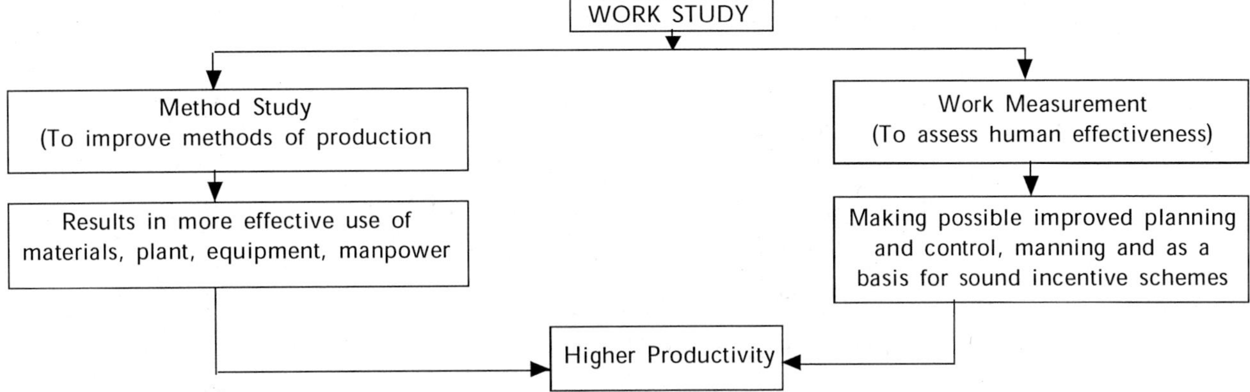

Method study as defined by British standard is:

"The systematic recording and critical examination of the factors and resources involved in existing and proposed ways of doing work, as a means of developing and applying easier and more effective methods and reducing costs."

Work Measurement is defined as:

"The application of techniques designed to establish the time for a qualified worker to carry out a specified job at a defined level of performance."

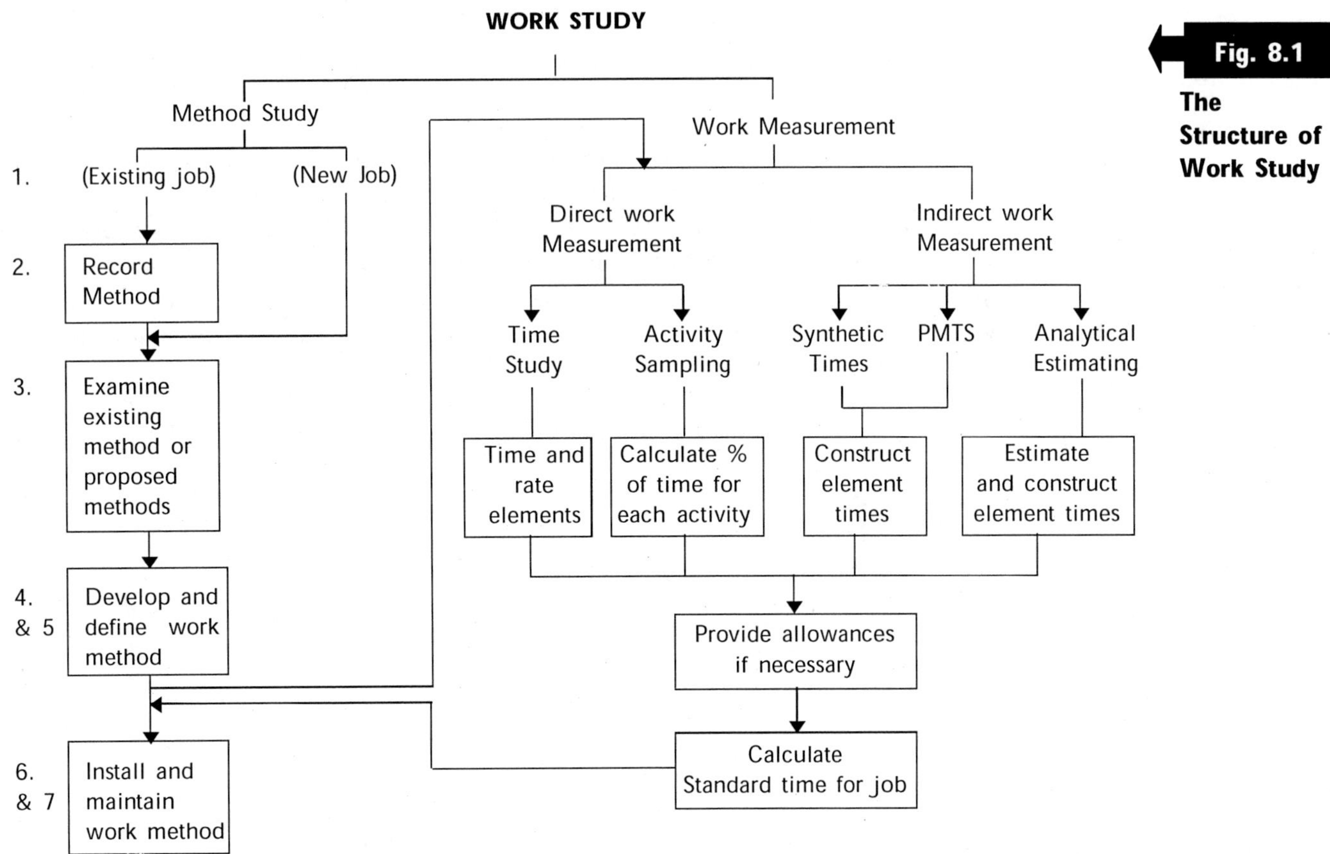

Fig. 8.1 The Structure of Work Study

Basic Work Study Procedure

WS consists of eight basic steps, some of which are common to both method study (MS) and work measurement (WM).

Sr. No.	Basic Step	MS	WM
1.	Select	✓	✓
2.	Record	✓	✓
3.	Examine	✓	✓
4.	Develop	✓	—
5.	Measure	—	✓
6.	Define	—	✓
7.	Install	✓	—
8.	Maintain	✓	—

Thus, Method Study (MS) has six steps:

1. SELECT the job to be studied.
2. RECORD how it is performed right now.
3. EXAMINE the existing method critically.
4. DEVELOP an improved method.
5. INSTALL the improved method.
6. MAINTAIN it in practice.

The acronym SREDIM will help you to remember the steps.

To conduct MS, we should have conducive human relations climate, top management support, supervisory co-operation. WS, if properly applied, tends to improve industrial relations. WS should not be conducted amidst an atmosphere of distrust. Skilled seniors may resist changes. WS results may render some workers redundant, leading to retrenchment/redeployment/ transfer. In developing countries, this causes the greatest anxiety. In the long run, however, the technique benefits all. WS is to be conducted by a properly qualified person, who can win confidence of both the supervisors and the workers. He should be able to deal with people. WS results are to be applied with tact.

Let us now examine MS, focusing our attention on those steps which improve effectiveness and productivity. We shall postpone the discussion of technicalities like physical environment, therbligs, motion economy etc. to a subsequent chapter.

METHOD STUDY

Diagrammatically, the Method Study (MS) procedure is illustrated hereunder:

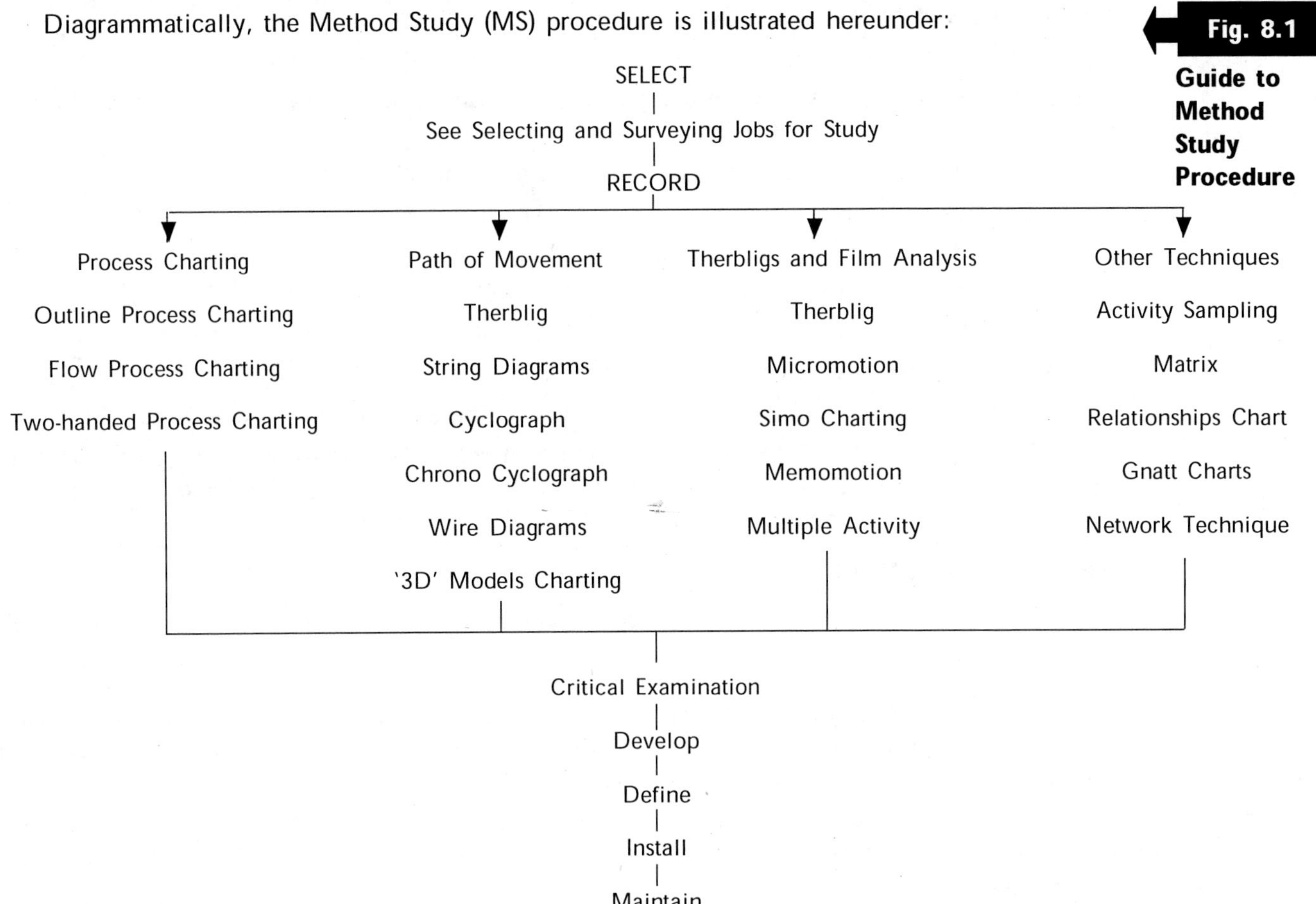

Fig. 8.1 **Guide to Method Study Procedure**

Introduction

There is always an improvement possible in a process.

Method study involves the breakdown of an operation into its component elements and the elements are analysed.

The Method Study Men should have

1. The desire and the determination to produce results.
2. The ability to produce results.
3. An understanding of the human factors involved.

Factors to be Considered while having Method Study

(*i*) Economic considerations

(*ii*) Technical considerations

(*iii*) Human reactions.

Analytically, method study involves basic procedure of SELECT — RECORD — EXAMINE — DEVELOP — INSTALL — MAINTAIN, sequence.

— The merit of the basic procedure is that, whatever be the job or its size, it can be approached and dealt with on a common pattern.

— The RECORD step is an important step and should be carried out with accuracy, because further study depends on the recorded data. If the recorded step is inaccurate, the whole process of critical examination and developed method may fail.

— The critical examination is the heart of the method study procedure.

Examination makes a systematic analysis of the purpose, place, sequence, person and means involved at every stage of the operation.

The following questions are considered for the examination step:

(*i*) (*a*) What (is achieved)? (*b*) Why (is it necessary)?

(*ii*) (*a*) How (is it done)? (*b*) Why (that ways)?

(*iii*) (*a*) Where (is it done)? (*b*) Why (there)?

(*iv*) (*a*) When (is it done)? (*b*) Why (then)?

(*v*) (*a*) By whom (is it done)? (*b*) Why (that person)?

The answer to the question why? leads to the consideration of other alternatives.

In this way methods will be adopted that are completely assured to be not only economically sound and technically correct, but are based on sound physiological and psychological principles and above all make a positive contribution to the value of the produce.

Method Study Objectives

The first step in carrying out a work study is the method study of the work under consideration.

Definition

Method Study is the systematic recording, analysis, and critical examination of the methods and movements involved in the performance of existing or proposed ways of doing work, as a means of developing easier and more productive methods.

Method study is essentially concerned with finding better ways of doing things, and it contributes to improved efficiency by getting rid of unnecessary work, avoidable delays and other forms of waste. **This is achieved through:**

(*a*) Improved layout and design of factory, plant and workplace, (*b*) Improved working procedures, (*c*) Improved use of material, plant and equipment and manpower, (*d*) Improved working environment, (*e*) Improved design or specification of the end product.

The Techniques of Method Study aim at doing three things

(1) To reveal and analyse the true facts concerning the situation, (2) To examine those facts critically, (3) To develop from the examination of the facts the best answer possible under the circumstances.

[The value of method study is due to the flexibility with which the technique may be used in different situations].

Basic Procedure

There is a simple framework for application in any circumstances.

SELECT: The work to be studied.

RECORD: All the relevant facts of the present (or proposed) method.

EXAMINE: Those facts critically and in sequence systematically.

DEVELOP: The most practical, economic and effective method having due regard to all contingent circumstances.

INSTALL: That method as standard practice.

MAINTAIN: That standard practice by regular routine checks.

The Function of Method Study

Method study does not replace the ability to make the best use of available information, the inventive genius or the organizing ability necessary to develop new methods. What the analytical approach of method study does, by its carefully planned sequence of analysis, **is to show where change is likely to be most effective by highlighting unnecessary activities and showing where improvements are possible.**

In this way thoughts are directed into channels likely to be profitable, and any inherent flair for improvements the members of the work study team may possess stands the best chance of finding full expression. **Thus, method study enables the ordinary man to improve methods and at the same time avoid the dangers of taking 'short cuts.'**

(1) Selecting Jobs for Study

Cost is the usual basis for the selection of operations, sections or departments likely to benefit from method study. **The following defects in an organization indicate where method study is likely to bring worthwhile savings:**

1. Poor use of materials, labour or machine capacity, resulting in high scrap and reprocessing costs.
2. Bad layout or operation planning, resulting in unnecessary movement of materials.
3. Existence of bottlenecks. Work begins to pile up.
4. Inconsistencies in quality.
5. Highly fatiguing work.
6. Employees' complaints about their work without logical reasons. Labour discontent.
7. Workload is unevenly distributed. Some workers are over-burdened, and get excessive over-time and some are under-loaded with a lot of spare time.
8. Areas of high accident rate.
9. Bad quality of work.

The question is whether a change is likely to achieve the following results sufficiently to make the cost of the study worthwhile:

1. Increase production and reduce costs.
2. Maintain it with less labour, materials or equipment.
3. Improve quality without additional labour or equipment.
4. Improve safety conditions.
5. Improve standards of cleanliness and house-keeping.
6. Reduce scrap.

When all these matters have been weighed up in the light of the economic importance of a task and its expected life, the manager should be able to select the work to be investigated.

The manager should also list the objectives for the study in order of priority. (Danger of going too far and carrying the study to uneconomic limits must be avoided).

Both in selecting objectives on the larger scale [*e.g.*, a whole company or plant] and in choosing the economically appropriate methods, mathematical techniques like "Operational Research" are used hand in hand with method study.

Once a job is selected for method study, we have to make an official record of:

(*i*) The name of the job to be investigated.

(*ii*) Objectives of this investigation.

(*iii*) Accountability for this investigation.

(*iv*) Resources available for this investigation.

(*v*) Person authorising the investigation.

Having selected the job and getting it approved for method study, we should communicate this to all concerned outlining the logic behind the study. Method Study becomes successful if everyone involved extends to it the necessary co-operation.

(2) The Need for Records

In order that the activities selected for investigations may be visualised in the entirety, with a view to improving them by subsequent critical analysis, it is essential to have means of placing on record all the necessary facts of the existing method.

A record is also essential if a before-and-after comparison is to be made to assess the effectiveness of the investigation and the subsequent installation of the new method.

It is tedious and costly to jot down every small detail about a particular job. It is, therefore, convenient to use charts and phonographic or electronic methods of recording.

Recording Techniques

According to the nature of the job being studied, and the purpose for which the record is required, the technique chosen will fall into the following categories:

1. Charts (for process and time records)
2. Diagrams and models (for path of movement records)

Charts

Charts are often used to record the facts due to their simplicity and economy.

1. Outline process chart — principal operations and inspections.
2. Flow process chart — activities of men, materials or equipment.
3. Two handed process chart — activities of worker's two hands.
4. Multiple activity chart — activities of men and/or machine on a common time scale.
5. Simultaneous motion cycle (simo) chart — activities of a worker's hands, legs and other body movements on a common time scale.
6. Travel chart — movements of materials between departments.

Diagrams & Models

1. Flow and string diagrams — path of movement of men, materials or equipment.
2. Two and three dimensional models — layout of workplace or plant.
3. Cycle graphs and Chrono cycle graphs — high speed, short cycle operations.

Whatever type of chart or diagram is prepared, great care should be taken to ensure that the information it portrays is easily understood and recognised. **The following information should always be provided:**

1. An adequate description of all the activities or movements entailed in the method.
2. Whether the present or proposed method is shown.
3. The specific reference to where activities begin and end.
4. The time and distance scales used, where applicable.
5. An explanation of any abbreviations or special devices.
6. The date of construction of the chart or diagram.

Process Charting

Process Charts

All process charts are recording procedures. In these charts, the sequence of events is represented by a series of symbols. The symbols used are:

○ Operation

⇨ Transportation

□ Inspection

▽ Storage

D Delay

An *outline process chart* records the main parts of the process, say operations and inspections. It is a preliminary step. A *flow of process chart* may be concerned with either *materials* or *workers* or both. In a sense, it is amplification of the outline process chart and shows, apart from operations and inspections, *transportations, storages* and *delays.* A *two-handed process chart* or *operator process* chart is the most detailed version of the flow process chart. It records the activities of the worker's hands in operation to one another. It is combined to activity carried out at a single place. Inspection symbol is omitted in this chart, as it is represented by movements of the hands, and storage symbol is now taken to mean *hold.*

The job or process under investigation often consists of a number of activities. It is with a view to listing them conveniently, we use symbols as a short-hand.

The modern system of process charting is an adaptation of one of Gilbreth's later developments in motion study technique. Originally Gilbreth used a large number of symbols, 'as a device for visualising a procedure as a means of improving it.' Later, in 1947, the American Society of Mechanical Engineers reduced the number of symbols and standardised the technique to its present form. The British definitions are as follows:

Process Charts: Charts in which a sequence of events is portrayed diagrammatically by means of a set of process chart symbols to help a person to visualise a process as a means of examining and improving it. We can devise our own symbols. However, we follow standardised symbols developed by A.S.M.E. since 1947.

Process Chart Symbols

Symbols used for recording the nature of events.

Operation	○	Indicates the main steps in the process, method, or procedure. Usually the part, material, or product concerned is modified or changed during the operation.
Transport	⇨	Indicates the movement of workers, materials or equipment from place to place.
Permanent	▽	Indicates a controlled storage in which material is received into or issued from a store under some form of authorization, or an item is retained for reference purposes.
Temporary Storage or Delay	D	Indicates a delay in the sequence of events, for example, work waiting between consecutive operations, or any object laid aside temporarily without record until required.

Inspection ☐ Indicates an inspection for quality and/or a check for quantity. (This covers measuring, weighing or looking for some aspect of quality).

Combined ☐ Combined activity occurs simultaneously. Various combinations are possible.

Activity ⇨ Combined activities can be shown by superimposing their respective symbols so that the outer symbol represents the major activity.

Types of Process Charts

Outline Process Chart (Operation Process Chart): It gives the bird's eye-view of the whole process by recording in sequence only the main **operations** and **inspections**. It, therefore, **uses only operations and inspection symbols.**

Fig. 8.2 gives an example of outline process chart.

Specify

1. Type of chart.
2. Job concerned and whether it is the present or proposed method.
3. Date of study and name of observer.
4. Where chart begins and ends.

Include

5. Adequate and accurate description of all activities on the right-hand side of the symbol concerned.
6. Number each activity for identification purposes by placing the number within the symbol. The convention for doing this is implied by the chart.
   (*a*) Each class of symbol is numbered in its own sequence.
   (*b*) Numbering begins on the main line of activities which is always placed on the right-hand side of the chart.
   (*c*) The numbering sequence continues until there is a junction with a subsidiary line, when it jumps to the top of this subsidiary and proceeds downwards from there. The same convention is applied when meeting all other junctions. When combined symbols are used, the first number applies to the outer symbol.
7. Date concerning time, distance, weight, or quantity are shown on the left-hand side of the symbol it refers to.
8. A summary of activities is shown at the bottom left-hand side of the chart.
9. Use the same scale of breakdown in the analysis of activities so that the comparison of present and proposed methods will not be distorted by appearances.
10. Neatness and clarity in the layout of the chart helps to simplify the process of critical examination.

The outline process chart gives an overall view of a process, from which it can be decided whether a further and more detailed record is needed. It is a graphic representation of the points at which materials are introduced into a process, and of the sequence of all operations and inspections associated with the process.

The chart does not show where work takes place, or who performs it, and since it is concerned only with operations and inspections, only two of the five recording symbols are used.

In the design stage, where it is increasingly the practice to use work study, outline process charts are often used to assist in the layout of plant, and in the design of the product or the machinery for making that product. The charts can be made to record the basic data, which can then be subjected to the complete method study procedure while still on the drawing board. Features in the design of a product which are wasteful of materials or labour can often be eliminated and it is frequently the case that expensive equipment, which otherwise might have been bought, proves unnecessary in the light of the investigation.

RECONDITIONING OF BRAKE SHOES: OUTLINE PROCESS CHART

Fig. 8.2 **Outline Process Chart**

Method: Present | **Location:**

Charted by: Name of the observer | **Chart begins:** Inspection Pit

Date | **Chart Ends:** Road test

RIVETS AND LINING

(4) Requisitioned

(5) Issued

WORN BRAKE SHOE

[1] Inspected on bus

(1) Removed from bus

(2) Cleaned

(3) Worn lining removed

(6) New lining fitted

SUMMARY

(2) Operations

[7] Inspections

RECONDITIONED SHOE

[7] Fitted to bus

[2] Road Tested

Construction of the Chart

A start is made by drawing an arrow to show the entry of the main materials, writing above the line a description of the component, and below the line a description of the condition.

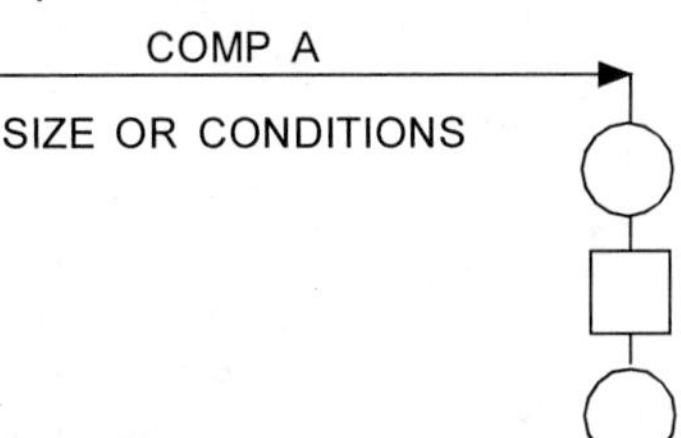

Fig. 8.3

As each operation inspection takes place, the symbol is entered and numbered in sequence, with a brief description to the right and if required, a note of the time taken on the left.

During an assembly process, the major process is charted towards the right hand side of the chart and subsidiary process on to its left. These are joined to each other and to the main trunk at the place of entry of the materials or sub-assembly.

Flow Process Chart

The flow process chart is an **amplification** of the outline process chart, in which it shows transports, delays and storage as well as operations and inspections. It gives a detailed picture of the process by showing all the activities in sequence. It can express the process in terms of the events as they affect the material being processed, or it can express the process in terms of the activities of the man or the use of certain types of equipment.

Flow process charts recording simultaneous activities of two or more subjects can be presented alongside each other on the same sheet of paper to indicate more clearly their interdependence.

It is essential however, that only the activities of the particular subject to which it refers, either man, materials or equipment, are recorded on any single chart.

Construction of the Chart

The conventions used in the construction of the chart and the method of construction are the same as for the outline process chart, except that all five symbols are used. It is usual for distance to be recorded on the left of the symbol for transport in the same way as time can be recorded against operations. The total distance can then be entered at the root of the chart.

Amplifying the Chart

The value of a flow process chart as record may be increased by making full use of colouring and hatching in order to show up some particular aspect of a process. The transport symbol may be used to show movement in one direction or another by altering the way it faces.

When a particular activity extends over a large area covering different workplaces, a clear understanding of what is done at each is obtained if they are separated on the chart. The movement between the sections concerned is also brought out.

Types of Flow Process Charts

(i) Material or Product type records what happens to material or product.

(ii) Man type which records what the worker does.

(iii) Equipment type which records show how the equipment is used.

The following diagram illustrates Material type of Flow Process chart:

Fig. 8.4 Flow Process Chart (Material)

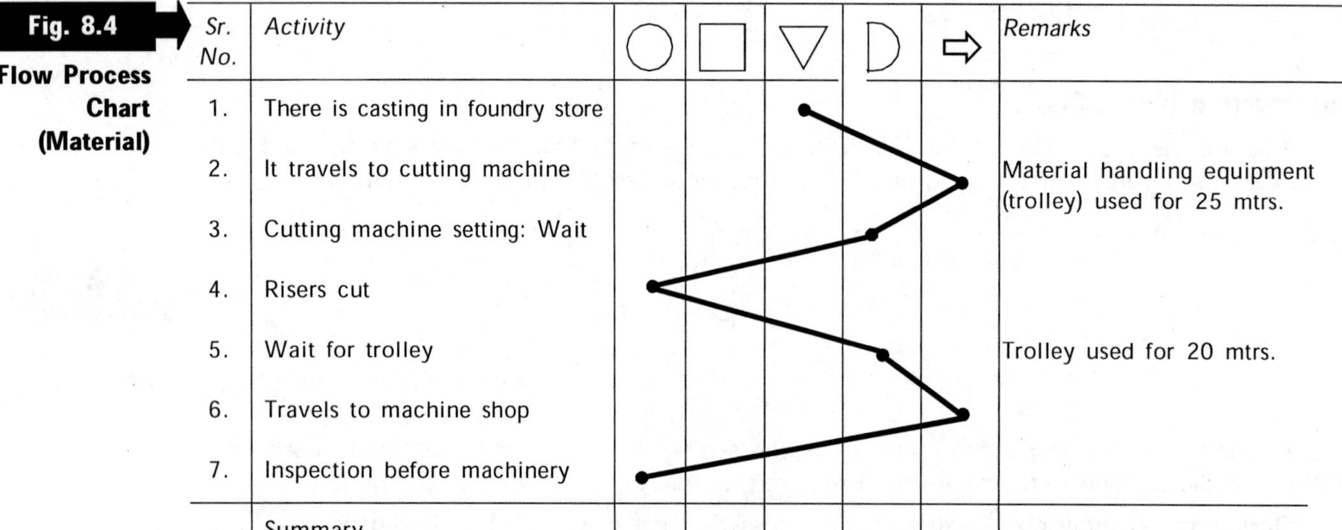

Sr. No.	*Activity*	○	□	▽	D	⇨	*Remarks*
1.	There is casting in foundry store			•			
2.	It travels to cutting machine					•	Material handling equipment (trolley) used for 25 mtrs.
3.	Cutting machine setting: Wait				•		
4.	Risers cut	•					
5.	Wait for trolley				•		Trolley used for 20 mtrs.
6.	Travels to machine shop					•	
7.	Inspection before machinery	•					
	Summary						

Mostly flow process charts are either man/material/equipment type, but there are some combined flow process charts making use of three resources — man, material and equipment.

One more process chart is used in Organization and Methods (O & M) called **Form Process Chart** which graphically represents the flow of paper-work form. The focus is on one or more forms. It shows operations, movement, storage, inspection, verification and disposal of all forms charted, and information flow between these forms.

Two-handed Process Chart

Work confined to a single workplace often consists of the use of hands and arms only, and the two handed process chart gives a **synchronized** and graphical representation of the sequence of manual activities of the worker. Recording is made by the ordinary symbols with **omission of the inspection symbol**, since inspection will be shown as movements of the hands. They can be labelled as inspection by bracketing such movements and writing the word in. The Ñ symbol implies **HOLD instead** of **storage.**

A two-handed process chart is made up of two columns in which are recorded the symbols representing the activities of the left hand and the right hand respectively. They are inter-related by aligning the symbols on the chart so that simultaneous movements by both hands appear opposite each other. A brief description of the activities represented by the symbols should be inserted.

Movements of the two feet can be recorded by making two additional columns.

The use of two-handed process charts is limited by the comparatively broad meaning of the symbols and the fact that neither paths of movement, nor detailed movements of hands and arms are shown. They do, however, help to assess whether the expense of the detailed micromotion analysis is justified.

Two-handed Process Chart — Operations Only

Where only an overall picture of the activities at the workplace is required, the activities of the hands will be described solely in terms of operations.

Two-handed Process Chart in Full Detail

If more detail is required for the study, then the symbols for transport and delay and hold will also be used.

The two-handed process chart is given below: (See Fig. 8.5).

Fig. 8.5 Two-Handed Process Chart

Two-Handed (LH – RH) Process Chart
Job: Dismantling of 15 ampere electric plug, +

Chart Begins: Hands empty plug top in carton
Chart Ends: Hands empty plug top dismantled

Details of present method
Charted by: ....
Date ....

	Left Hand		*Right Hand*
1	Delay	1	To carton on bench
		1	Pick up carton
1	To meet right hand		To meet left hand
1	Grasp carton		
1	Hold carton	2	Open lid and grasp plug
2	Draw off carton and toss aside		
3	To meet plug at right hand	3	Plug to left hand
2	Grasp plug-rotate to disassembly position	3	Release plug
2	Hold plug	4	To screwdriver on bench
		4	Pick up screwdriver
		5	Screwdriver to plug
		5	Remove-unscrew cover retaining screw
		6	Lay screwdriver on bench
		7	Empty hand to plug top
4	Draw off cover-lay aside on bench	1	Hold plug top
5	To plug	8	Plug to meet left hand
3	Grasp plug-rotate to disassembly position	6	Release plug
3	Hold plug	9	To screwdriver bench

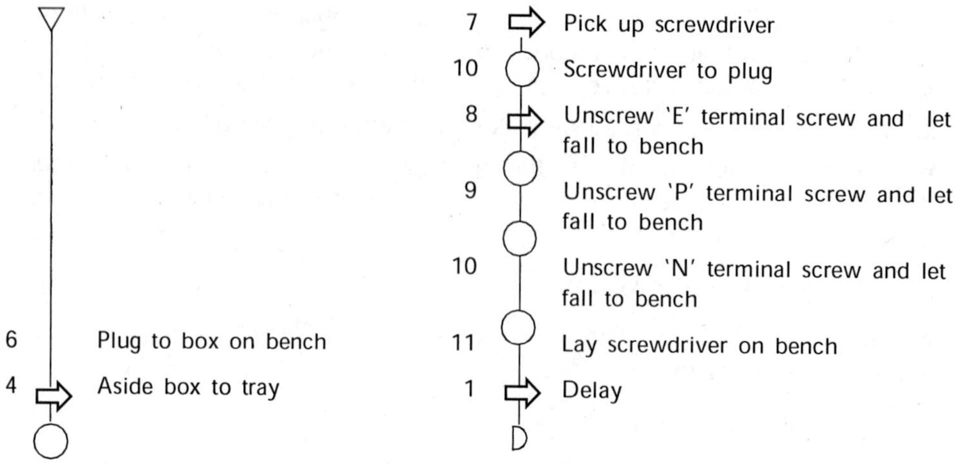

Left hand			Right hand		
	▽		7	⇨	Pick up screwdriver
			10	○	Screwdriver to plug
			8	⇨	Unscrew 'E' terminal screw and let fall to bench
			9	○	Unscrew 'P' terminal screw and let fall to bench
			10	○	Unscrew 'N' terminal screw and let fall to bench
6		Plug to box on bench	11	○	Lay screwdriver on bench
4	⇨	Aside box to tray	1	⇨	Delay
	○			D	

SUMMARY					
LEFT HAND			RIGHT HAND		
○	Operation	4	○	Operation	10
⇨	Transport	6	⇨	Transport	11
□	Inspection	0	□	Inspection	0
D	Delay	1	D	Delay	1
▽	Hold	3	▽	Hold	1

In the two-handed process chart, however, the symbols are used in a slightly different way.

▽ is used to represent **HOLD**. For example, the left hand might hold an electric plug while the right hand manipulates a screwdriver to tighten a screw. Thus, the activity of the left hand would be described by the **HOLD** symbol.

D the delay symbol is used to show that a particular hand is idle at a certain time.

The conventions peculiar to this type of chart are implied by Fig. 8.5. Exact identification of the symbol with the action it represents is essential, and if the observer desires, a sketch plan of the workplace layout can be included at the top of the chart to make the analysis of motions more meaningful. The chart itself shows a column of symbols for the left and right hand respectively. These symbols are positioned so that the simultaneous motions of the left and right hands are indicated by parallel symbols. Thus, in Fig. 8.5 operation 2 (L.H.) is carried out at the same time as operation 3 (R.H.)

Constructing the chart usually starts by plotting the activities of the hand that does the most work. Then, the observer turns his attention to putting the symbols for the other hand in their right places. Mostly the movements being recorded are small and fast, so it is preferable, with this type of chart, to start at the top, with the earliest activity and work downwards. Another example of two-handed process chart follows.

TWO-HANDED PROCESS CHART

Job: Assembly of 3 Pin Electrical Plug

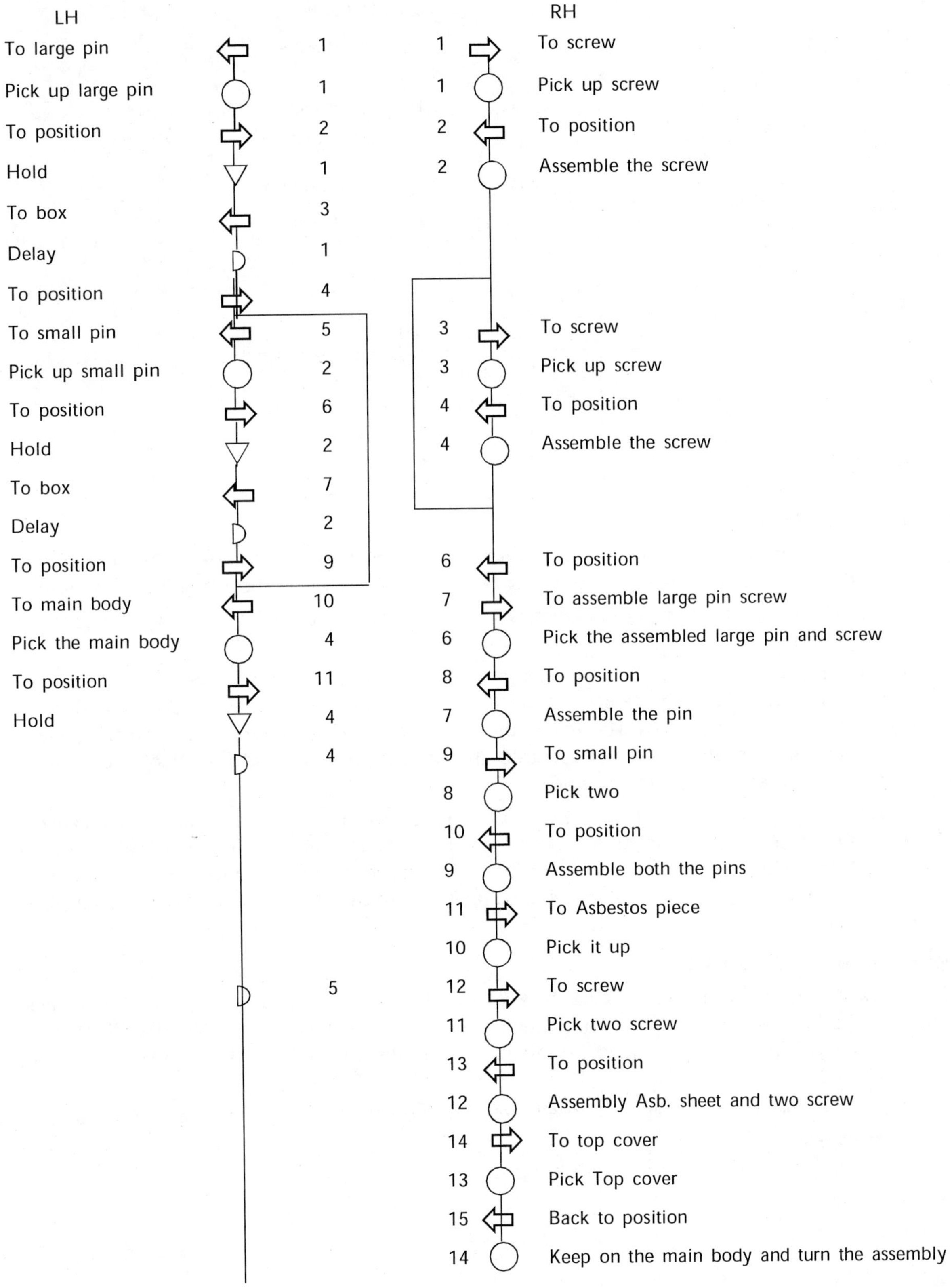

Fig. 8.6 **Two-handed Process Chart**

Chart begins: Hands empty: Material in boxes

Chart ends: Completed assembly aside to box.

LH			RH
To large pin	1	1	To screw
Pick up large pin	1	1	Pick up screw
To position	2	2	To position
Hold	1	2	Assemble the screw
To box	3		
Delay	1		
To position	4		
To small pin	5	3	To screw
Pick up small pin	2	3	Pick up screw
To position	6	4	To position
Hold	2	4	Assemble the screw
To box	7		
Delay	2		
To position	9	6	To position
To main body	10	7	To assemble large pin screw
Pick the main body	4	6	Pick the assembled large pin and screw
To position	11	8	To position
Hold	4	7	Assemble the pin
	4	9	To small pin
		8	Pick two
		10	To position
		9	Assemble both the pins
		11	To Asbestos piece
		10	Pick it up
	5	12	To screw
		11	Pick two screw
		13	To position
		12	Assembly Asb. sheet and two screw
		14	To top cover
		13	Pick Top cover
		15	Back to position
		14	Keep on the main body and turn the assembly

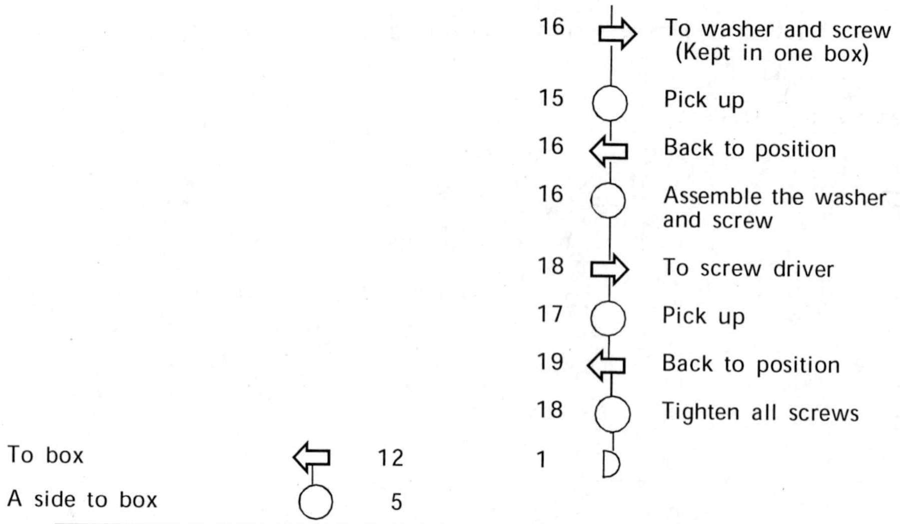

		16	⇨	To washer and screw (Kept in one box)
		15	○	Pick up
		16	⇦	Back to position
		16	○	Assemble the washer and screw
		18	⇨	To screw driver
		17	○	Pick up
		19	⇦	Back to position
		18	○	Tighten all screws
To box	⇦ 12	1	D	
A side to box	○ 5			

L.H.			R.H.		
Operation	=	5	Operation	=	18
Transport	=	12	Transport	=	19
Hold	=	4	Hold	=	0
Delay	=	5	Delay	=	1

Multiple Activity Charts

It is similar to process and two-handed charts. It is a chart where activities of more than one subject (worker or equipment) are each recorded on a common time scale to show their inter-relationship.

The multiple activity chart is used whenever it is necessary to consider on the same document the activities of a subject in relation to one or more others.

By allotting separate bars, placed against a common time scale, to represent the activities of each worker or machine during the process, the multiple activity chart shows up clearly periods of ineffective time within the process. This makes the avoidance of such time by rearrangement of work a much easier task. It is often useful to construct the chart so that the most important subject from the aspect of costs receives the major emphasis.

This type of chart is particularly useful for enabling maintenance and similar work to be organized so that the time expensive equipment out of commission is reduced to a minimum. It is also a useful means, when organizing team work, of deciding the number of machines workers should look after, and for other similar purposes. It enables complex processes to be recorded in a simple way for study at leisure.

Construction of the Chart

Worker and machine activities are normally recorded by shading the respective bars. The timings, which can be built up from previous measurements or by direct timing can ensure the chart to be effective. The activities are then plotted in sequence against the time scale within their own particular bar on the chart.

A summary of the present and proposed methods, showing the times and % use of all subjects should be made.

The following diagram illustrates Multiple Activity Chart.

Product: Punched cards

Process: Read in a deck of cards in Card Reader

Time in Seconds	Man	Machine
0	0	
3	Remove rubber band	
5	Picks up weight from hopper	IDLE
7	Places deck in hopper	
9	Replaces weight in deck	
12	Pushes start button	CARD
	IDLE	READER
20	Picks up deck from output stacker	READS
23	Replaces rubber band on the deck	THE DECK OF CARDS

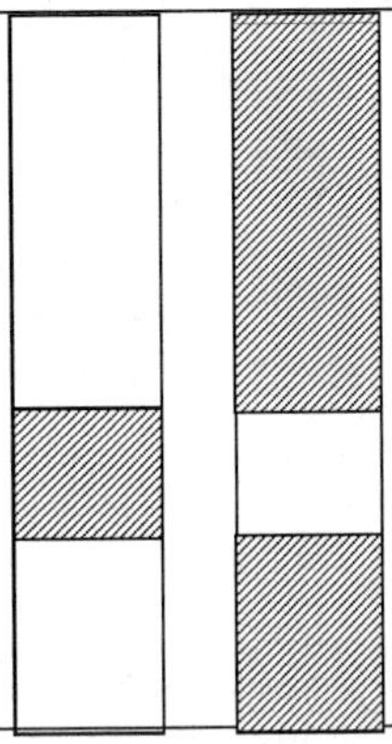

Fig. 8.7 **Multiple Activity Chart**

SUMMARY

	Man		*Machine*	
	Time (Secs)	***%***	***Time (Secs)***	***%***
Work	15	64	8	36
Idle	8	36	15	64

Diagrams and Models Showing Movement and Flow of Activities

Although the flow process chart shows the sequence and nature of movements, it does not show clearly the paths of movement. In the paths of movement there are often undesirable features such as back-tracking, congestion and unnecessarily long movements. To record these undesirable features, representations of the working area in the form of flow diagrams, string diagrams or two and three dimensional models can be made.

These techniques are useful when considering problems of plant layout and design and can be used effectively for demonstrating the improved method to both workers and management.

Flow Diagram

The flow diagram is a drawing, substantially to scale of the working area, showing the location of the various activities identified by their numbered symbols and is associated with a particular flow process chart, either man or materials or equipment type.

The routes followed in transport are shown by joining the symbols in sequence by a line which represents as nearly as possible the paths of movement of the subject concerned.

It is essentially a scale map of the workplace which shows the various activities in the places in which they occur and the routes followed by operators, materials or equipment.

Flow Diagram Elevations: As distances moved on the vertical plane can be just as significant as those on the horizontal plane, flow diagrams can be prepared to show an elevation as well as a plan of the area concerned.

Three-dimensional Flow Diagram: When a subject covers several floor levels as well as different parts of the factory, a three-dimensional flow diagram is particularly useful.

The flow diagram is illustrated in the following figure.

It depicts the scaled view of space roughly in its simplest form. It gives layout of workplace, and the travel routes of workers, materials or equipment.

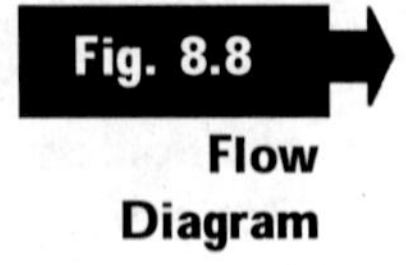

Flow Diagram

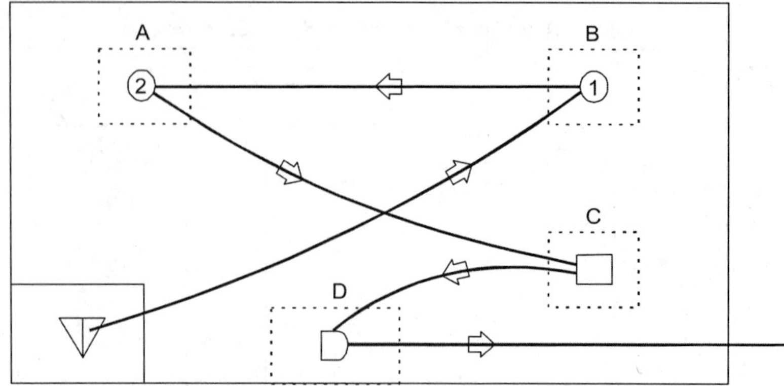

String Diagram

A string diagram also uses a scale drawing of the workplace, but here the routes taken by operators, materials or equipment are traced on the diagram by the use of a continuous thread fixed with pins. The string diagram is a scale layout drawing on which a length of string is used to record the extent as well as the pattern of movement of a worker or piece of equipment working within a limited area during a certain period of time. Although it can be used in places where the movement is a simple backward and forward one between two or three fixed points, it is of most value where the journeys are so irregular in distance and frequency that it would otherwise be difficult to see exactly what is happening.

Construction: Once the need for a string diagram has been established, the first step is to make a study of the movements in the task concerned.

The form of study sheet required is simple.

STRING DIAGRAM STUDY				
Man/matl/equip/ **Department** **Section** **Operator** **Operation No.**			**Study No:** **Sheet No:** **Date:** **Time started:** **Time finished:** **Study done by:**	
1 ***Time Dep***	***2*** ***Time Arrival***	***3*** ***Time Elapsed***	***4*** ***Destination***	***5*** ***Notes***

When the study is completed, a scale layout drawing is prepared of the area in which the recorded moves have taken place. Care should be taken to include in this drawing all building features, such as walls and doorways, block plans of machines and other equipment installed in the vicinity of the route.

The completed drawing should then be attached to a board and panel pins driven into it at each of the terminal points observed during the study. Terminal points will correspond to machines, storage racks, stacked material, loading docks and other similar places between which journeys are made.

A strong thread is then tied to the starting point pin and by reference to the study, taken round each of the other terminal points on the drawing in the sequence. In this way it is possible to record on the diagram any number of journeys between any number of points. Since thread is used instead of drawing lines, there is no risk that obliteration will occur. Also, if it is required to make several studies of the same task, each diagram may be photographed as soon as it is completed, and then the string can be removed and the layout can be used for the next study.

By using different coloured threads, diagrams can be prepared on which the movement of different work or equipment can be represented.

Thread of single colour can also be used to indicate movement under different circumstances, such as whether a truck is travelling empty or full, by attaching clips or flags or otherwise marking the lengths between certain terminal points.

Fig. 8.9 is an example of String Diagram.

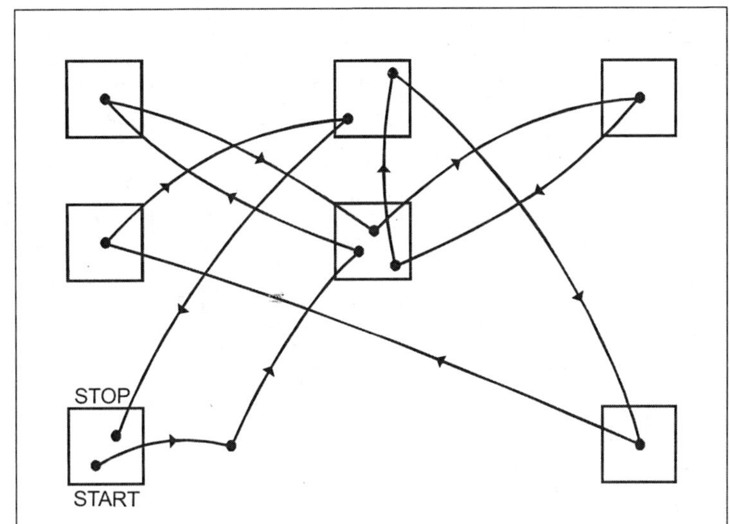

Fig. 8.9 String Diagram

Use: The primary function of a string diagram is to produce a record of an existing set of conditions so that the job of seeing what is actually taking place is made as simple as possible. Like other recording techniques, the string diagram is not an end in itself, and if it is to justify the time spent in its preparation it is important that it should be correctly interpreted and used.

As soon as it has been completed, the diagram should be carefully examined to see what facts it brings to light.

One of the most valuable features of the string diagram is the way it enables the actual distance travelled during the period of study to be calculated. Hence, it is possible to make a very effective comparison between different layouts.

It is useful to track excessive amount of back-tracking and whether the movement pattern is orderly and consistent. It is useful to locate bottlenecks and other unprofitable activities such as duplicated or unnecessary journeys.

Travel Charts

Travel charting is used to indicate which particular trips are made frequently. It consists of a number of columns representing possible destinations, and rows representing possible starting points.

In certain instances when it is required to examine complex interdepartmental or inter-section materials movement, the flow diagram becomes a maze of lines and difficult to follow. **In particular the flow diagram is not suitable when quantitative factors as distances, weight and frequency of movement have to be studied.** An alternative device is the Travel Chart.

The particular areas being studied are marked out along the horizontal and vertical axes as shown, both commencing from the same point. Movement is always plotted by reading from the horizontal to the vertical axis. If in the example it is assumed that the initial movement was from department 5 to department 3, the 'x' at the junction of the column, joining department 5 to 3 records this move.

The numbers of 'x' in each vertical column is then added up and the bar chart constructed. Similarly for horizontal columns.

These charts not only provide at a glance picture of the volume and nature of the movement to and from each department, but also form the basis for further analysis.

Substituting the 'x' for distance, with no. of journeys presents an even more realistic picture of the movement. The effect of rearrangement of machines and depart. to eliminate or reduce movement can readily be studied from this type of chart.

Fig. 8.10

Bar Chart

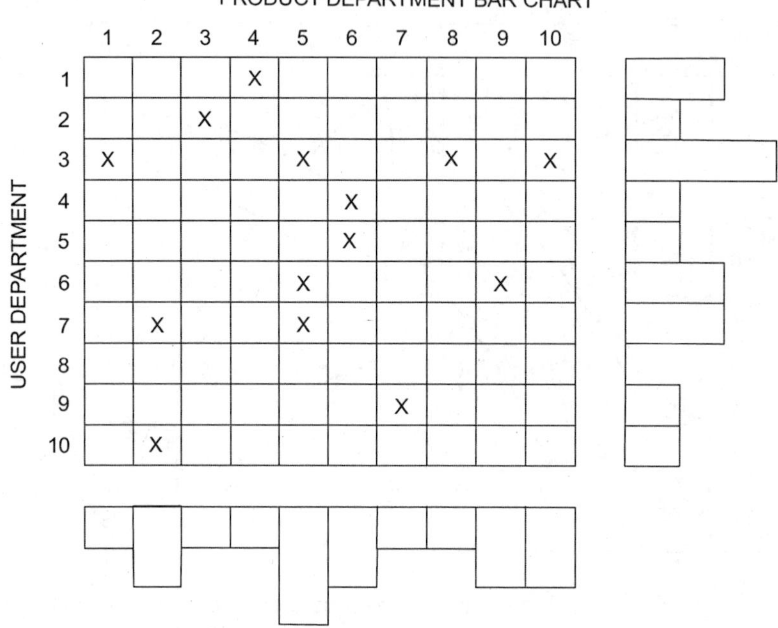

To Summarize

The principal uses of string diagrams are to investigate movement in the following circumstances:

1. When a team is working.
2. When one worker is tending several machines.
3. In processes where several sub-assemblies have to be moved to another assembly.
4. Where the process necessitates the worker moving from one workplace to another.
5. For testing the relative values of different layouts.

Use of Models

Models are always useful in assisting in the development of new layouts, and as visual aids to explain and discuss problems and proposals with other people. The desirability of using such refinements depends on the size of the job and the work such a model entails. Standard models and graphed planning boards can be bought and used repeatedly, but these standard parts cannot be expected to cover all requirements. Besides models, other aids are available such as templates and translucent planning materials.

Photographic and Cinematic Recording Methods

In the case of detailed investigation at a workplace where the operations may be of very short duration, or performed at a high speed or where several different jobs are being carried out simultaneously, the observer is frequently unable to perceive movements accurately enough for recording purposes. In such cases, photography can be used for recording and examining. It is also used when conditions like wetness or dirt make it difficult to write down a record. It is also used when there is an element of danger.

Both still and cine photography are employed for this work.

The following are advantages of photography:

1. A permanent record is obtained of the work being studied.
2. The record can be referred to at any time, in any place and by any number of people.
3. An excellent means is obtained of demonstrating differences in method. This is a valuable aid in training.
4. Reproduction of the original method is possible at any time after the improved method has been installed. (This is useful when the degree of improvement may be disputed).
5. Repeated study of worker's activities can be made without disturbing him at frequent intervals.
6. The examination of intermittent work can proceed when the work itself is not actually in progress.

The "Polaroid" type of camera which gives the finished print in a minute is very useful.

Use of Cine Films

Cine films possess a number of features as compared to visual inspection:

1. They can be projected to any required speed and can be stopped at any convenient point.
2. They can be run backwards, which sometimes enables clumsy or backward movements to be more easily detected.
3. Permit greater detailing than eye observation.
4. Provide greater accuracy than pencil, paper and watch techniques.
5. Are more convenient.
6. Provide a positive record.

The following are the ways in which films are employed

1. Micromotion Studies

Two-handed process charts, simocharts, cyclegraphs and chronocycle graphs are used for the study of operations at the workplace. The last of these four is main technique of micromotion analysis, which is concerned with the most detailed aspects of methods improvement.

Micromotion analysis is expensive to conduct, and should be undertaken, if it appears economically justifiable, only after large-scale improvement has been fully investigated as a result of using the other recording techniques.

In certain types of operations, particularly those with very short cycles which are repeated thousands of times (such as the packing of sweets into boxes or food cans into cartons), it is worthwhile to go in much greater detailed studies to determine where the movements and efforts can be saved and to develop the best possible pattern of movement thus enabling the operator to perform the operation repeatedly with a minimum of **effort and fatigue.**

The techniques used (usually filming) are collectively known as MICROMOTION STUDY.

The micromotion group of techniques is based on the idea of dividing human activities into divisions of movements or groups of movements according to the purpose for which they are made.

Therbligs

Therblig is the name given by Frank B. Gilbreth to each of the specific divisions of movement, according to the purpose for which it is made. These therbligs cover movements, or reasons for the absence of movement. Each therblig has specific colour, symbol, and letter for recording purpose.

Originally, Gilbreth created seventeen Therbligs, but later, in the 1940s, ASME revised this and added the therblig 'Hold.' With the exception of the letter code identification, which is not often used, these eighteen therbligs are shown in Fig. 8.11.

At first it may seem burdensome to employ therbligs in charting, but a little experience of their use soon shows that they have a number of advantageous properties not possessed by process charting. For instance, the standard colours enable each therblig duration to be charted to a time scale, and these colours not only assist in analysis by emphasizing the identity and time relationship of each movement, but also facilitates the synthesis of activities and durations on proposed charts. Thus, the estimated cycle time of the proposed method can be built up as essential therbligs are transferred from the old to the new chart.

Fig. 8.11 Therblig Chart Symbols

Symbol	Name	Description	Colour	Pencil No.
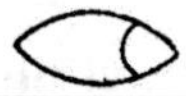	SEARCH	Locate an article	BLACK	67
	FIND	Mental reaction at end of search	GREY	69
→	SELECT	Selection from a number	LIGHT GREY	70
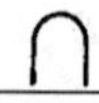 ∩	GRASP	Taking hold	RED	19
	HOLD	Prolonged grasp	GOLD OCHRE	58
	TRANSPORT LOADED	Moving an article	GREEN	45
9	POSITION	Placing in a definite location	BLUE	29
#	ASSEMBLE	Putting parts together	VIOLET	25
U	USE	Causing a device to perform its function	PURPLE	22
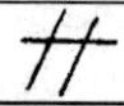 ++	DISASSEMBLE	Separating parts	LIGHT VIOLET	26
 0	INSPECT	Examine or test	BURNT OCHRE	60
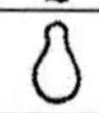 8	PREPOSITION	Placing an article ready for use	PALE BLUE	39
	RELEASE LOAD	Release an article	CARMINE RED	14
	TRANSPORT EMPTY	Movement of a body member	OLIVE GREEN	51
	REST	Pause to overcome fatigue	ORANGE	10
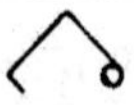	UNAVOIDABLE DELAY	Idle-outside person's control	YELLOW	6
	AVOIDABLE DELAY	Idle-within person's control	LEMON YELLOW	1
	PLAN	Mental process before action	BROWN	55

To help people become familiar with therbligs, the charts shown in this section require to be coloured in, using the coloured pencils indicated in Fig. 8.11. This activity will assist the process of memorising the standard notation and help to make the charts more meaningful. Given an equal facility with process charting and therbligs, the practitioner is better able to make a proper choice in what is the most efficient tool for his purpose. Sometimes, process charting is all that is necessary; at other times, a time scale may be desirable, or fine detail may have to be recorded, in which case therbligs have more to offer. The only technique that can be offered as suitable alternatives to therbligs in situations governed by human movement are a predetermined motion time system such as MTM, or Work Factor.

In its simplest form, therblig symbols can be used in place of process chart symbols, to produce a therblig chart. This can serve much the same purpose as a flow process or two-handed process chart, and although it may seem that greater detail can be portrayed in this way, the absence of a time scale makes this advantage dubious. On the other hand, a therblig chart is often used as a first step towards the construction of charts that do possess a time scale, in which case the method of gathering data must possess a means of identifying each therblig and its duration. The most convenient method for collecting such data is by recording the job on 16 mm cine film and then analysing the film picture by picture. When Gilbreth first did this, he had the sort of cine camera that was handcranked, and the time gap between each picture depended on how fast the handle was turned; hence, to measure the time of movements, a special clock was placed in the viewing field of the camera. Gilbreth designed his clock to have 100 graduations marked on a dial large enough to be photographed easily. Of the two hands on the clock, the small hand moved and at 2 rev/min and the large hand at 200 rev/min. Thus, when the large hand moved through one graduation on the dial it measured one upon two thousandth part of a minute. This unit of time Gilbreth called a WINK, and the clock itself a Wink Counter. Nowadays, either a wink counter or a microchronometer (decimal minutes) can be used, but the need for them mainly depends on whether the timing mechanism of the cine camera can be relied on as an alternative. Certainly, it is convenient to see the clock on each frame (picture of the film), but it is yet another piece of equipment that the worker is not used to setting up in the workplace. When a cine camera is being actuated by its own timing mechanism and run at 16 frames/second, it is often used for charting purpose, so that the time scale is plotted in frames and the duration of each therblig is indicated by the number of frames it occupies. At faster speeds, more detail can be recorded on the film, but there is also a greater footage of film to be analysed, the presence of a clock then saving trouble for the analyst and advancing accuracy. At slower speeds the clock becomes necessary for reasons to be given later.

Simultaneous Motion Charts

In India, Simultaneous Motion Charts (SIMO) are not very popular, since they are expensive.

Simultaneous Motion Cycle (SIMO) Chart

A Simo chart is a chart, often based on film analysis used to record simultaneously on a common time scale the therbligs or groups of therbligs performed by different parts of the body of one or more workers.

The simo chart is the micromotion form of the man type flow process chart. Because simo charts are used primarily for operations of short duration, often performed with extreme rapidity, it is generally necessary to compile them from films made of the operation which can be stopped at any point or projected in slow motion. It is recorded by a **'wink counter'** placed in such a position that it can be seen rotating during the filming.

To prepare such a chart, an elaborate procedure and the use of expensive equipment are required. Investigation in this degree of detail is only justified when the saving resulted from improved method will defray the cost of the work involved.

SIMO CHART

Drawing No. & Name: Film No.:
Operation Chart No.:
Operative Sheet No.:
Op. No. Date:
Charted by:

Wink counter reading	Left Hand Description	Time	Therblig	Time in 2,000/min	Time	Therblig	Right Hand Description

2. Memo Motion

There are many jobs that have activities, or an inter-relationship of activities which, although they do not need to be examined in fine detail, are still too fast or intricate to be measured and recorded accurately without the help of a film. The production quantities of some jobs may not justify the detail of micromotion analysis, the job cycle may exceed the 4-minute duration, or the efficiency of a cycle may depend on integrating the work of a team of people. The filming of these various classes of work can be performed economically and efficiently by Marvin E. Mundel's method of time lapse cine photography known as 'memo motion.' This is carried out by attaching an electric time lapse unit to the cine camera so that a picture is taken at an interval of time set at any convenient unit between 1/2 seconds up to 4 seconds in frequency. Usually, the time interval chosen is one from a second, which means that a 100-ft reel of film can record an hour's work. For a very large range and variety of jobs one frame a second misses very little detail of the information that is vital to a study, so that this technique is an extremely valuable tool possessing all the advantages of a film record, and the additional advantages of economic use of film and the ability to record longer periods of work. To avoid difficulties, however, it is necessary to set a wink counter or microchronometer in the picture and, also, to take supplementary notes of what is happening while the camera is running. Thus, if by some chance the time lapse unit falters, then time continuity will not be lost, or if the camera's view of an activity is momentarily obstructed, then the notes can be referred to.

Analysing such a film is much the same as for mocromotion, but the scale of analysis is broader and the therbligs are listed to suit the type of chart that applies. In teamwork, this would be a multiple activity chart.

Cyclographs and Chronocyclographs

In addition to the straight forward use of still photography to make permanent records of workplace layouts, string diagrams and models etc., a technique was originated by Gilbreth to enable comparatively short motion patterns to be recorded on a photograph of the workplace itself. The record can be made as a continuous or dotted white line, known as cyclograph or chronocyclograph reply.

Here we are particularly interested in the motions made by an operator while doing a job. A cyclograph is a technique employed to record of path of movement usually traced by a continuous source of light on a photograph. It is produced by attaching small lights to the worker's wrists (or where desired) and making a time exposure (on a small lens stop) while a single cycle of portion of cycle is performed.

A similar photographic procedure is used to make a chronocyclograph in which the light source is suitably interrupted at regular intervals so that the path appears as a series of pear-shaped spots rather than a continuous line. This enables both the direction of movement and the speed at any point along the path to be recorded. The shape indicates the direction of the movement and the space between the dots, the speed. This is achieved in following way:

(1) The interruption of the light source is arranged to take place at carefully controlled regular interval (usually 10, 20, or 30 times per second).

(2) The method of interruption is such that, when the light is being recorded on the film, the movement of the subject results in a pear-shaped dot being produced, distinctly tapering off at one end. This is achieved either by means of suitable equipment in the lighting circuit operating at the required frequency, or by exposing the film through a disc rotating at the appropriate speed and of suitably graduated density.

When the frequency of the interruptions is known, the speed and direction of movement at any point along the path can be easily calculated from the number and shape of dots recorded.

The main value of cyclographs and chronocyclographs, lies in the convenience with which different motion patterns can be compared for variations in the method of performing a particular operation.

3. Examination

After 'record' comes 'examine.' Critical examination of the facts collected and recorded in some form of process charts is needed to solve problems. The best known approach to 'examine' is the Questioning Technique.

Questioning Technique

The means by which the critical examination is conducted, each activity being subjected, in turn, to a systematic and progressive series of questions.

(a) Primary Questions: The first stage of the questioning technique which queries the fundamental need for the performance, place, sequence, person, and means of every record, and seeks a reason for each reply.

(b) Secondary Questions: The second stage of the questioning technique whereby the answers to the primary questions are subjected to further query to determine whether possible alternatives of place, sequence, persons and/or means are practicable as a means of, improvement over the existing methods.

There are five sets of questions about the purpose, the place, the sequence, the person and the means.

WORK STUDY

	PRIMARY QUESTIONS		*SECONDARY QUESTIONS*	
			Possible Alternatives	*Selected Alternatives*
1. PURPOSE	What is being done?	Is it necessary? Why is it being done?	What else could be done?	What should be done?
2. PLACE	Where is it being done?	Why there? Advantages: Disadvantages:	Where else could it be done? A: D:	Where should it be done?
3. SEQUENCE	When is it done? After: Before:	Why then? A: D:	When else could it be done? A: D:	When should it be done?
4. PERSON	Who does it?	Why that person? A: D:	Who else could do it? A: D:	Who should do it?
5. MEANS	How is it done?	Why that way? A: D:	How else could it be done? A: D:	How should it be done?

Fig. 8.12 Critical Examination Sheet

Notice the points brought out by this definition:

(1) Each activity, in its turn, is subjected to these questions, but remember the advantage gained by dealing with key activities first.

(2) When dealing with a particular activity, all primary questions are satisfied first, before the secondary questions are applied.

(3) The primary questions aim at reaching conclusions on five cardinal points, *i.e.*, Purpose, Place, Sequence, Person, Means. Once these conclusions have been reached they can be related and borne in mind when working on the secondary questions.

(4) The objective of the secondary questions is to discover all the possible alternatives for each of the five principal points and then finally, to reach a decision as to which alternative should be adopted for optimum results.

The order of the sets of questions is purposely designed so that we do not waste time. The question 'what should be done' moves us from an existing method to an improved one. This is a creative procedure and no text can give some definite rules which if followed will lead to improvements. One sure-shot way to improve methods is, however, the elimination of unnecessary work. It is also possible to simplify, change or combine them.

Summary of Conclusions

Primary Stage: The conclusions reached for each group of questions should be collated and written down at the end of the primary examination so that their relationship and effect on each other can be taken into account at the secondary stage. This narrows down the range of alternatives that will present themselves for consideration.

Secondary Stage: Most of what follows now depends on the thoroughness of the initial examination. Achievements and advantages that must be retained should be inherent in the various alternatives listed under the headings — Purpose, Place, etc. The unnecessary achievements and the disadvantages should be excluded wherever possible. The usual procedure is to refer to the primary work that has been done under a particular heading, together with the overall conclusions, and then to list the alternatives suggested by this information. Each alternative will have its advantages and disadvantages which will have to be evaluated against the intention of the investigation.

All this material should then lead us to the next stage in the investigation, *i.e.*, the 'development of the new method.'

4. Developing a New Method

At the end of the critical examination process, the examiner or examining team will have determined:

(*a*) What activities are vital to the objective.

(*b*) The order of their performance.

(*c*) What activities might be combined.

(*d*) Undesirable features that should be eliminated.

(*e*) Lists of alternatives for Purpose, Place, Sequence, Person and Means for each of the key activities.

Conditions and jobs vary so much that this list is not exhaustive. The development of a new method is simplified to a certain extent by extracting and working with the key activities that are suggested by the conclusions of the critical examination. These are the activities vital to the objective. Their order of performance is known, and the alternatives for their performance are listed against them. With the background factors in mind, alternatives for each activity need to be selected. One useful point to look for is the type of alternative that lends itself to a particular alternative in the activity that follows, the idea being that the method used in one key activity can often help minimise the support activities that make ready for the next. When the alternatives have been selected, their supporting links are established, and the proposed method can be charted. The purpose of the new chart is to:

1. Check for detail and further improvement.
2. Compare with any alternative method developed.
3. Compare with present method to help estimate savings.
4. Become part of the basis for defining the new method.

One aspect of the evaluation to be done at this state is to test vital features by experimentation. Mistakes can be made on paper but they must be discovered and corrected before they can do harm. Here are a few points that give purpose to such trials:

1. Prove that each feature is practical and safe.
2. Ensure that quality standards can be maintained.
3. Discover snags to be eliminated.
4. Modify or incorporate new suggestions.
5. Check services required to operate properly.
6. Check assessment of staffing and training requirement.

Where and how these experiments are carried out depends on conditions, but whether carried out in the shop or in a test area, there are going to be disadvantages that can only be offset by the quality of co-operation existing between the personnel involved. If people can see and agree with the need for the improvements and the type of trials taking place, then the danger of rumour and obstructive attitudes will be minimised.

5. Installation

This is the final stage. It has five stages:

1. Acceptability of change at the supervisory level.
2. Acceptability of change at the works/general manager level.
3. Acceptability of change at the workers/union level.
4. Retention of workers to operate new systems.
5. Continuous monitoring to see the application of new method.

Stage 5 falls under maintenance. Casual changes may occur due to so many factors. In order to maintain a method, we need to compare what happens in subsequent practice with the original specifications. They need examination and study.

We shall now examine another component of work study called work measurement.

WORK MEASUREMENT

Work measurement is concerned with the determination of the amount of time required to perform a unit of work. It answers the question 'how long should this job take to do?' It enables management to compare alternative methods, and also to do initial staffing. It makes available the data for planning and scheduling and becomes a basis for wage and salary administration, especially for devising incentive schemes.

The measurement of human work has always been a problem for management, as plans for the provision of goods or services to a reliable programme and at a predetermined cost are often dependent on the accuracy with which the amount and type of human work involved can be forecast and organized. While it has commonly been the practice to make estimates and state targets based on past experience, these too frequently prove a rough and unsatisfactory guide.

Work measurement, by enabling target times to be set, into which are incorporated rest allowances appropriate to the type of work involved, provides a far more satisfactory basis on which to plan.

It has been defined by the British Standard Institution as –

"The application of techniques designed to establish the time for a qualified worker to carry out a specified job at a defined level of performance."

The Objectives

Using as a target the times established for jobs at the defined level of performance, work measurement will be found to have the following uses:

1. To assist in method study by comparison of times for alternative methods, and for allocating labour to jobs in proportion to the work involved so that the labour on a job is properly balanced.
2. To enable realistic schedules of work to be prepared by relating reasonably accurate assessments of human work to plant capacity.
3. As the basis of realistic and fair incentive schemes.
4. To assist in the organization of labour by enabling a daily comparison to be made between actual times and target times.
5. As a basis for labour budgeting and budgetary control systems.
6. To enable estimates to be prepared of future labour requirements and costs.

Let us compare and contrast MS: Method Study and Work Measurement

Method Study	***Work Measurement***
(1) Method study is the principal technique for reducing the work involved primarily by eliminating unnecessary movement on the part of materials or operatives and by substituting good methods for poor ones.	(1) Work measurement is concerned with investigating and reducing and subsequently eliminating ineffective time. Not only can it reveal the existence of ineffective time, but it can be used to set standard times for carrying out the work, so that, if any ineffective time does evolve later, it will immediately be found out by the increased standard time.
(2) Method study can reveal shortcomings of design, materials, and method of manufacture and as such affects mainly technical people.	(2) Work measurement is more likely to show up the management itself and the behaviour of the workers.

Work Measurement

(*i*) Reduces ineffective time.

(*ii*) Suggests rest pauses and other allowances as a result of which the operators are in a position to maintain effective efficiency.

(*iii*) Provides a sound basis of giving incentive wage.

(*iv*) Calculates the correct manpower required for doing a job and hence aids in economising manpower.

(*v*) Aids in accurate production planning.

Work Measurement Techniques

For the purpose of work measurement, work may be regarded as:

(1) Repetitive work: The type of work in which the main operation or group of operations recurs continuously during the time spent at the job. This applies equally to work cycles of extremely short duration as light press work jobs, and to those of several minutes, or even hours duration.

(2) Non-repetitive work: It includes some types of **maintenance** and **construction** work, where the work cycle itself is hardly ever repeated identically.

The principal techniques of work measurement are:

(A) Time Study, (B) Synthesis from standard data, (C) Predetermined Motion Time System (PMTS), (D) Analytical estimating, (E) Comparative estimating, (F) Estimating, (G) Activity or Work sampling, (H) Rated Activity Sampling, (I) MOST.

The Practice of Work Measurement

It can be depicted as:

(*a*) The job is broken down into its elements.

(*b*) For the elements of human work, the records of basic or normal times are consulted for this time for each element.

(*c*) For those elements for which there is no basic time already available, the basic time is determined by the appropriate work measurement technique.

(*d*) The values so determined for any of the elements which could conceivably recur in another job are added to the records of basic times.

(*e*) The proportion of rest required is assessed and added to the basic time, to arrive at the time for doing the work at the standard rate of working and for recovering from the effort, i.e., the work content.

(*f*) The addition of relaxation allowance may be made element by element or the basic times for the elements may be summed and the relaxation allowance added job wise, again to give the work content.

(*g*) The necessary technical data are collected for any machine involved in the job.

(*h*) The values for the human work, the technical data and any other appropriate allowances are combined to arrive at the standard time for the job.

The records of basic times for elements are termed as **synthetic data** and the compilation of as much synthetic data is an important objective of any work measurement study programme. This is represented below.

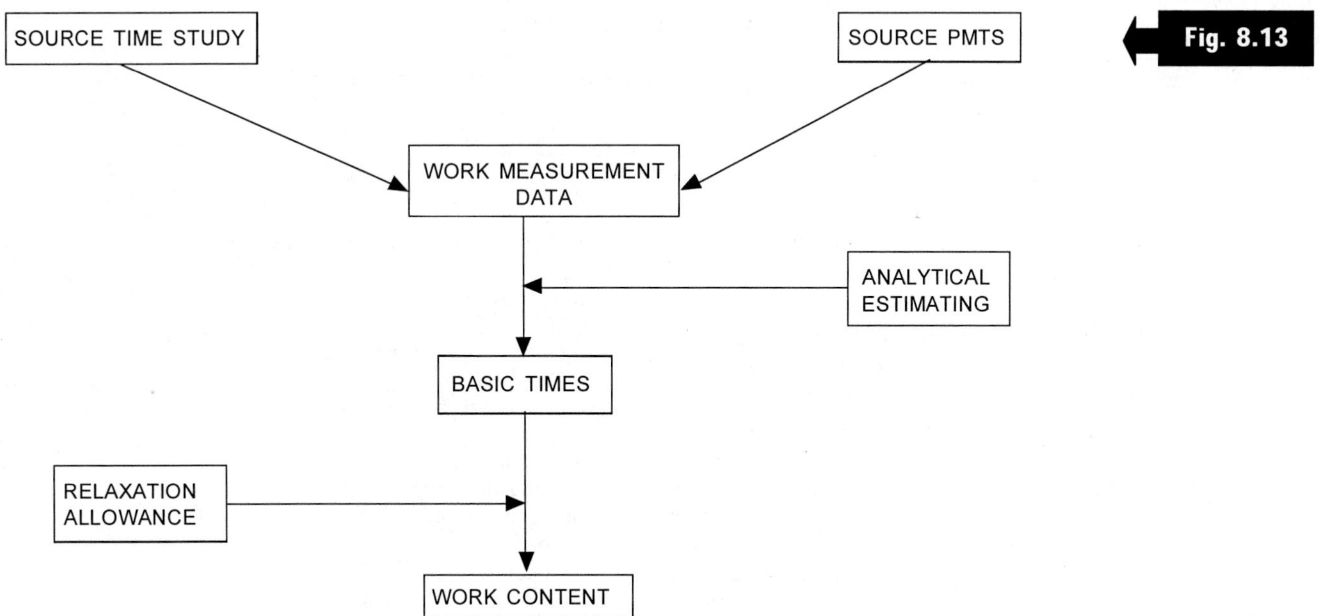

Fig. 8.13

Procedure

The basic procedure for work measurement is given below diagrammatically —

TRADITIONAL REPRESENTATION OF WORK MEASUREMENT PROCEDURE

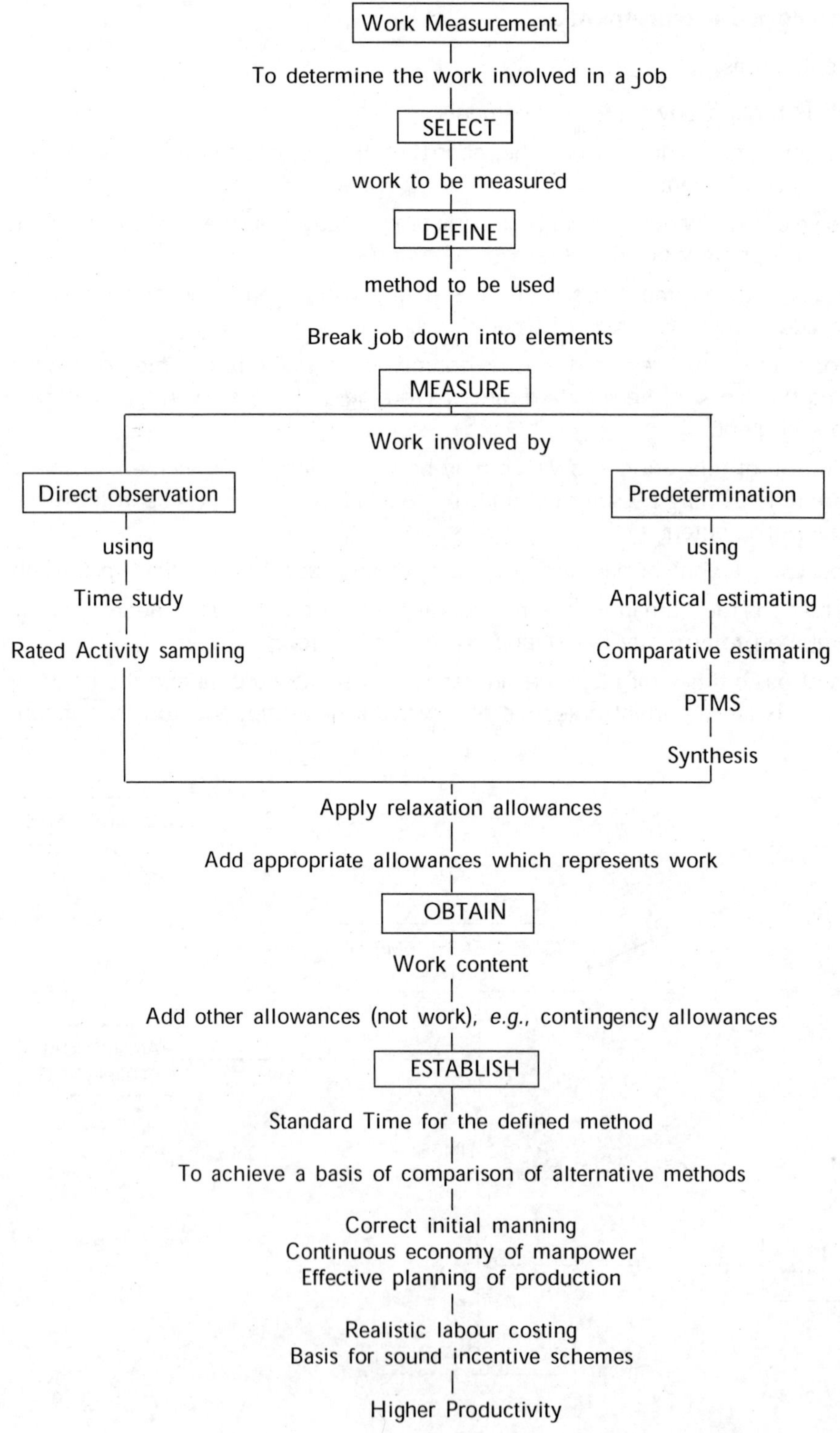

Time Study

A work measurement technique for recording the times and rates of working for the elements of a specified job carried out under specified conditions, and for analysing the data so as to obtain the time necessary for carrying out the job at a defined level of performance.

The basic steps in time study procedure are outlined below:

SURVEY JOB CONTENT

(Correct method, operating conditions, and quality. Assess nature of constituents to be measured)

↓

PLAN

(The programme by which all the constituents can be measured economically and accurately)

↓

DEFINE ELEMENTS

(Covering the whole job, selected for convenience of observation, measurement, analysis and synthesis)

↓

MEASURE

(Recording the rate and time for each element repeated in sufficient volume to provide reliable data covering all expected conditions)

↓

EXTEND

(To obtain the basic time for each element by the calculations)

$$\frac{\text{Observed time} \times \text{Observed rating}}{\text{Standard rating}}$$

↓

COLLATE DATA

(To establish a representative basic time for each element in the task)

↓

DETERMINE RELAXATION ALLOWANCE

(For each element in the task)

↓

ALLOW

(For other relevant factors, and summate to establish the)

↓

STANDARD TIME

(For the defined job)

THE NUMBER OF CYCLES TO BE TIMED

There should be enough readings for the accuracy of the results. Direct time study is a sampling process. Its accuracy is determined by the variability of the elements and the sample size. The number of observations depend upon:

- The variation in the times of the element.
- The degree of accuracy required.
- The confidence level needed.

A 95 per cent confidence level and an accuracy of ±5 per cent or ±10 per cent are usually adopted. It means that there are 95 chances out of 100 of the mean or average from observations being in error by ±5 or ±10 per cent of the true element time. A brief pilot study is conducted prior to calculating the number of observations to satisfy these requirements. The formulae used to calculate the number of observations are:

95 per cent confidence ± 5% accuracy

$$N' = \left(40\frac{\sqrt{N\Sigma x^2 - (x)^2}}{\Sigma x}\right)^2$$

95 per cent confidence ± 10 per cent accuracy

$$N' = \left(20\frac{\sqrt{N\Sigma x^2 - (x)^2}}{\Sigma x}\right)^2$$

Where N′ = required number of observations for given confidence level and accuracy

N = actual number of observation taken in the pilot study

x = each observed element time from the pilot study.

Selecting the Job to be Time Studied

Generally speaking there is a lot of pressure on time study section personnel to study no. of jobs and in a given well organized factory there may be 2 to 3 thousand time standard that had to be carried out. It becomes necessary to understand what are the reasons for which time study may be done. These are as follows:

1. The job in question is a new one not previously carried out.
2. Change in the method of existing time standard.
3. Complaint received from works or unions regarding the time standard.
4. A particular operation appears to be a "bottleneck" operation, which holds up a number of subsequent activities.
5. Change in the management policy regarding how time standards are used, *viz.,* when time standards are used for the wage payment, they are to be more accurate than when they are used for general planning purpose.

Various Steps in Making Time Study

(A) Obtaining and recording all information of job, operator, and surrounding conditions likely to affect the carrying of the work.

(B) Recording the complete description of the method and breaking down the operation into element.

(C) Measuring with timing device and recording the time taken by the operator to perform each element of operation.

(D) At the same time assessing the effective speed of operator, relative to predetermined normal speed.

(E) Converting the observed times, to **"normal times."**

(F) Determining the allowances to be made over and above the normal time for the operation.

(G) Determining the allowed time for the operation.

The information to be obtained is as follows:

- Study number, sheet number and job sheet.
- Name of the W.S. man, date of W.S.
- Name of the person approving the study.
- Name of product, drawing or specification number, part number, materials, quality requirement.
- Department or location where the operation is taking place, description of operation.
- Method study or standard practice sheet number.
- Plant of machine utilised, jigs used, tools used.
- Sketch of workplace layout.
- Operator's name and his clock number.
- Starting time and finish time of study.
- Duration of study.

Before recording the method, care should be taken that systematic method study has been carried out, if not, it should be done at this juncture. As has been made clear earlier, it is meaningless to talk of time study in absence of a properly defined method. Corresponding to each method there is one only one T. Standard Method study allows us to define the various possible alternatives of exacting a given task and choosing the best among them which is taken up for establishing the time study.

Methods of Measuring Work

There are four common methods.

Direct Observation Methods

(*i*) Stop-watch studies.

(*ii*) Activity (or work) sampling.

Indirect Work Measurement

Synthetic Methods

(*i*) Using standard data.

(*ii*) Predetermined motion time systems.

Measurement with a Stop-watch

Measure with a stop-watch for each element repeated for sufficient number of cycles, so as to give data for all possible conditions. We also have and do performance rating which is assessing the effective speed of working of the operator relative to a predetermined normal speed.

Methods of Using the Stop-watch

Basically, there are two ways of taking readings from a stop-watch, i.e., snap back (or flyback) timing, and cumulative (or continuous) timing.

Snap Back Timing

A method in which the hands of the stop-watch are returned to zero at the end of each element, and are allowed to restart immediately, the time of the element being obtained directly.

Fig. 8.14

Timing and Recording Practice

TIME STUDY SHEET (CONTINUATION)

SHEET . . . .

FINISH . . . .

START. . . . .

DATE . . . .

OPERATOR . . . .

Element	*Rate*	*Cumulative time*	*Subtracted time*	*Basic time*	*Element*	*Rate*	*Cumulative time*	*Subtracted time*	*Basic time*	
(1)		19			(1)		19	0.19		
(2)		53			(2)		53	0.34		
(3)		88			(3)		88	0.35		
(4)		1.07			(4)		1.07	0.19		
(5)		46			(5)		46	0.39		
(6)		80			(6)		90	0.34		
(7)		2.01			(7)		2.01	0.21		
(8)		26			(8)		26	0.25		
	A					B				

Cumulative Timing

A method in which the hands of the stop-watch are allowed to continue to move without returning them to zero at the end of each element, the time for each element being obtained subsequently by subtraction.

Rating

We have to adjust the observed time to arrive at a basic time for the job which represents the normal rate of working. This process of adjustment is called *rating.*

Different rates of working are expressed numerically according to the particular rating scale that the WSO has been trained to use.

Fig. 8.14 compares three of the most commonly used rating scales. The difference to notice is that the level set as a standard for the two older rating scales is not the same as the standard rating set for the British Standard Rating 0-100 Scale.

Standard Rating

The rating corresponding to the average rate at which qualified workers will naturally work at a job, provided they know and adhere to the specified method, and provided they are motivated to apply themselves to their work. If the standard rating is maintained and the appropriate relaxation is taken, a worker will achieve standard performance over the working day or shift.

British Standard 0-100 Scale: One common scale is 0-100 scale. Here 0 represents no work at all and 100 a normal rate. We rate a job on this scale after observing. A slow rate may be rated around 50 and a fast one around 125. The observed time is adjusted to a sensible basic time by using the formula.

$$\text{Basic Time} = \text{Observed Time} \times \frac{\text{Rating}}{100}$$

Relaxation Allowance (RA)

An allowance to the basic time, intended to provide the worker with the opportunity to recover from the physiological and psychological effects of carrying out specified work under specified conditions, and to allow attention to personal needs. The amount of the allowance will depend on the nature of the job.

Standard Time

Standard time has been defined as 'the total time in which a job should be completed at standard performance.' Standard performance can be defined as 'the rate of output which qualified workers will naturally achieve without over-exertion as an average of the working day or shift, provided they know and adhere to the specified method and provided they are motivated to apply themselves to work.'

Standard time expresses the total time a job will take at standard performance, i.e., work content, contingency allowance for delay, unoccupied time, and interference allowance, where applicable. The units used to state this time are either standard hours or, more usually, standard minutes. A unit of work consists partly of work and partly of relaxation, the proportion between them being dependent on the nature of the job. A standard minute (1 SM) expresses a unit of work in terms of the 100 BS scale. Standard performance is recognized as being 60 SMs an hour.

Standard time is broken into two parts:

(1) **Basic Time** which is actually spent on doing the job.

(2) **Allowances** to cover acceptable contingencies and relaxation.

Standard time is expressed in hours and minutes. Allowances are expressed as percentages which are added to the basic time.

Other Allowances

Within the work cycle or between cycles extra work of infrequent or irregular occurrence may exist, *e.g.*,

(*a*) Supplying own materials to the work station.

(*b*) Loading new coil strip onto a press to complete batch.

(*c*) Lubricating die occasionally in a forming operation.

(*d*) Bringing a machine to a certain temperature before it can operate.

Where it is impossible or undesirable to eliminate contingencies of this sort from the job, an allowance for them has to be made in the time standard. In other classes of work, delays of infrequent or irregular occurrence may be unavoidable and have to be regarded as an inherent part of the job. During the time study, enough readings of these infrequent happenings may appear to enable their average duration and frequency to be established; more often, though a special study has to be made specifically to measure such contingencies, either by means of a production study or by activity sampling. Standard time is obtained in four basic steps:

(*i*) Breaking down the job into elements.

(*ii*) Timing and rating each element.

(*iii*) Converting observed time into basic time.

(*iv*) Adding allowances.

Elements

Different elements of a job require different skills. It is difficult to rate a whole job or to apply overall allowances to the basic time. Each job is broken down into elements and each kind of work is given its own rating and allowances.

Element is a distinct part of a specified activity or task composed of one or more fundamental motions or machine activities, selected for convenience of observation, measurement and analysis.

Worker Rating

There are two measurements — the actual time taken to perform the elements of work, and the time the workers should take to do so. There is thus comparison between the actual rate and the standard rate. This makes it possible to convert observed time to basic times. (basic time is the time required to carry out an element of work at standard performance). Every observation must be rated, and the appropriate rating factor must be recorded.

Performance rating compares the actual rate of working against a defined concept of standard rating. Let us understand what is the standard rate. It is the average rate at which qualified workers will naturally work on a job, with specified method and a given level of motivation. The standard rating can be taken as 100, i.e. a rating of 50 being half the standard rate of working. The standard rate, however, depends on the situation and differs from company to company.

Several rating systems are in vogue. **Effort rating** is concerned with work speed of the worker with adjustments being made **for the adjustments being made** for the difficulty level of the task. **Objective rating** is concerned with speed and difficulty. The Westing House Company rated the skill used, the effort required, the conditions prevailing and the consistency required. This system rates the job, rather than its elements.

The following example gives separate rating for each element, and sums up the final rating for each element.

Observed (actual) element time	=	0.35 minutes
Element rating	=	+ 0.07 (skill)
	=	+ 0.11 (effort)
	=	+ 0.00 (conditions)
	=	+ 0.01 (consistency)
	=	+ 0.19
Basic time for element	=	0.35 (1.00 + 0.19)
	=	0.4165 minutes

The general formula for basic time is

Basic time for element or job

$$= \text{Observed time} \times \frac{\text{Rating}}{100}$$

- **Allowances**

Basic time does not contain any allowances to compensate for fatigue, personal requirements, contingencies etc. Therefore, a provision for allowances is made as a percentage of the basic time. These allowances could be:

Allowance	***Compensates for***
Relaxation	Fatigue allowance to recover from exertion. Allowance for personal needs, i.e., going to washroom etc.
Contingency	To perform additional and periodic activities.
Tool and Machinery	Time to adjust and set up equipment.
Reject	A proportion of defective items are inevitable.
Interference	Time lost by stoppage of two or more machines attended by one worker simultaneously.
Excess work	Extra work required on account of unforeseen or temporary changes in the standard conditions.

Total allowances are around 15-20 per cent.

- **Standard Time Calculation**

Standard time for either on element or job is —

$$\text{Standard Time} = \left(\text{Observed time} \times \frac{\text{Rating}}{100}\right) \text{Per}$$

cent total allowance.

- **Standard Minute**

It is the unit of measurement of work made up of partly work and partly relaxation. It indicates **the output in one minute** if the work is performed at the standard rate. SM is measure of work and not a measure of time. It relates to time only so far as it indicates one minute of time at 100 performance. SM can be used to calculate wages and performance.

$$\text{Performance} = \frac{\text{Output expressed in SMS}}{\text{Total Labour Time in Minutes}}$$

Work cycle is a complete sequence of elements necessary to perform a specified activity or task so as to yield one unit of production. It may also include elements which do not occur in every cycle. Following are the reasons for breaking up job into its constituent elements:

1. To ensure that productive work (and corresponding productive time) is separated from unproductive activity.
2. To permit the rate of performance to be assessed more accurately than would be the case if the assessment were made over a complete cycle. The operator may not work at the same pace and may be found to perform some operations faster than others.
3. To enable the elements involving light fatigue to be isolated and to make the allocation of the rest allowances more accurate.
4. To enable time standards to be checked so that the later omission or insertion of elements is quickly detected.
5. To enable a detailed job specifications to be produced.
6. To enable standards time values for frequently recurring elements such as the operation of machine controls of loading and unloading w/p from fixtures to be established. (For PMTS).

Various Types of Elements

(1) Repetitive elements are those elements which occur in every cycle of the given activity of task, *e.g.*, loading and unloading.

(2) Constant elements are those elements which may occur in every cycle or not, but they are identical in specification and time from cycle to cycle, *e.g.*, switch on machine, put cutting tool on post.

(3) Variable elements are those, in which the time of performance varies in relation with characteristics of the product equipment on the process, such as dimension, or weight of the object, *e.g.*, loading and unloading of trucks.

(4) Occasional elements are those elements which do not occur in every cycle of the task, but may take place either at regular intervals or randomly, *e.g.*, weaving in the textile will, replacing the bobbin (pern) (regular interval), (random) breaking of threads, help labour load and unload boxes of casting (10 per box 58 kg 2 men 1/30 cycles).

(5) Foreign elements: These are the elements observed during the study but do not form the necessary part of the given activity of the cycle, *e.g.*, the operator stopping the machine, and talk to his friend.

(6) Governing element: When two elements are going on simultaneously in a given cycle, the element that takes longer time is called governing element, *e.g.*, Boil kettle water, while setting out teapot and cups.

(7) Manual element is the element performed by the worker.

(8) Machine element is an element automatically performed by a machine, *e.g.*, pressing part.

Principles Guiding how to Break the Job into Elements

Selection of Elements

1. Elements should be easily identified and should have distinct beginning and distinct end. These beginnings and ends are many times to be recognised by a distinct sound, *e.g.*, stopping of the machine which creates a clinching sound; pressing of a tool on the table which will give a sound.

   Such clear points are known as break points and should be clearly described by breaking the job into elements and recording them on time study chart.
2. Elements should neither be too small in time variations (0.08 to 0.1 of a min. nor too large (not marathon 20 secs.). If the elements are too large the performing rate may vary during

the duration of the element, thereby causing loss in the rating accuracy. On the other hand if the element is too short it may become difficult to rate it properly.

3. Elements should be as unified as possible. This means, that a certain group of basic motions such as "reach for", "grasp", "move", may be combined together because they achieve a given purpose.
4. Elements of defining nature should not be combined together, *viz.*, variable elements should not be combined with constant, nor the man element combined with machine element, because such combining will lead to confusion and inaccurate time standards.
5. Measure each element in terms of time.

The next stage is concerned with the way the groups of activities in the job will be grouped together for timing. This is known as breaking the job down into elements.

The BST definition of an element is a distinct part to a specified job selected for convenience of observation, measurement, and analysis.

For the purpose of timing, the whole job is broken down into elements. In time study these elements will be anything between 0.05 to 0.5 of a minute in duration. Normally, a student is advised not to choose an element that is shorter than 0.1 of a minute but, of course, as he becomes more expert in timing and rating short elements, his choice would depend on his own expertise and the information to be obtained from the group of motions that have been brought together as an element. The reason why a cycle of work has to be broken down into elements arises from the need to be able to identify the causes of time variation that will appear in actual practice. Timing the overall cycle does not provide the opportunity for isolating these causes and measuring their individual effect. Element breakdown enables the WSO to:

(*a*) Account for variation in time — human, environmental, material and equipment;

(*b*) Separate unproductive from productive activities;

(*c*) Increase accuracy in rating;

(*d*) Increase accuracy in assessing relaxation allowances by isolating those elements containing different levels of fatigue;

(*e*) Produce a detailed work specification — easier to check for coverage, insertions, or omissions;

(*f*) Extract synthetic data for recurring elements.

Certain motions or activities should be grouped into an element with a definite purpose in mind, ease of measurement being only one part of this. The beginning and end of an element must consist of something that is clearly recognizable, so that the observer knows precisely when it starts and when it finishes. The instant at which one element in a work cycle ends and another begins is known as a break point. The best possible sort of break point to choose would be an activity that can be identified at a precise instant of time by the sound that it makes, a part falling into a bin, for instance, or the starting of a machine. But this, it must be understood, is a thing of convenience only. There may be more important reasons why the job should be broken down in another way.

If sound cannot be used as a break point, then a visual one has to take its place. Whatever clue is selected, it must be capable of precise recognition, otherwise one element overlaps into another.

The choice of element is influenced by a number of considerations:

(*a*) Ease of recognition — sound or vision.

(*b*) Separate evaluation of manual activities from machine activities.

(*c*) Ability to cross-check group activities from machine activities.

(*d*) Setting break points so that the effect of snags in the job can be isolated for measurement.

(*e*) Setting break points to facilitate differential timing, *i.e.*, a method of obtaining the time of one or more small elements. Elements are timed in groups, first including and then excluding each small element, the time for each element being obtained subsequently by subtraction.

(*f*) Separation of constant, variable, and intermittent elements.

(*g*) Separation of heavy work from light work for accurate evaluation of rating and/or fatigue content.

(*h*) Ease of timing 0.10 to 0.50 minute duration. When this is not possible, elements of longer duration should be timed and rated every half minute so that the effect of performance can be properly evaluated.

Each element can be given a number or letter to identify it so that the requirement for written material is minimised while the rates and times are being recorded.

Work Sampling or Activity Sampling

It was pioneered by L.H.C. Tippet in a British textile mill. Since then it has been used in different industries under various names.

Work sampling is a method of finding the percentage occurrence of a certain activity by statistical sampling and random observations.

It is also known as "activity sampling", "ratio delay study", "random observation method", "snap-reading method" and "observation ratio study."

The Need for Work Sampling

In order to obtain a complex and accurate picture of the productive time and idle time of the machines in a specific production area, it would be necessary to observe continuously all the machines in that area and to record when and why any of the machines were stopped. It would of course be quite impossible to do this unless a large number of workers spent the whole of their time on this task alone, which is unrealistic.

If it were possible to note at a glance the state of every machine in a factory at a given moment, however, it might be found that, say 80% of machines were working and 20% stopped. If this action were repeated 20 or more times at different times of a day and if at each time the proportion was always 80% working machine, it would be possible to say with some confidence that at any one time there were always 80% of machine working.

As it is not generally possible to do this either, the next best method is to be adopted. That of making tours of the factory at random intervals, noting which machine are working and which are stopped, and noting the cause of each stoppage. This is the basis of the work sampling technique. Here we use a sample of observations made at random moments during a working period to indicate what goes on all the time. When the sample size is large enough and the observations made are at random, there is quite a high probability that these observations will reflect the real situation, plus or minus a certain margin of error.

Advantages of Work Sampling in Comparison with Time Study

1. Many operations or activities which are impractical or costly to measure by time study can readily be measured by work sampling.
2. A simultaneous work sampling study of several operators or machines may be made by a single observer. Ordinarily an analyst is needed for each operator on machine when continuous time studies are made.
3. It usually requires fewer man-hours and costs less to make work sampling study than it is to make a continuous time study. The cost may be as little as 5 to 50% of the cost of continuous time study.
4. Observations may be taken over a period of days or weeks, thus decreasing the chance of day-to-day or week-to-week variations affecting the results.
5. It is not necessary to use trained time study analysts as observed for work sampling studies unless performance sampling is required.

6. A work sampling study may be interrupted at any time without affecting the results.
7. It may be made with a preassigned degree of reliability. (Results are more meaningful).
8. With work sampling the analyst makes an instantaneous observation of the operator at random intervals during the working day, thus making prolonged time studies unnecessary.
9. Work sampling studies are less fatiguing and less tedious to make on the part of the observer.
10. Work sampling are preferred to continuous time studies by the operators being studied. Some people do not like to be observed continuously for long periods of time.
11. A stop watch is not needed for work sampling studies. If an electronic data collector is used, results are shown on a computer printout.

Disadvantages

1. Ordinarily work sampling is not economical for studying a single operator or machine, or for studying operators and machines located over wide areas. The observer spends too much time walking to and from the workplace. Also, time study, standard data, or PTMS are preferred for short cycle respective operations.
2. Time study permits a finer breakdown of activities and delays than is possible with work sampling.
3. The operator may change his or her work pattern upon sight of the observer. If this occurs, the results of such a work sampling study may be of little value.
4. A work sampling study made of groups presents average results, and there is no information as to the magnitude of the individual differences.
5. Management and workers may not understand statistical work sampling as readily as they do time study.
6. In certain kinds of work sampling, no record is made of the method used by the operator. Therefore, an entirely new study must be made when a method change occurs in any element.
7. There is a tendency on part of some observers to minimise proper sample size, randomness of observation etc.

Three Main Applications

(1) Activity and Delay Sampling: To measure the activities and delays of workers, *e.g.*, finding out percentage delay of the total working time of machine or worker is not able to carry out its intended activity in terms of regular production.

(2) Performance Sampling: This is to measure working time and non-working time of a person on manual task and establish performance index or performance level for the person during his working time.

(3) Work Measurement: Under certain circumstances work sampling technique may be used to measure a manual task and to establish a time standard for an operation.

Theoretical Basis of Work Sampling

Work sampling is based on law of probabilities and more specifically on Binomial Distribution. This is so because work situation is basically defined in terms of 2 parameters

p = delay or idle time

$1 - p$ = working time

Thus while observing any work situation the person is either working or not working. The standard deviation of Binomial Distribution is given as:

$$\sigma_p = \sqrt{npq}$$

Since the whole population cannot be enumerated we take a sample size 'n' to estimate the S.D.

$$S = \sqrt{\frac{npq}{n}} = \sqrt{\frac{pq}{n}}$$

In order to obtain pre-determined accuracy of the value of 'p' this estimator by definition is taken as

$$S = S_p = \sqrt{\frac{pq}{n}}$$

Where S is relative accuracy

p = % idle time

q = % working time

n = no. of observations or sample size

The above formula is valid for 68.27% confidence level, i.e., out of 100 observations taken independently on a given population 68.27 observations will be within the specified limit.

$$= P \pm \sqrt{\frac{pq}{n}}$$

Generally speaking confidence limit is taken at 95% level.

∴ The formula becomes

$$S_p = 2\sqrt{\frac{pq}{n}}$$

$$\therefore n = 4\ \frac{pq}{s^2q^2}$$

$$= \frac{4P(1-P)}{s^2q^2} \quad \text{for 95\% confidence limit.}$$

S_p = absolute accuracy.

Sampling Procedure

The following steps are required in making work sampling study:

1. Define the problem.
   (*a*) State the main objectives or purposes of the project or problem.
   (*b*) Describe in detail each element to be measured.
2. Obtain the approval of the supervisor of the department in which the work sampling study is to be made. Make certain that operators to be studied and the other people in the department understand the purpose of the study and obtain their co-operation.

   These steps are **organizational** steps:
3. Determine the desired accuracy of the final results. This may be stated as a standard error of percentage of desired accuracy or as the absolute error of desired accuracy. The confidence level should also be stated.

$$S_p = {}^{2}\sqrt{\frac{P(1-P)}{N}} \qquad p = 20\% \ \therefore p = 20 \pm \text{error}$$

where s = relative accuracy $\qquad S_p$ = abs. accuracy

relative accuracy is 5 , ∴ S = 5%, p = 20%

$\therefore S_p$ = 1% 20 ± 1, i.e., 19 and 21

i.e., any value between 19 and 21.

Generally, S = 5% Now N = $4p(1-p)/S^2P^2$

4. Make a preliminary estimate of the percentage occurrence of activity or delay to be measured. This may be based on past experience. However, it is usually preferable to make one or two days preliminary work study sampling [pilot study].

Pilot Study

Department					**Authorised** by			
Work sampling data					**Carried out** by			
Objective					**Date**			
Men/machine/both					**Approved** by			
					Date			
Description of element	1	2	3	4	5	6	7	8
Working								
Not Working	IIII	~~IIII~~	~~IIII~~	III	III	~~IIII~~	IIII	IIII
Total	5	5	5	5	5	5	5	5

$p = \frac{7}{40} = 17\%$ 7 = not working

(5) Design the Study.

(A) Determine the no. of observations to be made, $N = \frac{4P(1-P)}{s^2p^2}$

Here s = Conventionally 5%

p = estimated from pilot study, ∴ N can be found out.

e.g., = Let p = 20% $\therefore N = \frac{4 \times 0.02\ (1-0.02)}{(0.05)^2\ (0.02)^2}$

$= \frac{16}{25} \times 10{,}000 = 6{,}400$

(B) Determine the no. of observers needed. Select and instruct these details to them.

For instance if six days are given and if one day is involved in pilot study, then 5 days are remaining.

Each day we have to make $\frac{6,400}{5}$ = 1,280 observations.

[complete calculations after each day]

One person can take 10-15 rounds per day.

If there are 10 stations, each observer after 10 rounds now will take 100 readings. Therefore, we will need approximately 16 observers.

Reading blueprint
Assembling tool (new)
Dismantling tool (new)
Trying out tool
Assy. tool (old)
Dismantling tool (old)

Instructions to be able to distinguish operations.

The persons selected should be familiar with the type of activity to be performed. Instructions are important because, each observer should record the same facts, get the same reading when observing a given activity or else the information may be wrong and misleading.

(C) Determine the no. of days or shifts needed for study.

It is fixed up by deadline within which one has to submit the final report.

(D) Make detailed plans for taking the observations such as the time and route to be followed by observer.

Two methods are employed:

(I) Random observation time: By taking out chits.

8.05	12.40	9.15	10.50	3.50
8.06	10.51	9.20	3.20	

(II) Random observed work station: By taking out chits or by mapping a route.

Random Time

There are 2 methods of making random times to prepare chits of all the times.

The chits will show the random time 8.30, 9.00, 9.01, 8.15, 10.15, 10.30, 11.30, 9.10.

Chits are preferred since the workers do not understand random tables.

Arrange the chits in chronological order.

2nd method: Here we have to refer to random numbers table [Barnes]

The random time study chits or numbers should be taken out on the preceding day of study.

(E) Design the observation from

WORK SAMPLING STUDY

Department **Men/machine/both** **Date** **Purpose**					**Observed** by **Checked** by **Date** **Sheet No.**:
Description of element	***1***	***2***	***3***	***4***	***5***
Working **Not working** **Miscellaneous**					

Suppose the study is done in *tool room*, the following elements occur:

Working	***Not Working***
(1) Reading blueprint	(1) Operator away
(2) Assembling tool	(2) Attending to personal need
(3) Inspecting tool/part	(3) Operator absent
(4) Dismantling tool	(4) Operators talking (Personal)
(5) Taking instruction	(5) Operator idle — no work
(6) Filing part	(6) Operator idle — no mats/sub std. mats.
(7) Marking part	(7) Operator idle — machine failure
(8) Machining part	(8) Operator idle — power failure

Miscellaneous are all those elements which have not been listed in working and not working.

It allows you to take care of 100% time.

If the study is well designed miscellaneous should not exceed 2 to 5%. During the progress of the study if it is found that a particular element is taking significant time, it should be transferred to relevant group (working/not working), so that miscellaneous does not exceed 5%.

Make the observations according to the plan. Analyse and summarise the data.

(*a*) Make the observations and record the data.

(*b*) Summarise the data at the end of each day.

Summary can be done horizontally or vertically on the Work Sampling Study Form. Plot daily summary control chart.

Fig. 8.15 Daily Summary Control Chart

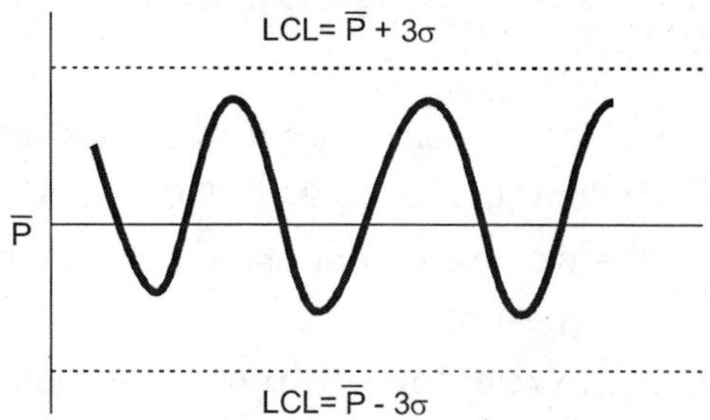

$$\sigma = \sqrt{\frac{p(1-p)}{n}}$$

where n = number of observations

(*c*) Determine the control limits.

(*d*) Plot the data on control chart at the end of each day.

If daily 'p' value exceeds UCL or LCL, it should be cancelled unless certain assignable causes are found and more readings should be taken.

[If the samples taken are not for the same population, 'p' is out of limits if assignable causes are not found.]

Check the accuracy or precision of data at the end of the study.

The calculated accuracy should be greater or equal to 5%.

Prepare the report and state conclusions, make recommendations if these are called for.

Results are presented by 2 methods

1. Bar chart method
2. π chart method [Popular method].

MOST Measurement System

MOST stands for Maynard Operation Sequence Technique, which was conceptualized in 1967 but was put to use in 1975. Displacement of objects, it is assumed here, is the common denominator to study an overwhelming majority of work. It concentrates on movement of objects in three modes.

The General Move Sequence for movement in air. The controlled move sequence for movement against a surface or attached movement.

The Tool Use Sequence for the use of common hand-tools.

In other methods of work measurement, the primary work units are basic motions. But in most they are fundamental activities (collections of basic motions).

Applications of WS

These techniques can be applied to a large number of situations, much beyond the shop floor, *e.g.*, office activities, agriculture, hospital, national and local government services, defence, hotels and housekeeping. WS personnel are a good asset in the design teams. They, together with VA: (Value Analysis) people contribute to design effectiveness.

There are two methods to derive synthetic time standards:

(*i*) by using standard data

(*ii*) by pre-determined motion time systems.

I. Standard Data

In engineering industry, suppose standard times are obtained from stop-watch studies and recorded. Though jobs are different, they have some common factors, *e.g.,* drilling. Over a period of time, we shall have data of standard time for drilling holes of different depths, to different tolerances, in different types of locations and into metals of varying hardnesses. Thus, we can relate the standard time and the various factors in the work, and derive standard data. The relationships can be converted into a chart or a mathematical formula. A 'library' of information can be developed. However, we cannot use data from other firms, because the environment may be different.

II. Predetermined Motion Time Systems (PMTS)

PMTS can be defined as a work measurement technique in which times established for basic human motions are used to build the time for a job at a defined level of performance.

A work measurement technique whereby times established for basic human motions (classified according to the nature of the motion and the conditions under which it is made) are used to build up the time for a job at a defined level of performance.

PMT systems are an important development within the field of time and motion study. Originally, F.W. Taylor's idea was to establish a library of predetermined element times so that the correct job method could be planned, and its time be established, before the job reached the production floor. As a pioneer, he managed to go only part way in this, for his approach was to establish element times by time study, with results that have some semblance to our synthetic data. F.B. Gilbreth's therbligs and filming techniques opened up another avenue with the possibility of identifying and timing the types of motions that are the fundamental ingredients of any manual element. It was seen that this could provide a greater potential for judging the effectiveness of a motion pattern structure, as well as determining the time required for its performance. American research in this field came to fruition after 1940. Now there are a number of systems in existence such as Motion Time Analysis, Basic Motion Time Study, Work Factor and MTM are the best known.

MTM itself came into prominence in 1948 on the publication of the American book 'Methods Time Measurement' by Maynard, Stegmerton, and Schwab. By their definition: 'Methods time measurement is a procedure which analyses any manual operation or method into the basic motions required to perform it and assign to each motion a predetermined time standard which is determined by the nature of the motion and the conditions under which it is made.'

The motion classifications and times for this system were derived from the analysis of many micromotion films taken at 16 frames a second on a cine camera actuated by a constant speed motor. From this research the essential data was set out in ten small tables with the captions: (1) Reach (2) Move (3) Turn and apply pressure (4) Grasp (5) Position (6) Release (7) Disengage (8) Eye travel and eye focus (9) Body, leg, and foot motions (10) Simultaneous motions.

Each table classifies the sub-divisions of its topic, and tabulates the time to be assigned according to the category of motion and the factor that causes the time to vary. These times are expressed in 'Time Measurement Units', where one TMU is equal to 0.00001 hour.

When using this system, the analyst may either establish the sequence of motions for the job by observation, or he may visualise what should take place and plan the best sequence or motions according to the data that gives simplest and economical movements. To enable him to pursue either course and to explore alternative sequences quickly, each category of movement possesses a letter code to give it a distinct identity, *e.g.,* R12ACD would mean 'Reach, 12 inches, Case A with Change Direction.' Using this code, a chart similar in principle to a therblig chart can be constructed. Given this the MTM tables can then be referred to and the relevant times calculated and assigned to their sequence on the chart.

Both Work Factor and simplified PMT operate in much the same way as MTM. Mainly, it is the classification of detail and the units recommend it in its simplicity and in the units of time used. Although simplified PMT system recognizes the BS rating scale and expresses its standards in milli-minutes, *i.e.,* 0.00001 minutes.

The advantages of such systems are numerous:

1. Evaluating time standards before the job is running.
2. Comparing method alternatives with the minimum need for experimentation.
3. Aiding tool and product design.
4. Setting targets and motion pattern in operator training, and so on.

There are, of course, limitations. These systems can deal only with the manual content of a job. If the manual activities control and dictate the time of a job cycle, then PMT can produce a standard for the job, otherwise it can contribute to different objectives only. Unfortunately, this is not the entire case, for there are instances where certain categories of movement are subject to a restraint not catered for in the data. An article may have to be moved with caution, or a controlled movement may be necessary to obtain a desired quality of finish. There are occasions, too, where it is difficult to decide the sequence of finger movements that will act on a job. These examples can be regarded as minor problems on some jobs because careful approximation is often a satisfactory expedient. The main disadvantage is the time it takes to analyse a job into its very small constituents, calculate the times that apply, find the necessary RA, and add all the data to reach a standard. If the job detail is established by observation, then there is additional difficulty of making an accurate recording of fast and intricate motions. This, too, may increase recording time, but the significance of the inaccuracy is far more important.

Synthetic Timing

Once the time studies are completed, the data of the elements are coded and stored. These data are examined time and again to see whether there is any consistency between times for similar elements. After obtaining enough consistent data, a database for future use can be created.

Machine element data is easy to generate as times are often constant or functions of known variables. Worker elements also involve equal times whenever the job or element is performed. It is difficult to deal with the variable elements. It is necessary to examine the variations in time due the nature of element itself or action of other variables. Wide variations indicate fundamental differences in the nature of the elements. Here the data cannot be assembled together. The rest of the variation could be due to mostly variables such as distance, size, weight. Afterwards graphs and tables can be constructed.

These synthetic data are reliable and consistent, as they have been generated after several studies over a period of time. Short-run work can be assigned time standards, because the time to conduct time study for these or to construct time standards for jobs not yet started is not enough. It is usual to synthesize basic times, and allowances are added thereto.

Synthesis

Stop-watch studies and activity sampling used direct observations of job in operation. However, sometimes, direct observations are not convenient. Under such circumstances, we may estimate a standard time on the basis of previous experience of similar jobs. Time standards arrived at this way are called *synthetics.*

A work measurement technique for building up the time for a job at a defined level of performance by totalling element times obtained previously from time studies on other jobs containing the elements concerned, from synthetic data.

Steps in Synthesis

Collect full details of job
(Dimensions, tools, methods, conditions)

|

Analyse job into constituent elements
(Activity grouping to enable synthetic elements to be applied if relevant)

|

Select appropriate basic times from synthetic data for all elements

|

Select and apply synthetics covering contingent factors

|

Verify detail of elemental analysis for job method and conditions

|

Total basic times, RA and allowance to establish the standard time for the job

Analytical Estimating

A work measurement technique whereby the time required to carry out elements of a job at a defined level of performance is established from knowledge and practical experience of the elements concerned.

Collect full details of a job
(Dimensions, tools, methods, conditions)

|

Analyse job into constituent elements
(Activity grouping to enable synthetic
elements to be applied if relevant)

|

Apply synthetic data and estimate basic times for the
remaining elements and contingencies

|

Apply the appropriate RA as a blanket allowance

|

Verify detail of elemental analysis
for job method and conditions

|

Total basic times, RA and allowances to establish
the standard time for the job.

Appendix - I

WORK MEASUREMENT SYSTEMS

Predetermined Time Systems: PMTS

A time standard for a job or an operation may be established by time study, by work sampling, or by the use of predetermined times.

Predetermined time standards (PTS) are advanced techniques which aim at defining the time needed for the performance of various operations by derivation from pre-set standards of time for various motion and not by direct observation and measurement. They are not normally considered suitable for the trainee to use until he has gained a real understanding of and considerable experience in work study practice.

Definition

A predetermined time standard is a work measurement technique whereby times established for basic human motions (classified according to the nature of the motion and the conditions under which it is made) are used to build up the time for a job at a defined level of performance.

Factors to be Considered in using a Predetermined Time System

1. The application of PTS requires that the operation being measured be divided into basic motions.
2. At the time a PTS is first adopted by a company the level of performance as represented by the time standards produced by the system should be determined and adjustments made, if necessary, in order to match the company performance level.
3. Most pre-determined time systems do not include allowances so these are added as they would be in a time study.

Advantages of PTS Systems

PTS systems offer a number of advantages over stop watch time study.

1. With PTS one time is indicated for a given motion, irrespective of where such a motion is performed. In stop watch study it is not so much a motion as a sequence of motions making up an operation is timed.
2. Timing by direct observation and rating can sometimes lead to inconsistency. A PTS system, avoids both rating and direct observation and hence can lead to more consistency in setting standard times.
3. Since the times for the various operation can be derived from standard time tables, it is possible to define the standard time for a given operation even before production begins and often while the process is still at the design stage. This allows the work study man to change the layout and design of the workplace and of the necessary jigs and fixtures in such a way that the optimum production time is achieved.
4. It is also possible before starting the operation to draw up an estimate of the cost of production, and this could be valuable for budgeting.
5. They are not too difficult to apply and can be less time consuming than other methods when time standards are determined.
6. They are particularly useful for very short repetitive time cycles such as assembly work in the electronics industry.

Disadvantages

PTS system took a long time to become part of general work study practice. The main reason for this delay is probably the considerable number and variety of systems that have been produced, together with the fact that many of them would be obtained only by employing consultants. At present, over 200 such systems exist.

1. Any PTS system is rather complicated. It is not easy to learn and a work study man needs a good deal of practice before he can apply it correctly.
2. The task of learning enough about the various systems to be able to judge their claims and their relative merits is an almost impossible one. For example, some systems do not go into sufficient detail in defining a certain motion.
3. PTS systems do not, as was claimed, eliminate the need for the stop watch, any more than they eliminate method study or work sampling.
4. Machine time, process time and waiting time are not measurable with PTS systems and occasional or incidental elements are often more economically measured by using other techniques.
5. In fact it is difficult to obtain 100% coverage in a plant using only a PTS system and for certain operations such as batch production or non-repetitive jobs the use of such a system can be an expensive proposition.
6. It is invalid to add up times for individual small motions in the way required by PTS systems because the time taken to perform a particular motion is influenced by the motions preceding and following it.

The main uses of PTS systems may be divided in the following two classes:

Work Methods

1. Improving existing methods.
2. Evaluating proposed methods in advance of actual production.
3. Evaluating suggested designs of tool, jigs requirement.
4. Aiding in the design of the product.
5. Training members of the staff to become motion-minded.
6. Aiding in training operators.

Work Measurements

1. Establishing time standards.
2. Compilation of standard data and formulae for specific classes of work.
3. Checking standards established by time study.
4. Auditing time standards.
5. Estimating labour costs.
6. Balancing production lines.

Nine predetermined time systems are as follows:

1. Motion Time Analysis (MTA) — A.B. Segur
2. Body Member Movements — W.G. Holmes
3. Motion-Time Data for Assy. Work — Harold Engstrom & H.C. Geppinger
4. The Work Factor System — J.H. Quick, W.J. Shea & R.E. Koehler
5. Elemental Time Standard — Western Electric for Basic Manual work
6. Methods Time Measurement (MTM) — H.B. Maynard, G.J. Stegements, J.L. Schwab

7. Basic Motion Times Study (BMT) — Ralph Presgrave, G.B. Bailey, J.A. Lowden
8. Dimensional Motion Times (DMT) — H.C. Geppinger
9. Predetermined Human Work Times — Irwin P. Lazarus.

The First Predetermined Time System

A.B. Segur developed the first PTS system, which he called Methods Time Analysis (MTA). He worked with Gilbreth during World War I using micromotion analysis of films. By 1924 Segur had perfected his system and made it available on a consulting basis. His data was never published. His system was very detailed and required a high degree of skill and training.

The Work Factor System

It is a widely and generally used PTM system. The first actual shop application was made in 1938 and time values published in 1945. The system includes

(*i*) Detailed work factor
(*ii*) Ready work factor
(*iii*) Abbreviated (using Form A)
(*iv*) Abbreviated (using Form B)
(*v*) Brief work factor
(*vi*) Detailed Mento factors.

This system makes it possible to determine the work factor time for manual tasks by the use of predetermined time data. First, a detailed analysis of each task is made, based on the identification of the four major variables of work and the use of work factors as a unit of measure.

Then the proper standard time from the tables is applied to each motion. The total may be increased by personal, fatigue and delay allowances.

Four Major Variables

There are four major variables which affect the time to perform manual motions

1. Body member used
2. Distance moved (inches)
3. Manual control required
4. Weight or resistance involved.

Standard Elements of Work

Work Factor recognizes the following standard elements of work:

1. Transport (Reach & Move) (TRP)
2. Grasp (GR)
3. Pre-position (PP)
4. Assembly (ASY)
5. Use (manual, process, or machine time) (US)
6. Disassemble (DSY)
7. Mental Process (MP)
8. Release (RL).

Work Factor Notation

The symbols employed for the body members and work factors are shown below:

Body Members	***Symbol***	***Work Factors (Written in this sequence)***	***Symbol***
Finger	F	Weight or Resistance	W
Hand	H	Direction Control (steer)	S
Arm	A	Care (precaution)	P
Forearm Swivel	FS	Change Direction	U
Trunk	T	Definitive Stop	D
Foot	FT		
Leg	L		
Head Turn	HT		

METHODS TIME MEASUREMENT (MTM)

The MTM system was developed from motion picture studies of industrial operations, and the time standards were first published in 1948. This system is defined as a procedure which analyses any manual operation or method into the basic motions required to perform it, and assigns to each motion a predetermined time standard which is determined by the nature of the motion and the conditions under which it is made.

Beginning in 1963, the first new member of MTM system called General Purpose Data (MTM-GPD) was introduced and at that time MTM-1 was used to designate the original basic MTM system. Today, the family of systems includes MTM-1, MTM-6PD, MTM-2, MTM-3, MTM-V, MTM-M, MTM-C, and 4M DATA.

MTM-1

It uses data tables. The unit of time used in these tables is 0.00001 hour, and is referred to as one time-measurement unit (TMU). Thus one TMU equals 0.0006 minutes.

The basic elements are:

1. Reach
2. Move
3. Turn
4. Apply pressure
5. Grasp
6. Position
7. Release
8. Disengage
9. Eye Times
10. Body, Leg and Foot Motions
11. Limiting Motions

MTM-2

Of the family of MTM system MTM-1 is the most accurate, provides the most detailed methods description, but requires the longest time for analysis.

MTM-2 was developed by constructing motion combinations from basic motions of MTM-1. It has a smaller number of distance ranges and fewer cases of control than MTM-1. Although the analysis can be made more quickly than with MTM-1, accuracy and method description are not as great. **MTM-2 is suitable for work that is not highly repetitive and for elements that are not less than 1 min long.**

The system consists of nine categories of manual motions.

	Motion	*Symbol*	
1.	Get	G	(Get and put are the only two variable categories and only 37 time standard appear on MTM-2 Data Card)
2.	Put	P	
3.	Apply pressure	A	
4.	Regrasp	R	
5.	Eye Action	E	
6.	Crank	C	
7.	Step	S	
8.	Foot Motion	F	
9.	Bend & Arise	B	

Speed of analysis with MTM-2 is twice as fast as with MTM-1.

MTM-3

It is the simplest of the MTM systems and is intended for use with long-cycle short-run operations. The MTM-3 system consists of four categories of motions.

	Motion	*Symbol*
1.	Handle	H
2.	Transport	T
3.	Step & Foot Motion	SF
4.	Bend & Arise	B

Of these, the two motions Handle & Transport have variable categories and only ten time standards appear on the MTM-3 data card.

Speed analysis with MTM-3 is seven times as fast as with MTM-1 and three times as fast as with MTM-2.

Limitations: MTM-3 should not be used for analysing manual motions with a frequency higher than 10 or a sequence of eye movements. In such cases MTM-2 or MTM-1 should be used.

MTM-6PD: It has been derived from MTM-1 time values for basic data. This is a **"building block process"** for development of standard data.

MTM-V: It is designed for use with machine tool operations including such items as setting machine tools, handling tools and work process, measuring and gauging, operating the machine and clearing work pieces and equipment.

MTM-M: It is a second level Functional System of original data designed for the analysis and measurement of manual assembly work performed under stereoscopic magnification of 5 to 30 power.

MTM-C: It is a two level data system synthesized from MTM-1 and is used for clerical related work. Its use includes desktop operation and such tasks as filing, typing, key punching and data entry.

4D Data (Micro-Matic Methods and Measurement): It is a computer-aided means of applying MTM-1. The computer takes over much of the work of the analyst and assists in standard data development, recalling elements, and mass changing standards.

LEARNING CURVE

While we instal the new work method, there should be appropriate training with expected learning. Learning is the process of acquiring skill and proficiency at a task leading to increased productivity in performance. Here learning is restricted to task learning and the speed with which a task can be accomplished. We are also concerned how learning contributes to accelerate the pace, and the factors which influence learning. The nature of the learning curve has been discussed here. The following diagram 8.16 illustrates the learning curve.

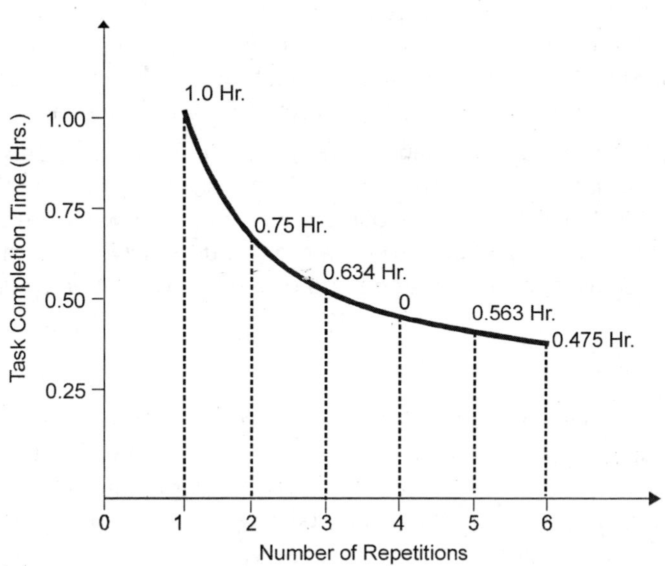

Fig. 8.16
75 Per cent Learning Curve

The learning curve shows an improvement of 75 per cent in performance on account of learning equivalent to a constant improvement of 75 per cent. In other words, the first performance of the task requires one hour, and each subsequent repetition shows 75 per cent improvement. Thus, the second performance require 1 × 0.75 = 0.05 Hrs. The fourth performance requires 0.75 × 0.75 = 0.56 Hrs. Learning a task is affected by:

1. the length of the task. The longer the task, the slower is the learning.
2. the complexity of the task.
3. the competence of the worker, and his familiarity with the work.
4. motivation of the worker, and personality traits.
5. learning methods and circumstances.

STANDARD DATA

Standard data is a form of work measurement that consists of time values for specific elements of work. The manual part of a task is broken down into groups of hand motions or body motions that can be precisely defined and that are applied only in connection with a particular machine or a specific operation. The elemental time values usually take the form of tables, formulas or graphs. Elemental time values for establishing **standard data** had been determined by stop watch time study until predetermined time systems became available. Through simple plans for combining motions into "elemental building blocks" and the further combination of these data, Deere & Company has developed a system of "Operational Data" which they have used successfully over a period of years.

The Deere plan consists of four parts of steps:

1. Predetermined time system (micromotion time)
2. Basic data (combination of predetermined times for motions)
3. Universal data (A combination of blocks of basic data)
4. Operational data (Time values for elements for a specific type of operation).

PHYSIOLOGICAL METHODS OF MEASURING WORK

Physical work induces changes in oxygen consumption, heart rate, pulmonary ventilation, body temperature, and lactic acid concentration in the blood. Although some of these factors are only slightly affected by muscular activity, there is a linear correlation between heart rate, oxygen consumption and total ventilation, and the physical work performed by an individual.

Of these three, heart rate and oxygen consumption are the most widely used for measuring the physiological cost of human work. When a person is at rest, heart rate and the oxygen consumption are at a fairly steady level. Then when the person does muscular work, i.e., when he changes from a "resting level" to a "working level" both the heart rate and the oxygen consumption increase. When work ends, recovery begins, and the heart rate and oxygen consumption return to the original resting level.

Heart Rate Measurement

The graph shown shows that initially the heart rate was 70 beats/min. and when the individual started working it gradually increased to 110 beats/min. and when he stopped working heart beat dropped off gradually to 70 beats/min. The increase in heart rate during working may be used as an index of the physiological cost of the job. The total physiological cost of a task consists not only of the energy expenditure during work, but also the energy expenditure above the resting rate during the recovery period, *i.e.,* until recovery is complete.

Each time the heart beats, a small electric potential is generated. By placing electrodes on either side of the chest, this potential can be picked up and transmitted by wire or radio transmitter to a receiver. There are individual heart beats that can be counted directly, or by means of a cardio-tachometer the impulses can be converted into heart rate. This data can be recorded continuously on ruled graph paper by a milliampere recorder.

Heart beat signals can also be obtained by means of an ear lobe unit. Information concerning rate of recovery also can be obtained simply by using a stethoscope and stop watch.

Fig. 8.17

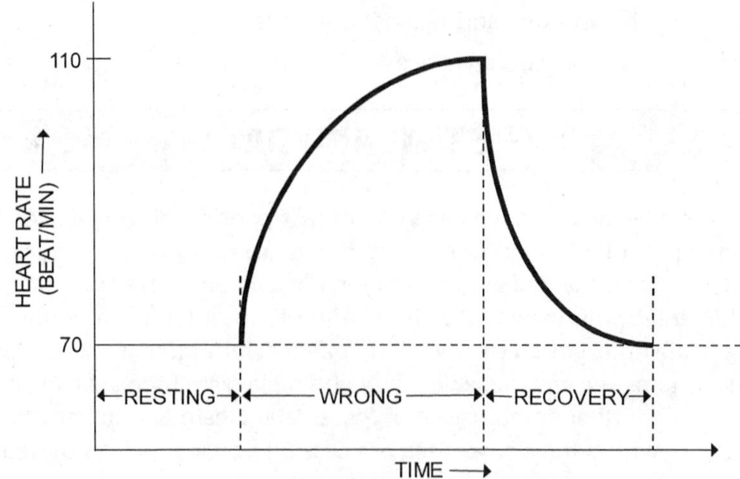

Portable Heart Rate Recorder

A compact, lightweight, two lead heart rate recorder which records signals up to 26 hours can be worn by the worker. This unit has a synchronous motor drive, integrated circuit and a rechargeable battery pack. An event marker button, when depressed by the worker records an event mark on the tape for precise time/event correlation.

An automatic tape scanning system, called Electro-cardioscanner, permits the recordings to be played back at real time recorded speed or at rapid speeds of 30, 60 or 120 times real time. Heart rate is shown as a trend line on oscilloscope and is automatically printed on a summary trend chart.

Measuring Oxygen Consumption

Change in the rate of oxygen consumption from the resting level to the working level is also a measure of the physiological cost of the work done.

A person extracts oxygen from the air breathed. In order to measure oxygen consumed per unit of time, it is necessary to measure the volume of air exhaled and the oxygen content of this air. Oxygen consumption may be defined as the volume of oxygen expressed in litres per minute which the individual extracts from the air inhaled. A common method of obtaining this information is by means of a portable respirometer.

A respirometer is a light wt. (5½ pounds) gas meter which can be worn on the back. The person is equipped with a mask and a 1-inch rubber tube which carries the exhaled air from the mask to the respirometer. This respirometer indicates directly the volumes of exhaled air in litres. A sample of the exhaled air is drawn off at random intervals into a rubber football bladder, and an analysis of its content is made. This permits a comparison of the oxygen content of the sample of expired air with that of the air in the room.

A curve showing energy expenditure before, during and after physical work would look much like the curve shown previously.

TAYLOR'S USE OF TIME STUDY

Time study began in the machine shop of the Midvale Steel Company in 1881 and Frederick W. Taylor was its originator. Taylor came from a well-to-do Philadelphia family, was trained at Phillips Exeter academy to enter Harvard, and passed the *Harvard entrance examinations* with honours but at the cost of seriously impaired eyesight. Forced to give up the idea of further study at the age of 18 he obtained a job in a machine shop. In 1878, when he was 22, he went to work at the Midvale Steel Works as an ordinary labourer. He was rapidly promoted to time clerk, journeyman, lathe operator, gangboss and foreman of the machine shop. At the age of 31, he was made chief engineer of the works. During his early years at Midvale, Taylor studied at night and in 1883 obtained a degree in mechanical engineering from Stevens Institute.

When Taylor was the foreman, he decided to make a determined effort to change the management system *"so that the interests of the workmen and the management should become the same, instead of opponents."* He further stated that "the greatest obstacle and harmonious co-operation between the workman and the management lay in the ignorance of management as to *what really constitutes a proper day's work for a workman.* Taylor obtained permission from the president of the Midvale Steel Company to spend some money in a careful, scientific study of the time required to do various kinds of work.

Two classes of experiments were made, one by physiologists who were studying the endurance of workers, and the other by engineers who were attempting to measure physical work in terms of horsepower.

Taylor started his study by employing two good steady workers who were physically strong. These men were paid double the wages and co-operated fully in the investigation. Taylor in these experiment was trying to learn what really constituted a full day's work for a first class man and not to find the maximum work that a man could do for a short period.

In this study, Taylor hoped to determine what fraction of horsepower a man could exert in a day. After several years Taylor was convinced that *there was no direct relationship between the horsepower that a man exerts and the tiring effect of the work on the man.* However, he discovered that, for very heavy work, the controlling factor in determining how much work a man could do in one day was the percentage of the day that the workman was underload, the percentage of day he was resting and the length and frequency of rest periods. *Taylor also developed the use of stop watch time study which is a great contribution.*

Taylor's Principles of Management

Taylor came up with questions *"which is the best way to do this job?" and "what should constitute a day's work?"*

Taylor explained his objectives in the following way:

First: The development of a science for each element of a man's work, thereby replacing the old rule-of-thumb methods.

Second: The selection of the best worker for each particular task and then training, teaching and developing the workman; in place of the former practice of allowing the worker to select his own task and train himself as best he could.

Third: The development of a spirit of hearty co-operation between the management and the men in the carrying on of the activities in accordance with the principles of the developed science.

Fourth: The division of the work into almost equal shares between the management and the workers, each department taking over the work for which it is the better fitted; instead of the former condition, in which almost all of the work and the greater part of the responsibility were thrown on the men.

Taylor's Investigation of Shoveling

In 1898, when Taylor went to the Bethlehem Steel Works, he undertook to improve methods in various parts of the plant. One task which came to his attention was shoveling. 400 to 600 men were employed in the year and much of their work was shoveling. Iron ore was shoveled the most and then nice coal came next in tonnage. Taylor found that each good shoveler in that yards owned his own shovel; he preferred to do this rather than to have the company furnish it. A foreman supervised 50 to 60 men, and they shoveled a variety of materials in the course of a day. *The yard was approximately 2 miles long and a quarter mile wide.*

Taylor found that shovelers were lifting loads of 3½ pounds when handling nice coal and up to 38 pounds when moving ore. He immediately set about to determine what shovel load permitted a first-class shoveler to move the most materials in a day. Taylor took two good shovelers, set them to work in different parts of the yard, and detailed two time study men with stop watches to study the work of these men.

At first large shovels were used so that heavy loads were taken. Then the end of the shovel was cut off to permit a smaller shovel load, and again the tonnage handled was noted. The results of this study showed that with a load of *21½ pounds* on the shovel, a man could handle a maximum tonnage of a materials in a day. Thus, a small spade shovel that would just hold 21½ pounds was provided for the worker when he handled ore, and a large scoop was provided for light materials such as ashes.

A tool room was established and special shovels were purchased and issued to the workers as needed. In addition Taylor inaugurated a planning department to determine in advance the work to be done in the yard. After 3½ years at the Bethehem plant Taylor was doing the same amount of the work in the yards with *140* men as was formerly done by *400 to 600.* He reduced the cost of handling material from *7 to 8 cents* to *3 to 4 cents* per ton. After paying for all added expenses, such as planning the work, measuring the output of the workers, determining and paying bonuses each day, and maintaining the toolroom, Taylor showed a saving during the last 6 month period at the rate of $ 78,000 per year.

Motion Study as it was Developed by the Gilbreth

Frank B. Gilbreth and his wife Lillian M. Gilbreth contributed a great to the motion study. Mrs. Gilbreth training as a psychologist and Mr. Gilbreth's engineering background fitted them in a unique way to undertake the work involving an understanding of the human factor as well as a knowledge of materials, tools and equipment. Their activities cover a wide range, including noteworthy inventions and improvements in building and construction work, study of fatigue, monotony, transfer of skill and work for the handicapped and the development of such techniques as the process chart, micromotion study and the chronocyclograph.

In 1885, Gilbreth, as a young man of 17, entered the employ of a building contractor. Gilbreth began by learning the bricklayer's trade. By the beginning of the century Gilbreth was in contracting business of his own. From the very beginning Gilbreth had noted that each craftsman used his own peculiar methods in doing his work and that no two men did their job in exactly the same way. He also observed that the workers did not use the same set of motions.

The bricklayer, for example used one set of motions when he worked rapidly, another set when he worked slowly and still a third set when he taught someone else how to lay bricks. These observations led Gilbreth to find the "one best way" of performing a given task. He made photographs of bricklayers at work, and from the study of these photographs he continued to bring about increased output among his workers.

Gilbreth invented a *scaffold* which could quickly and easily be raised a short distance at a time, thus permitting it to be kept near the most convenient working level at all times. This scaffold was also equipped with a bench or shelf for holding the bricks and mortar at a convenient height for the workmen. This saved the bricklayer the tiring and unnecessary task of bending over to pick up a brick from the floor of the scaffold each time he laid one on the wall.

Formerly bricks were dumped in a heap on the scaffold and the bricklayer selected the bricks as he used them. He turned or flipped each brick over in his hand in order to find the best side to place on the face of the wall. Gilbreth improved this procedure. As the bricks were unloaded from the freight car, Gilbreth had low priced labourers sort them and place them on wooden frames or "packets" 3 feet long. Each packet held 90 pounds of bricks. The bricks were inspected by these men and placed on the packet side by side, so that the best face and end were uniformly turned in a given direction. The packets were then placed on the scaffolds in such a way that the bricklayer could pick up the bricks quickly without having to disentangle them from a heap. He also placed the mortar box on the side of scaffold, so that the bricklayer could pick up a brick with one hand and a bowel full of mortar with the other at the same time.

These changes, along with others developed by Gilbreth increased the amount of work which a brick layer could do in a day.

Gilbreth's Work at the New England Butt Company

On *May 13, 1912* Gilbreth started an important consulting assignment at the New England Butt Company. This was a small, well organized unit manufacturing machinery for making braids for wearing apparel and shoe laces and coverings for insulated wires.

Gilbreth here made his first application of *micromotion* study in a manufacturing organization and eventually his work included the installation of the Full Taylor System. Gilbreth had the company build a special laboratory called "Betterment Room". Here problems were analysed, mock-ups were constructed, and better methods developed. Gilbreth also established a production planning department, improved the tool room and studied the flow and handling of materials by constructing a scale model of the factory and movable models of the machines. He first used the *process flow chart* in this connection. He also designed work tables of the proper height and provided chairs for the workers. He made use of the newly designed *"skid and lift truck"* method of mass handling.

Gilbreth made some, *2,00,000 feet* of film during his professional career.

Appendix - II

SCIENTIFIC MANAGEMENT

In order to appreciate how what goes by the name Work Study today has emerged from the contributions of pioneers of Scientific Management, we must recognise the major landmark created by F.W. Taylor, an American engineer and management consultant who progressed from an apprentice machinist through various supervisory levels to Chief Engineer at the Midavale Steel Works, Philadelphia. Taylor, who later became a management consultant, believed the employer-employee co-operation to be the foundation for any management scheme. To attain this, Taylor listed the following requirements:

(*a*) All aspects of work should be investigated on a scientific basis. (Result: rules, laws, formulae governing the best methods of working, and constituting *a fair day's task*).

(*b*) Select, train and develop each workman to attain the above objective.

(*c*) Create organisational climate to get the work done as per the objective.

(*d*) Divide the work so that the management and workmen share equally in the daily performance of each task. (Managers plan the work, and the workmen carry out the work as planned).

This, then, is the essence of Scientific Management. Any system needs acceptance, and Taylor was aware of the fact that acceptance, for scientific management needed a 'complete mental revolution on the part of both management and workers' Taylorism's success depended upon its acceptance which in turn depended upon the co-operation between managers and workers as a result of sharing prosperity by both the sides.

A Fair Day's Task

Taylor has discussed how the change in the way of working leads to improvements by recording a number of his investigations showing surprising results. He emphasised the need of trained investigators to discover the best way of doing the task and to determine who was best suited to perform it after training. He evaluated a fair days task by studying (*a*) fatigue and (*b*) the time a job should take. There are of course difficulties in measuring the time it took to do a job. Parronet (1708-94), a French Civil engineer, and Babbage (1792-1871), a mathematician and inventor advocated secret time studies, which today are unacceptable to us due to advances in knowledge. Taylor's time study had the following essentials:

1. A trained time-study observer, who would take his time observations on top-class men only.
2. A number of men would be timed, and having obtained the best time of a top-class man, a percentage could be determined to find out how much an average man would fall short of this maximum.
3. Method of timing: Split the job into elementary movements, discard unnecessary elements, and time the remainder being done by different men.
4. The final average time for each element was classified and filed for quick reference.
5. Percentage covering contingencies, fatigue, and special conditions were also computed, classified and filed in the same way.
6. This data was then used to help identify:
   (*i*) Best elements and
   (*ii*) Conditions for doing a job.
7. By adding the appropriate times and allowances, the time for the desired method was established.

Against this background, we will be in a position to appreciate the loop-holes to be plugged up and refinements to be made for the present-day time study.

Standardisation

The term standard is defined as "that which is set and established by an authority... for the measure of quantity, weight, extent value or quality."

We have many standards like ethical, legal etc., but in an industry these are classifiable as:

(*a*) Engineering Standards, (*b*) Administrative Standards.

The different source for standardisation are:

(1) Company, (2) Associations, (3) National, (4) International.

(1) Setting up specifications, (2) Simplification, (3) Numbering codification, (4) Preferred numbers, (5) Adoption of formats, (6) Discussions/liaison with other agencies.

The description of any item is indicated by specification. Specification is a standard of measure and a check over the quality of materials. It is the result of careful study and experience. It is a minute enumeration of materials services, jobs or contracts. It becomes a standard when applied to repetitive type of items. If specifications are once drawn to meet any tailored item, it cannot be said as a standard. To be a standard it must have general acceptability as to equality and other characteristics.

Simplification is reduction in variety.

The items essential are standardised and the rest weeded out.

Advantages and Approach

A few of the advantages of standardisation, may be listed as under:

1. Establishes specifications for materials.
2. Interchangeability of parts.
3. Reduction in variety of materials.
4. Easy review, as the items are fewer in number.
5. Establishes formals and eliminates confusion and communication gaps.
6. Ensures systematic provisioning and cuts the lead times.
7. Guarantees the quality and quantity aspects of the materials.
8. Obviates prior inspection.
9. Reduces the costs.
10. Co-ordination between departments is improved due to better understanding of materials.
11. Eliminates surpluses and obsolete items, minimises the rejections.
12. The buyer and seller knows the quality/quantity of items contracted for.
13. Allows proper store house maintenance and easy identification of materials and
14. Admits computerisation.

The Indian Standards Institution is contributing to maximum extent in co-ordination with the International Institute for Standards.

At the national level, Indian Standards Institute is doing a lot by drawing and publishing the standards for the different materials in co-ordination with the ISO and other Agencies, like DGMS, National Safety Councils. The materials having relation to each other are tied up to a chosen series. This applies to sizes, weights and areas. The ISI has published these series for guidance of industry. For any one company, establishment of standards for all items are impossible, however competent the technical personnel it has. It is, for these reasons desirable to have discussions with the outside agencies and exchange the views. The ISI has advisory/consultative committees, which may be made use of, by joining of big companies for adopting the standards.

Economic Influence of Standardisation

In the long run, an in-plant standardisation of production equipment is the factor which will reduce to the greatest extent the number of spare parts and maintenance materials in stock, and thus decrease the capital tied up in these articles.

The standardisation includes:

1. Complete machine units, as tool machinery, material handling devices, boilers, compressors, furnaces, etc.
2. Machine components, as electric motor pumps, valves, bearings, fittings, pipes, etc.
3. Regular consumed maintenance materials, as steel bars, plates, oil, metals, etc.

Organisation of Standardisation Background:

The basis for standardisation are international standards, national standards, (DIN-norms for instance) and standard dimensions set up by different manufacturers (SKF-ball bearing catalogue etc.)

An internal company standard or norm is a very limited fraction of standards mentioned above. In practice, this will turn out to be a book of norms.

Use of norms: The material collected in the book of norms will be used for:

1. Design of new production equipment, both in the companies' own drawing office and by a manufacturer or an engineering firm from outside.
2. Purchasing of materials and spare parts for the factory.
3. Registration of materials and spare parts from the storeroom.

It is not allowed to go outside the norms. Only people at a certain high level in the Company's organisation may authorise the use of off-standard dimensions under special circumstances.

Standardisation Office/Committee

There are two main possibilities for organising standardisation work:

1. A standardisation committee, consisting of people who, most of their time, are engaged in other types of work.
2. A standardisation office, with one man or a group of people working full time on this subject.

In additions, the office will operate with supporting and decision-making committees.

Book of Norms

As mentioned earlier, the product of the standardisation office is a steadily growing book of norms. This book will have one sheet for each type of material. In Fig. 8.17 is indicated a norm sheet for steel pipes of cast iron.

It contains the following information:

(*a*) Type of articles: Steel plate for boilers.

(*b*) Blade No.: Here 002.007 which identifies the sheet. It is different from any other norm sheet.

(*c*) Material used: Here H II Din. 17155, certified according to the standard German DIN norms. This is a precise description of the steel used in these plates.

(*d*) Example of ordering: is the description to be used when the company shall order material from the outside vendor.

(*e*) Stock term: The description to be used when the workshop shall order this material from the store. Note that the internal no. (002.007.03) is used in this requisition and not in the purchasing order.

(*f*) The date: This norm blade was official (4th January 2008).

(*g*) Material No.: thickness, dimensions, tolerances, weight, etc., which are all necessary technical information.

(*h*) Where in stock: The company has four factories, Rjukan, Eidnager, Glemfjord and Notodden (Norek Hydro). A mark in the last column REGN (the first letter in the factory names) will tell which factories have this material in stock.

STOCK NORMS

Article: Steel Plates for Boilers over 4.75 mm. Blade No. 002.007

Material: H II DIN 17155 certificate Date: 4, Jan. 2008

Example of Ordering: Steel plates for boilers 16 x 1250 x 2500 DIN 1543
H II DIN 17155, certificate

Stock term: Steel Plates for boilers 16 x 1250 x 2500 H II Material No. 002.007.09

Thickness and tolerance according to DIN 1543.

Mat. No.	Thickness t mm	Dimension w×1 mm	Tolerance			Weight	on stock by				
			t mm	w mm	1 mm	kg.pl.	kg/2	R	E	G	N
002.007											
.03	5	1250 × 2500	–0.3	+ 10	+ 12.5	125	40		X		
.04	6	1250 × 2500	–0.3	+ 10	+ 12.5	150	48		X		
.06	8	1250 × 2500	–0.3	+ 10	+ 12.5	200	64		X		
.07	10	1250 × 2500	–0.3	+ 10	+ 12.5	250	80		X		
.08	12	1250 × 2500	–0.5	+ 10	+ 12.5	300	96		X		
.09	16	1250 × 2500	–0.5	+ 10	+ 12.5	400	128		X	X	X

Fig. 8.18
Norm for Steel Pipes

Workplace Design

Elephant Design, Pune has installed a large-screen display (LSD), a live video-wall for Reliance Industries, Jamnagar for situational analysis of plant data. There are eight walls measuring 8 × 4 metres each which cover the operations of the entire refinery. They made a static prototype, and took it to the site. They consulted the employees, the contractor and project partner. There were 10,000 data points. They worked with the client's people. It took them six months. They created special dynamic objects which the operators could recognise. Design makes workplaces efficient, functional and safe. Elephant has also designed Venky's X-press retail outlets for chicken.

9

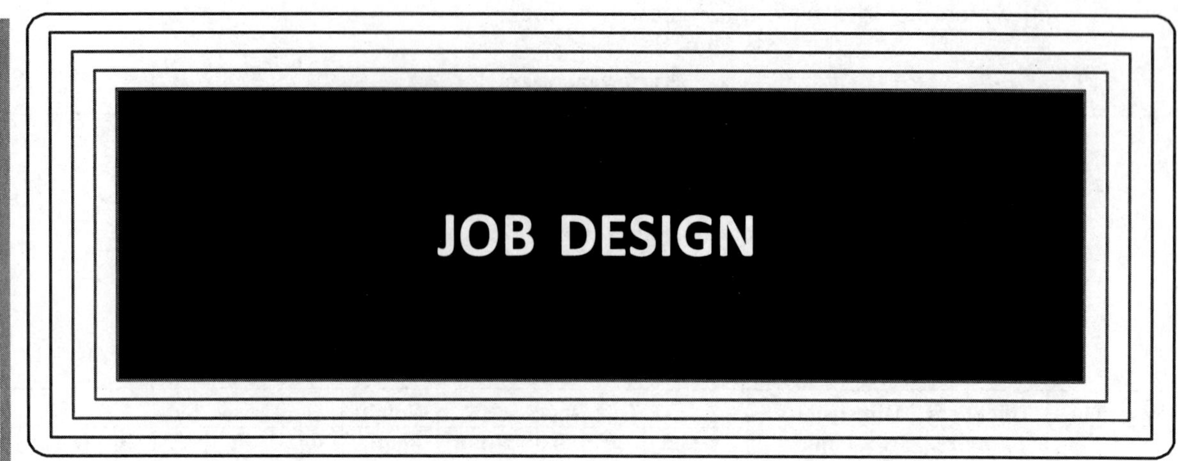

JOB DESIGN

Planned structuring of work is called job design. It answers the questions like what job is to be performed, by whom, at what place and time. It also seeks to justify the necessity of the job and spells out the way to perform it. The basic aim of job design is to minimise the amount of human exertion. In olden days, robust physical abilities were considered essential for a job. In modern times, most jobs are so designed that they suit the average worker, and abilities are more related to academic performance and experience.

In the context of an organization, a job has two basic elements — a human element and a work element. The human factors related to job design are physiological, social and psychological aspects. The work element has been considered in sufficient detail in the previous chapter though some points which are left out will be considered here.

Poor job designs affect a worker physically and mentally. Job design aims at developing work assignments to satisfy the organizational and technological requirements, and also simultaneously satisfying the personal individual requirements of the worker. The smallest elements of work activities — therbligs — which make up micromotions have been considered previously.

Task is made up by two or more elements taken together.

Job is made up of the set of tasks.

Job design is a complex topic since a host of factors affect the ultimate job structure.

Degree of Labour Specialisation

Specialisation has its pros and cons. On the positive side, it makes possible high speed and low cost of production. It, therefore, enhances our standard of living. On the negative side, it may have adverse effects on the worker like a feeling of ennui.

The chief merits of specialisation for the management are as follows:

(1) Speedy training of the workforce, (2) High output due to repetitive nature of work, (3) Ease in recruiting, (4) Low wages as labour is substitutable, (5) Close control over work flow/work loads.

The advantages for the workers are:

(1) Little accountability for output, (2) Little mental effort, (3) No need for higher education.

The disadvantages for the management are:

1. Difficult to exercise control over quality, as the job is broken down into several parts and no one could be held responsible for the final product.

2. Hidden costs of worker dissatisfaction on account of disruption of production process internally, absenteeism, turnover, tardiness and grievances.

The disadvantages to the workers are:

1. Monotonous job leads to boredom.
2. Overall contribution to the completed product insignificant and so there is no gratification.
3. Little or no control over workplace, leading to frustration.
4. No progress on the job due to postal learning.
5. Little opportunity to show initiative.
6. Muscular fatigue locally since the same muscles perform the same task.
7. Little opportunity of interacting with other workers owing to layout constraints.

However, the disadvantages of specialisation far outweigh the advantages. It was necessary to come forward with alternative approaches to job design. The result is approaches like human engineering, ergonomics, work physiology, job enlargement, job enrichment, job relation, social-technical system etc.

Ergonomics/Human Engineering

In a manufacturing company, there are two aspects — the physical facilities called hardware and the non-physical facilities called the software. The whole system is part of the physical environment of an organization. These components should be so arranged by the designer that there is harmonious operation. Ergonomics is an attempt to match the characteristics and abilities of people involved to the various parts of the system. Once ergonomics is applied, there are better opportunities for the designer to improve the system. Ergonomics is somewhat similar to human reactors with engineering. Human engineering is a field of study concerned with human capabilities and constraints in the design of tools, instruments and workplaces.

We shall now discuss the environmental and organizational factors affecting the Job Design.

DESIGN FACTORS

Layout of Equipment and Seating

It is most preferable to design the equipment used keeping in mind the operator who operates it. However, the equipment is designed first, and the operator is expected to cope with it, even though control and display are unsatisfactory. There is an inertia to change. This attitude keeps the equipment as it is for a long time. Some lathes may have work carried out far from the eye, and the operator's bent posture is therefore taken for granted. Can we not design a tilted centre lathe where the operator has not to stoop?

Similarly, vision in cranes formerly was unsatisfactory but newer models permit unrestricted vision.

For good design, the operator and his/her anatomy should be the basis for vision, controls, seating, leg room etc. Allowances are necessary for anthropometric differences of gender — male and female. Job design has to account for a standing job or a sitting job or a combination of both. Workers may have to leave the workplace for change of posture very often. Some seats are so uncomfortable for sitting for a long time, that workers often stand up to do the job.

Seating should not cause overstrain of certain muscles. Back rest must be provided to allow relaxation of back muscles. Seat should not press unduly the tissues of buttocks. It may be necessary to go to sleep by being too uncomfortable. Restricted blood flow may also cause numbness. Well-designed seat bears the weight of the body in a good posture on hips and not on thighs. Good seating depends upon the size, shape and height of the seat, the back-rest provided, and the material used. High chairs require foot-rests which are flat-surfaced, rather than bars which cause fatigue.

It is necessary at times to provide standing support called rump rest.

Some situations require floor level work, allowing greater freedom to anatomy, *e.g.,* cobbler's work, tailor's work.

Operatives may be provided by consultants a stool or a bench out of human consideration, to facilitate putting tiffin boxes, small bags, shawls and such personal belongings. They should not be misused for sitting.

In assembly work and controls, the renewal principles of motion economy as laid down by Gilbreth should be taken as guideline. (See the Appendix for principles of Motion Economy).

For controls, binary form information of yes-no type is preferred. Lights which alternate (green-red) can be used. For quantitative information, digital presentation is better than the reading of graded scales. Control panel instruments should have both audio and visual signals. Visual signals should not mislead. Centrally located lights are immediately visible and off-centre lights 30° from the centre are difficult to notice. Layout designs should anticipate future maintenance problems and hence those points that need frequent maintenance should not be inaccessible.

Diagnostic studies are conducted to identify causes of failure, and rectification accordingly should be done.

At various stages of design, ergonomic considerations are kept in mind.

Instrument Display Design

Display is a device that provides information about a situation which has occurred already or is just occurring. Sometimes this information cannot be seen/heard directly. We then make use of instruments, *e.g.,* pressure gauge. Instrumental displays may be auditory/visual type.

Visual Dial Displays : Graduated scale. Value given by a pointer used for both quantitative and qualitative reading. May be used with controls. Could be circular or linear.

Indicators : Off-on lights. They are used for display and control.

Warning Devices : They warn us about a situation. They are used for display and control.

Counters : Numerically displayed information. Use for quantitative and qualitative reading. May be used with controls. Superior since they give value directly in numerals.

Kinds of Visual Display

(i) Moving Index Display : Moving index with a fixed legend. Superior to fixed index displays.

(ii) Fixed Index Display : Fixed Index with a moving legend.

(iii) Open Window Display

(iv) Counters

(v) Shutters, Lights etc.

(vi) Computer Graphics : Pictorial displays with tables, graphic presentations, pictorial panels.

Auditory Displays

(i) Yes-No type : Provides warning signals.

(ii) Chiming clock : Gives additional quantitative information.

Compatibility

Movements should be natural, for instance, turning a knob clockwise or from left to right to switch on an equipment. Design should conform to naturalness in movements. Such compatibility makes mastery easier with less learning time. Incompatibility makes one accident prone and less productive.

All control knobs are either compatible with natural movements or all of them are not. Controls and dials on the same panel are laid out with the same spatial relationship, for instance left-hand dial is operated with left-hand controls. Most of the equipment is designed for the right-handed people, though the operator's preferred hand does make a difference.

Control Design Characteristics

In a non-computerized situation, controls communicate instructions of the operator to the machine. We have, therefore, to consider the design characteristics of control, *e.g.*, shape, size, friction characteristics, inertia etc.

Continuous adjustment calls for rotary or reciprocating type of controls. Rotary controls are cranks, hand wheels, knobs whereas reciprocating controls are levers and 'joysticks'; Levers are unidimensional and joysticks have two dimensions. Discreet movement calls for on-off type controls.

The following table summarises control mechanisms and their usefulness:

Control Mechanism	***Description***	***Utility***
Crank	Handle is offset from and parallel to shaft	For high turning speeds up to 200 r.p.m. For rapid control turns. For manual movement of heavy loads.
Hand Wheel	Circular control gripped by the rim preferably with both the hands	For low turning speeds (1 rpm or less) For very accurate partial turns For a torque above 15 inch/lbs. For turn not exceeding 90^0
Knob	Rotary control. Operated by gripping it freely on both sides with the fingers of one hand	For making fine adjustments For light loads (up to 22 inch/lbs) As rotary selector switch.
Lever	Rod-like Hand-operated Uni-dimensional Fulcrum	For small effective travel For fast movement which does not require accuracy For medium-heavy load.
Joystick	Lever which works in two directions	For continuous simultaneous control in two dimensions For rapid multiple switching operations
Toggle Switches	Miniature levers 30°-40° movement on either side of the central position Not useful for discreet adjustments	Used as selector switches. Should not be used for more than three switching positions.
Pedal Handgrip	Rotary lever Limited area of movement Gripped near the shaft	For rotary multiple switching
Rotary Lever	Attached to a shaft to allow complete turn	When a fairly high force is required For powerful force
Pedal	Reciprocating control Operated by one foot	For continuous controlling For on-off or start-stop switching
Push Button	Reciprocating control. Positive action in one direction only	Switching
Rudder Bar	Reciprocating control. Pivoted about its centre. Operated by foot. Example:Treadle	For accurate control and little force.

ENVIRONMENTAL FACTORS

Temperature and Humidity

High temperatures adversely affect the productivity of workers. They also increase the resting time of workers. Research studies show an increase in accidents both with decrease and increase of temperature from an optimum of 65°F, the increase with cold being somewhat the greater. Old people are adversely affected by higher temperatures. We should, therefore, provide a conducive environment to the workers for optimum efficiency.

For human body, there are gains as well as losses of heat; gain by convection (C), radiation (R) and basal metabolism (M) and loss by evaporation (E), convection (C) and radiation (R). The heat balance expression is given by:

$$M \pm R \pm E = 0$$

$$\text{or } E = M \pm R \pm C$$

Evaporation Rate depends on perspiration mechanism and the relative humidity or water pressure of the environment.

If the body's gains exceed the losses by evaporation there is a maximum body temperature rise of about 1°C (or 2°F). If this does not happen, there is severe heat stress, leading to heat stroke. Over a period of time, however, human body's tolerance to heat increases.

Heat afflicts us adversely under two conditions:

(*i*) Warm-moist — Heat is convected. Work becomes difficult because of high humidity which reduces perspiration.

Remedy: Proper ventilation and AC. If heat is radiated, workmen should be removed for some time to cool off.

(*ii*) Hot-dry — Warm-dry conditions do not pose a problem.

Vibration

The sources of vibration at the time of work are varied. The effects of vibration could lead to motion sickness, physical discomfort or physical damage. The tolerable limit of vibration between the amplitude (A) and frequency (F) of a vibration is

$AF^3 = 2$ for low frequency vibration: 1-6 cycles/second

$AF^2 = 1/3$ for medium frequency vibration: 6-60 cycles/second

$AF = 1/60$ for high frequency vibration: Over 60 cycles/second.

Tolerable limits of vibration cause no physical damage; though they may affect efficiency and may result in fatigue. Excessive vibration causes pulmonary damage, hematuria, rectal bleeding and constipation. Hand-held vibrating tools like drills may lead to 'white fingers,' dead hand, and Raymond's phenomenon.

Despite the above, we cannot lay down the specific design recommendation regarding vibrations lessening its effect. The operators feel they are compensable adequately to tolerate vibrational discomfort. They accept it so long as it does not affect them physically.

Noise

Noise is unwanted sound, and is irritating and fatigue-causing. Sound frequencies between 2400-4800 cycles/second may cause damage to the ear. As we advance in age, impairment of hearing is increased. Individuals exposed to high sounds also experience a hearing loss. Intermittent noise is considered a potential hazard. Deafness due to noise has been made compensatable in many countries.

Cotton wool in the external ear might protect the ears. Noise above 90 decibels makes us error-prone. Irritation also affects the work efficiency. High-pitched voices are more annoying than low-pitched voices.

Noise can also be meaningfully employed to break the barrier of quietness existing between workers in no-sound work situations. Music is soothing, though it might not be liked by some. High volume music also becomes irritating. Noise affects the oral communication. Raising the voice above the din, we can communicate but it is strenuous. In such situations, visual signs should be considered.

Noise can be reduced at the level of the source itself. Noise can be localised by surrounding structure around the source. Resonating parts should be given suitable damping devices. Damping material can be attached to cover surface of the sheet metal. In certain situations, acoustic absorption will have to be tried. Tree plantations around the factories reduce noise pollution for the residents in the neighbourhood.

VISUAL ENVIRONMENT

Lighting

It is estimated that 80% of the information required in doing a job is perceived visually. Good visibility of equipment, the product and the data in the work process is an essential factor in accelerating production, reducing the number of defective products, preventing visual fatigue.

Visibility depends on a number of factors:

1. The size of the workpiece
2. Its distance from the eyes
3. The persistence of the image
4. The lighting intensity
5. The colour of the workplace and contrasts of colour and lighting levels with the background.

Lighting should be adapted to the type of work. The level of illumination should be increased not only in relation to the degree of precision but also in relation to the worker's age. (Old people require a higher level of illumination).

Lighting intensity at workplace should be checked periodically and all lighting surfaces should be kept clean. In general the light should be uniformly diffused. Natural lighting should be used wherever possible.

Careful choice of interior colour schemes should be made. The glare is discomforting as it produces a feeling of strain. The disability glare causes a reduced ability to see. Both the glares are visual distractions. Planning for visual efficiency should start at an early state of job planning. As a general rule, sunlight is better than artificial light.

Ventilation

Ventilation is a dynamic parameter that complements the concept of air space, *i.e.*, for a given number of workers. The smaller the work premises the more intense should be the ventilation. (Ventilation replaces contaminated air by fresh air).

Workplace ventilation:

1. Disperses the heat generated by machines and men at work.
2. Dilutes atmospheric contamination
3. Maintains the feeling of air freshness.

When natural ventilation is inadequate, artificial ventilation has to be used (Blown air system and exhaust air system).

Organizational Factors

Rest pauses or breaks have engaged the attention of research workers. Work measurement techniques previously discussed are a good help. As a rule, the worker should not expend more than 3200 K cal/day. Heavy work results in heavy calories expenditure. In good health, physiologists recommend not to exceed 4800 K cal/day. A day is broken up into time spent in bed, work and non-work. A normal day's work takes about 2000 K cal; or 5 K cal/minute. The work and rest should be adjusted to accumulation of lactic acid where muscle fatigue sets in. Rest taken at such time remains short. When rate of work exceeds 5 K cal/minute, the work cycle consists of 10 minutes of activity and 7 minutes of rest to have optimum results. The working hours are to be interspersed with pauses, rest periods, tea breaks, meal breaks etc.

Just as in heavy work there is fatigue, in light work there is boredom. Jobs are to be redesigned so as to enlarge and enrich them. This leads us to a discussion of behavioural dimensions of job.

Behavioural Dimensions of Job Design

Conventionally, job designs aim at minimising the costs and maximising the productivity. Though economic criteria are important in designing jobs, behavioural dimensions also do affect them, and influence performance. Let us therefore discuss the concepts of job enlargement, job enrichment, job rotation and participative job design.

Jobs are a set of tasks. Varied tasks provide varied stimuli — auditory, visual and/or tactile. Routinised jobs usually provide few stimuli.

Job Enlargement

Very specialised jobs become monotonous and lead to job dissatisfaction. Workers are adversely affected where there is tardiness, absenteeism and labour turnover. Job enlargement is an answer to such situations. Jobs are enlarged in terms of:

1. Variety of skills used.
2. Autonomy to exercise controls over how and when the job is completed.
3. Task identity — opportunity to be responsible for an entire piece or programme of work.
4. Feedback — opportunity to receive on-line information.

Job Enrichment

Job enrichment has the above four dimensions. In addition, it stresses the dimension of task significance. Many jobs are highly specialised. Workers do not understand how significant their part of the job is. Tightening a nut allows the automobile to hold its wheel, and results in overall safety. Job enrichment involves re-assigning work-content to make the job more meaningful, more enjoyable. It involves employees in planning, organizing and controlling their work. The information regarding goals/performance expected must be given by the management.

Job Rotation

Some jobs cannot be redesigned to eliminate their undesirable features. They are not automated also. In such a situation, it is possible to move/rotate employees into the job for a while, and move them out again. Job enlargement and job enrichment might not work out in all situations. Here job rotation comes handy.

Any discussion of job design that overlooks the man behind the machine is incomplete. He has to participate in the process of job design.

SOCIO-TECHNICAL APPROACH TO JOB DESIGN

Traditional job designs have to modify their approach to take care of social aspects of work environment, while designing the jobs on the basis of production technology. In short, what is recommended is a socio-technical approach to provide high productivity and at the same time conducive work environment giving job satisfaction. This is an integrated approach that blends cost and quantity considerations to social consequences of work.

Tavistock Institute, London, was the first to offer guidelines on the job-design according to this approach:

1. Variety of tasks in the total job.
2. Significance of tasks in each job to constitute a single, overall task.
3. Work cycle optimisation.
4. Standardisation of quantity/quality of production and feedback of results.
5. Auxiliary/preparatory tasks are included in the job.
6. Making job respectable by introduction of elements of skill, knowledge and effort.
7. Significance of the job to make the product useful to the consumer.

   Some group-level guidelines are:

8. Inter-locking of tasks, job rotation or physical proximity.
9. Interlocked tasks have semblance of an overall task, scope for standardisation and control over boundary tasks.

Implementation of the above guidelines require care and caution, and of course, the top management support.

Appendix

PRINCIPLES OF MOTION ECONOMY

The principles of motion economy form a basis — a code or a body of rules — which, if applied by one trained in the technique of motion study and the problem solving process, will make it possible to increase the output of manual labour with a minimum of fatigue.

These principles have the following three sub-divisions:

(I) Principle of motion economy as related to the use of the human body.

(II) Principles of motion economy as related to the arrangement of the place.

(III) Principles of motion economy as related to the design of tools and equipment.

Principles of Motion Economy as Related to the Use of the Human Body

(1) The two hands should begin as well as complete their motions at the same time.

(2) The two hands should not be idle at the same time except during rest periods.

(3) Motions of the arms should be made in opposite and symmetrical direction and should be made simultaneously.

It is advantageous to arrange similar work on the left and right hand sides of the workplace, thus enabling the left and right hand to move together, each performing the same motions. The symmetrical movements of the arms tend to balance each other, reducing the stock and jar on the body enabling the worker to perform the task with less mental and physical effort. There is apparently less body strain when the hands move symmetrically than when they make nonsymmetrical motions, because of this matter of balance.

(4) Hand and body motions should be confined to the lowest classification with which it is possible to perform the work satisfactorily (Class I, II, III, IV, V).

General Classification of Hand Motion

(A) Finger motions.

(B) Motions involving fingers and wrist.

(C) Motions involving fingers, wrist and forearm.

(D) Motions involving fingers, wrist, forearm and upper arm.

(E) Motions involving fingers, wrist, forearm, upperarm and shoulder. This class necessitates disturbance of the posture.

Finger motions are more fatiguing, less accurate and slower than motions of the forearm. Forearm is the most desirable member to use for light work and that is highly repetitive work, motions about the wrist and elbow are superior to those of the fingers or shoulders.

(5) Momentum should be employed to assist the worker wherever possible, and it should be reduced to a minimum if it must be overcome by muscular effort.

The momentum of an object is its mass multiplied by its velocity. In most kinds of factory work the total weight moved by the operator may consist of 3 components — the weight of the material moved, the weight of the tools or devices moved, and the weight of the part of the body moved. It is often possible to employ momentum of hand, the material or the tool to do useful work. When a forcible stroke is required, the motions of the workers should be so arranged that the stroke is delivered when it reaches its greatest momentum.

In laying a brick wall, for example, if the bricks are conveyed from the stock platform to the wall with no stops, the momentum can be made to do valuable work by assisting to shove the joints full of mortar. If instead of being utilized, the momentum must be overcome by the muscles of the bricklayer, and fatigue will result.

(6) Smooth continuous curved motions of the hands are preferable to straight line motions involving sudden and sharp changes in direction.

The abrupt changes in direction are both time-consuming and fatiguing to the operator, *e.g.*, Folding paper.

(7) Ballistic movements are faster, easier and more accurate than restricted (fixation) or "controlled" movements.

Voluntary movements of hands may be grouped into:

(i) Fixation movement: Here opposing groups of muscles are contracted, one group against the other, *e.g.*, finger and thumb method of writing.

(ii) Ballistic movement: It is fast, easy motion caused by a single contraction of a positive muscle group with no antagonistic muscle group contracting to oppose it.

It is less fatiguing, for the muscles contract only at the beginning of the movement and are relaxed during the remainder of the movement. It is more powerful, faster, more accurate, and less likely to cause muscle cramp, *e.g.*, the skilled carpenter swinging a hammer in driving a nail. The carpenter aims his hammer, then throws or swings it. The muscles are contracted only during the first part of the movement, they idle along the rest of the way. The swinging curves of an orchestra conductor's baton is another example of ballistic movement.

(8) Work should be arranged to permit an easy and natural rhythm wherever possible.

(9) Eye fixations should be as few and as close together as possible.

Although some kinds of work can be performed with little or no eye direction, but where visual perception is required it is desirable to arrange the task so that eyes can direct the work effectively, *i.e.*, workplace should be so laid out that the eye fixations are as few and as close together as possible.

Principles of Motion Economy as Related to the Workplace

(10) There should be a definite and fixed place for all tools and materials.

The operator should always be able to find the tools and materials in the same location. Similarly, finished parts and assembled units should be disposed of in fixed places. It should not be that the operator will have to think where the materials are located. Definite stations for materials and tools aid the worker in habit formation, permitting the rapid development of automaticity.

(11) Tools, materials, and controls should be located close to the point of use.

Very frequently the workplace such as a bench, machine, desk or table, is land out with the tools and materials in straight lines. This is incorrect, for a person naturally works in areas bounded by lines which are arcs of arcs.

Normal Working Area

Considering the horizontal plane, there is a very definite and limited area which the worker can use with a normal expenditure of effort. The normal working area for the right hand is determined by an arc drawn with a sweep of the right hand across the table. The forearm only is extended, and the upper arm hangs at the side of the body in a natural position until it tends to swing away as the hand moves toward the outer part of the workplace. The normal working area for the left hand is determined in a similar manner. The normal arcs drawn with the right and left hands will cross each other at a point in front of the worker. The overlapping area constitutes a zone in which two handed work may be done most conveniently.

Maximum Working Area

There is a maximum working area for the right hand and for the left hand, working separately and for both hands working together.

The maximum working area for the right hand is determined by an arc drawn with a sweep of the right hand across the table, with the arm pivoted at the right shoulder (similarly for left hand).

The overlapping area formed by these two curves constitutes a zone beyond which two handed work cannot be performed without causing considerable disturbance of posture and accompanied by excessive fatigue.

Fig. 9.1

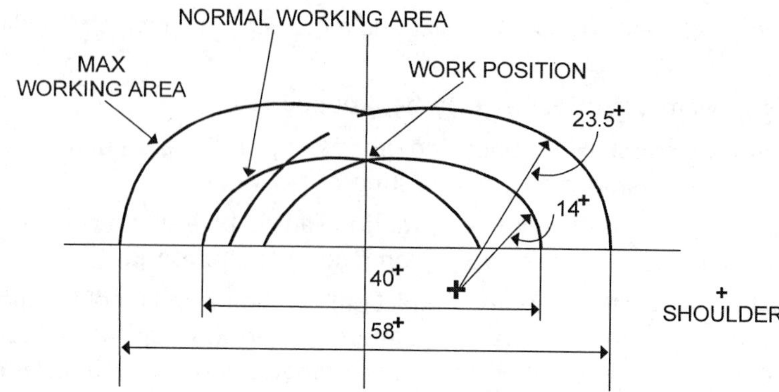

Each hand has its normal and maximum working area in vertical plane.

The use of a duplicate fixture and duplicate bins arranged symmetrically on each side of the fixture permits the two hands to make simultaneous motions in opposite directions in performing the operation. Such an arrangement facilitates natural, easy, rhythmical movements of the arm.

Those tools and parts that must be handled several times during an operation should be located closer to the fixture of working position than tools or parts that are handled but once.

Fig. 9.2

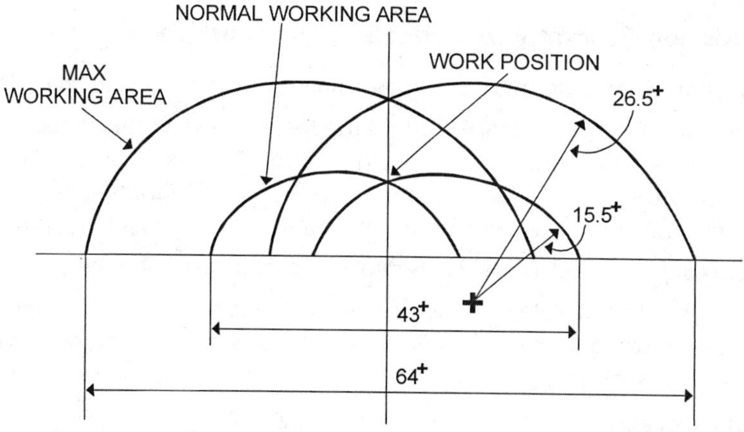

Arrangement of Machines: The following statement might be considered as a corollary to rule (11).

In the continuous type of manufacturing, machines, process apparatus, and equipment should be arranged so as to require the least movement on the part of the operator.

(12) Gravity feed bins and containers should be used to deliver material close to the point of use.

A bin with sloping bottom permits the material to be fed to the front by gravity thereby relieving the operator of having to dip down into the container to grasp parts.

(13) Drop deliveries should be used wherever possible.

The work should be arranged so that the finished units may be disposed of by releasing them in the position in which they are completed, thus delivering them by gravity. This saves time and also frees the two hands to begin another cycle. If a chute is used to carry the finished parts away, it should be located so that the parts can be released in the position in which they are finished.

(14) Materials and tools should be located to permit the best sequence of motions.

The material required at the beginning of a cycle should be placed next to the point of release of the finished piece in the preceding cycle. This arrangement permits the use of two hands to best advantage at the beginning of the new cycle.

(15) Provisions should be made for adequate conditions for seeing. Good illumination is the first requirement for satisfactory visual perception.

By adequate illumination is meant (A) Light of sufficient intensity for the particular task.

(B) Light of proper colour and without glare.

(C) Light coming from the right direction.

(16) The height of the workplace and the chair should preferably be arranged so that alternate sitting and standing at work are easily possible.

Workers should be permitted to vary their positions by either sitting or standing as they prefer. Such an arrangement enables an individual to rest certain sets of muscles and a change in position tends to improve the circulation.

It also produces less fatigue. To determine the average height of the workplace, the height of the worker's elbow above the standing surface is commonly taken.

(17) A chair of the type and height to permit good posture should be provided for every worker.

A good chair should have the following features. The chair should be adjustable in height. It should be rigidly built, preferably of steel frame with a lightly padded set and back rest. The edges of the seat and back should be rounded so that no sharp corners are present.

Swivel chairs and chairs with casters are not readily recommended for factory work unless the operator needs to work through an arc or move about.

Foot Rest: An adjustable foot rest should be provided wherever possible. It may be attached to the floor or to the work table.

Arm Rest: Arm rests are most effective on work that requires little movement of the forearms, with the hands working at approximately the same position, *e.g.,* light drilling, tapping and reaming.

The arm rest should be padded and must not interfere with the necessary working movement of arms and hands.

Principles of Motion Economy as related to the Design of Tools and Equipment

(18) The hands should be relieved of all work that can be done more advantageously by a jig, a fixture, or a foot-operated device.

(19) Two or more tools should be combined whenever possible.

It is usually quicker to turn a small two-ended tool end-for-end than it is to lay one tool down a pick up another.

For example, two ended wrench, pencil and eraser.

(20) Tools and materials should be pre-positioned whenever possible.

Pre-positioned refers to placing an object in a pre-determined place in such a way that when next needed it may be grasped in the position in which it will be used. For pre-positioning tools, a holder in the form of a socket, compartment, bracket, or hanger should be provided, into which or by which the tool may be returned after it is used, and where it remains in position for the next operation.

(21) Where each finger performs some specific movement, such as in typewriting, the load should be distributed in accordance with the inherent capacities of the fingers.

The normally right handed perform work with less fatigue and greater dexterity with the right hand than with the left. Although most people can be trained to work equally well with either hand on most factory operations, the fingers have unequal inherent capacities for doing work. The first and second fingers of the two hands are ordinarily superior in their performance to the third and fourth fingers.

(22) Levers, hands, wheels and other controls should be located in such positions that the operator can manipulate them with the least change in body position and with the greatest speed and ease.

The operator should not be required to leave his normal working position to operate machine. The controls should be placed in such a way that he need not bend over or twist his body in an uncomfortable manner when manipulating them.

☙❧ ☙❧

10

OPERATIONS/PRODUCTION PLANNING AND CONTROL: (OPC or PPC)

Introduction

The basic objective of creating the manufacturing organization is to make products. Thus, production is the nucleus or the centre of the entire business operations. Production planning and control functions look after the manufacturing activities. Production planning and control comprise the planning, routing, dispatching and follow-up functions in the manufacturing process so that the movements of materials, performance of machines and operations of the labour, however, subdivided, are directed and co-ordinated as to quantity, quality, time and place. Planning and control are two basic and interrelated managerial functions. They are so interrelated that they can be and often are considered as being one function. Planning is a pre-operation activity while control is a post-operation function. Both of them are so closely related that they are treated as Siamese twins. Planning sets the objectives, goals and targets on the basis of the available resources with their given constraints. For the translation of such objectives, goals and targets into reality, it is imperative to install control machinery for using the resources and assessing the performance. Such assessment can be made effectively only when some standards of performance are set in advance. Planning involves setting up of such standards. Controlling is made by comparing the actual performance with these preset standards and deviations are ascertained and analysed. Effective control presupposes some sort of planning. Thus, planning and controlling are intimately related. Production planning involves the decision on the resources (*viz.*, men, materials, machines, methods etc.) that the firm will require for its further manufacturing operations and allocation of these resources to produce the desired product in the required amounts at the minimum costs, while production control is the adjustment of the plans in response to the noted deviations from the plan arising out of the business uncertainties of the future.

Production Planning: Meaning

Production planning is an essential prerequisite to production control. Production planning is the very basis of manufacturing. It involves management decisions on the resources that the firm will require for its manufacturing operations and the selection of these resources to produce the desired goods at the appropriate time and at the least possible cost. According to Alford and Beatty, production planning is defined as, "The technique of foreseeing or picturing ahead, every step in a long series of separate operations, each step to be taken in the right place, of the right degree and at the right time, and each operation to be done at maximum efficiency."

Production planning is to determine in advance manufacturing requirements such as men, materials, machines, manufacturing process, money and order priority. It organises production of an item prior to the commencement of production.

Production planning and control is the process of planning production in advance of actual production.

Objectives: The basic objectives of production planning are as under:

1. On the basis of the sales forecast and its engineering analysis, to estimate the kind of the resources like men, materials, machines, methods, etc. in proper quantities and qualities. It also estimates when and where these resources will be required so that the production of the desired goods is made most economically.
2. It also aims to make all necessary arrangements so that the production targets as set in the production budget and master schedules are reached. While attaining these targets, adjustments are made for the fluctuations in the demand and customers.

Planning Procedure

The end product of the production planning efforts is the formulation of production plans. The plans are formulated in the light of the specified future period. The plans are to be implemented in the light of the estimated costs and agreed policies. The costs in this case include capital costs of assets and plant facilities, inventory cost, labour cost and cost of setting up the operations. The policies are framed in the light of the planning techniques and strategies which have been developed for the particular plan. The important steps in production planning are as under:

(1) Demand forecasts: The production planning function is geared to the estimated demand for the products. The demand forecasting represents an anticipated level of demand and it also reflects on the pattern of the demand. If seasonal or other kind of symmetry can be predicted, production can be planned to take advantage of the predicted pattern of the demand.

(2) Specification of production requirements: Though demand forecast provides the basis in production planning, it is not everything in production planning. The demand forecast must be converted into a specification of production requirements. The forecast demands are adjusted as under while planning the actual production:

(*a*) On the basis of available production capacity, the forecast demand is put on the calendar schedule.

(*b*) Reasonable allowances are made for possible errors in the forecast.

(*c*) The deficiency or surplus of the existing production capacity is ascertained in terms of machine capacity and labour force. On the basis of the temporary or permanent fluctuations in the demand, the adjustments in the machine capacity and labour force are planned well in advance.

(*d*) A schedule of materials requirements is prepared. While deciding the quantity of materials, due consideration is given to the seasonal advantage, cost of excess inventory carrying, cost of stock outs, etc.

The above type of production planning is made in the light of the specifications of the product or the customer orders within the prescribed tolerance limits.

(3) Requirements planning: Planning is seeing that all the required tools, machines, men will be available at the right time, in the right quantities and are of the right quality.

(4) Preparation of load charts: Load charts are prepared and are fitted with work orders. These are adjusted to the uncomitted time of the company's facilities.

(5) Setting of production rate: The production requirements are broken into periods and the schedule of production is prepared. The production at any point of time is the result of the prescribed rated capacity. In the light of the desired production, the production rate should be planned on the basis of the existing production capacity, overtime working, extra-shift working or new additions to the existing production capacity. The inventory levels should be geared to the production rates. On the basis of the set production rates, the schedule of the periodic production and inventory holding should be prepared. The production rate is set with the help of graphic techniques.

The setting of the production rate is relatively difficult in case of the seasonal demand. However, the adjustments can be made by continuing the average production throughout the year and by manipulating the inventories if it releases some cost advantages. Various mathematical programming methods are used in practice for planning the seasonal production requirements.

(6) Controlling production: Once the production plan is made and set to operation, it is likely that the actual stock of the finished goods inventory will fall below or exceed the planned balances due to the discrepancies in the estimated and actual sales. The marginal imbalances in the estimated and actual sales are solved by providing for certain safety stock level of inventories. The size of the safety stock depends on the promptness of production adjustments. In any way, such discrepancies would necessitate the periodic adjustments in the production with a view to bring the inventories into the line. The adjustments in the plan are made as under:

(*i*) Where only a short span of the planned cycle is over, the revisions in the original forecast should be made by adjusting the expected sales changes to the cumulative forecast for the remainder of the planned cycle.

(*ii*) Where the planned cycle is on the verge of completion, the forecast may be extended to cover the next planning cycle.

Control is a diffused activity and includes functions such as dispatching, progressing and expediting.

In short, production planning covers the following activities:

- Process selection for the product
- Break-down of parts/materials
- Make or buy decision
- Planning machines/equipment/tools
- Setting time standards
- Routing or the path of raw materials will travel to produce the desired output
- Create the production schedule.

The planner is influenced by the total quantity of output required and the frequency of re-orders. The type of order decides the manufacturing method and the type of machine shop — batch production, mass production etc.

Production Control: Meaning

Production planning strives to set the production targets and plans the availability of the resources to translate these targets into realities. While the production control constantly keeps a watchful eye on the production flow and use of resources along with the location, of any deviation from the preset action and to arrange for the prompt adjustment so that the productivity may run according to the original or revised schedules. It directs instructions to all parts of the factory to produce the desired output at the time specified. It is analogous to the central nervous system of the human body.

Production control is a facilitating service to manufacturing. It coordinates all the production operations by collecting the relevant information about various types of inputs and outputs and by making necessary adjustments in them. It directs and checks the course and progress of the work and closes the records on the completion of the work or order.

Objectives: The main objectives of the production control are as under:

1. To implement the production plans by issuing necessary orders to the persons who are supposed to implement them.
2. To ensure that the resources, *i.e.*, men, machines, materials, methods etc. which are required for the implementation of the production plans have been provided in the required quantity and quality, at proper time and proper place.
3. To see that the persons are carrying out the operations properly so that the production plans may be executed according to the schedules.

Scope of Production Control: Within the broad perspective of the production control, the following functions are covered:

(1) Activity control: Which involves the release of manufacturing orders and release of resources through dispatching.

(2) Control on inventory: Which observes proper ordering, receipt, storing, issue and movement of inventories.

(3) Control on tools: Which looks after the availability of proper tools as required by the specifications of the production.

(4) Control on timings of production: Which observes only stoppages, delays, rushes arising in each operation, and thus regulates the entire flow of production so that the orders may be executed on the delivery dates or in the vicinity of the dates.

(5) Quality control: Which involves the observation of in-process work at predetermined stages to determine whether the right quality of acceptable work has been processed.

(6) Replacement control: Which observes that the rejected raw materials and work-in-progress not fulfilling the quality standards are replaced by fresh inventories.

(7) Labour efficiency control: Which observes labour operations and records proper timings of labour operations. It attempts to maintain labour efficiency by comparing the time allowed and time taken for different operations.

(8) Control on machines and equipments: Which strives to attain the maximum utilization of installed capacity. It keeps the machines working through proper arrangements of cleaning, oiling, repairing and replacing.

(9) Control on methods: Which observes the methods set for various operations and devises the better methods in the course of the time.

(10) Control on progress of orders: Which requires the observation of the progress of orders and effects any adjustments, if required by the deviations. It closes the order on its completion and keeps a record for future reference.

Production planning and control is the function of looking ahead, anticipating problems and taking steps to overcome these before they happen. Production control is achieved through:

Dispatching which keeps the materials, tools and equipment moving. It keeps the work moving from machine to machine on operation to operation basis. It interfaces with scheduling.

Progressing collects data from the manufacturing shops, records the progress of wok and companies, progress against the plan.

Follow up which expedites the materials, in-process inventory and assembly.

Factors Determining the Production Control Procedure

The production control functions vary from organization to organization. Generally, the control procedure is governed by the following factors:

(1) Nature of the business: The control procedure required in a flour factory would be quite different from that required in an iron and steel industry.

(2) Scale of operations: The complexities of production control procedure are more in large sized manufacturing firms as compared to the smaller firms.

(3) Type of manufacturing: The control procedure in the intermittent production is very complex as compared to that in the continuous manufacturing system. The frequent changes in machine set-up, methods, specifications, sequence of operations, type of materials, operation instructions etc. in intermittent production increases the complexities of the control procedure.

(4) Degree of mechanization: Under the automatic production systems, the production flow is controlled automatically. The deviations are corrected through the feedback system. The materials are fed automatically to machines and move automatically throughout the process. The speed and other adjustments in the machines are done automatically. It needs less of human operation and they are regulated along with the mechanical operations. Due to all these factors, the control procedure in the automotive production system are more simple in relation to the non-automotive operations.

Production Planning	***Production Control***
(*i*) Preparation of production budget.	(*i*) To sub-divide the master schedule into manufacturing orders and subsidiary orders.
(*ii*) Devising manufacturing methods and sequence of processes.	(*ii*) Routing
(*iii*) Prescribing the type of machines and equipments.	(*iii*) Scheduling and machine loading
(*iv*) To set plant layout.	(*iv*) Dispatching
(*v*) To design tools.	(*v*) Follow-up or expediting
(*vi*) To prepare operation sheets and instruction cards.	(*vi*) Tool keeping
(*vii*) To undertake time and motion study for operations.	
(*viii*) To estimate material requirements.	
(*ix*) To estimate manpower requirements.	
(*x*) To prepare the master schedule of production.	

(5) Philosophy of the management: The production control is a service function to the manufacturing operations. The assignment of the control function and its splitting into various tasks largely depends on the realization of its importance by the management. Progressive organizations provide for exhaustive control procedure while traditional firms ignore or make insufficient provisions for control machinery.

(6) Organisation of production planning and control: The organisation of production planning and control differs from organization to organization. As noted above, production planning and production control are so interrelated that they can be and are often considered as being one function. However, the major areas of activities of production planning and production control can be segregated as shown.

The list mentioned broadly describes the various facts of production planning and production control. In actual practice the break-up of the total task varies significantly, *e.g.*, in the large organization the inventory control function is segregated from the production planning and is assigned to a separate head. It can still be bifurcated into general inventory control and traffic, the latter merely concentrating on the receiving, material handling and shipping functions. In some organisations some of the production planning functions such as production methods, procurement of machines and equipments, plant layout, tool design, instruction cards, time and motion study etc. are assigned to a separate division of industrial engineering.

Thus, the size of production planning and control and the division of activities in it largely vary from organization to organization on the basis of type of business, scale of operations, nature of manufacturing activity and degree of mechanization. The production planning and control department report to the works manager. The activities are split on the principle of cost-benefit analysis.

Typical Organisation Structure of the PPC Department

A medium-sized organisation's PPC department is illustrated below:

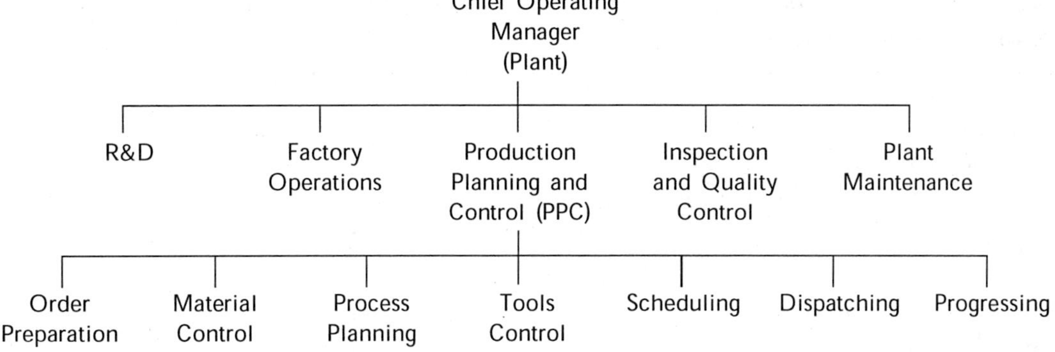

1. Work Order Preparation

The link between the sales function and manufacturing is the PPC department. The sales raises the sales order to the production department. It is a communication from the sales as well as an authorisation. The finished product stores raises the order for piece parts and sub-assemblies of a product. It is a formal request to the production department. There is a third situation when goods are manufactured to stock. Here the shipment order is raised by the sales, a copy of which is forwarded to the PPC department which oversees the inventory management. In batch production, there is a rolling sales programme and the PPC tries to meet the targets as per it.

One important function of the PPC department is to convert sales/stock order into work orders. A work order is an internal document of the PPC department. It is raised as an official authorization to different wings to initiate action.

The following diagram illustrates the procedure for raising the work orders.

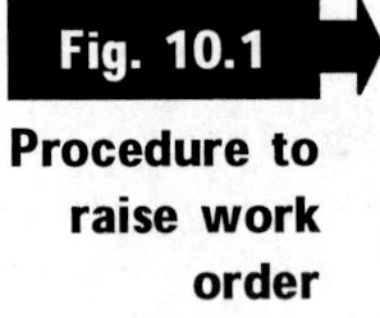

Procedure to raise work order

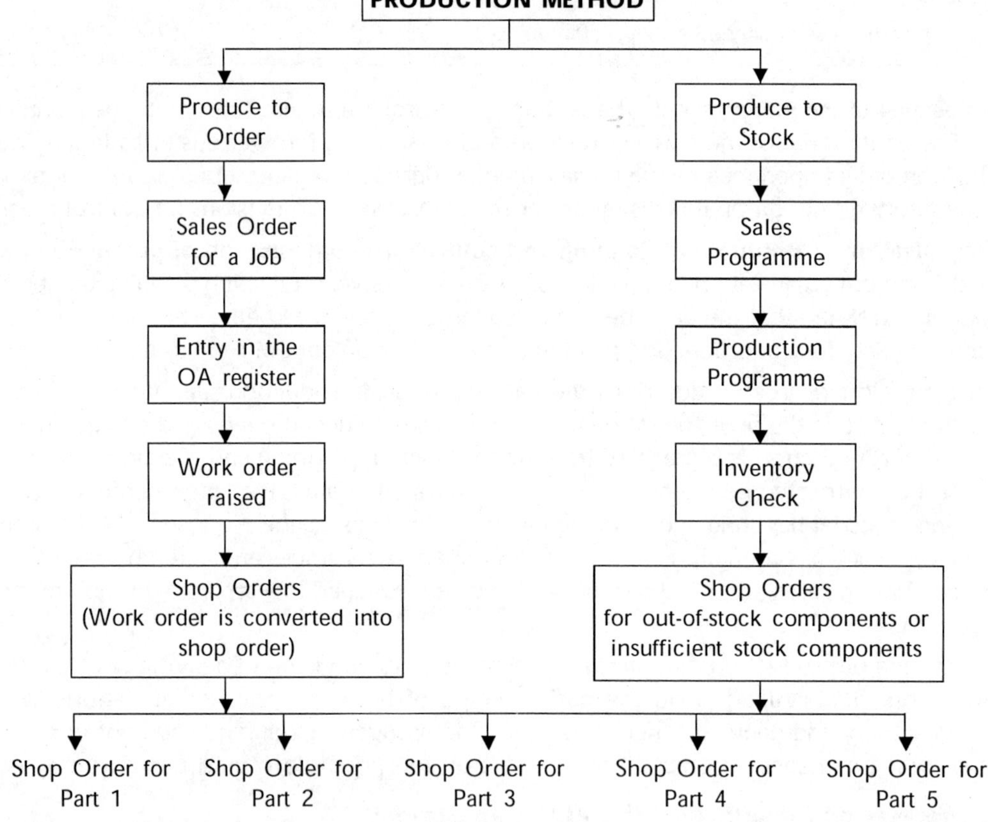

Work Order Documents

We have to acquaint ourselves with the usual format of these documents.

Work Order: It is illustrated below:

Fig. 10.2

Work Order

Work Order No.. ....
Customer .... Date: ....
Name of the Part ....
Quantity ....
Order No. ....
Part No. ....
Customer Part No. ....
Date to be despatched ....
Issued by ....

2. Process Planning

This is the method that traces the shortest and the most economical path of each part from the time it is procured to the time it leaves as finished product. It is, in other words, a list of operations and their sequence. It spells out machine tools for each operation and shows the necessary toolings required. The document that portrays all this is called Process sheet or Route Sheet

Functions of Production Planning and Control

There are four major functions of production planning and control — routing, scheduling, despatching and follow up. Routing scheduling are the planning functions, whereas despatching and follow up are the control functions.

Routing

Routing involves work planning — what work is to be done on material to produce the part or product, who will do it and where it will be done. It considers the path along which the work flows, and the necessary operations to be done on material along this path or route.

In routing, one important decision is regarding the quantity of materials for each individual part and for the whole order. Generally, explosion technique is used to do this. In this technique, the scheduled quantities of end products are split into the required quantities of component parts or raw materials. Synthesis is a method used when there is production to stock. A list of each part for future production schedule is made. As against this, in the analysis method, the end product material requirements are arrived at by breaking down it into sub-assemblies and parts, and then breaking sub-assemblies into its component parts. Analysis method is employed when producing on order.

Routing Documents

There are two important documents of routing — route sheet or route card and operation sheet. These documents spell out the sequence of the process used.

Route Sheet: Here, manufacturing operations are arranged in a proper sequence and related to the machine tools used for each part. It suggests the departments where the operations will be performed. The departmental movement of work is also indicated. The parts move in batches amongst the processes from one point to another. It is thus a travel sheet too. A typical route sheet is given below.

ROUTE SHEET

Part's Name .... Part No. .... Drawing No. ....
Product .... Product No............................. Quantity ....
Material ....
Economic Lot Size ....
Order No. .... Due Date ....

Operation No.	Description of the Operation	Machine/ Equipment	Department	Tooling

Fig. 10.3 Route Sheet

Operation Sheet: This sheet spells out the various operations carried out to make a part. The details keep on varying. A simple sheet specifies the operations and the machines on which these will be carried out. It is the discretion of the operator to set the cutting speed, depths of the cut and feeds needed. This is specially so if he is a skilled technician and is producing small quantities. Some operations sheets are elaborate and give the details of cutting speeds, feeds, depth of the cut and tools required. This sheet can carry the time analysis for each operation. A typical operation sheet is illustrated below:

Fig. 10.4

A Typical Operation Sheet

Part Name .... Part No. ....

Material .... Quantity required ....

Operation Number	Operation	Machine Tool	Cutting Tool	Cutting Speed mm/re	Feed mm/re	Depth of cut mm	Time Analysis

3. Materials Planning

Material planning is a part of production planning. It determines the requirements of materials. These include raw materials, bought out components and others. The material must come at the right time, in right quantity and with the least amount of capital tie-up. Materials Planning is done both for the direct and indirect materials.

One of the most widely used technique for materials planning is bill-of-materials (BOM). It is a document-generated at the design stage to spell out the structure of the product. It divides the final assembly into major assemblies, major assemblies into sub-assemblies and sub-assemblies into parts. These are details of part name, part number, description, quantity required, material etc. Each product is divided into its basic requirements with the help of BOM. The process of division or splitting is called explosion. The explosion chart can be prepared for an individual product or a group of products from a series of BOMs. In materials requirements Planning (MRP), the explosion is done by the computer level-by-level.

Bill of Materials: Bill of Materials specifies the names of the components or parts and/or raw materials that go into making a product. The quantities and description of each are given. All these components are identified by a code. The Bill is initiated by the process engineer or product designer or the engineering department. Bill of Materials is a necessary document for inventory management and control.

Fig. 10.5

Bill of Materials

Product .... Product No. ....

Prepared by .... Checked by ....

Approved by .... Date ....

Sr. No.	Part Code	Part Description	Specification	Weight/Qty.

4. Loading Scheduling

As an organisation is committed to the delivery data, each component entering the assembly must be made available in time. Scheduling determines the starting and completion date of each operation listed on the route sheet. Scheduling matches a shop order into the uncommitted available time for a machine or a group of machines in the production process, and such matching should not exceed the promised delivery date.

Scheduling is the time-table of the production plan. It spells out the commencement and completion dates of processing the products. It helps reduce congestion and idle machines during the operations. Scheduling aims at maximising the utilisation of resources, ensuring timely deliveries, and minimisation of costs and waiting times.

There are two types of schedules — Master Schedule and Shop/Production Schedule.

Master Schedule: It is the schedule that specifies which products are to be made, in what quantities and by which date. It also ranks the manufacturing orders in terms of their significance. The period used may be months. The constraint on Master Schedule is the production capacity. Master Schedule leads to the planning of individual components and sub-assemblies of each product. Master Schedule leads to purchase orders for raw materials and components. The Shop Schedules are prepared for parts to be made within the plant based on Master Schedule.

It is necessary to consider the delivery dates to arrive at the starting time. While doing so, the equipment is taken into account. It is also important to know the existing scheduled load. After deciding the delivery dates, the orders are sent to manufacturing section. The chart of product is split into its parts and sub-assemblies. The schedule is worked backwards. The starting dates are then decided.

There are two ways to schedule jobs — start manufacturing all the parts on the same date, and the past that takes longest to manufacture will decide the date of completion of the product. Other parts though finished earlier will have to wait; or else, start the production of various parts in sequence as per their manufacturing time. All the parts will be ready on one and the same date. This method is the preferred one.

The Master Schedule is a composite plan, prepared an monthly basis and extends into the future till all orders are fulfilled. It continues to roll month by month, a new month getting added as the previous one comes to an end. The schedule is adjusted for those activities that lag behind or as per sales forecasts.

Shop Schedule (Production Schedule): Production schedule is prepared after preparing the Master Schedule. It includes machines pertaining to that department and labour-load schedules. It also mentions the starting and finishing times of the production of various components to be made internally. The job is assigned to a scheduling clerk who jots down the delivery date, the availability of the capacity and the urgency of the task. The scheduling of orders is done as per the machine or labour capacity. When machines are independent, they are classified into types, and operations assigned to them are listed with the standard times to perform them. When a whole bunch of machines are used and they are dependent on one another, labour type is identified and capacity is noted in available labour hours. Thus, there is either machine type of loading or labour type of loading. The latter is easier to handle; as changes can be quickly factored in, and thus it comes on par to machine loading in terms of accuracy.

Production Schedule is a complex document as several hundred or thousand parts are involved, each having a separate process route through a large number of machines or limited machines performing multiple operations and myriad features. Besides, order priorities may be different, and cycle times are variable. There is a possible encounter of defectives and machine breakdowns.

Loading and Scheduling Devices

These indicate how the different operations begin and end. In a simple one operation, just a sheet for each operation is enough. When there are more than one operations, a sheet or card is prepared for each machine. If there are various operations on different machines in varying sequences, a separate sheet for each job is prepared. It is called *work schedule*. There could be another board which show different tasks against different work centres. Such a board is called *load chart*.

Machine Loading: It refers to job allocation to work centres. Job shopping refers to job allocation to the whole shop. In production planning, machine loading keeps production plan and costs in control, thus allowing optimisation of resources. The machine load capacity can be expressed in terms of pieces per unit of time or time in terms of pieces. The capacity is determined readily in either case by reference to standard time values of operations. Machine loads vary everyday, and records must reflect these variations. A new job increases the future load on a machine. The finished job decreases it. The work back-log is noted easily through these records. Jobs are so allocated that there is time optimisation.

Machine loads are received regularly to take care of underloading/overloading. Thus, any modification required in capacity, overtime, shifts can be effected. Machine load chart indicates work ahead for various machines and processes.

A typical machine load chart is given below:

Fig. 10.6 A Typical Machine Load Chart

Machine	Number of Operators	Hours/Week	April				May				June			
			1	2	3	4	1	2	3	4	1	2	3	4
	4	210												
	8	290												
	2	85												
	4	125												

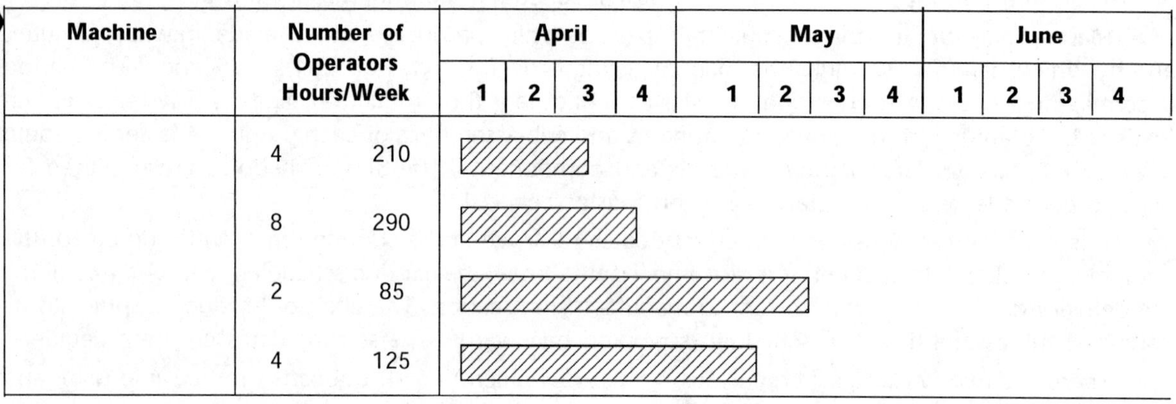

In the above chart, load is expressed in terms of hours for a given number of pieces. This chart is called *Bar Chart* or *Gantt Chart*. Each bar represents a task. It is indicated on the horizontal axis which indicates time scale. Gantt chart is developed by an American engineer, Henry L. Gantt.

Dispatching

Dispatching is concerned with the physical release of manufacturing order and job allocation to workmen on different machines. The materials and tools are delivered from the stores to the shop. The movement of material is facilitated. Records of idle time and spoilages during production is maintained. Control is exercised on work-in-progress.

Once the schedule is over, a master manufacturing order is prepared. It covers details about routing, finish dates within each department or on each machine and the engineering drawings. The departmental manufacturing orders are derived from the master document. These are required for each individual supervisor or foreman. This covers inspection tickets and approvals to move the work inter-departmentally. The departmental document authorizes the foreman to start work in his department. The despatch of the orders/instructions is the job of a dispatcher. Thus, despatching refers to issuance of orders/instructions that sets the production moving as per production schedules and routings. This is function clerical in nature and involves a lot of paper work.

A dispatcher issues the current work order instructions and drawings to the respective operational departments/work stations/operators/supervisors. The papers include machine schedules, route sheets, operation sheets, material requisition (MR) forms, machine loading cards, move or material ticket, etc. Against these, materials are released from the stores. Production toolings are also released. A dispatcher keeps records of the start and finish dates of each operation. He receives the feedback.

Machine Load Chart Symbols:

The following symbols are used in preparing a Gantt Chart

[	Opening bracket indicating the commencement of production activity.
]	Closing bracket indicating the completion of production activity.

— Thin bar indicates the progress of an activity.

⊠ This shows change over a period of time.

Machine Loading Chart: Gantt chart for machine loading is illustrated in Fig. 10.7.

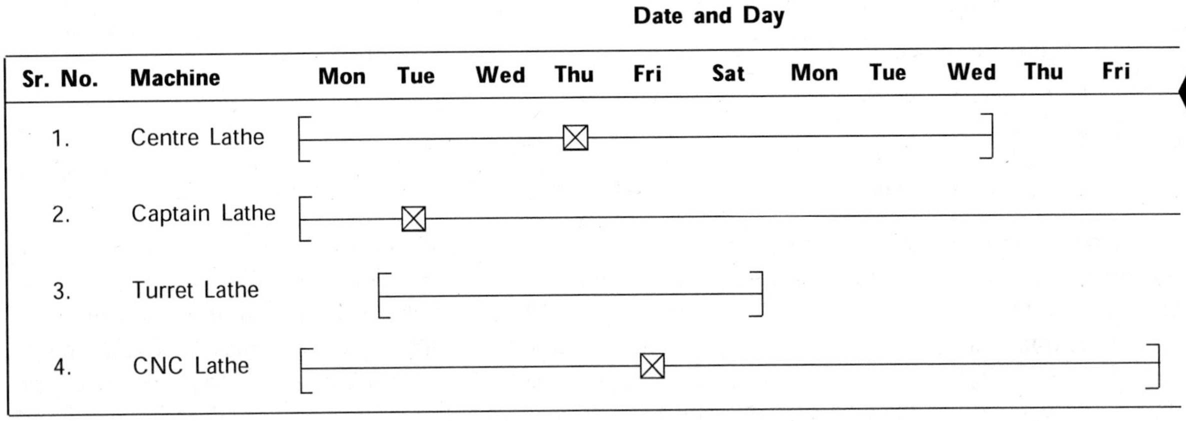

Date and Day

Sr. No.	Machine	Mon	Tue	Wed	Thu	Fri	Sat	Mon	Tue	Wed	Thu	Fri
1.	Centre Lathe											
2.	Captain Lathe											
3.	Turret Lathe											
4.	CNC Lathe											

Fig. 10.7 Machine Loading Chart

Material Requisition Form

The form outlines the material required for the job scheduled and the quantity to be issued. It is illustrated in the following diagram.

Part:	Part No.	Drawing No. ....
Product:	Product No.	
Material:	Material Code	Quantity ....
Quantity Authorized:	Quantity Issued	

Fig. 10.8 Material Requisition Form

Dispatching Functions

As observed already, the dispatcher prepares manufacturing orders consisting of:

- shop orders
- operational layouts
- stores-issue orders
- tool orders
- move orders
- inspection orders etc.

The documents are drawn from the respective files and are kept ready. The start of the job is authorised by raising a job card or time ticket.

Job order		Sr. No.	_____		
Employee	_____	Part Name	_____	Part No.	_____
Batch Qty.	_____	Qty. produced	_____		
Start time	_____	Completion line	_____		
Hours spent	_____	Hourly rate	_____		
Labour cost	_____	Std. Hours	_____		
Bonus	_____	Efficiency percentage	_____		

Fig. 10.9 Typical Job-card

The stores must issue the required quantity of materials and deliver it to the machine. The dispatcher has to raise a stores issue order.

STORES ISSUE ORDER

Fig. 10.10 **Typical Stores Issue Order**

Raw Material		Size	Specificatiion ....
Unit		Qty Needed	
Date required			
Charge it to			
Part Name		Part No.	
Shop Order No.			
Date	Entered by	Delivered by	Date of Delivery ....

Apart from raw materials, there should be tooling available to the work centre. The tools required may be consumable like reamers, drills, milling cutters etc. They could be machine aids such as chucks, collets, etc. There are work aid tools such as jogs and fixtures. There are inspection aid tools such as gauges, micrometers and Vernier callipers. Consumable tools and inspection tools are issued directly to workmen against tool vouchers. Machine aids and work aids are withdrawn by the dispatcher and issued some hours in advance of the commencement of the job.

Alternatively, a tool order can be prepared to document the tools issued directly to the workmen, and those issued to the dispatcher. There is record of the tool return date too in the tool order.

The internal material handling department is authorized by the dispatcher to carry materials to the work centre by raising the move order.

Move Ticket: It shows the travel path the material takes from the stores to the respective department, and then between departments or work stations. It is illustrated below:

Fig. 10.11 **Move Ticket**

Order No.:	Date: ....
From Dept.:	To Dept.: ....
Qty. Delivered:	Quantity Accepted: ....
Foreman:	Foreman: ....
Moved by:	
Remarks:	

The inspection department inspects the products against an inspection order from the dispatcher. The dispatcher also coordinates with the scheduler who has done the routing. Though the jobs are assigned by the foreman to the machines, this function could be performed by the dispatcher in collaboration with the foreman.

Ultimately, the material is forwarded to dispatch of finished parts stores. This is done by raising a forwarding note. At the end of the production run, the route sheets and operational layouts are collected by the dispatcher from the shop.

In short, the whole dispatching function raises the following documents.

- Job cards/Time tickets
- Stores issue order
- Tool order
- Move order
- Inspection order
- Machine set up order
- Forwarding note.

Inspection Ticket: This indicates the acceptance or rejection of the quantity of parts at each stage of operation. It is illustrated in Fig. 10.12.

Dept.: .... Order No.		Date: .... Charge to:	
Material	Quantity	Accepted Quantity	Rejected Quantity
Why Rejected? Operator's Fault:		Last Operation:	
Disposal			
		Inspector	

Fig. 10.12 **Inspection Ticket**

Dispatching function is present mainly in centralised control plants where production control's despatch office instructs what jobs are to be worked out. A shop order copy *travels* through the shop with parts from operation to operation. This copy carries the foreman's progress report. A copy of shop order is retained in the despatch department. Material comes back to the despatch office after operations are complete in the respective department. Material is routed to the next operation as per the sequence of operations. This system enables good monitoring and tracking of the material. After the entire work is over, the order is closed. In decentralised control, despatching is not very much prevalent. In such an organisation, the foreman passes out the jobs.

Progress Reporting and Follow up

In production, there could be several problems — shortage of parts or failure on the part of the supervisor to live up to production schedules. These could be attributed to faulty routing, scheduling and despatching. Moreover, there could be lack of raw material, breakdowns, lack of proper tools, jigs, fixtures, labour problems, too many rejections, etc. Such problems could be assigned to the system and communication problems. These delays make it necessary to have a system of progress reporting.

After production in a particular department is completed, there is an inspection to check conformance to the specifications and quality. The inspection ticket returns to the production department. Through this ticket, data is taken on the master control chart. This way production control is exercised.

Progressing is a process of comparing the actual performance against one production plan and identity the deviations, and take corrective action to set them right. It monitors the production function, recognises the delays and interruptions, expedites matter and keeps the customers updated. The documents used in progressing are the Daily Production Report/Job Card/Route Sheet, Progress Cards/Gantt Charts, and Revised Delivery Schedule.

Gantt charts were commonly used as production control tools. These charts as we know, are bar charts. The activities are listed vertically, and elapsed time horizontally. Symbolically, start and finish of a task can be represented on the chart. If these charts are updated regularly, it becomes a good visual aid to assess the progress of production. Gantt Charts, however, are not able to depict the inter-relationships of the separate tasks.

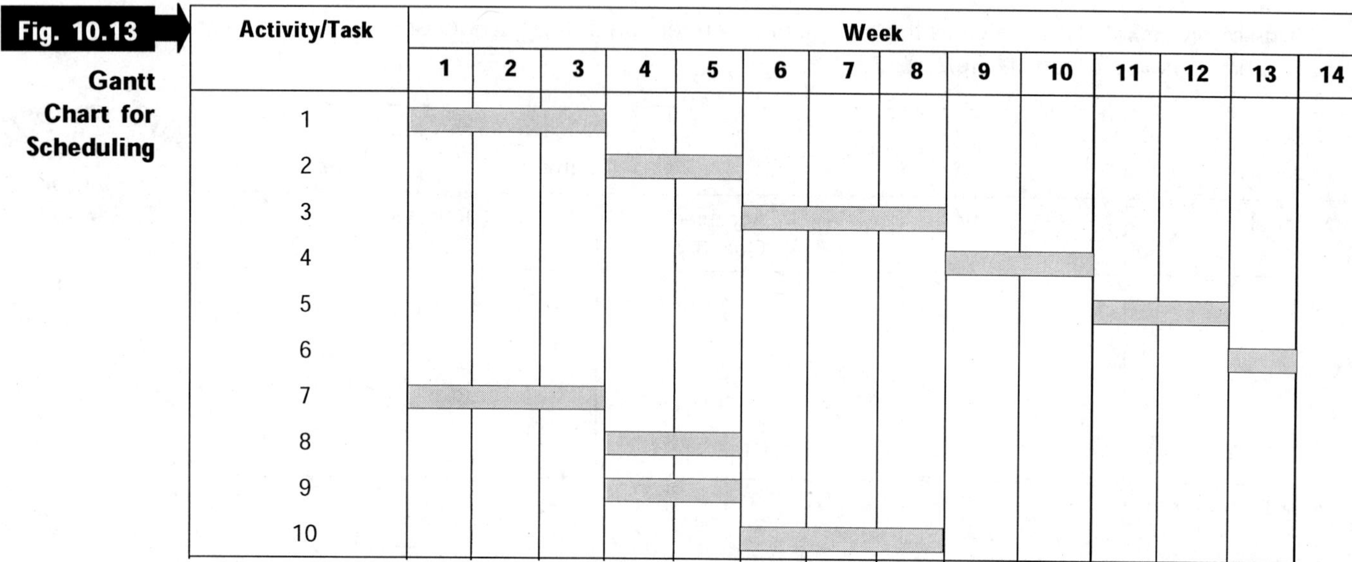

Fig. 10.13 Gantt Chart for Scheduling

Gantt Charts have been modified into graphic portrayals of production status and control. They offer work status visually. They are frequently updated.

A manufacturing and assembly flow chart can be prepared to facilitate scheduling, fabrication and assembly. Fig. 10.14 depicts parts and sub-assemblies, a collection of which leads to one finished assembled product.

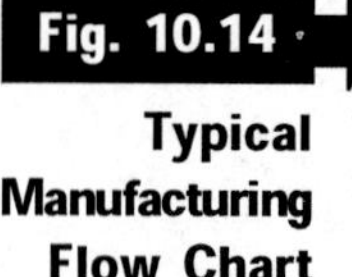

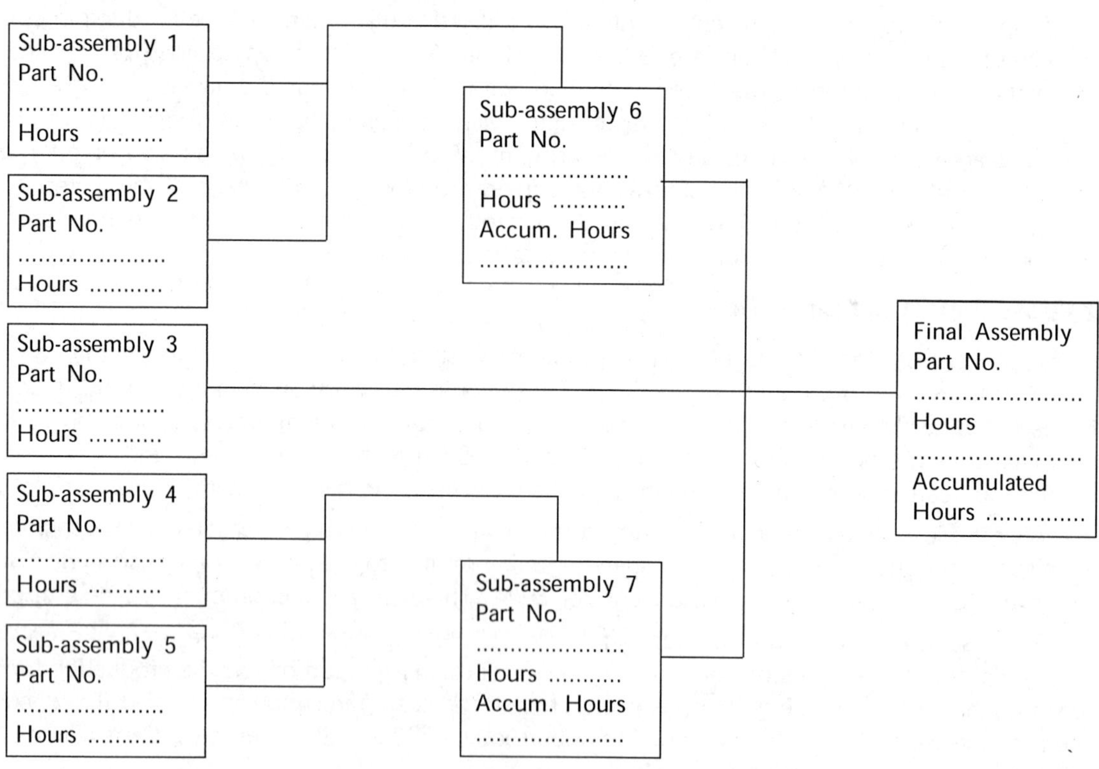

Fig. 10.14 Typical Manufacturing Flow Chart

The standard hours of each assembly are also indicated. Two or more sub-assemblies generated accumulated hours. The production cost can be assessed at any work station. The chart is also used to assess the lead time.

Follow up: Follow up people follow the through the jobs to expedite them and to locate lost jobs. They are called expeditors or stock chasers. They anticipate delays. The current status of the job indicates whether expedition is called for. It regulates the progress of materials and parts. The delays are overcome by suitable measures. The job is tracked within the plant and sourcing is looked into.

Follow up could be through customer orders which are followed throughout the plant. Follow up could be arranged department-wise. Follow up is both, *i.e.,* internal, within the plant and external, outside the plant at the supplier level. Internal follow up requires thorough understanding of operations. Outside expediting is through a representative deputed at the vendor's plant. He ensures a smooth flow of material from the vendor end to the plant.

CHARTS IN PLANNING

Pictorial and diagrammatic representation is always valuable, as it is a short-hand method of saying which we would have said in many words. Gantt chart is the simplest of all planning charts. It is diagrammatically given below:

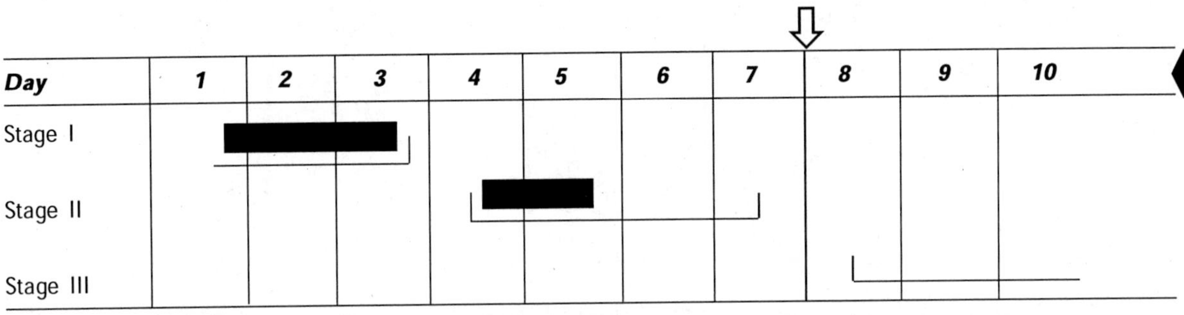

Day	*1*	*2*	*3*	*4*	*5*	*6*	*7*	*8*	*9*	*10*
Stage I										
Stage II										
Stage III										

Fig. 10.15
Gantt Chart

Imagine there are three stages in production. The time is shown horizontally. The unit could be hours, days or weeks. Vertically, we have shown the stages. The planned timing for each stage is shown by a bar or horizontal bracket. As the plan rolls on, we show the present point of time by an arrow. The progress of production is shown by second line or bar against the bracket. In the given diagram, the planned timings are 3 days for stage I, 4 days for stage II and 3 days for stage III. The bars indicate the completion of stage I and only half of stage II. We should have completed by now stage II as per the plan. In fact, we are lagging behind.

Gantt Chart has many forms. It is now a generic term for a variety of charts where times are charted horizontally and the actual progress is recorded as bars/brackets. While devising a production chart, we should emphasise clarity and flexibility.

Concept of Line of Balance

Line of Balance (LoB) is a planning technique which is of much use when we have to manufacture similar products over a period of time. Consider the following order:

Week	*1*	*2*	*3*	*4*	*5*	*6*	*7*	*8*	*9*	*10*
Quantity	2	4	4	10	10	20	20	10	10	10
Cumulative Total	2	6	10	20	30	50	70	80	90	100

Here, over a period of ten weeks, we have to deliver 100 units. The production has the following three stages:

Machine parts	:	3 weeks
Assembling the product	:	2 weeks
Testing the product	:	1 week

While the production is in progress, we have to ascertain how many units pass through each of these stages so that we can keep up the delivery schedules. At the end of 5th week, for instance, how many units must have completed machining. After machining, we require further three weeks for the next two stages, assembling and testing. At the end of the 5th week, we ought to have done machining as at the end of 8th week (5 weeks + 3 weeks). By the end of 6 weeks, we should have 80 units completed. Therefore at the end of the 5th week, a total of 80 units should have been machined.

Such computations can be made for any stage at a given point of time. The following is the bar chart of the position as at the end of week 5.

Fig. 10.16

Line of Balance at Week 5

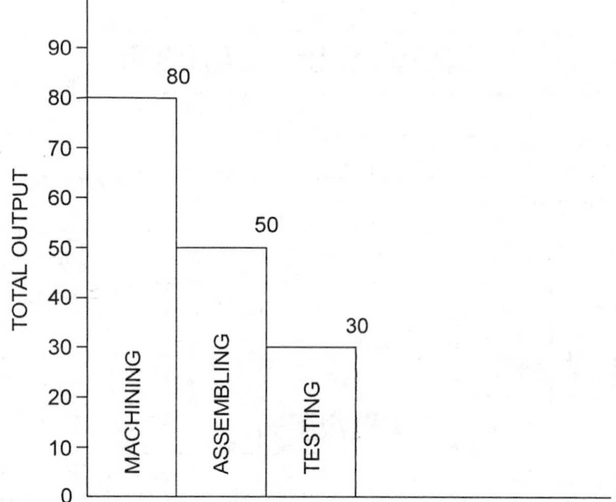

The planned position at a given point of time of the various stages of production is called the Line of Balance. If the actual output differs from this line of balance at any point of time, we have to set it right by rendering assistance to those stages where it falls below the plan, and de-emphasise the stages which are ahead of the plan. This can be achieved by deploying the resources like equipment and manpower properly.

Alternatively, instead of allowing products to flow through the stages progressively over a period of time, we can process all of them in one batch at each stage, and then proceed to the next. This is preferable where set-up time or preparation for production takes a long time. The alternative approach tends to accumulate inventories of work-in-progress, and hence, capital intensive.

Caselet: The Kanban Technique

It is a Japanese production control system invented and developed by Toyota that allows no surplus production and gives the workers the right to stop the line if they cannot keep up. It runs contrary to well-settled principle of the continuity of production. Kanban literally means a card. The only paper work issued by production control department consists of the final assembly schedule and two cards — travelling production authorisations. These cards stay with the container (or pallet) containing components throughout the production process. Each consuming department consumes the components in the container. The empty container and cards are returned to its preceding supplying department. There is immediate replenishment of the container, which is again sent to the consuming department (under strict lead time and delivery schedules). Kanban aims to achieve *just in time* production. It relies on the physical evidence of an empty container. It is not a time-phased approach. It is a 'pull' system of production authorisation. The secret of *just in time* production lies in the number of cards which are allowed to circulate on the factory floor at any one time. Kanban treats inventory as a liability rather than an asset. It believes in set ups where

(Contd...)

(Contd...)

there are fast changeovers, extra machines, off-line calibration. Kanban gives a significant competitive advantage to the Japanese industry. It moves towards stockless production by cutting EOQ and safety stocks. Japanese believe in building relationships with a hard core of suppliers. For effective working of Kanban, continuity of relationship with suppliers is essential, as these suppliers are expected to supply in smaller lots at less frequent intervals. In Kanban, a flexible organization with an educated workforce which concentrates upon the key problems such as the reduction of set-up times is really very helpful. Design rationalisation, rationalisation of parts and attendance to logistics are also equally important for the success of the Kanban. In Kanban, a 'bank' system is established between one process and another to adjust automatically the quality of in-process products and to reduce the down-time of the whole line. It is however to be noted that Kanban system cannot be applied to all manufacturing operations. Where there are large variations in day-to-day production levels, and frequent design changes, MRP (Materials Requirements Planning) is the best system. Sometimes, best results are obtained by combining Kanban and MRP.

Kanban is a cost reduction method of inventory management. Toyota maintains because of Kanban 0-3 day's inventory of spares. It also improves productivity (2,700 cars a day at Toyota's Takaoka plant, each completed in 1.6 man hours average. Compare with 3.8 hours in the U.S.A., 4-7 hours in Sweden and 2-7 in Germany). Kanban is only a contributory factor. Productivity in actuality results from the Japanese style of management with emphasis on 'work together concept' and a belief in 'people, not systems, produce the desired results.'

We wish you to examine critically the implementation of just-in-time production in a country like India.

Production Types

Production planning and control considers two types of production — production for stock and production for customer order.

Production for stock: Here, the finished products are available in inventory and customer orders are fulfilled from the available stock. The production is dictated by a forecast. The products are standardized.

Production for customer orders: Here, production is initiated on the receipt of a confirmed order. Sometimes it is difficult to deliver in time if no work is done prior to the receipt of an order. It is customary to carry some semi-finished or finished items to overcome this problem. Mostly, all orders received during a given period are grouped together for batch production of common parts.

Self-Managed Teams (SMTs)

Dr. Reddy's Laboratories is the pioneer of this concept by introducing it at their Yanam, Pondicherry plant in 2002. An SMT obviates the need for a supervisor, which is cost-saving too. Here the work schedule is defined by the planning department based on a fixed product mix. The schedule is forwarded to individual workers. The maintenance department stands by for support whenever there is a machine breakdown of any kind. The idea empowers the workers to deal with the planning and maintenance departments directly. It eliminates the need for a supervisor.

Workers are trained to hold meetings and plan their work accordingly. There are charts on the machines which tell them about the goals and the actuals. If the actuals are lower, the gap analysis is done to find out the root of corrective action thereafter. The disciplinary rules here are self-managed. The appraisals are on deliverables. This empowerment signals to the workers that they are not mere cog in the wheel. They were responsible. PepsiCo and RPG group too have adopted this concept. It ensures participative management.

ACTIVITY SCHEDULING

Activity scheduling has strategic significance, and affects the overall performance of the business. The operating system itself is the major point of consideration while scheduling the activities.

As the name itself indicates, it is the process of setting the time schedule or dates for all the activities to be performed. Once the schedule is drawn, we come to know how the items/customers will flow through the operating system. The times are decided in advance. How the problem is addressed depends on the nature of the demand. The schedules in anticipation of demand will be quite different from those which are designed considering the delivery date requirements. There are other factors too. It is a matter of choice for the operations manager to decide the appropriate solution for the problem on hand. Two major factors influence his decision — whether the scheduling is internal-oriented or external-oriented. Second, whether the demand is dependent or independent.

Internal-oriented and External-oriented Scheduling

As scheduling is concerned with the timing fo the activities, it has to be related to whether the customer has to be supplied a specific product by making it or the product is to be given from stock. A custom made specific product has a specific delivery or due date. The end product must be available by this date. In this situation, the customer has direct influence on the timing of the activities. In other words, the activity scheduling is external-oriented. The activities have to satisfy a particular external customer's timing requirements. In another situation, a product may be made and kept in stock in anticipation of the demand of the customer. The internal activities are thus not directly influenced by a particular customer. Customers are given products from stock and the stock is replenished as and when needed. This replenishment need influence the timing of the activities. Acitvity scheduling such as this is called internal-oriented. There is more latitude in fixing times and can be designed to maximise resource utilisation.

The orientation of scheduling in fact defines the scheduling problem. The structure of the operating system influences the choice of the scheduling strategy.

Just-in-Time (JIT) is an example of external-oriented scheduling. It has been discussed separately in this book.

The demand uncertainty in scheduling is to be managed. There is the problem of random arrivals — customers arriving randomly at service centres. To avoid waiting, the external scheduling is used with total excess capacity for capacity management. At hospitals, the demand is managed by appointments and reservations.

The activity scheduling resorted depends on the nature of the operating system — whether it is job production or project or batch production or project or batch production or flow production.

Reverse scheduling is used when there are external and date considerations.

Activity Scheduling Techniques

The production process involved generally tells upon the type of technique employed. If the production requirements are unique, the situation is one-off project type situation. Somewhere, the production is repetitive and the output satisfies the needs of a particular set of customers. *e.g.,* transport industry. There are intermediate situations in which batch processes are employed. There are overlapping areas between these production processes. The following table spells out the scheduling technique appropriate for a given situation.

Scheduling Technique	***Description***	***Processes where used***
Reverse scheduling (Gantt charts)	From the required completion date, duration of particular activities are subtracted. It is scheduling in reverse from the required due date.	It is used in project, jobbing and batch production.
Forward scheduling (Gantt charts)	The scheduled time of activities from a given date are carried forward till completion date is reached. It is the opposite of reverse scheduling	It is used in project, jobbing and batch production.
Sequencing	The best order for processing is decided to carry it through given facilities. The objectives are to optimise throughput times, queuing and idle time.	It is used generally in projects.
Dispatching	Here we have to identify a set of jobs to process next on available facility. The objective is to optimise throughput time, lateness etc.	It is used generally in jobbing.
Assignment	Available set of jobs are allocated to next available on an set of resources. It optimises throughput time, resource utilisation.	It is generally used in jobbing.
Time Tabling	A schedule or a time table to indicate when certain facilities/resources will be available to those who would like to avail them.	It is used in flow production.
MRP	A product structure is exploded and is checked against inventory. MRP is used for scheduling, for inventory management and capacity management. MRP II is broader in application.	It is mainly used for batch production. It is used in job and batch production.
Network Analysis	The project activities are schedules on the basis of their interdependence and slack is identified.	It is used for projects
Batch Scheduling	Optimum batch size is determined. A schedule for completion of batches is decided on a set of facilities.	It is used for batches.
Line of Balance (LOB)	It allows the calculation of quantities of particular activities/parts/components which are required to be completed by an intermediate date so that the delivery schedule is maintained. It is a scheduling and controlling technique.	It is used for batches.
Flow Scheduling	Appropriate facilities are used to allow the processing of the items/customers where each item passes through the same facilities in the same order.	It is used for job production.

The loan *forward scheduling* is used for an internal-oriented scheduling that decides the times/dates for subsequent activities, given the times/dates for an earlier activity (starting time).

Sequencing decides the optimal order for processing a set of jobs. It could be *static* sequencing when all jobs to be processed are known and are available. During this type of sequencing, additional jobs are not in the queue. In *dynamic* sequencing, the jobs arrive continuously in the queue.

In static sequencing, the given queue of jobs pass through a given set of facilities and each job passes through in the given order and time. The aim is time optimisation for all jobs or the throughput time. The aim in dynamic sequencing is minimisation of idle time, work-in-progress and conforming to the deadlines for each job.

PLANNING AND CONTROL FOR MASS PRODUCTION

Production process is essentially a transformation process of inputs to get outputs. There are three important classes of the production process: the flow shop, the job shop and the project. In a flow shop, the same operations are repetitively performed in a sequence. In job shop, a variety of jobs are performed in small batches. The project is a unique one-shot affair. It consists of many non-repetitive activities which consume time and resources, and which requires scheduling, co-ordination of activities and allocation of resources.

The flow shop equipment is a special purpose equipment designed to mass produce an item. The job shop carries the general purpose machines.

What is Mass Production?

Ford pioneered the concept of assembly line used for mass production. Mass production is wrongly equated with heavy production meant for teeming millions. However, mass production is a concept. It believes in break-up of a task into its simplest possible elements. These elements are then grouped as per production norms. Assembly line consists of work stations in sequence. At each work station, a carefully designed portion of work is done (in a soft drink plant, for example, filling of bottles). In this system, similar parts on assembly line are interchangeable and replaceable. This enables a production of a large quantity and maintenance too of large quantities.

On assembly line, the material moves continuously at a uniform average rate. It reaches the various work stations, where a portion of work is done. To illustrate, we have Premier Padmini Automobile assembly, Onida TV assembly, ICIM computers assembly, Leo toys assembly etc. The diagrammatic representation of an assembly is presented below.

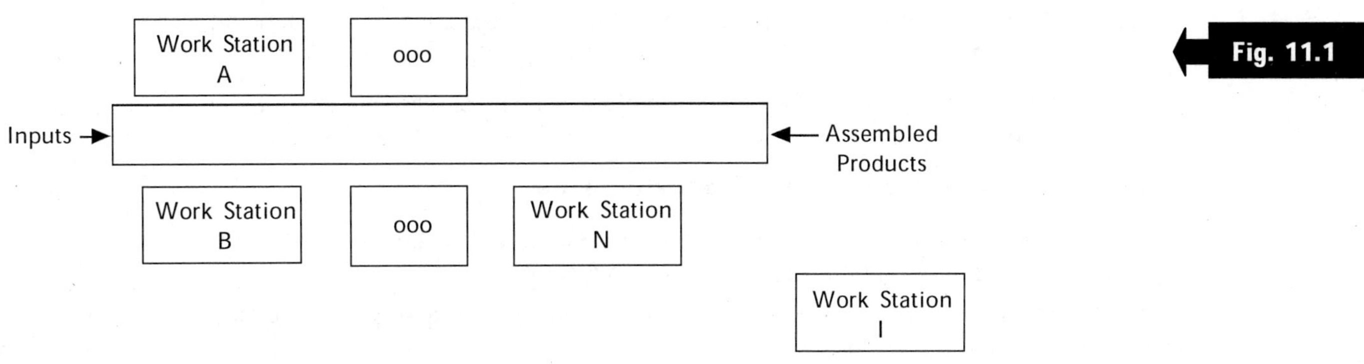

Fig. 11.1

Assembly line operations of materials can be manual or can be or conveyor belts carrying the part at pre-decided speed so that there is sufficient time at each WS to perform the allotted task. The conveyor belts are of belt type, chain type, overhead type, pneumatic type or screw type. Assembly lines on one hand can be 100% manual or on the other hand 100% automatic, with many different semi-automatic possibilities between these two extremes. The same principle however is at work in an automatic or non-automatic or semi-automatic process, changing only the labour content of the task.

Mass Production: Suitability

Mass production refers to a large quantity of production with standardised products having less variety. Ideally, it should be a single standard product (no changes in design) manufactured on a continuous basis over a period of time. So the determining factor is the demand which makes us opt either for continuous or batch type production. If there is a larger demand than the production rate, mass production can be sustained. But with a rate of demand lesser than the rate of production, batch production is called for. It gives us an inventory build-up.

Besides this, the economics of the assembly line must be attended to. When annual requirements are comparatively small, it is better to buy from outside. When they are moderate, it is better to produce on individual stations. For a higher demand, an assembly line is justified.

Characteristics of a Mass Production System

This system shows certain characteristics:

Merits

1. There is a smooth flow of material (from one WS to another WS) which is straight line, or L-type or U-type, or circular or S-type.
2. There are small WIP (work-in-process) inventories because output of one becomes input of the other process.
3. Production time/unit as a whole is short.
4. Closely spaced WS's reduce material handling.
5. No expertise necessary to operate the system. Less training costs.
6. PPC (production planning and control) is simple.
7. Less storage space for temporary storage and WIP.

Demerits

1. One machine failure results in a stoppage of the whole line following it. Maintenance is therefore challenging.
2. Assembly lines are not flexible. Great changes in layout are necessary when product design is charged.
3. Production speed is determined by the slowest machine. Line balancing is difficult.
4. It requires general rather than specific supervision.
5. Capital intensive owing to installation of special type of machines and their possible duplication along the line.

Concepts of Assembly Line and Fabrication Lines

Assembly line refers to a line where there are assembly operations — arrival of parts and departure of parts as an assembly (putting together) or sub-assembly.

Fabrication line refers to operations where a product undergoes physical/chemical changes, *e.g.*, machining, heat treatment etc.

Now line balancing in both these cases are though similar, it is to be appreciated that fabrication line is more difficult to balance as grouping and regrouping are difficult and the precedence restrictions are tighter. Operators on assembly line change jobs with ease, but on fabrication lines it is not so because there will have to be consequent changes in set-up and tools and machine tools.

Design of an Assembly Line

The assembly line balancing means to minimise the total amount of idle time. Alternatively, it means the reduction in the number of operators to accomplish a given task at a given speed of assembly line. In other words, we reduce the balance delay which is defined as the amount of idle time as a fraction of the total working time resulting from unequal task time assigned to given WS's.

The Precedence Diagram

It is dividing the assembly into parts (work elements). In this diagram, the order of performance of work elements is given. This ordering is in response to technological restrictions on the process or constraints of layout, safety or convenience. The precedence diagram is the foundation for grouping of work elements into work stations. The following precedence diagram shows 6 work elements.

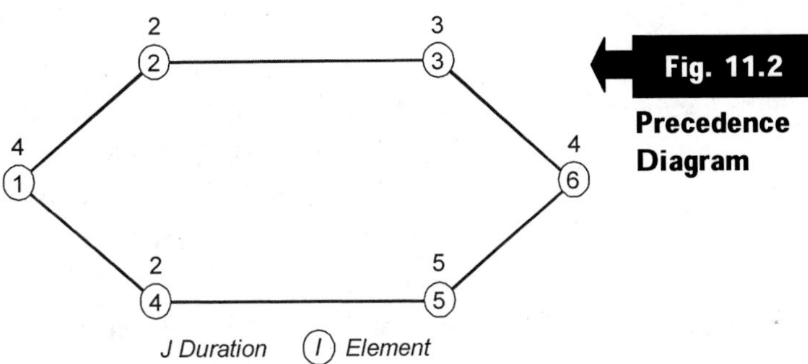

Fig. 11.2 Precedence Diagram

Grouping of Tasks for WS

Let us be familiar with Cycle Time (CT). It is the time taken between the completion of two successive assemblies. The Station Time (ST) is the sum of the times of work elements performed at a particular station.

ST does not exceed CT.

Precedence restrictions are not violated.

These two are important criteria for grouping work elements into WS. Possible ways of doing so are many, governed in general by line efficiency, balance delay, smoothness index.

$$\frac{\text{Line Efficiency}}{\text{(LE)}} = \frac{\text{Total Station Time}}{\text{CT} \times \text{Number of WS}} \times 100$$

$$\frac{\text{Balance Delay}}{\text{(BD)}} = \frac{\text{Total Idle Time of All Stations}}{\text{Total Available Working Time of all Stations}} \times 100$$

BD in other words is (100 – LE) as a percentage

$$\frac{\text{Smoothness Index}}{\text{(SI)}} = \sqrt{\sum_{i=1}^{K} \left(\text{Max. Station time} - \text{Station times of station } i\right)^2}$$

SI = O means a perfect balance. K, total number of WS cannot exceed the total number of work elements N. Also CT $\geq$ Maximum time of any work element, and < the total of all work elements

$$T_{max} \leq CT \leq \sum_{i=1}^{K} T_i$$

where

T_i = time for work element

N = No. of work elements

T_{max} = Max work element time

CT = Cycle Time

Line Balancing Methods

In the 1950s, the first analytical models of line balancing were developed. The assumptions were, however, too simple. Later, some authors developed 'neuristic' methods of line balancing. Here we deal with two such methods.First we shall discuss Kilbridge and Wester method.

Kilbridge and Wester Method[1]

Here, numbers are assigned to each operation to denote how many predecessors it has. Those operations showing the lowest predecessor number are first taken on WS. The steps are:

1. Draw the precedence diagram of work elements. Draw columns taking the starting elements first and then the succeeding events. Elements within a column are assigned to WS, after all the elements of the previous columns have been assigned.
2. Select CT which is feasible.

$$T_{max} \leq CT \leq \sum_{i=1}^{K} T_i$$

3. Assign work elements to WS. Sum of elemental times should not exceed CT while doing so. Proceed from Col. I to Col. II and so on. Break intra-column tie by using the norm of minimum number of predecessors.
4. Deduct assigned work elements from the total number of work elements. Repeat step 3.
5. If WS time is more than CT, identify the work element due to which this happens and carry it forward to next WS.
6. Repeat Steps 3 to 5 till all elements are fully assigned.

See how our precedence diagram is adjusted into columns.

We want to balance line with CT = 8.

Fig. 11.3

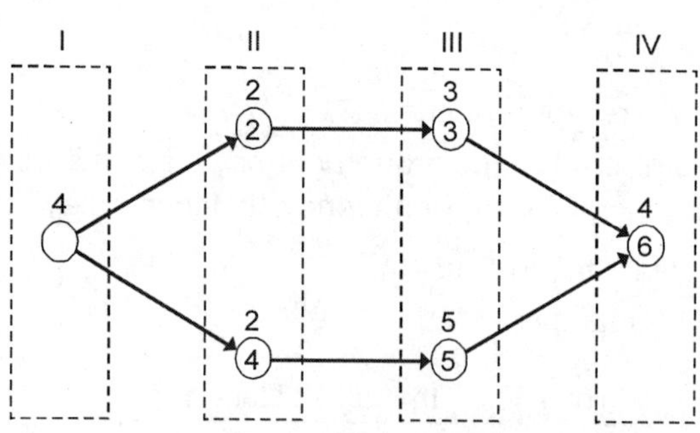

Table 11.1
Number of Predecessors for each Work Element

Work Element	***Number of Predecessors***	T_i
1	0	4
2	1	2
3	2	3
4	1	2
5	2	5
6	5	4

---

1. Kilbridge, K. and Wester, L. (1961) A Heuristic Method of Line Balancing, *Journal of Industrial Engineering*, 11(4), p. 292.

ASSIGNMENT OF WORK ELEMENTS TO WS
(Kibridge and Wester Method)

Station	*Element*	T_i	*Station Sum*	*Idle time*
I	1	4		
	2	2	6	2
II	4	2		
	5	5	7	1
III	3	3		
	6	5	8	0

$$\text{LE} = \frac{\text{Total Station Time}}{\text{CT} \times \text{No. of WS}}$$

$$= \frac{21}{8 \times 3} = \frac{21}{24} \times 100$$

$$= 87.5\%$$

$$\text{BD} = \frac{\text{Idle Time of all Stations}}{\text{Available Working Time of All Stations}} \times 100$$

$$= \frac{3}{21} \times 100$$

$$= 14.29\%$$

The solution is not optimum. K and W method is heuristic giving a reasonably good working solution.

Helgeson and Birnie Method[2]

Also known as Rank Positional Weight Technique, it is put forward by Helgeson and Birnie. The steps involved are as follows:

1. Precedence diagram is first constructed.
2. Each work element is assigned a positional weight, which corresponds to the time of the longest path from the commencement of the operation through the remaining network.
3. Rank the work elements in accordance with the positional weight, the highest coming first and so on.
4. Assign WEs to WSs (Work Stations). High ranking elements are assigned first.
5. If there is spare time at any WS after such assignment of an operation, the next in rank operation is then assigned to that WS. This, however, should not violate the precedence relationships and the station time should not exceed the CT.
6. Repeat the above two steps (4 and 5) until all elements are assigned to the WSs.

PROBLEMS AND PROSPECTS OF MASS PRODUCTION

Variable Work Element Times

In practice, work element times are not constant but vary randomly. The reasons for this are human element which is variable, fatigue factor and negligence of the operator. The set-up time of the components also result in variations in case of machine operations. The effect is dual: (*a*) there is greater idle time at some WSs. (*b*) There is reduction of the average production rate of the line. Deterministic balancing methods are modified to probabilistic balancing methods to account for this.

2. Helgerson, N.B. and Birnie, D.P. (1961) Assembly Line balancing using the ranked positional weight technique. *Journal of Industrial Engineering,* 12(6), p. 394.

Breakdowns at WSs

Operations in mass production system are carried out in a sequence and hence a failure or breakdown at one WS results in halting the whole production system till the snag is rectified. It affects the production rate. In practice, this problem is overcome by an efficient maintenance system and a storage of buffer semi-finished goods which can carry on from that stage onwards. How much buffer stock can be carried between the stages? It depends upon the production rate, the production cost and the availability of the production system. Technically, this is a problem of multi-stage waiting line.

Multi-product Lines

Assembly line is not given to flexibility, which is its major drawback. The line is for a standard design, and the changes in the design are difficult to be accommodated. However, there are similar products — in the sense that many of the tasks are common. There is a possibility here of using the same production line.

Line efficiencies depend upon the volume of products. Separate lines can be utilised for which a common precedence diagram is developed.

MODULAR PRODUCTION

In order to introduce variety amongst mass production system, the modular approach is used where a minimum number of parts or operations are designed, developed and produced. These are called modules. These can be combined in a number of ways to offer a wide variety of products and services.

GROUP TECHNOLOGY

Here there is specialisation in families of similar parts. Parts requiring a particular operation are assigned to different groups. These groups are the basis of group technology plant layout (a traditional process plant can be converted into group technology plant layout). Machines are arranged here in such a way that each individual machine is assigned to the production of one group of parts. Group Technology affects the component manufacture only.

AUTOMATION

Mass production is undergoing rapid changes, thanks to automation and robotics. Automation is an integration of three building blocks: machine tools, material handling and controls.

Multiple spindle machine is the first step where multiple operations are performed on a single machine. Automatic work piece indexing and transfer of work pieces from one WS to another is another step in this direction. The third step is robotics.

ROBOTICS

In the sixties, the electronics gave us numerically controlled machines (NCs) and computer numerically controlled (CNC) machines.

Machining Centres

The increase in speed of production process brought about by the application of computer to machinery, presented a problem in that the loading of parts to the machine and their movement from one machine to another consumed disproportionately more time than the production process. Two solutions were found. The 'Machining Centre' was developed which combined both rotational movement of the work piece with the three axis movement normally used in milling. This permitted a sequence of operations which had hitherto been done on a number of machines to be done on a single machine. The other development was a system of manufacturing cells in which groups of machines, the operations of which normally followed one another, were located together so that parts could be moved by the operator quickly from one machine to another.

Industrial Robots

The advent of industrial robots in 1970s allowed the manufacturing cells to be automated in a system which is called 'Flexible Manufacturing.' In flexible manufacturing a computer instructs the machines what to make and a robot moves the parts from one machine to another. The power of the central computer allows more than one type of part to be made at once, ensures that the machines are used as effectively as possible, and reduces the time taken for raw materials to be converted to finished products.

Originally robots were numerically controlled handling machines for picking and placing parts from one previously defined position to another. With the increase in their capability and the software operating them becoming more complex, they began to be adapted for other purposes such as spraying paint and welding.

Currently they are normally used in combination with other machinery such that messages are passed from the other machines to the robots indicating which operations are to be carried out and from the robot to the other machines, telling them when the job is complete. In this way they form a team with the other production machines, in which the robot may be either moving a part along its planned production path or alternatively executing one of the operations on that part. In both of these applications the robot replaces a human being in what is often a monotonous, uncomfortable and occasionally dangerous operation.

Worldwide Use

The applications for which robots are used today include: car production, die casting, spot welding, arc welding, forging, heat treatment, press transfer, machine tool loading and shell casting.

Once the problem of 'touch' is solved, the robots will have more use in batch assembly. A robot has to recognise the size and shape of a component and the work on this is in progress. Robot 'sight' using T.V. cameras would be more useful with camera on the 'hand' of the robot and the robot that explored the Atlantic after the Kanishka disaster had this arrangement.

Why robots? It is already known that the use of robot in hostile environments such as paint spraying in auto manufacturing is essential considering the health hazards involved. Further robots can also do away with boring jobs involving repetitive actions. Robotised operations are economical specially where the labour rates are high. New applications for which robots can be advantageous include order picking, packaging, textiles, and medical laboratory handling work.

Low budget assembly presents a tremendous challenge to robotics and the technology required to meet the challenge includes giving robots vision and tactile sensing. A mechanical solution for the latter is being worked out whereby strain gauges will be used to allow the robot to feel the shape in order to carry out 'bin picking' — picking out components at random from a bin in order to make up or assemble them.

In the very far future though, the possibility of robots collecting refuse, dispensing petrol, dispensing fast-food, carrying out animal husbandry, nuclear power plant maintenance and even conducting neurosurgery is not ruled out.

According to a Delphi study conducted in the U.S.A., by 1990, 25% of all robots in that country will have vision, 20% will have touch sensing and 40% will be a part of flexible manufacturing systems.

Industrial robots can be reprogrammed for different applications. Robot therefore represents *flexible automation,* rather than *hard automation.*

The basic components of a robot are a manipulator (series of mechanical linkages that provide movement), the controller directing these movements, and the energy source.

ଔଷ ଔଷ

PLANNING AND CONTROL OF PRODUCTION FOR BATCH PRODUCTION

Batch production is resorted to when a variety of products are to be made and the volumes are not large enough to demand a separate line for each product. In this method, general machines are used to turn out different products. The flow of materials is more complex in such a system. The layout is planned keeping the volume, flow and variety in mind. Batch production, however, is distinct from the job shop production. In batch production, there is a continuous demand. **However, the rate of production exceeds the rate of demand (P > D).** Hence, the batches of products. The scheduling here is that of the **batch sizes and their sequence.** In job shop production, there are a group of orders. They are processed on common facilities. Each job however is unique. It may consist of a single item or a collection of identical items. The scheduling here is that of sequencing the jobs at the common facilities.

Features of Batch Production

Batch production employs a process layout (unlike mass production system where there is product layout). In this system, similar machines are grouped into a department (like tabletting department, capsulation department, oral liquids department in a pharmaceutical unit). Different jobs follow their own routes. The flexibility of the system is much more.

Merits

1. Fewer machines are necessary, since machine utilisation is better.
2. Specialised supervision is possible.
3. Not-so-capital-intensive. Low investment in machines.
4. Flexibility with respect to personnel, equipment.
5. Job satisfaction for the operatives.

Demerits

1. Material handling is costlier since the flow is longer and irregular.
2. PPC is elaborate.
3. Production time is longer generally.
4. WIP (work in process) ties up large capital and space.
5. Skills of a higher order are necessary considering the variety.

The advantages apart, the basic question which puzzles the production man is the size of the production lot or batch and the sequencing of the different batches. Mostly these questions are settled by some rule-of-thumb methods. However, a rational approach can be adopted. It is discussed hereunder.

Batch Processing Decisions

Batch process planning requires basically decisions in three areas:

(*a*) *batch sequencing* or deciding the order in batches of different items will be processed.

(*b*) *batch sizes* to determine the quantities of each type of items (or customer) to be processed at one time.

(*c*) *batch scheduling* to decide the timing of the processing of batches of items or customers.

Batch sequencing

The total set up cost is a function of the sequence of the items. We have to decide an appropriate sequence to minimise the set up cost. Generally, the assignment method of linear programming is used to determine the optimum sequence for batches of items to be processed on mixed-model repetitive/ flow processing system.

Processing 'families' of items

There could be a situation in which several different types of items (or customers) require a similar, but not identical set up. Here, those items could be considered as a 'family' of similar items. In this context, it is prudent to process a batch of any one of the items in the family to take advantage of the set up and process a batch of all the items within the family. In short, the items of within a family are identified, and a processing cycle is determined for these. Then the optimum sequence for the remaining items is determined and these are processed as required between families.

Determination of Batch Sizes

Too large a batch quantity would tie up a large capital in inventory. High inventory will also lead to high carrying or holding costs. Too small quantities would b inadequate to meet large fluctuations in demand and the frequent processing of small batches. The batch quantity should, therefore, be optimum to minimise the total costs. We shall consider the model where the rate of processing and consumption are *known* and *constant*.

Consider the following notations

Nu = Optimum process batch quantity

S = Set up cost per batch

C = Carrying cost per item per unit of time

r = Consumption rate per unit of time

P = Processing rate per unit of time

Then

$$\text{Average stock level} = \text{Nu}/2$$

$$\text{Optimum batch size} = \text{Nu}^* = \sqrt{\frac{2Sr}{C}}$$

$$\text{Total cost/unit of time} = C$$

$$\therefore C^* = \sqrt{2rSC}$$

$$\text{Processing cycle time, } t = \frac{\text{Nu}}{r}$$

$$\therefore t^* = \frac{\text{Nu}^*}{r}$$

The model can be extended to include 'stockouts'. It introduces an additional cost factor C_2. The model assumes known and constant demand. The modified formula would be

$$Nu^* = \sqrt{\frac{2rS}{C_1}} \qquad \sqrt{\frac{C_1 + C_2}{C_2}}$$

$$C^* = \sqrt{2rC_1S} \qquad \sqrt{\frac{C_1}{C_1 + C_2}}$$

$$t^* = \frac{Nu^*}{r}$$

Let us consider the situation where the total processing batch is not delivered into stock at the same time. Instead, the items constituting the batch are delivered into the stock continuously throughout the process period.

$$\text{Average inventory} = \text{Buffer stock (B)} + \frac{Nu}{2}\ (1 - r/p)$$

$$Nu^* = \sqrt{\frac{2Cr}{C1(P - r/P)}}$$

$$C^* = \sqrt{2rSC_1}\ \sqrt{1 - (r - P)}$$

$$t^* = \frac{Nu^*}{r}$$

Production Range (Processing Range)

It is difficult to establish accurately C_1 and S. The total cost curve is therefore flat at minimum cost point. It means the total variable cost is not very sensitive to the Nu. It is possible to adopt a batch size that differs a bit from the optimal without affecting the costs. This gives rise to 'production range' concept. The quantities within this range are acceptable.

Economic Lot Size (or Batch Size)

We shall consider this with respect to ***a*** single product, and ***b*** multi-product case.

First let us get acquainted with three categories of costs in production function.

Set Up Cost

Batch production involves a set up cost, each time a batch is produced. Set up cost is roughly equivalent to the ordering cost per order. It consists of *engineering cost* of setting up the production lines or machines, *paperwork cost* of processing work order and authorizing production and *ordering cost* to provide raw materials for the batch or order.

Carrying Costs

These are incurred on the finished product from the time it is manufactured until it is finally sold.

Single Product: Optimum Lot Size

Let us be familiar with the symbols.

$$\frac{\text{Pr oduction Runs}}{\text{(Optimum No. Year)}}$$

A = Annual Sales of items in rupees

C = Carrying Costs as a per cent of finished goods

S = Set up cost per run

Nr = Optimum No. of runs per year.

Assumption

(1) End products are to be placed in stock.

(2) They are sold at a constant rate until some low level is reached.

(3) At that level, another batch will be produced.

Illustration

A company produces ₹ 40,000 worth of worm-gears at the factory each year. The carrying costs on finished stocks are 20 per cent per year and the set up costs per production runs is ₹ 80. Optimum number of production runs per year (N_r) for this item would be:

$$N_r = \sqrt{\frac{AC}{2S}} = \sqrt{\frac{₹\ 40{,}000\ (0.20)}{2\ (₹\ 80)}}$$

$$= \sqrt{\frac{₹\ 8{,}000}{₹\ 160}} = \sqrt{50} = \text{About 7 runs/year.}$$

The so-called *economic batch quantity* represents an attempt to calculate the best compromise on batch size, which also keeps the total costs to the minimum.

Production Lot Size: Simultaneous Production and Sales

Here the end products being produced are simultaneously being sold. In this case, the inventory of finished goods does not generate immediately to its maximum point. Instead, it builds up slowly as goods are produced faster than they are being sold, then it declines to its lowest point as production of a particular batch ceases although sales continue. The concept is illustrated in the following figure.

$$Nu = \frac{\text{Optimum Production Run Size (Units)}}{\text{Maximum Finished Goods Inventory (Production Stops)}}$$

The inventory formula for optimum number of units (Nu) under these conditions is:

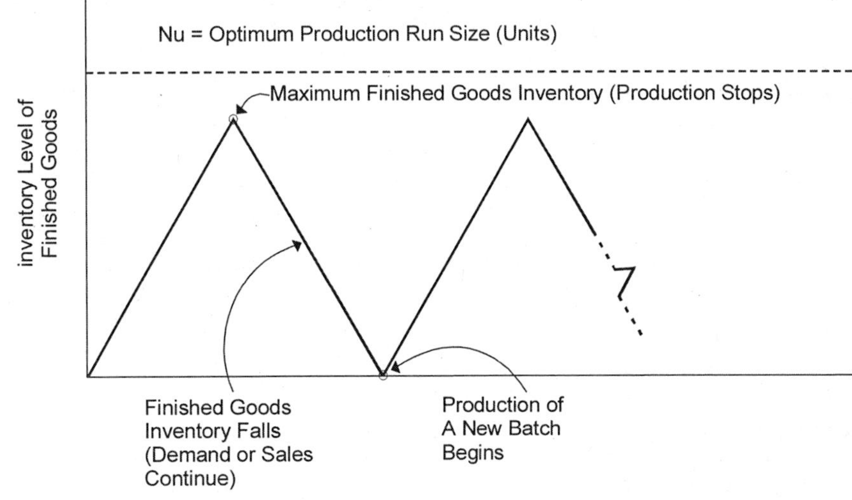

Fig. 12.1 **Simultaneous Production and Sales**

$$Nu = \sqrt{\frac{2US}{RC\ (1 - d/p)}}$$

where,

Nu = Production runs equation (Optimum units per batch)

U = Annual Sales in units

S = Set up cost per batch

R = Factory cost per unit

C = Carrying costs as a per cent of finished goods

d = Sales rate (demand rate) in units per day

P = Production rate in units per day.

We can put down total ordering and carrying costs as follows:

Nu = Optimum lot size in units

and

P = Production rate in units daily

then

$$\frac{Nu}{P} = \text{No. of days required to receive entire order}$$

If

d = Use rate in units daily

then

$$\frac{Nu}{P} \times d = \text{Number of units used during receipt period}$$

$$(Nu)\frac{-Nu}{P} \times d = \text{Maximum inventory which can be build up}$$

Since, average inventory is approximately half the maximum inventory, the average inventory in this case would be

$$\frac{1}{2}\left(Nu\frac{-Nu}{P} \times d\right) = \frac{1}{2}Nu\left(1 - \frac{d}{p}\right)$$

Let R represent cost per unit and C represent carrying costs. If carrying costs equal average inventory in units times cost per unit times carrying costs in per cent, we get

$$\text{Carrying costs} = \frac{Nu}{2}\left(1 - \frac{d}{p}\right) \times R \times C$$

$$= \frac{RCNu}{2}\left(1 - \frac{d}{p}\right)$$

And if the annual usage in units is denoted by U and set up costs as S.

$$\text{Number of lots per year} = \frac{U}{Nu}$$

$$\text{and Total Ordering Costs} = \frac{U}{Nu} \times S$$

We appreciate that the total ordering and carrying costs are minimum when the cost to order equals the cost to carry per year. Thus, we equate the two expressions we have already defined and solve for N:

$$\frac{US}{Nu} = \frac{RCNu}{2}\left(1-\frac{d}{p}\right)$$

$$RCNu^2 = \left(1-\frac{d}{p}\right) 2US$$

$$Nu^2 = \frac{2US}{RC\,(1-d/p)}$$

$$Nu = \sqrt{\frac{2US}{RC\,(1-d/p)}}$$

Multi-product Case

Supposing several items (n) are made on a single machine, with a common CT (cycle time), then these batches (n) are phased within the common cycle. Here the total cost per year is the summation of the individual costs. For resource feasibility check, the equation for time becomes

$$\frac{d_1}{P_1} + \frac{d_2}{P_2} + \ldots + \frac{d_n}{P_n} \leq 1$$

It can be determined whether all items (n) can be scheduled on a single machine. The optimum cycle time (CT) can be obtained by putting

$$\frac{d \times \text{Total Annual Cost} \times CT}{d \times CT} = 0$$

CT, therefore, becomes $\dfrac{\sqrt{2\sum_{j=1}^{n} \text{set up cost}}}{i\sum_{j=1}^{n} \text{variable cost per unit} \times d_j \left(1-\dfrac{d_j}{P_j}\right)}$

Once CT is obtained the Optimum batch sizes Nu_1, Nu_2, Nu_3 can be easily obtained by using $Nu_j = CT\ d_j$, $j = 1 \ldots. n$.

Scheduling for Batch Processing

We have to arrive at the most economical cycle that optimises the set up and carrying costs. As set up costs go up, the carrying costs goes down, and the number of cycles increases. However, to get the satisfactory solution, the cycle time for all items must be set simultaneously.

Line of Balance Technique

We have assumed a sequential batch processing consisting of several operations (1, 2, 3 etc.). The whole batch is completed on operation 1, and then passes on to operation 2, and so on. The operations control is easier here. It is iterative. However, the throughput time for any batch will be high. It calls for large storage space. The ideal solution would be to divide the batches, to start processing on the next operation prior to the completion of processing of the batch on the previous one. Still, we must exercise control.

The line of balance technique takes care of such situations. It follows the principle of 'management by exception', It considers only the crucial operations in a job. It establishes a schedule for these. It is useful for large batches of complex items. It is a sophisticated version of the Gantt Chart.

Line of Balance (LoB) for Control of Batch Production

LoB is useful when batches are split to study the progress of jobs periodically, and with reference to the delivery schedule. We begin with the delivery schedule, and construct an operations programme. While reviewing a programme progress chart is drawn. This chart shows the number of items which have been finished at each of the critical or important operations at a given date. Above this chart is drawn a line (LoB) which shows the requisite number of items which should have been completed at each operation at the review time. Analysis of progress is then done. Shortage and non-conformance to schedule are identified. LoB is management by exception.

Batch Scheduling

There are basically three batching methods:

(*i*) Individual batch size fixed for each part.

(*ii*) Aggregation of parts which are treated as one batch.

(*iii*) Fixed batch quantity for a product rather than of parts.

Irrespective of the batching method used, we have to decide the order of processing the batches at the various stages of production. Suppose a certain machine has to take four batches for processing. It means this can be done in twenty-four ways. The more the number of batches, the greater the ways of ordering the batches, *e.g.*, eight batches gives over forty-thousand ways. It is difficult to choose the particular scheduling sequence. We have to keep in mind the objectives of a schedule and its significance. Are we aiming to reduce the idle machine time or work-in-progress (WIP) or production costs? These may be desirable objectives, but in practice, they come in conflict. In a particular situation, we have to make assessment of their relative costs. The problems should be kept simple by scrutinising the product range and parts made for which a simple manufacturing process can be designed. Jobs which are troublesome are contracted out. Scheduling problems are eased by excess capacity. However, loading a plant fully increases the scheduling problems.

Problems and Prospects of Batch Production

Here, WIP and the lead times are large. Requirements Planning is a tool to overcome this. MRP, however, needs computerization. Kanbaan system of Japan emphasises the reduction in production lead time and WIP by using shorter production runs of a particular product.

FMS: Flexible Manufacturing system is also a tool to overcome problems of batch production. FMS machines though general purpose are versatile enough to perform different operations which are linked by material handling system. The machines and material handling are controlled by a computer system. FMS makes possible machining of desired mix of parts in a given time period. It reduces WIP and increases machine utilisation in small batch manufacturing.

Appendix - I

AGGREGATE PRODUCTION PLANNING

Demand from customers gets converted as units of product while considering the production system. The plan of the next few coming months has a demand schedule. It is to be met by developing the workforce and the machine time allocation which is called aggregate production planning. Aggregation results an overall production plan for all the products (*e.g.*, tonnes of soap). Individual product schedules, for example of toilet premium soaps, janta soaps, washing soaps are obtained by breaking up the overall plan (disaggregation).

While allocating workforce, there are two conflicting considerations. The inventory carrying cost is to be balanced against the cost of adjusting activity levels to variations in demand. The demand pattern of two alternative production strategies is seen in the following diagram.

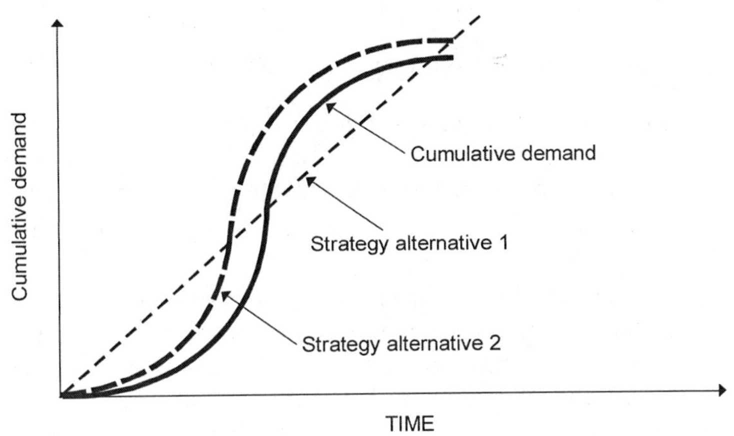

Fig. 12.2 Demand Pattern: Aggregate Production

Strategy Alternative 1

Workforce is constant. Production output rate is therefore constant. P is however greater than D (expected demand rate in earlier production periods), CP exceeds CD. It results in a high inventory carrying cost. The converse is also true. When CD exceeds CP, there is a high shortage cost.

Strategy Alternative 2

Here, the production is adjusted to demand to minimise the inventory carrying costs. The workforce level is constantly adjusted or is paid high O.T. during peak demand periods. Both these alternatives are extreme positions. Optimum alternative minimises the total cost of the inventory and the cost of adjusting the workforce level. As a result of this exercise, we generate a master schedule where the number of units to be produced per period and the workforce level corresponding to that are described.

Material Requirement Planning (MRP)

As we have seen the master schedule gives us the end products (final products) per period and the workforce levels. Given this, MRP calculates the timing of all sub-assembly, component and raw material production and purchasing activities necessary to satisfy the master schedule. MRP is done with a view to minimising WIP inventory. Because of voluminous data, most MRP systems are computerized.

The process of determining components and sub-assemblies from the master schedule of end products is called **Parts Explosion Requirements.**

13

PLANNING AND CONTROL FOR JOB SHOP PRODUCTION

Planning and Control for Job Shop Production

Job shops handle a variety of jobs, where each job is different. In batch production though there is a continuous demand for products, the rate of production exceeds that of demand, and hence there are batches. In batch production, jobs are predictable. Job shop is a different proposition, where jobs and demand both are unpredictable. Job shop handles the unique jobs each time with a unique set of operations and processing time.

Job shop machines are general purpose machines organized department wise. The sequencing of each job is unique, depending upon the technological requirement. Job shop is a complex waiting line system — a job exits from a machine to wait on a new machine because of other jobs. Each machine has a waiting line of jobs. The converse is also true. Machines may wait for the job but no job is forthcoming. (Idle Time). Planning here is a process of prioritizing the jobs at each machine to seek the desired objectives.

Problems of Job Production

The basic question here is that of scheduling. When there are ***n*** jobs awaiting processing on ***m*** machines, each job having a pre-decided sequence of operations and processing timings, then what should be the order of loading the jobs on machines so as to optimise the expected performance standards?

Expected performance standards could be:

1. Mean flow time.
2. Total processing time.
3. Idle time of machines.
4. Mean earliness and lateness of jobs (Job completed before due date is its earliness. Lateness — actual completion time — due date).
5. Mean tardiness of jobs. (Job completed after its due date).
6. Number of tardy jobs.
7. Mean waiting time.
8. Mean number of jobs in the system.

The factors affecting the solution are:

1. Total number of jobs for scheduling.
2. Total number of machines.
3. Manufacturing facilities — flow shop or job shop.
4. Nature of job arrivals — static or dynamic.
5. Evaluation criteria for scheduling.

If ***n*** (number of jobs) goes up and ***m*** (number of machines) also goes up, the problem of scheduling to that extent becomes more complex. Here there are no optimal solutions then.

We then adopt simulation and heuristic algorithms.

In this chapter, we restrict our initial discussion of simple job shop problems involving one or two machines, for which optimisation is possible. These are of use in many practical situations. There is a graphical method also. We at the end will appreciate some scheduling rules derived from simulation studies.

n Jobs, One Machine Situation

Several jobs are to be processed on a single machine or facility. Here prioritization or assignment is necessary. Several jobs remain waiting. The objectives are to optimise mean flow time (MFT), average WIP, average lateness, average waiting time, tardiness and total processing time of jobs.

Consider when *n* jobs whose processing times are known are to be processed on a single machine. New (job) arrival wait for their turn.

The following terms are commonly employed:

n = number of job.

t_i = processing time of any job i.

W_i = Waiting time.

F_i = Flow time.

C_i = Completion time.

d_i = Due delivery date.

L_i = Lateness.

T_i = Tardiness.

N_T = Number of tardy jobs.

Makespan or the total time to complete the job is fixed. It is equal to the sum of processing time for each job. ***n*** job, one machine situation demands optimisation of mean flow time.

SPT = Shortest Processing Time

Jobs are arranged in such a way that one which takes the least time is taken up first, followed by one with the next smallest possible time. This sequencing is called SPT and it achieves the following aims at a time.

1. Mean lateness minimised.
2. Mean waiting time minimised.
3. Mean flow time minimised.
4. Mean number of tasks in WIP minimised.

SPT is slightly modified by assigning weightages to the jobs as per their importance. WMFT — Weighted Mean Flow Time is given by

$$\frac{\sum_{i=1}^{n} W_i F_i}{\sum_{i=1}^{n} W_i}$$

While applying WSPT (Weighted Scheduling Rule) ***n*** jobs are sequenced such that

$$\frac{t_{[1]}}{W_{[1]}} \leq \frac{t_{[2]}}{W_{[2]}} \leq .... \leq \frac{t_{[n]}}{W_{[n]}}$$

Where bracketed figures refer to the position of the job in the optimal sequence.

Processing with Due Dates

SPT discussed above minimises the mean lateness of the jobs EDD, Earliest Due Date, rule states that the jobs are sequenced in the order of non-decreasing due dates. This helps in reducing the maximum job lateness as well as maximum job tardiness.

n Jobs, Two Machines Situation

Suppose ***n*** jobs are to be processed on two machines, M_1 and later on M_2. The processing times of all jobs on both the machines are known. The minimum time to complete all jobs require a particular sequencing. Johnson's algorithm is useful here:

(*a*) Job down processing time of all jobs on M_1 and M_2.

(*b*) Assess the minimum processing time.

(*c*) If the minimum processing time is on M_1, position the corresponding job first — as early as possible in the sequence. If it is on M_2, position the corresponding job last — as late as possible in the sequence.

(*d*) Eliminate jobs already assigned (as a result of step *c*). Keep on repeating *b* and *c* till all jobs are sequenced. Ties while applying step *c* can be broken arbitrarily.

Two Jobs, *m* Machines Situation

Consider two jobs, to be processed on *m* machines. The optimal sequencing so as to minimise the total processing time is derived graphically, where on *x*-axis, processing time and sequencing of job 1 on machines are plotted and on *y*-axis job 2 is plotted. The scale is kept the same for both the jobs. When a machine would be occupied by two jobs simultaneously, the areas in the graph are shaded. The processing of both the jobs is given by a continuous path having horizontal, vertical and diagonal segments. Diagonal segment means concurrent processing of the jobs. Feasible path (maximising diagonal movement) minimises the total processing time. Trial and error method decides the optimal path.

Scheduling Rules for Job Shops

The situations we have discussed are all very simplistic. For complicated situations, we rely upon her heuristic techniques. In practice, there are many machining centres and so many jobs. We have to adopt priority despatching rules for sequencing jobs at each machine centre.

Some of these priority despatch rules are as follows:

(*a*) **SPT** : Select the job that has shortest possible processing time.

(*b*) **EDD** : Select the job that has earliest due date.

(*c*) **FCFS** : Select on the basis of first come, first served.

(*d*) **SLACK** : Select the job with the minimum slack.

(*e*) **LRPT** : Select the job that has least minimum processing time.

(*f*) **RANDOM** : Select at random any job.

(*g*) **LCFS** : Select on last come, first served basis.

(*h*) **DS** : Select the job that has least dynamic slack. (Time remaining to due date — remaining expected flow time).

(*i*) **DS/PT** : Select the job with this minimum ratio. DS: Dynamic slack time to remaining processing time.

(*j*) **S/OPR** : Select the job with this minimum ratio: Job slack time/number of operations remaining.

Research observations indicate that **SPT** rule inclines towards the lowest mean flow time even for large shops. However, here the variance flow time tends to be large. **FCFS** scores on this count.

Job Shop Production: Problems and Prospects

The facilities in the job shop are limited, and the jobs crowd up demanding individual processing sequences. It gives rise to some peculiar problems: flow pattern problems, WIP inventories, counting of jobs, long completion time and certain unpredictable problems.

The work in this area mainly relates to static job or flow shop. However, in a large shop, the possible sequences are many. It requires further research work. More work has been in the area of dispatching rules using simulation in a dynamic environment. Scheduling has implications for both the costs and effectiveness. So right frequency of scheduling with these twin objectives is a major research area these days.

14

PLANNING AND CONTROL OF PROJECTS

To begin with, we shall understand the concept of a project. A project is a set of non-repetitive type of operations and activities. These activities once through are not repeated. Hence every project is unique. A project is a series of related jobs directed towards some major output and requiring considerable period of time to perform. Some examples of a project are: building a new skyscraper in Mumbai, designing a new motor car etc. There is no experience to guide, since nothing similar has been done under similar circumstances in the past. Project management is concerned with the planning, directing and controlling resources to meet the technical, cost and time constraints of the project.

PROJECT MANAGEMENT

As we have learnt, a project is any activity with a specific goal to be completed in specific period of time. A project by definition, is a finite activity, in terms of both time and the use of resources.

Project management is, therefore, concerned with the achievement of the specific goal, deploying the given resources over the defined period of time. It means we have to plan and establish an operating system, acquire the resources, schedule the activities and review the completed activity. Project management is different since it is concerned with a one-time activity rather than repetitive activities.

Projects are common in engineering, construction, transport, supply (aid distribution) and service areas. Major projects have large resources committed to them, and require long time periods. However, whether large or small, project management requires some specific activities associated with different stages. The following diagram 14.1 illustrates the three-phases of the life cycle of a project

Let us discuss the various stages.

Project Formulation and Definition

In case of R&D projects, we will select only a few for further work. There could be a number of possible project alternatives. There could be exploratory work on them. But only a few qualify for prototype development. Project selection is a very crucial stage. We have to consider the overall objectives of the organisation, its strengths and weaknesses, the competence available, the financial strength and cost estimates. Projects could be ranked. There is an initial feasibility test.

Organisation which work in response to customer enquiries, project selection may not be important. The emphasis here is on the interpretation, definition and formulation of project requirements. Tender conditions must be carefully interpreted. Outline specifications must be developed. There should be evaluation of alternatives. The whole thing must be discussed with the clients. This leads to an agreed project formulation for further work.

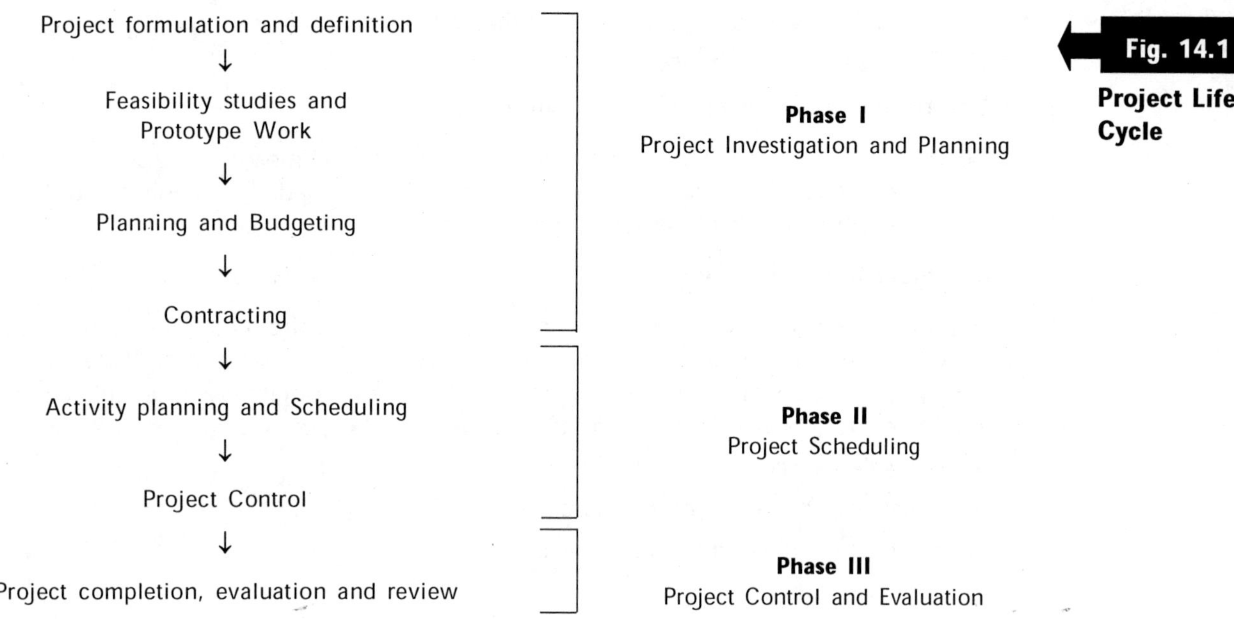

Fig. 14.1
Project Life Cycle

Feasibility Studies and Prototype Work

Excepting those projects which are undertaken against customer requirements, further feasibility studies leading to prototyping work are required. This work could form a part of an agreement between an organisation and its client. New product development requires translation of product concepts into a prototype. Here, there is concept testing prior to prototyping. Later, the prototype is tested for performance and market feedback.

Planning and Budgeting

Whether in-house or customer response generated, a project must be budgeted to control the expenditure. We have to estimate a cost sheet of the final product. The rough outline of the time estimates of the product and development of resources must be made. It is a pre-requisite for the budgetary preparation.

Contracting

When projects are undertaken for the clients, an agreement is entered into with them. It spells out all terms and conditions of the execution of the project. It also has specifications of the project work and detailed costing, There are clauses regarding payments and delivery. There may be separate agreements with the sub-contractors.

Activity Planning and Scheduling

We have to prepare a detailed plan. We have to decide the schedule of activities showing estimated start and finish times of all major tasks. We have to commit resources to carry out these tasks. As it is a project, most of the tasks are new; and so there is an element of uncertainty. There is an interdependence of tasks and sequential nature of certain tasks. But these two are also to be decided. Thus planning a project is frought with risk; and it this risk is to be dealt with. There may be revision and modification of the schedule and alternative allocation of resources.

Project Control

Project control continues along with planning. It is all the more important in the force of uncertainty. All activities must be closely monitored and controlled. There should be comparison of progress against the plans. There can be consequent modification of the schedules and redeployment of resources and redirection of efforts. The project manager has to manage the project team. Project work is ultimately the team work, and project manager has to provide the leadership. There should be proper recruitment and selection of the team members.

Project Completion, Evaluation and Review

Once the project is over, the final costs are calculated and compared against the budgeted costs. The project effectiveness is assessed. The project team is disbanded. The feedback guides the future projects, and establishes a database for future reference.

Role of Project Management

The project manager takes the overall responsibility of the entire project life cycle. Most projects are organised as matrix type structures. Activities across functions are to be co-ordinated. Each function is headed by an independent functional manager. The whole project is successful only when it is completed in time to the specifications and to costs decided. A successful project manager must have:

- attitude to succeed.
- objectives which can be measured.
- method to achieve these objectives.
- conducive environment
- adequate and appropriate resources.

To plan and control these projects, we have developed a tool called: PERT. (Project evaluation and Review Technique)

We shall therefore call a project a set of inter-related activities that are organized for a common goal or objective. Each **activity** in a project consumes **resources** and **time.** Let us take one example of a simple project, and see what activities constitute it.

All the projects are not one time occurrences. Many of them can be replicated or can be transferred to other contexts or products. There will be another project output.

Statement Of Work (SOW)

This is the beginning of the project. It spells out the objectives we have set for achievement. It also contains in brief the work to be done, and a proposed schedule of the start and the end periods. It generally carries a budget, milestones and the written reports.

Task

A project is subdivided into *tasks.* Generally, it is expressed in months and is performed by one group or organization. A project, if necessary, can be further sub-divided into *sub-tasks.*

Work Package

It is a group of activities put together, and assigned to a single organizational unit. There is a short description of what is to be done, when it is to be done, when it has to begin and end and its budget. It also carries performance measures to be reached at specific points of time (called milestones). Some milestones may be the development of the prototype and the product launch.

Work Breakdown Structure (WBDS)

When we create a hierarchy of project tasks, sub-tasks and packages, we get a work breakdown structure (WBDS). When a work package or packages are completed, it leads to the completion of a sub-task, and when one or more such sub-tasks are completed, ultimately leads to the completion of a project. An illustrative WBDS is shown here.

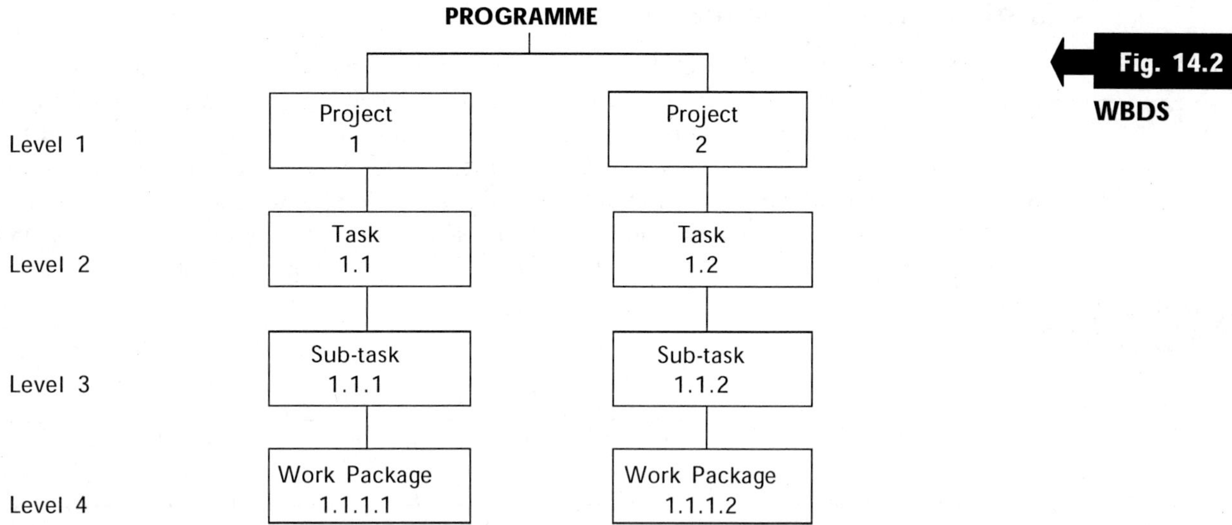

Fig. 14.2
WBDS

Project Control

Some programmes of control developed for defence purposes are available to the managers for the presentation of data.

Gantt chart, considered elsewhere in this book is a bar chart showing the sequence of activities and the time involved. We can plot a graph of cost breakdown by plotting labour cost, material cost and overhead cost against time. Total labour cost and total labour hours are inter-related. We can show allocation of labour hours to manufacturing, finance, engineering, overheads and personnel and the percentage of cost against each such allocation. A barchart of completion of these projects can be created.

Organization Structure

A project can be tied to the parent organization in three ways — pure project, functional project or a matrix project.

In the matrix form, the rows represent the projects which borrow resources from the columns representing the functional areas. A matrix can be balanced, weak or strong. It, in other words, indicates how the project managers are organizationally *vis-a-vis* the functional managers. It is to be noted that a project leader must have certain characteristics.

The three forms of project organization are discussed below.

Pure Project

It is a self-contained team which works full-time on the project. The project manager has the ultimate authority — responsibility for the project. All team members report to him. The communication is quick, and there is quick decision-making. As different projects require different teams there is duplication of resources. The team works autonomously, and is removed from its organization. It is thus likely to ignore the policies of the organization. The team may be apprehensive about life after the project, and may delay the completion of the project.

Functional Project

Different functions in the organization take over the project work too. For instance, engineering may handle project X, Y and Z. Similarly manufacturing may handle project X, Y, Z. R&D too may handle project X, Y, Z. A team member can work for a number of projects. A functional area gains from working on the project by acquiring technical expertise. The functional area continues to accommodate team members after the completion of the project. There are some drawbacks of this type of arrangement. Some aspects of the project not related to the respective function which is handling the project may get neglected. The teams are slow to respond. The motivation may not be high.

Matrix Organization for the Project

Here, there is a blending of the pure project form and the functional project form. Each project has people drawn from different functional areas. The project manager decides about the tasks to be performed and their timing, whereas the functional manager controls the people and technologies involved. It affords better communication. There is less duplication of resources. The policies of the parent organization are followed. However, matrix organization has to report to two superiors. A project manager must show good bargaining skills. As project managers may overcommit resources to their projects, they may harm the other projects. The following diagram illustrates a matrix organization.

Fig. 14.3

Matrix Organisation

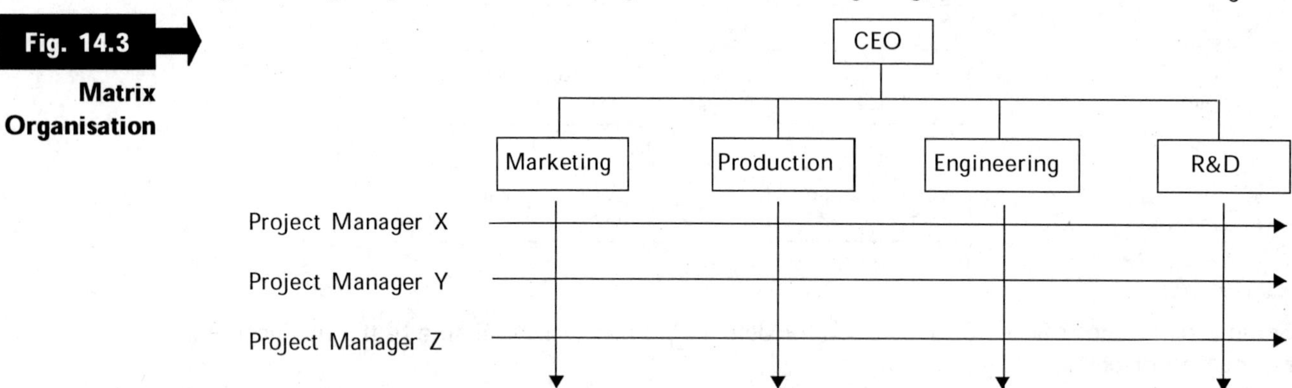

Some Key Concepts

Consider a situation where your college has decided to hold the Internal Evaluation Test. The college, therefore, will have to undertake the following activities:

(1) Design the question paper.

(2) Print the question paper.

(3) Make seating arrangements for the candidates.

(4) Distribute the question paper at the appointed day and time. Collect answer books.

(5) Make evaluation.

Thus, you can see that the Internal Evaluation Test consists of several activities listed above where each activity stands for the time-consuming part. Each activity is a job by itself. Let us jot down the time-estimate necessary for the completion of each activity.

Activity	***Time-Estimate***
Design the question paper	7 days
Print the question paper	1 day
Make seating arrangements for candidates	3 days
Distribute the paper	15 Minutes
Collect Answer books	15 Minutes

It is to be made clear that each activity here consumes some time and needs manpower, material facilities, space and other resources.

Some activities listed above are dependent on some other activities. For instance, we cannot print the paper unless it is first designed. Designing the paper therefore precedes its actual printing, and so it is called the *predecessor activity*. Where printing follows the designing it is called the *successor activity*. These activities are said to be *in series*.

We can start the printing work and make arrangements for seating at one and the same time. These activities are performed simultaneously, and are therefore said to be *in parallel* or are called *concurrent activities*.

In short, an activity is a time consuming effort that is required to perform a part of the work. An activity is shown on an arrow diagram by a line with an arrow head pointing in the direction of progress in the completion of work.

Events

Event represents the starting or the end-point of an activity or a job. It is also called a *node.*

Design the Question Paper: It is an activity. Start designing the paper is an event. Make evaluation is an activity. Evaluation completed is an event.

In PERT, the activities are denoted by arrows, and the events, by circles or rectangles. PERT is event-oriented, where the emphasis is on the start (S) or completion (C) of an event, rather than on activities themselves.

In short, an event

(*a*) must indicate a noteworthy or significant point in the project.

(*b*) is the start or completion of a job.

(*c*) does not consume time or resources.

The events are usually numbered 10, 20, 30, 40 and so on. Early events are assigned low numbers, and later events the higher numbers. If it is necessary to modify the network by adding more events, these can be numbered 11, 12 and so on. Activities are referred to by showing the events they connect *e.g.*, activity 10-20, activity 20-30 and so on.

Network Diagram

When all activities and events in a project are connected logically and *sequentially*, they form a network. While designing a network, the following problems are answered:

1. Which event or events must be completed before the particular event can start? (Predecessor Events)
2. What event or events follow this? (Successor Events)
3. What activities can be accomplished simultaneously? (Concurrent Activities)

The network progresses from left to right.

Drawing Project Network

We should have as input a list of activities and their precedence requirements to draw a project network. While listing the activities, the immediate predecessors are listed.

Consider the following project

Activity	*Immediate Predecessor*
A	–
B	A
C	A
D	–
E	B, D
F	C, E
G	F

From the above a project network diagram is drawn. In this diagram **activities are represented by arrows and events by circles (called nodes).** See the following diagrammatic representation of an activity.

Here one circle represents the start of the activity and the other circle represents the completion of the activity. The arrow represents the activity itself. Activity B as we see from the table above starts when activity A is completed. In other words, they are in series. See its representation.

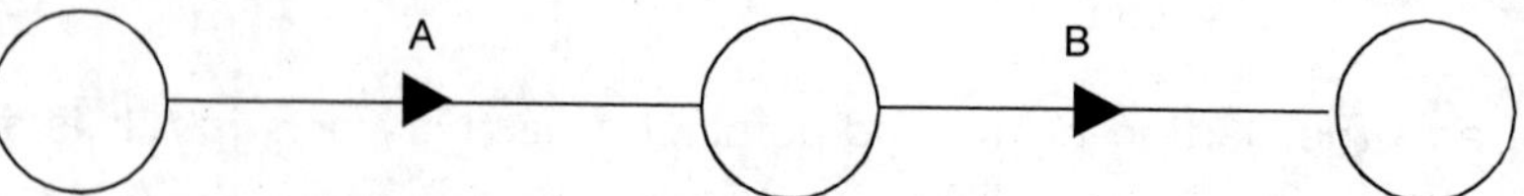

Now in this project, activity E has two predecessor activities. (B and D). The end points of these two activities (B,D) are merged into the starting node of activity E.

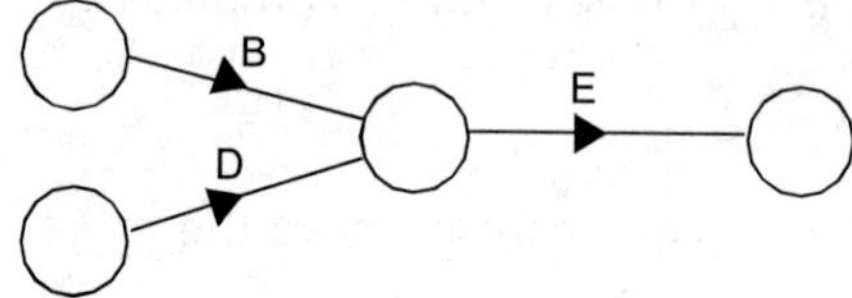

The whole project looks like.

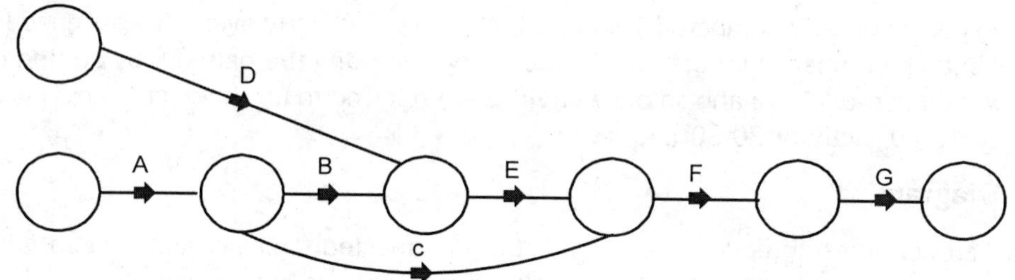

The starting activities are A, D. Their nodes can be joined together. They can start at any time together.

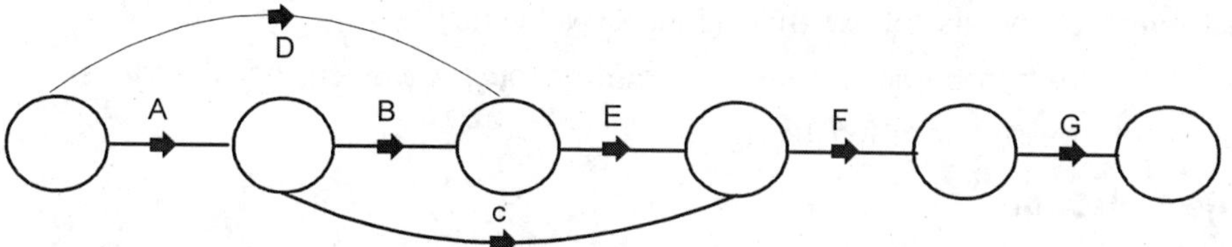

Now with this practice consider our Internal Test Example. The diagram will look like.

Some events are concurrent.

Fig. 14.4

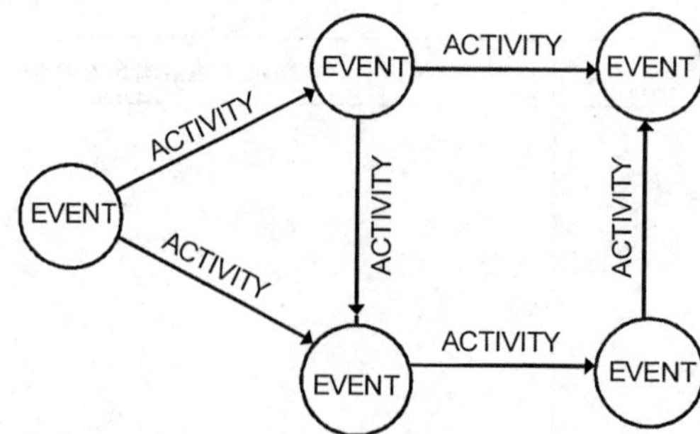

It is a graphical representation of events following logically and sequentially.

Some events are in series:

Fig. 14.5

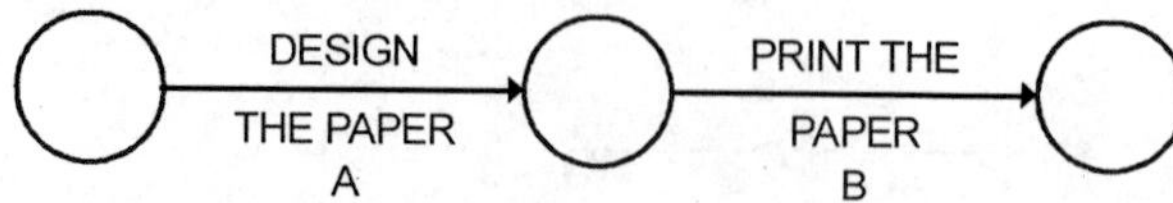

Some events are concurrent:

Fig. 14.6

Let us take another example.

Activity	Immediate Predecessor
A	—
B	—
C	—
D	C
E	A, B
F	E, D
G	D
H	F, G

The network looks as follows:

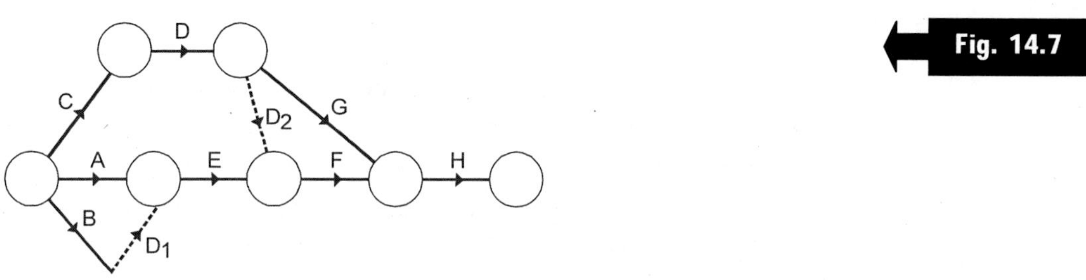

Fig. 14.7

Here we have shown for correct representation D_1 and D_2 as **dummy activity.** These activities are dotted, and do not consume time or any resources. These dummies are added to ensure that one pair of events connect only one activity.

Here our diagram till the activity F presents no problem. But correct representation of G is tricky. It has only D as its predecessor. The **dummies** are therefore necessary. Dummies ensure correct precedence relationship. They also ensured that **two events are joined at most by one arrow.**

Logical Sequence of Activities

An arrow network is an orderly representation of activities and events as per the logical sequence. The rules of network diagrams are as follows:

(*i*) An activity cannot start until its tail end is reached.

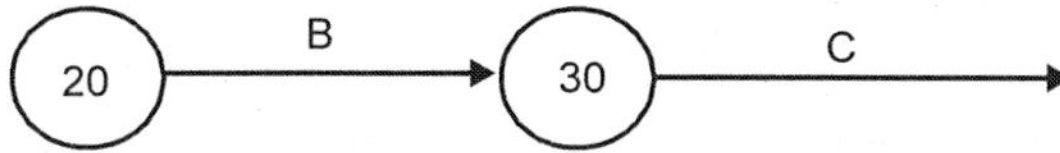

Thus activity C cannot start until activity C cannot start until activity B (20-30) has not been completed.

Similarly,

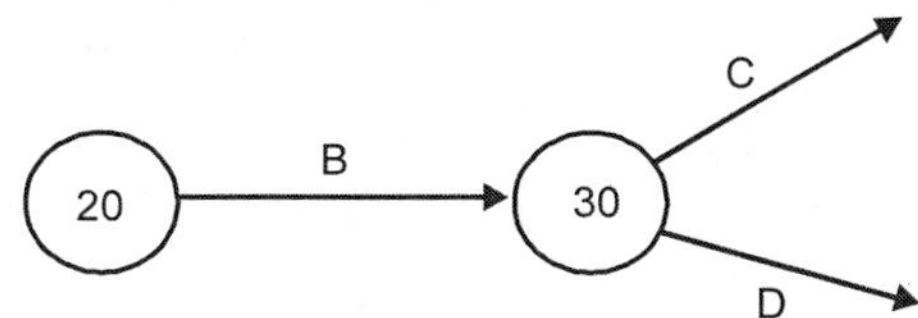

Activities C and D cannot start until activity B has been completed.

(*ii*) An event cannot be reached until all activities leading to it are completed. Thus in

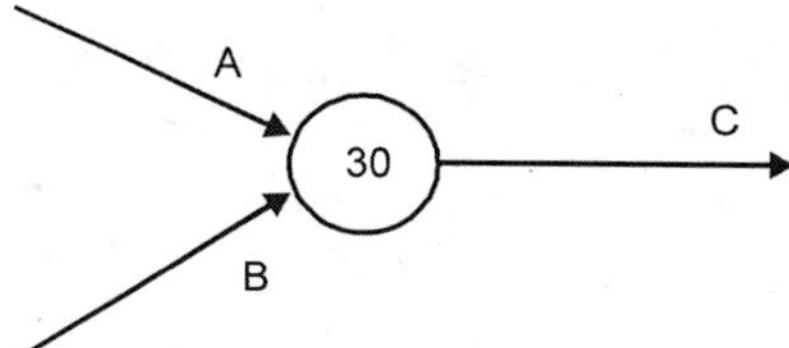

Activities A and B precede activity C.

(*iii*) Sometimes events are interdependent. This dependence is on the preceding event, even though these two events are not connected by an activity. These events which do not consume time and resources are called dummies, and the activity is represented by a dotted line.

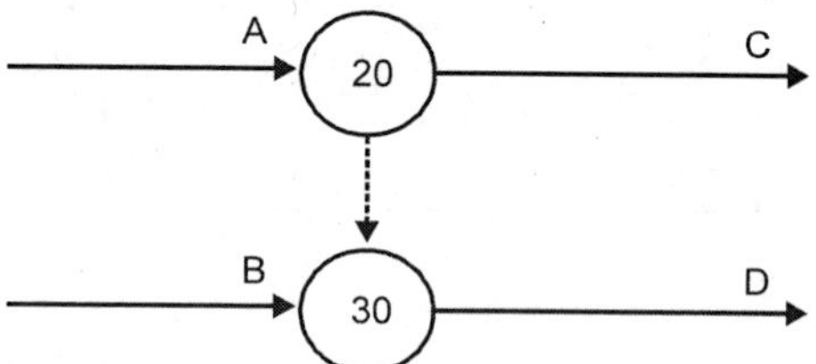

In the above diagram, activities A and B must be completed before activity D but activity C depends activity A and is independent of activity B.

(*iv*) All activities must both start and finish with an event.

(*v*) Any event, excepting the first and the last, must have at least one activity leading into it and at least one activity leading out of it.

(*vi*) Events are numbered in terms of the time of their occurrence.

(*vii*) Network should be drawn in such a way that event numbers increase progressively from left to right.

Node Labelling

Node labelling includes the numbering of events.

The event number should in some respect reflect their logical sequence. When a complicated network has been formed after numerous additions and deletions (which are unavoidable before a final acceptable network is obtained), the problem of assigning numbers to the events has to be considered. A rule devised by **D.R. Fulkerson** reduced this sequential numbering to the following steps.

(*i*) An "initial" event is one which has arrows coming out of it and none entering it. In any network there will be one such event. Number it "1."

(*ii*) Delete all arrows emerging from event 1. This will create at least one more "initial event."

(*iii*) Number these new initial events as "2, 3,..."

(*iv*) Delete all emerging arrows from these numbered events which will create new initial events.

(*v*) Follow step (*iii*).

(*vi*) Continue until the last event which has no arrows emerging from it is obtained.

Let us consider the network shown in Fig. 14.8 and apply Fulkerson's rule to number the events.

(*i*) Event A has no arrows entering, but only emerging arrows. Hence, we shall number it 1.

(*ii*) There are two arrows *a* and *b* emerging from this numbered event. Deleting these arrows yields two events B and H with no entering arrows, but only emerging arrows.

(*iii*) These will be numbered 2 and 3 respectively.

(*iv*) From these newly numbered events 2 and 3, arrows *c, d, e* and *f* emerge. Deleting these, we get events E and J which have only emerging arrows. Notice carefully that event K will have an arrow entering after deleting *e* and *f*, and hence cannot form initial events. Number events E and J as 4 and 5 respectively.

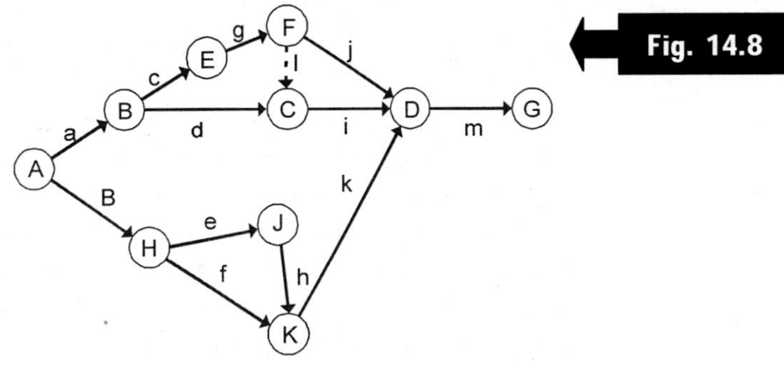

Fig. 14.8

(*v*) Delete arrows *g, d* and *h*. These give events F and K which will be numbered 6 and 7 respectively.

(*vi*) Delete arrows *i, j* and *k*. Events C and D will get numbers 8 and 9 respectively.

(*vii*) Finally event G which has no emerging arrows will form the end event and is numbered 10.

Fig. 14.9

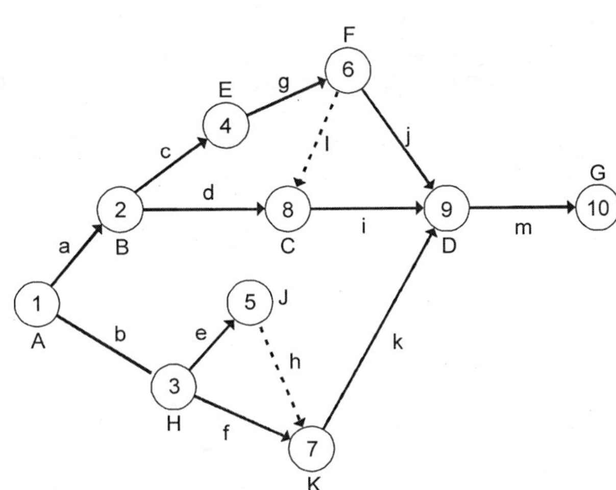

In the above example where there are only ten events, numbering them serially 1–10 is OK. But in large complicated networks, where extensive modifications may have to be made either before the network is finalized or as the project progresses, there must be scope to incorporate new events and number them without causing inconsistencies or loops. This can be achieved by what is known as skip numbering. Here, in the initial event numbering, use is made of only every tenth number, such as 10, 20, 30, 40 and 50. Any event added later would be assigned a number which lies between the number of the immediately preceding event (Predecessor event) and that of the immediately succeeding event (Successor event). Another practice would be to leave out such numbers as 8, 9, 18, 19, 28, 29 in the initial network and allot the left out numbers to the newly added events. Obviously, we can devise a variety of ways by which this kind of freedom is built into the system.

Time Management of Projects

We want to complete the project at the earliest. So time scheduling of the different activities is a pre-condition. We require data of time estimates for each activity. The duration of each activity is called activity time. There are two types of projects in terms of activity times.

1. Projects where sufficiently accurate estimation of activity time can be made.
2. Projects where estimation of activity time is difficult.

House building is 1st type. Launching of Agni missile is 2nd type.

Time management of type 1 projects is done by CPM. Time management of type 2 projects is done by PERT.

CRITICAL PATH METHOD (CPM)

Here an assumption is made that activity times are known to us with certainty. We have to compute here for each activity **earliest start time** and **latest start time**. Besides, the critical path is identified. **The critical path is the path which has the largest amount of time associated with it.** The length of the critical path determines the minimum time in which the entire project can be completed. The activities on the critical path are called **critical activities** or **bottleneck activities.** Any delay in the completion of these activities will delay the whole project. The critical path is important for two reasons. First, it highlights those activities which must be performed very rapidly if the total project completion time is to be reduced. Secondly, as we have already observed, any delay in these activities will delay the completion of the project whereas delays in non-critical activities may not delay the completion of the project. This is because there is slack (difference between earliest start time and earliest finish time). These non-critical activities can be delayed upto the amount of slack, without causing any effect on the total duration of the project.

Let us take the previous example, and show the time estimates for each activity.

Activity	***Immediate Predecessor***	***Activity Times (weeks)***
A	—	6
B	—	10
C	—	14
D	C	6
E	A, B	14
F	E, D	6
G	D	4
H	F, G,	4

The project network looks like:

Fig. 14.10

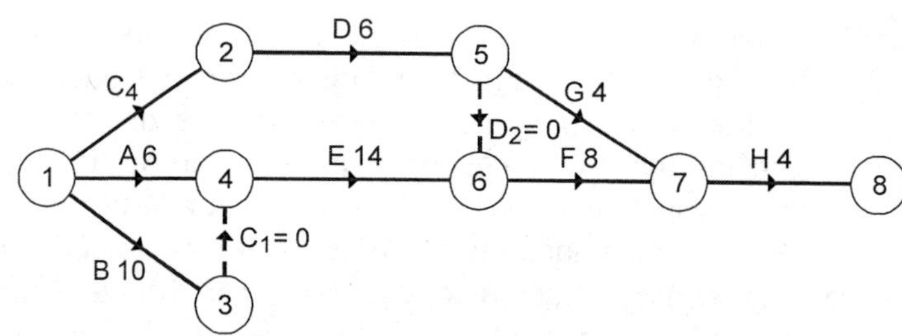

First let us acquaint ourselves with the definitions of the terms.

ES_i (Earliest Start Time for Activity i)

It is the earliest possible time that the activity can begin, assuming that all of its predecessor activities also started at the earliest possible time.

EF_i (Earliest Finish Time for Activity i)

It is the earliest possible time for the completion of the activity, assuming that all the predecessor activities did start at the earliest possible start time. The earliest finish time of an activity is the sum of the earliest start time and the estimated time to perform the activity.

$EF_i = ES_i + T_i$ (Activity Time)

LS_i (Latest Possible Start Time for Activity i)

It is the latest start time for an activity and is obtained by finding out the difference between the latest finish time and estimated time for the activity to be performed.

$LS_i = LF_i - T$ (Estimated Time)

LF_i (Latest Possible Finish Time for Activity i)

It is the latest possible time an activity can finish without delaying the project beyond its deadline, assuming all of the subsequent activities are performed as planned.

Computation of ES_i and EF_i for the Activities

For our network, we shall first set ES_i of the starting activity at zero. We shall then add the estimated time to perform the first activity to its *ES* (zero) thereby getting *EF* for the first activity. Since activity A takes 6 days, the *EF* for activity A is 6. Similarly *EF* for *B* and *C* activities will be

$EF_B = 0 + 10 = 10$

$EF_C = 0 + 14 = 14$

Please note that *EF* of predecessor activity becomes *ES* for the succeeding activity, to which *T* is added to get *EF*.

Activity *D* is dependent upon activity *C* and activity *E* is dependent upon activities *A* and *D*. We give the computations below.

$EF_D = ES_D + T_D$

Please remember the EF_C becomes ES_D

$\therefore = 14 + 6 = 20$

$EF_E = ES_E + TE$

Now A's *EF* becomes $ES_E = 6$ days

So also D_1's $EF = 10$ becomes *EF* for *E*.

But out of these two the greater value is accepted as the ES_E. The greater value is 10.

So $EF_E = 10 + 14 = 24$

Similarly,

$ES_G = EF_D$

$= 20$

$EF_G = 20 + 4 = 24$

$EF_{D_2} = 20 + 0 = 20$

$EF_F = EF_E$ or $EF_D + T$

Maximum is 24 and so

$= 24 + 6 = 30$

$EF_H = EF_G$ or $EF_F + T$

Maximum of these two is 30 (24 and 30)

$= 30 + 4 = 34$

Thus, Activity H will be completed in the 34th week and so project completion time will be 34 weeks from its start.

All activities summed up, you might have noticed, require 64 weeks but they can be finished in 34 weeks because some of them are carried out concurrently. However, since some activities are in series, the project cannot be completed before 34th week.

In short,

1. First set all the starting activities *ES* to zero.
2. Earliest finish time is *ES* plus *T*.
3. *EF* of preceding activity becomes *ES* of succeeding activity. To get again *EF* of this activity step (2) is repeated.
4. When the succeeding activity is dependent upon more than one preceding activity, *ES* of maximum value is chosen as *EF* for that activity.
5. A path is a network is a sequence of activities completed as such due to precedence requirements. In our network C, D, F, H is a path.

Similarly, (A, E, F, H), (B, D, E, F, H), (C, D, D_2, F, H) are paths. Time duration of a path is the sum of activity times of all activities on that path.

6. The path or paths with the largest time duration is/are called critical path(s). Activities on the critical path are called critical activities. The earliest time by which a project could be completed is the time duration of the critical path.

Computation of LS and LF Time of Activities

This is called backward pass. To obtain *LS* and *LF* for each activity, we start from the end of the network diagram. First we set the *LF* for the last activity *H* equal to *EF* for that activity, i.e., 34.

To get *LS* we have to subtract the activity time (T) from *LF*. So *LS* for *H* will be (34 – 4) = 30. Activity *G* is the preceding activity. So its *LF* is given by the *LS* for activity *H*. Similarly activity *F* is also the preceding activity and its *LF* is given by the LS of activity *H*. Now consider an activity like *D* whose *LF* is either *LS* of D_2 (hence *F*) or *LS* of *G*, whichever is smaller. The following table gives *ES, LS, EF, LF* for all activities. In the last column, the difference between *LS* and *ES* is recorded as *Slack*.

Table 14.1
Activity Times

Activity	*Duration*	*ES*	*EF*	*LS*	*LF*	*S*
A	6	0	6	4	10	4
B	10	0	10	0	10	0
C	14	0	14	4	18	4
D	6	14	20	18	24	4
E	14	10	24	10	24	0
F	6	24	30	24	30	0
G	4	20	24	26	30	6
H	4	30	34	30	34	>0
D_1	0	10	10	10	10	0
D_2	0	20	20	24	24	4

From the table it is obvious that activities B, G, E, F, H are critical activities since they show **zero slack value.** They together form the critical path.

In short,

1. Set *LF* of last activity equal to its *EF*.
2. *LF* – *T* gives *LS*.
3. Make it *LF* of preceding activity, and subtract *T* again to set *LS*.
4. Continue this backward pass. When there are two *LS* values out of which one is to be made *LF*, the smaller value is chosen.

Slack (Float)

It is the difference between ES_i and LS_i or EF_i and LF_i. Slack is defined as the difference between the latest event time and earliest event time. It is by this amount of difference that we can delay, some activities without delaying the whole project. It refers to the number of days an activity can be delayed without forcing the total project to be delayed beyond its deadline. There will be zero slack for those activities which are on the critical path. When the slack for an event is zero, it means any delay in the occurrence of that event will cause delay in starting subsequent activities. Any activity which has positive slack may be delayed beyond its *ES* by an amount of time up to the amount of slack; without causing any effect on the duration of the total project. Slack enables us to have better management of projects. If we operate under resource constraints, we first allocate resources to activities with zero or small slack.

PROGRAMME EVALUATION AND REVIEW TECHNIQUE (PERT)

Critical Path Method (CPM) which we have already studied is an instrument to plan and control projects where activity times are known with certainty. However, projects like R&D are such where time durations of activities cannot be assessed with certainty. At such times PERT is used. Whereas CPM uses a single time estimate for all activity durations, PERT uses three probable time estimates, namely,

Time Estimates

After the planner has decided on the network, the next attention is to estimate time required for carrying out each activity or job. Unfortunately, today's environment, because of the various uncertainties involved, is such that an exact estimation of the time a job will take is very difficult. There is always a pressure to get the job done in the minimum interval of time. This is the usual impatience of the manager. However, the uncertainties may tell upon the timely completion of the job. To take these uncertainties into account three kinds of time estimates are generally obtained.

These are:

(a) The Optimistic Time Estimate: This is the estimate of the shortest possible time in which an activity can be completed under ideal conditions. In arriving at this estimate no provisions are made for delays or setbacks. Better than normal conditions are assumed to prevail during the execution of the job. We shall denote this estimate by *a*.

(b) The Pessimistic Time Estimate: This is the maximum possible time it could take to accomplish the job. If everything went wrong and abnormal situations prevailed, this would be the time estimate for the activity. Of course, major catastrophes like labour strikes or unrest, acts of God, etc. are excluded from this estimate. This time estimate is denoted by *b*.

(c) The Most Likely Time Estimate: This is the time estimate which lies between the optimistic and the pessimistic time estimates. It assumes that things go in the normal way, with a few setbacks, usual lapses in deliveries, no dramatic breakthrough and so on. It reflects a situation where "things are as usual; nothing exciting." The most likely estimate is represented by *m*.

These three estimates are stated in days, weeks or months and represent calendar dates and not actual working days. Once these estimates are made, they should be held valid unless a change in resources demands a corresponding revision in them.

Estimated Time:

a : optimistic time
m : most likely time
b : pessimistic time

σ^2 : variance, calculated from $\dfrac{(b-a)^2}{6}$

t_E : expected time, calculated from $\dfrac{a+4m+b}{6}$

Fig. 14.11

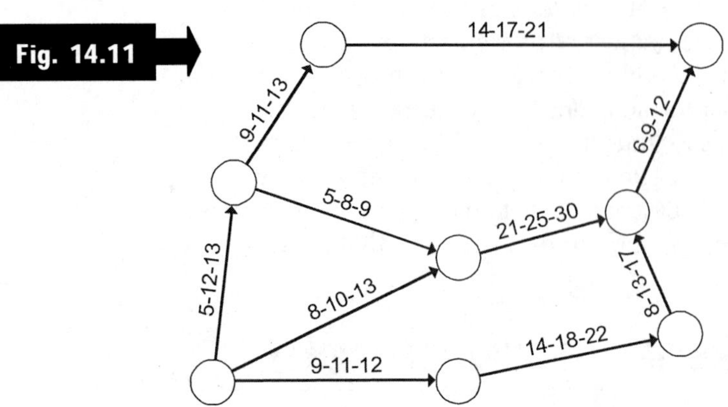

Example 1:

For the network shown in Fig. 14.11 the optimistic, the most likely and the pessimistic time estimates are given on the arrows representing the activities. The events are to be properly numbered according to Fulkerson's rule, the variance is to be calculated and the expected time is to be determined for each activity.

Applying Fulkerson's rule, the first circle on the left-hand side is the initial event since no arrows are entering it. We shall number it 10. Delete all arrows emerging from event 10. That leaves only two circles with no arrows entering. These shall be numbered 20 and 30 as shown in Fig. 14.12. Deleting the arrows emerging from events 10, 20 and 30 gives us events 40, 50 and 60. Notice that event 50 could not be given a number when the arrow connecting 10-50 was deleted, because of the arrow connecting 20-50. Proceeding this way, we arrive at events 70 and 80, the latter being the end event. The sequentially numbered network is shown in Fig. 14.12.

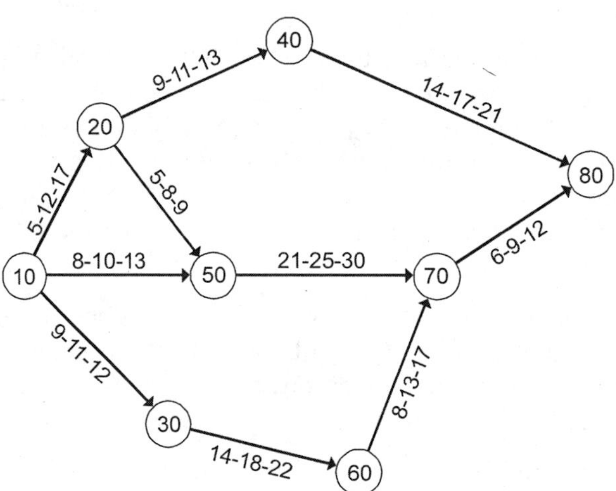

We shall now enter the data as shown in the following table:

Predecessor event	***Successor event***	***a***	***m***	***b***	σ_2	t_E
10	20	5	12	17	4.00	11.67
10	30	9	11	12	0.25	10.83
10	50	8	10	13	0.69	10.17
20	40	9	11	13	0.44	11.00
20	50	5	8	9	0.44	7.67
30	60	14	18	22	1.78	18.00
40	80	14	17	21	1.36	17.17
50	70	21	25	30	2.25	25.18
60	70	8	13	17	2.25	12.83
70	80	6	9	12	1.00	9.00

In entering the event numbers, first the number of the start event is entered in the predecessor-event column. Next, in the successor-event column the events connected to the start event (10 in this case) are entered with the numbers in the ascending order. For example, events 20, 30 and 50 are connected to 10. After exhausting all the events connected to 10, we go to the next higher number, *i.e.*, 20 in the predecessor-event column. This event 20 is connected to 40 and 50 which are entered in the successor-event column. This process is carried on until such time as all the events are entered.

The values of the variance σ^2 and the expected time t_E are entered in their respective columns and their calculations are straightforward. The significance of the calculation for σ^2 will be clear from the example that follows about introduction of Himalaya's Detergent Powder.

Notes: Characteristics of the distribution used to express the variation in time.

1. A small probability (1 in 100) of reaching the most optimistic time (shortest time), symbolized *a*.
2. A small probability (1 in 100) of reaching the most pessimistic time (longest time), symbolized *b*.
3. One and only one most likely time which would be free to move between the two extremes mentioned in 1 and 2 above, symbolized *m*.
4. The ability to measure uncertainty in the estimating.

The beta distribution was picked because it has all four of these attributes. The following figure illustrates a beta distribution with the time designations under the curve.

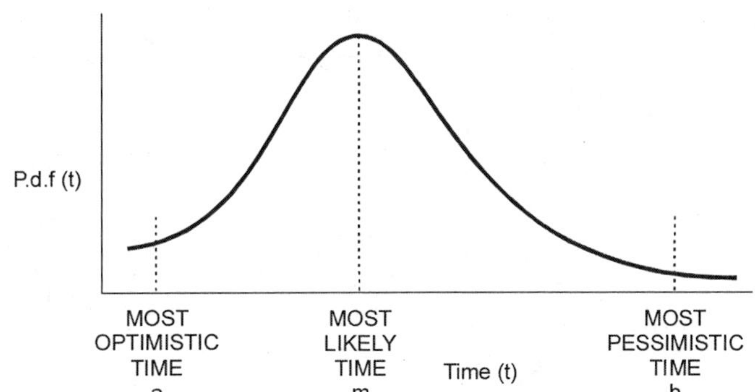

Fig. 14.13

After these three time estimates have been made, they must be combined into a single workable time value. This is done algebraically, using a weighted average.

$$t_E = \frac{a+4m+b}{6}$$

where t_E equals the expected time for the activity.

Studies have been made of the accuracy and validity of ***t*** computed by formula. One study shows that in most **PERT** situations, the error in form calculating it with equation of t_E was small enough to make the method quite satisfactory in most cases.[1]

To describe the variation or dispersion in the uncertain activity, times in a **PERT** network, we used the standard deviation of the activity times. Because we have three time estimates for each activity we can calculate a standard deviation for that activity. The difference between the ***a*** time and the ***b*** time represents the distance from the extreme left-hand end to the extreme right-hand end of a distribution of possible activity times. This distance is about ± 3 standard deviations: therefore, ***b* – *a*** = 6 standard deviations.

$$\text{Thus, 1 std. deg. for an activity} = \frac{a+4m+b}{6}$$

1. K.R. MacCrimmon and C.A. Ryavec, "An Analytical Study of the PERT Assumptions," Memo RM 3408 – PR RAND Corporation, Santa Monica, Calif., December 1962.

Fig. 14.14

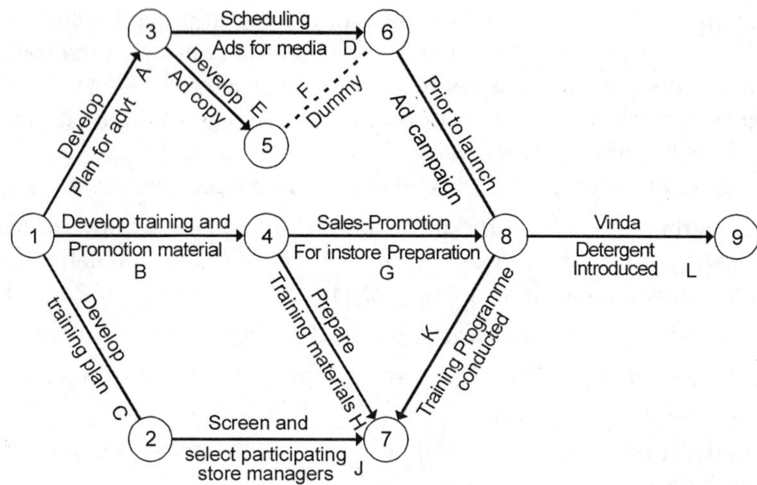

In the above example we have found out the square of 1 standard deviation for each activity.

PERT Network: Introducing Himalaya Detergent Powder in the market.

The following table summarises the Expected Time and Standard Deviation for activities in the above project:

Activity	*a*	*m*	*b*	$\frac{a+4m+b}{6}$	*s*
A	1	2	3	2	0.33
B	1	2	3	2	0.33
C	1	2	3	2	0.33
D	1	2	9	3	1.33
E	2	3	10	4	1.33
F	—	—	—	0	0
G	3	6	15	7	2.00
H	2	5	14	6	2.00
I	1	4	7	4	1.00
J	4	9	20	10	2.67
K	1	2	9	3	1.33
L	4	4	4	4	0

In the following table, we have tabulated *LF, EF, LS, ES,* and slack for all activities for the network of introducing Himalaya's Detergent Powder.

Activity	*ES*	*LS*	*EF*	*LF*	*Slack (LS – ES or LF – EF)*	*Activity on Critical Path*
A	0	5	2	7	5	
B	0	4	2	6	4	
C	0	0	2	2	0	yes
D	2	8	5	11	6	
E	2	7	6	11	5	
F	—	—	—	—	—	
G	2	8	9	15	6	
H	2	6	8	12	4	
I	6	11	10	15	5	
J	2	2	12	12	3	yes
K	12	12	15	15	0	yes
L	15	15	19	19	0	yes

Critical Path in Terms of Slack

From the above table, it can be seen that activities C, J, K and L do not have any slack and any delay here will delay the total project. These activities C, J, K, L form the critical path. Delay in noncritical activities (activities with slack) like A, B, D, E, G, H, and I will not delay the completion of the project, unless the delay is greater than the slack time an activity has. For instance, activity H can be delayed by 4 weeks, which is its slack, without affecting the total project time of 19 weeks.

In a more formal manner, critical activities are those activities which have zero slack value, and the path on which critical activities fall is called critical path.

Probability Estimates in PERT

We have already learnt to calculate a standard deviation for each activity. It helps to assess the effect of uncertainty in time estimation process. In Himalaya's Detergent Powder Network, the critical path is C-J-K-L with an expected total time of 19 weeks. If the activity times on the critical path are statistically independent, the standard deviation of the earlier finish time of the network is given by the following formula.

Standard deviation of the earlier finish time of the Network

(of the critical path on that network)

$$\sqrt{(\sigma)^2 + (\sigma)^2 + (\sigma)^2 + (\sigma)^2}$$

First Critical Activity C	Second Critical Activity J	Third Critical Activity K	Fourth Critical Activity L

From the table, we substitute the values of Standard Deviation.

$$= \sqrt{(.33)^2 + (2.67)^2 + (1.33) + (0)^2}$$

$$= \sqrt{0.1089 + 7.1289 + 1.7689 + 0}$$

$$= \sqrt{9.0067}$$

$$= 3$$

Imagine Himalaya would like to know:

What are the chances to complete the project in 20 weeks?

PERT assumes normal distribution of project time. *EF* for the network is 19 weeks, and Himalaya has now a completion of 20 weeks on mind. We have calculated above the Standard Deviation of critical path which is 3 weeks. Thus the distance from the mean to 20 weeks is:

$$\frac{20-19}{3} = 0.33 \text{ standard deviation.}$$

Refer the table of Standard Normal Probability Distribution for areas under the normal curve from the left hand tail to a point .33 S.D. above the mean. We get an answer 0.62930. Thus there is a brighter than 60 per cent chance that Himalaya will complete the project in less than 20 weeks.

Distinction between PERT and CPM

We have already learned that PERT is an event-oriented network where there is a planning and control of time. Now we shall learn CPM (Critical Path Method) where the concept of cost is introduced in the planning and control process. The CPM user is assumed to be on firmer ground when estimating the time required for the performance of each activity. When time can be estimated fairly well and when costs can be calculated in advance, CPM is preferred to PERT. On the other hand, when there is an extreme degree of uncertainty and when control over time is more important than control over cost, **PERT** is a better choice.

Time Cost Relationship and Project Crashing

In this system, two time and cost estimates are indicated for each activity in the network — these two are a ***normal*** estimate and a ***crash*** estimate. The normal estimate of time more or less represents the most likely time estimate in PERT. Normal cost is the cost associated with finishing the project in normal time. The crash time estimate is the reduction in time attained by diverting more resources to the activity which is speeded up. Crash cost, therefore, is the cost associated with doing the job on a *crash basis* in order to minimise completion time.

In other words, crashing means reducing times taken for an activity by the expenditure of more money. For example, overtime work is possible but it increases the direct labour cost. Secondly, we might work seven days a week instead of five or six which could increase direct labour cost. Thirdly, we might put on a night shift for certain work involving higher labour cost. Fourthly, we can put more manpower to do a certain activity again involving a higher cost. Fifthly, we can put more machinery and equipment to do the same activity again involving a higher cost. All this is done if it is necessary to expedite the project, though it means more costs. **CPM is an attempt in crashing project to its lowest possible time at the minimum possible cost.** The method is illustrated in the following example.

Activity	*Normal Time (Weeks)*	*Crash Time (Weeks)*	*Normal Cost (₹)*	*Crash Cost (₹)*	*Cost to Expedite (₹/week)*
1–2	18	6	12,000	36,000	2,000
1–3	24	9	9,000	18,000	600
2–4	21	12	8,400	12,000	400
3–4	36	24	27,000	33,000	500
4–6	9	3	30,000	39,000	1,500
5–6	15	6	14,700	21,000	700
3–5	21	9	5,400	15,000	800
5–7	33	15	19,800	36,000	900
6–7	30	18	12,000	25,200	1,100
			1,38,300	2,35,200	

Fig. 14.15

Network using normal times

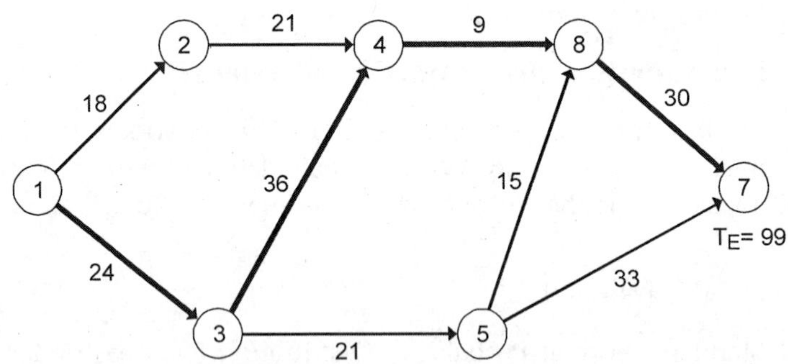

Consider two networks, developed on the basis of data given in the table using all normal times for the activities and the other using all crash times. (See Figs. 14.14 and 14.15). The critical path in each figure is shown by a heavy line. If the project is completed on a normal basis, the completion time is 99 weeks and the project cost is 1,38,300. If all activities are crashed the project completion time reduces to 54 weeks with a completion cost of ₹ 2,35,200.

Problem before Management

Can we reduce project time to 54 weeks without spending ₹ 2,35,200 as direct total costs?

Yes, we can do this by following the logical process, consisting of several steps, each step is an improvement over the preceding step.

Process of Crashing Activities

Step No. 1

Let us first mark the critical path in Fig. 14.16. It is 1–3–4–6–7. Find out which is the least expensive critical activity. In our example it is activity 3–4 (₹ 500 per week). We crash this activity to its minimum time of 24 weeks at a total cost for this action of (12 weeks × 500 per week) ₹ 6,000. When we crash this activity, it creates a new critical path which is shown in Fig. 14.17 by a heavy line.

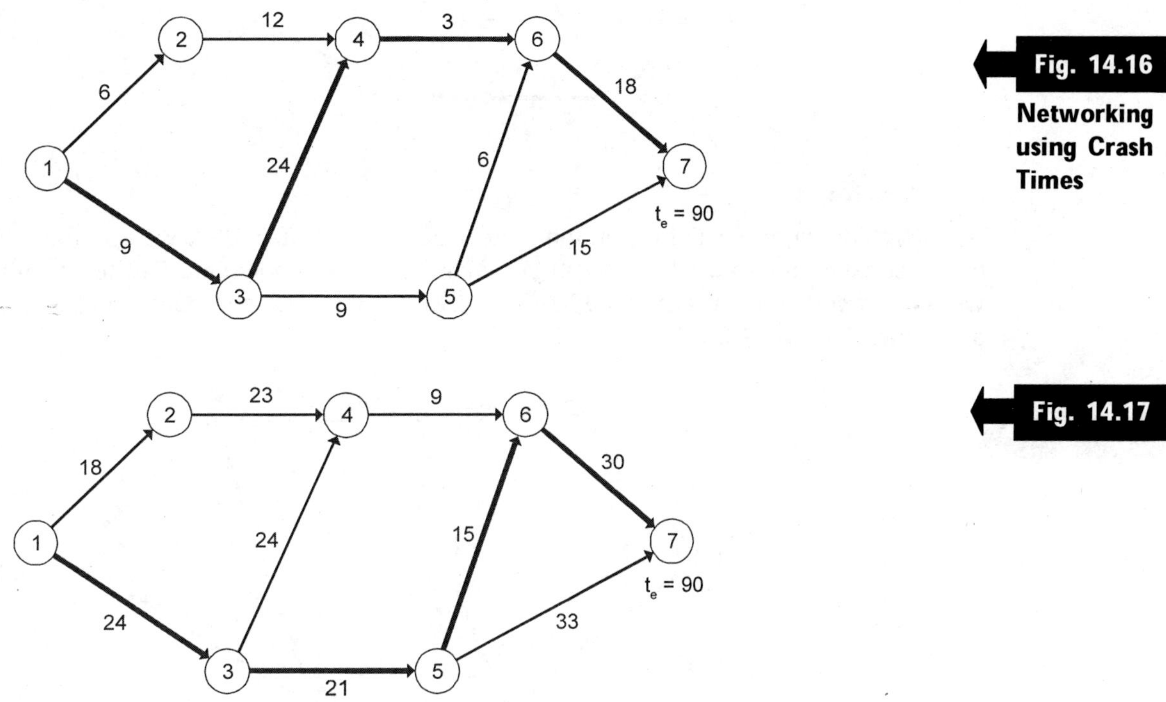

Fig. 14.16 Networking using Crash Times

Fig. 14.17

Step No. 2

The new critical path is 1–3–5–6–7 with a total completion time of 90 weeks. As in step No. 1, we crash that critical activity which is least expensive to reduce, which in this case is activity 1–3. Let us reduce activity 1–3 from 24 weeks to 9 weeks for which the cost incurred will be ₹ 9,000 (15 weeks × ₹ 600 per week). The new network is given by Fig. 14.18. In this network we get a new critical path 1–2–4–6–7.

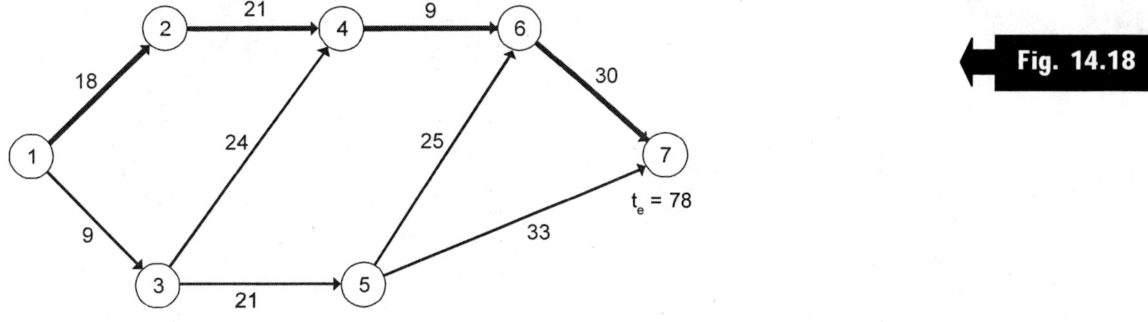

Fig. 14.18

Step No. 3

On this critical path activity 2–4 is the least expensive to crash at ₹ 400 per week. Proceeding as before we crash this activity from 21 down to 12 weeks, thereby incurring a cost of (9 weeks × ₹ 400 per week ₹ 3,600. This creates a new network and a new critical path as given in Fig. 14.19.

Fig. 14.19

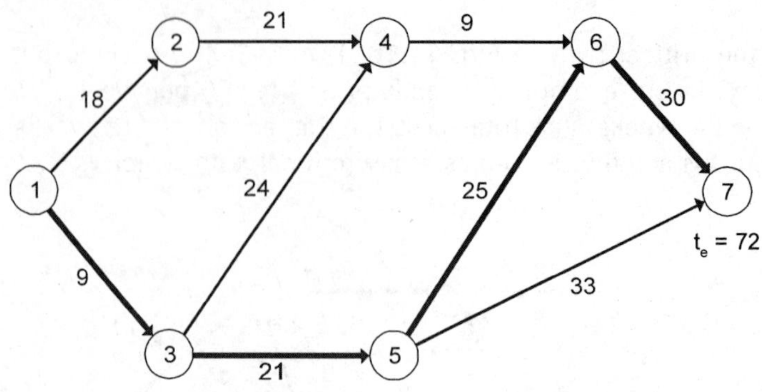

Step No. 4

Considering the activities on the new critical path 1–3–5–6–7, we observe that activity 5–6 is the least expensive to crash, at ₹700 per week. Let us crash activity 5–6 to its minimum time of 6 weeks at a cost of (9 weeks × ₹700 per week) ₹6,300. The consequent network and critical path are shown in Fig. 14.20.

Fig. 14.20

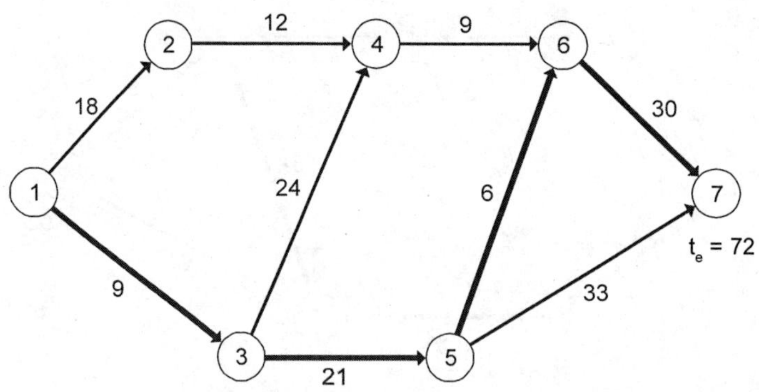

Step No. 5

Out of the activities on the new critical path 1–3–4–6–7, activity 6–7 is the least expensive to crash at this point and can be crashed to 18 weeks, at a cost of (12 weeks × ₹1,100) ₹13,200. As a result we get the new network and critical path as shown in Fig. 14.21.

Fig. 14.21

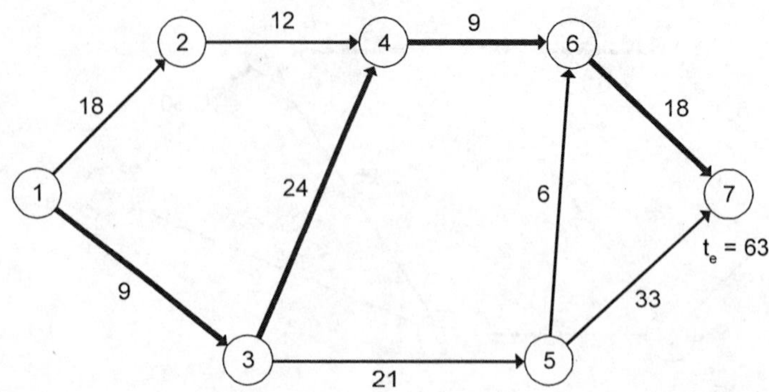

Step No. 6

Of the activities on the new critical path 1–3–5–7 activity 3–5 being the least expensive is crashed to 9 weeks at a cost of (12 weeks × ₹800) ₹9,600. The resultant critical path is illustrated in Fig. 14.22.

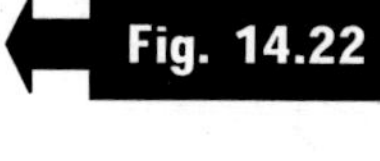

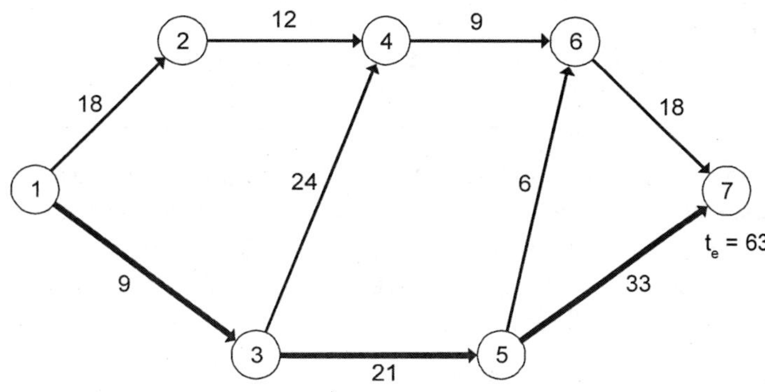

Step No. 7

While examining the new critical path 1–3–4–6–7, we notice that all activities have been crashed except activity 4–6, which we now proceed to crash to 3 weeks at a cost of (6 weeks × ₹ 1,500) ₹ 9,000. The results of this action are shown in Fig. 14.23.

Fig. 14.23

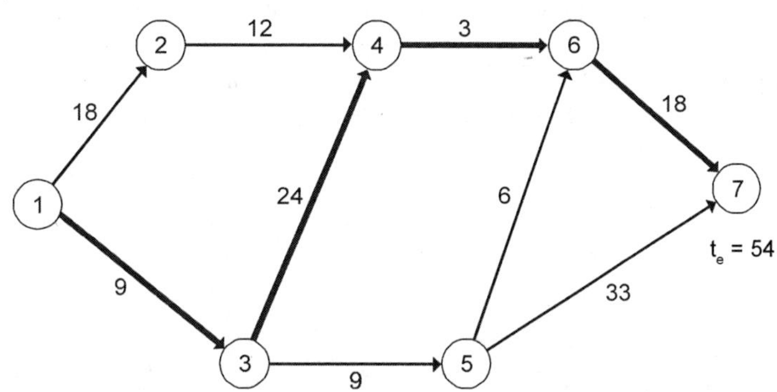

None of the activities of the critical path can now be further crashed. In other words, we have defined the longest reducible path through the network. The project can't be completed in less that 54 weeks at this stage. Let us calculate our expenses of crashing some of the activities commencing with step 1. The following table shows the results of our crashing programme:

We have successfully reduced the project completion time of 54 weeks without increasing the cost to the old crash figure of ₹ 2,35,200.

The next question is to explore the possibility of reducing project cost even further but without increasing the time beyond 54 weeks. In order to do this, we shall learn the concept of *Decrashing or Uncrashing.*

Results of the Crashing Actions (Figs. 14.15 to 14.21)

Original all-normal project costs	1,38,300
Crash activity 3–4 to 24 weeks	6,000
Crash activity 1–3 to 9 weeks	9,000
Crash activity 2–4 to 12 weeks	3,600
Crash activity 5–6 to 6 weeks	6,300
Crash activity 6–7 to 18 weeks	13,200
Crash activity 3–5 to 9 weeks	9,600
Crash activity 4–6 to 3 weeks	9,000
	56,700
Normal cost	1,38,000
Total cost of crash network	1,95,000

Uncrashing the Network

Consider Fig. 14.22 after crashing. There are only four activities on the critical path. We can attempt, therefore, the uncrashing of the Non-critical Activities (in other words, we can increase the time of the non-critical activities) which amounts to reducing the project cost further.

First consider the most expensive activity that has been crashed. It is activity 1–2 at ₹ 2,000 per week. We can reduce project cost more if we uncrash it. Later, we proceed to the next most expensive activity to uncrash it, and continue till we reach a point where no further uncrashing is possible. In other words, this stage gives us the least project cost with the time period of 54 weeks. The uncrashing is tabulated below:

Non-critical activity	***Cost of crashing (₹)***	***Action taken***	***Net gain obtain (₹)***
1–2	2,000	None, can't be uncrashed further	0
5–7	900	None, cannot be uncrashed further	0
3–5	800	Time extended to 12 weeks Path 1–3–5–7 will not permit further extension	2,400
5–6	700	Time extended to 15 weeks is the normal for this activity	6,300
2–4	400	Time extended to 15 weeks path 1–2–4–6–7 will not permit further extension	1,200
		Total gains from uncrashing non-critical activities	9,900

We can see this is the minimum project cost, with 54 weeks as project completion time. The resulting network is shown in Fig. 14.24.

The project cost for crashed network is ₹ 1,95,000 from which we can subtract ₹ 9,900 being the total gains of uncrashing to give us a minimum project cost of ₹ 1,85,100. Please note that all the paths in Fig. 14.24 are critical paths.

Fig. 14.24

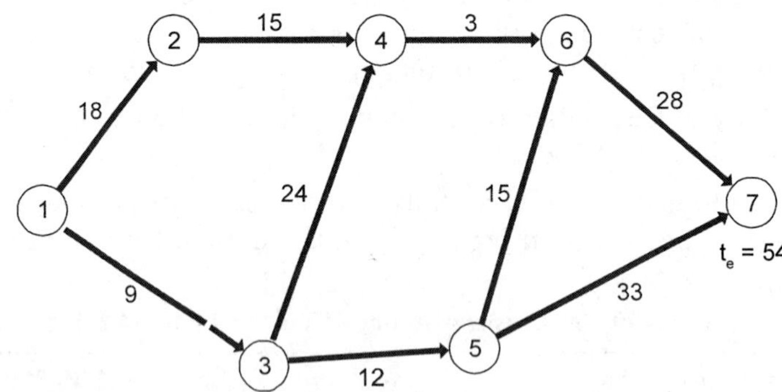

To Sum up:

1. Locate the critical path of normal network.
2. Crash the least expensive activity on the critical path to get a new critical path with its least expensive activity to crash. Proceed in the manner till we get a critical path on which all activities are at their crash time. (Non-reducible critical path).
3. Reverse the procedure by considering the non-critical activities and begin uncrashing by choosing the most expensive activity and proceeding to the least expensive activity, allowing uncrashing to the extent of critical path or to their normal times whichever is shorter.

Indirect Costs

So far, we have considered only the direct costs. Indirect costs are expenses for equipment rent, supervisory salaries, cost of payment and performance bonds on projects. In the following example, we have introduced indirect costs to find the optimum project cost.

Illustration:

The normal and crash duration with cost for various activities involved in a repair work is given below. The indirect cost for supervision of the work is also indicated.

Activity	*Time*	*(days)*	*Cost*	*(₹)*	*Expediting Cost per day (₹)*	*Indirect (₹)*
	Normal	*Crash*	*Normal*	*Crash*		
1–2	6	2	4,000	12,000	2,000	—
1–3	8	3	3,000	6,000	600	—
2–4	7	4	2,800	4,000	400	—
3–4	12	8	9,000	11,000	500	2000 per day
4–6	3	1	10,000	13,000	1,500	—
5–6	5	2	4,900	7,000	700	—
3–5	7	3	1,800	5,000	800	
5–7	11	5	6,600	12,000	900	—
6–7	10	6	4,000	8,400	1,100	—
			46,100	78,400		

(*a*) Draw a network diagram for these activities indicating the earliest start and latest finishing time at each node.

(*b*) What is the normal and ultimate crash duration of the project? Relax the compressed activities without changing the above crash duration. Draw a fresh network with costs.

(*c*) Considering the effect of direct and indirect cost find the optimum project cost for a duration of 26 days. Satisfy that the compression is followed by relaxation of optimum cost.

Solution:

(a) The network diagram is indicated below: (Fig. 14.25)

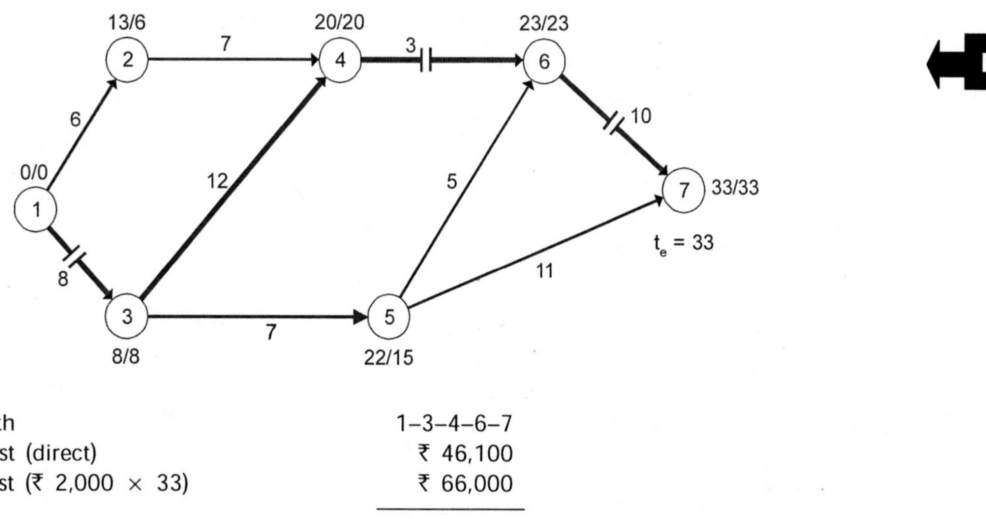

Fig. 14.25

Critical path	1–3–4–6–7
Normal cost (direct)	₹ 46,100
Indirect cost (₹ 2,000 × 33)	₹ 66,000
Total cost	₹ 1,12,100

Normal duration of the project is 33 days.

(b) 1st Stage of Crashing:

Slope of activity 3–4 (₹ 500) is the minimum along the critical path. So we crash it firstly by 3 days (Fig. 14.26).

Fig. 14.26

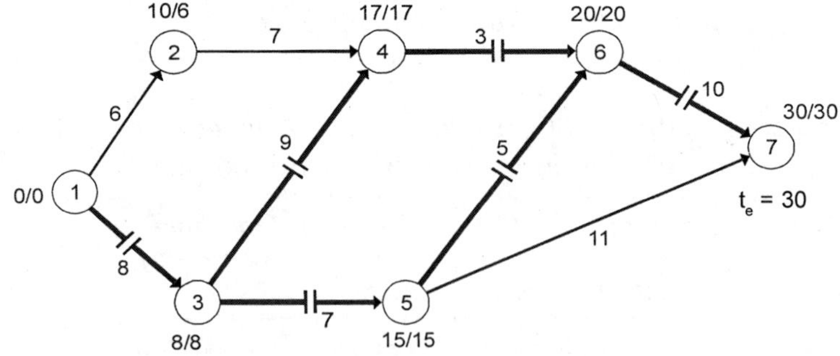

Decrease in indirect cost (₹ 2,000 × 3)	₹ 6,000
Increase in direct cost (₹ 500 × 3)	₹ 1,500
Saving in cost	₹ 4,500

Critical Paths

(*i*) 1–3–4–6–7 (*ii*) 1–3–5–6–7

(c) 2nd Stage of Crashing: (Fig. 14.27)

(*i*) Crash 3–4 along with 5–6 (Slope ₹ 500 + ₹ 700 = ₹ 1,200) or (*ii*) Crash 1–3 (Slope ₹ 600) by 4 days.

Decrease Indirect Cost (₹ 2,000 × 4)	₹ 8,000
Increase in Direct Cost (₹ 600 × 4)	₹ 2,400
Savings in Cost	₹ 5,600

Critical Paths (*i*) 1–3–4–6–7 (*ii*) 1–3–5–6–7

Fig. 14.27

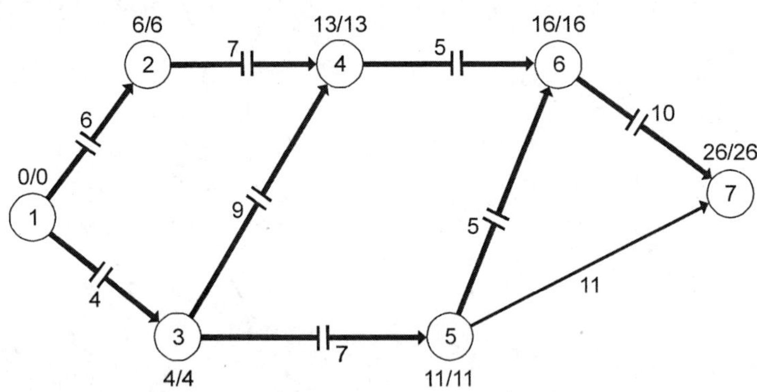

(d) 3rd Stage of Crashing: (Fig. 14.28)

Fig. 14.28

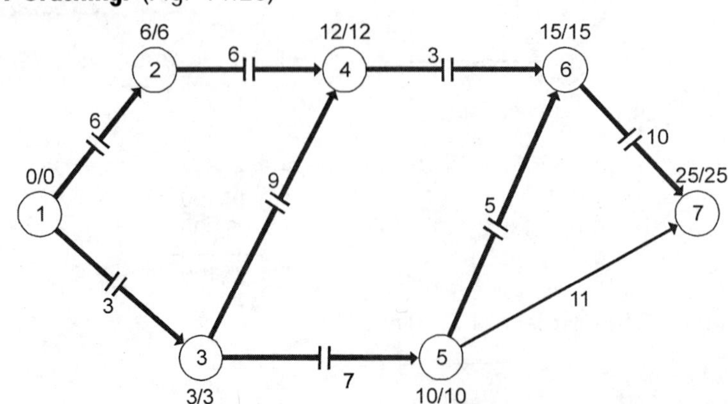

Crash 2–4 alongwith 1–3 by one week.
(Slope ₹ 400 + ₹ 600 = ₹ 1,000)

Decrease in Indirect Cost (₹ 2,000 × 1)	₹ 2,000
Increase in Direct Cost (₹ 400 + ₹ 600)	₹ 1,000
Savings in Cost	₹ 1,000

Critical Paths remaining the same.
Activities 1–3 is fully crashed here.

(e) 4th Stage of Crashing: (Fig 14.29)

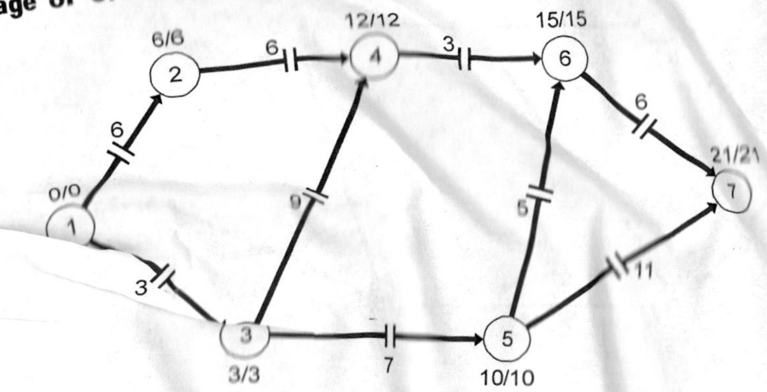

Fig. 14.29

(*i*) Crash 2–4 along with 3–4 and 5–6
(Slope ₹ 400 + ₹ 500 + ₹ 700 = ₹ 1,600) or
(*ii*) Crash 6–7 (Slope ₹ 1,100) by 4 days

Decrease in Indirect Cost (₹ 2,000 × 4)	₹ 8,000
Increase in Direct Cost (₹ 1,100 × 4)	₹ 4,400
Savings in Cost	₹ 3,600

Activity 6–7 is fully crashed here.

(f) 5th Stage of Crashing: (Fig. 14.30).

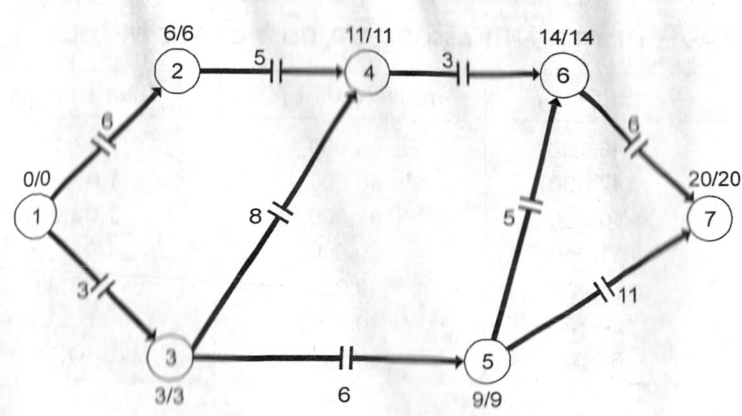

Fig. 14.30

(*i*) Crash 2–4 with 3–4 and 3–5
(Slope ₹ 400 + ₹ 500 + ₹ 800 = ₹ 1,700) or
Crash 3–5 along with 4–6
(Slope ₹ 800 + ₹ 1,500 = ₹ 2,300) or

(*ii*) Crash 5–7 along with 5–6 and 4–6
(Slope ₹ 900 + ₹ 700 + ₹ 1,500 = ₹ 3,100)

PRODUum is crashed by one day

Therefore: (i) being is

Decrease in | ₹ 2,000
Increase in | ₹ 1,700
| ₹ 300

Savings ircal and activity 3–4 is fully crashed here.

All the path ashing: (Fig. 14.31)

(g) 6th Sta

Fig. 14.31

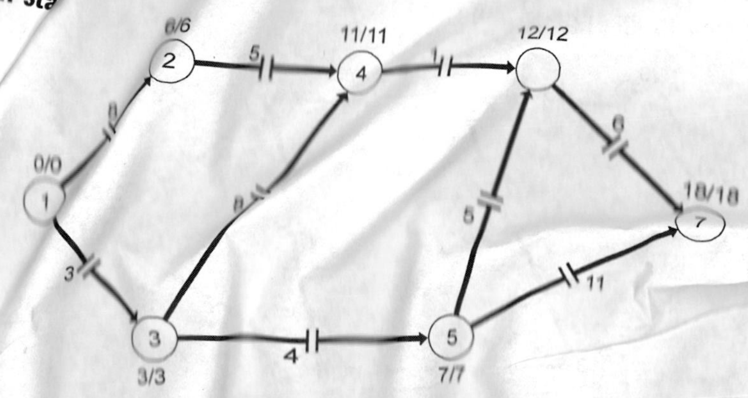

(i) Crash 5–6 along with 4–6 and 5–7

(Slope ₹ 700 + ₹ 1,500 + ₹ 900 = ₹ 3,100) or

(ii) Crash 3–5 and 4–6 by 2 days

(Slope ₹ 800 + ₹ 1,500 = ₹ 2,300)

Therefore:

Decrease in Indirect Cost	₹ 4,000
Increase in Direct Cost	₹ 4,600
Increase in Cost	₹ 600

All the paths are critical and activity 4–6 is fully crashed here.

SCHEDULE OF TIME AND ASSOCIATED COST OF THE PROJECT

Days	*Direct Cost (₹)*	*Indirect Cost (₹)*	*Total Cost (₹)*
33	46,100	66,000	1,12,100
30	47,600	60,000	1,07,600
26	50,000	52,000	1,02,000 *
25	51,000	50,000	1,01,000
21	55,400	42,000	97,400
20**	57,100	40,000	97,100 ***
18	61,700	36,000	97,700

* Optimum cost for 26 days

** Optimum duration.

*** Optimum Cost.

N.B.: As per the question the crashing should have been done up to 26 days in order to get the optimum cost on the 26th day (*i.e.*, ₹ 1,02,000). But by further crashing cost can be further reduced till 20th day (₹ 97,100) beyond which the cost will rise. The cost on the 20th day is the optimum Project Cost.

Normal duration is given in (a) which is 33 days. Ultimate crash duration is 18 days.

Critical Path 1–3–4–6–7. (Fig. 14.32)

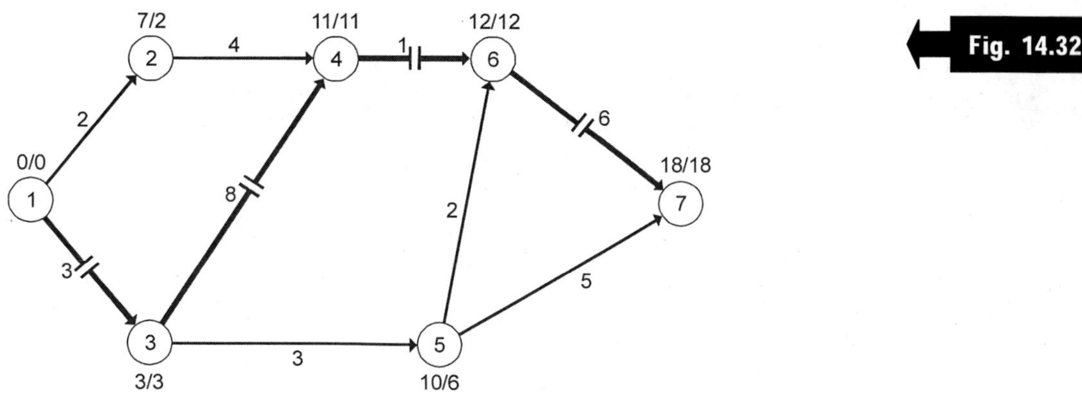

Fig. 14.32

1st Stage of Relaxing the Compressed Activities: (Fig. 14.33)

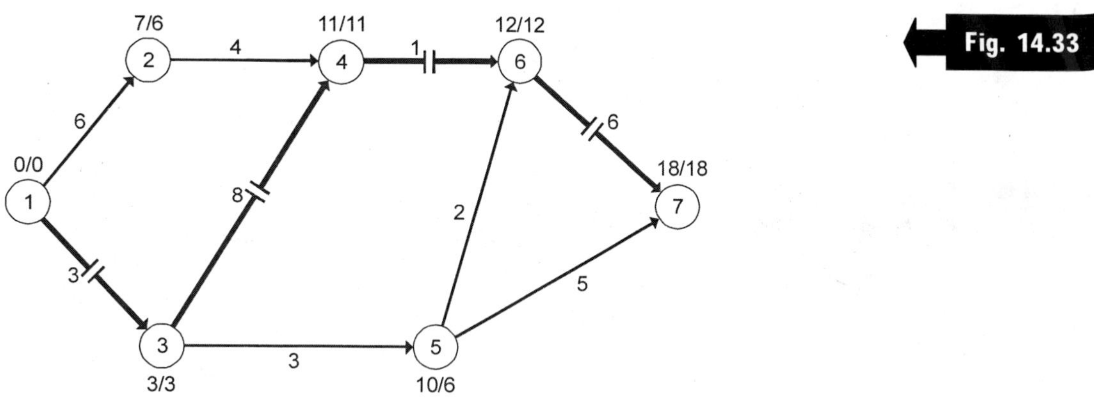

Fig. 14.33

1st relax the activity which has got the maximum slope along with the non-critical paths.

Relax activity 1–2 by 4 days – (Slope ₹ 2,000)

Saving in Direct Cost ₹ 8,000

(₹ 2,000 × 4)

Critical Path remains the same.

2nd Stage of Relaxation or Decrashing: (Fig. 14.34)

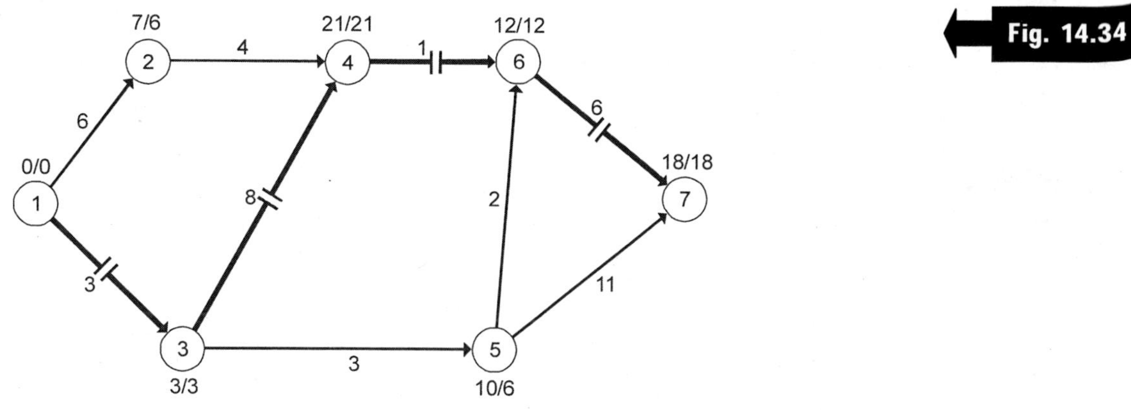

Fig. 14.34

Relax 5–7 by six days.

Savings in Direct Cost ₹ 5,400

(₹ 900 × 6)

Critical Path remains the same.

3rd Stage: (Fig. 14.35)

Fig. 14.35

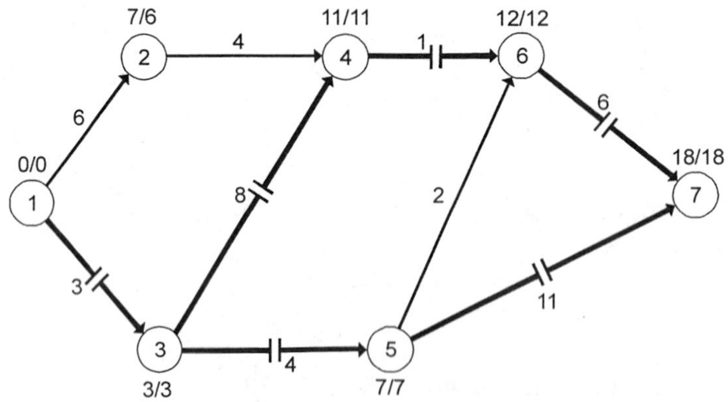

Relax 3–5 by one day.
Saving in Direct Cost ₹ 800
Critical Paths – (*i*) 1 – 3 – 4 – 6 – 7 (*ii*) 1 – 3 – 5 – 7

4th Stage: (Fig. 14.36)

Fig. 14.36

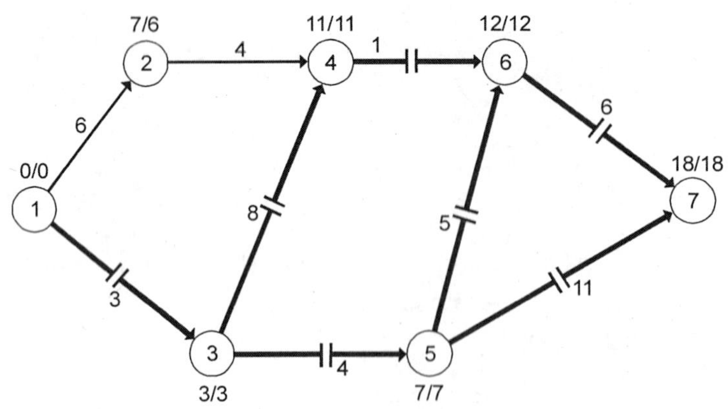

Relax 5–6 by 3 days
Saving in Direct Cost ₹ 2,100
(₹ 700 × 3)
Critical Paths (*i*) 1 – 3 – 4 – 6 – 7 (*ii*) 1 – 3 – 5 – 7 (*iii*) 1 – 3 – 5 – 6 – 7

5th Stage: (Fig. 14.37)

Fig. 14.37

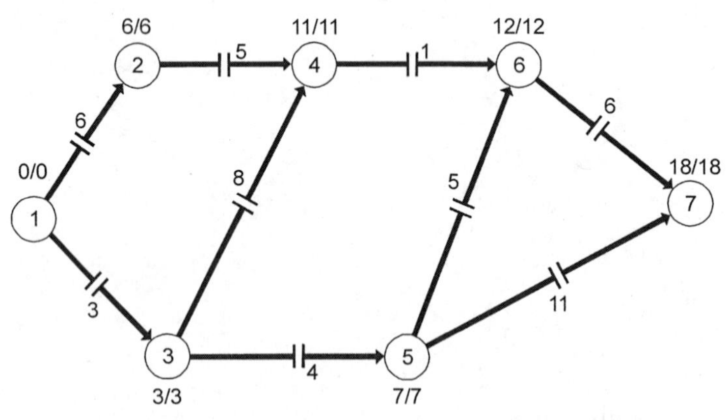

	₹
Relax 2–4 by one day	
Saving in Direct Cost	400
All the Paths are Critical.	
Crashed Cost as given in the problem less savings in direct cost as above	78,400
(₹ 8,000 + 5,400 + 800 + 2,100 + 400)	16,700
Minimum Direct Crash Cost	61,700
Add Indirect Cost ₹ 2,000 × 18	36,000
Minimum Total Crash Cost	97,700

Crashing a Programme: Illustration

The normal and crash duration with cost for various activities involved in a repair work is given below. The indirect cost for supervision of the work is also involved.

Activity	*Time (days)*		*Cost (₹)*		*Expecting cost/day*	*Indirect cost*
	Normal	*Crash*	*Normal*	*Crash*	*(₹)*	*(₹)*
1-2	6	2	4,000	12,000	200	
1-3	8	3	3,000	6,000	600	
2-4	7	4	2,800	4,000	400	
3-4	12	8	9,000	11,000	500	2000 per day
4-6	3	1	10,000	13,000	1,500	
5-6	5	2	4,900	7,000	700	
3-5	7	3	1,800	5,000	800	
5-7	11	5	6,600	12,000	900	
6-7	10	6	4,000	8,400	1,100	
			46,100	78,400		

1. Draw a network diagram for these activities indicating the earliest start and latest finishing time at each node.
2. What is the normal and ultimate crash duration of the project? Relax the compressed activities without changing the above crash duration. Draw a fresh network with costs.
3. Consider the effect of direct and indirect cost and find the optimum project cost for a duration of 26 days. Satisfy that the compression is followed by relaxation of optimum cost.

Solution

(a) The network diagram is given below:

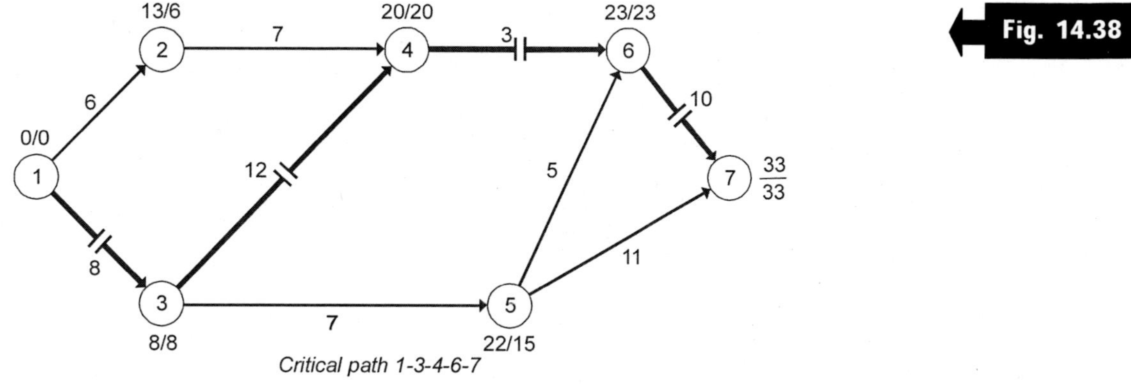

Fig. 14.38

Critical path 1-3-4-6-7

Normal cost (direct)	₹ 46,100
Indirect cost	
(₹ 2,000 × 33)	₹ 66,000
Total Cost	₹ 1,12,100

Normal duration of the project is 33 days.

(b) First Stage of Crashing

Slope of activity 3 – 4 (₹ 500) is the minimum along the critical path. So we crash it firstly by 3 days.

Fig. 14.39

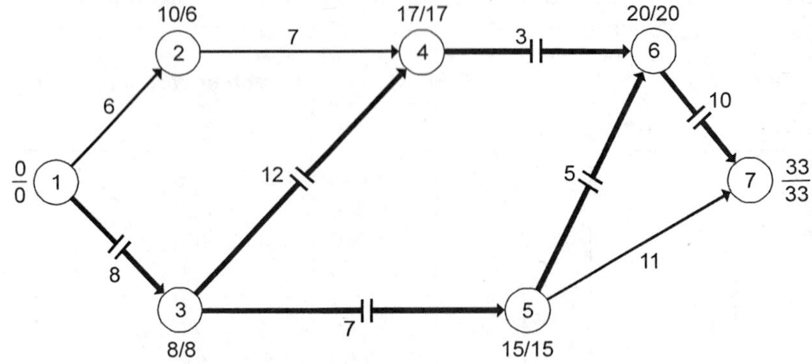

Decreases in Indirect cost	
(₹ 2,000 × 3)	₹ 6,000
Increase in Direct cost	₹ 1,500
(₹ 500 × 3)	
Saving in costs	₹ 4,500

Critical Paths

(*i*) 1 – 3 – 4 – 6 – 7

(*ii*) 1 – 3 – 5 – 6 – 7

Second Stage of Crashing

Fig. 14.40

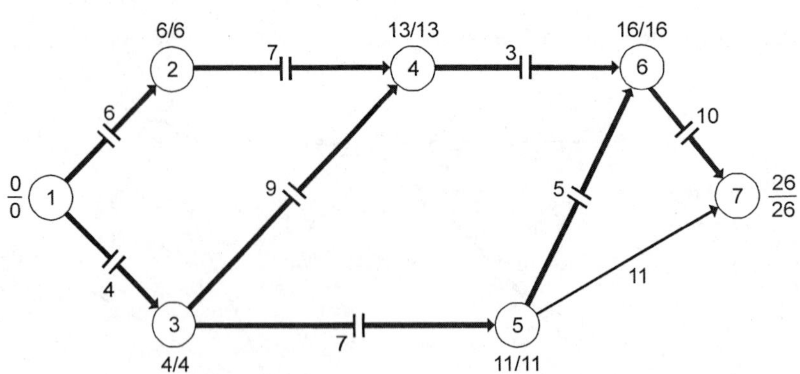

(*i*) Crash 3-4 along 5 – 6

Slope ₹ 500 + ₹ 700 = ₹ 1,200

or

(*i*) Crash 5-6 along with 4-6 and 5-7.

Slope ₹ 700 + ₹ 1,500 + ₹ 900 = ₹ 3,100

or

(*ii*) Crash 3-5 and 4-6 by 2 days.

Slope ₹ 800 + ₹ 1,500 = ₹ 2,300

Therefore,

Decrease in Indirect cost	₹ 4,000
Increase in Direct cost	₹ 4,600
Increase in cost	₹ 600

All the paths are critical and activity 4 – 6 is fully crashed here.

Schedule of Time and Associated Cost of the Project

Days	*Direct costs (₹)*	*Indirect cost (₹)*	*Total (₹)*
33	46,100	66,000	1,12,100
30	47,600	60,000	1,07,600
26	50,000	52,000	1,02,000
25	51,000	50,000	1,01,000
21	55,400	42,000	97,400
20	57,100	40,000	97,100
18	61,700	36,000	97,700

The optimum cost for 26 days is ₹ 1,02,000. The optimum cost is ₹ 97,100 and optimum duration is 20 days. Beyond 20th day, the cost will rise. The cost at 20th day is the optimum project cost.

Normal distribution as given in (a) is 33 days. Ultimate crash duration is 18 days.

Critical path 1 – 3 – 4 – 6 – 7

1st Stage of Relaxing Compressed Activities

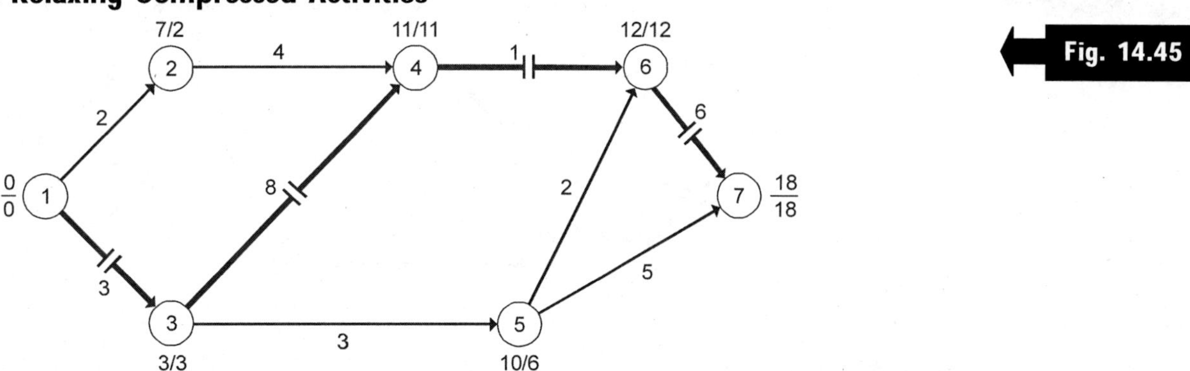

Fig. 14.45

First relax the activity which has the maximum slope along with the non-critical paths,

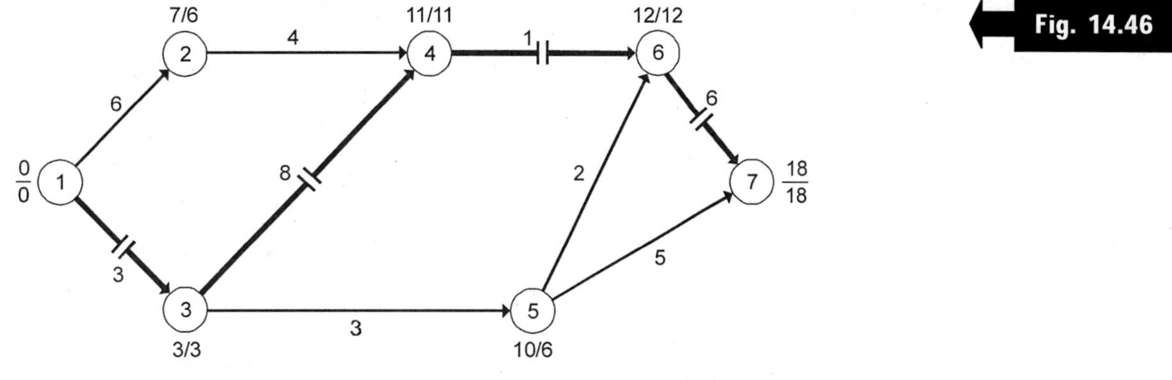

Fig. 14.46

Relax activity 1 – 2 by 4 days.

Slope ₹ 2,000

Saving in Direct cost ₹ 8,000
(₹ 2000 × 4)

Critical path remains the same.

Second Stage of Relaxation or Decrashing

Relax 5 – 7 by six days.

Fig. 14.47

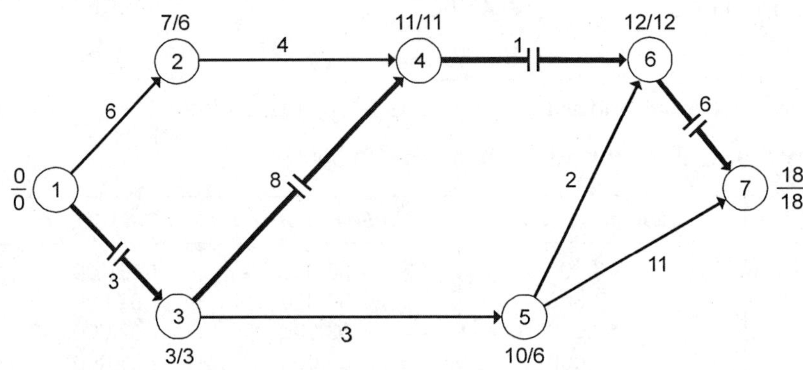

Saving in Direct cost
(₹ 900 × 6) ₹ 5,400

Critical path remains the same.

Third Stage

Fig. 14.48

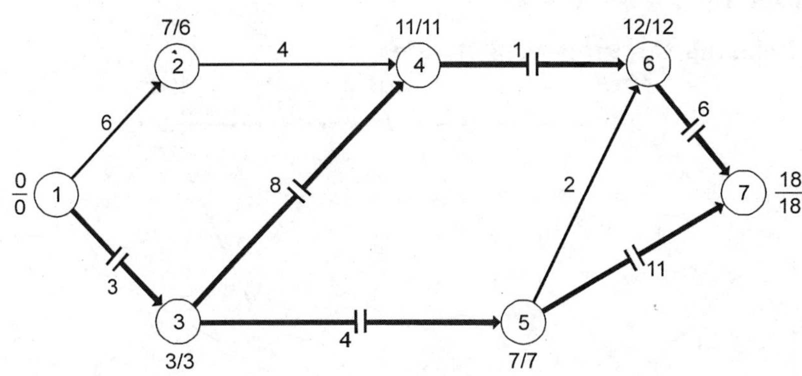

Fourth Stage

Fig. 14.49

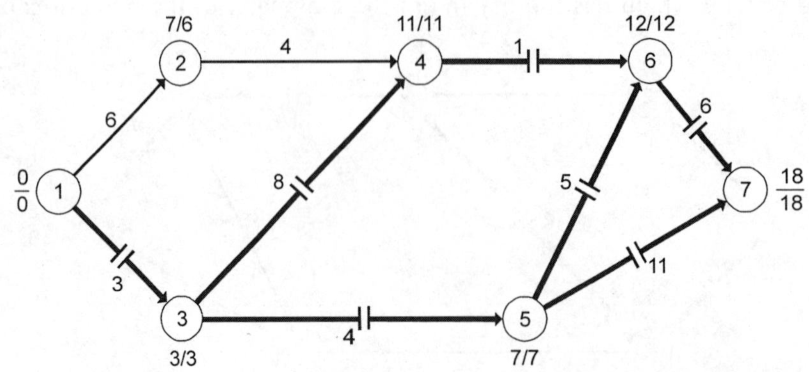

Relax 5 – 6 by 3 days.

Saving in Direct cost ₹ 2,100

(₹ 700 × 3)

Critical Paths

(*i*) 1 – 3 – 4 – 6 – 7

(*ii*) 1 – 3 – 5 – 7

(*iii*) 1 – 3 – 5 – 6 – 7

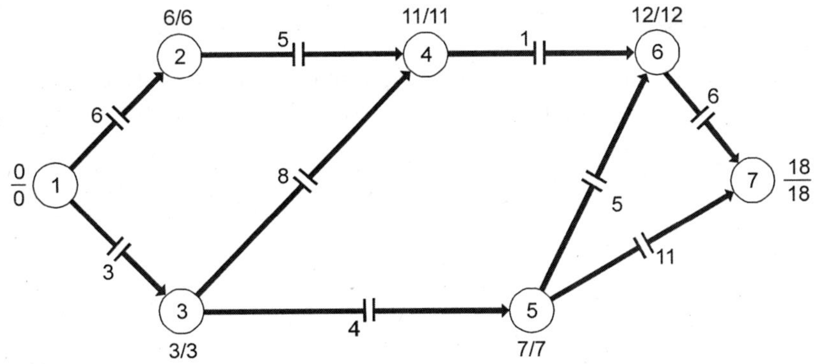

Fig. 14.50

Fifth Stage

Relax 2 – 4 by one day.

Saving in Direct cost ₹ 400

All the paths are critical

Crashed Cost (As given in the problem) less savings in ₹ 78,400

Direct cost (As above)

(₹ 8,000 + ₹ 5,400 + ₹ 800 + ₹ 2,100 + ₹ 400) ₹ 16,700

Add Indirect cost ₹ 36,000

(₹ 2,000 × 18)

Minimum Total Crash cost ₹ 97,700.

The relationship of direct cost and indirect cost and total cost can be plotted on a graph.

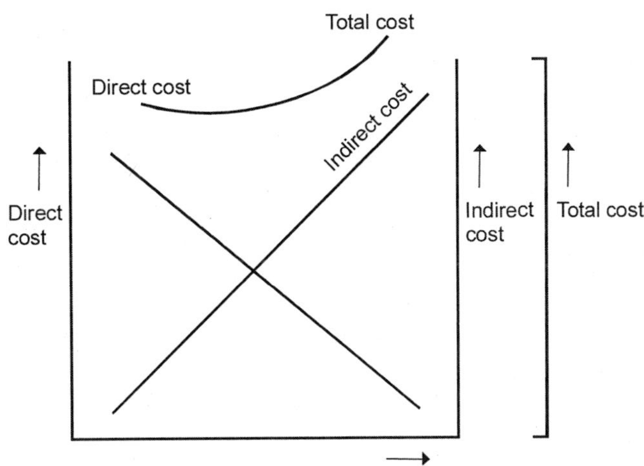

Fig. 14.51

Heuristic Method of Resource Allocation

Though an ideal solution of resource allocation is not possible under this method, certain simple rules can be kept in mind.

1. Allocate resources serially in time.
2. Give preference to activities with least slack when there are competing activities for the resources. Re-calculate the slacks of all the activities.
3. Reschedule non-critical activities to liberate resources for scheduling critical or non-slack activities.

Constant Reviewing of Projects

To be of help, the network techniques are to be updated along with the progress of the project. Computer software for network techniques enable us to do crashing/resource allocation with ease.

VALUE ENGINEERING OR VALUE ANALYSIS

Introduction

Value analysis aims at a systematic identification and elimination of unnecessary costs resulting in the increased use of alternatives, less expensive material, cheaper designs, less costly methods of manufacturing etc. to provide the same performance, quality and efficiency and in a decrease of overall unit costs and consequently greater profits. We can convert a stainless steel part into steel or even fibre-glass and thus save costs. TVS Suzuki's choice of fibre-glass for Spectra scooters has reduced its product-cost.

Suppose a housewife is out shopping for vegetables. There are four varieties of tomatoes to choose from, costing ₹ 15, ₹ 20, ₹ 25 and ₹ 30 respectively. Which will she buy? Quality? All are of good "quality." Price? Obviously not. Then the vegetable vendor won't be able to sell the other three qualities.

The answer is simple. She will buy that quality which serves her purpose. For example, if her husband's boss is coming for dinner and tomatoes are required for the salad, the ₹ 30 variety will be the obvious choice. If she wants to make tomato-rasam, then she will purchase the ₹ 15 quality. In other words, her choice will depend on the function the tomato is to perform. Each of the four varieties has a value and this value depends on the function it is expected to accomplish. This small example illustrates the approach of Value Analysis.

Value Analysis is, in essence, a study of function. The function of a part, or material, or service is the job it does. Value is the price we pay for a product process, material or service required to perform a specific function in an efficient way. We get the best value when we incur the least cost for an essential function or service with the required quality and reliability. The task of Value Analysis is to ensure that all the elements of cost whether for labour, for material, for designing or for services, contributes proportionately to the function.

Value analysis is a cost reduction technique and perhaps the most potent of all such techniques. Cost reduction is a very dynamic concept unlike, for example, cost control. In cost control we are aiming to keep cost within predetermined standards while in "Cost Reduction" our objective is to attack the costs themselves and eliminate them where possible. Value analysis parses a product into the functions performed by different components — and then looks for the cheapest way to have that function performed.

Definition

There are various definitions of Value Analysis. Stated very simply: "Value Analysis is an organized procedure for efficient identification of unnecessary cost." Another definition states: "Value Analysis is the study of the relationship of design, function and cost of any product, material or service with the object of reducing its cost through modification of design or material specification manufactured by a more efficient process, change in source of supply (external or internal), or possible elimination or incorporation in a related item."

A more elaborate definition of Value Analysis as given below throws more light on the subject.

"Value Analysis is the organized and systematic study of every element of cost in a part, material or service to make certain it fulfils its function at the lowest possible cost; it employs techniques which identify the functions the user wants from a product or service; it establishes by comparison the appropriate cost for each function; then it causes the required knowledge, creativity and initiative to be used to provide each function for the lowest cost."

Value Analysis (VA) is also known as Value Engineering (VE), Value Assurance and Value Management (VM). It is an approach for improvement in the performance of the products, systems or procedures and reduction or elimination of costs, without affecting the function. L.D. Miles defined VA "as an organized creative approach which has for its purpose the efficient identification of unnecessary cost, *i.e.,* cost which provides neither quality, nor use, nor life, nor appearance, nor customer features." VA was traditionally used in the area of hardware projects but is nowadays applied in software projects too. In non-traditional areas like customer service plans in banks, slum development, motivational techniques, VA can be of great use.

Historical Perspective

During the Second World War, one of the most serious problems faced by companies engaged in the war effort was the shortage of materials. This led to experimenting with substitutes, quite often in very unorthodox ways. In many cases, the experiments clicked and surprisingly there were a large number of instances where the substitutes were much cheaper and functioned more efficiently than the original material.

After the war, Harry Erlicher, the Vice President of Purchasing, General Electric Co. (U.S.A.) felt that this problem of finding out substitute could be done in a more scientific way and as a deliberate approach, rather than by an ad hoc crisis approach. He entrusted this job to a team of engineers headed by Lawrence Miles. In fact, it was Miles who coined the term Value Analysis and its synonym, Value Engineering. This team under his stewardship pioneered this technique and perfected it and, it is said, saved their company $ 200 million over a period of 17 years. In America, the technique is very widely used and is given a great deal of importance.

In fact, the US Defence Department insists that Value Analysis should be applied in all contracts in excess of $ 1,00,000. Mr. McNamara is on record as having said that in the year ending July 1965, the Defence Department saved $ 4.6 billion by using Value Engineering "without any adverse effect in our strength and combat readiness."

In India, the technique is catching on, but slowly. The basic difference between us and the Americans is that when they see something that is useful to them, they grab it. We are less enthusiastic in accepting change.

L.D. Miles, the father of this concept, wrote in 1961, a book, **Techniques of Value Analysis and Engineering.** Navy Bureau of Ships was the first organization to use VA in 1954. Society for American Value Engineers (SAVE) was established in 1959. VE programs came in vogue in many companies of the US, UK and Japan. In India, now we have Indian Value Engineering Society (INVEST) to create awareness of this approach and to propagate this concept.

VALUE AND FUNCTIONS

Types of Value

It is usually difficult to specify value mainly because values change from person to person. Generally speaking, there are seven classes of value — economic, moral, aesthetic, social, political, religious and judicial.

Of these, only the economic classification can be considered to be objective. It is the only one which can be measured. The others can be evaluated only subjectively.

Within the class "Economic Value", there are four subdivisions:

1. Use Value	Properties which accomplish a use, a work or a service.
2. Esteem Value	Properties which make the ownership of the object very desirable.
3. Cost Value	Properties which are the sum of the labour, materials, overheads and other costs required to produce that object.
4. Exchange Value	Properties that make the object possible of being trades for other items.

It is apparent that only "Use Value" is objective.

In almost everything we buy, we relate what we get to what we have paid for in terms of performance, reliability, appearance etc.

If we can collectively term these as "function" then we can express value in a mathematical way, *i.e.*,

$$\text{Value} = \frac{\text{Function}}{\text{Cost}}$$

By cost, we mean the total cost (*e.g.*, of material, labour, overheads etc.) required to produce the article. If we keep the function constant, we see that we get greater value when our costs come down.

Value can be increased —

1. When we reduce costs
2. When we improve function
3. By (1) and (2) together
4. When we increase function by a disproportionately low increase in costs.

Usually, most of us lack the ability to measure value. In industry most of us are performance or delivery oriented and we hardly search for or get cost information. Practice of value analysis sharpens this latent ability to determine worth and measure value and more than all to eliminate unnecessary costs.

Types of Function

It is the use value of a product — its functional utility. Functions can be of two types:

(*a*) **Basic Functions:** the primary purpose of a product.

(*b*) **Secondary Functions:** other purposes not directly contributing to the primary purpose but supporting it or resulting from a specific design approach.

Poor value may result from lack of understanding of functions, or an imposition of unnecessary functions.

Value Tests and Value Areas

The following is a check-list of ten tests for value complied by the purchasing department of General Electric Co. U.S.A. and it is considered most desirable, if not absolutely essential for every material, every part and every operation to satisfy these tests:

1. Does its use contribute value?
2. Is its cost proportionate to its usefulness?
3. Does it need all of its features?
4. Is there anything better for the intended use?
5. Can a usable part be made by a low-cost method?
6. Can a standard product be found which will be usable?
7. Is it made on proper tooling considering quantities used?
8. Do material, reasonable, labour overhead, and profit, total its cost?
9. Will another dependable supplier provide it for less?
10. Is anyone buying it for less?

Value analysis seeks answers to the following questions which may be asked about a complete product, a component or process:

1. What must this item or process do? What is its function? (This can usually be expressed in two words, *e.g.*, a bulb "provides light" or a paint "provides protection", or "enhances appearance."
2. What else does the item do? (If the item performs functions that are not needed, then it may be a symptom worth investigating to find out if there is a waste).
3. What does it cost?
4. What else could perform the same function?
5. What will be a possible substitute's cost?

It is usually said that one of the most important reasons for the success of Japanese business is the word "WHY"? Having a constructive discontent of everything around them, it is said, is a part of the Japanese character. The result is that they want change. This is exactly the philosophy of Value Analysis. Someone has described this philosophy by the following parody of the famous poem:

Ours is not to do or die,
Ours is to question WHY.

Add to this, Kipling's famous six honest serving men: What, Why, When, How, Where and Who and the profile is complete.

VALUE ENGINEERING JOB PLAN

VA process is in called VA job plan. Miles Job Plan was a modified version of work study. Later, several approaches have emerged. Some typical steps of a job plan are:

(1) Preparation, (2) Problem Selection, (3) Information, (4) Evaluation, (5) Creation, (6) Selection and presentation and (7) Implementation and Follow-up.

Mudge proposes the job plan in the following seven steps:

(1) General phase, (2) Information phase, (3) Function phase, (4) Creation phase, (5) Evaluation phase, (6) Investigation phase and (7) Recommendation phase. Each phase has a set of techniques, carried in the work sheets. VA is to be applied for those products where cost reduction potential is substantially high. It is the general phase which acts as a frame-work for other phases. The brief description of these phases follows.

The resistance is generally of the following types:

1. "We tried this a couple of years ago but it was not successful." (Conditions change. Why not try again now?)
2. "It can't be done." (If it has not been tried how does one know?)

3. "The customer is satisfied with the price as it is." (If this is so, he will be more satisfied and so will many others if the price is reduced.)
4. "Sampling is not as accurate as 100% inspection." (This is not always true but in any case, does it need to be that accurate?)
5. This way processing would produce too "many rejects to the specification." (Then, are the design limits too tight?)
6. There is no other technique. (Have you looked for one?) People have a natural resistance to change which may be further conditioned by experience, but favourable experience will help to reduce the resistance.

While thinking of doing VA, we must exercise good business judgement by being resourceful, thinking and innovative. The general phase is the foundation. We then enter the next phase the information phase.

General Phase

It is the most demanding phase of a VA Job Plan. It creates the right environment for successful VA. In this phase, emphasis is placed on human interactions to seek co-operation of the team to implement VA. Work is done on specifics, rather than on generalities. The resistance to change is to be overcome. Some typical beliefs, habits and attitudes are given below.

- "It will set a nasty precedent."
- "It won't work."
- "Cost too much."
- "The Public won't touch it."
- "It is impracticable."
- "The Production Dept. will have none of this."
- "Why change it — it works."
- "There is no other source of supply."
- "That is not our responsibility."
- "The Management will not accept it."
- "It's company policy."

Information Phase

Here an attempt is made to assess the potential of value improvement. Project is studied in detail and all important facts are gathered and considered. In this phase, facts which are in the form of technical specifications or environmental specifications are considered. Also, the engineering drawings, production sample, production data are all kept in mind. The cost data and work specifications are secured. Consumer preferences are jotted down. Development and testing are studied. Quantities and scrap are taken into account. A relationship is to be established between costs and specifications or requirements. Next stage is the functions phase. You will appreciate that lack of information is overcome in this phase.

Lack of Information

Most people who design a product are quite often not too sure of the real needs of a user and usually over-design the product by providing it with features that the user just does not use.

One of the facts of the manager community is that they lack cost information. Most of them feel that they have a rough idea, but how rough is rough?

The world is advancing exceedingly fast and new technology, new products, new materials and new processes are coming up almost every day. They create obsolescence in respect of the old materials or processes. Costs which were considered satisfactory yesterday become unnecessary today. In the face of competition the royal road to ruin is to adopt the methods of yesterday to the business of today.

Function Phase

Here the product is defined in terms of its functions, in terms of its performance expectations. These functions are co-related with costs and their worth.

Most of the times, an attempt is made to define functions with only two words — a verb and a noun. It makes the definition pretty sharp. It introduces an element of rationality into the exercise, by trimming the frills. Some examples will make you familiar with this approach.

SOME FUNCTIONAL DEFINITIONS

Product	*Function*
Tea Cup	Hold tea (liquid)
Light Bulb	Emit light
Gas Lighter	Provide ignition
Fan Regulator	Regulate speed
Match Box	Provide ignition
Mirror	Reflect light
Brake	Arrest motion
Screwdriver	Transfer torque

Another technique which is used under this phase is to evaluate function relationship by ranking functions in descending order of importance. Simultaneously, relative value of their importance is determined.

Paired comparison method is fairly common amongst researchers. It determines numerical value of various functions. Here pairs of functions are compared to know their importance and to assess the degree of variation (major, medium or minor).

Functions are defined for the products as a whole and for all their components. Functions are either basic or secondary. Generally a product's basic function is one, but it may possess several secondary functions. Basic functions can be restated in more ways than one.

Creation Phase

Lack of Ideas

A survey done in the United States shows that most people use less than 5% of their creative abilities. "We have hardly any time" (to think?).

Most of us want previously tried out materials, designs, processes and procedures. We jump at the first ideas that work and usually do not bother to find out if better methods are possible.

These days to give a fillip to creative ideas, brainstorming technique is used. To nurture creativity, positive thinking is established. Creative ideas are also developed by a number of check-lists and idea-stimulators.

Evaluation Phase

Creative ideas generated during the above phase are screened for their feasibility, cost effectiveness and practicability at this stage. For this purpose, ideas are further refined or combined together. Cost of all ideas and savings resulting from their implementation are studied. Decision-matrix can be set-up to evaluate on the basis of various criteria.

Investigation Phase

It is a virtual extension of the previous phase. Ideas accepted are here converted into acceptable and workable solutions to perform the desired functions at the least cost. It may be necessary to standardise, to consult vendors and specialists, and to use specialty products, processes and procedures.

Recommendation Phase

It is the ultimate phase of VA. Finally, selected value alternative here is presented for implementation on acceptance. Acceptance is the key to success of VA. Sometimes, acceptance is a result of presentation, or a combination of both. All the relevant data is kept before management to enable it to take suitable decision.

Alternatives of Job Plan

Instead of the above described method, we can adopt FAST or DARSIRI, which is an acronym for Data Collection (D), Analysis (A), Record of Ideas (R), Speculation (S), Investigation (I), Recommendation (R), and Implementation (I). All these steps have been explained above. So let us now concentrate on FAST (Functional Analysis System Techniques) as a value engineering technique.

FAST as VE Technique

Developed by Charles W. Bytheway (1965), FAST is a visual representation of functions and identifies the areas of greatest impact of these functions on costs. It is an interaction between function and cost.

FAST is like a network diagram.

The following steps are followed for construction FAST:

1. Use verb and noun for describing functions.
2. These functions are written on small cards.
3. First select the Basic Function card. Arrange other cards by answering the following questions:
   (*i*) How is this function performed?
   (*ii*) Why is it performed?
   (*iii*) When is it performed?

The logical sequence of functions (basic and secondary) generate a critical function path. It consists of only critical functions. FAST is bounded on both ends by scope lines.

BATTERY CABLE

1. Case Study

Battery cable was used in quantities of 50,000 for connecting battery to the starter. The cable was made of 90 mm^2 $\times$ 1.5 metre. Copper, with brass lugs on both ends. The cost was 52 units each.

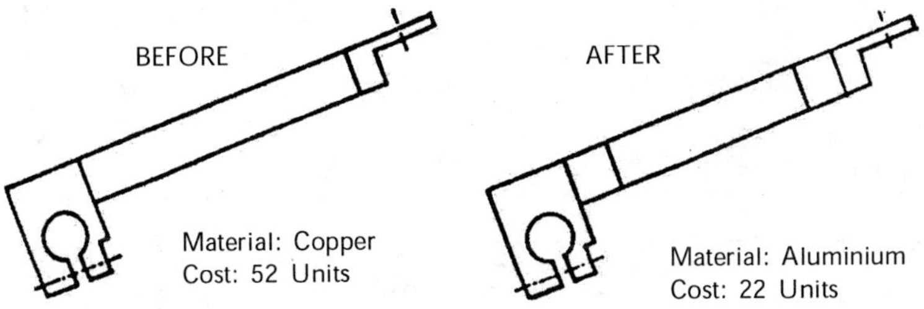

BEFORE

Material: Copper
Cost: 52 Units

AFTER

Material: Aluminium
Cost: 22 Units

Fig. 15.1

Data Collected	***Function, cost, current (450 amps) C/Section, other conductors and their costs, etc.***
Function	Conduct Electricity
Cost	52 Units per cable.
Worth	17 Units (steel cable with increased cross section could also conduct at cheaper cost).
Value Index	52/17 = 3 (More than 1, hence good potential for V.E.)
Creative Phase	Ideas to use cast iron, steel, aluminium, Nicro-alloys, silver, etc. generated.
Evaluation	After analysing different ideas aluminium was considered best and investigated regarding its feasibility, economy and related problems like bi-metallic corrosion between aluminium and brass lugs etc.
Recommendation	Aluminium cable of 120mm^2 $\times$ 1.5 metres with zinc alloy sleeves and brass lugs recommended.
Saving	30 units per cable (57% cost difference between copper and aluminium + cost increase due to addition of zinc alloy sleeves). = 30 $\times$ 50,000 = 15 Lakh units per year.

Courtesy: Sharma, M.K., Mgr. (Std.) TELCO, Jamshedpur, Vide INVAVE Vol. VI, Issue 1.

PIPE COUPLING

2. Case Study

PIPE COUPLING of a 5 component design was used in quantities 12,00,000 per year. The cost was 8 units per coupling.

Fig. 15.2

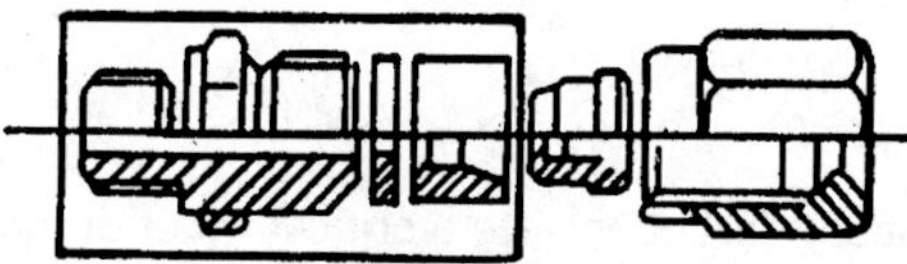

No. of Parts : 5
Cost : 8 Units

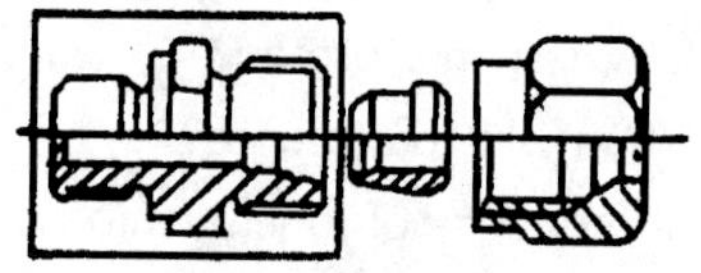

No. of Parts : 3
Cost : 7 Units

Data Collected	***Function of each part, material, cost, other coupling designs, etc.***
Function	Connect Pipe.
Cost	8 Units.
Worth	2 Units (cheapest way is to weld/braze).
Value Index	8/2 = 4
Creative Phase	To weld, use clips, use threaded pipes, combine functions of parts, etc.
Evaluation	After necessary analysis of function of each component of the coupling the functions of three parts were combined into one part.
Recommendation	Use of pipe coupling with 3 parts eliminating two parts and also reducing length of cap nut.
Saving	1 unit per coupling (12%) 12 lakh units per year.

THIN CASTLE NUT

3. Case Study

Thin castle nut M36 $\times$ 1.5 (with across flat 55) used in quantities 40,000 per year was imported at a cost of 33 Units per nut.

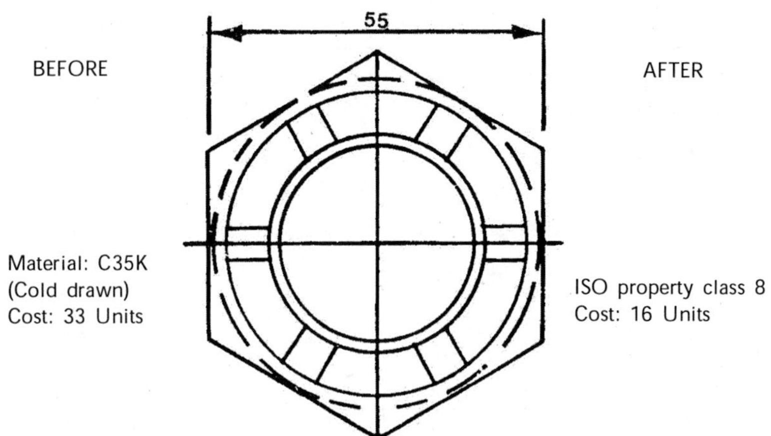

Fig. 15.3

Data Collected	***Function, cost, source of supply etc. Parts were procured as per drawing since material specified was C 35 K. Cold drawn bar of 55 Across flat, which was not made in India.***
Function	Fasten Steering Gear Box Accommodate Split-Pin
Cost	33 Units.
Worth	12 Units (similar nuts procured as per standard indigenously cost 12 units).
Value Index	33/12 = 2.7
Creative Phase	Ideas to change material to alloy steels, hot rolled bar with heat treatment, to use a standard Thin Castle Nut with ISO property class etc. were generated.
Evaluation	After analysis, use of standard nut with ISO property class 8 was investigated.
Recommendation	To use standard thin castle nut to IS 5368 with ISO property Class 8.
Saving	17 Units per nut (52%) 6.8 Lakh units per year (An import substitution)

CASTLE NUT WITH COLLAR

4. Case Study

Castle Nut with collar was used in quantities of 1,60,000 per year. The cost was 4.4 units each.

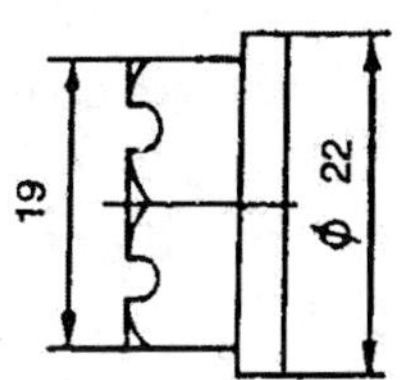

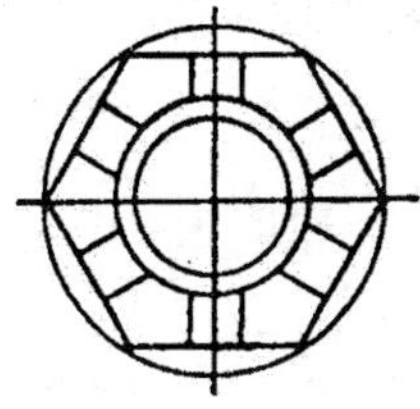

Cost: 4.4 Units

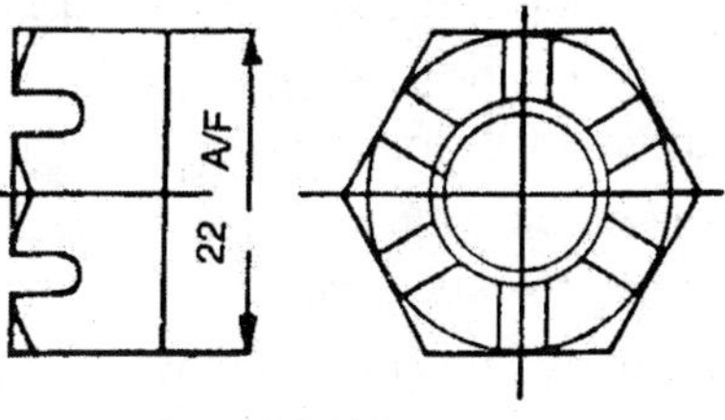

Cost: 2.8 Units

Fig. 15.4

Data Collected	***Function, cost, consumption, material, other similar items used etc.***	
Functions	1. Fasten Screw	
	2. Provide More Area	
	3. Accommodate Split Pin	
Cost	4.4 Units.	
Worth	Fasten + Accommodate Split Pin (Cost of castle nut)	1.2
	Provide more area (cost of a washer)	0.2
		1.4
Value Index	4.4./1.4 = 3.1 (more than 1).	
Creative Phase	Use of castle nut and washer, round nut with flats and slots, hex nut with large across flat & slot etc.	
Evaluation	Use of hex nut with large across flat and slots was analysed for cost and feasibility, discarding others due to certain limitations.	
Recommendation	Hexagon slotted nut with increased across flat (equal to the collar dia to previous nut) and without collar was recommended. This simplified manufacturing.	
Saving	1.6 Units per nut (36%) 2.5 lakh units per year.	

Organizational Aspects of VA

At the outset, let it be clear that VA requires top management support. The VA also requires team work. The VA function can be organized as per the needs of the organization — its size, operations, product-line etc. It can be administered by the staff at the corporate office or it may be run on decentralised basis or a balanced combination of both. A decentralised and local VA group is accepted as a helpful service. This is specially effective when manufacturing units are set up on product line basis and are autonomous cost and profit centres. VA however is not as firmly entrenched as marketing, finance and other corporate functions. There are frequent resistance problems to VA. Its endorsement at the top level leads to acceptance at lower levels. VA is also affected by the management level to which it reports — it must be wide enough to cover all areas affecting the validity of the study, high enough to communicate with decision-makers responsible for implementation, powerful enough to control and take responsibility for the administration and assignment of VA group.

Benefits from Value Analysis

There are several direct and indirect benefits which can accrue from the introduction and practice of Value Analysis. Some of these are:

1. A reduction in cost of existing products or systems.
2. Prevention of unnecessary cost in new products or systems. These two are quantifiable and can be easily measured.
3. The introduction of Value Analysis leads to overall cost consciousness and a general attitude change toward costs.
4. Product Value gets improved and the quest for new materials and processes get encouraged; it provides a great boost for import substitution.
5. Systems relating to cost and estimating usually benefit from reorganization necessitated by the wider use of cost information.
6. Finally, a greater return of investment results. In other words, greater profits accrue.
7. Value Analysis is a very important tool in contracts, and it is good to have a VE Incentive Clause to encourage a contractor to reduce the costs. There could be sharing of resultant benefits in a fair manner.

V.A. Through Vendors

Some materials managers claim that VA is an M.M. technique. However, when it comes to actual application of VA by material professionals in their various functional areas; the record is not exactly impressive. Even in organizations which take VA seriously, the involvement would appear more from other disciplines — industrial engineering, production, R&D, etc. — than from materials management.

Against this backdrop, C.K. Karunakaran, the M.M. Consultant suggests vendor's involvement for V.A. In the USA it is obligatory for defence contracts above certain value to include a VA clause. This is a highly desirable step, not necessarily confined to defence orders. There is a strong case to involve vendors in VA for major contracts, particularly in new projects and top their innovative skills. The benefit of any cost reduction brought about by vendors. VA efforts must be shared fairly between them and buyers' organization. The former ought to get preferences in the placement of orders and other concessions. This approach need not be limited to work contracts. Whenever the specifications are not rigid or critical and depending upon the value, volume and frequency of demand, this practice is relevant and beneficial. Beneficial to both vendors and buyers.

Incidentally, many materials managers do not seem to be aware of a national body functioning in India to promote V.A. We are referring to the Indian Value Engineering Society (INVEST) with headquarters in New Delhi at 9 Commercial Centre (North), Panchshila Park, New Delhi 110 017. Its quarterly organ, THE INVAVE publishes interesting articles and Indian case studies on the subject. This society, affiliated to the world body, has been doing excellent work in spreading the concept of VA in this country.

Weight Reduction for VE

Mahindra engineers propose to build an SUV that weighs less than a tonne. Their latest offering XUV 500 weighs 1750 kg, well under two-tonne benchmark for SUVs. They have reduced the weight of Scorpio by 60 kg in three years by saving in the weight of sheet metal and re-engineering the power train. Each kg saved amounts to a reduction in cost of ₹ 80-90 per vehicle. They propose to reduce weights of existing vehicles by 200-240 kg in a span of 30 months. Downsizing of engines also improves fuel efficiency. Metal is replaced by plastic in building up a vehicle wherever possible. Light-weight vehicles are examined for their technical feasibility and commercial viability. Maruti has undertaken 'one gram, one component' weight reduction programme. The new Swift is 20 kg lighter by using high strength steel. Their K series engines are aluminium engines with plastic, resin-coated piston to reduce friction. Instead of a metallic fuel tank, Maruti uses a six-layer polymeric fuel tank which leads to 10-15 per cent weight loss. Ideally, weight reduction means cost saving, but not always, as the substitute materials may be costlier.

16

MANAGING QUALITY

QUALITY

In both production and materials management, one of the important objectives is to manage quality. Quality is cross functional in nature and permeates the whole organization, especially production and materials. Materials that go into production ultimately determines what the quality of the ultimate output is going to be. Operations has the responsibility of producing a quality product for the customer. Quality management envelops the whole organisation. In this chapter, we examine how to manage quality. In the next chapter we shall study quality control.

In the recent times, there is focus on quality. We hear about quality awards, ISO 9000 and six-sigma quality.

Quality management evolved over a period of time. To begin with, in early 1900s, quality was related to inspection; a method to ensure quality. In the 1940s, quality acquired statistical connotation and quality came to be managed within the natural variation of the process. Shewhart, Dodge, Romig and Nelson contributed statistical control charts and other methods. The main objective was to keep the process within a state of statistical control and thus reduce the amount of inspection necessary. Quality management then amplified its scope in 1960s to cover the entire organisation as each function has something to contribute to quality design. Quality these days is taken to mean a process of continuous improvement. It gives competitive advantage and makes an organisation customer oriented.

Quality Definitions

Quality is defined in terms of something meeting or exceeding customer requirements. These requirements may be present requirements or future requirements. It makes a product fit for customers use. This fitness is related to the benefits derived by the customer and customer satisfaction. Customer satisfaction is a relative concept. Each person has a separate definition of quality consistent with his needs and means at a particular point in time. Thus quality is defined as the degree to which the product or service satisfies the customer requirements.

To a producer, quality is defined with respect to specifications, the variation from which cannot be tolerated. A producer specifies quality attributes and tries to meet them while improving process over a period of time. The manufacturing based definition of quality implies 'conformance to requirements.' Whether such a product meets the consumer expectations or not is for the consumer to decide.

Producers try to improve quality continuously by doing a better job of meeting customer needs and by product innovations.

The central idea about quality is 'continued improvement' or 'performance excellence.' Quality is defined as doing the right things right the first time and every time. Quality as a movement, as an organised teaching methodology for how an organisation should function, began in Japan in the 1950s and 1960s. Quality is also the value perceived by the customer. The user-based definition of quality is that it fits the purpose.

The following dimensions of quality deserve our attention.

- Quality of design
- Quality of conformance
- Availability, Reliability, Maintainability
- Field service

In other words, quality is the totality of features and characteristics of a product that influences its utility to satisfy the customer.

Quality of Design

It is the degree to which the specification of the product or service satisfies the customer requirements. This is the intended quality in the design of the product. It is thus decided prior to the production. It is a cross functional effort of the product design team. This team has members from engineering, operations, marketing and other functions. Quality of design is facilitated by research specifications and design concept. Research assesses the customer needs. These are translated into a concept. This concept leads to certain specification for the product. It involves identifying the right product, spell out its features, prepare its specifications so that it provides satisfactory service to the consumer at optimum cost.

Quality of Conformance

This is the extent to which the quality of design is achieved in production. Quality of conformance maintains the quality of design. In other words, it means producing a product to meet specifications. It is also called process quality. It is the degree to which the product or service conforms to specifications. It refers to the extent to which the product conforms to the laid down design.

Availability

It refers to the continuity of service. A product is said to be available if it is in operational state, and not down for repairs or maintenance. Maintaining availability refers to combat readiness. Mathematically,

$$\text{Availability} = \frac{\text{uptime}}{\text{uptime} + \text{downtime}}$$

Reliability

It is the probability that a product or a part or a system or requirement will perform satisfactorily for a given time under normal conditions of use. A product of better quality may not be reliable. Quality is related to the initial performance of a product or service but reliability is related to continuation of performance over a period of time. When the maintenance or replacement of a product or a part or a component is easy, simple, quick and cheap, the reliability becomes less important. The failure of an important part not available easily is considered serious.

The reliability of a product is also related to the mean time between failure (MTBF) which is the average time that the product functions from one failure to the next. The longer the MTBF, the more is the reliability of the product.

Maintainability

It refers to the restoration of a product or service that has failed. A product that can be restored quickly is said to have high degree of maintainability. Maintainability can be measured by the meantime to repair (MTTR) of the product. Availability is a composite concept which combines both reliability and maintainability A product high on reliability and maintainability will also be high on availability. This could be rephrased in terms of MTBF and MTTR:

$$\text{Availability} = \frac{\text{MTBF}}{\text{MTBF} + \text{MTTR}}$$

Field Service

It represents warranty, repair or replacement of the product after sale. It is also called after-sale-service or customer service or just service. A customer expects high level of customer service. It should be prompt too.

The following diagram captures these dimensions of quality.

Fig. 16.1

Types of Quality

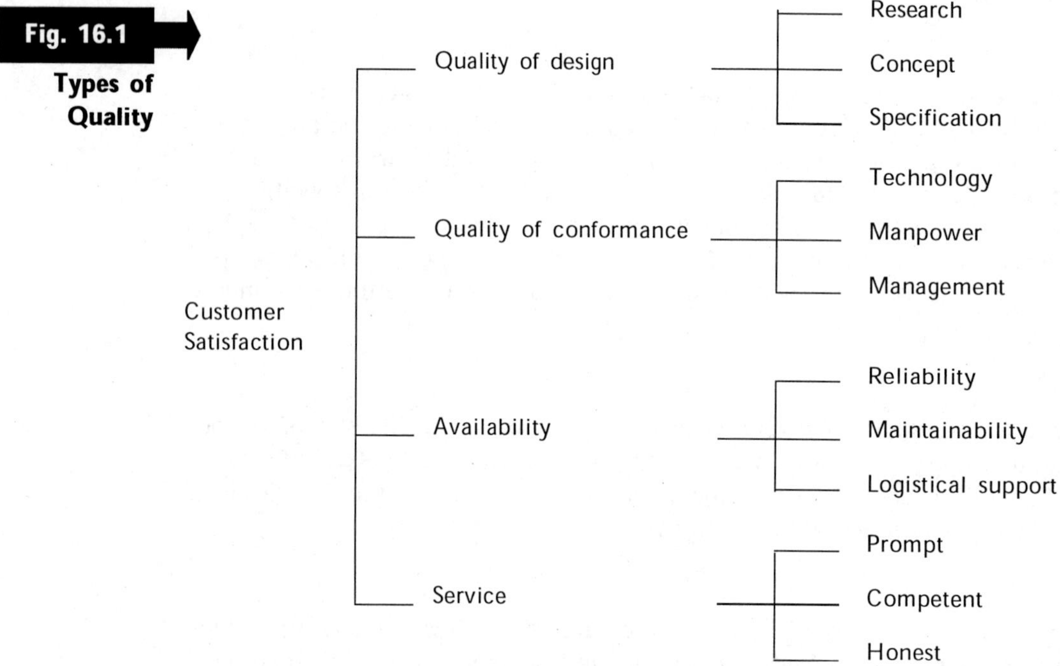

Quality concerns begin at the raw material procurement and design stage prior to production, continue during the progress of the production process and do not end with the sale of the finished product but thereafter too as after-sale-service.

Quality Planning, Control and Improvement

Quality planning and control requires constant interaction amongst the customers, operations and other areas of the organization. **Quality cycle** is the mechanism for these operations.

Fig. 16.2

The Quality Cycle

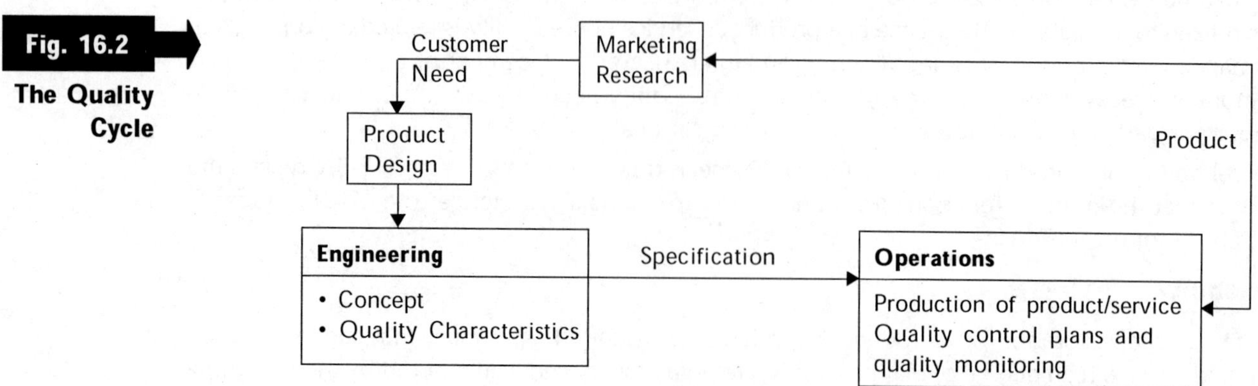

Marketing research assesses the customer needs. These need are conceived as product design by a cross-functional team. Engineering department examines the feasibility and spells out the specifications which match the production capability. The product is produced as specified, keeping quality of conformance in mind. Process variance is kept under control. Quality improvement is kept continuous over a period of time.

The whole process can be put into the following steps:

1. Definition of quality attributes in response to customer needs
2. Measuring each attribute
3. Set quality standards
4. Testing for each standard
5. Detecting causes for poor quality and correcting them
6. Continue making improvements.

Quality control is the mechanism that ensures the products conform to specifications derived from consumer research. It has to control systematically the variables in a manufacturing process which tell upon the excellence of the final product.

Quality Gurus

Here we shall consider the holy trinity of quality consisting of three persons — W. Edwards **Deming**, Jospeh M. **Juran** and Philip **Crosby**. We shall also mention in passing Prof. Shoji Shiba who diversified from researching salmon populations to breakthrough management practices. He is the present day Japanese quality meister. We shall also examine the work of Ishikawa and Taguchi.

We shall then turn our attention to ISO 9000 and the Balridge approach to quality management.

W. Edwards Deming

Deming first convinced the Japanese in 1950 about the importance of quality in product. He advocated management's role in quality improvement. To Deming, quality is continuous improvement of a stable system. Here stable refers to stability in the statistical sense. This involves measuring quality attributes throughout the company and keeping track of them over a period of time. If these measurements manifest a constant variance around a constant average, the system is stable. There is one more aspect to Deming's philosophy — improve the various systems to reduce variation and meet customer needs better. Deming said that quality could only be defined in terms of customer satisfaction.

Deming articulated his philosophy to quality in his **14-points** shown in the panel below.

The 14 Points

Deming developed the following 14 points to improve management of quality. These are taken from *The Deming Management Method* by Mary Walton (Pedigree Books, N.Y. 1986)

1. *Create constancy of purpose* for improvement of product/service.
2. *Adopt a new philosophy* which does not accept poor workmanship and sullen service.
3. *Cease dependence of mass inspection.* Quality comes not from inspection but from improvement of the process.
4. *End the practice of awarding business* on price tag alone. Purchase from the lowest-priced vendor may lead to low quality purchase.
5. *Improve constantly and forever the system of production and service.*
6. *Industrial training.*
7. *Institute leadership.*
8. *Drive out fear.*

9. *Break down barriers between staff areas.*
10. *Eliminate slogans, exhortations, and targets for the wok force.*
11. *Eliminate numerical quotas.*
12. *Remove barriers to pride of workmanship.*
13. *Institute various programmes of education and retraining.*
14. *Take action* to accomplish the transformation.

Deming advised executives not to opt for short-term profits compromising quality. He expected management not to bank upon mass inspection to achieve quality and recommended prevention of defects instead. Deming expected to achieve quality by training, supervision and statistical methods. Deming believed that the quality problems are a consequence of poor systems. It should not be attributed to workers.

Deming, along with Juran, improved quality in the Japanese industry. America woke up to his genius 30 years after Japan had begun facing Deming's line. Deming was hired by Ford in 1983 to effect turn around. He worked thereafter to spread his quality mission in American industries such as GM, AT & T, Western Electric.

Deming passed away at the age of 93 on Dec., 20, 1993.

Joseph Juran

Juran sparked off quality revolution in Japan in 1954. He believes in the trilogy — planning, control and improvement of quality. He recommended annual quality goals as a part of planning. These goals must be met. He believed that improvement of quality follows careful planning. He wanted to attack on the vital few for quality control. Juran, like Deming, believed in statistical quality control. He wanted the employees to be trained and their participation to ensure continuous quality improvement. He put forward the concept of 'quality of design' implying product features and 'quality of conformance' implying freedom from deficiencies. He believes there are two dimensions to quality — one concerned with matching customer requirements, one with building the products and services correctly. Juran was also responsible for Pareto analysis as applied to problem solving and the idea of Quality Council within the organisation.

Philip Crosby

Quality, according to Crosby, means getting it right for the first time rather than merely laying down acceptable standards of quality. Companies must price their product on this proposition and then quality costs no more. It is virtually free.

The key to quality is conformance to requirements. It is the first absolute on quality. He laid emphasis on prevention of defects. He advocates quality performance which has zero defects — do it right for the first time. He is of the opinion that quality should be measured by the price of non-conformance.

He concentrated on quality philosophy, particularly related to management. His must popular phrase is 'quality is free' and his four absolutes of quality are well-known. They state: The definition of quality is conformance to requirements, the system of quality is prevention; the performance standard is zero defect and the measurement of quality is the price of non-conformance.

Prof. Shoji Shiba

He is the practitioner of 'breakthrough management.' Godrej and Boyce in India has adopted the 'Shiba way' by introducing value stream mapping. The work flow is studied to identify waste in the system. Shiba streamlines processes and plant layout. He also transforms the human factor. He is the disciple of W. Edward Deming.

Kaoru Ishikawa

He developed the quality circles approach. He also introduced the term Company Wide Quality Control (CWQC). He felt that the Total Quality Management (TQM) approach focused on non-specialist inputs.

Genchi Taguchi

He developed the concept of Quality Loss Function (QLF). QLF is a measure of the economic loss or penalty suffered by the customer after receiving an item that fails to meet the larger specified quality. These losses include higher maintenance costs, higher operating costs, adverse environmental costs etc. The greater the variation, the greater such costs. QLF is tool to quantify quality improvements. He introduced the idea of quality by design which deals with specifications.

Nariaki Kano

He introduced the Kano model that relates to three factors is the degree of implementation. The three factors are — Basic, Performance and Delighter factors.

Christian Gronroos

He has produced a list of seven criteria for good perceived service quality. These are Professionalism, Attitudes, Trustworthiness, Service scape, Credibility, Accessibility and Recovery (PATSCAR).

ISO 9000 Standards

Today, the most talked about quality initiative is ISO 9000 quality system standards. It is recognised internationally as a benchmark for measuring quality. It is oriented towards conformance quality and does not include design quality. It is an entry-level quality approach.

ISO 9000 quality system was developed by International Standard Organisation (ISO) and approved in its present form in 1987. These standards were revised in 1994. ISO 9000 is considered minimum acceptable level of standards. Since 1987, several countries have adopted it as their national quality standard. Its Indian equivalent is commonly referred as IS 14000 series.

ISO 9000 expects a company to have a quality assurance system in place together with procedures, policies and training. A quality manual is usually required as a part documentation. The assessor audits the quality manual, the written procedure, the practices, the documented records to assess whether certification may be given. The product itself is not certified as having high quality, only the process for making the product is certified.

ISO 9000 has been accepted by the European community as a standard of selling in their markets.

ISO 9000 ignores strategic planning, leadership, customer satisfaction, continuous improvement and business results. It is not a complete quality system. Even a company, the product of which is not liked by the customers can have ISO 9000 certification as long as the quality system is in place, to ensure conformance to its specifications. ISO 9000 is just the first step to ensure quality. Much more is required.

Malcolm Baldrige Award

This award was established by the US Congress in 1987 to promote quality movement in American industry. The criteria against which the award is given have become quality standards The award is given each year in three categories — manufacturing, service and small business.

There are seven award criteria which include leadership, strategic planning, customer and market focus, information and analysis, HR focus, process management and business results. The total points are 1000 against these seven criteria. These criteria have become a comprehensive framework for quality management. Each company has the freedom to choose special techniques and approaches within the overall criteria. There is a great variety amongst the past winners. Baldrige awards recognise that quality cannot be isolated from enlightened management and enlightened management is required to produce products meeting customer needs, right now and in the future.

Complete Quality Process (CQP)

The best quality in any field is achieved by 100 per cent employee involvement from CEO to any hired labourer. It should be from the outset of the process. The process is complete by having every person involved and by structuring it using the quality tools available. CQP is the superset. Six Sigma, ISO, Lean, Kaizen etc. are the subsets. Total Quality Management (TQM) concentrated on beneficial set of steps. At best it invites everyone to take part in quality management. TQM was virtually never 'total.'

Cost of Quality (COQ)

To decide an acceptable cost of quality we consider the value offered by the finished product. While increasing the quality of the product, we tend to increase its cost, but the value added to the final product tends to grow less rapidly. Consider the following graph. (Fig. 16.3)

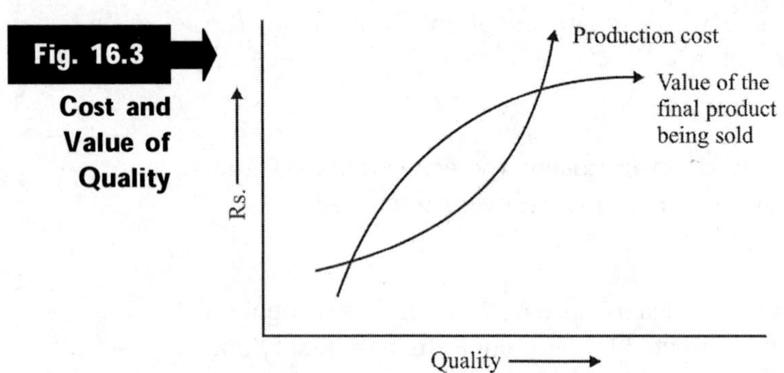

Fig. 16.3
Cost and Value of Quality

We would rather have a level of quality at which the value of the product exceeds its production cost. While ascertaining the cost of quality, we have achieved a trade-off between the losses on account of defects and the cost of inspection and quality control.

We are interested in increasing the value of the ratio R, given by —

$$R = \frac{\text{Quality}}{\text{Cost}}$$

It is necessary to prepare quality-cost framework for our company's processes and activities. Costs are classified into three categories. Prevention costs help us in preventing flaws and defects, creating stable designs, educating workers, and investing in preventive maintenance. Appraisal costs consist of expenses on measuring the level of quality through testing, sampling etc. Failure costs arise from re-working, rejections, machine downtimes, worker downtime, replacements, warranties given to the customer after sale etc. Failure costs are of two types — Internal Failure Costs are generated before a product is dispatched as a result of non-conformance to requirements. External Failure Costs are generated after the product is dispatched as a result of non-conformance to requirements. Rework is an example of internal failure costs, whereas complaints and returns are an example of external failure costs. We have to minimize the last two costs; appraisal costs and failure costs. This may result in an increase in prevention costs.

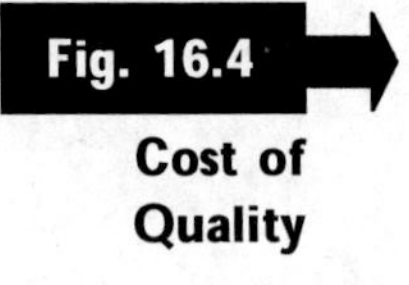

Fig. 16.4
Cost of Quality

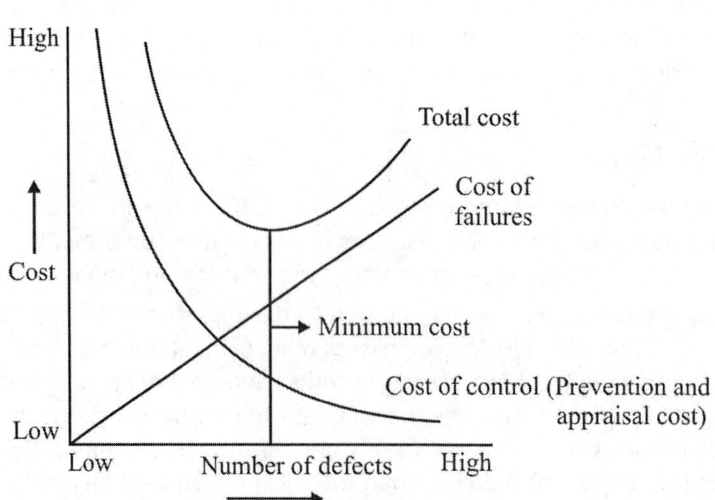

Prevention costs and appraisal costs are control costs since they are related to those activities that remove defects from the production system.

The total cost of quality can be minimized by plotting the cost of quality and the degree of conformance, and observing the relationship between the two. When the degree of conformance is high *i.e.,* low defects, the cost of failures are low but the costs of control are quite high. When the degree of conformance is low, that is defects are high, the opposite situation prevails. Between these two extremes lie an optimum level of conformance where the total costs are minimized. (see Fig. 16.4)

The optimal point is nearer to zero defects in many cases.

It is also necessary to reduce the cost of quality by revising the production system including technology, training, attitudes and management. Consequently, both the control costs and failure costs are reduced. This is shown in Fig. 16.5.

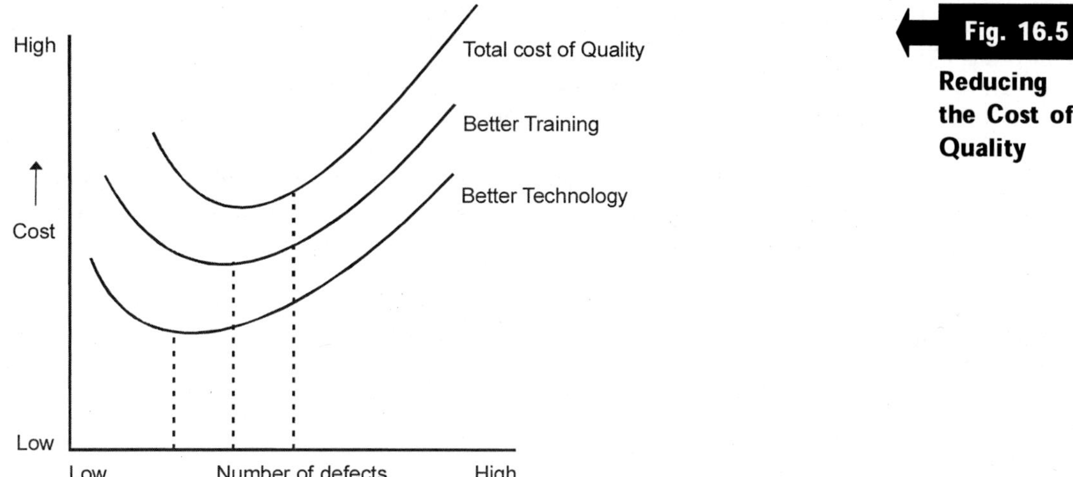

Fig. 16.5

Reducing the Cost of Quality

The cost of quality is an effective tool for quality improvement. This leads to improved profitability.

Appendix - I

RELATIONSHIP BETWEEN QUALITY AND COSTS

Fig. 16.6

Quality and Cost Relationship

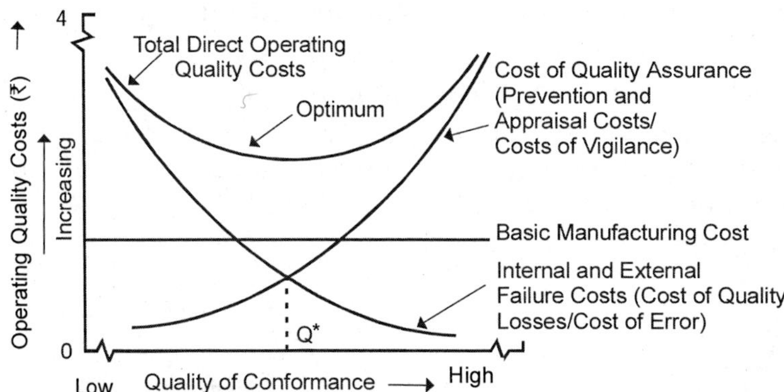

The three quality costs we have discussed, *viz.*, prevention costs, appraisal costs and failure costs are the *direct* quality costs. There are certain *indirect* quality costs such as customer-incurred quality costs, customer dissatisfaction costs and loss of reputation costs. The following diagram shows the relationship between the direct, indirect and total quality costs.

Fig. 16.7

Relationship Between Quality and Cost

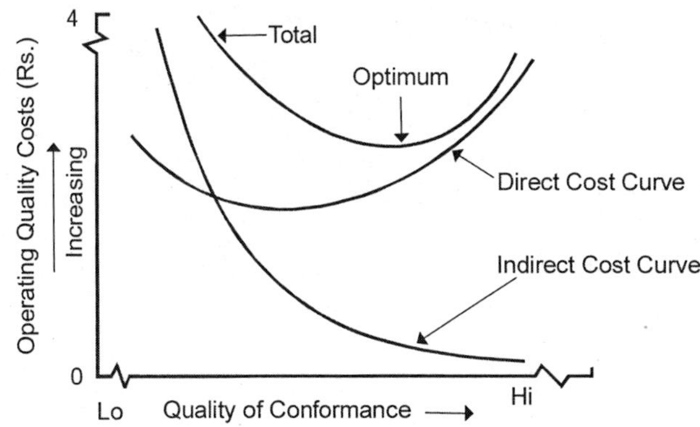

The horizontal axis shows the quality of production expressed in terms of the percentage of work which is defective. Extreme left indicates lot of defectives and extreme right gives no defectives in production. An organization may decide to prepare *quality cost report* giving a break up of the three types of quality costs.

Alternatively, we can classify costs on the lines of Crosby. *Price of Conformance (POC)* measures costs in getting things right for the first time. Price of Non-conformance (PONC) is the price the company has to pay for not doing that in terms of re-work. We here concentrate on inefficient process. PONC traces back to the design of the processes — whether there is any flaw here. When the business or production process or the specifications set by the customer have any flaw, it becomes a cost. PONC can account for 25 per cent of a company sales, as compared to 2-3 per cent for POC. The obvious lesson is that prevention is much better than cure.

Traditional accounting may not guide us much in identifying the costs of non-conformance. Just considering costs of labour, capital, plant and machinery and inventories is not enough. If there is non-conformance, workers will have to re-work, and the salary cost is involved. Similarly, we are using machine-time, and costs are involved. Sales people spend their time dealing with customers who complain about poor quality. Thus all these costs associated with non-conformance remain concealed, and are not eliminated.

Economics of Quality (Quality Cost)

There are three types of costs associated with quality.

System costs to set up the operating system to deliver appropriate quality.

Control costs to monitor checking and correcting activities during the operations.

Consequent costs are incurred after the completion of operations. The nature of these costs throw the following cost categories.

Investment costs: Costs incurred before operational to set up facilities and systems.

Prevention costs: To prevent poor quality in products and services.

Appraisal costs: To measure, evaluate, audit products or services to assure conformance to quality standards or performance requirements.

Failure costs resulting from non-conformance to requirements. They may be internal or external.

Crosby associates quality costs with the conformance or non-conformance.

Closer to Total Quality Management (TQM) philosophy.

A. Importance: Today the existence of any manufacturing or trading unit depends on the quality of product or services it manufactures or supplies. The image or goodwill of any unit is closely related to the quality of products or services made or supplied by that unit. The position of a unit in the industrial world depends on the quality of its products or services. Even the status of the employees, of a particular manufacturing or trading unit, in society, is affected by the performance and appearance of the products manufactured or supplied by that particular unit. Employees of certain units get high respect in the society to which they belong. The employees themselves are also proud of their connections as the employees with certain units, *e.g.,* employees of Tata concerns or certain Birla concerns or foreign drug companies or certain engineering concerns etc. considered themselves lucky enough for getting chances to serve in such companies. Society also considers their workplace as prestigious. Customers also prefer products of certain companies because according to the customers such companies rank high so far as the quality is concerned. In short, one can say that the company is known by the products it manufactures or services it gives.

A manufacturer of a quality product can certainly earn the expected profit and can hold a big share of the market. It all depends on the quality standards of the products manufactured by the firm. Today each manufacturer is required to give great importance to the quality factor so far as his products are concerned because there are many manufacturers of the same type of products and more and more numbers are entering into the field to manufacture the same type of products. Moreover, the consumers' taste-pattern also shows rapid changes day-by-day. Consumers' taste has become an ever changing factor in the market. Under such circumstances a manufacturer, who wants to exist with profit and to make his position sound in the market, must have to be quality conscious. In the case of a seller's market, a manufacturer can sell goods of whatever quality. But in this age of keen competition, it is not possible.

Now the level of quality is the mirror for a manufacturer, which reflects the design of the product, skill of the manpower employed, types of equipment, tools and machinery in use, amount of testing and inspection done, proportion of defectiveness or number of defective products produced etc. High level of quality reflects lower proportion or small number of defective products, high skill level of manpower, use of standard equipment and tools and better machinery, existence of effective testing and inspection methods etc.

Quality is very important for a manufacturer of products or services, because the very existence of a manufacturer depends on the quality level. Good quality ensures higher profitability, creates goodwill, and makes the employment of highly skilled manpower with better wages possible. And therefore to maintain as well as to improve the quality standards, each and every manufacturer spends a certain amount of money, the total cost of which may sometimes exceed the selling cost or production cost depending upon the type and nature of a product. For this purpose, a manufacturer maintains a separate inspection and testing department with trained and experienced inspectors or maintains a research and development wing or laboratory with the latest equipment and trained technical personnel. Moreover, a quality conscious unit gives technical assistance to the suppliers and also sends its official to the suppliers' factories frequently to check their facilities and to see whether the facilities are adequate for the production of quality products required by them. Samples are also evaluated by various concerned departments — inspection, design, engineering and production. Large units maintain service stations or field repairing shops and spend a big amount for the purpose. This is all done to satisfy the customers.

Poor quality or high proportion of defective products results in the extra cost to a producer/ manufacturer/supplier. A manufacturer/supplier/producer sometimes has to bear losses also due to poor quality. This can be explained as under:

1. Poor quality results in reduction in sales, which ultimately results in lower production, increase in the cost of production and decrease in the profit as well as the profitability. A manufacturer may have to incur heavy losses also for continuation of activity. Cost of loss in sales may prove detrimental to the existence of the manufacturing unit.
2. Manufacturer's or supplier's goodwill is also affected. Goodwill is created as a result of good performance over a long period. Re-establishment of goodwill once lost is a very difficult task. It is a time-consuming and costly process.
3. A manufacturer or a supplier becomes liable to indemnify the customer for any loss sustained by him due to poor quality, if he or she has guaranteed for the same.
4. A manufacturer or a supplier may be required to replace any part or the whole product, if it proves to be of inferior quality or if it fails to give rated performance. Sometimes, a manufacturer may also be required to get the product replaced at the customer's end.
5. A manufacturer or a supplier may have to sell the defective or substandard products at a discount or as seconds at a low price.
6. Defective products may cause delays and stoppages in production processes, which may thereby result in the loss of production and increase in the cost of production per unit.
7. Sometimes, a manufacturer or a supplier has to incur the cost for rework on defective products.
8. Sometimes, it also becomes necessary to spend extra money for servicing and repairing the products.
9. A rejected or defective product represents a loss to a manufacturer not only equivalent to the cost of materials used in that product but it includes over and above, the cost of direct labour and overhead expenses also incurred up to the final stage, *e.g.*, a defective or rejected product worth ₹ 5 at the raw material stage, after going through a number of operations may cost ₹ 100 at the final stage. So that if it is rejected at the final stage due to poor quality, the cost is not ₹ 5 but ₹ 100.
10. High proportion of defective products or rejection makes it necessary for the firm to spend an extra amount for more vigorous inspection and testing.
11. Nobody wants to take the responsibility for high proportion of defectives or rejection. One department shifts the responsibility to the other. Such type of activity on the part of various departments affects the morale of the working force badly.
12. Sometimes, investigation to find out the causes for failures or high rate of defective products etc. becomes necessary. A manufacturer or a supplier has to spend money also for such investigation.

Now-a-days, a manufacturer or a supplier has to consider 'legal costs' also. There are specific laws which provide for the liability for defective products. Courts award a much higher level of damages in case of litigation. Moreover, a manufacturer or a supplier has to spend a good amount for defending the firm against suits filed by various customers. Formerly legal actions were very rare but today the position has changed with the introduction of Consumer Protection Act (CPA), 1986.

A manufacturer may be forced by the law to withdraw certain products or certain batches of products from the market due to substandard quality or other defects, *e.g.*, when on the basis of research it is proved that certain drug is injurious to health or it has side effects, the government warns the users and forces the manufacturer to withdraw that product from the market and to discontinue the production of such items. Sometimes misuse or improper use of a product may cause personal injury to a customer. This may be due to the absence of proper instructions on the label or in the leaflet, which is generally put with a bottle inside the packing. Informative labelling and leaflets with operating instructions have assumed much more importance.

B. How does a manufacturer decide the quality?: The assessment or the study of customer's needs is generally made by the marketing department in terms of quality, quantity and price. This information is provided to the design engineering department of a firm. On the basis of such information a committee consisting of representatives of various concerned departments, headed by a design engineer prepares detailed specifications of the product planned for production. Specifications are a detailed description or listing of the characteristics of materials parts and components used in making a product. They describe the quality of a product desired, in a brief or precise manner. The cost of production and the ability of the product to function are also considered while developing proper specifications. Thus, the specifications are the detailed description of product's design in quantitative terms. Now the design process is a continuous process because with the change in customers' taste, it becomes necessary to change the specification for customers' satisfaction. The products with standard specifications, manufactured by different manufacturers will be the same. When products or goods are ordered on the basis of standard specifications, the buyer as well as the seller know what is required.

Generally, three types of specifications are used: (*i*) Technical specifications, (*ii*) Performance specifications and (*iii*) Brand name. Technical specifications state the physical and chemical properties desired in the product. When the desired properties are in measurable terms, they are called dimensional specifications. This type of specifications can be checked easily. Sometimes materials to be used and method of manufacture are also prescribed. Performance specifications describe, in words, the performance or use of the products or materials to be purchased or the services that a product will give. Here the customers give importance to the performance of the products and not to the detailed analysis of the products, stating details of physical and chemical properties of the products. The conformance to the performance specifications can be determined by use of the product. Performance specifications, thus indicate the needs of the customers for satisfactory performance. Performance specifications are extensively used in purchasing highly technical military and space products and also complicated machines and machine tools with sophisticated technology. When it becomes very costly to develop performance or technical specifications or if such a practice does not prove satisfactory, purchases are made on the basis of brand names.

It should be noted that on the basis of strict specifications, materials, parts, tools etc., may not be available continuously. Moreover, production or procurement of parts or products or components etc. with exact size or dimension, *i.e.,* with exact specifications may prove very costly. It may also result in a higher rejection rate. Most of the vendors may not have adequate facilities to manufacture materials, parts etc., with strict specifications. In such circumstances, if a slight difference in specifications does not affect the quality of the final product or the performance of the product materials or parts or products should not be rejected. Considerable judgement should be applied while taking decision of acceptance or otherwise.

A manufacturer must instil a sense of pride in every employee in the work that he does. The Taj and the Meenakshi temple must have been treated by workmen who took extreme pride in their work. When they must have worked, all must have lost to them. Only their art remained.

Reasons for the Failure of Quality Efforts

Quality efforts do benefit companies financially, though at times they are not effective enough to provide substantial benefit. It all depends upon the approach and the implementation process. It is a question of changing organizational philosophy and values. Management should not be obsessed with short term gains, thus undermining quality efforts. Quality efforts should have the back up of management and these cannot be left to the lower level employees. Some managers are not ready to bear the cost of quality. Quality is team work and not an individual's work. Sometimes, the systems and procedures are antiquated. Quality efforts must be supported by organizational culture (OC). Quality efforts require training the employees and leading them by example.

Total Quality Management (TQM)

Total Quality Management (TQM) is an organisational philosophy which believes in the commitment to and involvement in quality assurance and control by the *whole* organisation. It also believes in *life cycle quality management.*

The life cycle approach aims to manage all stages which influence the quality and sustains this interest even when the product is in use. It is a strategic commitment for the organisation to survive in the competitive environment.

In TQM, quality does not remain just a concern of the quality department but it is a responsibility of all and one. It is an organisation-wide commitment.

QUALITY CONTROL AND IMPROVEMENT

Industry set up formal quality control departments in recognition of its tremendous importance in early 1900s. Walter A. Shewhart (1924), an American engineer and statistician developed a statistical quality control chart as a part of Statistical Process Control (SPC). Dodge and Romig improved the statistical theory further in 1930s. The World War II required military supplies to be subjected to quality control which led to the adoption of statistical quality control in industry in early 1940s. However, these methods were given up later, again to be rediscovered in 1980s. Though manufacturing industry adopted these methods, service industry has lagged behind. In 1946, American Society for Quality was formed. Quality movement expanded to include customer needs, total quality control or management (TQM) and continuous improvement. Quality control is exercised in an organisation at three levels — input control, process control and output control. These stages are complementary. If there is inadequate control at one level, there should be greater effort at the next level. The following diagram illustrates the procedures for quality control at different levels.

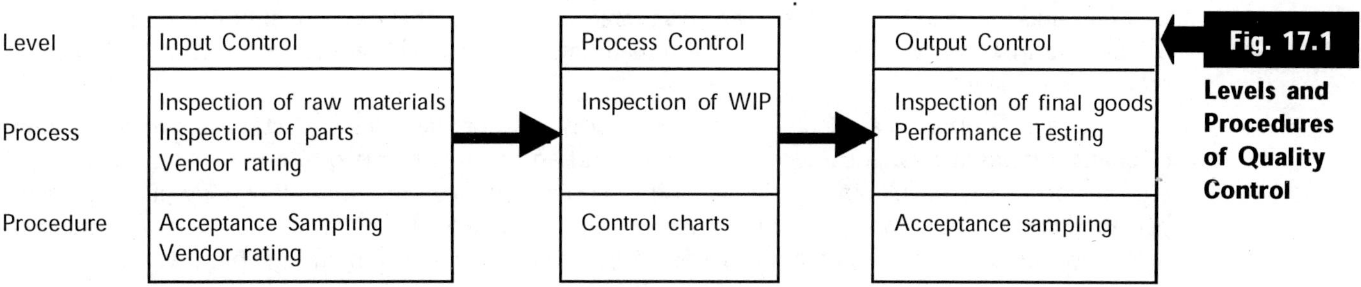

Level	Input Control	Process Control	Output Control
Process	Inspection of raw materials Inspection of parts Vendor rating	Inspection of WIP	Inspection of final goods Performance Testing
Procedure	Acceptance Sampling Vendor rating	Control charts	Acceptance sampling

Fig. 17.1

Levels and Procedures of Quality Control

We shall examine in this chapter process definition, statistical quality control (SQC) and continuous improvement.

Design of the Quality Control Systems

A process of production is the starting point for any quality control system. A production process can consist of many sub-processes each with its intermediate output

A process may consist of one single machine or a group of machines. In non-manufacturing system, it can be just some clerical activity or administrative activity. Each process caters to the needs of its internal customers by offering products and services. The customer is the starting point of the next process or processes which receives output from the preceding process. To illustrate, design department submits designs to the machine shop. Thus, machine shop is the customer for the design department. In its turn, the machine shop produces an output of parts which becomes input for the assembly department.

A larger process is thus sub-divided to exercise quality at each point of sub-division. Amongst these points, some are **critical points** where inspection or measurement is necessary. Management has to decide who will inspect, either the workers or separate inspectors. Usually, it is inspection by operators. These decisions together contribute to the development of a system of quality control and continuous improvement of a stable system.

Vendor selection and certification are crucial to avoid inspection, since certified vendors do have quality control system in place. Quality control is exercised on raw materials at the vendor's premises also to reduce the cost of inspection later. Inspection at the stage of arrival and storage is done. Defects in finished products are detected and corrected before the final output is turned out. Inspection has been dealt with length in at stores management chapter elsewhere in this book.

The second step is to decide the type of measurements at each inspection point — based on variables or attributes. **Variable measurement** uses a continuous scale for dimensions such as length, height, weight, viscosity, time taken etc. **Attribute measurement** uses a discrete scale by counting the number of defective items or the number of defects per unit. In case of TV, colour can be used as an attribute. For cloth, the flaw in the material can be taken as attribute. These, measurements can be taken by using certain devices also.

We have to decide the proportion of inspection and statistical process control. Statistical process control reduces the amount of inspection needed.

However, when human life is at stake, 100 per cent testing and process control — both can be used. This is the third step in defining the quality control system.

The last step in the design of the quality control system is the delegation of responsibility of quality control — whether the workers would do it, or the inspectors or the customers.

Statistical Process Control for Quality

Statistical Process Control (SPC) is a method that incorporates a set of statistical tools and techniques to monitor and measure the stability and predictability of a process. It takes risky guesswork out of quality control. It is a scientific data driven methodology. Process quality control is exercised when the product is being produced. Samples are drawn from time to time from the output of the production process. When it is observed that process quality characteristics have changed, the process is brought to a halt and the search is made for an **assignable cause**. The change in quality can be assigned to the change in operator, the machine or the material. The necessary adjustments are made, and the process is resumed.

There are always no assignable causes for process variation. Even the perfect process shows **random** or **chance variations**. Chance is really inherent and an inevitable part of the manufacturing process *e.g.*, material may have minor differences in composition, working conditions may affect workers performance, machine may perform erratically. In process control, we try to find the natural random or chance variation of the process and ensure that the production remains within this range.

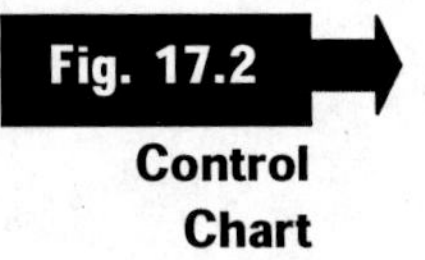

Control Chart

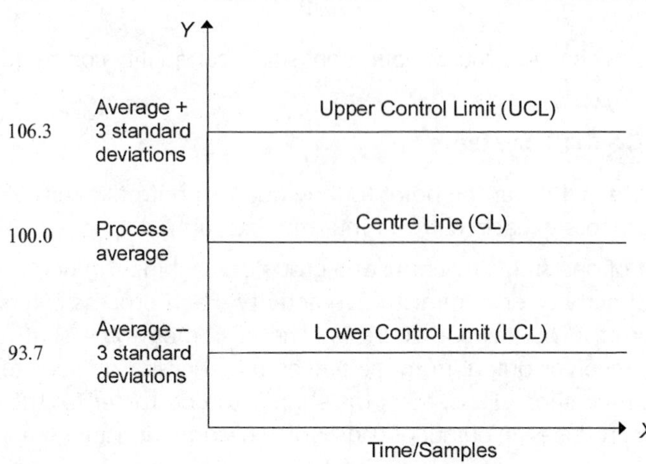

Production processes are, therefore, out of control either due to chance factors or some special causes called assignable causes. The quality control managers try to correct the variations due to assignable causes and bring the process under statistical control. The rest of the variation is due to random causes.

The same principles could be applied to administrative processes such as accounting, HR, finance, sales and marketing.

A process is brought to a **state of control** through control charts. In the control chart the **centre line** shows the average quality characteristic being measured or process average. The *Y*-axis represents the quality characteristic being controlled. The *x*-axis represents time or a particular sample drawn from the process. The upper control limit (UCL) represents the maximum acceptable random variation. The lower control limit (LCL) represents the minimum acceptable random variation. Both UCL and LCL are set when a state of control exists. Usually, UCL and LCL are set at ± three standard deviations from the mean. Assuming a normal probability distribution, these control limits will include 99.74 per cent of random variations observed.

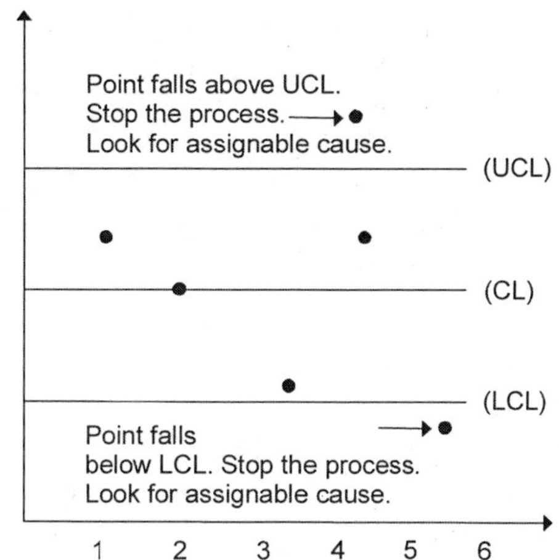

Fig. 17.3 **How Control Chart is Used**

From a steady-state process, periodic samples are drawn. If the measurement points are within the control limits, the process is continued. If some points cross the control limits, the process is stopped, and we look for the assignable causes. This is the procedure to keep the process in control, and there is only random variation in process output.

Quality is measured for the control charts by variables or attributes. We shall examine them one by one.

Control Charts

A control chart turns time-ordered data for a particular characteristic, such as product volume or the time it takes to prepare a pizza after the order is placed into a picture that is easy to understand. Control charts serve to warn us when unusual shifts in a process occur. Strictly speaking, control charts help us detect non-random sources of variation in the data. In other words, they separate variation due to common causes from variation due to special causes.

Frequency Distribution

It is an accepted fact that in any manufacturing method, no two parts are identical and for every part, there are always variations from the established standards. These variations can be attributed to slight differences in successive units of raw materials, wear and tear of tools, power fluctuations, temperature changes and so many other causes. All these variations can be broadly put into two categories.

(Contd.)

(Contd.)

Chance or Usual Variables

These variables or causes occur at random and so they are difficult to avoid. These causes lead to insignificant variations, and their elimination cannot be justified economically. Some of these causes are:

- Raw material variations
- Imperfect machine design
- Imperfect manufacturing process
- Inaccuracies of inspection instruments
- Human error on the part of operator due to sensory judgement

Assignable or Unusual Variables

These occur less frequently and can be traced to some external cause.

These causes include:

- Machine malfunctioning or process malfunctioning
- Incorrect sequence of operations
- Machines/instruments require repair due to excessive wear and tear
- Varying temperatures
- Vibrating affecting machine functioning.
- Wear on tools and faulty materials.

Assignable causes lead to large variations in the quality of the product. These should be identified and eliminated if possible.

Chance variations only keep the product within the limits set. These occur randomly and can be described by the normal probability distribution. The process is said to be in control. If assignable causes start operating, the part variations exceed the specified *limits*. The process is then said to be out of control.

Quality controller define *limits* within which variations are acceptable and beyond which either they are unacceptable or require some examination such limits are called *control limits*. For instance, for a normal probability distribution, 99.73 per cent of all chance variations would be expected to occur within limits placed three standard deviations larger or smaller than the mean value of the variable. If any variation crosses this limit, it could have resulted from the assignable causes and require investigation.

Part variations are recorded by two methods of inspection. *Inspection by variables* check the part against a graduated tool/instrument to assess how far it varies from the ideal value. *Inspection by attributes* is go-no-go type of inspection to assess whether it lies within limits of variability established for it.

The recorded data enables the establishment of frequency distribution. The frequency distribution is an arrangement of numerical data according to size and frequency. The frequency distribution can be described by two characteristics — central tendency and dispersion..

Central tendency is the most representative value, and spread or distribution shows how far it varies from the central tendency. The most valuable measures of central tendency are the average and the median.

Average

It is obtained by dividing the sum of the value in a series of readings by the number of readings *i.e.,*

(Contd.)

(Contd.)

$$\bar{X} = \frac{x_1 + x_2 + x_3 \ldots X_n}{n}$$

where x_1, x_2, ... x_n are the values of each reading and n is the number of readings. In case there are many readings, the readings can be grouped in suitable cells and then these cells are summed up. This simplifies the calculation of average.

$$\bar{X} = \frac{\sum fX}{n}$$

When values of the average of each series in a number of series are calculated, we can compute the average of these different averages calling it the grand average (X)

$$\bar{X} = \frac{\sum X}{k}$$

where k = number of series or subgroups.

Median

The median is that value which divides a series of readings (arranged in order of their magnitude of their values) so that an equal number of values lie on either side of the centre of the median value. For instance in a set of readings 22, 24, 26, 30, 32, the value of the median is 26. In another set of readings, 16, 18, 18, 20, 22, 24, 24, 26, 26, 26, 30, the value of the median is 22.5.

Standard Deviation

The standard deviation is the root of the mean square deviation of the readings in a series from their average. It is denoted by σ.

$$\sigma = \frac{\sqrt{\left(X_1 - \bar{X}\right)^2 + (X_2 - \bar{X})^2 + \ldots (X_n - \bar{X})^2}}{n}$$

or

$$\sigma = \sqrt{\frac{\Sigma\left(\bar{X} - X^2\right)}{n}}$$

If there are many readings, they are conveniently grouped together by putting the readings of the same value in individual cells. Then

$$\sigma = \sqrt{\frac{\Sigma fX^2}{n} - \bar{X}^2}$$

Range

It is the difference between the lowest and highest readings in a series. Thus

$R = Xmax - X_{min}$

Normal Distribution

Several types of frequency distributions occur, *e.g.*, Binomial and Poisson. To engineers and management students, normal or Gaussian distribution is of importance. It is a bell-shaped symmetric distribution. It is symmetrical about its arithmetic

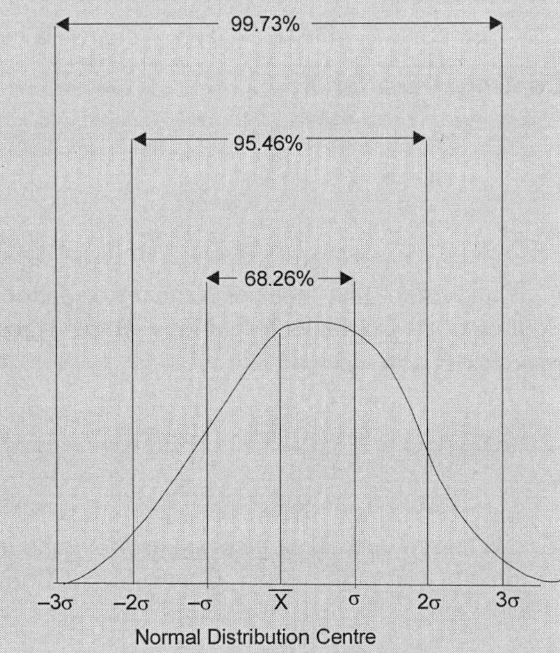

Fig. 17.4 **Normal Distribution Curve**

mean. In other words, values which are at equal distances from the arithmetic mean have equal frequencies.

Mathematical analysis shows a definite pattern of the percentage of items located at various distances from the arithmetic mean measured in terms of standard deviation. Thus, 99.73% of the items of normal distribution lie within $\pm 3s$ on either side of arithmetic mean. This is the reason why the control limits of a quality control chart are usually located at $\pm 3\sigma$. It means that only 0.27% of parts would not conform to specifications.

There are two categories of control charts: Attribute and Variables. Variable control charts monitor process parameters or product features. Attribute control charts are used to monitor an organisation's progress at removing defects that are inherently present in a process.

Variable Control

Variable control charts include:

- X Bar and R charts
- Individual Moving Range (IMR) charts
- Multi-vari chart

Here the control charts are used to measure variables. During inspection a continuous variable is measured. Two values are calculated from the sample — a measure of central tendency, usually the average and a measure of variability (the range of standard deviation). These two values lead to two control charts — control chart for central tendency ($\overline{X}$ chart) and control chart for variability of the process (R chart). Mostly these charts are used in combination. ($\overline{X}$ – R Chart).

The $\overline{X}$ – R chart is a valuable tool for troubleshooting. It provides information on three counts — basic variability of the quality characteristic, consistency of performance and average level of the quality characteristic. Variability as we know, may be due to chance or assignable causes. If the process is out of control on either $\overline{X}$ or R it is stopped and a search for assignable cause is made.

Samples are drawn at regular intervals and measurements are taken. Such samples are called sub-groups. The size of sub-groups is such that within the sub-groups, the variation is due to chance alone. The variation, if large, from one sub-group to another is due to other causes. A sub-group of the size 4 or 5 is generally preferred and more than 25 sub-groups are examined.

The control limits for $\overline{X}$ and R chart are computed as follows:

Control Limits for $\overline{X}$:

$$CL = \overline{X}$$

$$UCL = \overline{X} + A_2 \overline{R}$$

$$LCL = \overline{X} - A_2 \overline{R}$$

Where $\overline{X}$ is the grand average of past $\overline{X}$ averages and $\overline{R}$ is the average of several past R values. A_2 is a constant that includes standard deviation in terms of range. It is obtained from the Table of Control Chart Constants for various sample sizes.

Control Limits for R

$$CL = \overline{R}$$

$$UCL = D^4 \overline{R}$$

$$LCL = D^3 \overline{R}$$

Where D_3 and D_4 are constants providing three standard deviations for the range. These values are obtained from the Table: Control Chart Constants.

No of observations in sub-group n	*Factors for $\bar{X}$ Chart*	*Factors for R Chart*	
	A_2	D_3	D_4
2	1.88	0	3.27
3	1.02	0	2.57
4	0.73	0	2.28
5	0.58	0	2.11
6	0.48	0	2.00
7	0.42	0.08	1.92
8	0.37	0.14	1.86
9	0.34	0.18	1.82
10	0.31	0.22	1.78
11	0.29	0.26	1.74
12	0.27	0.28	1.72
13	0.28	0.31	1.69
14	0.24	0.33	1.67
15	0.22	0.35	1.65
16	0.21	0.36	1.64
17	0.20	0.38	1.62
18	0.19	0.39	1.61
19	0.19	0.40	1.60
20	0.18	0.41	1.59

Table 17.1

Control Chart Constants

The example below illustrates how to compute control limits and how to determine whether a sample is in control.

Example

From a machine set-up to produce glass-beads each of 20 gm, a sample of 5 beads are taken every two hours and the data obtained is as follows:

Sample No.	1	2	3	4	5	6	7	8	9	10
Mean wt. Kg.	2	2.10	2.15	2.19	2.04	2.05	2.0	2.15	2.17	2.1
Range in kg.	0.2	0.25	0.3	0.2	0.2	0.25	0.2	0.3	0.25	0.15

Draw a control chart of mean and examine whether the process is under control. You are given that for n = 5, the μ control factor for mean is 0.58.

$$\bar{X} = \frac{\Sigma X}{N} = \frac{20.85}{10} = 2.085$$

$$\bar{R} = \frac{\Sigma R}{N} = \frac{2.3}{10} = 0.23$$

For control chart of $\bar{X}$:

$\bar{X}$ = 2.085 and A_2 = 0.58 for sample size of 5 from table of control chart constants.

$$\begin{aligned} UCL &= \bar{X} + A_2\bar{R} \\ &= 2.085 + (0.58 \times 0.23) \\ &= 2.0850 + 0.1334 = 2.2184 \end{aligned}$$

$$\begin{aligned} LCL &= \bar{X} - A_2\bar{R} \\ &= 2.085 - (0.58 \times 0.23) \\ &= 2.0850 - 0.1334 = 1.9516 \end{aligned}$$

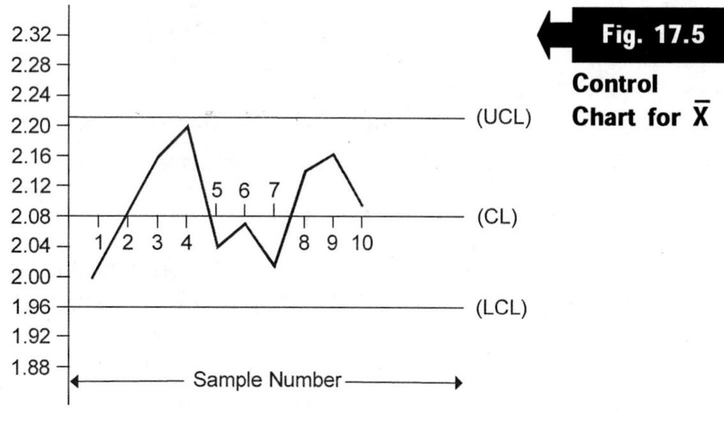

Fig. 17.5

Control Chart for $\bar{X}$

Fig. 17.6

Control Chart for $\bar{R}$

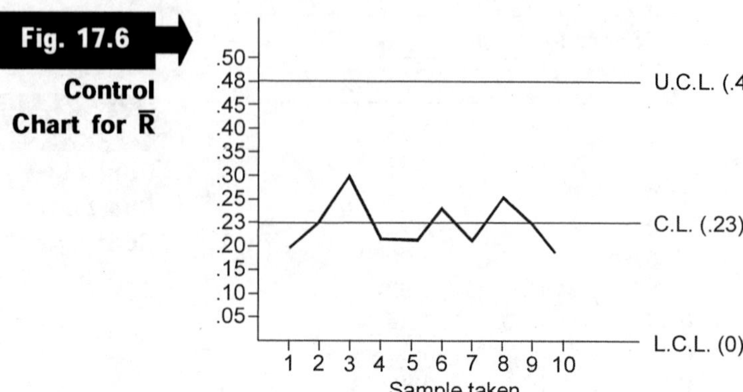

For control chart of $\bar{R}$:

$\bar{R}$ = 0.23 and $D_3 = 0$ and $D_4 = 2.11$ from table for n 5

$$UCL = D_4 \bar{R} = 2.11 \times 0.23 = 0.4853$$

$$LCL = D_3 \bar{R} = 0 \times 0.23 = 0$$

Attribute Control

Attribute control charts include:

- p-chart: Proportion of no-conforming units in a sample.
- np-chart: Number of non-conforming units in a sample.
- c-chart: Number of defects per unit where the sample size is 1.
- u-chart: average number of non-conformities per unit.

As we know, the characteristics which cannot be measured are called attributes. The inspection is visual or by go-no-go gauges where the product is classified as either good or bad. For example, defects such as crack in a part or bubbles in glassware cannot be measured. We can only note whether there is any defect or not. If any defect is seen, the product is to be rejected; otherwise it is accepted. When quality is measured by attributes, the quality characteristic is the percentage of defective units in the process. Control charts prepared to control the portion of defective units or the number of defects in a unit come under this category.

This percentage is estimated by taking a sample of n units at random from the process at specified time intervals. From each sample, the observed per cent defective (p) in the sample is calculated. These values of p are plotted on a chart one for each sample. This type of chart is called p-chart. Control charts for *proportion* or *per cent defective* are known as *p-charts.*

The fraction defective (p) is calculated for each sample by using the formula:

$$p = \frac{\text{Number of defectives}}{\text{Total number inspected}}$$

Thereafter the averaged $\bar{p}$ value of all samples is calculated.

$$\bar{p} = \frac{\text{Total number of defectives in all the samples combined}}{\text{Total number of units inspected in all the samples combined}} = \frac{\Sigma P}{N}$$

$$\text{or} = \frac{\text{Sum of number of defectives}}{\text{Total number inspected}}$$

For Control Chart $\bar{p}$:

Central line = $\bar{p}$ since it represents the best available estimate of the true average per cent defective in the process. The UCL and LCL are calculated using as follows:

$$UCL = \bar{p} + 3\frac{\sqrt{\bar{p}(1-\bar{p})}}{n}$$

$$LCL = \bar{p} - 3\frac{\sqrt{\bar{p}(1-\bar{p})}}{n}$$

The standard deviation of the process is under square root. Three standard deviation are added and subtracted to and from the mean to get control limits. These limits assume the distribution of proportion of defectives is binomial.

The following illustration shows how a $\bar{p}$-chart is used.

Example

Draw a control chart for the following data and state your conclusion.

Sample No. (each of 100)	1	2	3	4	5	6	7	8	9	10
No. of defectives	12	10	6	8	9	9	7	10	11	8
Fraction defectives	0.12	0.1	0.06	0.08	0.09	0.07	0.1	0.1	0.11	0.08

(1) Find $\bar{p}$, the average fraction defective

$$\bar{p} = \frac{\text{Total Number of defective items}}{\text{Total number of items inspected}}$$

$$= \frac{90}{1000} = 0.09$$

(2) For control chart of Fraction Defectives:

(*a*) Central line = $\bar{p}$ = 0.09

(*b*) UCL $= \bar{p} + \sqrt{\frac{\bar{p}\bar{q}}{n}} = +$ where $= \bar{q} = 1 - \bar{p}$

$$= 0.09 + 3\sqrt{\frac{0.09 \times 0.91}{100}}$$

$$= 0.09 + 0.0858 = 0.1758$$

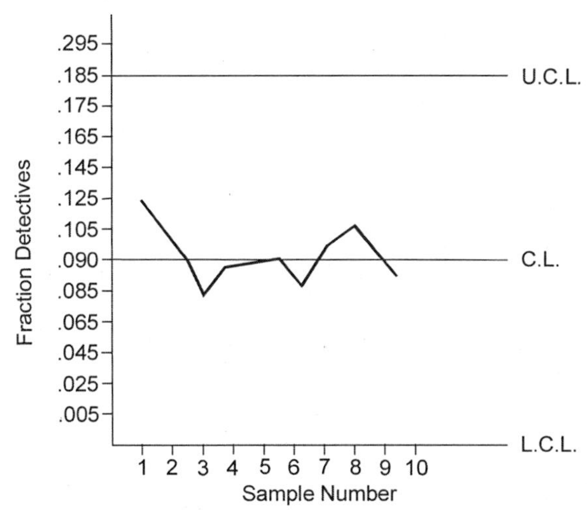

Fig. 17.7 **Control Chart for $\bar{P}$**

(*c*) LCL $= \bar{p} - 3\sqrt{\frac{\bar{p}\bar{q}}{n}}$

$$= 0.09 - 3\sqrt{\frac{0.09 \times 0.91}{100}}$$

$$= 0.09 - 3\sqrt{0.000819}$$

$$= 0.09 - (3)\ (0.0286)$$

$$= 0.09 - 0.0858$$

$$= 0.0042$$

Control Chart for Number of Defectives (np Charts)

In the previous example, we have taken the fraction or proportion of defectives. If we are interested in the number of defectives, then *np* chart is used. The number of defectives equals sample size multiplied by fraction defective (which is *np*).

First $\bar{p}$, the average number of defectives is calculated.

$$\bar{p} = \frac{\text{Total number of defective items}}{\text{Total number of items inspected}}$$

Control Chart of Number of Defectives

Centraline = $n\bar{p}$

UCL = $n\bar{p} + 3\sqrt{n\bar{p}(1-\bar{p})}$

LCL = $n\bar{p} - 3\sqrt{n\bar{p}(1-\bar{p})}$

The above chart is more convenient since the number of defectives can be plotted directly from the inspection report. The following example illustrates the use of *np* chart.

Example

Construct a suitable control chart for the following information and comment on the result to control chart.

Sample No. of 100	1	2	3	4	5	6	7	8	9	10
No. of defectives	12	10	6	8	9	9	7	11	11	9

$$\bar{p} = \frac{\text{Total number of defective items}}{\text{Total number of items inspected}}$$

$$= \frac{92}{1000} = 0.092$$

$$n\bar{p} = 100 \times 0.092 = 9.2$$

$$q = 1 - \bar{p} = 1 - 0.092 = 0.908$$

$$\text{UCL} = n\bar{p} + 3\sqrt{n\bar{p}\bar{q}}$$

$$= 9.2 + 3\sqrt{9.2 \times 0.908}$$

$$= 9.2 + 3\ (2.890)$$

$$= 9.2 + 8.67$$

$$= 17.87$$

$$\text{LCL} = n\bar{p} - 3\sqrt{n\bar{p}\bar{q}}$$

$$= 9.2 - 3\sqrt{9.2 \times 0.908}$$

$$= 9.2 - 8.67$$

$$= 0.53$$

There is no observed point which has gone beyond the two limits *i.e.,* LCL and UCL. So the process is said to be under control.

Control Chart for the Number of Defects (c-Chart)

This chart is used to control the number of defects. In certain industrial products, it is the number of defects in an article or in a unit. That makes the article useless. If the number of such defects are within the specification specified by engineers, the product is accepted or else it is rejected. The number of defects is denoted by $\bar{c}$. For instance, the number of faulty rivets can be counted, or the number of defects in the roll of cloth can be counted. Conditions such as these enable the Poisson distribution to be used.

The average number of defects ($\bar{c}$) is given by

$$\bar{c} = \frac{\text{Total number of defects in all the samples}}{\text{Number of items inspected in all the samples}}$$

$$= \frac{\Sigma C}{N}$$

For c-Chart

Central line = $\bar{c}$

UCL = $\bar{c} + 3.09\sqrt{\bar{c}}$

LCL = $\bar{c} - 3.09\sqrt{\bar{c}}$

These control limits are based on the assumption that Poisson distribution tends to be normal distribution with mean C and standard error $\sqrt{\bar{c}}$

The following example illustrates the use of c-chart.

Example

Draw a suitable control chart for the following data pertaining to the number of foreign threads (considered as defects) in 15 pieces of cloth 2m × 2m of a certain make of synthetic fibre and state your conclusions.

7,12, 3, 20, 21, 5, 4, 3, 10, 8, 0, 9, 6, 7, 20

(1) Central line $\sqrt{\bar{c}} = \frac{135}{15} = 9$

UCL = $\bar{c} + 3\sqrt{\bar{c}}$
$= 9 + 3\sqrt{9}$
$= 9 + 3 \times 3$
$= 9 + 9 = 18$

LCL = $\bar{c} - 3\sqrt{\bar{c}}$
$= 9 + 3\sqrt{9}$
$= 9 - 3 \times 3 = 0$

Using Control Charts

The sample size should be in the range of 50-300 observations for attribute control to allow for the detection of defective unit. In case the process produces 1 per cent defective units, the samples size should be at least 100. Variable control requires smaller samples in the range of 3-10 items.

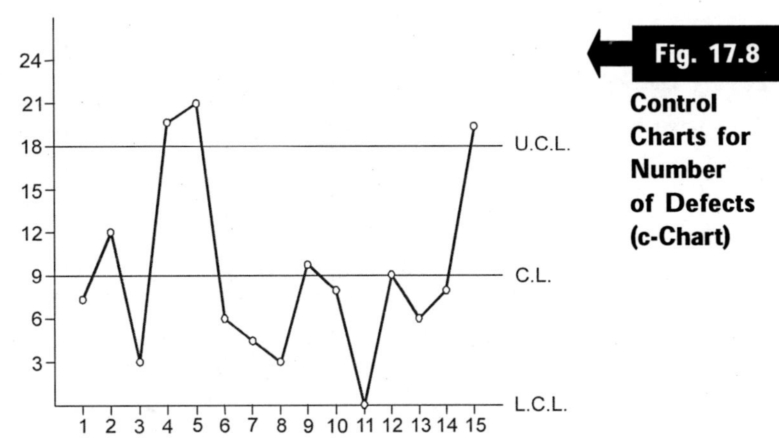

Fig. 17.8 **Control Charts for Number of Defects (c-Chart)**

Frequency of sampling is another issue. The factors considered are the production rate, the cost of producing defects and the cost of inspection. If the production volume is high, the frequency of sampling should be more because these is a possibility of a large number of defective units to be produced in between samples. If cost of producing defective units is high with respect to inspection cost, there should be frequent sampling.

One more issue merits attention. It is about control limits and specifications. The process may be in control and yet, many units do not meet the specifications. Either the specifications must be relaxed or a better process should be used. In this situation, 100 per cent inspection can be instituted till either the specifications or process is revised.

Continuous Improvement

Continuous improvement reduces the variability of the product or process. The approach is that of problem solving or revising the design of the product or process itself. Continuous improvement is effected by using three techniques:

- Pareto analysis
- Cause-and-effect diagrams
- Process capability charts.

Pareto Analysis

Pareto Analysis: It is a very simple tool for quality control. Rejections can be reduced by the use of this simple but powerful tool. The main principle working behind this method of quality control is 'to concentrate on a vital few and ignore the trivial many'. Under this method, data relating to the causes of rejections are collected, analysed and tabulated to find out the effect of the causes on rejections. In many cases of rejections, may be the same or four-five causes may have resulted in major rejection. There may be other causes, the share of which in total rejection may be very negligible. Therefore, to improve the process or quality, it is very necessary to concentrate on 4 to 5 major causes, instead of many less important causes.

Suppose the rejection in a factory is 20% and the number of causes responsible for rejection and the share of each cause in total rejection are as under:

Table 17.2

Cause No.	*Share in Rejection (%)*
–1	0.04
–2	0.12
–3	0.03
–4	0.05
–5	0.01
–6	5.60
–7	0.30
–8	0.10
–9	0.05
–10	0.01
–11	0.02
–12	6.00
–13	0.02
–14	0.13
–15	0.07
–16	0.12
–17	0.03
–18	2.30
–19	0.20
–20	1.90
–21	0.50
–22	0.80
–23	1.40
–24	0.14
–25	0.06
Total 25	20.00

By tabulating this information, as under, we can get the information regarding the share of each cause and the cumulative share of various causes in order of their share in total rejection.

Table 17.3

Cause No.	*Individual Share*	*Cumulative Share*
0.12	6.00	6.00
0.6	5.60	11.60
0.18	2.30	13.90
0.20	1.90	15.80
0.23	1.40	17.20
0.22	0.80	18.00
0.21	0.50	18.50
0.7	0.30	18.80
0.19	0.20	19.00
0.24	0.14	19.14
0.14	0.13	19.27
0.2	0.12	19.39
0.16	0.12	19.51
0.8	0.10	19.61
0.15	0.07	19.68
0.25	0.06	19.74
0.4	0.05	19.79
0.9	0.05	19.84
0.1	0.04	19.88
0.3	0.03	19.91
0.17	0.03	19.94
0.11	0.02	19.96
0.13	0.02	19.98
0.5	0.01	19.99
0.10	0.01	20.00

The above table shows that out of 20% rejections, 18% rejections are due to only 6 causes (No. 12,6,18,20,22 and 23) and 19% of rejections are due to only 9 causes. Therefore, efforts should be made to eliminate or to minimize the effect of these 6 or 9 causes only. If the control department tries to remove the effect of all the causes, it will require much more labour and money. To remove the effect of 6 to 9 causes will be much more economical than to remove the effect of 25 causes.

Cause and Effect Diagram

Kaoru Ishikawa is credited with the development of the 'Fishbone' diagram. It is a cause and effect diagram showing the various possible causes of a quality problem and their inter-relationship.

In this diagram the causes are shown along the spine of the diagram. The effect or the problem is shown on the right side of the diagram. It looks like a fishbone.

The causes are broken down into detailed causes. CE diagram brings out the potential causes of the problem vividly. These are evaluated to find the real causes.

CE diagrams are sketched by the quality or problem-solving teams. Brainstorming is used to arrive at possible causes.

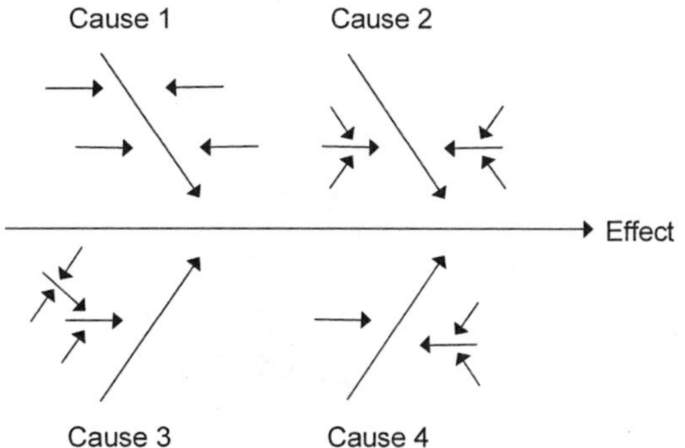

Fig. 17.9
Fish-bone Type Cause and Effect Diagram

Pareto analysis and CE diagrams make it possible to reduce defects and thus improve quality.

Process Capability

A process may be statistically under control depending upon the inputs of materials and outputs generated. In a highly reliable process, the limits are set close to the arithmetic mean. Years later, the same process may become unreliable owing to a number factors. i.e., normal wear and tear. The normal variability shown then will be greater, *e.g.,* the dimensions of the items produced. Thus, the limits will be set further away from the overall mean.

The limits set in the chart and the specifications set for the item have no direct co-relation. The process may be reliable but the design specifications may not be tight. There is a possibility that the use of control charts may result in the rejection of items which are acceptable under the original design specifications. The converse is also true. The process may turn out items to fine tolerances, yet the design specifications are narrow. Thus, the use of control chart may lead to the acceptance of items which otherwise would not be unacceptable under the original design specification.

Thus, it is necessary to understand the relationship between the control chart limits and design specifications. There emerges the question of *process capability.*

Process Capability Index

The performance potential of a manufacturing process is given by the process capability. It is measured by the proportion of output that complies with the specified tolerances. Process capability index C_p is the ratio of the specification width to the process width:

$$C_p = \frac{\text{Specification width}}{\text{Process width}}$$

If the process is centred within the specification range $C_p \geq 1$ is a good indicator of the process capability since the process width is within the specification width.

In practice, the specification width is computed by the difference between the upper and lower limits of specification (USL – LSL). The process width is computed by using 6 standard deviations of the process measurement being monitored (6σ)

$$C_p = \frac{USL - LSL}{6\sigma}$$

Just when (USL – LSL) > 6σ and the process is in control following normal distribution, we can infer the process is capable of meeting the specifications presented.

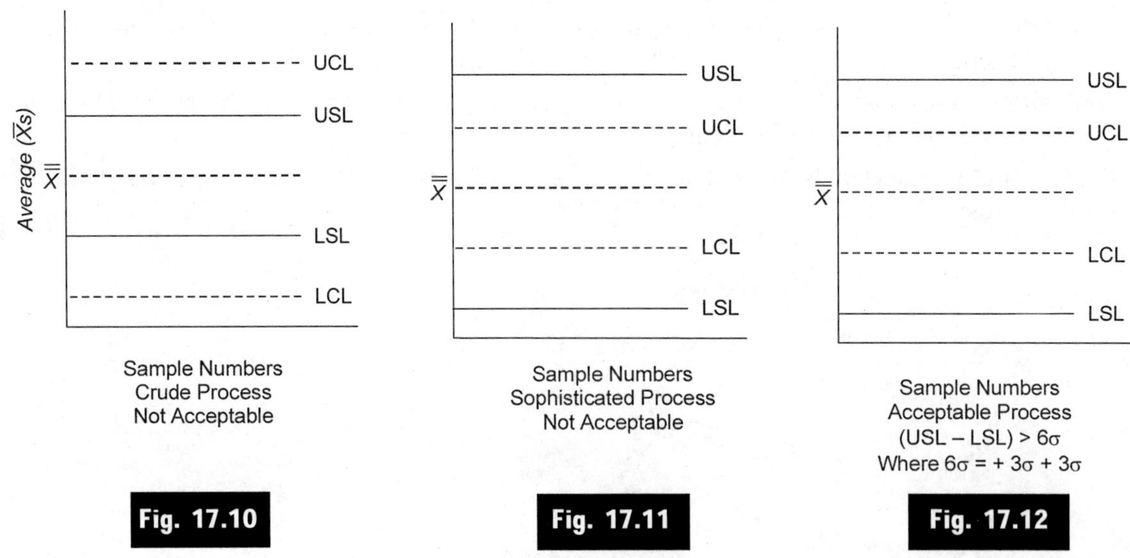

Fig. 17.10 **Fig. 17.11** **Fig. 17.12**

There can be three types of situations:

1. In situation one, the process is so crude that the specification lie within the control limit
2. In situation two, the process is so sophisticated that the control limits lie within the specification limits.
3. This is an acceptable situation where the CLs and SLs are close to each other. In fact, the CLs lies within the SL.

Six Sigma Management Technique

This technique is the latest and highest form of quality management, and surpasses ISO 9000. Six Sigma means faultless quality right across the company management. GE, US practises this. One of the reasons why we know so much about six sigma is the tool's association with Jack Welch, former CEO of GE. Some computer software companies have also adopted this technique. The Greek letter Sigma is the statistical short-hand for standard deviation and is an indicator of degree of variation. Mathematically, to attain efficiency of one sigma is to have around 30 per cent efficiency, but it increases drastically when we move from one sigma to six sigma, *i.e.*, 30% to 99.9997%. It really refers to the extent to which a process is capable of deviating from pre-set specifications without causing errors. The higher the sigma rating, the greater is this capability.

Six Sigma allows variations of up to 6 times the standard deviation without causing flaws. In theory, there would be approximately two failures per million attempts. But in practice due to drift of plus or minus, 1-5, six sigma status means 3.4 failures per million. Six Sigma philosophy is the same as that of TQM — reducing defects. The following table gives the defect rate per million and cost of poor quality in terms of sales.

Sigma	***Defect Rate PPM***	***Cost of Poor Quality (% of Sales)***	***Competitive Level***
Six σ	3.4	Less than 10%	World Class
Five σ	233	10-15%	World Class
Four σ	6210	15-20%	Industry Average
Three σ	66,807	20-30%	Industry Average
Two σ	308,537	30-40%	Non-competitive
One σ	6,90,000	More than 40%	Non-competitive

It must be puzzling for you to settle for six sigma level of 3.40 defects per million part, though three sigma level of 6,210 flaws is the corporate average. Just appreciate that even 3.4 defects per million in a product with10,000 different components amounts of 34 defective products out of every 1,000. In other words, it mean 34 out of every 1,000 customers will still be not entirely satisfied with your product. It explains why even six sigma is not the ceiling. The cost of poor quality for a six sigma company is less than 10 per cent, as against 15-20 per cent at four sigma levels.

Sigma as a mathematical term was coined by Walter Stewart in 1920. It was commercially applied by Motorola. It was introduced by Bill Smith.

It is one of the best tools that is tied to actual financial benefits. It helps companies avoid sub-optimization and see benefits in revenues and profits. There are recurrent savings. There is 6 per cent savings on total revenues in the first six-eight months itself. In 3-5 years, a manufacturing company can achieve savings of up to 20-30 per cent on its total revenues. In case of services, the swings could go up to 30-40 per cent.

Two Approaches to Implementation of Six Sigma

The DMAIC approach consist of Define, Measure, Analyse, Improve and Control. The DMADV approach consists of Design, and Verify instead of Improve and Control.

The Mathematics of Six Sigma

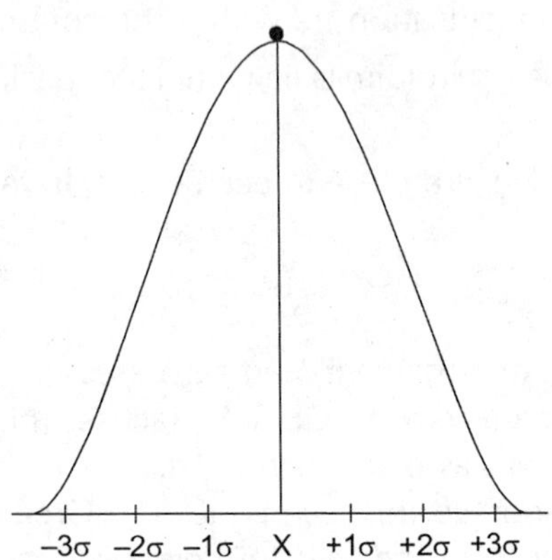

Most of the output of a process will meet your specification (call it X). But some will deviate, to vary in extents, measured by the standard deviation (σ). So, some units will have a specification of X ± 1σ, some, X ± 2σ, and some X ± 3σ.

Fig. 17.13

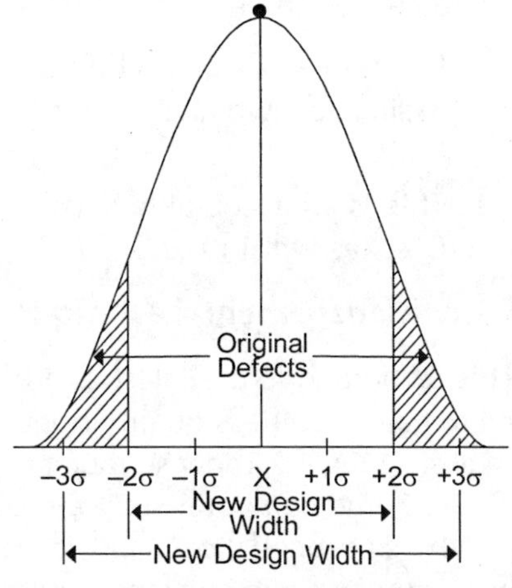

The Six Sigma methodology tackles this problem in 2 ways. First, it widens the design width, stretching the upper and lower specifications limits so that even if the product ranges between X − 3σ and X + 3σ, it will function perfectly.

Fig. 17.14

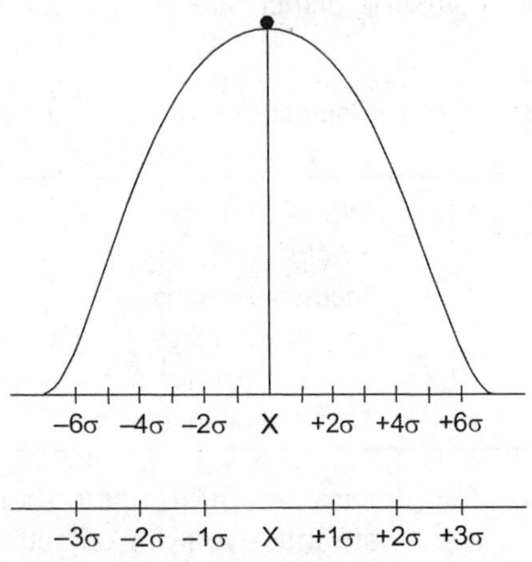

The second step: Analyzing and re-engineering the process so that the value of sigma drops. Thus, if the upper and lower specification limits originally stood at ± 3σ, they will automatically stand at ± 6σ now.

Fig. 17.15

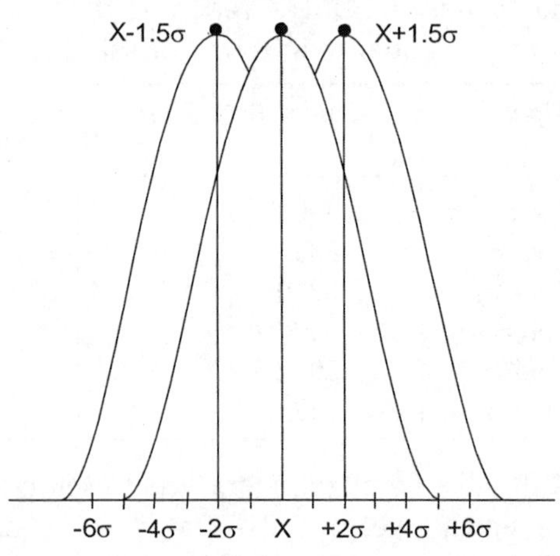

A Six Sigma process should actually generate no flaws at all. But since, over the long run, every process shifts by ±1.5σ, 3.4 parts out of every million will go even beyond the 6σ level, generating a few defects.

Fig. 17.16

Wipro's Six Sigma Programme

Wipro is dedicated to six sigma quality initiative. In simple terms, this means reducing the firm's error-level from 6,90,000 mistakes every million opportunities (one sigma) to 34 mistakes per million (six sigma). Wipro's several critical business processes are today (1999) below three Sigma. By March 2000, the company achieved four Sigma and by December 2002, Wipro reached six Sigma in most of their key processes.

QUALITY MANAGEMENT

Using one quality tool will only yield limited results. These tools work best when used in an integrated way. To be a world class organisation, a mix of tools is used.

Quality assessment is a probe of the level of quality being achieved. *Quality Control* starts with quality assessment, and includes action taken to do away with unacceptable quality. A typical QC programme is based on periodic inspection, later followed by feedback on results, and the adjustments made where found necessary. Quality Control is a system of setting the quality standards, appraising conformance to these standards, actions taken when standards are not met, and planning changes in these standards. *Quality Assurance* is quality control, but with an emphasis on quality in the design of the products, processes and jobs and in the selection of personnel and their training. *Total Quality Control (TQC)* refers to a total commitment to quality in all its aspects, to commitment of quality in all functional areas of work and makes use of behavioural techniques like QCs (quality circles), zero-defect programmes etc. The biggest misconception that people have about TQC is that it is restricted to product quality. It is not. It is about the quality of all business processes.

Total Quality Control (TQC) works on the basis of the following functions:

- Quality of design
- Quality of planning
- Quality of production
- Quality of shipment
- Quality of field service (market)

The above functions are integrated to the quality objectives. TQC concept was first put forward in 1957 by Dr. A.V. Feigenbaum who advised to take quality beyond the shop floor and wanted the process to start at the planning and design stage and continue it till the product reaches the consumer. Its philosophy is 'do it right the first time, everytime.'

Total Quality Management: TQM takes quality from the shop floor to every conceivable activity in an organization, with the customer at the centre of all thoughts, processes, decisions. ISO has defined TQM as "management approach of an organization centred on quality based on participation of all its members and aiming at long-term success through customer satisfaction and benefits to all members of the organization and Society." TQM is an integrated organizational approach in delighting customers by meeting their expectations on a continuous basis through everyone involved with the organization working on continuous improvement in all products, services and processes along with proper problem solving methodology.

Total Quality Management (TQM) is one of the techniques, along with others like supply-chain management, re-engineering, cellular manufacturing and bench-marking, which seek to improve a company's operational effectiveness (OE). TQM and other OE techniques can elevate a company's operations to a level that cannot be surpassed, unless there is alternative superior technology. This could be a short-term competitive advantage. It is necessary to appreciate that rivals can also adopt the same OE techniques, including TQM. TQM thus cannot replace strategy.

Green has put forward the concept of Global Quality — modified version of TQM. As we know. TQM is not restricted to just statistical and process improvement techniques, but covers knowledge-management, group dynamics, customer understanding, innovation and commitment. It is now proposed that organization culture (OC) is an integral part of post-TQM paradigm. TQM is now viewed as a tool for organizational and attitudinal change. Green has already put intellectual capital, innovation and understanding customers as components of a strategy. Thus, there is a tenuous link between TQM and strategy.

Hamel feels a good strategy is recognised only in hindsight. A successful strategy, according to his hypothesis, is not created but it evolves. Thus, an organization creates an organization context which facilitates the emergence of this strategy. The catalysts are participatory style, encouraging individual's talents and knowledge to utilise it for new strategies, organization — wide dialogue or open culture and a test-run of the strategies so as to derive more learning. Hamel establishes that TQM can create this type of culture.

TVS ELECTRONICS AND TOTAL QUALITY CONTROL (TQC)

Total Quality Management (TQM) aims at doing things better and avoiding wastes. TVS Electronics has eliminated on the shop-floor all non-value added activities of manufacturing. Value engineering is used as a key cost-reduction and elimination tool. The target is to reduce costs by 10 per cent every year. The assembly-line has been replaced by cellular manufacturing. They have adopted a lean production system. In cellular manufacturing system, each team has been assigned complete responsibility of assembling an entire product. This curtails the production-related costs. A suggestion scheme has been introduced at the shop-floor level. Cost-saving suggestions attract cash incentives. Wasteful activities are identified by video-filming. Delivery schedule is maintained 100 per cent. Scrap is reduced.

Quality assurance is a modern day concept. **SQC – Statistical Quality Control** came on the scene in 1924 in the States. **Quality Circles (QCs)** are very popular these days. QC is a group of employees whose task is to identify problems, formulate solutions, and present their results to management with suggestions for implementation. Just recently, we had an international convention of Quality Circle Forum — an organization devoted to this cause in India.

Quality Organization

Quality is not only the concern of the manufacturing department. Quality is everyone's business. Each department has to contribute to quality. Quality is built into the product at the product concept stage and is ubiquitous all throughout its life. Poor quality can occur because of organizational problems anywhere, or even outside the organization. Top management's commitment to quality is a proper beginning. Quality improvement is to be viewed as a positive effort. Continuous training is thus a key to Quality Control. Quality function can be organized in several alternative methods, keeping the above principle in mind.

Quantification of Quality

As opposed to quantity, we have the abstract concept of quality which by definition is not amenable to quantification. But in the absence of quantification, how is it possible to measure either (*i*) quality improvement or (*ii*) quality deterioration? Anything that cannot be measured cannot be controlled. It is, therefore, necessary to quantify quality by relating it to costs. There is a vast difference between the actual operating cost and operating cost prevailing in a situation where things are done right the first time — avoidance of rejections, re-working, re-processing, delays etc. It is this gap that provides the potential to increase profits.

Quality Manual

This is a document which gives details of the quality systems followed in an organization. It outlines the company's policy on quality.

Setting Targets for Quality Improvement

Quality is measured in terms of cost. Quality improvement represents the savings. Quality improvement targets specify the maximum permissible level of non-conformance cost (NCC) at a given point of time.

We have to set realistic target in terms of C_2 and T_2. This is possible if we have prior knowledge of NCC level (C_1) prevailing before quality improvement efforts were taken (T_1).

There are two dimensions of quality costs — positive and negative.

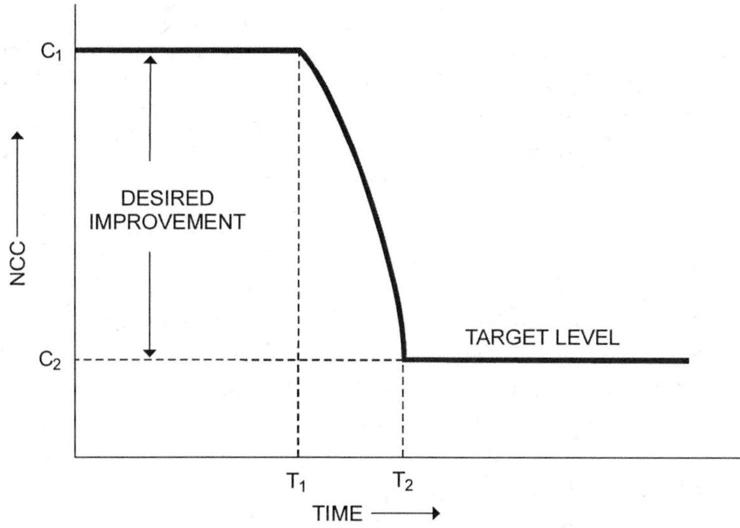

Positive Costs

These costs are attributed to having to spellout optimum quality right from procurement of raw materials to the delivery of the finished product to the final customer.

These costs have two aspects, costs for formulation of strategic policies for total quality. There is also an attempt to prevent problems, and solve them when they arise. There are training costs to have a quality culture. Another aspect of positive cost is the inspection cost. Both these aspects are investments which no organization can avoid. The positive costs should not exceed 6% of total turnover, which is a trivial cost to bear considering the benefits which accrue therefrom.

Negative Costs

Negative costs fall in three categories:

(*i*) Costs attributable to defects creeping in the manufacturing process.

(*ii*) Costs due to rectification of defects like after-sales service costs.

(*iii*) Costs on account of rejection of a consignment by a customer for sub-standard quality goods, especially by an importer.

Many a time, non-production departments contribute a great deal to the negative costs, *e.g.*, purchase department, maintenance department, design and engineering department.

QUALITY ASSURANCE

Meaning and Importance

Quality assurance refers to the assurance to customers that the products, parts, components, tools etc. contain specified characteristics and are fit for the intended use. Quality assurance is concerned with determining the procedures to be used and frequency of checks or tests to be made within the system so as to ensure that the system is meeting the specification incorporated in the product/service design. In today's competitive industrial world, no business unit can exist for a long time without adhering to the quality. Now, the assurance of quality is not a responsibility of a single person or a department only. Only the inspection department or its personnel cannot be held responsible for assurance of quality. It is the responsibility of everybody connected with the production, directly or indirectly, *e.g.*, each and every department connected with production — from design and raw materials stage to despatch and transportation stage, *i.e.*, from the designing of the product to the sales and delivery of the finished product — is responsible. Thus design engineering department, purchasing department, inspection department, materials handling department, maintenance and repair department, stores department, production department, sales department etc. are all equally responsible for assuring the quality. They all play an important part for providing a customer a product of acceptable quality. Therefore, everyone has to be alert and everyone should perform one's duty efficiently, because everyone's activity is directly or indirectly related to the quality of a product which their company is manufacturing. Employees of the unit must be made quality conscious. They should be motivated, if the unit wants to get best results from them. This can be done by explaining to them, why the quality is important for themselves as well as for their unit.

Factors Affecting Employees' Morale

Increase in morale results in improvement of quality. If workers are dissatisfied or working conditions are poor, employees' morale will be at a low level and cases of rejections will increase in any manufacturing unit right from the consumption stage to the finished product stage. Efficiency of any unit as a whole can be increased only by minimising the chances of rejection, which in turn results in better quality. Employees may not be able to work or may not work or generally do not work efficiently because of many factors which can be classified as under:

Psychological Factors

(i) Monotony and boredom: When a person is required to perform the same type of work a number of times repeatedly over a long time, he gets bored or tired. He works only to spend time without having interest in his work. He gets dissatisfied and a dissatisfied worker cannot discharge his duty efficiently and effectively. This ultimately badly affects the quality of a product, resulting in higher rejections.

(ii) Frustration: Employees get frustrated due to various reasons. They may not find any chance of promotion or scope for self-development. The boss may not be cooperative or may be ill-tempered. Management may not have trust in the employees, under such circumstances, employees may not work with interest.

(iii) Absence of incentives: Absence of incentives in the form of wages linked with productivity, incentive wage rates, prizes for quality work etc. makes the employees dissatisfied and it becomes difficult for anyone to get the work done by such dissatisfied employees. Employees become careless, thereby affecting badly the quality of a product resulting in higher rate of rejections.

Physiological Factors

After working for a certain period continuously, a worker experiences stress, which leads to fatigue. If fatigue is severe, it will affect the quality as well as the quantity of production.

Technical Factors

(i) Unclear specifications and faulty design: The specifications must be well defined and the design of a product must be faultless because ambiguous specifications and faulty design make the products unfit for use, quality of the products suffers heavily and it results in higher proportion of rejection.

(ii) Improper or unsuitable or substandard tools and equipment: Tools and equipments, which are not proper or suitable or of standard quality, affect the quality badly even if the workers are efficient and sincere.

(iii) Complex or unsystematic operations or processes and improper maintenance and repairs of tools and machines: Operations and processes must be planned and designed systematically and scientifically. Timely repairs and proper maintenance may result in higher productivity and production of defective products in small number.

Other Factors

Working conditions in a factory should be satisfactory. Absence of (*i*) Proper ventilation, (*ii*) Sufficient light, (*iii*) Normal temperature, (*iv*) Subsidised canteen facilities, (*v*) Urinals and latrines in sufficient numbers, (*vi*) Provision of safety gloves, safety glasses, helmets etc. for workers, if found necessary etc. result in decreased efficiency. Possibilities of accidents and absenteeism show upward tendency with the passing of time. Unsatisfactory working conditions bring into existence conflicts between employees and management thereby resulting in decreased productivity and increased number of rejections.

How to Motivate the Employees?

In the preceding section on "Factors affecting employees' morale", we have discussed various factors affecting the efficiency of employees. To motivate the employees for increasing their efficiency, it is necessary for the employer to consider these factors and to take necessary steps as corrective measures. The following are some of the important corrective measures, which may prove to be useful for motivating the employees:

(*i*) An employee should be moved from one work to another at a regular interval. This type of job rotation reduces monotony and boredom. If a worker is given liberty to work in his own way without affecting quality and productivity, he will work with interest. Job design should be changed, if it is found necessary to simplify the operations or processes. Unnecessary interference by a supervisor, while a worker is performing his job, should be avoided as far as possible.

(*ii*) Suggestions from employees for improvement of quality should be encouraged and prizes should be awarded for good suggestions. Certain progressive companies run suggestion schemes very successfully.

(*iii*) Quality campaigns should be initiated and continuously promoted. Moreover, progress against predetermined standards should be examined regularly to find out variances if any. Quality work should be appreciated and incentives in form of prizes, early promotions, higher wage rates etc. should be given for quality work.

(*iv*) Reasonable wage rates linked with productivity and quality should be implemented to encourage the workers to work sincerely and carefully.

(*v*) Provision for adequate training to workers should be made for improvement of quality and productivity. Workers should be made known about the use of parts, components, products etc. which they are making or are going to make. If they know the use and importance of the result of their hard labour, they will work with great care.

(*vi*) Promotion policy should be framed in such a way, which can provide an incentive to honest, sincere and hardworking employees in terms of comparatively early promotions at regular intervals. The officers or heads should be co-operative and capable of motivating their subordinates. Each head should work in such a way so that the workers under each head do feel that the head is their own man and also that he is one important member of the team. The boss should take care of his subordinates. Such a practice makes the relations between heads and their subordinates cordial and workers work sincerely with full confidence in their superiors.

(*vii*) After working for a certain number of hours continuously, workers get exhausted physically as well as mentally. Therefore, sufficient rest period during working hours should be provided. Now the span of working period after which rest period is to be allowed depends on the type of work. If the work requires comparatively more physical and mental exercise, the rest period to be allowed should be kept comparatively long and it should be allowed after a comparatively short span of working period. Heavy work should be mechanised as far as possible to reduce the strain on body and brain. In large factories, where the materials to be handled are very heavy and in large quantity, latest mechanised materials handling devices, *i.e.*, most modern materials handling equipment (conveyor belts, etc.) are used.

(*viii*) Drawings, designs, operations, methods of production, etc. should be simple, well-defined and technically practicable as far as possible. Process sheets should be simple so that operators do not find it difficult to understand the working of a process. Specifications should not be stringent, because no two products coming out of the same process will be identical. There may be a slight difference between any two units that have come out of the process. If stringent specifications are to be followed, number of defective/rejections will be too much. Now workers also get frustrated, if they know that the defective or rejections are excessive, even if they have put in their best efforts. Therefore, to minimise rejections, tolerances (with upper and lower limit) should be prescribed, instead of following the specifications rigidly. Variations in dimension, weight etc. should be permitted up to a certain limit (upper or lower), which do not affect the quality.

(*ix*) Employees should be provided with suitable tools and equipment of standard quality. If this is done, the employees will work with pleasure and quality products will come forth. Proper maintenance and timely repair of the tools and equipment are also important to ensure continuity in production.

(*x*) Better working conditions encourage the workers to put their best efforts for quality work. Better working conditions generate healthy relations between workers and employers thereby resulting in industrial peace which is a must for increased productivity and better quality work.

What should be done for Quality Assurance?

(a) General: For quality assurance, first of all, *quality specifications* for the product should be established, so that it can meet the requirements of a customer. Suitable *quality standards* for raw materials, parts, components, tools and equipment, production process etc. are also determined in advance so as to manufacture quality products as per the predetermined standard. This all should be done at the initial (design) stage.

Secondly, proper *inspection and testing* procedures and methods should be evolved to check the quality specifications of raw materials, parts, components, tools and equipment, production processes and methods and also final product. With the help of inspection and testing, a manufacturer can determine whether they all conform to the predetermined quality standards or design specifications or not.

Lastly, *periodical evaluation* of methods and procedures of inspection as well as quality control is a must to measure their efficiency and effectiveness. On the basis of such evaluation, if it seems that some changes are necessary in the procedures and methods for quality improvement, changes should be made without unnecessary delay. Under such circumstances delay proves to be dangerous. To evaluate the efficiency and effectiveness of inspection as well as control methods, random checking and testing of the products at various stages of production and also random checking and testing of tools, equipment etc. should be done.

As we have seen earlier, quality assurance means *assurance of the existence of physical and chemical properties* in a product as prescribed in advance, *assurance of the fitness* of a product for intended use and *assurance of the rated performance* by a product as claimed. Assurance of all these three is called '*Quality Control.*' Even though the products, processes, machines, equipment, tools, parts, components, raw materials, inspection and testing methods and procedures etc. are all standardised, the product which comes out may not be of a standard quality, because of various reasons. Therefore, it becomes necessary to exercise control at various stages to assure quality.

(1) Inspection Method: To assure the quality of materials, parts, components, tools, equipment, finished products, process or methods of production, etc. inspection and testing is done by component personnel called inspectors. It is a type of policing action that sorts out given lot or batch into two categories — good or bad, low quality or high quality, acceptables or non-acceptables etc. It is essentially a *sorting process*. It is not a *preventive process*. The responsibility of inspection and testing rests with the inspection department. The inspection department sees whether:

(*i*) the purchase department has procured materials, parts, components, tools, equipment etc. as per the specifications or standards,

(*ii*) the production department has produced standard quality products and standard processes, methods of production and tools and equipment are used in that department, (*iii*) the repair and maintenance department has worked properly to repair and maintain the tools and equipment used in the factory, and

(*iv*) the stores department has taken proper care in storing materials until they are used and finished products until they are sold.

On the basis of information given and suggestions made by this department, after the inspection and/or testing is over, the concerned department takes corrective steps to improve the defects.

Technological development has made the work of inspection and testing more complicated. Inspectors have to apply considerable judgement for taking proper decision. Absolutely correct decision is not possible, but the decision should be perfect as far as possible. Therefore, the inspectors have to be very careful, while performing their duties. In no case, should the inspection department accept substandard goods etc. or reject the goods etc. on simple grounds. No doubt, it may be very difficult to decide whether the goods procured conform to the specifications or not, but the problem can be solved by proper justification of the facts. The efficiency of a manufacturing firm depends on the decisions of this department.

Acceptance of substandard or defective goods (*i*) spoils the quality of products, (*ii*) increases customers' dissatisfaction due to inferior quality, (*iii*) results in loss of trade or markets, (*iv*) increases cost of production in the form of higher rate of spoilage and defective, rework on defective etc., (*v*) results in production stoppage due to poor quality of material, parts, components, etc., (*vi*) increases servicing, repairing and replacement costs, etc.

On the other hand, acceptance of materials, parts, components, tools, equipment etc. on the basis of strict specifications also increases the cost of production. It may also result in stoppage of work for want of materials etc. as per the strict specifications. It is very difficult and moreover costly to procure materials etc. on the basis of strict specifications.

Now the products during the process, *i.e.*, while they are in making, are also inspected. It saves the cost of further work in defectives. 100% inspection of finished products does not serve the purpose fully, because defects or troubles in processes may result in the production of substandard or defective products or scrap, even though the materials are of standard quality and inspection procedure for finished products is satisfactory. Therefore, inspection of products during the process, assumes great importance. Nowadays for quick and reliable inspection special automatic inspection devices are built into the machines, which reduces the work of inspection to a great extent. When something goes wrong during a process, *e.g.*, a machine may not work, defective products may come out, defective goods may have been received from the preceding process etc., in most of the cases it becomes possible for the workers connected with that process to find out the fault and to determine the responsibility for that fault. The workers, themselves, may be at a fault. A worker is the best judge of his own work but it is not advisable to allow him or to expect him to serve as his own judge. It may create unnecessary conflict and may give rise to groupism. Therefore, for impartial and effective inspection to assure the quality at this stage, inspection department should be entrusted with the responsibility of inspecting the products during the process.

Finished products are also inspected and if found necessary tested before they are delivered to the stores. Testing may be necessary to measure performance or chemical properties of the products. Sometimes, testing may destroy the whole product, *e.g.*, a gun shot or a missile or a rocket. In such circumstances only samples are tested. Products should also be inspected or tested while delivering the same to customers, so as to minimise the rejections.

While inspecting the products during the process, the following points should be considered for better results:

1. When costly operations are to be performed on the materials, inspection should be carried out before such operations, so that cost of such operations on materials which are found defective can be saved.
2. In the same way, when there are chances of breaking or jamming the machines by faulty products, inspection should be carried out before the products are passed on to such machines for further operations.

3. When the possibility of covering up of defect by subsequent operation is there, inspection should be carried out before such operation, *e.g.*, a defect, crack etc., in steel tubes or wood can be covered up by painting. Therefore, they should be inspected before painting is done.
4. When operations are of such type, which may produce defective items, inspection should be done after such operations, so that no more work may be done on such defective items.
5. When as a result of assembling or mixing process different products are so mixed up that they cannot be separated, inspection should be carried out before such process, *e.g.*, when two types of chemicals are mixed up to prepare a certain product, without prior inspection or test of such chemicals and if the final product is found faulty, the error or the defect cannot be located. Either chemical 'A' or chemical 'B' may be defective.
6. When automatic or semi-automatic machines are used, first and final and occasionally, in between products should be inspected.

Centralised *vs.* Decentralised Inspection

Inspection may be carried out at the job place or in a separate inspection department. The location of inspection, *i.e.*, place of inspection depends on various factors, *e.g.*, types of materials to be inspected, process flows, types of inspection and testing machines and equipments, etc. When the testing and inspection machines are to be kept in special rooms with various facilities — air conditioning, maintenance of temperature at certain level etc. and they cannot be taken to the job place, materials, products, parts, components etc. which are to be inspected, are taken from the normal flow to the inspection department or to such a place where such machines and equipment have been kept or installed. Thus, when materials, parts, products, components etc. are sent to the inspection department for inspection, it is called as central inspection. It is so because inspection is carried out at one central place only. Central inspection saves the time of inspectors, because they have not to move out in various departments for their work, but they receive in the inspection department, what they have to inspect. They have not to wait for the jobs to inspect. Moreover, the inspectors can work freely without any pressure from the people, whose work they inspect. It makes possible the use of special inspection and testing machines and equipment.

But central inspection cannot be used to inspect very heavy items and also huge quantity such as casting of 25 tonnes, an airplane, tonnes and tonnes of materials etc. It cannot be used in case of such products also, which pass continuously and automatically from one process to another or from one operation to another operation and the maintenance of continuous flow is a must. In such circumstances, inspection is done at the job place.

Moreover, in case of central inspection, materials are inspected, only when inspectors are available and therefore many a time, persons from various sections have to wait for a long time, to get the materials etc. inspected. This lengthens the production cycle, because without inspection, the materials etc. cannot be taken back for further operations. Materials, products etc., are required to be taken to and from central inspection department several times, which increases the cost of handling and transportation. It also causes delay in production and it may happen that a large number of defective units may be turned out before the defect is discovered or final decision regarding acceptance or rejection is taken.

Inspection at the job place is used to resolve the problems mentioned in the preceding para. It is known as 'floor' or 'patrolling' or 'roving' or 'first piece' inspection. Here the inspectors move from one place to another place, or from one department to another department, or from one machine to another machine or from one process to another process etc., to inspect materials, parts, components, tools, equipment, products during the various stages of production and the finished goods. They get the machines set right before production starts and also they catch defective work before a large quantity has been produced. Products of semi-automatic machines are also checked from time to time and results are recorded. If operations are found out of control, inspectors can advise to stop the machines before heavy losses have occurred. Corrective action is immediately taken to set the machines right.

This type of inspection saves time, money and labour. Materials, parts, semi-finished and finished products etc. are not required to be handled and transported very often to and from central inspection place. Persons from various sections have not to wait in inspection department for getting materials, parts, products etc. inspected. Thus time of production cycle becomes short to some extent.

But the persons of various sections, who want to get materials, parts, products etc., inspected, have to wait till the inspectors come. The workers on the job have to wait for a green signal till the inspectors come and inspect their jobs, or work or production or machines. They can start their work or machines after inspection is over and a green signal is received. Moreover, inspectors have to move to different places for inspection work with inspection tools. If the measuring or testing equipments are delicate, it is not advisable and also not possible to carry them everywhere. In such circumstances, only central inspection is advisable.

Government agencies, responsible for quality and safety of regulated services, make use of 'roving' inspectors considerably. Such inspectors have to visit various units situated at different distant places and therefore central inspection is not practicable in such cases.

For proper and reliable inspection and testing, the equipment and tools used for the same, should also be checked periodically and maintained properly. If this is not done, the results of inspection and testing may misguide the users and may prove useless. Sometimes, production is continued, even though the proportion of defective items in the total production is very high. Continuous production becomes necessary when (*i*) the item is badly needed for own use or (*ii*) the item is badly needed for timely delivery to customers or (*iii*) the defects can be removed by rework with a small cost.

Now, the suppliers for materials, parts, equipment etc. are selected with great care after considering their past history, their reliability, volume of business, goodwill in market etc. If after inspection and testing of number of lots received from them, it is found that the lots are satisfactory, inspection can be reduced for goods received from such suppliers. It will save the cost of inspection and also the transportation and handling cost for returning the defective goods etc. It is not advisable to do away with inspection and testing of materials etc., received from such suppliers, but occassional inspection should be done. If during the occasional inspection, it is found that number of defective products are increasing with each next lot supplied, then the lot in which proportion of defects is beyond the upper limit, is rejected. Instead of occasional inspection of lots, each lot received from such suppliers is inspected.

Sampling *vs.* Total Inspection

Sampling is the kind of inspection where all the pieces are not subjected to inspection but only a certain proportion or percentage of pieces taken from each lot are inspected. The quality of the whole lot is judged depending upon this sample.

Samples are viewed with suspicion as statistics has often been abused. However, in certain situations, there is no alternative to sampling. Total inspection is not desirable in the following situations:

(*i*) When testing an article means its total destruction, *e.g.*, crackers, ammunition, measuring the breaking strain of belting, etc.

(*ii*) When a large number of low cost articles are being made, it is costlier to inspect each and every piece, *e.g.*, plugs, caps, etc.

(*iii*) When total inspection does not guarantee that there will be no defective articles.

When the cost of failure is not high (*e.g.*, loss of life), it is better to resort to sampling, rather than total inspection. Sampling is, however, successful if the production is under control to show consistent behaviour, and there is a large enough number to draw samples. Sampling has the following advantages over cent per cent inspection:

(*i*) Sampling saves time and costs.

(*ii*) Less tedious for the inspectors.

(*iii*) Does not disrupt production flow.

(*iv*) Trend becomes obvious. 100% inspection might make it difficult to see the trend.

Types of Inspection		
Process Inspection	Inspection of goods in process Floor Inspection Patrol Inspection First piece Inspection	Set adjustable limit gauges; and fixed gauges. Check work by patrolling from machine to machine. Inspect operations. Check batches on completion. The first few pieces are inspected after the production commences. Tells us if tools, etc. have been set properly.
Key Point Inspection	Preventive inspection during manufacturing process at key points of manufacture.	Key points are those points beyond which the product may not be capable of being reworked or where re-working would be costlier or critical.
Working Inspection	Pieces are checked at definite intervals of time.	
Shop Centralised Inspection	Inspection of conveniently arranged percentage.	
Operation Inspection	It is applied at the completion of an operation.	Most commonly used.
Final Inspection and Testing	Any attribute is chosen, e.g., finish of the product. Performance inspection Endurance inspection.	On random sample.
Tool Inspection	Inspects tools, jigs, fixtures and gauges.	Conducted prior to the commencement of production.

SAMPLING APPROACHES

Sampling can be resorted to when production process is in progress so as to assess the quality of the product being produced. Here we are concerned with *process* control. However, when we are to assess the quality of goods already produced, we resort to *acceptance sampling*.

Acceptance Sampling: This approach to quality control is used when a batch of product already exists and we wish to decide whether to accept it. This is likely when the products are made elsewhere and when sampling is preferred to total inspection. When materials are purchased in a large quantity or articles are produced on a large-scale, there may be few defective items in each lot of materials, parts, components etc. Purchased or the finished products manufactured by complete inspection of the whole lot, *i.e.*, by 100% inspection acceptance and use or production of defective items can be avoided. But because of the following reasons, 100% inspection (piece to piece inspection) is not done:

(*i*) It proves to be uneconomical as compared to the cost of inspection with the value and importance of the product.

(*ii*) Sometimes, inspection or testing of the product destroys the product itself or makes the product useless. It means that 100% inspection or testing of such products is equal to 100% destruction of the products before they are used. No wise man will insist that all the blood in his body should be checked. Therefore, fixation of a limit or the number of products to be inspected or tested, is necessary. Each shot fired reduces the number available and therefore, the supplier will add the cost of shots fired in the bill.

(*iii*) 100% inspection is a time-consuming procedure and requires more labour.

(*iv*) 100% inspection makes the inspectors careless. To satisfy the boss as well as themselves, they generally in most of the cases, throw out few items now and then from the materials and products received for inspection. They consider inspection as throwing out or rejecting some items now and then. Their carelessness may result in the rejection of a good lot or acceptance of a bad lot. Under such circumstances, 100% inspection does not guarantee that there will be no defective items in materials, components, parts and products inspected. Hence, such inspection becomes useless.

(*v*) Handling the products may cause deterioration. Moreover, handling the large quantity is not an easy task.

Therefore, to assure better quality on one hand and to come out of the difficulties as mentioned above, acceptance sampling method, *i.e.*, method of sampling inspection is used. When the decision regarding acceptance or rejection of an entire lot of products or materials or parts or components is taken on the basis of number of defectives in a sample, it is called acceptance sampling. Acceptance sampling is a process of evaluating a portion of production or material from the whole lot for either accepting or rejecting the material on the basis of whether it conforms or does not conform to the set quality standard. A sample is drawn from each lot for inspection. If the amount of defective is less than the prescribed minimum, the lot is accepted. If not, the lot is rejected as being below the standard. Here, decision is taken without going through 100% inspection of the entire lot. Acceptance sampling reduces the work of inspection and the quality standards. The maximum limit of the number of defectives in a sample, to consider it acceptable, is determined first, and on the basis of this limit, decision regarding acceptance or rejection is taken. If the number of defects in a sample is less than the prescribed number, the lot is accepted and if the number of defects is more than the prescribed number, the lot is rejected. Acceptance sampling is used to determine whether (*i*) to accept or reject a particular lot of materials etc. purchased or (*ii*) to pass or not to pass a particular batch of finished products for despatch to the customers or (*iii*) to pass or not to pass a particular lot of materials in process. Most often it is used in receiving inspection department where materials, parts, components etc. bought are inspected. It is used less at the plant level because control charts are used right at the operations in so many places. Large lots of products are never produced and made complete first and then inspected. A few at a time are inspected as they are being made. Sampling inspection can be carried out either as sampling by attributes or sampling by variables.

Acceptance sampling is mostly attribute inspection rather than variable inspection. And even more than in the case of operation control charts, acceptance sampling is a matter of calculated risks, because it deals with large quantities of already finished products. There is always a slight chance that bad lots will be passed or that good lots will be rejected. Always, when there are large quantities of products, there are going to be at least a few defective pieces in every lot. Thus acceptance sampling does not eliminate the risks of getting the good lots rejected and bad lots accepted or passed. Both buyer and seller understand that there will be some defective products and contracts are drawn accordingly. In fact, the number of expected defective products will be reflected in the price. If the buyer wants the products he buys to have a very low percentage of defective, he pays more than if he is less demanding.

When the products arrive at the buyer's plant, he inspects them and accepts or rejects them depending on whether the rejects in the sample he looks at are above or below the ratio allowed. Both buyer and seller take some risks. The consumer runs the risk that now and then he will accept a lot with too many defectives. The sample might not have its share of defectives. The producer (seller) runs the risk that now and then a good lot will not pass inspection (if the sample happens to contain more than its share of defectives). Acceptance sampling does not get rid of these risks, but it allows us to decide how much risk to run and to inspect accordingly. The more determinate you want to be, the bigger sample you must inspect (and pay more for inspection costs).

The first step, it is obvious, is to assess the possibility of accepting the lot. Mathematically, it is given by Poisson Distribution which is defined as

$$e^{-2} + ze^{-2} + \frac{z^2e^{-z}}{2!} + \frac{z^3e^{-Z}}{3!}, \text{ etc.}$$

Each of the items of distribution gives the probability of occurrence of 0, 1, 2, 3, etc. defectives, where z is the average number of defectives.

With acceptance sampling unlike with control charts, it is not necessary to make our own tables of sample sizes and rejection numbers for our inspectors. Statisticians have whole sets of them, all figured out and published in booklets. We can, however, figure out our own plan, if those published do not suit our needs. Statistics books explain how to do this.

There are two main sets of published tables, the Dodge-Roming tables and Military Standard 105C. Dodge-Roming System includes plans for single and double sampling. There are plans classified by LPTD: Lot Tolerance Per cent Defective and plans classified by AOQL — Average Outgoing Quality Limit. The LTPD values range from 0.5 to 10 per cent and AOQL values 0.1 to 10 per cent. The plans are calculated to give the minimum necessary amount of inspection for different levels of average fraction defective. To use the system correctly, the average fraction defective must be known. Dodge-Roming System is suitable for process inspection and final inspection. MS 105C also gives figures for several 'levels' of inspection. The most widely used sampling system is ISO 2859 which is also known as MIL-STD 105D and is classified by AQL: Acceptable Quality Level. It has seven inspection levels of which I, II, and III are general levels, and the remaining four are special levels — S_1, S_2, S_3 and S_4. We inspect normally until a vendor sends us several satisfactory lots. Then we cut out parts of it and inspect only now and then. But if a lot is rejected, we resort to more frequent inspection for a while. The unscrupulous suppliers sometimes make sampling inspection a farce. They put defective items or materials inside and low down in the load, so that it becomes difficult to get a representative sample. Now when materials or parts or components come in metal containers or big boxes or other containers, they put defective materials etc. in the centre and low down, so that when a sample is taken, it does not contain defective materials etc. Sometimes, the supplier sends the rejected articles again and again in the succeeding lots and such a practice becomes helpful to him in getting all the defective articles accepted. Few of the defective items get through with the first lot and remaining defective items are sent back to the supplier, who again sends them back in the second lot. This time also few of the defective items get through and remaining defective items are sent back to the supplier. The supplier and the buyer play the game until all the defective items are accepted.

Sometimes, inspectors also make acceptance sampling a farce. An inspector, if he finds that the number of defectives in a sample is more than the prescribed limit, must reject the lot. Now, instead of rejecting the lot, he takes another sample with the hope that it will contain less number of defectives. If second sample also shows more defectives, he takes the third. Thus he goes on taking samples until he finds that the proportion of defectives items is less than the prescribed limit. Such a practice results in a poor quality.

Risks Involved in Acceptance Sampling

There are two types of risks involved while taking decisions of acceptance or rejection on the basis of sample inspection.

- A bad lot may be accepted because the sample drawn from it was good.
- A good lot may be rejected because the sample drawn from it was bad.

Acceptance Sampling

Hundred per cent inspection is a desirable procedure, as probably that will ensure that no defectives pass unnoticed barring some error in the inspection process itself. However, this is not practical since inspection may damage the products. The accuracy too falls down due to fatigue factor. It is too expensive and even hazardous. Instead of cent per cent inspection, some form of *sampling inspection* is used as an alternative.

Acceptive sampling uses a sample or a portion of items drawn from the batches to decide about the quality of these batches. If the sample conforms to the quality norms, the whole batch passes and is accepted. If the sample fails to satisfy the quality norms then the whole batch is rejected or subjected to further inspection. Sampling makes the decisions about quality easier, quicker and economical.

There is a risk involved in either such acceptance or rejection. There is a possibility that the sample withdrawn from the batch may not represent the quality of the whole batch from which it was withdrawn. A greater proportion of defectives in the sample may lead us to attribute a lower quality level to the batch and *vice versa.*

Sampling Plans

Acceptance sampling plans may take a *single* sample from a batch or *multiple* samples from the same batch. Plans do change as per the measurements involved. The simplest plan, and most extensively used, classifies items as good or bad or as acceptable or unacceptable. This is called *acceptance sampling by attributes.* The less frequently used plan uses *variables* where the inspection focuses on the exact measurements of the dimensions. It is called *acceptance sampling by variables.* Here we shall highlight the usual *single acceptance sampling by attributes.*

Acceptance Sampling by Attributes

It very well suits those items whose critical features cannot be precisely measured, *e.g.,* the illumination of incandescent lamps or the finish of furniture. It may also be useful for those items where inspection is geared to dimensions which are either acceptable or not. *e.g.,* the dimension or size of a hole. It could either be within the upper or lower tolerance limits, and hence be acceptable or if it violates the same, it stands rejected. Here go/no go gauges are used to check the acceptance.

As we have observed previously, 100 per cent inspection is not practical. Hence, some lower quality level is agreed upon.

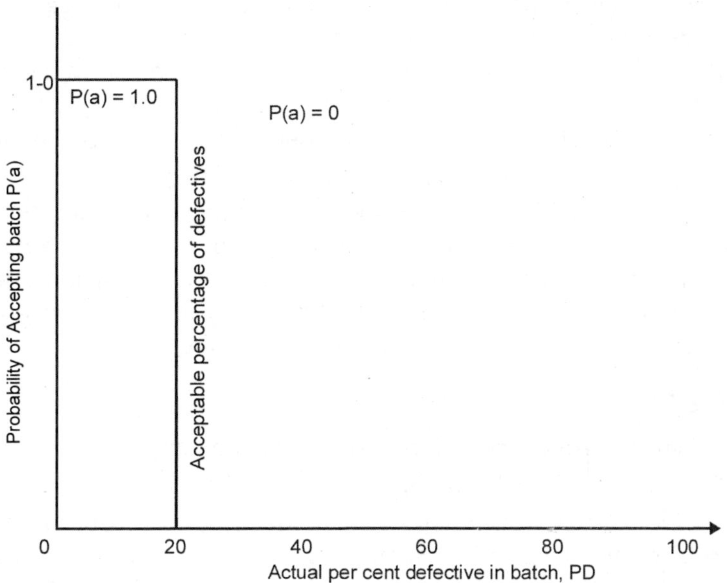

Fig. 17.18 **The probability of accepting batches, with 100 per cent inspection. Acceptable percentage of defectives 20 per cent**

In Fig. 17.18, there is 100 per cent inspection to ensure 100 per cent certainly about quality conformance of the batches, which is set at a maximum of 20 per cent defectives per batch. The assumption is that the inspection is flawless:

Let us now arrive at a curve at a curve that shows the probability of accepting batches with different percentage defectives. This curve is called *operating characteristic curve* (OC) and could be drawn for any sampling plan if we specify the sample size (*n*) and the acceptance number, *i.e.,* the maximum allowance number for defects in the sample C.

An OC curve is shown as an illustration for a sampling plan with $C < 1$ and $n = 10$ in Fig. 17.19.

Fig. 17.19

Operating Characteristic Curve (n=10, c≥1)

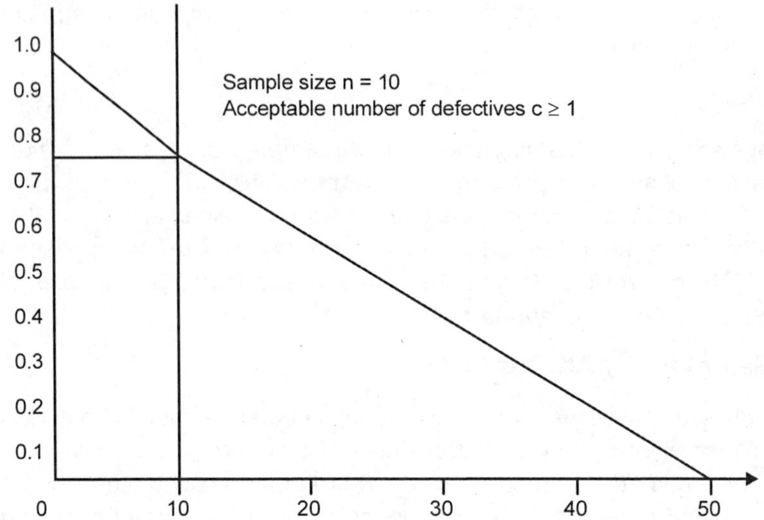

Types of Acceptance Sampling

Acceptance sampling is of two types:

(1) *Attribute acceptance sampling:* Here decision regarding acceptance or rejection is based on a number of defectives found in a sample. A sample is taken from a lot and good items and defective items are separated. Then the number of defective items is compared with the allowable limit stated in a sampling plan. If the number of defective items is less than the allowable limit, the lot is accepted, otherwise rejected. This type of sampling is used widely, because of its simplicity.

(2) *Variable acceptance sampling:* Here decision regarding acceptance or rejection is based on 'average' (mean) and 'spread' of a number of individual measurements specifying the quality characteristics of a sample. Here a sample is taken, quality characteristics of each unit are measured, and average is worked out. The average value worked out is compared with the allowable value stated in a sampling plan, to decide whether to accept or reject a lot. A sampling system for inspection by variables is ISO 3951 which is based on MILD-STD-414. It is classified by AQL.

Types of Sampling Plan

Sampling plan may be of three types. It may be (*i*) a single sampling plan or (*ii*) a double sampling plan or (*iii*) a multiple (continuous) sampling plan.

(*i*) *Single sampling plan:* In such a type of plan, decision to accept or reject a lot is taken on the basis of the results of the first sample. Here, generally a large sample is used. When the lots are extremely good or bad or contain high proportion of good or bad items, decision can be taken on the basis of even a small sample. A large sample unnecessarily increases the cost of inspection in such a case.

Each of the sample items (n) are either acceptable or defective. Such a sampling plan is known as sampling by attributes.

In single sampling plan, one sample is drawn randomly from the lot, and acceptance/rejection decisions are taken on the basis of inspection of this sample.

Consider the following data:

Lot size (N) = 18,000
Sample size (n) = 600
Acceptance Number (C) = 14

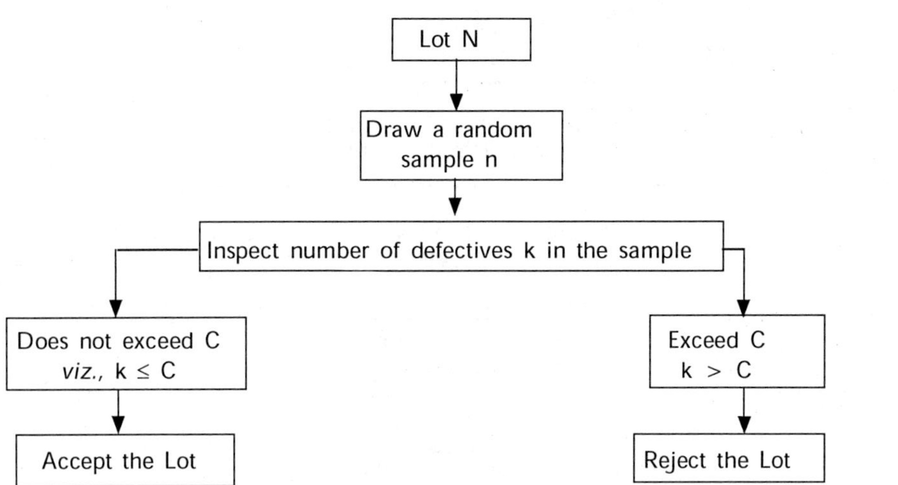

Fig. 17.20 Single Sampling Plan

Here a sample of 600 units is drawn randomly from a lot of 18000 units. These 600 units are inspected and if fourteen (14) or less than that defectives are found in the sample, the lot is accepted. If fifteen (15) or more defectives are found in the sample, the lot is rejected. The working of the single sampling plan is diagrammatically given in Fig. 17.20.

(*ii*) *Double and Multiple Sampling:* Inspection involved to get a certain quality level output could be curtailed if *double* or *multiple* sampling is used. The OC curve discussion was based upon a single random sample. In double sampling, the decision to either select or reject the batch could be delayed till a second sample is taken. Sometimes it becomes difficult to decide, on the basis of first sample, whether a lot is good or bad. This happens in case of borderline cases. Number of defectives may be very close to the upper control limit. Under such circumstances, it becomes necessary to inspect another sample. A second sample, therefore, is drawn, inspected, added to the first sample and then on the basis of the combined result, decision regarding acceptance or rejection of the lot is taken. This is called double sampling plan, because here two samples are taken to arrive at the decision. The following procedure is followed under this plan:

(1) Take first sample. Find out the number of defectives in that sample. Compare the number with two acceptance numbers C_1 and C_2.

(2) If the number of defectives is less than C_1, accept the lot and if it is more than C_2, reject the lot.

(3) If the number of defectives is between C_1 and C_2, take a second sample. Find out the number of defectives in the combined sample. Compare the number with two acceptance numbers C_1 and C_2.

(4) If the number of defectives is less than C_2, accept the lot and if it exceeds C_2, reject the lot.

This can be explained in Fig. 17.21.

Let us consider the following example:

Lot size (N) = 18,000
Sample size – First sample (n_1) = 120
Acceptance number – first sample (c_1) = 2
Rejection number – First sample (r_1) = 10
Sample size – Second sample = 300
Acceptance number for both samples (c_2) = 12
Rejection number for both samples (r_2) = 14

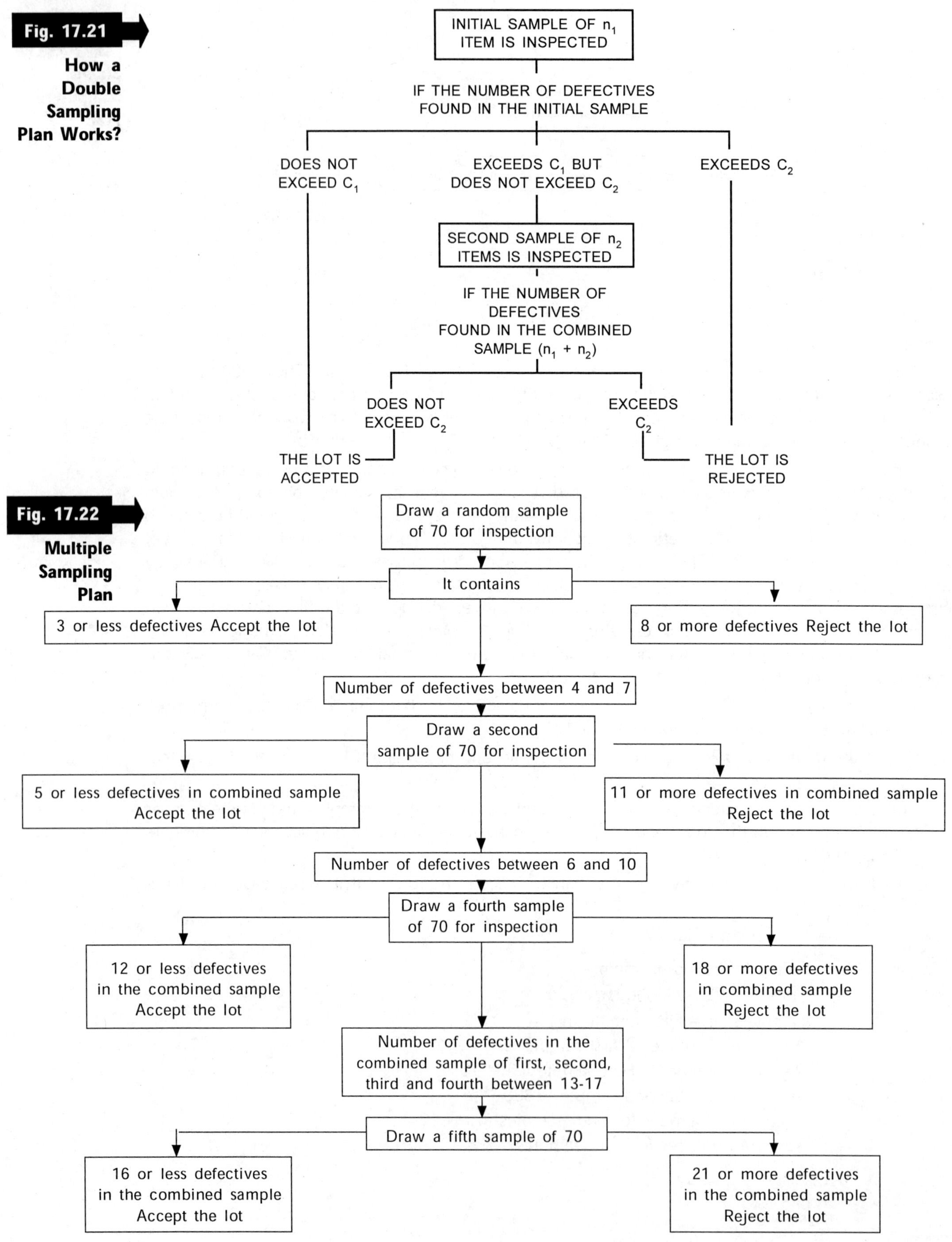

Fig. 17.21 How a Double Sampling Plan Works?

Fig. 17.22 Multiple Sampling Plan

If (n_1) is the initial sample of 120 from a lot of 18,000 (N) chosen for inspection, we can take any of the following judgements:

- If there are 2 or less defectives, the lot is accepted.
- If there are 10 or more defectives, the lot is rejected.
- If there are 3, 4, 5, 6, 7, 8 or 9 defectives, no decision is taken, and a second sample is drawn.

A second sample of 300 (n_2) is drawn from the lot, and is inspected, and one of the following judgements is made:

- If there are 12 or less defectives (C_2) in the combined sample, the lot is accepted. This number is obtained (12 or less) by 4 in the first sample and 8 or less in the second sample, by 6 in the first sample and 6 or less in the second sample, by 8 in the first sample and 4 or less in the second sample.
- If there are 14 or more defectives (r_2) in both the samples, the lot is rejected. This number (14 or more) is obtained by 4 in the first sample and 10 or more in the second sample, by 6 in the first sample and 8 or more in the second sample or by 8 in the first sample and 6 or more in the second sample.

Advantages of Double Sampling Plan

The very first sample may be enough to take the decision. It is of small size, and thus the amount of inspection is less than the single sampling plan. It provides enough psychological back up as two samples are chosen to arrive at the decision.

(*iii*) *Multiple sampling plan:* In multiple sampling, the procedure is similar. However, there is a possibility of drawing more than two samples from the same batch. Under this plan, several samples are taken until a decision to accept or reject a lot is reached. It should be noted that if the first few items are found defective, the lot could be rejected without further inspection.

In this plan, we can draw as many samples as we want, each sample of a small size. It is an extension of the double sampling plan. We can either stop the multiple sample plan at a particular stage or can continue till the lot is exhausted or a decision is arrived at.

The following example illustrates this plan:

Consider a lot size of 1500 units (N) of a particular product for which the following multiple sampling plan is drawn:

Sample Number	***Sample Size***	***Combined Samples*** ***Size***	***Acceptance No.***	***Rejection No.***
1	70 (n_1)	$n_1 = 70$	$C_1 = 3$	$r_1 = 8$
2	70 (n_2)	$n_1 + n_2 = 140$	$C_2 = 5$	$r_2 = 11$
3	70 (n_3)	$n_1 + n_2 + n_3 = 210$	$C_3 = 8$	$r_3 = 14$
4	70 (n_4)	$n_1 + n_2 + n_3 + n_4 = 280$	$C_4 = 12$	$r_4 = 18$
5	70 (n_5)	$n_1 + n_2 + n_3 + n_4 + n_5 = 350$	$C_5 = 16$	$r_5 = 21$

The multiple sampling plan for the above data is worked out in the following diagram:

Sequential Sampling Plan

Here we draw the units randomly from the lot and inspect them one by one. It is to be decided whether to accept the lot or reject it or to continue sampling after each inspection. The sampling process is continued till ultimately we either accept or reject the lot. A sequential sampling plan for two different cases (case 1 and case 2) is shown in the following figure.

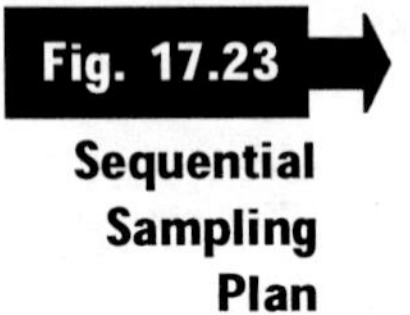

Fig. 17.23

Sequential Sampling Plan

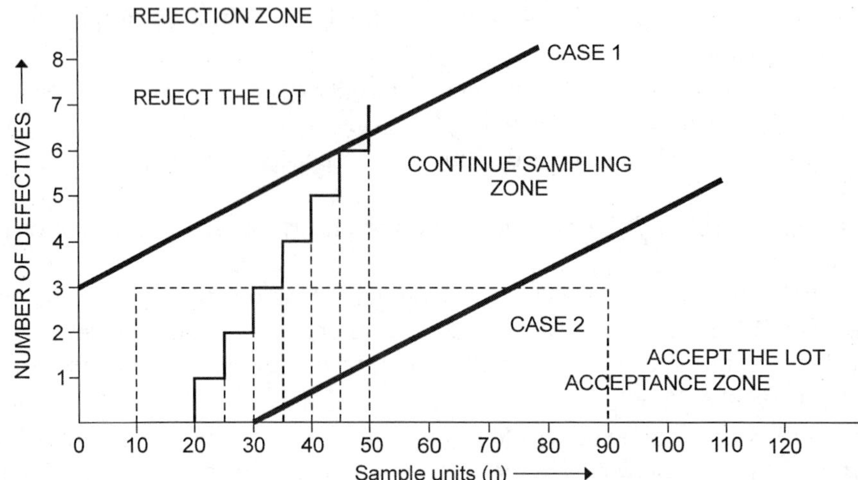

In the diagram, in case 1, the first defective is seen after 20th sample, second after 25, third after 30th, fourth after 35th, fifth after 40th and sixth after 45th. Uptil this point, we are in the continue sampling zone or the indecisive zone. We, therefore, cannot take a decision whether to accept or reject the lot. We detect 7th defective at 50th sample, which lies in the rejection zone. Hence, the lot is rejected. In case 2, we detect 3 defectives till the 90th sample. As per the plan, the lot is acceptable and sampling is to be stopped. The decision to accept or reject is taken on sequential basis.

Whichever may be the sampling plan, selection of a sample is made at random, so that all the items in a lot have an equal chance of selection in a sample. Acceptance sampling plan specifies the sample size (number of items in a sample) for a specific lot size and the number of allowable defects in the sample, on the basis of which decision regarding acceptance or rejection of the entire batch or lot is made.

OPERATING CHARACTERISTICS CURVES (OCCs)

As we have observed, when there is sampling, the cost of inspection decreases, though the risk of accepting the defective items increases. It tends to move us in favour of larger samples. The OC curve represents the probability of accepting the batches with more than the acceptable number of defectives as well as the probability of rejecting the batches with fewer than the acceptable number of defectives.

There are two desires here. The consumer's desire is to reduce the probability of accepting batches containing too many defectives. The producer's desire is to reduce the probability of rejecting batches containing an acceptable number of defectives. The first is called the *consumer's risk or* β and the second the *producer's risk or* α.

Thus the design of acceptance sampling plans have these two values plus two more points.

Acceptable Quality Level (AQL)

The desired quality level at which the probability of acceptance is high.

Lot tolerance per cent defective (LTPD)

The quality level below which batches are considered unacceptable and at which the probability of acceptance is low.

These four values are plotted on the OC curve as shown in Fig. 17.24.

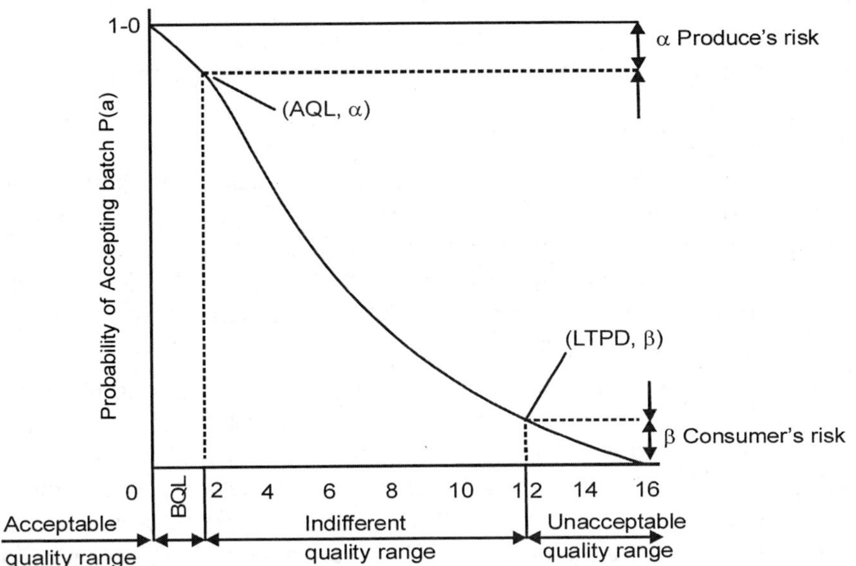

Fig. 17.24

OC Curve and points specifying a sampling plan

The four values are taken as follows:

Consumer's risk (β)	10 per cent
Producer's risk (α)	5 per cent
Acceptable quality level (AQL)	2 per cent
Lot tolerance per cent defective (LTPD)	10 per cent.

The OC curve passes through the two points - AQL, α and LTPD, β. Trial and error method is used to select values for the sample size (n), acceptable number of defectives (c) and substituting these into binomial probability formula till an acceptable curve is arrived at. Alternatively, Thorndike chart can be used.

The OC curve thus plotted decides the sample size *n* and the value of *c* to be used in acceptance sampling procedure. Defectives in the sample can either be rectified or replaced. If the inspection shows that the samples drawn have more than the acceptable number of defectives, we can either reject/scrap the whole batch or subject it to 100 per cent inspection to rectify and replace the faulty items.

Operating Characteristics Curve is a tool to show the strength of a given sampling plan. It graphically presents fraction defective or per cent defective in a lot against the probability of acceptance. It is a graphical relationship between percentage defective in the lots being submitted for inspection and the probability of acceptance. It is called operating characteristic of a particular sampling plan.

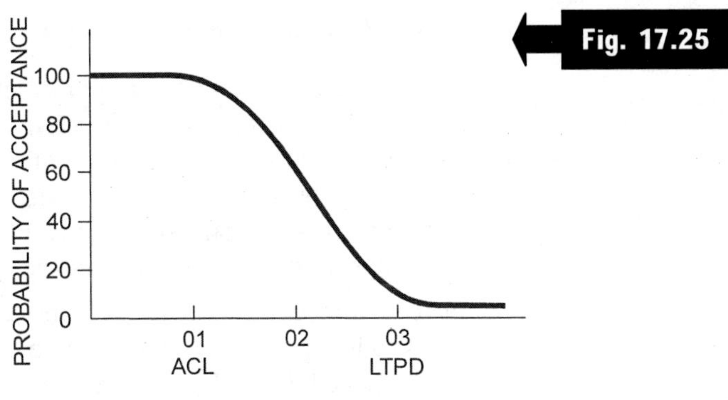

Fig. 17.25

Every acceptance sampling plan has an 'operating characteristics' (OC) curve that shows how it works or how effective it is in discriminating between a good lot and a bad lot.

Suppose that we first set up a plan and then look at its OC curve. We'll start by deciding the producer's risk. (Sometimes called the a or alpha risk). This is the risk that the producer takes that a very good lot of acceptable quality might, by chance, be rejected. It is called the acceptable quality level (AQL) and is, generally, set at 5 per cent.[1]

1. Both Martin Company and Ford Motor are among a growing number of companies which have adopted a policy of 'zero defects', meaning that no defectives are allowed in the sample. This is essentially the same as setting the AQL at zero. Praiseworthy as such is a goal, it will in many cases increase costs. On the other hand, zero defect users say that 'doing it right — the first time', has resulted in better workmanship and smaller scrap losses.

AQL is defined as the maximum per cent defective or the maximum number of defects per 100 units. For sampling inspection, this can be considered as a process average. This means that quite good lots will pass 95 per cent of the time.

Next we will set the consumer's risk, or the lot tolerance per cent defective (LTPD). This is sometimes called the lot tolerance fraction defective LTFD. It is also sometimes called the b or beta risk. LTPD is the maximum proportion of defectives that will make the lot definitely unacceptable. Consumer's risk (β) is the risk consumer is willing to take that lots of LTPD quality level will be accepted even though they are unacceptable. The consumer's risk is generally set at 10 per cent, which means that the consumer wants a plan which will reject lots with the maximum proportion of defectives (the LTPD) 90 times out of every 100 such lots.

The plan that will accomplish the objectives we want is an instruction to the inspector guiding him how many to include in his sample and also the maximum number of defectives that will let the lot pass.[2] If the lot is 10,000 or more than he should inspect a sample of 400 and reject all lots whose sample contains eight to more rejects. With seven or fewer defectives he accepts the lot. But if the lot is only 1,000, we get the same quality assurance by having him inspect a sample of only 275 and accepting the lot if he finds no more than five defects. If the whole lot is 200, he should inspect 125 and accept if he finds two or fewer rejects. Our 'plan', therefore, for each size lot, tells the inspector how big a sample to take and how good it has to be.

Size of Required Acceptable

Universe	*Sample*	*Defectives*
∞	400	7
10,000	400	7
1,000	275	5
200	125	2

Fig. 17.19 is the particular plan's operating characteristics curve. On this chart, the horizontal line at the bottom is an 'If' line. 'If' a lot submitted has 1,2,3,4, etc., per cent defectives, then we can read up to the curve and across to the left to see what the chances are that we will accept such a lot. Lots which actually contain 1 per cent defectives will pass about 95 per cent of the time. Lots with 2 per cent defectives will pass 40 per cent of the time. Lots containing 3 per cent defectives will get by only 10 per cent of the time and poorer lots have very little chance of getting by.

Every acceptance inspection plan has its own operating characteristic curve. The shape of the line depends on the quality we want and the extent to which we want to be certain that we will get this quality. The slope of the curve depends upon the size of the sample and on its proportion of the parent lot. For any given size lot, the larger the sample, the steeper the curve.

Degrees of Defects in Acceptance Sampling

Many products can have major or minor defects or both at the same time. If so, we might like our receiving inspectors to be using two or more inspection plans at the same time and on the same sample. We might, for instance, allow no defects at all in the sample for critical or major defects. The curvature of a spring for an automobile door lathe might be critical. If it curves too much and puts on too much pressure, it might break and let the car door swing open. So if one finds even one defective in the sample one would reject the lot.

We would also want to have very few or no major defects even when danger isn't involved. If an automatic seat adjuster in an automobile doesn't have enough pull, the seat won't adjust. Sometimes, we need to watch for defects because they will jam machinery. The head diameter on a driver installed by automatic assembly machine, if it is too big, will jam the machine. The defect is unimportant functionally,

2. For the method for calculating OC curves see Statistical Quality Control, by Eugene L. Grant (3rd ed.: New York; McGraw Hill Book, Co., Inc. 1964) pp. 333-67.

yet it is important in keeping production moving. Again, we might use an inspection plan that allows for no defects in the sample.

But minor defects which won't affect the product's operation aren't so serious. We could accept lots with a few minor defects. Probably you'd use a plan that would accept the lot even if the sample had 10 per cent minor defectives. Our inspectors could be applying two or three inspection plans when they inspect a sample. The rejection number would be low for serious defects and high for minor or trivial defects.

The Average Outgoing Quality Level (AOQL)

The average outgoing quality is the quality that leaves the inspection operation. If rejected lots were always scrapped, then your average quality of products used would probably be about halfway between the AQL and LTPD.

But the items from a bad lot can be 100 per cent inspected and the lot's quality improved just by taking out the bad items. This means that you end up getting good quality — and the worse the quality of lots first submitted, the better the quality you end up with. If most lots are rather bad, SQC will catch nearly all of them and, after 100 per cent inspection, they will end up nearly perfect. Average these in with the good lots that passed plus the few bad lots that got through and you'll have a better quality than if most lost were just good enough to pass.

In a sampling plan, we assume that any rejected lots are inspected 100 per cent to eliminate the defectives, and the rectified lots then carry 100 per cent good product. The acceptance sampling plan automatically adjusts inspection level to the quality of lots being inspected, since rejected lots are inspected 100 per cent. The performance of the plan is given by the plans average outgoing quality (AOQ)

$$AOQ = \frac{p.P_a\,(N-n)}{N}$$

where p = Fraction defective

P_a = Probability of acceptance

N = Lot size

n = Sample size.

Summarisation of the Design of a Sampling Plan

The sampling plan (n, c) has an OCC to meet certain pre-set requirements. More often, the design is based on the probability of making one of the following errors:

(1) Probability of accepting a bad lot (β)

(2) Probability of rejecting a good lot (α).

Subjective criteria are laid down, but they reflect the cost of accepting a bad lot or rejecting a good lot. It goes without saying that we've to define beforehand what is a good lot and a bad lot before putting the value for α and β. These values are with respect to the specified lower and upper limits of fraction defective *(f)* as given below.

AQL (Acceptable Quality Level) is the fraction defective *(f)* that the user considers acceptable. In other words, a fraction defective equal to AQL in a batch makes it acceptable. The probability of accepting lots with AQL value varies between 0.88 and 0.99. It increases with the lot size.

LTPD (Lot Tolerance Per cent Defective) is the fraction defective that defines a bad lot (or a lot which should be rejected). No doubt, AQL must be less than LTPD.

Producers' Risk (α) is the largest allowable probability of rejecting a good lot (due to some statistical error). It is to be appreciated that when AQL is set at 5 per cent, a good lot has a fraction defective less than or equal to AQL.

Consumers' Risk (β) is the largest allowable probability of accepting a bad lot (due to some statistical error). This risk is generally set at 10 per cent (LTPD). A bad lot as fraction defective is greater than or equal to LTPD.

In practice, Thornkike Chart (Dodge and Roming Sampling Inspection Tables, Wiley) can be used to do the calculations. The chart gives the probability of *c* or less detectives P(a) on the vertical axis for given values of PD × n/100 on the horizontal axis where PD is the actual per cent defectives in a batch and *n* is the sample size.

The sampling procedure has the ability to distinguish between the good and bad batches on the basis of sample size. Consider 3 sample processes for which the acceptable quality level is 1 per cent or less defectives. Here the process that uses the largest sample would be more accurate than the ones with percentage defectives in a batch is high. Fig. 17.26 shows three OCC_3. Here curve three is superior. As the sample size increases, the curves become steeper.

Fig. 17.26 **Operating Characteristic Curves**

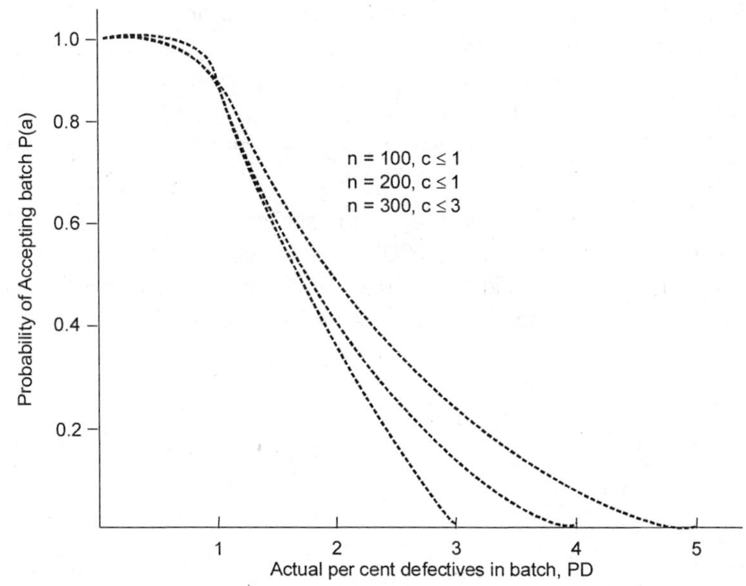

QUALITY CONTROL CIRCLES

QC circles are an important contributor to Japan's success in improving product quality and in achieving technological innovation. Initially established two decades ago, when foremen and workers were first taught quality control concepts, today more than 1,00,000 circles are registered at QC circle headquarters in JUSE. These circles can have a significant impact on a firm — there are 1,800 at Toyo Kogyo, involving half of the total 27,000 workers and can be found in almost every department from personnel to sales.

QC circles enable Japanese companies to harness the creative talent and intellectual energy of all their employees in order to compete more effectively. At the same time, in a society that emphasizes consensus, circles give individuals with ideas an institutionalized way to change their working environment without rocking the boat. Comments JUSE's Noguchi, "QC circles are based on the idea that everyone would like to use his brain in addition to his labour." Adds Mazda's Watanabe, "People appreciate growth through work."

Basically, a QC is a small group of employees — the advantage number is nine who volunteer to meet regularly in order to undertake work related projects designed to advance the company, improve working conditions and spur mutual self-development, by using QC concepts. Originally circles formed around foremen. Now circles coalesce from groups of co-workers or even individuals who share recreational interests. Many companies encourage circle leadership to rotate within the group.

According to a 1979 JUSE survey, circles tend to be most common in production, with maintenance, procurement, administration and engineering, respectively, the next most frequent. In the majority of cases, circles meet once or twice a month, usually for about an hour, and most often during the working day.

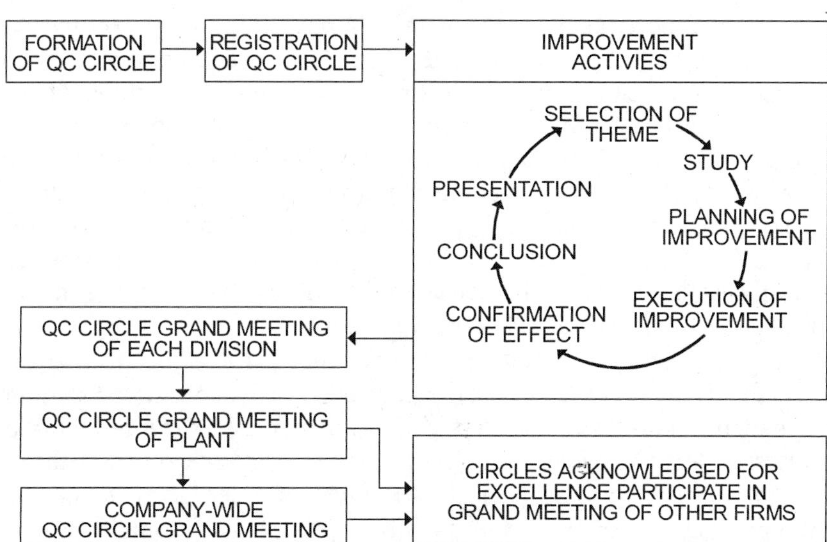

Fig. 17.27

Approximately 75% of all circle projects are selected by the members themselves. About 30% of the projects deal with quality improvement and 45% with cost reduction. But circles sometimes range further. Topics such as improvements in tooling, safety measures and environmental protection, are becoming more common. And at least one circle decided to examine itself: finding its members in poor health, the circle instituted a physical fitness programme that brought results so striking — in terms of the group's physical wellbeing and work output — that the programme is to be extended throughout the company.

Indeed, circle accomplishments often are remarkable. No one usually knows more about the strengths and weaknesses of a system than those who have to operate it. Noguchi cites a Japanese steel company that attributes a quarter of its profits to circle initiatives. The JUSE survey reveals that 40% of the managers polled saw significant gains in quality and safety, while 276 responding plants reported a 1:80 average cost-benefit ratio for circle activities.

However, Noguchi emphasizes that QC circles were not created in Japan to increase productivity. Higher output, greater efficiency, lower costs are, in a sense, by-products, of improved quality. For circle members, quality is the primary motivating force, not productivity — even though in the TQC system the two are almost the same.

Although circle participation often counts for promotion and in some firms is reflected in bonus pay, there are usually non-direct cash incentives. Personal satisfaction comes from achievement. Recognition is given at annual plant, company regional and national QC meetings, when circles report on projects successfully completed.

QC circles have spread around the world — to the U.S.A., Britain, Brazil, Indonesia, and more. There are 40,000 circles in Korea alone. But noting the differences that exist between cultures and countries, Noguchi advises: "In order to introduce the QC circle, you must first start the spadework for adaptation. For this everybody's understanding, especially top management's understanding, and co-operation are imperative. You should expect that it will take your much time." (Purchase)

Quality Circles in India

Quality Circles as a concept has taken root in India only recently. The pioneering move was made by BHEL in Hyderabad in 1980. Many managements are now enthusiastic about introducing QCs in their plants. QCs can be introduced in any organization. There are certain misconceptions about QCs which are sometimes called 'The Magic Circles.' These must be removed.

RELIABILITY

Meaning and Importance

The term reliability was developed during the late 1940s and early 1950s by American manufacturing and research organizations to test and improve the life of electronic components, particularly radio valves used in civilian and military aircraft applications. Reliability is something different from quality. It is related to quality but it is something more than that. It is the probability that a product or a part or a system or equipment will perform satisfactorily for a given time under normal conditions of use. A product of better quality may not be reliable according to the customers. Quality is related to the initial performance of a product or a service, but reliability is related to the continuation of performance over a period of time. A product with better initial performance may fail to give the same performance afterwards. In such a case a product is not considered reliable. Therefore, the manufacturers should produce not only quality products but also reliable products.

Today reliability tests are also specified to ensure that the specifications are not met initially only, but also maintained over some specified period. Reliability is considered most important in case of various latest weapons and electronic equipment of military use, because failure of a single small part may cause disaster. Imagine what would be the result, if a tank on the battlefield fails or if a bomber plane has to land in enemy's place due to failure of a certain small part?

Failure of the product or a small part of the whole product may sometimes cause a great harm to the user. Failure of a brake or steering mechanism of a car or truck results in a fatal accident. As the number of critical parts in a particular whole product increases, its reliability decreases, because with the increase in number of parts, probability of failure also increases. Failure of any one of these parts makes the whole product less reliable. There are also 100 chances of failure of a product having 100 parts, while there are only 25 chances of failure of a product having 25 parts, considering one chance of failure for each part. Several years ago, the United States submarine 'Thresher' sank and 129 men lost their lives because one pipe joint — out of 8,000 — failed.[†]

When the maintenance or replacement of a product or a part or a component is easy, simple, quick and cheap, the reliability becomes less important, so far as that product or part or component is concerned. Electric bulb, when it burns out, can be replaced easily and quickly. And, therefore, its failure is not considered too serious. But the failure of an important part used in power generating machine in a thermal power station, which is not available within the country, is considered very serious, because it results in the closure of the power generating unit for a long period, *i.e.,* until that part arrives and fitted in place of an old part in the machine and the machine starts working. Quick and easy maintenance does less harm. Breakdown of a machine can cause a great harm in terms of a production loss, if it cannot be repaired or replaced quickly. But, if a machine can be repaired or replaced easily and quickly, actual harm in terms of production loss will be much less.

How can it be measured?

Reliability can be measured, only if it is expressed in quantitative terms. For the measurement of reliability, two points (1) probability and (2) time need consideration. Reliability must be maintained throughout the process of manufacture and the useful life of a product. If a product is not found reliable, while it is used, it becomes useless. Whether a product is reliable or not, depends on the probability of its failure during a given period and the length of time for which it gives the rated performance. The information relating to the failures or defectives during a given period of time is collected, analysed and corrective actions are taken to improve reliability. The measurement of reliability depends on the type of products. For example: (*i*) certain products function only on one occasion, (*ii*) certain products have a long life, but if they fail they cannot be repaired, and (*iii*) certain products have a long life and if they fail they can be repaired and then again can be put to use.

† *Production/Operations Management* — F.G. Moore, & T.E. Handrich, 122, Ed. 1982. D.B. Taraporewala & Sons Pvt. Ltd., Mumbai.

A guided missile or a bomb or a gunshot can function only on one occasion. If such a product functions successfully only on one occasion, it is considered to be 100% reliable. Products like an electric bulb, a radio valve etc. have a long life, but if they fail, they cannot be repaired. It means that when they fail any time during the period of their use, they fail completely at the same moment. If the expected life of a bulb is 1,000 hours and if the probability of failure is 3 bulbs out of 100, it can be said that the bulbs have the reliability of 0.97. The reliability of such products is measured through the life tests. Batches of the products are tested and how long each unit functions successfully is recorded and the results are compared with predetermined goal or standards. A product such as a motor truck, a scooter or a car has a long life and if it fails it can be repaired and again can be put to use. Here to measure the reliability, the time of each failure is recorded during the useful life. The useful life of such type of products is stated in terms of kilometres. The time and number of failures during the useful life of such type of products indicate to what extent they are reliable. Thus time is the most important factor to be considered while measuring the reliability. Reliability of a shot fired on one occasion successfully and a failure of a scooter once during its journey of 1,000 kilometres cannot be compared because of the time factor. A shot can be fired only once and therefore its successful functioning on one occasion is not the proof of its 100% reliability. A scooter has a useful life of thousands of kilometres and therefore its failure during its journey of 1,000 kilometres cannot be considered as its 100% failure or "Zero"% reliability, because it can be used again after its repairing is done.

While measuring the reliability of a product, one has to consider the conditions of use also. A product or a part or a component, if not used properly or if it is not well maintained, its useful life may be shortened. Its reliability may decrease, now the fault is of the user. A motor car, having an useful life of say 100,000 kilometres, cannot be used continuously for the journey of 100,000 kms. If a bulb, having expected useful life of 1,000 hours, if used continuously, may not last even for 800 hours.

The reliability information illustrated in form of charts or curves becomes very much useful in taking certain important decisions. The following questions can be easily solved with the help of charts or curves:

(*i*) What changes should be made in the design of a product to improve its reliability?

(*ii*) Which item should be inspected and when should it be inspected?

(*iii*) Which part or machine should be inspected or replaced and when should this be done?

(*iv*) How far a particular investment proposal would prove to be financially strong?

(*v*) How far a product or a process or a machine or a part is reliable and how can its reliability be improved?

(*vi*) How should the plant and machinery, tools, equipment etc., be maintained for its maximum efficiency?

Presentation of the reliability information

To illustrate the reliability information in the form of charts or curves, the following data relating to the number of failures and time of failure of a given product or part or component or machine etc. are calculated.

(1) Number of failures during a given period as a proportion of the total is calculated. It is called the failure probability rate. Suppose out of 200 timebombs, 2 bombs fail. The rate of failure, *i.e.*, the failure probability, here is 0.01 or say 1%.

(2) Total number of failures up to a given period, expressed as a proportion of the total is calculated. Here, cumulative total is considered. For example, if during the first, second and third period, the number of bombs failed per 100 is 2, 4 and 3 respectively, the cumulative total of bombs failed comes to 9 and the proportion of failures comes to $\frac{2+4+3}{100+100+100} = 0.03$ or say 3%. This is called the cumulative failure probability rate.

(3) Total number of survivors up to a given time expressed as a proportion to the total is calculated. It is called the cumulative survival probability rate.

(4) Sometimes, the total number of failures during a given period is expressed as a proportion of the total number of survivors. This rate is called the conditional failure rate.

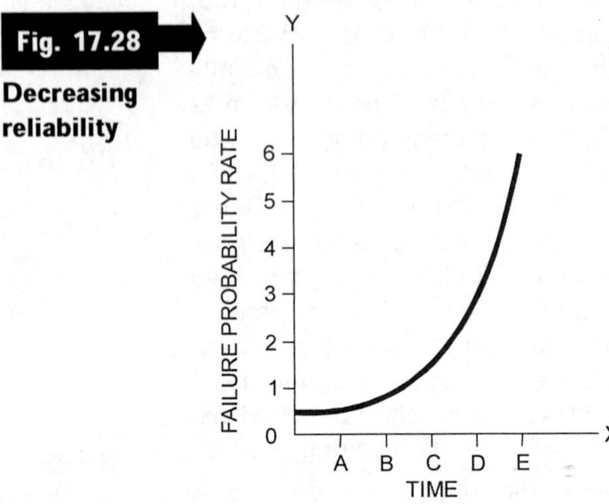

Fig. 17.28

Decreasing reliability

Fig. 17.29

Increasing reliability

The curves drawn from the data given in (1) and (2) above, may show the following shape depending upon the trend in reliability.

Figure 17.28 indicates that the rate of failure increases as the time goes on. It means that the reliability of a product or a part or a component decreases as the time goes on.

Figure 17.29 indicates that the rate of failure decreases as the time goes on. It means that the reliability of a product or a part or a component increases as the time goes on.

(D) How can it be improved? Reliability is measured to see to what extent a product or a part or a machine or a component or a process is reliable. If the reliability shows decreasing trend, corrective actions to improve the reliability are taken.

Reliability of a product depends on the reliability of parts or materials used in manufacturing that product and also on the reliability of tools and equipment, machines, methods or production process etc., used for the manufacture of that product. Therefore, to improve the reliability of a certain product:

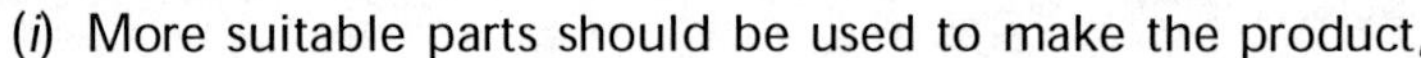

(*i*) More suitable parts should be used to make the product,

(*ii*) Standard quality materials, purchased from the reliable suppliers should only be used,

(*iii*) Plant and machinery, tools and equipment must be repaired and maintained properly. A car, if checked after a journey of every 500 kms. and if properly maintained, may not put the owner in difficulty in the middle of the way,

(*iv*) Standard and suitable tools and equipment should only be used,

(*v*) Parts or tools or machines should be replaced before they become unreliable. For example, if a bulb with an estimated useful life of 1,000 hours is replaced at the interval of every 800 to 900 hours, there will be no possibility of its failure.

Use of Computers in Quality Control

These days there is software available for QC. There is a provision for controlling the process online. The software packages are likely to make QC work much more comfortable than it previously ever was.

Strategic Role for Quality

Juran's concern for quality went beyond made to specifications products; and inspecting them for defectives. His strategic role for quality was implemented by the by taking the following steps:

1. Senior Japanese executives were placed in charge of this function.
2. Quality management training was imparted to the entire managerial hierarchy.
3. They did improve quality at revolutionary pace, and the pace was maintained year after year.
4. Deming's 1950 lectures inspired them to use SQC. They later invented QCs.
5. Each company spelled out quality goals.

US and Quality

During 1950s US products were generally competitive with European and were superior to Japanese products. The Europeans, and the Japanese held an advantage in price. Their labour costs were lower. The US however responded to this price competition. Anti-dumping laws and tariff barriers were used. 'Buy American' — a patriotic appeal was used. The American mindset considered Japanese as copyists and not as innovators. They can do price competition, but never quality competition.

The quality function in the US was delegated to the quality control department, and the top management was divorced from the quality function totally.

Xerox revolutionized copying and was very successful in the 1950s. Xerox however had no mechanism to measure customer satisfaction. Their machines malfunctioned/broke down regularly. The response of the Xerox executives was to send technicians in the field to repair them. The customers did not want this curative maintenance. They wanted machines that did not break down in the first place. The Japanese rushed in to produce exactly the type of machines the customers wanted — machines that did not break down so often. In addition, the Japanese machines gave better copies and low cost copies. Xerox machine had the data of product failures but the same faults were not rectified by the design engineers which Xerox had in plenty. Rather the same faults were carried over, model after model, like genetic disorder. The decisions were taken by Product Managers (mostly sales oriented) who prodded the designers to add more and new product features to increase the sales. But the failure-prone features were retained. Their priorities were wrong.

The Xerox case was typical of America's other industries too. American TV companies who produced quality TVs during 50s were overtaken by the Japanese in the 80s. The auto industry is another example where the Japanese caught up and then surpassed the US by 1975 in terms of product quality by working towards it for 20 years.

When the third edition of *Quality Control Handbook* of Juran was being published, he approached Toyoda, M.D. Toyota Motors to request him to contribute a chapter on quality (1972). This chapter focused on customer needs rather than on mere conformity to specifications.

The 1970s and 1980s were the years of slippage for the US in terms of quality. But by the 1990, there was a silver lining. It all started from the 80s when a small number of US companies could attain world-class quality. Motorola is one example. It became a leading seller of communication equipment in Japan. Xerox took measures to improve the quality and restored the market share it had lost.

Last century could be described as the century of productivity, but the 21st century is the century of quality.

US has instituted Malcolm Baldrige National Quality Award. The visibility of quality has been raised as an essential discipline. The National Institute of Standards and Technology (NITS) administers this award.

US companies who have attained world-class quality insist on vendors developing the same quality for their supplies. The recruitment and selection policy will put more emphasis on a candidate's mastering Total Quality Management from business schools.

By 1993, Juran found that his lectures are heard by CEOs — a watershed event that compares with what happened in Japan when Juran first addressed them four decades ago. The critical variable in Japanese quality leadership is the extent of active participation by senior managers. The loss of America's quality leadership is attributable to the senior manager's isolation from the quality function.

'Made in US' will soon be a symbol of world-class quality.

How Juran Learnt about Process Control?

In 1924, Juran became an engineer at Western Electric, the manufacturing section for the Bell system where he analysed a tiny circuit breaker being made in millions, but being rejected to the extent of 15 per cent in inspection as they could not meet the specification for electric resistance. On analysis, Juran found uniform electric resistance in any given reel but variations were observed from reel-to-reel. A length of wire from each reel equal in resistance to the mean specification limits was taken. Then the entire reel was cut into pieces of the same length. All these cut wires showed uniform resistance, despite the reel-to-reel variation. This led to a slight drop in defect rate.

Quality Moves Ahead	
Year	*How quality moves ahead*
	Informal Inspection
1800	Formal Inspection
	Instrument used: gauges
1922	Concept of conformance quality by G.S. Radford
1931	SQC pioneered by W. Schwhart. It is a precursor to Total Quality Control (TQC)
1942	Quality Control Section set up by US War Department.
1946	American Society for Quality Control founded.
1950	Cost of quality concept put forward by Joseph Juran
1951	Deming arrives in Japan. Believer in SQC
1952	Deming propagates the principles of TQC to Japanese industry
1954	Reliability engineering introduced as a discipline the by US army
1956	Total Quality Management (TQM) emerges as a new concept at the hands of Armand Feigenbaum
1961	Zero Defect Concept comes forward from Martin Co.
1979	Crosby puts forward four absolutes of quality
1987	ISO 9000 series approved in its present form
1990	Paradigm shift after TQM
Future Trends	Customer Centred Quality Control Expert Systems for TQM etc.

Juran then measured and plotted resistance of the finished circuit breakers. They were quite uniform. The average resistance was not at the mean of the specification. The average resistance shifted to the minimum. They then observed the manufacturing process closely. The difficulty was located. The operatives were soldering the wire to the units at a point about 2″ from the end of the wire and then cut off the excess. They were required to provide two more inches to the specified length of each piece of wire before it was cut off. The defect-prone process then became defect-free.

QUALITY AND DESIGN

Quality is a virtue of design. Customer satisfaction is derived from:

- Quality of design
- Quality of conformance to design

In the literature, conformance has been emphasized more than the design. However, design is more important, as design itself determines the features which either satisfy or dissatisfy the customers. Besides, conformance is easy to achieve with a good design.

Achieving an attractive good design on paper is one thing. This should however be translated into reality. Taguchi defines quality as the loss imparted to society once a product is delivered. A good design minimises the loss. A shirt imparts a loss every time it is washed and ironed. A scooter that has to be serviced every 5,000 kms imparts greater loss than the one that is to be serviced after 20,000 kms. Certain forms of loss are scandalous. Loss emanates from functional variations or harmful effects. Sources of loss include power consumption, life expectancy, maintenance reliability and trouble, space requirements or occupation with volume and positioning or set-up time.

According to Taguchi, a good design reflects an optimal trade-off between cost and performance. It is easier to make a more complicated design but it takes genius to simplify designs. A product which functions satisfactorily over a wide range of conditions is more useful. Good design has a customer focus. However, it must also integrate to the organisation's technology, culture, market-orientation and so forth. Design takes into consideration the process capability of an organisation. Process capability basically refers to **what we can do.**

The manufacturing process was analysed to locate the difficulty. By improving the process, they not only improved the quality (of the circuit breakers) but also reduced the cost of producing (them).

The superior, however, told Juran that process improvement was the job of a production department, and not of the inspection department where Juran was working! Juran realised this organizational barrier to quality management and warned the Japanese against this pitfall.

What a CEO should do to Initiate Quality Revolution?

Juran recommends the following:

- Set up a company quality council. The CEO should be its member.
- Establish quality goals for the whole organization. Also establish quality improvement goals. These should be a part of a corporate plan.
- Establish the means to measure quality results against quality goals.
- Review results against goals continuously.
- Give recognition to performance on quality front.
- Revise the reward system to respond to the changes demanded by world-class quality.

'Zero Defects' Programmes

In the US, Martin-Marietta Corporation initiated the pioneering 'Zero Defects' programme around 1962 to improve product quality beyond that achieved by the statistical procedures. Mainly, it was a motivational package offered to the operators combined with a prevention package that removed causes for errors.

Appendix - I

A MEASURE OF QUALITY

Launched in 1987, the ISO series has now been accepted by national standards bodies of 90 countries, including India and all EU member countries.

Issued by one of the several national standards bodies accredited to the International Organisation for Standardisation (IOS). ISO certificates are increasingly gaining acceptance around the globe as the hallmark of quality.

The specialised international agency has been set up to promote development of standardisation to facilitate international exchange of uniform quality goods and services. The ISO comprises 180 technical committees, each responsible for one of the several areas of specialisation.

The ISO Series

ISO	Indian Standards	European Norms	Scope
9000	IS 14000	EN 29000	Selection and use: Quality management and quality assurance standards.
9001	IS 14001	EN 29001	Model for quality assurance in design/development, production, installation and servicing.
9002	IS 14002	EN 29002	Model for quality assurance in production and installation.
9003	IS 14003	EN 29003	Model for quality assurance in final inspection and testing.

Source: CII-TQM Division.

The word ISO (pronounced as ice-o) has been derived from the Greek word *isos* which means equal.The ISO series consists of six standards: a standard terminology on definition and concepts known as ISO 8402 and five quality standards (ISO 9000-4) popularly called the ISO series.

Each certificate specifies that a company possessing it conforms to and implies quality aspects as specified by the IOS. The company's name is subsequently registered with the agency awarding the certificate. Over 30,000 companies around the world have been certified under ISO standards so far.

Appendix - II

SOFTWARE ENGINEERING INSTITUTE'S CAPABILITY MATURITY MODEL (SEI CMM)

Indian company Wipro has received level 5 certification from SEI, USA and has become one of the six high-quality organizations across the world. Wipro has also initiated the Six Sigma programme. The following diagram illustrates the five levels of maturity in the SEI-CMM model.

Level 1	Initial	Ad hoc activities. Few processes defined. A few individual's contributions define success.
Level 2	Repeatable	Disciplined processes. Majority understand them and follow them.
Level 3	Defined	Standardised defined processes.
Level 4	Managed	Measurement of processes and prediction of results controlled.
Level 5	Optimisation	Ability to change the processes for improved results. Assessment and improvement continuous.

Each maturity level is further sub-divided into several key process areas. There are 17 key process areas from level 1 to level 5. Such as software project planning, software project engineering and software quality management. Each process area has several key practices. These define infrastructure and activities which contribute most to the effective implementation and institutionalisation of the key process areas.

Appendix - III

HISTORICAL MILESTONES IN QUALITY MOVEMENT IN JAPAN

Period	Happenings	Remarks
1945-50	Quality control study group was formed under the sponsorship of civil communication section (CCS) of the allied forces. Japan Standard Association (JSA) was formed. Standardisation law was passed.	—
1950-55	In 1950, W.E. Deming, the US statistician, lectured in Japan on the virtues of QC. Japanese Union of Scientists and Engineers (JUSE) and JSA started training programmes on statistical methods.	There was simultaneous social change after introduction of literacy campaigns and compulsory education.
1955-60	J.M. Juran, another American brought home the importance of QC. Training courses by JUSE and JSA for middle and top managers.	QC is not restricted to just quality control department, but permeates the whole organization. QC seminars were extended to purchase and sales departments.
1960-65	The QC training reached the foremen and frontline supervisors. Ishikawa (1963), recommended that foremen should establish book reading circles within their work-groups to promote quality concept. The work-based groups soon moved from theoretical study to problem solving.	His suggestion was gradually taken up across the whole country. This emerged into Quality Circles (QCs). It emphasised decentralisation and participative decision making.
1965-70	A distinct Japanese style of quality control emerged, and permeated the whole organization. Quality Control Audit was introduced. Computers were used for QC. National quality circle activities were organized.	

Appendix - IV

COMPARISON OF DIFFERENT CHARTS

Factor	X-R Charts	p-charts	c-charts
Data	Variable data	Attribute data	Attribute data
Application	Individual characteristic is controlled.	Overall fraction defective of a process is controlled.	Overall number of defects per unit is controlled.
Advantages	1. Provides maximum utilisation of information drawn from data. 2. Provides detailed information on process average and variation of control for individual dimension.	1. Data drawn from the inspection records. 2. Easy to understand. 3. Provide overall picture of quality.	1. Data drawn from inspection records. 2. Easy to understand. 3. Provide overall picture of quality. 4. Focus is on defectiveness in units of products.
Disadvantages	1. Trained personnel necessary for implementation.	1. Control of individual characteristic not possible.	1. Control of individual characteristics not possible.
	2. Confusion between control limits and specification limits.	2. Degrees of defectiveness not recognised.	2. Different degrees of defectiveness of units of a product not reorganized.
	3. Cannot be used with go-no-go type of data.		

The following table summarises the points of comparison of the three types of control charts.

ꕥ ꕥ

18 MAINTENANCE MANAGEMENT

Since the dawn of civilisation, man has used machines and equipment and tools to fulfil his daily chores and to eke out his livelihood — be it tilling the farm, producing the construction materials, conveyance of the loads and drawing out of water from wells and lakes. Man has always tended to keep up these equipment of use with care, and mend them wherever necessary, till the useful life of these assets got exhausted. In other words, it was the job of upkeep and maintenance which lengthened the life of an asset. We, in India continue to make heavy capital investments, but are not careful to maintain these. Proper maintenance leads to better capacity utilisation of the same asset, avoiding thus the investment in additional facilities. So far, industries had a tendency to neglect maintenance function, thinking it to be a not so important job, howsoever necessary. It has been taken just for granted.

The maintenance policy is framed to answer questions like —

- What we plan to do about breakdowns of machines?
- What steps are we going to take to prevent the breakdowns?

The two dimensions to maintenance are preventive maintenance before breakdowns and maintenance after the breakdown happens. Though preventive maintenance reduces the number of breakdowns, it is no guarantee against total elimination of breakdowns. We have to take into consideration the cost of prevention against the cost of failing to prevent. Maintenance is a sort of quality control problem, but as applied to the standard of service expected of the machines.

Introduction

The efficiency of the production function solely depends on the functional reliability of the production facilities which are nothing but a package of land, building, plants and equipment, tools and plant services such as materials handling, power plant, gas and steamlines, water supply, fire fighting facilities etc. All these facilities are subject to wear and tear either simply by elapse of time or by the frequency of their use. For the maintenance of the functional reliability of all these facilities, plant maintenance is considered as an important services function of modern production management. The basic objective of plant maintenance is to keep all the production facilities in a constant and smooth servicing condition. It is a service function and thus involves indirect costs of production activity.

Scope of plant maintenance: The plant maintenance services spare a lopsided attention for the maintenance of machines and equipment due to their frequency of use and strategic position in the entire production function. A machine is nothing but a mechanism consisting of the services of sequential components, each performing its specific function which is a part of the whole mechanism, *e.g.,* in a simple typewriting operation, when the typist strikes a key on the keyboard, it causes a mechanical action of the type to strike the ribbon which gives an impression on the paper arranged on the carriage. The type linkage returns to its original position and simultaneously the carriage moves one space to make the way for the next cycle. Some parts of the machine are fixed while some are replaceable. Such mechanical devices and their parts need constant and continuous services like cleaning, lubricating, repairing, replacing, etc. so that their operational efficiency can be maintained. It should be noted that the plant maintenance service is not confined only to the machines and equipment. Under the wide spectrum of the plant maintenance service, the maintenance of the ground, building, power plant, materials handling equipment, transport services, water supply, steam and gas pipelines, fire fighting facilities etc. are also covered. The frontiers of the plant maintenance service also extend to include the provision of maintenance equipment and the stocking up of the repair parts and maintenance materials. Thus, it is a broad and exhaustive function which covers the wide range of production facilities contributing to the production either directly or indirectly.

In other words, maintenance is not just a repair function, but 'is a combination of any actions carried out to retain an item in, or restore it to an acceptable condition.' This function keeps an eye on the entire production system and facilities. These days, National Productivity Council (NPC), is spreading the message of good maintenance management. In fact, these days a comprehensive tero-technology approach is adopted which looks after the physical assets right from design to discard stage through various angles — managerial, financial, technical and maintenance.

Importance of plant maintenance: Plant maintenance is an important and inevitable service function of an efficient production system. It helps in maintaining and increasing the operational efficiency of plant facilities and thus contributes to the revenue by reducing the operating cost and increasing the quality and quantity of the production. As a service function it involves the incurrence of certain costs. The important components of this cost centre are — employment of maintenance crew and other incidental administrative expenses, investments in maintenance equipment and stocking up of repair parts and maintenance materials. However, the absence of planned maintenance service proves costlier. Absence of plant maintenance results in machine breakdown and failure of certain production services which in turn result in production stoppages, idle machine-time, idle direct and indirect labour time, dislocation of the subsequent processes, poor quality of production, increased scrap, failure to meet the promised delivery orders, industrial accidents endangering the life of workers, payment of workmen's compensation, the resultant effects on morale of workers etc. The plant maintenance services should be provided in the light of the cost-benefit analysis. As it is a service function, it should be provided at the least possible cost.

Objectives of Maintenance

1. One of the most important objectives of maintenance management is to improve functional reliability of the production facilities.

Functional reliability of the production facilities: The functional reliability refers to the consistency of the degree of performance of the machine, equipment or service operation. When it is generally stated that the machine is having a 97% reliability, it means that 97% of the machine time is utilized in performing the standard production for which it is meant for. For the remaining 3% it is not performing its standard production either due to breakdowns or sub-standard performance. The plant maintenance service strives to maintain and increase the functional reliability of the production facilities. The functional reliability of the production facilities can be maintained or improved as under:

(*i*) To employ sufficient maintenance staff and to provide adequate repair and maintenance facilities.

(*ii*) To provide for reasonable slacks in the production system so that the parallel paths can be developed in a critical situation.

(*iii*) To provide for the stand-by (extra) equipment for key operations.

(*iv*) To decouple the rigid sequential stages of production by maintaining the reservoir of materials between the operations.

(v) To adopt the preventive maintenance system so that the critical parts can be replaced before they fail.

It should be noted that each of the above suggestions involves some costs. So its incurrence should be justified on the basis of cost-benefit analysis, *i.e.*, the cost of attaining reliability must be lower than the cost advantage available out of the production stoppages, idle machine and labour time, scrap, poor quality, loss of goodwill due to failure to keep delivery promises etc.

2. Maintenance extends the useful life of assets by reducing wear and tear. In developing countries, replacement of assets is not always economical, and hence the importance of maintenance.
3. Maintenance keeps up operational readiness of all equipments required for emergencies.
4. Maintenance contributes a great deal to safety of manpower using the facilities.
5. It prevents wastage of spares, tools and materials.
6. More automation calls for sophisticated maintenance.

Maintenance in modern plants requires a multi-dimensional approach in these days of computer controls.

Failure Analysis

In order to have better maintenance planning and control, it is important to learn about the nature and occurrence of failures over a period of time for the equipments. The graph of the failure pattern, called Weibull distribution graph after Weibull who developed it, is shown below. It is called commonly a Bath Tub Curve (BTC) because of its shape.

As commonly experienced, newly installed equipment shows a very high rate of failure. Greater failure rate is common during the initial phase, let us call it infancy. Once this phase is over, the failure rate dips relatively. The behaviour comes close to hyper-exponential distribution. It is a result of poor design and poor installation. The equipment's initial run allows those failures which were inherent in it. May be, we can better remember this by calling it *infant mortality*.

The other extreme is that of wear and tear on ageing of the equipment. There may be a failure, a total failure or death which comes about at 'mean' or 'average' time, may be a little earlier or later. This ageing failure comes close to a bell-shaped normal distribution pattern.

Now between these two extremes also equipment do fail, but reasons for these failures are neither inherent design or installation anomalies or ageing wear out. The cause here is external to the equipment, and so the probability of failing is constant. It is represented approximately by a negative exponential distribution. Weibull distribution or Bath Tub Curve is a combination of these three distributions: Hyper exponential, negative exponential and normal. These graphs are available so that we can compute Mean Time Between Failure (MTBF), thus indicating system reliability, availability, anticipated life etc. When there are recurrent failures, the failure statistics come handy as a diagnostic tool. As you have learnt now, maintenance has to ensure the availability and reliability of an equipment. The availability (A) is given by

$$A = \frac{T_{up}}{T_{up} + T_{down}}$$

where, T_{up} = the cumulative time of operation in the normal working condition and

T_{down} = the cumulative down time.

Breakdown time distributions: The information about the breakdown time distributions provide the basic data for the formulation of plant maintenance policies. These distributions indicate the frequency of the maintenance-free performance of the machine during a specified time. The shape of these frequency distribution curves will vary according to the characteristics of the equipment. In a simple machine with few moving parts there will be symmetric breakdowns with minimum variability in their breakdown time distributions. The shape of the frequency distribution curve will be like curve 'A' as depicted in Fig. 18.2. The dotted line T_a on the X-axis represents the average breakdown time. For the machines

Fig. 18.1

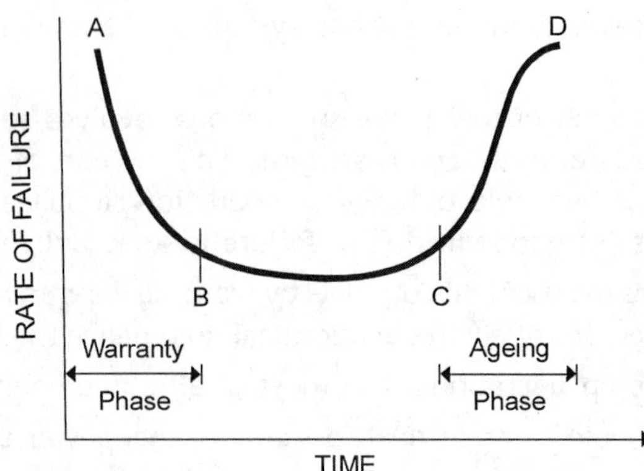

representing the situation like curve A, the large percentage of breakdowns occur near the average breakdown time and very little at the extremes.

For the machines involving complex mechanism with many parts, the chances of breakdown of any part would be great. The aggregate picture of the distribution of the breakdown time would be like curve B as shown in Fig. 18.2. The variability of the breakdowns would be very great as it can breakdown at any time with the breakdown of any of its part. As a result of this, there would be a much wider variability of breakdown time for the same average breakdown time T_a as shown in the figure.

For the machines requiring tricky adjustments and repairs, the chances of the breakdown time of such machines would be like curve C of Fig. 18.2. The breakdown in such machines occurs immediately after the repair or readjustment; or after a long span of time after the repair or readjustment; depending upon the quality of the repair or adjustments. Considering the same average breakdown time T_a, such machines will face greater degree of variability as shown in the Fig. 18.2.

Fig. 18.2

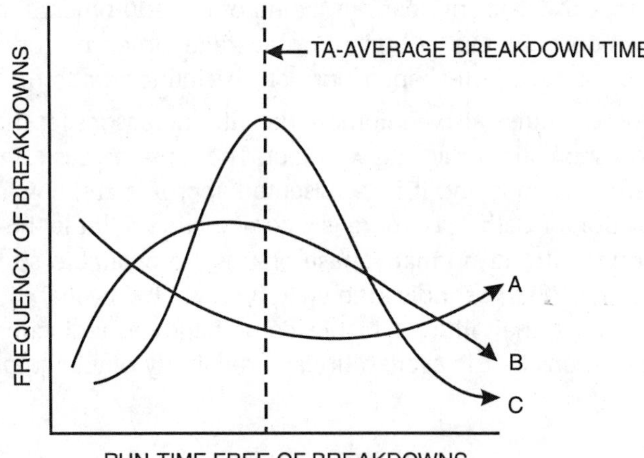

The above-mentioned data can be recast as shown in Fig. 18.3 converting the information into the breakdown time distributions and the percentage of breakdowns that exceeded a given run time.

It can be observed from Fig. 18.3 that curve A shows lower degree of variability, curve B exhibits moderate variability while curve C indicates greater degree of variability from the average breakdown time T_a.

Types of maintenance system: These days the ad hoc unplanned emergency maintenance is not recommended. We recommend a planned maintenance, which could be of two types:

(1) Repair Maintenance; (2) Preventive Maintenance.

(1) Repair Maintenance: When any sudden breakdown occurs in any machine or plant service, the repair maintenance staff endeavours to locate any mechanical, electrical or some such fault and

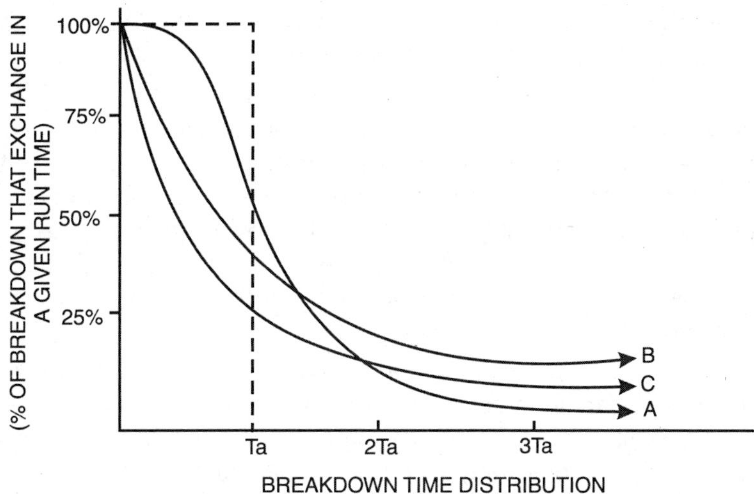

to correct it immediately. The repair maintenance function presupposes previous breakdowns. This function involves the disassembling of the equipment, to locate the fault if it has occurred through any broken part, then to find out that part and to replace it, to reassemble the equipment and then to check the equipment to ensure that it has restored its functional capacity. The repair maintenance function may be of a major nature or it may be a minor one. It may extend, to a few minutes, a few hours in a day or even a few days depending upon the size and complexity of the equipment, the nature of the fault and the availability of repair staff and equipment.

In other words, it is corrective maintenance. It restores an item to acceptable condition again.

(2) Preventive Maintenance: Repair maintenance attempts to repair the breakdowns, while preventive maintenance attempts to prevent any probable breakdowns resulting in production stoppages. It follows a slogan that "prevention is better than cure." It is also said that, "preventive maintenance is a stitch in time that saves nine." Preventive maintenance ensures smooth and continuous production flow. It eliminates any chances of breakdowns and industrial accidents. It controls vibration and noise transmission, and thus prevents any adverse effect on the morale of workers.

Preventive maintenance in other words is prophylactic, diagnostic or predictive maintenance, periodically carried out to reduce the probability of an equipment's condition falling below a required level of acceptability. Preventive maintenance can be made while the machines are running or when they are shut down.

Preventive maintenance is carried on as under:

(*i*) Elimination of overloading on equipment or plant services.

(*ii*) Regular cleaning, greasing and oiling of the moving parts.

(*iii*) Replacement of worn out parts before they fail to operate.

(*iv*) Periodic overhauling of the entire machine.

(*v*) Parts or equipments which are liable to sudden failures should be installed in duplicate, *e.g.*, pumps, transformers, compressors, motors etc.

(*vi*) For the key and critical machines, stand-by (extra) machines should be provided.

The preventive maintenance function is subdivided as under:

1. Preventive maintenance of production departments:
   (*i*) Anticipatory inspection and servicing of equipment.
   (*ii*) Routine maintenance.
2. Preventive maintenance of plant services.

Let us examine (1) Preventive maintenance of production department and (2) Preventive maintenance of plant services.

(1) Preventive maintenance of production departments: Production departments are directly contributing to the production operations and so the maintenance is strategic in nature. It is done as under:

(i) Anticipatory inspection and servicing of equipment: Anticipatory inspection is a time-scheduled inspection of all production departments conducted with a view to detect any wear and tear of the equipment or any plant. A predetermined schedule is prepared for the inspection of each part of the machines and equipment. Such scheduling is generally done by the plant engineer who is well conversant with the characteristic features of each machine and equipment. Generally, the inspecting and service functions are conducted during night, week-end days, holidays or slacks so that the production flow may not be interrupted.

(ii) Routine maintenance: The routine maintenance of the production department involves the cleaning of work-bench; cleaning, greasing and oiling of machines; tightening the bolts, recharging of batteries, replacing all the light bulbs in the plant area at some regular intervals etc. It is routine in the sense that it does not require any technicality. It is of a repetitive nature and is done more frequently than anticipatory inspection.

(2) Preventive maintenance of plant services: Preventive maintenance is equally important for the various types of plant services. Though they do not directly contribute to the production like other production departments, they play a key role in the production operations. The important plant services requiring preventive maintenance are ground and flooring, buildings, power plant, materials handling equipment, fleet of transport vehicles, water supply, waste disposal systems, storeroom, toolroom, timekeeper's office, fire fighting facilities etc.

It should be concluded that preventive maintenance is many times desirable than repair maintenance. Preventive maintenance does reduce the repairs, however, it cannot eliminate them because wear and tear is a common phenomenon. The time required for preventive maintenance and repairs should also be taken care of. If it takes just as long as to perform a plant maintenance as it does to repair the machine, there is no advantage in plant maintenance reducing the amount of time that the machine can work.

Preventive maintenance can be time-based or condition-based. The condition-based analysis uses a technique of 'Signature Analysis' which is nothing but a systematic record of signals or information emanating from the equipment which can give a clue to impending breakdown. Instruments are used to record various signals like vibrations, the condition of roller bearings etc. Condition-based preventive maintenance helps us avoid major disasters and accidents. However, this maintenance method is costly and requires specialist manpower. It is also not easy to monitor certain parameters.

Planned Maintenance

Preventive maintenance is the basis of planned maintenance. This is the best option where spare capacity is limited or non-existent. In flow-type production, the whole line can stop due to one single breakdown. It is, therefore, desirable to bear the cost of preventive maintenance. In batch-type production also, preventive maintenance is justified where some flexibility in the use of machines is possible.

When there is no spare capacity or very little spare capacity, maintenance becomes a must. Spare capacity whenever available can be exploited while the machines are under repair. This makes sense when expensive machines are in use. Spare parts are kept in stock if they are of importance. Their importance becomes obvious only if proper maintenance records of each machine is kept.

Preventive maintenance involves servicing the machines in advance. Maintenance plan guides us as to when this should be done, and at what frequency.

Maintenance Plan

1. First, the work to be done is defined. The statutory maintenance to prevent fire, pollution control, maintenance of elevators, cranes, disposal of wastes etc. is separated from other maintenance. Later, maintenance of plant and machinery is defined. Past records are used as guidelines. If no such records exist, we have to undertake work study and industrial

engineering to arrive at an estimate of frequency of routine maintenance required. This is integrated to future production plans.

2. Future work-load of maintenance operations is tackled by the use of suitable methods.
3. Work study indicates the potential maintenance capacity of our maintenance staff.
4. Maintenance plan is a bridge between potential work-load and our competence to carry it out. It is drawn for a year. Allowances are to be made for more breakdowns which occur in spite of preventive maintenance. The plan is revised in the light of feedback.

Maintenance Planning and Control

It is necessary to devise appropriate maintenance systems. In planned maintenance, maintenance request emanating from production staff details the defect and the possible rectification required. There is an Assets/Facilities Register where there is detailed description of each physical asset: name, code, vendors, spares vendors, interchangeable parts etc. The register is maintained on the basis of asset classification in terms of usage, technical category and maintenance methods.

(1) Scheduling of maintenance work: Scheduling refers to the timings and sequences of operations. It is an important segment of the production planning and control activity. However, it is equally important for the service operations like plant maintenance. The scheduling of the plant maintenance is desirable for the following reasons:

(*i*) Scheduling facilitates the optimum use of the highly paid maintenance staff. Proper scheduling reduces the idleness of maintenance crew.

(*ii*) The plant maintenance equipment can be utilised effectively through scheduling their uses.

(*iii*) It eliminates undue interruptions in the production flow. Maintenance works scheduled on night, week-end day, holiday etc. can ensure smooth flow of production operations.

(*iv*) Proper scheduling of the maintenance service eliminates the chances of abrupt breakdowns and equipment failures.

(*v*) It is sometimes necessary to maintain the sequence in providing the plant maintenance service, *e.g.*, clearance of clogged pipes and waste disposal. Scheduling facilitates the proper sequence in the maintenance service.

Maintenance schedules lead us to work/job specifications. It is a link between the engineer and the tradesman. It gives guidance in respect of method, and presents a work-load.

These are important steps for programming the annual and weekly maintenance programmes. After maintenance, an Inspection Report is produced. Other historical records are also kept pertaining to maintenance on manual or EDP basis for better planning.

Maintenance calls for planned lubrication, where what is to be lubricated, when it is to be lubricated, the lubrication of operation or how it is to be lubricated is decided.

Planned maintenance reduces emergency cases (they remain hardly 10 p.c.). We also have to determine work priority into several classes, facilities priority into several classes and arrive at Priority Index for any job (work priority × facilities priority) and can be expressed as a percentage.

Safety is always an important consideration. It is ensured by providing guards, protective clothing, power isolation fuses, safety valves for pressure systems, and issue of a permit to work on a particular machine by the maintenance staff.

Cost control of plant maintenance: Plant maintenance is an inevitable service function and so it should be provided with the lowest possible costs. Generally, plant maintenance cost is controlled through budgets. The amount of the budget provision largely depends on the management policy to have either over-maintenance or under-maintenance. The policy of under-maintenance reduces the cost of maintenance but increases the chances of breakdowns and the resultant losses. While the policy of over-maintenance increases the over consciousness of maintenance at high cost, efforts should be made to strike a balance between the two with a view to have the optimisation of this service. The distinction should be made between the revenue expenditure and capital expenditure on maintenance.

The foreman of each department should try to keep his revenue maintenance cost within the budgeted limits. The complete records of the maintenance cost should be maintained. The actual maintenance cost should be compared with the budgeted one and the discrepancies should be found out. Any significant adverse discrepancy should be investigated thoroughly so that the causes can be traced and their recurrence can be checked. Maintenance cost is nothing but an insurance against the future cost. It saves the future cost arising out of the breakdowns and the resultant losses. A reasonable comparison should be made between the current maintenance cost and the probable cost advantage arising out of the prevention of breakdown. According to **H. N. Broom,** in the light industry, the average maintenance cost should be 3% of sales income and in heavy industry, it should be 4% or more of the sales income. However, it would be proper to relate the maintenance cost of the scale of activity rather than the sales volume. It is generally found that too much emphasis is given to the reduction of the maintenance cost. This is not a wise policy. It is true that there is a possibility of savings in maintenance cost in certain respects, *e.g.,* painting of the building. However, as a policy, the maintenance cost should be saved in the light of the calculated risk.

Maintenance crew — size, remuneration, supervision and organization: The diversity of the maintenance functions is very large. Various types of maintenance staff are required to perform each of these functions. The type of the worker ranges from highly skilled to unskilled covering inspectors, mechanics, electricians, cleaners, plumbers, carpenters, painters, blacksmiths, pattern makers, welders, masons to ordinary labourers. The organization must try to define each function of maintenance and to spell out its responsibilities. Sufficient care should be taken to avoid any gapping or overlapping in defining the maintenance functions. The size of the maintenance crew will largely depend on the type of maintenance work, frequency of maintenance and other specific requirements of the unit. The specialist or generalists or operator-cum-repairer can be employed according to the need of the organization.

Generally, the maintenance staff is rewarded on time basis. As the maintenance work is of highly non-repetitive nature, it is difficult to set any standard of performance and so the payment of remuneration on piece-rate system is not feasible. Moreover, there is no ensured regularity of work like production departments. So mostly they are paid on time-rate method. However, a study conducted by the Du Pont Company of U.S.A., revealed that the maintenance staff is working below their capacity in relation to the operating staff, and so there is a case for implementation of wage-incentive plans for tapping the ability of the maintenance staff which is beneficial to both the company as well as the maintenance staff.

Where the workers are paid on the time-rate basis, it becomes highly essential to supervise their operations. The supervision of the maintenance staff poses a special problem. As their work assignments involve the scattered visits of extensive plant area, they go beyond the watchful eye of the supervisor. So the maintenance supervisors need a special type of skill and vision to handle the situation. Generally, the plant maintenance function is put under the control of the plant engineer. A plant engineer reports to the works manager and he generally heads the two main departments—"workshop" and "plant maintenance." The plant maintenance can again be sub-divided into building services, machine maintenance, other plant services according to the need of the organization.

Plant maintenance is continuous production and automation: In the continuous production, the production activity consists of the series of sequential operations, however, the whole system operates like a single large machine. There is a situation like everything in operation or everything idle. A delay of even few minutes proves very costly to the organization. Thus, preventive maintenance is very important in continuous production. In such a production system, some of the operations are designed with removable sections, which can be replaced immediately with spare sections or parts. For certain critical operations, the stand-by (extra) equipment are provided. However, this is possible only where the equipment is not very costly. The periodic checking and overhauling should be made for the whole system rather than the maintenance of the machines and equipments on piecemeal basis. Automation is an advancement of the continuous production system. The preventive maintenance is equally or a bit more important because here also the production system works on the full-working or nil-working basis. In continuous production, there is possibility of some flexibility because the stoppage of one part for few minutes can be tackled without the entire production stoppage. But under automation, the entire system is managed through push-button control. The machines are relatively more complex controlled through electronic devices. The maintenance supervisors are not called in case of need. In fact, they have to attend all the time as long as the system is in operation. They are required to patrol in anticipation of any required repairs.

Critical Analysis

Critical analysis is possible after a sufficient data-base is established about maintenance. It is generally observed that maintenance problems also follow the well-known Pareto's maxim (of the significant few and trivial many).

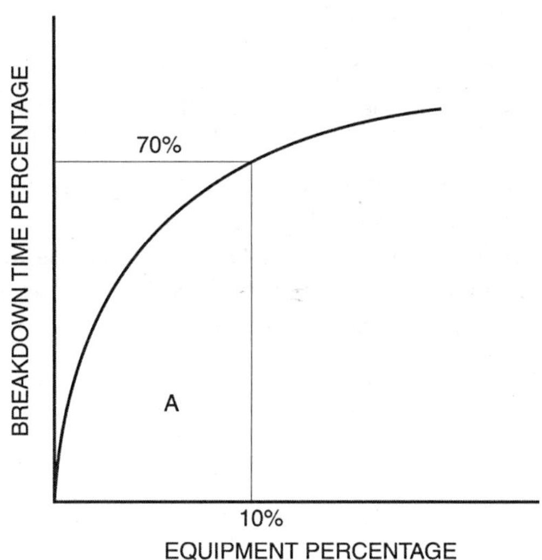

Fig. 18.4

A small percentage (about 10–15%) of equipment, as seen from the graph, contributes to about 70-75% of breakdown time. Let us call this equipment, A category equipment. In a similar fashion, a defect analysis also can be done, again proving that a small percentage of defect (10-15%) contributes to about 70% of breakdown time. We have to concentrate our control over A type of equipment, and A type of defects, since they are critical to the functioning of the system. Preventive maintenance for these A items is of utmost importance. We can try to eliminate or simplify or improve these items. Lubrication, though of great importance formerly, has been minimised due to better designs. There is an automatic lubricator also these days.

Maintenance Performance Ratios

Some ratios which could be used for measuring the effectiveness of maintenance function are:

$$\text{Waste Index} = \frac{\text{Waste Quantity (WQ)}}{\text{Output Quantity (OQ)}}$$

$$\text{Productivity of Maintenance} = \frac{\text{Output (product)}}{\text{Maintenance cost (product)}}$$

$$\text{Maintenance Cost Index} = \frac{\text{Maintenance cost}}{\text{Capital cost}} \times 100$$

$$\text{Breakdown Maintenance Index} = \frac{\text{Breakdown hours}}{\text{Manhours available}}$$

$$\text{Downtime Index} = \frac{\text{Downtime hours}}{\text{Production hours}} \times 100$$

Total Productive Maintenance (TPM)

Maintenance is the key to zero loss, zero breakdowns, zero accidents, zero defects. It is in short a zero-sum philosophy. This concept was put forward by the Japanese management expert Seiichi Nakajima in his gospel *Introduction to Total Production Maintenance* in 1984. The ultimate aim was to maximise the output-to-input ratios. It aims to improve capital productivity. Maintenance is no longer considered as reactive problem fixing but as pro-active planning and management. When we adopt TPM, maintenance no longer remains confined to the maintenance department, but spreads as company-wide culture. It aims at better capacity utilisation. It ensures total effectiveness of the plant by tackling utilization, quality and down-time. At Bajaj Auto plant in Pune, they follow the idea of Total Productive Maintenance (TPM) for many years.

TOTAL PRODUCTIVE MAINTENANCE (TPM) AND TQM

Two Japanese gurus Yoshikazu Tsuda (64) and Sueo Yamaguchi (52) have been proponents of total quality. Tsuda is a retired professor of mathematics. He is now a counsellor at the Union of Japanese Scientists and Engineers (JUSE). Yamaguchi works at the Japanese Institute of Plant Management (JIPM) which is a temple of Total Productive Maintenance (TPM). Tsuda goes top-down, and Yomaguch bottom up. Yamaguchi is teaching TPM to Indian companies. The steps in TPM programme are:

1. Plant audit and assessment
2. Company commitment
3. Formation of committees and sub-committees
   - TPM promotion committee
   - TPM steering committee
   - Jishu Hozen sub-committee
   - Kaizen sub-committee
   - Planned maintenance sub-committee
   - Quality maintenance sub-committee
   - Office TPM sub-committee
   - Planning and design sub-committee
   - Education and Training sub-committee
   - Safety and Environment sub-committee
4. Selection of pilot line(s)
5. Focus on eight pillars
   - Autonomous maintenance
   - Improvement activities
   - Zero loss
   - Zero defect
   - Efficiency of support services
   - Institution of flow control systems
   - Zero accidents
6. Raise levels and select other areas
7. Focus on eight pillars in new areas.

What Leads to TPM Excellence?

1. Promotion, monitoring and reviewing
2. TPM results
3. Raising levels and revising standards.

Based on the study of American Preventive Maintenance (PM) techniques between 1950 and 1970, Yamaguchi crafted the concept of TPM in 1971. TPM and TQM complement each other. There is never a conflict. Many companies implement TPM after TQM in India.

Tsuda is teaching TQM to Indian companies. The basic steps are:

1. Plant audits and assessments
2. Good housekeeping practices
3. Selection of pilot line
4. Emphasise worker safety
5. Focus on 5-S which define standards of cleanliness and housekeeping
   - Seri (Clearing)
   - Seiton (Organizing)
   - Seiso (Cleaning)
   - Seiketsu (Standardising)
   - Shitsuke (Training)
6. Sunrise/sunset meetings
7. PDC Cycle introduced
8. Gap analysis/standardisation
9. Management system.

Tsuda examines the vision and strategy of a company, and current practices of quality. He organizes learning companies into clusters.

Yamaguchi tries to change the mind-set about the real value of TPM. He expects personal commitment of the CEO. He wants middle-management participation.

TPM Companies in India

India can now boast of 141 TPM (total productive maintenance) companies that have been certified by the Japanese. The operational equipment efficiencies of these companies are of a very high order of 85 per cent.

☙ ❧

19

JOB ANALYSIS, JOB DESCRIPTION AND JOB SPECIFICATION

Introduction

Scientific management has brought about a great change in the industrial atmosphere. A few questions which were considered to be of no great importance in the past have come to be recognised as no less important than anything else. Let us see one or two of such questions. Which type of person should be selected for a particular position? How should a particular work be done so that it is performed in the best manner? Managers no more reply to this question with authoritarian approach. Each job is systematically studied to answer all such questions. The thorough study of the job will find out the nature of the job, qualifications necessary to be possessed by a person to do the job effectively, etc. The study of the job can also give comparative value of each job and the proper pay for each job can also be indicated by the study. Let us first of all be familiar with different words used in scientific study of work.

Job

Job is an activity involving a particular set of duties and functions and which can be assigned to an individual employee, for example typing is a job. Many employees may be doing one type of job (*i.e.,* there may be a number of typists in a firm).

"A job is defined as an assignment of work calling for a set of duties and conditions that are different from those of other work assignments."[1]

Job Analysis

The personnel tool with which the duties, responsibilities, operations, conditions and organizational aspects of a particular job are studied, specified and clearly enumerated is job analysis. The job analysis is a procedure by which the facts with respect to each job were systematically discovered and noted.[2]

Job Description

The information gathered by job analysis is very much detailed. When this information is presented in a concise form and in an orderly manner, it becomes job description. Here, the name of the job, its functions, the machines and instruments used, hours of work, conditions of work, and personnel requirements of the job are mentioned.

Job Specification

Job description prepared on the basis of job analysis gives complete details about the job. But, all this information is not necessary for selection of employees. From the job specification, the portion

1. *Dynamic Personnel Administration* — M.N. Rudrabasavaraj, p. 99.
2. *Dynamic Personnel Administration* — M.N. Rudrabasavaraj, p. 100.

stating skills, abilities and qualifications expected of the employees is prepared separately which is known as job specification.

Job Evaluation

A comparative study of all the jobs is made to determine the value of each job when compared with other jobs. This is known as job evaluation. The idea of wages payable for each job can be gathered by job evaluation.

Merit Rating

In job evaluation, only the job was thought of; but in merit rating the attention is given towards the employee performing the job. Here the importance of the employee in the business, his abilities, intelligence, training, education, etc., are compared with the other employee and amount payable to him in the form of wages/salary can be determined.

Now, after knowing the introductory part, let us study each of the above listed things in detail.

Job Analysis

(a) Meaning and Definition

Job analysis is a process by which minute details of a job are accurately collected. It includes the functions and conditions of the job as well as personnel requirements of the job. In the words of ***Mr. Milton Blum,*** "Job analysis is an accurate study of the various components of a job." Job study is another name of job analysis. "Job analysis is the process by which data in regard to each job is systematically observed and noted. It provides information about the nature of the job and the characteristics or qualifications that are desirable in a job holder."[3]

Dale Yodar says that job analysis can be helpful in getting information regarding the following matters:

(1) The requirements of the job. For example, the job requires polishing semi-finished goods.

(2) The method of doing the job. The machines and instruments used for the job and the order of doing the work.

(3) What types and amount of skill is required to perform the job effectively, can also be known by job analysis. For example, a typing speed of 50 w.p.m. is one of the requirements for the job of a clerk.

(4) The amount of experience necessary for the job, the opportunities for promotion, etc.

Moreover, matters like the information of raw materials used, the amount of risk involved in the job, geographical atmosphere of the working place, hygienic conditions, etc. are also studied under job analysis.

The above discussion clarifies one point, that in job analysis two factors are observed: (*i*) To get detailed information about the job itself; and (*ii*) To get information about the employees, *i.e.,* what should be skills, abilities and qualifications of the employee who is supposed to perform the job. Here one point should be clearly noted. In job analysis, qualities of an individual employee are not to be studied. In fact, no employee is considered as far as job analysis is concerned. Job analysis is solely concerned with the job and the personnel requirements of the job. The necessary physical, mental and intellectual qualities expected of the employee who is to be assigned the job are enlisted.

In the 'Guide for Analysing Jobs' prepared by War Manpower Commission of United States, a four-point formula is given to get information of job analysis. The four points are in the following questions form:

1. What is done by the employee?
2. How does the employee perform the job?

---

3. *Personnel Management* — Arun Monappa, Mirza S. Saiyadin.

3. Why does he perform the job?
4. What skills are necessary for performance of the job?

After understanding the meaning of the job analysis, let us see the types of job analysis.

(b) Types of Job Analysis

Two types of job analysis can be found considering the objective of the job analysis. They are: (*i*) Single-purpose job analysis; and (*ii*) Multi-purpose job analysis.

(i) Single-purpose job analysis: If the job analysis is meant to fulfil one single purpose, then the job analysis will be known as single-purpose job analysis. Such job analysis is done to assist in solving some particular problem.

(ii) Multi-purpose job analysis: As the name itself indicates such job analysis is meant to serve a number of purposes. The objective may be better selection of employees, better training programme, better control, etc. Obviously, multi-purpose job analysis is of far more importance than the single-purpose analysis.

(c) Process of Job Analysis

The entire process of job analysis can be divided into following stages:

1. To determine the objectives.
2. To decide what information is to be gathered.
3. To collect the required information.
4. To present properly the collected information.
5. To analyse the collected information and take decisions.

Let us see each of these stages one by one in their respective order.

(1) To determine the objective: It is impossible to decide on the mode of journey before we know where we want to go. Similarly, before undertaking any activity we should be clear about its objective. Job analysis is no exception from this canon. Thus, we should first of all decide the objectives of the job analysis before we proceed any further. The clarity of objective will help in stopping waste of time, money and energy and will direct the entire process of the right path.

(2) To decide what information is to be gathered: What information is necessary to fulfil our objective should also be decided so that time, money and energy spent on collecting information doesn't go in vain. We saw the job analysis formula given by 'War Man-power Commission' of U.S.A. earlier in the chapter.

The formula includes the nature and conditions of the job (WHAT), the process of job, machines and instruments used and the process for their use (HOW), the objective of the job (WHY) and the qualities required from the employee (SKILLS).

(3) To collect the required information: One or more of the following methods can be used to collect the required information:

(*i*) Questionnaire.
(*ii*) Interview.
(*iii*) Observation.
(*iv*) Other Methods.

(i) Questionnaire

This is an old and well-known method of collecting information. A questionnaire containing the questions pertaining to the job is given to the employee. Some directions are given and the employee is asked to reply the questions. Sometimes this method is known as self-analysis. In small firms, the number of questions is limited. However, in big concerns questionnaire sometimes extends up to five or six pages. Two types of questions are asked in questionnaire. The following questions constitute the first part:

(*a*) Description of the job.

(*b*) What special knowledge is necessary for the job.

(*c*) How much experience is necessary for performance of the job.

(*d*) How much time does the employee have to work for successful performance of his job.

The second part will include questions relating the following things:

(*a*) What is his daily work.

(*b*) What is his weekly work.

(*c*) What is his monthly work.

(*d*) The detail of his special duties, if any.

(*e*) Criticism of the job.

The filling of questionnaire by the employees themselves saves time and money. But this method is useless for illiterate employees. However, special employees can be kept to question the illiterate employees and fill up the questionnaire.

(ii) Interview

In this method, a trained analyst interviews the employees and gathers the required information. This is a relatively expensive method. Interviews can be held in two ways. The interviewer may go to the spot where the employees are working and take their interviews; or he may call the employees one by one or in groups of twos and threes in his office and take their interviews.

(iii) Observation

Instead of questioning the employees, here, the analyst goes on the shop-floor, observes the working of the employees, and gathers the first hand information. However, he may ask the supervisor or the employee himself regarding certain complex matters. This method can help in collecting far more accurate information; but the basic requisites are that the analyst should know the job pretty well and he should have enough time for his observations.

(iv) Other Methods

One of the methods not discussed above is the conference method. In this method, a conference of workers, supervisors and related officers is held, and information is gathered by discussions. However, this method may interrupt the regular functioning of the organization.

Moreover, combinations of different methods may be formed. For example, the employees may be asked to fill up a questionnaire; supervisors may be interviewed to check the validity of the information given in the questionnaire; and finally a conference may be held.

After collection of the information the step which will logically follow is the presentation of the information.

(4) To present the information: The heap of the collected information will not serve any purpose. The information should be properly arranged in a certain order. Only after proper arrangement of information it would be possible to gather some meaning from the information. The inter-related information should be put together and a certain order should be maintained to present the information.

At this point, it will be fair to switch over the goal of doing all this exercise, *i.e.*, taking decisions on the basis of the information collected.

(5) To analyse the collected information and take decisions: Now, we arrive at the end-point of the job-analysis process, the aim of all the labour. The information collected should be interpreted properly and necessary decisions should be taken. However, the interpretation of the information would be affected by the objective of the job analysis and so the objective of the job analysis remains in the centre while making decisions.

(d) Utility (Advantage) of Job Analysis

(*i*) Job analysis makes the work of personnel department scientific and more efficient. For example, as job analysis determines the skills of the jobber, proper kind of employees can be recruited. So, the problems of misreplacements don't arise. As a result, productivity of employees will increase and they will achieve greater job satisfaction. Similarly, it will be equally helpful for promotions, transfers, etc.

(*ii*) Control of the work of employees also becomes easy. The administrative decisions taken after knowing all the details of the job are bound to be better. Moreover, the management can also have an idea of how much each employee should work.

(*iii*) The deficiencies of motion of the worker can be noted and corrected. This will help in reducing the exhaustion of workers and for improving the methods of working. Thus, productivity can be raised.

(*iv*) Job analysis can give an idea about the risks and possibilities of accidents for a job. Steps can be taken to eliminate these chances and accidents' rate can be brought down. In other words, it is helpful for security programme of the company.

(*v*) As the detailed information about the job is available it will help to understand the job better. This will assist in making decisions as to what the employees should be taught and how should they be taught. Thus, job analysis is helpful in preparing training programmes.

(*vi*) Job analysis can also be useful for scientific wage and salary administration. It provides information regarding the efforts necessary for performance of job, skills required, experience essential and risks involved in the job. On the basis of all this a scientific wage and salary policy can be decided.

(*vii*) Job analysis is also very important for professional guidance. It specifies the requirements of each job and would help in determining for which job a particular person is suitable. This will provide professional guidance to that person.

(*viii*) The job analysis helps in establishment of scientific wage and salary administration policy, which will reduce the scope of industrial dispute.

(*ix*) In short, job analysis is useful to keep up maximum efficiency in an industrial unit and better manpower planning.

We end our discussion on job analysis and proceed on to job description.

Job Description: Meaning and Explanation

To present properly the lot of information gathered by job analysis in a manner that will help in selection of employees is job description. In short, it is the concise form of job analysis.

The following information is given in job description:

1. Title of the job.[4]
2. Description of the job in brief.
3. Functions of the job.
4. The instruments, machines and tools used for the job.
5. The working conditions (*i.e.,* lighting, temperature, ventilation, etc.).
6. Training necessary for the job and facilities of the training.
7. The interrelationship of this job with other jobs. (From which position can a person be promoted to this position and the position where employee can be promoted from this job.)

4. Dictionary of Occupational Titles — prepared in the U.S.A. contains descriptions of more than 20,000 jobs.

8. What are the requirements for the performance of the job?
   (*a*) Physical qualities.
   (*b*) Intellectual qualities.
   (*c*) Experience.
9. What salary is paid for the job?

The following points should be kept in mind for job description:

1. While doing job description special care should be taken towards our language. The reader can't understand anything or misunderstands something if the language is ambiguous. For the same reason, technical jargon should not be used in job description.
2. No exaggerations should be made while listing job requirements. For example, if the education up to S.S.C. is sufficient for the performance of the job, it should not be mentioned that the education up to graduate level is required for the job.
3. If the job description is designed for the purpose of division of work, special care should be taken so that there is no conflict between the employees regarding their areas of duties. It should be clearly mentioned in the job specification that the duties of each job can be expanded, when felt necessary. Thus, no employee will be able to say that he is not required to do a certain work.

Difference between Job Analysis and Job Description

1. In job analysis all the information regarding the job is collected. Whereas in case of job description the collected information is clearly, concisely and systematically stated.
2. Job description is meant for some special purpose. When a part of the detailed information gathered by job analysis is systematically presented for some purpose, it becomes job description.
3. The above discussion clearly explains that job analysis is in a detailed form; whereas job description is in a condensed form.

Utility of Job Description

1. Job description helps in getting the idea of the nature of the job and its functions. Particularly it enables the new employees to understand their duties and responsibilities.
2. Job description makes the work of personnel department easier. It helps a lot in matters like recruitment, training, transfers, etc.

Job Specification

Job specifications describe the job, the minimum requirements in relation to the workers' qualifications and abilities to perform the job, and the working conditions.

The 'Job specification, a product of job analysis and a refined form of job description, may contain the duties of the job and the type of employee required, in terms of skill, education, experience, special aptitude, etc.'[5]

Details: Generally job specification should contain the personnel requirements of job. But, sometimes description of the job is also given to give an idea of the job to the employee.

1. First of all, the nature of the job is explained in the job specification.
2. The required skills for the performance of the job are mentioned, particularly the following information is given:
   (*a*) Intellectual requirements.
   (*b*) Educational qualifications.
   (*c*) Physical requirements — like height, weight, sight, age, etc.
   (*d*) Necessary skills and the amount and type of training necessary.

5. *Dynamic Personnel Administration* — M.N. Rudrabasavaraj.

3. The working conditions of the job are also mentioned. However, the greater emphasis is put on the required skills from the employees.

The main objective of job specification is to help in personnel management. It is particularly helpful in recruitment of right person at the right place. It is also useful for promotions and transfers.

Difference between Job Description and Job Specification

1. Job description describes the job, while job specification specifies the skills expected of the employee for the performance of the job.
2. The aim of the job description is to get brief information about the job; whereas the objective of job specification is to determine the qualities of the employees.
3. Job description is concerned with the job and not with the employee; while the job specification is concerned with employee and not with the job.

Standardisation in India

The Indian national standards body is BIS. It has formulated more than 15,000 standards. It operates BIS Certification Marks Scheme. It is operated under the Bureau of Indian Standards Act. Those manufacturers who meet these standards on verification get licence to use Standards Mark. There are periodic inspections of the factory and testing of samples drawn. BIS has adopted ISO 9000 series of standards on quality.

☙ ❧

20

JOB EVALUATION AND COMPENSATION PLANS

Introduction

The widely accepted financial incentives to employees in most of the organizations are conceptualised as wages and salaries. Obviously, monetary incentives are meant for the satisfaction of primary needs as well as the secondary needs. As individuals organize mainly to fulfil their personal needs it is important that they are compensated fairly. The very first problem in wage and salary administration is the setting up of the base compensation for jobs, assigned to individuals. To keep organization running and to attract and retain required personnel, there should be methods available to rate jobs for equitable reward. Job evaluation is the method used for comparing all the jobs within the organization and for obtaining internal and external consistency in wages and salaries.

Job Evaluation

There is considerable ambiguity among the terms job evaluation, job analysis, job description and job specification. Job analysis is the collection of data and the critical evaluation of the operations, duties and relationships. Job description is the written record of duties, responsibilities and requirements of a particular job. While job specification, is written statement showing the aptitude, qualification, experience etc. that would be necessary to perform a particular job. Another result of job analysis is job evaluation. The concept of job evaluation has altogether different meaning. Strictly speaking, job evaluation is the method of precisely fixing the relationships between jobs and wage rates. In the simplest words, job evaluation is the rating of jobs according to their worth.

Different authors have dealt with the definition of the term in their own way. To define it in a concise manner we can say "job evaluation is the systematic, analytical scrutiny of all the jobs in the organization, with a view to compare all the jobs among themselves and to rate them according to the requirements." The main purpose of job evaluation is to maintain the consistency in wage rates, *i.e.,* a senior foreman should be paid more than a shift foreman.

The rationale behind job evaluation is to reward employees fairly, which helps the organization to attract and retain them. On the part of employees it provides them the motivation for the betterment of performance and their effectiveness. Equitable compensation relates to the problem of attracting and retaining employees which motivation directly refers to the monetary and non-monetary incentives.

Equity and justice coincide according to natural law. It is clearly experienced that greater the feelings of equity, the more will be the equilibrium. When the employee receives compensation, his equity perception is affected by two factors: (1) Effort-output ratio, *i.e.,* what are the inputs given by employee in terms of physical and mental effort, training, education and how he works and furnishes task and how they are rewarded. Thus, compensation to the work accomplished by employee has great impact in the future performance and it also shows an impact on the mental adjustment. If numerator is low and denominator is high, *i.e.*, if the ratio is low, it leads to dissatisfaction which results in low performance, less effectiveness and low productivity. On the other hand, high ratio can also lead to overall dissatisfaction arising out of overpayment. Employee will feel guilty and try to work more to show that he actually deserves. So equity concept balances these two extremes and accordingly gives a rational basis to work out the wages and salaries. (2) The comparison of above ratio with other person's ratio with whom he has direct contact.

The dynamics of contribution and pay may clearly be understood from Fig. 20.1.

Fig. 20.1

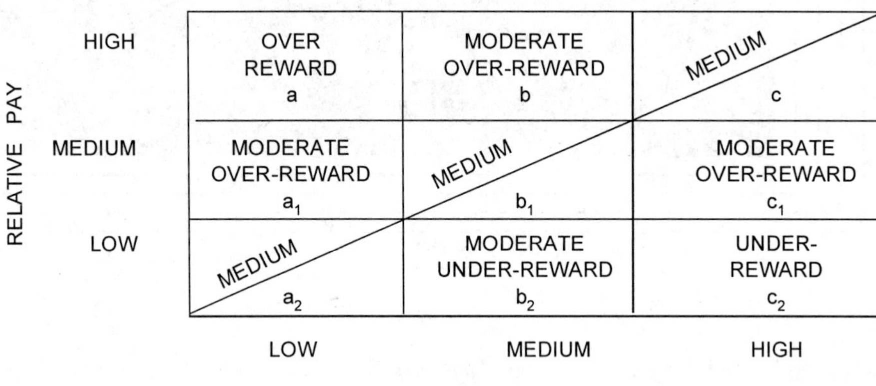

Cells, a_2, b_1 and c would result in perception of equity. The remaining cells show feeling of disagreement. Apparently, there should be lower level of satisfaction in cell c_1, b_2 and c_2 than equity or overpaid cells. Generally, cells a, b, and a_1 would lead to guilt and discomfort which induce employee to work more to reduce imbalance. So, in general, grouped under a, b and a_1 cells are less dissatisfied than group under cells c_1, b_2 and c_2. Individuals in cell b, a_1, c_1, b_2 are more satisfied as they are near equity line. Even any change in working condition, or environment change would not raise productivity of dissatisfied group. ***Herzberg*** concluded that the pay is not the motivator of employee behaviour. However, the equity concept indicates that more often than not, it (the problem) is not the inability of pay to motivate but it is problem of improper design of a wage plan.

'Earth is round' — the same way, we have come at the point where we left the discussion of job evaluation. So job evaluation is that system which decides the equitable compensation to the employees by keeping in mind the common wage structure of industry. Job evaluation always intends fair reward with an aim to raise productivity, efficiency etc. There is every possibility, in practice, that after application of the system some may get high pay, while others may not. This fact, however, does not undermine the importance of job evaluation. It would therefore, be useful to discuss various techniques available for job evaluation. But rather than going straight to that point, what type of role trade union plays in working out the system, should also be seen.

Contribution of Trade Union to Job Evaluation

Trade union is an organized group of employees who come together to strengthen their bargaining position and to put group efforts towards realisation of management goals. 'Trade unions' of workers, supervisors etc., exist but generally, in India workers' union is a more common phenomenon.

Workers, who have main objective to fulfil their personnel needs through organizing and rendering services, expect reward in terms of money. So directly, the trade union is concerned with job evaluation.

Usually, workers carry a biased view when analysing the role of management, *i.e.*, management is our boss and boss is always concerned with how to cut the benefits given to the workers and in turn reduce labour cost. Obviously, one of the objective is to cut the costs. However, an understanding of the healthy relation between management and trade union helps to ease the cut-off rate idea.

Economic and other motivational factors lead people to work. Economical needs motivate people to work to get something in return for the services rendered. So, establishment of the fair wage rate is necessary and as such union's attitude toward job evaluation is very significant.

The only weapon in the hands of trade union is collective bargaining, which the union thinks is taken away by applying the job evaluation system. In India, collective bargaining, which is mainly brought to the fore to deal with wage fixation, the application of job evaluation lessens the chance for unions to gain strength as they feel it would defeat the very objective of the existence of trade unions.

Some unions argue that job evaluation weakens the bargaining strength and makes it impossible to work out adjustments matched to individual needs. It is interesting to note that the concept of job evaluation is well recognised among unions even before management has given serious thought to this system. Unions agree that the jobs having the same requirement should be given equal wage and thus believe in equity-centered approach. So job evaluation for trade union is merely a systematic framework for negotiation. It reduces grievances and disputes.

Well designed job evaluation helps business firm in more than one way.

(*a*) Being a systematic process, job evaluation fixes the wage rate for each job.

(*b*) It is considered to be simple as it is easily understood by all.

(*c*) It establishes the equitable wage rate for all the jobs, according to the job requirements.

(*d*) Company training programme, placement, recruitment selection and long range manpower planning always follow job evaluation.

(*e*) It enables company to get data for incorporation in local wage surveys to establish job classification.

All these contribute to healthy, sound and equitable wage structure in organization. But in practice, the role of trade union varies from outright opposition to complete participation. In many cases unions involve and provide full participation. In such a case, local unions select members who are trained by management and form a joint union-management committee to work out and install a job evaluation system.

The main reason for unwillingness on the part of trade union is that they feel it is not their job. There is always dispute among the members to settle status.

When several unions exist in an organization, it becomes even more difficult to apply this system. Thus, one of the primary objectives of job evaluation is to devise a fair wage structure that workers would accept. So, relations between two parties are significant and depend on how flexible the management is towards its policy. Thus, for the success of any job evaluation system it is absolutely imperative that the system gets the support of unions.

Techniques of Job Evaluation

Many techniques are used for the measurement of jobs. All forms of job evaluation are designed to enable management to determine how much one job should be paid as compared to others.

Basically, all systems of job evaluation can be classified under two broad categories: (1) Non-quantitative and (2) Quantitative. Simple ranking and grading are placed in non-quantitative category while point system and factor comparison methods are under quantitative category. The most widely used method is point system and the least is ranking system. One company can apply two methods for two different types of jobs. But, generally, all the four methods are useful and real effectiveness of any method would depend on how best they are applied. ***Thomas Atkinson*** and ***Wendell French*** tried to inter-correlate these four systems and found intercorrelation to be as high as 0.94.

(a) Simple Ranking: This method is widely used in small organizations. Being a very simple and not expensive method, it also consumes less time and promises enough potential in its usefulness. Before actual ranking, brief job descriptions of all the jobs are taken. Then a job-evaluation committee is asked to place all the jobs in the order of their relative worth, without any other consideration. In the beginning of process, the highest and lowest jobs are determined which serve as the bench marks for the ranking of the remainder. The second method is the paired comparison techniques in which each job is to be compared with all other jobs.

Once the comparison is done, jobs are arranged according to their worth. In this technique, the main idea is to rank jobs in the order of their worth. The simplicity of this method is rather deceptive.

The defects of the simple ranking method are great:

(*i*) Simplicity is one of the disadvantages as it tends to make measurement somewhat crude.

(*ii*) Measurement of whole job, *i.e.*, all the factors affecting the job are not considered.

(*iii*) Absence of predetermined yardstick leads to personal bias.

The end product of this method is a list of jobs, in order of their worth, *i.e.*:

Rank	***Job***
1	A
2	B
3	C
4	D
5	E

Here, the main assumption is that the difference between A and B is equal to that between B and C, which does not always hold good. To avoid this limitation, key jobs are selected and plotted on the graph against the money value of these jobs. Then all the remaining jobs are relatively compared with the key jobs and the money worth of these jobs is determined.

(b) Job Grading: In ranking we do not have pre-decided scale of value, but here there is one yardstick consisting of job classes. In this approach, job factors approach is not considered. Jobs are rather measured as a whole.

A scale of values consisting of grades and grade descriptions is prepared. Job grades are determined for a category of jobs. From this, the grade descriptions are prepared which should be broad enough to include several jobs. Such grade descriptions cover job descriptions as well.

Two approaches are used in preparing grade descriptions which help to create a single scale of values for measuring the worth of a job. For example, in an enterprise, job A and B are of similar nature and job X, Y, Z are of similar nature. Another, approach is to give grade definitions by a committee in advance. Such definitions are then compared with some known key jobs.

When the yardstick is established, the next step is to read out job description, the grade description and allocating the jobs to one particular grade. The jobs falling under the same grade get the same wage scale.

No doubt it is an improvisation, yet this method suffers from some defects:

(*i*) Being broad generalisation of jobs, there are chances of dissatisfaction among certain group of job-holders.

(*ii*) Grading system requires multiple-system because grading of clerical job may be quite different from that of operative jobs.

But besides these defects, this method is otherwise simple and inexpensive. One benefit of this system is that the grading arrives at a series of clauses.

Point System

This system is widely used in job evaluation. It is quantitative, analytical and detailed approach hammered out to derive a balanced wage structure with least dispute among employees. This method consists of the following steps:

(*a*) Select job factors or features.

(*b*) Prepare yardstick of value for each job factor.

(*c*) Decide the value of all the jobs against the predetermined yardsticks.

(*d*) Build a wage survey for selected key jobs.

(*e*) Design the wage structure.

(*f*) Adjust and operate the wage structure.

(a) Selection of Job Factors

Ranking system and grading system measure job as a whole. This is the first approach which breaks down jobs into several essential or salient characteristics. The number of characteristics vary with the organizations. A job factor is defined as a specific requirement levied upon the jobholder, which he must endure. To say, if a person occupies a position as a supervisor, he is expected to work, to supervise, to motivate employees. Thus, he has to put some physical effort, besides mental. His responsibility is much more than that of a worker. Job factors are generally enumerated as follows:

(1) Efforts (2) Responsibility

(3) Skill (4) Working conditions

These abilities are input of employees for which they get compensation. There can be many sub-divisions within each of these factors.

Skill	***Responsibility***	***Effort***	***Working Condition***
Education Experience Initiative	Equipment or process Material or product Safety of others Work of others	Physical effort Mental effort	Work condition Hazards

Usually the number of such sub-factors are kept at 10 or 11. But the more the number of sub-factors, the greater will be accuracy due to detailed specification. The measurement of skill is achieved by taking into account education, experience and ingenuity. Responsibility refers to the accountability for the time and value of things. Effort refers to the putting and applying physical and mental efforts on the job. While working condition obviously deals with what one may call safety precautions.

These factors are decided from the job contents. But job contents alter as technology and level of automation change in the organization. In other words, job evaluation system should change with the change in technology. As the degree of automation is increased, the job evaluation should give more weightage to higher education, higher responsibility, higher mental efforts.

The new concept is suggested by Elliott Jacques. It takes into account the various key factors that will tell on the overall performance of a job.

In spite of several job factors, only one factor 'time span of discretion' is used. The actual meaning is this — the longest period of time during which employees are allowed to work without any supervision by superior. Allowance of work includes the exercise of discretion, initiative and judgement. Thus clearly, the time span of discretion is weighted in respect of responsibility, which is common for all the jobs. The essence behind this approach is, those employees who enjoy equal time span of discretion should be rewarded equally.

(b) Construction of the Yardsticks

The construction of yardsticks is done by deciding the total points assigned or to be utilized in a system. The most important decision to be taken is what proportion of total points to be allocated to skill, effort, responsibility and working condition. That is to say, a decision is taken that if the total point in a system would be 1,000, then what could be the percentage contribution of each factor.

The determination of this will depend upon the nature of the organization, *i.e.*, an enterprise with high automation technology should assign more points for responsibility since the manual skill is translated into machine skill. But generally, skill is given more weightage than responsibility, efforts and working conditions. If we decide 1000 point for a system, then it could be divided as:

Factor	*Number of Points*	*Percentage*
Skill	500	50
Responsibility	200	20
Effort	150	15
Working condition	150	15
Total	1000	100

Skill and responsibility will vary with the situation. Assignment of points to the various factors is subjective. After the yardstick is developed the composition of points and degrees of the particular factors are worked out. For example, let us consider that of the total value 140 points are allocated to education. Then a **seven**-point scale could be developed as follows:

Education

1. Read write add and subtract 20
2. Two years high school or equivalent 40
3. Four years high school or two years Univ. or equivalent 60
4. Four years high school plus 2–3 years trade training 80
5. Four years high school plus 4 years trade training 100
6. Two or three years college plus 4 years trade training 120
7. Four years college degree plus 4 years trade training 140

This type of job evaluation manual is prepared by an outside agency or by the individual engineering experts of the company. To prepare a manual is a tiresome and time-consuming process. So most of the companies like to use ready-made manual prepared industry-wise by external agencies. Here the defect is that the agency prepares manual keeping in mind the industry as a whole and because of this, a company may find some deviations in factors or degrees. But still the manual is the best for most of the companies.

(c) Evaluation of the Job

Evaluation of job demands the construction of reliable yardstick and detailed job specifications. Now the process of evaluation is very simple. The process consists of reading the job specifications carefully and comparing the information with the degree on yardstick and placing it accordingly. Adding up all the points give the points worth of that job.

In reality, a committee is appointed to evaluate jobs. The participants should have familiarity with the job to be rated. The degree of familiarity has impact on:

(*a*) Adaptability (*b*) Decision-making

(*c*) Mental work (*d*) Working conditions

(*e*) Managerial requirements.

The more detailed the job specification, the higher are the chances of accurate rating. Thus job specifications do much and they are preventive tools to check in case of any differences of opinions among the members of rating committee.

(d) Wage Survey

Once jobs have been evaluated and all the points have been summed up, the next step is placing of all evaluated jobs according to points in terms of money. This is the point when rated jobs are translated into monetary values. To conduct wage survey the existing rates are taken for comparison. The main purpose of wage survey, is to find out the fair rate for various jobs in order to establish the entire wage structure. Selection of key jobs whose duties are clearly defined, not unstable and mostly representing all level of jobs worth, is the very first step in building a wage survey. For the wage survey, two types of samples are needed. First, sample of key jobs and second, a sample of firms in the labour market. Jobs require different personnel, in terms of skill, ability, etc. and thus it varies from local to regional level. Selection of a sample of firms should be from those firms which operate under similar market conditions.

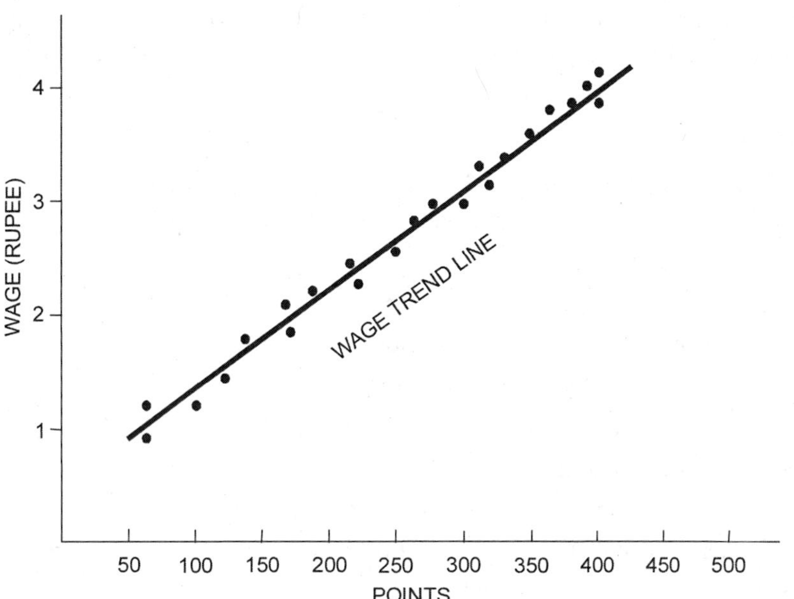

Fig. 20.2

The job content and available data are carefully analysed and averaged out, and in this way the rupee values of jobs are prepared and plotted on the chart.

By plotting key jobs against their existing wages, we get a wage-trend line which lies close to all the jobs plotted on the graph. The wage-trend line should be drawn in such a way that it covers most of the points. Those which lie below the line should be paid more to come on the line of best fit. But simultaneously the authority and responsibility should also be increased in line with the wage increase. And as all those which are above the best fit line cannot be paid lower than the existing wage rate, all such rates should be freezed.

If we want to know what are the deviations, slopes of X-axis and Y-axis are taken. To calculate accurately and to forecast, regression analysis can be applied, in which one is dependent variable and another is independent. From this regression, the expected value of Y can be obtained, when X is known.

(e) Designing the Wage Structure

In construction of wage structure similar jobs are grouped and treated as a job class. All the jobs, which come under that job class are paid the same wage. In the point system, suppose, 120 points to 150 points make a job class. In such case, all the jobs which fetch total between 120 and 150 would carry the same monetary compensation. The purpose of grouping of jobs is to facilitate wage administration.

Factors affecting the designing of the wage structure are:

(*a*) Labour market condition: If supply of labour is higher than demand, the wage would be relatively low.

(*b*) Economic condition of the country: That is, if standard of living is high it calls for higher wage.

(*c*) Wage structures of other firms in the same industry directly affect the company's wage structure.

(*d*) Sometimes, even though the competitors pay relatively higher wage, due to weak collective bargaining power of the trade union, management may settle wage at a relatively low rate.

(f) Adjustment and Operation of Wage Structure

These factors lead to adjustment in the wage structure. All wages should be paid within limits which is given by the standard set through a wage structure. A cardinal principle of wage and salary administration is that wage rate shall not be cut, as a result of installation of job evaluation. So, red circle rates should be placed at proper place by means of appropriate measurement. Adjustments in the total rate structure should also be akin to the percentage increment in order to maintain equitable relationship.

Factor Comparison System

Improved method of ranking system is known as factor comparison system where job factors are compared rather than the whole jobs. It consists of the following steps:

(*a*) Selection of job characteristics.

(*b*) Selection of key jobs.

(*c*) Determination of correct rates of key jobs.

(*d*) Ranking of key jobs under each job factor.

(*e*) Allocation of correct rate to each key job.

(*f*) Evaluation of all other jobs.

(*g*) Designing, adjusting and operating the wage structure.

The first three steps are quite similar to that of point system. While the fourth one, is the ranking of all the key jobs, to a particular factor at a time. For example, suppose job A, B, C, D, E constitute key jobs. They are ranked in such a way that one factor is considered at a time.

Skill	***Responsibility***	***Effort***	***Working Condition***
A	B	D	D
B	A	C	E
C	C	E	C
D	D	A	B
E	E	B	A

After preparing this table, the key jobs are to be rated in money worth. How much worth should be given to job A for say skill factor is determined by the evaluation committee.

The following table gives the yardstick for determining the rate in Rupees for each factor.

Correct Job rates	***Skill***	***Responsibility***	***Efforts***	***Working Condition***
A 20.00	A 12.00	B 8.50	D 2.50	D 3.00
B 18.00	B 7.00	A 5.50	C 2.00	E 2.80
C 14.00	C 5.20	C 4.40	E 1.80	C 2.40
D 10.00	D 3.20	D 1.30	A 1.50	B 1.50
E 7.00	E 1.40	E 1.00	B 1.00	A 1.00

When we have constructed a yardstick, the next step is to compare other jobs against these factors. That is, if job Z is to be evaluated, then how much skill is required. If it is similar in skill to A (12.00 ₹) and responsibility similar to C (4.40 ₹), efforts similar to B (1.00 ₹) and working condition is similar to E (2.00 ₹) then the value of job would be equal to 12 + 4.40 + 1.80 + 2.80 = 21.00 ₹ The last step of adjusting, operating a wage structure is somewhat similar to the preparation of wage structure under the point system.

Human Relations and Job Evaluation

Job evaluation is technically not simple but rather a complicated system because of the involvement of human beings. The emergence of job evaluation is directly referred to the grievances and difference about existing wage rates among the employees. High degree of reliability is necessary and can be determined but validity of the process can be determined only through employee satisfaction. Job evaluation is not only a scientific process but it is an analytical and systematic approach. Consequently, we must be concerned with employee and labour union reactions.

The second problem which comes from job evaluation is that it lessens the grievance more rapidly. It is argued on this point that there is always some confused conditions in the organization which become more clear and distinct, as job evaluation gives clear definition of wage structure.

And finally, the most common platform for the conflict between management and workers, is in relations to skill, responsibility, efforts, working conditions and the compensation for these factors. The solution to this problem is that management has to be flexible.

To conclude, we can say that though the conflict between employer and the employee cannot be totally eliminated, it is possible to minimise it if both employer and employees agree to the usefulness of job evaluation methods in fixing the worth of a particular job.

Concept of Wage

A very common terminology 'wage' does not demand an explanation. A need to define 'wage' hardly arises. The term wage has been defined under the Minimum Wages Act, 1948. According to it, 'wages' means all remuneration capable of being expressed in terms of money, which would, if the terms of the contract of employment, express or implied, were fulfilled, be payable to a person employed in respect of this employment or of work done in such employment. It includes house rent allowance but does not include:

(*i*) the value of (*a*) any house accommodation, supply of light, water, medical attendance or (*b*) any other amenity or any service excluded by general or special order of the appropriate government.

(*ii*) any contribution paid by the employer to any pension fund or provident fund or under any scheme of social insurance.

(*iii*) any travelling allowance or the value of any travelling concession.

(*iv*) any sum paid to the person employed to defray special expenses entailed on him by the nature of his employment, or

(*v*) any gratuity payable on discharge.

But this definition created more confusion than simplifying meaning. Thus for our purpose, we can say that 'wage' is a reward to the employees for services rendered. It is necessarily that reward which is in monetary terms plus any extra benefits. The wage normally consists of basic wage, dearness allowance, bonus and other incentives. Basic wage directly depends upon the internal economic conditions, whereas the other two components namely, the dearness allowance and bonus are affected by external factors. Financial incentive which is a major constituent of any wage plan is worked out in accordance with the wage incentive system which the enterprise may decide to adopt. The type of wage incentive system that the enterprise chooses to operate depends upon the company's wage policy. Here it is important to emphasise that basic wage is not generally amenable to change and therefore, is kept more or less constant. The increase in wage is therefore, effectuated through changes in the dearness allowance and other incentives.

Wage Policy

The Bhootalingam Committee report on Wage, Income and Prices had once again revived the questions of the need and the importance of a sound wage policy. How far has the government been successful in this direction in the past? Have we ever had a rational and sound wage policy? To answer these questions, one will have to look at the attempts made in the past and the achievements accrued thereof. Soon after independence the Government of India, in its economic policy emphasised on the twin goals of achieving economic growth and social justice. In practice, however, these two goals are found to be inherently conflicting. Though time and again attempts have been made to strike a balance between these two inherently conflicting goals, little could be achieved.

Emergence of wage policy: During the period 1948 to 1966, the emphasis was on the concepts of minimum wage and fair wage. The determination of minimum wage and fair wage felt necessary in order to provide the worker with a wage that would be necessary for the fulfilment of the basic needs of an average family. The Fair Wage Committee suggested three layers.

A living wage: Which should provide for a standard of living.

Minimum wage: The minimum wage suggested by the Fair Wage Committee was different from the minimum wage defined under the Minimum Wages Act, 1948.

Fair wage: In between minimum wage and a living wage, a third stage was introduced, called 'Fair wage.'

Though this concept fascinated many people, it failed to produce any significant result. Failure in its implementation was largely due to the lack of uniformity of application as no clear-cut norms were laid down by the Fair Wage Committee. In 1957, the National Commission on Labour tried to quantify the basic needs of an average family. This was termed as *Need Based Minimum Wage*. The N.C.L. suggested that the following factors should be taken into account while calculating the N.B.M.W.

(*a*) The N.B.M.W. must be calculated assuming that a family consists of three adult units.

(*b*) It must provide for food enough to produce 2700 calories of energy per adult unit.

(*c*) Perks must provide for reasonable house rent allowance, etc.

The government failed to implement the N.C.L.'s recommendation mainly because in most of the cases the N.B.M.W. worked out to be more than what was being paid to the workers. Though the government was willing to implement the N.C.L.'s recommendation, it has failed in its endeavour because neither the firm nor the government was prepared to bear the extra cost.

Importance and Need of a Rational Wage Policy

A sound wage policy should be aimed at social justice which eventually means that the working class gets its due share. This is important because even after five decades of Independence, more than 50 per cent of the urban population and nearly 38 per cent of the rural population live below the poverty line.

So a rational wage policy must be able to furnish a standard of living and must be able to eliminate the relative poverty. Here it is important to clarify the concept of relative poverty. It refers to the relative share of income accruing to the working class. Relative poverty is concerned with the inequality in distribution of income. A study on wage differentials has shown that forty per cent of the lowest earner gets only sixteen per cent of the total national income, whereas the share accruing to the top twenty per cent of high income earners is as high as fifty-two per cent of the total national income.

Thus in the present condition, a rational wage policy must effectively deal with the following components:

(*a*) Fixing minimum wages.

(*b*) Fixing ceiling in wage incomes.

(*c*) Wage structure.

(*d*) Price stability.

There is a need to fix the minimum wage which in the absence of a Central directive may be very low. Thus there is a need for policy to provide a wage which would be necessary for the fulfilment of subsistence level needs. According to *Turner*: "The protection of workers against exploitation or unduly low wages has been wage policy's major preoccupation in any underdeveloped country."

Similarly, the need for a wage ceiling is advocated to check the upward inflationary trend of the wages. It is argued that the wage should be related to productivity. In order to achieve the objectives stated above, a policy must provide for a wage structure. According to *Dayal*, it refers to a set of relationships between rates of pay for different groups of similar occupation. The past efforts in this direction were not very encouraging mainly because of the wage differentials that exist in our country. According to *Turner*, "the spread of wage and salaries in underdeveloped countries is extremely wide." The wages structure must also contribute to price stability.

Thus it is clear that a rational wage policy must concentrate on raising the incomes and employment of specific socio-economic groups in India. The one important goal that usually wage policies seek to achieve is to control the inflationary trend. The economists have strongly advocated that hike in prices is the result of the inflationary trend and it can be established only by curbing inflation, which is caused by higher wages. However, according to *A.S. Mathur*, "This conventional wisdom can hardly be justified as the higher wage may be consequence rather than a cause of inflation. What they actually ignored is the fact that inflation might have been caused by several other factors like reckless deficit financing, easy credit policy and inelasticity of output of the essential goods."

Thus, only a tight control over wages may not have any significant impact on curbing inflation which is too often caused by multiple factors. At best, such control over wages can only moderate the speed of inflation.

The rational wage policy, therefore, should aim at reducing the relative poverty of the working class. It is, however, in this direction that our achievements have been least impressive of all.

It is proposed that for the unskilled workers. The minimum wage per day would be ₹ 115. It will be called National Floor Level Minimum Wage. After the proposal gets the approval of the Parliament, it will be a statutory, and will become binding on all states. The states will have the liberty to prescribe a minimum wage higher than that fixed by the Centre. The proposal will ensure uniformity in wage structure. The national floor is linked to the Consumer Price Index Number for Industrial Workers and is revised from time to time. Currently, agricultural workers are paid low wages. According to the NSO survey, the labour in agriculture is paid wages ranging from ₹ 61 to ₹ 227 per day. Though minimum wages benefit the workers from the organised sector, it is difficult to monitor workers in the unorganised sector.

Indian Working Class Movement

Indian labour movement has a glorious past. It is a part of national movement. The movement has contributed a great deal to the freedom struggle of India. The Britishers had repressed the labour movement in industries owned by Indians. There were industries owned by the Britishers. The labour used to agitate against the British authorities. The Factory Act was enacted in 1892 to regulate the factories. Narayan Meghaji Lokhande (1948-1897) initiated the labour movement even prior to this. He is the father of this movement. His 115th anniversary day is being celebrated on 9th Feb. 2012.

Lokhande and his associates demonstrated that labour can organise 128 years ago. There is a large pool of unorganised labour even today.

Lokhande was an associate of Mahatma Jyotirao Phule. He started a journal *Deenbandhu* to ventilate the grievances of the mill workers. The Britishers had appointed factory commission. To put across the thinking of the workers, Lokhande started Bombay Millhands Association. It was the first union in Mumbai. Lokhande aired his views in Girangaon and held a public meeting of 4000 workers at Supari Baug, Parel on 23rd September, 1884. Another public meeting was held at Mahalaxmi Race Course which was attended by ten thousand workers. The objective was to agitate against the reluctance of the mill owners to declare Sunday as holiday. In this meetings, even the women workers made speeches. The owners realised the power of organised labour. They decided Sunday as holiday on 10th June, 1890

The worker of those days was patriotic and willing to sacrifice. When Tilak was imprisoned by the Britishers in 1908, the whole working community in Mumbai went on strike for six days. The strike was not to have their grievances redressed but to have Tilak freed.

There was a unilateral strike on 20th June, 1920 by the Port Trust workshop workers to get wage rise, bonus rise and DA rise. It was the first strike in Mumbai Port. There was a compromise after 15 days strike, and the workers resumed duties on 5th Feb. 1920. This gave rise to B.P.T. Employees Union on 3rd May, 1920. It was a union of dock workers. This was a strike before the enactment of Trade Union Act, 1926. The Union was also established prior to this Act. Port trust workers have always contributed positively to the labour movement.

India got freedom on 15th August, 1947. BPT Employees Union submitted a charter of demands to Mumbai Port Trust on 15th September, 1947. The objective was to ensure that the worker should at least have a standard of living on par with the common man. The charter had demands related minimum wages, scales of pay, free quarters, DA, promotion etc. The authorities did not pay heed, and the workers from the workshop and crane department started a sit-in strike from 24th Dec. 1947. The work came to a standstill. The ships were detained. The government tried to break the strike. The strike was declared illegal. The government took the steps contrary to the spirit of the 1926 Act. The Port Trust declared a lock out on 2nd January, 1948. The army was called in thousands of participating workers were dismissed on 23rd Jan., 1998. It became a prestige issue. Achyutrao Patwardhan and Sane Guruji extended cooperation to hold a public meeting of all the workers who expressed solidarity with the port workers. Jayprakash Narayan took the Secretary of BPT Union Dr. Shanti Patel to Mahatma Gandhi. Gandhi understood the position and took the responsibility of persuading the central ministers. After Gandhi's assassination, the chief labour commissioner intervened to end the strike. The dismissed workers were taken back unconditionally. On 9th February, 1948, the workers resumed. The strike of port worker's of 47 days is historic. It led to the enactment of Dock Workers Regulation and Employment Act. The toliwalla method of contract labour ended, and all the workers were regularised.

Strike is a tool in the hands of the workers. It is a way to highlight their problems. There were instances when the striking workers were chucked out. They lost their jobs. However, their struggle continued. The society supported the movement. The leaders were drawn from the freedom movement. Apart from Lokhande, there were leaders such as Lala Lajpat Rai, Pandit Jawaharlal Nehru, Lokmanya Tilak, Subhaschandra Bose, Com. Shripad Dange, N.M. Joshi etc. The pre-independence support continued post-independence too till the strike of the railway workers in 1974 under the leadership of George Fernandes.

Dr. Datta Samant led the strike of textile workers of 62 mills in 1982. The number of striking workers was two and a half lac. It was the longest strike. In 2012, a period of 30 years has elapsed since that strike.

The labour movement faced a set back after liberalisation. Organised retail has replaced mills and factories. The employment opportunities have diminished, small and medium scale enterprises who could not survive the competition close down. Bigger organisations initiated VRS schemes. Many workers left their jobs without adequate social security.

There are challenges before the labour movement — the insecurity of jobs, outsourcing, poor implementation of laws and exploitation of the unorganised sectors workers. The weakening factors are the multiplicity of unions in one industry and political unionism. The movement is dissipating. Indian population is 121 crore. The labour constitutes 40 per cent of this population. Out of these, only 3 per cent labour is organised, and 97 per cent unorganised. It means that almost 37 crore unorganised workers in India must be organised. Rather than wage rise, retaining a job is a major problem. All unions must come together in the interest of the workers.

In today's globalised economy, there is some rethinking again on labour reforms. It becomes difficult for an industry to exit. There are areas where apprentices are necessary. Some flexibility is needed to employ contract labour who are paid equal to what the permanent labour gets. The present government is considering amendments to the factory Act. Winds of change are blowing.

COMPENSATION PLANS

Wage Incentive Plans: Wage as monetary reward is paid to an employee for the services rendered by him. One of the important components of any wage plan is the incentive bonus paid to the operative personnel. There are a good number of incentive plans that have been devised. All the incentive plans are based on the fundamental factors such as the standard time, time actually worked, time saved and the output level attained. Some of the wage incentive plans have been discussed below. They are:

(*a*) Halsey Premium Wage Plan
(*b*) The Rowan Plan
(*c*) Straight Piecework Plan
(*d*) Taylor Differential Piecework Plan
(*e*) D'Gant Incentive Plan
(*f*) Emerson Premium Plan
(*g*) 100 per cent Time Premium Plan
(*h*) The Bedaux Plan

The standard notations used throughout this chapter are:

r = Rate per unit
T = Actual time worked
S = Standard time

$$= \frac{T \times \text{Number of units produced}}{\text{Production standard}}$$

N = total number of units produced
P = premium percentage
E = total employee earnings.

(a) Halsey Plan: It takes into account the total time saved by the employee, and is a useful method for computing the incentive, when accurate performance standards have not been established. The value of time saved by the employee is computed and the earning is shared by the employee and the organization. The total earning of the worker is computed by the formula given below:

$$E = rT + P(S - T)r$$

Suppose, a worker should produce 50 units in 8 hours and he is paid at the rate of ₹ 3 per hour. If he produces 100 units in 8 hours, his total earnings for the day would be —

$$E = 3 \times T + 1/2\ (16–8) \times 3 = 24 + 1/2 \times 8 \times 3 = 24 + 12 = ₹\ 36$$

where r = ₹ 3
T = 8 hours
P = 50%

$$S = \frac{8 \times 100}{50} = 16 \text{ hours}$$

E = Total earnings of the worker.

(b) Rowan Plan: It was devised in Glasgow, Scotland. In this plan the bonus is calculated on the basis of the time worked. Thus the premium paid to the worker is a percentage of the time worked. If we consider our previous example, then the total earnings of the worker under the Rowan Plan would be:

$$E = rT + \frac{S-T}{S} \times rT$$

$$= 3 \times 8 + \frac{16-8}{16} \times 3 \times 8$$

$$= 24 + \frac{8}{16} \times 24$$

$$= 24 + 12 = ₹\ 36$$

Thus, the total earnings of the employee would be ₹ 36/-.

It is worth noting that this plan is not easy to understand by the operative personnel and it also involves more clerical work.

(c) Straight Piecework Plan: This is a common system and is easily understandable. The rate per unit, at which the worker should be paid for the number of units produced, is determined by past records.

If we consider our previous example again, the total earnings would be:

$E = rN$

Here r is the piece rate and is equal to 48 paise.

Therefore, $E = 0.48 \times 100 =$ ₹48.

(d) Taylor's Differential Piece Rate Plan: Taylor's piece rate plan can be applied when the job is clearly defined and when the conditions are such that it would be possible for the average worker to attain the performance target. The important features of Taylor's plan are:

(*a*) It does not guarantee a day rate;

(*b*) It calls for two piece rates;

A high one when the worker attains or exceeds the standard and a low one when he fails to attain the standard. It means a worker would be paid high for achieving the standard and would receive a low pay in case he fails to achieve the standard. The one advantage of Taylor's incentive plan is that it motivates the worker to exceed or at least maintain the standard. At the same time, it also places a heavy responsibility on management to establish the work standard carefully so that the worker would not feel that he is unjustly penalised. The formula for computing his earnings under this system is same as the straight piece rate system, the only difference is that it provides for two rates, namely —

$E = rN$ when the worker fails to attain the standard.

$E = r_1N$ when the worker exceeds or attains the work standard.

(e) D'Gant Incentive Plan: This incentive plan was given by *Henry L. Gant* and it is the only incentive plan that pays an incentive (bonus) percentage multiplied by the value of standard plan. Just like the Taylor's Differential Piece Rate plan it also provides for a substantial differential between standard and substandard work. However, it does guarantee a day rate to the worker. The Gant's system allows various premium percentage for bonus payments, however, Gant often used $33^1/_3$%. The Gant system allows the worker to draw more than what he would receive under straight piecework plan or 100% premium plan. The formula used for the computation of the total earnings under the Gant plan is given by —

$$E = r.\ S + p.\ rS$$

Using the original problem the total earnings of the worker in this case would be equal to,

$$E = 3 \times 16 + 1/3 \times 3 \times 16$$
$$= 48 + 16$$
$$= 64$$
$$= ₹64$$

(f) Emerson Premium Plan: This plan, which is like Rowan plan, is based on index of efficiency multiplied by the value of work. The Emerson plan ensures wage for the standard time work plus an incentive for performance above standard. Emerson used a sliding scale of bonus for performance from $66^2/_3$% of the standard up to standard. The Emerson plan exerts a steady pull on the worker to reach the standard performance. The important element of this plan is that it allows the worker to receive a full pay for all his standard time above task but the premium is calculated on the actual time worked. The computation of formula is given below —

$$E = r \times T + p(rT)$$

The percentage is determined from a table constructed especially.

(g) 100% Time Premium Plan: Under the 100% Time Premium Plan the worker is paid the full value of the time saved. This plan calls for the determination of accurate time standard through time and motion study. This plan also guarantees day rate to the worker.

The formulae for computing worker's earnings are:

$$E = r \times T$$

When the worker fails to attain or just attain the standard.

$$E = r \times S$$

above standard.

Taking our original example, the worker's earnings under this plan would be —

E = 3 × 8 = ₹24 at or below standard

E = 3 × 16 = ₹48 above standard

(h) Bedaux Plan: This is also time saving bonus plan. Each job is rated on the basis of standard work unit allowed for its performance. The base rate for each job is guaranteed and incentive is paid for performance above standard. When the worker is paid for the full allowed time, the computation of earnings would be as follows:

$$E = rT + P(S - T)r$$

B represents unit of work. 1B stands for 1 standard work minute and it includes working time and rest allowance. A worker earning 60B in an hour reaches 100 of standard output. A bonus is paid to worker who earns more than 60Bs in one hour.

Group Incentive Plan

Effective contribution of worker cannot be measured, although it can measure related output of others. All workers are equally skilled. Procedure: (*i*) evaluate the collective performance of the group (*ii*) calculate the total incentive and working (*iii*) Divide the earnings in equal or any other proportions amongst workers depending upon qualities possessed by each worker. The group leader may be given bigger share, because he is responsible for the co-ordination and successful completion of job. If division is carried out unwisely then it deteriorates the team spirit.

Advantages: (*i*) Team spirit is built (*ii*) less skilled worker learns from skilled worker (*iii*) supervision is less (*iv*) less clerical work.

No one incentive system of itself is the safe instrument for increasing efficiency. The value of every plan depends upon its implementation and administration.

The fact which should be borne in mind while adopting any incentive system or while devising one's own system is that the plan must possess certain characteristics such as:

(*a*) It should be simple to understand by those who are going to be affected by the introduction of such systems.

(*b*) It must provide for higher earnings with increased output and efficiency.

(*c*) Work standard should be established through time and motion study.

(*d*) The base rate should be guaranteed irrespective of the daily output.

ꕥ ꕥ

ORGANIZATION AND MANAGEMENT OF SAFETY IN A FACTORY

Introduction

The twentieth century has been characterized as the age of the common man. There has been an increasing appreciation of the importance of human needs, a widespread recognition to improve the working and living conditions of the workers engaged in the productive process.

There is evidence of great technological revolutions in every field with serious amazing discoveries. It has been found that engineering can prevent accidents. It has also been found that workers could be reached through educational techniques and brought to a greater awareness of the problems and methods of combating accidents. Through trial and error, it has also been discovered that safety rules could be established and enforced. In this discovery of what is called the four "Es" of safety — Engineering in design, Enforcement of the factory inspectorate, Education and Enthusiasm — industry has found the means to make a drastic improvement in the prevention of accidents.

An attempt is made in the following write-up to formulate some typical characteristics of organized safety and, on the basis of these 4 characteristics, to build up a picture of how safety could best be promoted in the various types of operations encountered in different types of industrial units in our country.

Irrespective of the type of activities, one finds a common pattern of approach continually increases safety in all respects and at all levels. In a condensed form, this could be expressed as:

1. Make safety a way of life for everyone working in the unit.
2. Organize the safety effort because it does not happen by itself.
3. Exchange findings and experiences to mutual benefit.

Today, every industry, in order to exist, has to be concerned with the value of its services. The value of a particular activity in any industry may be indicated in a variety of ways but the most effective, usually, is increased sales or decreased costs.

Safety, in relation to cost, stands in a peculiar position because for every industrial operation, some element of safety is essential. If this is lacking, operations do not remain under control and schedules and unit costs can't be counted upon. Breakdowns involving costs, and sometimes substantial costs, become frequent. Compensation amounts go up, supplies of skilled people with the right attitude and motivation becomes difficult, labour relations become strained and efficiency and productivity stand impaired. Management must seek efficient operations if it is to manage at all and create enough enthusiasm in safety.

The main driving force behind the industrial safety movement is the fact that accidents are expensive. Substantial savings can be had by preventing them.

Workers' attitudes in industrial safety are dependent upon a whole array of factors ranging from the social and environmental background to their own circumstances and character. A good safety organization therefore, constantly helps the workers in promoting safety education in various forms which will pay good dividends in preventing accidents.

Knowing what makes people tick will uncover many accident causes. Safest is a factor which deals with the influencing of an employee's mind, resulting in a proper attitude that governs his behaviour at work. If we can understand human behaviour, and through effective leadership get the main ideas of safety psychology among the workers, not only will morale improve, but correspondingly be reflected in smoother working of the industrial organization.

The key to a successful safety programme in any plant, large or small, is leadership by the management and its guidance and help to the supervisors to do the same for their men. They should adopt and practise safe habits and ensure that the safety and security of those with whom they work is constantly maintained.

Goal of Safety

When we consider organized safety, the most important point to bear in mind is the prime goal of safety. This can be stated as: "to reduce the number of all types of accidents which may cause loss of life, personal injury, loss or damage to equipment or loss of operating efficiency."

We encounter two distinctly different groups of accidents:

(*a*) Those accidents emanating from failure of equipment on plants or from unrecognised danger in process or operation or from "acts of God."

(*b*) Accidents caused by personnels' unsafe acts, ranging from carelessness and negligence to poor craftsmanship, lack of instruction and inadequate instructions.

It might help to elucidate this with a few examples. We all know examples of failure of equipment — disintegration of high speed rotating equipment, bursting of pressure vessels or pipes, collapse of structures which cause loss of life, injuries and material damage — none of which were the "fault" of the operators or users involved. The same applies to many "operational" accidents, resulting in fires, explosions, poisoning etc., where only experience and analysis of circumstances taught us better procedures for safe future operations (static electricity as a cause of tank fires, explosions, safe handling of TEL, tank cleaning). Even those accidents, which are indicated as "acts of God", can be analysed and studied, resulting in reduced or no damage in case of recurrence (extreme wind velocities during hurricanes or typhoons and excessive wave heights in offshore drilling operations, earthquake damage etc.).

This category of accidents, if we wish to reduce their occurrence and effects, requires the gathering of reliable information on what happened, careful analysis of basic causes and resulting from that: the built-in safety, in future, for similar equipment or plants.

The second group, in which by far the largest number of accidents have to be classified, are those caused by the "operating individual" and this group covers all the range from minor mishaps (hitting your own nail instead of the nail) to major catastrophes due to mismanipulations. In it we find the lackadaisical attitude of "this won't happen to me" (grinding without goggles, not using safety belts).

This category of accidents, therefore, can only be tackled by working on the individual, by providing good training, by issuing complete operating instructions and by the realisation of where the danger lies. And, however regrettable, it is unavoidable, too, by "Policing" the adherence to established safe practices.

Scope

From the above it is clear that the task of safety promotion is a team work which has to penetrate the entire company from the very start of our idea on development till the final execution of an operation — be it the transport of oil or gas by ship, the drilling of a well, the loading and unloading of cargo, a process in chemical or refining activities or distributing, storing and selling products. In all instances it requires the joint application of the experience, knowledge and know-how of a number of specialists, experts in their own field of activity.

We must, therefore, provide a concept of organization in which it becomes routine to gather all knowledge and experience to ensure safety in operations. Finally, the organizations should provide for the dissemination of information collected.

The Safety Unit in a Company

The management of a company will undoubtedly wish safety to be pursued in each phase of the operation for which it is responsible. The management will also need information on how safely the work is being performed, how that could be improved, how safety consciousness can be spread. In short, it will, in any operation of some size, feel the need for a central point where the gathering of such information can be effected and which can be allocated the task of promoting safety. The organization needs a "Safety Unit", a 'Safety Department' or "Section", even if it is a one-man effort.

There is, therefore, the need for:

1. Specially allocated people with a basic understanding of what is generally indicated as Industrial Safety.
2. Intimate co-operation between safety units and other specialists whether designers, medical men, process engineers, transport people, plant or machine operators etc.
3. Continuous contact with those departments in the company which deal with personnel in all its aspects of employment.
4. Realisation of the benefits which can be reaped from experience gained in one's own organization as well as elsewhere.

Mode of Operation

This leaves us to establish in some detail what such a safety unit is expected to do, what its responsibilities are and what place it should most effectively have in the organization. But, we should also attempt to describe the type of personnel which is needed to staff such a unit; the question of a safety budget has to be dealt with and, finally, the lines of contact.

Safety Programme

It is not good enough to earmark one or more people as Safety Officers and tell them to spread safety in the organization. You may find them standing in the cold very soon.

Long-standing experience in industry, in general, has proved the need for a "safety programme" which really comprises strategic planning against the enemy. Such a programme should be set up to suit the operations in the company. It should be designed by a man trained in basic principles of safety in consultation with management, so as to ensure that the proposed activities crossing the borders to various operating departments, as they do, will not clash with any policies and responsibilities as earlier laid down by management.

Although top management has top responsibility for establishing definite safety policies, procedures and safe working conditions, most of what is planned and established must reach the employee on the job through the first line supervisors who are in frequent and close association with the employees.

The works supervisor, in discharging his responsibilities for safety, has, among his principal duties, the following:

1. To teach each employee the hazards of his job and how to avoid them.
2. To impart to each employee the understanding that the violation of established safety rules will not be tolerated.
3. To see that needed safety equipment is provided and used for each job.
4. To take prompt corrective action whenever unsafe conditions and unsafe acts are noted.
5. To teach employees that accidents are caused but can be prevented.
6. To investigate and find causes of all accidents, even those which result in minor injuries.
7. To see that all injuries are reported and properly treated.
8. To instil a safety awareness in each employee through personal contacts and by safety meetings.
9. To conduct regular safety appraisals of his section.
10. To give full support to all safety activities and safety procedures.

It is the works supervisors and not the soldiers or our army who are the safety people. Efforts should therefore be directed towards training these supervisors.

Another basic step in the safety programme is the establishment of safety rules. No rule must be introduced unless there is need for it and the intention is to enforce it. Enforcement of rules is a necessary step to ensure the complete success of any safety programme. Disciplinary action should be avoided until management has thoroughly discharged its safety obligations and every effort has been exhausted in securing voluntary co-operation. However, in the final analysis, disciplinary action for failure to follow a rule must be taken or the rule will cease to exist. Here again, the works supervisors are in the middle of the battle, firstly in assisting to establish the proper rules, and later on making them adhered to.

Among the duties of the works supervisor regarding safety, two specific duties, where his initiative is required, are emphasized.

(*a*) He has to investigate accidents and take corrective action.

(*b*) He has to inspect and prevent unsafe conditions.

Thus, correction and prevention go side by side in every safety programme dealing with either minor hazards or major dangers and catastrophes.

Summarizing, we can say that such a programme has to implement the basic principles in (1) Safety rules, (2) Safety inspection, (3) Safety training, (4) Accident analysis, (5) Recommendation for correction, (6) Recording and reporting.

Duties of Safety Personnel

The foregoing discussion of the safety programme brings us, in logical sequence, to the duties of the safety personnel.

Their's is a staff responsibility. They advice and assist the entire operations, but do not operate themselves. A survey done in America indicated that in some 300 industrial enterprises, the Safety Supervisor functions in an advisory capacity in 90% of the cases. There is however, a recent trend in large enterprises of an intricate structure whereby safety becomes both a staff and a line function; a person co-ordinates the programme enterprise-wise (a "Safety Director" or "Safety Manager") with specialists (Safety Supervisors, Safety Engineers) allocated to the actual operating force.

Very much in line with what we have seen as typical safety functions for the works supervisor, we can define the duties of the Safety Personnel as:

1. Set up, develop and administer the Safety Programme.
2. Establish safe practices.

3. Study accident causes.
4. Investigate accidents.
5. Train supervisors.
6. Initiate corrective action.
7. Inspect.
8. Develop safety rules.
9. Study accident trends and keep accident records.
10. Initiate safety meetings.
11. Arrange safety meetings.

As already indicated before, many of these duties require the assistance or even guidance from experts whose combined experiences and knowledge cannot possibly be expected to be found in any one Safety Officer.

The study of accident causes and the investigation will, in particular cases, ask for much specialised knowledge. Likewise, the development of safety rules and the establishment of safe practices require intimate contact with people who are fully conversant with every angle of the operation under consideration.

The training of Supervisors is high on the list of duties of Safety Personnel and it is through the Supervisors that safety has to be spread.

Place in the Organization

It is already indicated that safety could well be a staff function, in some cases modified into a combination of staff functions with personnel allocated in line positions of the actual operations. No hard and fast rule can be made. However, the safety unit is of considerable importance.

A survey in the U.S. of some 300 firms gives a result that in 33 per cent, the safety unit is a separate department directly reporting to some management level. In 67 per cent the unit is either amalgamated with another department (26 per cent) or subordinated to another department (41 per cent).

We must study the reporting aspect with care.

With regard to contact of the safety unit, the most frequent ones are undoubtedly with the operating departments via training sessions, safety talks, accident investigations, safety inspections and proposals for prevention of accidents, as well as setting up safety rules.

There is also large front of contact, with personnel and medical departments and also with I.R. Department. There are a number of aspects where I.R. and Safety have common grounds.

I.R. Department contact comes in more at the time of issuing warning letters to workers for violation of safety. Also with regard to reporting accidents to the Factory Inspectorate, I.R. and Safety have common grounds.

Against combining the safety unit with any one of the operating departments, I can say that the influence of that safety unit could tend to become restricted to that particular department, whereas it is intended to cover the entire operations in the company. There is moreover, the undesirable chance of an operating department too readily dominating the subordinate safety unit.

Weighing these various possibilities, one is strongly inclined to advocate, for large companies, an independent safety department reporting to management, preferably to the Technical Manager in a staff of functional capacity. In the case of a widespread operating company the safety supervisors could then be allocated to particular areas reporting either to the local head of operations or preferably to the local I.R. representatives. In either case a strong functional contact should be maintained between the head of the Safety Department and the Safety Supervisors providing the latter with a direct channel to management.

In smaller operations with less variety of activities, a safety section in the Industrial Relations Department might well prove the most efficient and most economical to run.

Safety Personnel

The personnel to be recommended for selection of the safety functions should as for any other job, qualify for a number of minimum requirements if they are expected to do this work successfully, for this work is not easy. The safety man has to inspect, teach, propose changes and guide investigations. In short, he has to do a lot of things which by their very nature are apt to provoke resentment in others as he is poking his nose into their business. And this is valid for the whole range of safety personnel from Department Head to Junior Safety Supervisor.

We can thus conclude, that the man must have a personality which combines perseverance with the gift to compromise when this is not to the detriment of safety. He must have ideas, enthusiasm and an ability to "sell" safety, but, also, he must be responsible and ready to give advice so that he will avoid being considered "The Secret Police."

With regard to his education and background, it is generally appreciated that he should have a technical upbringing and experience in factories. Better and faster results are expected by giving specialised safety training to an experienced man of the right personality out of the same company than trying to add experience to a total outsider who has not lived with the company.

The safety man of the future should at least be an engineering graduate with sufficient knowledge, both spoken and written, of the local language. He should be able to preside over meetings or act as secretary to meetings. Besides that, knowledge of English would be very welcome. Finally do not choose a man who has no ability to write a comprehensive report or keep records.

The special training that should be given to the candidate for safety work, comprises, in the first instance, of the basic techniques to promote safety and prevent accidents. There are several books and courses available by now to achieve this, some treating general aspects, others going into great detail of specialised applications.

Equally important, with the training techniques, however, is the use of visual aids and how to prepare them, the use of statistics and the Factories' Act as well as various Safety Codes.

Safety Budget

It is always sound to know how much an activity costs. Therefore, a budget should be made for safety just as for any other activity. It should be comprehensive, covering not only the salaries of the staff but also what is expected to be spent on training, publications, lectures, demonstrations, incentive schemes, firms, visits abroad, etc.

Lines of Contact

The only thing which has such importance that it might be repeated here is that in any company safety should have a free channel to management, so that it cannot be overruled or subdued without the possibility of appeal.

Different lines of contact, however, are required to ensure interchange of experience, increased knowledge and new developments. Here we have to establish a communication whereby companies within a group make available their recorded and classified findings, and the logical central point to receive and distribute such findings is a Central Safety Committee.

The information received by the Central Safety Committee should serve a three-fold purpose:

1. It should provide the designer with ideas for the introduction of new techniques and operations.
2. Such experience gained is often of benefit to all companies in that group.
3. It also forms the major source of experience on which to base the constant review of safety codes.

The information collected readily provides an indication where the enemy struck most frequently. Accordingly, changes should be made in the design of equipment, in plant layout, in the size and shape of steps, protective guards, etc. This should ensure greater safety in the future for the outlay of a new plant.

Finally, to conclude, a company should arrange for group contacts between safety officers of various companies.

For safety work, many items of safety promotions have to be tested against experience with employees. For example, safety posters and illustrated booklets with safe practices which are most effective in one country or region mean nothing in another country or region. The attitude *vis-a-vis* injury and death is very different in various places in the world. Training techniques must differ greatly in order to be effective.

These are only a few of a range of problems which the safety man has to deal with. It seems logical that repetition of misdirected effort can be prevented when the safety people from various companies operating in certain areas can freely exchange their opinions and findings. This type of contact, which can never be covered efficiently by a company, should therefore be established by national conferences on Industrial Safety.

Safety Laws

In all, there are 25 separate Central legislations pertaining to safety ranging from battery handling to managing hazardous waste. The laws also safeguard workers against accidents sustained with agricultural machinery. The proliferation of laws by itself is a hazard. These are all piecemeal legislations and are occupation-centric. A large proportion of population still remains outside the ambit of safety laws.

Labour falls in the concurrent list of subjects and so while the centre frames the laws, the states have the responsibility of implementing them. There is absence of a single comprehensive safety law. The regulations change from state to state. These cause problems of compliance.

Various Acts

India's 25 laws relating to health, safety and environment

- The Factories Act, 1948 (amended in 1987 and 2001)
- The Mines Act, 1952
- The Oilfields (Regulation and Development) Act, 1948.
- The Dock Workers (Safety, Health and Welfare) Act, 1986
- The Indian Boilers Act, 1923 (amended in 1986)
- The Building and Other Construction Workers (Regulation of Employment and Conditions of Service) Act, 1996
- The Dangerous Machines (Regulation) Act, 1983
- The Motor Transport Workers Act, 1961 (amended in 1986)
- The Plantation Labour Act, 1951 (amended in 1982)
- The Beedi & Cigar Workers (Conditions of Employment) Act, 1966 (amended in 1993)
- The Shops and Commercial Establishments Acts enacted by respective state governments.
- The Explosives Act, 1884 (amended in 1983)
- The Petroleum Act, 1934
- The Inflammable Substances Act, 1952
- The Environment Protection Act, 1986 (amended in 1991)
- The Water (Prevention and Control of Pollution) Act, 1974 (amended in 1988)
- The Water (Prevention and Control of Pollution) Cess Act, 1977 (amended in 2003)

- The Air (Prevention and Control of Pollution) Act, 1981 (amended in 1987)
- The Public Liability Insurance Act, 1991 (amended in 1992)
- The Motor Vehicles Act, 1988 (amended in 2001)
- The Atomic Energy Act, 1962 (amended in 1987)
- The Insecticides Act, 1968 (amended in 2000)
- The Electricity Act, 2003 (replaced The Indian Electricity Act, 1910)
- The Disaster Management Act, 2005
- The Energy Conservation Act, 2001

Source: National Safety Council of India.

22

BUDGETARY CONTROL

Introduction

Business planning is an essential feature of all progressive managements. Generally, the long-range as well as the day-to-day business operations are planned in accordance with the expectations of the future. Much of the planning in business boils down to the quantitative figures and those related to the profit realization into the rupee values expressed in terms of costs. The quantitative sketch of the business operations over a specified period of time is a **budget**. A budget is a planning tool for shaping profits and economic growth of an enterprise. Most of the planned activities are expressed in the quantitative terms in some organized form which is known as a budget. A budget is also considered as a control technique because budget sets the pre-operation quantitative targets with which the actual performance data are compared and any positive or negative variations between actual and budgets are ascertained and they are analysed for control purposes. Thus, a budget is a management tool which incorporates organizational and financial plans, analyses the behaviour of various costs, sets the objectives and evaluates the performances. The budget expresses the responsibilities delegated to the various organizational sub-divisions of a company. It spells out quantitatively what is expected of each member of management at every level in terms of expected goals and the cost expected to be incurred to accomplish the tasks assigned. The accounting and budgeting are closely related. In fact, a budget uses the language of accounting and in a real sense it gives added purpose to accounting by increasing its effectiveness in day-to-day control of business operations. The accounting system and budgeting are built around the same organizational structure and both are information systems concerned with same operations and financial situations. Accounting reports quantify information on actual past events and conditions while budgets reflect what those values were expected to be and what is expected in the future. All budget data are arranged to conform with the existing accounting system or to agreed changes, in order to make possible the periodic comparison of actual performance with the projected figures.

Definitions

The various terms, budget, budgeting and budgetary control are defined as under:

(1) Budget: A budget is a plan which shows how the resources will be acquired and used over a period of time.

According to **Dickey,** "a budget is a written plan covering projected activities of a firm for a defined time period."

Heiser defines budget as "an overall blueprint of a comprehensive plan of operations and actions expressed in financial terms."

Thus, the following characteristics of a budget should be noted:

(*a*) It outlines the projected activities;

(*b*) The expressions are made in quantitative terms, and in most of the budgets in financial terms, *i.e.,* rupee value, and

(*c*) It relates to a fixed periodicity say, a day, a week, a month, a year etc.

(2) Budgeting: Budgeting is a term which is used to describe the act of preparing the budgets.

According to the terminology of Cost Accountancy, Institute of Cost and Works Accountants, U.K., budgeting refers to "the establishment of budgets relating to the responsibilities of executives to the requirements of a policy, and the continuous comparison of actual with budgeted results either to secure by individual action the objective of that policy or to provide a basis for its revision."

(3) Budgetary Control: When budgets are used as a means for the control of various business activities, such techniques are treated as "budgetary control."

Walter R. Bunge defined **budgetary control,** as "the exercise by line management of control over costs through continuous appraisal of actual expenditure, using as a guide the planned costs as expressed in budget."

The interrelationship of **budget, budgeting** and **budgetary control** is well explained in the following definitions given by *More and Jaedicke.*

"A plan showing how resources will be required and used over a specified time interval is called a **budget.** The act of preparing a budget is called **budgeting,** and the use of budget as a means of controlling activity is called **budgetary control.**

Types of Budgets

Generally, budgets are classified on following two bases:

(1) On the basis of type of expenditure:

(*i*) Capital expenditure budget, and

(*ii*) Operating budget.

(2) On the basis of level of activity:

(*i*) Fixed budget, and

(*ii*) Flexible budget.

(1) On the basis of type of expenditure: Budgets are the financial plans which make the allowances for different types of expenditures to be incurred for the projected business operations and the generation of revenue out of them. The expenses are broadly classified into two, capital expenditure and operating expenditures. The budgets are classified on the basis of these two types of expenditure as under:

(i) Capital expenditure budget: Capital expenditures are those expenditures the benefits from which are deferred over a longer period of time, *e.g.,* purchase of plant and machinery. The expenditures on such items are relatively higher and the benefits from them are derived till the economic life of such assets. Such expenses result in creation of assets and are shown in the balance sheet of a company. Capital expenditure budgets are prepared for the purchase of new assets or for the replacement of existing assets. The budget period is generally longer as compared to operating budget, usually 3 to 5 years or even more.

(ii) Operating budgets: Operating budgets are the most common types of business operations. They relate to sales revenues and various operating costs. The results of the revenues and costs are reflected in the yearly profits and losses and are recorded in profit and loss accounts. Unlike capital expenditures, operating expenses are recurring expenditures the benefits from which are derived for a relatively shorter period, *e.g.,* salary to the administrative staff, consumption of raw materials etc. Operating budgets are usually prepared on the annual basis and they are broken into still shorter time-spans say, half-yearly, quarterly, monthly etc.

The principal operating budgets are as under:

(*i*) Sales budget

(*ii*) Manufacturing budget consisting of:

(*a*) Direct material cost budget

(*b*) Direct expenses budget

(*iii*) Administrative expenses budget

(*iv*) Sales and distribution expenses budget

(*v*) Profit plans

(*vi*) Cash budget etc.

(2) On the basis of the level of activity: On the basis of the level of activity, the budgets are classified into two: (*i*) Fixed budget and (*ii*) Flexible budget.

(i) A fixed budget is prepared on the basis of certain fixed pre-determined level of activity. In the fixed budget, certain fixed monetary allowances are made which do not vary along with the changes in the conditions. Fixed budgets are suitable only for such enterprises whose quantity and quality of production as well as sales during the budget period can be pre-determined with reasonable accuracy. The government budgets are mostly fixed budgets. In case of government budgets fixed appropriations for specific projects or programmes which have not been completed during the fiscal period are generally required to be expanded during the particular year. In business, where fixed budgets are used, and where some significant variations occur, the fixed budget loses its importance as a control technique. Some companies solve such situation by rebudgeting. They revise the budgeted figures for the remaining period. The other alternative method is to establish a series of fixed budgets set at incremental level of activity. This is nothing but a variant of flexible budget and it is more cumbersome than the flexible budget.

(ii) The flexible budget reflects the actual behaviour characteristics of the costs. Fixed budget assumes that the cost incurrence is a function of time. They vary with the passage of time irrespective of the volume of production. While flexible budget segregates the cost into two parts: (1) those costs which vary with the passage of time and (2) those costs which vary with the volume of production. The former are fixed costs (*e.g.*, salary of executive) and the latter are variable costs (*e.g.*, consumption of direct materials). Thus, unlike fixed budget, the flexible budget assumes that the cost will vary with the volume of activity. The flexible budget makes varying allowances for the different levels of operating conditions, say budget at 50%, 60%, 75%, 90%, and 100%, level of operating conditions.

Illustration 1:

The production capacity of one plant is 10,000 units per annum. The cost components are as under:

Direct materials	₹ 3 per unit
Direct labour	₹ 5 per unit
Overheads:	
Variable	₹ 1 per unit
Fixed	₹ 20,000

Prepare the fixed budget and also flexible budget for 60%, 75%, 90%, 100% and 120% production capacity.

Solution:

Annual Fixed Budget — Production: 10,000 units

(At 100% operating level)

Element of cost		*Amount* ₹
Direct material cost		30,000
Direct labour cost		50,000
Overheads:		
Fixed	₹ 20,000	
Variable	₹ 10,000	30,000
Total cost		1,10,000

(B) Annual Flexible Budget — Rated capacity 10,000 units (100%)

Element of cost	*Production as a percentage of rated capacity*				
	60%	*75%*	*90%*	*100%*	*120%*
Direct material	18,000	22,500	27,000	30,000	36,000
Direct labour	30,000	37,000	45,000	50,000	60,000
Overheads:					
Fixed	20,000	20,000	20,000	20,000	20,000
Variable	6,000	7,500	9,000	10,000	12,000
Total cost	74,000	87,500	1,01,000	1,10,000	1,28,000

The Master Budget and the Operating Budgets

A budget may be prepared for any activity that management considers critical. As the business activity is the system consisting of various sub-systems, separate budgets are prepared for different activities which are integrated into one master budget. A master budget tends to emphasise the relationship between the expected outputs and the optimum level of inputs required to achieve these outputs. The primary function of the master budget is that it relates all the activities of an organization in terms of profits, net cash flows and changes in the composition of assets and liabilities during a specified budget period. The first problem in preparing the master budget is the selection of the starting point. Usually, the forecasted sales are treated as the starting point. The sales are the basic figure around which the entire production facilities are arranged, and sales being the varying figure the entire budget function becomes continuous and flexible. The sales forecast serves as the basis for developing a production budget for the given budget period. Once the production budget is agreed upon, the estimates are made for the cash and non-cash expenditures needed to produce the budgeted output. The important items of expenditures are purchase of materials, direct labour costs, manufacturing overheads, selling and administrative expenses etc. For ascertaining the cash flow during the budget period, cash budgets are prepared which record the sales revenues (cash sales and collections from credit sales) and various types of aforesaid cash payments like payments for cash and credit purchases, labour cost, manufacturing overheads etc. A capital budget is also prepared for any required capital expenditure during the budget period. Thus, a master budget is an integration of the following types of budgets:

(1) Sales budget, (2) Production budget, (3) Materials purchase budget, (4) Direct labour budget, (5) Manufacturing overhead budget, (6) Administrative expense budget, (7) Selling expense budget, (8) Cash budget, (9) Capital expenditure budget etc.

The budget data are cast in the projected income statement and the projected balance sheet covering the budget period, which generally coincides with the accounting period.

The concept of the master budget and various types of operating budgets is explained in the following exhaustive illustration.

Illustration 2:

The Perfect Manufacturing Co., Ltd., manufactures two standard products, Alpha and Beta. The following types of raw materials are used:

Plastic (5/8" sheet); Steel (1/4" sheet); Wood (2 × 4" × 10")

The production is carried on in three manufacturing departments A, B, and C, each with 40,000, 55,000 and 50,000 annual machine hours capacity respectively. The products are marketed in the three territories, X, Y and Z.

The relevant budget data for the year ending on 31st December 2001 are provided in the respective budgets.

Some important budget data for the year 1981 will appear as under:

(1) Sales Budget:

The Perfect Manufacturing Co. Ltd.
Sales Budget for the year ending on 31.12.2001

Quarter	*Territory X*		*Territory Y*		*Territory Z*		*Total*	
	Units	*₹*	*Units*	*₹*	*Units*	*₹*	*Units*	*₹*
				Product Alpha (₹ 3 per unit)				
1	7,000	21,000	10,000	30,000	9,000	27,000	26,000	78,000
2	8,000	24,000	11,000	33,000	9,000	27,000	28,000	84,000
3	11,000	33,000	14,000	42,000	9,000	27,000	34,000	1,02,000
4	9,000	27,000	9,000	27,000	8,000	24,000	26,000	78,000
Total	35,000	1,05,000	44,000	1,32,000	35,000	1,05,000	1,14,000	3,42,000
				Product Beta (₹ 4 per unit)				
1	40,000	1,60,000	75,000	3,00,000	50,000	2,00,000	1,65,000	6,60,000
2	50,000	2,00,000	80,000	3,20,000	70,000	2,80,000	2,00,000	8,00,000
3	55,000	2,20,000	75,000	3,00,000	80,000	3,20,000	2,10,000	8,40,000
4	50,000	2,00,000	60,000	2,40,000	75,000	3,00,000	1,85,000	7,40,000
Total	1,95,000	7,80,000	2,90,000	11,60,000	2,75,000	11,00,000	7,60,000	30,40,000

(2) Production Budget:

The Perfect Manufacturing Co. Ltd.
Production Budget for the year ending on 31.12.2001

	No. of units in Quarter			
	1	*2*	*3*	*4*
Product Alpha				
* Units to be sold	26,000	28,000	34,000	26,000
Plus: Budgeted ending inventory	1,000	1,300	1,000	1,200
Less: Beginning inventory	700	1,000	1,300	1,000
To be manufactured	26,300	28,300	33,700	26,200

Total = 1,14,500 units

	No. of units in Quarter			
	1	2	3	4
Product Beta				
* Units to be sold	1,65,000	2,00,000	2,10,000	1,85,000
Plus: Budgeted ending inventory	10,000	12,000	15,000	20,000
Less: Beginning inventory	5,000	10,000	12,000	15,000
To be manufactured	1,70,000	2,02,000	2,13,000	1,90,000
* As per the sales budget			Total = 77,500 units	

(3) Materials Purchase Budget:

The Perfect Manufacturing Co. Ltd.
Materials Purchase Budget for the year ending on 31.12.2001

Type of Material	*No. of units in Quarter*			
	1	2	3	4
	Plastic (5/8" sheet) at ₹ 0.50 per unit			
To be used	1,00,000	3,00,000	2,00,000	50,000
Plus: Budgeted ending inventory	10,000	15,000	5,000	10,000
Less: Beginning inventory	20,000	35,000	9,000	4,000
To be purchased (units)	90,000	2,80,000	1,96,000	56,000
Value (₹)	45,000	1,40,000	98,000	28,000
Total Purchases = ₹ 3,11,000				
	Steel (1/4" Sheet) at ₹ 0.75 per unit			
To be used	1,00,000	1,00,000	1,75,000	15,000
Plus: Budgeted ending inventory	10,000	7,500	10,000	10,000
Less: Beginning inventory	10,000	11,500	5,000	8,000
To be purchased (units)	1,00,000	96,000	1,80,000	15,200
Value (₹)	75,000	72,000	1,35,000	1,14,000
Total Purchases = ₹ 3,96,000				

Type of Material	*No. of units in Quarter*			
	1	2	3	4
	Wood (2"× 4" × 10") at ₹ 0.40 per unit			
To be used	1,00,000	1,00,000	50,000	50,000
Plus: Budgeted ending inventory	10,000	10,000	8,000	20,000
Less: Beginning inventory	15,000	10,000	10,000	8,000
To be purchased (units)	95,000	1,00,000	48,000	62,000
Value (₹)	38,000	40,000	19,200	32,800
Total Purchases = ₹ 1,30,000				

(4) Direct Labour Budget:

The Perfect Manufacturing Co. Ltd.
Direct Labour Budget for the year ending on 31.12.2001

	Quarter 1	*Quarter 2*	*Quarter 3*	*Quarter 4*
	Product Alpha: (Rate 1 hour/unit)			
Required hours	26,300	28,300	33,700	26,200
Direct Labour cost at ₹ 0.50/hr. (₹)	1,31,150	14,150	16,850	13,100
Total = ₹ 57,250				
	Product Beta: (Rate 0.5 hour/unit)			
Required hours*	85,000	1,01,000	1,06,500	95,000
Direct labour cost at ₹ 0.40/hr. (₹)	34,000	40,400	42,620	38,000
Total = ₹ 1,55,020				
Total direct labour cost (Alpha and Beta) = ₹ 2,12,270				

* On the basis of total units to be manufactured as indicated in the Production Budget.

(5) Manufacturing Overhead Budget:

The Perfect Manufacturing Co. Ltd.
Manufacturing Overhead Budget for the year ending on 31.12.2001

Particulars	*Quarter 1* ₹	*Quarter 2* ₹	*Quarter 3* ₹	*Quarter 4* ₹	*Total* ₹
Power	5,765	6,235	6,400	6,095	24,295
Light	3,200	3,000	2,800	3,000	12,000
Supplies	7,895	6,460	4,700	7,240	26,295
Maintenance	12,000	13,000	15,000	12,300	52,000
Rent	15,000	15,000	15,000	15,000	60,000
Indirect Labour	3,820	4,600	4,935	4,320	17,675
Depreciation	23,500	23,500	23,500	23,500	94,000
Insurance	1,000	1,000	1,000	1,000	4,000
Total	72,180	72,765	73,335	72,455	2,90,765
Less: Depreciation*	23,500	23,500	23,500	23,500	94,000
Cash overflows	48,680	49,295	29,835	48,955	1,96,765

* The depreciation is apportioned evenly throughout the year. Depreciation is an important item of manufacturing overheads and so is added in the total cost. However, it is not an actual payment like other expenses, rather it is an accounting adjustment. As it does not involve any cash payments, the net cash outflows is reduced by the amount of the depreciation in the above budget.

It should be noted that the manufacturing overheads expenses are indirect in nature. So on the basis of budgeted production and the budgeted manufacturing overheads, the overhead recovery rate is applied to the actual production to trace the proportionate manufacturing overhead to the actual production. In our illustration, the manufacturing overhead recovery rate will be calculated as under:

Budgeted production: (As per Production Budget)

Product Alpha	1,14,500 units
Product Beta	7,75,000 units
Total Production	8,89,500 units

Budgeted manufacturing overhead
(as per manufacturing overhead budget) = ₹ 2,90,765

$\therefore$ Manufacturing overhead recovery rate = $\frac{₹\ 2,90,765}{₹\ 8,89,500}$

= ₹ 0.325 (approx.)

Here the average recovery rate is ascertained for the purpose of simplicity. Separate recovery rate for individual product can also be ascertained on the same principle.

(6) General and Administrative Expenses Budget:

THE PERFECT MANUFACTURING CO. LTD.
General and Administrative Expenses Budget
for the year ending on 31.12.2001

Particulars	*Quarter 1* ₹	*Quarter 2* ₹	*Quarter 3* ₹	*Quarter 4* ₹	*Total* *A*
Salaries	72,500	72,500	72,500	72,500	2,90,000
Stationery & Printing	2,000	2,000	2,000	2,000	8,000
Rent	9,500	9,500	9,500	9,500	38,000
Postage and Telephones	1,000	1,000	1,000	1,000	4,000
Light Charges	3,000	500	500	2,000	6,000
Sundry expenses	500	500	500	500	2,000
Audit fees	8,000	—	—	—	8,000
Depreciation:					
On Furniture	1,500	1,500	1,500	1,500	6,000
Taxes	14,000	14,000	14,000	14,000	56,000
Total	1,12,000	1,01,500	1,01,500	1,03,000	4,18,000
**Less:* Depreciation	1,500	1,500	1,500	1,500	6,000
Total cash outflows	1,10,500	1,00,000	1,00,000	1,01,500	4,12,000

* Depreciation is an accounting adjustment and it does not involve any cash payments.

(7) Selling Expense Budget:

The Perfect Manufacturing Co. Ltd.
Selling Expense Budget for the year ending on 31.12.2001

Particulars	*Quarter 1* ₹	*Quarter 2* ₹	*Quarter 3* ₹	*Quarter 4* ₹	*Total* ₹
Salaries	25,000	25,000	25,000	25,000	1,00,000
Commissions*	22,140	26,520	28,260	25,740	1,02,660
Travelling	16,000	17,000	17,000	16,000	66,000
Advertising	50,000	50,000	50,000	50,000	2,00,000
Telephone	1,000	1,000	1,000	1,000	4,000
Office rent	6,250	6,250	6,250	6,250	25,000
Stationery	3,820	4,560	4,880	4,220	17,480
Delivery exp.	4,000	5,000	6,000	5,000	20,000
Total:	1,28,210	1,35,330	1,38,390	1,33,480	5,35,140

* The commission is a variable expense and it is generally allowed as certain percentage on sales. In this illustration the commission is allowed at 3% on the total sales of the products. The sales data as budgeted in the Sales Budget are used as a base to calculate the amount of the commission.

As this is an illustrative problem the preparation of cash budget, the capital budget, the projected profit and loss account and projected balance sheet are excluded in this illustration as their presentation would require substantial details.

The actual production, sales revenues and costs data are compared with the budgeted figures and the variances are ascertained. The area of inefficiency is located and attended to by the management. For the effective control the expenses are divided into fixed and variable expenses. The fixed expenses are period costs which tend to remain static per unit of time while the variable expenses are the product costs which may vary with the volume of production or sales. Thus, budgets are considered as an important control technique.

Mechanics of Budgetary Control

Budgetary control is a technique which controls the business operations with the help of various types of budgets or financial forecasts. The main facets of the budgetary control mechanism are as under:

1. Projection of the sales forecasting for the future period. For the budget purposes, usually the annual sales forecast are considered. It should be noted that sales forecasting is the basic data to which all other activities of the business are geared.
2. Preparation of the master budget for the specified future period, usually one year, on the basis of the sales forecast. On the basis of the master budget all other functional annual budgets will be prepared covering every activity.
3. Approval of every budget with a view to ensuring commitments of the management team and the operating staff for the quantitative data outlined in the budget.
4. The "breakdown" of the approved annual budget into short-period budgets such as daily, weekly, monthly budget etc.
5. Presentation of information at the end of every period about the actual performance. The deviations will be ascertained by comparing the actual figures of the specified period with the budgeted figures of the period.
6. The deviations will be analysed immediately and prompt corrective action will be taken to reduce the chances of such deviations in future. The responsibilities will be located for negative controllable deviations.

CAPITAL BUDGETING

Introduction

The essence of the business activity is to spend money on certain heads with a hope to realize some returns out of such investments. The spending activity which is popularly known as investment function is broadly divided into two parts: (*a*) Operating expenditure, the benefits of which are expected to be realized within a short span of time, usually not more than a year, *e.g.*, expenditure on materials, labour etc.; (*b*) Capital expenditure, where benefits are realized over a period longer than a year, *e.g.*, Expenditure on purchase of a machine, construction of a building etc. It should be noted that the choice of one year is arbitrary and it is considered as a convenient cut-off time for distinguishing between the operating and the capital expenditure.

Capital budgeting fundamentally deals with the planning of the capital expenditure. As the time horizon extends beyond a year, capital budgeting decisions involve long-range planning.

Capital budgeting is an important area of financial management. Financial management manages the "financing decisions" (*i.e.*, fund raising functions) and the "investment decisions" (*i.e.*, the decisions about the application of funds). The financing decisions prescribe the "cost of capital", while the investment decisions consider the "rate of return on investments." Both these decisions are important as well as interrelated. The wealth of the owners can be maximised by reducing the cost of capital or by increasing the rate of return on investment. Capital budgeting is an integral part of the investment decisions. Only those capital expenditure proposals are entertained whose rate of return on investment exceeds or at least equates the cost of capital.

Meaning

Capital expenditure means to spend something today with a view to get benefits out of it in future. It is the present sacrifice for future returns. Thus, in capital budgeting decision, substantial cash outflow occurs today and cash inflows occurs gradually in future years, *e.g.*, when a decision to buy a machine is taken, we pay the price of the machine today, and yield the benefits out of this machine over a period of time. Such decision is known as capital budgeting decision.

The following definitions will clarify the meaning of the term "capital budgeting."

1. "Capital budgeting involves the entire process of planning expenditure whose returns are expected to extend beyond one year." — **J.F. Weston** and **E.F. Brigham.**
2. "Capital budgeting is concerned with the allocation of the firm's scarce financial resources among the available market opportunities."

The consideration of investment opportunities involves "the comparison of the expected future streams of earnings from the project with the immediate and subsequent streams of expenditure for it." — **G.C. Philipratos.**

Significance of Capital Budgeting

The capital budgeting decision is considered to be one of the most important and strategic managerial decisions due to the following elements, involved in it.

1. It involves huge initial cash outflow. This necessitates the arrangement of financial resources affecting the capital structure and the resultant financial risk of the unit.
2. The initial cash outflows (*i.e.*, the investments) are certain while the cash inflows (*i.e.*, future returns arising out of the investments) are uncertain.
3. It is a long-term commitment and the decision once taken cannot be reversed or can be reversed at a great loss.
4. The capital budgeting decision changes the overall riskiness of the firm. The capital expenditure made on expansion and diversification are exposed to certain types of business risks.
5. The investments in fixed assets like plant and machinery are subject to the obsoletion losses caused by the technological development.

Types of Capital Expenditure

Resource constraint is a common phenomenon of all economic activities. Moreover, sometimes when a firm is able to spend on certain items, it is not willing to do so. So, a systematic screening process is employed to accept or reject the investment proposals. For the purpose, the investment proposals are broadly divided into two groups: (*a*) Mutually exclusive proposals and (*b*) Independent proposals.

Mutually exclusive proposals are nothing but the alternative methods of doing the same thing. If one method is selected, the other must be rejected, *e.g.*, if in-plant material handling facilities are needed, they can be arranged either through conveyor belt or through the fork-lift truck. The economic benefits of each of the proposals are evaluated and the one contributing maximum economic benefits is selected while the rest are rejected. **Independent proposals** are those items of capital expenditure that are being considered for different types of projects which are required to be accomplished. All independent proposals are independent of each other and are worthy to be implemented. However, due to certain financial constraints, priorities are assigned to each of the proposals according to the gravity of the need of the organization, *e.g.*, along with the material handling facilities, the investments may be required for weighing machines, stamping machines, packing machines etc. For the 'mutually exclusive proposals' the decision criterion is 'accept' or 'reject' while for the 'independent proposals' it is 'ranking.' This decision is taken on the basis of the methods of evaluating the capital budgeting decisions.

The nature of the capital expenditure proposals are broadly classified thus: (1) Replacement, (2) Expansion, (3) Diversification, (4) Strategic proposals.

(1) Replacement: Capital expenditure involves the replacement of an old machine by a new one. The replacement becomes necessary due to wear and tear or due to obsolescence. It results in more production, better quality production and reduction in operating costs. As the investments are made in the same line of production, it is not exposed to business risks.

(2) Expansion: This involves the capital expenditure to increase the production capacity in the same line of production. As the investments are made in the known area of activity, it involves lesser business risk as compared to diversification, however, a bit greater risk than the replacement expenditure.

(3) Diversification: Here the investments are made in a new line of production. Such investments are exposed to the greater degree of business risk due to the non-familiarity of the production and sale area.

(4) Strategic: These investments indirectly contribute to the revenues. Such investments may be of following nature:

(*i*) Investments in plant services like material handling, storing facilities etc.

(*ii*) Investments in personnel services like investments for provision of canteen, parking area, office air-conditioning etc.

(*iii*) Huge expenditure on advertisement campaign.

(*iv*) Expenditure on marketing of securities etc.

It should be noted that capital budgeting is customarily considered with reference to the investments in plant and machinery. However, principally, it can be applied to all types of investments mentioned above.

Components of Project Evaluation

Capital budgeting decision involves the rigorous evaluation of each investment proposal in quantitative terms. The comparison is made between the cash inflows and the cash outflows of each proposal.

Cash flows: In the capital budgeting decisions, cash flows out of the investments are considered rather than the accounting profits generated out of the investments. The cash inflow and the accounting profit do not represent the same figure because cash inflow is the excess of cash receipts over cash payments while accounting profit is a periodic profit ascertained on the basis of the accrual principle of accounting involving certain accounting adjustments, *e.g.*, provision of depreciation on fixed assets reduce the accounting profits, but it is not an actual outflow of cash. Thus, the cash inflow and the accounting profits hardly tally with each other. In the capital budgeting analysis, cash flows rather than the accounting profits are considered because for the purpose of making additional profits one must have cash to reinvest and there is no assurance that one will have the accountant's reported profits available in the form of cash.

The cash flow statement is prepared with the help of the following three steps:

1. Estimated initial cash outflows
2. Expected cash inflows
3. New cash inflows.

(1) Estimated Initial Cash Outflows: Capital budgeting decision involves huge cash outflows. The initial cash outflows are ascertained as under:

Invoice price of the new machine	...	xxx
Add: Freight and installation charges	...	xxx
Add: Additional working capital required due to the operations on the new machine	...	xxx
Less:		
1. Scrap value of this plant at the end of its economic life	xxx	xxx
2. Recoupment of the additional working capital at the end of the economic life	xxx	xxx
Initial cash outflow		xxx

It should be noted that in case of the decision involving the replacement of an old machine by a new one, following two additional items will be deducted while ascertaining the initial cash outflows.

(*i*) Tax savings arising out of the disposal of the old machine.

(*ii*) Realization of the salvage value of the old machine.

(2) Expected Cash Inflows: We have analysed the nature of the capital budgeting decision that it is the present sacrifice with a view to yield returns out of it in future. The initial cash outflow [*i.e.*, above (1)] is the present sacrifice, while here we will consider the expected cash benefits out of such sacrifice which will be available till the economic life of the investments, say 10 to 12 years. The cash inflow statement will be prepared for each year as under:

	Sale			xxx
Less:	Operating costs	...	xxx	
	Depreciation	...	xxx	
	Income before tax	...		xxx
Less:	Income tax	...		xxx
	Income after tax	...		xxx
Add:	Depreciation	...		xxx
	Net cash inflow of the year	...		xxx

N.B.: (*i*) As depreciation is an accounting adjustment and not an actual outflow of cash, it is added back for ascertaining the net cash inflow of the year. Depreciation is allowed as a deductible business expenditure for tax purpose, so it is initially deducted while ascertaining the taxable income. Thus, the tax advantage arising out of the depreciation provisions gets incorporated in the cash inflows.

(*ii*) It is assumed that the entire sales are on cash basis and all the operating costs have been paid in cash. As this is a cash flow statement, only cash receipts and cash payments are considered.

It should be carefully noted that the 'Sales' and the 'Operating costs' components of the cash flow statement involve some element of uncertainty in the sales forecast of each year till the economic life of the investment. The entire analysis of the project evaluation will be vitiated if the sales forecasts are not made carefully. Similarly, the operating costs of certain inputs like materials, labour, infrastructure facilities etc. are subject to price changes. Reasonable cost escalations should be made to increase the reliability of the cash inflow data for the purpose of evaluating the capital budgeting decision.

Net cash inflow for replacement decision: There lies a fundamental difference between the fresh capital budgeting decision and the replacement decision. When an old machine is replaced by a new one, the estimated cash outflows arising out of the new machine will be affected by the tax savings on disposal of an old machine as well as realisation of the salvage value of the same.

Similarly, the replacement decision will also affect the expected cash inflows in terms of increased production and the resultant rise in sales, economy in the operating expenses, the tax benefits on the depreciation etc. This phenomenon is explained in the following illustration.

Illustration:

The Precision Tools Ltd., purchased a machine on 1st January 1994 at a cost of ₹ 7,500. The machine's estimated economic life is 15 years and it will not fetch any salvage value at the end of its economic life. The machine is depreciated on a straight line method and on 31st December 1998, its written down value was ₹ 5,000. The company is considering a proposal to replace this machine by a new one from 1st January 1999. The details of the proposal are as under:

Acquisition cost of the new machine —
(including installation) ₹ 10,000

Economic life of the new machine 10 years

Increase in sales — from ₹10,000 to ₹11,000

Reduction in operating costs — from ₹ 7,000 to ₹ 5,000

The salvage value of new machine is estimated to be zero.

On 1st January 1999, the realizable value of the old machine is ₹ 1,000/-.

The company falls in the 50% tax-bracket.

Prepare the comparative statement showing the effect of the replacement decision on the cash flows.

Solution:

The cash flow calculations are made in the three steps as discussed in the above paragraphs:

(1) Estimated initial cash outflow:

		₹
Acquisition cost of the new machine —		10,000
Less: (1) Tax savings	2,000	
(2) Realization of salvage value of the old machine	1,000	3,000
Estimated initial cash outflows		₹ 7,000

N.B.: (1) The written down value of the old machine on the date of replacement is ₹ 5,000. The salvage realizes ₹ 1,000. So the unabsorbed loss of the old machine ₹ 4,000 (₹ 5,000- ₹ 1,000) is allowed as the deductible item for the tax purposes. As the company falls in the 50% tax bracket, the company will enjoy the tax advantage of ₹ 2,000 (*i.e.*, 50% of ₹ 4,000). As this tax benefit is arising out of the new machine, the initial investment of the new machine will be reduced to that extent.

(2) The realization of the salvage value of the old machine reduces the cash needs for the new machine and so it will also be deducted for ascertaining the estimated initial cash outflows.

(3) *Expected cash inflows:* The benefits arising out of the investment in new machine will be available up to ten years. The yearly cash inflows out of the replacement decision will be calculated as under:

COMPARATIVE CASH INFLOW STATEMENT

	Old machine (without replacement) ₹	***New machine (with replacement)*** ₹
Sales	10,000	11,000
Less: Operating costs	7,000	5,000
	3,000	6,000
Less: Depreciation	500	1,000
Profit before tax	2,500	5,000
Less: Income Tax (50%)	1,250	2,500
Profit after tax	1,250	2,500
Add: Depreciation	500	1,000
Cash inflow (per annum)	1,750	3,500

N.B.: (1) The new machine is depreciated on a straight line method. As its scrap value is estimated zero the capital cost of ₹ 10,000 is divided equally among 10 years.

(2) As depreciation is an accounting adjustment and it does not involve any cash outflows, it is added back while ascertaining the cash inflows.

The replacement decision avails the following advantage:

Cash inflow with replacement	₹ 3,500
Less: Cash inflow without replacement	₹ 1,750
Increase in cash inflow due to replacement decision	₹ 1,750

₹ 1,750 is the yearly advantage. The life of the new machine is 10 years. So the total cash inflow would be ₹ 17,500 (₹ 1,750 × 10 years).

(3) Net Cash Inflow: The replacement decision involves certain cash benefits (*i.e.*, cash inflows).

The net advantage of the replacement decision will be as under:

	Expected total cash inflow of 10 years	₹ 17,500
Less:	Estimated initial cash outflows	₹ 7,000
	Net inflow arising out of replacement decision	₹ 10,500

The third step in the analysis is the ascertainment of the net cash inflow. With the help of the estimated initial cash outflow [above (1)] and the expected cash inflows [above (2)], the net cash inflow is ascertained as under:

	Expected cash inflows	—	(Benefits)
Less:	Estimated initial cash outflows	—	(Sacrifice)
	Net cash inflows	—	(Net benefits)

Thus, net cash inflow is nothing but the excess of expected cash inflows over the estimated cash outflows. Only those capital projects should be selected which yield the maximum net cash inflows.

It should be noted that the expected future cash inflows is closely related with the economic life of the project. In the capital budgeting decision, the length of the period during which the project is expected to yield economic benefits (*i.e.*, expected future cash inflows) is an important input. Here, we are concerned with the "economic life" of the project. By economic life, we mean the periodicity during which the cash inflows are estimated. Economic life is largely commanded by the rate of technological development.

The economic life of the project is an important component of the analysis for the following reasons:

(*i*) It prescribes the number of years during which the cash inflow all occur.

(*ii*) Longer the life of the project, higher will be the uncertainty in cash inflow estimates, because the precision in the estimation is inversely related to the length of the time.

(*iii*) Money has the time value in terms of compounding advantages. A rupee received today is valuable than a rupee received after five years because compounding interest on money is received at later stage. The concept of the time value of money is explained in detail in the following paragraph (F) on "PRESENT VALUE."

The "cost of capital" is another important component required in evaluating the capital budgeting decision. The cost of capital is the cost of raising the funds. The firm's cost of capital is decided on the basis of the capital structure, *i.e.*, mix of the long-term funds. Cost of capital is a cut off rate for capital budgeting decision, the yield from the project must not be less than the cost of capital, *i.e.*, the ROI is calculated on the basis of the total investments in the project and total net cash inflow from the project. Considering cost of capital and ROI of each project, only those projects are accepted whose ROI exceeds or at least equates the cost of capital. The logic is simple to understand. We raise funds for a project which costs us 10%. So we must employ these funds in a project which yields at least 10% to meet the cost of funds. If the project yields less than 10% it is better not to go for the project rather than to go for it to reduce the wealth of equity shareholders.

Present Value or Discounted Value

Money has a time value. A rupee received today has more value than a rupee received after five years. A rupee received today can yield some returns if it is invested in the bank for five years. Thus, the present rupee is definitely more valuable than a rupee received after five years. It is interesting to note that the present value of a rupee received after 25 years and discounted at 20% rate of interest is just 1 paisa. Thus, a rupee received today and a rupee received after 25 years cannot be put at par.

The time-value of the money is explained through the ready-made "Compound Interest Tables" and the "Present Value Tables." It should be noted that discounted value (or the present value) explains the same phenomenon of the time value of money. As used in the common parlance of the banking transactions, a rupee of today gets the compounded interest till five years and the aggregate value at the end of the fifth year would be greater than ₹ 1. Conversely, the bills maturing after three months can be discounted today which will fetch the lesser value than the value to be received on the maturity of the bill. Thus, compounding process, is exactly the opposite of discounting process. In the compounding process, today's rupee is compounded at some future date, while in discounting process tomorrow's rupee is discounted today to ascertain its present value. Thus, the compounded value is always greater than "1" while the discounted value is always lesser than "1." As the discounting process ascertains the discounted value on today, *i.e.*, the present time, it is also known as **present value.**

The concept of compounded value and the discount value can be explained with the help of the formula and the graph as under:

Compound Value

The compound interest formula is as under:

$$A = P(1 + i)^n$$

where, P = Principal or beginning amount.

i = Rate of interest.

n = No. of years during which the compounding is to be done.

A = Aggregate amount at the end of the period, *i.e.*, Principal plus aggregate interest, *e.g.*, ₹ 1,000 are deposited for 3 years at 10% compound interest. How much amount will they fetch at the end of 3rd year.

$$A = P(1 + i)^n$$
$$= 1{,}000\,(1 + 10\%)^3$$
$$= 1{,}000\,(1.1)^3$$
$$= ₹\ 1{,}331$$

It should be noted that ready-made compound interest tables are available which are prepared on the basis of the aforesaid formula. The columns prescribe the rate of interest while the rows indicate time in years. Such tables are prepared on "Per Rupee basis." Referring to the "compound interest table of ₹ 1," the intersection of the 10% column and 3rd year's row, gives the value of 1.331. This is the compound value of ₹ 1. Therefore, the compounded value of ₹ 1,000 would be ₹ 1331.

The ready-made tables are also available for the compound value of an **"annuity."** An annuity is defined as a series of payments of fixed amount for a specified number of years. Thus, under the annuity, a specified fixed amount is added every year which is compounded along with the historical investments, *e.g.*, if ₹ 1,000 are invested every year up to 3 years 10% compound interest, the aggregated value at the end of 3rd year will be as under:

The compound value is calculated with the help of the graph as under:

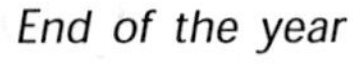

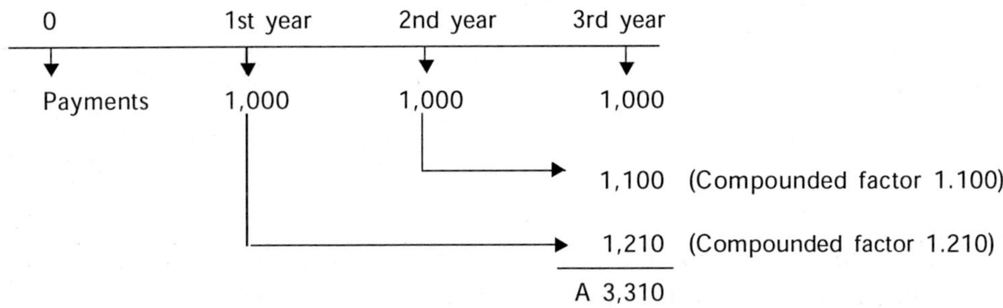

The use of the annuity tables eliminates the need for ascertaining the compounded factor for each year from the simple "compound interest table of ₹ 1." Referring to the "compound interest table of annuity of A 1" we directly get the compounded factor of 3.310 at the intersection of 10% and 3 years and thus for ₹ 1,000, we get ₹ 3,310 which is exactly the same amount ascertained on the basis of the "compound interest table of ₹ 1" which requires the separate calculation for each year.

Present Value: The present value is just the opposite to the compound value. It is also popularly known as the Discounted Cash Flow (DCF). The use of the compounding value is very popular in the banking sector. However, for the evaluation of the capital budgeting the present value concept is very useful. The concept of present value is explained in the following paragraphs with the help of formula and graph. The present value formula can be divided as under from the compound interest formula:

$$A = P(1 + i)^n$$

If the equation is solved for the value of P, we get the present value formula as under:

$$P = \frac{A}{(1+i)^n}$$

where, P = Present value

A = Aggregate value at the end of the period

i = Rate of interest

n = Economic life of the project in years during which the cash flows occur.

The ready-made present value tables are available which are prepared on the basis of the aforesaid formula. In the "present value table of ₹ 1" the columns indicate various rates of interest at which ₹ 1 received in future is required to be discounted and the rows indicate the time in years, *e.g.*, for ₹ 1,000 received after 3 years, the present values at 10% discount rate will be ascertained as under:

$$P = \frac{A}{(1+i)^n} = \frac{1{,}000}{(1+0.10)^3} = ₹\ 751.30$$

The present value can also be obtained with the help of the present value tables. The intersection of 10% column and 3rd year row gives the discount factor of 0.7513. It is the present value of ₹ 1 received after 3 years. So, the present value of ₹ 1,000 received after 3 years and discounted at 10% will be ₹ 751.30 (1,000 × .7513).

The ready-made "Present Value Tables of Annuity of ₹ 1" are also available. With the help of the annuity table, the present value of the fixed amount received on annual basis during a specified future period can be calculated very easily, *e.g.*, if ₹ 1,000 are received every year up to 3 years, and are discounted at 10% the present value (*i.e.*, today's value) is ascertained with the help of the graph as under:

END OF THE YEAR

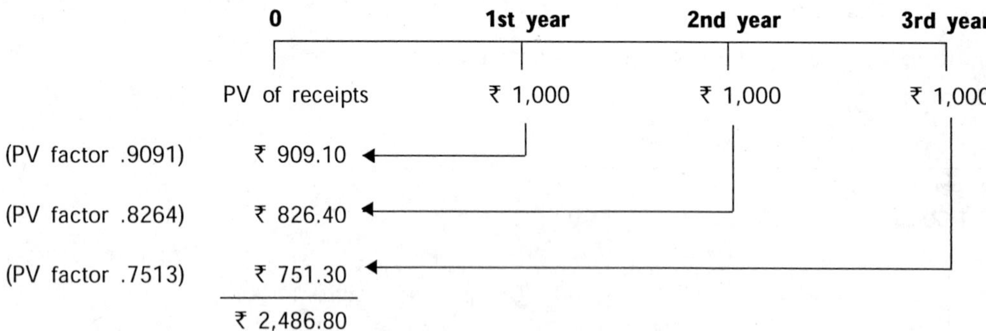

The use of the "Present Value Tables of Annuity of ₹ 1" eliminates the need for calculating the discount for each year from the simple "present value table of ₹ 1." For the above example, if we refer to the annuity table, we directly get the present value of the annuity of ₹ 1 received up to 3 years. The present value factor at the intersection of 3rd year and 10% is 2.4869.

The present value tables are very useful in evaluating the capital budgeting decisions. Capital expenditures involve the initial cash outflow (*i.e.*, project cost) today and the recurring cash inflows in future years till the economic life of the project. The cash inflows of the future period are discounted at the specified rate of interest, which is usually the company's cost of capital. The present values so ascertained are compared with the project cost which is nothing but the present value of the cash outflows. From this, the Net Present Value (NPV) is ascertained which indicates the merit of the project. Projects with negative Net Present Value (NPV) are rejected while those with the highest NPV are selected.

The calculation of the aggregate present value of the cash inflows received in future years is mathematically presented as under:

$$PV = \frac{C_1}{(1+i)} + \frac{C_2}{(1+i)^2} + \frac{C_3}{(1+i)^3} + \dots \frac{C_n}{(1+i)^n}$$

where, PV = Aggregate present value of cash inflows

C = Cash flow of the respective years

i = Rate of interest at which the cash flows are to be discounted usually the cost of capital

n = Number of years during which the cash inflows occur

As this is nothing but a summation of different values, it can be presented as under:

$$PV = \sum_{t=1}^{n} \frac{Ct}{(1+i)^t}$$

The application of the present value technique is explained in detail in the following paragraphs dealing with the "method of evaluating the capital budgeting decisions."

Methods of Evaluation

Following methods are employed in evaluating capital budgeting decision:

(*i*) Pay-back period (PBP)

(*ii*) Accounting rate of return on investment (ROI)

(*iii*) Net Present Value (NPV)

(*iv*) Internal rate of return (IRR)

It is to be noted that in the first two methods (*viz.*, PBP and ROI), the time value of money is not considered and so the discounted cash flow technique is not applied, while the other methods (NPV and IRR) are based on the discounted cash flow technique.

(i) Pay-back period method (PBP): Pay-back period method is one of the most widely used methods of evaluating capital projects. Surveys show that it is widely used in U.S.A. and U.K. especially for foreign investment. In India also it is widely used. Many State Financial Corporations use this method to evaluate the projects falling within the limits of ₹ 5 lakhs.

Pay-back period is the length of the period required to recover the original investment. In this method following two aspects are considered:

(*i*) Original project cost, and

(*ii*) Cash inflows in subsequent years.

Pay-back period will be considered on the basis of following nature of cash inflows.

(a) PBP under even cash inflows: When annual cash inflow is same for all the years, then payback period will be found out as under:

$$PBP = \frac{\text{Investment}}{\text{Annual Cash Inflow}}$$

Illustration:

	Project A ₹	Project B ₹
Project cost (*i.e.*, investment)	30,000	40,000
Cash inflows:		
1st year	10,000	15,000
2nd year	10,000	15,000
3rd year	10,000	15,000
4th year	10,000	15,000

$$\text{PBP for project 'A'} = \frac{30,000}{10,000} = 3 \text{ years}$$

$$\text{PBP for project 'B'} = \frac{40,000}{15,000} = 2.67 \text{ years}$$

(b) PBP under uneven cash inflows: Where annual cash inflows are fluctuating, PBP can be obtained as under:

$$\mathbf{I = Y_1 + Y_2 + Y_3 ... Y_n}$$

where, I = Project cost or investment
Y = Yearly cash inflow
n = Number of years.

Illustration:

Find out PBP of the following project:

Project cost = ₹ 50,000

Cash inflow = 1st year ₹ 10,000
2nd year ₹ 30,000
3rd year ₹ 20,000

PBP is I $= Y_1 + Y_2 + Y_3 ... Y_n$

$$\therefore 50,000 = 10,000 + 30,000 + \frac{10,000}{20,000}$$

$= 2\frac{1}{2}$ years

In the PBP method, project having the **Shortest PBP** and which is falling within the cut-off PBP prescribed by the management is selected.

Merits:

1. It is simple to understand and easy to calculate and communicate.
2. It is good for such projects where the rate of technological change is very high. As it emphasizes a speedy recovery of original investments, it minimises the chances of losses arising out of obsolescence.
3. It indirectly emphasises the value of money. Project having speedier recovery of original investments are considered good.

Demerits:

1. It ignores the total profitability of the project. Profitability beyond pay-back period is not considered. Consider the following projects:

	Project A ₹	Project B ₹
Project cost	10,000	10,000
Cash inflows		
1st year	6,000	3,000
2nd year	4,000	4,000
3rd year	2,000	3,000
4th year	1,000	10,000
Total cash inflows	13,000	20,000
PBP	2 years	3 years

Though overall profitability of project 'B' is high (total cash inflows are A 20,000), project 'A' having shorter PBP (2 years) will be selected under PBP method.

2. It does not consider the time value of money. A rupee received today is more valuable than a rupee received after five years. Consider the following case:

Project	*Project Cost* ₹	*Cash Inflow* 1st year ₹	2nd year ₹	3rd year ₹
A	12,000	3,000	6,000	9,000
B	12,000	9,000	6,000	3,000

Both the projects A and B have got some **PBP,** *viz.,* **3 years**. So under PBP method both are ranked equally. But if we consider time value of money, project B is definitely superior to project A because in the first year project B yields ₹ 9,000 while project A yields only ₹ 3,000. The additional **6,000** rupees over project A has the advantage of compound interest.

(3) The cut-off PBP prescribed by the management for the investment decision is not decided scientifically. It is based on subjectivity and thus makes the entire analysis unscientific.

(ii) Accounting rate of return on investment method (ROI): Unlike PBP method, here the total profitability over the entire economic life of the project is considered. In this method capital projects are ranked in order of their earnings or returns. Project yielding the highest earnings is selected.

In ROI method following two variables are considered:

(*a*) Original project cost or initial investment.

(*b*) Annual income after taxes. (Here instead of cash inflows, the after tax net profits as disclosed by financial accounting are considered).

The ROI is calculated as under:

$$\text{ROI (in \%)} = \frac{\text{Average annual income}}{\text{Average project cost}} \times 100$$

The average annual income is ascertained dividing the total income from all the years by the number of years. The average project cost is nothing but the 'total project cost' ÷ 2. The reason for considering average project cost is that, the original project cost gets depreciated over the life of the project and reaches to zero value at the end of the project. So, the average investment will be nothing but just half the original investments.

Illustration:

Project	Annual Income in a year					Total Income ₹
	Project cost ₹	1 ₹	2 ₹	3 ₹	4 ₹	
A	5,000	1,000	1,500	2,000	2,500	7,000
B	5,000	2,000	3,000	1,000	2,000	8,000

Solution:

The ROI of the project is ascertained as under:

$$\text{ROI (in \%)} = \frac{\text{Average annual income}}{\text{Average project cost}} \times 100$$

Now, Average Annual Income

= total income of all years ÷ total number of years.

Thus for project A, average annual income

$$= \frac{(1{,}000 + 1{,}500 + 2{,}000 + 2{,}500)}{4} = \frac{7{,}000}{4} = ₹\ 1{,}750$$

For project B, Average annual income

$$= \frac{(2{,}000 + 3{,}000 + 1{,}000 + 2{,}000)}{4} = \frac{8{,}000}{4} = ₹\ 2{,}000$$

The average project cost for both the project A and B

$$= \frac{5{,}000}{2} = ₹\,2{,}500$$

$$\text{Thus, for Project A: ROI} = \frac{1{,}750}{2{,}500} \times 100 = 70\%$$

$$\text{for Project B: ROI} = \frac{2{,}000}{2{,}500} \times 100 = 80\%$$

The project B with higher ROI will be selected under this method.

Merits:

1. It is simple to calculate and easy to understand and communicate.
2. This method considers the total profitability of the project which is ignored under the **PBP** method.

Demerits:

1. It uses the after tax income as disclosed by the accounting data and not consider the cash inflows. Accounting income is calculated on accrual basis.
2. It ignores the time value of money. Profits earned in different periods are valued equally. Consider the following situation:

Project	Annual Income in a Year		
	1	2	3
	₹	₹	₹
A	10,000	15,000	20,000
B	20,000	15,000	10,000

The average annual incomes of project A and B are same, *viz.*, ₹ 15,000. So the rate of return calculated on average income will rank both the projects on equal footing. However, project B is superior as it generates ₹ 20,000 in first year (₹ 10,000 more than project A) which has time value.

3. It does not consider the length of the life of the project. It assumes that 25% accounting rate for five years is better than 20% for ten years.

(iii) Net Present Value Method (NPV): This method takes into account the time value of money as well as total profitability of the project. Net present value means present value of cash inflows less present value of cash outflows. The inflows and outflows are discounted at the firm's cost of capital.

NPV = PV of cash inflows — PV of cash outflows.

Following steps are involved in NPV method:

1. Ascertain the appropriate rate of interest. Generally, firm's cost of capital is the discounting rate.
2. Discount the cash outflows at this rate. Cash outflows is nothing but the project cost. Generally, it is given that the project cost is incurred initially (*i.e.*, at time zero). So, as project cost represents today's worth, it will not require any discounting. Thus, the present value of cash outflow will be nothing but the project cost.
3. Discount the cash inflows at the given discount rate, *i.e.*, at firm's cost of capital. Cash inflows occur every year. So, present value of each year's cash inflow shall be found out with the help of PV tables.
4. To get the net present value, subtract the PV of outflows from that of the aggregate cash inflows of all the years.

The accept-reject rule will be as under:

i.e., Accept if NPV ≥ 0

Reject if NPV < 0

Illustration:

Calculate the net present value for project X and project Y from the following data:

Project	***Project cost***	***Cash Inflows after Tax***			
		1st year	***2nd year***	***3rd year***	***4th year***
	₹	₹	₹	₹	₹
X	7,000	2,000	5,000	2,000	2,000
Y	7,000	3,000	2,000	2,000	3,000

The project costs are to be incurred immediately. Firm's cost of capital is 10%.

Solution:

The PV of cash inflows will be as under:

Year	***PROJECT X***			***PROJECT Y***		
	Cash inflows ₹	***DCF factor at 10%***	***Present value*** ₹	***Cash inflows*** ₹	***DCF factor at 10%***	***Present value*** ₹
	(1)	(2)	(3) = (1) × (2)	(4)	(5)	(6) = (4) × (5)
1	2,000	0.909	1,818	3,000	0.909	2,727
2	5,000	0.826	4,130	2,000	0.826	1,652
3	2,000	0.751	1,502	2,000	0.751	1,502
4	2,000	0.683	1,366	3,000	0.683	2,049
Total PV			8,816			7,930

The PV of cash outflows is nothing but project costs because they are incurred today so their discounting would not be necessary.

Now NPV of both the projects will be as under:

NPV = PV of Inflows – PV of outflows

For Project A: NPV = 8816 – 7000 = ₹ 1,816

Project B: NPV = 7930 – 7000 = ₹ 930

Thus, both the projects have got positive NPV, and hence should be selected. If both the projects are mutually exclusive (*i.e.*, only one out of the two is to be selected) then project X will be selected as it yields higher NPV.

Profitability Index: In the above problem, we have considered two projects having equal project cost, *viz.*, ₹ 7,000. But when project costs are unequal, then profitability index is used as selection criterion.

$$\text{Profitability index} = \frac{\text{Total PV of inflows}}{\text{Total PV of outflows}}$$

For project X profitability index will be as under:

$$\text{Profitability index} = \frac{8{,}816}{7{,}000} = 1.259$$

Project having the highest profitability index will be selected.

NPV Formula: NPV can also be expressed by the following equation. In this formula, it is assumed that all cash outflows are made in initial year, *i.e.*, at time t_0.

$$\text{NPV} = \left(\frac{C_1}{(1+i)} + \frac{C_2}{(1+i)^2} + \frac{C_3}{(1+i)^3} + \ldots \frac{C_n}{(1+i)^n}\right) - I$$

where, C = Cash inflow of respective year

i = Discount rate, *i.e.*, firm's cost of capital

n = Number of years

I = Initial outflow, *i.e.*, project cost

The above formula can also be expressed as under:

$$\text{NPV} = \sum_{t=1}^{n} \frac{C_t}{(1+i)^t} - I$$

Merits

1. It recognizes the time value of money which is ignored in PBP and ROI methods.
2. It considers all cash inflows during the entire life of the project, while in PBP method cash inflows beyond the pay-back period are ignored.
3. It permits the direct comparison between the returns from the methods.
4. It gives due consideration to uncertainty and risk in returns. Returns arising remotely are assigned less values.

Demerits

1. It is difficult and complicated, as it is involves cumbersome calculations. However, this is not a forceful argument.
2. It presupposes that the discount rate, *i.e.*, firm's cost of capital is known. Discount rate plays a pivotal role in entire calculation. However, this rate (*i.e.*, firm's cost of capital) is difficult

to ascertain in reality. Internal rate of return (IRR) method is superior to this method only on this ground that IRR does not consider any predetermined discount rate.

3. It does not give a satisfactory answer when project costs are unequal. However, in such a situation we can come to a conclusion on the basis of profitability index.
4. Similarly, sometimes it misleads when projects have unequal lives. In such a situation sometimes judgement under NPV and IRR are contradictory.

(iv) Internal Rate of Return Method (IRR): Like NPV, this method also considers the time value of money and the total profitability over the entire life of the project. It is also known as "time adjusted rate of return." Economists describe it as the efficiency of capital. **Internal rate of return is the rate which equates the present value of cash inflows with the present value of outflows. In other words, it is the rate at which the net present value is zero.**

Like NPV, it does not use any outside rate but a built-in rate is ascertained which will equate the PV of both the cash flows, inflows and outflows. Internal rate is the maximum rate that can be paid for the capital employed over the life of the project without any loss on it.

It is difficult to get the IRR at first attempt. The ascertainment of IRR involves many attempts under the trial and error method. If the IRR is falling between the two ranges, the precise IRR is found out with the help of interpolation.

The decision criterion is to accept project if IRR ≥ firm's cost of capital and reject if IRR ≤ the cost of capital. Thus, IRR is compared with the firm's cost of capital. If selection is to be made among the mutually exclusive projects, the project with the highest IRR, is selected. IRR can be found out by solving the following equation:

$$I = \left(\frac{C_1}{(1+r)} + \frac{C_2}{(1+r)^2} + \frac{C_3}{(1+r)^3} + \dots \frac{C_n}{(1+r)^n}\right)$$

where, I = Initial project cost or investment

C = Yearly cash inflows

r = Internal rate of return

n = Number of years

It can also be expressed as under:

$$= \sum_{t=1}^{n} \frac{C_t}{(1+r)^t}$$

The equations under NPV and IRR are the same. The only difference between them is that under NPV method "i" (*i.e.*, discount rate or firm's cost of capital) is known while under IRR, "r" (*i.e.*, the discount rate or IRR) is to be found out.

Illustration:

Calculate the internal rate of return from the following data:

Project cost	₹ 16,200
Cash inflows:	
1st year	₹ 8,000
2nd year	₹ 7,000
3rd year	₹ 6,000

Solution:

The solution will be sought under the trial and error method. So it should be done in the following sequence:

(*i*) First of all discount the given cash flows at any discount rate. Under the trial and error method, the most crucial decision is from where to start so that the calculations are minimized. Here following rule be followed:

Find out the annuity factor as under —

$$\text{Annuity factor} = \frac{\text{Project cost}}{\text{Average cash inflow}}$$

$$= \frac{16,200}{7,000}; 7,000 = \frac{(8,000+7,000+6,000)}{3}$$

$$= 2.31$$

We know that the life of the project is 3 years. So, now refer to the PV table titled as "present value of an annuity of ₹ 1" and pick up the **3rd year column** and move horizontally to different interest rates and locate the table value which is near to 2.31 (*i.e.,* the annuity factor). For this problem at 14% interest rate the value is 2.322 which is nearer to 2.31. So, first of all start with 14% discount rate and find out the net present value as under:

NPV AT 14% DISCOUNT RATE

Year ***(1)***	***Cash inflow*** ***(2)*** ₹	***PV factor at 14%*** ***(3)***	***PV (2 × 3)*** ***(4)*** ₹
1	8,000	0.877	7,016
2	7,000	0.769	5,383
3	6,000	0.675	4,050
Total PV			16,449
Less PV of cash inflow			16,200
(*i.e.,* project cost) NPV			249

(*ii*) We know that the IRR is rate where NPV is ZERO. Now at 14% discount rate calculated above, the NPV is + 249. So, we shall have to try some other discount rate so that we can eliminate the positive value of NPV. For the second try following rule be followed:

Rule: NPV and the discount rate are **inversely** related, *i.e.,* if we want to reduce the NPV, increase the discount rate. Now at 14% discount rate, the NPV is + **249**. So, to reach to ZERO NPV (as IRR is a rate at which NPV is ZERO), we shall have to reduce the value of NPV. To reduce NPV, increase the discount rate. So, from 14% the second try will be made at 16%. Now find out the NPV at 16% discount rate.

NPV AT 16% DISCOUNT RATE

Year ***(1)***	***Cash inflow*** ***(2)*** ₹	***PV factor at 16%*** ***(3)***	***PV*** ***(4) = (2 × 3)*** ₹
1	8,000	0.862	6,896
2	7,000	0.743	5,201
3	6,000	0.641	3,846
Total PV =			15,943
Less PV of outflow =			16,200
(*i.e.,* project cost NPV)			–257

At 16% discount rate the NPV is negative (– 257). So we can conclude that the IRR is not above 16% and below 14%. It is falling between 14% and 16%. The exact value of the IRR will be obtained with the help of interpolation as explained in step (iii) below.

(*iii*) We know the range of IRR, *i.e.*, it is falling between 14% and 16%.

The interpolation between 14% and 16% will be made as under to arrive at the precise IRR.

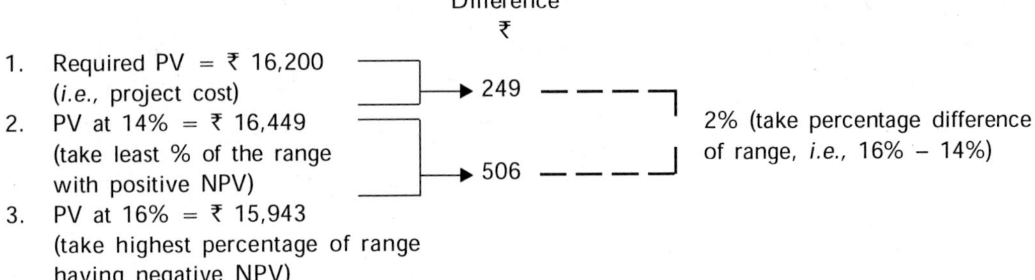

Now, from the above-mentioned differences of value and % age, find out the IRR as under:

IRR = Least discount rate

$$+ \text{ Differential percentage in the discount rate} \times \frac{\text{Upper difference}}{\text{Lower difference}}$$

$$= 14\% + 2 \times \frac{249}{506}$$

$$= 14\% + 2 \times \frac{1}{2} \ldots \left(\frac{249}{506} \text{ is approximately } \frac{1}{2}\right)$$

$$= 14\% + 1$$

$$= 15\%$$

Thus, at 15% IRR, the NPV will be ZERO, which can be verified as under:

NPV AT 15% DISCOUNT RATE

Year (1)		*Cash inflows (2) ₹*	*PV factor at 15% (3)*	*PV (4) = (2 × 3) ₹*
1		8,000	0.870	6,960
2		7,000	0.756	5,292
3		6,000	0.658	3,948
	Total PV	=		16,200
	Less PV of outflows	=		16,200
	i.e., Project cost + NPV	=		00

Merits:

1. Like NPV method, it considers the time value of money.
2. Like NPV, this method also considers the cash flow over the entire life of the project.
3. It prescribes the floor limit below which the funds should not be employed. Because of this characteristic, it has appealed rigorously to the business community and financial institutions.
4. In NPV method, the discount rate (*i.e.*, cost of capital) is a pre-condition for the calculation. IRR method does not pre-suppose any such discount rate. However, for the purpose of selection, **IRR** is compared with the cutoff rate (*i.e.*, cost of capital) and to that extent cost of capital should be known.

Demerits:

1. It is complex to calculate and difficult to understand. It requires substantial calculations under trial and error method.
2. It assumes that the cash flows generated during the life of the project, will be re-invested at the same rate, *i.e.,* IRR. In reality this may not be the case at all times.
3. NPV and IRR methods sometimes give conflicting results especially when project costs are unequal or project lives are not similar.

SUPPLY CHAIN MANAGEMENT

In operations management as well as materials management, one topic has recently invited attention of all businesses — it is supply chain management (SCM). The difference between the conventional thinking and SCM is that SCM treats the whole flow of information, materials and services from the suppliers through factories and stores to the final customer as a business system. These core activities require management on day-to-day basis so as fulfil the demand.

Supply chain actually represents the inter-linkage of an organization with other organizations which in turn are also having their own inter-linkages. Let us make the purchase or materials department as the central department. If we consider how the suppliers are received by the purchase department, we find it has a number of suppliers, and each supplier itself has its own set of suppliers, and so on. It is thus a network or series of chains. In the following diagram, we show one such network or supply chain, where three suppliers have been connected to the purchase department. If there are more suppliers, the supply chain becomes quite a complex thing.

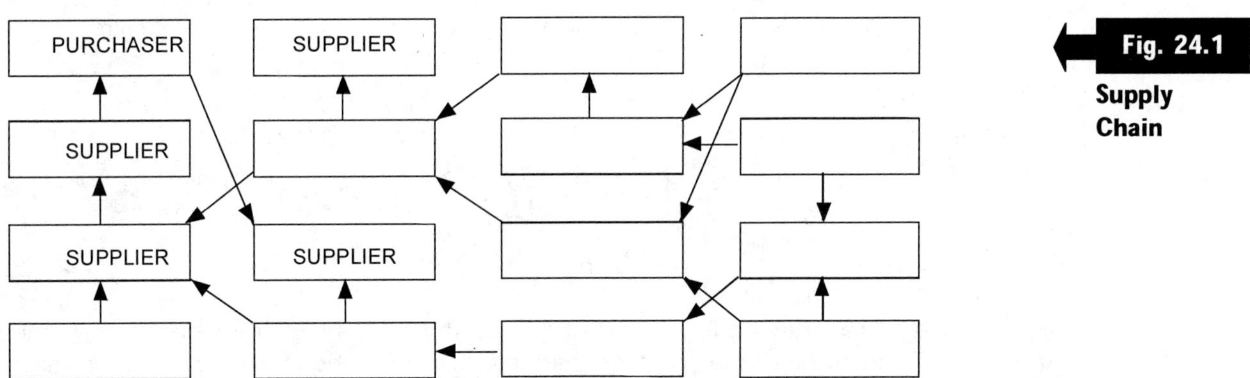

Fig. 24.1
Supply Chain

The major objective of supply chain management (SCM) is to minimise uncertainty and risks associated with the supply chain. This by itself positively affects inventories, cycle time, processes, and customer service. SCM is another name for systems optimisation. The tools for this system management are forecasting, aggregate planning, inventory management and scheduling. These have been discussed elsewhere in the book.

Fig. 24.2 **Tools for SCM**

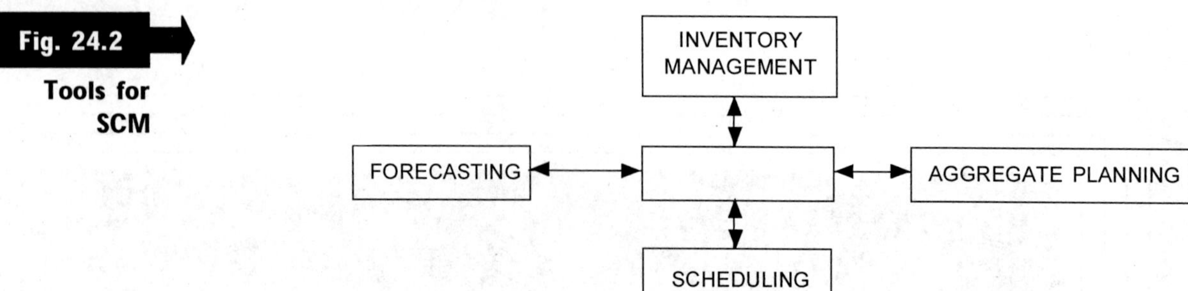

It is to be appreciated that a forecast becomes input to aggregate planning, which affects inventory planning, which ultimately leads to schedules of workforce and equipment.

Any decision taken at one stage of supply chain affects the other stages. To illustrate, if we plan to make 2 lakh scooters this week at our plant, we expect our supplier to provide us 4 lac tyres in time at our plant so as to reach our goal. This does not happen just as we wish. It has to be planned in terms of manpower, materials and time.

Fig. 24.3

Supply Chain Management

The supply chain is a network of facilities and distribution options that perform the functions of procurement of raw materials, transformation of these materials into intermediate and finished products and the distribution of these finished products to customers via the distribution channel that would normally include distributors, stockists and retailers.

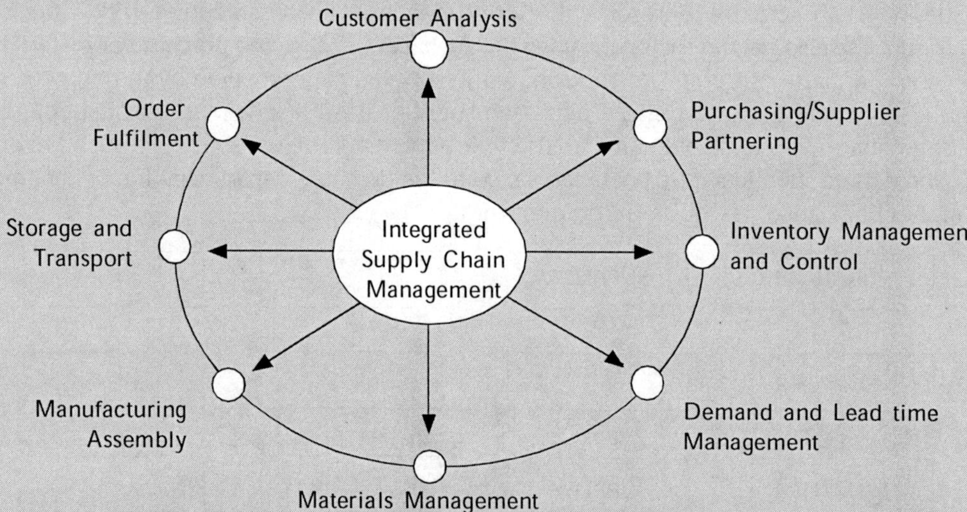

A typical broad supply chain may incorporate the supplier of raw materials (vendors), transporters, manufacturing plant or manufacturer, warehouse, wholesaler, retailer and finally the consumer. Each participant in the supply chain has a supply chain of its own that seamlessly integrates into the entire network.

Till recently, all these departments functioned independently. There was internal computerisation of these departments. But still they were islands. Data sharing was not practised. As demand showed variations, the procurement of raw materials which was based upon the demand also was erratic. As distribution data was not available on tap, it resulted in huge inventories and equally huge, instances of wastage. Sometimes, when demand was overestimated, huge quantities of consumables with short shelf life had to be discarded.

These days we reap the benefits of networking. SCTM is now internet based or extranet-based. Data are accessible in real time. It cuts down time and costs. If there is scarcity of raw materials, manufacturing gets immediate alert, which in turn alerts packaging and distribution. Thanks to retailer-manufacturer linkage, production and inventory planning improves greatly. Point of sale information is captured online. The number of days inventory then is benchmarked. Production schedules are designed accordingly. It matches the distributors' demands.

SCM solutions are implemented through internet using servers or through closed proprietary networks. Internet is very economical. Physical presence is not required. We can access the system even while on the move. Instructions can be given to plant people. Convergence has further enhanced the utility of SCM.

OUTSOURCING

Materials constitute a large percentage of costs in manufacturing — from 60 to 70 per cent. Outsourcing means procurement of materials, assemblies and other services from outside sources, rather than doing them inside the company. Outsourcing enables a company to focus on its core competencies — do what it excels in doing. It gives the company a competitive advantage.

The co-ordination of outsourcing is done by the materials management or production management function. We use materials management and logistics as synonyms. Basically, these terms represent all those activities which support the complete cycle of material flow — procurement and control of materials, planning and control of work-in-progress, despatch and distribution of the finished products. Supply contracts are generally handled by the purchase department.

In this chapter, we shall discuss the components of supply chain — make or buy decisions, outsourcing, purchasing, vendor selection, and information flow.

OUTSOURCING

In consumer electronics segment, Philips, BPL or Videocon outsource parts such as battery chargers, batteries and even complete finished products like transistor radios and B&W TV sets. Titan does not make the complete watch at its works, but outsources parts from other manufacturers. In pharma industry, almost 50% of the finished products sold are manufactured at external facilities.

Make or Buy

Components that go into the production of many items are either made by the factory owner or are purchased from outside suppliers. No car is a 100 per cent work of one factory, and no watch that appears on the market is without parts that are not made by the maker, but are purchased from outside. What considerations are uppermost in management's mind when taking a crucial make-or-buy decision? Some important ramifications of this engaging problem are delineated here.

Management in action is decision-making and some important decisions are made in respect of the feasibility of producing materials within one's own plant rather than purchasing them from outside sources. It is an option of make or buy. Apart from this, the organization may decide either to do processes of manufacturing in their own plant or to have part of the work done by outsiders. It is a practice of sub-contracting, and presents another form of the make or buy decision.

Make-or-buy decisions are policy decisions arrived at after deliberations with several functional heads. However, the purchase department, best-informed as it is about various issues involved, takes an active part in making such decisions. In most of the cases, it communicates information and data to the upper management for chalking out a policy.

Factors Affecting the Make-or-buy Decision

Generally, four important issues merit attention in all purchasing decisions; quality, quantity, cost and service. These basic issues, as they affect the make-or-buy decision, would be elaborated to give a proper perspective.

Quality Considerations

Compare the quality of the purchased item and the quality that the company could have achieved, had it made it on its own. If there is no possibility of a very wide variation, quality considerations do not weigh heavily in making a make-or-buy decision.

If there is a possibility of very wide variations between the two alternatives, quality factor becomes crucial in making one decide either in favour of make or in favour of buy. If a better quality could result when the company produces the item on its own, and therefore takes to making it rather than buying, should probe the matter further. How is it that no supplier has taken to making the desired quality soon after a temporary period of shortages? Is the company competent to undertake the production of desired quality in its own plant?

Absence of quality desired for in the market may indicate a situation where suppliers have not thought it worthwhile to make it considering the meagre, non-recurring demand for it. So economic viability of producing the desired item should also be considered by the manufacturer who takes a 'make' decision.

If the specifications of the engineering department regarding quality are more fastidious than necessary for the proper operation, or expected life for commercial standards of the item, there is room for relaxation in the specifications so that the purchase of the item as available from outside becomes possible. However, this is a matter of expert review involving value analysis.

An item for a new product is bound to be in short supply initially. But the situation is temporary. And so make-or-buy decision should be taken in this light, or else heavy financial commitment to making the item that results after taking make decision out of temporary shortage would be reversed after much loss.

The concern's own production facilities should be taken into account when any 'make' decision is taken. Are we technically competent to produce a better quality than can be bought? There must be some technical hitch, when the specialist suppliers fail to meet the desired quality standards. Is it possible for the concern to do better by overcoming the technical difficulties which even the specialist suppliers could not overcome?

Make decisions are also the outcome of a legitimate apprehension that an outsider, having no financial stake in the finished product may compromise with the quality of his supplies. When outside suppliers are chosen for supplying the components of a product there should be a procedure of quality control, rigid enough to eliminate substandard components. The concern should also come forward to provide technical know-how to smaller ancillary units to produce the component to desired standards. If the outside supplies are defective, it would jeopardise saleability of an otherwise good finished product.

Unpatented designs or processes are generally not entrusted with outsiders to protect business interests by preventing others copying them for a prolonged period of time.

Buying from outside has several reasons:

1. To take advantage of specialised activity of the buyer.
2. To take advantage of quality resulting from patents or production methods that the supplier controls.
3. To introduce flexibility with respect to quality of the part being purchased.

Quantity Considerations

Quality and quantity considerations differ with reference to one important issue — Quality is fairly specifiable whereas it is not so with quantity. Quantity is always in a state of flux and it is related with time element. The correct quantity under given condition at a given time may not be valid at another time under changed circumstances. How much to buy — quantity is a variable whereas, what to buy — assortment — is not.

Considering upon the basis of quantity, the make decision is taken when the supplies are likely to be too small to interest an outsider. However, it should be considered whether the order can be made large enough to interest outsiders or a corresponding large inventory can be maintained to meet production needs. It is also seen if sundry small use items can be ordered with common specifications.

It is also worthwhile to consider the economics of making a small use item on one's own, when the outsider has not thought it unprofitable to venture production on such a small scale.

Based on quantity, another decision of making rather than purchasing is the possibility of closer co-ordination between quantity produced and quantity required. PPC thus becomes an easy activity.

Quantity required may be so high that either a decision is taken to make it or to split the requirement among several suppliers. However, when the product is made with the help of dies or patterns, split purchases are ruled out completely. Each supplier in such a case cannot be given dies or patterns. Its costs are very heavy. Thus, a large quantity requirement often has a slant towards make-decisions.

On the contrary, an exceptionally large quantity may hamper production of the regular product line. It then becomes advisable to buy from a supplier rather than to make the item.

Cost Considerations

Cost has relevance in make-or-buy decisions when all other factors are equal, or else reasonable cost estimates of the variations should be included to make up for any inequality.

Let us consider quality, quantity and service factors to be equal. Then the decision of make-or-buy rests on a comparison between a known cost and an estimated unknown cost. The known cost is the price charged by the vendor, and the unknown estimated cost is the cost of making. If there is negligible difference between the two costs, the item should be purchased. In most cases, a known cost is rather more reliable than a slightly lower estimated cost.

How is the cost of making estimated? It is a skilled job and the estimate is more reliable when it is calculated with skill and care. When the item is smaller, value-wise and quantity-wise, the task of accurate estimation becomes difficult.

The estimation of the cost accurately becomes difficult when overhead costs are to be allocated on an item that is made in the plant from the materials and on the machines being used for other items. If the item is such as stands out in a class by itself, the overheads are easy to allocate.

Then there is a problem of the current level of production in the plant. A plant operating at or near capacity gives a different cost sheet of the item now being purchased than a plant having idle capacity would give. Idle capacity results in a high ratio of fixed costs to total costs. Therefore, additional output can be obtained with only a nominal increase in total cost. On the other hand, a firm operating at full capacity gives additional output at substantially increased costs.

A plant with excess capacity can increase production by merely adding incremental costs that are variable in nature. A plant working at capacity, however, can give additional output only by increasing its capacity, thereby adding incremental costs of both fixed and variable nature. BEC (break-even-chart) would make the point clear.

A firm raises its output from 100 to 110% incurring thereby incremental costs of ₹ 30 (₹ 120 to ₹ 150 per unit) as a result of increase in fixed and variable costs. However, the same firm could have raised its output from 70 to 80% and incurred incremental costs of only ₹ 8 per unit (₹ 91 to ₹ 98), since the latter output range keeps fixed costs constant and increases merely direct costs.

When the plant works below capacity, the cost of making should be determined by dividing the estimated volume into the increased variable costs. The purchase decision then would be taken for the item if its unit purchase cost equals or is less than the unit increase in variable costs. At any higher price, the decision is in favour of making, because it would be contributing something towards overhead costs.

The plant operating at capacity presents a different situation. The options now open are to expand the facilities or go in for an outside purchase. In such a situation it is right on the part of the company to purchase from outside at any price less than the unit total costs making the item. If the requirement is meagre, the buyer may even be justified in paying an enhanced price rather than committing funds to expansion of facilities that may be left partly utilised and partly unutilised.

The above analysis of cost considerations, though apparently simple, involves difficult assumptions in practical situations. The time element looms large in any decision. A firm having a plant operating at 70% of capacity errs in changing from buying to making if projected sales of product line will require capacity production in a few years. Besides this, there is a difficult problem of classifying costs into fixed and variable expenses, exclusive of each other, whereas in practice, many costs are partly fixed and partly variable.

Suppose we take a decision to make an item whose raw materials have not been previously purchased. In such a case, procurement costs in the short run are going to be fairly high. If the product being made is different from the regular product line, a line change in existing facilities is necessary sometimes along with trained manpower.

Another consideration is the future trend of prices.

Opportunity costs should not be lost sight of in any make or buy decision.

Sometimes, for an item that is made, there is only self-consumption and so the production should be high enough to allow economies of scale. An outside supplier with a regular clientele can enjoy many production advantages. Inventory is high when the item is internally made than when it is purchased from outside.

Economic ordering quantity formula can be applied to a 'make' decision.

$$ECQ = \sqrt{\frac{2us}{ID}}$$

Where u = Expected usage in units over time

D = Cost per unit (direct production cost when inplant production is involved)

I = Carrying charge as a percentage (including value of money invested, insurance, and other overheads)

s = Set up costs or purchase costs (materials and supplies)

Assuming no significant discount for volume and the same cost irrespective of whether the item is purchased or made, the economic lot size of manufacture will be greater than Economic lot size of purchase, resulting in a heavier carrying cost for the 'make' item. The illustrations that follows stresses the higher EQO quantity required for an item with the same purchased cost and make cost.

Computation of Economic Lot size

Annual consumption	:	100 pieces
Purchase	:	₹ 10
Cost to make	:	₹ 10

Manufactured Lot:		Purchased Lot:		
Carrying charge	= 25%	Carrying charge	:	25%
Set-up costs	= ₹ 100	Purchase costs	:	₹ 10

$$EOQ = \sqrt{\frac{2\times 100\times 100}{0.25\times 10}} \qquad EOQ = \sqrt{\frac{2100\times 10}{0.25\times 10}}$$

$$EOQ = 89 \qquad EOQ = 28$$

The higher the set-up costs to prepare for production, the greater the variation between the quantities for making versus buying.

Transportation cost is one more element that may be higher in making than in buying. Raw materials may be bulky, contributing thereby to higher transport costs as compared to finished products which may involve less transport costs as they are lighter.

One offsetting consideration is the fact that transport costs per 100 pounds of raw material is usually less than those for processed goods.

Service Considerations

The guarantee of supply is an important service consideration. Generally it can be said that supply is more assured when a company makes an item than when it buys it. Assured supply to the assembly line is often a reason for making rather than buying. Such decisions are valid for large industrial concerns where uninterrupted supply is necessary to prevent a breakdown in the supply line.

Making rather than buying items may enable a firm to give more assured and regular employment to its employees.

Unfair practices of the suppliers may force a company to make rather than buy. The existence of a monopolistic condition provides a strong stimulus to make rather than to buy. Sometimes, a company is compelled to devise a substitute for a patented item so as to protect against a "legal monopoly."

One more factor merits consideration. A company may stop purchasing one item and start making it. But the company purchases several other items from other suppliers. The other suppliers may develop an apprehension that even the other items will finally be made by the company. The suppliers are not sure of a constant business relationship and so there is a risk that the quality of service and the assurance of supply may be affected.

One more consideration is about the effect of the make or buy decision on the buyer's flexibility. While purchasing negotiations with various suppliers are possible and the suppliers can be selected as the occasion demands to get the right quality, the right quantity at the right time and for the right price. Once a company starts making an item, this flexibility is lost. It becomes difficult to adjust quantity, quality, or price (cost).

Other Considerations

While deciding to make an item, attention should be paid to the availability of technical know-how. Even if technical know-how is available, its cost should be considered.

Taxation policy of the Government should be considered while deciding to make the item. The contingency of war is another consideration bearing on the make or buy decision.

In general, a new company that is still growing will tend to buy more items than a company that has reached maturity.

With the desire to make the company growth-oriented, the management may decide to make items it formerly bought. Industrial relations are reflected in make or buy decisions. Trade unions often attempt to include in their contract clauses that prohibit management from buying or sub-contracting items that can be manufactured in its own plants.

Sub-contracting

Sub-contracting involves hiring another firm to perform some of the manufacturing process or to give subassemblies that will be incorporated into the end product. Sub-contracting, in other words, is one method of buying instead of making and hence many of the factors discussed above, influence the sub-contracting decision. The term of subcontracting has come to be particularly associated with contractual arrangements between industrial concerns and governmental agencies.

Sub-contracting has several advantages. It is the fastest method of increasing output. The buyer uses manpower where it is located instead of shifting that manpower into his own plant. It enables him to use technical and management skills, already existing as a functioning unit instead of developing new units. It may avoid the need for new plants and equipment on the part of the buyer, since he in effect, borrows existing facilities.

Sub-contracting checks over-expansion of productive facilities. Such over-expansion can create serious over capacity if the demand is temporary.

Sub-contracting will generally save the buyer from incurring investment costs in specialised machinery and tooling which may not be usable for his regular production requirements. However, since the sub-contractor does incur such costs, his operating costs still reflect them, and to some extent, the savings may be more nominal than real. It is called the comparative cost factor to be considered prior to making the subcontracting decision. Another factor to be considered is the availability of the "market."

Collaborative Manufacturing

There was a time when manufacturing was considered as the single most important activity and companies like Ford and General Motors preferred to make all the components that went into their vehicles. The idea was that if we do not make, we cannot control the price, the supply and the quality of these components. These days, however, manufacturers have realised that making everything is not only expensive but also inefficient. Manufacturing strategies have been redefined because of the vendor development programmes and quality control one can exercise over them. The issue now is whether to make or outsource. It is understandable if manufacturing-intensive units outsource some activities. But these days companies like Sara Lee marketing Kiwi and Brylcreem have divested all its manufacturing operations. Its focus is now on marketing and brand-building. Many auto and pharma companies will take this route in future. There will be a shift from mass production to mass customization.

But that does not make manufacturing irrelevant. It becomes even more critical. There is pressure on shop-floor efficiency and flexibility. It leads us to the concept of *collaborative manufacturing*. Here an OEM will not rely on its vendor network. It can source a component from the most competitive supplier. The same machinery will be used to make different products. Such machines must have a higher intelligence to minimise human failure.

Information is the most important resource that flows through the value chain. We have to leverage this resource to meet customer needs. The factory will have to be wired for the seamless flow of information. Customers will be able to custom-build a car or computer or music system or home furniture on the Internet, striking a best bargain. Remotely-hosted software will keep track of operations. E-manufacturing will no longer remain science fiction. OEM may shift from production to mere assembly. Vendors would not supply discrete parts, but fully built up modules, e.g., brake and wheel assembly, the entire chasis.

Lastly, there is a factor of relative cost between doing one job in the plant and subcontracting for it. Some practical questions should be answered. To what extent the subcontractor permits his facilities to be committed to the buyer? To what extent should a buyer assist a sub-contractor in procuring materials, supplies and tools? To what extent should technical assistance be extended? To what extent a sub-contractor is financed? It is important to raise these questions and to answer them in the light of the particular situation and sound business principles.

Outsourcing

In the 1990s, outsourcing has emerged as a major type of make-or-buy decision. When organizations buy from outside what they were formerly producing inside, it is called outsourcing. Outsourcing is a reversal of a previous make decision. Some activities have been traditionally outsourced, e.g., janitorial, food, and security services. More and more activities are being outsourced to downsize or right size, to emphasise on value-added activities and to focus on core competencies. Such outsourcing leads to cost savings, survival and prosperity.

Information systems have been chosen as a target of outsourcing recently. Other outsourcing candidates are mailing, copying and travelling.

We can outsource the whole function or a part of it. Some elements of information technology may be of strategic significance. Some may be routine. Some may be critical. We have to break up a function into its parts, and see which part is of strategic importance or critical and should be performed in-house, and which can be outsourced.

Lean inventories mean better compliance with the delivery schedule. Transport companies have added logistics aspect to their function. They just do not move goods from one point to another. They manage all despatches over a period of time. They have tracking technologies to reduce risks. In just-in-time system, such logistical support is crucial.

Outsourcing has one disadvantage. It results in lay offs. The problem can be mitigated if the service provider is in a position to absorb the laid-off employees. Outsourcing is not liked by the unions.

Purchase function is closely associated with outsourcing decisions. But there are cases where purchase is not involved while outsourcing, *e.g.*, outsourcing of the information systems. In outsourcing of services, purchase may not play a major role.

Business Process Outsourcing (BPO)

C.K. Prahlad's core competency theory advocated focus on our core strengths, and get rid of everything else. It later gave birth to Business Process. Outsourcing where functions that added no value were outsourced to specialist firms, leaving the organization free to concentrate on more basic functions such as manufacturing, product management or marketing. Besides, outsourcing is a cost effective method because outside firms perform the same operation at a fraction of a cost of what it cost the company to run an inhouse department. Outsourcing service provider, at the top scale, acts like a consultant for that function.

Even a call centre handling customer enquiries is BPO but such a function is at the bottom of the BPO pyramid. BPO can be used to perform complex tasks such as pay-roll processing, insurance underwriting, loan processing, marketing research. These jobs require diverse skills. Some organizations outsource even the entire HRD function. BPO work was formerly concentrated in the US and Europe. But as technology advanced, BPO centres started across the globe to avail of the cheaper costs. India has attracted a sizeable proportion of BPO work. MNCs started their own BPO centres as call centres some 6-7 years ago, but soon they graduated to far more complex outsourcing operations.

The following table illustrates the BPO companies and their clientele in India:

Many more BPO companies will pitch their tents in India in years to come. The company-owned or company-created contact centres were the first to set up shop. Now even specialist outsourcing firms and consultants have begun eyeing India as a base.

BPO has infinite market. Anything not forming part of core operations can be outsourced to a specialist — the advantages being time savings, low costs and improvement in processes.

Ernst and Young is setting up a tax computation and processing firm in Bangalore. Apart from MNCs, indigenous firms have also started entering this market.

Some BPOs are bypassing call-centres altogether and are directly entering at the higher end of the ladder.

eFunds provides processing service of Deluxe, the largest cheque book printer in the US. It processes cheque book requests to the tune of 1.75 lakhs to 2.0 lakhs per month. A requisition is filled in the US, which reaches Deluxe or US-branch of the Bank. It is scanned and image is retained on the server. Here an agent accesses the image and processes the request. This involves ensuring accuracy in name, address, spelling, font and any specific design request of the customer. This input is transmitted to the US for printing and delivery.

Let BPO Work

Though very popular these days, BPO must be carefully handled. The objectives of outsourcing must be clear, and must be explained to the vendor. There should be proper vendor selection, and subsequent checks and balances. S. Kumar learnt this the hardway when they entered ready-to-wear apparel with its brand Tamarind by outsourcing the manufacturing from 20 companies. These suppliers were not deadline conscious and they were not exclusive to S. Kumar's. They were exporters too and their priorities shifted quite often. This affected the supply chain.

Services Outsourcing

We in India concentrated on the services, neglecting manufacturing. We adopted outsourcing of services, thus creating a whole new industry of IT and ITES. However, there were opportunities of outsourcing even in manufacturing, which China tapped. We were prevented by our leftist ideals, skepticism and outdated labour laws. Apple and Boeing could have entered India. It would have spawned many ancillaries.

The present NDA government elected in 2014, has made 'Make In India' as its basic tenet.

Case: Outsourcing by Tata Motors

Tata Motors, an automobile company, so far manufacturing trucks, has diversified into car manufacturing. It has now started thinking about the activities which should be outsourced, and which should be retained in-house. There is a transitional dilemma. Tata Motors' commercial vehicle division was vertically integrated in its operations. It not only designed and assembled the vehicle, but also made a large number of components in-house. When the market conditions are good, this seems to be a good strategy to get all the financial benefits. But when the conditions are not so conducive, the in-house making decision does a lot of harm. While doing all things in-house, Tata Motors does not utilise its assets efficiently. ROI of 14-15 per cent is not so impressive. After launching Indica, winds of change have started blowing. They propose to move out their axle, forgings and some components operations. How should this be done? It is yet to be decided. One way is to have 'a factory within a factory' — the partner is allowed to carry out these operations on Tata Motors campus. Another way is to transfer these assets to a joint venture. There are problems of workforce deployment — whether to retrench them or transfer them? They have formed TACO — Tata Automobile Component Company. It is forging alliances with component manufacturers. Outsourcing will free a lot of capital for Tata Motors. A cash surplus of ₹ 400-500 crores is estimated if the axle, crankshaft, forgings and metal components operations are moved out. This capital can be used to upgrade design and marketing.

In automobile manufacture, the company that makes the vehicle is called OEM — original equipment manufacturer. OEMs to begin with did everything — designing, component manufacturing, assembly. They were also in distribution and customer service. Today both the supply and distribution ends of the chain are occupied by the third parties. More and more activities are being outsourced. One day, even assembly may be outsourced. In some countries, assembly is being undertaken for several OEMs. Leading component firms also supply to several OEMs. At the distribution end, the dealers have become independent. They have marketing and customer-service expertise.

If outsourcing on a massive scale is occurring at both the manufacturing and distribution level the OEMs have recognised that their main role is to build a brand and deliver the promise it makes. Brands provide the power to the OEM to control what has been outsourced.

The Concorde chain of dealerships (joint venture with Jardine International Motors) will serve as extension of the manufacturer.

Outsourcing by Pfizer

Pfizer India has outsourced a large number of its functions — from housekeeping of its Headquarters to cash management, pay roll operations, share registry and manufacturing. It outsourced maintenance to Knight Frank to get one-window redressal for all maintenance issues. It outsourced its payroll to India Life Hewitt. There are tax charges and constant update is necessary. It is a non-value adding activity. The shareholding registry function has been outsourced to Tata Share Registry. Pfizer has outsourced its manufacturing for more than a decade. Though manufacturing is a core activity, the reasons why it is outsourced are as follows:

- DPCO imposed price controls and there is a large gap between price allowed and the cost of manufacturing in-house, *e.g.,*

Becosules, Pfizer's best-selling multi-vitamin. By outsourcing, Pfizer sustains the product makes it competitive and manages to get margins.

- Third party manufacturing facilities of superior capabilities and approval are available.
- There are a large number of stock-keeping units (SKUs) in pharma business. Pfizer has some 300 SKUs. It is impossible to make all these in one plant. Even if there are specific plants, there are problems of capacity.

Pfizer knows that in manufacturing service providers may not meet requirements, and their forecast metrics can be poor. Even they may have poor inventory management. In other functions, service providers may not meet the requirements and the quality of their documentation tends to be poor.

It is precisely for this reason that Pfizer enters into short-term service contracts with service providers. In case of cash management services, treasury operations including signing and issuing cheques have been outsourced. Pfizer trained the service providers for fulfilling these obligations. Such training was also given for payroll functions.

OUTSOURCING FOR INDICA CAR (Tata Motors)

Part	***Make***	***or Buy***	***Vendor who Supplies it***	***Remarks***
Cylinder Head and Block Transmission	✓	—	—	Critical
Piston		✓	Goetze India, Faridabad	High-tech
Piston		✓	India Pistons, Chennai	Parts which
Piston Ring		✓	IT Rings, Chennai	are proprietary
Piston Ring		✓	Escorts Mahle, Faridabad	
Radiator		✓	Tata Toyo, Pune	
Batteries		✓	Exide Batteries, Mumbai	
Carburetter		✓	Purolator, Delhi and Shimla	
Filter		✓	Ucal Fuel, Chennai	
Bearings		✓	SKF, Mumbai	
Bearings		✓	ABC, Pune	Widely available
Fuel Injection System		✓	Lucas-TVS, Pune	High-tech parts
Alternator, Starter		✓	Lucas-TVS, Chennai	
Wiper motor and Lamps		✓		
Instrument Cluster		✓	Premier Instrument Controls, Coimbatore	
Trim Linings		✓	BTR, Pune	
Wind shield and Glass		✓	Asahi, Delhi and FAG, Baroda	
Head and Tail Lamps		✓	Lumax, Delhi	Widely available
Brakes		✓	Kalyani Brakes, Pune and Brakes India, Chennai	low-tech parts
Power Steering		✓	Rane TRW, Chennai	
Manual Steering		✓	Rane, Chennai	
Dashboard		✓	Tata Auto Plastic Systems	
Seats		✓	Harita, Chennai and Tata Jhonson Controls, Pune	Listed Vendors
Shock Absorbers		✓	Gabriel India, Shimla	
Rear View Mirrors and Control Cables		✓	Tata Ficosa, Pune	
Paint		✓	Perfect Coatings, Pune	
		✓	Goodlass Nerolac, Mumbai	
Sheet Metal Parts		✓	Jay Bharat Maruti, Gurgaon	
Plastic Fasteners		✓	Tata Nifco, Pune	
Springs		✓	Tata TC Springs, Pune	

Part	*Make*	*or Buy*	*Vendor who Supplies it*	*Remarks*
Wiring Harness Wheels Tyres		✓ ✓ ✓	AMP India, Pune Wheels India, Pune Bridgestone, Baroda Goodyear, Delhi J.K. Tyres, Delhi	
Transmission		✓		High-tech

There should be trust between the organization and vendor. The vendor should be careful about confidentiality of data. There should be accountability. The control must be delegated.

In hospitality industry, the vendor ethos and values must match that of the company's. In-house training and inspection are critical to ensure that the service producers' systems are robust. In India, there is no tort regime for outsourcing companies. When such a regime develops, the vendor will be held accountable, and his liabilities will be unlimited in case of a mistake. It will make insurance compulsory. The tort regimes of developed countries spread their jurisdiction to wherever the outsourcing organization is located.

FUNDAMENTALS OF PURCHASING

Purchasing and Supply Management (PSM)

PSM programme has the potential to improve the bottom-line of industrial companies by 20-50 per cent. A company must determine its requirements of goods and services approximately. It must define its purchase costs carefully. It must define the role of suppliers. It should introduce organisational changes to optimise costs. PSM adoption makes companies aggressive in setting cost reduction targets on a continuous basis. They should identify and monitor non-personal expenses. We should consider the total cost of ownership (TCO). Total costs include purchase price, internal costs such as yields, wastage, inventory, joint costs such as R&D costs. This understanding gives an edge to the company in negotiations with the supplier. A supplier must state his value proposition in relation to the competitors. To reap the full benefits of PSM, a purchase organisation must be built with an agenda of reducing the total cost of ownership of all purchased goods and services. Instead of reactive buying, there should be proactive sourcing strategies for every commodity. World-class PSM requires supplier management and development capability that ensures virtual integration with selected suppliers. Here suppliers are positioned as strategic partners. This helps in lowering costs, especially due to information sharing and joint problem solving.

Introduction

Purchasing is one of the core activities of any economy. All types of organizations, whether merchandising, manufacturing or even non-profit, are continuously engaged in purchasing certain goods or services. In the business world purchasing is broadly classified into two groups: *mercantile purchasing* and *industrial purchasing.* Mercantile purchasing refers to the commercial activities wherein the buying of items is intended to their resale at a profit. Industrial purchasing involves the procurement of items for the purpose of consumption or conversion. The industrial purchasing encompasses the wider area and opens the avenues for their microscopic studies.

Industrial purchasing deals with the efficient procurement and management of issues incidental to it in respect of the following items:

(*i*) *Raw materials:* Raw materials are the items which are purchased in their natural or fabricated state which needs further processing and fabrication, *e.g.*, iron ore, crude oil, rubber, leather, yarn, granules, etc.

(*ii*) *Components:* Components are the finished products which are sub-assembled or assembled to form finished products, *e.g.,* a tyre in automobile industry.

(*iii*) *Consumable stores and supplies:* These are the items which are required in the manufacturing operations but which normally do not enter into the finished products. They are also known as indirect materials, *e.g.,* lubricants, abrasives, paper, cleaning compounds, etc.

(*iv*) *Office supplies:* The office supplies are the indirect materials which are consumed in the office. They include office stationery such as writing paper, carbon paper, stencil paper, duplicating ink, pins, pens, pencils, etc.

(*v*) *Office appliances:* Office appliance refers to office machines such as typewriters, duplicating machines, calculators, intercom system, air-conditioning equipments, etc.

(*vi*) *Spares and tools:* They include tools and parts required for repair, replacement and maintenance, such as bolts, nuts, hammers, pumps, wrenches, bearings, different types of tools, etc.

(*vii*) *Machines and equipments:* Various types of machines and equipments are required for different types of manufacturing operations and services. They include lathe, driller, cutter, furnaces, boilers, trucks, material handling equipment, etc.

Meaning

Purchasing is one of the most common at the same time a strategic activity of the business. The success of any business activity is contingent upon having materials and parts, stores and supplies, machines and equipment available in proper quantity, with proper quality, at the proper place and time and at the proper price, popularly referred to as five R's of efficient procurement. Failure to satisfy any of these criteria adds to the cost and reduces the profit margin. It is as good as conducting the manufacturing operations with obsolete machines and outmoded methods of production and institution sales efforts with inefficient selling techniques.

In a narrow sense, the term purchasing merely refers to the acquisition of some kind of property and giving of an accepted price on consideration in return. The broader meaning of purchasing is described as under by Westing, Fine and Zeng. "Purchasing is a managerial activity that goes beyond a routine act of buying, and includes the planning and policy activities covering a wide range of related and complementary activities. Included in such activities are the research and development required for the proper selection of materials; sources from which those materials may be brought; selection of the supplier on the scientific basis; order placing on expressly classified terms and conditions; the follow-up to ensure proper delivery; the inspection of incoming shipment to ensure that both quantity and quality comply with the order; the development of proper procedure, methods and formats to enable the purchasing department to carry out the established policies efficiently; the co-ordination of the activities of the purchasing department with such other internal divisions of the concern such as receiving, store-keeping, traffic and accounting so as to facilitate smooth operations; and the development of a technique of effective communication with the top management of the company so that a true picture of the performance of the purchasing function is presented." Till the middle of this century, purchasing was not considered as a major business activity. The entire complexion of this activity has undergone a sea change since last two decades. The clerical order placers have given way to value conscious purchasing personnel, skilled in price and cost analysis, product reliability, economic ordering quantity determination, learning curves, purchasing research, economic forecasting, supplier selection, contract negotiation, evaluation of supplier performance, value analysis, material studies and the logistics of supply management. The modern concept of purchasing is effectively presented in a presidential speech made in 1966, before the shareholders of the Bethlehem Steel Company, Inc. (U.S.A.) that his company's purchase department was headed by a vice-president who is a member of the Board of Directors and the Executive Committee of the Company. There are about 1,000 people in the purchasing department dealing with more than 30,000 vendors to whom are issued 25,000 to 30,000 purchase orders per month. These suppliers are located in 50 states and 60 foreign countries. More than one billion dollars are spent annually for materials and services. Average inventories carried amounts to approximately 400 million dollars. These figures indicate the role of purchasing in a large corporate sector. Such views are also expressed by John H. Hill in a speech made before the National Association of Purchasing Agents (NAPA-U.S.A.) describing "purchasing traditionally has been considered a service function, a place where money was spent....Recent developments have shaken this point of view. Good purchasing is essential to good profits. The difference between good purchasing and poor purchasing can be the difference between outstanding results and mediocre performance."

Purchase function enjoys a key role in the modern organization because it manages the basic inputs — raw materials and components, stores and supplies and machines and equipment. Of these only raw materials and components account for more than 50% of the sales value. The cost of materials in different industries ranges from 50% to 85% of the unit cost. On an average about one-third of the total assets of a company represents the sustained investments in inventories. A slightest efficiency in the management of these items, releases substantial absolute advantage. A saving of 5% to 10% in the cost of purchase in a company absorbing more than 50% of the sales value, will result in the monetary advantage of 2.5% to 5% of the sales value. Efficient procurement of inputs not only avail the monetary advantages as described above, but it also ensures better quality of output and thus helps in building a long-term image of the company.

Objectives of Purchasing

Purchasing is an important and inevitable activity of any business or non-trading activities. Progressive organizations recognize it as an important function and organize a separate purchase department to look after the purchase function. The objectives of the purchase function must be spelt out clearly for the justification of its independent existence. Moreover, purchasing being the part of the total management activity must see that its objectives are in conformity with the overall objectives of the organization. Identification of objectives encourages the imaginative personnel to accelerate their efforts in attaining them efficiently and economically. Objectives are set by the head of the purchasing department either in consultation with the top management or on the line of the broad policies outlined by the top management.

The objectives of the purchase department can be outlined as under:

(1) To avail the materials, supplies and equipment at the minimum possible costs: These are the basic inputs in the manufacturing operations. The minimization of the input cost increases the productivity and resultantly the profitability of the operations.

(2) To ensure the continuous flow of production: Purchasing department helps in ensuring the uninterrupted production flow through continuous supply of raw materials, components, supplies, tools etc. and good equipment with repair and maintenance services.

(3) To increase the asset turnover: The efforts of purchase department result in formation of fixed assets and maintenance of a certain level of investments in inventories. The investments in fixed assets and also in the inventories should be kept at minimum in relation to the corresponding volume of sales. This will increase the turnover of the assets and thus the profitability of the company will get enhanced.

(4) To develop the alternate sources of supply: Exploration of alternate sources of supply of materials increases the bargaining ability of the buyer, minimization of cost of materials and increases the ability to meet the emergencies.

(5) To establish and maintain the good relations with the suppliers: Maintenance of good relations with the supplier helps in evolving a favourable image in the business circles. Such relations are always beneficial to the buyer in terms of charging of reasonable price, preferential allocation of materials in case of material shortages, intimation about forthcoming shortages, information about the newly developed substitute, prolonged payments in case of temporary liquidity crisis, etc.

(6) To achieve maximum integration with other departments of the company: The purchase function is related with the following other departments of the company:

(*i*) *Production department* regarding the material specifications, flow of materials, suggested supplies for certain items etc.

(*ii*) *Engineering department* for the purchase of tools, machines and equipment.

(*iii*) *Marketing department* regarding the forecast sales and its impact on procurement of materials, impact of quality of inputs on quality of outputs and sales.

(*iv*) *Finance department* for the purpose of maintaining levels of materials, pledging and hypothecating the materials for meeting working capital needs, tapping the quantity discount, scheduling the investments in capital assets such as materials and equipment.

(*v*) *Personnel department* for the purpose of manning and developing the personnel of purchase department, maintaining the vendor relationships, etc.

(7) To train and develop the personnel: Purchasing department is manned with varied types of personnel. The company should try to build the imaginative employees force through training and development. This will ensure management succession and a contented workforce who are provided with an opportunity to fulfil their aspirations through getting promotions on higher positions.

(8) Efficient record-keeping and management reporting: Paper processing is inherent in the purchase function. Such paper processing should be standardized so that the record-keeping is facilitated.

The periodic reporting to the management about the purchase activities is also one of the important activities which justifies the independent existence of purchase department. The management is interested in knowing the following aspects of the purchase functions which provides them the valuable data for shaping certain important policies:

(*i*) To know the volume and value of the purchase broken into raw materials, supplies, spares, components, machines and equipment, etc.

(*ii*) To know the departmental cost of the purchase department according to the important heads of expenditure.

(*iii*) Analysis of the work performed in the purchase department.

(*iv*) Information about the cash discount and quantity discount earned and lost.

(*v*) The trend about the price changes in the foreseeable future and its impact on the cost of inventories.

(*vi*) The predictions about the availability of materials and the development of the strategy against such predictions.

(*vii*) The information about the new materials and processes which may reduce the manufacturing costs.

(*viii*) Exploration of new sources of supply.

Purchasing Principles

The success of any manufacturing activity is largely dependent on the procurement of materials of right quality, in the right quantities, from the right source, at right time and at right price — popularly known as five 'Rs' of the art of efficient purchasing. They are also described as the basic principles of purchasing as under:

1. To purchase the right quality of materials;
2. To purchase the materials in right quantities;
3. To make the materials available at right time;
4. To purchase the materials at right price;
5. To purchase the materials from the right source.

They are briefly explained as under:

(1) Right quality: The materials are the basic input and the quality of the output. It should be noted that best quality is not always the right quality. The right quality is determined by the cost of the materials and the technical characteristics as suited to the specific requirements. The right quality should be defined clearly and should be described in terms of specifications. Generally the quality decisions are made by the technical staff. The quality specifications are controlled before the materials are issued for the manufacturing processes. The quality testing is done through the inspection either at supplier's plant or at buyer's plant.

(2) Right quantity: The right quantity of the materials is determined on the basis of economic ordering quantity (E.O.Q.). It is advantageous to purchase the materials on the basis of EOQ lots. The EOQ describes the size of the order at which the ordering cost and the inventory carrying cost will be the minimum. The ordering cost consists of the cost of paper processing such as paper, typing, postage, filing, cost of personnel, the costs incidental to order placing such as follow-up, receiving, inspection, etc. If the size of the order is large, the annual requirements will be met with little of the ordering cost as the number of orders placed would tend to be less. Conversely, storing cost consists of interest on funds locked up in storing, cost of storing, cost of insurance and taxes, etc. If few orders involving large quantities are placed, the carrying cost will increase; however, the ordering cost will decrease due to less number of orders. Thus ordering cost and carrying cost are mutually exclusive. At EOQ level both these costs equate each other and at this point, the total inventory cost would be at the minimum. The EOQ is calculated on the basis of the following formula:

$$EOQ = \sqrt{\frac{2RD}{CS}}$$

where R = Annual requirements of the materials in units

D = Ordering cost per order

C = Cost per unit

S = Storing cost as the value of materials stored.

(3) Right time: The materials should be purchased at right time so that it may not result in either excess investment in the stocks or may result into stock-outs. Efforts must be made to replenish the materials at a point where they are reaching at the reordering level. The purchase action is initiated at a time when the material reaches to its predecided reordering level. The reordering level is decided on the basis of the rate of consumption and the lead-time. It should be decided on the basis of the probability of maximum periodic consumption and maximum lead-time. As stock-holding is directly related with the lead-time, efforts should be directed towards the reduction of the lead-time so that the carrying costs can be reduced to the minimum.

(4) Right price: The investments in inventories is determined by the prices charged for them. All attempts should be made to procure the materials at right price because a slightest reduction in the price results in substantial absolute monetary gain. It should be noted that the low bidder is not always the best bidder. The right price can be availed through searching for the proper sources of supply and comparing all such sources on some scientific basis. The quotations of various suppliers are compared after bringing them all on some common footing. Due considerations are also given to the factors such as regularity of supply, character of the supplier, his financial standing etc. The price is an agreement between the buyer and the suppliers, the former considers his utility while the latter takes into account his cost of production. The market conditions greatly effect the price determination. In a monopolistic condition (*i.e.*, sellers' market) the chances of price reduction are very low for the buyer. On the contrary, he has to maintain good relations with the supplier so that the regular supply can be assured in scarcity. In case of perfect market, the individual buyer and supplier cannot have any say in the price determination. Under such situation buying decision should be made on the basis of the price-trends and demand forecasting. Under the imperfect competition, which is the common phenomenon of the market, price is the result of negotiations and haggling. The negotiating skills help in availing the right price.

(5) Right source: The right source is a key consideration in purchasing as all other 'Rs.' The suppliers are not only supplying the required materials but they also supply the information such as probable market conditions and the resultant price trends, general industrial climate and the business environment. Such information is of immense use to the buyer in making strategic buying decisions. The selection of right source involves the considerations such as search for the more and more sources, selection of the appropriate source through some scientific analysis, negotiating with the selected supplier and post-purchase rating of the supplier.

(E) Significance of Purchasing: Purchasing is the single most important activity of the materials management in most of the companies. Efficient purchasing can reduce the cost considerably. Now let us enumerate the advantages we can get by efficient purchasing function.

(1) Efficient administration: The function of purchasing is equally important to every type of organization, whether it is manufacturing unit, trader or government or charitable institution. It directly effects the quality of the final product, extra productivity, delivery time, etc. If the function of purchasing is made efficient the better quality goods can be acquired at reasonable price. Thus it helps management to be efficient.

(2) The quality of the final product: Manufacturers are extra careful about the quality of their final product. If the product is faulty or defective there would be direct impact on the reputation of the company. Brand loyal customers are very much conscious about their favourable brand. Quality aspect requires more attention when the market is competitive. Hence, the purchasing department has to be extra careful about incoming goods. Due to defective raw materials many problems may arise. It would be wastage of time to rectify the errors emerged due to improper quality.

(3) Delivery in time: Timeliness is one of the important characteristics of the industrial activities. Many companies had to forgo their lucrative business due to lack of sense of timeliness. Moreover, continuous and regular flow of raw materials are the requisite conditions for an uninterrupted production process. Purchase department should have the idea of their inventory. They should also know the time a new order is to be executed. Purchasing department should have thorough control over time element with a view to delivering the goods in time.

(4) Increase in profitability: The field of purchasing encompasses the issues which directly affect the profitability of the company. It has to decide whether purchase should be made in bulk or not. They have to be alert in the market which may be fluctuating. For example, a textile unit has to be vigilant during the season of cotton as cheaper procurement reduces the total cost substantially.

Moreover, the man-hours can also be reduced by proper quality and in-time receipt of the goods. It increases production and so profitability. It is now clear that the decisions of purchase department do affect the profitability of the company.

(5) Optimum utilization of capital: Proper purchasing avoids unnecessary investment of the capital. Thus, the saved capital can be utilized for more profitable purposes. This objective can be achieved by the purchase of right quantity of right quality at the right time from the right source. The purchase department can also try to get maximum discount from the supplier.

Thus, effective purchasing enables the company to function smoothly and profitably. And this fact is reflected in the selection of head of the purchase department. Highly qualified and highly paid executives head the department of purchasing.

Purchasing Procedure

The procedure describes the sequence of steps leading to the completion of an identified specific task. Thus purchasing procedure describes the sequence of steps by which a purchase function is carried through from its inception to its completion. The purchasing procedure starts with the realization that something is required, the need is then spelt out either in the form of requisition or in a bill of materials. Then attempts are made to identify their sources, the appropriate supplier is selected on the basis of some scientific analysis, the purchase order is placed with the selected supplier, it is checked to ensure that the delivery is made as per the agreed terms, the invoice of the vendor is checked and paid out and finally all relevant records are filed and maintained. Generally, the professionally managed organizations prepare their own "Purchase Manual" which details out the purchase procedure. It is not desirable to prescribe any standard purchasing procedure due to the existence of wide range of variations that exist among industries, companies, products, personnel, etc. Generally, organizations should devise their own procedure on the basis of their specific needs. However, the following basic steps are considered while prescribing the full-proof purchasing procedure:

Steps of purchasing procedure: The purchasing procedure generally comprises the following steps:

1. Recognition of the need.
2. Selection of the supplier.
3. Placing the purchase order.
4. Follow-up of the order.
5. Receiving and inspection of the materials.
6. Payment of the invoice.
7. Maintenance of the records.
8. Maintenance of the vendor relations.

Purchasing is a continuous and recurring phenomenon. The prescription of procedure simplifies and expedites the operation. Similarly various types of forms are designed to simplify the purchasing procedure. The popular forms which are used in the purchasing procedure are: Purchase Requisition, Purchase Order, Purchase Contract Form, Follow-up Form, Receiving Slip, Inspection Report, Test Certificate, Rejection Form, etc.

Following paragraphs briefly describe the various steps involved in the purchasing procedure:

(1) Recognition of the need: The initiation of procedure starts with the recognition of the need by the needy section. It may be either manufacturing department, stores department or the office section. The demand is lodged with the purchasing department in the prescribed Purchase Requisition Form forwarded by the authorized person either directly or through the Stores Department. It is also called Purchase Indent. The three most common types of purchase requisitions are:

(*a*) Standard purchase requisition

(*b*) Travelling purchase requisition

(*c*) Bills of materials

Fig. 24.4

Proforma Purchase Requisition

STANDARD PURCHASE REQUISITION

PURCHASE REQUISITION/PURCHASE INDENT

Serial No. .... Date: ....

Please arrange to procure the following items

Name of Department: .... Order No.: ....

Date of Requirement: .... Present Stock:............................

Usage Rate: ....

No.	Code No. or Symbol	Description	Required Quantity	Remarks

Signature:. ....

Designation: ....

(For purchase department),

Purchase Order No. .... Name of supplier: ....

Date of order placed: .... Delivery date: ....

Signature of purchase officer

The purchase requisition clearly specifies the details such as specification of materials, quality, quantity, suggested supplier, etc.

The company should specify by way of policy that who can make out the purchasing requisition and who can authorize the expenditure by counter-signing it. If the requisitions are directly sent to the purchase department by the needy section, then a list of the authorized signatories should be made available to the purchase department. The extent of the authority of each signatory should also be specified, *e.g.*, the supervisor may be authorized to sign the requisition requisitioning the tools up to ₹ 200, and above this limit, it must be countersigned by the higher authorities such as Works Manager. The Stores department makes the requisition for those items which have reached to the re-order level.

Travelling Purchase Requisition

It is used by stores for requiring requirements of materials and standard parts. It is in the format of a card for a simple item, and is used for many requisitions, when the stock level drops to or below the re-order point. A sample of the format is shown.

TRAVELLING REQUISITION FORM

Material Description: . ... Order Quantity: ....

Part No.: .... Re-Order Level: ....

Annual usage: .... User Departments: ....

Vendors:. ....

Requisitioned			Received		Remarks
Date	***Qty. on hand***	***Qty. requested***	***Date***	***Qty.***	

Fig. 24.5 Travelling Purchase Requisition

Bill of Materials

(1) In a jobbing industry wherein production is undertaken according to the specifications of the customers, "the bill of materials" serves as a requisitioning document. A "bill of materials" is a comprehensive list of all items which are required in completing one specific order. It is prepared at the time of engineering drawing of the product. Generally, the low value sundries and items of common use are purchased for stock while costlier and special items are purchased according to the production programmes. The purchases of machines and equipment and such capital expenditure items are treated in different manner. Generally, the corporate level executives are the authorized signatories to such demands. Such purchases are approved by the Board of Directors. The reference of the approval is made on requisition and a copy of the requisition is sent to the secretary for the purpose of overall planning and budgeting.

(2) The selection of the supplier: The process of selection of supplier involves two basic aspects — searching for all possible sources and short-listing out of the identified sources. The complete list of prospective suppliers is maintained and updated. The information about the supplier is available from various sources such as trade directories, advertisement in trade journals, direct mailing by the suppliers, interview with supplier's salesman, suggestions from business associates, visit to trade fair, participation in industry convention, etc. Identification of more and more sources helps in selecting better and economical supplier. However, it increases the task of shortlisting.

SCHEDULE OF QUOTATIONS

Name of Goods: .... Date: ....

Code: .... File No.: ....

Name of Supplier	***Rate (Price)***	***Quantity***	***Amount***	***Period of receipt of goods***	***Other conditions***	***Remarks***

Fig. 24.6 Proforma Schedule of Quotations

Shortlisting out of the existing sources is made on the basis of past experience with the suppliers. This is done either through inferences or on the basis of scientific evaluation of suppliers. In case of new sources, it is done through inferences only. The scientific evaluation of the past performance brings in objectivity in the decision. Various methods have been devised to evaluate the performance of the supplier, such as categorical method, weighted-point method and cost-ratio method. The selected suppliers (few in number) may be asked for their latest quotations of price, delivery and other terms and conditions. A "comparative statement of quotations" should be prepared to eliminate the variations in quotations so that a meaningful comparison can be made among varying quotations. The keen study of the comparative statement will reveal the best supplier out of the available ones. It should be noted that the low bidder is not always the best bidder. When everything except price is equal, the low bidder would be selected. The important considerations in the selection are the price, ability to supply the required quantity, maintenance of quality standards, financial standing, etc. It should be noted that it is not necessary to go for this process for all types of purchases. For the repetitive orders and for the purchases of low-value, small-lot items, generally the previous suppliers with good records be preferred. In a research conducted by Hugh Bucknet on "How British Industry Buys", it was revealed that, "Approximately half the persons involved in purchasing would not change from their best supplier to buy an identical product from a new supplier for a price reduction of less than 5%. Approximately one-fifth would not change for less than 10% reduction in price." In principle, the rigour of analysis should be confined to the trade off between the benefits arising out of best selection and the cost of processing the selection. The supplier selection authority should rest with the purchasing department and under no circumstances the requisitioning department should part with it, as otherwise it will result in friction between the two, the morale of the purchasing department will be affected adversely and the control on the purchase function will be lost.

(3) Placing the purchase order: The purchase order is placed with the selected supplier. It indicates an official announcement of the intention of the buyer addressed to the supplier to receive the specified materials. Generally, printed forms are used for the purpose and specifications such as name of the supplier, item specifications, quality, quantity, price, date of requirement, mode of delivery and other relevant terms are made in the purchase order.

Generally, all purchases are made through purchase order. When emergency purchases are made through telephone or telegram, the purchases are confirmed by sending a regular purchase order, following the telephone or telegram. Such purchase order should be made as "confirmation" so that any misunderstanding on the part of the supplier treating it as a fresh order can be eliminated. It is not proper to specify the preparation of the number of the copies of the purchase order. The number of copies is closely related with the complexities of the purchase organization.

However, the copies of the purchase order are generally required as under:

The original copy is sent to the supplier. Sometimes an additional copy is also sent to the supplier who is supposed to return the same signifying his acceptance. Such procedure ensures that the supplier has received the order and that he accepts the buyer's terms and conditions. Copy may be sent to the receiving department, the accounting department, the initiating department, the stores department, the inspection department and the follow-up department. One copy is, of course, retained by the purchase department for record. It should be noted that the outstanding orders should be separated from the completed orders. They should be filed properly. Generally the outstanding orders would be filed alphabetically while the completed orders should be filed numerically. It is highly essential to develop a system for tackling the small orders as quickly and as cheaply as possible.

As it would not be desirable to institute control on all items bought, the principle underlying the ABC analysis should be followed. 'A' items are about 20% of the total number of items which account for 80% of the total purchase expenditure. More than 75% of the total items tends to account for less than 20% of the total expenditure. Such items are denoted as "C" items. The rest are the "B" items. Rigorous control be exercised on "A" items only.

The buying practice for the low-value, small order items can be devised as under:

(*i*) To buy from the intermediaries like wholesalers or retailers, rather than from the manufacturers.

(*ii*) To place a standing order with the supplier. Standing order is an arrangement under which the supplier continues to supply the article at regular intervals until he is told to stop.

(*iii*) To place a blanket order with the supplier. The blanket order is a period contract made with the supplier to supply the items at agreed terms against the requisition made by the buyer.

(*iv*) The arrangement of cash limit purchases. Under this system, the staff is authorized to make the direct purchases up to certain limit, *e.g.*, special order pads marked "Not valid for orders over ₹10" can authorize the subordinate staff to order directly for meeting the routine requirements.

(*v*) The junior executive or the order clerk can be delegated the authority to handle all types of purchases of this nature.

Generally, it is the usual practice that all purchases should be made through the purchase department. However, sometimes the authority is delegated to certain key staff for the emergency purchases, *e.g.*, the maintenance foreman should be empowered to make emergency purchases to meet any unforeseen breakdown in the machines. However, the usual practice is to limit the authorized persons, occasions and amount of emergency purchases, and it should be confirmed by the purchase department at a later stage.

(4) Follow-up of the order: Getting the materials at right time and right place are the important ingredients of effective purchasing. Simply the placing of the order with the supplier does not ensure that the materials will be made available where and when they are wanted. So follow-up or expediting the purchase order is considered as an essential step in the purchasing procedure. It should be noted that it is not necessary to chase all types of purchase orders. It would be sufficient if the follow-up function is confined to the key components and materials which directly affect the smoothness of the production flow. It is not worthwhile to follow up the purchase of standardized items which can be procured at eleventh hour and from an alternate source. Similarly the items of low-value having no direct bearing on the production process can be precluded from the costly follow-up procedure. As a principle, follow-up procedure should be employed wherever the costs and risks resulting from the delayed deliveries of materials are greater than the cost of follow-up procedure. The follow-up procedure

PURCHASE ORDER

(Please quote in all correspondence)

Code: ....

Phone:. .... Requisition No. .... Order No. ....

Gram:. .... Date .... Date ....

Messrs ....

....

Please supply the following materials to our Stores Department at 5, Lucknow Road, Delhi- 110 007, in accordance with the terms and conditions mentioned overleaf. This has reference to your quotation/under No................ dt. ....

Sr. No.	*Identification*	*Description*	*Quantity Required*	*Rate*	*Value*	*Remarks*

Date: ....

Terms and conditions overleaf

Signature.......................................

Designation ....

Fig. 24.7 Proforma Purchase Order

tries to see that the purchase order is confirmed by the supplier and the delivery is promised. It is also necessary to review the outstanding orders at regular intervals and to communicate with the supplier in case of need. Generally, a routine urge is made to the supplier by sending a printed post-card or a circular letter asking him to confirm that the delivery is on way or will be made as per the agreement. In absence of any reply or unsatisfactory reply, the supplier may be contacted through personal letter, phone, telegram or even a personal visit.

The follow-up function varies from company to company. It is handled through recording relevant particulars on the copy of the purchase order or maintaining a desk diary for the follow-up or handling of the outstanding orders with the help of progress-card or by establishing a separate position of expediter in the purchase organization. The timings of the follow-up also depend on the circumstances of each case. It may be the due date of the order, a week earlier to that or at each stage of the implementation of the purchase order till its execution.

(5) Receiving and inspection of the materials: The receiving department receives the materials supplied by the vendor. The quantity is verified and tallied with the purchase order. The receipt of the materials is recorded on the specially designed receiving slips or forms which also specify the name of the vendor and the purchase order number. It also records any discrepancy, damaged condition of the consignment or inferiority of the materials. The purchase department is informed immediately about the receipt of the materials. Usually a copy of the receiving slip is sent to the purchase department.

If the materials require any quality control or inspection, they are sent for such testing. The inspection department tries to verify that the incoming materials comply with the standard quality as specified in the purchase order. It may involve mechanical, electrical, chemical or such types of testing. The accept-reject decision may be taken on the basis of either sample testing or testing the entire lot. The inspection may involve in-house testing or testing done at the vendor's plant.

The inspection report along with the Test Certificate, and the recommended acceptance or rejection should be sent to the purchasing department. On the basis of the recommendations made by the inspection department, the purchase department arranges for the segregation of the rejected materials. They are sidetracked from the normal flow towards the stores or production departments. If they involve some further shipments at supplier's end, they are suspended immediately. The concerned departments such as stores department, production department, accounting department, scrap and waste disposal section etc. are immediately informed about the rejections. If the defectives are within the established tolerance limits, they may be accepted as their returning to the vendor may disrupt the production schedule. However, the vendor should be informed about this and if possible, the credit should be claimed from him.

Receiving function is usually of a routine nature and sometimes it is kept independent of purchase department. However, it is desirable to treat the receiving department as a subordinate function of purchase department due to following reasons:

1. Before the settlement of the invoices, the purchase department has to verify that the consignment agrees with the purchase order in all respects. This can be verified only with the help of the receiving department.
2. When the shipment is received in damaged condition, the purchase department must have first hand prompt information about this, so that it can initiate immediate legal action against the vendor or the carrier. It can also take necessary action for tapping the substitute sources of the supply for the urgently needed materials.
3. In case of the short-shipment from the suppliers, the rush orders can be managed so that the work stoppages caused by the lack of materials can be eliminated.

(6) Payment of the invoice: When the goods are received in satisfactory condition, the invoice is checked before it is approved for the payment. Generally, the invoice is checked to see that the goods were duly authorised to purchase, they were properly ordered, they are priced as per the agreed terms, the quantity and quality conform to the order, the calculations are arithmetically correct etc. It is a matter of controversy, whether the invoice should be checked by the purchase department or by the accounting department. The popular arguments in favour of purchase department are:

(*i*) It is the purchaser who can accurately verify that the consignment is billed properly.

(*ii*) As he is familiar with the routine details and terms and conditions of the order, he can correct and adjust any discrepancy in the execution of the order before an invoice is paid.

(*iii*) It allows the purchaser to watch the price of the materials closely increasing his consciousness for the future purchase.

The arguments in favour of the invoice checking by the accounting department are as under:

(*i*) Invoicing is an accounting procedure which can be handled efficiently by the accounting department.

This is not a sound argument because invoice checking is not merely a routine clerical checking but it also involves certain constructive checking like quality of materials, terms of the purchases etc.

(*ii*) It facilitates the internal checks. The accuracy of purchase department is verified by the accounting department. However, where the system of internal auditing is in operation, such type of internal checking would not serve any purpose because such verification is bound to be undertaken by the accounting department at some later time. After the proper verification of the invoice, it is approved for the payment. It is the duty of the accounting department to make the payments in time. In case of the damaged consignment or short supply or supply of inferior goods, the adjustments should be made with the supplier before the payments are made for the invoice. The usual adjustments are to return the goods to the supplier at his cost, to scrap them on the site, to accept the damaged goods at reduced price with the consent of the supplier, to correct the goods at the cost of the supplier. The payment of the invoice should be made only after the settlement is made with the supplier.

(7) Maintenance of the records: Maintenance of the records is an important part and parcel of the efficient purchase function. In the industrial firms most of the purchases are repeat orders and hence the past records serve as a good guide for the future action. They are very useful for deciding the timings of the purchases and selecting the best source of the supply. The maintenance of the records is advantageous as under:

(*i*) It acts as a guide for future action. The person may change, however, the system prevails.

(*ii*) It provides the authentic records about the inventory which is essentially needed for the inventory control.

(*iii*) The maintenance of the records is also desirable for the viewpoint of legal proceedings which may take place in future. The purchase order and its acceptance are legal documents and hence should be preserved till they possess any legal significance. Purchase requisitions are also important documents so they should be preserved because they constitute the authority on the basis of which the purchase department initiated the buying action.

(8) Maintenance of vendor relations: The quantum and frequency of the transactions with same key suppliers provide a platform for the purchase department to establish and maintain good relations with them. Good relations develop mutual trust and confidence in the course of the time which is beneficial to both the parties. The efficiency of the purchase department can be measured by the amount of the goodwill it has with its suppliers.

(9) Specialized purchasing procedures: The material requirements are broadly classified into two: (*i*) direct materials and (*ii*) maintenance, repair and operating suppliers. The characteristics of these two groups of materials differ substantially and hence their procurement efforts need distinct treatment. The purchasing procedure described in the above paragraph mostly deals with the purchase of direct materials while "the specialized purchasing procedure" describes the procurement of indirect materials such as stores and suppliers. It is highly desirable to have a distinct treatment for the procurement of suppliers because:

(*i*) The cost of paper processing for placing the order is very high. Such costs can be reduced by placing a large order for the non-recurring items such as suppliers.

(*ii*) The inventory carrying costs is another consideration. It is the cost of interest on locking-up of the funds in inventories, storing cost, insurance cost etc. It represents some 15% to 20% of the value of the average stock holding.

(*iii*) Like direct materials, their needs are not directly affected by the research and development. They are more or less standardized commodities.

(*iv*) Under the "principle of exception" the efforts of the buying staff can be saved for the purchase of such items which can be utilized effectively for the purchase of some important items.

The following are certain specialised procedures which are employed in buying the standardized indirect materials such as stores and supplies:

(1) Blanket order.

(2) Stockless buying.

(3) Systems contracting.

(4) Small order purchases.

(1) Blanket orders: The blanket order is a type of standing order with the supplier for the supply of the materials according to the requirements of the buyer. The deliveries are scattered over the contractual period, usually one year. The blanket order procedure is advisable for materials of low value but having a high annual usage, the rate of usage of which cannot be planned precisely.

Some important terms of the blanket order needs special considerations. Regarding *the type of materials* to be supplied, the clarification should be sought as under:

(*i*) Specific description of materials.

(*ii*) General category of the materials.

(*iii*) All materials that the supplier is able to furnish.

Regarding the price, the agreements should be sought on any of the following lines:

(*i*) Fixed price contract during the contractual period.

(*ii*) Market price at the time of delivery.

(*iii*) The specification of ceiling price which cannot be crossed without fresh negotiations.

The *timings of delivery* can be agreed upon as under:

(*i*) Delivery of standard quantity at regular time intervals, *e.g.*, 500 units on 1st day of every month.

(*ii*) Delivery as per the specified schedule.

(*iii*) Delivery as per the demand from the buyer.

(2) Stockless purchasing: As the name suggests, the buyer is not required to maintain the stock of these items. The onus of the maintenance of the stock rests with the supplier. The financial incidence of the storing and inventory carrying is borne by the supplier. The supplier locates the materials at his own plant or at buyer's plant. If the inventories are maintained at supplier's plant, the physical distance of supplier's plant should be considered while deciding about the supplier. Where the materials are located at buyer's plant, it is known as "consignment buying."

The buyer identifies the materials to be obtained under such arrangement. They are properly described and clubbed into related groups along with their rate of usage. Negotiations are made with the supplier accordingly. Generally, the price of the materials is a bit higher than the usual prices because the storing and carrying costs are borne by the supplier. However, the actual cost incidence on the buyer is less than the alternative arrangements because, the supplier is expert in handling such type of stock and the maintenance of safety stock is much less as the supplier is developing such contracts with many buyers and mutual adjustments among the buyers is possible.

(3) System contracting: A system contracting incorporates the characteristics of blanket order and stockless buying, still it is different from them. Like blanket contract, the periodic contract is made with the vendor, and like stockless buying, the buyer is not required to maintain the safety stock. The system contract is unique in the sense that it is a long-term contract as compared to blanket order or other types of arrangements.

According to Ralph A. Bolton, "A system contract is a total corporate technique designed to assist the buyer and seller to improve reordering of repetitive-use materials or services with an absolute minimum of administrative expense and with the maintenance of adequate business controls."

The system contractor is a large supplier at the competitive price. He assists the buyer to spell out his needs more scientifically, the delivery schedules and standard sized shipments are developed. The purchasing procedure like order placing, follow-up, receiving, payments are excessively simplified. The system contract results in substantial cost advantage to the buyer. The companies which have adopted this system of purchasing have reduced their costs substantially because this arrangement eliminates the need for stocking the non-essential items while inventory carrying of the key items is reduced to the minimum.

(4) Small order purchases: It is a common experience of all companies that they need certain items of non-recurring nature which involve very insignificant cost. Such items are sometimes available from some corner supplier and hence they cannot be clubbed with some other large orders. Moreover, they cannot be pent up for the purpose of accumulating the need for forming a sizable order. It is also not wise to stock them for future needs. The cost of the materials to be purchased does not justify the paper cost of the purchasing. So such items are purchased without undergoing the formal purchase procedure. Such purchases are also known as "paperless purchasing." The popular methods of such purchases are — (*i*) Purchases under the petty-cash system where indirect cash purchases are for small items, (*ii*) Purchasing through telephone orders wherein no formal purchase orders are sent to the supplier, (*iii*) Purchasing under the cash on delivery (COD) system wherein the purchases of certain major items are made on cash basis. The cost of order placing, invoicing and account processing is reduced substantially.

Centralized versus Decentralized Purchasing

The issue of centralization versus decentralization of purchase function is basically concerned with decision about the purchasing policies defining the purchasing authorities and the resultant responsibilities. This issue is highlighted in the situations such as a single plant with diversified production, geographically scattered multi-plant with diversified production, geographically scattered multi-plant with single product, scattered multi-plant with diversified products, ubiquitous availability of basic raw materials etc.

Centralized purchasing is a method of procurement of all types of materials, supplies, equipment etc. through a single department (not necessarily centrally located) under the direct control and superintendence of one responsible person. He is directly accountable to the top management for all duties falling within the broad area of purchase function. A single-plant company with centralized operating facilities readily recognizes the efficiency and profitability of those arising from the centralized purchasing. In a single-plant company with diversified products or in a scattered plant company with a single product, the issue of centralized purchasing would become relatively difficult. However, in a scattered plant company with diversified products, the issue of centralized purchasing would become increasingly complex. The complexity will be directly related with the number of plants, size of the plant, geographical dispersal and diversification of product range.

Under the policy of centralized purchasing all types of purchases in a single-plant organization are made by the central buying section, who are authorized to decide on the sources of supply, negotiate with the vendor, place the order and instruct the mode of delivery. In a multi-plant organization with scattered plant locations, all purchases are made by the central buying section of the head office. In such organizations sometimes regional or branch purchasing agents are employed to make purchases in local markets. They are doing so under the superintendence and control of the centralized purchasing department. Materials which are used by more than one plant are purchased by the centralized purchase department. If the sources of the supplies are scattered, then the suppliers are instructed to canalize the deliveries at various centres on the basis of freight advantages available from such deliveries. In such organizations, the regional or branch purchase agents are allowed to buy the materials from the local market if they are available and involve freight advantage. They are also authorized to make emergency buying. However, this should be restricted to the minimum. The degree of decentralization should be reduced to the minimum. According to *Lee and Dobler,* "If 97 per cent or more of the purchasing is performed by the purchasing department, decentralization should not be considered a problem. However, the correct extent of decentralization must be determined for each firm from an analysis of the individual factors involved in its operations." Though centralization avails certain advantages, certain degree of decentralization is desirable under the following conditions:

(*i*) Where the unit uses single natural raw material which is available at local markets, it is desirable to have decentralized buying. The price of such commodities fluctuates at various markets, the grades differ as per the localized climatic conditions, the deals are completed through auction in local mandis, *e.g.,* cotton, tobacco, groundnuts etc.

(*ii*) Sometimes certain low-value technical items are obtained from local vendor. The exact specifications of the materials are decided after the series of trials and tests. The buyer has to be himself in close touch with the vendor.

(*iii*) The purchase of certain non-technical odd items are allowed to be purchased from local markets. The reason is that the cost of paper processing from placing an order sometimes exceeds the cost of such items.

(*iv*) Particular decentralization of purchase function would be highly desirable in a scattered multi-plant unit manufacturing diversified products.

Advantages of Centralized Purchasing

The centralized purchasing avails the following advantages:

(*i*) As the duplication of efforts in buying function is eliminated, its cost will be relatively less and it will be managed efficiently.

(*ii*) The superintendent of manufacturing departments, departmental heads and office managers are relieved from the responsibility of purchasing their own requirements. They can concentrate in their assigned areas of activities in a better way.

(*iii*) It is possible to tap the advantage of the specialized skill of the buying staff.

(*iv*) Bulk buying strengthens the bargaining position of the buyer. Moreover, the advantage of the quantity discount can be tapped. Direct contact with the suppliers will be possible which will eliminate the link of the intermediaries.

(*v*) It enables to develop and maintain good relations with the suppliers. Moreover, it facilitates the supplier to maintain relations with few buyers and thus it enables him to pass over some benefits on buyers.

(*vi*) It will enable the purchase of standardized items through standardized procedure.

(*vii*) It will reduce the inventory carrying costs. The minimum level of inventories are not maintained at different centres but at centralized centre which reduces investments in inventories along with the other incidental storing costs. The central buying staff manages the stock levels, recording material usage, lead time and prices effectively.

(*viii*) The receiving of large supply through consolidated orders reduces the transport cost per unit.

(*ix*) The cost of order processing such as order placing, receiving, inspection, accounts etc., are reduced substantially due to few orders of large quantities.

(*x*) As the responsibility centre is fixed on one departmental head, the shifting of responsibility for wrong decisions is eliminated.

(*xi*) The inter-section requirements of the materials can be easily adjusted. Scarce materials can be allocated according to the economical advantage.

Disadvantages

The centralized purchasing suffers from the following limitations:

(*i*) The specific requirements of the individual items may not be attended successfully. At times, it may result in absence of matching of mind between the needy section and the buying section resulting in wrong buying.

(*ii*) The centralized standard procedure may result in delays in receiving the materials.

(*iii*) It is likely that the centralized buying staff may not be expert in buying varied types of items.

(*iv*) In case of multi-plant units located at distant places and receiving their requirements from centralized storing, it may not be possible to tap the local resources. However, this situation can be handled effectively authorizing the regional purchase agent to make local purchases if they involve cost advantage.

(*v*) It adversely affects the employee morale. It can be concluded that the company should centralize all policy matters, the purchase of major raw materials and capital equipment should be made by the head office, while the individual divisions should be allowed to make their own purchases in accordance with the policies established by central office. If the company adopts the "profit centre decentralized" set-up, the decentralization should be made accordingly.

Purchasing Manual

The purchasing manual is an important means of effective purchasing. It outlines the policies and procedures to be followed by the purchasing personnel. It contains the approved statement of policies and thus provides standing answers to recurring questions.

Purchasing manual sometimes becomes a source of irritation and conflict. Many purchasing managers consider it to be restrictive. In fact such situations can be eliminated if the following aspects are considered while preparing the manual:

(*i*) The purchase authorities should be clearly defined.

(*ii*) It should clarify the relationship with other departments.

(*iii*) The co-operation of the personnel should be sought while preparing the manual.

(*iv*) It should be drafted clearly.

(*v*) The policies and procedures should be segregated. Generally, policies are of permanent nature while procedures are subject of frequent changes.

Purchasing manual is an important tool for managing the purchase function efficiently. It is not only useful to the large organization, but is required in small organizations as well. In the large organization, the purchase function is relatively complex and can be eased with the help of the purchasing manual. In the small organization, it is essentially required because in such organization, purchasing function becomes a one-man show and the absence of such key man may paralyse the purchase activity. Purchasing manual attempts to reduce such over-dependence of one man.

Contents: A representative purchasing manual should contain the following:

(*i*) The foreword by President or other top man — this gives authority to the manual as a statement of policy.

(*ii*) Objectives of purchase department.

(*iii*) Scope and responsibilities.

(*iv*) Chart of organization — A chart showing position of purchase department in the company and the detailed organization of the department itself.

(*v*) Limitations — A statement concerning the authorization to purchase, the final determination of quality and list of certain classification of purchase that are exempted (for example: insurance, advertise, rentals etc.)

(*vi*) Sources of supply: A statement of policies for selecting suppliers such as dealing with only reliable suppliers, requirements of competitive bids, criteria used in evaluating sources, and reciprocity.

(*vii*) Policies of making commitments — this section covers areas concerned with placing purchase orders. For example, all negotiations are to be conducted and concluded by the purchasing department, no commitments will be valid except as authorized by the purchase manager. Conditions for acceptance of the supplier's sales contract forms would be included here.

(*viii*) Relations of purchasing department with other departments.

(*ix*) Policy on personal purchases — it should be made clear whether the company allows employees to purchase items that are to be charged to the company and if so, how the money is to be allocated?

(*x*) Plant visitations.

(*xi*) Relations with suppliers — policy on acceptance or non-acceptance of gifts or gratuities.

(*xii*) Reports required.

Advantages derived from the use of Purchasing Manual: The compilation of purchase policies and procedures are useful as under:

(*i*) It clearly defines the authorities and relationships with other departments and thus eliminates the conflicts and confusions in the administration of the purchasing function.

(*ii*) It prescribes policies and procedures and thus eliminates the need of communication for recurring phenomena; thus it relieves the staff from contracts, communications and decision-making.

(*iii*) It is a useful tool for training the new personnel.

(*iv*) It is a useful guide to the internal staff as well as outside suppliers.

(*v*) It helps in developing and improving the policies and procedures. In the course of time, it results into standardized practices.

(*vi*) It provides written and approved policy statements which are valuable as compared to incomplete, inaccurate and misunderstood verbal instructions.

(*vii*) A manual tends to ensure greater consistency in handling the controversial matters such as reciprocity.

Organization of the Purchasing

Organization is a structure manned by human beings who are arranged under the defined relationships. The organization structure establishes the authority and responsibility relationships among its personnel. Peter Drucker opined that, "Organization is not an end in itself, but a means to the end of the business performance and business results. Organization structure is an indispensable means; and the wrong structure will seriously impair business performance and may even destroy it." The departmentation of activities, the line of superior-subordinate relationship is generally decided on the basis of the nature, spread and quantum of work involved in type of tasks and operations. However, the attitude of the management has a deciding role in the establishment and amendment of any structure. Which activity should be clubbed with whom, who should report to whom are the key decisions of the management which give shape to the organization. As far as the purchase function is concerned, the following two alternatives are open for deciding the location of the purchase function in the overall organization structure:

(1) To consider purchase function as a major area such as production, marketing, finance, personnel etc., directly reporting to the management. The nature of the organization under such situation would be as under:

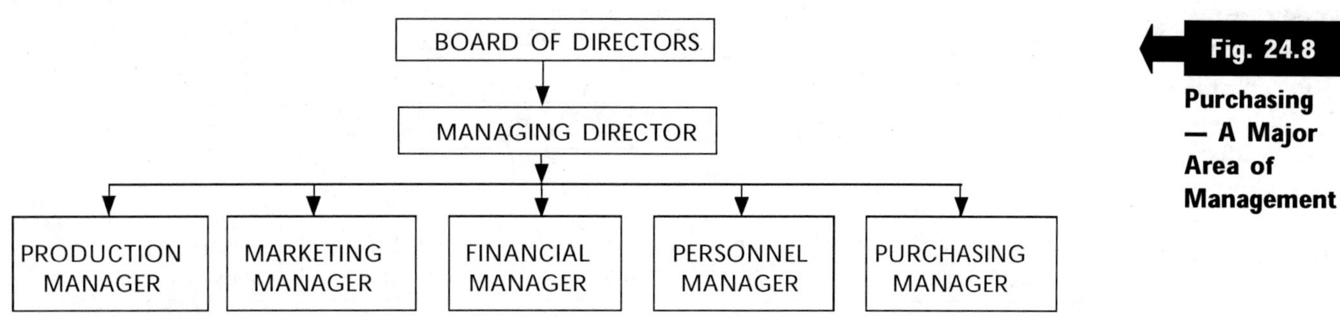

Fig. 24.8 Purchasing — A Major Area of Management

(2) To consider purchase function as a subsidiary to some major area of management, such as production, marketing, finance, personnel, etc. It is a matter of judgement whether it should be made subordinate to production or marketing. However, the general practice is to keep it under the direct control and superintendence of production department. The usual structure under this philosophy would appear as under:

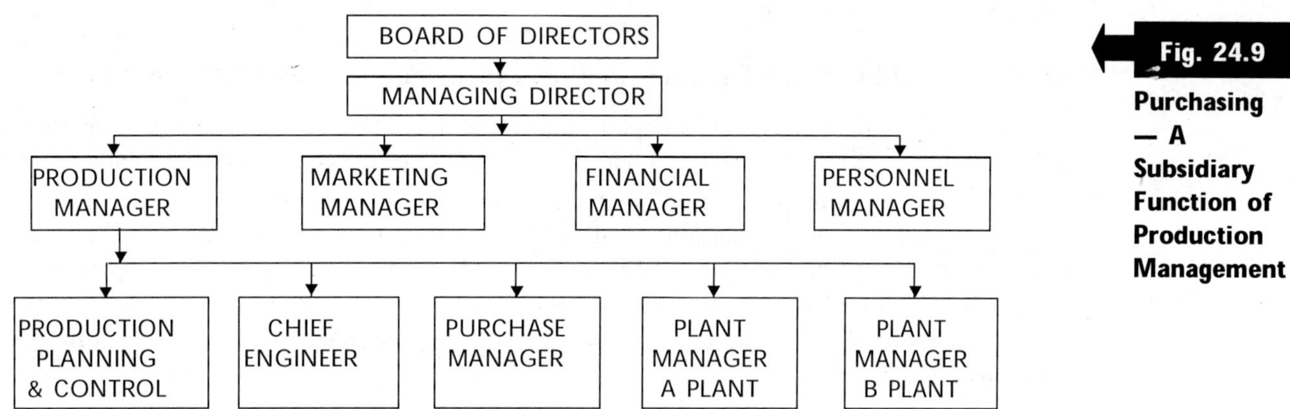

Fig. 24.9 Purchasing — A Subsidiary Function of Production Management

The position of the purchase department is largely decided on the basis of how management considers it in the overall operations which is supported by the phenomenon such as absolute rupee value of the purchase in the total budget, share of the material cost in the total product cost, complexities involved in the buying of certain items — materials as well as equipment. Purchase function is assuming greater importance in the modern management. Recent trends supported by certain surveys indicate that in a large organization, management considers it worthwhile to treat it as a major area of management on par with other areas such as production and marketing. In the medium-sized organization purchase function is treated as subordinate to the production department.

Purchase Function and Materials Management

The purchase function within its wide range includes the purchases of materials along with purchase of equipments and appliances. The characteristics of purchase of materials and that of machines and equipment differ substantially. Moreover, the purchasing of materials is a continuous and recurring phenomenon while purchase of equipment and appliance is a special and sporadic activity. So, on the basis of the materials budget in the total purchases, due consideration is given to the materials management. Where materials assume predominant role, the position is designated as materials manager instead of purchasing manager. The status of the materials manager is same as the purchasing manager as described in the above paragraphs. Under such organizational set-up, purchase section looks after the purchases of materials only and it works under the direct control of materials manager. The purchases of equipment and appliances are made by the respective line managers. The services of materials purchase section is made available in case of need. The typical organization structure under such arrangements would appear as under:

Fig. 24.10 Purchasing — A Subsidiary Function of Materials Management

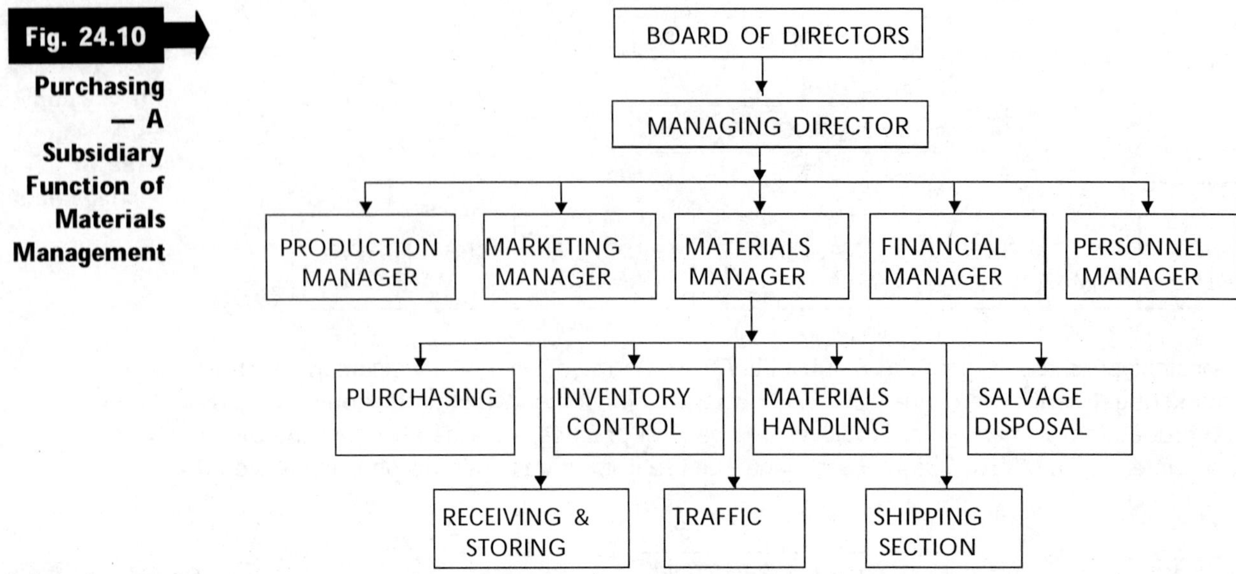

Organization of Purchase Function in Single-plant and Multi-plant Company

In a single-plant large-sized company the benefits of specialisation can be had through the functionalisation of the purchasing. Generally, the purchase function would be divided into:

(*i*) **Buying function:** This would be the core function, which would be headed by the buying officer. If the size of buying of certain individual items necessitates specific attention, buying function may be arranged according to individual items such as buying officer — wood, buying officer — steel, buying officer — chemicals etc. Such sub-divisions should be co-ordinated by the buying supervisor.

(*ii*) **Other ancillary functions:** The buying function results in receiving and inspection, follow-up and record maintenance.

(*iii*) **Purchase research:** The complexities and magnitude of buying makes it difficult for buying officers to concentrate on the in-depth investigations about the commodities to be purchased. The specialized research staff conducts the exhaustive purchasing research and thus helps the buying officer in making effective purchases.

In a single-plant with diversified products, the division of the actual buying function can also be arranged according to products or projects instead of individual material items as described above. The typical organization structure under this type of situation will as under:

Fig. 24.11 Purchasing — A Subsidiary Function of Materials Management

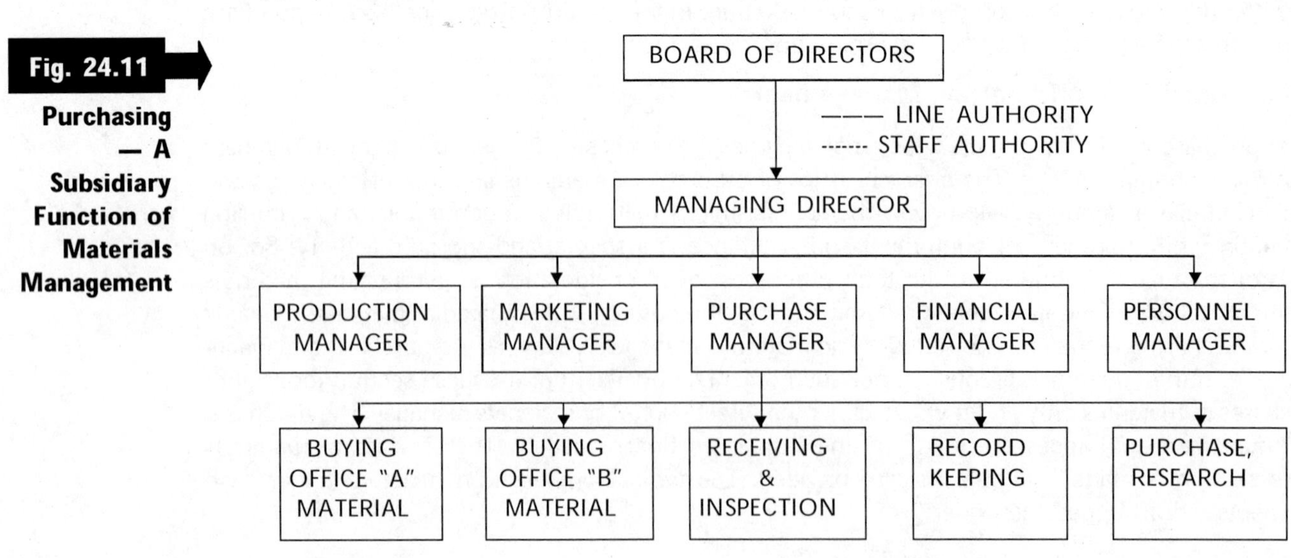

The organization of the purchase function in a scattered *multi-plant* company will be similar to that under the single-plant company except the policy regarding the centralized authority, the actual buying function and the staff research function would be controlled at the head office, while the receiving, record keeping and such other ancillary function will be performed by the respective divisions under the control of the central office. The problem of centralization and decentralization of purchase authorities is discussed at length elsewhere in this chapter.

Departmentation of the Purchase Function

In the above paragraphs, the role of the purchase function in the overall organization has been discussed. Purchase function itself represents a cluster of varied activities. The internal organization of the purchase department in a large-sized organization can be described as under:

Fig. 24.12

Purchase Function — in a Typical Large Organization

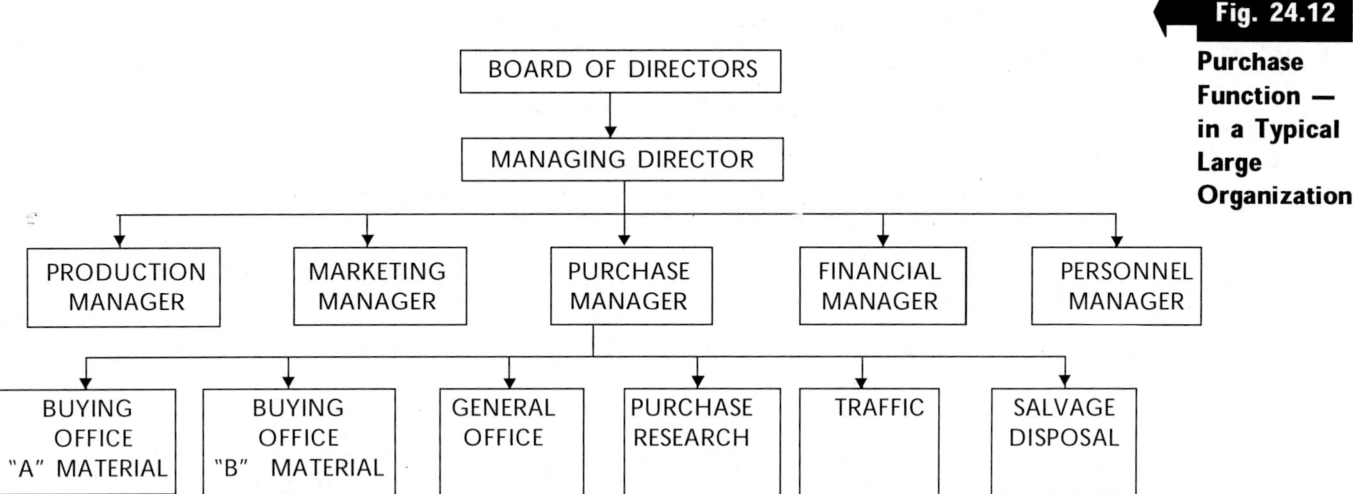

Generally the purchase department is organized on the line basis, and it is headed by the purchase manager. In practice the head of the purchase department is designated differently, like purchase manager, purchase officer, purchase agent, director of purchasing, materials director etc. The split-up of purchase department is made in the light of the activities mentioned in the following structure. The further split-up or combination is decided on the basis of the need, cost and convenience of the organization.

The functions of each section are described as under:

(*i*) **Buying section:** This is the core function of the purchase department and requires specialized skill in buying. It is sub-divided according to specialized lines in terms of materials, products or projects.

(*ii*) **Follow-up section:** The follow-up of the purchase is an important function. This can be a separate section in large organizations.

(*iii*) **General office section:** This section performs the routine clerical work incidental to purchase activities such as order placing, inward and outward posts, typing, records and filing, invoice checking etc.

(*iv*) **Purchase research section:** This section is generally organized in large companies. It mainly looks after the development of sources of supply, development of substitute materials, technological developments and its cost impact on manufacturing activities etc.

(*v*) **Traffic section:** In the large organizations, the problems of incoming materials and outgoing shipments require special attention which is usually handled by the traffic section.

(*vi*) **Disposal of salvage section:** In the large organizations, the responsibility of the disposal of the salvage is attached to the purchasing department. This section handles the entire salvage work, starting from collecting the salvage and scrap, their reconditioning and subsequent disposal.

Materials Management Education

The Indian Association of Materials Management began conducting the graduate diploma course in materials management (two years for part-time students, and three years for distance education students) in 1980. It was recognised by the Ministry of Education, Union Government for recruitment to superior posts. Indian Association of Materials Management on entering the academic field converted itself to Indian Institute of Materials Management (IIMM) in April 1983. IIMM also conducts one-year Studentship Course in MM. The IIMM has 26 branches.

There is a negligible percentage of girls doing an MM course. But abroad, there are 20-25 per cent women in materials management.

Till 1987, about 1100 students have passed out from the IIMM. The IIMM is affiliated to the International Federation of Purchasing and Materials Management (IFPMM) which has 60,000 members.

The IIMM also conducts a national convention of materials managers every year. It organizes MDPs to upgrade the knowledge of practising managers.

Mr. Madhav Capoor was the first Indian and the first Asian to hold the office of the President of the International Federation of Purchasing and Materials Management. Mr. Capoor is an ex-Dunlop executive. It shows the recognition of Indian professionals.

Materials management consultancy is a paying field; a good consultant averages a billing of ₹15 to ₹ 20 thousand per month. There are about 100 materials management consultants in India.

Annamalai University, Annamalainagar and Punjabi University, Patiala also offer correspondence courses in Materials Management.

PURCHASING DECISIONS

Materials Specifications

Meaning

Specifications are a detailed description or listing of the characteristics of materials, parts and components used in making a product. Specifications describe the quality of the product desired, in quantitative terms, through specifications. It should be noted that compiling specifications is a difficult task and it requires a good deal of time. It is a costly method of informing the suppliers about what is desired of the product, so far as the amount and labour to be spent for compiling specifications is concerned. But it is a better method of informing the customers what a product contains, *i.e.,* what are the characteristics of the product and how it differs from the same type of products of other manufacturers. The following are the examples of specifications:

(A) Specifications for "dome tweeters" used in stereo systems — made by Peico Electronics and Electricals Ltd., Kolkata.

Type No.	—	IPD 01630
Rated imparlance	—	4, 8, 15 ohms
Frequency response	—	1500 Hz to 20000 Hz
Operating Power	—	3 watts
Magnet dia.	—	72 mm.
Dome material	—	Textile
Sensitivity	—	3 watts input for 90 cl B sound level.
Power handling capacity	—	50 watts in enclosure.

(B) Engine specifications for the Peugeot XDP 4.90 diesel engine fitted in Mahindra NL 665 DP Mini Truck, Pick-up Van and Ambulance manufactured by Mahindra & Mahindra Ltd.

No. of Cylinders	—	4
Bore — mm	—	90
Stroke — mm	—	83
Bore/Stroke Ratio	—	l08
Displacement — cc	—	2112
Compression Ratio	—	22.4 : 1
R.P.M. (Max.)	—	4500
Max B.H.P.	—	75
Max Torque Kg.m. @ 200 r.p.m.	—	13.3
Weight Kg.	—	184

On the basis of such specifications comparison of the same type of products manufactured by different manufacturers can be made. Buying by specifications has become a very common practice for most of the business units because it is the easiest way of describing their needs.

Importance

The profitability and competitiveness of the product depends on the design of the products. The design depends on the specifications fixed in advance. Thus development of proper specifications is very very important for any management. Only properly fixed specifications can contribute to a great extent to the firm's profitability. It is very difficult to reduce the cost of production by adopting labour saving devices or other devices resulting in increased productivity because of the expected labour resistance or strong protests from them. Cost reduction by way of changes in design may also invite some pressure from labour force but it may not be too severe. Control at the design stage really helps in reduction of material costs because it is the first stage. If the cost is not controlled at this stage, it will continue to be incurred until somebody else finds out the defect, *e.g.,* if 40 parts are used instead of 30 parts (which would have become possible if strict control had been exercised at the design stage) to make a product, use of 40 parts will become a permanent feature, because once the design is fixed for a particular product, generally it is not changed, unless and until the manufacturers think otherwise. Thus the cost of 10 parts will be incurred unnecessarily. Sales volume also depends on the design. Thus design is very important for proper specification.

It is very difficult to fix proper specifications because conflicting views of various departments are to be considered for this purpose, *e.g.,* sales department desires that the product should be unique with special features, to increase the sales, while the engineering department considers design excellence as important which may make the production process more complicated and sales may not increase. Production department prefers such design which is very simple to work out which reduces the cost of production per unit and also the quantity of materials or number of parts used per unit. All departments must work with full co-operation among them, in the interest of the unit. When design engineer prepares specifications without consulting any other department, the specifications become very stringent, which may create many problems. Skillful management can motivate the departments and solve various problems that may arise against fixation of proper specifications. Proper specifications must serve the following objectives:

1. Specifications must be, as far as possible, simple and economical to produce.
2. Materials should be available easily in required quantity at reasonable prices.
3. Specifications must be such so that the product becomes acceptable to consumers. A best product may not have buyers in the market.
4. Specifications must ensure smoothness in production activity. The factory must function well without any obstacle.

5. It must be possible to check the conformance to the specifications.
6. It must be possible to substitute materials when it becomes necessary.

Proper/right specifications result in increased sales, decreased costs and stronger competitive position. The following points should be considered while preparing the specifications:

(*a*) Specifications must be as clear and explicit as possible, so that buyers and sellers both may understand the same thing in the same way.

(*b*) Specifications should be written in such a way so that maximum number of suppliers can bid and misunderstanding can be avoided. If specifications are not practicable very few suppliers may bid, which minimises competition thereby making the choice by the buyers limited.

(*c*) Specifications should not be written keeping in view a certain product only, because the competition will become very, very limited, *e.g.*, suppose only one company makes a particular type of part called 'A'. Now a manufacturer states in specifications that his/her firm will use that particular part (*i.e.*, 'A') in making a machine. Here the firm restricts the competition by making it clear that the firm will be using that part, which only one company makes. Here the firm will have no other alternative than only to purchase that part from that sole manufacturer (company) only.

When and how specifications should be prepared?

Generally a committee consisting of representatives of various concerned departments should be formed. The committee should include a design engineer, a production engineer, a quality controller, a purchasing officer, a sales officer etc. The design engineer should prepare the design of the product. Production department will consider the practicability of its production and cost of production. Purchasing department will consider whether the materials for its production will be available or not and the sales department will consider sales potential considering consumers' acceptability. Quality control section should see whether the products have certain chemical and physical properties or not. Thus only after approval of the committee, the design is finalised with or without some changes. If design department only is made responsible for preparing the designs, it may prepare unnecessarily stringent specifications, which may cause a great harm to the firm. Once the design is finalised, the specifications are reduced to writing with great care so that buyer as well as seller can have an idea about what they want or what they understand and it helps in making good purchasing. Efficient working of various departments such as design engineering, production, purchase, sales, stores, quality control etc. depends on good specifications written in clear and understandable terms.

Sometimes the manufacturers prepare specifications for their products, *e.g.*, different manufacturers of trucks, tractors, cars, scooters etc. have their own specifications. It is not possible to manufacture such items as per the specifications of buyers. In case of military purchases or purchases of the items of special use, the buyers prepare specifications as per their needs and they inform suppliers/manufacturers, so that the suppliers/manufacturers can supply as per buyers' specifications. Buyers and suppliers prepare specifications when standard specifications do not exist.

In case of most widely used and highly competitive items, standard specifications are available. The products with standard specifications, manufactured by different manufacturers, will be the same. When products or goods are ordered on the basis of standard specifications, the buyer as well as the seller know what is required. Such items are available at reasonable prices. There exist many users and therefore the producers can sell their whole production at reasonable price. Standard specifications specify the standard of materials to be used, the process of manufacture, the quality of workmanship, performance standard, method of checking the quality and performance etc. Standard specifications prove to be most helpful in simplifying the design and purchasing procedure. Moreover, inventory control and cost reduction become easy. Copies of standard specifications can be obtained from various sources such as manufacturers, government departments, testing laboratories, standard institutes etc. and therefore buyer and seller has not to spend time, money and energy for preparation of such specifications.

Types of Specifications

Generally, three types of specifications are used, *i.e.,* technical, performance and brand name. Technical specifications state the physical and chemical properties desired in the product. When the desired properties are in measurable terms they are called dimensional specifications. This type of specifications can be checked easily. Generally in case of oil, paints and metallic raw materials this type of specifications are used. Sometimes materials to be used and method of manufacture are also prescribed. This is another form of technical specifications. This happens generally in case of military purchasing, because military purchases are made as per the needs of the defence department, where standard specifications do not exist. Now the military requirements is a confidential matter and therefore the supplier/manufacturer has to follow the instructions and specifications provided by the defence department. In case of industrial purchasing, it is not so, unless and until the requirements of a particular unit are of special type or say unique. In case of industrial purchasing, generally the supplier/manufacturer knows what the buyer wants or what performance he/she expects from the articles purchased and therefore the supplier/manufacturer uses the materials and methods of manufacture accordingly.

Performance specifications describe in words the performance or use of the items to be purchased or the services that the product will give. Here the buyer gives importance to the performance of the product and not to the analysis of materials used or the dimensions of the product or the components used. It should be noted that the conformance to performance specifications can be determined by use of the product, while that of technical specifications can be determined by tests in laboratory. The supplier/manufacturer is not advised about the type of materials or the process/method of manufacture to be used. The supplier is free to use materials and process/method of manufacture which he/she thinks suitable and he/she may take advantage of most up-to-date knowledge of technological development to provide the best product at the lowest cost. When a buyer gives a supplier free choice to select materials as well as the process/method of manufacture, the buyer must be sure of the supplier's reliability and capability. Unreliable and incapable supplier may cause a great harm. A supplier, not fully reliable, may suggest another more expensive and better materials than needed or he/she may not be able to supply the materials in required quantity. Only the reliable suppliers can supply the materials or products at reasonable prices and can therefore transfer the benefit of advanced technology to the buyers, because only they make use of advanced knowledge. Performance specifications are extensively used in purchasing highly technical military and space products and also complicated machines and machine tools. Sometimes buyers advise the suppliers to use specific methods or process of manufacturing and materials. Such practice is not advisable except in case of military purchases. Here the buyer becomes fully responsible for the performance of the products, so long as his specifications were met by the suppliers. Moreover, the benefits of advanced technology in form of new and improved methods of production etc., with which only the suppliers are familiar, may not be available to the buyer. Further, it is also very costly and time-consuming to prepare specifications and to inspect for compliance. But when the buyers want to meet their specific needs or when the suppliers are too small to have research and development facilities, such practice can be adopted by buyers.

Now sometimes specifications take the form of blueprint. "The blueprint is the most accurate form of description and is used when close tolerance or high degree of mechanical perfection is required. Its use is expensive not only because of the cost of the blueprint, but also it usually describes an item of special design that is costly to manufacture." This method is the most feasible method of description for items like castings, forgings, tools, fixtures, punchings, machine parts, etc., where extreme accuracy is a must. Moreover, blueprints provide the basis for an accurate check on compliance, with specifications by the inspection department, when material is received.

When it becomes very costly to develop performance or technical specifications or if such a practice does not prove satisfactory, purchases are made on the basis of brand names, *e.g.,* in case of items like trucks, scooters, tractors, cars etc. It is not feasible for the buyers to develop specifications. There would be a small difference in each brand of different manufacturers, even though each product might be designed to provide almost identical performance at the same or slightly different prices charged for the competing brands, *e.g.,* prices of different brands of scooters — Bajaj, Priya, Allwyn-Pushpak,

Falcon, Avanti, Vijay Super, Girnar, etc., are not the same. Price of an Ambassador car is different from that of Premier Padmini. In case of such type of products each manufacturer would claim that his product is the best of all. But the buyer can judge the performance of each brand after using various products over a number of years and can decide the most satisfactory brand. The reliable and progressive manufacturer creates goodwill for his firm by ensuring the best performance of his products over a number of years. But the buyers have to keep a close watch over the working of different manufacturers and their products. The best product of the past may have become inferior due to change in quality, specifications, etc., while the new manufacturers with most modern machinery may have come out with better products than the best products of the past.

Advantages of Specifications Buying

1. When a buyer has to purchase or is required to purchase a particular type of goods from more than one supplier, specifications ensure the identity of goods purchased. Thus, the materials with identical nature can be purchased from different suppliers on the basis of specifications only.
2. Specifications provide an exact standard to the inspection department of the buyer against which incoming materials can be inspected or measured or tested with great accuracy and this ensures uniformity in quality of materials purchased.
3. Specification buying includes more suppliers to bid an offer because all of them know exactly what is required and they also know what the other suppliers are bidding for. Now increased competition proves very economical to the buyer in form of lower prices.
4. Specifications are prepared considering various factors such as quality, sales potential, availability of raw materials, consumers' acceptability etc. This may result in simplification of design, reduction in the quantity of materials used, increasing the productivity, decreasing the cost of production, lower selling price etc. Thus, buyers are more benefited by specifications, if the benefits mentioned as above are passed on to them by the suppliers.
5. If the suppliers combine specifications with quality control measures, the buyers have not to worry much about the testing or inspection of the products purchased and in such circumstances buyers save money and time both, by doing less complete inspection.
6. Specifications buying is a necessary step towards industry-wide standardisation and standardisation helps a lot in cost saving.

Disadvantages

1. Specifications become inappropriate in case of patented items or items with brand names or items manufactured by patented process. Product of each manufacturer shows slight difference, even though each of them might be designed to provide same type of service, *e.g.*, trucks, tractors, scooters etc. Product of each manufacturer is unique and the buyers purchase the products of a particular manufacturer because they have confidence in the unique skill of that manufacturer, *e.g.*, Telco Trucks, Bajaj Scooters, Premier Padmini cars etc.
2. Items purchased to specifications require detailed inspection to decide whether they are in conformity with specifications prescribed or not. This proves costlier. While items with brand names require only a casual check.
3. When specifications become very stringent, many problems arise. In case of very stringent specifications, the buyers have to pay more than necessary for the items.
4. Specifications buying proves economical only in case of large purchases. It is not a wise or advisable step to prepare specifications for small purchases. Moreover, where the buyer has to purchase many types of items in small quantity, it may prove very harmful to prepare specifications for such items.
5. When a buyer purchases items as per his/her specifications and if the product does not prove satisfactory even though the supplier has complied with the terms of the purchase, the responsibility rests with the buyers for unsatisfactory performance.

6. Now once the specifications are fixed, it is in the interest of the buyer to review them. If the buyers do not review the specifications once fixed, considering technological developments, they may be thrown out of the markets by the consumers.

SOURCES OF SUPPLY: VENDOR SELECTION AND RATING

(A) Introduction: Scientific purchasing involves identification, development and at times creation of the appropriate sources of supplier of materials their evaluation and selection of the capable and willing vendor. This is a challenging task because it is not easy to discover all the sources that exist at a particular point of time. Even if all the sources are identified, some sources may not be feasible to be tapped due to time, distance, quantity and quality constraints.

Selection of the suitable supplier is both a right as well as a responsibility of the purchase department. It can contribute substantially to the fundamental objectives of the business enterprise. It is a continuous job. The decision is not to be taken once for all. The decision tends to be a complex one. It is not that the supplier bidding the lowest price is the best supplier. In fact varied economic and non-economic factors are considered while evolving the optimum decision.

Different strategies are developed for acquiring different types of materials. The selection of supplier for standardized products will differ substantially from that for the non-standardized products. A different consideration would be involved in acquiring the capital equipment, indirect materials, tools, stationery etc.

(B) Sources of Supplier: The best buying is possible only when the decision maker is familiar with all possible sources of supply in general, and their respective terms and conditions in particular. The purchase department should try to locate the appropriate sources of the supplier of various types of materials. This is also known as the "survey stage." A survey of the following will help in developing the possible sources of supply:

(*i*) Specialized trade directories;

(*ii*) Regional directories of chambers of commerce or such organizations;

(*iii*) Assistance of professional bodies or consultants;

(*iv*) The purchaser's handbook or the buyers' guide;

(*v*) The manufacturers' and/or distributors' catalogue;

(*vi*) Direct mailing of advertising literature;

(*vii*) The advertisement in dailies such as "buyers' guide" section;

(*viii*) The advertisement in specialized journals;

(*ix*) The new product and process announcements as published in dailies (*e.g., Economic Times*) and magazines (*e.g., Purchase*);

(*x*) Visit by supplier's agent;

(*xi*) Film slide or movie;

(*xii*) Trade fair exhibitions.

The survey should be conducted by the purchase department in consultation with the Engineering, R&D, Inspection and such other departments which may contribute to a refined decision. It should be noted that this task is not confined to mere identification of existing sources. Sometimes, it becomes necessary even to develop a source where none had been previously available. The survey stage is a positive function in the sense that it attempts to add more and more suppliers in the list, while the development of the approved list of suppliers is the negative process in the sense that a short-listing is made out of the available exhaustive list of the suppliers that match to the requirements of the buyer.

(C) Development of Approved List of Suppliers: The survey stage highlights the existence of the source. A business inquiry is made with the appropriate supplier. It is known as an "Inquiry Stage."

Here a shortlisting is made out of the given sources of suppliers in terms of production facilities and capacity, financial standing, product quality, possibility of timely supply, technical competence, manufacturing efficiency, general business policies followed, standing in the industry, competitive attitude, interest in buyers' orders etc.

The exhaustive details about the supplier can be obtained from the advertisement, trade reference, direct business inquiry or through a personal visit. The objective of the inquiry stage is to locate those few suppliers who are capable of supplying the item in required quality and quantity, who can be relied on as a continuous source of supply, who will keep their delivery promises and other incidental commitments and who offer competitive price and other conditions of supply.

In case of critical items involving huge economic values and high degree of technicality, the evaluation and selection of the prospective supplier will be made in a group decision. The group or a supplier survey team should consists of members from the purchasing department, production department, engineering department, quality control department, R&D Department. The supply survey team should conduct the exhaustive survey about the suppliers which will result into the preparation of the "approved list" of suppliers.

The size of the approved list largely depends on the circumstances of each case. However, there must be more than one vendor because there may be no one best source in practice. The inclusion of more suppliers in the approved list facilitates the competitive advantage. It also ensures the availability of adequate supply. However, the policy of approved list restricts the choice only to the selected suppliers included in the approved list. Moreover, those who are not included in the approved list develop a feeling of a members of the black list. As this is a self-imposed discipline, the addition to the approved list should be left to the purchase department which will try to up-keep the list of highest standards.

(D) Evaluation and Selection of the Supplier: The purchase policy and procedure differ according to the type of items to be purchased. The evaluation and selection of the supplier differ accordingly. For the stores and supplies, the selection is more simplified. The selection of the supplier of the capital equipment requires distinct considerations and are discussed in a separate chapter on "Capital Budgeting." The evaluation and selection of the supplier of the critical items of high value requires detailed and exhaustive considerations. The bids are invited from the approved suppliers. The bid must specify the quantity description or specification of items to be purchased, required time of delivery, required point of delivery, mode of transport, mode of payment and of course price and all other special conditions having a bearing on the price.

In the "Purchasing Handbook" edited by Aljian, it has been suggested that the following variables be considered while evaluating the quotations of the suppliers:

(1) Cost Factors

(*a*) Price

(*b*) Transport cost — if not included in the bid, to be calculated by the buyer.

(*c*) Installation cost, if any.

(*d*) Tooling and other operation cost.

(*e*) Incidence of sales-tax and excise duty.

(*f*) Terms of payment and cash discount.

(*g*) Price basis if multiple deliveries are involved.

(*h*) Price subject to acceptance within certain specified days.

(*i*) Price protection conditions such as fixed price, protection against reduction in price, price subject to escalation etc.

(2) Delivery

(*i*) Routing: It is the privilege of the owner of the goods.

(*ii*) F.O.B. terms are extremely important in determining (*a*) the point at which the title to the goods passes from the vendor to the buyer, and (*b*) the responsibility for the payment of freight charges.

(3) Design and Specification Factors

(*a*) Specification compliance.

(*b*) Specification deviation.

(*c*) Specification advantages.

(*d*) Important dimensions.

(*e*) Weights.

This should be considered in line with the demonstration of sample, experience of other users, reputation of the supplier, after-sale service, availability of technical personnel, availability of parts etc.

(4) Legal Factors

(*a*) Warranty

(*b*) Cancellation provision

(*c*) Patent protection

(*d*) Public liability and workmen's compensation protection

(*e*) Federal Law and reputation compliance.

Evaluation of the Supplier

The suppliers are rated on the basis of their past performance with the company. Purchasing is a repetitive and continuous process. The supplier once selected should be continued or dropped is a matter of judgement. The evaluation of supplier or popularly known as "vendor rating" provides valuable information which helps in improving the quality of the decision.

In the vendor rating generally three basic aspects are considered — quality, service (*i.e.,* timely delivery) and price. How much weight should be given to each of these factors is a matter of judgement and is decided according to the specific need of the organization, *e.g.,* quality would be the main consideration in the manufacturing of the electrical equipment while price would be the prime consideration in a product having a tense competitive market. For a company procuring its requirements under the blanket contract with agreed price, the suppliers rating would be done on the basis of two variables only, *viz.,* quality and delivery.

The Development Project Committee of the National Association of Purchasing Agents (U.S.A.) has suggested following three methods for evaluating the past performance of the supplier:

(1) The categorical plan; (2) The weighted-point plan; (3) The cost-ratio plan.

(1) The Categorical Plan: Under this method the members of the buying staff related with the supplier like receiving section, quality control department, manufacturing department etc. are required to assess the performance of each supplier. The rating sheets are provided with the record of the supplier, their products and the list of factors for the evaluation purposes. The members of the buying staff are required to assign the plus or minus notations against each factor. The periodic meetings, usually at the interval of one month, are held by senior men of the buying staff to consider the individual rating of each section. The consolidation of the individual rating is done on the basis of the net plus value and accordingly, the suppliers are assigned the categories such as "preferred," "neutral" or "unsatisfactory." Such ratings are used for the future guidance.

This is a very simple and inexpensive method. However, it is not precise. Its quality heavily depends on the experience and ability of the buyer to judge the situation. As compared to other methods, the degree of subjective judgement is very high as rating is based on personal whim and the vague impressions of the buyer. As the quantitative data supported by the profits do not exist, it is not possible to institute any corrective action with the vendor. The rating is done on the basis of memory, and thus it becomes only a routine exercise without any critical analysis.

(2) The Weighted-Point Method: The weighted-point method provides the quantitative data for each factor of evaluation. The weights are assigned to each factor of evaluation according to the need of the organization, *e.g.*, a company decides the three factors to be considered — quality, price and timely delivery. It assigns the relative weight to each of these factors as under:

Quality	...	50 points
Price	...	30 points
Timely delivery	...	20 points
		100 points

The evaluation of each supplier is made in accordance with the aforesaid factors and weights and the composite weighted-points are ascertained for each supplier. To develop the problem further, assume that three suppliers — A, B and C — are rated under this method. First of all the specific rating under each factor will be made and then the consolidation of all the factors will be made for the purpose of judgement.

Quality Rating: The quality of the materials is judged on the basis of the degree of acceptance and rejections. For the purpose of comparison, the percentage degree of acceptance will be calculated in relation to the total lots received, *e.g.*, from A, B and C the number of lots received were 80, 60, and 50 respectively, while the accepted lots were 76, 54 and 48, respectively. The acceptance rate will be ascertained on the percentage basis $\left(\frac{\textit{i.e.,}\ \text{Accepted lots} \times 100}{\text{Total lots}}\right)$ and will be multiplied by the weighted-point of quality factor (in this problem quality is assigned 50 points) to get the quality rating of each supplier as under:

QUALITY RATING

Supplier 1	*Total lots received* 2	*Total lots accepted* 3	*Percentage acceptance* 4	*Weighted point* 5	*Quality rating (6)=(4) × (5)* 6
A	80	76	95%	50%	47.5%
B	60	54	90%	50%	45.0%
C	50	48	96%	50%	48.0%

Price Rating: The price rating is done on the basis of net price charged by the supplier. Assume that A, B and C are as under:

Supplier	**Terms of agreement**
A	₹ 10 per unit with 5% discount plus 50 paise transportation charges.
B	₹ 11 per unit with 10% discount plus 40 paise transportation charges.
C	₹ 10.50 per unit with 10% discount plus 60 paise transportation charges.

From the above data, the net price of each supplier will be ascertained as under:

ASCERTAINMENT OF NET PRICE

Supplier ₹	*Unit Price in* ₹	*Discount in*	*Transportation charges* ₹	*Net price (5)=(2) – (3)+(4)*
A	₹ 10	0.50 (5%)	0.50	10.00
B	₹ 11	1.10 (10%)	0.40	10.30
C	₹ 10.50	1.05 (10%)	0.60	10.05

For the purpose of comparison the aforesaid net price will be converted into percentage on the basis of the lowest price $\left(i.e., \frac{\text{Lowest net price}}{\text{Respective net price}} \times 100\right)$ and this percentage will be multiplied by the weighted-point of price (in this problem price is assigned 30 points) to get the price rating of each supplier as under:

PRICE RATING

Supplier	*Lowest net price in* ₹	*Respective net price in* ₹	*Percentage of (2) to (3)*	*Weighted point*	*Price rating (6) = (4) × (5)*
A	10	10.00	100%	30%	30%
B	10	10.30	97%	30%	29.10%
C	10	10.05	99.5%	30%	29.85%

Rating of timely delivery: Timely delivery is a key consideration. The delayed deliveries should be discounted on the basis of timely delivery as shown in next page:

Delivery	*Points*
Timely delivery	100%
1 day late	98%
2 days late	95%
3 days late	90%
4 days late	83%
5 days late	75%

In our problem, let us assume that the average performance of the suppliers was as under:

Supplier	
A	Timely delivery
B	2 days late
C	1 day late

Here the percentage value of the specific delays, will be multiplied by the assigned weighted-points of timely delivery (in this problem 20 points), to ascertain the rating of timely delivery as under:

RATING OF TIMELY DELIVERY

Supplier 1	*Actual rating of delivery* 2	*Weighted point* 3	*Rating for timely delivery (4) = (2) × (3)*
A	100%	20%	20%
B	95%	20%	19%
C	98%	20%	19.60%

Then at the end the consolidation of the individual ratings will be made as under:

CONSOLIDATED RATING SHEET

Rating	***Supplier A***	***Supplier B***	***Supplier C***
Quality (50 points)	47.5%	45%	48%
Price (30 points)	30%	29.10%	29.85%
Timely delivery (20 points)	20%	19%	19.60%
Consolidated total Rating	97.5%	83.10%	97.45%

Here supplier A with highest rating of 97.5% will be selected, because the selection is made on the basis of the maximum consolidated total rating. The supplier indicating the maximum rating is not necessarily the best supplier. The cut-off rate for the maximum rating can be prescribed by the company. A supplier with the maximum score, but falling below the cut-off rate, should not be selected.

(3) The Cost-Ratio Plan: Under this method, the vendor rating is done on the basis of various costs incurred for procuring the materials from various suppliers. The cost-ratios are ascertained for the different rating variables such as quality, price, timely delivery etc. The cost-ratio is calculated in percentage on the basis of total individual cost and total value of purchase, *e.g.*, the total delivery cost is ₹ 5,000 and the total purchases are ₹ 1,00,000, then delivery cost-ratio will be

$$\frac{5{,}000}{1{,}00{,}000} \times 100 = 10\%$$

At the end, all such cost-ratios will be adjusted with the quoted price per unit. The plus cost ratio will increase the unit price while the minus cost ratio will decrease the unit price. The net adjusted unit price will indicate the vendor rating. The vendor with the lowest net adjusted unit price will be the best supplier and so on.

Under this method, the most strategic issue is the identification of various costs and their allocation among different variables and suppliers. Certain important heads of quality costs and delivery costs can be listed as under:

Quality Costs	***Delivery Costs***
(*i*) Visit to vendor's plant for approval of samples etc.	(*i*) Postage and telegrams.
(*ii*) Inspection costs	(*ii*) Telephones.
(*iii*) Cost of defectives	(*iii*) Visit to vendor's plant for expediting the delivery.
(*iv*) Reworking costs	(*iv*) Extra cost for getting quick delivery, e.g., costlier means of transportation.
(*v*) Manufacturing losses on rejected items.	

All the cost-ratios are calculated for all the suppliers on individual basis. On the basis of the value of the each cost-ratio, the consolidated rating of each supplier is done in the manner as explained in an earlier discussion.

Buyer-Seller Relationship

The continuity of buyer-seller relations helps in fostering the mutual benefits. The development and maintenance of satisfactory supplier is beneficial to both the dealing parties — the buyer and the seller. In fact, purchase and sale are the two facets of a single transaction; however, it is possible to fulfil the mutuality of interest. The selection of the supplier is basically an impersonal action, but intimacy develops in the course of time. Such a relationship can be created and maintained through the following actions:

(*i*) Complete and clear communication as regards need, application and usage of the item; the scope of the product; and technical speciality of the product; limitation of the product; schedule of the probable requirements etc.

(*ii*) Reciprocal understanding for each other's problems and constraints.

(*iii*) Mutual confidence in statement and intent of both the dealing parties.

(*iv*) To be considerate of each other's reasonable demand and elimination of undue demands.

(*v*) Extended relationship beyond merely the contract fulfilment such as to suggest for cost reduction in manufacturing, packing, despatch, usage, accounting etc.

(*vi*) Elimination of all chances of avoidable inquiries and unnecessary expedition.

(*vii*) Continuous improvement in ordering method at buyer's end and supplier services at seller's end.

(*viii*) Cultivation of personal contacts through liaison activities.

The natural culmination of such warm relations is that representative of the seller becomes a member of the "buyer's team" and conversely the buyer becomes an esteemed member of the "vendor's family." It should be noted that such mutual relationship does not weaken the position of either party but in fact it helps in identifying the area of integration of objectives of both the parties which helps in serving the interest of each other.

The loyalty towards the vendor always reaps some benefits in the long run. In fact, loyalty begets loyalty. The opportunism in buying or buying through "shopping around", may generate some short-term economic benefits. But in the long run such opportunism results in development of ill-feelings and dissatisfaction in the course of time. The vendor assures the uniformity of supply, assurance of supply, preferential allocation of quota under scarcity, valuable suggestions as regards probable position of supply and price, sympathetic treatment in case of crisis at buyer's plant etc. The vendor loyalty does not mean that the area of competition is eliminated or the search for the better source is abandoned. It simply means that the established supplier is given an opportunity to work out the best terms of the deal that are consistent with the requirements of the buyer, without sacrificing the interest of the buyer. In fact, continuous change in the supplier not only increases the cost of buying, but it also indicates the lack of reliability of buyer from the supplier's viewpoint which definitely proves costlier in subsequent buying.

The legitimate buying and selling do not leave any room for the dishonesty in buyer-seller relations such as bribery, offer of gift articles, misrepresentations etc. However, it is very difficult to put a line of demarcation between fair or foul tactics in buying and selling, and it merely becomes a matter of degree and intent. The development of the personal relationship with the salesman of the supplier is good, but the loyalty must rest with the supplier because when salesman joins the competitor's firm, the business should not go with him. In fact, some salesmen hold a good command over certain key buyers and accordingly, they bargain their position. Similarly, the purchase officer should be made free from pressure of superiors in exercising the buying decision. If this is not maintained then purchase officer should not be held responsible for any form of failure of purchase function. The superior may not always act in the interest of the organization and thus may not be inclined to adhere to the standards. The purchase function should be handled autonomously through the independent purchase organization.

BUYER-SELLER NEGOTIATIONS

Introduction

Negotiation is an important, interesting, costly and complex mechanism in the buying and selling process. Generally it is confined to the high value and/or large volume buying. It is superior to competitive bidding, another popular technique employed in high value and/or large volume purchases because unlike bidding, negotiation is a two-way process. In fact, negotiation provides a legitimate and ethical means for setting the transaction between the buyer and seller through the give and take tactics. It is not a process of stripping or trapping any of the party by other party but a healthy activity which eliminates the injustice to any of the parties of the deal. In reality, the successful negotiations result in satisfaction to both the parties. At the end of the deal, the dealing parties feel that they have reached to an agreement which is mutually beneficial.

Negotiation means deliberations between the parties leading to an agreement. It is a business session between the buyer and seller for the purpose of settling some business transaction. ***Webster*** defines negotiation as, "conferring, discussing, or bargaining to reach agreement in business transactions." It is also defined as, "the process of working out a procurement and sales programme together, to the point of reaching a mutually satisfactory agreement." As competitive parties deal through the negotiation, the purchase deal of one party results into the sales deal of the other.

Many times negotiation is considered as a price haggling, and thus is considered unethical. In reality, price is not the only, but one of the considerations in the negotiation. Moreover, it does not amount to exploitation of one party by the other, but it results in an agreement which is mutually beneficial.

Objectives of Negotiation

The negotiation is an objective oriented process. All types of negotiations strive to attain one or more of the following objectives:

1. To settle a fair price.
2. To perform the contract in agreed time.
3. To exert control on the fulfillment of the agreed terms.
4. To seek maximum co-operation from the supplier.
5. To develop sound and sustained relationship.

(*1*) ***To settle a fair price:*** To get price settlement is the core part of the negotiation. Both buyers and sellers consider their respective cost analysis of the product. Cost-data is the factual data, of course, it is subject to some adjustments during the deliberations. However, the utility factor of the buyer (*i.e.*, the intensity of the need) and the profit margin of the seller, provides sufficient leeway in the price settlement. Both parties have their respective ranges of the price. Negotiation strives to develop a fixed point on these ranges which is considered satisfactory by both the parties. It should be noted that price fixing is sometimes qualified by the quantity of purchase, sustained buying from the negotiating supplier, transportation and other allied costs, insurance, etc. Clarification should be sought on all these issues while developing a fair price.

(*2*) ***Timely delivery:*** The objective of buyer and seller gets integrated on the issue of timely delivery because for the buyer it eliminates the situation of stock outs and the resultant losses, while for the seller, it enables him to liquidate his stock and the paraphernalia of costs attached to storing and to utilise his production capacity more effectively. Timely delivery is endangered when buyer fails to plan his requirements, or the planned requirements are not communicated to the seller. Seller fails to deliver in time when there is no commitment or there exists any ambiguity in commitment. Negotiation attempts to bridge such gaps on the side of both the dealing parties.

(*3*) ***Fulfilment of the terms:*** Any negligence on the part of the supplier as regards quality, quantity, time of delivery, mode of delivery, pricing etc. greatly affects the interest of the buyer. Specific conditions can be deliberated at the time of negotiations and can be expressly provided in the agreement. Such type of effective plugging is not possible in any other form of contracting. It should also be noted that the conditions of the agreement are not always static. In fact, they change over the period of time. A prudent buyer never allows his agreement to be filed once it is agreed upon, he keeps it alive throughout the contractual period. He will remain alert on all issues and may also initiate the possibility of reopening the negotiations in case of need, considering the interest of his company.

(*4*) ***To seek maximum co-operation from the supplier:*** Generally the supplier is put to a positive situation as compared to the buyer. So the buyer should try to develop all such tactics through which the maximum co-operation of the seller can be obtained. Co-operation begets co-operation. To get the maximum co-operation from the supplier, the buyer should try to co-operate with him in all respects, *e.g.*, if all other things are equal or if the change in the supplier is marginally and temporarily beneficial, the supplier should not be changed. The environment of contented relations, permits the supplier to reduce some of his operating costs and he willingly passes over some part of such benefits over to the buyer.

(*5*) ***To develop sound and sustained relationship:*** The sound relationship between the buyer and seller can be developed through the frequency of transactions and the behaviour during the fulfilment of specific transactions. Such relations can be developed through courteous behaviour and recognizing the adversities of the other party and if possible, adjust to it accordingly, *e.g.*, to help in meeting the financial crisis of the supplier by making prompt payments or advance payments, rescheduling of orders due to some accident at supplier's plant etc. A good supplier will definitely recognize the importance of such considerate buyers and will try to help them in all respects such as giving priorities of supplies in case of shortages, special concessional price offer, advance intimation about the forthcoming supply position, the information about the offing technological changes and its impact on the buyers' production etc. The negotiation involves the two-way communication and it is not once and for all but it should be more or less of a permanent nature. Whether one buys from the previous seller or not, the relations should be established on a sustained basis.

Need for the Negotiation

Negotiation is a costly affair. It may involve a short-lived telephone talk to a series of discussion sessions consuming substantial time. Due to this, the negotiations should be confined to the needy occasions only. Negotiation would not be desirable under following types of purchases:

(*i*) Minor purchases.

(*ii*) Purchase of low, very non-recurring items.

(*iii*) Sporadic purchase of a fairly high value item.

(*iv*) Branded items which are stocked by the supplier and are sold at the catalogue prices.

(*v*) When supplier's proposals are considered satisfactory by the buyers.

Negotiations would become necessary under following conditions:

1. Where situation is not conducive to competitive bidding such as lack of explicit clarity in the minds of buyers and sellers regarding specifications, existence of less number of sellers, urgency of the need etc.
2. The variables other than price such as quality, time of delivery, mode of delivery, incidence of transportation costs etc., are required to be agreed upon.
3. Where the buyer desires to contract for the unused capacity of the seller rather than for the products manufactured by him.
4. Where the business risk involved in the deal cannot be determined accurately, negotiation should be preferred. Under such situation, generally, sellers charge high prices for the purchase of compensating against such business risks. When such risks do not materialise, the buyer stands loser under the deal. Mutual negotiation eliminates or minimises such incidences on the buyer.
5. When the deal is for capital equipment and its tooling and set-up costs represent a large percentage of total costs, negotiation would be desirable for the beneficial deal.
6. When a long period of time is required to produce the items purchased or services performed, negotiation would become inevitable, *e.g.*, deal for the turnkey projects, civil construction of some chemical plants etc. Under such deals it becomes highly necessary for the adjustment of prices according to the changing environment.
7. When frequent production interruption, occur due to the changing conditions, a series of negotiations would become necessary, *e.g.*, change required in the contractual obligation caused by technological developments.
8. When seller is required to sub-contract a part of the deal and agreement of the buyer is necessary for such sub-contracting work, negotiation is the only means for settling the deal.

9. Where seller is the exclusive supplier of the materials, it becomes necessary to negotiate on prices and other terms for the purpose of preventing any unreasonable dictation by the seller.
10. Negotiation is necessary under jobbing contracts wherein individual needs are required to be settled.
11. It is desirable to negotiate for the items which are subject to price-fixation under the law. Under such situation price advantages can be tapped under the technique of "Concealed price cut", *e.g.,* where two items, one being subject to price control are purchased from the same supplier the benefits can be adjusted in non-control items without distorting the price regulations.

Area of Negotiation

Negotiation is a two-way communication wherein the dealing parties always have some issues on which the settlement is sought. All such issues provide the subject matter for the negotiation. It should also be noted that negotiation is possible only for those issues which are subject to settlement under various alternative sources. There cannot be any negotiation for an issue which has the one and the only solution.

The popular areas of negotiation are:

1. Price
2. Quality
3. Quantity, and
4. Service.

(1) Price: Price is the key as well as complex consideration in the negotiation. The buyer strives to prove that there exists keen competition in the market and so supplier should offer the most competitive price while the supplier would try to prove his indispensability and hold in the market and thus will try to strengthen his bargaining position. While negotiating on the price, each break-up of the price should be negotiated separately. In case of conditional price (*e.g.,* f.o.b. price), the incidence of each condition on price should be measured accurately. Sometimes instead of price negotiations, cost negotiations are carried on. Under such negotiations, deliberations are made on each element of cost. The usual break-up of the price along with the elements of the cost is as under:

	Material cost		x x
+	Labour cost		x x
+	**Overheads:**		
	Fixed	x x	
	Variable	x x	x x
	Cost of production		x x
+	Profit margin		x x
	Price		x x

The ascertainment of each element of cost is a technical matter and is subject to substantial deliberations. Especially the overhead part of the cost is most debatable. However, reasonable agreement is possible on all these issues.

(2) Quality: The quality considerations are also subject to debate and deliberations. The quality will be largely affected by the factors such as the dimensions of raw materials, material mix, quality control, processing method and even primary and secondary packing. All these issues should be deliberated and agreed upon expressly.

(3) Quantity: The quantity considerations involve the negotiation on the issues such as quantity discount, commitment of the supplier to meet the future requirements, the guarantee from the buyer to place orders in future etc.

(4) Service: The service aspect of the negotiation involves the considerations such as timely delivery, after-sales services, treatment of defectives and rejections etc.

As settlement of agreement is a composite deal, the impact of all these factors should be weighed individually before finalizing the final deal.

Principles of Successful Negotiation

Negotiation requires a specialized skill. The essential element in the negotiation is the bargaining between the individuals or groups of individuals, so the negotiation process involves the personalities, their motives, their strengths and weaknesses and above all a great deal of psychology. The following rules should be observed in carrying a successful negotiation:

1. The issues of the negotiations should be organized properly.
2. The buyer should carry on the negotiation on his home ground and as per his own arrangements.
3. The buyer should try to put himself in supplier's shoes.
4. The buyer should allow the supplier to do most of the talking.
5. Only one point be taken up at a time.
6. The talk should be directed towards proper person.
7. The discussion issues resulting in sustained conflicts be postponed for next session, if possible.
8. One should not get fumbled with excessive facts and figures.
9. One should try to avoid the emotional reactions to the presentations of the other, at the same time emotional touch to the presentation should also be eliminated.
10. If any party has to retreat on a point, allow it to do it gracefully.
11. The objective of any negotiation is to come at some conclusion so try to avoid premature and hasty conclusions.
12. One should try to satisfy the emotional needs of the persons who are negotiating during the session.

Paul R. McDonald has described the following attributes of a good negotiator:

(*i*) He must be a clear, rapid thinker.
(*ii*) He must express himself well and easily.
(*iii*) He must possess the ability to analyse.
(*iv*) He must be impersonal.
(*v*) He must be patient.
(*vi*) He must be able to consider the other person's ideas objectively.
(*vii*) He must be tactful, have poise and self-restraint.
(*viii*) He must possess a sense of humour.

The Strategy and Tactics of Negotiation Process

The negotiation involves the communication between the buyer and seller either in short-lived or extended sessions. The parties to the negotiation must define the objectives of negotiation. In the line of the objectives, they should spell out the issues to be considered, and the degree of importance to be given to each issue. Negotiation is a game between two parties. The weakness of one is the strength of the other. Pre-negotiation preparations and good homework help in increasing the bargaining position of the party.

The complete knowledge about the issues covered under the negotiation helps the party in developing the strategies and the tactics during the negotiation. Strategies and tactics are the integral parts of the negotiation. The strategy deals with the planning for the negotiation and directing the negotiations so as to reach a defined goal, while tactics deal with moves and manoeuvres which are employed in implementing the strategy. The strategy and tactics can be employed successfully only when the dealing parties become aware about the strengths and weaknesses of each other.

Seller's Strength	***Seller's Weaknesses***
(*i*) Absence of competition in terms of number of sellers or superiority of technical competence of seller's product. (*ii*) The seller's certainty of getting the contract. (*iii*) The intensity of the need of the buyer, *e.g.*, short lead time, the need to balance the capacity etc. (*iv*) The scarcity of the products in relation to its growing demand.	(*i*) The intensity of the need to have the contract. (*ii*) The existence of keen competition in the market. (*iii*) Dealing with the buyer who provides assured market for the products of the seller. (*iv*) The general economic conditions and industry trends adversely affecting the business of the seller.
Buyer's Strength	***Buyer's Weaknesses***
(*i*) The extent of competition in the market. (*ii*) Ability to analyse the cost data effectively with special reference to seller's constraint, *e.g.*, to hire supplier's idle capacity. (*iii*) Large size of the order utilizing the substantial part of seller's production. (*iv*) Economic conditions and its adverse effect on the industry of which seller is a member.	(*i*) Dealings with the seller employing the monopoly in the market. (*ii*) Compelling forces on the buyer to turn to the specific seller only. (*iii*) The intensity of the need of the buyer to get the materials as quick as possible, *e.g.*, emergency buying. (*iv*) The scarcity of the products in relation to its demands.

The strategy and tactics should be developed on the basis of the knowledge about the strength and weaknesses of the dealing parties. The information highlighting the strength and weaknesses of the parties can be had from the published data about general economic conditions as well as data about specific conditions of the industry and the company, pre-negotiation talks and behaviour of the parties, strength disclosed or errors committed during the negotiation sessions. During the negotiation session one should try to recognize the strength of the other party but at the same time should not succumb to it. Conversely, the party with the bargaining strength should be graceful to the other and should not hit hard on its weaknesses.

Legal Environment and Negotiation

The business houses are required to honour the laws and regulations enacted by the Government. Some legal enactments encourage the negotiations while some provisions restrict the area of negotiation. In India, the Monopolies and Restrictive Trade Practices Act (MRTP Act), discourages the further growth of large houses or firms controlling the production of certain items. Such facilities encourage the competition in the market and thus the bargaining position of the buyer is strengthened. The MRTP Act also discourages certain restrictive and unfair trade practices. Such environment puts the negotiation on a sound footing. On the other hand, the Patent, Trade Mark and Copyright Acts ensure the monopoly to certain firms and thus strengthen their bargaining power. The price control measures of the Government imposed on certain essential commodities, restrict the area of negotiation on the price variable. However, there are certain tricks which open the avenues of negotiations even on fixed price items, *e.g.*, concealed discount offer, as referred in the above paragraphs.

PRICING DECISIONS

Product's unit price is contributed by its purchase price plus transportation cost, handling cost, inspection cost, insurance and administrative cost (variable). To an organization, the right price might near that price which satisfies its requirements and yet is low enough.

Prices are determined through published price lists, competitive bidding and buyer-seller negotiations. Competitive bidding is most applicable to standardised products. Here the lowest bidder, generally sets the order. For high value purchases, where even specifications are valued, the negotiations are a great help.

Some terms used in pricing when a consignment is shipped (transported) need classification.

F.O.B. Buyer's Plant: F.O.B. means Free on Board. Here the goods are delivered to buyer's plant. The transportation charges are borne by the supplier. The buyer takes the title in delivery only, and so all claims for damages/losses during transit are borne by the supplier.

F.O.B. Seller's Plant: Here the title is transferred to the buyer as soon as goods are loaded onto the carrier. The transportation charges are therefore borne by the buyer. The buyer has to lodge claims against the transporter for damages/losses if any.

F.O.B. Seller's Plant Freight Allowed: It is similar in legal sense to the above but the seller pays the freight charges.

C.I.F. Contracts: The price aggregates cost of materials + insurance + freight.

F.A.S.: It stands for Free Alongside Ship. Here in export trade, the supplier has to get the goods up to the ship. Therefore, the buyer takes the title as well as all responsibilities.

In the previous chapter, we have studied the various types of purchase contracts. Some important terms relating to discounts are explained below.

Trade Discount: The distributor gives this discount to the buyer. It makes buying from the distributor economical.

Quantity Discount: It is offered when we purchase beyond a certain value of money.

Seasonal Discount: It is offered for purchases made in off-season.

Cash Discount: It is offered for full/cash payment.

PURCHASE TIMING DECISIONS

Purchase timing in an unstable price market situation is critically important. The organization responds to the market conditions by any of the following responses:

(a) Speculative Buying: Buying here is to take advantage of rising prices so that profits can be made through these rising prices.

(b) Forward Buying: Buying in quantities which exceed current requirements, but are within actual forcible requirements. It is an approach adopted in situations where prices are stable over a period of time. This approach gives the following advantages:

1. A favourable price.
2. Quantity discounts.
3. To exploit availability.
4. To protect against shortages.

The inventory carrying cost is high and so working capital is tied up.

Hand-to-Mouth Buying: It satisfies only our current requirements. It is uneconomical. It can be used for certain high value items.

To reduce the financial risk the following two techniques are in vogue:

Time Budgeting Purchases: Items are frequently purchased over a long period with cyclical fluctuations very close to average market price. This is achieved by purchasing small quantities over short operating periods of equal length. In other words a purchase budget is prepared in terms of quantity required and to be purchased and the amount to spent on purchases during a particular period. This method is useful when the price fluctuations are somewhat or extremely irregular; but if they show only one-sided trend (*i.e.*, continuous downward or upward trend) month after month, this method will do more harm.

Hedging: The buyer uses this method to protect his organization from the losses rising out of wide fluctuations in prices. The buyer can protect this company hedging in futures market. Here the buyer enters into two contracts at the same time — one for purchase of materials for spot (ready) delivery and other for sale of materials for future delivery. This is the concept of hedging. It is used in organized commodity markets or exchanges.

PURCHASING BY GOVERNMENT

Government as a purchaser wants to take advantage of centralised purchasing for which purpose an agency called Directorate General of Supplies and Disposal (DGS & D) has been created under the ministry of supply. It is headed by a director, and is responsible for all purchase of materials of all kinds. It functions as a purchase and inspection agency on behalf of:

1. All ministries, attaches and subordinate offices of GOI.
2. All State Governments and their departments.
3. All local bodies (municipalities, corporations, district boards).
4. All quasi-public institutions, statutory corporations, PSUs who may also avail of the services of DGS & D.

The DGS & D has the wings of supply, inspection, progress and disposal. The suppliers have to register with DGS & D.

Government as a purchaser also purchases apart from DGS & D by the following two methods:

(*a*) Tender Method (Advertised bidding method).

(*b*) Negotiation Method (Negotiated purchase method).

Electronic Information Flow

A supply chain is essentially a linkage of the stages starting from raw materials through production to its distribution to the consumer. Some operating systems such as MRP push the product to the user. Some others pull it to the producer such as JIT. In any system, what matters is the flow of information — its frequency and speed. It affects the inventory level efficiency, costs and so on. Information flow has been streamlined by making it electronic. Several manufacturers share information with the customers electronically. Such sharing pertains to processing of product orders, invoicing and despatch instructions. Electronic data interchange (EDI) may be initiated either by the customers or manufacturers. Such interchange is 'paperless.' Retailers and vendors communicate electronically through Quick Response (QR) and Efficient Consumer Response (ECR). Its main aim is to develop a JIT replenishment system. ECR is just a variation of QR adopted by supermarkets. Here the distributors, suppliers and grocers co-operate closely to bring products to consumer.

Efficient Consumer Response (ECR)

The ECR (Efficient Consumer Response) is a global movement in fast moving consumer goods industry focussing on supply chain management. The beginning of this movement is an example of collaborative management along the supply chain — suppliers, manufacturers, wholesalers, retailers and 3P service providers. By working together they meet the changing demands of the consumers better, faster and at lesser cost.

ECR has been facilitated by global movement of goods and advances in information technology. Its aim is to deliver the right products to the consumers at the right price. We have to avoid non-standardised operational practices, *e.g.,* lack of standardisation in packaging products. There should be standardised bar codes on all the SKUs as well as outers. There should not be rigid separation between manufacturer and the retailer. It can block the supply chain unnecessarily. It fails to exploit the synergies from IT and planning tools. ECR breaks down the non-productive barriers. The ECR Group in India monitors stock-outs at retail level. The overlapping and duplication of software is being avoided. The use of XML standards would allow the various elements of the supply chain to interact digitally with one another. The costs saved could be passed on to consumers by rendering them better service; and by introducing product differentiation. There should be assortment guidelines at the retail level which manufacturers understand easily. There should be new product introduction guidelines at the retail level. There should be data sharing between manufacturers and retailers. There should be collaboration between the manufacturer and the retailer for better inventory management.

BS 7799: Protecting Customer Data

BPOs handle sensitive information on behalf of its customers. Information assets of clients include customer lists, account, and credit information, personal information, health records, project plans, details of the most profitable customers etc. It is therefore, necessary to create a company-wide policy on data security.

BS 7799 is, unlike ISO series, prescriptive in nature, and defines what a BPO needs to do in order to establish, implement and document an effective security management system (ISMS). There are three primary components to BS 7799: Confidentiality, Integrity and Availability of data (CIA). According to the certification, there are 10 guiding principles for an effective ISMS.

The 10 Mantras of BS 7799

1. ***Define*** security policy, so that all employees know about it.
2. ***Organize*** resources and assets to manage information security.
3. ***Classify*** data into different categories of sensitivity.
4. ***Pay*** attention to physical and environmental security.
5. ***Provide*** personnel security to reduce opportunities for theft.
6. ***Communicate*** security policy across the organization.
7. ***Control*** access to sensitive zones to prevent leakage of data.
8. ***Build*** security into information systems.
9. ***Plan*** disaster recovery for continuity of business activities.
10. ***Comply*** with legal requirements to avoid breach of obligations.

It takes anywhere between nine and 12 months before a company can qualify for the certification, which is valid for three years. There are at least three kinds of audits a vendor must go through — internal, external (by certifying agency) and customer-led.

Work stations are set up with more care. Disk drives and print commands are disabled.

Desktops are 'hardened' to ensure that no unauthorised software can be loaded. Internet access is not available. Internal LAN cannot be accessed from a customer terminal. Cell phones are banned on the 'floor' of most BPOs.

What makes the system fool-proof is, however, employee education.

Aircraft Purchasing

Aircraft is an expensive product. The average list price of a brand new Airbus A320 (in 2011) is $85 million. Boeing 737-800 is listed for $84.4 million. Aircrafts, however, do not sell at the listed price. There is bargaining if the order is large and after negotiations, discounts from 10 to 40 per cent are offered. All depends on the type of aircraft ordered, delivery dates requested, the engines selected and the interior options specified.

At the time of signing the deal to buy the aircraft, only one per cent of the cost of the aircraft is paid by the airline. They pay small percentages of the cost to the manufacturer at pre-determined intervals before the delivery date. The deal is financed by the banks by way of long-term loans at pre-determined rates.

The role of the leasing companies such as GECAS (General Electric group) and ILFC (International Lease Finance Corporation, of AIG group) is important. They buy the aircraft from the manufacturer and then lease them to the customers. This happens prior to delivery. In India, the leasing deal is concluded before delivery. The leasing company pays the cheque, which is used to pay the manufacturer. The ownership papers are given to the airline. These are then transmitted to the leasing company. The airline can sell an aircraft to the leasing company at a higher price and make a profit.

The aircraft engine may not be bought from the aircraft manufacturer. There are separate deals with engine manufacturers. There are 'per hour' basis deals with engine companies. Engines can be swapped around the aircrafts.

The lease agreement factors in the profit made by the airline. The lower the profit, the lower the lease rental. The average lease rental on a brand new A320 or 737-800 ranges between $500,000-750,000 per month. There is no depreciating asset on airline's books. The lease payments are operational expense.

25

INVENTORY MANAGEMENT: INDEPENDENT DEMAND INVENTORY

Concept of Inventory

Inventory is defined as a usable resource which is physical and tangible such as materials. In this sense, our stock is our inventory, but even then the term inventory is more comprehensive. Though inventory is a usable resource, it is also an idle resource, unless it is managed efficiently and effectively.

Inventory management boils down to maintaining an adequate supply of something to meet the expected demand pattern subject to budgeting considerations. Inventory could be raw materials, work-in-progress (WIP), finished products or the spare parts and other indirect materials. Effectiveness of the materials and production functions depend to a large extent upon inventory management. Inventory turnover ratio $\frac{\text{Annual Demand}}{\text{Average Inventory}}$ is an index of business performance. Sound management gives a higher inventory turnover ratio.

Inventories have to be procured, stored and carried for a production system, since a situation when they can be instantaneously available is difficult to assume in Indian setting. Inventories are, therefore, a necessary evil to stay.

Importance of Inventory

Inventories constitute the largest component of current assets in many organizations. Poor management of inventories therefore may result in business failures. A stock-out creates an unpleasant situation for the organization. In case of a manufacturing organization, the inability to supply an item from inventory could bring production process to a halt. Conversely, if a firm carries excessive inventories, the added carrying cost may represent the difference between profit and loss. Efficient inventory control, therefore, can significantly contribute to the overall profit-position of the organization.

What Function Does Inventory Perform?

Functions that inventory performs

In any organization, inventories add an operating flexibility that would otherwise be lost. In production, work-in-process inventories are an absolute necessity unless each individual part is to be carried from machine to machine and those machines set up to produce that single part. The many functions inventory performs can be summarized as follows:

(a) Regularising Demand and Supply

Harvest of tobacco is carried out during the concluding part of the summer, but the manufacture of tobacco products such as cigarettes and cigars continues throughout the entire year. In cases like this sufficient raw materials must be purchased during the tobacco-producing period to last the entire year. It compels the manufacturer to carry inventory.

In a simple sense, because a commercial vehicle can be driven 100 miles without passing a petrol pump, its tanks must carry enough petrol to avoid run-outs.

(b) Economising Purchases or Productions by Lot Buying or Batch Production

If the product does not have the demand sufficient to sustain its continuous production round the year, it is usually produced in batches or lots, on an intermittent basis. During the time when the item is not being produced, sales are made from inventory which is accumulated while the item is being produced. Similarly, a super-bazar selling men's clothing does not purchase a new shirt from Double Bull each time they sell one. Rather they choose to carry with them an inventory of these shirts so that purchasing can be done in larger quantities, thereby allowing lower costs and less paper work.

(c) Allowing Organizations to cope with Perishable Materials

Organizations selling canned foods, particularly fruits and vegetables, operate at peak production capacity only for a few months each year. They must store up inventory to supply sufficient to last them through a year's anticipated demand until the next season. They give thoughtful consideration to the rate of inventory accumulation and depletion throughout the peak production and sales periods each year.

(d) Inventory can Store Labour

Though it may sound abstract to talk of "Inventorying" labour, it has been done as a matter of routine. Levin and Kirkpatrick illustrate this by a lively example. "The peak demand for the installation of replacement heating units comes in the fall, just after the old units have been operated for the first time. The manufacturers of heating units store up excess labour by having their workers produce at a designated rate all year long, then having converted labour into finished heating units, they hold them in inventory until the point when demand increases rapidly. Even if demand exceeds current productive capacity, a manufacturer can supply the difference out of inventory at that time."

Inventory Decisions

Executives decide two basic issues while dealing with inventories. These two decisions are made for every item in the inventory.

(*a*) *How much* of an item to order when the inventory of that item is to be replenished.

(*b*) *When* to replenish the inventory of that item.

We will introduce you to the more commonly used inventory models which managers use to make the two decisions enumerated above.

Inventory in common parlance is called stock of any time or resource used in an organization. Since so much capital is committed to inventory and it affects the delivery of finished products to the consumers, inventory management is an important operation. Inventory management influences several other functions such as operations or production, marketing and finance.

By definition, inventories facilitate production or satisfy customer demands. **Inventory system** is a set of policies and controls which monitors and determines the levels of inventory. Inventories conventionally include raw materials, work-in-process, component parts, supplies and finished goods. Operations is a transformation process in which the inputs are raw materials and the output is the finished goods.

Suppliers → Raw material → [Production work-in-process] → Finished goods → Customers

Inventories here are equated with stock of materials. This is a narrow view. Broadly speaking, inventory is an idle resource that has potential economic value, thus taking in its ambit idle workers as inventory. But apart from materials, other idle resources are considered as capacity. Inventory is a product at some point in conversion and distribution process, whereas capacity is the potential to produce.

In the service industry, inventory refers to the tangible goods to be sold and supplies necessary to administer the service.

In the production process, inventory stocks are located at various points. These are inter-connected through flows. A stock is replenished at a particular rate which is called the supply capacity. The rate of stock depletion is called demand. Inventory is a buffer between the different demand and supply rates. The analogy of a water tank illustrates the concepts of flows and stocks.

Fig. 25.1

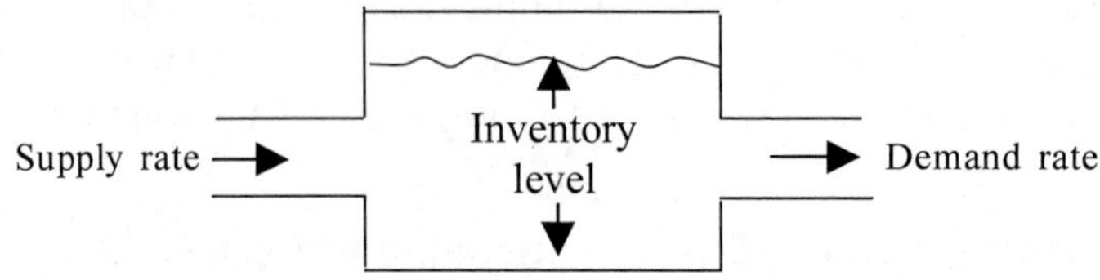

Just as the water enters the water tank, supply enters the productive process. The flow of water from the tank is analogous to demand. The water level is equivalent to inventory. It is a buffer between demand and supply. If the demand is greater than supply, the water level goes down till the demand and supply rate balance each other or till the water is depleted. If the supply is greater than demand, the water rises up. One can also imagine a series of inter-connected water tanks with varying inputs and outputs.

Fig. 25.2

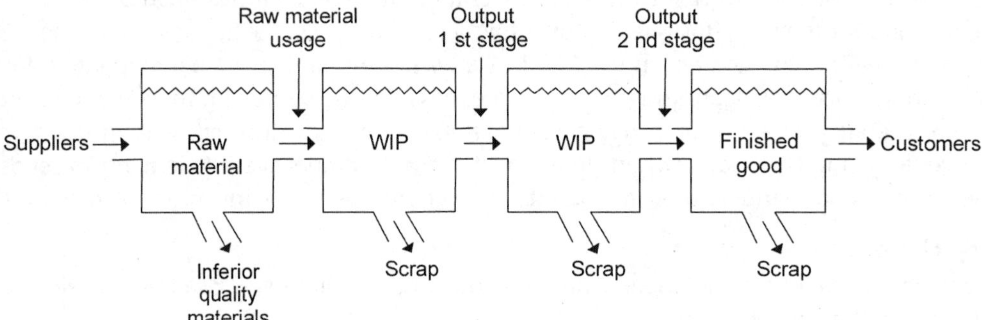

Why do we study inventory management? We have to answer two questions (1) When should we order the items? (2) How large our order should be? If there is an yearly contract given to a supplier, the 'how many to order' becomes 'how many to deliver'.

Purpose of Inventory

There are several reasons to carry inventory.

1. To protect against uncertainties in supply, demand and lead time
2. To maintain independence of operations *e.g.*, a supply at work centre allows it flexibility of operations.
3. To allow flexibility in production scheduling.
4. To allow economic production and purchase.
5. To provide for transit.

Inventory Costs

The following four types of costs are considered in calculating inventory size:

(1) Holding (or carrying) costs: These relate to those costs which are incurred to carry the inventory items in stock for a period of time. It is expressed as a percentage of rupee value per unit of time. An annual holding cost of 15 per cent means that it will cost ₹ 15 to hold ₹ 100 of inventory for a year. This broad category includes costs for storage, handling, insurance, pilferage, breakage, obsolescence, depreciation, taxes and the opportunity cost of capital. When items are carried in inventory, the capital is tied up and is not free to be invested in other things — a case of foregone opportunities for other investments. This is assigned to inventory as an opportunity cost.

(2) Set up (or production charge) cost: Production of different products requires procurement of the necessary materials, arrangement of specific equipment set-ups, filling of the required papers, charging time and materials and moving out previous stock of materials. It means paperwork costs and the costs to set up production equipment for a run.

When set up costs are heavy, there is an economy in having large runs. Set up time can be reduced by changes in production system and product. Though set up cost is considered fixed, it can be changed by changing the design and management of operations.

Were there no costs in changing from product to product, it would have been possible to produce smaller lots leading to lowering of inventory levels and saving in costs.

(3) Ordering costs: These are the costs associated with the placement of an order. This cost remains the same irrespective of the items ordered. These costs include clerical costs of making an order, expediting it, receiving it and so on. Transportation costs are a part of ordering costs. Even if the item is produced within a firm, there are ordering costs. Tracking an order is also a part of the ordering costs.

(4) Stock-out costs: There is an economic cost when we run out of stock. If the customer has to wait because of back logging an item for the customer, there is loss of future business. It is an opportunity loss. If the material is not on hand, there can be a lost sale with consequent loss of current and future profits.

When the item is depleted, we cannot entertain its order till the stock is replenished. There is a trade off between carrying cost to satisfy demand and costs resulting from stock out. This is what is known as shortage costs.

Inventory management is cross functional. Marketing tends to avoid lost sales. Finance tends to minimize capital costs. Production tends to keep inventory at level that assures smooth scheduling and production control. These objectives may run counter to each other. We have to take a cost optimization approach from the combined effects four individual costs. Besides cost consideration, there is time consideration which impinges on inventory cost.

Independent *vs.* Dependent Demand

While studying inventory management, it is important to understand the distinction between independent and dependent demand. Demand can be attributed to the end item or can be attributed to the item itself. The predictions of inventory are based on how demand is attributed. **Independent demand** is influenced by market conditions outside the control of operations. The demand in other words, is **independent of operations.** Finished goods inventories and spare parts for replacement have usually independent demand. **Dependent demand** is related to the demand for another item. When a product is made up of parts and components, the demand for these are dependent upon the demand for the final product.

In an automobile company, the demand for cars is an independent demand decided by the market forces and the demand for tyres is a dependent demand decided by the production of the cars.

Sales forecast is an essential input to decide the quantity of independent demand. The forecast is adjusted by certain extra quantity. In this chapter, we will examine models to take care of the independent demand. The approach to inventory is based on the demand pattern. Replenishment philosophy is appropriate for independent demand. As the stock depletes, it is replenished. When the inventory starts to run out, an order is placed for more material, and the inventory is replenished.

On the other hand, requirements philosophy is employed for dependent demand items. The amount of stock ordered is based on requirements for higher level items. More material is ordered only when required by the need of the end product or higher level items. More depletion would *not* lead to the order of raw material or work-in-process.

Classifying Models

Inventory systems are of two types — **fixed-order quantity models or fixed-time period models.**

Fixed-order quantity models are also called the **economic order quantity (EOQ) and the Q model.**

Fixed time period models are referred to as the **periodic review system and P model.**

Q models are related to an event and P models are related to time. In Q models, order is initiated when the event of reaching a specified re-order level occurs. This event depends upon the demand for the items and can occur any time. In P models, the order is placed at the end of a pre-decided time period. What matters is the passage of time.

While using Q models, the inventory must be continuously monitored. It is a perpetual system. Here records of inventory are updated on every addition to or withdrawal from the inventory. In P models, inventory is counted only at the end of the review period.

There some more differences between the Q and P models.

- In P models, the average inventory size is larger to protect against stock out during review period.
- Since average inventory is lower in Q models, it favours more expensive items.
- Q models are suitable for critical items because of close monitoring and quick response to stock out.
- Q models record additions and withdrawals and so are time consuming.

The following table shows the distinction between the Q and P model:

Point	***Q*** ***Fixed-Order Quantity Model***	***P*** ***Fixed-Time Period Model***
Order-quantity	Constant	Variable
Time	When inventory drops to recorder point—R	When the review period arrives—T
Record	Each time the addition or withdrawals made	Counted only at review period
Size of inventory	Less than P	Larger than Q
Maintenance	Time-consuming since monitoring is perpetual	—
Types of items	Expensive, critical, vital items	—

Q Systems

As we know by now, that in this system the inventory is continuously reviewed — therefore, it is also called as continuous review system. When the stock position drops to a predetermined order point, a fixed quantity is placed on order. As the order quantity is fixed, the interval between orders will vary depending upon the random nature of demand.

The stock position or inventory position is defined as:

On-hand + On-order – back ordered quantities

We have to see whether the stock position is less than or equal to the record point. If yes, we issue an order for exactly Q units, not more or less. In the Q system, there are two parameters Q and R. It is assumed in the simplest model that all aspects of the situation are known with certainty. The annual demand, the setup costs, the holding costs are all known. It is a good basis to understand inventory models, though in practice, the assumption of complete certainty is not valid.

The optimal order quantity model assumes:

(*i*) Constant demand and uniform demand throughout the time period

(*ii*) Constant lead time (time between the order is placed and goods received)

(*iii*) Price per unit of product is constant

(*iv*) Inventory holding cost is based on average inventory

(*v*) Order/setup costs are constant

(*vi*) All demands for the product will be satisfied (no backorders).

Saw-tooth Effect

The following diagram illustrates the saw-tooth effect relating Q and R. (see Fig. 25.3).

Fig. 25.3

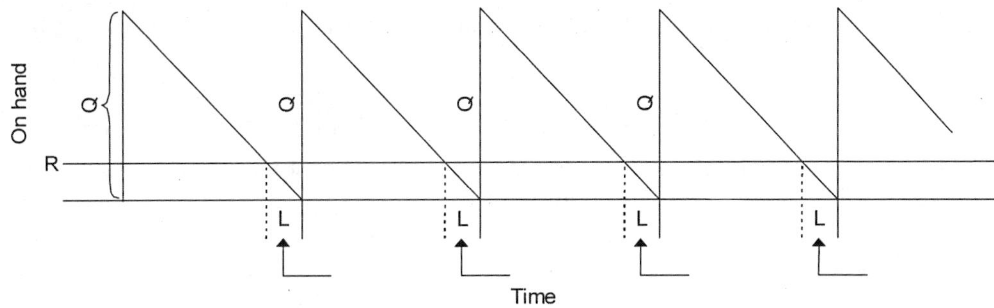

In the above diagram, we can see that when the inventory position drops to point R, a recorder is placed. This order is received at the end of period L which is constant here.

Economic Order Quantity (EOQ)

This celebrated model was developed by F.W. Harris in 1915 and came to be extensively used through the efforts of a consultant named Wilson. It is known after Wilson, though it is originally developed by Harris. EOQ and its variations are still popular for independent-demand inventory management.

Trade-off between Ordering Frequency and Inventory Level

If we order small lots, the ordering frequency will increase but there will be low average inventory. If we order larger lots, the ordering frequency will decrease but there will be more inventory to carry. The trade-off between ordering frequency and inventory level can be represented by a mathematical equation using the following symbols:

D = Annual demand rate

S = Cost per order placed or setup cost

C = Cost per unit

H = Annual holding cost per unit of average inventory. Often, holding cost is expressed as percentage of the cost of the item. As such, H = *i*C where *i* carrying interest rate (per cent carrying cost)

TC = total of ordering cost plus holding cost per year

The annual ordering cost is:

Ordering cost per year = (Cost per order) (orders per year)

= SD/Q

In this equation D is the total demand annually. Q units are ordered at a time. Thus D/Q orders are placed in a year. This is multiplied by S, the cost per order placed.

The annual holding/carrying cost is:

Holding/carrying cost per year = (annual carrying rate) × (unit cost) × (average inventory)

$$= \frac{Q}{2}H$$

$$= \frac{iCQ}{2}$$

In this equation the average inventory is Q/2. A maximum of Q units is carried just as a batch arrives in inventory. The minimum amount carried is zero units. The depletion rate of stock is constant, and therefore the average inventory is Q/2. The carrying rate per year (*i*) multiplied by the unit cost (c) gives the holding cost of one unit in inventory for a year. This unit charge multiplied by the average inventory level gives the total holding/carrying cost per year.

The total annual cost of inventory then —

Total cost per year = ordering of cost per year + carrying cost per year.

$$TC = \frac{SD}{Q} + \frac{iCQ}{2} \qquad \text{...(1)}$$

In this equation, the annual purchase cost or procurement cost DC is ignored since it is constant independent of Q. It will not affect the minimum TC.

Fig. 25.4

Graphical Representation of EOQ Formula

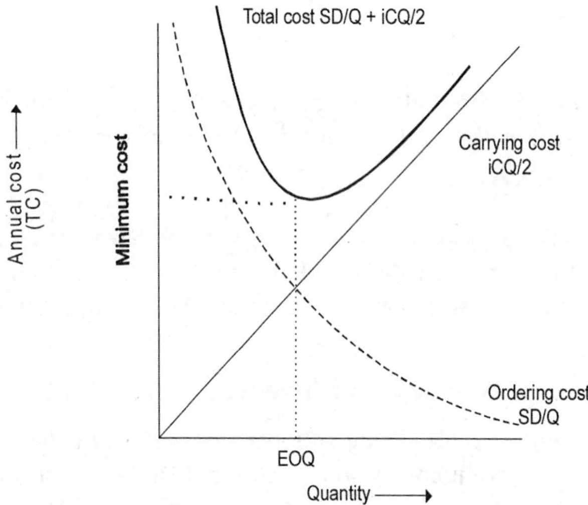

In Fig.25.4, TC vs Q are plotted. Each component of TC is shown separately along with the total. As Q rises, the ordering cost falls as fewer orders are placed per year. At the same time, the carrying cost rises as more average inventory is held. Thus, ordering and carrying costs are offsetting — one falls while the other rises This is the tradeoff between ordering and carrying costs, because of which TC has a minimum. Here the slope of the curve is zero.

We can find the value of Q that minimizes TC by using calculus. We take the derivative of TC and set it equal to zero, and then solve for the resulting value of Q.

$$TC = \frac{SD}{Q} + \frac{iCQ}{2}$$

$$= -\frac{SD}{Q^2} + \frac{iC}{2} = O$$

$$= \frac{SD}{Q^2} + \frac{iC}{2}$$

$$Q^2 = \frac{2SD}{iC}$$

$$Q = \sqrt{\frac{2SD}{iC}} \qquad \text{...(2)}$$

This equation 2 is the classic Wilson economic order quantity (EOQ) which minimizes the cost of operating the inventory. We have taken minimum cost on annual basis but any unit of time can be taken, provided D and *i* are compatible. For instance, if D is expressed in months then *i* should also be expressed in months.

This simple model assumes constant demand and lead time. Hence, no safety stock is necessary. The reorders point R is therefore,

$$R = \bar{d}L \qquad ...(3)$$

Where,

$\bar{d}$ = average daily demand (constant)

L = lead time in days (constant).

Average Inventory

The order quantity and the average inventory shows a constant ratio of 1:½ and is maintained uniformly. This is because we have assumed a constant depletion of inventory between two periods over a period of time. The following diagram illustrates this.

Let us suppose that by one single order we receive the total annual requirement. It is received on 1st January. It is consumed uniformly over the year. On 31st Dec. we will have no stock. Our average inventory holding during the year will be ½Q.

Let us again suppose we will hold the inventory during each of the twelve months. We shall place our orders in such a way that supplies are received on the 1st of every calendar month. In other words, supplies come in twelve equal instalments. Here we hold maximum inventory at the beginning of the month *i.e.,* 1st of every month. There is depletion at uniform usage rate till it reaches zero at the end of the month. In this case also the average inventory is half the order quantity.

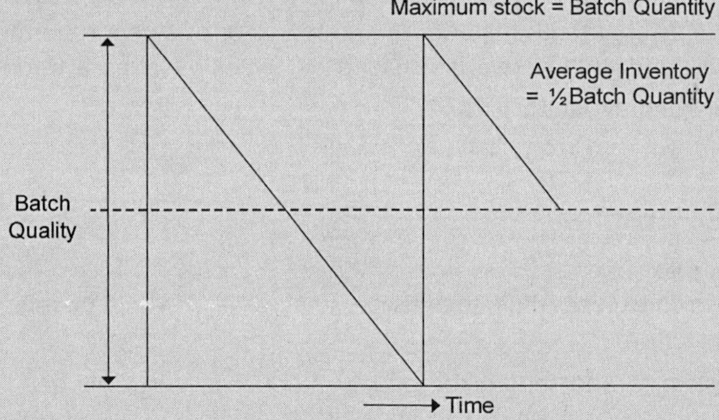

Fig. 25.5 **Inventory Holding at a Constant Rate of Depletion**

Let us imagine a third situation where supplies are received twice a year *i.e.,* 1st Jan. and 1st July. Here also the average in inventory is ½ Q over the six months period.

Average inventory is thus always half the order quantity or delivery size.

Example: **Economic Order Quantity**

Find the EOQ on the basis of the following data:

Annual demand = 1200 units
Ordering cost = ₹ 10 per purchase order
Cost per unit = ₹ 1
Holding costs per unit = 24% per year *(contd.)*

(contd.)

$$EOQ = \sqrt{\frac{2DS}{iC}}$$

$$= \sqrt{\frac{2 \times 1200 \times 10}{1 \times \frac{24}{100}}} = 316 \text{ units approx.}$$

Limitations

The EOQ derived in equation 2 has limitations on account of the restrictive assumptions made. The cost assumptions are rational and are not found in real life. The unit cost of purchase varies in practice. The lead times are not constant. The demand is erratic. The rate of consumption is not uniform. The application, therefore, of this formula, as it is, is not possible. Discounts on quantity also distort the formula. Lead time variations are pretty common. If the usage rate is not uniform there will be stock outs. Buffer stocks are, therefore, necessary. The formula will have to be adapted to meet these limitations, but then it becomes complicated.

The significant idea that emerges from this discussion is that of the total cost. Whatever may be the situation, if one arrives at the total cost, then EOQ can be found. The idea of minimizing the total-cost equation is basic to all lot-sizing formulas and situations.

Fixed-Order Quantity Model with Usage During Production

The total cost equation 1, assumes the receipt of the ordered quantity in one lot, which is not true always. In several situations, there is production of an inventory item and its usage at the same time. It is relevant when the output of one part becomes input of the other part of the production system *e.g.*, aluminum extrusions being produced to turn out aluminum windows. There are also contractual arrangements with the suppliers *e.g.*, six month material requirements or one year requirements being covered through one single order and with deliveries spaced out weekly or more frequently.

The total cost equation for such situation is:

$$TC = \frac{SD}{Q} + \frac{(p-d)QH}{2p}$$

Where d = constant demand rate

p = production rate (which exceeds the rate of usage. Otherwise Q would be infinite, resulting in continual production)

Differentiating with respect to Q and setting the equation equal to zero, we get

$$EOQ = \sqrt{\frac{2SD}{H} \cdot \frac{p}{(p-d)}} \qquad ...(4)$$

Graphically this model is shown below:

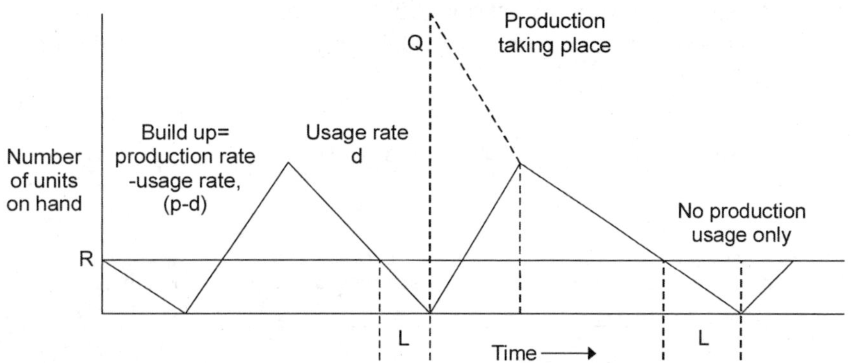

Fig. 25.6

Fixed Order Quantity Model with Usage During Production

Example: **Optimal Lot Size**

A component of product x (let us call it x_1) is produced in another department. x_1 is produced at the rate of 200 units per day. The assembly line uses x_1 component at the rate of 80 units per day. Considering the following data, what would be EOQ of component x?

Daily usage (d) = 80 units
Annual demand (D) = 20000 (80 units × 250 working days)
Daily Production (P) = 200 units
Cost for production set up (S) = ₹ 100
Annual Holding cost (H) = ₹ 1 per unit
Cost of component x_1 (c) = ₹ 14 each
Lead time (L) = 7 days

The EOQ would be

$$EOQ = \sqrt{\frac{2SD}{H} \cdot \frac{p}{(p-d)}}$$

$$= \sqrt{\frac{2(20000)\,100}{1} \cdot \frac{200}{200-80}}$$

$$= 2581 \text{ units}$$

We can find the recorder point R by

$$R = dL = 80(7) = 560 \text{ units}$$

It means that an order for units of component x should be placed when the stock drops to 560 units.

Safety or Buffer Stock

We have assumed in the above discussion a certain demand at constant rate. Mostly, demand varies from day-to-day and is not constant. Safety stock has to be maintained to protect against stockouts. Safety stock is defined as the additional amount of stock carried to meet more than the expected demand. But if more and more additional stock is carried, it means holding of unnecessary additional inventories. When less is carried, there are chances of a stock out. Management then faces the risk or production hold ups. Such uncertainties require precise treatment of safety stocks. The following diagram illustrates the situation.

There are two causes of stockouts. Stockout could be a result of the major rate of usage or excess consumption. Stockouts could be due to delayed delivery. Stockouts could be the result of both of these two factors.

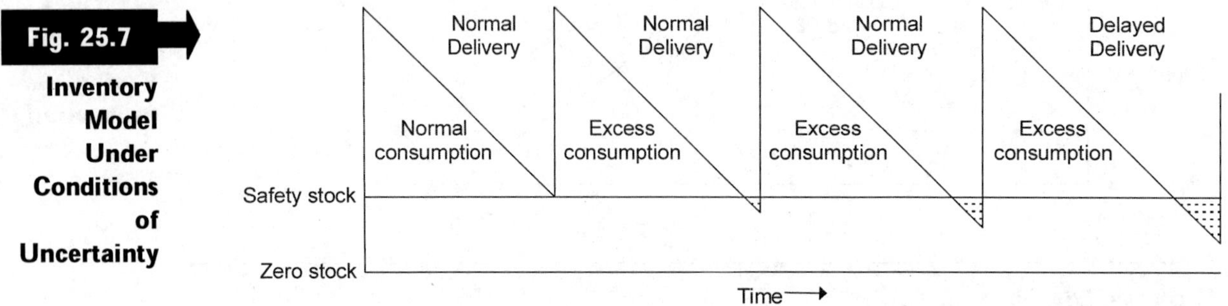

Fig. 25.7 **Inventory Model Under Conditions of Uncertainty**

Safety stocks provide the necessary cushion when consumption is at a higher rate or the normal delivery period is exceeded.

Probability Approach

Safety stocks are treated with two approaches — **probability approach** and **expected number** approach. Probability approach considers the probability that demand will exceed some specified amount. The inventory objective could read, 'the safety stock is set at a level where there is 6 per cent chance that the demand will exceed 100 units.' The expected number approach considers the expected number of units which will be out of stock. The inventory objective could read 'inventory level is to be set such that we can meet 96 per cent of the orders for the unit (or be out of stock 4 per cent of time).' In the first approach, the probability of exceeding a value is considered. In the second approach, we are concerned with how many units we fall short of.

The value of R can be based on either stockout cost or stockout probability. Stockout based on cost formulations are cumbersome. Therefore, **stockout probability** is commonly used as a basis to determine R.

The probability of a stockout over a period of time is determined by plotting a normal distribution for the expected demand and see where the amount on hand lies on this curve.

If the demand is expected to be 100 units, and the standard derivation is 20 units, the probability of being stocked out with an opening stock of 100 units is 50 per cent. Half of the month the demand is expected to be greater than 100 units, and half of the months less than 100 units. If the order of 100 units is received at the commencement of the month, in the course of time there will be a stockout for six months of the year. As a precautionary measure, we might carry an additional 20 units. Though the monthly requirements would be ordered the same way, the delivery would be so scheduled that the items arrive while 20 units are still in stock. This is the concept of safety stock which provides the cushioning against probability of stockout.

Look at the appendix Standard Normal Distribution. Move 1 standard deviation right to the mean. It gives a probability of 0.3413. We need to add 0.5 to this. It comes to a probability of .8413. Therefore 84 per cent of time, we would not expect to face a stockout, and .16 per cent of time, we would face a stockout. If our ordering frequency is every two months, the expected stockout would be (.16 × 12) = 1.9 months or approximately 2 months.

The companies commonly set 95 per cent as the probability of not stocking out. It means they carry about 1.64 standard deviations of safety stock or 33 units (1.64 × 20 = 32.8). It does not mean an additional order of 33 units each month. It means scheduling of the receipt of the item at a time when 33 units are still in inventory. The expected stockout is approximately 6 months per year or a stock out in 1 month of every 20 months.

Service level

Service Level is an extensively used concept in inventory management. A 100 per cent service level indicates, that all the demands of the customers would be met from inventory. The stockout percentage is equal to 100 minus service level.

If an annual demand for an item is 10,000 units and the service is 95 per cent, it means that 9,500 items can be supplied immediately from the inventory and 500 units are short.

Service level can be expressed in three ways:

(1) Service level is the probability that all orders will be filled from the stock during the replenishment lead time of one recorder cycle.

(2) Service level is the percentage of demand filled from stock during a given period of time (say a year).

(3) Service level is the percentage of time the system has stock on hand.

Each of these definitions would lead to a different recorder point. To simplify the matter, the first definition is accepted.

The recorder point is based on the probability distribution of demand over lead time.

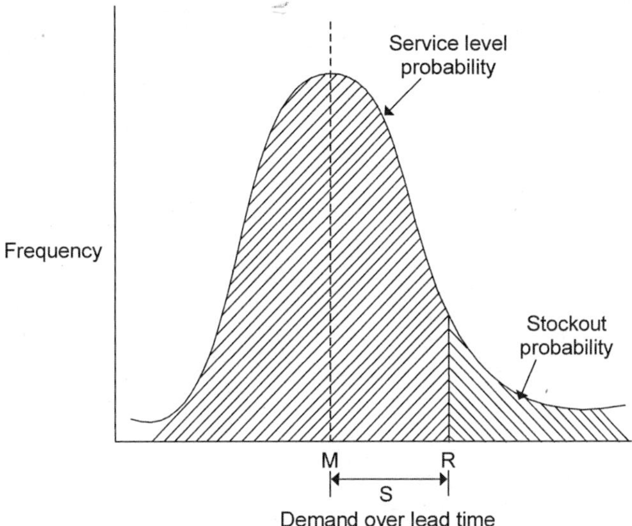

Fig. 25.8 **Probability Distribution of Demand Over Lead Time**

The reorder point is set high (greater than zero) to reduce the stockout probability. We assume normal distribution of demand as it is realistic for independent demand inventory problem.

The reorder point is

$$R = m + S$$

where, R = reorder point

m = mean (average) demand over the lead time

S = Safety stock

Safety stock is given by

$$S = z\sigma$$

where z = Safety factor

σ = Standard deviation of demand over lead time

We can then rewrite as:

$$R = M + z\sigma$$

Reorder point is set equal to the average demand over lead time m, plus a specified number of standard deviations σ is to protect against stockout.

Even service level is controlled by controlling z and the standard deviations used.

A high level of z leads to a high reorder point and a high service level.

If we know the service level desired, we can determine z and m from the table give here.

Table 25.1

Normal Demand Percentages

z	*Service Level (%)*	*Stockout (%)*
0	50.0	50.0
.5	69.1	30.9
1.0	84.1	15.9
1.1	86.4	13.6
1.2	88.5	11.5
1.3	90.3	9.7
1.4	91.9	8.1
1.5	93.3	6.7
1.6	94.5	5.5
1.7	95.5	4.5
1.8	96.4	3.6
1.9	97.1	2.9
2.0	97.7	2.3
2.1	98.2	1.8
2.2	98.6	1.4
2.3	98.9	1.1
2.4	99.2	.8
2.5	99.4	.6
2.6	99.6	.5
2.7	99.6	.4
2.8	99.7	.3
2.9	99.8	.2
3.0	99.9	.1

Example:

Consider the following data:

Average demand = 100 units per day
Lead time = 4 days of supply from the vendor
Standard deviation of daily demand = 75 units
Desired service level = 95 per cent
S = ₹ 100 per order
i = 20% per year
C = ₹ 100 per unit.

Continuous review system is used to manage inventories. The warehouse is open five days a week, 50 weeks a year or 250 days a year.

Average annual demand = 250 (100) = 25,000 units per year.

The EOQ is

$$\text{EOQ} = \sqrt{\frac{2(100)(250)100}{100(.20)}} = 500 \text{ units.}$$

(Cont.)

(Cont.)

The average demand over the lead time is 100 cases a day for four days. Therefore m = 4 (100) = 400 cases. The standard deviation of demand over lead time is $\sqrt{4}$ (75) = 150 units.

Note: The standard deviation of demand over the five day lead time can be arrived at from the daily standard deviation assuming that the daily demands are independent. In the present case, the variance is additive. The variance for 4 days is 4 times the daily variance. This equates to $\sigma^2 = 4(75)^2$ or $\sigma = \sqrt{4}(75)$.

The 95 per cent level requires a safety factor of z = 1.65 (see the table). Thus, we have

$$R = m + z\sigma$$
$$= 400 + 1.65 (150)$$
$$= 648$$

The Q-system decision rule is to place an order for 500 units whenever the stock position drops 648 units. On an average 50 orders will be placed per year, and there will be an average 5 working days between orders. The actual time between orders will vary however, depending on demand.

P System

There are systems in which finished goods are not reviewed continuously, but periodically. A supplier may make deliveries periodically, say every fortnight. The delivery van comes once a fortnight, and order is placed if materials are needed. There is an assumption that the demand is random. The previous EOQ assumptions are valid, except those of constant demand and no stockouts.

At the time of review, the stock is brought by ordering to a target level which covers demand till the next periodic review, plus the delivery lead time. The ordered quantity varies with the target level set. P system, as this is called, is also known as the fixed-order-interval system or fixed-order-period system or just the periodic system.

In a formal way, periodic system reviews the stock position (on hand plus on order) at fixed periods P and orders an amount equal to target inventory T less the stock position at each review.

The following graph illustrates the P system.

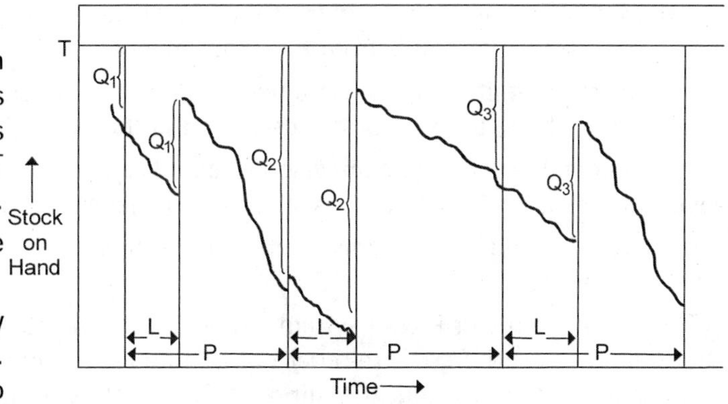

T
Q1 Q1 Q2 Q2 Q3 Q3
Stock on Hand
L P L P L P
Time

Fig. 25.9
Periodic Review System

The stock position drops erratically until the fixed review time is reached. At this point, a quantity is ordered to upgrade the stock to the target level. The order comes later, after a lead time L. The cycle of usage, reorder and stock receipt is repeated.

In the Q system, there is reorder point R. In P system, there is no R but target inventory T. There is no EOQ in P system since the ordered quantity changes according to demand.

In the P system, the order interval is fixed and not the order quantity. There are thus two parameters, P and T.

The relationship between optimal value of P and EOQ is as follows:

$$P = \frac{Q}{D}$$

Substitute this in the EOQ formula.

We then have

$$P = \frac{Q}{D} = \frac{1}{D}\sqrt{\frac{2DS}{iC}} = \sqrt{\frac{2DS}{iC}} \quad \dots (5)$$

The above equation 5 provides an approximate optimal review interval P. In case of highly irregular demand, this approximation is very poor.

The target inventory level is set by a specified service level. It is so set that it covers demand over lead time plus review period. Such coverage is necessary as the stock would not be ordered till the next period and it will take lead time to arrive. A service level is achieved by covering demand over time P + L at the average level plus a safety stock. We thus have

$$T = m' + s'$$

Where T = target inventory level

m′ = average demand over P + L

s′ = safety stock

The safety stock is so set that the desired service level is assured.

Safety stock is given by

$$s' = z\sigma'$$

Where s = the standard deviation over P + L

z = safety factor

In order to control the target inventory and consequent service level, we have to control z.

Choice between P and Q Systems

Both these systems are in vogue for independent demand inventory management. The choice between them depends on management practices and economics. P is however chosen when

- Orders are placed and delivered at specified intervals, *e.g.*, orders of beverages to a grocery or general stores.
- Multiple items are ordered from the same source and are to be delivered in one consignment *e.g.*, shades of paints from the same manufacturer.
- Inexpensive items not maintained on perpetual inventory system. *e.g.*, nuts and bolts to fill up the bins; the size of bin determining the target inventory.

In P system, there are no cumbersome records and there is scheduled replenishment. P system, however, carries a larger safety stock than the Q system.

Q system is used for expensive items where there is a need to hold down the investment in safety stock inventory.

These are hybrids of P & Q systems in practice. One such system uses min-max decision rules and periodic review. There is a re-order point (min) and a target (max). At the periodic review, there is no order if the stock exceeds the min and if it is below min, the order is placed so as to shoot up the stock position to the max level.

Special Purpose Models

In both the Q and P models we have discussed so far, the common characteristics are the constant cost of the units irrespective of the order size and the continuous reordering process.

We shall consider two new models. In the first model, the unit price changes with the order size. In the second model, there is cost-benefit analysis.

Price Break Models

Here the selling price varies with the size of the order. This is a discrete charge. The larger the order size, the lower the price. For instance cost per unit would be ₹ 5 for orders between 0-499 units, ₹ 4.5 for orders between 500-999 units and ₹ 3.90 for orders of 1000 and above. In such a situation, EOQs can be calculated for each price and at the point of price change. But all EOQs may not be feasible, *e.g.,* some EOQ may suggest a quantity where cost per unit would be higher.

The total cost of each feasible EOQ and the price break order quantity is tabulated and the Q with the minimum cost is chosen. If the holding cost is expressed as a percentage of a unit price, it is not necessary to compute EOQ at each price. The largest order quantity or the lowest unit price is solved first. If it gives a valid Q, it is the answer or else the next largest order quantity or second lowest price is derived. If this is feasible, the cost of this Q is compared to that of the price break Q above. The lowest cost decides the optimum Q.

Single Period Models

These problems pertain to short-lived items purchased frequently or placing orders to cover just one demand period. A news boy has to order papers every day — the question is how many he should. Here the classic economic approach of marginal analysis can be used. The optimal decision is one where the benefits derived from stocking an additional unit are less than the costs for that unit. Of course, benefits and costs are based upon the problem. e.g., marginal profits and marginal costs.

When stocked items are sold, the optimal decision is to stock that quantity where the profit from the sale or use of the last unit is equal to or greater than the losses of the last unit, if the last unit remains unsold.

Symbolically, it is MP ³ ML

where MP = Profit from the nth unit if it is sold.

ML = Loss from the nth unit if it is not sold.

We can introduce probability of occurrence in the marginal analysis without affecting its validity.

$P\,(MP) \geq (1 - P)\,ML$

where P = Probability of the unit being sold.

(1 – P) = Probability of the unit remaining unsold.

Solving of P, we get

$$P \geq \frac{ML}{MP + ML}$$

According to this equation, the inventory size can be increased till the probability of selling the last unit added is equal to or greater than the ratio ML/(MP + ML)

Miscellaneous System

Many of the assumptions in the inventory models are unrealistic. There are two challenging tasks in inventory management — maintaining adequate control over each item and record keeping. In practice, three simple systems are used — optional replenishment system, one-bin system and two-bin system. Two more techniques are used for better control — ABC analysis based on analysis of items in terms of their contribution to value and cycle counting for improving record accuracy.

Optional Replenishment System

Here inventory level is compulsorily reviewed at fixed frequency, say weekly and items are ordered to replenish the stock which night have dropped below some cutoff.

The maximum inventory level (M) is computed based on demand, ordering costs and shortage costs. Since ordering takes time and costs, a minimum order size (Q) can be established. Inventory position (I) is subtracted from the replenishment level (M) when the item is reviewed. This gives us *q*.

$q = M - I$

If q is equal to or greater than Q, order q, or else ignore it till the next revision.

If $q \geq Q$, order q.

Two Bin System

This is the earliest system of inventory control. The items are placed in two bins out of which one is emptied first before using the second one. The second bin contains such a quantity that ensures replenishment of the first bin. The replenishment arrives when the second bin Q is empty. When delivery arrives, both the bins are again filled in. Both the bins are located together. There can be just a dividing line between the two bins. Inventory here is so separated that part of it is held in reserve until the rest is used first.

When the quantity is finished in the first bin, a re-order is placed for a fixed quantity, generally based on EOQ. During the lead time, the second bin supplies the required item. The total level is equal to the mean expected demand during the lead time plus the safety stock.

Fig. 25.10 **Two Bin System with Automatic Review of Re-ordered Point with Usage**

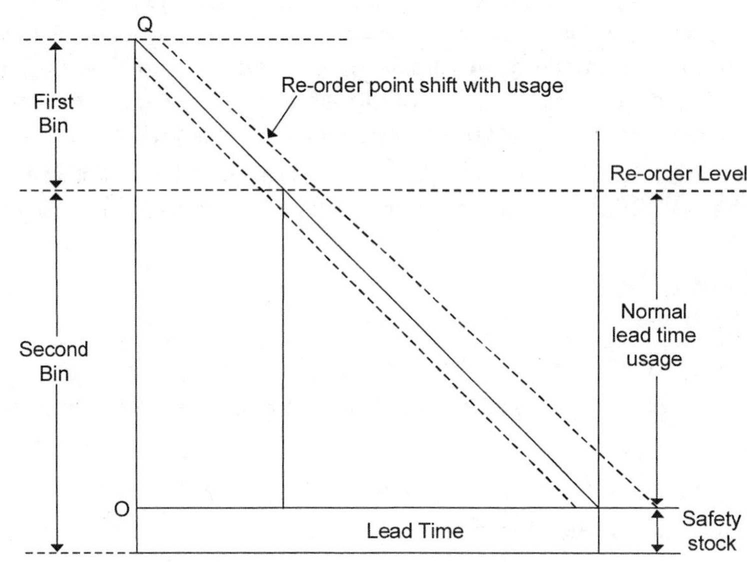

In the above diagram, we see how a re-order point is self regulated. The re-order point is reached earlier if the rate of consumption is higher than normal. The reorder point is reached later if the rate of consumption is less than normal.

In practice, the two bins or parts or lots may not be maintained. There should be some tangible dividing line. The two quantities can be separated on the bin card itself, and the re-order point is prominently marked on it.

The order quantity is fixed. It is, therefore, easy to know when to reorder. The operation of the system can be allotted to junior functionaries. The system is also called *minimax system.*

One-bin System

Here inventory is replenished periodically (say weekly) to its predecided maximum level. In the optional replenishment, the re-order is only when q ≥ Q. In the one-bin system, one bin is always replenished. It is a P model.

ABC ANALYSIS

It was in 1906 that Vilfredo Pareto observed in a study of distribution of wealth in Milan that 20 per cent of the people controlled 80 per cent of the wealth. This principle of 80:20 can be extended to many situations in life, say 20 per cent of customers contribute 80 per cent to sales or a few people in an NGO do most of the work. This principle is thus broadened to sort out the significant and the insignificant. It is also true for the inventory system — a few of the items account for the bulk of our investment.

ABC analysis underlines a very important principle 'VITAL FEW – TRIVIAL MANY'. In inventories, a few items account for most of our inventory values as measured by rupees usage (demand times cost). If these few vital items are controlled closely, we can control most of the inventory value. ABC analysis indicates that a large number of items account for a small rupee volume. ABC analysis puts the items into three categories — A items constitute the top 15 per cent of the items, B items the next 35 per cent and C items the last 50 per cent, thus B and C items though many in number contribute less to the value. ABC analysis segregates all items of inventory on the basis of rupee value or annual usage. Such categorization enables one to pay the right amount of attention, effort and expenditure as merited by each items. The segregation has been plotted in the following diagram.

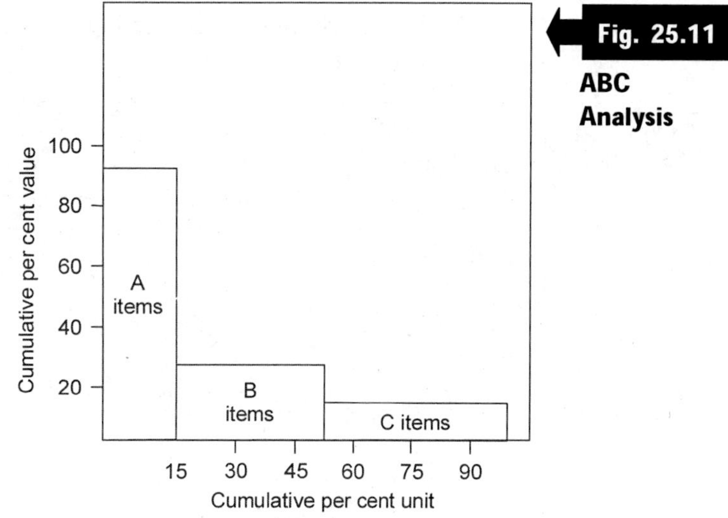

Fig. 25.11 **ABC Analysis**

The above analysis enables a manager to exercise appropriate control over each item. A items merit a tightly controlled inventory system with constant attention. B items require formal inventory system with periodic attention. C items use a simpler system designed to cause the least trouble to the purchase and stores department.

The following table illustrates the treatment of these categories:

A items	*B items*	*C items*
High consumption value	**Moderate value**	**Low consumption value**
1. Very strict control	Moderate control	Low control.
2. No safety stock	Low safety stock	High safety stock.
3. Frequent ordering	Once in 3 weeks	Bulk ordering once in 6 months.
4. Weekly control statement	Monthly control reports	Quarterly control reports.
5. As many sources as possible for each item	Two or more reliable sources	Two reliable sources for each time.
6. Rigorous value analysis	Moderate value analysis	Minimum value analysis.
7. Accurate forecast in materials planning	Estimate based on past data on present plans	Rough estimates for planning.
8. Minimization of waste obsolete and surplus	Quarterly control over surplus and obsolete items	Annual review over surplus and obsolete materials.
9. Maximum efforts to reduce lead time	Moderate efforts	Minimum clerical efforts.

Procedure for Making ABC Analysis

The entire procedure for making ABC analysis can be summarized in the following steps:

1. Calculate rupee annual issue for each item in inventory by multiplying the unit cost by the number of units used in a year.
2. Sort all items by rupee annual issues in descending order.
3. Prepare a table showing item No., Unit cost, annual units issued and annual rupee value of units issued.

4. Starting at the top of the list, compute a running total item-by-item issue value and the rupee value of consumption.
5. Compute the cumulative percentage for the item count and cumulative annual issue value.

The normal items in most organizations show the following pattern:

1. 5% to 10% of top number items account for 70% of total consumption value. These items are 'A' class.
2. 15% to 20% of the number of items account for 20% of total consumption value. They are 'B' class.
3. The remaining number of items account for the balance 15% of total consumption value. They are 'C' class items.

Table 25.2

◆ **Illustration:**

The following is the table which gives you the list of materials used by one industrial unit. Classify the items into A, B and C categories.

Symbol	***Item***	***Annual Consumption (Units)***	***Price (Per Unit) in Rupees***
A	Benzyl Penicillin	5,000	10
B	Dexamethasone	650	10
C	Mannitol	1,800	18
D	Chlorxylenol	4,200	1
E	Ampicillin	60	8
F	Gentamycin	6,500	6
G	Tetracycine	2,500	5
H	Triflyperazine	4,200	1
I	Imipramine	50	10
J	Diazepam	100	7
K	Streptopenicillin	100	35
L	Oxytetracycline	50	8
M	Phenobarbitone	2,000	0.25
N	Analgin	20	10
O	Prednisolone	30	6
P	A.P.C.	80	0.15
Q	Sulphone	200	0.50
R	Vitamin C	750	4
S	Aluminium Hydroxide	300	7
T	Aspirin	20	10

❖ **Solution:**

The first step is to construct a Ranking Table by assigning ranks in descending order to annual usage of the inventory items. (Starting which the highest annual usage value)

Table 25.3

Symbol	***Annual Consumption Unit***	***Price per unit (₹)***	***Annual Usage (₹)***	***Ranks***
A	5,000	10	50,000	1
B	650	10	6,500	5
C	1,800	18	32,400	3
D	4,200	1	4,200	6
E	60	8	480	14
F	6,500	6	39,000	2
G	2,500	5	12,500	4
H	4,200	1	4,200	7

(contd.)

(*contd.*)				
I	50	10	500	12
J	100	7	700	11
K	100	35	3,500	8
L	50	8	400	15
M	2,000	0.25	500	13
N	20	10	200	16
O	30	6	180	18
P	80	0.15	12	20
Q	200	0.50	100	19
R	750	4	3,000	9
S	300	7	2,100	10
T	20	10	200	17

Soon thereafter, cumulative annual usage and cumulative percentage are calculated in the 3rd and 4th columns. Items A, F, C account for 75.5 per cent of total annual consumption and are therefore A category items (15 per cent). Items G, B, D (another 15 per cent) contribute approximately 15 per cent to annual usage. The remaining 70 per cent items contribute roughly 10 per cent to annual usage, and are therefore, C category items.

Table 25.4

Items	***Annual Usages***	***Cumulative Annual Usages***	***Cumulative Usage Percentage***	***Category***
A	50,000	50,000	31.12	A
F	39,000	89,000	55.39	A
C	32,400	1,21,400	75.55	A
G	12,500	1,33,900	83.34	B
B	6,500	1,40,400	87.38	B
D	4,200	1,44,600	89.99	B
H	4,200	1,48,800	92.61	C
K	3,500	1,52,300	94.79	C
R	3,000	1,55,300	96.66	C
S	2,100	1,57,400	97.96	C
J	700	1,58,100	98.40	C
I	500	1,58,600	98.71	C
M	500	1,59,100	99.02	C
E	480	1,59,580	99.32	C
L	400	1,59,580	99.57	C
N	200	1,60,180	99.69	C
T	200	1,60,380	99.82	C
O	180	1,60,560	99.93	C
Q	100	1,60,660	99.99	C
P	12	1,60,672	100	C

◆ Explanatory Note on Cumulative Percentage

Total cumulative usage is equal to 100%

Annual cumulative consumption = 1,60,672

Annual cumulative consumption for A item = 50,000

1,60,672 : 50,000: :100

$$\frac{50,000 \times 100}{1,60,672} = 31.12$$

Annual cumulative consumption for B item 1,40,400

1,60,672 : 1,40,400 : : 100

$$\frac{100 \times 1,40,400}{1,60,672} = 87.38$$

Other Versions

There are other versions of ABC analysis which are discussed here briefly

VED Analysis

The possible consequences of material stock outs when demand arises from the basis of VED analysis. The cost of shortage depends upon the seriousness of the situation. Items are grouped as V (Vital), E (Essential) and D (Desirable).

Items	*Remarks*	*Strategy*
V	Very critical and therefore high opportunity cost of shortage. Must be available in stock whenever demanded.	Percentage of risk should be quite small. High level of service is called for.
E	Quite critical. Substantial opportunity cost of shortage. Should be available in stock by and large.	Can take a relatively higher risk of shortage.
D	No serious consequences of non-availability. Can be stocked.	Risk that can be taken is even higher.

A.T. Kearney's Classification

In an industry, the components can be put into three categories. The first category consists of vital but not critical components. The buyer can leverage large volumes for lower costs using strategies like centralized purchasing. The second category consists of critical components. Here, a few vendors supply these components. The bargaining power of the buyer, is therefore, weak,. Mostly negotiations are carried out for a long-term deal to obtain lower prices. The third category consists of commoditised inputs. Here there is little to choose by way of price or equality. It is, therefore, necessary to reduce the transaction costs. It is necessary to identify which raw materials are vital, critical and commoditised. We can design the strategies to deal with them accordingly,

FSN Analysis

All items are not required with the same frequency — some are required regularly, some occasionally and some once in a while. FSN Analysis places the items in three categories : Fast Moving (F), slow Moving (S) and Non-Moving (N). Inventory policies and models for these three groups are different.

Theoretical modes have validity for F items with regular consumption. Spares are slow moving (S), and requires special management. Disposal policies are designed to control dead-stock.

SDE Analysis

This classification runs like this.

S = Scarce items

D = Difficult (to procure) items

E = Easy (not difficult to get) items

HML Analysis

This analysis is based on the cost of the item.

H = High Cost Items

M = Medium Cost Items

L = Low Cost Items

Inventory Accuracy and Cycle Counting

There can be a discrepancy between the actual inventory and the inventory records. Though the physical count and records must tally within some specified range, there are several reasons for their not tallying.

- Access to inventory to both authorized and unauthorized persons.
- Misplaced inventory.
- Removals in a hurry are left unrecorded.
- Records are lost.
- Location not recorded properly.
- Storage at several locations.
- Replacement of inventory on account of cancellation of customer's order.

Several Steps are taken for Record Accuracy

- Store-room is locked.
- Record accuracy becomes a criteria for performance appraisal.
- Record-keeping mechanism for in-store and production floor inventory.
- Educating personnel about the significance of record-keeping.
- Only authorized transactions are allowed.
- Count inventory frequently and see their agreement with the records. One of the methods used is cycle counting

Cycle counting is an inventory counting method. Here inventory is counted frequently rather than once a year or twice a year. It is necessary to decide which items deserve counting, when they will be counted and by whom they will be counted. In a computerized environment, the computer generates a counting alert when

- Inventories are low and counting is easier.
- A back order is written.
- Post-activity counting where activity is specified.
- Using ABC analysis.

A period of counting is carefully chosen, say weekends when there is less activity in the stores. Counting cycle depends on the manpower availability. Counting can be outsourced. Full time cycle counters can be set up devoted to this task only. Some firms aim at 100 per cent accuracy, whereas some allow a variation between 1-3 per cent. Of course, for A items the variation between physical count and records must not exceed $\pm$ 0.2 per cent It can be $\pm$ 1 per cent for B items and upto $\pm$ 5 per cent for c items. Safety stock may be provided to factor in the variation.

Inventory Control in Services

We shall examine how inventory control works in service organizations such as a big retail outlet having many inventory items called stock-keeping-units (SKUs). SKUs of each item run into a large number, say socks are available in two fabric varieties — cotton and synthetic, three sizes (extra large, medium, small) and four colours. Thus, there are 24 ($2 \times 3 \times 4$) different items. SKUs run into thousands in a big departmental store.

Manually EOQ cannot be computed for each item. How then is the inventory managed? The department is divided into major product lines — say shirts and trousers. Items are classified according to prices. The items are sourced from the distributor who handles the products of many manufacturers. This way orders and despatch time are minimised. The distributor's salespeople visit the store and take the count of inventory available.

The distributor's salespeople take the order as per the replenishment level decided by the buyer. This saves time. The typical lead time is 2-3 days. The safety stock is therefore low. The lead time demand plus expected demand are covered by the replenishment level.

There is no formal method of assessing the stockout and establishing safety stock. It is because the items are far too many. The department's items are counted in terms of value. The replenishment level is set as rupee allocation.

Each department plans monthly values for inventory. Inventory balance, monthly sales, items on order are tabulated. That gives us **open-to-buy** figure — the unspent figure of the budget. This is the amount available to the buyer for the following months. When seasonal increases are expected in demand, there is a large open-to-buy position. The replenishment levels are raised creating a higher stock of goods on hand.

Practically, open-to-buy is utilized at the commencement of the month. Some funds are reserved by the buyer for special purposes and to restock fast moving items.

COMPUTER-BASED INVENTORY SYSTEMS

The inventory is of three types — raw materials, work-in-progress (WIP) and finished goods. The inventory should be sufficient for manufacturing and sales — it is called Working Stocks, and is often referred to as Lot Size Inventory. There are fluctuations due to demand pattern and lead time. Safety stock takes care of these. It is also called reserve or buffer or stabilization stock. If a large demand is anticipated or short supply is apprehended, the inventories are increased. It is called Anticipation Stock. Transportation or pipeline stock means a product's movement during the manufacturing process or shipment to the customer.

There are stock outs, because of which demand is lost. Inventory lead time can be considered in four periods — review, order, manufacturing or purchasing and receiving.

There are three types of inventory costs — Ordering or Set-up cost, Inventory Carrying Cost and Stock-out cost.

Ordering or set-up cost includes the following bought-in items — cost of actual purchase requisition by inventory control, cost of issuing a purchase order, any follow-up time by the purchasing department and cost of order processing by the receiving department.

Set-up costs for the manufactured items include cost of generating the manufacturing requisition by inventory control, cost of planning, scheduling, loading and expediting the item by production control, machine set-up time, any one-time cost e.g. start up, scrap etc.

Inventory carrying cost includes all expenses required to maintain a volume of inventory. It is expressed as a proportion of the value of the inventory per unit of time. Stock-out cost includes all expenses from running out of stock. If there is expediting, stock out cost would represent back order cost plus loss of profits due to lost sales. Back order costs include paper work, loss of return on capital, loss of customer goodwill. It is difficult to monetise the stock out costs. Stock outs are controlled by adopting service levels.

Purpose of Computerised Inventory Control System

Inventory control's primary objective is to monitor the stock levels by recording the stock movements. Inventory acts as buffer to take care of the variations in supply and demand. In inventory control we try to achieve the avoidance of excessive stocks and shortages and optimisation of ordering and carrying costs.

Inventory control parameters are re-order level, economic ordering quantity, safety stock, maximum stock and average stock.

Computerised inventory control enables the reduction of WIP inventory, elimination of duplicate holdings and order status information. It makes inventory function efficient.

The following table describes the applications of computerised inventory control systems in order of ascending complexities. Coding of inventory is a pre-requisite for computerised inventory system. There should be bill of materials and purchasing records also before computerised inventory system can be implemented.

Computerised Inventory Applications

Least Complex			***Most Complex***
Stock reports (Weekly) Stock reports (daily)	Use reports	Forecasts of Requirements	Continuous updating of inventory
Catalogue of items	Reports of requirements	EOQ	Status reporting of items automatically
ABC Analysis	Time series reports		Initiation of POs automatically
Net returns analysis	Procurement requirements Physical inventory accounting and cycle count		

Inventory System Design

Let us take the inventory system of a mass retailing outlet. Inventory system requires data files. One file called master file records the quantity of each item available in stock. Besides, there could be record of the location of each item in the warehouse, the cost of the item, the recorder point, present order status and the vendors through whom the item is sourced.

The system is user-friendly and helps us in locating the item quickly. It also points out the items required to be ordered and generate orders automatically. It performs similar other inventory control tasks.

Transaction files record each individual transaction. One such file monitors sales transactions. Another file records the incoming inventory. The relationship between the transaction files and master file could be seen in the diagram below.

Master file summarises all activities in the two transaction files.

Key Fields

Key fields relate the various files to one another. A key field is unique for every item in the master file and it exists there as well as the transaction files with identical name, type and width.

Master file

Part No. _____
Name of the Item ____
Stock Cost ____
Amount on Order ____
Warehouse location ____
Vendor details ____
Order date ____

Sales/Issues

Part No. ____
Quantity issued/sold ____
Selling price ____
Date ____
Customer ____

New Stock Transaction File

Part No. ____
Quantity received ____
Purchase price ____
Date ____
Vendor details ____

Fig. 25.12 **Key Fields Relations**

The key field is expressed in terms of an identifying code, which is part number in our inventory example. Each inventory items carries a unique part number. In the absence of the key fields, it is very difficult to manage the data.

In this system, suitable for SMEs, every new inventory item is assigned a unique part number, and added to the master file.

The user receives reports about the inventory stock, items requiring re-orders, and items on order. The system also generates POs automatically. It also keeps the user updated about the sales transactions and receipt of inward stock. The receipts and issues update the master file.

While designing the system, each file will be designed first. Then the input menu or screens are designed.

The system should allow the different users to perform the various functions. The stores manager is responsible for the stores and master inventory. The sales clerks enter the individual sales transactions at the point-of-sale. The warehouse clerk records the inward stock. There are three separate but inter-related systems whose overall structure would look like as shown in the diagram.

Fig. 25.13

Menu Sub-systems

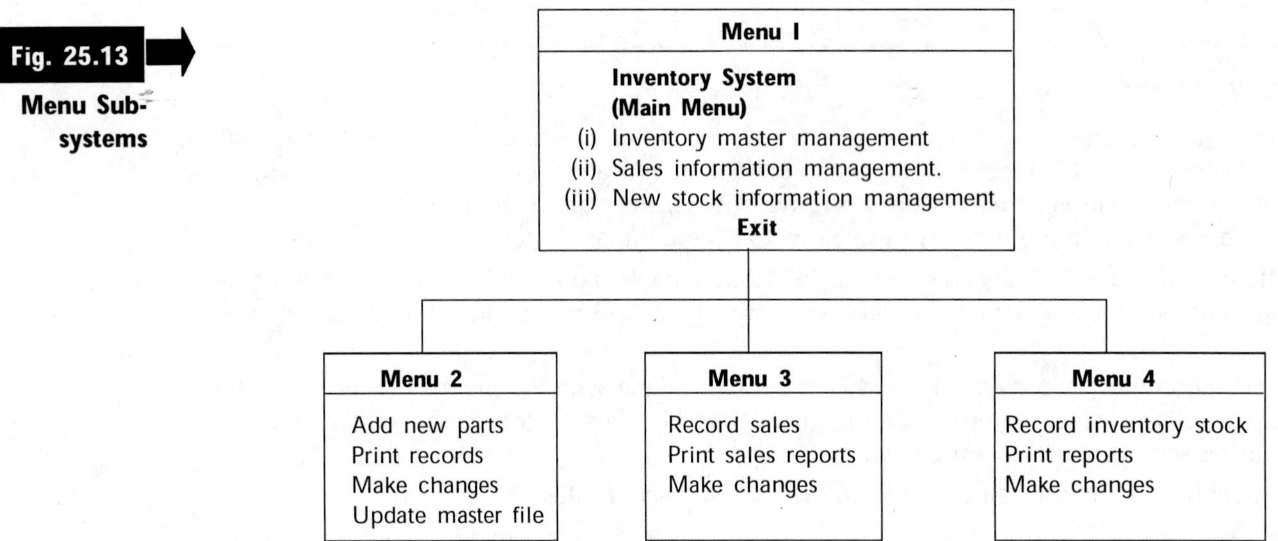

The above system has four menus. There is one main menu and several sub-programmes of secondary menus. The main menu provides access to inventory, sales or stock master files. The secondary menus have options to add new parts, report printing and record revision. Suitable programmes can be developed to perform these desired functions.

Some software packages available for inventory control are OMAC (ICL), PCS (Burroughs), MAPICS (IBM). There are several packages available for PCs from Indian software companies.

Appendix - I

LEAN DOES NOT MEAN ZERO INVENTORY

Daniel T. Jones and James P. Womack wrote a book on Toyota '*The Machine that Changed the World*' in 1990. It first introduced *lean* to the world. Lean is practised more in auto industry as Toyota spread in every other country. In the U.S., the aerospace industry has practised it successfully. Supermarkets are also practising it. In Canada and Denmark, post offices practise it. Lean is not restricted to factories. It can be extended to services and retailing.

Though lean does not mean zero inventory, there are organizations who make purchases on the basis of the sales the day before, *e.g.,* a brewery in South Africa which makes beer. Everyday one can buy what one needs. Here demand is highly predictable. In a supermarket, there are inventories at various levels, as they cannot predict demand. But it is not possible to have an inventory-less business.

Fig. 25.14 **Lean Evangelists: Jim Womack (left) and Dan Jones**

Lean has grown fast over the last five years, since it helps an organization to become a global manufacturer. Indian companies like SRF, Sundaram Brake Linings, and Sona Koyo Steering are also practising Lean.

Appendix - II

UNIFORM LOT DELIVERY

Inventory can be delivered in instalments, rather than in one single lot. A producer may build up inventory at a constant production rate, or a retailer may receive consignment in several lots. The following diagram illustrates this.

Fig. 25.15

Uniform Lot Delivery

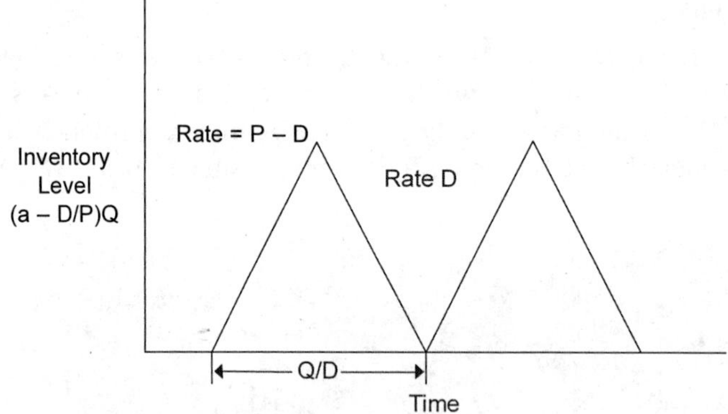

There is both production and consumption. There is slow build up of inventory. The inventory is then depleted as only consumption occurs. Imagine units being produced at the rate of P units per year and consumed at the rate of D units per year, where P > D. Then the average inventory level would be,

$$\frac{Q}{2}\left(1-\frac{D}{P}\right)$$

Minimizing the resulting expression for TC, the EOQ would be,

$$Q = \sqrt{\frac{2SD}{iC(1-D/P)}}$$

There the EOQ would be somewhat greater than the ordinary EOQ, since (1 – D/P) is less than 1. As P approaches D, EOQ becomes greater, which in other words, indicates a continuous production. When P is very large, the above EOQ formula is closer to the ordinary EOQ. While deriving ordinary EOQ, we assumed one lot delivery of inventory which is tantamount to an infinite production rate P.

Appendix - III

JUST-IN-SEQUENCE (JIS) OR JIT (JUST-IN-TIME) SYSTEM OF INVENTORY

Just in sequence or time is an 'inventory' and 'right first time' strategy adopted by manufacturers to align their delivery of component parts in a way that they arrive at the production shop floor moments before the sequencing phase. This reduces the stock pile up of component parts in the production area for every possible variant, and aims at eliminating likely errors using, 'Poka-Yoke' or error proofing systems. JIS can be implemented once there is sufficient JIT. It is a coordination between internal inventory handling and external supply chain.

It is also called zero-inventory operation. It is actually a philosophy which can be installed after eliminating all unwanted operations and waste. It is a continuous process. It seeks to eliminate raw material stock and finished stock. It has to adhere to other norms of manufacturing excellence like right time delivery every time, perfect quality and right implementation of plan. It presupposes complete cooperation between management and workers.

JIT cannot be maintained if quality components are not continuously made available. Rejections of substandard components or faulty production operation leads to disrupted production. It consequently leads to non-delivery of finished product.

In India, it is difficult to get specified materials at the right time and at the right place. There is a factor of ancillarisation where ancillary industry feeds the parent industry. In absence of proper tooling and equipment, ancillaries face rejections at their level or at the buyer's level. The internal and external suppliers are the key to success in JIT system. Quality and timely supply schedule are necessary for it. JIT has been successfully employed in Taiwan, Korea and Japan. On installing JIT, they have reduced inventory level of only 2 days in place of 8-12 weeks inventory levels. Overseas supplies in a country like India also impede the installation of JIT. JIT reduces inventory carrying costs. There is scope to implement JIT in integrated companies where there is no reliance on external sources.

JIT in our situation, therefore, can be installed if suppliers carry stocks for us, which make them participators in our JIT programme. Perhaps, this is easier said than done in our situation. Even a slight trend towards JIT will be a big step forward.

Companies often mistake JIT for inventory elimination, missing delivery schedules and increasing machine idle time.

Just-in-Time Philosophy

The basic concept is not to make anything till it is needed. It further extends to producing anything needed to the highest level of quality. JIT is not restricted however to manufacturing, but can be extended to distribution, sales, marketing and finance. It is applicable to both manufacturing and service industries. In JIT, we have to meet customer's requirements of quality, cost and delivery time. The factors which affect these requirements are wasteful, and so must be eliminated. For instance, factors like interest, unnecessary equipment and holding large inventories tend to increase costs, and so must be eliminated. JIT teaches us an effective method of manufacturing. A working definition of just-in-time is that it is a *structural* approach in a manufacturing organization focussed on improving *timeliness, quality, productivity* and *flexibility* utilising various methods of *work simplification* and *waste reduction*. We shall be able to appreciate JIT better if we compare it with traditional methods of manufacturing.

Just-in-Time at Maruti Suzuki

Storage is an obsolete term at Maruti Suzuki plant at Gurgaon. The company has 230 plus vendors. Their transport vehicles e.g. trucks and tempos line up outside the shed. They bring in the exact quantity of components required for the day's production. These are hauled inside in bins, which go back to the vendors. This is the supply just-in-time, eliminating the storage completely. The plant is directly responding to daily shifts in demand.

Factor	***Traditional Method***	***JIT***
Quality	Quality has cost.	Quality is free Do things right first time. It leads to good quality and also lowers cost. TQC and total employee involvement. *Kanban*.
Workers-Managers-Engineers Relationship	Managers-engineers are experts. Workers execute their orders.	Workers are experts. Managers-engineers are facilitators.
Errors	Errors are to be eliminated by inspection.	Stepping stones to success. One must learn from them. They are not to be repeated. Closer to the concept of zero defects.
Inventories	Always in-stock to keep production process continuous.	Inventories hide our inefficiencies. Low inventories (does not necessarily mean zero-inventory). Practise JIT selectively for big-budget items and not for all items.
Lot Size	Mass production Large-lot production	Small lot sizes, preferably one. It means do a little bit of everything everyday. Study set-up times and reduce them. Modify some equipments.
Queue	Queues at work production stations lead to better machine utilisation.	Against queue formation. Small lot sizes and low inventories result in small or no queues.
Automation	Substitutes labour	Preferred for consistency in quality.
Cost Reduction	*Tools:* High machine utilisation High rate of production Labour reduction	*Tools:* Accelerated flow of product due to reduction in lead times.
Lead times	Increase in delivery lead time	Decreases delivery lead time.
Flexibility	There is flexibility at the cost of excess capacity, general purpose equipment, accumulation of inventories, and overheads	Flexibility by reducing all lead times.
Line and staff functions	Separated	Line workers perform the minimum staff functions like maintenance and job-rotation.
Labour	Retrenchment when demand falls	Relocation to other areas, e.g., sub-contracting.
Breakdowns	Accepted as routine	Preventive maintenance.
Procurement	From multiple vendors	Development of one vendor. Participation in vendor development process.
Purchasing	—	Purchase in small lots. Supplier evaluation is stringent. Makes inspection on arrival redundant. Over-specifications are avoided. Delivery-time insisted upon. Minimum paper work. Packaging in small standard containers with required quantity. Simple purchase agreement.
Implementation	Depends on attitude towards work	Depends on attitude towards work.

Samsung, Noida

At Noida plant of Samsung, there was no perfect supply chain prior to 2003-04. If it were to make 5000 TV sets a day, and an assortment to be made, it would decide on the process 24 hours in advance and inform the vendors accordingly. Today, the company has a three-day fixed plan in place. It is globally accepted, and none has the authority to change the three-day sequence. This keeps the people on their toes, and enable the plant to carry on with the minimum required inventory on the production line.

Waste Definition

JIT is achieved through work simplification and waste reduction. Waste is anything other than minimum amount of equipment, material, parts and working time absolutely essential to production. Absolute minimum resources mean for example:

- One supplier.
- No people, equipment or space dedicated to work.
- No safety stock.
- No excess lead times.
- No people doing jobs that do not add value.

CASELET: KANBAN SYSTEM OF INVENTORY MANAGEMENT IN JAPAN

In this system, there is 'just-in-time' inventory arrival — the inventory arrives just a couple of hours before it is needed for production process. It is in other words zero-inventory system, eliminating carrying costs altogether and making the industry highly competitive. This system was developed by Taiichi Ohno, a vice-president of the Toyota Motor Co. However, the system which operates successfully in Japanese environment may not prove effective in other environments. This system failed miserably in General Motors, USA. The factors like the spread of vendors over vast geographical expanse, the failure of vendors to adhere to strict delivery deadlines, the transport bottlenecks affected the system's successful implementation. In a country like India, which is a shortage economy in terms of raw material availability, power and other infrastructural inputs, this Japanese system may not find any application.

What do you think about the implementation of *Kanban* in India?

KANBAN

A Japanese word that means 'Display Cards.' This term is used for any means of communicating a demand for material either within the process or from the process to the supply point.

KANBAN

SIGNAL FOR REPLENISHMENT

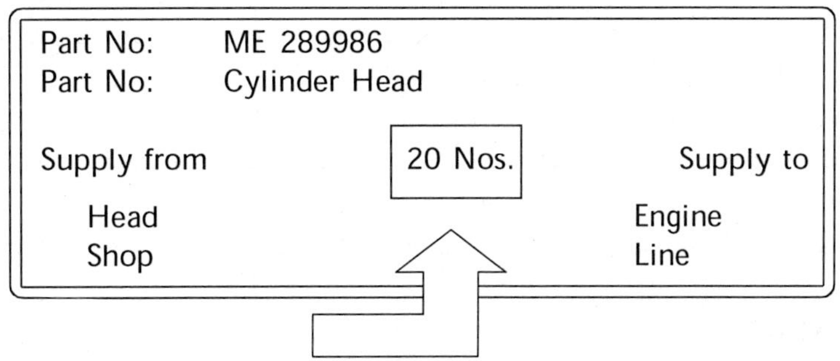

KANBAN SIZE — STANDARD SUPPLY QUANTITY

Rules for Kanban

- Do not send defectives to the subsequent process.
- The subsequent process comes to withdraw.
- Produce only the quantity withdrawn.
- Equalise production.
- Kanban is a means to fine tuning, stabilization and rationalization of the process.

Reference: KANBAN; *Management Begins at the Work Place,* Japanese Management Association.

Just in Time in TVS-Lucas

Lucas-TVS embarked upon JIT in 1985. Their operations are based at Padi. It had a fat workforce of 3105 in those days. It turned out components worth only ₹ 61 crores. The rejection rate was 10 per cent. JIT was pioneered by Toyota Motor Company in the late 50s. After introducing JIT, TVS-Lucas has made surprising gains. Sales per employee shot up to 13.80 lakhs from 1.96 lakhs then. The workforce is downsized to 2230. Rejection rate is down to 1 per cent from the previous 10 per cent. Scrap has almost been eliminated at 0.8 per cent. Sales have quintupled to ₹ 308.6 crores.

Lucas-TVS has become the first company outside Japan and Korea to bag the prestigious Japanese award, JIT Grand Prix, from JIT Management Laboratory Co.

When JIT was introduced, the company had to create an awareness about it amongst the employees. This was step 1. In step 2, they focused on housekeeping by using the 5 Ss: Seiri, Seiton, Seison, Seiketsu and Shitsuke.

Seiri focuses on sorting out parts and supplies on the shopfloor. The objective is to keep only those parts and supplies which are needed on the factory floor. Seiton is about assigning a permanent place for everything on the shop-floor. Seison or shine urges operators to keep the machines and workplace spick and span.

The workplace must look neat and tidy. After these 3 Ss, the attention moves to manufacturing. Seiketsu emphasises standardisation — a set way of doing everything. At the end, Shitsuke ensures that there are continuous improvements in all other four Ss.

In step 3, the flow between processes was created. In mass production factories, we have a layout according to shops, each devoted to cutting line, grinding line, welding line and so on. This is OK till the demand is predictable and a limited variety of products are turned out. But as environment changed, mass production gave way to mass customisation. Smaller lots of greater variety of components are required not just everyday, but several times a day. The process layout is not suitable for this. Each shop here completes its part of the job, and stocks up components. These components have to crisscross the shopfloor. Obviously, there would be in-process waiting time. Sometimes, the required parts are not available. As a result, precious capital was tied up to inventory. There was high wastage. The customer satisfaction was affected.

The shop floor was reconfigured into product-centric layout — according to products manufactured. They created cells for starter motors, alternators, distributors and wiper motors. They implemented a card-based material requisition system called *Kanban* where each process would *pull in* only the requisite amount of parts. For instance, the wiper motor cell would receive parts like the motor and casing only when it sent the *kanban* card to the internal supplier.

There is no inventory between processes. When there is no order, parts are manufactured. It saves several crores every year in inventory cost. There is less rejection and scrap, since first time quality is emphasised.

It is a leaner and more efficient system. The company is better prepared to absorb sudden changes in demand.

There are four benefits — it enables a mass manufacturer to produce a wide variety of products at low volumes. It increases first time quality by creating systems that capture defect at every stage of manufacture. Equipment effectiveness goes up. Low set up time allows manufacturing to react faster to market changes.

The company wants to upgrade the cells by housing machines closely, and wants to integrate its 400-odd suppliers into JIT.

The Change Chronicle

Lucas-TVS' step-by-step journey to JIT

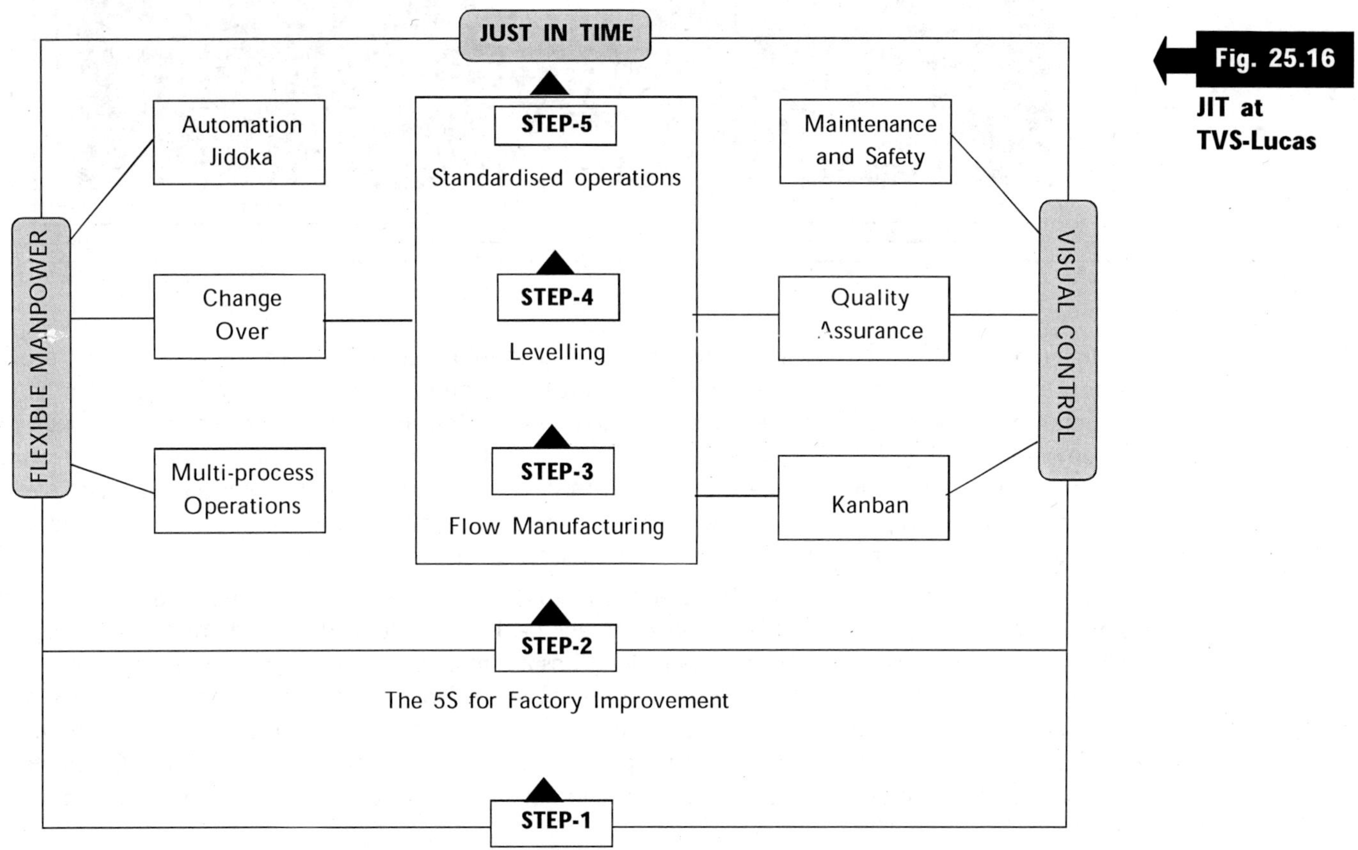

Fig. 25.16 JIT at TVS-Lucas

The Hero group uses JIT along with other Japanese techniques like Kaizen and Kanban. Hero plant in Ludhiana practises JIT. Some resist JIT on the grounds of infrastructure and transport bottlenecks. They could start with Near-in-Time, and then work their way closer to JIT. Some cite vendor weaknesses. However, a company should seriously work towards vendor development and incentivisation.

26

INVENTORY MANAGEMENT: DEPENDENT DEMAND INVENTORY: MATERIALS REQUIREMENT PLANNING (MRP)

In a manufacturing organisation, inventory management is very complex in view of the numerous products, processes, parts and uncertainties. Priorities keep on changing. The demand is erratic. Still, managers do not give up. They use a computerized planning and control system called materials requirement planning (MRP). Even service, organisations such as restaurants, hospitals, power-generating companies can also benefit from the use of MRP. MRP is most valuable in fabrication industries. MRP is moderately useful in process industries. In MRP, Master schedule for end products is converted into a detailed schedule for raw materials and components used in the end product.

In the previous chapter we have studied the distinction between the independent and dependent demands. Independent demand pertains to the demand decided by the market conditions for the finished products and spare parts. Inventories in such situations are managed by the Q and P systems discussed previously. Dependent demand inventories are dependent on demand for higher level parts and components upto and including master production schedule. To illustrate, raw materials and work-in-process are used in manufacturing organisation to support the manufacturing process itself. In a restaurant the ingredients used in recipes depend upon the menu offered. These inventories are managed by MRP or just-in-time (JIT).

Simple MRP Model

Materials requirements planning is basically concerned with the scheduling of activities and the management inventories. It is very useful. The final product uses components, items and sub-assemblies. These are the lower level provisions for the final output. These lower level provisions are considered to be *dependent* on the customer's final requirement.

Against the forecast, the demand at lower level can be obtained. The MRP is used precisely for this purpose. It takes the forecast demand as the input. It breaks down this demand into component parts, compares the requirement against existing inventories, and seeks to schedule the parts against available capacity.

Let us take a product A made up by three parts of B and two parts of C. Diagrammatically it looks like

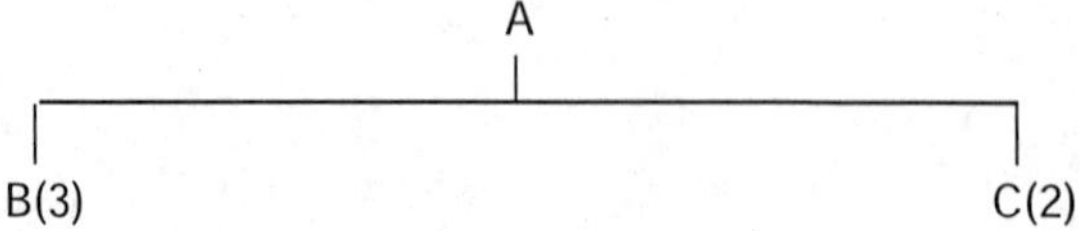

Further, let us suppose B itself is made of one part of D and two parts of E. Similarly part C is made of 3 parts of D and 3 parts of F. The product structure then looks like:

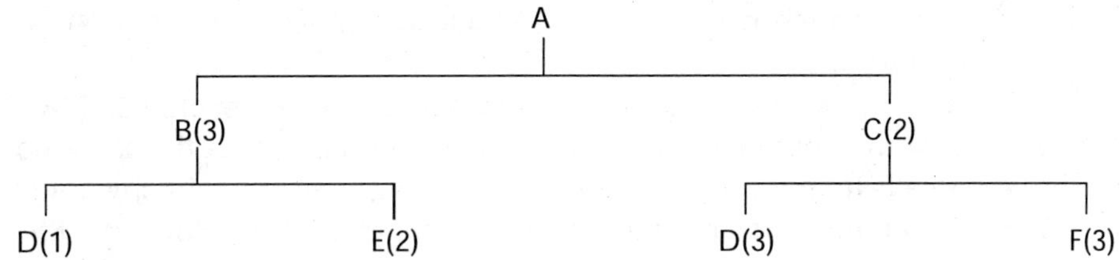

Let us suppose we require 100 units of A. We therefore need:

Part B	3 × Number of As	3 × 100 = 300
Part C	2 × Number of As	2 × 100 = 200
Part D	1 × Number of Bs + 3 × Number of Cs +	1 × 300 3 × 200 } = 900
Part E	2 × Number of Bs	2 × 300 = 600
Part F	3 × Number of Cs	3 × 200 = 600

Let us consider the procurement time for these items (either making it or buying it from outside). Suppose these parts are produced as under:

Product/Part	***Time to Produce (in weeks)***
A	1
B	2
C	2
D	3
E	1
F	1

We can then produce a time schedule chart showing when all materials must be ordered and received to meet demand for A. The following is the MRP for 100 units of A.

Fig. 26.1

MRP for 100 Units of Product A in Period 7 weeks

		Week							
		1	***2***	***3***	***4***	***5***	***6***	***7***	
A	Required date							100	A = lead time
	Order placement						100		= 1 week
B	Required date						300		B = lead time
	Order placement				300				= 2 weeks
C	Required date						200		C = lead time
	Order placement				200				= 2 weeks
D	Required date				900				D = lead time
	Order placement	900							= 3 weeks
E	Required date				600				E = Lead time
	Order placement			600					= 1 week
F	Required date				600				F = lead time
	Order placement			600					= 1 week

The MRP chart shows which items are required and when. We know how A is made and the time required to produce each part.

This example makes it obvious how cumbersome it would be to develop an MRP for thousands of items. It is practically ruled out. We require a great deal of data about the stock position and the product structure. This calls for the use of a computer. The emphasis, therefore, would be on the files required for a computer programme and the architecture of the system. However, the MRP remains the same as in our simple example.

In India, MRP has become popular after the computerization process started in full swing post 60s. It is a precise schedule of priorities of production and a re-scheduling mechanism for revising plans, as changes occur keeping inventory at a low level and still meeting the demands as they arise.

MRP is a computer-based time-phased production planning and inventory control system.

Basic Elements

MRP consists of four basic elements:

1. The master production schedule which drives the MRP.
2. The bill of materials (BOM) or product structure file.
3. The inventory status file which carries the necessary data.
4. The MRP software package that contains the necessary logic.

We shall examine all these four elements or files one by one.

Master Production Schedule

It is based on known or forecast demand for a specified future period. The schedule shows the quantity of each end item and time they are wanted. It is essentially a delivery schedule for each product expressed in terms of the quantity and timing.

It deals with the end items or output of the production function. All further demand for work-in-process and raw materials are dependent on the master schedule. Past demand does not always get extension in future and this is kept in mind while planning for raw materials and work-in-process.

Master schedule allows management to control customer service, inventory level and manufacturing costs. Master scheduling is delegated to a cross functional team.

Aggregate plan indicates general operational range. Master schedule specifies exactly what is to be produced. These decisions have interface with other functional areas of business. First trial master production schedules are run through an MRP programme. The planned order releases generate the detailed production schedules. They are checked to ensure the availability of resources and reasonableness of completion time. Master schedules feasibility is thus checked. Sometimes, it can be resource hungry after product explosion. It then requires modification. MRP programme is then run again.

The parts explosion process assumes that master schedule is feasible with respect to capacity. Master schedule is an input for parts explosion to produce shop orders and purchase orders. The shop orders are put into a capacity planning routine and checked by materials planner to determine the availability of sufficient capacity. If it is not available, either capacity or master schedule is not feasible.

Master schedule should not be inflated and should reflect realistic capacity constraints. Inflationary schedules expect more output under pressure, which makes due dates invalid, thus breaking down the system.

The following diagram illustrates the aggregate plan and the master production schedule for bedsteads.

Month	1	2
Bedstead Production	800	850

	1	2	3	4	5	6	7	8
Type I	200			350		150	100	
Type II		100	75		125		100	
Type III			75			175	200	

Fig. 26.2
The Aggregate Plan and Master Production Schedule for Bedsteads

In the upper portion of the diagram the aggregate production plan of bedsteads by weeks has been given. The lower portion shows a master production schedule classifying the bedsteads and the quantity planned by week This will be followed by an MRP programme. Master production schedule is the starting point for the disaggregating process. It states how many and when each of the bedsteads are required.

Time-fencing MPS

MPS should have an element of flexibility. Many factors decide this — production lead time, commitment of parts and components to a specific item, buyer-seller relationship, excess capacity available and the tendency to make or not to make changes.

Time-fencing ensures a reasonably controlled flow through the production system. Time fences are shown in the following diagram.

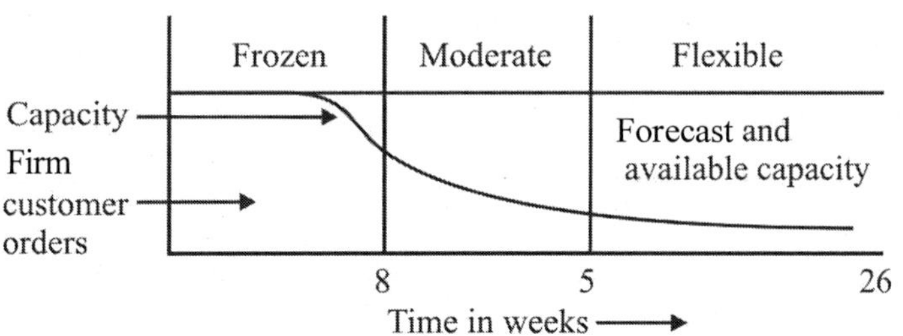

Fig. 26.3
MPS Time Fencing

There are opportunities to introduce changes. MPS in the above diagram is frozen till 8 weeks, with no changes or minor changes. A moderate period allows changes in specific products if parts are available. A flexible period allows any variation in products, provided that the capacity is maintained constant, and no long lead times are involved.

Master schedule developed on weekly output requirements is based on what are called **weekly time buckets**. When master schedule is updated weekly, a parts explosion programme is run to generate new requirements. It is called **regenerative MRP System.**

Bill of Materials (BOM)

A particular finished product is made up of materials, parts and components. They are arranged sequentially. The BOM is a structured list of all this. It contains the complete product description. The BOM file is an important input to the MRP programme, the other inputs being MPS and inventory records file.

What a recipe is to a cooking dish, the BOM is to the product. It is also called product structure file or product tree. The BOM should be error-free, otherwise proper materials would not be ordered, and the product would not be assembled correctly, and would not be dispatched. Consequently, the available parts will wait in inventory and the missing parts will be expedited. It is very expensive to have a flawed BOM. Some companies have different BOMs used by departments such as engineering, manufacturing and costing. The BOM fed to the computer must be fault-free, and must represent the structure of the product faithfully. In organizations where the BOM is used just for referencing and not as material planning tool, it becomes difficult to have a single BOM.

BOMs are constantly revised in the light of product redesign and this is facilitated by having **engineering-change-order** (ECO) system.

The following diagram illustrates a BOM for product S.

Fig. 26.4

BOM for product S

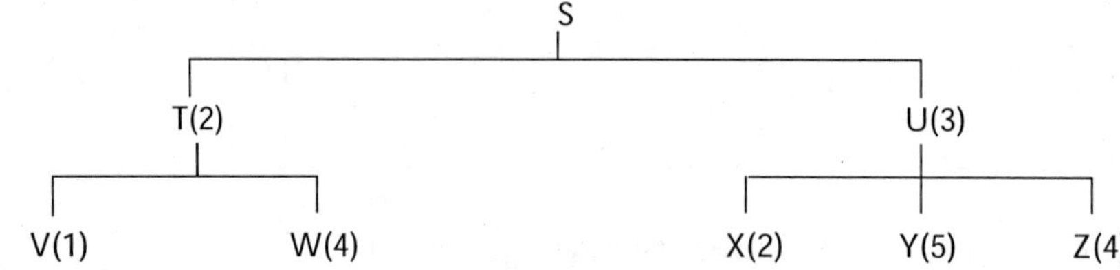

Consider product S which is made of two units of part T and three units of part C. Part T in its turn is made of one unit of part V and four units of part W. Part U is made of two units of part X, five units of part Y and four units of part Z.

Previously BOM files have been tested as an indented file. Indentation signifies components of the item. This is not suitable for computerization. The amount of each item needed at lower levels is computed by expanding (exploding) each item and summing it. A more efficient system is to store parts of data in a single level explosion.

Fig. 26.5

Parts List in Indented Form in a Single-level List

Indented Parts List			***Single Level Parts List***	
S			S	
	T (2)			T (2)
		V (1)		U (3)
		W (4)	T	
	U (3)			
		X (2)		
		Y (5)		
		Z (4)	U	
				X (2)
				Y (5)
				Z (4)

Fig. 26.6

Product D Hierarchy (a) Expanded to the Lowest Level of Each Item in (b)

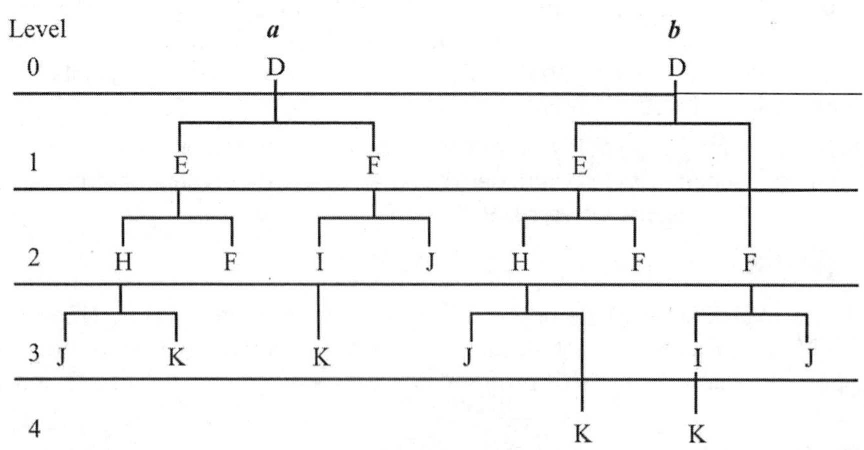

In single level explosion, each item and component is listed showing its parent and the number of units needed per unit of its parent. It obviates duplication. Fig. 26.6 shows both the indented parts list and the single-level parts list for product S.

Low Level Coding: If the identical parts appear on the some level for each end product, material requirements can be arrived at easily. Consider a product D shown in Fig. 26.7(a).

Consider for instance item F in Fig. 26.7(a) which is an input to both D and E. Item F therefore needs to be lowered down to level 2 (see Fig. 26.7(b)) to bring all Fs to the same level. If all identical items are at the same level, computer scanning across each level becomes easier and summarization is also easier.

Inventory Status or Records

Each item of inventory forms a separate file in computerized inventory. It can carry a very wide range of information about an item. Some of the details attached to an inventory item are given in the following diagram.

Fig. 26.7 **Inventory Status Record**

<table>
<tr><td rowspan="3">Item master data segment</td><td colspan="11">Part No. Description Lead time Std. Cost Safety Stock</td></tr>
<tr><td colspan="11">Order Qty. Setup Cycle Previous Usage Class</td></tr>
<tr><td colspan="11">Scrap Allowance Pointers Other details</td></tr>
<tr><td rowspan="6">Inventory status segment</td><td rowspan="2">Allocated</td><td rowspan="2">Control Balance</td><td colspan="8">Period</td><td rowspan="2">Total</td></tr>
<tr><td>1</td><td>2</td><td>3</td><td>4</td><td>5</td><td>6</td><td>7</td><td>8</td></tr>
<tr><td>Gross requirements</td><td></td><td></td><td></td><td></td><td></td><td></td><td></td><td></td><td></td><td></td></tr>
<tr><td>Scheduled receipts</td><td></td><td></td><td></td><td></td><td></td><td></td><td></td><td></td><td></td><td></td></tr>
<tr><td>On hand</td><td></td><td></td><td></td><td></td><td></td><td></td><td></td><td></td><td></td><td></td></tr>
<tr><td>Planned order releases</td><td></td><td></td><td></td><td></td><td></td><td></td><td></td><td></td><td></td><td></td></tr>
<tr><td rowspan="4">Subsidiary segment</td><td>Order details</td><td colspan="10"></td></tr>
<tr><td>Pending action</td><td colspan="10"></td></tr>
<tr><td>Counters</td><td colspan="10"></td></tr>
<tr><td>Tracking</td><td colspan="10"></td></tr>
</table>

Source: Joseph Orlicky, *Materials Requirement Planning,* New York: McGraw Hill, 1975.

The MRP programme accesses whenever needed the status segment as per the specific time period or time buckets.

The MRP programme travels downwards from product structure, and explodes requirements at each level. Sometimes, identification of the parent item which caused material requirement is called for. The MRP programme creates a **peg record** file; which allows us to trace the material requirement upwards in the product structure through each level, identifying each parent item that caused the demand.

MRP Computer Programme

This programme works on the inventory file, the master production schedule and the BOM file. MPS provides a list of end items in specified time period. BOM describes the materials and parts needed to make each item. The stock position is shown by the inventory file. The MRP programme accesses the segments of the inventory file, and at the same time refers to the BOM to compute the quantities of each terms required. This figure is corrected by taking into consideration the on-hand amount. The net requirement to offset or set back in time is to factor in the lead time for acquisition of the material.

The present BOM and inventory files of the company may require modification to suit the MRP system.

The MRP programme may ignore the capacity constraints, in which case, the capacity is balanced by the master scheduler manually. The output is examined in terms of feasibility. The MPS is adjusted to correct imbalances. The programme is run again. This process is reiterated till the output is acceptable.

There can be multiple master schedulers for each major product line, and they compete for resources. As a whole, they have to optimise resource utilisation and due dates for the system.

Output Reports

MRP accesses the BOM, MPS and inventory file, and generates a wide variety of reports. These are classified as primary and secondary reports.

Primary Reports: These are the usual reports for production and inventory control such as **planned orders** to be released, **order release notices** to execute the planned orders, **changes in due dates** to accommodate **rescheduling, cancellations** or **suspensions** on MPS and inventory **status data.**

Secondary Reports: These could be **planning reports** for inventory forecasting, **performance reports** to point out inactive items, and to determine lead times — actual and programmed, and quantity usage and cost — actual and programmed and **exception** reports to point our discrepancies.

As MRP has expanded into MRP II, there are several additional reports.

Net Change System

It is a form of MRP where changes can be made as they occur on a real time basis. Here constant updation of the system is called for. It is preferred to a regenerative MRP system. Net change systems however are 'nervous' sometimes because of constant order changes. Suppose a customer cancels an order for week two, consequently leading to cancellation of all purchase orders (POs) and shop orders. Suppose another customer enters the scene and places an exactly similar order for week two. There is immediate addition of POs and shop orders into the schedule. This is what is known as the nervous system.

Net change systems can be modified to respond to unplanned or exceptional occurrences.

Structure of the MRP System

The typical MRP system is shown in the Diagram 26.8.

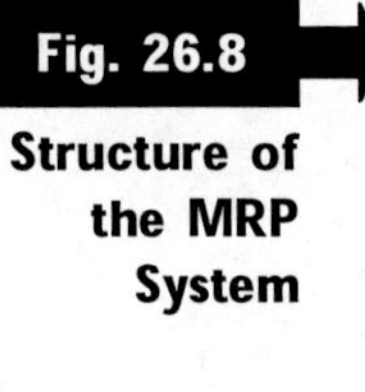

Structure of the MRP System

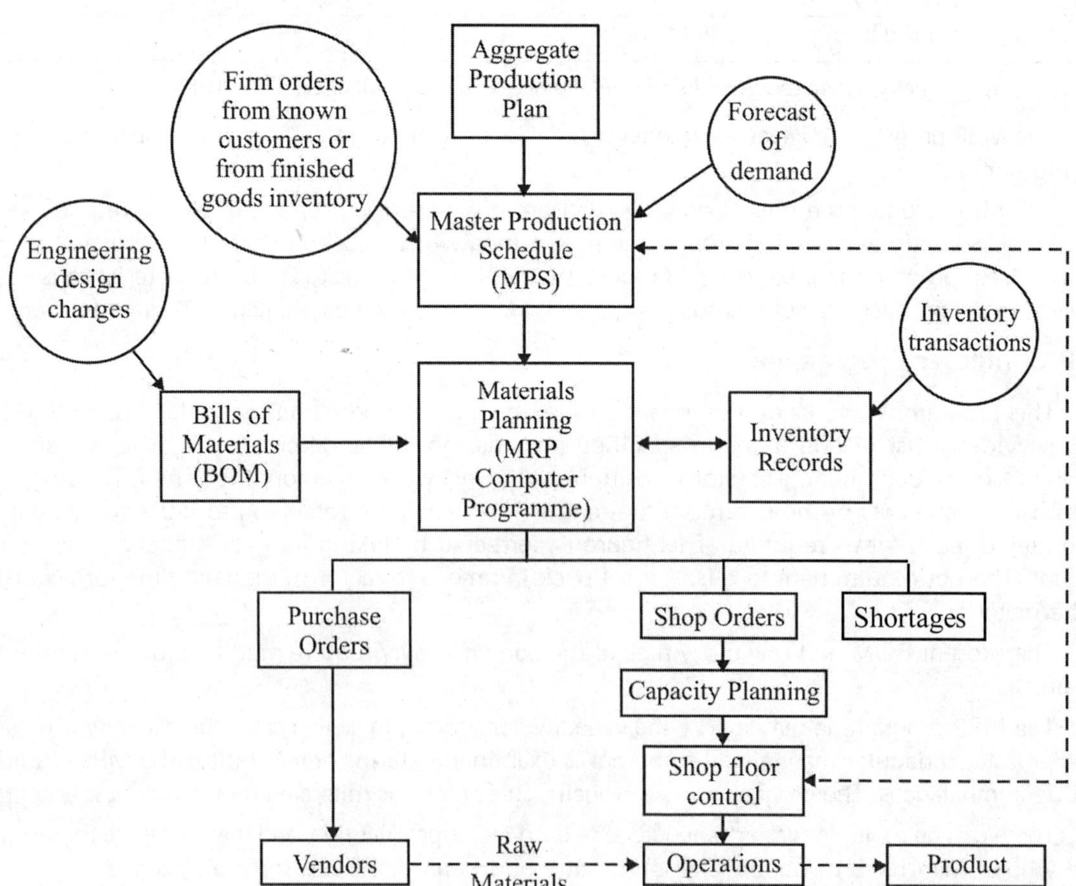

Master production schedule (MPS) is at the top of the diagram. It is determined by the customer orders, aggregate production planning and forecasts of demand. The MRP programme is at the heart of the system. It is driven by three inputs — MPS, BOM and inventory records. There are two types of output — purchase orders going to the vendors and shop orders going to the factory. Before the execution of the shop orders, it is checked whether sufficient capacity is available. If so, the shop order is placed under the control of the shop floor control system. If the capacity is not available, a change must be made in the capacity or the MPS through the feed-back loop shown. The orders under shop floor are monitored to make sure they are completed on time. Shop Floor Control (SFC) consists of three software modules — order release, order schedule and order progress. Order release is basically documentation such as route sheet, material requisitions, job cards and parts list. Order schedule assigns the orders to various machines. It consists of machine loading and job sequencing. In sequencing, the priorities are given by first-in-first-out rule, earliest delivery rule, shortest processing time rule and least slack jobs rule. Order progress monitors shop order status, and maintains information on work-in-progress and production output data for capacity control.

Diagram 26.8 repreents an MRP system to control inventories and capacity.

Though computerized inventory system were in use for years, **they were independent of the scheduling system.** MRP links them together. It creates specific schedules to identify the specific parts and materials required to produce the end items, the quantities needed and the dates when orders for these materials should be released or be received or completed within the production cycle.

Purposes of MRP

Joseph Orlicky in his seminal work on MRP (1975) has defined three principal functions of MRP as follows:

Inventory

- Order the right part.
- Order in the right quantity.
- Order at the right time.

Priorities

- Order with the right due date.
- Keep the due date valid.

Capacity

- A complete load.
- An accurate load.
- An adequate time to view future load.

If the MRP system given in Fig. 26.8 is used appropriately, all the three functions described by Orlicky can be achieved.

Philosophy of MRP

Materials should be expedited when their lack would delay the overall production schedule. Materials should be de-expedited or delayed when the schedule falls behind and postpones their need. Behind schedule orders are traditionally got back on schedule. When an order's completion date is delayed, there is not appropriate rescheduling. As a result, later orders are expedited, but easier orders are not rescheduled for later.

Advantages of MRP

- Competitive pricing
- Reduced sales prices

- Reduced inventory
- Reduced setup costs
- Reduced sale time
- Better customer service
- Better response to market demands
- Guides when to expedite and de-expedite
- Delays or cancels orders
- Changes order quantities
- Changes order due dates
- Helps capacity planning.

Disadvantages of MRP

MRP may not get top management support. It is considered just a manufacturing system, rather than a business plan. Top management should recognise MRP as a strategic planning tool. MRP has been sold as a standalone system, rather than a part of the total system. MRP should be integrated to JIT. MRP requires accuracy to function correctly. MRP is criticised for being too rigid in scheduling, deviation from which is quite difficult.

Three Different Types of MRP

MRP can be used in a variety of ways. It leads to three different types of MRP systems.

Type I: An inventory control system: It releases manufacturing and purchase orders for the right quantities at the right time to support the master schedule. Work-in-process and raw material inventories are controlled through proper timing of order placement. This system does not control capacity planning and shop-floor modules.

Type II: A production and inventory control system: It is used to plan and control inventories and capacities. Here orders are checked to see if there is, sufficient capacity available. If it is not available, either the capacity or MPS is modified. It has a feedback loop between the orders launched and MPS. It is also called a closed-loop system.

Type III: An enterprise resource planning system (ERP): It is a companywide system to plan and control all resources — inventory, capacity, cash, personnel, facilities and capital. MRP is integrated to other sub-systems — accounting, sales and marketing, HR, finance through common database. As the same information is used for working, co-ordination is possible amongst all resources — not just materials and capacity. ERP is discussed separately.

MRP *vs.* Order-point Systems

Order-point systems are not suited to manage dependent demand inventories. Before the advent of MRP, there was no alternative but to use order-point systems. The distinction between order-point systems and MRP is summarised in the following table.

Table 26.1

Comparison of MRP and Order Point Systems

Point of distinction	*MRP*	*Order Point*
Demand	Dependent	Independent
Ordering Philosophy	Requirements	Replenishments
Control	All items to be controlled	Follow ABC analysis
Forecast	Master Production Schedule-based	Past experience
Lot size	Discrete	EOQ
Demand	Predictable	Random
Inventories controlled	WIP and raw materials	Finished products and spare parts.

The basic difference is that MRP is based on requirements dictated by production schedule, whereas order point systems believe in replenishment as and when the inventories get depleted. In manufacturing, this is relevant since the demand for components is lumpy. Suppose a lot is scheduled. Components are needed then for that lot, but demand is then zero, until another lot is scheduled. Had we used the order point systems for such lumpy demand pattern, there would have material on hand even during long periods of zero demand. Order point systems extrapolate the past into the future, to have a forecast used to replenish stocks. In MRP system, the requirement in the MPS are used to order materials. It is future-oriented. MRP is not based on ABC classification. An item is not complete till even a small trivial part is available. It is necessary to control all the parts in MRP, even C parts. In view of the lumpy demand, lot sizing is discrete in MRP systems. Order-point systems are outward-oriented because the objective is to provide a high customer service level at low inventory operating costs. MRP on the other hand is manufacturing-oriented or inward-oriented, as it is based on the requirement of the MPS.

27 STORES MANAGEMENT

Introduction

The aim of any business activity is to increase the value of the original resources which are risked by the owners in the venture. The aim of the manufacturing operation, which is an important facet of the business activity, is the timely manufacturing of the desired products of specified quality, in proper quantities at least possible cost resulting in the increase in the value of the resources. The efficiency of the manufacturing operations largely depends on the efficient functioning of the receiving and stores operations. Receiving and storing are the service functions and involve much of the paper work. The benefits out of an efficient receiving and storing are bound to outpace the cost of administering them. Moreover, there is an ample scope for simplifying and standardizing the paper work involved in these functions. Receiving and storing are the key considerations in the materials management because (*i*) the quality of the end product largely depends on the quality of materials received, (*ii*) the smooth and uninterrupted production flow is dependent on the efficient stores function, (*iii*) the stores organization acts as custodian of stock items and (*iv*) above all these functions directly as well as indirectly affect the production cost. The direct production cost is reduced by strategic location of stores ensuring quick issue and elimination of production stoppages caused by waiting for materials. It indirectly reduces the production costs in terms of reduced investments in materials, storage space and insurance, elimination of pilferage and theft, obsolation, reduced handling cost, etc.

Stores Functions

The important function of the stores are as follows:

- **(a) Receipt** : It receives and accounts inventories.
- **(b) Storage** : It stores and preserves the inventories protecting them from damage, pilferage and deterioration.
- **(c) Retrieval** : It helps easy accessibility to materials and ensures optimum space utilisation. Materials can be located and retrieved with ease.
- **(d) Issue** : It satisfies the demands of consuming departments by proper issue of inventories on receiving the requisitions.
- **(e) Records** : It keeps proper records of the issue and receipts.
- **(f) Housekeeping** : The space is kept neat and clean so that material handling, preservation, storage, issue and receipts is done satisfactorily.
- **(g) Surplus Stock** : Scrap and surplus disposal management is a function of stores.
- **(h) Verification** : Physical verification and purchase initiation to avoid stockouts.

(i) Coordination & Cooperation : To interface with production inspection and inspection department.

Receiving of materials: Receiving is an important control point in the material control system. It is sometimes considered that receiving is a routine clerical work where the materials shipped by the supplier are received, unpacked, checked and compared with the packing slip. In fact receiving is something more than this. **Lee and Dobler** in their **"Purchasing and Materials Management",** stated that, "any problem or error in specific purchase transaction should come to light during the receiving operation." If the problem (shortage in quantity, damaged material, wrong item shipped etc.) is not detected and corrected during the receiving operation, the cost to correct the mistake later is much higher. Many hours are frequently spent in determining what really happened and rectifying the situation. Hours are required to correct the error that could have been corrected at the receiving station in minutes.

Receiving procedure: The receiving involves much of the paper work and it varies from firm to firm. However, the key issues involved in the receiving function are commonly described in the following standard procedure:

The receiving division unloads the goods at the delivery bay and verifies the condition of the consignment to satisfy that it is not received in a damaged condition. The receiving clerk opens the consignment and verifies the contents with the packing slip and the purchase order. The details are recorded in the separate report which is popularly known as **"the goods received note or GR note."** The goods received note is an important document because it is the only document with the firm which signifies the details of the materials it has received. This document is used as the basis for invoice payment, for continued purchase negotiation and for closing the order. Generally, the receiving clerk counts or weighs the physical volume and the apparent condition of the goods. If there is discrepancy between the physical volume and packing slip or purchase order particulars, it is recorded on the goods received note. The condition of the consignment is also recorded. The copy of the goods received note is sent to the purchase department and other needy departments. The next step in the receiving process is the inspection of the materials.

Goods Received (GR) Note		S. No. .______________	
Dt.	Consignor		Consignor's advice
Transport Mode			Order No.:
Material Code	Description	Qty. Recd.	Invoice No. & Value
The above stores have been received. Damage/ shortage report no. ...... applies subject to acceptance and taken into stock. Signature ______________ (Storekeeper) Dt. ____________		The above stores are in accordance with the terms and conditions of the order as regards quality. Signature ______________ (Inspector) Dt. ____________	

The inspector compares the quality of the incoming materials with their specifications with the help of gauges, visual tests, chemical, electrical or mechanical tests, laboratory tests and such other tests. He reports his findings on the receiving report. The inspection report may be a separate form or it can be a part of the goods received note. The inspection report is sent to the purchase department and such other departments.

If the materials are rejected, the purchase department immediately informs the supplier and seeks his instructions about the mode of their disposal. The supplier may ask for the return of materials for reworking or he may scrap them. If the returning of the rejected materials involves high transport cost, the supplier may prefer to have the buyer either rework or scrap them at buyer's plant at supplier's cost. The supplier is not given any credit for the rejected materials or it is adjusted to the terms agreeable to the parties. Rejection should be considered in the light of the accounting adjustments only. In fact, it poses a distinct problem of non-availability of materials. Prompt action should be taken to replenish the rejected items with a view to eliminating any chances of production stoppages caused by stock-outs.

When the materials are accepted, they are sent to the stores section for their proper recording and storing. All relevant departments are informed about the receipt of the materials.

The damage/shortage report is given separately to the transporter and the consignor. The following proforma can be used.

Damage/shortage Report

S. No. ____________
Dt. ____________

To
The Consignor
____
____

To
The Transporter
____
____

Ref. Order No.__________

Dt. ____________

With reference to the above quoted order and your advice no. __________ dt. ________, we would like to inform you that the following discrepancies have been observed against the goods (short/damaged/correct) (tick any one of these).

Material Code No.	Description	Qty. Advised	Discrepancy

Signature ______________
(Storekeeper)
Date: ____________

The stores can send a material inspection report as to quality and standard to the suppliers:

Material Inspection Report

S. No. ________________
Order No. ______________
Dt. ________________

To:
The Supplier
____
____

The supplies received against our above quoted PO have been inspected, and the materials have been found in the following conditions.

S. No.	Code No.	Description	Quality		Details of Defect
			Received	Rejected	

Instruction:

1. Arrange replacement within ______ days.
2. Quality and standards not satisfactory. (tick any one)

Signature ______________
(Inspector)
Dt. ________________

Store-keeping: *Need for storing*: In stores room, the inventories — like raw materials, work-in-progress, finished goods, bought-out components, consumable stores, spares and scraps— cost heavily to the organization. Moreover, the inventories, which are stored in the stores room, represent the idle investments of the capital resources. So sometimes, it is argued that can one do away the storing function? The answer is in the negative. The store-keeping has proved its indispensability in the modern business world due to following reasons:

Type of inventory	Reasons for holding the inventory
(1) *Raw materials*	(*i*) Hand-to-mouth buying is not feasible due to the quantum and frequency of use and the distantly located source of supply. (*ii*) Pre-operation seasoning. (*iii*) To reap the price advantage available on seasonal raw materials. (*iv*) To safeguard against the stockouts caused by prolonged lead time or high rate of consumption. (*v*) Large order placing avails certain economies like cost of order placing. (*vi*) The imported raw materials or materials received under quota system are generally purchased through a single order and are stocked till their use.
(2) *Work-in-progress*	(*i*) To balance the production flow. (*ii*) To eliminate the ideal capacity of machines. (*iii*) To even out the imbalance in the demand and supply position.
(3) *Consumable stores*	(*i*) The daily consumption is too insignificant to have daily purchases.
(4) *Spares*	(*i*) The rate of consumption is very low and so they are purchased in bulk and are stored for future requirements.
(5) *Ready-made components*	(*i*) When the components are bought rather than made, it is essential to buy them in advance of their requirements so that the production flow may not be interrupted due to lack of components.
(6) *Scraps*	(*i*) They are disposed of in bulk.

As noted above, the store-keeping is a service department, so the principal objective of the stores function is to provide that service most economically. The fundamental considerations of providing this service economically is to maintain the value of the stores in the stock at the lowest possible level and to make the required inventory available at all times. These two aspects are mutually exclusive in nature. If more inventories are stocked, they will be available at all times. However, such action will fail to keep the value of the stocked items at the lowest possible level. Conversely, if less inventories are stocked, such action will keep the value of the stocked items at low level, but it may equally create the chances of stockouts. The disadvantages of high level of inventories and lower level of inventories are as under:

High level of inventories	Low level of inventories, it will result in stockout resulting into,
(*i*) Locking up of working capital	(*i*) Production stoppages.
(*ii*) High insurance charges	(*ii*) Idle production capacity.
(*iii*) More storage space	(*iii*) Idle labour time.
(*iv*) Deterioration in the quality of materials	(*iv*) Liability of fixed overheads.
(*v*) Chances of theft and pilferage	(*v*) Failure to meet delivery order etc.
(*vi*) Evaporation of alcoholic materials.	

As maintenance of high-level or low-level inventories is mutually exclusive, the efficiency of the stores function lies in the skill that strikes the balance between the two.

Identification system of materials: When innumerable items are stocked in stores room, it is essential to codify them for their quick identification.

Codification is a technique of assigning brief names to the items stocked in the stores room, decided on some scientific basis, *e.g.,* when "BS 24, 25" is used to describe "the round brass rod of .25 inch, in diameter", one can understand the importance of codification in describing the items. The materials codification is advantageous as under:

(*i*) It describes the item briefly, thus saving the time in writing and describing.

(*ii*) It facilitates the quick identification of the item in the store-room, *e.g.,* when we write BS, we talk of brass. The first digit "2" represents metal, second digit "4" speaks about round bars etc. When materials codification is accompanied by location codes, it facilitates exact location of the materials inside the storeroom.

(*iii*) It facilitates the matching of minds between the production department, stores department and various divisions of the same organization.

Generally, alphabets, numbers or combination of alphabets and numbers are used as the codes. In numerical codes, the 3 to 4 elements of numbers, the binary code with 1 and 0 element or the decimal codes are used. In the alphabetic codes twenty-six alphabets are used as elements. The alphabets are used as pure alphabetic symbol or as mnemonic code which serves as an aid to memory, *e.g.,* BS for Brass Screw. It is also possible to use both letters and numbers as 2 for general class (rod) and 4 for specific class (round) code elements, *e.g.,* BS 24.75 which describes the brass metal round rod with .25 inch diameter. It is also possible to use the colour scheme for the quick identification of materials. Generally, colour codes are used to distinguish the various grades of metals like steel, brass, copper, bronze. The objective of the codification is quick identification and short description. However, the brevity should not be at the cost of clarity. This is achieved through the construction of the codes on some scientific basis. Generally, code construction is made on any of the following methods:

(*i*) *Mnemonic method:* Under the mnemonic method, the alphabets are used as an aid to memory, *e.g.,* BS for brass screw. They can be applied effectively only when the stock items are few in number. Its application becomes difficult as the number of items increases.

(*ii*) *Random method:* Under this method, the numerical and/or alphabetic codes are assigned on random basis. It is flexible, as it is possible to add the new number or letter in sequence in case of addition of new item. However, the codes are constructed arbitrarily rather than on any scientific basis.

(*iii*) *Scientific method:* Under this method, the codification is done by dividing the total stock items into a number of groups or classes and then to assign a symbol to each class. The class is then divided and sub-divided again until the individual item is identified, *e.g.,* first digit for metal (say 1). Second digit for type of metal (say 3 for aluminium). Third digit for the shape (say 2 round rods). The additional digit with decimal point may describe the size of the metallic item.

Thus coding will be done as under:

11 — Steel
12 — Brass
13 — Aluminium.

and 132.75 for aluminium round rods of .75 inch diameter. Generally, block system is used to describe the main class and the subclass, *e.g.,* 11 to 20 for metals, 21 to 30 for liquid items and so on.

Location and Layout of the Stores

The storeroom is commonly described as a "place for everything and everything at its place." The first part of the phrase refers to the provisions of adequate space for the materials while the latter part highlights on the scientific location and layout of the storeroom. The point of receiving the material and the point of use are not always the same. In between them, the materials are housed in the storeroom. The storeroom provides the space for materials. The storage space may be in the form of constructed buildings or godowns, temporary structures or even in the form of vast open yards. The size and the type of the storage space is dependent on varied factors such as number of items to be stored, quantity, characteristics of the materials to be stored such as liquid, fragile, weight, dimension, cost, chances of evaporation etc. While deciding the storage space, due consideration should also be given to the space required for the movement of material handling equipment inside the store area. The ways inside the storeroom are divided between the main tracks and side streets. The main track must provide for two-way movement and the side streets for one way.

Every cubic inch of the storeroom costs the organization. For the economic use of the stores area, vertical stacking within the limits of the height of the ceiling, weight of the materials, capacity of the container etc., is done. For the economic use of the space and efficient handling of the materials, various types of stores equipment are used.

Lee and Dobler have mentioned that the following eight types of equipment are commonly used in storing materials:

1. Pallets and skids.
2. Open and closed shelving.
3. Cabinets (with or without counters).
4. Bins.
5. Stacking boxes.
6. Special storage racks.
7. Gravity feed racks.
8. Outdoor platforms and racks.

The location of the stores is also an important consideration which has a direct bearing on the product cost. The basic principles of stores location are — straight line movement with minimum of backtracking, minimisation of handling, rehandling and internal transportation costs, minimisation of waste motion for personnel and reduced human hazards, efficient utilization of storage space and provision for the flexibility and expansion of the store area.

The materials are stored at one central godown or in the godown located at distant places. Where the materials are stored is distantly located godowns, receiving materials from various suppliers and issuing materials to remotely located production centres. The optimum stores location is decided on the basis of clearly defined objective function with the help of quantitative techniques or through the computer programming.

The stores location will differ according to the divisibility of the total storage space, type of business activity say multi-product operations, manufacturing operations carried on at multi-plants located at distant places, type of production processes such as continuous processing, job-order production, assembling etc. Fundamentally, the *raw materials* should be stored in the vicinity of the starting point of the production operation, *work-in-progress* between first and following operation, *finished inventories* near the shipping area, *spares, tools and stores* somewhere in the central storage area.

Stores Organization

The stores manager assisted by storekeeper manages the stores. He either reports to the materials manager or to production controller/manager.

The problem of centralized storing versus decentralized one should be decided on the basis of their undermentioned relative merits and demerits which are mutually exclusive in nature.

Merits of Centralized Storing

1. Bulk buying in few orders with the advantage of quantity discount and transportation cost.
2. Possibility of standardization of materials reducing the variety of items stored.
3. Reduced investments in inventories.

4. Reduction in administrative cost.
5. Reduction in the requirements of the personnel.
6. Reduced storage space and other incidental expenses.
7. Greater safeguard against pilferage and theft.

Demerits of Centralized Storing

1. Increase in the material handling cost.
2. Possibility of bottlenecks and the resultant delays.
3. Possibility of communication gap between the user of the item and its supplier.
4. In absence of proper designing of the routine work, the administrative cost may go up.
5. Greater danger of loss by fire.

Principles of Efficient Layout of the Stores

The following aspects should be considered while administering the layout of the stores:

(*i*) The floor area should be adequate and should suit to the specific characteristics of the materials stored, *e.g.*, liquid, inflammable, fragile etc.

(*ii*) The floor load must be adequate.

(*iii*) The gangways should be wide enough to take any stores trolleys and must allow articles to be withdrawn from bins and racks.

(*iv*) Weighty items should be stored as low as possible.

(*v*) The items which are used most frequently should be located near the issuing windows.

(*vi*) Obstructions such as poles, partitions, staircases etc. should be reduced or eliminated.

(*vii*) The stores racking should not prevent the normal movement of air and temperature distribution.

(*viii*) Water-proofing must be assured in the stores area. In the production area, a leaking roof is immediately observed while in the stores area, it may be so obscured due to stored materials and that considerable damage might be done before it is discovered.

(*ix*) In the vertical stacking, the load should be distributed evenly and should be broken by intervening shelves. It should not touch the ceiling height otherwise it will prove a hindrance in case of fire fighting.

(*x*) The stores area should be equipped with the handling equipment such as cranes, lifts, hoists etc. and the computing and weighing scales.

(*xi*) It must provide safety to the personnel and security to the items stored.

(*xii*) A location system should be devised so that it may pinpoint the position of any item stored inside the storeroom.

Approaches to Stores Location

The problem of the materials inside the storeroom is tackled with the help of the following three approaches:

(1) Fixed location; (2) Random location; and (3) Zoned location.

(1) Fixed location: Under this approach, a specific fixed place is assigned to each item of the material. The allocation of the space is made on any of the following basis:

(*i*) On the basis of supplier.

(*ii*) On the basis of similarity of the item.

(*iii*) On the basis of the joint issue of the items.

(*iv*) On the basis of the size and frequency of the use.

The last basis is more efficient and economical. Under this approach, the fast moving items are stored nearest the point of issue, and the slow moves in the remote areas.

(2) Random location: Under this approach, the materials are stored at any vacant place available in the storeroom. This approach is workable where the stores function is operated by one or two persons and the storing is required for only few items. The location is memorized by the store-keeper. This is the most unscientific method with its many drawbacks.

(3) Zoned location: This approach divides the total storage space into different zones. Popularly there can be three zones — (*i*) for bulk stock, (*ii*) for reserve stock and (*iii*) indirect materials like spares and consumable stores.

Zones can be devised on certain other basis also like, liquid materials, metal bars, inflammable materials, costly materials, dangerous materials etc. Zone approach attempts to avail the maximum benefits out of the available space and other storing facilities.

Location coding: As the materials' codification helps in identifying and describing various items of the materials, similarly the location coding also helps in locating the specific material item in the stores area. Location coding is desirable especially where the large number of items are stocked in big godowns located at different places. The same principles of code classification are followed while constructing the location code. The location is identified in terms of number of warehouse (if more godowns are maintained) row, column, racks, shelf, bin etc.

Storing of Materials

It is commonly observed that a storeroom is "a place for everything and everything at its place." As we have noted that there exists a time gap between the point of receiving and the point of the issue of materials, it becomes inevitable to store the materials. The materials are stored in the storeroom and the storage space may be in the form of constructed godown, temporary structures or even open yards. Various types of stores equipment such as pallets, skids, shelves, bins, boxes, drums, tanks, racks are used for the purpose of economic use of the storage space and efficient handling of the materials. The materials are stored till they are requisitioned by the production departments or the specific jobs. The stored materials are issued to the respective production department or job against the authorised materials requisition.

The stored materials are pending for issue. They should be preserved till they are issued. The materials represent the money value, so they should be safeguarded against fire, deterioration of quality, mixing, evaporation, theft, pilferage etc. Proper and adequate storage facilities should be provided for all types of materials according to their specific requirements.

The materials should be physically verified periodically with the stores records, the storage space should be cleaned regularly, the storage facilities should be checked frequently and the entry to the storage area should be restricted to the authorized persons only.

Record-keeping of Materials

Materials represent the money value. It is nothing but the application of financial resources and hence their proper records as regards the quantity as well as value should be maintained properly and efficiently. Proper record-keeping becomes inevitable even for accounting and costing purposes. Up-to-date stores records help in determining the quantity of respective material items on particular point of time which provides the guideline for the fresh purchase or disposal of the materials, the valuation of stock on any particular point of time representing the asset value locked up in stores items and provides the basis for charging the various production departments or jobs who have received the materials from the storeroom against materials requisition.

The store records can broadly be classified into two:

(1) The bin card and (2) the stores ledger.

(1) The Bin Card: The bin card or the stock card is usually attached to each bin, shelf or other form of containers. The bin cards of the items stored in the open yards like coal, are kept at the desk of the store-keeper. They are used as record of the quantities of each type of material received, issued and on hand each day. They contain only the quantity column and they are not considered for accounting the price of the materials. The pricing is recorded in the stores ledger card which is discussed in the following paragraphs. Usually the bin card specifies the location; the description of materials, maximum, minimum and reorder level; date; receipt; issue and balance specifying only the quantity etc.

Fig. 27.1

Bin or Stock Card

BIN CARD

Bin No......................... Max. Qty ....

Material Code No............................ Ordering Level ....

Stores Ledger Folio .... Minimum Qty. . . . .

Date	*Qty. Received*	*Qty. Issued*	*Balance*	*Remarks*

It is used as basis for verifying the physical stock and the stores ledger accounts.

(2) The Stores Ledger: The objective of the stores ledger is to keep the proper record of the respective materials specifying their quantity as well as value. It is a record which charges the respective departments or the job at the price of the materials issued to them. Generally, stores ledger is maintained on the loose-leaf card basis and separate card is kept for each material item. The stores ledger card specifies the account number, location, description of the materials, unit measurement, maximum, minimum and reorder level, debit, credit and balance columns under the description of receipt, issue and balance specifying both the quantity and the rupee value. It is also a practice to keep the column such as outstanding order, units reserved or units appropriated for special jobs. The outstanding order column helps in reviewing the actual and the probable supply picture which serves as a guide in scheduling the production. The reserved column earmarks the materials for strategic needs and is not considered for ascertaining the stock in hand for the purpose of recording. The appropriated column ensures the execution of certain specific orders without any interruption. The provision of these and other columns is decided on the basis of the need of the organization.

When the store-keeper issues materials to any department or job against the material requisition, a copy of material requisition is sent to the stores ledger clerk. He makes entry in the "issue" section of the card, specifying the date, requisition number, the department or job, the quantity, the unit cost and the total cost. Finally, the new balance is calculated and entered in the balance column.

Issue of Materials

The materials stored in the stock-room are issued to various jobs or production departments against the authorized materials requisitions. The issues are recorded in the store ledger and the respective jobs or production departments are debited with the price of the material issued. As the time of purchase and the time of issues are mostly different and the market price of the materials tends to vary, the problem of pricing the materials issued necessitates certain policy formulation. It is an important consideration not only under stores management but also for costing and pricing policies. The fundamental consideration is whether to price the issues at historical price, *i.e.*, the original purchase price, at the replacement price, *i.e.*, the prevailing market price at the time of issue or at some other price.

MATERIAL REQUISITION

Fig. 27.2 **Material Requisition**

Material required for .... No. ....
(Specify Job or Process)
Department .... Date ....

Sr. No.	*Description No.*	*Code*	*Quantity*		*Rate*	*Amount*	*Entered on Stock Register Page No.*
			Demand	*Supplied*			

Requisitioned by Approved by Material Issued by Received by

The various methods are used for pricing the material issues which are based on different principles. The following are the important methods of pricing the material issues:

(1) First In First Out Method (FIFO Method): FIFO method, as its name suggests, is governed by the principle that the materials which are received first are issued first. The issues are priced at the cost price of the oldest consignments till it gets exhausted. As soon as the oldest lot is exhausted, the issues are priced at the cost price of the next of oldest lot in the sequence, *e.g.*, the following transactions occurred during the first week of April, 1993:

April 1 : 200 units purchased @ ₹ 5 per unit

April 3 : 500 units purchased @ ₹ 6 per unit

April 5 : 300 units issued to Job No. 1001

The issue of 300 units will be priced as under	₹
From the first lot: 200 units @ ₹ 5 =	1,000
Remaining 100 units from second lot = 100 units @ ₹ 6	600
	1,600

The value of the closing stock of 400 units (*i.e.*, second lot 500 units less 100 units issued) will be costed @ ₹ 6, *i.e.*, the value of closing stock would be ₹ 2,400.

(2) Last In First Out Method (LIFO Method): LIFO method reverses the procedure as followed under FIFO. The cost of the last lot of materials received is used to price the issues until that consignment is exhausted, then the next lot of pricing is used and so on through the successive lots. This method is based on the premises that the materials which are issued to the jobs should carry the cost of the most recently purchased materials, and that is why it is also known as the "replacement cost" method. It should be noted that like FIFO method, the actual physical handling of the material in the bins and shelves in the sequence of purchases is imaginary. It is considered only for pricing the issues made from the stores, *e.g.*, the following transactions occurred in the stores department during the first week of April, 1991.

April 1 : 500 units purchased @ ₹ 5

April 3 : 300 units purchased @ ₹ 6

April 6 : 400 units issued to Job Order No. 1086

The issue of 400 units on April 6, will be priced as under:

First 300 units @ ₹ 6 =	₹ 1,800
Remaining 100 units @ ₹ 5 =	₹ 500
	₹ 2,300

The closing stock of 400 units will be priced @ ₹ 5, *i.e.*, ₹ 2,000.

(3) Average Cost Method: Under this method, the issues are charged at a price ascertained from the common pool made up of the varied prices of a several lots. It is advantageous to use this method when the prices are subject to constant changes. In the periods of rise or fall of material prices, an average cost tends to even out the extreme price changes. The upward and downward trends are moderate as contrasted with the steep rise or fall under the FIFO and LIFO methods. The average price is calculated in different ways as under:

(1) Simple average of the stock on hand at the price of the issues.

(2) On the basis of the simple average cost of each kind of material on hand at the close of the month, and to apply it for all issues made during the following month.

(3) On the basis of the simple moving average wherein the earliest price is dropped the moment the new purchases are made and cost of such fresh purchases will be included while arriving at the new average.

It should be noted that instead of the simple average wherein only the unit cost is considered for calculating the average cost to be charged to the issues, weighted average cost can also be used. Under the weighted average cost, along with the unit cost the quantity of the units is also considered, e.g., the following two lots were purchased during April, 1993:

(1) 1,000 units @ ₹ 3

(2) 5,000 units @ ₹ 5

The simple average cost would be ₹ 4 only (*i.e.*, ₹ 3 + ₹ 5 + 2) while the weighted average cost would as under:

	Unit cost ₹	*Weight*	*Weighted cost* ₹
(1)	3	1,000	3,000
(2)	5	5,000	25,000
		6,000	28,000
Weighted average cost		=	$\frac{28,000}{6,000}$
		=	4.67

(4) Replacement Price Method: This method is also known as market price method under which the material issues are priced at the prevailing market price on the date of the issue. This method is based on the principle that the materials issued for any job on a particular day should be charged at the rate at which they could be replaced immediately from the fresh purchases on the same day. In short, material issues are priced at the prevailing market price on the date of its consumption. This method is applicable to the raw materials of standardized grades which are traded at the commodity exchanges such as cotton, cereals, certain metals etc., because the prices of such items are quoted in the newspapers and it is relatively easier to ascertain the current market price. The main advantage of this method is that it considers the current market price which is more significant for the purpose of the pricing policies. It enables the comparison of the operating efficiencies with those of the competitive units. The comparison between the purchase price and the issue price (*i.e.*, the market price) reflects on the efficiency or otherwise of the purchase department. The main drawback of this method is that it distorts the data for the accounting purpose which necessitates the adjustments in the Stores Ledger. There is bound to be a discrepancy between the purchase price and the issue price. The difference between the market price and the purchase price is adjusted to the 'Price fluctuation reserve account' which indicates the efficiency or inefficiency of the purchase department.

(5) Standard Price Method: Under this method, the material issues are charged at a predetermined, budgeted or estimated price which reflects a normal or an effected future price. Generally standard price is fixed after the careful examination of the current market price, trend of the price, market conditions etc., so that a fairly correct average standard price may be predetermined. The standard price is made applicable for a definite period say a month, a quarter or a year. The material receipts are recorded at the actual price while the material issues are costed at the predetermined standard price. So there is bound to be the discrepancies between the standard and the actual price. The difference between the actual price paid and the standard price charged is recorded to a separate 'Price Variance Account.' The standard price is revised periodically, if the discrepancies go beyond a particular limit. The main advantage of this method is that the pricing of issues becomes a simplified function. Like FIFO, LIFO and average cost method, the issue price need not be ascertained after each receipt or issue of materials. However, it is not advised if the materials involve frequent and substantial price fluctuation.

(6) Actual Price Method: Under this method the material issues are priced at the actual acquisition cost of the respective materials. This method is applicable where the purchases are made for the specific jobs and are kept physically separate in the storeroom. Each material receipts is recorded in separate stores ledger card and the material issues are costed at the actual acquisition cost. This method is relatively awkward, however, it is advised where few costly items are used in the processing and where non-standardized materials are purchased to meet the customer's specification. It is more suitable to the jobbing industries.

(7) Inflated Price Method: This method of pricing is based on the principle of uniform spreading of normal wastage on the residual units. There are certain types of normal wastage which are incidental to materials usage, *e.g.,* loss of breaking the bulk, evaporation etc. The cost of such normal wastage is absorbed by the good units through charging the material issues at inflated price, *e.g.,* 100 units at ₹ 15 were purchased. This material is subject to 10% normal wastage, so the total cost of ₹ 1,500 (100 units × ₹ 15) will be spread over 90 (100 units – 10 units normal wastage) good units, and the issue of the materials will be charged at an inflated price of ₹ 16.67 (₹ 1,500 × 90 units) instead of ₹ 15.

In conclusion it should be noted that the material pricing should be on the basis of the acquisition cost of the materials. The acquisition cost should consider the net invoice price of the supplier and the transportation charges which are 'the visible costs.' They should also consider certain invisible costs like the cost of ordering, receiving, unpacking, inspection, insurance, storing etc. The precise cost analysis of these aspects requires exhaustive treatment which is beyond the scope of this book.

Replacement of Materials

Receiving and issuing of inventories are the common and recurring phenomena in a manufacturing organization. When the inventories fall below a particular level, they are replenished by the fresh purchases. The prescription of reorder level (ROL) is an important technique of inventory control. It fundamentally deals with "when to order" to replenish the inventories. Reorder level is a predetermined point, and when the existing stock of inventories reaches this point or falls below it, the purchase action is initiated to replenish them. The ROL is mentioned in the bin-card of each inventory item. What should be the quality of replenishment order is also a matter of policy. Generally, size of the order is determined on the basis of the economic ordering quantity (EOQ), which is also an important technique of inventory control.

The reorder level is decided for each important item of inventory on the basis of the following considerations:

(*i*) Lead time, (*ii*) Average periodic consumption (say, daily consumption), (*iii*) Safety stock.

Reorder level is decided as under:

ROL = (Lead time × Average daily consumption) + Safety stock.

Illustration:

The following data relate to one basic raw material item:

Average daily consumption	50 units
Lead time	4 days
Safety stock	average 2 days' consumption
Size of the order	300 units

Solution:

ROL = (Lead time × average daily consumption) + Safety stock

= (4 days × 50 units) + 100 units

= 300 units.

The minimum level of the inventory will be the safety stock. The re-order level (300 units) is 200 units above the safety stock (*i.e.*, 100 units). The order will be placed for 500 units when the stock reaches to 300 units, *i.e.*, ROL. As it takes four days to get materials after placing an order, the fresh stock of 500 units will arrive at a time when the stock had reached to 100 units, *i.e.*, the safety stock. Thus, the safety stock will be the minimum level of inventory.

The maximum level of inventory would be as under:

Maximum level = Safety stock + Reordering quantity

= 100 units + 500 units.

The ordering level is controlled through the following techniques:

(1) *Two-bin System:* Under this system, the inventory item is divided into two parts. One part is active one from which issues are made. The other part is kept reserved and touched only when the active part is exhausted. It is also known as the "bin reserve" system. When the reserve part is touched, a fresh order is placed to replenish the stock. The reserve part becomes active and the earlier active part which is exhausted is replenished with the fresh stock. The fresh order is placed for the fixed quantity. The quantity in the reserve part serves as a reordering level. It is not necessary to provide for two separate bins. It is a notional presentation. The two parts can be segregated even by the line. This method is applicable to low-cost, high-volume items which have consistent usage. This method does not involve any record keeping.

(2) *Mini-Max System:* Under this system, when the inventory item reaches to a predetermined minimum level, it is replenished by the fresh purchase up to the predetermined maximum level. The minimum level serves as a reordering point. The fresh order is placed for that much quantity which shows deficiency in maximum level. Thus, the size of the order is variable rather than fixed. Like the two-bin system, this method is applicable to low-cost, high-volume parts with consistent usage.

(3) *Imprest System:* Under this system, the reordering is made at regular time intervals. The maximum level of each item is predetermined. At a particular fixed period, say after one week, a fresh collective order for all the items will be placed. The size of the order will be decided on the basis of the shortage indicated by the existing stock in relation to the maximum level. Thus, the quantity of replenishment will exactly equate the quantity consumed during the period. The size of the order will vary considerably.

Physical Verification of Materials: Proper stock records are kept in the bin-card as well as the stores ledgers. When the materials are received or issued, they are properly recorded and the new balance is struck at the end of every transaction. Principally, the bin must contain the quantity which is shown in "balance" column of the bin card. But sometimes, the book-balance and the quantity physically does not tally. The important reasons for such discrepancies are as under:

1. Wrong recording in the bin card.
2. Placement of the material in the wrong bin.
3. Mixing in adjacent bin.
4. Loss due to breaking the bulk.
5. Evaporation of alcoholic materials.
6. Pilferage etc.

However, such situation emphasises the need for physical verification of the materials stocked in the stores room.

There are following two popular methods of the stock verification:

(A) Periodic inventory verification, and

(B) Perpetual inventory verification.

(A) Periodic Inventory Verification: Under this method, all items of the storeroom are verified through counting, weighing, measuring etc. at the end of the specific period, usually the last day of the accounting year. They can also be verified at the end of every quarter or six months. However, in the light of the huge task of verification, usually they are verified only once and that too on the last day of the accounting year. It is also required by the accounting system to value the stock-in-hand on the last day of the year for the purpose of preparing the annual accounts. The issues are not made during the verification to the size of the inventory. Additional staff is employed for the huge verification task. This method gives correct picture of the stock-in-hand on the last day of the accounting year.

(B) Perpetual Inventory Verification: Under this method, the verification function becomes a continuous function rather than a year-end function. All the items are verified rotatively on the continuous basis. Under this system all items are not verified at a time like year-end verification. Generally, those items which have reached a minimum level are selected for the verification. This policy reduces the burden of verification. The verification work is arranged in such a way that every item is verified twice or thrice during the year on rotation basis. This system does not necessitate the employment of any special staff for verification. The store-keeper carries on the verification work according to his convenience. Moreover, it is easy to locate the reasons for the discrepancies promptly. In fact, it serves as a deterrent to pilferage. Such control is not possible under year-end verification. The main limitation of this method is that the valuation of the ending inventory is made on the basis of book figures rather than on the basis of actual physical verification.

Disposal of Waste and Scrap

The waste and scrap consist of the following:

(*a*) Spoiled raw materials.

(*b*) Rejected components.

(*c*) Defective parts.

(*d*) Obsolete stores and equipment.

(*e*) Wastes from the production departments, like cut-pieces of metals, scraps, chips, etc.

(*f*) Non-returnable containers and packing cases.

Such wastes and scraps involve some commercial values. They should be disposed of periodically and proper credit of the amount realized should be taken in the books of the accounts. Such disposal also releases the space in the storeroom.

Automated Storage/Retrieval

Technology has been applied to storage function where automatic material handling systems are used for the unit load type storage retrieval system. When different quantities of different materials are to be retrieved, semi-automatic system of handling is used. The operator undertakes a tour of the stores and fills up the required stores. To facilitate this system, items like nuts and bolts are stored in pairs, location is made scientific, a picking list is carefully prepared, a single operator moves along an aisle, sequencing is done of stops in a single picking tour optimally.

Caselet: Computerisation of Stores

Let us recapitulate a case of Minolta Photo Co. Ltd., Mizuno plant. Since a large inventory of parts tie down a large amount of capital and expenditure on maintenance, Minolta has adopted the Minimum Inventory System. Here a bare minimum amount of parts is kept in automated computerised store. The supplier delivers a day's requirements according to a strict schedule during the day. In case a part falls below a certain level, the concerned employee gets the necessary supply by pushing a button. It increases the overall competitiveness of the product.

What do you think India should learn from Minolta?

28

RATIONALISED CODIFICATION SYSTEM

The system to be adopted for accurate identification of materials should be the allotment of a numeral to each item. In materials management terminology this is known as 'Codification.' The objective of codification is to provide a common language for identification of every single 'input' item in the inventory for all transactions within the organization, *i.e.,* within its constituent units. All input materials, irrespective of the source of procurement, whether from external sources or manufactured by the organization itself, are to be codified.

Codification, to be successful, must be based on a simple system.

Step I

The large number of items and the variety involved even in a moderate sized inventory present a formidable task for code planning. The entire inventory needs to be classified under major groups known as 'Generic' groups. The principles for classification may be either prime composition of materials, *e.g.,* ferrous metal, non-ferrous metal, rubbers, plastic, timber, textiles, oil and lubricants etc., or usage-wise, *e.g.,* electrical, mechanical, structural, electronic, chemical, ceramic, miscellaneous, etc. A certain amount of overlapping may be inevitable. For example, where prime composition of material is the criterion, the problem will be where to place items of a mixed composition. The decision may be to place such items in the category in which a particular material is predominant, or in the group where the major user shops, or, in some cases just allow a judicious mixture of both the 'composition' and 'usage' principles. For instance, if the generic grouping includes both 'Ferrous Metal' and 'Mechanical Engineering' there would be no problem to place an item of mechanical engineering in the mechanical engineering group even though the metallic composition of the item be ferrous metal.

Step II

Items under each generic group should then be further classified into distinct sub-groups according to the type of the material. These are known as 'Specific' groups. For example, under the generic group 'General Engineering' one of the specific groups may be 'Bearing.' This specific group will cover all the present and also the anticipated future holdings of Bearings Ball, Bearings Roller, Bearings Tapered Roller, etc.

Step III

The next step would be to classify and to list out, firstly, in alphabetical order and then in size chronology, all the items under each specific group. For instance, in the case of Bearings, all Bearings Ball should be listed size-wise to be followed by a similar list of Bearing Roller, and a list of Bearing Tapered Roller, etc. Each item should then be allotted consecutive numerals. The code numbering is now complete.

Precautions

While consecutive numbers are allotted care should be taken to leave few serial numbers vacant, rather liberally. These numbers will be required later for allotment to new items inducted in the inventory from time to time. At the time of preparation of the code lists it would pay to involve the R&D and the user divisions whose guidance about probable induction of new items or new sizes in the period ahead would be of immense value. It would help in deciding the appropriate stages where the serial numbers may be left unutilised and the quantum of such numbers.

Reading the Code

(1) The code number of each item would consist of the generic group number, the specific group number and its own code serial number in that order. In most cases, the generic group and the specific group are expressed in two digit numbers each, and the individual item code number is expressed in seven digits. For example, code numbers may read like 00 04 018, 02 01 009, 06 02 065 etc. All the seven digits should not be written continuously. To express the generic code number, and the specific code number distinctly a one-digit space should be left blank after each group number.

The coding system envisaged is illustrated on next page.

Item Code:

001 – Beaker, Griffin Low Form with spout 1 ml capacity, size 12 × 16 mm.
002 – do –5 ml capacity, size 20 × 25 mm.
003 – do –10 ml capacity, size 25 × 32 mm.
004*
005*
006 – do –250 ml capacity, size 68 × 95 mm.
007 – do –500 ml capacity, size 83 × 109 mm.
008*
009*
010*
011 – Bottles, Aspirator outlet for tubing 250 ml capacity, size 65 × 10 mm.
012 – do –500 ml capacity, size 80 × 170 mm.
013*
014*
015*
016 – Bottles, Reagent Plain Narrow Mouth 250 ml capacity, size 65 × 140 mm.
017*
018*
019*
020 – Burette for Pinchcock with tip class BIS 1997: 1967 50 ml. graduation 0.1 ml.

* Provisions left for code numbering new items anticipated to be received in the inventory in future.

(2) Some organizations having a large number and large variety of items in their inventory use four digits as the item code number. The disadvantage in the increase in digits is that the more the number, the more will be the possibility of human error. The three digit code numbering allows serial numbering up to 999 to cover all items under each specific group. However, if the number of items under any specific group is estimated to exceed 999, the three digit system will be inadequate and the organization will have no alternative but to adopt the four digit system for all the items in the inventory.

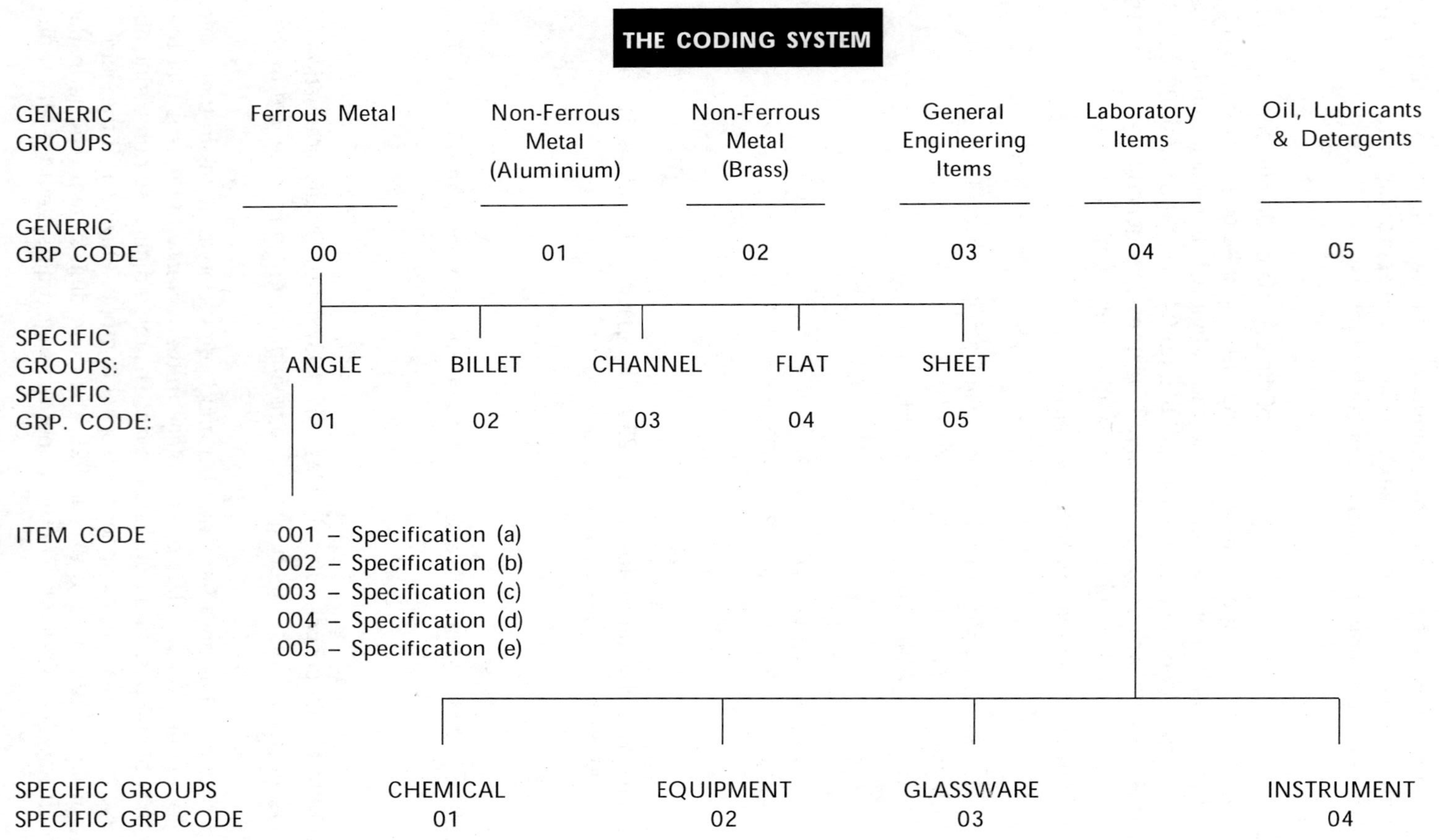

GENERIC GROUPS	Ferrous Metal	Non-Ferrous Metal (Aluminium)	Non-Ferrous Metal (Brass)	General Engineering Items	Laboratory Items	Oil, Lubricants & Detergents
GENERIC GRP CODE	00	01	02	03	04	05

SPECIFIC GROUPS:	ANGLE	BILLET	CHANNEL	FLAT	SHEET
SPECIFIC GRP. CODE:	01	02	03	04	05

ITEM CODE

001 – Specification (a)
002 – Specification (b)
003 – Specification (c)
004 – Specification (d)
005 – Specification (e)

SPECIFIC GROUPS	CHEMICAL	EQUIPMENT	GLASSWARE	INSTRUMENT
SPECIFIC GRP CODE	01	02	03	04

(3) Code serial numbers are to be allotted following the 'next size' dictum. If a certain size or sizes are not expected to be inducted in the inventory in the foreseeable future, no serial number need be left vacant for those. It is advisable to leave a few unutilised numbers before going over to the next foremost alphabet.

(4) For convenience in handling, a separate Code Book is to be prepared for each generic group. The generic group code number and the specific group code number should both be displayed boldly on the cover of each booklet, and should also be shown inside the booklet, to precede each item code. The columns of the Code Book may be as follows:

Generic Group Code No.	***Specific Group Code No.***	***Item Code No.***	***Nomenclature with full Specifications (and manufacturers Part No. in brackets)***	***Acctg. Unit***	***Drawing No.***	***Amend-ment No.***	***Amend-ment Date***
1	**2**	**3**	**4**	**5**	**6**	**7**	**8**

Objectives of Codification

The objectives of a rationalized Material Coding system are:

1. Bringing all similar items together.
2. To enable putting up of any future item in its proper place.
3. To classify an item according to its characteristics.
4. To give a unique code number to each item to avoid duplication and ambiguity.
5. To reveal excessive variety and promote standardization and variety reduction.
6. To establish a common language for the identification of an item.
7. To fix essential parameters for specifying an item.
8. To specify item as per national and international standards.
9. To enable computerised data processing and analysis.

A codification system must aim at satisfying as many of the above-mentioned objectives as possible and the codes evolved will depend upon the nature of industry, items of stores and the management policy.

Important Codification Systems

The two important coding systems are the *Kodak* and the *Brisch* system.

Kodak System: It is developed by Eastman Kodak Co. of N.Y., U.S.A. It is a system of 10 digits numeric code with 100 major classifications and each class divided into 10 such classes. The classification is based on procurement consideration.

The Brisch Classification: The codes in Brisch Classification are wholly composed of numbers, are of constant length and generally contain six to eight digits. The first digit covers a broad classification of all the materials into 10 main classes and the value ranges from Zero to Nine and indicate the classes concerned. For example, in an engineering organization, the classifications are:

0. Organization and operation
1. Primary materials
2. Brought out commodities
3. Components to user's own design
4. Sub-assemblies and assemblies
5. Tools and portable equipment
6. Plant and Machinery
7. Building and Utilities

8. Scrap
9. Reserved.

Each of these divisions are broken into sub-classes, and each of the sub-classes are divided into finer classes till the final symbolic description of an item is complete.

An Example of a Significant Code:

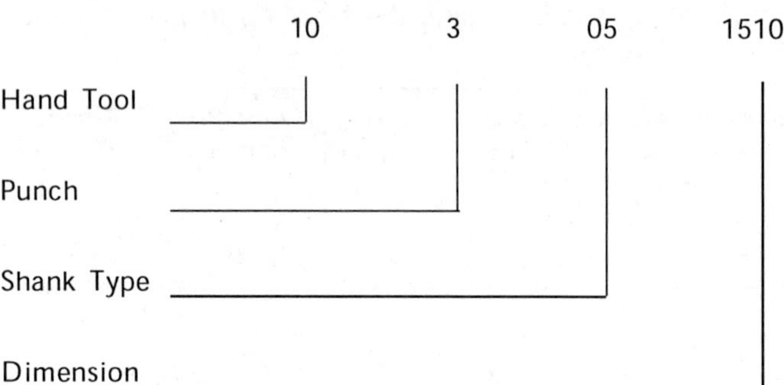

In the above example, the first two digits denote the major group. The major group can accommodate 100 classifications.

1st and 2nd digits	— Major Group
00	— Raw Materials
01	— Vacant
02	— Packing Materials
03	— Lab Chemicals
04–05	— Civil Stores
56–49	— General Stores
90–96	— Spares
97	— Scrap
98	— Stationery
99	— Finished goods

now 06–49 can be classified as:

06–13	— Tools
14–39	— Hardware and Consumables
40–49	— Electric item
06–13	— Comprises of the following groups:
06	— Cutting tools
08	— Finishing tools
10	— Hand tools
12	— Measuring tools
07, 09, 11, 13	— Vacant groups

3rd Digit: Sub-groups of Major Group (for Hand tools)

0	— Hammers
1	— Chisels
2	— Blades
3	— Punches
4	— Wrenches and Spanners
5	— Pliers
6	— Screw Drivers
7, 8, 9	— Vacant sub-groups

4th and 5th Digits: Type (for Punches)

00 — Neck Punch
01 — Eyelet Punch
02 — Handnail Punch
03 — Nail Punch
04 — Strating Punch
05 — Shank Punch
06–99 — Vacant

6th, 7th, 8th and 9th Digits denote the dimension of the Punch, 10th digit may be included as a check digit which can be computed in many ways. For example, multiply the first digit by 9, the second by 8 and so on and sum the product. Divide the values by 9 and the remainder is the check digit which can assume values from 0–9.

In the end, it must be added that the task of assigning codes to new items must be centralized and consistent, so that uniformity is ensured.

29 WASTE MANAGEMENT

Waste Management (WM) has several dimensions — engineering, economic, geographic, social and management. Its basic purpose is to minimise the overall waste in a given system. Waste here refers to waste of all kinds of resources, but especially the material resources which constitute a significant portion. Some waste is inevitable in any conversion process of inputs into outputs. To reduce waste, we have therefore to maximise the use of resources. Resource Management and Waste Management are thus supportive to each other.

Classification of Waste

Waste can be classified on the basis of:

1. Resources wasted
2. Origin
3. Property
4. Recoverability

Waste Resources: Material resources like solids, liquids, and gases can be wasted. Energy resources like physical, human and solar energy can be wasted. Time resource can be wasted. Capital in the form of capacity, equipment, machine hours and inventory can be wasted. Services like communication, transport, health etc. can be wasted. Life or human resources, data and information may also suffer wastages.

Origin of Waste: It could be industrial, residential, commercial, office, municipal, construction and demolition, agricultural etc.

Property: Materials wasted are either hazardous or non-hazardous.

Recoverable: Wastes can be recovered into some useful resource, material waste recycled. Non-recoverable wastes are lost with time.

Waste exists in myriad forms — non-workable components, excess inventory, machine downtime, re-work, non-conformance, warranties. Any activity that does not add value is a waste. Re-work is the biggest non-value added activity that a company performs. If we reduce the unnecessary activities or eliminate them, costs will come down drastically.

Measurement Of Waste

$$\text{Wastivity} = \frac{\text{Waste (W)}}{\text{Input (I)}}$$

$$\text{Gross Wastivity} = \frac{\text{Total Waste}}{\text{Total Input}}$$

Net Waste = Total Waste – Waste Recycled within the system

$$\text{Net Wastivity} = \frac{\text{Net Waste}}{\text{Total Input}}$$

Wastivity and Productivity

Waste is an indirect measure of productivity. If wastivity is checked, the effect, productivity will be automatically improved.

Causes of Waste

Various causes are responsible for wastes. An illustrative list is given below. The highest waste causing factors are considered to be critical.

Table: Causes of Waste

1. Faulty planning and policies, systems and procedures
2. Faulty organization structure
3. Environmental pressures
4. Tardiness
5. Lack of accountability
6. Unawareness of technological advances
7. Non-responsiveness to automation/computerization
8. Wrong specifications, standards, codes
9. Wrong raw materials
10. Lack of inventory control
11. Lack of proper storage, layout of facilities, handling of material
12. Communication gaps
13. Faulty work-method
14. Less emphasis on PPC
15. Lax supervision and control
16. Wrong recruitment/selection policies
17. Lack of motivation/incentives
18. Poor working conditions
19. Unsafe practices
20. Poor IR: Industrial Relations
21. Maintenance failure
22. Power failure
23. Distribution problems
24. Less attention to waste segregation and collection
25. Technological obsolescence
26. Miscellaneous cause

Systematic Approach to Waste Reduction

1. First of all, the total waste in the whole system is recognized.
2. Then, the stages at which waste is generated are identified.
3. Then, the sub-stages are identified in which above wastes can be put.
4. Then, waste-reduction programme is implemented at each stage by planning correcting action and eliminating the cause.

Waste Collection System

Wastes affect the environment, the organization and the public health. Waste collection consists of transporting the waste. It is a major cost element, and if efficiently handled, may reduce the overall cost of WM. Waste collection consumes 80 p.c. of waste reduction programme.

The following factors govern the waste collection:

1. Separate the waste at source.
2. Make arrangement to collect it in suitable containers of the right material and right size.
3. Depending upon the generation rate of waste, make arrangements to collect waste from time to time.
4. Offer incentives to segregate waste at source.
5. Carry the waste to the salvage industry for ultimate reuse.
6. Make suitable arrangements to collect both the organic and inorganic wastes.

Recycling of Wastes

The wastes can be recycled/reused. For this purpose, suitable recycling projects are created. In **recycling,** the waste is used as input to the same process/system, *e.g.,* recycling of foundry scrap. In **reuse,** the waste is used as input to some other process/system, *e.g.,* sugarcane bagasse is used to prepare paper. In reuse of waste, we may generate power or by-products, *e.g.,* bio-gas generates electricity/fuel and molasses produces alcohol. In reclamation, the damaged, rejected or undesired outputs are converted by repair or processing. Recovery is a general term to indicate gain of resources from wastes.

Waste Disposal System

Waste can be classified by two categories in terms of its disposal

(*i*) Salvable waste — They have the salvage value, *e.g.,* scrap rejected goods, surplus and obsolete items.

(*ii*) Non-salvable waste — They have no salvage value, but need further processing and treatment for disposal.

Disposal of Salvable Waste — Management of Surplus and Scrap

Introduction

Eventually surplus is usually not an inspiring word, every manufacturer unwillingly and yet unavoidably manufactures surplus. To make matters worse, surplus is more-often-than-not, associated unglamorously with 'Junk' and 'Scrap' heaps. Consequently, surplus is seldom considered an enchanting business activity and therefore, it rarely receives the management attention it deserves. This is highly deplorable because the total cost of production is the sum of cost outlays on labour, materials and direct overheads less any return from the successful sale of all kinds of surplus materials. Strikingly enough, often scrap volume is high enough for the proceeds of sale to rank as an appreciable secondary income source. Hence, profits can be maximized when all elements affecting cost are fully controlled.

What is Surplus?

Industrial surplus is defined as those materials which are in excess of the reasonable operational requirements of the concern. Surplus is the state of an item when stock is likely to last longer than a reasonable period or when it is no longer required for use.

Surplus stock generally arises on the following occasions:

1. When purchases have been made in larger quantities than the usual requirements. However, when inventory control is pursued with one diligence, such situation will not generally occur.
2. When operations are suddenly curtailed. This applies mostly to production materials, specially, raw materials and components although tools and certain general stored items also may become surplus in this manner.
3. When, at the materials procurement, on account of some error or miscalculation that has crept in, of course, inadvertently, the wrong item has been purchased.
4. When the usual materials are rendered useless due to change in materials specifications to illustrate, if the specification normally used for manufacturing a component is EN3B2" dia steel bar and that has been changed to EN3B3" dia or something else, the original material is, naturally turned surplus.
5. When a project is completed, some quantities of the items, used for the commissioning of the project are bound to be left out, this is surplus. To illustrate, if a building is constructed by the concern itself, it is most common to find that certain quantity of material used for the purpose, *e.g.*, cement, steel bar, wire mesh, etc., are left unutilized — they are termed surplus.

In this connection, surpluses emanate from three primary sources:

(*a*) Scrap and waste.

(*b*) Surplus, obsolete or damaged stock items.

(*c*) Surplus, obsolete or damaged equipment.

Let us explore each of the above components of surplus.

(A) Surplus from Scrap and Waste

Wastage, spoilage, empty drums and bags which are not returnable to suppliers, broken and worn-out tools which are beyond repairs, irreparable parts of machinery, turning and borings from machines are all commonly termed as 'scrap.'

Wastage

A residue or pieces cut of raw materials during the manufacturing process is wastage. Since, not all the materials injected into production processes are converted into finished products, surplus from production process are inevitable and common feature in every concern. To illustrate, take a company that stamps disks from the copper strip. During the operation, 10 to 15 per cent of copper is left out and that cannot be used elsewhere in production operations. This residue is called "wastage" and must be disposed of as surplus-scrap item.

It is highly impossible for any firm to get rid completely of this type of surplus; however, effective and intelligent production planning, handling of issue from stores and control can sizably contribute to reduce it. To illustrate, if there is a requisition for a piece of 3' × 1' size steel sheet. It should be issued from cut pieces if available, instead of a large sheet. Similarly, a 2' × 3' piece should be issued from 3' × 6' sheet instead of from that of 4' × 8' and so on.

Spoilage

Surplus that is generated from inefficient use of production machinery, carelessness and poor purchasing are spoilage (wastage) of resources. Items spoiled among the course of manufacture or storage are also spoilage. Spoilage may involve loss of machine hours as well as man-hours. Special care should be extended particularly during storage of perish-at-time items, so that spoilage is avoided.

(B) Surplus, Obsolete or Damaged Goods (Stocks)

Items which are degenerated out-of-date — mostly superseded by a better design and sophisticated technology — are known as obsolete items. It is quite unreasonable to expect sales forecasting and production planning to match exactly in reality. It is a variety, though not absolutely impossible.

In case of over-anticipation, enthusiastic and optimistic sales forecasting, excess materials are found in the stores. Further, constant, continuous, sweeping, successive and rapid changes take place with its sky-rocketing pace in the designs and specifications of the materials and components. So the slow-moving items are surplus in this fast moving society. As a consequence, obsolete products and their parts constitute a continuing source of surplus materials.

Besides, the lag between production planning and its actual commencement as well as commencement of production and its completion is very vital. The longer the time period in between there are more chances that either technical or product changes neatly sweep the schedule of materials. The ease with which technology can generate surplus is highlighted by the single but very eye-catching fact that in many concerns today over 50% of the products sold did not even exist just 10 years ago.

Moreover, excessive forward buying as well as planned over-buying are another common and yet profound source of surplus materials. These entail the hazard of surplus from obsolescence, deterioration and errors in stock-taking and record-keeping.

(C) Surplus, Obsolete or Damaged Equipment

All machines and equipment at some point in their life become surplus for two primary reasons — one, they wear out with passage of time and secondly, they become technologically obsolete with the invention of better technology machines. It is, however, a normal and yet noteworthy experience of all that, in today's rapidly advancing technological system, it is the second factor above that counts for surplus rather than first one. In this sense, machines or tools are seldom worn out, they have to be replaced in view of changed circumstances to avail better functioning and efficiency.

In addition, the steady improvement has been a greater change particularly for capital expenditure programmes. The capital investment conceded the best and prudent in light of present state of technology is obliterated, preposterous and non-sensical with the years succeeding in future. Every manager, therefore, has been at his wit's end and makes haunting efforts to prolong the life of its capital equipment as long as possible. But for the fact of the reasons of obsolescence, breakdowns, introduction of new products or new methods of production, replacement of major capital assets even buildings becomes mandatory.

For the fact that these obsolete equipment or components can be modified to the latest design or sold to the original user of the original design, they prefer but to dispose of them as surplus — even as scrap in some extreme cases.

Disposing of Surplus

When the material has been categorised as surplus, it is the Reclamation Department or Purchasing Department to take charge of it. Unlike sale of other items of the organization, disposal function is entrusted under the purview of Purchasing Department rather than Sales Department. The reason lies in that the Purchasing Department that undertakes buying of diversified materials, parts, tools equipment etc., has reasonably better knowledge of who else uses the same material, that what can be the alternative uses, and how and where the same can be put to use in own concern. Based on this set of precise and ready information, Purchasing Department comes out with disposal function with utmost efficiency and profitability. To put more Sales (Marketing) Department has much to look after its major products and in these days of keen competition, it can't afford to divert its efforts for such second grade sales function. So disposal of surplus if thrown to Sales Department would mean overburdening the back that has already been at its full swing. Doubtless to say, the Purchase Department can serve well in this regard.

The information regarding the surplus item can be well served to the authority concerned in the specified form. A model of it is annexed as Annexure 1.

Disposal — Where to be made

Disposal of surplus can take the following routes, to enlist the possible channels:

(A) Circulation within the concern.

(B) Return to supplier.

(C) Direct sale to another firm.

(D) Sale to dealers or brokers.

(E) Sale to scrap consultants.

(F) Sale to employees.

(G) Donations to educational institutions.

Each of the above is discussed as under:

(A) Circulation within the Concern: Circulation of surplus items, if surplus can be put to some alternative productive use, in the same concern is best of all the disposal programmes. This channel has some added features. Use of surplus items on the concern itself negates all possibilities of 'Bargain Loss' or 'Deal Reduction' that is a common phenomenon in other disposal programmes. Further, the administrative cost is saved to a greater extent, when the surplus item(s) is (are) put to use somewhere also within the concern, that otherwise would have been a must to get rid of these surplus in the profitable manner.

(B) Return to Supplier: If the surplus materials are not found useful in the concern, the next best method is to return these to the suppliers. Most often, suppliers as a courtesy to good account allow return of surplus materials. This may particularly be allowed for the items which do not perish with time and are not rendered obsolete so swiftly. Depending upon the account to trace, size of the order, material's intrinsic value, its degree of contamination etc., even scrap items are also allowed to be returned to the suppliers.

This method finds favour particularly with precious materials whose residue quality (*i.e.,* surplus to the concern) is capable of same definite use somewhere else. The sum that such deed fetches mostly covers the original cost for surplus items and equals a reasonable compensation for scrap items.

(C) Selling to Other Firms: Alternatively, the firm may resort to open market and find out some concerns using the same materials that is lying with the concern as surplus stock. The clients for surplus items encompass mostly the competitors, although some users in other spheres of activities can't be ignored. For scrap items, sales is said to be ideal when the production surplus-scrap is the raw material of another concern.

Compared to the first outlet of surplus and scrap, this channel is a bit costlier, since the sincere efforts to identify the alternate potential users of the concern's surplus items, to be in touch with them, to persuade and to sign the deal inevitably involves a cost outlay in items of administrative cost and human efforts.

(D) Selling to Dealers-Brokers: Where the concern is not in a position to lay its access to the potential users of the surplus materials directly, the sale of such item to the dealers or agents is the best channel open to it. The dealer acts as an intermediate agency to relieve the concern of its surplus accumulation and to acquire the requirements for the users.

The inlet of funds under this channel is reduced to the extent that the dealer or broker or agent charges commission. However, this method does not necessitate the cost of finding out and entering into the deal with the customer from the open air. In spite of that, such dealers constitute an excellent outlet for surplus materials.

Such disposal may be effected by

1. Inviting offers from time to time.
2. Public Auction.
3. Annual Contract.

When the concern adopts first method — Inviting offers at a regular interval (say quarterly, or half yearly) or as and when it thinks necessary, it releases the advertisement for the sale of surplus, in the local dailies, on 'WHERE IS AS IS' basis. The tenders from the parties interested are invited. On the basis of comparative study of the tenders received, and the organization's specific requirement the most suitable tender is accepted.

At the public auction, dealers bid against each other and the highest bidder is sold the surplus. Unlike inviting tenders, public auction may not be found suitable for it proves danger of bidding on mutual understanding.

The annual contract system is the best and cheapest of all the methods. Under this method, a contract is entered into with the carefully selected dealer to off-take the entire surplus as may be generated from time to time during the year for the terms and conditions negotiated at the time of contract. This method has a definite and conspicuous advantage that the concern is relieved of both its rations to dispose of the surplus items in the sense that the surplus will be automatically removed from time to time. There will be no large accumulation of surplus overcrowding scrap with all possible fire and pilferage or deterioration hazard. At the same time, the valuable space in the factory will be saved. Besides, the cost and efforts of the concern to trace out the most suitable dealer each time are commendably saved.

(E) Sale to Scrap Consultants: The salient aspect in management of scrap and surplus items is that it is the buyer who is more well-versed and informed regarding the items than the seller. But on the other hand, though revenue received of scrap and surpluses is a sizable sum, it is quite negligible in comparison with that of the company's regular product line. Further the varieties of surplus are so diversified in grades and kinds that it is practically difficult, though not (totally) absolutely impossible for any concern to deal with them.

As a solution to this, the services of scrap consultants come as a rescue. The scrap consultant renders the services of his preliminary survey for scrap and surplus items and their handling procedures. He then, on the basis of his wide experience in the profession, recommends in his report for segregating, grading, handling, weighing and accounting for the company's accumulated surplus stock. The programme is implemented under direct audit and periodic survey of the consultant by the supervisor (the person-in-charge) of its scrap and surplus programme. The negotiations from time to time with suitable parties bring a ready disposal of the company's surplus. In return, the consultant is paid a commission on sales of scrap and surpluses. This channel, though not invaded in its right perspective, can be a better outlet for surplus items.

(F) Sale to Employees: Some scrap items or scrap items at times, are sold to the employees. If surplus is the result of overstocking or technical obsolescence and the materials are in new or good condition, or if they are odds and ends of scrap described by do-it-yourself employees, this can be a satisfactory method of disposal of surplus stock. On the other hand, if the surplus are not in fully satisfactory condition, such sales, regardless of their attractive price, can be a source of resentment on the part of employees towards the employer.

Most of the concerns do not find this method favourable because of its inherent potential disadvantages. Many sophisticated firms do not sell used surplus to their employees. Especially scrap tools and equipment should not be sold to the employees, since such a concession might encourage scrapping of serviceable tools and equipment. Besides, the dissatisfaction is commonly witnessed among the employees emanating such sale. Further, it often entails a high cost of paper work and imposes an administrative burden on ensuring complete impartiality in the sale.

(G) Donation of Educational Institutions: At present time, schools and colleges and even university departments actually need machine tools and other type of industrial materials for instructional use in laboratories. The disposal of surplus in this direction is a rare phenomenon in the industrial realm. Though this alternative does not yield anything for the surplus or scrap items, it earns a favourable public image in the community. This is an evidence for the company's enlightened, concern with its social responsibility. This sense, the sum that a concern has to forgo in respect of any such surplus item gifted to the educational institutions, can be very well treated as the premium to avail of higher community confidence.

Conclusion

On the whole, the management of surplus and scrap has its unique features particularly for the manufacturing units which require high usage of consumable items. Processing materials are so frequently likely to be confronted (affected) with the grave problems — how to yield best of the surplus items? The industries which suffer swiping and swift generation of its plants and equipments, machinery and tools on account of rapidly developing technologies from time to time are also the victims of high stock of surplus and even scrap heaps. So much so with this, scrap industry is characterised by a market of its uniqueness. In the true sense, scrap is usually, intended to be bought rather than sold. The practical bias to the management of surplus and scrap accumulation reveals that no market or regular demand can be created for such surplus stocks as it is a common phenomenon with regular trade commodities. No means of advertising, howsoever effective in its application, can do well in this typical industry. The reason underlying rests that the demand is a delivered demand completely dependent on the sale of firm's products and conversely for the raw materials. As a result, when the requisitionists knock at the door, the items must be ready on hand to be delivered. Once missed the opportunity, it is incumbent upon the manufacturing unit to maintain the large inventories till another indent is received for the items from the user dealer.

Annexure - I

Surplus Plant Equipment				
*No.			Date:	
*Name of Equipment			From Whom?	
*Model-Size:				
*Capacity:				
*Location:				
*Additional information				
How does it operate today? (See on the back for instructions)	Excellent	Good	Fair	Poor
* Why is to so surplus/discarded/demolished/obsolete Reasons:				
Purchase Price A			Value Today (₹)A	
*If Modernised, what would it cost? A				
*What would it cost to replace? (₹)			When will it be available?	
*Estimated cost to scrap (₹),				
*Reviewed by	Remark		Date	
Store-keeper				
Departmental head				
Accountant				
Works Manager				
Divisional Manager				
Mode Recommended				
Hold for future	Transfer		Sale	Donate
Final Decision				
Date:			Purchase No.	

Annexure - II

DISPOSAL OF NON-SALVABLE WASTE

These are processed to reduce storage, facilitate disposal to recover resources, to get conversion products and energy and to minimise the environmental effects. All wastes with no further value are ultimately disposed by the following techniques.

Mechanical Processing

Volume is reduced by compaction and baling. Size is reduced by shredding. Components may be mechanically separated, especially from solid wastes.

Thermal Processing

Thermal Processing reduces volumes and generates energy and by-products. Incineration converts toxic gases into harmless gases. Solid wastes are subjected to destructive distillation.

Bio-Processing

Composting, fermentation and hydrolysis are commonly employed.

Ultimate Disposal

Left-over wastes with no value are disposed on or in the earth (land filling) or at the bottom of the sea.

Annexure - III

SCRAP DISPOSAL

Item	Categories	Method of Disposal
M.S. Scrap	(*i*) Heavy melting scrap (*ii*) Structural and fabricated scrap (*iii*) Cast iron scrap (*iv*) Pipe and light scrap (*v*) Machine shop turning and boring scrap	Scrap is segregated in different categories to realise better value rather than selling it as mixed scrap.
Gunny Bag Scrap	Cement Bags	Can be sold to manufacturers directly.
	Sugar Bags Nylon Bags Mixed Bags (other than nylon and cement) Torn bags	Segregation is essential.
Cable Scrap	Copper Aluminium Miscellaneous	Clean and burn insulation segregate. Can be given to cable suppliers to adjust its value or can be sold as scrap.

Item	Categories	Method of Disposal
M.S. Cut and Rusty Drums	In Chemical industries, corroded drums of different sizes.	Sell them with light scrap.
	Good drums	Cut and spread them in sheets and sell as corrugated sheets.
Waste Material	Filter cloth	Segregate into cotton, nylon and torn categories. Dispose in separate lots.
	Polythene bags White Black Paper	Bundle them size-wise, pre-weigh them.
	Fibre-drums	Remove food drums and sell them separately. From the rest, remove the plywood, steel ring and sell them separately. Press the drums and sell them as fibre drum paper scrap.
	Scrap wood — Good wood from machinery packing	Keep for repacking, sell the rest
	Waste-firewood.	Sell separately.
Stainless Steel Scrap	(*i*) New plate and pipe cut pieces scrap from workshop (*ii*) Used pipe and other non-magnetic scrap (*iii*) M.S. and S. St. mixed scrap (*iv*) S.St. turning and boring scrap (*v*) Equipment scrap (*vi*) M.S. and S. St. mixed equipment and spares scrap.	Segregate into different categories to realise better value.

Annexure - IV

MSTC — TRIED, TRUSTED AND PROVEN AGENCY FOR SCRAP DISPOSAL

For the past 20 years, Metal Scrap Trade Corporation Ltd. (MSTC) has developed expertise in the field of scrap disposal by studying the market variables, the price trends, the categorisation of scrap and the demand pattern of the actual users and emerged as a pivotal body engaged in the disposal of ferrous and non-ferrous scrap in the domestic market.

Today, MSTC besides acting as selling agents to the integrated steel plants arranges the disposal of scrap, surplus and obsolete stores of over 30 public sector companies and with good reasons. MSTC arranges prompt disposal of all types of industrial, re-rollable and melting scrap, miscellaneous surplus items including machinery and equipment, barges, locomotives, vehicles, motors, bearings, tools, high-speed steel and non-ferrous scrap, etc. and thus helps in generating liquidity for the units.

For speedy and efficient disposal MSTC itself conducts auction. MSTC has an up to-date set-up for collating market intelligence and price data and keeps track of supply/demand patterns.

Located in Kolkata, the nerve-centre of steel and scrap, MSTC has 3 strategically located regional offices that give you an opportunity of availing of its assistance and expertise. MSTC also has a subsidiary — FSNL specialising in scrap recovery from slag dumps.

The addresses are as follows:

Metal Scrap Trade Corporation Ltd.
(A Government of India Company)
225-F, Acharya Jagadish Bose Road, Kolkata-700 020.
Gram: METSCRAP.

Regional Offices at:

Raheja Centre, Flat No. 607 (6th Floor), Nariman Point,
Mumbai-400 021.
Sucheta Bhavan (4th floor), 11A, Rouse Avenue,
New Delhi-110 002.
11 Block, Kormangala, Bangalore-560 034.

30

INDUSTRIAL PRODUCTIVITY

Introduction

The welfare of individuals, the growth of enterprises and the development of the national economies are largely dependent on their comparative productivity. There may exist the differences among the various countries of the world based on political ideologies, economic systems or some such reasons, but all unanimously recognize the importance of the improvement in the productivity levels. Productivity is a ratio between the output of the wealth produced and the input of resources used in the process of any economic activity. There always exists a scarcity of input of resources and each input processes certain inherent "input creativity" which is translated into output. The "input creativity" can yield greater amount of output through "conversion efficiency."

Here lies the importance of improvement in productivity levels. The concept of productivity, of course, with some degree of confusion, has remained a continuous and challenging area of study. The changes in the productivity levels greatly influence a wide range of human, economic and social considerations, such as higher standard of living, rapid economic growth, improvement in balance of payments, control of inflation, culture of the nation etc.

Meaning

The productivity in a most simple way may be defined as a ratio of output to input. It is expressed as under:

$$P = \frac{O}{I} \text{ or Productivity } = \frac{\text{Output}}{\text{Input}}$$

According to **Oxford Illustrated Dictionary**, productivity is defined as "efficiency in industrial production" to be measured by some relationship of outputs to inputs.

Productivity is a relative measure as it becomes meaningful when compared with something else, by comparing itself with similar operations in the industry or measuring it over a period of time so as to compare between different time periods.

According to Encyclopaedia Britannica: "Productivity in economics is the ratio of what is produced to what is required to produce it. Usually, this ratio is in the form of an average, expressing the total output of some category of goods divided by the total input of say, labour or raw materials. In principle, any input can be used in the denominator of the productivity ratio. Thus one can speak of productivity of land, labour, capital or sub-categories of any of these factors of production."

It should be noted that, the concept of productivity is so closely attached to the labour input that the term 'productivity' is almost used as the synonym of "productivity of labour." International

Labour Organization (I.L.O.) defined productivity as, 'the ratio between the volume of output as measured by production indices and corresponding volume of labour input as measured by employment indices.' The most important reasons why labour is used as the commonest factor in measuring productivity are: (*i*) It is easy and precise to measure the units of labour inputs as compared to other inputs like materials, capital etc. The productivity can be very easily measured in terms of output per man, output per man-hour or output per unit of labour time. (*ii*) Labour input is universally applied to all types of plants, and processes and productions. (*iii*) It has become a common practice to link wages, with the productivity.

However, the consideration of the concept of productivity with reference to the labour only suffers from the following limitations:

(*i*) The output ascertained per man-hour does not measure the productive efficiency as a whole, or even the productive contribution of the labour.

(*ii*) An increase in output per man-hour may or may not be desirable. Moreover, it may or may not reduce the unit labour cost.

(*iii*) If the increase in output per man-hour is accompanied by only a proportionate increase in hourly wage rate, the production costs are more likely to increase than to remain unchanged in capital-intensive industries like iron and steel industry.

(*iv*) Output should not be considered in terms of tangible work but the aspects such as pleasure and work satisfaction which the workers derive from the work should also be considered. So also, under the input considerations, due weightage should also be given to the factors such as fatigue, effect on health, monotony, ability to enjoy the leisure time, recreation etc. The measurement of such factors is difficult and may result into subjective consideration.

The difference between the following terms will help in clarifying the concept of productivity:

Productivity and Production: The concept of productivity and that of production are totally different. Production refers to the absolute output, while productivity is a relative term wherein output is always expressed in terms of input. The production may rise without the corresponding rise in the productivity and *vice versa*. If inputs remain the same and the production of output increases, there is a rise in the level of productivity. If the output rises in greater proportion than the increase in the input, there is still a proportionate rise in the level of the productivity. But if the output rises at a slower rate than the input, there will be a fall in the productivity even though there is an increase in production on the whole.

Productivity thus refers to the efficient utilization of resources. The improvement in the level of productivity refers to the efficient utilization of various types of inputs contributing to the output.

Productivity and Cost: The concept of 'productivity' and 'cost' have gained great popularity, during and after the Second World War. Both are so closely related that they are sometimes treated as the Siamese twins. They are virtually inseparable and as a result if one of them is being referred to, the inference of the other, by implication is unavoidable. Productivity in its ultimate analysis, does not simply mean higher production divorced from cost. We always talk in terms of: How to increase productivity so as to reduce costs, or how to reduce costs so as to increase productivity.

There exists misconception about the productivity in the minds of the labour class. The workers mean that greater productivity means bigger work loads, greater efforts and increase in the profits of the owners. They also mean that it results into displacement of labour. However, these are not the correct observations. In fact, productivity integrates the objectives of the owners and workers. Greater productivity increases production through efficient utilization of inputs rather than the exploitation of workers. In principle, it emphasises that due share in the increased production and profits must go to the workers who are the key contributories to the productivity. Productivity strives to minimize the human hazards and human efforts with a view to utilizing them to those areas where they can contribute maximum to the output. At times, the techniques employed to increase the productivity may result into replacement of labour. However, the retrenchment of the workers can be minimized through effective manpower planning.

Importance of Productivity

The productivity consciousness has increased in all types of activities because it avails the following advantages:

1. It emphasises the efficient utilization of all the factors of production which are scarce universally. It attempts to eliminate the wastage of every kind.
2. It facilitates the comparison of the performance of the firm with that of its competitors or related firms, both in terms of aggregate results and in terms of major components of performance.
3. It enables the management to control the performance of the firm by identifying the comparative benefits rising out of the use of different inputs, or varying proportions of the same inputs, currently and over longer periods, as the basis for considering alternative adjustments over future periods.
4. It also provides a reliable data for certain managerial decisions such as collective bargaining regarding the wages with the trade union, effective presentation before the Government against the imposition of prospective restrictions etc.
5. At national level also the concept of productivity is useful as under:

The statistical data about the productivity assist, the Government in framing certain economic policies regarding business community, trade unions, employment, hours of work, wages, price control, protection to industries, technological developments, taxation and fiscal policies, allocation of scarce natural resources, extension of labour welfare and social extension schemes etc.

The Indices of Productivity

The productivity is expressed in terms of ratio between output and input, and it is measured in terms of the output per unit of input. There exists a well-defined relationship between output (O) and the input (I) in a particular industry. In fact, the output is a function of the input and so mathematically it can be expressed as $O = f(I)$. The output is nothing but the "value added" in various types of inputs such as labour, capital etc.

As productivity measures the output per unit of input, theoretically there are as many indices of productivity as there are inputs. However, for the purpose of simplicity, they can broadly be classified as under:

(*i*) Labour productivity;

(*ii*) Capital productivity;

(*iii*) Raw materials and fuel input productivity, and

(*iv*) Total factory productivity index.

(i) Labour Productivity: The labour productivity is obtained by dividing the gross value added by the average daily employment.

$$\text{Labour Productivity} = \frac{\text{Gross value added}}{\text{Average daily employment}} \text{ or } \frac{\text{Output}}{\text{Labour}}$$

The gross value added (*i.e.,* numerator) is obtained by subtracting raw material inputs and fuel, electricity and lubricants consumed from the ex-factory value of the output. The depreciation is not deducted. The average daily employment (*i.e.,* denominator) is obtained by the total attendance of the persons in all the shifts in all working days and dividing it by the number of days worked.

(ii) Capital Productivity: It is obtained by dividing the gross value added by the fixed capital.

$$\text{Capital Productivity} = \frac{\text{Gross value added}}{\text{Fixed capital}} \text{ or } \frac{\text{Output}}{\text{Capital}}$$

In the denominator only the fixed capital investments are considered, such as land, buildings, plant, machinery etc. The working capital is excluded because under inflationary business conditions, the components of working capital, *viz.*, inventories, receivables, cash holdings etc. are more often determined by the supply and the market expectations rather than by the purely technological pipeline requirements of the working capital.

(iii) Raw Materials and Fuel etc., Input Productivity: It is obtained by dividing the gross ex-factory value of output by the combined value of inputs like raw materials, fuel, electricity, lubricants etc.

Raw materials and fuel input productivity

$$= \frac{\text{Gross ex-factory value of output}}{\text{Combined value of raw materials, fuel etc. inputs}} \text{ or } \frac{\text{Output}}{\text{Materials}}$$

(iv) Total Factory Productivity Index: It is a ratio between output and the sum of combined inputs of labour and capital.

$$\text{Factory Productivity Index} = \frac{V_t}{W_o L_t + R_o C_t} \text{ or } \frac{\text{Goods and service produced}}{\text{All resources used}}$$

where V_t = Gross value added in year 't'

W_o = Base year wage rate

R_o = Base year return on capital

L_t & C_t = Labour and Capital inputs in year 't'

The indices of productivity focus on the measurement of output and various types of inputs and thus they help in determining which particular output-input comparisons are most relevant in evaluating the performance of various operations and units of concern to management and to interpret such findings with giving due regard to the influence of internally controllable and externally imposed factors.

Tools of Productivity

All progressive units strive to attain the higher level of productivity. The productivity is a key factor which brings success to any establishment. The level of the productivity can be increased through the following means:

(*i*) Application of the scientific management techniques.

(*ii*) Devising better methods of operating the things with the help of time, motion and method studies.

(*iii*) Implementing simplification and standardization in operations.

(*iv*) Application of the principle of division of labour and specialization.

(*v*) Effectivating the control techniques, such as production control, quality control etc.

(*vi*) Improvement in the plant-layout and material handling facilities.

(*vii*) Provision of better working conditions, plant and personnel services.

(*viii*) Provision of the effective plant maintenance services.

(*ix*) Proper selection and training of workers.

(*x*) Amicable industrial relations.

(*xi*) Provision of fair wages and industrial relations.

(*xii*) Philosophy of management.

Factors Affecting the Industrial Productivity

Productivity is a technique of extracting greater output from the inherent "input creativity" of various resources through the "conversion efficiency." The "conversion efficiency" which changes the level of productivity is largely affected by numerous factors. All these factors affect the level of productivity either individually or jointly. Some important factors are classified as under:

(1) Technological, (2) Managerial, (3) Financial, (4) Natural, (5) Sociological and (6) Government.

(1) Technological factors: The technological advancement always strives to achieve the increased production with minimum of costs and efforts, which always result into increased productivity; *e.g.*, application of mechanized power, automation etc.

(2) Managerial factors: Progressive and imaginative managerial skill always taps greater output of the human and non-human resources. Good organizational relationships, delegation of authority, true recognition of human factor, imaginative judgement results into increased productivity and contended labour force.

(3) Financial factors: The availability of financial resources enables the organization to spend money for the research and development, employment of professional executives, adoption of latest technology, provision of amenities, effective stock piling and material control. All these factors directly affect the level of the productivity. The low level of productivity and poor industrial growth of the underdeveloped countries is due to poor capital formation and constraints on the financial resources.

(4) Natural factors: The natural resources like geographical, physical and climatic conditions directly affect the level of the productivity. The effect of these factors is confined to certain type of industries and the possibility of bringing them within the control; *e.g.*, humidification in textile industry, quality, thickness and depth of the mineral resources; climatic effect on the labour efficiency etc.

(5) Sociological factors: The genetic characteristics, racial quality etc. has a great impact on the productivity of the labour. The productivity is also affected by the attitude of the workers towards the work and the approach of the management towards the working force and the provision of working conditions.

(6) Government policy: The Government policy regarding financial incentives, taxation policy, tariff policy, industrial licensing, labour laws etc. also affects the productivity; *e.g.*, provision of concessional loans for modernisation, tax incentives for the expenditures on research and development etc. help in increasing the level of productivity.

Productivity Movement in India

Productivity in industrial undertakings has assumed greater importance in recent years, especially due to increased national and international competition and limitation of resources. It encourages efficient utilization of scarce resources.

After independence Government of India intended to increase productivity consciousness in the country. So in 1952 and 1954, it invited the team of experts of International Labour Organization (I.L.O.) with a view to establishing Productivity Centre in the country. In 1957, Government of India appointed a Committee on Productivity under the Chairmanship of Dr. Vikram Sarabhai. It visited Japan to study the constitution, administration and working of Productivity Centre of Japan. The Committee submitted its report in March, 1957. On the basis of the recommendations of the Committee, the National Productivity Council (NPC) was established in India in February 1958. NPC is registered as an independent autonomous body under the Societies Registration Act, 1860.

The main objects of the NPC are:

(*i*) To promote productivity consciousness in all sectors of national economy.

(*ii*) To disseminate the knowledge of the concepts and techniques of productivity and demonstrate their value and validity in the practical application.

NPC is an autonomous national body having 75 members representing various groups as under:

(*a*) Central Government (12 members);

(*b*) Representatives of employers (12 members);

(*c*) Representatives of employees (12 members);

(*d*) Representatives of Local Productivity Councils (12 members);

(*e*) Representatives of several national, professional and technical organizations.

The administration of the NPC is done by the *Governing Body.* The Governing Body is elected from among the members of the NPC with 25 members. It is represented by five members each of Central Government, employers and employees plus representatives of *Local Productivity Councils.* It is a policy-making body and meets once in a quarter.

The Headquarter of the NPC is at New Delhi. Moreover it has established nine regional directorates and two sub-regional directorates in the important industrial centres of the country. It has also fostered the establishment of local productivity councils in the important industrial cities of the country. At present more than 50 local productivity councils are working; *e.g.,* Ahmedabad Productivity Council, Baroda Productivity Council etc. The regional directorate of the NPC looks after the Local Productivity Councils falling in its jurisdiction. Local Productivity Councils are constituted on the model as designed by the NPC. LPCs represent the State Government, employers, employees and other professional bodies.

The main activities of the NPC are as under:

(*i*) To organize training programmes directly or through Local Productivity Councils. Training is given to the participants in various courses like, work study, industrial engineering, inventory control, preventive maintenance, plant layout, fuel and heat utilization etc. It has designed more than 1,000 courses in different subjects.

(*ii*) It organizes national and regional **seminars** and **conferences**.

(*iii*) It conducts productivity surveys in different units and areas of management. This activity was introduced from 1963. It is more or less same as consultancy services. This provides general and specific investigation of organization, management, technical procedure etc. of the individual units with a view to detect differences and discover areas of improvement. NPC has conducted many such surveys.

(*iv*) It sponsors management and technical personnel for training abroad under the scheme of **technical assistance**. Under the scheme of technical assistance, NPC has sent many personnel for training at U.S.A., West Germany, U.K., France, Japan, etc. They are trained in the areas like industrial management, industrial engineering, production management, personnel management, industrial relations, quality control and allied subjects.

(*v*) It sponsors study teams for the productivity studies abroad.

(*vi*) It disseminates the informations and increases productivity consciousness through various **publications** as under:

(*a*) Productivity Journal (quarterly);

(*b*) NPC Informations (Monthly);

(*c*) Publication of reports of study teams on various subjects.

(*d*) Publication of training manuals and case examples of the impact of productivity techniques.

(*vii*) It also maintains libraries at Headquarter, regional directorates and Local Productivity Councils. It also develops audiovisual aids (films) on productivity.

(*viii*) It helps in establishing and developing Local Productivity Councils and guides and supports their activities.

(*ix*) It guides and promotes efficient utilization of fuel and heat in industry. For this purpose **Fuel Efficiency Service** was established by NPC in 1964.

(*x*) It supports the activities of **Asian Productivity Organization**. A.P.O. has its Head quarters at Tokyo. NPC assists the study teams sponsored by A.P.O. visiting India. NPC has conducted and organized many programmes in collaboration with A.P.O.

The Government of India observed the year 1982 as **"Indian Productivity Year"** for nation-wide movement on productivity consciousness.

ICOR: Incremental Capital Output Ratio

Efficiency in the use of capital is measured by the incremental capital output ratio (ICOR) which means:

How many units of capital are needed to give one unit of output? We can ask the converse of this question: What is the percentage of additional output per unit of investment?

If we could lower our ICOR of 6.5, to what it was when we began planning, we should get a growth rate of above 7 per cent, even with the present level of investment.

Productivity of capital is low for two reasons: (*i*) We have relied on capital as the principal resource. (*ii*) We have paid scant attention to land and labour. Our agricultural productivity is low. Our labour productivity is low as our industries are labour intensive, though we started with capital intensive industries. Capacity utilization is low in small sector. Large capital outlays are deployed for the backward region development. Capacity is split up amongst plants. There is more capital investment as a result.

Productivity Index

Labour productivity or 'output per hour' is recognized as one of the standard guidelines.

Labour productivity can be found out by dividing the company's total annual labour output by the total hours worked.

The labour output is the "real" annual sales. The labour input is the average number of employees multiplied by the average number of hours worked during the year.

Many companies compute their labour productivity index annually and keep a continuous record, making comparisons with other companies in their industry and with the national index.

Fig. 32.1 **An Input Output Model of Firm**

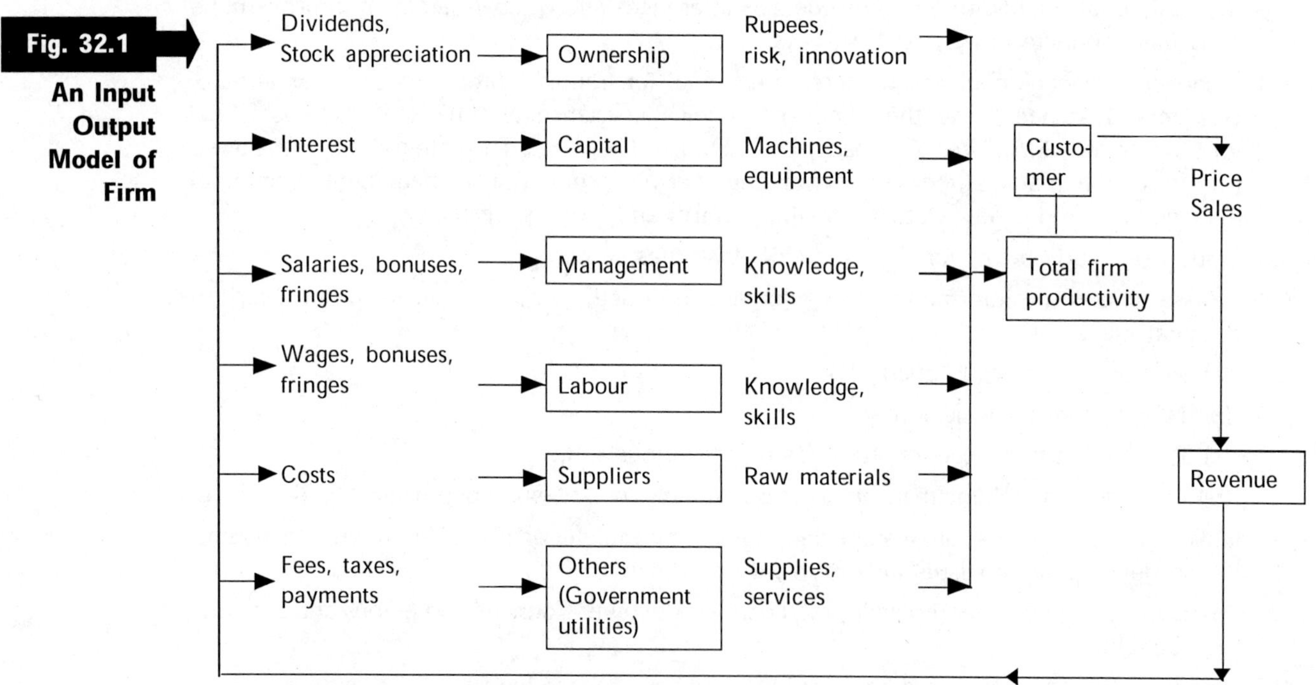

Factors Affecting Productivity

1. Nature and quality of raw materials
   — better methods to eliminate wastes and to provide efficient handling.
2. Basic nature of processes employed.
3. Amount of plant and equipment employed.
4. Efficiency of plant and equipment employed.

5. Volume, continuity and uniformity of production.
6. Utilization of manpower.

The Six Lines of Attack

The six lines of attack to improve productive efficiency are:

1. Improve basic processes by research and development 2. Provide more and improved physical means of producing	Long-term — will require capital
3. Simplify and improve the product and reduce the variety	Intermediate — may require capital
4. Improve methods of operation 5. Improve organization, planning and control 6. Increase manpower effectiveness at all levels	Short-term — will require little or no capital

Standard of Living

"Standard of living" means the degree of material well being available to a person or class or community which is necessary for sustaining and enjoying life.

Requirements for a minimum satisfactory standard of living

(1) Food (2) Clothing (3) Shelter (4) Security (5) Essential services.

The greater the amount of goods and services produced in any community, the higher its average standard of living will be.

There are two main ways of increasing the amount of goods and services produced, *viz.,* (1) To increase employment (2) to increase productivity.

We can have

(A) More and cheaper food by increasing the productivity of agriculture.

(B) More and cheaper clothing and shelter by increasing the productivity of industry.

(C) More security and essential services by increasing all productivity and earning power, leaving more from which to pay for them.

Productivity in general may be defined as the ratio of output to input.

In simple terms, productivity is the ratio of amount produced and the amount of any resources used in the course of production.

These resources are:

(1) Land (2) Material (3) Plant, Machine tools (4) The services of men.

An increase in production does not indicate an increase in productivity. If the input resources go up in direct proportion to the increase in output, the productivity will remain the same and if input increases by a greater amount than output, higher production will be achieved at the expense of a reduction in productivity.

In short, higher productivity means that more is produced with the same expenditure of resources.

(1) Labour productivity = Output per unit of time

$$= \frac{\text{Units produced}}{\text{Hours worked}}$$

(2) Capital productivity $= \dfrac{\text{Output}}{\text{Capital input}}$

(3) Material productivity $= \dfrac{\text{Output}}{\text{Material input}}$

Role of Work Study in Raising Productivity

Method study increases productivity because it

(*i*) cuts down the work content of the job by eliminating unnecessary and unproductive work,

(*ii*) develops the best method of doing job which imparts less fatigue to the operator,

(*iii*) results in more effective use of machinery, manpower and materials,

(*iv*) improves design of workplace layout,

(*v*) gives rise to wholesome working conditions,

(*vi*) modifies tools and equipment design to the advantage of operator.

Appendix

ELTON MAYO'S HAWTHORNE STUDIES

At the Hawthorne plant, the researchers used illumination to see its effect on output. There were two groups — an experimental group and a control group. The experimental group worked under varying degrees of light. The control group worked under normal illumination conditions of the plant. As the lighting power was increased, the output of the experimental group increased on expected lines. However, surprisingly the output of the control group too increased — though there was no change in the illumination conditions.

These test results prompted the researchers to probe further. It was felt that apart from the physical conditions, some behavioural considerations must be explored. The management, therefore, commissioned Elton Mayo and his associates to do further research.

Mayo and his group started the experiments with a group of women who assembled telephone relays. Mayo and his associates, for more than a year and a half, improved the working conditions of the women by introducing —

- scheduled rest periods
- company lunches
- shorter working weeks

They too uncovered astonishing results just like the illumination experiment. The researchers then decided to withdraw the benefits, and restored the previous working conditions. It was expected that this would have negative psychological impact on the women with a consequent decrease in the output. Instead, their output reached on all-time high.

The answers were not found in the physical or production aspects. They were found in the human aspects. The group was lavished upon with attention. The women got a sense of importance. They were just not isolated individuals. They formed a congenial and cohesive group. They developed feelings of affiliation, competence and achievement. All these needs remained unsatisfied at the workplace. These were now fulfilled. The women were motivated to work harder and better.

After discovering this interesting result, the researchers extended their research. They started subjecting more than 20 thousand employees to a structured interview to find out about their jobs — the working conditions, the supervisors, the company, anything that bothered them They tried to relate these to productivity. The researchers after several interview sessions came to the conclusion that the structured question-answer type interview was not useful to elicit the requisite information. They discarded the questions, and allowed the employees to speak freely. These interviews were therapeutic — they gave workers an opportunity to open up. This brought about a change in attitude. They felt that organisation values them as their suggestions were being implemented. They got a sense of importance both as individuals and as a group. They were participating in the operations of the company and the future plans. They were not just performing unchallenging, unappreciated tasks.

In these experiments, the significance of informal groups was recognised. The relationships among people do matter, not just the pay and working conditions. Whenever the informal groups identified with the management, the productivity rose. This enhanced productivity reflected workers feelings of competence — a sense of mastery over the job and work environment. Whenever the group felt that their own goals were in opposition to those of management, productivity remained at low levels or declined. This often happened when workers were closely supervised and had no significant control on job and environment.

These findings induced management to involve workers in planning, organising and controlling their own work.

The emergence of informal groups is a reaction to the society's insensitivity towards human beings who are treated as insensitive machines with only economic self-interest. Workers, therefore, treat work just as exchange of labour for money. Workers were to work mechanically and had no control on what they were doing. Work was monotonous. The esteem and self-actualisation needs were not addressed. Just the physiological and security/safety needs were being satisfied. It created tension, anxiety and frustration in people. The workers felt they were the victims of their own environment. Mayo called these feelings of helplessness *anomie.* What was observed in society was extended to industrial scene by managers who felt workers were interested in maximising their wages for the least possible work. The work was organised on this assumption of workers being a contemptible lot. Mayo called this assumption *republic hypothesis.*

In this experiment, the significance of feedback was recognised. There was feedback from management on the importance and the role of workers in the organisation. It created more productive work environment. Though feedback is not the panacea for solving interpersonal problems, its absence does make it extremely unlikely to sort out the interpersonal problems.

Introduction

In the modern business world, profitability, growth and survival are considered as the basic economic goals of any business organization. Among these, profitability is the key goal because growth and survival are incidental to the profitability. No enterprise can survive if it does not prove profitable in the long-run. Similarly, there is a case for growth only when the existing and the proposed projects seem profitable. Without undergoing into certain technical controversies about the terms "cost" and "profit", it can plainly be put that profit determination is dependent on cost. From the revenue and cost data expressed in monetary value, the profit is determined as under:

$$\text{Revenue} - \text{Cost} = \text{Profit}$$

Thus, profit is the positive difference of revenue and cost. Profit is a derived rather than a direct figure. The margin of profit can be increased by the maximisation of revenue or reduction of cost or maximisation of revenue along with the reduction of the cost.

The revenue can be maximised either by charging the higher price or by increasing the volume of sales. In the *capitalist economy,* it is not possible to charge higher price due to existence of keen market competition. Moreover, the existence of cut-throat competition makes it extremely difficult to increase the volume of sales. Similarly in a *controlled economy,* the prices are regulated by the government agencies and so it is not possible to increase the revenue economy by charging higher prices. Thus, one alternative of maximisation of profit, *viz.,* increases in revenue is curbed in capitalist as well as controlled economy. The other alternative to the goal of maximization of profit is the cost reduction. The cost reduction can be managed effectively only when the costs are clearly defined and identified and are ascertained on the basis of some units of production. Due to such specific need of the cost studies, cost accounting has evolved as an off-spring of the traditional accounting system since the First World War.

In fact, the traditional financial accounting system failed to fulfil the need of the professional management which gave way to the development of cost accounting. Cost accounting provides the data to the management required for the following key purposes:

1. Planning and policy decisions for non-routine functions.
2. Planning and controlling routine operations.
3. Valuation of inventory and determination of income.

In the modern times, the development of the science of cost accounting is sufficient enough to treat it as a separate branch of science of accountancy. The specialized cost accounting institutes are training the professional cost accountants to cater to the needs of the business world. In India, the

Institute of Cost and Works Accountants (ICWA), Kolkata is a professional body striving for preparing the professional cost accountants and development and dissemination of the science of cost accounting. Practically such institutes work in all the progressive countries of the world.

Meaning

Certain important terms are defined as under:

(1) Cost: Cost may be defined as resources sacrificed or foregone to achieve a specific objective. Cost signifies an expenditure or monetary outlay (actual or committed) to secure some benefits. When the cost from which the benefits are derived (and sometimes failed to derive any benefits) are recognised and recorded, it is known as "expired cost" or "expense", *e.g.,* payment of wages to a worker. When the cost is recorded before the sufficient benefits are derived, it is known as "deferred cost", *e.g.,* purchase of a machine with a longer operating life. The deferred cost becomes expired cost in course of time.

(2) Costing: Costing is a technique and a process of determining the cost of doing something, e.g., the cost of manufacturing an article, rendering a service or performing a function.

(3) Cost objective: The objects of costing are always activities. The article manufactured, service rendered or function performed is known as object of costing. Cost objective is defined as, "any activity for which a separate measurement of cost is desired."

(4) Cost accounting: Cost accounting is a specialised branch of accounting which deals with classification, recording, allocation and control of costs. It is a formal mechanism which scans out the accounting information into systematic cost data required by the management for various purposes. Its spread of activities ranges from the routine collection of costs for statements and budgets to the specialized cost studies required for certain specific purposes.

(5) Cost accountancy: The Institute of Cost and Works Accountants of U.K. has defined Cost Accountancy as "The application of costing and cost accounting principles, methods and techniques to the science, art and practice of cost control and the ascertainment of profitability as well as presentation of information for the purpose of managerial decision-making."

(6) Cost unit: The cost units are the bases in terms of which the costs are ascertained and expressed. The important cost units are quantity of the product, *e.g.,* number of fans, tonnes of coal, bales of cotton etc.; a group of identical products or batch; a unit of service, *e.g.,* power consumption in units, number of beds in hospital, passenger mile in transport services etc., a job or contract.

(7) Cost centre: A cost centre is a department or a part of the department, a machine or an item of a machine, a group of the persons or a person, in respect of which the costs are ascertained. The whole organization is artificially divided and sub-divided into cost centres for the purpose of cost ascertainment and cost control. Such division enables in ascertaining the precise unit cost and it also helps in locating the responsibilities for cost control. The cost centres may be production departments, service departments, person or group of persons, operating unit consisting of machines and operators or a whole process. Generally the cost accountant in consultation with the management devises the cost centres according to the need of the organization.

Elements of Cost

The cost of any product or service is the sum of various segments of the cost. Such segments are treated as elements of cost, *e.g.,* the cost of a chair prepared out of a piece of wood involves following cost elements:

Cost of raw materials (piece of wood)

Labour cost (wages paid to operator)

Overhead cost (building and other services required for manufacturing chairs)

In general, all types of manufacturing involves the following elements of cost:

(1) Direct material cost, (2) Direct labour cost, (3) Direct expenses, (4) Overhead cost: (*i*) Factory overheads, (*ii*) Administrative overheads, (*iii*) Selling and distribution overheads.

(1) Direct material cost: Direct material cost in the cost of material (may be raw material, unprocessed material fully or partly processed material, component etc.) used for the manufacture of the units. It is directly traceable to the production units. The direct material cost includes the purchase price as well as incidental expenses such as freight, insurance, loading and unloading expenses, octroi, import duties etc. The expenses incurred for the primary packing materials are also treated as direct material cost. The expenses incurred for grease and oil, nails, cleaning materials, other consumable stores etc., are of common nature which are not traceable to any point of production. So, they are treated as indirect material cost which forms a part of the overhead cost.

(2) Direct labour cost: Direct labour cost consists of wages paid to the operators directly engaged in the manufacturing of the product. It also includes the wages paid to all such workers who are solely engaged in a particular type of production, job or contract which are directly attributable to that specific cost unit, e.g., wages paid to the worker engaged in handling the product inside the department. Wages paid to the time-keeper, watchman, sweeper etc. are common nature expenses and are treated as indirect labour expenses. They are treated as indirect expenses and are treated as overhead costs.

(3) Direct expenses: Direct expenses are such expenses other than those incurred on direct material and direct labour which can be directly attributed to the cost unit. Such expenses are specially incurred on a particular job, contract or work order, *e.g.,* cost of trial runs, cost of special designs, drawings, moulds of patterns, cost of hiring special tools and equipment, consultancy for a specific job etc.

It should be noted that direct cost, direct labour cost and direct expenses are collectively known as "prime cost."

Prime cost = Direct material + Direct labour + Direct expenses (if any).

(4) Overhead costs: Overhead costs are the "indirect" costs which cannot be directly attributed to any particular cost unit (*i.e.,* a product, a job, a contract etc.). They are also simply referred as "overheads." Aforesaid direct material, direct labour and direct expenses are treated as direct cost and all expenses other than direct cost are treated as "overheads" or "indirect expenses."

Overheads are classified into the three groups: (*i*) Factory overheads, (*ii*) Administrative overheads, and (*iii*) Selling and distribution overheads.

(*i*) *Factory overheads:* Factory overheads include all indirect expenses which are incurred in connection with the manufacture of a product. They are also known as works overheads, or factory burden or works burden. Factory overheads may be fixed or variable. Fixed factory overheads are those costs which do not vary with the volume of production, *e.g.,* rent on factory building, salary of watchman, time-keeper, supervisor, expenses on labour welfare activities etc. Variable factory overheads vary directly with the volume of production. They include cost of fuel and power, cost of repair and maintenance, cost of normal idle time, cost of normal wastage and spoilage etc.

(*ii*) *Administrative overheads:* Administrative overheads include all those indirect expenses which are incurred in respect of general administration and management of an enterprise. These expenses are of common nature and are incurred for the business as a whole. They are apportioned among cost units on some appropriate basis. Like factory overheads, administrative overheads also tend to be fixed and variable. The fixed administrative overheads include rent and rates on office buildings, salaries to clerical staff, salaries to executives, salaries to managing director and directors, legal charges, audit fees etc. The variable expenses may include items like stationery, postage, telephone charges, lighting and heating expenses. They are more of a semivariable nature.

(*iii*) *Selling and distribution expenses:* Selling and distribution expenses are indirect costs which pertain to marketing the product or services. They are not strictly related to the cost of the products, jobs, contracts or services. Sometimes, selling and distribution costs are separated with a view to apportion these overheads on some accurate basis. Like other overheads, they also comprise fixed and variable elements. Some illustrations of these overheads are as under:

❖ Distribution expenses

Fixed — Rent, rates and taxes of finished goods warehouse; maintenance of delivery vans; salary of dispatch staff.

Variable — Secondary packing; Loading expenses; Carriage outward.

❖ Selling expenses

Include all such expenses which are incurred for creating and enhancing the demand for the products. Some important selling expenses are as under:

Fixed — Cost of advertising and publicity; Rent and rates of sales office; Salary to permanent sales staff; Show-room and display expenses; Market research expenses etc.

Variable — Commission to sales force; Cost of after sale services; Bad debts; Discount allowed to trade debtors.

The inter-relationship of various elements of cost along with their cumulative effect is presented in the typical cost sheet as under:

Cost Sheet		
(A)	Direct materials	. . . . .
(B)	Direct labour	. . . . .
(C)	Direct expenses	. . . . .
	PRIME COST	. . . . .
(D)	Factory overheads or expenses or operations overheads	. . . . .
	FACTORY COST	. . . . .
(E)	Administrative overheads or expenses	. . . . .
	COST OF PRODUCTION or MANUFACTURING COST	. . . . .
(F)	Selling and Distribution expenses	. . . . .
	COST OF SALES or TOTAL COST	. . . . .
(G)	Profit margin	. . . . .
	SELLING PRICE	. . . . .

Thus **Factory Cost** = Prime Cost + Factory expenses

Factory cost is also called Works Cost.

Manufacturing Cost or Cost of production is given as

Manufacturing cost = Factory cost + Administrative expenses

Total cost is given as

Total cost = Manufacturing cost + Selling and Distribution expenses.

Selling Price is given as

Selling price = Total cost + Profit

The above mentioned cost sheet is diagrammatically represented below:

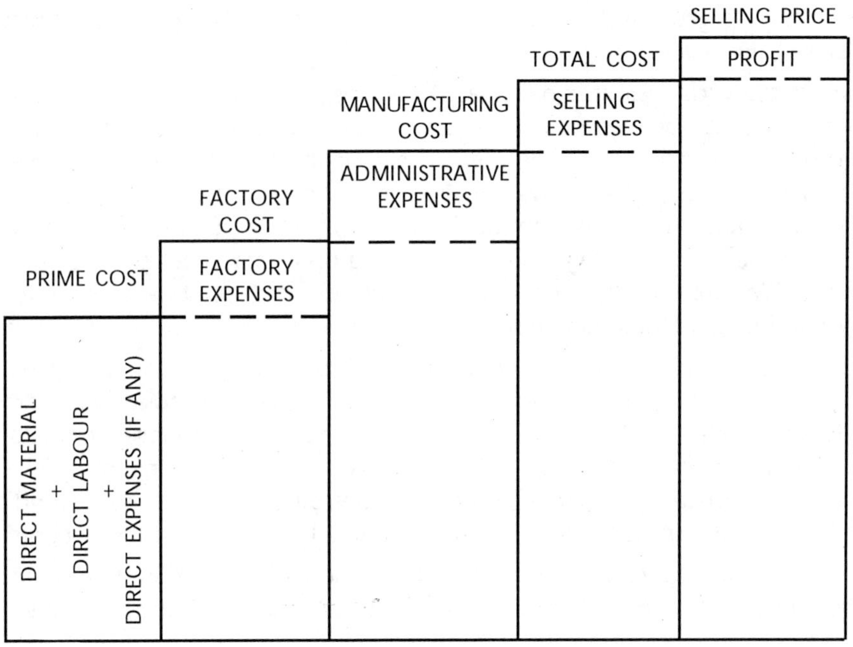

SELLING PRICE
TOTAL COST | PROFIT
MANUFACTURING COST | SELLING EXPENSES
FACTORY COST | ADMINISTRATIVE EXPENSES
PRIME COST | FACTORY EXPENSES
DIRECT MATERIAL + DIRECT LABOUR + DIRECT EXPENSES (IF ANY)

Fig. 31.1
Cost Structure

Cost Control

As noted in the earlier paragraphs the profitability of any business organization can be maximized through widening the gap between the cost and the revenue, *i.e.,* the decrease in cost and increase in revenue. There exist some constraints in increasing the revenue in the capitalist as well as controlled economies. So, the profits can be maximized mainly through cost control. Cost control is an important and clearly spelt out objective of the cost accounting system.

Cost control is attained through the guidance and regulation by the executive action on those who are responsible for the incurrence of expenditure in the course of business operations. Cost control presupposes the element-wise cost ascertainment. The measures of cost control are sensible only when one knows in advance what the cost "should be" for a particular unit of output. Similarly, cost of production is the sum of various elements of cost like direct materials, direct labour, overheads etc. The element-wise cost estimation helps the management in locating the major areas of inefficiencies and to institute preventive, corrective and at times punitive actions.

Steps in Cost Control

Cost control is an important executive function. Effective cost control can be attained successfully with the help of the following steps:

(1) *To set up the target:* The expense target should be set in advance for a specific period. This is properly known as budget. Proper budgeting should be done for all important spending centres. They should be related to the production targets. Meticulous care should be taken while fixing the targets for the variable expenses.

(2) *To measure the actuals:* The detailed information about the actual performance should be collected on a regular basis. As the actuals are to be compared with the targets, they should be measured on the same basis as the targets; *e.g.,* if the targets are set on weekly basis, the actual data should also be made available on the weekly basis. Moreover, the actual data must be made available frequently otherwise, it is likely that the time lag might make it difficult to institute any prompt corrective action.

(3) *To compare the actuals with the target:* The actuals are compared with the targets with a view to ascertain any discrepancy between the two. Such discrepancies are known as deviations or variances. It is a simple arithmetical exercise and can be presented as under:

$$V = T - A$$

Where T indicates target, A indicates actual, and V indicates variance. The variances are expressed as favourable or (+) and averse or (–).

(4) *To analyse the variances:* It is necessary to analyse the variance to find out the facts behind the figures. The discrepancy between the target and actual is due to some reasons. The variances are analysed to find out the reasons for the difference, *e.g.,* if the direct material cost per unit is ₹ 2.10 instead of the targeted ₹ 2.00, it is essential to find out whether this extra cost of 10 paise per unit is due to price fluctuation, inefficiency in purchasing, usage of wrong material, excessive usage of material with greater degree of wastage, incorrect setting up of machines producing more defectives etc. Unless the specific cause for the higher cost is identified, it will not be possible for the executive to institute any guiding or regulating action.

(5) *To locate the responsibilities for unfavourable variances:* The adverse variances arise due to either controllable or uncontrollable factors. The responsibilities for the controllable factors should be located properly and should be treated severely because they indicate lapses, omissions, negligence or carelessness, *e.g.,* in the above example, high direct material cost resulting from the excessive usage of material is a serious matter to be attended to. Uncontrollable factors are beyond the control of management. However, the strategic decision may mitigate the severity of the uncontrollable factors.

(6) *To take action for the correction of variances:* The variances should be detected as early as possible and they should be corrected immediately. This is done through the preventive and corrective action.

Cost Accounting and Managerial Decision-making

Cost accounting as a branch of accounting, has developed out of the need of management to have some precise and reliable data than can be used in shaping proper and effective decisions. Cost accounting data help in following types of managerial decisions:

(1) *Cost ascertainment:* It provides reliable cost data in respect of materials, wages and other expenses which help in ascertaining the cost of production precisely. Detailed cost data regarding materials, labour and overheads reveal actual and potential sources of cost savings and cost reduction.

(2) *Cost control:* Cost accounting provides the element-wise cost for each product, process, department, job, contract etc. Thus the profitable and unprofitable areas are identified in the organization. This information serves as a good guide to the management for either shutting down the unprofitable activities or enhancing their profitability through changes in the technology, methods, machines or such other measures. The scarce resources are utilized efficiently with the minimum of costs and wastages.

(3) *Pricing decisions:* Cost accounting provides accurate cost data which serve as a good guide in the pricing decisions. Various types of pricing policies can be evolved on the basis of the cost data, e.g., "cost plus" pricing in contract business, wherein certain agreed profit margin is added in the cost of job; special offer of reduced pricing to tap unused capacity; incorporation of the escalation clause in the contractual business etc. The cost-volume-profit analysis serves as a basis in pricing decisions.

(4) *Quotations and tenders:* Historical cost data serve as a good guide for estimating the cost of future production. Such data as adjusted to the expected changes help in preparing quotations and submitting tenders. Due to the accurate cost ascertainment, the unprofitable commitment arising of the low-tendering is eliminated. Conversely, the chances of rejection of tenders resulting from higher-tendering are minimized.

(5) *Planning and control:* Cost accounting provides the valuable data for planning, budgeting and thus controlling the costs. It is highly essential to plan and control the activities so that the desired volume of production can be secured at minimum costs. Cost accounting attempts to ascertain actual historical cost as well as the estimated costs under the given situation and constraints. The pre-determined budgeted costs serve as the standards for judging whether the actual costs are what they should have been.

(6) *Specific managerial decisions:* The cost data provide invaluable information which help in sharpening some following types of important decisions: (*i*) to make or buy the component,

(*ii*) to own or hire the fixed asset, (*iii*) to replace the existing plant before its useful life, (*iv*) to continue or shut down the whole or any part of the business.

In these recessionary times, there is a need to go beyond cost control to cost reduction. Cost control is the control of actual costs, by comparing them with pre-set standard costs identifying variances analysing reasons and taking necessary actions to bring the actuals back in line with the standards. But in a recession, meeting the standards is not enough. One has to beat the standards by significant amounts. This requires the use of many management techniques such as work study, industrial engineering and value engineering.

Nirmalya Kumar quotes Warren Buffet who said, "You only find out who is swimming naked when the tide goes out." The slowdown will require companies to tighten their belts.

Estimation of Cost Elements

We have to estimate the prime cost elements by following a proper procedure. The overheads or indirect expenses are decided by the costing or management accountancy department.

Direct material cost is obtained from the purchasing or materials management department. Drawings do help in determining the weight of the part. Irregular part is divided into sections to compute the volume. Volume multiplied by density provides the weight. Weight multiplied by cost gives material cost. The bulk losses and handling costs are taken into account to arrive at the correct material cost.

Direct labour cost is estimated by dividing the jobs into operations assigned to machines. Operation time is estimated. Total time multiplied by labour rate gives the direct labour cost. Time is broken down into:

Set up time: Time required to prepare for the operation *e.g.,* studying the drawing, do the paperwork, get the tools, install them.

Man or handling time: The time to load and unload the work taken by an operator. The time taken to manipulate tools and machines. The time to measure during each cycle.

Machining time: The time machine continues to work during each cycle of operation. The time the tools take to cut.

Tear down time: The time necessary to remove the tools from the machine and clean them and clean the machine itself. Tear down time is short lasting 10 minutes on an average. Exceptionally, it goes up to 30 minutes when there are large machines involved.

Down or lost time: The time lost by breakdowns, waiting for the tools, materials etc. It is unavoidable.

Allowances: The whole operation cycle has to account for the personal needs of the operator, time to change or resharpen the tools. It accounts for 20 per cent of the total time.

Personal allowance is for personal needs of the operator and is usually 5 per cent of the total time.

The efficiency of the worker decreases due to fatigue which accounts for 5 per cent of the normal work, and could be more depending upon the nature of the work.

The time taken to change or resharpen the tools varies from machine to machine.

There is inspection or checking allowance depending upon the specifications.

Setup time and tear down time are performed for each batch/lot.

$$\text{Set up time/piece} = \frac{\text{Setup time for the machine}}{\text{Number of pieces produced in the lot}}$$

Setup time, handling time and tear down time are estimated from past records. By conducting a time and motion study, the elements of work on each type of machine are standardised. Machining time is obtained using the formulae. The sum of machine time and handling time is called *run time* or *unit operation time.*

The total time to produce a piece is one way to estimate the direct labour cost. The total time is broken into the set up time, machining time, non-machining time and down time. The tear down time could be considered as a part of set up time. The non-machining time is represented by the man or handling time, personal needs of the operator, tool sharpening time, fatigue, inspection, cutting time etc. The man or handling time has been defined already.

Set-up Time and Economic Lot Size

The setup time is with reference to a batch/lot. The number of setups required for a product depend upon economic lot size. It is that quantity in each setup that optimises the cost. The comparison is between cost of set up, tooling, handling and carrying cost (interest, taxes, insurance, obsolescence etc.) and the cost of storage of the product.

$$N = 5\sqrt{\frac{AS}{KC}}$$

where A is the average monthly requirement of pieces

S = Set up cost per lot

C = Cost per piece

K = Carrying charge factor in percentage — 5-30 per cent.

The set up time S per lot is $S = \frac{NS}{A}$

Tool Change and Sharpening Time

Machining and tool life are the key factors that determine the frequency of tool sharpening. The formula for unit time to change tools is

$$t = \frac{T'cTk}{T}$$

where T'c = Cutting time tool is in use during operation cycle

Tk = Total time to change the tool

T = Tool life

Inspection and Checking Time

These timings are a function of the type of operation, the type of surface and the kind of measuring device. The time allowance for checking a specific dimension is given by

$$tc = \frac{Tc}{N+1}$$

where Tc = Total time needed to check this dimension for all the parts.

N = Number of parts

or the equation can be put as

$tc = F \times Tc$

where F is the frequency of checking a dimension.

If Tc is calculated for other dimensions, the sum total is taken

$Tc = tc\ (N + 1)$

Performance Factor: This factor takes cognisance of the 'downtime' based on historical studies. The considerations are for the actual time and the estimated time to do the job. As it is non-production time, it lies between 1 and 2, and is always more than 1. Performance factor ratio is denoted by R.

$$R = \frac{Ta}{Tc}$$

where Ta = actual time to do the job

Tc = estimated time to do the job

Indirect Expenses: These are also called overheads, and cannot be easily attributed to a specific operation or part. They are apportioned on the operational units such as machines, plants, etc. which are given weightages. The methods of estimating overheads are as follows:

(i) Percentage of direct labour cost: Overheads are apportioned on the basis of direct labour cost. Labour burden ratio of annual total indirect expenses to the annual direct labour cost is considered assuming that it represents the hourly overheads costs to hourly labour costs.

$$\text{Overhead rate} = \frac{\text{Total overheads in ₹ for a period}}{\text{Total direct labour in ₹ for a period}}$$

Overhead cost = Overhead rate × Direct labour/Unit

(ii) Percentage of direct labour hours: Here Overhead costs = Operation time × Overhead rate

The rate is represented by the total indirect costs applicable to a production unit for a period of time by the total number of hours of direct labour during the same period.

$$\text{Overhead rate} = \frac{\text{Total overheads for a period}}{\text{Total hours of direct labour for a period.}}$$

(iii) Machine hour method: The overhead rate is given by the total annual overhead costs chargeable to a machine by the number of hours the machine is used.

$$\text{Overhead rate} = \frac{\text{Charges applied to a machine over a period}}{\text{Number of hours of the operation of the machine during this period}}$$

(iv) Direct material method:

$$\text{Overhead rate} = \frac{\text{Total overhead expenses in ₹}}{\text{Total direct material costs in ₹}}$$

(v) Unit of production method:

$$\text{Overhead rate} = \frac{\text{Overhead expenses in ₹ over a period}}{\text{Quantity of production over a period.}}$$

(v) Space rate method: The amount of space occupied by a machine (in terms of total area in sq. mtrs.) has an obvious relationship with overhead expenses.

(vii) Combination of labour hour and machine hour method

(viii) Percentage of Prime cost

$$\text{Overhead rate} = \frac{\text{Total overheads over a period}}{\text{Prime cost over a period}}$$

Methods of Estimating

The cost of a new product can be estimated by a variety of methods.

Conference Method: A conference is held of key functionaries from materials, process engineering, design and time and method study and a cost estimate is arrived at. The data is collated by the cost/ management accountants and manufacturing cost is estimated. The method requires meticulous work sheets of costs and its success depends upon the accuracy of the data.

Delphi Method: This is a version of the conference method where experts put forward their estimates, but their identity is withheld.

Past experience: The estimate of costs of similar products in the past provides a framework to estimate costs of new products. The variations in these products and their manufacturing are adjusted.

Detailed Analysis Method: It is one of the most accurate and reliable methods of cost estimation. However, it is time consuming. The analysis pertains to the cost of raw material usage, processing involved, labour cost involved, equipment and tools required, inspection involved and packaging and transport costs.

The data required for estimation are design specifications, quantity of production, production rate, layout of the plant, drawings bill of material, operational analysis, time study, equipment and tools required, testing and inspection procedures, packaging and transport, plant area, land and buildings.

The cost estimates involves analysis of cost request, analysis of part or product, manufacturing process study, material costs, production time for each operation, labour and burden rates. All these costs are summed up to arrive at manufacturing costs. The selling price is arrived at after applying profit.

ଔଈ ଔଈ

32 COST ACCOUNTING SYSTEMS

Introduction

The basic economic objective of any business organization is the maximization of profits. If profit is defined as a positive difference between the selling price and the cost per unit, it can be concluded that profits can be maximized by any or all of the following actions:

(*i*) Reduction in the cost per unit.

(*ii*) Increase in the selling price per unit, and

(*iii*) Increase in the volume of production and sales.

The increase in the selling price (*i.e.,* above (ii) action) is not within the exclusive control of the management unless it is a monopoly firm with guaranteed (*i.e.,* elastic) demand. Even in such a situation they are subject to the imposition of price controls through the government. Similarly, the volume of production and sale (*i.e.,* above (iii) action) is a situation which is mostly dictated by the outside factors. The only effective course of action within the ambit of the management is the reduction in the cost per unit (*i.e.* above (i) situation). The reduction in the cost presupposes the ascertainment of cost per unit. The cost accounting systems help in ascertaining the cost per unit of the production. It should be noted that the cost is ascertained for each element of cost, *viz.,* the direct material cost, direct labour cost and the overheads. The aggregation of these three elements gives the cost per unit of the product.

Cost accounting is nothing but an extension of financial accounting. The cost accounting attempts to develop some meaningful information from the financial accounting records which serve as a basis for certain managerial decisions. In fact, the financial accounting system mostly attempts to cater the needs of the *external decision makers* such as shareholders, banks, financial institutions, suppliers, other creditors, government bodies etc. While the cost accounting system strives to fulfil the needs of the internal decision makers, *i.e.,* the management. Cost accounting data provide the valuable information which help in sharpening certain basic decisions like cost control, pricing policy, profit to planning, evaluation of divisional performance, break-even analysis, cost-volume-profit analysis, to continue or to shut-down, to make or buy the components etc.

Cost Accounting Systems

The cost accounting systems for the manufacturing firms provide the means whereby cost information can be developed within the framework of the financial accounting records. Basically the cost systems are classified into following two groups:

(1) Historical cost system. (2) Standard cost system.

(1) Historical cost system: The historical cost system records the actual costs as they are incurred. The ascertainment of the actual direct material cost and direct labour cost can be easily traced to any unit of the production and hence the overheads are apportioned to the production at some predetermined rate, *e.g.,*. "Job A" will be cost as under:

1. Direct material cost	₹ 10	
2. Direct labour cost	₹ 8	
3. Overheads	₹ 3	(at predetermined rate say 30% of direct material cost)
Total cost per job	₹ 21	

As this systems considers the actual cost incurred, it is also known as the actual cost system.

The historical cost system is further divided into two broad groups of manufacturing activities, *viz.,* job order production and continuous mass production.

(*i*) *Job order costing:* The job order cost system ascertains the cost of each job or order. Under the job-order type of production the size of the order and the specifications of each order differ from job to job and the production is distinguishable into different lots. Job order costing is generally applicable to the manufacturing activities such as printing shops, construction companies, machine tool manufacturing, repair-shops etc.

(*ii*) *Process costing:* The process cost system is applied to the continuous mass production. The continuous mass production is characterized by the quality production of uniform standard product. The production process continues under the given machine set-up to manufacture large volume of identical products. The products are of uniform nature and so are interchangeable in size and form which are manufactured according to the standard specifications. It is true that even in continuous production, sometimes the production varies in styles with certain changes in the specification. However, for the costing purpose it is possible to maintain the records for the total number of units of each style manufactured in each process. Process cost system is applicable to the industries like textile mills, chemical plants, foundries, paper and pulp mills, dyes and colour factories, tyre and rubber factories, canning factories, mining, oil refineries etc.

(2) Standard cost system: Under the standard cost system, unlike the historical cost, the cost is ascertained on the basis of some predetermined standards for each element of cost. The standard cost is predetermined scientifically for direct material, direct labour and overheads. The cost of the unit of production is ascertained on the basis of such present standards of each element of cost. It is true that the actual cost will differ from the standard, however the difference between the predetermined standard cost and actual cost is isolated in the accounts. Such differences are known as variances. Various types of variances are computed for each element of cost and their analysis serves as the basis for managerial decision. As specified in the above paragraphs, the main cost system can be classified as under: (1) Job order costing; (2) Process costing, and (3) Standard costing. Each system is explained in brief in the following paragraphs:

(1) Job Order Costing

The job order costing or at times referred as "job costing" is applicable to the manufacturing activities which carry on the production according to specifications of each order. This system operates under the assumption that each job is physically identified during each step of manufacturing process and so it is directly charged with the direct materials consumed by it, direct labour employed on it and the fair share in the overheads calculated on the basis of some predetermined overhead absorption rate.

The difference elements of cost for each job will be ascertained as under:

(*i*) *Direct materials:* The materials are issued to the various jobs from the storeroom upon the presentation of the authentic material requisition. The requisitioning department or the job is charged with the cost of the direct materials issued to it. All the materials issued to particular job during a specific period of time signifies the total direct material cost traceable to that particular job. The entries of the materials specifying the date, quantity and amount are recorded in the "production cost sheet" which is prepared for each job.

(*ii*) *Direct labour:* Under the job costing it is essential to keep the detailed records relating to the labour time, rate of pay and the number of the jobs on which the employee worked. This is done through the "time cards" which are maintained for each employee. The time card provides the information pertaining to the direct labour time each employee worked on a particular job. At the time of the completion of the job, the sorting of the time cards according to job number in a summarized statement provide the information about the total amount of the direct labour cost chargeable to that particular job. The total direct labour cost is entered in "the Production cost sheet" maintained for that particular job.

(*iii*) *Manufacturing overheads:* The manufacturing overheads are of common nature and hence are not directly traceable to various jobs in a precise manner. The examples are costs of service departments like power plant, storeroom, materials handling cost, rent on factory building, cost of time-keeping office, lighting, supervision, insurance, depreciation etc. So they are allocated to the various jobs on some acceptable predetermined absorption rates which are devised scientifically. The popular basis for determining the absorption rates are certain percentage of direct material cost or direct labour cost, or labour hour rate or machine hour rate etc. As the allocation of the overheads may distort the precision of cost ascertainment, it is highly desirable to devise the absorption rate based on the past experience, technical factors, changes in the situation etc., e.g., the particular job may be allocated the manufacturing overheads at 30% of the direct material cost. As ascertainment of direct materials for each job is easily traceable, the allocation of the overheads to such job on the basis of certain percentage on direct materials would not pose any problem. The relevant overheads will be recorded in the "production cost sheet" on the completion of the job. The details of the production cost sheet will provide the break-up of each element of cost and the total cost of the job on its completion. The specimen of the production cost sheet is given as under:

Fig. 32.1
Production Cost Sheet

Production Cost Sheet

Job No.: 2225 — Production Order: 221
Product: XLS Turbines — Date Begun: 4th June
Date Completed: 20th Sep.

Date	*Materials*		*Direct Labour*	*Overheads*	*Summary*	
	Quantity units	*Amount ₹*				₹
7/6	400	4,000			Materials:	10,000
10/7	500	5,000			Labour:	8,000
2/8	100	1,000			Overheads:	3,000
					Total:	₹ 21,000
20/8			8,000	3,000		
Total		10,000	8,000	3,000		

❖ Illustration:

The Bharat Engineering Company Ltd. manufactured and sold 1,000 "Asha" sewing machines in 1990. The following particulars relate to the year 1990:

Cost of materials		₹	80,000.00
Direct labour		₹	1,20,000.00
Overhead	— Fixed	₹	24,000.00
	— Variable	₹	30,000.00

The company plans to manufacture 1,200 "Asha" sewing machines in 1991. You are required to ascertain the unit cost of the "Asha" sewing machine for the year 1991 considering the following estimated changes in the cost structure:

(*i*) The price of the material will rise by 20%

(*ii*) The cost of direct labour will go up by 5%

(*iii*) The variable overheads will step up by 10%.

Solution:

	1990 (1000 Units)		***1991 (1200 Units)***	
	Total ₹	***Per Unit ₹***	***Total ₹***	***Per Unit ₹***
Cost of materials	80,000	80	1,15,200	96
Direct wages	1,20,000	120	1,51,200	126
Overheads				
Fixed	24,000	24	24,000	20
Variable	30,000	30	39,600	33
Total	2,54,000	254	3,30,000	275

The unit cost which was ₹ 254 in 1990 on the volume of production of 1,000 units will go up to ₹ 275 in 1991 even on the increased volume of production to 1,200 units. Though there is cost advantage of ₹ 4 per unit in case of absorption of fixed overheads due to increase in the volume of production, the cost of production has increased due to the rise in the cost of direct inputs. On the basis of the cost data, the company can decide its selling price by adding its profit margin on the product.

(2) Process Costing

The process costing is applied to the continuous mass manufacturing system where uniform standard units are produced on large scale. Like job costing, there is no necessity of maintaining the detailed records for each job because the total production consists of identical units. Here the unit cost is ascertained on the basis of average calculations. Under this system, all the costs for a period are accumulated by departments or other cost centres. The unit cost is ascertained dividing the number of units produced during the period by the total accumulated costs for that period. It should be noted that in the denominator, the units which are completed during the year are considered. But in reality there can arise following three types of situations:

(*i*) Uncompleted units of the prior period completed during the current period. (Such units are shown as the work-in-progress in the beginning).

(*ii*) Units started and completed during the current period.

(*iii*) Units started during the current period but remain uncompleted at the end of the current period. (Such units are shown as the work-in-progress at the end of the year).

We have noted above that for the purpose of ascertaining the cost per unit, only the completed units are considered. So the beginning work-in-progress [*i.e.*, above (*i*)] and the ending work-in-progress [*i.e.*, above (*ii*)] are converted into the equivalent completed units on the basis of their stages of completion. For such calculation, the information about the stage of completion is very important, *e.g.*, at the end of the period say 1,000 units are in process and the processing on them have been completed only up to 40%. In this case, 1000 uncompleted units will be treated as 400 completed units for the purpose of ascertaining the cost per unit.

It should be noted that if the units are lost or spoiled during the processing in any department, such loss in borne by the units complete and remained uncompleted in that department. Thus, the cost of lost units is spread over the remaining units on some equitable basis.

In case where the products are processed in more than one department, the costs of one department are transferred to the next department and the total cost and the total units are accumulated till the stage of completion.

The ascertainment of various elements of cost is made as under:

(*i*) *Direct material cost:* The cost of materials used for the period is determined by totalling the material requisitions of that period. The total represents the cost of materials consumed which are charged to the producing department as a whole rather than the individual job as in the case of job costing.

(*ii*) *Direct labour cost:* Direct labour cost is determined by the total paybill of the respective departments. Sufficient care should be taken to see that wages considered for these calculations are for those employees whose work can be specifically identified with the actual production in the respective departments.

(*iii*) *Overheads:* The overheads are apportioned to the various production departments on some scientific basis. Generally, it is the practice to apply the predetermined overhead rates in proportion to the direct material, direct labour, labour hour rate, machine hour rate, or some other reasonable basis. It maybe desirable to use different overhead rates for each producing department since the various departments may not incur overheads in the same proportion.

Illustration:

A product passes through two distinct processes — A and B. The output of process A passes directly to Process B at the end of which it is treated as finished product. From the following information, you are required to prepare the process accounts and to ascertain the cost of the finished product.

	Process A ₹	***Process B*** ₹
Raw materials (10,000 units @ ₹ 2.00)	20,000	—
Other materials	2,000	6,000
Direct labour	14,000	8,000
Manufacturing expenses	4,000	4,000
Output	9,400 units	8,300 units
Normal wastage	500 units	940 units

The normal wastages of process A and that of process B were sold for ₹ 40 and ₹ 94 respectively.

Assume that no opening or closing stock is held in process.

Solution:

'Process A' Account

	Units	₹		***Units***	₹
To raw materials	10,000	20,000	By normal wastages	500	40
To other materials	—	2,000			
To direct materials	—	14,000	By abnormal wastages	100	420
To manufacturing expenses	—	4,000	By transfer to Process B A/c	9,400	39,540
Total	10,000	40,000		10,000	40,000

N.B.: (1) The abnormal wastage in units is the balancing figure ascertained from the Input (output + normal wastages).

(2) The cost of the abnormal wastages is calculated as under:

The total cost of all inputs =	₹ 40,000
Less: Realization from normal wastages	₹ 40
	₹ 39,960

Normal production in units = Total units – Normal wastages

= 10,000 – 500 = 9,500 units

Now, cost per unit of normal production

$$= \frac{39,960}{9,500} = ₹\ 4.20 \text{ approx.}$$

∴ The value of the abnormal wastages of 100 units valued at normal cost, of ₹ 4.20 per unit will be ₹ 420.

(3) The cost of the materials transferred to Process B is calculated as under:-

(Units transferred to Process B) × (Unit cost of normal production) = 9,400 units × ₹ 4.20 = ₹ 39,540.

₹ 39,540 is nothing but the balancing value of the Process A account.

'PROCESS B' ACCOUNT

	Units	**₹**		***Units***	**₹**
To Inputs transferred from Process A	9,400	39,540	By Normal wastages	940	94
To Other materials	—	6,000	By Abnormal wastages	160	1,087
To Direct labour	—	8,000	By Finished Stock	8,300	56,359
To Manufacturing expenses	—	4,000			
Total	9,400	57,540		9,400	57,540

N.B.: (1) The abnormal wastages in units are ascertained as under:

Input – (Normal wastages + Finished Stock)

= 9,400 – (940 + 8,300) = 160

(2) The cost of the abnormal wastages is calculated on the basis of the unit cost of normal production:

Cost of normal production

= Total cost – Realisation from normal wastages

= ₹ 57,540 – ₹ 94 = ₹ 57,446

Normal production in units = Input – Normal Wastages

= 9,400 units – 940 units = 8,460 units.

$$\text{Now cost per unit of normal production} = \frac{₹\ 57,446}{8,460 \text{ units}}$$

= ₹ 6.79

∴ Cost of abnormal wastages = 160 units × ₹ 6.79

= ₹ 1,087 approx.

(3) The cost of the finished product is ascertained as under:

= (Finished stock in units) × (Unit cost of normal production)

= 8,300 units × ₹ 6.79 = ₹ 56,359

which is nothing but the balancing figure.

Hybrid Costing Systems

We have seen that the cost systems based on the historical costs are broadly classified into two — Job costing and Process costing. But in practice, the cost systems of many firms do not exactly fit in the category of either job costing or process costing. Some important variants from these two basic systems are as under:

(*i*) *Batch Costing:* In many firms like pharmaceutical, engineering etc. the production of certain uniform identical units is continued up to certain quantity which is popularly known as a batch. After the completion of a particular batch production, the machines are reset according to the specifications of another batch production. Such production system falls somewhere between the job production and continuous production. The total cost of each batch is averaged out on the basis of batch production to find out the cost per unit.

(*ii*) *Multiple Costing:* The multiple costing is applied to a production system where the finished product is obtained through the assembling and sub-assembling of the parts and components. The cost of each part or component is ascertained individually either on job costing, process costing or on some other costing method and the individual cost of each part or component is summed up to ascertain the cost of the finished products.

(*iii*) *Operating Costing:* The output of some of the manufacturing activities is a service rather than the physical product like transportation, electricity, gas, etc. The operating costing, which is also known as the service costing, is applied to describe the system which is used to ascertain the cost of performing the service by each servicing unit.

(*iv*) *Contract Costing:* The contract costing is a special type of job costing which is applied in the building and construction business. The cost is ascertained for each item of construction on its completion, *e.g.,* cost of house, dam, bridge, etc. It is also known as terminal costing.

(3) Standard Costing

The historical costing attempts to ascertain the cost per unit on the basis of the historical (*i.e.,* actual) costs those have been incurred during the manufacturing activity. It breaks up the total cost into various elements of cost like material, labour and overhead. Such break-up does provide some valuable information for the managerial decision-making, but it does not focus any light on the desirability of particular cost which is the basis for the cost control. It simply tells "how much" costs have been incurred, but speaks nothing about "how much costs should have been incurred" for the production of a particular item.

The standard costing system attempts to prescribe the standards for each element of cost which are predetermined on scientific bases. Standard cost accounting makes use of predetermined standard cost relating to each element of cost — material, labour and overhead — for each line of product manufactured or service provided. The actual costs are compared with such predetermined standard cost and the differences between the two, which are described as "variances" are found out. The variances are further analysed into favourable and unfavourable. The unfavourable variances are again analysed into controllable and uncontrollable. The favourable variances are also analysed to verify whether they are arising out of any leniency in prescribing the standards. The causes are found out and the concerned persons are informed immediately so that the appropriate action of either elimination of inefficiency or revision of standard may be taken as early as possible. It should be noted that the standard costing can be applied to any type of production activity, either job order production or continuous mass production. In fact, it is considered as a complementary system to the ordinary costing system like job costing and process costing. The crux of this system is that it sets the standards for each element of cost — material, labour and overhead and such predetermined standards are considered as the yardsticks for measuring the efficiency or otherwise of the actual performance. The most strategic part of the standard costing is the prescription of standard for each element of cost. The material cost is prescribed in terms of quantity, ideal material mix, standard price etc. The standards of the labour cost are prescribed in terms of standard time, standard mix of labour, standard efficiency, standard wage rate etc. In case of the prescription of standards for overheads, there is a possibility of the subjective opinions of the policy makers. However, attempts are made to ascertain the costs for the given stated conditions. Generally, the standards are prescribed on the basis of past performance, test runs, use of certain tested formulaes, technical estimates etc.

Variance Analysis

The variance is a difference between the standard and the actuals (*i.e.,* V = S – A). It may be positive or negative. Various types of variances are computed for each element of cost. The detailed variance analysis is beyond the scope of this book, so only following important variances are explained in brief:

(A) *Material cost variance* is divided into following two parts:

(1) Price variance. (2) Usage variance.

(B) *Labour cost variance* is divided into following two parts:

(3) Rate variance. (4) Efficiency variance.

(C) *Manufacturing overhead variance* is explained under the following head: (5) Overhead variance.

(A) *Material cost Variance:* The material cost generally consists of two parts: the price of the material multiplied by the usage of the material. So the material cost variance is sub-divided into:

1. *Price variance* is the difference between Actual Price (AP) and the Standard Price (SP) multiplied by the Actual Quantity (AQ).

   Thus, Price Variance = AQ (AP – SP)

2. *Usage variance* is a difference between the Actual Quantity (AQ) and the Standard (SQ) of the materials used, valued at Standard Price (SP).

   Thus, Usage Variance = SP (AQ – SQ).

(B) *Labour cost variance:* The labour cost is the result of the wage rate and the efficiency of the labour measured in terms of labour hours. So the labour cost variance in made-up of following two sub-variances:

3. *Rate variance* is the difference between the Actual Rate (AR) and the Standard Rate (SR) of the worker employed multiplied by the Actual Hours (AH)

   Thus, Rate Variance = AH (AR – SR).

4. *Efficiency variance* is the difference between the Actual Hours (AH) and Standard Hours (SH) valued at the Standard Rate (SR).

   Thus, Efficiency Variance = SR (AH – SH).

(C) *Manufacturing overhead variance* is difference between the actual and the standard overhead. It is ascertained under the overhead variance as under:

5. *Overhead variance* is the difference between the Actual overhead (AO) and the Standard overhead (SO).

   Thus, Overhead variance = (AO – SO).

Illustration:

Asha Engineering has developed the following standard costs for a unit of production:

Material cost 5 lbs. @ ₹ 2	₹ 10
Direct labour 6 hrs. @ ₹ 3	₹ 18
Manufacturing overhead	₹ 3
Standard cost per unit	₹ 31

During April 1981, 1000 units were manufactured. The following is the summary of the transaction which occurred during the month:

1. Purchases 6,000 lbs. of materials at a price of ₹ 2.10 per lb.
2. The time card data revealed that 8,000 hours of labour were required during the month and the average rate paid per hour was ₹ 2.75.
3. Actual manufacturing overheads for the period was ₹ 2,500.

Find out the following variances: (1) Material price variance, (2) Material usage variance, (3) Labour rate variance, (4) Labour efficiency variance, and (5) Manufacturing overhead variance.

Assume that there was no any stock of opening or closing inventories.

Solution:

1. *Material Price Variance (MPV)*
   = AQ (AP – SP)
   = 6,000 lbs. (₹ 2.10 – ₹ 2)
   = 6,000 × ₹ 0.10
   = ₹ 600 unfavourable
2. *Material Usage Variance (MUV)*
   = SP (AQ – SQ)
   = ₹ 2 (6,000 lbs – 5,000 lbs.)
   SQ is 5,000 lbs. for 1000 units or 5 lbs. per unit.
   = ₹ 2 × 1,000 lbs.
   = ₹ 2,000 unfavourable.
3. *Labour Rate Variance (LRV)*
   = AH (AR – SR)
   = 8,000 hrs. (₹ 2.75 – ₹ 3)
   = 8,000 hrs. × ₹ 0.25
   = ₹ 2,000 favourable
4. *Labour Efficiency Variance (LEV)*
   = SR (AH – SH)
   = ₹ 3 (8,000 hrs. – 6,000 hrs.)
   = (∴ SH for 1 unit is 6 hrs., so for 1,000 units, 6,000 hrs.)
   = ₹ 3 × 2,000 hrs.
   = ₹ 6,000 unfavourable
5. *Manufacturing Overhead Variance (MOV)*
   = AO – SO
   = ₹ 2,500 – ₹ 3,000
   ∴ 'SO' for one unit is ₹ 3, so for 1,000 units, ₹ 3,000
   = ₹ 500 favourable.

Reasons for the variances: Various variances are analysed by reasons for the control purposes. The possible reasons for certain importance variances are as under:

I. Reasons for material price variance

(*i*) Change in the price.

(*ii*) When quantity discount is considered while setting the standard price and it is not tapped while making the purchases.

(*iii*) Similarly, where cash discount is not tapped.

(*iv*) Excessive inward transport cost, purchasing and store-keeping expenses which are debited to purchase account.

(*v*) Purchase of materials other than standard material.

II. Reasons for material usage variance

(*i*) Poor workmanship resulting into greater wastages.

(*ii*) Purchase of defective or sub-standard materials.

(*iii*) Greater degree of rejection during inspection.

(*iv*) Use of materials other than standard material.

(*v*) Deviation from the standard material-mix.

(*vi*) Pilferage, theft etc.

III. Reasons for labour rate variance

(*i*) Changes in wage rates.

(*ii*) Employing highly or poorly paid operator than a standard operator.

(*iii*) Where standards have ignored overtime operations and a part of the production is carried on over-time basis.

IV. Reasons for labour efficiency variance

(*i*) Employment of sub-standard operator.

(*ii*) Inefficient operations caused by poor working conditions, inefficient supervision, poor machines, equipment and tools, inefficient production planning resulting into waiting and rushing.

(*iii*) Idle labour time.

V. Reasons for manufacturing overhead variance

Decrease in the production resulting into the burden of fixed overheads, which arises due to production stoppages caused by:

(*i*) Machine break-downs; (*ii*) Power failures; (*iii*) Materials stockouts; (*iv*) Labour trouble; (*v*) Accidents etc.

(4) Direct Costing

The conventional cost accounting systems like job costing, process costing and standard costing are based on the concept of full costing, *i.e.*, all the manufacturing costs were allocated among the units produced either completed or semi-processed.

Instead of such full absorption of the manufacturing costs, the technique of direct costing considers only those costs which are directly related to the production. Such direct costs vary with the volume of production. Direct costing is the American version. In Britain and other countries, this technique is described as "*marginal costing.*" It is also referred as "*incremental costing*" or "*differential costing.*"

The essential feature of the direct costing is that it divides the total manufacturing costs into two groups: (1) Variable costs or direct costs and (2) Fixed costs.

(1) *Variable costs* are those costs which directly vary with the volume of production. Such costs are direct material, direct labour, electric power, factory supplies etc. As they vary with the production, they are also termed as the "product costs." The per unit incidence of cost remains unchanged at any level of output.

(2) *Fixed costs* are those costs which remain fixed irrespective of the volume of production. Such costs are factory rent, depreciation, insurance charges, taxes on property, salary of the permanent staff etc. Such costs are committed costs. As they arise simply by effluxion of time, they are treated as "period costs."

The per unit incidence of fixed cost is inverse to the volume of production.

It should be noted that direct costing is a technique which supplements the other conventional cost accounting systems. Direct costing provides the valuable information for analysing certain important managerial decisions. The principles of direct costing are applied to the break-even analysis and "the cost-volume-profit relationships."

It is true that the profit is a key variable in the business operations however, for the purpose of planning and decision-making, it is "the contribution" rather than the profit which serves as a key factor. "The contribution" is an essential outcome of the direct costing. The contribution (C) is nothing but the difference between the sales (S) and the variable cost (V).

Thus, C = S – V

The contribution can be calculated on the unit basis or on the basis of the total sales revenue. It is termed as contribution, because its positive difference contributes towards the fixed costs. Any surplus remaining after the absorption of the fixed costs, is the profits. Where the business operations result into negative contribution, it indicates that prompt action is required. Negative contribution arises when the selling price is below the variable cost. Variable cost by its nature is a postponable cost. The negative contribution gives a signal regarding the contribution or shutting down of production operations. The concept of contribution is also very important for the multi-plant or multi-product business operations. The contribution of each product or division be ascertained on individual basis and their relative efficiency can be judged. The aggregation of the individual contribution will create "a contribution pool" which will be utilized to wipe off the fixed costs of the whole organization.

Illustration:

The ABC Ltd. is manufacturing only one Standard Product. The per unit cost data of this standard product is as under:

Direct material ₹ 12; Direct labour ₹ 7; Direct expenses ₹ 3.

During the year, the company manufactured 1,000 standard products. The entire production was sold at a price of ₹ 50 per unit. There were no opening or ending inventories. The fixed overheads of the company for the year were ₹ 15,000.

Calculate the amount of the contribution and profits for the year under review.

Solution:

			₹
Sales (1,000 units @ ₹ 50)	=		50,000
Less: Variable costs:			
Units		₹	
(*i*) Direct material (1,000 × 12)	=	12,000	
(*ii*) Direct labour (1,000 × 7)	=	7,000	
(*iii*) Direct expenses (1,000 × 3)	=	3,000	22,000
Total contribution (C = S – V)			28,000
Less: Total fixed costs			13,000
Profits			15,000

The total profits on the sale of 1,000 units is ₹ 15,000. Therefore, the profit per unit comes to ₹ 15 (₹ 15,000 ÷ 1,000 units) at the sales volume of 1,000 units. Due to the existence of the fixed element in the cost structure, the per unit profit will change along with the change in the volume of production and sales.

Introduction

These days, a great deal of importance is attached to cost-volume-profit relationship which, as its name itself implies, is an analysis of three distinct factors — cost, volume and profit. In a scheme of cost-volume-profit analysis, an attempt is made to study the general effect of the different levels of activity upon total revenue and total cost with the help of revenue-output function and cost-output function respectively. Ultimately, this technique measures profits corresponding to the different levels of output.

The study of cost-volume-profit relationship is frequently referred to as "Break-even Analysis." In the opinion of some, it is a mere misnomer, since the break-even analysis is just incidental to the cost-volume-profit analysis. Contrary to this view, others interpret the term "break-even-analysis" in two senses, narrow and broad. In its narrow sense, it refers to a system of determining that level of operations where total revenue exactly equals total expenses, *i.e.,* the level of operation where the undertaking neither earns a profit nor incurs a loss. Considered in its broad sense, break-even analysis denotes a system of analysis that can be used to determine the probable profits at any level of activity.

In a nutshell, break-even analysis is a technique that represents the relationship of costs and revenues to output.

As stated above, an understanding of the interrelationship between these three forces, and of the likely effect that any change in sales volume would generate upon the business is extremely helpful to management in a broad variety of problems involving planning and control. Through the knowledge and information obtained from the break-even analysis, complicated budgeting and profit-planning issues can be made easy and possible. Thus, the break-even analysis is a vital tool of financial planning and control. However, the accuracy of results would largely depend upon the reliability of the data and validity of the assumptions on which the technique functions.

Assumptions

Unless some conditions prevail in the undertaking, the break-even analysis cannot be expected to create significant results. Therefore, the break-even analysis to be a vital and meaningful aid in management decision-making requires the following basic assumptions:

1. The total cost can be divided into two watertight components — fixed cost and variable cost. That is to say, all costs are either perfectly variable or absolutely fixed over the entire range of volume of production.

2. Fixed cost remains constant for a specified level of activity. Although the total volume of production may vary from zero to the projected full capacity, the fixed cost does not change in amount.
3. The variable cost varies directly and proportionately with the volume of production. Thus, double the level of activity, the variable cost would be twice that before.
4. The selling price does not change with a change in the volume of sales. Since all revenue techniques assume a single price for all the units of production, it is variable with the physical volume of production. The revenue earned from the first unit and that from the last unit is equal. This gives a straight line to the total revenue curve.
5. The firm deals in only one product or in the case of multiple products, all the products have the same contribution margin (explained hereafter), or the sales mix remains unchanged.
6. There is perfect synchronization between production and sales. This assumes that everything produced is sold and so there is no change in the inventory of finished goods.

Presentation of Break-even Analysis

Usually, a break-even analysis is presented graphically, as this method of visual presentation is particularly well-suited to the need of managers to appraise the situation at a cursory glance. The graphical representation of this technique avoids the danger of unnecessary details cropping up in the representation and presents the data and information in the most lucid and simplified manner. When presented graphically, the break-even analysis takes the shape of a break-even chart (See Fig. 33.1).

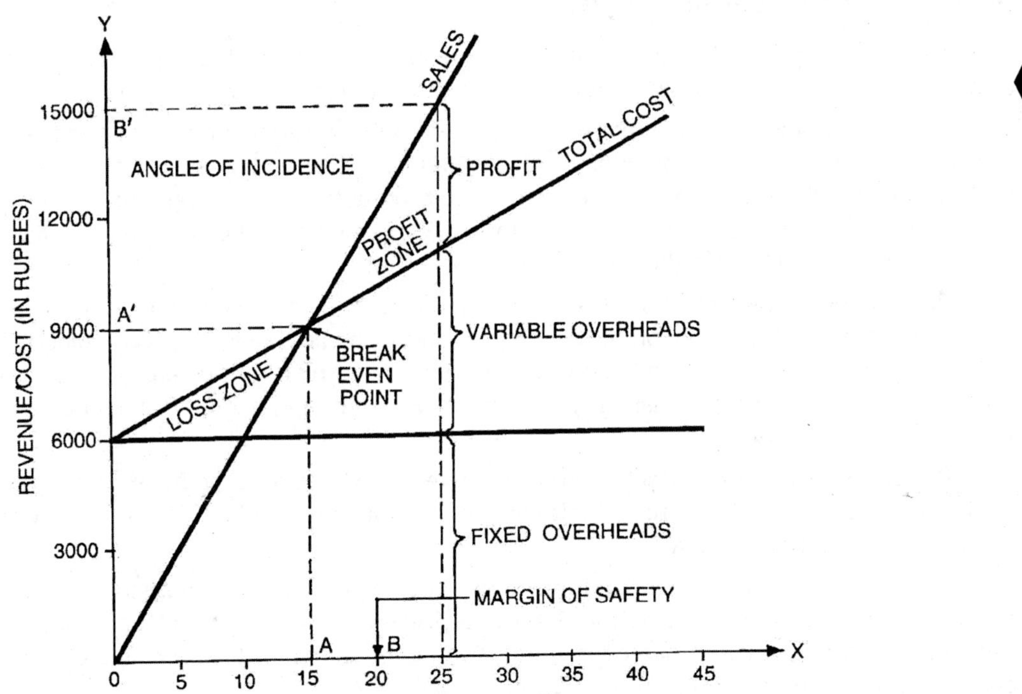

Fig. 33.1
Break-even Chart

A break-even chart shows the profitability or otherwise of an undertaking, corresponding to the different levels of activity and as a result, depicts the point at which total revenues meet total costs exactly. This point is known as the break-even point. The break-even point is the level of activity where the undertaking neither earns profits nor incurs losses. Hence, it is also known as "NO-PROFIT-NO-LOSS-POINT."

Given the following information, a break-even chart for ABC Co. Ltd. may be presented as follows:

(*i*) Fixed overheads remain constant ₹ 6,000.

(*ii*) Variable cost ₹ 200 per unit.

(*iii*) Selling price ₹ 600 per ton.

(*iv*) The tonnage produced and sold is 25 tons.

Explanation

In the graph, the following information is summarised:

1. Quantity (sold and produced) has been plotted along the horizontal (x) axis.
2. Revenue and costs have been plotted along the vertical (y) axis.
3. Fixed overheads being constant from zero to projected capacity have been shown by a parallel line to the horizontal axis (₹ 6,000).
4. The line representing variable costs is shown from the point where fixed the costs end so as to constitute the total cost curve.
5. Break-even point has been obtained at the intersection of the lines representing sales and total cost.
6. At the point of intersection perpendiculars, if drawn on vertical and horizontal axes, give the break-even point in terms of sales revenue (₹ 9,000) and quantity produced (15 tons) respectively.
7. The margin of safety is the difference between the existing level of output and the level at the break-even point (here it is 10 tons — 25 tons — 15 tons) between A and B.

Mechanics of Break-even Analysis

Here it is required that certain items frequently used in this technique be introduced and the calculations of break-even point made with the derivation of various formulas.

1. Break-even Point: The break-even point is at which the total cost line and the sales line (*i.e.,* total revenue line) intersect one another on the graph. The spread to the right of the point shows the profit potential while to the left represents the loss potential. This is the level of activity where the undertaking neither earns profits nor incurs losses. Since total revenue and total cost are exactly equal, the break-even point is also the "no-profit-no-loss point."

2. Angle of Incidence: This is the angle at which the sales line cuts the total cost line. The larger the angle, the higher the rate of profit would be. A narrow angle shows that even though fixed overheads are recovered, the profit accrued shows a low rate of return. This indicates a larger part of variable costs in total cost. In all, the management aims at widening the angle of incidence and improve the rate of the profitability.

3. Contribution Margin: Contribution margin refers to the difference between the sales and variable overheads. If both the items are on unit basis, it is Unit Contribution Margin, otherwise it is known as Gross Contribution Margin.

The contribution margin is the fund or pool out of which fixed overheads are to be met and if that leaves any sum, it would be the Break-even Analysis 141 profit. So the contribution margin is the excess of the unit sales price over the unit variable overheads that contributes to the recovery of fixed overheads and share of profit.

Then, again, profits realised on one individual product cannot be compared with that of other products since apportionment of fixed overheads is not possible for each product. A comparison of the relative contribution margin of each product serves the purpose. Higher the contribution margin in percentage, the product would be more profitable. This concept helps to determine the profitability of different products or departments in an undertaking and arriving at the best possible sales mix.

Contribution Margin (unit) = Unit Sales Price – Unit Variable Costs

Gross Contribution Margin = Total Revenue – Total Variable Costs

4. Margin of Safety: This represents the amount by which the volume of sales exceeds one at break-even point. The margin of safety in a way connotes the extent to which the undertaking can afford to lose the sales or lower the prices and yet remain in business. So it is very important that a reasonable level of margin of safety should be there, otherwise a reduced level of activity may prove disastrous and even endanger the very existence of business.

A high margin of safety usually connotes a low level of fixed overheads. So firms with such a situation are invulnerable in times of reduced level of activities, especially in a recessionary period. On the other hand, a low margin of safety is not sufficient to absorb even fixed overheads in most recessions. This puts the firms out of business.

Algebraically, the margin of safety is,

$$\frac{\text{Sales} - \text{Sales at BEP}}{\text{Sales}} \times 100$$

or $$\frac{\text{Operating Profit}}{\text{Gross Contribution Margin}} \times 100$$

Here, Operating profit = Total Revenue – Total Cost

= Total Revenue – Variable Cost – Fixed Cost

= Gross Contribution Margin – Fixed Cost

$$\therefore \text{Margin of safety} = \frac{\text{Gross Contribution Margin} - \text{FC}}{\text{Gross Contribution Margin}}$$

5. P/V Ratio: Profit Volume Ratio (P/V Ratio) measures the profitability in relation to sales. So it is a measure to compare profitability of different products. Higher the P/V ratio, the high yielding is the product.

$$\text{P/V Ratio} = \frac{\text{Contribution (p.u.)}}{\text{Sales (p.u.)}} \times 100$$

Algebraic Representation of BEA

Basically, there are two approaches to the break-even analysis:

(1) Equation technique and (2) Contribution margin technique.

(1) Equation Technique: A simple equation that represents the relationship of income statement is considered here. For any break-even or profit estimate situation, the equation reads:

Sales = Variable Overheads + Fixed Overheads + Profits

(2) Contribution Margin Technique: Here, with the help of the concept of contribution margin, the break-even point is calculated. The unit contribution is divided into total fixed expenses to arrive at the number of units to be sold to break-even. So the equation reads:

Unit Sales Price – Unit Variable Overheads = Unit Contribution.

With this, we compute the break-even point as under:

1. $$\text{BEP (units)} = \frac{\text{Fixed Overheads}}{\text{Per Unit Contribution}}$$

2. $$\text{BEP (₹)} = \frac{\text{Fixed Overheads}}{\text{Per Unit Contribution}} \times \text{Per Unit Sales Price}$$

   Or = BEP (Units) × Sales Price (p.u.)

3. $$\text{BEP (₹)} = \frac{\text{Fixed Overheads} \times \text{Total Revenue}}{\text{Gross Contribution Margin}}$$

(4) $$\text{BEP (₹)} = \frac{\text{Fixed Overheads}}{\text{P/V Ratio (\%)}}$$

Illustration:

XYZ Ltd., plans to sell a toy motor at the Gujarat Diwali Fair. The motors are purchased at ₹ 5/- each on the express condition that all unsold motors shall be returned. The booth rent at the fair is ₹ 2,000/-, payable in advance. The motors will be sold at A 9/- each. Determine the number of motors which must be sold:

(*a*) to break-even (*b*) to earn ₹ 400/- as profits.

We shall solve it with both the aforesaid methods.

(1) Equation Technique: Here,

Sales = Variable Overheads + Fixed Overheads + Profits

In the case (*a*):

Profits = 0 (since it is BEP)

Variable overheads = ₹ 5/- p. a.

Fixed overheads = ₹ 2,000/-

Sales price = ₹ 9/- p.u.

Suppose the number of motors sold is A. Then,

$$9A = 5A + 2,000 + 0$$
$$\therefore 4A = ₹\ 2,000$$
$$\therefore A = 500 \text{ (units)}$$

In the case (*b*):

Apart from other information, profit is expected to the tune of ₹ 400/-. Then,

$$9A = 5A + 2,000 + 400$$
$$\therefore 9A - 5A = ₹\ 2,400$$
$$\therefore 4A = ₹\ 2,400$$
$$\therefore A = 600 \text{ (units)}$$

(2) Contribution Marginal Technique: Here, in the case (a):

$$\text{BEP (units)} = \frac{\text{Fixed Overhead}}{\text{Unit Contribution Margin}}$$

$$= \frac{\text{Fixed Overhead}}{\text{Sales Price (p.u.)} - \text{Variable Overhead (p.u.)}}$$

$$= \frac{2,000}{9-5} = \frac{2,400}{4}$$

$$\therefore \text{BEP (units)} = 500 \text{ units}$$
$$\text{and BEP (A)} = \text{BEP (units)} \times \text{Sales Price (p.u.)}$$
$$= 500 \times ₹\ 5 = ₹\ 2,500$$

In the case (b): To earn ₹ 400/- as yield, we must obtain ₹ 400/- over and above the fixed overheads. So now,

$$\text{BEP (units)} = \frac{\text{Fixed Overhead} + \text{Expected Profit}}{\text{Per Unit Contribution}}$$

$$= \frac{2,000 + 400}{9-5}$$

$$= \frac{2,400}{4}$$

$$\therefore \text{BEP (units)} = 600 \text{ units}$$
$$\text{and BEP (₹)} = \text{BEP (units)} \times \text{Sales Price (p.u.)}$$
$$= 600 \times ₹\ 5$$
$$= ₹\ 3,000.$$

In case XYZ Ltd., sells 750 motors in the fair, find (I) Margin of Safety. (2) Profits at 750 units.

(1) Margin of Safety $= \dfrac{\text{Sales} - \text{Sales at BEP}}{\text{Sales}} \times 100$

$$= \frac{750 - 500}{750} \times 100$$

$$= \frac{250 \times 100}{750} = 33.33\%$$

OR

$$\text{Margin of Safety} = \frac{\text{Operating Profits} \times 100}{\text{Gross Contribution Margin}}$$

$$= \frac{(\text{Gross Contribution Margin} - \text{FC}) \times 100}{\text{Gross Contribution Margin}}$$

Now, here, at the level of 750 units:

Gross Contribution Margin

= Total Revenue — Total Variable Overheads
= (750 × 9) – (750 × 5)
= ₹ (6,750 – 3,750) = ₹ 3,000

Now, margin of safety

$$= \frac{(3{,}000 - 2{,}000) \times 100}{3{,}000}$$

$$= \frac{1{,}000 \times 100}{3{,}000} = 33.33\%$$

and (2) to calculate profits at a sale of 750 motors,

Profit = Total Revenue – Total Cost
= Total Revenue – Total Variable Cost – Total Fixed Cost
= Gross Contribution Margin – Total Fixed Cost
= ₹ 3,000 – ₹ 2,000 = ₹ 1,000.

Practical Applications of BEA

To the management, the utility of break-even analysis lies in the fact that it presents a microscopic view of the profit structure of an undertaking. The break-even analysis not only highlights the areas of economic strength and weakness in a business organization but also focuses upon certain averages which can be obtained to enhance profitability. The break-even analysis has a dual role to play — one as a tool of financial planning and the second as an instrument of control. In the light of these two facts, the managerial uses can be as follows:

(1) Safety Margin: The break-even chart helps the management to know at a glance the profits at different levels of activity. Besides, the management considers the margin of safety associated with it. Here, the safety margin refers to the extent to which an undertaking can afford to lose its sales, before it starts incurring losses, with the help of the formula.

$$(\text{Safety Margin}) = \frac{(\text{Sales} - \text{Sales at BEP})}{\text{Sales}} \times 100$$

In an example, sale is 10,000 units and sale at BEP is 7,000 units,

$$\text{Safety Margin} = \frac{(10{,}000-7{,}000)}{10{,}000} \times 100$$

$$= \frac{3{,}000 \times 100}{10{,}000} = 30\%$$

But if in the next year, sales decline to 8,000 units

$$\text{Safety Margin} = \frac{(8{,}000-7{,}000)}{8{,}000} \times 100$$

$$= \frac{1{,}000 \times 100}{8{,}000} = 12.5\%$$

This means that the firm's resistance capacity to avoid losses has become poorer.

(2) Volume Needed to Attain Target Profit: Sometimes, the firm may aim to generate a particular amount of profit in a specified period. For this purpose, with the help of contribution margin concept under the break-even analysis, it is very convenient to calculate the volume of sales necessary to achieve the targeted profit. For instance, a firm furnishes the following information. Let us calculate the target sales for ₹ 4,000 profit.

Fixed overheads	₹	20,000
Selling price (p.u.)	₹	100
Variable overheads	₹	60

Then,

$$\text{Target sale volume} = \frac{\text{Fixed overhead} + \text{Target profits}}{\text{Contribution margin (p.u.)}}$$

$$= \frac{20{,}000 + 4{,}000}{40}$$

$$= \frac{24{,}000}{40} = 600 \text{ units.}$$

So the undertaking can plan its efforts to ascertain the least sales to accomplish the target profit of ₹ 4,000.

(3) Submitting undue Quotations and Accepting Special Orders — Dumping in Foreign Markets, etc.: A decision in each of the aforesaid situations basically depends upon the contribution theory of the analysis. The situation arises only when the firm has sufficient excess capacity, *i.e.*, if the decision is taken, the firm need not go in for commissioning any new plant or machinery. So fixed overheads for additional orders undertaken is zero.

For instance, ABC Ltd., undertakes a special order for 5,000 units at ₹ 10 each. The product costs ₹ 9.50 to ABC Ltd. So the contribution (Gross) is 5,000 (0.50) = ₹ 2,500. So the job is accepted.

(4) Reduction in sales price in competition and/or Depression or Additional sales volume required to maintain a particular level of profit: In this case, on account of the adverse market situation, it is imperative that prices must be reduced. If the firm wishes to maintain the level of profit as before with the use of formula as,

$$\text{Expected Sales Volume} = \frac{\text{Fixed Overhead} + \text{Target Profit}}{\text{Contribution (p.u.)}}$$

can be derived more easily and likewise the firm can employ its strategies. For instance, ABC Ltd., furnishes the following information:

Fixed cost ₹ 20,000

Variable cost ₹ 6

Selling price ₹ 10 units sold 15,000 as,

Selling price (reduced) ₹ 8

In this case, originally, the firm had a total profit of ₹ 40,000 as,

Profit = Gross 'C' Margin — Fixed Overhead

= 15,000(4) — 20,000

= ₹ 40,000.

Now, with the reduced prices, it is required to attain the sales volume of 30,000 units to attain ₹ 40,000 as profits.

$$\text{Expected volumes of sales} = \frac{\text{FC + Targeted Profits}}{\text{Contribution (p.u.)}}$$

$$= \frac{20{,}000 + 40{,}000}{8 - 6}$$

$$= \frac{60{,}000}{2} = 30{,}000 \text{ units}$$

So with the reduced price of ₹ 8, the firm must make efforts to sell 15,000 more units.

(5) To Decide — Continue or Shut Down: In the case of serious marketing constraints, the firm may be confronted with the problem whether to continue or shut down a particular unit of production for the time being with the help of break-even analysis. It can be easily saved.

If the contribution from the product is positive, that is, contribution of the product will contribute something to cover the fixed overheads, then it would be in business prudence to continue the unit rather than shut it down. Since the contribution is positive (+ve), it reduces the burden of fixed overheads to the extent of contribution. To take an illustration:

In ABC Co. the department D has following results:

Fixed cost ₹ 10,000

Selling price ₹ 5.00 (p.u.)

Variable cost ₹ 4.80 (p.u.)

Units sold 1,000 units

In such a situation, the contribution is ₹ 0.20 p.u. So, gross contribution comes to ₹ 200. If department D is shut down temporarily, interest on ₹ 10,000 must be borne by company. But if continued, the company would have to bear ₹ 9,800.

(6) To Decide— Make or Buy: The question most often confronted by industries, especially the assembly industry, is whether to make the particular component or part within the factory itself or purchase it from outside sources. This can be solved judicially with the help of break-even analysis.

There can be two situations:

(*a*) The firm has sufficient excess capacity to procure the component from within, so no fixed overheads are to be created.

(*b*) Secondly, the firm has to undertake installation of new machines and equipment necessary for the purpose of making the particular components at home.

In the case of (*a*), the contribution theory helps a lot. If the prices at which it is available from the market are higher than the cost of making at home, then one must go in for making it.

A part can be procured from inside at ₹ 10 and can be made at home for ₹ 8. Since no fixed overhead is involved, the contribution is positive and the decision is to make it.

In other cases, the component must be procured from outside dealers.

In the case of (*b*), it should be seen whether the volume required meets with the volume at break-even point or not. If the requirement exceeds the volume to break-even, it would be advisable to make the component within the factory, otherwise it should be bought from outside agencies.

For instance, the firm requires 5,000 units of component A.

Fixed cost	₹ 8,000
Variable cost	₹ 10 (p.u.)
Selling price (offered by outside agencies)	₹ 12 (p.u.)

Then,

$$\text{BEP (units)} = \frac{\text{FC}}{\text{Purchase Price} - \text{Variable Cost}}$$

$$= \frac{8{,}000}{12-10} = 4{,}000 \text{ units.}$$

Here, to undertake the production of component A at the factory would be beneficial. However, one must note that other factors like secrecy of design, desire to exert control over production, technical competence, etc., have a significant bearing upon the decision.

(7) To Decide — Add or Drop: The issue whether to incorporate a particular item in the sales unit in place of some other item can be well settled with the use of break-even analysis.

Here, for the given items of products we are to get the combined (total) contribution ratio for the different mix. The mix that yields a higher total contribution ratio is to be selected.

(a) Here are the proposals before ABC Ltd. — advise it.

	Particulars	***Price***	***Variable Overheads***	***Percentage of Sales***
(*a*)	A	60	40	30
	B	100	60	20
	C	200	120	50
(*b*)	A	60	40	50
	D	160	60	10
	C	200	120	40

For these two proposals, the contribution ratio is as follows:

$$\text{Contribution Ratio (P/V Ratio)} = \frac{\text{Price} - \text{Variable Cost}}{\text{Price}} \times \text{Percentage of Sales Contribution Ratio}$$

For proposal (*a*):

$$A - \frac{60-40}{60} \times 30 = 10\%$$

$$B - \frac{100-60}{100} \times 20 = 8\%$$

$$C - \frac{200-120}{200} \times 50 = 20\%$$

Total Contribution Ratio = 38%

For Proposal (*b*):

$$A - \frac{60-40}{60} \times 50 = 16.66\%$$

$$D - \frac{160-60}{160} \times 10 = 6.25\%$$

$$C - \frac{200-120}{200} = 40 = 16.00\%$$

Total Contribution Ratio 38.91%

So, here proposal B carries a higher total contribution ratio, so from proposal (*a*), drop the product B and add D. That would give better results.

(b) To Choose Promotion Mix

For firms with multiple products, the break-even analysis guides to select the combination of the products and their proportionate share. The one that gives a higher P/V ratio is the best one considering cost-benefit factors:

For instance:

Products	***Sales price*** ₹	***Variable cost*** ₹	***Mix Weightage***
A	10	2	4/1
B	20	12	1/4

For weightage (4 : 1) The P/V ratio is,

P/V ratio	***Weight***	***Total P/V ratio***
A $-\frac{10-2}{10} \times 100 = 80\%$	4	320%
B $-\frac{20-12}{20} \times 100 = 40\%$	1	40%
		$\frac{360\%}{5} = 72\%$
For weightage (1:4) the situation is		
A $-\frac{10-2}{10} \times 100 = 80\%$	1	80%
B $-\frac{20-12}{20}$	4	160%
		$\frac{240\%}{5} = 48\%$

So have the first mix, A : B 4 : 1 is the best yielding, and so is accepted.

Likewise, the production mix can be obtained and production planning can be done.

(c) To Decide Expansion

When the firm feels its present capacity is not meeting the demand the expansion programme can be undertaken. But the manager must know the situation with all the care to avoid further difficulties in business. The business may have to suffer afterwards, because the margin of safety with any expansion programme gets reduced. So the estimate of demand must be made and if there is to be sufficient demand to meet the break-even point after the expansion, expansion can be undertaken. Otherwise the firm should resort to over-timing, double-shifts or even sub-contracting to make the best of the opportunity.

To take an example.

The firm has the capacity for	500 units
Likely demand	700 units
Total fixed cost	₹ 2,000
Total fixed cost (after expansion)	₹ 2,500
Variable cost (p.u.)	₹ 1.50
Selling price (p.u.)	₹ 5.50

The connotation in brackets shows situation after expansion programme.

As the Fig. 33.2 shows, the break-even point after expansion programme goes up to 625 units, and correspondingly, the demand is probably 700 units. If expansion programme is undertaken, it would be the best of the decisions to exploit the opportunity.

Improving Profit Performance: BEA and Leverage Effect

We have so far seen the break-even analysis is a major tool in profit planning. There are four ways in which profit performance of a business can be improved:

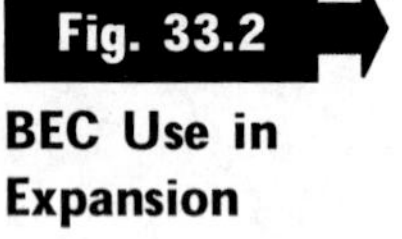

Fig. 33.2

BEC Use in Expansion

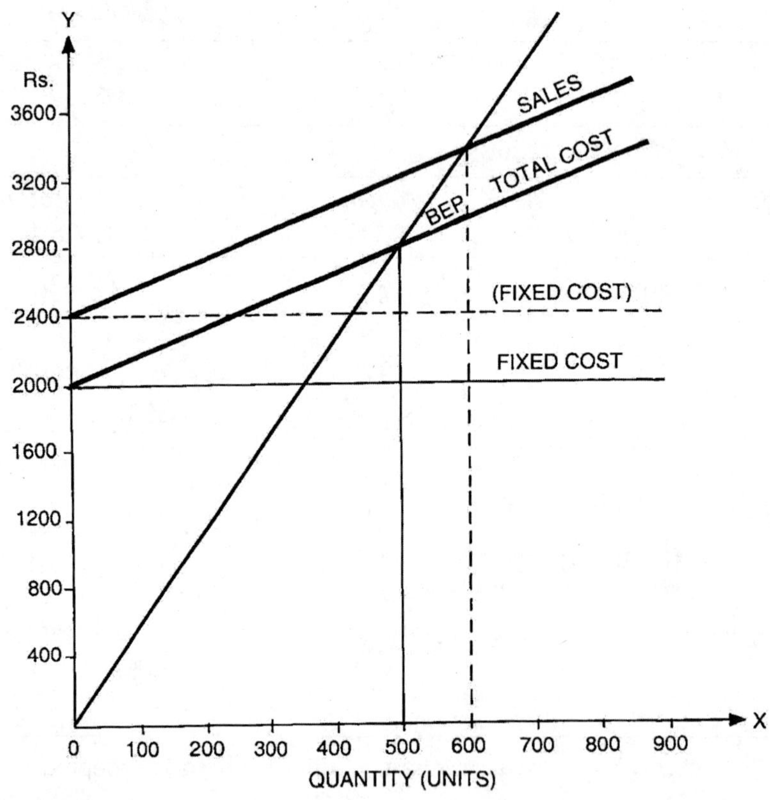

(1) Increasing volume of sales.

(2) Increasing selling price.

(3) Reducing the variable expenses.

(4) Reducing the fixed cost.

1. Increasing Volume of Sales

If the volume of sales is increased within the projected production capacity, such promotional companies are likely to enhance the rate of profitability since only variable overheads are to be incurred for the additional production. This improves the P/V ratio and ultimately the profit uptake, as shown in Fig. 33.3.

In Fig. 33.3, the firm operates at 4,000 units capacity and if the sales volume is increased to 5,000 units, it offers additional profits as shown by the shaded area. Here, however, the break-even point remains unaffected, because since the level of activity has increased, the margin of safety also has increased.

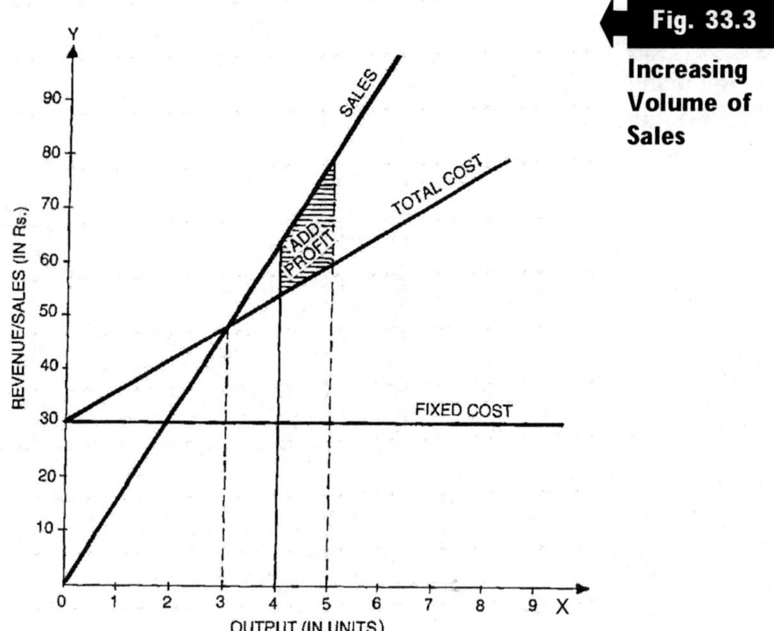

Fig. 33.3 **Increasing Volume of Sales**

2. Increasing Selling Price

Keeping the other factors constant, if the selling price is increased it gives an increased, contribution per unit to the extent the price has increased. Moreover, as a result, the angle of incidence that depict higher P/V ratio also widens and ultimately better profitability. The curve is seen in Fig. 33.4.

The break-even point as shown moves to its left (from B to B′) and makes the addition of profit to the extent as shown in the figure.

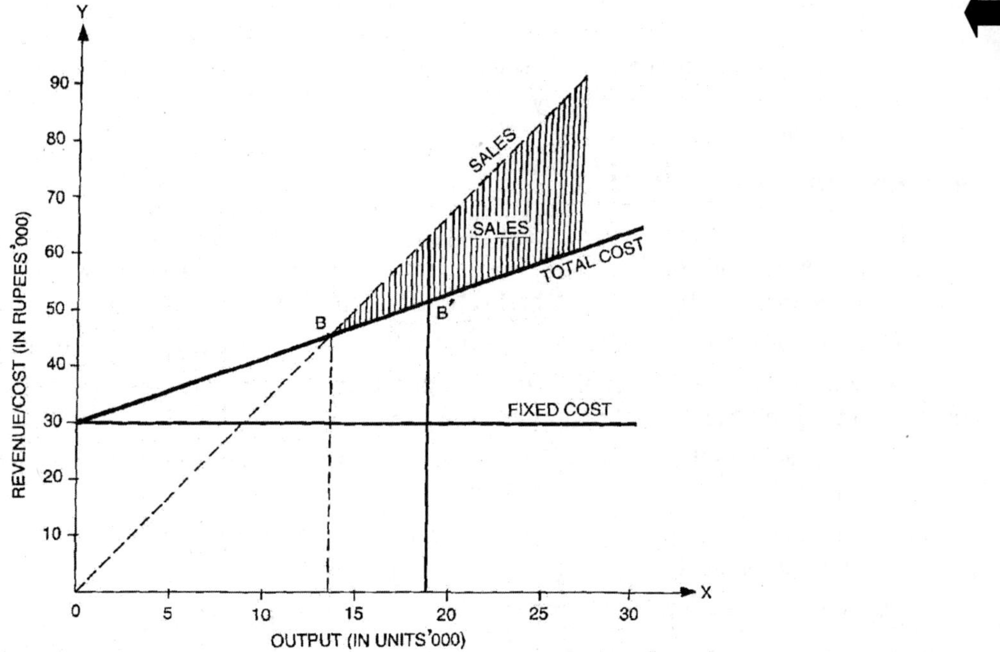

Fig. 33.4 **Increasing Selling Price**

3. Reducing the Variable Cost

Here, the concentration is upon the major constituents of total cost. Profits can be enhanced by lowering the cost. Here, we take only one ingredient of it — total variable cost with the reduced variable cost. The total cost curve becomes a flatter one. This has the following implications.

(1) The reduced variable cost makes the total cost curve flatter. On account of this, the break-even point is reduced to a lower level.

(2) The reduced level of break-even point increases the margin of safety.

(3) The flatter total cost curve widens the angle of incidence and thereby profitability per unit is increased, *i.e.*, P/V ratio is improved. The same is presented in Fig. 33.5.

Fig. 33.5 Reducing the Variable Cost

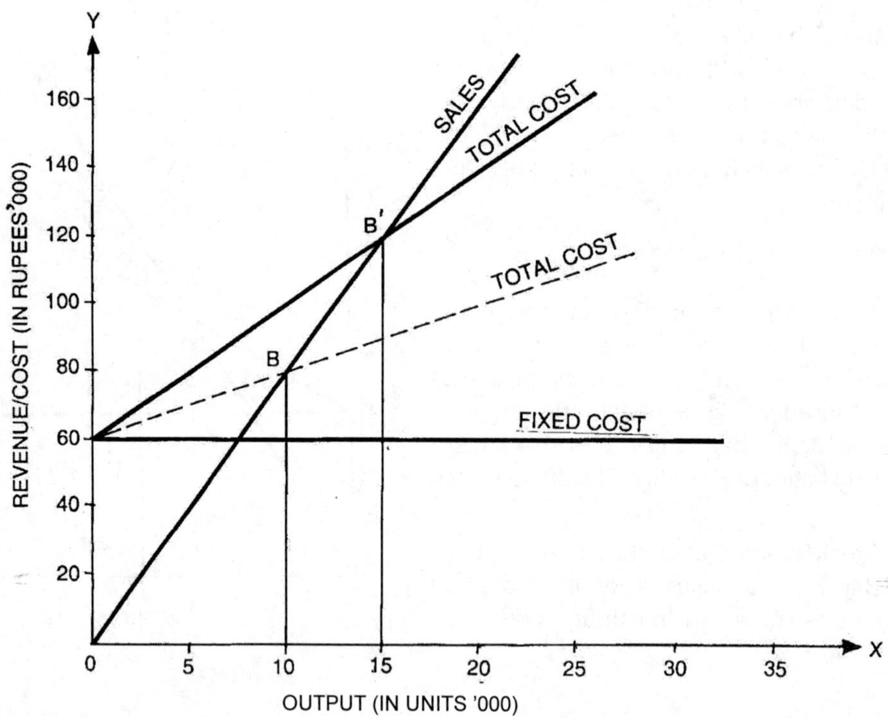

In the case of the above three instances, a change in any of the three variables — sales, selling price or variable cost — is followed by a greater change in the profits. This is called the leverage effect of break-even analysis.

4. Reducing the Fixed Costs

Fixed costs, as the other constituent of total cost, if reduced can also contribute significantly to the betterment of profit results. Here, however, no leverage effect is witnessed, since the change in fixed costs is followed by exactly a proportionate change in profits.

This is because fixed costs remain constant for any level of activity, from zero to projected capacity.

A reduction in fixed costs enhances the profits to the tune of the reduction of fixed costs. The graph showing this has the following implications:

1. The slope of the total cost curve remains the same and so the angle of incidence is unaffected in connection with this decision.
2. In relation to the reduced fixed costs, the break-even point is lowered that avails of a highest margin of safety.

This can be seen from Fig. 33.6.

Limitations of Break-even Analysis

We may now mention here certain important limitations which ought to be kept in mind while using break-even analysis.

1. In practice, all the means of costs are not always either fixed costs or variable costs. There are some semi-variable overheads. Moreover, in the long-run, all costs are variable. So the break-even analysis holds true only for short-run requirements.
2. A straight line total revenue curve presumes that any quantity can be sold at that one price. To be realistic, there is always a quantity ideal, especially for bulk orders.
3. The area included in the break-even analysis should be pointed. If too many products, too many departments or too many plants are lumped together and graphed in a single break-even chart, both good and bad performance can conveniently be buried in the total picture.

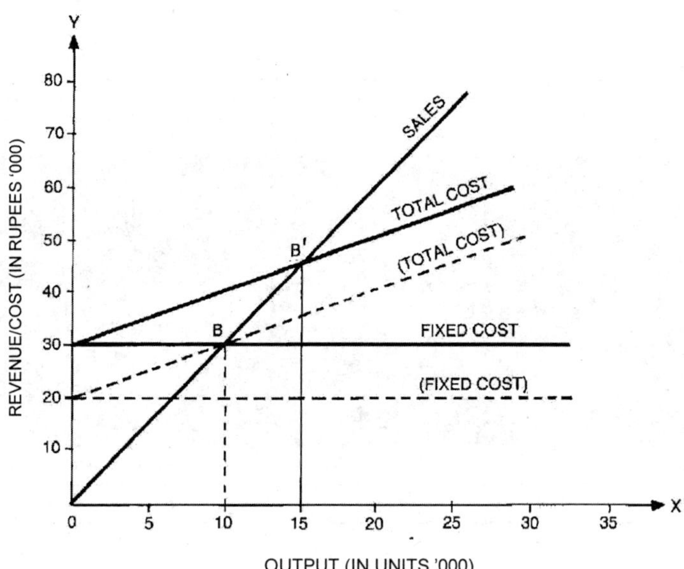

Fig. 33.6
Reducing the Fixed Cost

So firms with many products with different contribution (P/V) ratios cannot avail of the application of break-even analysis.

4. The break-even analysis is based upon accounting data. As it happens, it may suffer from various limitations of such data. The inter-firm management policy, arbitrary depreciation estimated and an appropriate allocation of fixed overheads, etc., in accounting area distorts the data, and thereby the comparative value of this technique.
5. Break-even analysis assumes that profits are a function of output ignoring the patent fact that they are also caused by other factors such as technological changes, improved management, changes in the scale of the fixed factors of production and so on.

On the whole, if we look simultaneously to the limitations of the break-even analysis and the assumptions underlying the analysis, it is apparent that the basic assumptions upon which the break-even analysis operates itself are the limitations of the analysis. However, the analysis is meaningful and a vital aid in management decision-making.

ꕥ ꕥ

34

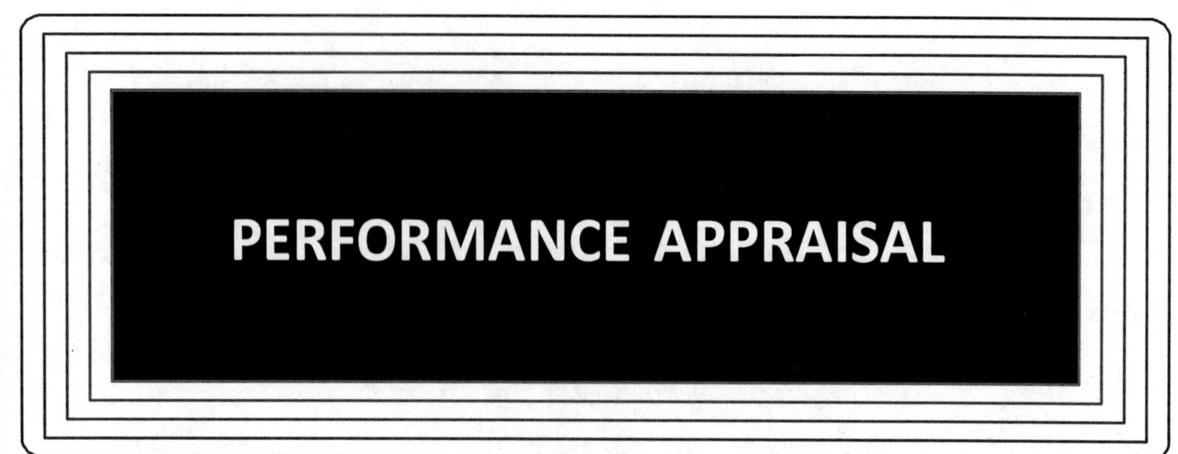

PERFORMANCE APPRAISAL

Performance Appraisal

In almost every company, every executive, supervisor and workers are subjected to periodic appraisal of their performance. This is particularly important if the enterprise's training and development objectives are to be realised, if the enterprise wants to make best use of its manpower available and if the organization wants to have a scientific and rational compensation system. An effective performance appraisal system brings rationality in management. If it wants to maximise its effectiveness then the enterprise must have tool by which it can discriminate between an effective manager and a not-so-effective manager. Today, appraisal is not something of a choice left to the wishes of the corporate bosses, nor it is a privilege to be enjoyed by few business conglomerates. Today, it is a must for every organization for its survival and growth.

In fact, performance appraisal is not something new. The appraisal system existed as early as 221 A.D., though the nature of appraisal was not so formal and the tools used were not so extensive. In fact the appraisal gained momentum in the post-world war period with the advent of professionalisation in management. At the earlier stages the performance appraisal was done just on the basis of the degree to which a person possesses certain traits which were considered essential for the effective performance of a particular task.

Towards a Definition of Performance

Performance appraisal is the systematic assessment of an employee in terms of the performance, aptitude and other qualities which are necessary for successfully carrying out the job.

Definition

'Merit rating is the evaluation of any employee by his supervisor or any other person familiar with the employee.'

The above definition brings out the following characteristics of merit rating.

1. Employee is evaluated on the basis of his skills and potentialities.
2. For evaluation, help of a supervisor or any other person familiar to the employee should be taken.
3. Its objective is to be helpful for the purpose of transfer, promotion, etc. of employees.

PURPOSE OF PERFORMANCE APPRAISAL

1. To assist in making decisions for promotion, transfer, etc.: A scientifically done appraisal provides vital information which can greatly help in making and enforcing decisions regarding promotions, pay increases, terminations and transfers. It permits each individual to be considered on the same basis as everyone else. It reduces the chances of nepotism, motivates individuals to put in their best. A sound performance appraisal system can be of great use to a manpower planner when confronted with the task of preparing a succession planning scheme.

2. To establish comparable and reliable records: Systematic performance appraisal provides information on which performance comparison can be made.

3. To stimulate and guide employee development: It is but the human nature to know how they are doing. A good performance appraisal system helps in employee development. A good appraisal reveals the performance of an employee which then can be communicated to the employee. The weaknesses, once identified, can be removed either by providing necessary training or through proper placement.

4. To provide counselling: Appraisal results may be used to counsel with each employee about his future development. This can be accomplished when the supervisor reports on the evaluation and tells each individual how he is doing and how he can improve. Admittedly this counselling and coaching procedure is difficult. It is hard to talk to a man about his weaknesses and it is even more difficult to do it in such a way that he is motivated to try to improve himself.

Counselling is a difficult art, not born out of textbooks and manuals. For the supervisor, as also for the subordinates, it is a point of self-improvement and growth.

When the evaluation is thoroughly discussed in a friendly private conference, the immediate superior has an opportunity to:

— recognise the individual's outstanding accomplishments,

— tell him exactly where he stands,

— show him exactly in what areas it is felt he can improve,

— explain why it is to his advantage to undertake the improvement.

This counselling step should help the employee improve his present job performance, point the way for qualifying to higher jobs and help him develop those broad characteristics important in top management position.

5. To provide a basis for the development of personnel: Another major use of performance appraisal is to provide a basis for the development of personnel. This can be done by constructing a development guide for each person. This guide should include identification of the individual position for which he seems best qualified, the limitations or training needs derived from a comparison of appraisal results with position requirements, and recommendations for training to fill out the person's competence. A schedule showing the development programme should also be provided. This schedule will disclose when the candidate can be promoted to the next higher position with promise of successfully carrying out his duties.

Hence the training programme for each management employee can be developed from appraisal results. The appraisal results therefore provide a basis for training — tailoring sound development programme to suit the company's needs.

Ethical Basis for Performance Appraisal

While appraising, the appraiser has certain responsibilities towards employees whom they appraise. It is, therefore, necessary to define the ethics involved; otherwise, the executives may overlook the fact that even a single wrong appraisal would mean the violation of integrity of personality. Marion and Kellogg pointed out at least ten norms which a manager (appraiser) should follow while appraising the performance of an employee.

1. Before appraisal is made it is important for the appraiser *to know the reason.* This would allow him to ask for specific and pertinent information.
2. Appraisal should be done on the basis of information which are representative in nature. It is highly unethical to appraise an employee on the basis of hearsay evidence as there is every chance that it would present a distorted picture of the performance.
3. The appraisal should be based on *sufficient information.* This would mean that all the relevant facts should be gathered before the appraisal is made.
4. Appraisal should be on the basis of *relevant information.*
5. *The appraisal must be an honest one.* An appraisal which is not made honestly may mislead others who go by such reports.
6. *The written and oral appraisals must be consistent.* Any inconsistency in this regard may prove very disastrous and may cause considerable frustrations and agony to the employee at a later stage.
7. An appraisal should always be presented as *an opinion than* as a fact.
8. The appraiser should not share the information he has collected about an employee with everyone. He must keep the assessment to himself and should share with only those who have a good reason to have it.
9. The appraiser should not imply the existence of an appraisal that has not been made at all.
10. The appraiser should not accept other's appraisal without knowing the basis for it. Before any such appraisal is accepted it is important to look for the facts and probe into the basis on which the appraisal is made.

To sum up, it is enough to say that if one recognises the basic values of the human being, if one recognises every employee as an 'Individual' then one must acknowledge that making and communicating appraisal of an employee involves ethical considerations.

Techniques of Performance Appraisal

1. Ranking
2. Man-to-man Comparison
3. Grading
4. Graphic scales
5. Check-list
6. Forced-choice
7. Critical Incidents

(1) Ranking: The oldest and simplest system for formal rating is to compare one man with all other men and place him in a simple rank order. In doing this, the appraiser considers the man and his performance as an entry. He makes no attempts systematically to fractionize him or his performance, but compares a whole man with another whole man.

One of the objections to the ranking process is that we are asking the rater to perform rather an impossible feat. The analysis of an individual's performance is not simple. Yet we are asking the rater to compare several people simultaneously and turn out an accurate rank order. Can the human mind handle all these variables at one time? To simplify this problem, the paired comparison technique of ranking can be used. Each man can be compared with every other man, one at a time. For example, suppose there are five employees. Employee A's performance is compared to that of B's, and decision is made concerning whose is the better performance. Then A is compared to C, D and E in order. Next, B must be compared with all others individually. The same approach is used for the other personnel. Thus, the use of the paired-comparison technique with these five employees would mean a total of ten decisions, only two people being involved in each decision. The number of decisions can be determined by the following formula:

$$\text{Number of Comparisons} = \frac{N(N-1)}{2}$$

In this formula, N equals the number of personnel to be compared. The results of these comparisons can be tabulated, and a rank can be made from the number of times each person is considered to be superior.

(2) Man-to-man Comparison: One of the first attempts to break the person's performance apart and analyse its components was the man-to-man rating system, used by the Army during World War II. Certain factors, such as leadership, initiative, and dependability, were selected for purposes of analysis. A scale was designed for each carefully defined factor, instead of defining varying degrees. The rater had developed his own scale by evaluating the leadership qualities of persons he had known. The person who demonstrated the highest degree of leadership that he had encountered was placed at the upper end of the scale, and particular men were assigned to the lowest and intervening degrees. Thus a scale was created for each selected factor.

It is apparent how the title 'Man-to-man' is derived. Instead of comparing whole men to whole men, personnel are compared to key men of one factor at a time. This system considering measurement is utilised today in job-evaluation, being known as the "Factor comparison" system. Though it is highly useful in measuring jobs, it is of very limited use in measuring people. The devising of scales would evidently be extremely complicated. Besides if each rater must use, for different degree definitions, particular men he has known, the ratings should not be comparable from one department to another.

(3) Grading: In the grading system, certain categories of worth are established in advance and are carefully defined. In the Federal Civil Services, for example, there are three categories of personnel; outstanding, satisfactory, and unsatisfactory. Employee performance is then compared with these grade definitions, and the person is allocated to the grade which best describes his performance. The employee can receive only O, S and U performance. There can, of course, be more than three grades. This is the same basic system called 'Grade description.' The Federal Civil Services is consistent, in that it uses the grading approach for both men and jobs.

The grading system is sometimes modified into forced distribution system, in which certain percentages are established for each grade. For example, 10 per cent of the total personnel must go into the top grade, 20 per cent must to the second grade, 40 per cent to the middle, 20 per cent to the fourth and 10 per cent to the bottom grade. It has the advantage of forcing a separation of the personnel in the group, so that the rater cannot relax and judge them all as average, superior or below average.

(4) Graphic Scales: This is the most widespread method of merit rating. A line is drawn for each factor to be evaluated. At one end of the line the name and description of the factor under consideration is given. Different classes are mentioned at intervals on the line. The line starts with the best class and ends with the worst. An example is given below:

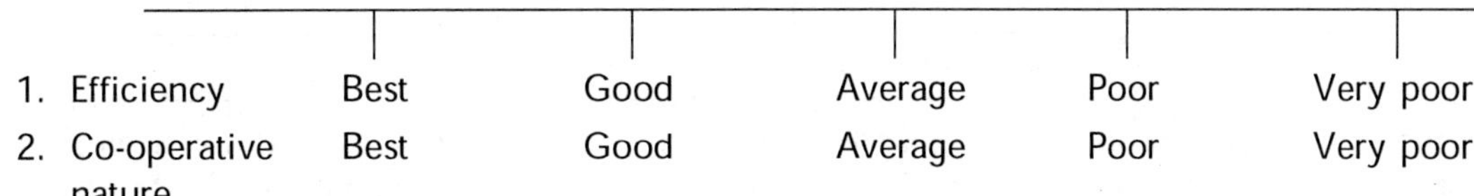

Now, if the employee's efficiency is 'average', a ✓ mark is put besides the word 'average' on the scale. Suppose, he shows extraordinary co-operation, a ✓ mark is put besides the word 'best' on the scale indicating the factor co-operative nature.

Two methods, the modifications of this method, are also popular. They are: (*i*) Adjectival method; and (*ii*) Numerical method. Let us see each of these methods.

(i) Adjectival method: Here, different adjectives are used for each factor to be evaluated. For each employee, a mark is made in the column of the adjective which best suits him. The total marks of the employees are counted from the total of marks assigned to each adjective. The main advantage of this method is that it is very simple. However, the same is its limitation it is deceptively simple. The different raters may perceive the adjectives differently.

(ii) Numerical method: This method is very similar to the above method. The only difference is that instead of adjectives, numbers are used. The number of marks for each point are decided. The rater makes a mark in the column of the number which he thinks suitable for the employee. These numbers are summed up and employee is evaluated. The advantage of this method, again, is simplicity. The main drawback is that the rater may use the number; according to their own beliefs about the marks.

SPECIMEN OF THE ADJECTIVAL MERIT-RATING METHOD

Factors	*Extra-ordinary*	*Fine*	*Good*	*Normal*	*Poor*	*Very poor*
1. Quantity of work						
2. Quality						
3. Ability						
4. Understanding of the work						
5. Loyalty						
6. Cooperation						
7. Leadership						
8. Health						

Date: Total marks Signature

SPECIMEN OF A NUMERICAL MERIT RATING METHOD

Characteristics	*1*	*2*	*3*	*4*	*5*	*6*	*7*	*8*	*9*	*10*
1. Quantity of work						✓				
2. Quality							✓			
3. Ability					✓					
4. Understanding of the work						✓				
5. Loyalty								✓		
6. Cooperation									✓	
7. Leadership virtue		✓								
8. Health	✓									

Date Total marks 46 Signature

The most commonly used system of performance appraisal is that of establishing scales for a number of fairly specific factors. It is an approach similar to that of the man-to-man system except that the degrees on the factor scales are represented by definitions rather than by key men. Exhibit shows such a rating form which utilizes four factors. Five degrees are possible for each factor. General definitions appear at points along the scale. It is interesting to note that this same basic approach is the most commonly used system for measuring the worth of jobs — the 'Point system' of job evaluation.

The selection of factors to be measured is a crucial part of the graphic scales system. As indicated previously, they are of two types: (*i*) Characteristics such as initiative and dependability, and (*ii*) Contributions such as quantity and quality of work. Since certain areas of job performance cannot be objectively measured, it is likely that graphic scales will continue to use a mixture of characteristics and contributions, with the emphasis upon the latter.

Conventional Rating Form

Name : O. P. Malhotra

Position : Assistant Director, Research and Development

Date rated : 8-9-2001

	Unsatis-factory	*Fair*	*Good*	*Very good*	*Excep-tional*	
Job knowledge Extent of theoretical knowledge and practical know-how as related to present job.	**1**	**2**	**3**	**4**	**5**	**5**
Organizing ability Effectiveness in planning own work and that of subordinates.	1	2	3	4	5	3
Judgement Ability to obtain and analyse facts and apply sound judgement.	1	2	3	4	5	4
Attitude Enthusiasm shown for job, loyalty to accept criticism and changes in company policy.	1	2	3	4	5	3
Dependability Reliability in carrying out assignments conscientiously and with effectiveness.	1	2	3	4	5	4
Creativity Ability to apply imagination to job, to develop new plans, work out costs etc.	1	2	3	4	5	5
Dealing with people Ability to assign work to others and to co-ordinate others through distribution of work load and responsibility.	1	2	3	4	5	3
Leadership Ability to stimulate subordinates to perform their jobs effectively.	1	2	3	4	5	2
Personal Efficiency Speed and effectiveness in carrying out duties not assigned to subordinates.	1	2	3	4	5	4
					Total points	33

(*a*) In the order of importance, state three performance characteristics which need improvement with respect to his present condition:

1. Emotional stability.
2. Dealing with subordinates.
3. Cost control.

(*b*) What might he do to improve his job performance? Should he try harder to get along with other people? Should he more practical?

(*c*) Are there any factors in the health, personal life or the outside influences which may have effected his performance during this appraisal period?

Divorced last month.

Comment: A very able researcher who finds at times difficult to get out of the clouds. His subordinates respect his ability though many are irritated by his moodiness. Possibly he may settle down when he solves his family problems.

Unsatisfactory	:	10.16 points	Evaluated by	:	Prasanna G. Apte
Fair	:	16.25 points	Title	:	Director, Research and Development
Good	:	26.35 points	Approved by	:	Kiran Shah
Very good	:	35.44 points	Title	:	(R&D) Manager
Excellent	:	45.50 points			

The number of factors ordinarily used varies from nine to two and is adjusted to the particular occupational category being considered, e.g., hourly personnel, sales and financial personnel etc. Commonly used factors are quantity and quality of work, co-operation, personality, versatility, leadership, safety, job knowledge, attendance and loyalty.

Though popular in use, graphic scales impose a heavy burden upon the rater. He must report and evaluate the performance of his subordinates on scales involving as many as five degrees on twelve different factors for perhaps twenty to thirty men. The fact that he reports a division for each factor in all cases does not necessarily mean that accurate decision can be made. For such reasons as these, other systems of appraisal have been developed.

In this variety of rating scales, the overall score is determined by adding up the scores given to specific factors (as in the upper portion of the form illustrated.) In spite of its deceptive simplicity, this approach has severe limitations. Note, for example, some of the basic assumptions lying behind it. One is that each of the factors (cost control, judgement, so forth) is of equal importance and that this holds true for all jobs. Yet clearly, on some jobs creativity is more important than effectiveness in dealing with people, and on others just the reverse is true. Another assumption is that these qualities are 'additive', for instance, strength in knowledge will offset lack of leadership.

Human Errors in Rating: All forms of numerical ratings are subject to certain human evaluative errors.

Clarity in Standards: Unless all raters agree on what terms such as " Good" or " Excellent" mean, their final ratings simply cannot be computed. To cite an extreme example, the rating scale in one hospital included excellent, very good, fair, satisfactory and unsatisfactory. Several head nurses objected to using the term "satisfactory" on the grounds that "no nurse is ever really satisfactory." To them "Satisfactory" meant "better than excellent."

Differing Perceptions: People differ in their standards of judgement. Even where there is no conscious prejudice, unconscious factors may bias a supervisor's evaluation of his subordinates. Even the fairest of people find it difficult to be impartial when judging the actions of individuals who differ greatly from themselves in terms of background values and style of behaviour. More than obvious factors, such as racial discrimination, are involved here. The man who is accustomed to making quick and deliberate decisions and *vice versa*. An appraisal also requires that we ask people who are perhaps not themselves good managers, to rate the managerial competence of others who may have more managerial competence than that of their bosses.

Excessive Leniency or strictness: As every student knows, there is a big difference between hard and easy graders. Supervisors in industry often hesitate to give low ratings for fear of antagonising their subordinates and making them less cooperative. Furthermore, the supervisor may be afraid that low-rating will reflect on his own ability. There is always a chance that his boss will say, 'If your subordinate is as bad as all this, why don't you do something about it?' Some executives regularly rate new employees very low, then gradually raise them, thus making the employee feel good and displaying to their superior their excellence as trainers. In many organizations there is a tendency for average rating to raise over time.

Effect: There is a natural tendency (sometimes called the 'Blending tendency') for the rater to be influenced in rating one factor by the kind of rating he gives to another. In fact, the individual rater tends to give each man approximately the same rating on all facts. If a supervisor has a general feeling that a man is good, he will rate him high on all factors and *vice versa*. On his rating on the first factor listed or on the factor he thinks most important may 'contaminate' his ratings on all others.

Influence of a Man's Job: Performance rating is designed to evaluate how well a man does on a particular job. Although in theory it is vastly different from job evaluation (which rates the job, not the man), in practice there is a common tendency to put a man on a higher rating just because of his position.

Newer Rating Methods: As a consequence of these criticisms of traditional rating scales, personnel researchers have tried to develop new rating procedures that are less affected by raters' personal biases and less concerned with imponderables such as traits. Among the best known of these new forms of rating are forced-choice, the critical incident technique and the check-list method.

(5) Check-list: To select a statement most applicable to the employee from the given statements is the essence of check-list. Two such methods are popular. They are: (*a*) Behaviour check-list method; and (*b*) Forced-choice method. It will be worthwhile to consider both the methods separately.

(a) Behaviour check-list method: Here, descriptive statements are given about the qualities and behaviour of the employees. The rater will see which statement is most appropriate to the employee, and make a mark under that statement. Marks are assigned to each statement. On the basis of this, the personnel department evaluates the employees.

A specimen of behaviour check-list method is given on the next page.

(b) Forced-choice method: In forced-choice method a series of groups of statements is given, and the rate decides how effectively the statement describes each individual being evaluated. Each statement carries some weight or scope which is not known to the rater.

This method is used in different ways. Sometimes all the statements may be either favourable or unfavourable or from four statements, two are positive and two negative. The rater is asked to pick up the most appropriate and the most inappropriate statement for the person being rated.

The forced-choice method attempts to make performance evaluation more objective. It prevents the rater from deliberately checking only the most favourable statement for those employees whom he wants to favour.

The U.S. Army used this method during Second World War. The task of forming the groups of statements is a very difficult one, and only an expert can carry out this work properly. One such group is given below:

1. Flees from responsibility.
2. Creates a feeling of pride in the organization.
3. Lacks the sense of humour.
4. Makes suggestions.

Many other methods are also used over and above those mentioned above. When the scientific methods weren't invented, most of the employers evaluated their employees on the basis of their knowledge about them. The famous Scottish mill owner Mr. Robert Owen adopted the method of keeping 'Character books.' He put a colourful block on the working place of each employee to indicate the rating of the employee.

(6) Forced-choice Techniques: A newer method of appraising which is gaining prominence is the forced-choice scale. It eliminates much of the criticism of subjectivity in rating forms. It was developed for the U. S. Army during World War II and subsequently has been adopted for use with management and supervisory personnel.

Specimen 1

MERIT RATING REPORT

Name of the employee .... Department ....

No. of the employee .... Type of the job ....

1. Is the employee conscious about security?	Many times breaks security rules.	Is careless in doing jobs.	Works with care.	Obeys security rules.	Is very conscious about security.
2. How is his working efficiency?	Unsatisfactory	Ordinary	Average	Above average	Extraordinary
3. Is the employee trustworthy?	Is lazy, wastes time.	Is leisurely needs supervision.	Is a good worker.	Trustworthy	Very much hardworking, needs no supervision.
4 How does he behave with other employees?	Cannot work in good condition with others.	Occasionally quarrels with others.	Works properly with others.	Helps others who are facing some difficulty.	Can work very well with others.
5. What is his knowledge about the work?	Insufficient. So cannot work satisfactorily.	Knows a little but not sufficient.	Has sufficient knowledge to carry on his work.	Has good knowledge of his work and related things.	Has very good knowledge of his work and related things.
6. How is his grasping power?	Has to be told more than once about the work.	Works only as much asked to.	Works as much he should. Sometimes makes suggestions.	Seizes the opportunity for improvements.	Creates and seizes opportunities.

Special abilities and inabilities ....

Rate .... Signature ....

How Forced Choice items are made: Forced choice rating element are sets of four phrases or adjectives pertaining to job proficiency or personal qualifications. The rater indicates which of the four is most characteristic of the ratee, and which is least characteristic; and repeats this selection for each of the sets included. A sample set is the following:

(*a*) Commands respect by his actions.

(*b*) Cool-headed.

(*c*) Indifferent.

(*d*) Overbearing.

It is at once obvious that two of these are relatively favourable. One of the two favourable terms, checked as most characteristic, gives plus credit; selecting the other gives no credit. In the same way, picking one of the two unfavourable items as least characteristic add credit whereas the other adds nothing.

The construction of these tetrads and the determination of the scoring key are the crucial problems in the development of a rating scale of this type. Rundquist outlined 6 steps in the process.

1. Collection of brief essay descriptions of successful and unsuccessful officers.
2. Preparation of a complete list of descriptive phrases or adjectives called from these essays, and the administration of this list to a representative group of officers.
3. Determination of two indices for each descriptive phrase or adjective, a preference index and a discrimination index.
4. Selecting pairs of phrases or adjectives such that they appear of equal value to the rater (Preference index) but differ in their significance for success as an officer (discrimination index).
5. Assembling of pairs so selected into tetrads.
6. Item selection against an external criterion and cross-validation of the selected items.

Construction of Forced-choice Tetrads: The scaling and selection of the rating elements to compose the forced choice tetrads is the hub of the problem. The basic assumptions underlying the method can be stated as follows:

1. Any real differences which exist between officers, in competence or efficiency can be described in terms of objective, observable items of behaviour.
2. These "behaviour items" differ in the extent to which people in general tend to use them in describing other people, *i.e.*, in general favourableness, and this tendency can be determined statistically.
3. These items also differ in the extent to which they characterise officers at one extreme of the scale of competence as opposed to officers at the other extreme. The index of this difference, the "discriminative" value can also be determined statistically.
4. Pairs of items can be selected such that they are equal in preference value but different in discriminative value. A rater forced to say which item is most (or least) characteristic of a ratee is thus unable to select solely on the basis of prejudice for or against him. (Since the preference values are equal). The rater is compelled to consider both alternatives and theoretically at least to do a more objective job of reporting.

The first step in the process of constructing the tetrads of items, as stated above, is obtaining brief descriptive essay of good and poor officers. These essays serve as the source of the behaviour items pertinent to the job — in this case, the job of being an Army Officer. This step is essential, not to focus agreement on the nature of the traits involved, but also to ensure that the behaviour items are worded in the language familiar to those who will later be using the scale.

In the second step, a large pool of behaviour items called from these essays is prepared in list form and submitted to another group of officers — a group numbering in the neighbourhood of 300 is generally used. Each man in the group is asked to select from among his acquaintances — one officer whom he knows well enough to rate with confidence, and to indicate for that officer the extent to which each of the items in the list applied to him. The following key is used for this purpose:

1. to an exceedingly high or to the highest possible degree.
2. to an unusual or outstanding degree.
3. to a typical degree.
4. to a limited degree.
5. to a slight degree, or not at all.

After completing the entire list in this fashion, each man is asked to evaluate the officer he is rating on a scale showing his position with respect to overall competence in a representative group of 20 officers of the same grade.

All lists are collected, arranged in order of the rating of overall competence, and separated into upper (U) and Lower (L) thirds. An analysis is then performed on each of the items, and a determination made for the three groups separately, of the frequency with which each of the five alternatives was chosen for that item. The values are then computed for each item.

1. Preference Value

Assume that there are exactly 300 officers in the group checking the lists, and consequently 300 officers rated, are divided into the three groups of 100 U, 100 M and 100 L. For each item, the frequencies of each alternative, are summed across the three groups (U, M, and L) multiplied by the alternative weight (one less than the number preceding that alternative in the key presented above) and these five weighted alternative frequencies in turn added to yield a weighted total sum for the item. This weighted total sum (which has limits of 0 to 1200 where N is 300) is divided by N and multiplied by 100 to give the preference index. As indicated this value (with limits of 0 to 400) indicates the tendency of raters to mark people high or low on the particular behaviour item. As here computed low values of the index indicate a tendency to mark the item as applying to a high or outstanding degree, high values indicate little or no applicability for the item.

2. Discriminative Index

For each of the alternatives of a given item, difference between its frequencies in the upper and lower groups is computed. These five differences are then added, without regard to sign, to give the discriminative index. At one extreme, where the distribution of alternative frequencies is identical for the upper and lower groups, this index will be zero. At the other extreme, where the two frequency distributions have no overlap the value will (in this case) be 200. Low values of the index, obviously indicate that the item is equally applicable to good and poor officers and consequently does not discriminate. High value, on the other hand, indicates gross differences among the groups in applicability of the item, and suggests that it represents behaviour which has significance for success (or failure).

The following chart illustrates the method of calculating these two indices for a typical item.

Alternative ***Weight (w)***	***1*** ***0***	***2*** ***1***	***3*** ***2***	***4*** ***3***	***5*** ***4***	
Frequency (F)						
Upper (U)	1	0	6	6	87	(N : 100)
Middle (M)	3	5	13	15	64	(N : 100)
Lower (L)	4	11	27	23	35	(N : 100)
f	8	16	46	44	186	(n : 300)
	0	16	92	132	744	(fw: 984)
d = (L – U)	3	11	21	17	52	(d: 104)

Preference index: $\frac{fw}{n} \times 100 : \frac{984 \times 100}{300} : 328$

Discriminative Index : d : 104.

Item pairs are made up by selecting in so far as possible two items equal in preference value and widely different in discriminative value. This selection is facilitated by plotting each item (identified by its number in the list) on a double entry table with preference values along the abscissa and discriminative values along the ordinate — both in suitable intervals. By entering any row in this role, two items close in preference can be picked that are widely separated on the ordinate scale. It is wise to avoid choosing items which are opposite in meaning since this eliminates the forced choice element. Also though the same item may be used in several pairs, it is wise to avoid too much repetition of this sort, since it tends to reduce the "scope" of the scale and necessarily raises the item intercorrelation; it may also inject an extraneous factor if the rater strives for "consistency."

Finally, pairs of items are combined to form tetrads. One pair with low preference indice (favourable) is combined with second pair having high (unfavourable) preference indices. There is no logical basis for this step, but experience has demonstrated that if single pairs are used with instructions to indicate the most characteristic, there is a considerable rater resistance to those pairs that have high (unfavourable) preference indices. By combining high and low preference pairs with instructions to choose the most and the least characteristic, rater resistance is materially reduced. The same can be achieved by presenting high and low preference pairs (as pairs) separately with appropriate instructions for each.

Scoring Forced Choice Rating Scale

Tetrads are formed from two pairs of items. The members of each pair are matched for preference value. One member of each pair differentiates good from poor officers. The other does not. It is possible, because, of the way items are thus combined into tetrads, to key forced choice scales by assigning a point (plus or minus as the direction of the discrimination indicates) to each of the two discriminating members of each tetrad.

Forced-choice items may, however, act differently in combination with other items than they do by themselves. Consequently it is always desirable to establish the key on the final set of tetrads. In doing this, it is necessary to include enough tetrads so that those which fail to stand up on the final cross-validation can be eliminated from the scoring key. Needless to say, the cross validation should employ an external criterion.

In one experiment on a group of 24 tetrads (96 items each of which could be marked as most or as least characteristic of the ratee) 75 per cent of the items were scored in the same way after cross-validation as they would have been scored by a predetermined key based on original preference and discrimination values. It should be noted that while items which had discrimination value (either positive or negative) in the predetermined key may have lost their value, and while some items which did not discriminate in the original study came to do so in the cross-validation run, there was not an instance in which an item which discriminated in one direction in the first experimental situation later on reversed its direction of discrimination in cross-validation run.

Critical Incident Technique

A new approach has been developed which is designed to place a much heavier emphasis on the study of the behaviour of the worker on the job. It aims to collect representative sample of observed behaviour which can be used as basis for obtaining objective, quantitative data regarding the job. It is hoped that instead of opinions and hunches, activity analysis can be made to yield the type of sampling data which can lead to inference and predictions of data reliability and validity.

The essence of this new procedure is to establish the critical requirements of a job or activity through direct observation by participants in or supervisors of the job or activity. A critical requirement is defined as a requirement which is crucial in the sense that it has been responsible for outstandingly effective or definitely unsatisfactory performance of an important part of the job or activity in question. Thus a critical requirement differs from requirements which appear important but in practice have no significant bearing on performance with respect to the specific activity. Observation to personnel engaged in a specific activity leads directly to critical requirements in terms of what workers actually do on the job. In addition, such critical requirements of the work such as aptitude training information, attitude, habits, skills and abilities are also considered. Critical requirements of these latter types must be based on inferences and hypotheses. These inferences and hypotheses may be checked by empirical studies.

It is believed that the determination of critical requirements in terms of behaviour is a necessary condition to an adequate definition of the job in terms of behaviour. Such a definition of the job must include the identification of the aspects of behaviour to be included, standards of satisfactory performance for these, and estimates of their relative importance. It is also clear that a definition of the job in terms of objectively described and evaluated behaviours of this type provides an almost complete statement of an adequate criterion measure of effectiveness of the job. Similarly no criterion or evaluation system which ignores these definitions of standards and of relative importance can be satisfactory. Thus it follows that the problem of definition, job requirements, and criteria of success necessarily reduce to one and the same problem, at least with respect to their major outlines.

It should be emphasized at this point that observations of the behaviour of the individual, or of the effectiveness of this behaviour in accomplishing the desired results in a satisfactory manner, constitute 9not just one source of data but the only source of primary data regarding critical requirements of the job in behaviour. Success and failure in the activity are nothing more or less than a series of actions leading to observed results.

Granting that objective data are more important than opinion, then the next problem is how can satisfactory data be obtained. Experience in establishing critical requirements indicates that five specific conditions must be satisfied.

These are as follows:

1. It is essential that actual observation be made of the on-the-job activity and the product of such activity.
2. The aims and objectives of the activity must be known to the observer. Unless this condition is fulfilled it will be impossible for the observer to judge or to identify success or failure. For example, foreman might be rated as very successful if the objectives of his activity were taken as getting along well with the workmen under him. At the same time, he might be rated as very unsatisfactory if the objective is to produce materials.
3. The basis for the specific judgement to be made by the observer must be clearly defined. The data can be objective only if all observers are following the same rules. All observers must have the same criteria for judging satisfactories. The definition must clearly state whether or not a minor imperfection will be regarded as an evidence of failure or whether a product must be completely unusable to be classified as unsatisfactory.
4. The observer must be qualified to make judgements regarding the activity observed. Typically the supervisor on the job is in a much better position to make judgement as to whether or not behaviour is outstanding or unsatisfactory, than is the job analyst or psychologist. On the other hand, the supervisor on the job is ordinarily quite lacking in the training essential to make an inference as to the particular mental trait which caused the behaviour to be successful or unsuccessful.
5. The last necessary condition is that the situation be such that reporting is accurate. The principal problem here are those of memory and communication. It is also important that the observer's attention be directed to the essential aspects of the behaviour being observed.

In order that the critical requirements accurately reflect the data collected, the process of reducing several thousand specific observations of behaviour to a fairly small number of critical requirements must be competently done. The synthesis of the critical requirements from a variety of specific behaviour must be such that judge will agree that each of the specific behaviours should be classified under the summary statement which has been developed to include it. For maximum usefulness the critical requirements also should be structured in such a way that they provide a coherent picture of the activity.

In conclusion, a few of the devices which have been found effective in establishing critical requirements will be listed.

(1) The critical incident technique which consists in getting incidents of extreme behaviour, either outstanding or unsatisfactory, has been found very effective in collecting data where adequate records regarding data are not available. This procedure has considerable efficiency because of the use of only the extremes of behaviour. It is well-known that extremes can be more accurately identified than behaviour which is more nearly average in character. It must be verified that the five conditions noted above are satisfied so that there will be no biasing of the sample of incidents, due either to selective memory or to inadequate definition of the type incident to be included.

(2) A second device which has been found very helpful is the evaluation and classification of incidents at the time of observation. It is much simpler to evaluate sample of behaviour at the time it is observed, when all relevant details may be noted or checked, than it is at some later time when further examination of the behaviour is impossible. If an incident is evaluated and classified at the

time of its occurrence and a mental recording of this is made, it is greatly improved in accuracy and the time necessary is considerably reduced.

(3) Another device which has been found to save much time is the preparation of a complete observational record form which contains practically all the types of incidents which are likely to be observed. Incidents may be reported on such a form by merely tallying in the appropriate space.

(4) A final use of such data is the direct conversion of frequencies into statistical estimates for purposes of prediction and evaluation. In situations where the observations can be accurately classified and where also an adequate representative sample of behaviour can be obtained, it is possible to obtain fairly accurate, unbiased estimates of the importance of a particular critical requirement with relation to the other requirements. Where the requirements are independent this can be converted into correlation coefficient by using the usual formula for estimating correlation attributable to common elements in the variables.

The critical incident technique has been successfully used in a number of situations. One of the first uses was in establishing the critical requirements for the United States Air Force Officers. In this instance the incidents were obtained by interviewing officers who had considerable amount of military experience. The procedure has been used in determining the critical requirements for research workers in scientific laboratories. In this situation, also, experienced supervisory personnel were requested to provide the incidents. Recently the procedure has been applied to hourly wage workers in one of the divisions of a large industrial corporation. In this situation the foremen supplied the incidents from which the critical requirements were developed. The Committee on Ethical Standards of the critical incident techniques is obtaining a survey of practical problems in that area.

In the course of these studies a substantial amount of research and developmental work has been accomplished and it is believed that there has now been sufficient experience with the critical incident technique to demonstrate that the critical requirements of a job can be established through the direct observations of personnel engaged in the activity.

Guidelines for Merit-rating

The following suggestions may prove to be useful for making most of merit-rating:

1. The rater should be selected with utmost care. He should be familiar with the methods of rating. Moreover, for the sake of uniformity in rating, he should be instructed properly. Rating requires special skills, which are not found in abundance. At most times the personal beliefs, prejudices, etc. are reflected in his rating. He must be impartial in evaluation of employees.
2. If the merit-rating methods are properly planned, the best results can be achieved.
3. The qualities to be evaluated should be properly interpreted and explained to the rater.
4. The rating plan should be as simple as possible so that the employee as well as supervisor can understand it properly.
5. The rater should be knowing the employee personally so that reliable information can be gathered. The opinion of a foreman regarding an employee will be more reliable than the opinion of managing director regarding the employee.
6. If possible, more than one rater should evaluate an employee.
7. Rating should be objective.
8. The objective of the rating should be constructive.
9. The employee should be given his tally in merit rating and his mistakes should be mentioned. The employee should also get a chance to appeal against the rating.

Utility and Advantages of Merit-Rating

The National Industrial Conference Board of United States conducted a survey in 1954. The following were the results of the survey. Forty-six per cent of the companies employing more than 1,000 persons were using merit-rating. 61 per cent of big companies and 45 per cent of small companies had implemented merit-rating. The popularity of merit-rating is because of its following advantages:

1. It is helpful in deciding whether the services of the employee should be made permanent, after his probation period. The rating of employee in the beginning and at the end of the probation period will indicate whether continuity of his service is in advantage of the company.
2. The merit-rating is also helpful in maintaining high level of morale among the employees. If the system is just, it will encourage the employees to improve their performance.
3. The introduction of merit-rating develops an ability in supervisor in noting the merits and demerits of the employees. This will help in increasing the efficiency of his department.
4. Merit rating can be considered an important yardstick for making decisions about promotions.
5. Merit rating will highlight the presence and absence of different skills in the employee. This would help taking decisions like transfer, demotion and dismissal of employees.
6. Merit-rating will manifest qualities and deficiency of an employee. This information will help in planning training programme.
7. The employees can be guided properly if we have knowledge about their plus points and minus points.
8. The management will get information about the capability of employees, by merit-rating. This is useful in management.
9. Rating will give birth to healthy competition among the employees. Each will try to improve his performance. Consequently there will be favourable impact on the production of the firm.

Limitations of Performance Appraisal

The surveys conducted by IPM in 1973 and again in 1976-77 or appraisal schemes in which some 24 major organizations were involved in the 1973 survey, and some 288 organizations in 1976-77, have indicated that in majority of the cases the assessments were purely subjective and were largely based on individual judgements and opinions of one person — usually the immediate superior. Thus the fact that appraisal schemes flourish outwardly does not mean that all is well within. There are many reasons which contribute to the failure of appraisal system. Some of these are:

- Failure to consult those who will use the scheme or to involve them clearly in its formative stages;
- Lack of commitment from the top;
- Over elaborate paperwork — too much documentation or forms of such complexity that they can only be understood by the designer are liable to arouse resentment in the line managers and may ultimately defeat their own purpose;
- Unequal standards applied by different raters together with the lack of any systematic monitoring of ratings;
- Inadequate feedback and lack of follow up;
- Lack of training of appraisers.

Difference between Job Evaluation and Merit-Rating

Though, the aims of both the processes — job evaluation and merit-rating — are different, their final aim is to improve the efficiency of the firm. They differ in following ways:

1. Job evaluation evaluates the job while merit-rating gives the relative importance of different employees.
2. Job evaluation is not at all concerned with the changes in efficiency of the employees; whereas merit-rating is solely concerned with these changes.
3. The aim of job evaluation is to set up a just and proper wage and salary structure, while the objective of merit-rating is to measure the skills of the employees for purposes like recruitment selection, promotion, transfer, training, remuneration, etc.

Conclusion

Appraisal is an essential part of a manager's task. It is through this subjective evaluation that he determines the individual's ability to perform something. It is most likely to be useful if its purpose is clearly defined and when appraisal is made on the basis of specific, accurate and relevant information. If however, we look back, over the last few decades hardly any progress has been made in this direction. On the brighter side we do find greater emphasis on relating appraisal to the objectives of the job. But on the negative side, it still seems to linger on trait readings and there is reluctance to devote enough time and effort in training the appraiser. Similarly most of the managers do not want to validate their existing appraisal system. It must be borne in mind that a bad appraisal system is worse than no system at all. Thus, if we want to see that the performance appraisal survives in the eighties not simply as a moribund return but as an essential part of effective management, then a sincere effort must be made to build appraisal system on the positive achievements.

35

Introduction

I. What is a Transportation Problem?

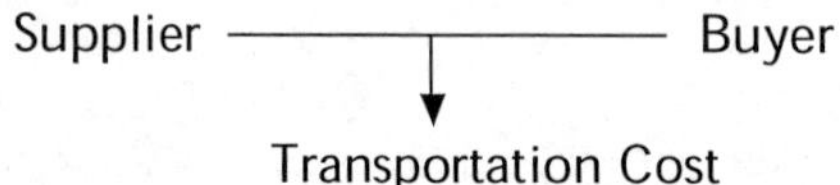

In a business transaction, products would have to be carried from the supplier to the buyer. This is possible by transportation only. However, any of the various means of transportation can be used. But, the main thing is that the transportation would involve a certain cost. Transportation cost is a cost which cannot be eliminated. It is immaterial who bears the cost the buyer or the supplier.

Transportation problem is the problem of minimizing the transportation cost. This problem is not so acute where there is one source (supplier's place) and one destination (buyer's place). But the problem becomes acute when the supplier has various plants and the buyer has various warehouses. Here, the necessity of forming combinations of plants and warehouses would arise to minimise the transportation. The least expensive method of transportation should be found out. This is known as *Optimisation* of transportation problem.

II. Transportation Matrix

Matrix is nothing but a combination of various mathematical numbers arranged in different rows and columns.

Now, to see how a transportation matrix is formed, we would take a practical example. Further discussion on solving of transportation matrix would be done keeping this example in the center. There is one assumption made, while taking the example, that supply and demand are equal. However, in practice, in many cases, these two may be different. We would consider such situations at a later stage in this chapter.

Example:

T. C. Mallet Trucking Company has a contract to move 115 truckloads of sand per week among 3 sand-washing plants W, X and Y, and 3 destinations A, B and C. Cost and volume information are given below:

Destination	Requirements Truckloads/Week	Plant	Capacity Truckloads/Week
A	45	W	35
B	50	X	40
C	20	Y	40
	115		115

Cost Information:

Cost per Truckload (A)

From	To Destination A	To Destination B	To Destination C
Plant W	5	10	10
Plant X	20	30	20
Plant Y	5	8	12

Based on this data we want to form a transportation matrix. Transportation matrix can be prepared as shown in Fig. 35.1.

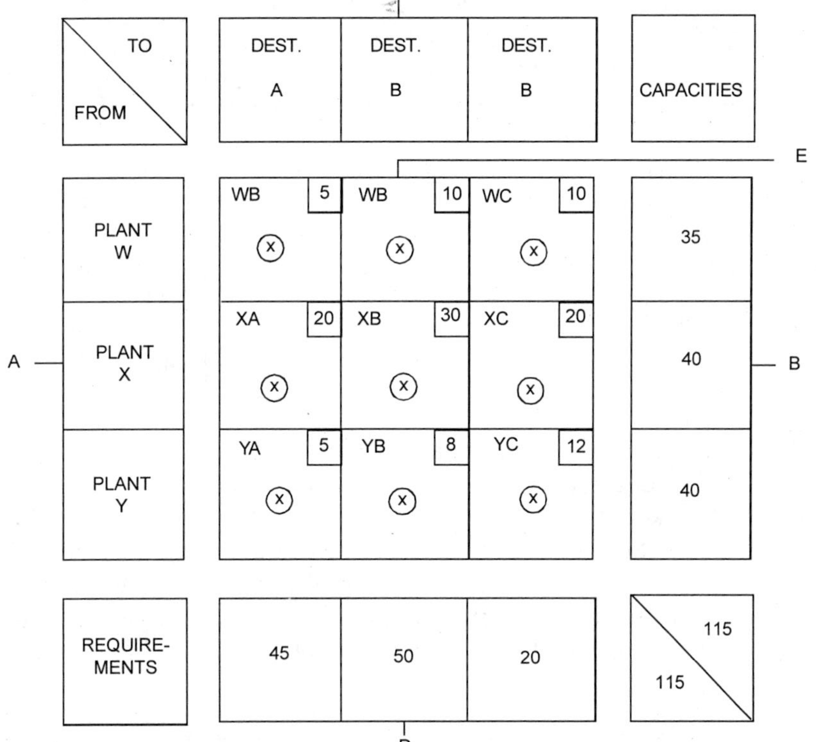

Fig. 35.1

In Fig. 35.1, A represents different places from where the goods are to be transported, *i.e.,* plants W, X and Y in our example. B represents the capacities of each plant. C represents different destinations and D represents the requirements of each particular destination.

E consists of different squares, each of which represents a combination of a plant and a destination, *e.g.,* square WA represents the combination of plant W and destination A. In round circles, quantity to be transported from a particular plant to a particular warehouse are to be written 'X' because until now, we don't know the quantities to be transported from each warehouse to different destinations. In each of these squares, on right-hand corner at the top, cost figures would be written, *e.g.,* in case of square WA, 5 is written because transportation cost per truck-load from plant W to destination A is ₹ 5.

In this way, the transportation matrix would be formed.

III. North-West Corner Rule

Now actual solving process of the transportation problem starts. For this purpose, North-West Corner Rule is applied. North-West Corner Rule states: "Start with the North-West corner of the matrix. Do not move till all the rim-requirements of that row are exhausted. And while moving to the right to the next column exhaust all the rim requirements of that particular column."

Following this rule, we would fill up the quantities in the squares of the transportation matrix. The matrix would now be as shown in Fig. 35.2.

Fig. 35.2

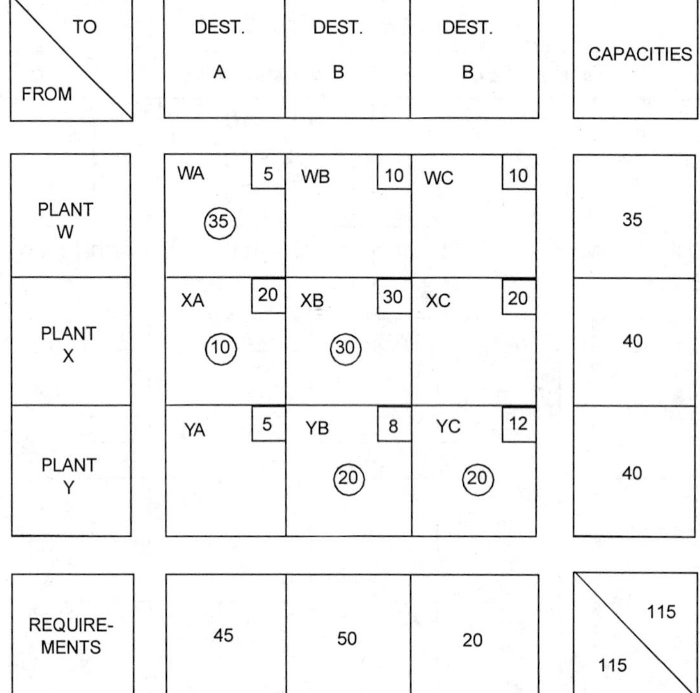

The squares in which there is some quantity are known as used squares. The others are said to be unused squares. The number of used squares should be equal to total rim requirements. If it is not equal to this, then a condition known as degeneracy comes into existence. We would consider the problem of degeneracy at a later stage in this chapter. We find that in our problem, there is degeneracy and so we proceed further now. We would now form a total cost schedule to see that each of the steps as we go further, brings us to some reduction in price. So, let us form a total cost schedule in accordance with the quantities we have allotted to different combinations of plants and destinations.

Total Cost Schedule

From Plant	*To Destination*	*Quantity (in truck-load)*	*Cost (₹ per truck-load)*	*Total Cost ₹*
W	A	35	5	175
X	A	10	20	200
X	B	30	30	900
Y	B	20	8	160
Y	C	20	12	240
				1,675

We can solve transportation problem by two methods: (1) Stepping stone method; and (2) MODI method. We would see either of them one after another. Let us first see stepping stone method.

IV. Stepping Stone Method

In this method, we suppose that a unit of quantity is taken from a used square and placed in an unused square. We see whether there is any reduction in total cost by this. The cost of squares which are now provided by an additional unit would be added and the costs of the squares from which a unit is taken off are substracted.

The path thus traced out by the exercise of addition and substraction is known as closed path. The result of the addition and subtraction is known as improved index for that square.

Let us take an example.

We transfer one truck-load from W to B. So one truck-load would be provided less to A from W. Now to fulfil the rim requirement one more truck-load should be provided to A from X. This would satisfy all rim requirements.

Let us see the change in cost by this.

Addition to costs:

From W to B	₹ 10
From X to A	₹ 20
	₹ 30

Deduction in costs:

From W to A	₹ 5
From X to B	₹ 30
	₹ 35

Net change in cost = ₹ 30 – 35 = – 5

This means that this business of additions and subtractions of quantities would reduce your cost by ₹ 5 per truckload.

–5 is known as improvement index for square WB.

We can also do this directly WB – XB + XA – WA

10 – 30 + 10 – 5 = – 5

Now, let us write the closed paths and improvement indices of all the unused squares of our problem.

Unused square	***Closed Path Improvement***	***Index***
WB	WB – XB + XA – WA 10 – 30 + 20 – 5	– 5
WC	WC – YC + YB – XB + XA – WA 10 – 12 + 8 – 30 + 20 – 5	– 9
XC	XC – YC + YB – XB 20 – 12 + 8 – 30	– 14
YA	YA – XA + XB – YB 5 – 20 + 30 – 8	+ 7

Now, we should select an unused square with highest negative improvement index, and make it a used square. Here, XC is such a square. We would add to and subtract from squares mentioned in closed path a fixed quantity. This quantity would be the minimum quantity from all the squares bearing negative signs.

In Fig. 35.3 (a) the squares on the closed path are drawn with their respective positive and negative signs. The inspection of these four squares would show that 20 truckloads are to be added and subtracted.

The Fig. 35.3(b) shows the quantity in the four squares after the addition and subtraction operations are carried out. A new matrix would be found (Fig. 35.4) with these changes in quantities in different squares. Fig. 35.4 would be said to be the first, improved solution. Let us see the reduction in cost by this improvement.

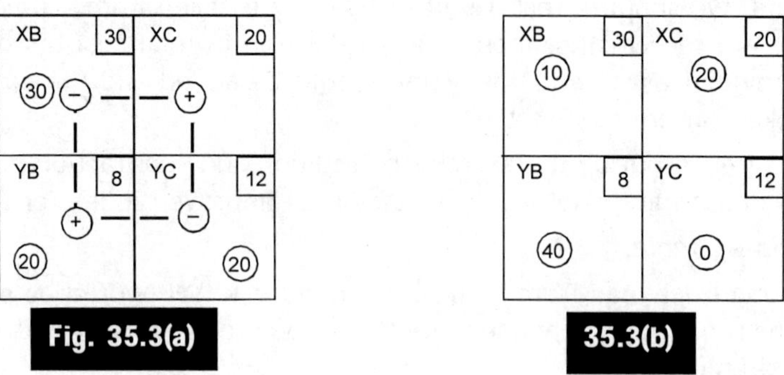

Fig. 35.3(a) 35.3(b)

Cost Schedule:

From Plant	*To Destination*	*Quantity (truckload)*	*Cost (₹/truckload)*	*Total cost*
W	A	35	5	175
X	A	10	20	200
X	B	10	30	300
X	C	20	20	400
Y	B	40	8	320
				1,395

Fig. 35.4

TO / FROM	DEST. A	DEST. B	DEST. C	CAPACI-TIES
PLANT W	WA 5 (35)	WB 10	WC 10	35
PLANT X	XA 20 (10)	XB 30 (10)	XC 20 (20)	40
PLANT Y	YA 5	YB 8 (40)	YC 12	40
REQUIRE-MENTS	45	50	20	115 / 115

So, now the cost has reduced from ₹ 1,675 to ₹ 1,395, *i.e.*, reduction of ₹ 280.

Now let us see whether further reduction in cost is possible. Till we get negative improvement index for any unused square, we must assume that further reduction in cost is possible. So, now let us find out closed paths and improvement indices of each of the unused squares first improved solution.

Unused square	*Closed path*	*Improvement Index*
WB	WB – WA + XA – XB 10 – 5 + 20 – 30	– 5
WC	WC – WA + XA – XB 10 – 5 + 20 – 20	+ 5
YA	YA – YB + XB – XA 5 – 8 + 30 – 20	+ 7
YC	YC – XC + XB – YB 12 – 20 + 30 – 8	+ 14

Now we would select the unused square WB (as it has highest negative improvement index) and do additions and subtractions as we had done while obtaining first improved solution. As a result second improved solution would be obtained (Fig. 35.5).

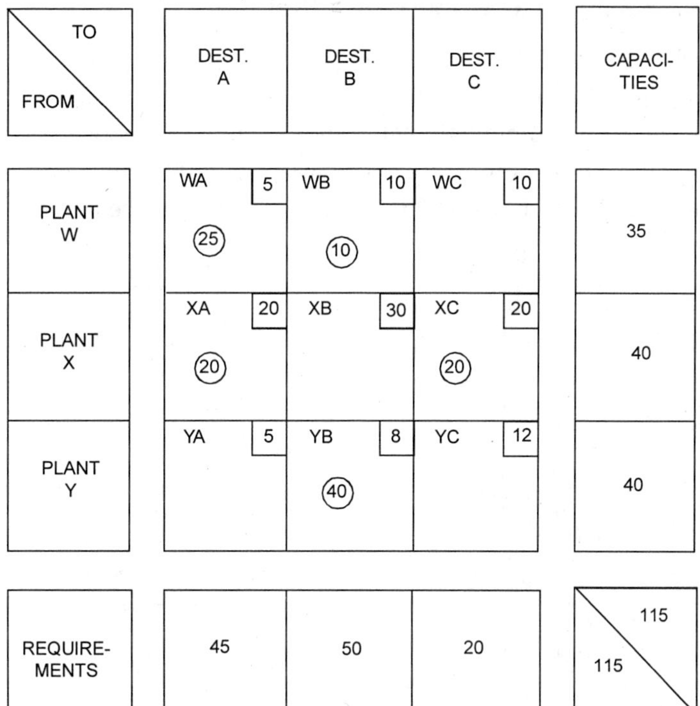

Fig. 35.5

Again, we would have to calculate the total cost.

From Plant	*To Destination*	*Quantity (truckload)*	*Cost (₹/truckload)*	*Total cost*
W	A	25	5	125
W	B	10	10	100
X	A	20	20	400
X	C	20	20	400
Y	B	40	8	320
				1,345

So, here again we have reduced the total transportation cost.

Now, let us calculate improvement indices for unused square to determine whether any further improvement can be done.

Unused square	***Closed path***	***Improvement Index***
WC	WC – WA + XA – XC 10 – 5 + 20 – 20	+ 5
XB	XB – WB + WA – XA 30 – 10 + 5 – 20	+ 5
YA	YA – YB + WB – WA 5 – 8 + 10 – 5	+ 2
YC	YC – XC + XA – WA + WB – YB 12 – 20 + 20 – 5 + 10 + 8	+ 9

Here, none of the unused squares has negative improvement index. So our second improved solution is the optimum solution. Minimum transportation cost would be involved if the combination of plants and destinations is done according to that solution. In this way we can solve transportation problem by stepping stone method. Let us now see the other method of solving it — MODI Method.

V. MODI Method of Solving a Transportation Problem

MODI means 'Modified Distribution.' MODI method can be defined as "computationally" more efficient method for solving transportation problem.

MODI method is said to be computationally more efficient method because only one closed path is to be traced and we can find improvement indices by putting values of unknown variables.

A Russian mathematician Charnce, who had developed stepping stone method in 1953, developed MODI method in 1955.

Fig. 35.6

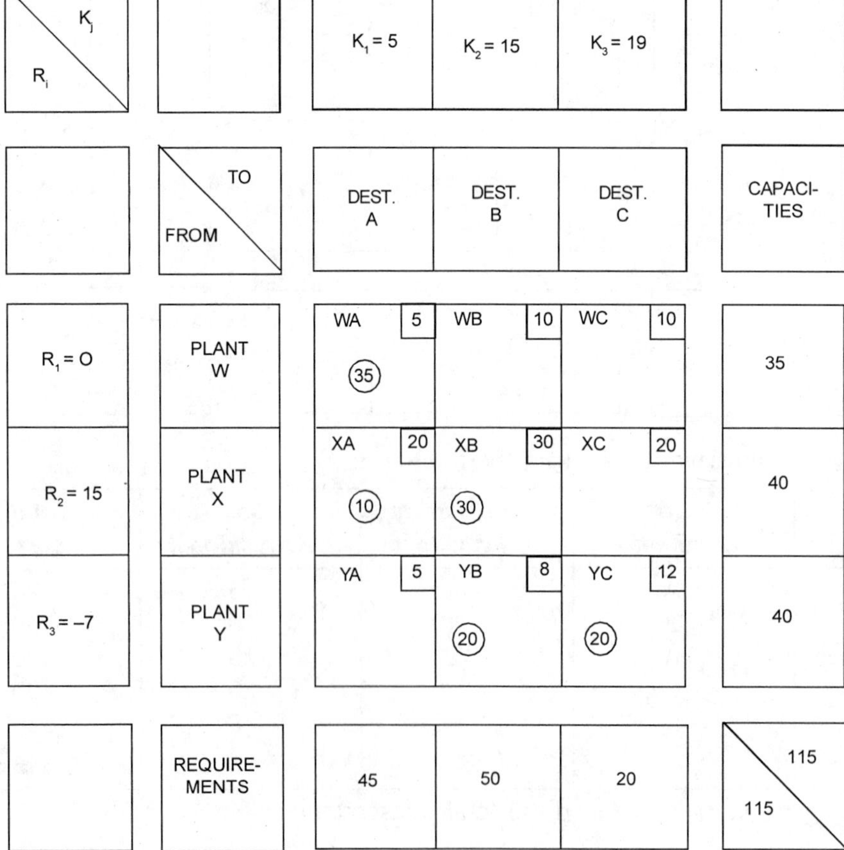

We would take the same example which we took when we saw stepping stone method. Now we would solve it by MODI method.

First of all, a matrix as seen in Fig. 35.6 will be prepared from the given data. The new variables introduced in the matrix are R_1, R_2, R_3 and K_1, K_2, K_3.

R_i is defined as a value assigned to a row.

K_j is defined as a value assigned to a column.

$R_i + K_j = C_{ij}$, where C is the cost of the square on the particular row and column.

We have implied the North-West Corner Rule in putting quantity in squares as we had done in the previous method also. Now, let us find the values of R_i and K_j. We would utilise used squares for this purpose.

Used squares	$R_i + K_j$	C_{ij}
R_1K_1	$R_1 + K_1$	5
R_2K_1	$R_2 + K_1$	20
R_2K_2	$R_2 + K_2$	30
R_3K_2	$R_3 + K_2$	8
R_3K_3	$R_3 + K_3$	12

We are not interested in absolute numerical values of unknown variables. We are only interested in their comparative values.

So, let us take $R_1 = 0$

As	$R_1 = 0$,	$R_1 + K_1 = 5$;	$K_1 = 5$
"	$K_1 = 5$,	$R_2 + K_1 = 20$;	$R_2 = 15$
"	$R_2 = 15$,	$R_2 + K_2 = 30$;	$K_2 = 15$
"	$K_2 = 15$,	$R_3 + K_2 = 8$;	$R_3 = -7$
"	$R_3 = -7$,	$R_3 + K_3 = 12$;	$K_3 = 19$

Now, we should prepare following table to find important indices of all unused squares.

Unused square	***Cost***	***Row Value (R_i)***	***Column Value (K_j)***	***Improvement Index***
R_1K_2	10	0	15	– 5
R_1K_3	10	0	19	– 9
R_2K_3	20	15	19	– 14
R_3K_1	5	(–7)	5	+ 7

Fig. 35.7

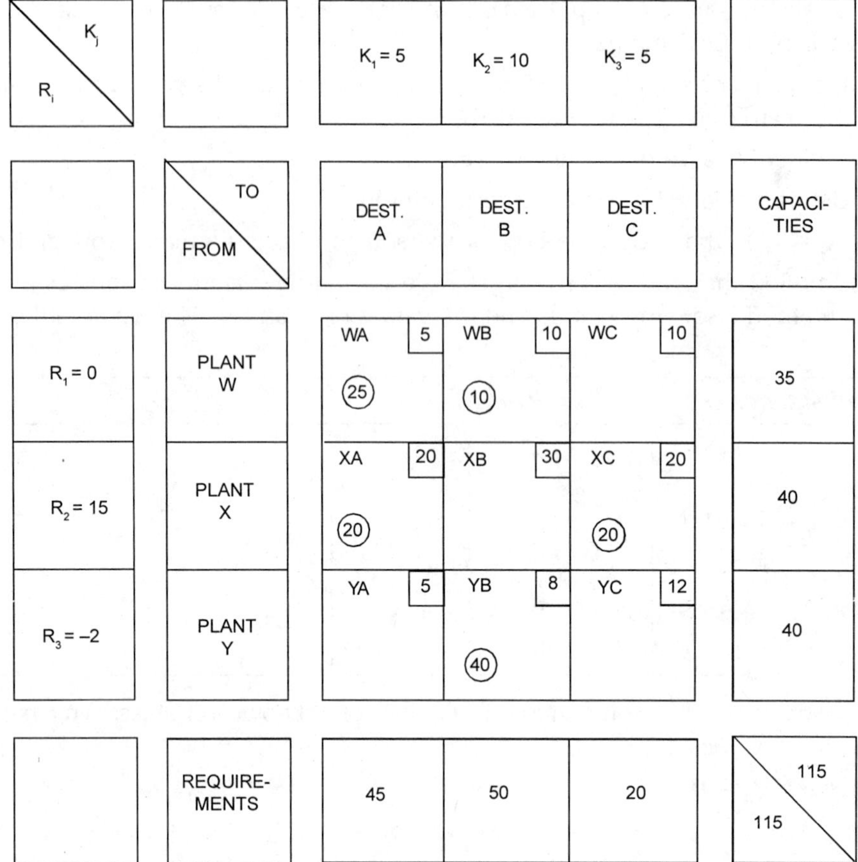

Now, we would select the unused square with highest negative value (R_2K_3) and trace its closed path. We would do additions and substractions as we had done in the stepping stone method and find out first improved solution (Fig. 35.7). We add and subtract 20. We can see that the improved solution is same as that was in stepping stone method. So it is not necessary to find the costs because they would be the same as we had calculated when we were solving this example by stepping stone method.

Now again, new values of R_i and K_j are to be found.

Used Square	$R_i + K_j$		C_{ij}
R_1K_1	$R_1 + K_1$	=	5
R_2K_1	$R_2 + K_1$	=	20
R_2K_2	$R_2 + K_2$	=	30
R_2K_3	$R_2 + K_3$	=	20
R_3K_2	$R_3 + K_2$	=	8

Let us take $R_1 = 0$

As	$R_1 = 0$	$R_1 + K_1 = 5$	$K_2 = 5$
"	$K_1 = 5$	$R_2 + K_1 = 20$	$R_2 = 15$
"	$R_2 = 15$	$R_2 + K_2 = 30$	$K_2 = 15$
"	$R_2 = 15$	$R_2 + K_3 = 20$	$K_3 = 5$
"	$K_2 = 15$	$R_3 + K_2 = 8$	$R_3 = -7$

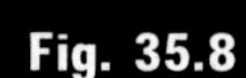

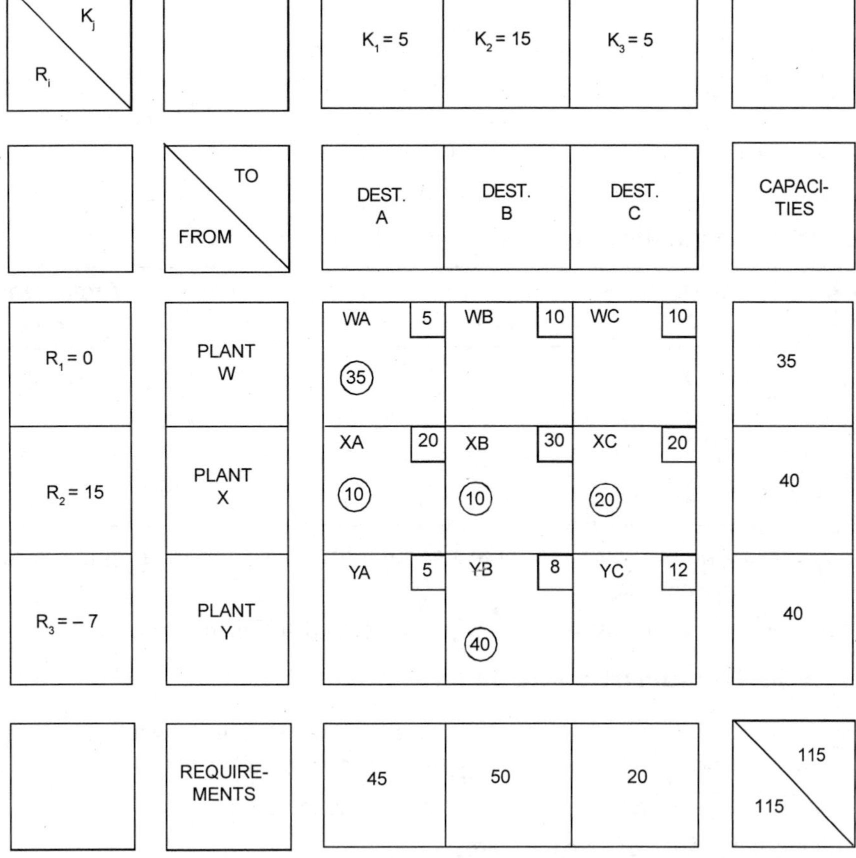

Now, we have to find improvement indices for all the unused squares.

Unused Square	***Cost***	***Row value (Ri)***	***Column value (Kj)***		***Improvement Index***
R_1K_1	10	0	15	=	– 5
R_1K_3	10	0	5	=	+ 5
R_3K_1	5	(–7)	5	=	+ 7
R_3K_3	12	(–7)	5	=	+ 14

Now, select the unused square with highest negative value (R_1 K_2) and do the same process as we had done previously. We would now come to a new matrix as shown in Fig. 35.8.

Now, again new values of R_i and K_j would have to be found using unused squares for the purpose.

Used Square	$R_i + K_j$		C_{ij}
R_1K_1	$R_1 + K_1$	=	5
R_1K_2	$R_1 + K_2$	=	10
R_2K_1	$R_2 + K_1$	=	20
R_2K_3	$R_2 + K_3$	=	20
R_3K_2	$R_3 + K_2$	=	8

Let us take $R_1 = 0$

As		
$R_1 = 0$	$R_1 + K_1 = 5$	$K_1 = 5$
$R_1 = 0$	$R_1 + K_2 = 10$	$K_2 = 10$
$K_1 = 5$	$R_2 + K_1 = 20$	$R_2 = 15$
$R_2 = 15$	$R_2 + K_3 = 20$	$K_3 = -5$
$K_2 = 10$	$R_3 + K_2 = 8$	$R_3 = -2$

Now, calculate improvement indices for all the unused squares.

Unused Square	***Cost***	***Row value (Ri)***	***Column value (Kj)***		***Improvement Index***
R_1K_3	10	0	(5)	=	+ 5
R_2K_2	30	15	10	=	+ 5
R_3K_1	5	(–2)	5	=	+ 2
R_3K_3	12	(–2)	5	=	+ 9

Here, we find that no unused square has negative improvement index and the second improved solution is the optimum solution.

In this way we can solve transportation problem by MODI method.

VI. Degeneracy in Transportation Problem

While solving a transportation problem, if the number of used square is not equal to total rim requirements – 1, a condition known as degeneracy is said to exist.

Now, degeneracy may occur in any of the following ways:

(A) Insufficient number of used squares.

(*i*) At initial stage

(*ii*) In improved solution.

(B) Excessive number of used squares.

Let us see each of these one by one.

(A) Insufficient number of used squares

(i) At initial stage: Let us take an example which will illustrate such a situation.

Illustration:

There are three plants, W, X and Y. Every week these plants produce 55, 25 and 35 units of a product, respectively. There are three projects, A, B and C which require this product. Their respective requirements per week are 35, 45 and 35 units respectively. Cost information is as follows:

Cost per unit (in ₹)

From Plant	***To Project A***	***To Project B***	***To Project C***
W	4	8	8
X	16	24	16
Y	8	16	24

Now, form a transportation matrix and apply North-West Corner Rule. The resulting matrix would be as shown in Fig. 35.9. We find that the number of used squares is 4, but we should have 5 used squares so as to eliminate the condition of degeneracy.

Fig. 35.9

TO / FROM	PROJECT A	PROJECT B	PROJECT B	CAPACITIES
PLANT W	WA 4 (35)	WB 8 (20)	WC 8	55
PLANT X	XA 16	XB 24 (25)	XC 16	25
PLANT Y	YA 8	YB 16 (0)	YC 24 (35)	35
REQUIRE-MENTS	35	45	35	115 / 115

In such a case, we will choose an unused square (chosen normally in such a way that used squares appear in a staircase form) and put the quantity zero in that square. This is merely a computational device. We would treat this square as a used one. (Square YB in our example).

After doing this we would proceed further and solve the problem by either of the methods discussed earlier.

(ii) In improved solution: Let us take an illustration where such a situation would arise.

Illustration:

There are three plants W, X and Y. Every week these plants produce 90, 60 and 30 units of a product, respectively. There are three warehouses A, B and C where these products are to be transported. Every week 45, 75 and 60 units are to be transported to the three warehouses respectively.

Cost information is as follows:

TRANSPORTATION COST PER UNIT (in A)

From Plant	*To Warehouse A*	*To Warehouse B*	*To Warehouse C*
W	4	8	8
X	16	24	16
Y	8	16	24

Now, let us form transportation matrix and apply North-West Corner rule. The resulting matrix would be as shown in Fig. 35.10. Now, after finding improvement indices of all the unused squares (You can use any method), we find that improvement index for square YA is – 20, which is higher negative index than all other unused squares.

Find closed path for this square and do additions and substractions accordingly. You will get a new matrix as shown in Fig. 35.11. We can see that how there is degeneracy in the problem. Now, we would solve the problem in the same way as we had done when there was initial degeneracy — by treating an unused square as used square, by putting quantity zero in that square (we have taken square XB in our example).

Fig. 35.10

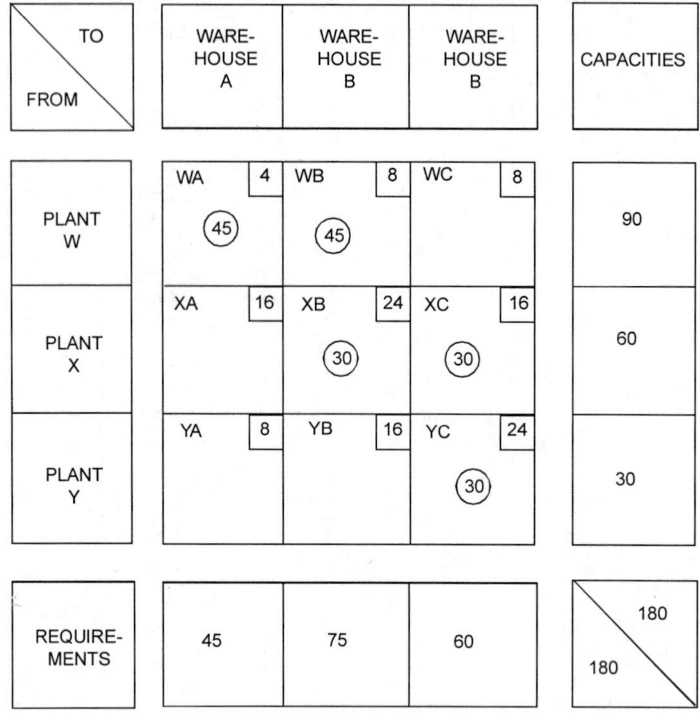

FROM \ TO	WAREHOUSE A	WAREHOUSE B	WAREHOUSE B	CAPACITIES
PLANT W	WA 4 (45)	WB 8 (45)	WC 8	90
PLANT X	XA 16	XB 24 (30)	XC 16 (30)	60
PLANT Y	YA 8	YB 16	YC 24 (30)	30
REQUIREMENTS	45	75	60	180 / 180

After doing this, problem can be solved in usual manner.

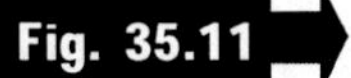

Fig. 35.11

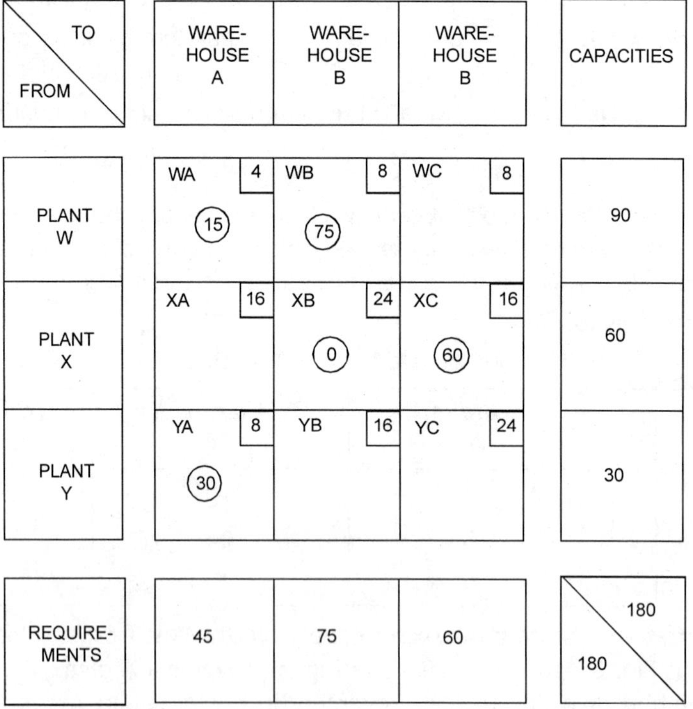

FROM \ TO	WAREHOUSE A	WAREHOUSE B	WAREHOUSE B	CAPACITIES
PLANT W	WA 4 (15)	WB 8 (75)	WC 8	90
PLANT X	XA 16	XB 24 (0)	XC 16 (60)	60
PLANT Y	YA 8 (30)	YB 16	YC 24	30
REQUIREMENTS	45	75	60	180 / 180

(B) Excessive number of used squares

You will face such a problem only when you have done some error in solving the transportation problem. So, when such a situation arises, check up all the processes you have carried out so far.

VII. Unbalanced Condition

Until now we have seen the cases where demand and supply are equal. But, in real life situations demand and supply may not be always in balance. So, let us consider the unbalanced conditions.

Unbalanced condition can be of two types —

(*i*) Supply is greater than demand.

(*ii*) Demand is greater than supply.

Let us see each of these conditions one by one.

(1) Supply exceeds demand

Let us take an illustration illustrating such a situation.

Illustration:

There are three plants W, X and Y producing 76, 82 and 77 units of a product per week, respectively. Three destinations A, B and C require 72, 102 and 41 units per week, respectively.

Cost information is as follows:

TRANSPORTATION COST PER UNIT (A)

From Plant	*To Warehouse A*	*To Warehouse B*	*To Warehouse C*
W	4	8	8
X	16	24	16
Y	8	16	24

Here we can see that total capacities exceed total requirements. In such a case we should add one more destination, *i.e.*, one more column. This column is known as dummy column. As the quantities in this column are not to be transported anywhere actually, transportation cost would be zero in such a column. The matrix formed with dummy column would be as shown in Fig. 35.12.

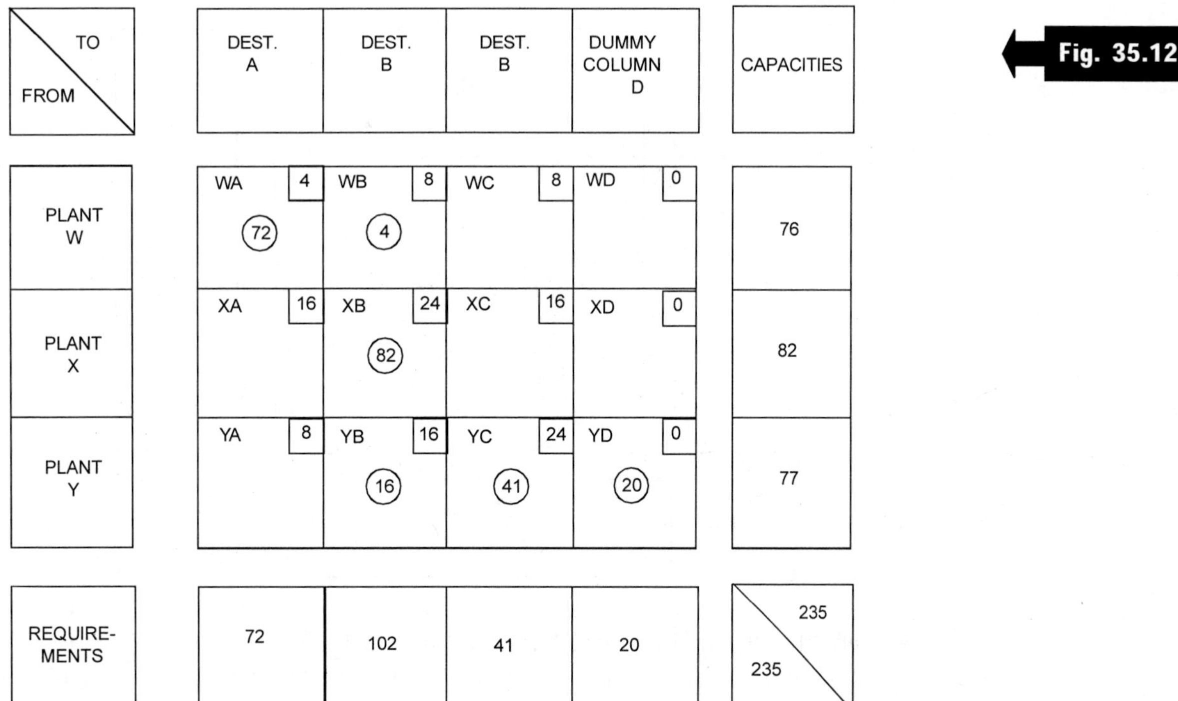

Fig. 35.12

After doing this, the problem can be solved in the usual manner. When you reach optimal solution, the quantities in dummy column would serve as a guideline as to how far the capacities of each of the plants are to be utilized.

(2) Where demand exceeds supply

Let us take an example.

Illustration:

Capacities of three plants, per week, W, X and Y are 56, 82 and 77 units respectively. Requirements of three projects, A, B and C are 82, 102 and 61, respectively.

Cost information is as follows:

TRANSPORTATION COST PER UNIT (in A)

From Plant	*To Warehouse A*	*To Warehouse B*	*To Warehouse C*
W	4	8	8
X	16	24	16
Y	8	16	24

Here, we can see that total requirements exceed total capacities. In such a case we should add one more row. This row is known as dummy row. As the quantities in this row are not to be actually produced there would be no transportation cost involved. The matrix formed with the dummy row would be as shown in Fig. 35.13.

Fig. 35.13

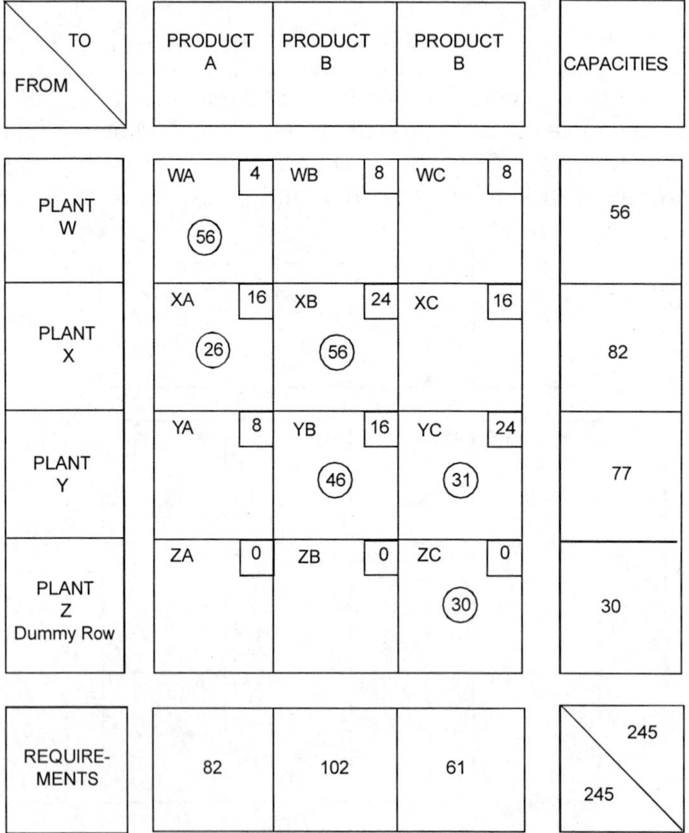

After doing this the problem can be solved in usual manner. The projects to which quantities are supplied by a dummy row would be getting that much quantity less than their requirements.

In this way, transportation problem of unbalanced conditions can be solved.

36

RE-ENGINEERING FOR THE 21ST CENTURY

Though re-engineering concept emerged at the beginning of the last decade of the last century, it has not lost its relevance even in this millennium; in spite of the presence of the so-called 'new economy' that co-exists with the 'old economy.' Re-engineering is being increasingly used to transform major operational chunks. The notion of a single person operation while handling customer service is in fact re-engineering. Similarly cross-functional teams, product made to fulfil customer orders rather than as a response to demand forecasts, decentralised low-cost purchasing and such other manifestations of re-engineering are seen everyday.

Re-engineering is not a panacea for slothful management. It came to be used as a generic term for change. Re-engineering has benefited those companies which implemented it faithfully. However, its full potential is yet to be realised. It was applied to back office in its early days. It also was applied to the factory and the warehouse. It has now come to be applied to the front-office. It touches the bottom-line by being applied to product development, sales and marketing. It is a close partner of IT. ERP is a re-engineering related technology. Internet must be integrated to re-engineering to realise its full potential. E-Commerce must be supported by solid re-engineered processes. Such re-engineered processes are easy to 'web-enable.'

In its first phase, re-engineering removed interfunctional boundaries. In its second phase, which is Internet-enabled, the inter-corporate boundaries are being removed, where processes do not stop at corporate doorsteps.

The basic motivations for re-engineering are the three Cs of customers, competition and change (Hammer and Champy).

Evolution of Corporation

Organizations of today are patterned after the concept of division of labour propounded by Adam Smith in his book *The Wealth of Nations* (1776). Here, each worker performs a part of a task, and becomes specialised in it, thereby improving productivity dramatically. The larger the organization, the more the work gets divided and the more specialised the worker becomes. Division of labour principle is not only relevant in manufacturing but in service industries too. Transportation gave a big fillip to the growth of organizations. Business bureaucracy was practised by the rail-road companies. Here people conformed to the procedures set. The command-and-control system was introduced. Assembly-line introduced by Ford brought work to the worker. Though each job of car making was made simpler, the co-ordination of people and combining their efforts became complex. Sloan of GM created smaller decentralised divisions to be managed from corporate HQ. Sloan extended the division of labour to management. The planning and control function became prominent after the World War II. The organization which evolved in the US later got duplicated in Europe and Japan. In those days, whatever was produced was consumed irrespective of quality and service. Capacity build up was the main concern. In this high-growth environment, pyramidal organization structure evolved. It can allow for expansion by adding the rank and file at the bottom or managers in the middle or top. As the work-load was divided into parts, each part was supervised properly. A scalar chain was created to introduce accountability.

The organizations however, became fat with several layers, and many people. The distance between the top and the bottom was too much. This is the genesis of the modern day corporation.

However, the organizations so evolved must adapt to the changing environment of today. We live in a different world. Business cycles are not predictable. Every other component of environment is changing. Adam Smith's idea is a matter of bygone era.

Competition, customer and change have affected the organization structure tremendously.

Competition

Competition is prolific, generic and specific. So many companies produce products which compete with our products. Besides, there is specific competition when the same product competes with us, say one tea brand and another tea brand, and generic competition when tea competes with other beverages like cold drinks. There is niche competition where similar products sell in different markets on different bases, say price or equality or service. Multinational competition is a fact of life in post-WTO regime. Competition sets benchmarks for others to follow.

Innovations of next generation may be introduced by pioneers, thus unsettling the established organizations. Pioneers author their own rules. Technology influences competition. Distribution and inventory functions are upgraded to confer more benefits. CRM or customer relationship management has increased interactions between the customers and the companies. It raises the expectations of the customers of all companies.

Customers

Customer-driven businesses are the norm today. They decide what they want and organizations have to cater to them. They also decide when and how they want it and how they will pay for it.

Mass market assumed that customers are all alike and are satisfied by a standard product. In mass market they had little choice. They had imperfect knowledge of the market. Now we realise that customers are not all cast in the same mould. They have varying needs and wants. We have to make products to satisfy these. Mass market is broken into many segments till we come to one single customer. Product innovations and competition changed the expectations of the customers. They demand more, knowing well that they will get it. Customer tracking has made companies more sensitive to what they want. The power has shifted from the producers to customers. Customers have better information thanks to Internet, communication facilities and advertising. Companies should shed their production-oriented and mass-market mentality. Each customer is a unique individual and he counts. Today, it is not a shortage but surfeit economy. People have high aspirations. They can afford to choose. Business is conducted on their terms. They do not like the organizations which are not ready to do so.

Change

As we have observed, competitive scene and customers have changed. So also there is a change in the very nature of change. Change has become a way of life. It is all pervasive and consistent. The rate at which change takes place has accelerated. Globalisation means more of global-level competition, with more of new products. Technological advances encourage innovations. Product Life Cycles (PLCs), have shortened, e.g., computers become obsolete in a matter of months. The new product development process must be hastened. Companies must be alert to changes taking place all around them. Maybe, our brands satisfy the customers. But still we may experience the decline in sales. Perhaps, the way we fill our orders may be wrong. There may be a change in an altogether unexpected component in the environment, and that may affect us.

Companies must adapt to the three components — customers, competition and change. Organizations geared to mass produce, stability and growth are not accustomed to a changing environment which calls for quick responses and flexibility.

Some managements place the blame at the door of the factors beyond their control. But the environment is successfully managed by some companies, and they move ahead. These examples undermine the external factor argument.

Companies in the red think that a wrong product portfolio is responsible for their troubles. But product portfolio is not a fixed thing. Most products have a short life cycle and they will fade out. Products *per se* do not bring success. The processes which create these products bring long-term success.

More change in corporate strategies is thought to be the remedy for sickness. There are mergers and acquisitions, changing the asset portfolio. But they should pay more attention to the operational processes — inventing, making, selling and servicing.

Management techniques by themselves also do not guarantee success — MBO, zero-based budgeting (ZBB), quality circles (QCs), portfolio management etc. Automation also considered an essential element of success.

A company becomes successful only when its operations are better managed than those of others. We should know how to work better. How best to get the work done is a formula for success.

Order-fulfilment, as per division of labour principle, becomes a task-oriented job which is not relevant in today's world. There should be someone to oversee the whole process. Many a cook spoils the broth. Task-orientation makes it error-prone. It is slow too. There is no element of customer service. Piece-meal approach wouldn't make it better. The whole process must be re-designed. Companies must learn to organize work around process. Process fragmentation leads to many problems — creativity and innovative spirit get killed. Hierarchy creates many problems. There are diseconomies of scale, seen in overheads in fragmented organizations. Putting disjointed pieces of task together takes its toll in terms of manpower and resources.

We thus have an organization operating in the current 21st century with its structure developed in the beginning of the 20th century and work processes at the end of the 20th century. We need an alignment between an organization and its environment.

What is Re-engineering?

Informally, we can understand against the above background, that re-engineering means reinvention of the company right from scratch in view of the current environment. It is just a restart, shedding all old systems. We have to find a better way of doing work.

How do we go about re-engineering? Which is the starting point? How people are involved? How re-engineering thinking is fashioned?

Some techniques have been developed empirically for re-engineering. These techniques are used to reinvent the way the work gets done.

Let us now define re-engineering formally.

"Re-engineering is the fundamental re-thinking and radical redesign of business processes to achieve dramatic improvements in critical, contemporary measures of performance such as cost, quality, service and speed." (Hammer and Champy)*

Some key concepts from the above definition are explained here.

Fundamental

What is our mission? Why this mission? How do we fulfil it? Why do we fulfil it this way? The whole process of conducting business is questioned. Many rules and assumptions may be out of place.

* Jim Champy and Michael Hammer are both systems engineers from MIT. They first wrote *Reengineering the Corporation.* It was on the *New York Times* best seller list for almost a year. It is reprinted in 25 languages worldwide. Champy has since gone on to write other books on related topics like *Reengineering Management* and *X-Engineering the Corporation: Reinventing Your Business in the Digital Age* and *Outermost.*

These assumptions are embedded in most processes. Things should never be taken for granted. We are not concerned with what *is* but with what *should be*.

Radical

We have to go to the root of things. Just superficial tinkering won't do. Cosmetic changes do not mean re-engineering. It is just not improvement or enhancement or modification. It is a total reinvention.

Dramatic

The aim is not to achieve some marginal improvements. We want a quantum jump in performance. Marginal improvement can be made by just fine tuning. Re-engineering comes on the scene when full blasting is called for.

Three categories of company need re-engineering. First, those companies which are in deep trouble. Second, companies which foresee trouble. Third, companies now healthy but desirous of even more robust health in future.

Processes

This happens to be the most important word in the definition of re-engineering. Most businesses so far were task-oriented rather than process-oriented, or people-oriented or structure-oriented. A business process is a series of activities requiring inputs and creating output which provides value to the customer. In order fulfilling process, the order is an input, there are a series of activities to fulfil it, and the output is the delivery of the ordered product to the customer. This placement has created value. The objective is to place the goods in the hands of the customer. We just can't concentrate only on the individual tasks. They are important, but still they are meaningless if the final outcome is not realised properly.

The above examples illustrate how re-engineering examines the whole process cutting across the organizational boundaries to bring about dramatic improvements, breaking rules traditionally followed and by using IT creatively.

IBM Credit Corporation used four different specialists before approving a credit proposal thereby lengthening a process. Instead, they put one generalist with access to data and techniques, the specialists used to process the application. It was a radical redesign. It shattered the assumption that you need specialists to process credit proposal. The performance improved drastically.

Ford had over-staffed accounts payable department which made the payment to the suppliers after tallying the purchase requisition, goods arrival note and invoice, consuming time and cost. This process of payment authorisation was changed. The procurement process incorporated the payment aspect too. The goods requisitioned were computer-fed, and the receiving department checked the goods arriving with the computer record, and if they tallied, at a specified date the payment was released. It reduced the manpower. It bypassed the receipt of invoice, and reconciliation of three documents in accounts payable. The point to be appreciated is that the process has been redesigned. It may change the nature of the organization. But that is incidental. This redesigning was enabled by the use of IT.

Kodak's rival Fuji introduced a sort of disposable camera, and Kodak had to act fast by re-engineering its product development process which would have taken 72 weeks to produce a similar camera. Kodak changed its traditional process to concurrent engineering. Engineers develop product at computer work station. They all connect to product design data base. Each day, this database is fed by individual engineer's work so as to make it a cohesive whole. Next morning, the participants in the development process see whether their individual work has distorted the overall design. The problem is sorted out immediately. Tooling starts at the early date. This cut the development process time by 50 per cent, from 72 weeks to 36 weeks. Even tooling and manufacturing costs are reduced by 25 per cent.

Re-engineering is not downsizing or automation or software engineering. It also does not mean organizational restructuring. It is also not just quality management, though both have some common features. In TQM existing processes are re-examined to enhance them. It does not aim at breakthroughs, as we do in re-engineering.

Re-engineering starts on a clean slate. It bids good-bye to conventions and time honoured assumptions. It seeks to reinvent new approaches to processes. It just reverses the industrial revolution.

Business process re-engineering or BPR is not just about reducing cost but also improving quality, speed to market, and changing the consumer experience. (Jim Champy)

CHARACTERISTICS OF RE-ENGINEERED PROCESSES

Re-engineered processes show certain common characteristics.

Combination of Several Jobs

In a re-engineered process, some jobs are integrated. The process compression may result into a single person handling the task from end-to-end called case worker, or a team called case team whose members are brought together at one location. This increases the speed and reduces the overheads.

Workers Decide

In re-engineered process, there is vertical integration, and the workers decide themselves as a part of their work, rather than expecting their superiors to do so. The horizontal and vertical integration makes the work cost effective, empowers workers and provides better customer service.

Natural Order Sequencing

There is no linear sequencing in a re-engineered process. It follows a natural precedence. When a process is freed from linearity, there are two advantages — concurrent performance of several jobs, and reduction in time between earliest time and latest time. It results into less delays.

Multiple Versions

Re-engineering ends standardisation observed in mass marketing of mass production. We have several versions of same process to adapt to the environment, but still the processes have economies of scale. A three-prolonged approach can be adopted in a multiple version process, e.g., credit appraisal for straightforward cases wholly computerised, appraisal for medium cases by an officer and for difficult cases by an officer assisted by specialists. One process for all makes the matter complicated. Multiversion process makes it simpler since each version deals with only the appropriate cases.

Sensible Work

Work is performed in a meaningful way. In a traditional organization, even trivial things like pencils will be purchased by the purchase department. However, it makes sense to allow the accountants who use these pencils to make their purchases. Customers can be encouraged to attend to minor repairs by counselling. Service technicians call on only when the problem is too complex. Sometimes, it makes sense to perform functions on behalf of the customer. A truck manufacturer may ask a tyre supplier to carry and manage inventory on its behalf.

Reduced Checks and Controls

In re-engineered processes, controls are sparingly used. Stricter control in a conventional organization means more time and more cost. In re-engineered processes, control is exercised over aggregate patterns rather than on individual cases. An insurer can settle claims for small accidents by paying the actual costs of repairs without sending assessors. Overbilling is avoided by studying the repair processes for different jobs and formulating an idea of standard charges. Thus a pattern is studied to take a decision.

Even though the process may be abused, by some, the excess cost is compensated by an economically streamlined process.

Minimal Reconciliation

In the re-engineered process, the external contact points reduced. In payment of purchases, the accounts department avoids the reconciliation of three documents — requisition, goods arrival note and invoice. The goods arrival point authorises the payment. In inventory management, the re-ordering decision can be shifted to the manufacturer who can ship the inventory to a retailer after approval. Here work has been relocated over organizational boundary. The supplier can add value to the product by taking over the functions of inventory management.

A Single Contact Point

A manager acts as a link between the process and customer. He provides all the information a customer needs.

Centralisation-Decentralisation Combination

In the re-engineered processes, companies can avail of the advantages of the combination of centralisation and decentralisation. Sales process is re-engineered by using IT advantageously. Sales people can connect to HQ through notebooks to access information. The software exercises controls so the sales people are immune to unreasonable prices and conditions of contract. Thus on one hand, autonomy is allowed to the sales people, and on the other hand due control over the process is exercised.

Though the re-engineered processes may show some characteristics listed above, their design is not a simple matter. It requires a great deal of creativity and innovativeness.

ORGANIZATIONAL SUPPORT

Re-engineering generates many changes in the organization.

Process Teams

Instead of functional teams spread across the whole spectrum of organization, the re-engineered organization brings forth process teams assigned one particular process; say fulfilling the orders. Work becomes integrated. The artificial separations are dispensed with. Such process teams can come for a short period too, say the new product development team, which is dismantled after the new product becomes a reality.

Job Restructuring

In assembly line work, each individual performs a particular task, in which he becomes a specialist. In re-engineering, process team workers are responsible for the overall process and are expected to have generalist skills. Individuals continue to perform certain tasks, but may perform several other tasks too. It becomes a multidimensional work. Work becomes more broad-based process performance borders on entrepreneurship. Work becomes rewarding. We can grow with work. More time is spent on work which adds value. Work is upgraded, and becomes more challenging and complex.

Empowered Team Members

In re-engineered processes, teams are given authority to take the decisions. Red-tapism is cut. It is a team that is self-directed. If they have to get supervisional sanction to proceed, they are not process teams. Recruitment and selection in a re-engineered organization become crucial. Job specifications just do not spell out the qualifications. They are equally emphatic about character. Self-discipline and motivation are important.

Training *vs.* Education

A team has to exercise judgement by having an insight and understanding of the problem. This comes after education. Training just improves skills.

Efficiency *vs.* Effectiveness

In traditional organization, efficiency matters though it may not lead to improved process performance. Effectiveness means doing the right things. It creates value. Re-engineering is result-oriented. In re-engineered organization, the criteria of measuring performance and compensation change. Persons are not paved in re-engineered organization on the basis of their position. They are valued for their contribution and performance.

Promotion

Promotion is based on ability and compensation on performance. We may make a good salesman a sales manager. The assumption is that a person who is good at sales will make a good manager of sales people. Often, this is not true. We may get a bad sales manager at the cost of a good salesman. Promotion or advancement should always be related to ability.

Values

In traditional organization, there is commitment to loyalty towards the boss. Though consumer-orientation is given top sympathy, it is not practised. In re-engineered organization, the bonus is paid on the basis of customer satisfaction. Managers then shift their focus. The organizational systems decide the values and beliefs. Management itself must be committed to these values. Changing process by itself would not work. It must be accompanied changing values. There should be realisation that we exist because of our customers. Value statements are meaningless without supporting management systems.

Less Supervision, More Loading

In a re-engineered organization, simple jobs become complex, and complex processes become simple. Process teams have no need to have close supervision. They require coaching for advice. Managers in a re-engineered organization are facilitators. They provide the conducive environment. They must have good HR skills.

Flat Structures

Work is organized around process and teams which perform these process. Communication is need-based. Control is vested in the people performing the process. Organizations tend to become flat after re-engineering. Structures are not rigid. They become flexible.

Leadership

As managers enable the workers to perform, their leadership role acquires greater importance. They influence and reinforce employee's values and beliefs.

An organization, follows a business system 'diamond' (Hammer and Champy). The business process changes, and consequently jobs and structure change. It also changes the personnel aspects — measurement of performance and compensation. These influence the values and beliefs of the employees which in turn support the business process. The integration of these four elements is important. A re-engineered organization replaces the existing diamond by a new diamond.

Information Technology

Information Technology plays an enabling role in re-engineering. Just automation or computerization of existing processes is not enough. It throws before us solutions which then seek problems it could solve, problems which perhaps remain hidden so far. It is inductive thinking. Technology should be utilised to do things which we are not doing rather than what we are doing. IBM did not envisage a market for PCs. But once PCs appeared, they brought a whole new class of applications.

Even scientists are given to deductive thinking. Edison thought the recording capability of phonograph is useful just to record dying statements of people. Telephone was thought to be a tool to reduce a sense of loneliness. IBM thought photocopying is not a great improvement upon carbon papers. Xerox ultimately tapped photocopying for convenience copies and not as a replacement of carbon paper. Technology makes a latent need relevant and tangible. People relate technologies to their existing frames of reference, and do not go beyond that. Needs and aspirations are shaped on the basis of what exists. Breakthroughs bring about an altogether new set of activities and actions unheard of so far. Teleconferencing has not reduced travel, but is has changed the way the work is performed. Technology breaks old rules and creates new styles — it re-engineers.

Technology, in other words, has disruptive power of breaking the existing system. IT makes information available at several places. An expert system enables a generalist to take the decisions of experts. Telecom allows business to avail of the advantages of centralisation and decentralisation. Decision making is not just the preserve of the managers. It becomes everyone's job. Information can be transmitted and received by persons in the field. Interactive videocontacts are substitutes of personal interaction. Tracking gives an idea where things are. Management Information Systems have an in-built feature that revises plans instantaneously.

We must be aware of what technologies are being developed, and plan smartly how best we can use them once they are available.

RESPONSIBILITY OF RE-ENGINEERING

In an organization, it is the people who re-engineer. In implementing re-engineering we come across a leader, who is a motivating force, and has enough clout and authority. He assigns re-engineering to a *manager*, and a *re-engineering team*. The strategy of re-engineering is formulated by a *steering committee*. An individual who develops re-engineering tools and techniques and co-ordinates the projects is called a *re-engineering czar*. (Hammer and Champy)

We shall discuss the roles of the people mentioned above one by one.

Leader

Re-engineering happens because of him. He is the senior executive, or a CEO, having enough authority to see re-engineering through. Tools and techniques of re-engineering are okay but if no leader supports these the efforts will go waste. Mostly a leader just emerges rather than appointed. He is a visionary and a motivating force. He sets goals for the followers, and gives them a feeling that these are their own goals. He triggers off the re-engineering efforts. He appoints managers to be in charge of the re-engineering process. He translates his own vision into reality through the re-engineering manager and his team. He creates a conducive environment for the team to operate. His leadership is just not positional, he draws strength from his character. He sets an example and leads from the front. He communicates through signals, and reinforces these by symbols, *e.g.*, he assigns talented people to the re-engineering job. He uses management systems to reinforce the re-engineering message. He rewards creativity and understands failures are stepping stones to success. He uses a fraction of his quality time to monitor re-engineering but he lives by re-engineering and makes it apparent in all his actions. Most re-engineering failures are failures of leadership. Sometimes the followers identify a potential leader.

Process Manager

He is a line manager sufficiently senior who is put in charge of the process which is being re-engineered. He is appointed by the leader after identifying the major processes. As a manager, he gets things going. He manages the team doing re-engineering. On the completion of the project, his job does not come to an end.

Re-engineering Team

They do the actual re-engineering. It is in charge of one process at a time. If several processes are being re-engineered, we will have more than one re-engineering teams. It consists of generally five to ten people. It is made up of some insiders and some outsiders. Insiders are a part of the organization, performing some activities involved in the process. They know the process and they build the confidence of the co-workers. But they have a narrow perspective; and would like to perpetuate the status quo. They may just be satisfied by some tinkering of the existing process. Outsiders disrupt the existing process, and are brought in for their dispassionate approach. They may be inside the organization in functions such as engineering, IT and marketing. They might be sourced externally. Insider-outsider ratio maybe 2 or 3 to one. Insiders and outsiders will discuss the issue threadbare. The discussions are likely to generate heat, but the aim is to generate light at the end. A team has to work in one place. A re-engineering team is quite comfortable with ambiguity. A team may have a captain who sets agenda for the team meeting. Team members must devote fully to the task, continue their association with the team all through the implementation and should be loyal to the process being re-engineered. The team has an inner core, and is surrounded by an outer ring of part-time and occasional contributors — they being the specialists in such areas as IT, PR or HR.

Steering Committee

Many companies opt for a steering committee for re-engineering which decides the priorities amongst the different re-engineering projects and resource allocation.

Re-engineering Czar

He is an individual who supports and enables the re-engineering effort and co-ordinates all the re-engineering activities.

RE-ENGINEERING OPPORTUNITIES

What we re-engineer are the processes, and not the departments. Processes may cut across several departments. Sometimes they remain invisible. Processes are what the companies do. Manufacturing process is essentially a procurement-to-despatching process. Some other recurring processes are sales starting from prospecting to ordering, product development, from concept to commissioning, order fulfilment from order to payment and service, from enquiry to satisfactory solution.

A process map is a chart of work flow through the company. A big organization may have just a handful of processes, *e.g.*, strategy development process, product development process, customer support process, manufacturing process, customer communications process. Some processes may not appear on the process map as we expect them but as a sub-process, *e.g.*, manufacturing can be a sub-process of order fulfilment. Sometimes sales may be just a sub-process of order acquisition in the overall order fulfillment process.

CHOOSING THE PROCESS TO RE-ENGINEER

From the map, we have to choose one or more processes which are to be re-engineered. Those processes which have become dysfunctional, which leave a major impact on our customers and which are feasible are chosen. A dysfunction process is in trouble, *e.g.*, a product development process that takes years to turn out a new product. Some of the symptoms of distress in a process are data redundancy, extensive information exchange and re-keying. It shows a fragmented process. Inventories management has a lot uncertainty, which must be removed. Many things do not contribute to added value. There is rework and iteration. Processes become complex over a period of time. Processes are prioritised on the basis of their importance in terms of the impact on outside customers. We can ask the customers what issues they care about strongly, which are then correlated to the processes. Feasibility indicates the likelihood that a particular re-engineering effort will succeed.

Some companies often chop the wrong product or process. This happens when the teams work in isolation. That is why we need a cross-functional teams. Most times, if changes are made in one process, others are affected. Besides, BPR is not a short-term measure. In order to be effective, it has to be an ongoing process.

Understanding the Process

After deciding which process is to be re-engineered, an attempt is made to understand it as it is carried out now. The intention is to take and the overall view, rather than a detailed analysis. The whole idea is to get an insight. Ideally, a process is best understood at the end of the customer. What do our customers want? What do they really need? What they feel about the gap between their need and want? What problems do they face? What do they do with the output? We try to understand the goals and problems of the customers. Just interrogation will not work. The re-engineering team must be observant. It must work with the customers. After understanding what the customer requirements are, we should examine what the process provides. It will indicate the direction for the new process.

Benchmarking is another tool that is available to the re-engineering team. Best is benchmarked in other companies. We have to take off from there. But benchmarking just makes you catch up with others. It is not a tool to excel. But it can be a source of ideas. Benchmarking can be from outside our own industry.

Process Redesign

The first step in the re-engineering is the process redesign using imagination, inductive thinking, and an off-beat approach. The conventional is questioned. Belief is suspended. A bold approach is advocated. It is not a step-by-step routine approach.

Though re-design is a creative approach, there are examples to adopt and adapt from other companies. Even in non-traditional processes, there are recurring characteristics and themes. Non-traditional characteristics are not obvious, as they are still not in practice. They are not a part of the collective traditional wisdom.

In passing an accident claim, an insurance company faces claims on two counts — medical and non-medical, say fixing a damaged car. The whole process of claim settlement can be re-designed by allowing an agent to settle claims of some lower amounts outside the company's administrative office, and by appointing authorised workshops for repair jobs. Process redesign starts by classifying claims into large and small exposures. In re-design, steps can be taken to settle claims fast. People like to deal with as few people as possible in the performance of a process. They don't like to deal with different people. While re-designing, several existing assumptions are questioned. We can harness the power of information technology to rethink the process, *e.g.,* check the credit rating of a customer who applies for a personal loan or claim-filing history of a customer.

It is not true that re-design is an expert's job or an insider's job. Being an outsider, on the contrary, helps. Everything is examined from customer's view-point. Redesign is a team effort and can be quite a funny experience.

Re-engineering Implementation

The most challenging task is to make people either accept or at least not oppose the re-engineering effort. You have to involve people. People must be educated about it. In fact, we have to sell the idea to them. First of all, they should understand why re-engineering is needed. We should spell out what we need to become, and how we can strive for that. A company prepares a 'case for action' and a 'vision statement' to articulate these concerns. If there are going to be job cuts, tell them so. Also tell them if they are willing to retool and relocate. They may be accommodated elsewhere in business.

A case for action of a pharma company may state the problem of long time taken to develop new drugs, while others have shorter development cycles. It raises concern about a decentralised R&D

effort. A saving in R&D expenditure is substantial. A case in action thus provides the background, states the problem, the competitive environment and the diagnosis. A case in action is thus, 'let us change' part.

The vision statement leads to 'what we change to.' It is the destination to be reached on re-engineering. A vision statement is our intention for the future, our operations in future and the results we intend to achieve in future. It is both qualitative and quantitative. It provides a focus and a sense of direction. It is a benchmark against which re-engineering effort can be judged. A vision statement is not just wishful thinking. It should be a powerful statement, capable of changing the basis of competition in the industry.

How to Succeed at Re-engineering?

While re-engineering, we have to avoid some common pitfalls to ensure our success.

1. Just tinkering with an existing process is not re-engineering. The temptation is great because using the existing process is more comfortable than using a radically new process. But this is the sure way to fail at re-engineering.
2. Sometimes, we focus on subsidiary issues like team work and innovation. But these emanate from processes and are the consequences. We have to shift focus to business processes. If we don't, we fail.
3. Re-engineering triggers off many changes while redesigning the process. We have to cope with these.
4. Re-engineering must go simultaneously with the change in mindset.
5. We should not be satisfied by marginal results, but should aspire for big results.
6. Some companies abandon re-engineering too early at the first sign of trouble.
7. We should not place constraints on the scope of the re-engineering effort.
8. A company's existing culture must not come in the way of re-engineering.
9. Re-engineering is not a bottom up approach. It is a top management job.
10. We should choose the right people for re-engineering.
11. Meagre resource allocation may come in the way of re-engineering.
12. Re-engineering should be a top priority. It just cannot be one middle item of corporate agenda.
13. We should concentrate on just a few re-engineering projects.
14. Re-engineering requires some time, and a CEO who is too close to retirement may not be a suitable candidate to put it in practice.
15. Re-engineering is not just another business improvement programme.
16. Re-engineering is not just redesigning. The redesigned process must be put into practice.
17. Re-engineering may pinch a few employees.
18. People may resist changes. But we must persist.
19. As re-engineering is stressful, it should be accomplished in a reasonable period of time.

Re-engineering fails or succeeds to the extent of the top management commitment. Those who embark upon re-engineering, with understanding, commitment and a strong desire to implement are sure to succeed at the re-engineering effort.

❧ ❧

37 WAITING LINES

Introduction

A new movie release at a cinema hall draws in a lot of crowd. People are enthusiastic and are eager to watch the new movie. They go to the ticket counter to purchase tickets. However, as there are many takers for the tickets, a queue is formed. We have to stand in the queue and await our turn before we get service. Like the cinema hall, there are many real life situations where we have to wait in queue, before getting service. Railways, Airport, banks, toll gates, library, traffic signal on the road, an assembly line in the factory are all examples of queuing systems.

Queuing theory is the study of a queuing system by developing a model of the system, and then running a simulation of the system. The simulation model of a queuing system is very useful tool in analyzing and studying the performance of a queuing system. For example, if we develop a model of Bank Teller's window, we can roughly find, for what time the teller remains busy, average number of customers in the queue, average waiting time of the customers etc. By studying these performance measures, we can attempt to improve the existing queuing system, or design a new queuing system. For simple systems, these performance measures can be computed analytically. But for realistic complex systems, a simulation is required.

Elements of a Queuing System

- **Customer:** A customer is the one, who is in need of service. Customers are people at a bank, cars in a parking lot, raw materials in a factory, students at a library, and airplanes on the runway.
- **Calling Population:** The customer is said to be generated from a common pool of entities called the calling population. For example, a bank may have 40,000 account holders. This is its calling population. But at any given, only a few them are likely to deposit or withdraw money from the bank. These likely few are the customers.
- **Waiting Area (Queue):** When a customer arrives at a bank, and finds that the teller is busy, he enters the queue or waiting area.
- **Server:** One who provides service to the customer is called the server. The bank teller, doctor at a clinic, robot at an assembly line, CPU in a computer, mechanic at the garage are examples of servers.

Costs involved in a Queuing System

Cost of Waiting Customers: Customers can impose a cost on the system. Suppose employees spend time waiting for photocopying to be done. This is called waiting cost.

Fig. 37.1
Queuing System

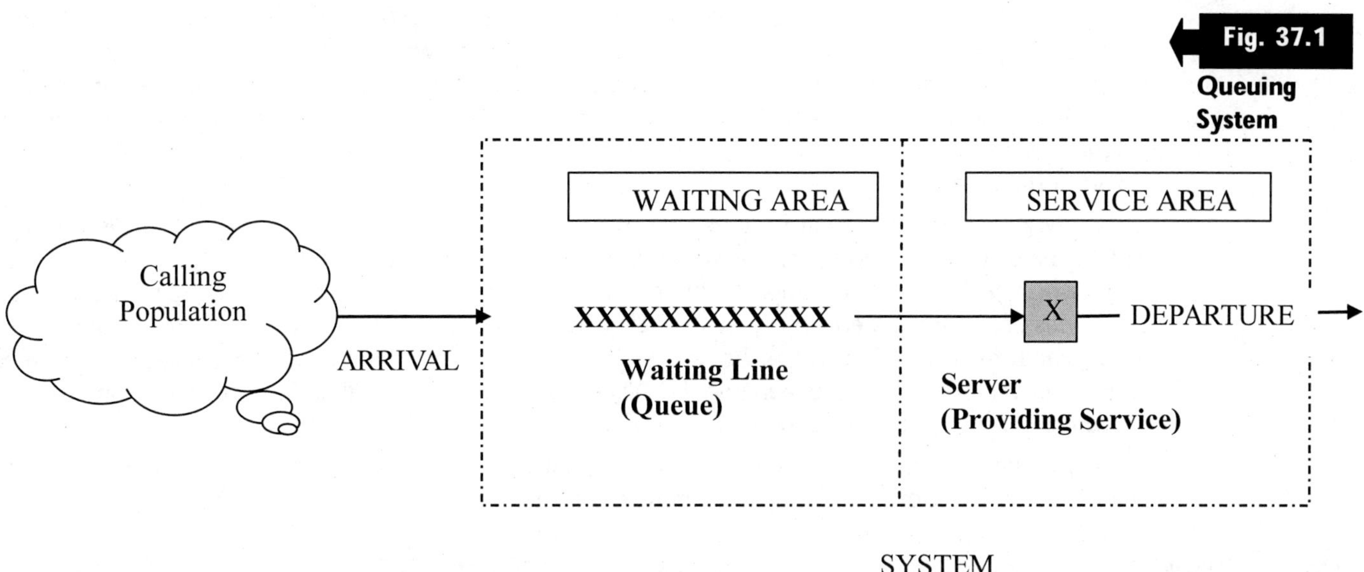

Cost of Servers: Servers may also impose a cost on the system. To provide quick photocopying service, and satisfy every customer, we may consider increasing the number of servers. This is called the cost of servers.

If the photocopying is not done quickly, it imposes a high waiting cost. This time could have been utilized in doing other productive activities. If the number of photocopier machines is more, the waiting cost goes down, but consequently the service cost shoots up.

Fig. 37.2
Plot of Cost *versus* Service Capacity

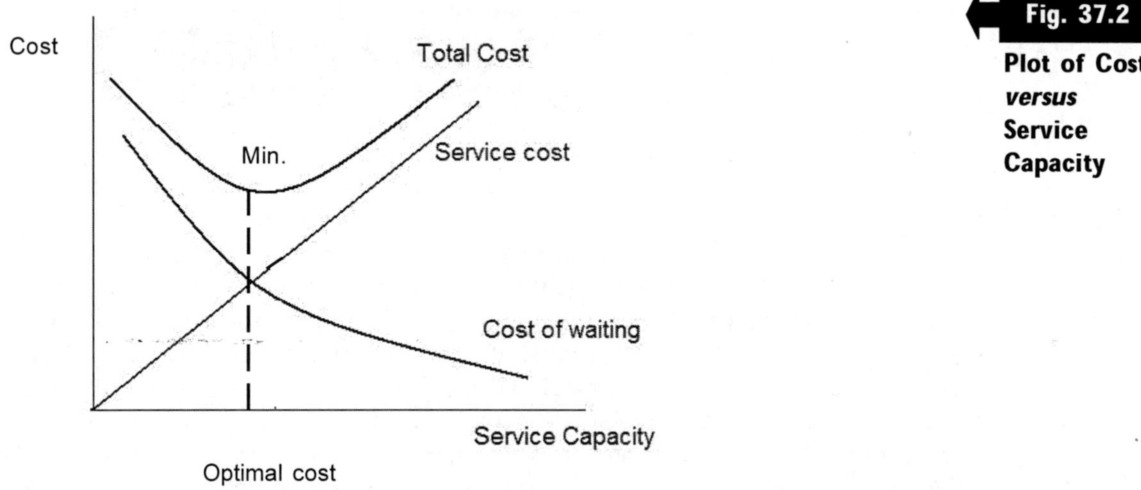

The cost of installing one additional photocopier can be compared to the value of the employee time saved. The waiting cost and service cost counterbalance each. If we try to reduce the waiting cost, the service cost rises. On the other hand, if we try to reduce the service cost, the waiting cost goes up. Thus, we need to find the optimal quality of service, at which the total cost becomes minimum.

Characteristics of a Queuing System

Calling Population: Calling population can be finite or infinite depending upon the situation. If the calling population is pretty large, for example the account holders in a bank, we assume it to be infinite. On the other hand, consider a bank with five machines. There is a worker to repair a machine in the case of a breakdown. Here the calling population is considered to be finite, because at the most five machines would be down at the same time.

System Capacity: System capacity can also be finite or infinite. In many queuing systems there might be a limit on the number of customers that can be in the waiting area. If an arrival occurs when the system is full, that arrival is turned away and cannot enter the system. For example, a barber shop has one barber, and five chairs in the waiting area. Thus, a maximum of six people can be accommodated into the system. On the other hand, some systems like railway reservation counters can be assumed to have infinite capacity.

Arrival Process: By arrival process, we mean the way the customers arrive in the system. The arrival process could be uniform, for example, customers arrive every 1 minute. Arrival process can be random, which means customers arrive randomly at any given time. This typically happens when the arrivals are unscheduled. In the case of unscheduled arrivals, the arrival rate (No. of arrivals in 1 hour) can take any random value. Arrival rate is said to be a random variable. Because, arrival times and inter-arrival times (Time between two arrivals) are unpredictable, we therefore talk about the **averages** and **statistical distributions** of these times.

A research group goes to a bank and carries out a study. They record the number of customers arriving at the bank every hour. They summarized the results in the form of a histogram.

Fig. 37.3

Frequency Distribution

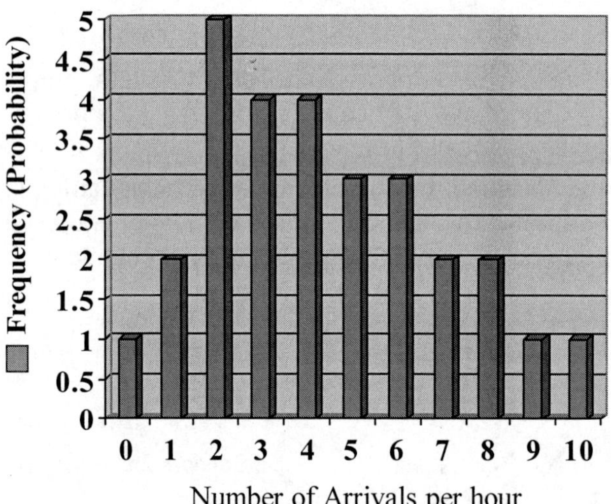

It can be seen from the graph that, the chances of 2, 3 or 4 customers arriving in an hour are the highest. It happens very rarely, that no customers arrive at all, or 10 customers come together. Thus, although the arrivals occur at unscheduled times, the possibility of 2 – 4 customers arriving in an hour is more likely than, the possibility of 10 customers arriving in an hour. Hence, the arrival process is said to follow a **statistical distribution.** There is a probability (likelihood) associated with each value of the random variable – Arrival rate. When customers in a given period of time, arrive at random, the distribution of arrivals is shown to follow the Poisson Distribution. In Poisson distribution, the arrivals are independent of each other, that is, the arrival time is unaffected by preceding or future arrivals. If arrivals fit into a Poisson distribution, we call the arrival process as a Poisson Process.

As an alternative to arrival times, we can also use inter-arrival times to describe a queuing system. As a thumb-rule, if the arrival process is Poisson, the inter-arrival times follow an exponential distribution.

Queue Behaviour and Queue Discipline: It refers to the behavior of customers waiting in a queue for service.

1. **Balking:** Customers refuse to join the queue, by seeing the length of the queue.
2. **Reneging:** Customers wait in queue for a long time, ultimately get tired and leave the queue, before getting service.
3. **Jockeying:** Customers switch between waiting lines.

4. **Combining or dividing:** Combining or dividing queues at certain queue lengths.
5. **Cycling:** Return to the queue immediately after obtaining service.

Queue discipline is the method that is followed when selecting the next customer to be served. Queueing discipline can be priority based, First In First Out (FIFO), Last In First Out (LIFO).

Service Times: Service time is the time between the customer entering the service area, getting served, and then departing from the system. It is the time spent by the customer in the service area. Service times may be constant or of random duration. In the latter case, we can model the service times using identically, and independently distributed random variables.

Service Facility: There are two ways of providing service:

1. Single Server (such as a barber's chair).
2. Multiple or parallel servers either with a single queue, or with multiple queues.

The six characteristics namely, Arrival rate, Service time, Number of servers, Queue discipline, System capacity and Calling population size are the basic parameters that can be used to describe any type of queue.

Kendall's Queuing Notation

There are many different types of queuing systems. Kendall has introduced a notation to describe any queuing system formally. The notation is used to describe the six different parameters of a queue.

A = Arrival process

B = Service time Distribution

C = No. of servers

X = Queuing discipline

Y = System capacity

Z = Size of the calling population.

Every queue can be described by this six parameters using the notation (A/B/C):(X/Y/Z).

The basic queuing models using Kendall's notation are:

(*i*) (M / M /1) : (FCFS / ∞ / ∞) — Single Server Queue with Poisson arrivals, exponential service times, unlimited capacity and infinite calling population.

(*ii*) (M / G /1) : (FCFS / ∞ / ∞) — Single Server Queue with Poisson arrivals, unknown service time distribution, unlimited capacity and infinite calling population.

(*iii*) (M / M /C) : (FCFS / ∞ / ∞) — Parallel Server Queue with Poisson arrivals and service times, unlimited capacity and infinite calling population.

(*iv*) (M / M /∞) : (FCFS / ∞ / ∞) — No. of servers is infinite.

(*v*) (M / M /C) : (FCFS / N / ∞) — Multi-server Queue with Poisson arrivals, Exponential service times and limited service capacity.

Long-run Measures of Performance (Operating Characteristics)

A queuing system is evaluated by one or more measures of performance. There are several measure of performance of queuing systems. They are stated below:

The Average Waiting Time, W

The average time the customer spends in the system, waiting in the queue plus being served is said to be the average waiting time.

The Average Waiting Time in the Queue, W_q

This is the average time a customer will wait in the queue, before he gets service.

The Average Number of Customers in the System, L

The number of customers in the system, those in the queue as well as those being served on an average.

The Average Number of Customers in the Queue, L_q

The number of customers in the queue on an average.

The Probability of the System Being Empty, P(0)

The probability that there are no customers in the system (that is the server is idle).

The Probability of Being in the System Longer than Time t, P{T > t}

The probability of waiting for a time period T, which is larger than a designated time t.

Probability of Finding Exactly N Customers in the System, P(N)

It is the likeliness of finding exactly N customers in the system, at any given point of time.

Probability that the Number of Customers in the System, N, will be Larger than a Specified Number of Customers, n

This measure can be used to find out whether balking would take place. That is, if a system can accommodate six people at a time, then when customers arrive, they see that there is no more room to wait, and leave. Thus, the probability of finding more than six people in a such a system will be the *balking rate* of the system.

Information flow in Queuing Models

The long run measures of performance of queuing models can be computed from three input variables:

Inputs and Outputs of a Queuing Model

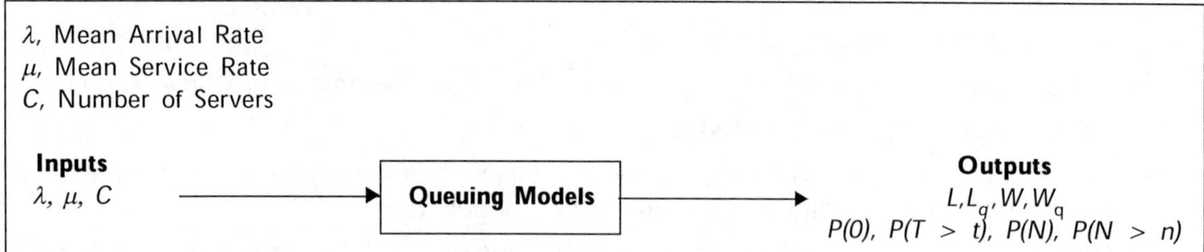

1. SINGLE SERVER QUEUE (*M* / *M* / 1): (FCFS / ∞ / ∞) MODEL

The following assumptions are made in this model:

(*a*) Arrival rate follows Poisson Distribution

(*b*) Service rate follows Poisson Distribution

(*c*) Number of servers is one

(*d*) Queue discipline is FCFS

(*e*) System capacity is infinite

(*f*) Calling population is infinite.

Little's Equations

J.D.C. Little has developed three relationships between the performance measures L, Lq, W, Wq. Given any one of these measures in terms of input parameters (λ, μ) we can find the other three using

Little's equations.

Little's equations are:

$L = \lambda W,$

$L = \lambda W_q$

$W = W_q + \frac{1}{\mu}$

Deriving the parameters L, Lq, W, Wq

(*i*) The average number of customers in the System L, is given by

$$L = \frac{\lambda}{\mu - \lambda}$$

(*ii*) The average waiting time of the customers, W will be:

Plugging in $L = \frac{\lambda}{\mu - \lambda}$ into Little's equation,

$$L = \lambda W$$

$$\left(\frac{\lambda}{\mu - \lambda}\right) = \lambda W$$

$$\therefore W = \frac{1}{\mu - \lambda}$$

(*iii*) The average waiting of the customers in the queue, Wq is given by,

Plugging in the value of $W = \frac{\lambda}{\mu - \lambda}$ into Little's equation we get,

$$W = W_q + \frac{1}{\mu}$$

$$\left(\frac{1}{\mu - \lambda}\right) = W_q + \frac{1}{\mu}$$

$$W_q = \frac{1}{\mu - \lambda} - \frac{1}{\mu}$$

$$W_q = \frac{\lambda}{\mu(\mu - \lambda)}$$

(iv) The average number of customers in the queue, Lq is given by,
Using Little's equation, $L_q = \lambda W_q$

$$L_q = \lambda\left(\frac{\lambda}{\mu(\mu - \lambda)}\right)$$

$$L_q = \frac{\lambda^2}{\mu(\mu - \lambda)}$$

Other Measures of Performance

(*i*) Utilization factor of the server $\rho = \frac{\lambda}{\mu}$

(*ii*) Probability of finding N customers in the system, $P(N) = (1 - \rho)\rho^N$

(*iii*) Probability of finding more than n customers in the system, $P(N > n) = \rho^{n+1}$

(iv) Probability of being in the system longer than time t, $P(T > t) = e^{-(\mu-\lambda)t}$

Cost Analysis

Queuing systems can be compared on the basis of their total cost (TC), which is composed of two components: Waiting Cost (C_W) and Service Cost (C_S). The total cost is the sum of the waiting cost and the service cost.

$TC = C_W + C_S$

Suppose each customer incurs a total cost of wait at the rate of ₹ A/hr. Each customer on an average waits for a time W. Therefore, average cost of waiting/customer is,

Average cost of wait/customer = ₹ AW

The mean arrival rate of customers is λ. So, the average cost of wait can be computed as follows:

Average cost of wait = ₹ $AW(\lambda)$ = ₹ $A(\lambda W)$ = ₹ AL

The cost of service can be composed of fixed costs as well as variable costs. The cost can be proportional to time, per hour. It can be proportional to per customer served, or per unit capacity, for example a facility can serve upto 10 customers per hour.

Example 1:

The arrival rate of papers at a printing press follows Poisson distribution with a mean of 45 reams per hour. The service rate of the press also follows Poisson distribution with a mean of 60 reams per hour.

(*i*) What is the utilization factor of the press?

(*ii*) What is the probability that the press will remain shut?

(*iii*) What are the chances of waiting longer than 10 minutes in the system?

(*iv*) Compute the measures of performance L, L_q, W, W_q.

(*v*) Each ream of paper imposes a cost of ₹ 200. Compute the waiting cost.

(*vi*) The press imposes a cost of ₹ 10,000 per hour. Hence, compute the total cost.

Solution:

We have the following data :

Arrival rate, λ = 45 per hour

Service rate, μ = 60 per hour

(*i*) Utilization factor $\rho = \frac{\lambda}{\mu} = \frac{45}{60} = 0.75$

(*ii*) Probability of the press remaining idle, $P\rho(0)$

We have, $P(N = 0) = (1 - \rho)\rho^N = (1 - \rho)\rho^0 = (1 - \rho)$

$P(0) = 1 - 0.75 = 0.25$

(*iii*) Chances of waiting longer than 10 minutes, $P(T > \frac{1}{6}\text{ hr})$

$P(T > 0.5) = e^{-(\mu-\lambda)t} = e^{-(60-45)(0.166)} = 0.08$ = 8 per cent

(*iv*) $L = \frac{\lambda}{\mu - \lambda} = \frac{45}{60 - 45}$ = 3 reams of paper

$$L_q = \frac{\lambda^2}{\mu(\mu - \lambda)} = \frac{(45)^2}{60(60 - 45)} = 2.25 \text{ reams of paper}$$

$$W = \frac{1}{\mu-\lambda} = \frac{1}{60-45} = 0.067 \text{ hours} = 4 \text{ minutes}$$

$$W_q = \frac{\lambda}{\mu(\mu-\lambda)} = \frac{45}{60(60-45)} = 0.05 \text{ hours} = 3 \text{ minutes}$$

(*v*) C_w = AL = (200)(3) = ₹ 600 per hour

(*vi*) C_S = ₹ 1,000 per hour.

Total Cost TC = $C_W + C_S$ = ₹ 1,600 per hour

Example 2:

A car manufacturer is considering the purchase of industrial robots for welding of cars on the production line. Robot A is capable of processing 20 jobs per hour, at the cost of ₹ 1,000 per day. Alternatively, robot B is capable of processing 30 jobs per hour at the cost of ₹ 1,500 per day. The robot is going to be installed at a factory, which is open 12 hours a day, with an average arrival rate of 15 jobs per hour. Each job incurs a cost of ₹ 30 per hour. Should the company purchase robot A or robot B?

Solution:

The solution will be based on the cost analysis and comparison of the queuing systems.

Comparing Measures of Performance

Parameters	***Robot A***	***Robot B***
λ, given per hour	15	15
μ, given per hour	20	30
Utilisation Factor $\rho = \frac{\lambda}{\mu}$	0.75	0.5
L customers	3	1
W hours per customer	0.2	0.067
P(0)	0.25	0.5

Robot A

Each job spends W = 0.2 hours in the factory, and because 180 jobs arrive at the factory (15 jobs every hour for 12 hours), there will be total waiting time of 0.2(180) = 36 job – hours. At ₹ 30 per hour, this waiting time will cost the company 30(36) = ₹1080 a day. The total cost is thus,

₹ 1,080 + ₹ 1,000 machine cost = ₹ 2,080 per day.

Robot B

Each job spends W = 0.067 hours in the factory, and because 180 jobs arrive at the factory (15 jobs every hour for 12 hours), there will be total waiting time of 0.067(180) = 12 job – hours. At ₹ 30 per hour, this waiting time will cost the company 30(12) = ₹ 360 a day. The total cost is thus,

₹ 360 + ₹ 1,500 machine cost = ₹ 1,860 per day.

Thus, Robot B is cheaper than Robot A, by ₹ 220 per day. Note that, even though Robot B is utilized only 50 per cent of the time, it is still the better machine to purchase (considering costs only).

COST COMPARISON FOR THE INDUSTRIAL ROBOTS

System	Cost of Service	Cost of Waiting				TC	TC
	Service Cost, Cs	λ	W	C	$C_w = \lambda WC$	(₹ per hour)	(₹ per day)
Robot A	₹ 1,000 per day = ₹ 84 per hour	15	$\frac{1}{5}$	30	90	84 + 90 = 174	2080
Robot B	₹ 1,500 per day = ₹ 125 per hour	15	$\frac{1}{15}$	30	30	125 + 30 = 155	1860

2. MULTI-SERVER QUEUE (M/M/C) : (FCFS/∞/∞) MODEL

The parameters of this model are as follows:

(*i*) Arrival rate follows Poisson Distribution

(*ii*) Service rate follows Poisson Distribution

(*iii*) Number of servers is C

(*iv*) Queue discipline is FCFS

(*v*) System capacity is infinite

(*vi*) Size of the calling population is infinite.

Unlike a single server queue, a multi-server queue consists of multiple servers. Each server has its own utilization factor ρ. So, we define the effective utilization factor of the system as,

$$\text{Effective utilization, } \bar{\rho} = \frac{\rho}{C} = \frac{\lambda}{C\mu}$$

Some of the most common measures of performance are:

1. *The probability of finding no customers in the system (an idle system):*

$$P(0) = \frac{1}{\dfrac{\rho^C}{C!(1-\bar{\rho})} + \displaystyle\sum_{i=0}^{C-1} \frac{\rho^i}{i!}}$$

2. *The probability of finding exactly N customers in the system:*

$$P(N) = P(0)\frac{\rho^N}{N!} \quad \text{when } N \le C \text{ (No. of customers is less than no. of servers)}$$

$$= \frac{P(0)\,\bar{\rho}^N C^C}{C!} \quad \text{when } N > C \text{ (No. of customers are more than the no. of servers)}$$

3. *The average number of customers in the waiting line:*

$$L_q = \frac{P(0)\,\rho^C \bar{\rho}}{C!(1-\bar{\rho})^2}$$

The remaining measures of performance can be computed using Little's equations.

Example 3:

In a machine shop, mechanics repair small electric motors which arrive according to a Poisson process at a rate of 15 per week (5-day 40 hours work week). Analysis of the past data indicates that engines can be repaired on an average, in 2.5 hours. There are 3 mechanics in the shop.

(*i*) What is the probability that the mechanics will sit idle?

(*ii*) How many hours should a customer expect to leave a motor for repair in the shop on an average?

Solution:

We have the following data:

Mean Arrival Rate, $\lambda = \frac{12}{40}$ per hour

Mean Service Rate, $\mu = \frac{2}{5}$ per hour

Server utilization factor $\rho = \frac{\lambda}{\mu} = \frac{\left(\frac{12}{40}\right)}{\left(\frac{2}{5}\right)} = \frac{12}{40} \times \frac{5}{2} = \frac{3}{4}$

Effective Server Utilization $\bar{\rho} = \frac{\lambda}{C\mu} = (1/3)(3/4) = 1/4$

(*i*) Probability that the mechanic will sit idle,

$$P(0) = 1\bigg/\left[\frac{\rho^C}{C!(1-\bar{\rho})} + \sum_{i=1}^{C-1}\frac{\rho^i}{i!}\right]$$

$$= \left[\frac{0.75^3}{3!(1-0.25)} + \sum_{i=0}^{2}\frac{0.75^i}{i!}\right]^{-1}$$

$$= \left[\frac{0.4218}{4.5} + 1 + \frac{0.75}{1!} + \frac{0.5625}{2!}\right]^{-1}$$

$= (2.125)^{-1} = 0.47$

(*ii*) To calculate W, we have to first calculate Lq.

$$L_q = \frac{P(0)\rho^C\bar{\rho}}{C!(1-\bar{\rho})^2} = 0.0146 \text{ motors}$$

$$W_q = \frac{L_q}{\lambda} = 0.0488 \text{ hours} = 3 \text{ minutes}$$

$$W = W_q + \frac{1}{\mu} = 2.5473 = 2 \text{ hours } 33 \text{ minutes}$$

Example 4:

Cars arrive at a service centre at random for a car-wash, at an average rate of 5.8 per hour. The service centre estimates that an average car-wash followed by blower/drying process lasts 10 minutes. However, the service centre is concerned about the possibility of a long queue and wonders if it needs to install more car-washing and drying machines.

Solution:

We have the following data:

λ = 5.8 per hour

μ = 6 per hour

(*i*) If there is only one washer and dryer machine installed, then it is a system with a single server.

Therefore:

$$L = \frac{\lambda}{\mu - \lambda} = 29 \text{ cars}$$

$$L_q = \frac{\lambda^2}{\mu(\mu - \lambda)} = 28.03 \text{ cars in the waiting line}$$

$$W = \frac{1}{\mu - \lambda} = 5 \text{ hours average time in the service centre per car}$$

$$W_q = \frac{\lambda}{\mu(\mu - \lambda)} = 4.83 \text{ hours average wait per car.}$$

Obviously, the service has to be concerned about the waiting period of the customers, an expected line length of 28 cars, and a total time of five hours before they may leave for home.

(*ii*) Solution with two washer-cum-dryer machines installed

Utilisation factor ρ = 0.967

Effective utilisation factor $\bar{\rho}$ = 0.4835

P(0) = 0.3514

$$L_q = \frac{0.3514(0.967)^2(0.484)}{2!(0.516)^2} = 0.216$$

L = 0.216 + 0.967

W_q = 0.216/6 = 0.036 hours = 2.16 minutes

W = 1.183/6 = 0.197 hours = 11.82 minutes

By increasing the number of servers, the waiting time of the customer is brought from many hours to just a few minutes. Hence, the service centre should consider adding another washer-cum-drying facility.

Example 5:

The arrival rate of vehicles at the toll plaza follows Poisson Distribution with a mean of 40 per hour. The service rate of toll-collector at the toll-gate also follows Poisson distribution with a mean of 30 per hour. The waiting cost of a vehicle in queue is ₹ 200 per hour. The labour rate per hour is ₹ 50. Determine the optimal number of toll gates to be made to collect the toll, such that the total cost is minimized.

Solution:

The following data are given:

Arrival rate, λ = 40 per hour

Service rate, μ = 30 per hour

Waiting cost = ₹ 200 per hour

Labour cost = ₹ 50 per hour

Since, $\lambda > \mu$, a minimum of 2 toll gates will be required. Therefore,

$$\rho = \frac{\lambda}{\mu} = \frac{40}{30} = 1.33$$

Case 1: When C = 2, $\bar{\rho}$ = 0.667

$$P(0) = \left\{\frac{\bar{\rho}^C}{C!(1-\bar{\rho})} + \sum_{i=0}^{C-1}\frac{\rho^i}{i!}\right\}^{-1} = \left\{\frac{(1.33)^2}{2!(1-0.667)} + \frac{1.33^0}{0!} + \frac{1.33^1}{1!}\right\}^{-1}$$

$$P(0) = 0.2$$

$$L_q = \frac{P(0)\rho^C\bar{\rho}}{C!(1-\bar{\rho})^2} = \frac{0.2(1.33)^2\,(0.667)}{2!(1-0.667)^2} = 1.08 \text{ customers}$$

Therefore, Waiting cost per hour = 1.08 × 200 = ₹ 216

Service cost per hour = 2 × 50 = ₹ 100

Total cost per hour = 216 + 100 = ₹ 316

Case 2: When C = 3, $\bar{\rho}$ = 0.445

$$P(0) = \left\{\frac{\rho^C}{C!(1-\bar{\rho})} + \sum_{i=0}^{C-1}\frac{p^i}{i!}\right\}^{-1} = \left\{\frac{(1.33)^2}{3!(1-0.445)} + \frac{1.33^0}{0!} + \frac{1.33^1}{1!} + \frac{1.33^2}{2!}\right\}^{-1}$$

$$P(0) = 0.255$$

$$L_q = \frac{P(0)\rho^C\bar{\rho}}{C!(1-\bar{\rho})^2} = \frac{0.255(1.33)3(0.445)}{3!(1-0.445)^2} = 0.144 \text{ customers}$$

Therefore, Waiting cost per hour = 0.144 × 200 = ₹28.90

Service cost per hour = 3 × 50 = ₹150

Total cost per hour = 28.90 + 1.50 = ₹178.90

Case 3: When C = 4, $\bar{\rho}$ = 0.334

Here, the total wages for 4 toll-collectors itself if 4 × 50 = ₹ 200. Hence with respect to 4 servers will be greater than ₹ 200.

Thus, the minimum total cost is ₹ 178.90, when the number of toll-gates is 3. Therefore, the optimal number of toll-collectors to be employed is 3.

SIMULATION

Simulation is an imitation of a real-world process or system, for the purpose of studying the behaviour of the system. Simulation is not strictly a model. A model represents reality. A simulation imitates reality. Simulation is a technique for conducting experiments. Simulation whether by hand or computer simulation, it is used only when the model in consideration is too complex to be solved by using analytical or mathematical techniques.

Model

A model is an abstract representation of the real-world system. It is usually a set of assumptions, which are stated in the form of mathematical or logical relationships. Once a model is constructed, we can obtain standard results like:

- Percentage utilization of servers
- Average number of waiting customers
- Average waiting time of customers.

All real world systems have different properties, which are of interest. Broadly, these properties fall into two categories: fixed and varying. Fixed properties of a system are called **Parameters**. For example, in a simple inventory system, if the people in a bank arrive at scheduled times, the arrival times are known and fixed. Thus, arrival time would be called a parameter. Properties that keep varying, as the system progresses in time, are called **Variables**. For example, the demand of a product varies over time. Hence, demand would be called a random variable.

Types of Simulation Model

- **Deterministic Simulation Model:** A deterministic simulation model has no random variables as inputs. Deterministic models have a known set of inputs and result in a fixed set of output. Deterministic arrivals occur at a clinic, if all the patients arrive at scheduled appointment times.
- **Probabilistic Simulation Model:** A probabilistic (stochastic) simulation model has one or more random variables as inputs. This means that each variable has an element of chance associated with it. People arriving randomly at a bank can be considered as a probabilistic system.

Monte Carlo Methodology

Real-world systems that exhibit an element of chance in their behaviour, can be simulated with the help of a technique called Monte-Carlo method. Thus, Monte-Carlo method is used to simulate probabilistic system. We can generate random samples (random numbers) to simulate the random inputs to the probabilistic systems. Before we study the crux of the Monte-Carlo technique, let's get familiar with a few basic terms.

Uniform Distribution:

Considering an experiment, where we roll a dice. The number that appears on the dice can be anything, 1, 2, 3, .., 6. In other words, its outcome is unknown and random. Thus, number that appears on the throw of a dice is a random variable that takes values in the range of {1, 2, 3, 4, 5, 6}. A dice has six faces. Thus, the chances of getting a 1, are the same as the chances of getting a 2, and are the same as the chances of getting a 3, 4, 5, 6. Each face of the dice is equally likely to appear. The chances of getting any face on the throw of a dice are 1/6th. Let X be the random variable that represents the number that appears on the roll of a dice. So,

Probability(X = 1) = Probability(X = 2) = Probability(X = 3) = ... = Probability(X = 6).

In other words, the random variable X is said to be distributed uniformly. Each of the values that X takes is equally likely to appear on the roll of a dice.

Random Number:

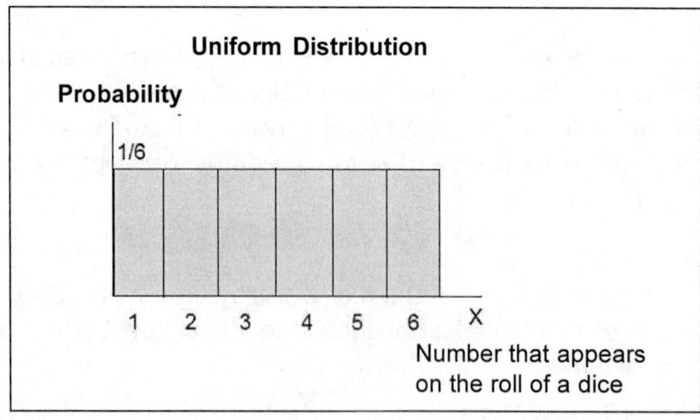

A random number is a number picked at random from a population of uniformly distributed numbers. Thus, each number in such a population has an equal chance of being drawn. Each number is equally likely to be picked up. Random numbers are chosen in different ways, depending upon the population.

Table 37.1

Random Digit Assignment

Population	*Random Number*
0 to 1	Decimal - 0.62
0 to 9	Single digit - 6, 8, 0
0 to 99	Two digits - 16, 83, 42
0 to 999	Three digits - 132, 602, 027

If the population under consideration is 1000, we generate three digit random numbers. If the population under consideration is of size 100, we generate two digit random numbers and so on.

Table of Random Numbers:

We can use a table of random numbers to generate pseudo-random numbers. Such a table is given at the end of the chapter.

Monte-Carlo Process

Step 1. Construct a cumulative probability distribution

We first have to assume the probability distribution of the random variables in question. Once the probabilities of the random variables are known, we find the cumulative probability distribution.

Step 2. Assign a range of RNs

Using the cumulative probabilities, we assign a range of random numbers to each of the values that the random variable takes.

Step 3. Generate a RN

Generate a random number using the random number tables.

Step 4. Predict a specific value of the variable of interest

Take the generated RN, and find the range in which the RN falls. Thus, we can predict the value of the input variable. These predicted values are then used in the simulation process.

Simulation of Waiting Lines

Example 6:

Consider an assembly line which assembles a product of considerable size, such as Television set. There are two workstations on the assembly line managed by Able (*first*) and Baker (*second*) respectively. The inter-arrival time of jobs has the following distribution:

Inter-arrival time (minutes)	*Probability P(x)*
3	0.1
4	0.15
5	0.35
6	0.25
7	0.15

A data-collection form was used to observe the performances of Able and Baker. The following are the service-distributions of Able and Baker.

Service Distribution of Able		Service Distribution of Baker	
Service time (minutes)	**Probability P(x)**	**Service time (minutes)**	**Probability P(x)**
2	0.3	3	0.35
3	0.28	4	0.25
4	0.25	5	0.2
5	0.17	6	0.2

Find by using simulation:

(*a*) Average performance time of each worker.

(*b*) Output rate of product through this line.

(*c*) How much time does Able wait for Baker?

(*d*) How much time does Baker wait for Able?

Solution:

Step 1. For product k, generate an inter-arrival time A_K. Add it to the previous arrival time T_{K-1} to get the arrival time of the product k as, $T_k = T_{K-1} + A_K$.

Step 2. If Able is idle, product k begins service with Able at the current time T_{now}. Able's service completion time, $T_{fin,A} = T_{now} + T_{SVC,A}$ where $T_{SVC,A}$ is the service time generated from Able's service time distribution.

Once Able completes his service, Baker can start servicing the product. Again, Baker's service time is generated from Baker's service distribution table. The total service time of the product Able' service time +Baker's service time.

Note that, Able can be idle or busy. Baker can also be idle or busy. Thus, this gives rise to 4 different possibilities. We shall investigate all of these while studying the simulation table.

We will now calculate cumulative probabilities and assign random digits to the Inter-arrival distribution and Service distributions of Able and Baker.

INTER-ARRIVAL TIMES OF PRODUCTS ARRIVING ON ASSEMBLY LINE

Time between Arrivals (Minutes)	*Probability*	*Cumulative Probability*	*Random-Digit Assignment*
3	0.1	0.1	00-09
4	0.15	0.25	10-24
5	0.35	0.6	25-59
6	0.25	0.85	60-84
7	0.15	1	85-99

SERVICE DISTRIBUTION OF ABLE

Service Time Arrivals (Minutes)	*Probability*	*Cumulative Probability*	*Random-Digit Assignment*
2	0.3	0.3	00-29
3	0.28	0.58	30-57
4	0.25	0.83	58-82
5	0.17	1	83-99

SERVICE DISTRIBUTION OF BAKER

Service Time Arrivals (Minutes)	*Probability*	*Cumulative Probability*	*Random-Digit Assignment*
3	0.35	0.35	00-34
4	0.25	0.6	35-59
5	0.2	0.8	60-79
6	0.2	1	80-99

(*a*) Utilization of Able = Total Service Time/Total time = 35/49 = 71.4 per cent

Utilization of Baker = Total Service Time/Total Time = 41/52 = 78.8 per cent

Average performance time of Able = 1.4 minutes

Average performance time of Baker = 1.26 minutes

(*b*) Output rate of the product = Total time/No. of units

= 56/10 = 5.6 minutes per unit

(*c*) Average time Able waits for Baker = 1.6 minutes

(*d*) Average time Baker waits for Able = 1.3 minutes

Item Number	Random Number	Clock				Able					Baker				
		Inter-arrival time	Arrival Time	When Able Available	When Baker Available	Start time	Random Number	Service Time	Finish Time	Wait Time	Start time	Random Number	Service Time	Finish Time	Wait Time
1	—	—	0	0	0	0	58	4	4	—	4	25	3	7	4
2	64	6	6	4	7	6	86	5	11	—	11	91	6	17	4
3	92	7	13	11	17	13	62	4	17	—	17	4	3	20	—
4	87	7	20	17	20	20	91	5	25	—	25	90	6	31	5
5	47	5	25	25	31	25	6	2	27	4	31	42	4	35	—
6	46	5	30	27	35	30	36	3	33	2	35	51	4	39	—
7	49	5	35	33	39	35	7	2	37	2	39	98	6	45	—
8	16	4	39	37	45	39	91	5	44	1	45	7	3	50	—
9	22	4	43	44	50	44	45	3	47	3	50	15	3	53	—
10	1	3	46	47	53	47	6	2	49	4	53	30	3	56	—

Random Number Table

13962	70992	65172	28053	02190	83634	66012	70305	66761	88344
43905	46941	72300	11641	43548	30455	07686	31840	03261	89139
00504	48658	38051	59408	16508	82979	92002	63606	41078	86326
61274	57238	47267	35303	29066	02140	60867	39847	50968	96719
43753	21159	16239	50595	62509	61207	86816	29902	23395	72640
83503	51662	21636	68192	84294	38754	84755	34053	94582	29215
36807	71420	35804	44862	23577	79551	42003	58684	09271	68396
19110	55680	18792	41487	16614	83053	00812	16749	45347	88199
82615	86984	93290	87971	60022	35415	20852	02909	99476	45568
05621	26584	36493	63013	68181	57702	49510	75304	38724	15712
06936	37293	55875	71213	83025	46063	74665	12178	10741	58362
84981	60458	16194	92403	80951	80068	47076	23310	74899	87929
66354	88441	96191	04794	14714	64749	43097	83976	83281	72038
49602	94109	36460	62353	00721	66980	82554	90270	12312	56299
78430	72391	96973	70437	97803	78683	04670	70667	58912	21883
33331	51803	15934	75807	46561	80188	78984	29317	27971	16440
62843	84445	56652	91797	45284	25842	96246	73504	21631	81223
19528	15445	77764	33446	41204	70067	33354	70680	66664	75486
16737	01887	50934	43306	75190	86997	56561	79018	34273	25196
99389	06685	45945	62000	76228	60645	87750	46329	46544	95665
36160	38196	77705	28891	12106	56281	86222	66116	39626	06080
05505	45420	44016	79662	92069	27628	50002	32540	19848	27319
85962	19758	92795	00458	71289	05884	37963	23322	73243	98185
28763	04900	54460	22083	89279	43492	00066	40857	86568	49336
42222	40446	82240	79159	44168	38213	46839	26598	29983	67645
43626	40039	51492	36488	70280	24218	14596	04744	89336	35630
97761	43444	95895	24102	07006	71923	04800	32062	41425	66862
49275	44270	52512	03951	21651	53867	73531	70073	45542	22831
15797	75134	39856	73527	78417	36208	59510	76913	22499	68467
04497	24853	43879	07613	26400	17180	18880	66083	02196	10638
95468	87411	30647	88711	01765	57688	60665	57636	36070	37285
01420	74218	71047	14401	74537	14820	45248	78007	65911	38583
74633	40171	97092	79137	30698	97915	36305	42613	87251	75608
46662	99688	59576	04887	02310	35508	69481	30300	94047	57096
10853	10393	03013	90372	89639	65800	88532	71789	59964	50681
68583	01032	67938	29733	71176	35699	10551	15091	52947	20134
75818	78982	24258	93051	02081	83890	66944	99856	87950	13952
16395	16837	00538	57133	89398	78205	72122	99655	25294	20941
53892	15105	40963	69267	85534	00533	27130	90420	72584	84576
66009	26869	91829	65078	89616	49016	14200	97469	88307	92282
45292	93427	92326	70206	15847	14302	60043	30530	57149	08642
34033	45008	41621	79437	98745	84455	66769	94729	17975	50963
13364	09937	00535	88122	47278	90758	23542	35273	67912	97670
03343	62593	93332	09921	25306	57483	98115	33460	55304	43572
46145	24476	62507	19530	41257	97919	02290	40357	38408	50031
37703	51658	17420	30593	39637	64220	45486	03698	80220	12139
12622	98083	17689	59677	56603	93316	79858	52548	67367	72416
56043	00251	70085	28067	78135	53000	18138	40564	77086	49557
43401	35924	28308	55140	07515	53854	23023	70268	80435	24269
18053	53460	32125	81357	26935	67234	78460	47833	20496	35645

38

FUTURE HR TRENDS RELEVANT FOR PRODUCTION/OPERATIONS

We have already a large number of people who work off-site. There is a different kind of work-life balance, and it will change further in the future. The very nature of work will change. All these aspects merit the attention of all the managers, especially the production and operations executive. These trends have been considered in this chapter so that there is further debate and discussion on these.

THE FUTURE WORKER

Organisations in future would no longer be the places which people visit for works. They will be convergence centres where multiple careers flourish to achieve a dynamic corporate goal. Today, the organisation pays for a set of skills, which may or may not contribute to its bottom-line. In future, a worker would have to run his own profit centre. Rigid hierarchies and functions will be a thing of the past. A matrix of collective competencies will emerge instead. Along with the anticipated changes in the organisation, the worker will have to change too.

Career

A future corporation will have three types of people on pay-roll. Professionals with relevant qualifications, contractual employees and organisations, and flexible labour force, indulging in job hopping. A future worker will concentrate on self, and choose employers, either one or many, depending on the payment fetched for his skills. Skill itself would keep on changing, ranging from generalist in the small organisation to specialist in the complex big organisation. A worker will have to upgrade the skills constantly to avoid being threatened by obsolescence. A worker may move across industries, functions and boundaries. A worker will demand handsome remuneration, and a better work-life balance. A worker will be mobile and not bound to any physical place. Work will be viewed as a series of experiences, and the total tenure would depend upon the quality of this experience.

Career Models

Technical expertise will be the hallmark of the new worker. He will be an innovator. Like an *intrapreneur*, he will organise the work in line with the corporate goals, bidding good bye to nine-to-five work day. As the *specialist-consultant*, the worker will be sought after for his unique skills. There will be flexibility in terms of who you work for, the work pattern and the fee. He will have the freedom to choose multiple employers. As *connected worker*, there will not be any need to remain physically present at the workplace. As *interim worker*, he would be a super specialist whose expertise is sought for a finite period in a particular industry or function.

New Career

A *concentric career* will be specialist, with specialisation built around a business, service or product. A *concurrent career* will have two or more major activities in tandem. A *combination career* would include a mix of activities, say a series of short-term projects. A *contingency career* allows for work only when there is need for money.

New Skills

Behavioural competency will be in demand, *e.g.,* the ability to work from home, the ability to work in an unstructured organisation. Self-motivation will be a desirable trait. Teamwork would be a plus point. The other preferred skills would be coping with different organisational contents, openness to learning, global perspective and cross-cultural sensitivity. Adaptation to new skills will be a key to success. Decision making skills will be valued, especially the quick decisions without any reference point. A worker will have to be a risk taker and should have emotional resilience. Companies will not provide security of service, and the employee will have to learn from his mistakes. Managerial skills will be industry specific.

Empowerment of Workers

Companies are cutting down on hierarchies and creating a level playing field for both workers and executives. At cafeteria, the same food is served to both the managers and workers *e.g.,* Nokia plant at Chennai. A shift supervisor is now equivalent to a deputy manager at Maruti Suzuki plant. At recruitment stage itself, trained personnel are absorbed at the supervisory level.

FUTURE OF WORK

Work was formerly considered just a physical activity. Brawn rather than brain was used to execute a task. In the concluding part of the last century, there emerged suddenly electronic technology which has changed the nature of work itself. Brain power has replaced muscle power. Job entails a variety of activities like operating more than one machine, reading control chart, for quality, maintain the machines and so on. Even the white-collar job has shifted from paper pushing to co-ordination and communication. However, infotech will take care of both the co-ordination and communication. A lot of information will be generated. The employee has to see how best he can use this information. A knowledge worker of the future will seek to add value to the task on hand. Jobs will be treated as entrepreneurial assignments. These internal entrepreneurs must have greater responsibilities, with a combination of a strategic and operational rate. Such a role will not be the preserve of the higher echelons of management.

Work will be considered as strategy, ownership, synthesis and leadership.

As a strategy, the emphasis would be to add higher value to the organisation. As a consequence work will be cerebral, specialised and not easily duplicable. Knowledge-based work will change the skill profiles. Work profile will change on account of the technological influence which makes higher skills necessary. Leverage of knowledge will give competitive edge to the organisation. Mechanical jobs will decline at a faster rate. Competitive nature of business calls for greater understanding of the markets and consumers. Constant innovation and improvement will become the order of the day. Innovativeness will be an added responsibility of the company's employees.

NATURE OF WORK

Work as ownership is a result of the knowledge economy. The worker owns the 'tools of production' — the ideas. As we know, in the old economy, the resources were owned by the employer. In future, the raw material of work itself will change. The employee will be in total charge of the work, and ensure optimum utilisation. A future company will be a lean company, with fewer employees processing higher skills. They are likely to 'own' their functional responsibilities. A team will have the total responsibility for a full process. Instead of the functional or departmental targets, there will be partnership, blend of strategic and operational responsibilities, role shuffles and seamless teams. Work has been organised as projects even now, with its own cost, quality parameters and time frame. In future, work will be a series of small projects. People will move from one project to another constantly. Projects will have to generate profits. Even third party projects can be taken to convert a division into a profit centre.

Work will be synthesized. The divide of strategic and operational divide will be lesser. There will be a multiplicity of roles in a job, and connectivity between functions. Managers will move across functions and industries effortlessly. Work will be carried out not only by the physical teams, but by virtual teams due to advanced communication technology. So far people go out to work, but in future work will come to people.

Work synthesis will allow people to match long-term personal goals to the choice of work. e.g., choosing career that allows retirement by the age of 45. Flexibility in work will be possible because the need of the employer in the knowledge economy will be greater than need of the employees. Physical presence and location will no longer remain relevant.

Work as leadership will change the leadership parameters. The CEO will be a facilitator and a team player. But at the same time, he will not lose focus on performance and shareholder value. He will lead by example. He will have to relate and participate. As a leader, he will empower the employees. Decisions will no longer be the preserve of the top team. Competence will count. There will not be imposition from the top leaders will just create the right environment. A future leader will be young in years and will operate in a technology-driven environment. He will have to break rules and traditions. He should be energetic and infectious. Though leaders will participate, coach and break rules, still they will not lose focus on performance. In AmEx, a leader is rated on ideas, relationships, result-orientedness and people leadership, along with an appraisal of leadership competencies. But the future leader will also take care of profits and shareholder value. A leader will have to be an entrepreneur and all managers will be micro-entrepreneurs. A new leader will combine roles.

FUTURE WORKPLACE

Technology will bring about a massive change in the workplace. More work, and better quality work will result from such a change. The overall productivity will increase. The elements which will change are the way we work, the way we interact, and the physical parameters of the workplace. Internet has brought about already a change in the business environment. Technology has killed the distance. Telecommuting will increase, and will account for 20 per cent of all work done. Performance appraisal will be in terms of the results achieved, rather than the number of hours put in. Employees will have access to databases, and there will have to be shared vision amongst employees who may never meet face-to-face. Remote working will have to tackle the problem of the employee's need to have social interaction. On-campus work is preferred, and so there will be a need to change the structure of the workplace making it more an area of debate and discussion rather than that of compiling information. An office cannot afford to be totally impersonal, and a balance must be struck. Teleworking will increase. Wireless connectivity is influencing the workplace substantially. E-mailing will soon give way to voice and later videomailing. A large portion of work will centre around communication. Our interactions will be affected by flatter and decentralised organisations of future. People will have access to information, not necessarily on a need-to-know basis. Future organisations will be characterised by flexibility and fluidity. The physical place of work will have more relaxed, open and friendly atmosphere. Work will be done on the concept of campus, while involving employees in the process of deciding what the work environment looks like. Comfort will be emphasised. Face-to-face meetings will be reduced. Pitstops are the places where employees can gather and talk. This is where the grapevine buzzes. According to some futurologists, the concept of permanent seating will disappear.

LIFE AND WORK

In this competitive age, and liberalised economy, people seek to work and work and work, keeping no time for other activities in life. Laptops, mobiles and technology has sneaked in to make people work even when they are away from the workplace. Some people have become workaholics, enjoying more while being at work rather than being at home. We have to strike a balance between increased work and life. True, jobs have become more demanding in lean organisations and competitive environment. There are many families where both parents work. There are more women in the workforce. Leisure activities are as much important as work. Work and personal life have become interdependent. Personal factors influence job performance. Organisations now devise methods to strike balance between work and life to reduce employee burnout and enhance productivity. Employees should also avoid overworking to save their homelife. There is a greater pressure on employees to perform, and perform 100 per cent. Anything less than that is simply not acceptable. Technology has also increased the workload by making people accessible. Work has tended to become more intrusive. Globalisation adds to the work-life imbalance. Time-zone differences make co-ordination quite challenging. Companies arrange with concierge services organisations to help employees in chore management. ATM facility is made available on company premises. Free telephone facilities are provided to keep family members in touch. Companies arrange leisure for its employees, *e.g.,* evening at a pub once a month. Organisations will have to formulate their leisure policy. They will have to assess the leisure needs of the employees and devise means to provide them. Though company can help to a certain extent in work-life balance, ultimately it is an individual issue. Companies must respect the individual space of their employees. There should be a clear demarcation between personal and private time. Business must be transacted during business hours. Beyond that, it is another realm. Women employees get a raw deal in work-life balance. Offices and houses should not be wide apart. Women can be allowed to work from home. Lever considers each case on its merits. Part timing and flexi-timing are possible solutions for both, men and women. Working hard does not mean 'working long.' One must learn to use time effectively.

FUTURE WORK SYSTEMS

In future corporations, we shall need systems which aggregate and leverage the critical resources such as competence, knowledge, relationships, capital and physical assets. Information system in future must be excellent. Work system will have to adapt to not only the current goals but future goals too. A future corporation will have stakeholders spread all across the globe. Besides, adaptations to present and future, goals would require multi-dimensional flexibility — strategic, organisational, operational, financial and marketing. As there will have to be seamless transfer and sharing of information, the systems must integrate and allow real-time updation and access. This by itself will become a crucial element of strategy. There should be cross-organisational sharing of market information. There will be cross-rotation of human beings. This too will require a supportive information system. Organisation's key asset are its people and work systems will have to be tailored around them. There are changes anticipated in the three R's of human capital — recruitment, rating and reward. In recruiting the manager in this millennium will conduct a global as well as a local search. Recruitment will not be only need-based, it will also be opportunity-led. Talent search will be far more aggressive. Searches will be global. There may be some niche searches. Recruitment may be outsourced through customised selection processes. Niche recruitments will be driven by employee referrals and networking. Appraisals would be speedier. They would be rigorous in the sense that wider performance linkages will be incorporated into them. Appraisals will be led by soft skills, and based on milestones. Some reviews will be weekly, monthly or quarterly. Exceptional performance in the short-run will be recognised. Rewards will also correspond to the review period. Parameters of rating could include volume growth, operating margins and customer satisfaction specially for senior positions. Ratings will be driven by skills, and to the extent the individual exercises them. Skill profile will undergo a change in idea-driven organisations, rather than process or product-led organisations. Change management, networking and knowledge management are soft skills today. They will be hard skills tomorrow and will form part of appraisals. Ability to develop and retain talent will be a major rating criterion. Appraisal would be task-specific, project-led and team-driven. The focus would shift to output and large tasks. Tracking would be milestone-led rather than being determined by the end-result. Criticality of processes would be rated too. Pay will be based on performance, followed by skills, competence, wealth-creation, organisational life-style and the demand-supply situation. Variable pay, now 10-30 p.c., could go upto 70 p.c. Negative pay or disincentive would be a feature of compensation system. Companies would offer a generalist career path to performers. Super-specialists will be rare, would command a higher price due to unique skills e.g., turnaround skills. Wealth-creation would drive the salaries in a big way. ESOPs will be the norm. There will be short-term wealth-creation options like sign-on bonuses, asset-building opportunities like housing and car-loans. Agreements will have *golden parachute* clauses which allow 3-6 months salary on being redundant. Competitive parity however, would be outdated. Compensation would be strategic. Benchmarking would be practised to remain competitive. Packages will be individualised. Specialist element would make the salaries cash-heavy. Work systems in HR would be smart selection, frequent appraisal, fat salaries, fatter options and the training and development of people. People will have to be made employable. The development will be largely left to the managers. They will have to relearn, reskill and retool.

Information Age

The future age will be obviously information age. The workplace will be full of Knowledge Workers (KWs). There will be knowledge factories all manned not by human but by bots. Humans will look after the well-being of KWs and bots. In service industry where personal interface is required, we shall need humans. KWs will be patched to a server in return for money. There will be KW work day. The work will transit from the realm of physical to that of cerebral. Every business will be a knowledge business.

Loose Organisation

Martin Thomas has written *Loose: The Future of Business is Letting Go.* He promotes the concepts of flexibility, agility and readiness to improvise. Successful and not-so-successful organisations will be set apart on these concepts. Yes, some basic structure is needed in any organisation. But even within this structure or framework, we can promote loose thinking and working. The structure that is called for depends upon the nature of business. A pharma company cannot afford to be highly loose, as it has to operate under FDA regulations and its products can either save or threaten life. However, a consumer products company can afford to be loose to operate in the present day environment. Some degree of looseness can be built into any organisation. It is just an issue of balancing the loose-tight elements or defining the freedom within an organisational framework. Google has adopted this philosophy which determines precisely the amount of management it needs, and then use a little less. This embodies the spirit of loose philosophy — freedom within a framework. It is difficult to be loose, rather than to be tight. As Sir Martin Sorrell has rightly said, 'The 21st century is not a place for tidy minds.'

Bring Your Own Device (BYOD): Workplace Revolution

The company hardware is considered old-fashioned. The IT departments get requests to support the new devices. The new policy is to allow employees to Bring Your Own Device (BYOD) to work. Wipro, Citrix and CISCO have started employing this policy. Wipro covers 5000 senior executives, including its own salesforce, under BYOD programme. It supports iPhone and iPod. The service can be further extended to all employees in Wipro. They could support devices based on Android and Windows Phone 7 Mango. It is a part of employee energization exercise. Citrix allows employees to buy any lap top of their choice by paying up to $ 2100 and most of them buy Macs. Many companies allow employees to access emails and some web-based applications on their personal devices. The issue of security is resolved by desktop virtualisation. Corporate data resides only in the company data server and never in your device. The log in into the data server is through a two-factor authentication process. Once the official work is done, one has to lot out. Then there is no trace of the company data on your device. Desktop virtualisation also means that your interface will look the same in whichever device you use. BYOD is cost saving too. The device can be fixed if there is a glitch by collective solutions, *e.g..*, there is a Mac Wiki for Mac users in CISCO.

MANAGEMENT INFORMATION SYSTEM (MIS) AND PRODUCTION MANAGEMENT

Management Information System is defined by Kelly as the combination of human and computer-based resources that results in the collection, storage, retrieval, communication and use of data for the purpose of efficient management of operations and for business planning. The information system is a means to process data which are then used for decision making. The following figure illustrates this concept:

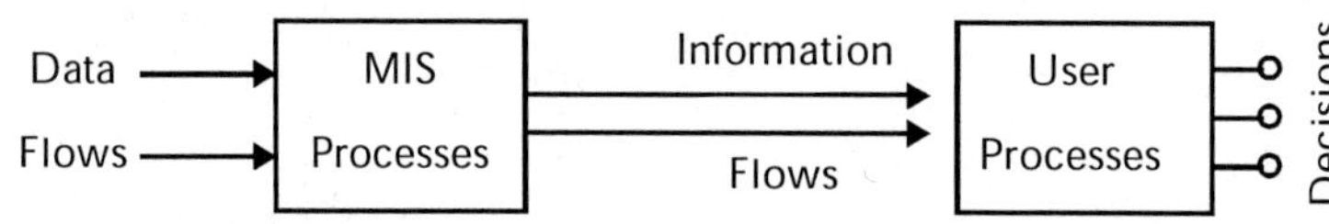

Fig.39.1 MIS in Decision Making

If there is no management interface, the system is just pure data processing. It becomes MIS when it is used by the management. The processed data is called information and the emphasis is on information generation, and not on the method of its generation.

A system viewed in totality is the holistic approach. It means the whole is greater than its parts. Systems consists of sub-systems and these parts interact with each other and are interdependent. The individual parts of the system can be studied separately — it is a reductionist approach.

Organisations have certain overall objectives, and they adapt to the changing environment. MIS in organisations help them to attain the objectives set, and to plan and control processes and operations.

Management process consists of planning, organising, directing and controlling. These elements are to be coordinated. The emphasis on different elements varies according to the level an executive occupies in the organisation. At the top level, conceptual and HR skills are required. At the middle level, there is a need to have communication, supervisory and HR skills. At the lower levels, we require technical skills. At the top level, we do not need a highly structured MIS. At the departmental level, the managers need an MIS pertaining to the functions they perform, *e.g.*, MIS for operations manager, MIS for Human Resources, MIS for finance, MIS for marketing, etc.

As managers, people are decision makers, and make two types of decisions, routine programmed decisions and strategic non-programmed decisions. MIS designers have to understand the decision making process.

As the assigned tasks are to be controlled, a system must have a provision for feedback. Thus, a system has input — process — output — control and feedback loop to correct the system. Thus, we have inventory control, production control, budgetary control and so on. It is an important feature of MIS.

IT and MIS

IT is a generic term which refers to computers, telecom and electronics. IT affects many areas of life including organisations and MIS. Hitherto, organisations concentrated mainly on accounting data; but now have extended the use of IT to other areas of management. IT is used for data or transaction processing, office support systems and end-user systems.

There is a turbulent environment these days. There are changes which affect the organisations. There is more competition, faster pace and increased globalisation. There is more emphasis on productivity and quality. The demographic profile of employees have changed. All this calls for the institution of a suitable MIS.

Data and Information

Data are transactions, facts, events and so on. Data are in the crude form or raw material form. When data is processed, it is converted into usable or meaningful information. MIS is a formal system that makes available to the management information from data generated externally or internally so as to make decisions regarding their functions.

A System

A system consists of some basic elements — inputs, processes and outputs

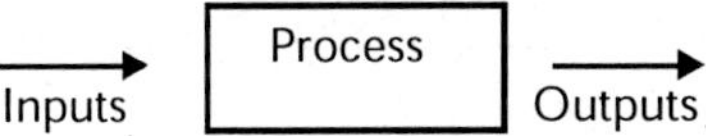

To illustrate, a production system has inputs such as raw materials and labour and outputs such as finished product. The manufacturing or production process converts the raw materials into finished products.

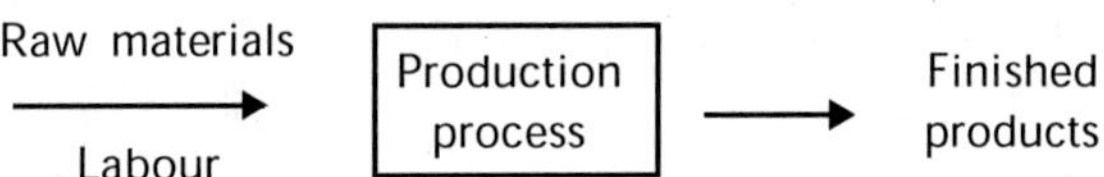

In all the systems excepting the physical/mechanical ones, the transformation process is controlled by information. The output of the system is used as a basis of control for the input of the system. This is called feedback.

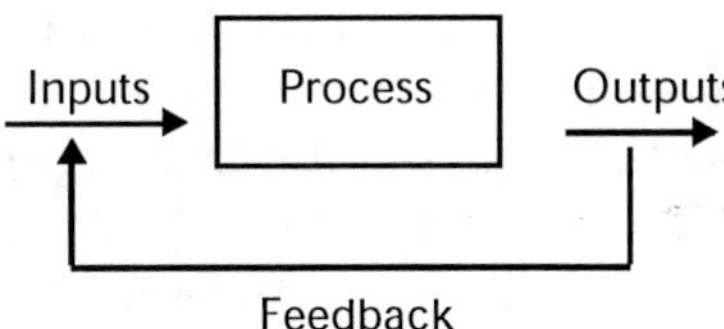

System Boundaries

The system's extent is given by its boundary. Physical and biological systems have well-defined boundaries. Social organisations have porous boundaries, and there are transfers across boundaries of information, people, materials and ideas. The internal boundaries within the organisations are decided by the management, *e.g.*, whether billing will be handled by the sales department or accounting department.

System Environment

The external elements to any system constitute its environment. They affect the state of the system and the system too affects them. The environmental elements have relationship with the system. To illustrate, an organisation is surrounded by social, technological, economic and cultural environment. Then, there is an interface between the organisation and the government — whether local, state or central.

A *closed system* is isolated from its environment e.g., physical systems, a production sub-system etc. An open system interacts with its environment. All social organisations are open systems.

Adaptability

Organisations survive and grow when they adapt to the changes in the environment. Adaptation occurs as a result of management decisions and actions.

Socio-Technical Systems

Trist and Tavistock Institute developed this view of the organisations. A production system has a technological organisation consisting of plant and machinery, production processes, methods, etc. It also has a work organisation or social system. Here, the necessary tasks are carried out. This requires structuring human activities around various technologies.

Different technologies spell out different technical sub-systems. The machinery, equipment, the layout and skills are differently patterned. This is obvious when we consider an automobile company, a hospital, an IT company. The social sub-system considers the aspirations, motivations, interactions and value system of the people. There is a close link between the technical and social sub-system. The following diagram illustrates an integration of the four elements of the socio-technical system.

Fig. 39.2

Social-technical View of the Organisations

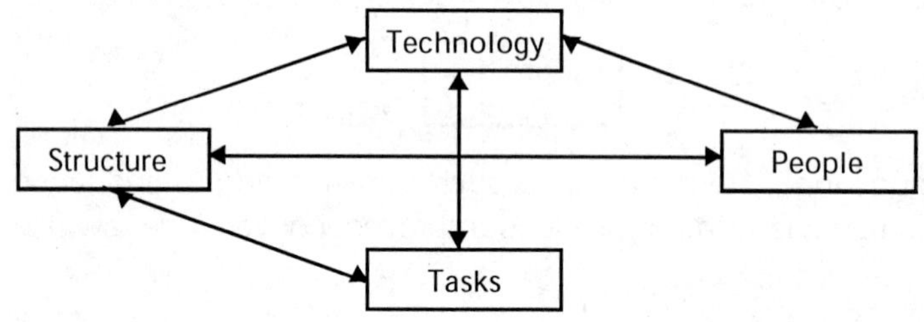

Organisational Structures

The classical organisation theory emphasises the structures. It focuses on detailed analysis and control of production methods. Taylor, Gantt, Gilberth and Fayol are the major contributors to this theory. It is a mechanistic view. Later Taylor's scientific management caught on after a series of experiments to improve labour productivity at the Bethlehem Steel Works, USA. His emphasis was on an ideal method of doing the task, selecting the best man to do it, and train him, and marry the scientific method to the selected and trained worker. The work is responsible for the performance, but the planning and preparatory part is the management's responsibility. Departmentalisation or grouping of work is inherent in the classical approach. A common functional break up divides the organisation into finance, production, marketing, materials, HR and R&D departments. Fayol contributed 14 management principles — scalar chain, unity of command, division of work, authority, centralisation, right man in the right place, unity of dissection, esprit de corps, initiative, stability of tenure, equity remuneration, organisational *vs.* individual interest and discipline. The HR school of organisational theory were pioneered by Mayo who conducted the Hawthorne Experiments at Western Electric, Illinois. The effects of physical factors were studied on productivity. It was seen that productivity was influenced by factors beyond the physical ones. The emphasis shifted to attitudes and motivation of individual workers. Social factors and the changes in supervisory attitudes did influence the work performance. This study was a turning point in organisational theory. An organisation is both a social system and techno-economical system. Informal grouping affects the organisational work. Social skills are as much necessary as technical skills. Organisations just cannot remain autocratic and authoritarian. They have to be democratic too. It focused on an participatory style. Motivational theories such as Maslow's Need Hierarchy and Hertzberg's dual factor theory were a major influence on organisational design. Vroom advocated expectancy-valence theory of motivation. The systems or contingency approach to the organisation think an organisation to be a complex system that interacts with the environment and responds to various interdependent variables such as people, tasks, technology, structure and environment. There is no one ideal way to organise.

The way we organise depends on or contingent on the prevailing conditions. Lawrence and Lorsch, the American researchers first used the term contingency approach.

Formal and Informal Organisation

The formal organisation depicts the relationships as they exist officially and could be seen on organisation charts. An organisation is also affected by the behaviour of people working in it. People form small informal groups and interact with each other. These groups exist in any formal organisation.

Matrix Structure

Organisation structures keep on evolving. The matrix structure is borrowed from high tech industries. There are project teams, each headed by a project manager. They are combined with the traditional formal structure. Each project team has its own goals. The project leaders coordinate with the functional heads for services. The functional heads provide the technical expertise and facilities. Apart from functional relationship, the project manager has a line relationship with his subordinates and superiors.

The following diagram illustrates the matrix organisation of a manufacturing company:

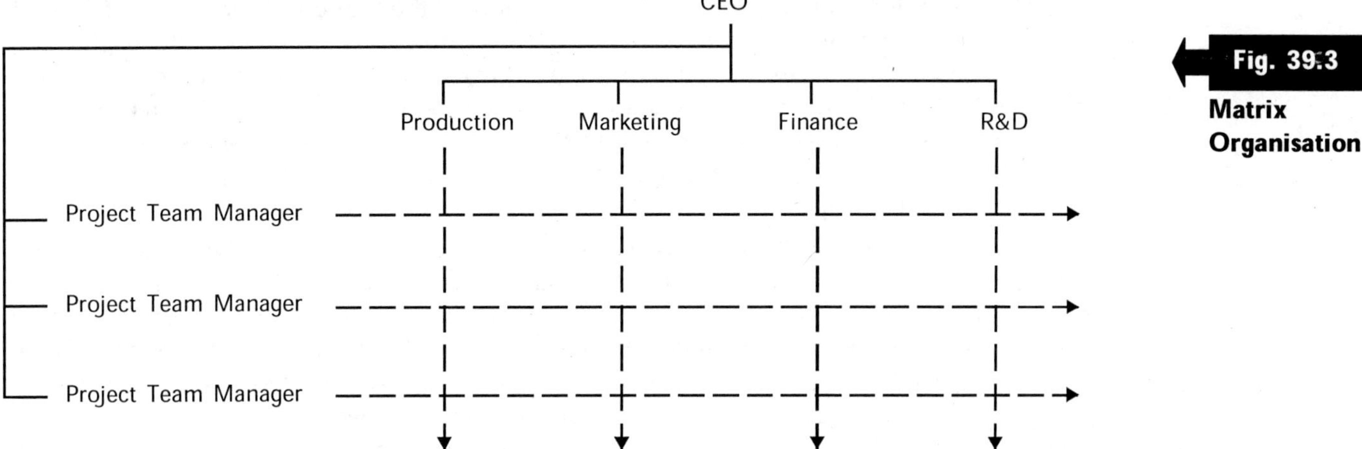

Fig. 39.3 Matrix Organisation

Span of Control

The number of subordinates over which a manager has direct control is called span of control. A narrow span means lesser number. A wide span mean higher number.

Levels

An organisation may have just one or two levels of management, and it is called a flat structure or several levels, and it is called a tall structure.

Centralisation and Decentralisation

An organisation can keep authority centralised at the top or can disperse it widely, and make the organisation decentralised. Some functions like finance can be centralised, and some decentralised such as production and marketing..

MIS must be appropriate to the organisation, or else it is useless.

Management by Objectives (MBO)

This term was coined by Drucker to mean that the individual objectives and organisational objectives must be coordinated. This calls for participatory style of management. An organisation as a whole has overall objectives, which are split into functional or departmental objectives. These in turn are broken down into individual objectives. The optimal approach is to harmonise individual and organisational objectives. The MBO organisation has key performance areas (KPAs) well-defined. There is participation of the superiors — subordinates in goal setting which are measured both quantitatively and qualitatively. Monitoring is done through performance appraisal. MBO process is linked to the planning process.

Business Process Re-engineering (BPR)

This was initiated by Hammer and Champy in 1993 and has been discussed earlier in the book. It involves radical redesign of business processes. It is a systems-oriented approach. Some typical processes are manufacturing, ordering, delivery and invoicing.

Planning

Planning is a function of management that decides what is to be done in future, how to do it, when to do it and who will do it. It consists of mission, objectives, individual plans or strategies and policies. Mission indicates the purpose of the organisation. Objectives are the aims or goals to be achieved, say a particular level of production or sales. Plans are specific actions and activities to achieve the objectives, e.g., production plan. Policies are guidelines to actions for recurrent decisions. The entire planning process is decision making exercise. In planning, the *end* results are objectives. Strategies or plans are used to achieve these objectives — in short, they are the *means.* Policies are *statement of conduct.* At the top-level, the objectives are overall general objectives. Lower down in the organisation, they become detailed and specific. Long-term planning for 5 years and more is strategic planning. It shows where the organisation is headed. It also spells out how the future projects will be financed. It also envisages the organisation structure to undertake these projects. It thinks about the deployment of resources. Medium term planning is tactical planning. It considers the product planning, the capital budgeting, the pricing and the production facilities required to meet the strategic planning requirements. Short-term planning for a year considers the production and marketing plans, the raw materials and manpower needed, and the way the operations are organised. Strategic planning at the top-level is also called corporate planning.

MIS of an organisation is facilitates planning and decision making. It makes use of models where reality is abstracted by considering certain critical variables. Computer-based models are of two types — optimisation models e.g., linear programming or simulation models which mimic different conditions to be explored. Simulation models can be deterministic or probabilistic. Deterministic models assume single point estimates and certainty. Probabilistic models use multipoint estimates to introduce uncertainty. With most models, it is possible to assess risk by undertaking *sensitivity analysis.* All the variables are held constant, except one, and it is altered step by step to record the effect on the result. This way, *critical* or *sensitive* variables are identified.

Decision Making

As we know, management is decision making. Routine and repetitive decisions are programmed decisions. Non-routine decisions with a lot of uncertainty are non-programmed decisions. At the top level of management, strategic long-term decisions with deployment of resources are taken. At the middle level, medium term tactical decisions are made. The day-to-day decisions are made at the operational level. Mergers and acquisitions (M&A), new product development, financial planning are strategic decisions. Price planning, capacity planning, budgeting, purchase planning are tactical decisions. Scheduling, maintenance, inventory control, credit rating are operational decisions. The decision models are either prescriptive or descriptive. A prescriptive model automatically selects the best options, *e.g.,* decisions such as LP, Break Even Analysis, Capital Budgeting. Descriptive models are behavioural in nature. In rational decision making, a decision objective is chosen and expressed in quantitative terms, *e.g.,* maximisation of profit. All alternatives are examined. They are ranked. The best alternative is chosen.

Decision Making and MIS

MIS provides information and explores alternatives to facilitate decision making by the management. MIS can by itself make the decision where routine operations are involved.

At the top level, management makes strategic decisions by installing Executive Information Systems. At the middle level, there are decision support systems and expert systems for making tactical decisions. At the operational level, there is Transaction Processing System, Automatic Decision Making System and Accounting Models.

Feedback Loops

Control is exercised through feedback loops. Here, the actuals are compared with planned performances. In feedback, the sensors are as mechanical devices or paper work. They measure the performance. The comparator is the software to compare the actuals and planned performance. The effectors are the supervisory mechanisms to take corrective action. The physical flows are compared and adjusted by one feedback coop. The information flows are linked to higher levels where corrective actions initiated. This is another feedback loop. Thus, there is double loop in organisations. Negative feedback dampens or reduces fluctuations around a standard or norm. Feedback system can be closed loop when it is based on output or open loop where control is based on externals. As opposed to feedback which monitors the past, feed forward looks ahead. The threats are scanned by feed forward and adjustments are made in advance.

Control in Organisations

There is operational control at the lower level. There are management control systems where top level policies are translated into action at the middle level. The strategic planning is control at the top level.

The example operational control system is production control system having sub-components like inventory control, scheduling job/process control and so on. The production control reports are generated by the system.

The management control system covers financial management control, production management control, R&D management control, marketing management control and HR management control. Here, control refers to the implementation of processes and procedures to influence the behaviour of people so as to attain the objectives set. The Key Result Areas are identified such as productivity, profitability, market position, HR development, etc.

There are interfaces of four factors in management control — the manager, the subordinates, the task and the environment.

Total Quality Control (TQC)

The quality is to build in right at the design stage and extends to production engineering, manufacturing, supply chain management.

Total Quality Management (TQM)

It refers to a culture where there is awareness of quality and quality improvement at all levels throughout and in all processes. Quality is considered to be the core value of an organisation.

IT and MIS

IT deals with information of any nature — pictorial, textual, vocal or numeric. IT involves processing storage and dissemination of such information through micro-electronics based computing and telecom. In IT, computers are used administratively in organisational context. Though management information system does not require computers essentially, they are useful. Computers do the processing fast and accurately. They are good at storage. They are good at retrieving the information. They handle large amounts of data. They can do repetitive operations.

IT-based information systems can be Office Support Systems, Data processing or Transaction Processing System or End User Computing. Word Processing, Image Processing are examples of Office Support Systems. Ledger, File and Transaction Processing are examples of Data Processing Systems. Decision Support System, Executive Information Systems are examples of End User Systems.

Designing Information System

First, project is initiated by deciding what to do and for which reasons. The system is then defined by agreeing to what is to be done. The next step is system design which works out how to do it. The system production is the actual work being done. The system acceptance and maintenance provides for its acceptance and unhindered running. The last stage is learning how effective the system is and how to improve it.

The following diagram illustrates this:

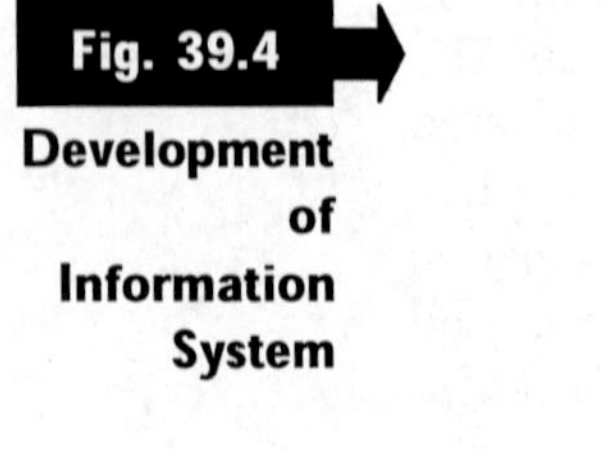

Fig. 39.4 Development of Information System

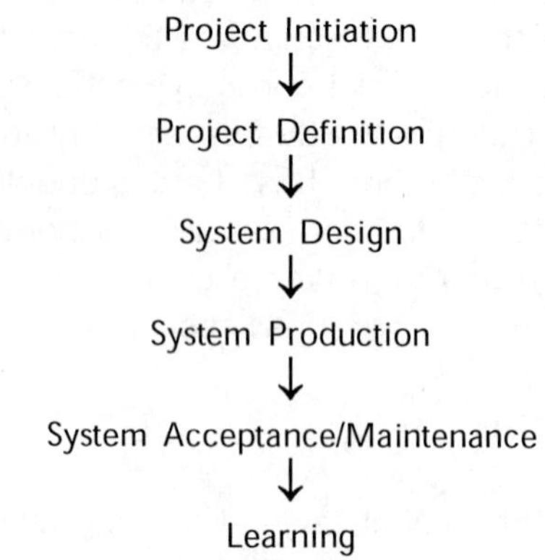

Structured System Design Methodology (SSADM)

This is a system followed in designing computerised systems. The main stages are the analysis of the status quo systems, specification of required system, selecting technical option, logical design and physical design. These correspond to the discussion we had on system design. However, it does not over-emphasise problem definition. SSADM is most suited for structured problem. One device used in SSADM is Data Flow Diagram. It represents the flow of information. The symbols used in data flow diagrams are:

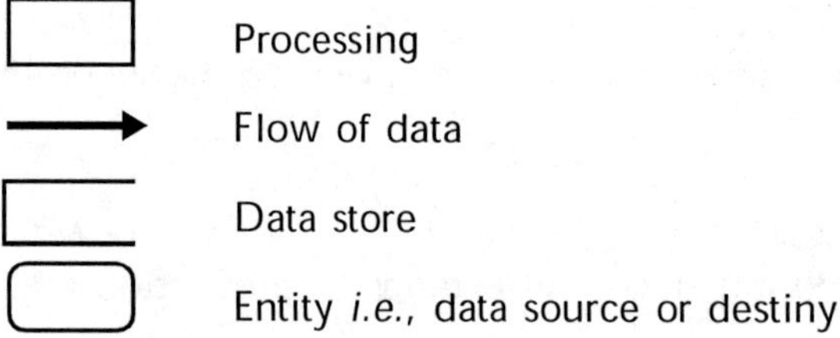

Data Flow Diagrams (DFDs)

They represent the flow information through a system. These can be used either for a manual or computerised system. They use the above four symbols. They can be put into physical and logical data flow diagrams. The physical DFD precedes the logical one.

A book store taking mail orders is shown below:

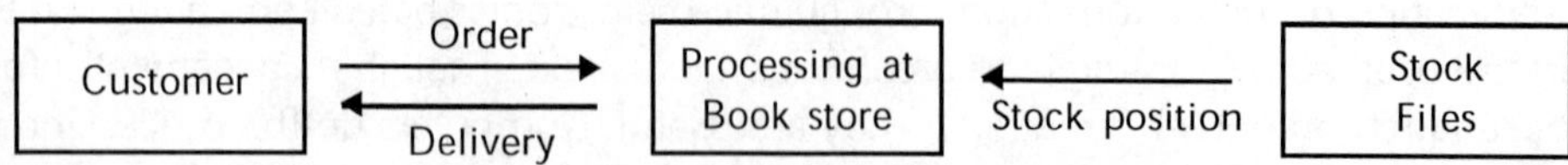

Decision Information Flow Diagrams are another version of DFDs. The symbols are the same but they portray individual decisions and the data flows

Data Processing

Computers are used for routine processing of day-to-day transactions which is called data processing or transaction processing. In addition, computers are used by the end-users *e.g.,* say managers. Transaction processing can be current activity processing (Issues → Activity Processing → Order Replenishment), report processing (report processing automatically at month end → Materials usage classified) or enquiry processing (whether item is in stock → Enquiry processing → enquiry response). Though such routine transaction processing is not MIS by itself, it is the foundation upon which MIS is built.

Databases

It is a structured collection of data, independent of any particular application. The programmes are written round the database. The database grows, and can comprise several databases, each providing relevant information for logically related information systems. DBMs or Data Base Management System is a software that deals with data structures and relationships. DBMs is the link between the user and the data in the base. It has three components — definition, processing and enquiry.

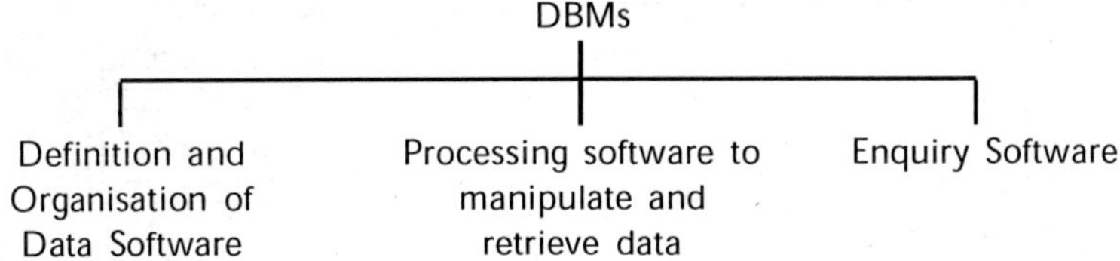

Decision Support Systems (DSS)

These overlap both, the database systems and the office support systems. These are facilitative systems for the managers. Mainly these are used for planning and decision making. Here the computers are an aid to the managerial decision making, but do not replace them. They are suited to semi-structured problems. DSS require a database, the software to handle it and support systems like modelling, spread sheets, analysis packages, export systems, etc.

Information Centres (IC)

These centres provide help to computers users within the organisation. They facilitate the software development for users. They are a link between organisation's DP department and outside suppliers. They are useful when there is distributed data processing.

Data Life Cycle

Data has several stages in its life cycle — data generation, data manipulation, data transmission, data storage and retrieval and reproduction of data.

Data is *generated* either internally in the organisation or externally. This data is captured through records such as purchase orders (POs), sales slips, vouchers, personnel Forms etc.

Such data when captured is *stored* in the memory of the person's brain or as a document or in any electronic/mechanical device. Such stored data is operated upon or utilised later.

Stored data is *retrieved* by search or access to the specific data elements from the medium it is stored in.

Retrieved data is *converted* or *reproduced* into a different form of storage or presentation format *e.g.,* a report.

Data is constantly on the move — it comes to the user in processed form. It is transferred to storage from the source. It is processed and passed on to the user. The user sends it back to the storage after working on it. It is then available for further retrieval.

Data is *sorted* and *classified* to reveal appropriate information. Data can be *synthesized* by aggregation to present a meaningful holistic picture.

Data processing subjects the data to manipulation based on arithmetical operations or on certain formulae. There are computations involved *e.g.,* salary elements of an employee. Quantitative techniques such as economic order quantities, aggregate planning can be used.

Data is for use, or else it is useless to keep it. It is used for decision making. Data is *verified* and *evaluated* to know what it costs to process it and how much valuable the information is. Data is destroyed after such cost-benefit analysis. Destruction constitutes the end of the data cycle.

The data cycle is given in the following diagram.

Fig. 39.5

Data Life Cycle

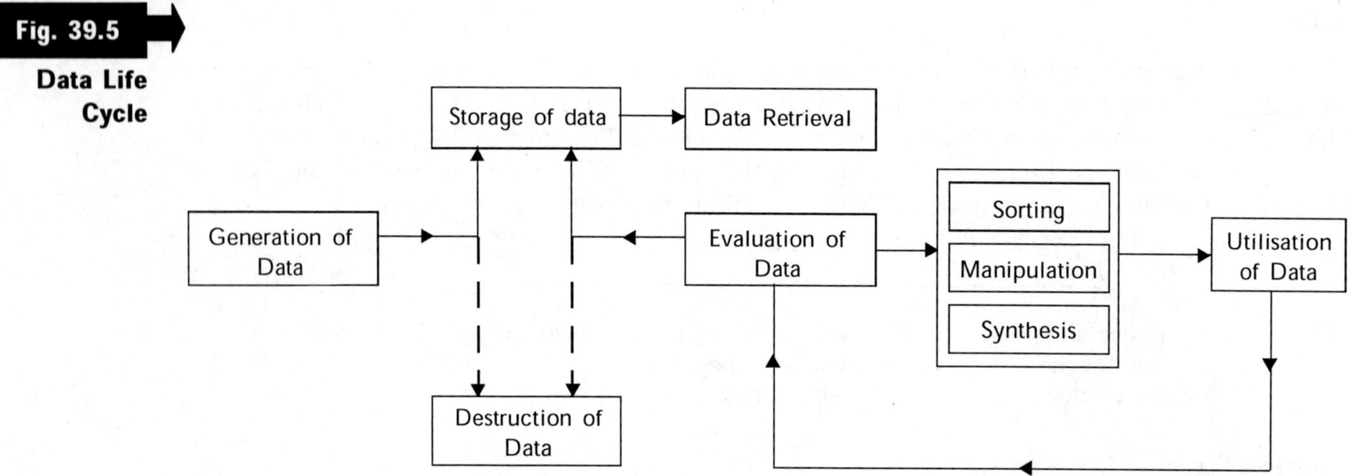

Adapted after Murdick and Ross, Management Information System, Prentice Hall.

NAME AND SUBJECT INDEX

A

B

C

D

E

F

G

H

I

J

K

L

M

N

O

P

Q

R

S

T

U

V

W

Z